A-Z MERSEYSIDE

REFERENCE

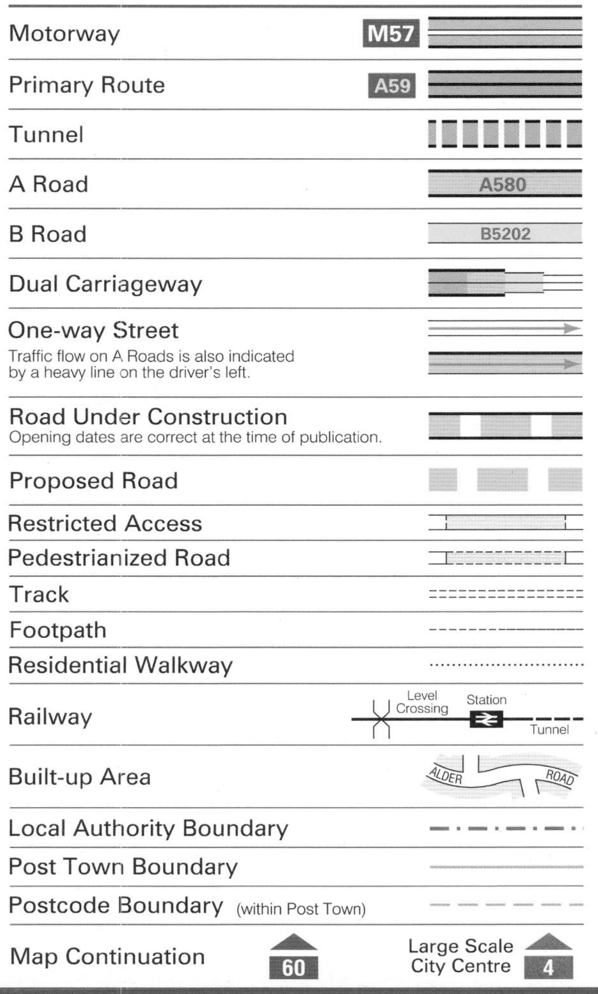

Motorway	**M57**
Primary Route	**A59**
Tunnel	
A Road	**A580**
B Road	**B5202**
Dual Carriageway	
One-way Street Traffic flow on A Roads is also indicated by a heavy line on the driver's left.	
Road Under Construction Opening dates are correct at the time of publication.	
Proposed Road	
Restricted Access	
Pedestrianized Road	
Track	
Footpath	
Residential Walkway	
Railway	Level Crossing / Station / Tunnel
Built-up Area	ALDER ROAD
Local Authority Boundary	
Post Town Boundary	
Postcode Boundary (within Post Town)	
Map Continuation	**60** / Large Scale City Centre **4**

Airport	✈
Car Park (selected)	**P**
Church or Chapel	†
Cycle Hire Docking Station	(Large Scale City Centre) 🚲
Cycleway (selected)	🚲
Fire Station	■
Hospital	**H**
House Numbers (A & B Roads only)	21 — 65
Information Centre	**i**
National Grid Reference	^{4}45
Park and Ride	Lea Green **P+R**
Police Station	▲
Post Office	★
Safety Camera with Speed Limit Fixed cameras and long term road works cameras. Symbols do not indicate camera direction.	(30)
Toilet: without facilities for the Disabled with facilities for the Disabled Disabled use only	▽ ▽ ▽
Viewpoint	⋇ ※
Educational Establishment	▢
Hospital or Healthcare Building	▢
Industrial Building	▢
Leisure or Recreational Facility	▢
Place of Interest	▢
Public Building	▢
Shopping Centre or Market	▢
Other Selected Buildings	▢

SCALE

Map Pages 4-5 1:9,500

0 — ⅛ — ¼ — ⅜ Mile

0 — 100 — 200 — 300 — 400 — 500 Metres

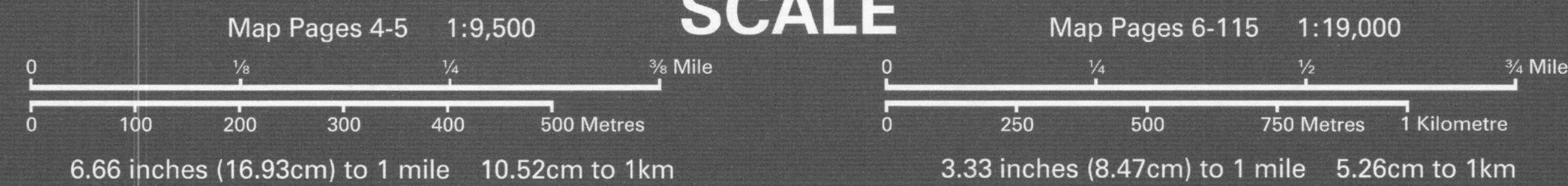

6.66 inches (16.93cm) to 1 mile   10.52cm to 1km

Map Pages 6-115 1:19,000

0 — ¼ — ½ — ¾ Mile

0 — 250 — 500 — 750 Metres — 1 Kilometre

3.33 inches (8.47cm) to 1 mile   5.26cm to 1km

EDITION 5 2017

Copyright © Geographers' A-Z Map Co. Ltd.

© Crown copyright and database rights 2016 OS 100017302.

Safety camera information supplied by www.PocketGPSWorld.com.
Speed Camera Location Database Copyright 2016 © PocketGPSWorld.com

A-Z Az AtoZ
registered trade marks of
Geographers' A-Z Map Company Ltd

www./az.co.uk

IRISH SEA

LIVERPOOL BAY

LARGE SCALE
4 **5**
LIVERPOOL CITY CENTRE

6 SOUTHPORT
7
8
9 Holmes
Banks
Marshside
Crossens
Churchtown
Mere Brow
Holmeswood
High Park

10
11 Hillside
Birkdale
12
13 Bescar
14 Smithy Lane Ends
15 Rufford
Shirdley Hill
Scarisbrick
Burscough Bridge
Hoscar
Ainsdale-on-Sea
Ainsdale
Woodvale

16
17
18 Halsall
19 Pinfold
Hurlston Green
20
21 Lathom
Freshfield
Haskayne
Bangor's Green
Primrose Hill
Clieves Hills
ORMSKIRK
Ring o'Bells
Burscough

24
25
26 Downholland Cross
27 Town Green
28 Aughton Park
Westhead
Scarth Hill
29 Blaguegate
Hightown
Lady Green
Ince Blundell
Great Altcar
Lydiate
Aughton
Royal Oak
Bickerstaffe

32
33
34
35
36 Melling Mount
Tower Hill
37
Little Crosby
Great Crosby
Thornton
Sefton
Netherton
MAGHULL
Homer Green
Lunt
Moss Side
Melling
Waddicar
KIRKBY
Barrow Nook

42
43 BOOTLE
44
45 Fazakerley
46 Southdene
Croxteth Park
47 Knowsley
Waterloo
Seaforth
CROSBY
Litherland
Orrell
Aintree
Walton
Norris Green
West Derby

FORMBY
Formby Point
Crosby Channel

WALLASEY
New Brighton
Kirkdale
Anfield
Everton
Old Swan
Knotty Ash

54
55
56 Liscard
Egremont
57 (Kingsway)
58 LIVERPOOL (Queensway)
59
60
61 HUYTON
Leasowe
Moreton
Seacombe
Mersey Tunnel
Wavertree

HOYLAKE
Meols
Greasby
Upton
Woodchurch
BIRKENHEAD
Oxton
Claughton
Toxteth
Sefton Park
Childwall
Gateacre

70
71 Newton
Frankby
72
73 Tranmere
Rock Ferry
74 Dingle
75 Mossley Hill
Aigburth
76 Allerton
Woolton
77
WEST KIRBY
Grange
Prenton
Storeton
New Ferry
Otterspool
Grassendale
Halewood
Caldy
Irby

Thurstaston
Pensby
Barnston
Thingwall
Brimstage
BEBINGTON
Port Sunlight
Spital
Garston
Hunt's Cross
Speke

86
87 HESWALL
88
89
90
91
92
93
Gayton
Thornton Hough
Bromborough
Eastham Ferry
Liverpool John Lennon
Brookhurst
Eastham

Parkgate
Raby
Willaston
Hooton
Little Sutton
Overpool
ELLESMERE PORT
Ince

100 NESTON
101
102
103
104
105
Little Neston
Ness
Burton
Whitby
Wolverham
Whitbyheath
Stanlow
Elton
Thornton-le-Moors
Stoak

Capenhurst
Woodbank
Backford
Picton

110
111
112
113

Point of Ayr

Greenfield (Maes-glas)
Holywell (Treffynnon)
Bagillt
Flint (Y Fflint)

ENGLAND
WALES
Shotwick

CONNAH'S QUAY

RIVER DEE (AFON DYFRDWY)
RIVER MERSEY

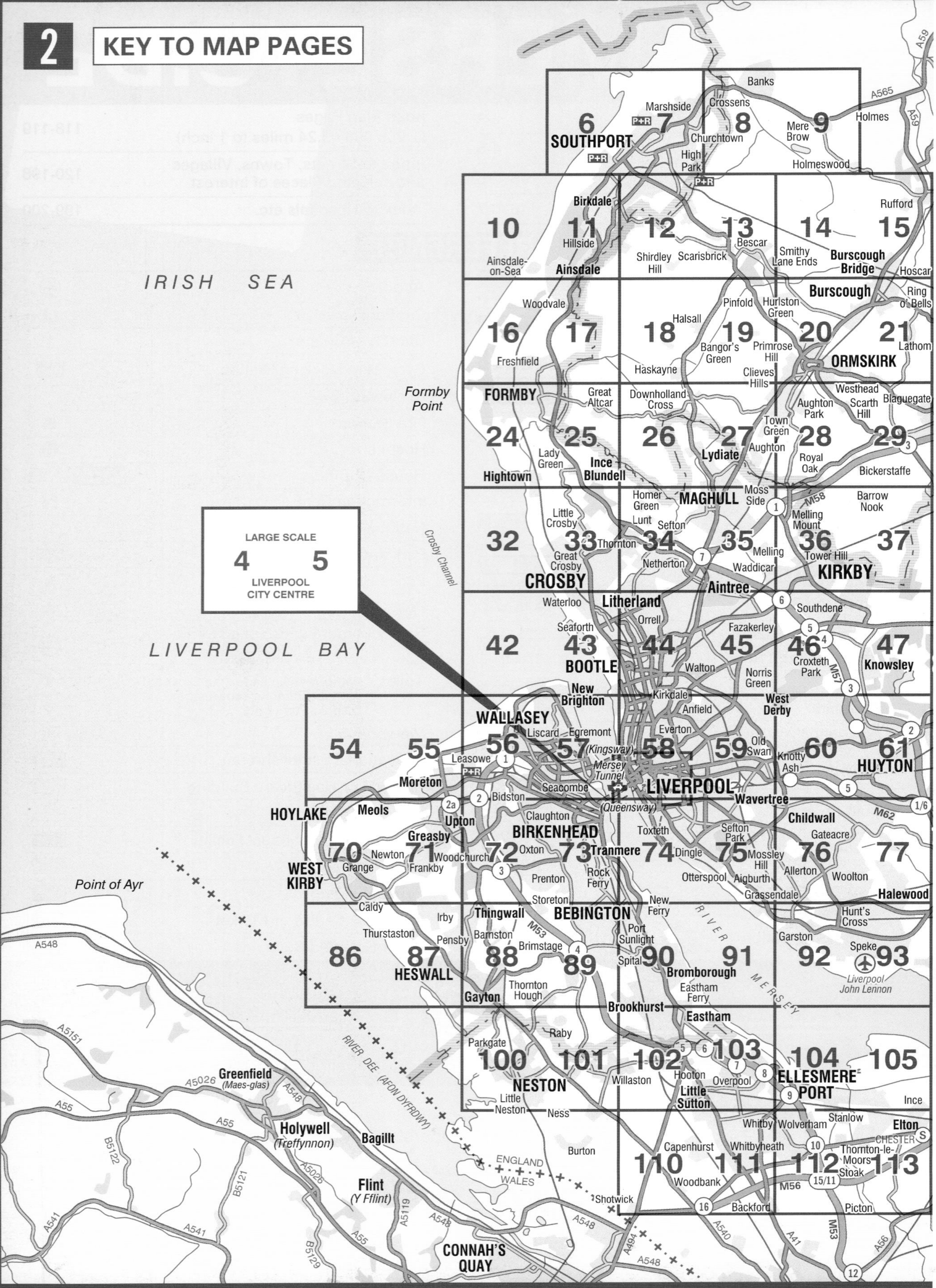

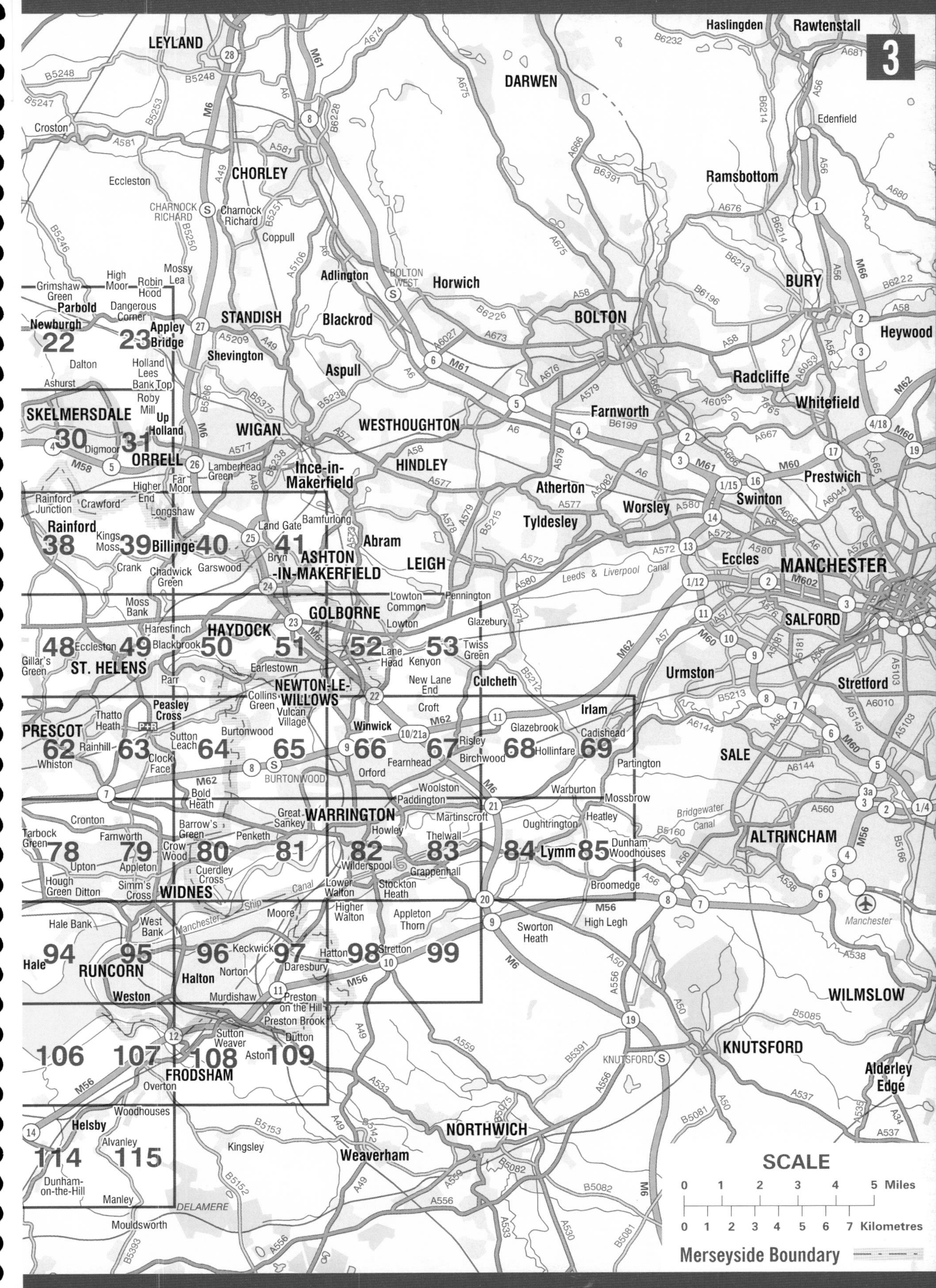
LEYLAND
Haslingden
Rawtenstall
DARWEN
Edenfield
Croston
Eccleston
CHORLEY
CHARNOCK RICHARD
Charnock Richard
Coppull
Ramsbottom
BURY
Adlington
BOLTON WEST
Horwich
Grimshaw Green
High Moor
Robin Hood
Mossy Lea
Parbold
Dangerous Corner
Newburgh
Appley Bridge
STANDISH
Blackrod
BOLTON
Heywood
22
23
Dalton
Shevington
Aspull
Holland Lees
Ashurst
Bank Top
Roby Mill
Radcliffe
SKELMERSDALE
Up Holland
Whitefield
WIGAN
WESTHOUGHTON
Farnworth
30
31
Digmoor
ORRELL
Lamberhead Green
Ince-in-Makerfield
HINDLEY
Prestwich
Higher End
Far Moor
Atherton
Swinton
Rainford Junction
Crawford
Longshaw
Worsley
Tyldesley
Rainford
Kings Moss
Land Gate
Bamfurlong
Abram
38
39
Billinge
40
41
Bryn
ASHTON-IN-MAKERFIELD
LEIGH
Eccles
MANCHESTER
Crank
Chadwick Green
Garswood
Leeds & Liverpool Canal
Moss Bank
Lowton Common
Pennington
GOLBORNE
SALFORD
Haresfinch
HAYDOCK
Lowton
Glazebury
48
Eccleston
49
Blackbrook
50
51
52
Lane Head
Kenyon
53
Twiss Green
Gillar's Green
ST. HELENS
Earlestown
Urmston
Parr
New Lane End
Culcheth
Stretford
NEWTON-LE-WILLOWS
Collins Green
Peasley Cross
Vulcan Village
Croft
Irlam
Thatto Heath
PRESCOT
Sutton Leach
Burtonwood
Winwick
Glazebrook
Cadishead
62
Rainhill
63
Clock Face
64
65
66
67
Risley
68
Hollinfare
69
Whiston
Fearnhead
Birchwood
Partington
SALE
BURTONWOOD
Orford
Bold Heath
Woolston
Paddington
Warburton
Mossbrow
Cronton
Great Sankey
WARRINGTON
Martinscroft
Heatley
Tarbock Green
Farnworth
Barrow's Green
Penketh
Howley
Thelwall
Oughtrington
Bridgewater Canal
ALTRINCHAM
78
79
Crow Wood
80
81
82
83
84
Lymm
85
Dunham Woodhouses
Upton
Appleton
Cuerdley Cross
Wilderspool
Grappenhall
Hough Green
Ditton
Simm's Cross
WIDNES
Lower Walton
Stockton Heath
Broomedge
Canal
Manchester Ship Canal
Higher Walton
Hale Bank
West Bank
Moore
Appleton Thorn
High Legh
Swarton Heath
Manchester
94
Hale
95
RUNCORN
96
Keckwick
97
Daresbury
Hatton
98
Stretton
99
Halton
Norton
Weston
Murdishaw
Preston on the Hill
WILMSLOW
Preston Brook
Dutton
Sutton Weaver
KNUTSFORD
106
107
108
FRODSHAM
Aston
109
KNUTSFORD
Alderley Edge
Overton
Woodhouses
Helsby
NORTHWICH
Alvanley
114
115
Kingsley
Weaverham
Dunham-on-the-Hill
Manley
DELAMERE
Mouldsworth
SCALE
0 1 2 3 4 5 Miles
0 1 2 3 4 5 6 7 Kilometres
Merseyside Boundary

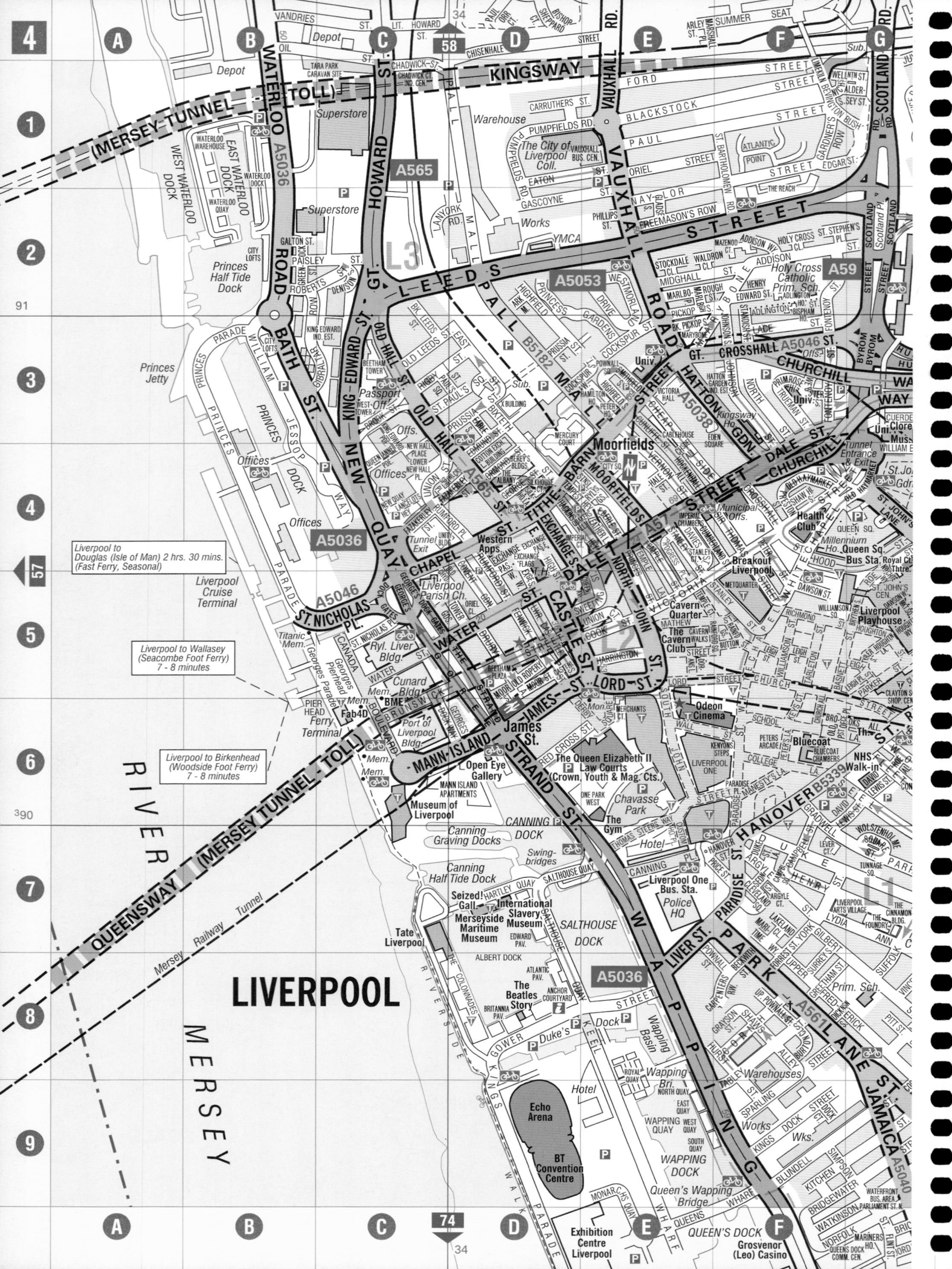

LIVERPOOL
RIVER MERSEY
Liverpool to Douglas (Isle of Man) 2 hrs. 30 mins. (Fast Ferry, Seasonal)
Liverpool to Wallasey (Seacombe Foot Ferry) 7 - 8 minutes
Liverpool to Birkenhead (Woodside Foot Ferry) 7 - 8 minutes
57
58
74
KINGSWAY
(MERSEY TUNNEL - TOLL)
QUEENSWAY (MERSEY TUNNEL TOLL)
Mersey Railway Tunnel
WATERLOO ROAD
BATH ST.
NEW QUAY
GT. HOWARD ST.
LEEDS STREET
VAUXHALL RD.
SCOTLAND RD.
GT. CROSSHALL ST.
CHURCHILL WAY
DALE ST.
TITHEBARN ST.
MOORFIELDS
CHAPEL ST.
WATER ST.
JAMES ST.
CASTLE ST.
NORTH JOHN ST.
LORD ST.
STRAND ST.
MANN ISLAND
WAPPING
HANOVER ST.
PARADISE ST.
PARK LANE
JAMAICA ST.
ST. NICHOLAS PL.
A5036
A565
A5053
A59
A5046
A5038
A57
B5182
B5339
A561
A5040
Princes Half Tide Dock
Princes Jetty
Liverpool Cruise Terminal
Titanic Mem.
Georges Pierhead
Pier Head Ferry Terminal
Cunard Bldg.
Ryl. Liver Bldg.
Port of Liverpool Bldg.
Museum of Liverpool
Open Eye Gallery
Liverpool Parish Ch.
Moorfields
Cavern Quarter
The Cavern Club
Breakout Liverpool
Odeon Cinema
Bluecoat
Liverpool One
Liverpool One Bus. Sta.
Police HQ
Chavasse Park
The Queen Elizabeth II Law Courts (Crown, Youth & Mag. Cts.)
Canning Dock
Canning Graving Docks
Canning Half Tide Dock
International Slavery Museum
Merseyside Maritime Museum
Tate Liverpool
Seized! Gall.
Salthouse Dock
Albert Dock
The Beatles Story
Duke's Dock
Wapping Basin
Wapping Dock
Queen's Wapping Bridge
Echo Arena
BT Convention Centre
Exhibition Centre Liverpool
Grosvenor (Leo) Casino
Queen's Dock
Warehouses
Holy Cross Catholic Prim. Sch.
The City of Liverpool Coll.
Queen Sq. Bus Sta.
Liverpool Playhouse
Millennium Ho.
Municipal Offs.
Health Club
NHS Walk-in
Tunnel Entrance & Exit
Superstore
Warehouse
Works
YMCA
Depot
Offices
Passport Off.
Western Apps
Mercury Court
Kingsway Ho.
Univ.
Hotel
The Gym
Swing-bridges
Prim. Sch.

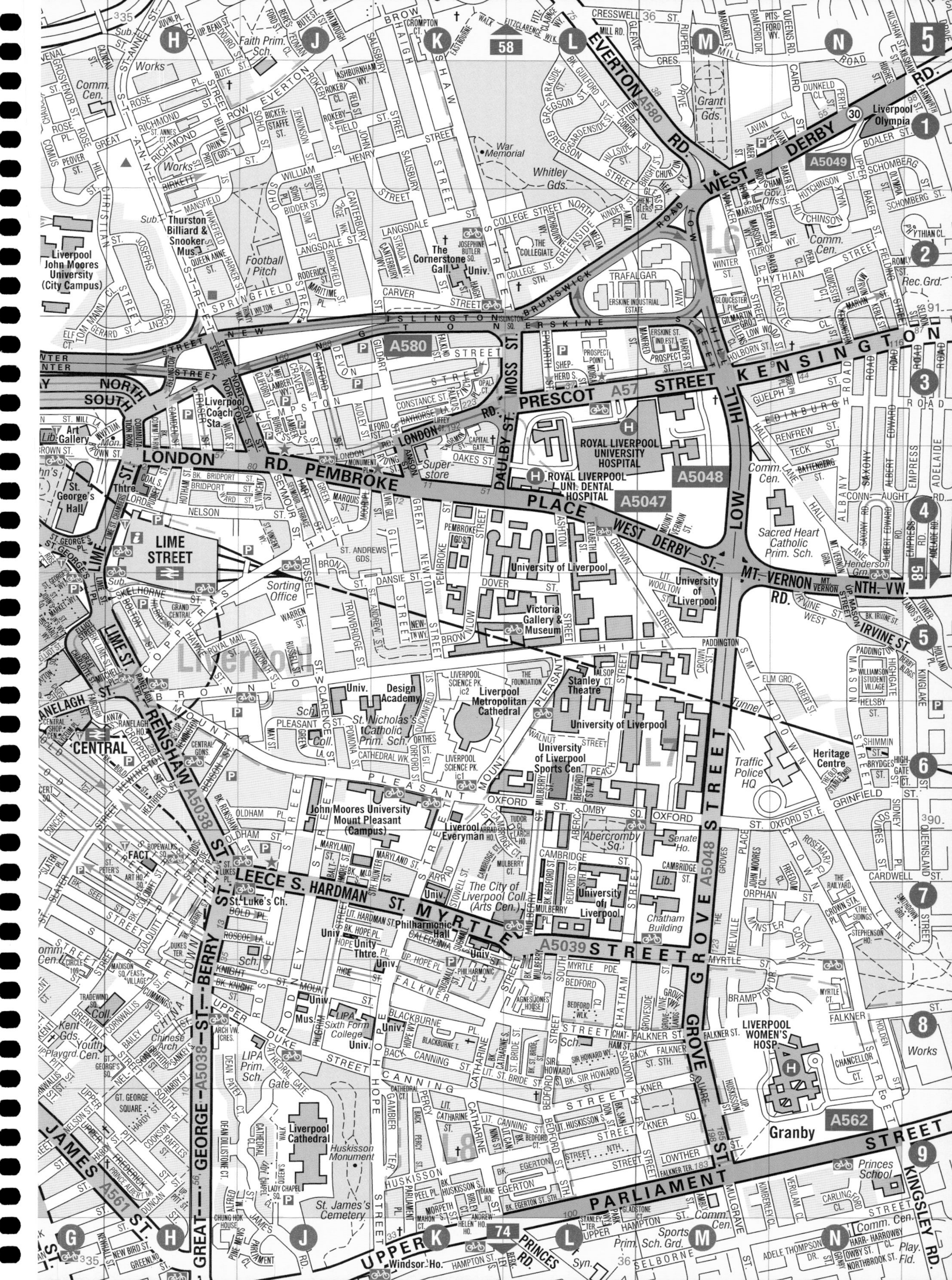

58
Faith Prim. Sch.
Works
Comm. Cen.
EVERTON RD.
A580
Grant Gds.
Liverpool Olympia
WEST DERBY RD.
A5049
War Memorial
Whitley Gds.
Thurston Billiard & Snooker Mus.
Liverpool John Moores University (City Campus)
Football Pitch
The Cornerstone Gall.
Univ.
THE COLLEGIATE
TRAFALGAR WAY
ERSKINE INDUSTRIAL ESTATE
L6
Comm. Cen.
Rec. Grd.
ISLINGTON
ERSKINE ST.
A580
PRESCOT STREET
A57
KENSINGTON
NORTH
SOUTH
Liverpool Coach Sta.
Art Gallery
LONDON RD.
PEMBROKE PLACE
Superstore
ROYAL LIVERPOOL UNIVERSITY HOSPITAL
ROYAL LIVERPOOL UNI. DENTAL HOSPITAL
A5048
A5047
WEST DERBY ST.
St. George's Hall
Thtre.
LIME STREET
LIME ST.
Sacred Heart Catholic Prim. Sch.
University of Liverpool
Sorting Office
Victoria Gallery & Museum
University of Liverpool
MT. VERNON RD.
IRVINE ST.
Liverpool
Design Academy
Liverpool Metropolitan Cathedral
Stanley Theatre
University of Liverpool
Tunnel
CENTRAL
St. Nicholas's Catholic Prim. Sch.
University of Liverpool Sports Cen.
Traffic Police HQ
Heritage Centre
RENSHAW ST.
A5038
John Moores University Mount Pleasant (Campus)
Liverool Everyman
Abercromby Sq.
Senate Ho.
Lib.
GROVE STREET
A5048
FACT
LEECE S.
HARDMAN ST.
MYRTLE STREET
A5039
St. Luke's Ch.
Philharmonic Hall
Unity Thtre.
The City of Liverpool Coll. (Arts Cen.)
University of Liverpool
Chatham Building
L7
LIPA Sixth Form College
Chinese Arch
Youth Cen.
Kent Gds.
LIPA Prim. Sch.
Gate
LIVERPOOL WOMEN'S HOSP.
Works
Liverpool Cathedral
Huskisson Monument
St. James's Cemetery
L8
Granby
A562
PARLIAMENT ST.
STREET
Princes School
KINGSLEY RD.
GREAT GEORGE ST.
A5038
JAMES ST.
A561
UPPER
74
PRINCES RD.
Windsor Ho.
Sports Grd.
Comm. Cen.
Syn.
Play. Fld.
G
H
J
K
L
M
N
1
2
3
4
5
6
7
8
9

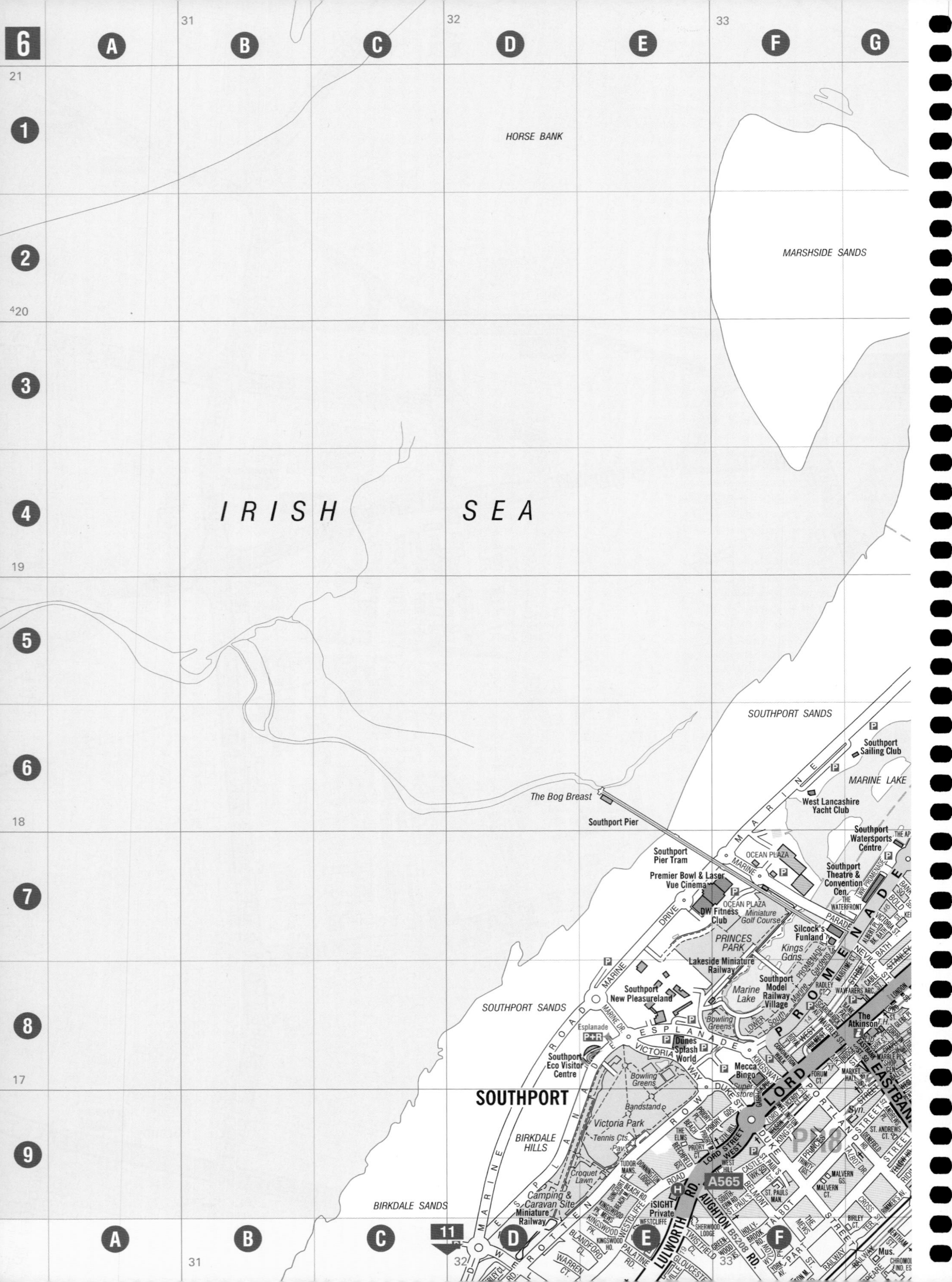

A   B   C   D   E   F   G

6

31   32   33

21

1

HORSE BANK

2

MARSHSIDE SANDS

⁴20

3

4   I R I S H   S E A

19

5

SOUTHPORT SANDS

P

Southport
Sailing Club

6   P

MARINE LAKE

West Lancashire
Yacht Club

The Bog Breast

18   Southport
Pier   Southport
Watersports
Centre

Southport Pier   THE AP

P

Southport
Pier Tram   OCEAN PLAZA

7   Premier Bowl & Laser
Vue Cinema   Southport
Theatre &
Convention
Cen

THE
WATERFRONT

P   OCEAN PLAZA

DW Fitness   Miniature
Club   Golf Course

Silcock's
Funland

PRINCES
PARK   Kings
Gdns.

P

Lakeside Miniature
Railway

Southport
Model
Railway
Village

Southport
New Pleasureland   Marine
Lake

The
Atkinson

8   SOUTHPORT SANDS   Bowling
Greens

P

Esplanade   P+R   P
Dunes
Splash
World

Southport
Eco Visitor
Centre   P   Mecca
Bingo

17   Super
store

Bowling
Greens

EASTBAN

SOUTHPORT

Bandstand

Victoria Park

9   BIRKDALE
HILLS   Tennis Cts.

St. Andrews

Croquet
Lawn

Camping &
Caravan Site
Miniature
Railway   **11**   iSIGHT
Private

A565

Mus.

BIRKDALE SANDS

A   B   C   **11**   D   E   F

31   32   33

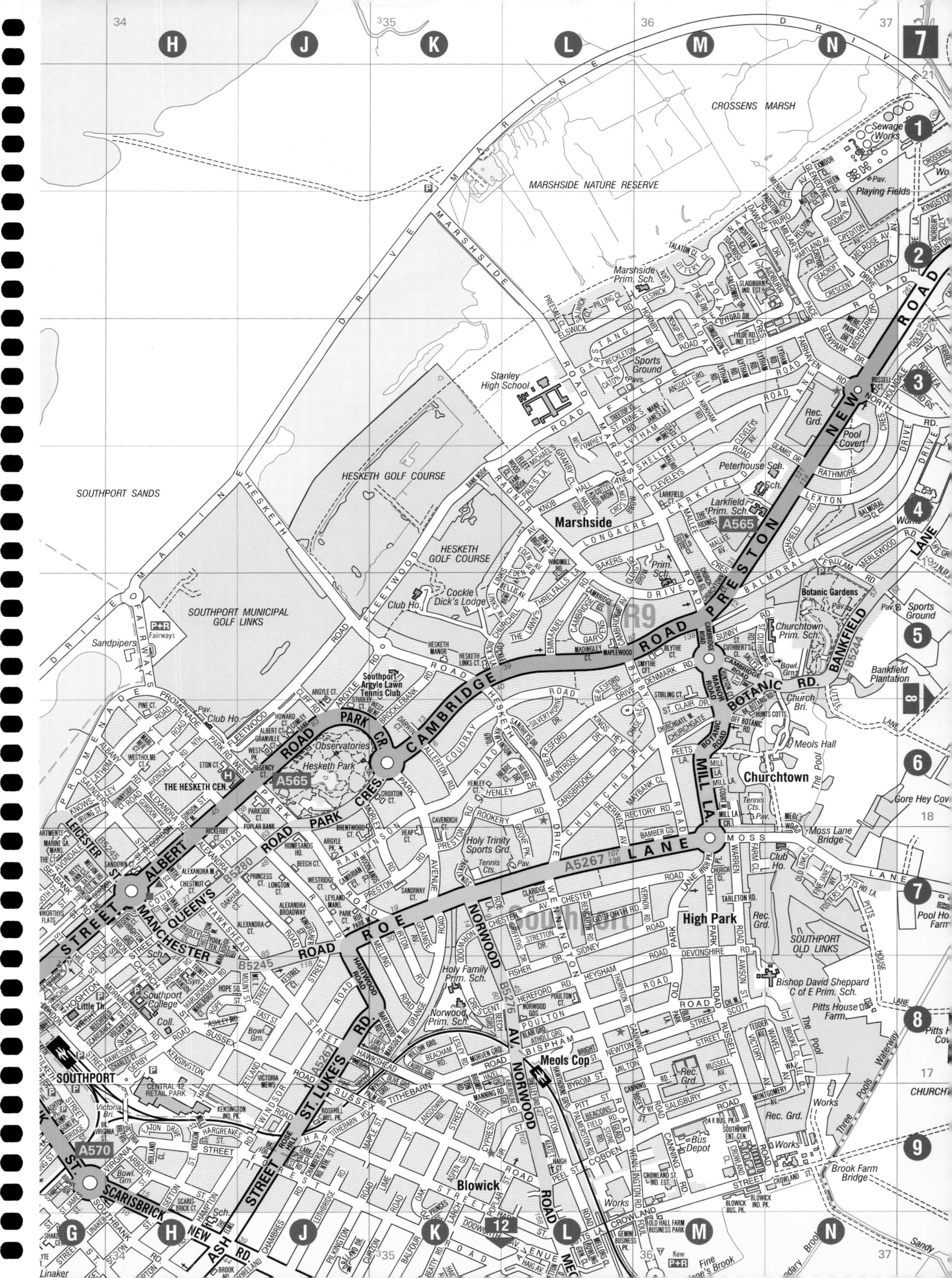

H
J
K
L
M
N
G
34
35
36
37
1
2
3
4
5
6
7
8
9
12
CROSSENS MARSH
Sewage Works
MARSHSIDE NATURE RESERVE
Playing Fields
MARINE DRIVE
MARSHSIDE ROAD
Marshside Prim. Sch.
Stanley High School
Sports Ground
FYLDE ROAD
NEW ROAD
PRESTON NEW ROAD
Rec. Grd.
Pool Covert
Peterhouse Sch.
Larkfield Prim. Sch.
SOUTHPORT SANDS
HESKETH GOLF COURSE
Marshside
A565
HESKETH DRIVE
FLEETWOOD ROAD
Club Ho.
Cockle Dick's Lodge
SOUTHPORT MUNICIPAL GOLF LINKS
Sandpipers
P+R Fairways
Botanic Gardens
Sports Ground
Churchtown Prim. Sch.
BANKFIELD LANE
B5244
Bankfield Plantation
BOTANIC RD.
Church Bri.
Meols Hall
Churchtown
The Pool
Gore Hey Cov.
Moss Lane Bridge
MOSS LANE
CAMBRIDGE ROAD
Southport Argyle Lawn Tennis Club
Observatories
Hesketh Park
PARK CRES.
THE HESKETH CEN.
ALBERT ROAD
A565
PROMENADE
LEICESTER ST.
B5245
B5280
QUEEN'S ROAD
Holy Trinity Sports Grd.
A5267
ROE LANE
MANCHESTER ROAD
CHURCHGATE
MILL LA.
High Park
Rec. Grd.
SOUTHPORT OLD LINKS
Bishop David Sheppard C of E Prim. Sch.
Pitts House Farm
Pool Ho. Farm
Southport
NORWOOD ROAD
B5276
Holy Family Prim. Sch.
Norwood Prim. Sch.
Southport College
Little Th.
ST. LUKE'S RD.
SOUTHPORT
CENTRAL 12 RETAIL PARK
KENSINGTON IND. PK.
Meols Cop
Bus Depot
Works
Rec. Grd.
Three Pools Waterway
Brook Farm Bridge
Blowick
A570
SCARISBRICK NEW RD.
ASH STREET
NORWOOD ROAD
CROWLAND ST.

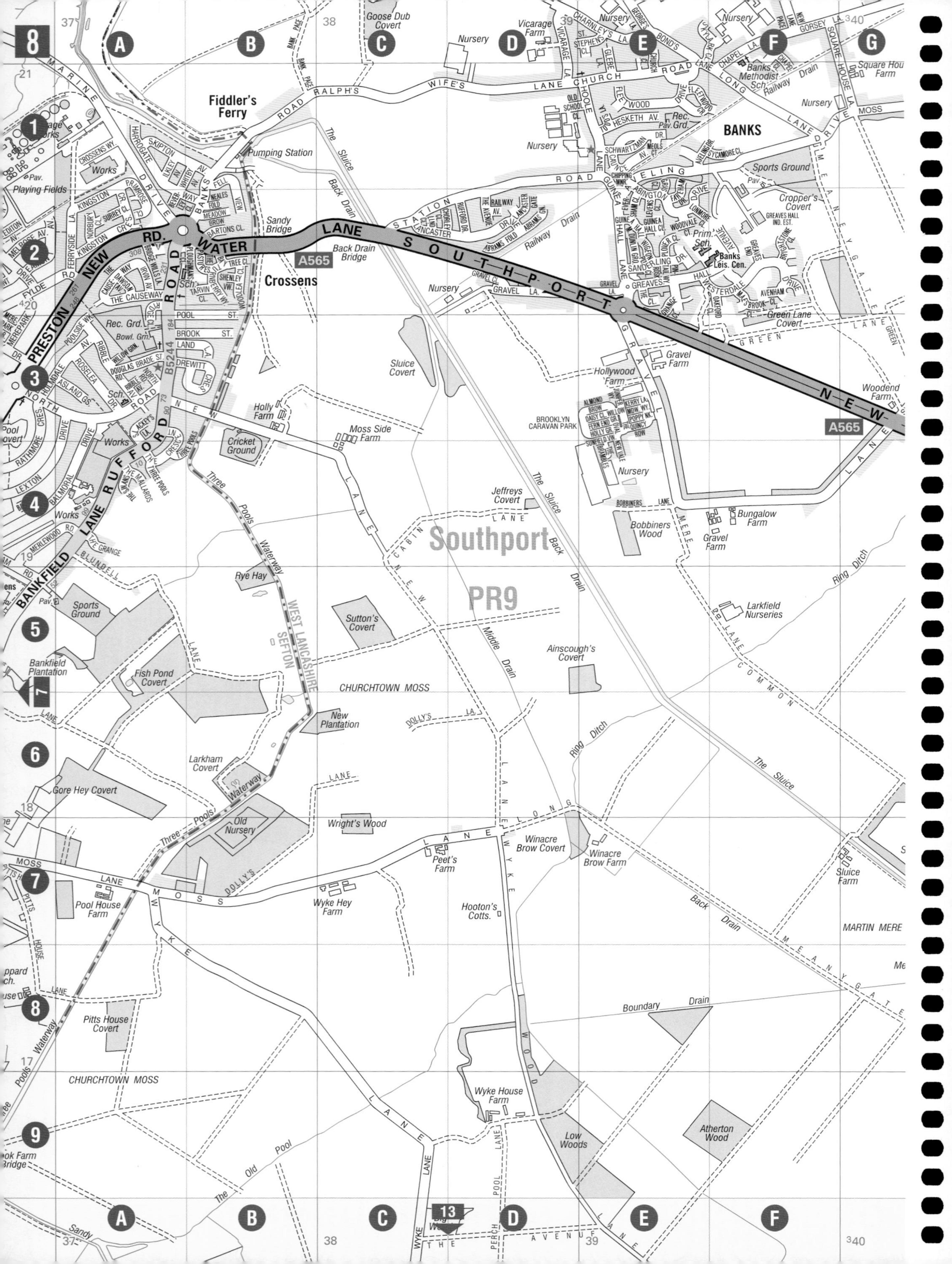
8
Fiddler's Ferry
Crossens
BANKS
Southport
PR9
A565
B5244
Pumping Station
Sandy Bridge
Back Drain Bridge
Goose Dub Covert
Vicarage Farm
Nursery
Banks Methodist Sch.
Square House Farm
Sports Ground
Cropper's Covert
Green Lane Covert
Gravel Farm
Hollywood Farm
Woodend Farm
BROOKLYN CARAVAN PARK
Holly Farm
Moss Side Farm
Cricket Ground
Sluice Covert
Jeffreys Covert
Bungalow Farm
Bobbiners Wood
Larkfield Nurseries
Rye Hay
Sutton's Covert
Ainscough's Covert
CHURCHTOWN MOSS
New Plantation
Larkham Covert
Fish Pond Covert
Bankfield Plantation
Gore Hey Covert
Old Nursery
Wright's Wood
Winacre Brow Covert
Winacre Brow Farm
Peet's Farm
Wyke Hey Farm
Hooton's Cotts.
Pool House Farm
Pitts House Covert
Sluice Farm
MARTIN MERE
Boundary Drain
Wyke House Farm
Low Woods
Atherton Wood
The Sluice
Back Drain
Middle Drain
Ring Ditch
Three Pools Waterway
WEST LANCASHIRE
SEFTON
The Old Pool
SOUTHPORT NEW LANE
WATER LANE
PRESTON NEW RD.
RUFFORD ROAD
BANKFIELD LANE
RALPH'S WIFE'S LANE
CHURCH ROAD
STATION ROAD
GRAVEL LANE
CABIN LANE
LONG LANE
WYKE LANE
WYKE WOOD LANE
MOSS LANE
DOLLY'S LANE
MEANYGATE
COMMON LANE
MERE LANE
BOBBINERS LANE
MOSS LANE
THE AVENUE
POOL LANE
Works
Playing Fields
Rec. Grd.
Sch.
Banks Leis. Cen.
Prim. Sch.
7
13

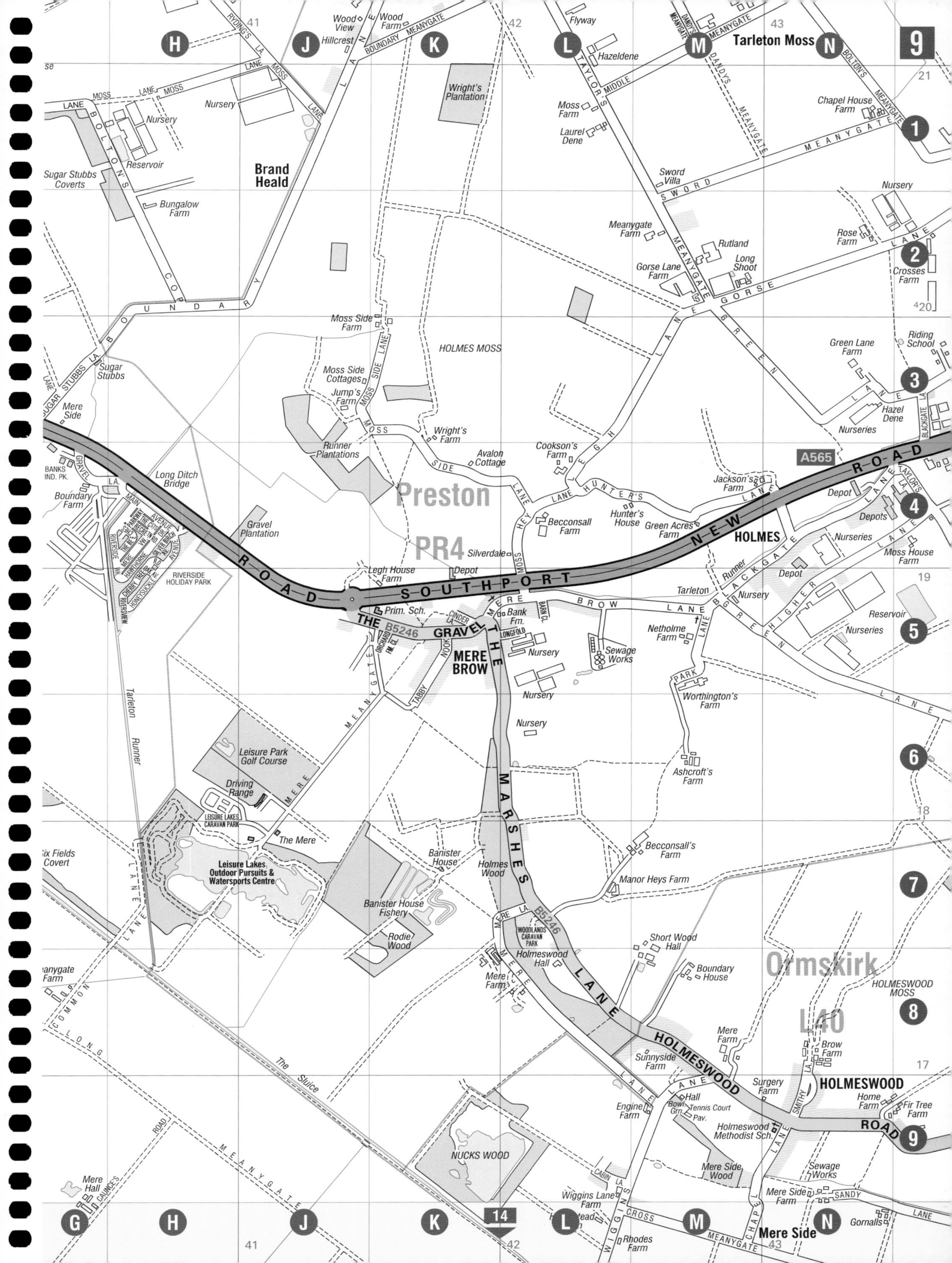
Tarleton Moss
Brand Heald
Preston
PR4
HOLMES
MERE BROW
Ormskirk
L40
HOLMESWOOD
Mere Side
HOLMESWOOD MOSS
HOLMES MOSS
NUCKS WOOD
SOUTHPORT NEW ROAD
A565
B5246
THE GRAVEL
THE MARSHES
HOLMESWOOD ROAD
BOUNDARY LANE
BOLTON'S COP
MEANYGATE
GORSE LANE
GREEN LANE
Leisure Lakes Outdoor Pursuits & Watersports Centre
Leisure Park Golf Course
Driving Range
The Mere
Banister House Fishery
Rodie Wood
Holmes Wood
RIVERSIDE HOLIDAY PARK
Tarleton Runner
The Sluice
Sugar Stubbs Coverts
Wright's Plantation
Gravel Plantation
Runner Plantations
Long Ditch Bridge
Sewage Works
Reservoir
Nurseries
Depot
Holmeswood Methodist Sch.
Prim. Sch.
Tennis Court
14

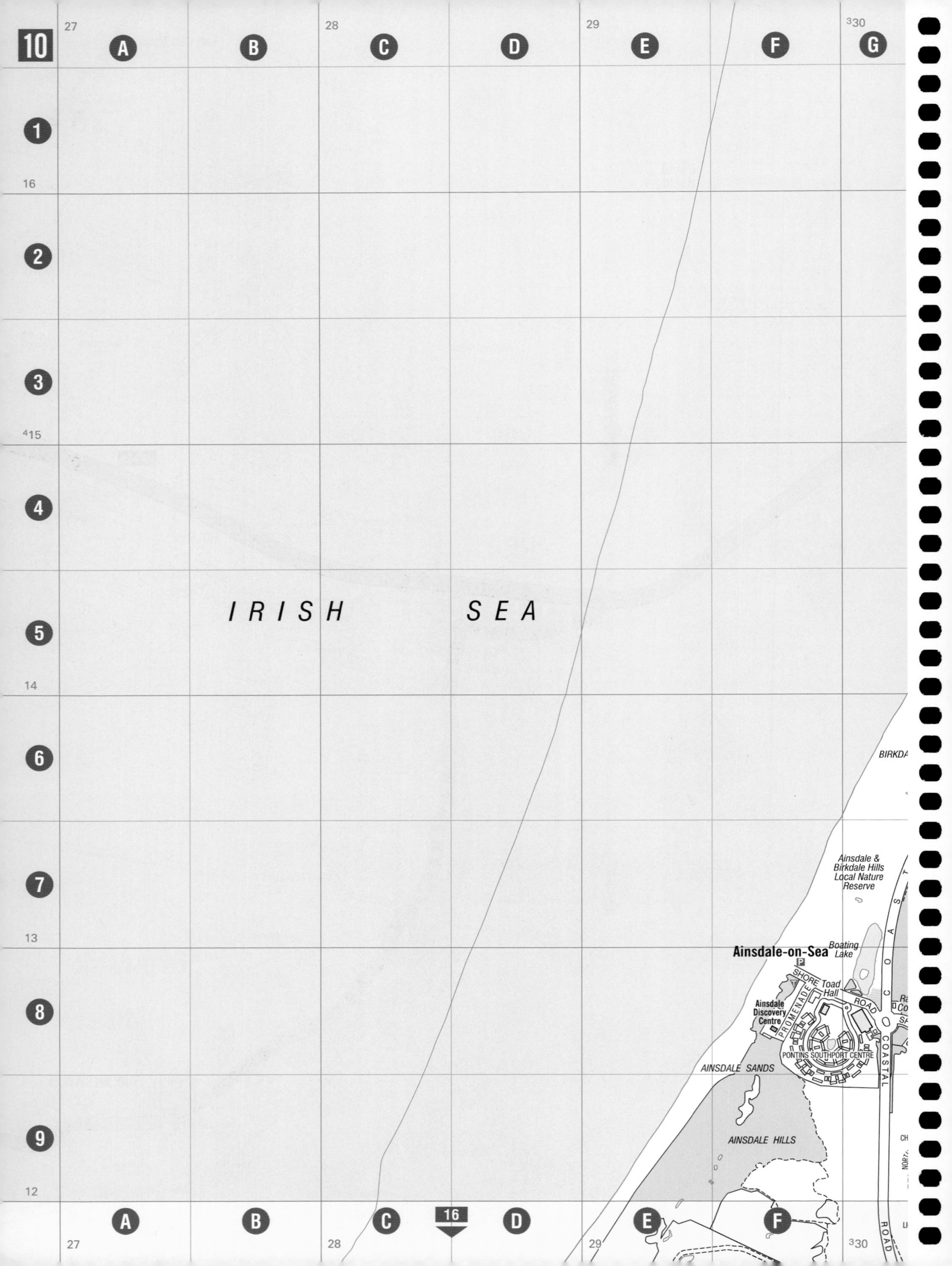

10

27 **A** 28 **B** **C** 29 **D** **E** 330 **F** **G**

16

415

14

I R I S H   S E A

13

BIRKDA

Ainsdale &
Birkdale Hills
Local Nature
Reserve

*Boating
Lake*

Ainsdale-on-Sea

SHORE   Toad
Hall

Ainsdale
Discovery
Centre

PONTINS SOUTHPORT CENTRE

AINSDALE SANDS

AINSDALE HILLS

12

A 27 **B** **C** 28 **16** **D** 29 **E** 330 **F**

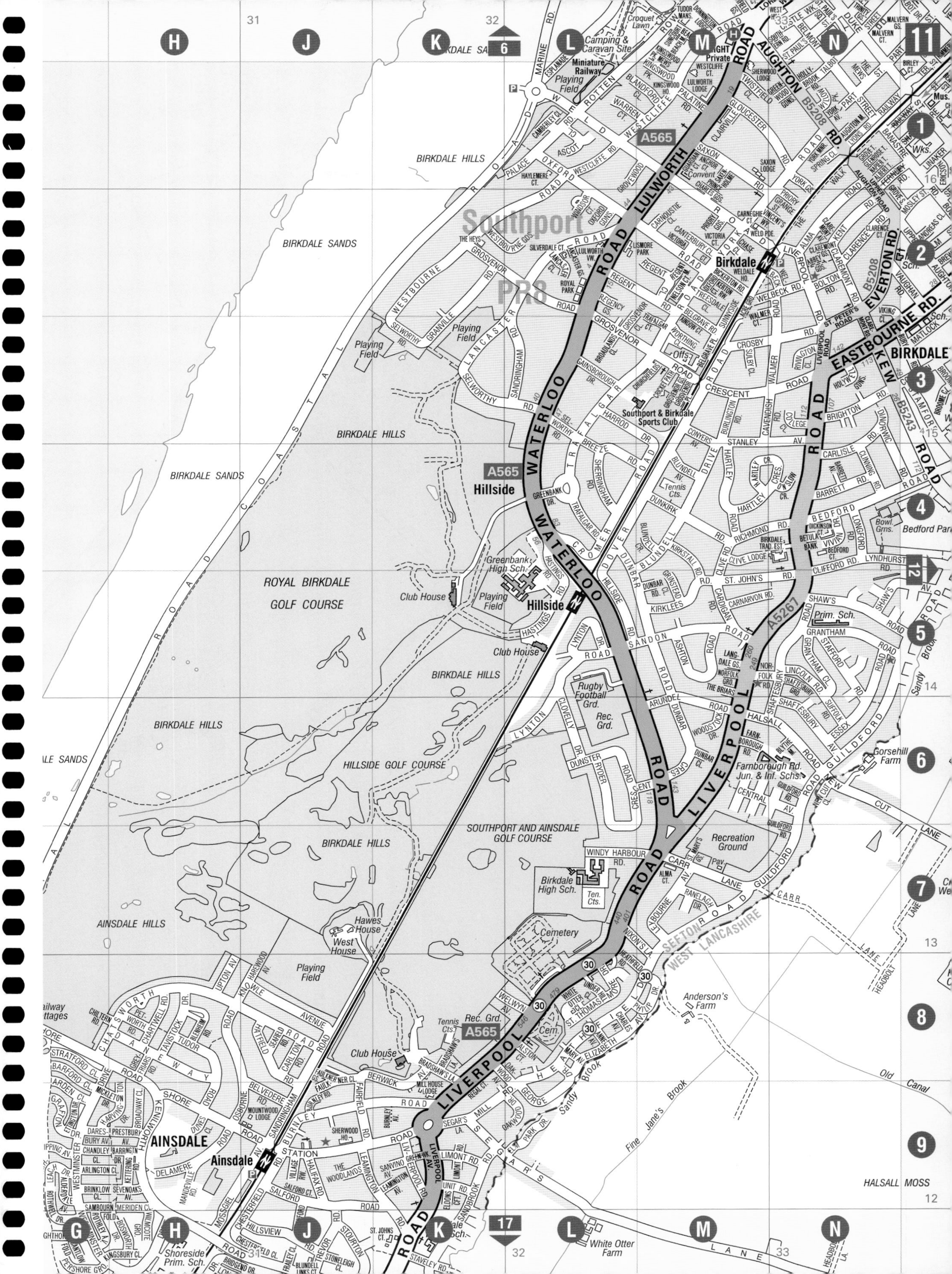

11
6
17
12
H
J
K
L
M
N
G
1
2
3
4
5
6
7
8
9
31
32
33
Southport
PR8
BIRKDALE
AINSDALE
Birkdale
Hillside
Ainsdale
BIRKDALE SANDS
BIRKDALE HILLS
AINSDALE HILLS
ROYAL BIRKDALE GOLF COURSE
HILLSIDE GOLF COURSE
SOUTHPORT AND AINSDALE GOLF COURSE
COASTAL ROAD
WATERLOO ROAD
LULWORTH ROAD
LIVERPOOL ROAD
EASTBOURNE RD.
KEW ROAD
EVERTON RD.
AUGHTON RD.
A565
A5267
B5208
B5243
Southport & Birkdale Sports Club
Greenbank High Sch.
Birkdale High Sch.
Club House
Playing Field
Rugby Football Grd.
Rec. Grd.
Recreation Ground
Cemetery
Hawes House
West House
Anderson's Farm
White Otter Farm
Gorsehill Farm
Farnborough Rd. Jun. & Inf. Schs.
Shoreside Prim. Sch.
Camping & Caravan Site
Miniature Railway
SEFTON
WEST LANCASHIRE
HALSALL MOSS
Old Canal
Fine Jane's Brook
Sandy Brook

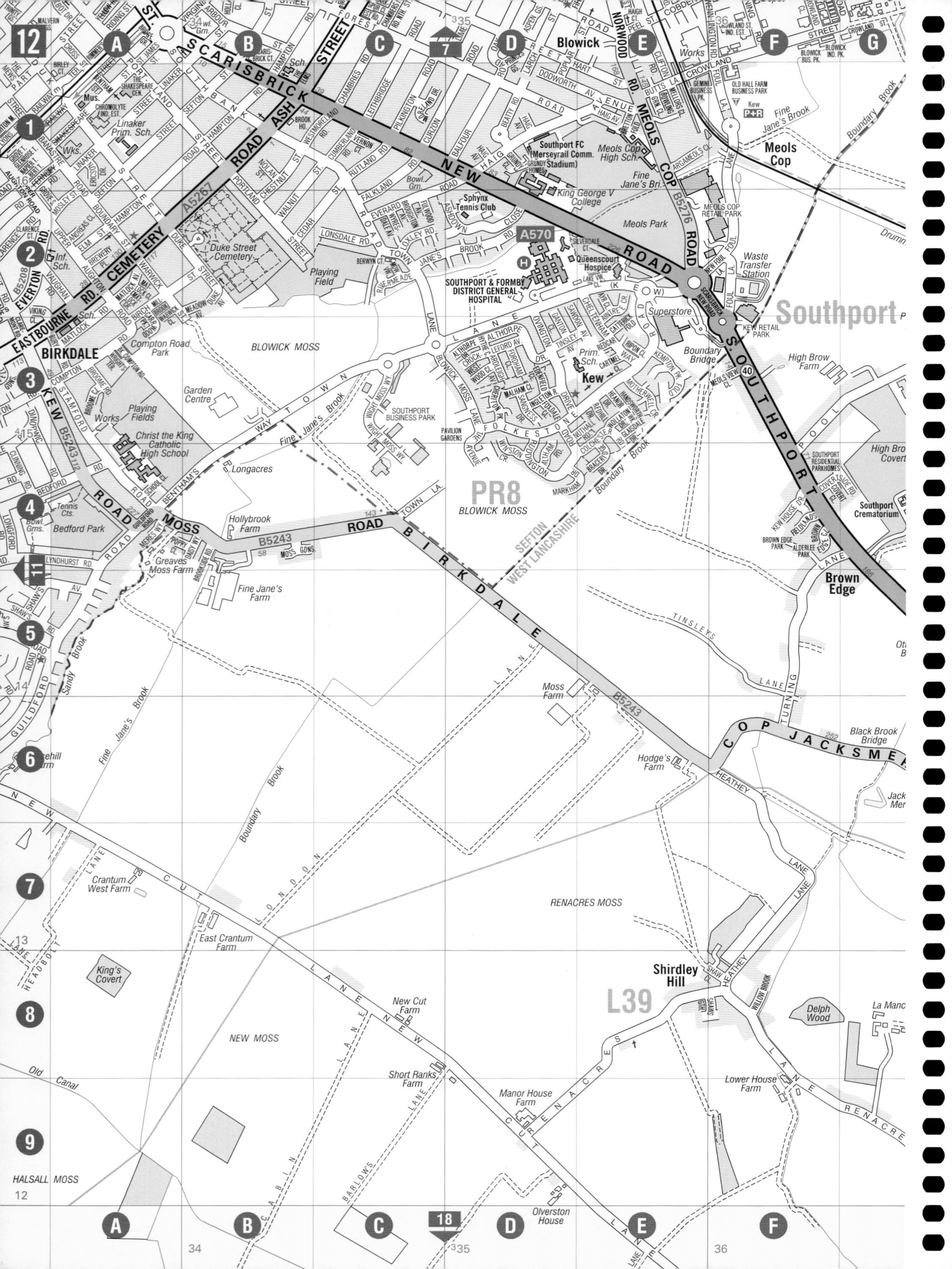
Blowick
Meols Cop
Southport
BIRKDALE
Kew
PR8
BLOWICK MOSS
Brown Edge
Shirdley Hill
L39
RENACRES MOSS
NEW MOSS
HALSALL MOSS
SCARISBRICK NEW ROAD
SOUTHPORT ROAD
BIRKDALE ROAD
MOSS ROAD
MEOLS COP RD.
NEW CUT LANE
RENACRES LANE
COP JACKSMEAD
Southport FC (Merseyrail Comm. Stadium)
King George V College
Meols Park
Queenscourt Hospice
SOUTHPORT & FORMBY DISTRICT GENERAL HOSPITAL
Duke Street Cemetery
Compton Road Park
Christ the King Catholic High School
Bedford Park
SOUTHPORT BUSINESS PARK
MEOLS COP RETAIL PARK
KEW RETAIL PARK
Waste Transfer Station
Southport Crematorium
SEFTON
WEST LANCASHIRE

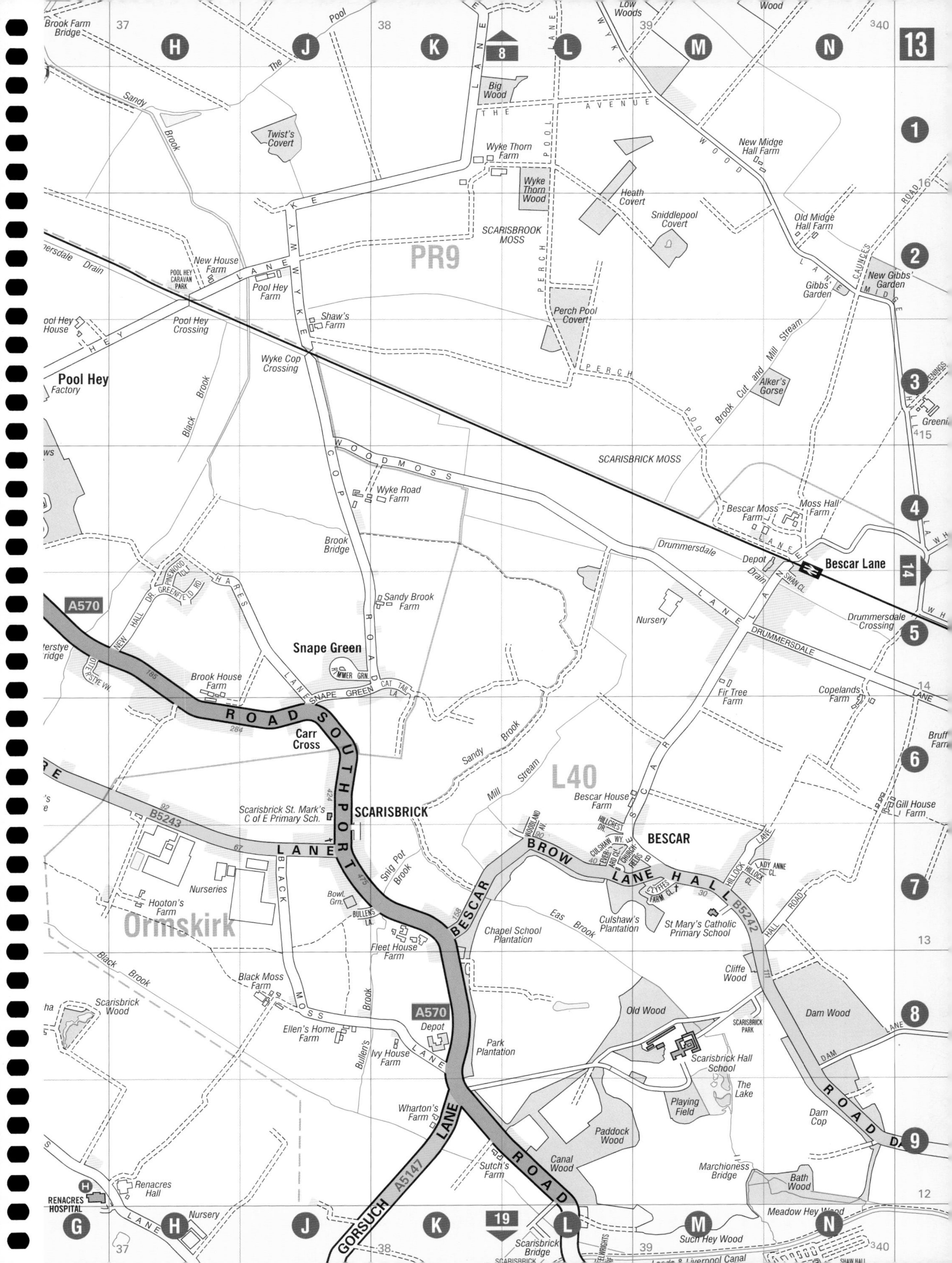

Brook Farm Bridge
Pool
The
Sandy
Brook
Twist's Covert
Big Wood
THE AVENUE
Wyke Thorn Farm
Wyke Thorn Wood
Heath Covert
Sniddlepool Covert
New Midge Hall Farm
Old Midge Hall Farm
SCARISBROOK MOSS
PR9
New House Farm
POOL HEY CARAVAN PARK
Pool Hey Farm
Pool Hey Crossing
Shaw's Farm
Perch Pool Covert
New Gibbs' Garden
Gibbs' Garden
Wyke Cop Crossing
Pool Hey
Factory
Black Brook
Alker's Gorse
Brook Cut and Mill Stream
SCARISBRICK MOSS
WOODMOSS
Wyke Road Farm
Bescar Moss Farm
Moss Hall Farm
Brook Bridge
Drummersdale
Depot
Bescar Lane
Nursery
Sandy Brook Farm
A570
Drummersdale Crossing
Snape Green
Brook House Farm
SNAPE GREEN
CAT TAIL LA
Fir Tree Farm
Copelands Farm
Carr Cross
SOUTHPORT ROAD
Sandy Brook
Mill Stream
L40
Bescar House Farm
Gill House Farm
B5243
Scarisbrick St. Mark's C of E Primary Sch.
SCARISBRICK
BESCAR
BROW LANE
HALL
B5242
Snig Pot Brook
Nurseries
Hooton's Farm
Ormskirk
Bowl. Grn.
BULLENS LA.
Chapel School Plantation
Eas Brook
Culshaw's Plantation
St Mary's Catholic Primary School
Fleet House Farm
Cliffe Wood
Black Brook
Black Moss Farm
Scarisbrick Wood
Old Wood
Dam Wood
A570
Depot
Ellen's Home Farm
Ivy House Farm
Park Plantation
SCARISBRICK PARK
Scarisbrick Hall School
The Lake
Playing Field
Wharton's Farm
Dam Cop
Paddock Wood
Canal Wood
Sutch's Farm
GORSUCH LANE
A5147
ROAD
Marchioness Bridge
Bath Wood
Renacres Hall
RENACRES HOSPITAL
Nursery
Meadow Hey Wood
Such Hey Wood
Scarisbrick Bridge
Leeds & Liverpool Canal

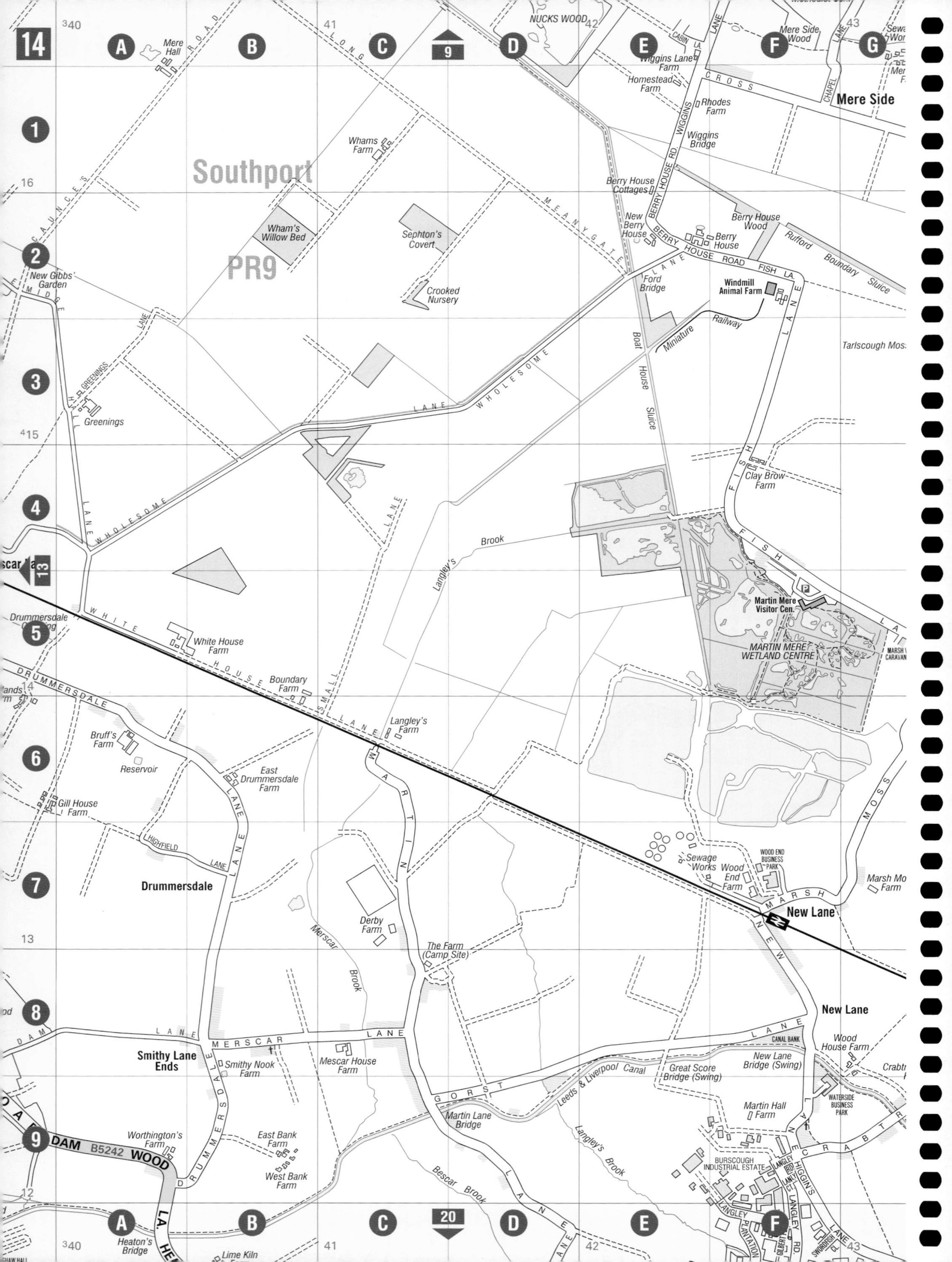

14
Southport
PR9
Mere Hall
Whams Farm
Wham's Willow Bed
Sephton's Covert
Crooked Nursery
New Gibbs' Garden
Greenings
NUCKS WOOD
Wiggins Lane Farm
Homestead Farm
Rhodes Farm
Wiggins Bridge
Mere Side
Mere Side Wood
Berry House Cottages
New Berry House
Berry House Wood
Berry House
Ford Bridge
Windmill Animal Farm
Miniature Railway
Boat House Sluice
Rufford Boundary Sluice
Tarlscough Moss
Clay Brow Farm
Langley's Brook
Martin Mere Visitor Cen.
MARTIN MERE WETLAND CENTRE
White House Farm
Boundary Farm
Langley's Farm
Bruff's Farm
Reservoir
East Drummersdale Farm
Gill House Farm
Drummersdale
Sewage Works
Wood End Farm
WOOD END BUSINESS PARK
Marsh Moss Farm
New Lane
Derby Farm
The Farm (Camp Site)
Mescar Brook
Smithy Lane Ends
Smithy Nook Farm
Mescar House Farm
Wood House Farm
New Lane Bridge (Swing)
Great Score Bridge (Swing)
Leeds & Liverpool Canal
Martin Hall Farm
WATERSIDE BUSINESS PARK
Martin Lane Bridge
Worthington's Farm
East Bank Farm
West Bank Farm
BURSCOUGH INDUSTRIAL ESTATE
Bescar Brook
Heaton's Bridge
Lime Kiln
WHOLESOME LANE
MEANYGATE
WHITE HOUSE LANE
SMALL LANE
DRUMMERSDALE LANE
HIGHFIELD LANE
MARTIN LANE
MERSCAR LANE
GORST LANE
MOSS LANE
MARSH LANE
NEW LANE
CANAL BANK
CRABTREE LANE
HIGGIN'S LANE
LANGLEY RD.
B5242
DAM WOOD LANE
FISH LANE
BERRY HOUSE ROAD
CROSS LANE
WIGGINS LANE

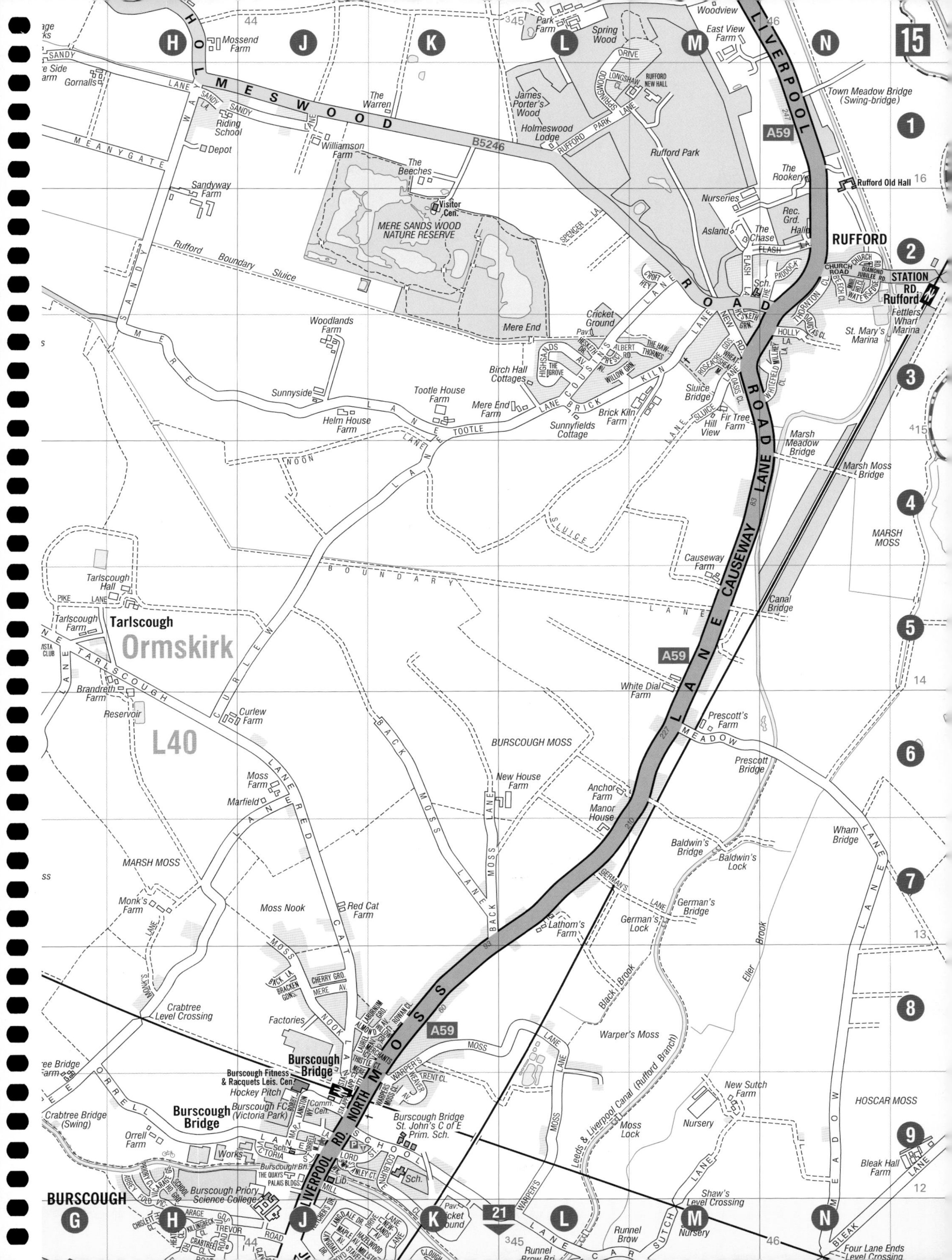

15
H
J
K
L
M
N
G
1
2
3
4
5
6
7
8
9
44
45
46
16
15
14
13
12
HOLMESWOOD
B5246
Mossend Farm
Gornalls
SANDY LANE
Riding School
Depot
MEANYGATE
Sandyway Farm
The Warren
Williamson Farm
The Beeches
Visitor Cen.
MERE SANDS WOOD NATURE RESERVE
Rufford Boundary Sluice
Mere End
Woodlands Farm
Sunnyside
Helm House Farm
Tootle House Farm
TOOTLE LANE
MERE LANE
NOON
Mere End Farm
Birch Hall Cottages
Sunnyfields Cottage
Brick Kiln Farm
BRICK KILN LANE
Cricket Ground
Park Farm
Spring Wood
James Porter's Wood
Holmeswood Lodge
RUFFORD PARK LANE
Rufford Park
RUFFORD NEW HALL
Woodview
East View Farm
LIVERPOOL ROAD
A59
Town Meadow Bridge (Swing-bridge)
The Rookery
Rufford Old Hall
Nurseries
Rec. Grd.
Hall
Asland
The Chase
RUFFORD
CHURCH ROAD
STATION RD.
Rufford
Fettlers Wharf Marina
St. Mary's Marina
Sluice Bridge
Hill View
Fir Tree Farm
Marsh Meadow Bridge
Marsh Moss Bridge
MARSH MOSS
CAUSEWAY LANE
Causeway Farm
Canal Bridge
BOUNDARY LANE
SLUICE
Tarlscough Hall
PIKE LANE
Tarlscough Farm
Tarlscough
Ormskirk
TARLSCOUGH LANE
Brandreth Farm
Reservoir
L40
CURLEW LANE
Curlew Farm
Moss Farm
Marfield
RED CAT LANE
MARSH MOSS
Monk's Farm
Moss Nook
Red Cat Farm
BACK MOSS LANE
BURSCOUGH MOSS
New House Farm
White Dial Farm
Prescott's Farm
MEADOW LANE
Prescott Bridge
Anchor Farm
Manor House
Baldwin's Bridge
Baldwin's Lock
Wham Bridge
GERMAN'S LANE
German's Bridge
German's Lock
Lathom's Farm
Black Brook
Eller Brook
Crabtree Level Crossing
Factories
Burscough Bridge
Burscough Fitness & Racquets Leis. Cen.
Hockey Pitch
Burscough FC (Victoria Park)
Burscough Bridge
NORTH MOSS
MOSS LANE
Warper's Moss
Burscough Bridge St. John's C of E Prim. Sch.
Leeds & Liverpool Canal (Rufford Branch)
New Sutch Farm
Nursery
Moss Lock
HOSCAR MOSS
Bleak Hall Farm
Crabtree Bridge (Swing)
Orrell Farm
ORRELL LANE
Works
Burscough Priory Science College
BURSCOUGH
LIVERPOOL RD.
SCHOOL LANE
Sch.
Lib.
Cricket Ground
21
WARPER'S
Shaw's Level Crossing
Nursery
Runnel Brow
CAR SUTCH LANE
Runnel Brow Bri.
BLEAK LANE
Four Lane Ends Level Crossing

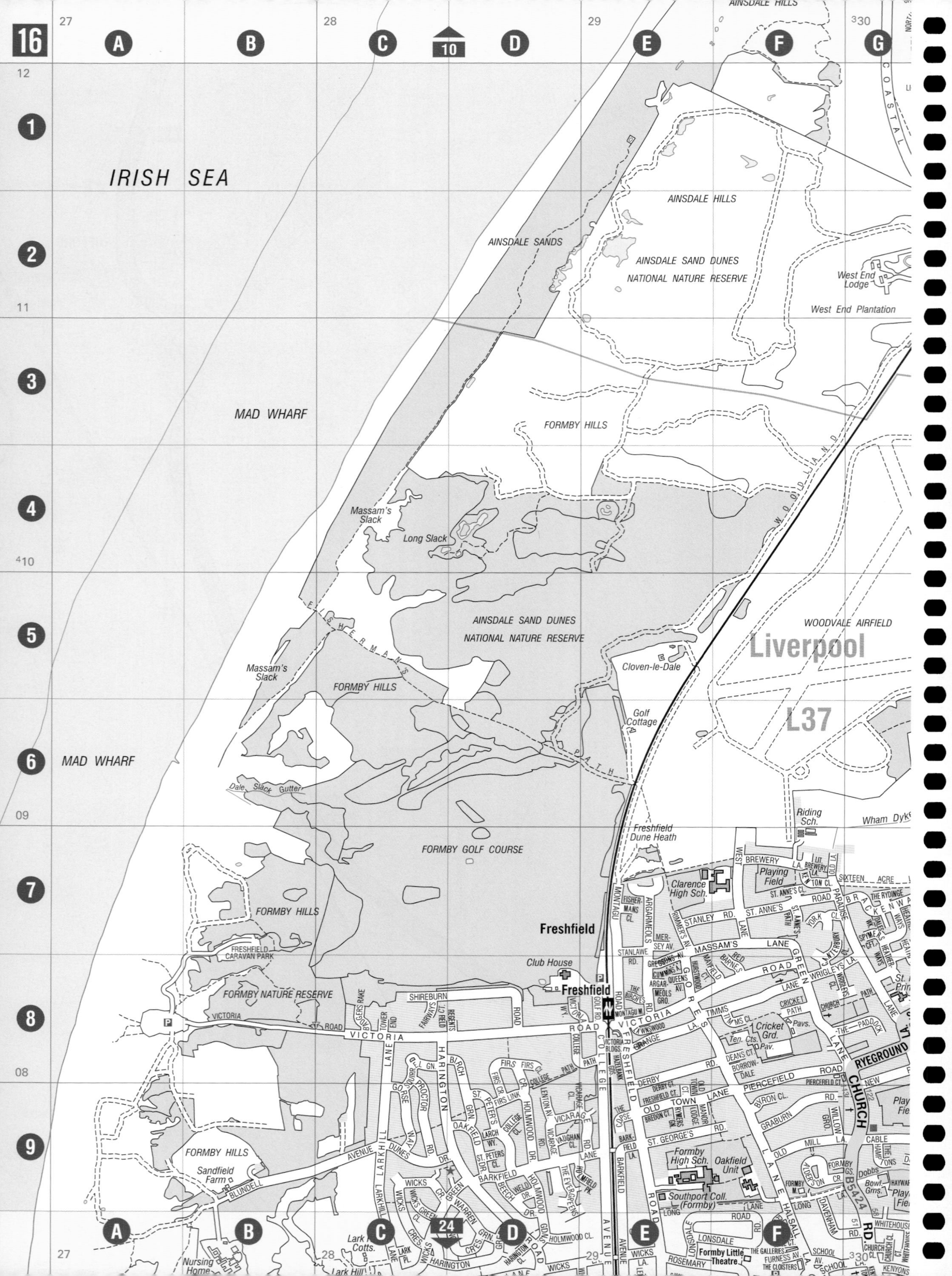

16

27   A   28   B   C   **10**   D   29   E   F   330   G

12

1

2 *IRISH SEA*

2   AINSDALE SANDS   AINSDALE HILLS

AINSDALE SAND DUNES
NATIONAL NATURE RESERVE   West End Lodge

11   West End Plantation

3   MAD WHARF   FORMBY HILLS

4   Massam's Slack   Long Slack

410

5   Massam's Slack   AINSDALE SAND DUNES   WOODVALE AIRFIELD
FORMBY HILLS   NATIONAL NATURE RESERVE   **Liverpool**
Cloven-le-Dale   **L37**

Golf Cottage
6 MAD WHARF   Riding Sch.   Wham Dyke
Dale Slack Gutter
09   Freshfield Dune Heath   BREWERY   Playing Field

7   FORMBY GOLF COURSE   Clarence High Sch.
FORMBY HILLS   **Freshfield**   STANLEY RD.

Club House
FRESHFIELD
8 CARAVAN PARK   ♦ **Freshfield**   Cricket Grd.
FORMBY NATURE RESERVE   SHIREBURN
P   Victoria   RYEGROUND
ROAD   VICTORIA   ROAD

08

9 FORMBY HILLS
Sandfield Farm   Formby High Sch. Oakfield Unit
BLUNDELL   Southport Coll. (Formby)   Formby Little Theatre

A   B   C   **24**   D   E   F   RD.
27   28   Lark Cotts.   29   330
Nursing Home   Lark Hill

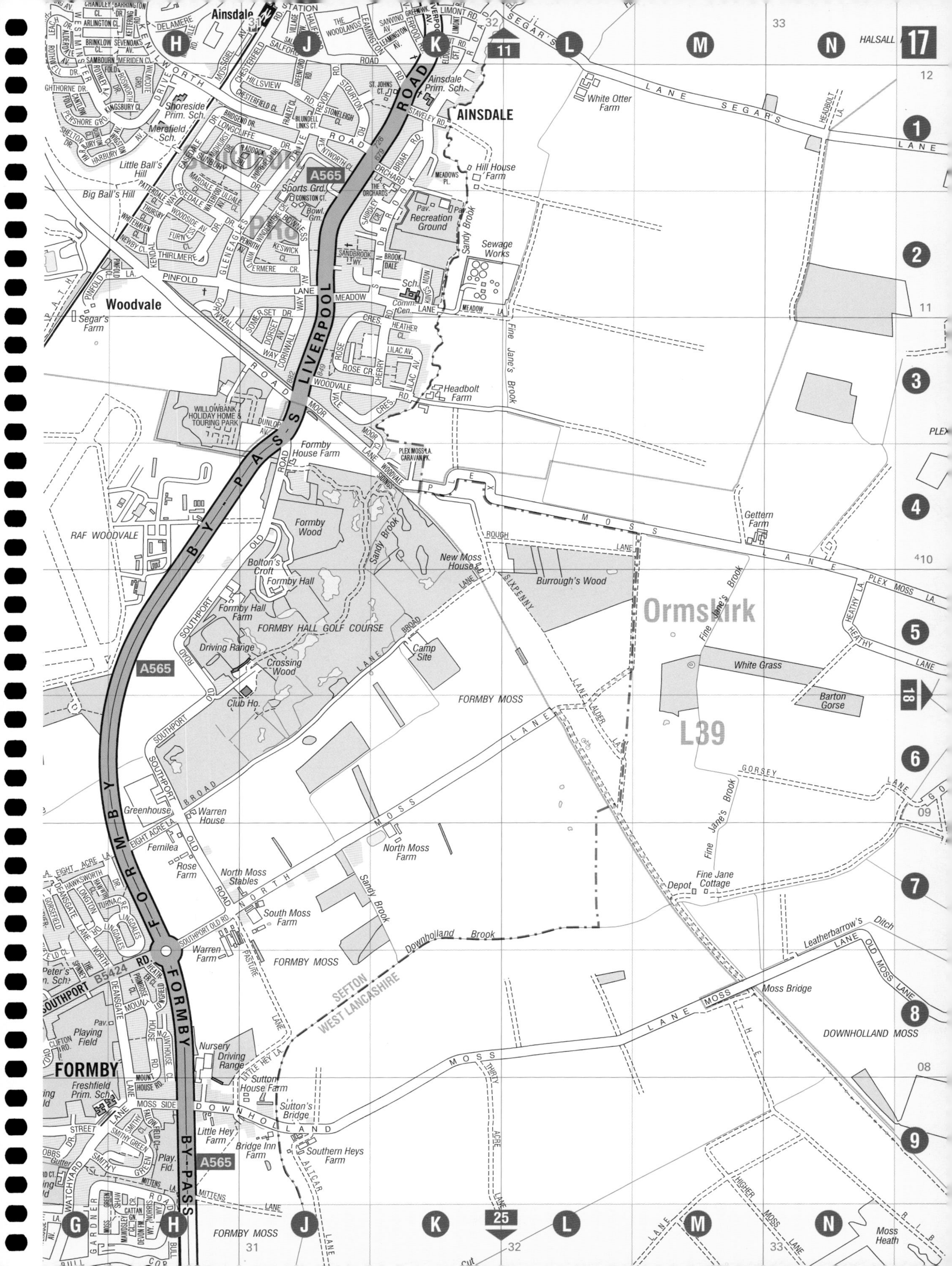

Ainsdale
AINSDALE
Woodvale
FORMBY
Ormskirk
L39
LIVERPOOL ROAD
FORMBY BY-PASS
A565
B5424
SEGAR'S LANE
PLEX MOSS LANE
Ainsdale Prim. Sch.
Shoreside Prim. Sch.
Merefield Sch.
Little Ball's Hill
Big Ball's Hill
Sports Grd.
Recreation Ground
Hill House Farm
White Otter Farm
Sewage Works
Headbolt Farm
Segar's Farm
RAF WOODVALE
WILLOWBANK HOLIDAY HOME & TOURING PARK
Formby House Farm
PLEX MOSS LA. CARAVAN PK.
Formby Wood
Sandy Brook
New Moss House
Burrough's Wood
Gettern Farm
Bolton's Croft
Formby Hall
Formby Hall Farm
FORMBY HALL GOLF COURSE
Driving Range
Crossing Wood
Club Ho.
Camp Site
FORMBY MOSS
White Grass
Barton Gorse
Fine Jane's Brook
Greenhouse
Warren House
Fernlea
Rose Farm
North Moss Stables
North Moss Farm
South Moss Farm
Warren Farm
Downholland Brook
SEFTON
WEST LANCASHIRE
Depot
Fine Jane Cottage
Leatherbarrow's Ditch
Moss Bridge
DOWNHOLLAND MOSS
Nursery Driving Range
Sutton House Farm
Sutton's Bridge
Little Hey Farm
Bridge Inn Farm
Southern Heys Farm
Freshfield Prim. Sch.
Playing Field
Play. Fld.
Moss Heath
HALSALL
11
25
18

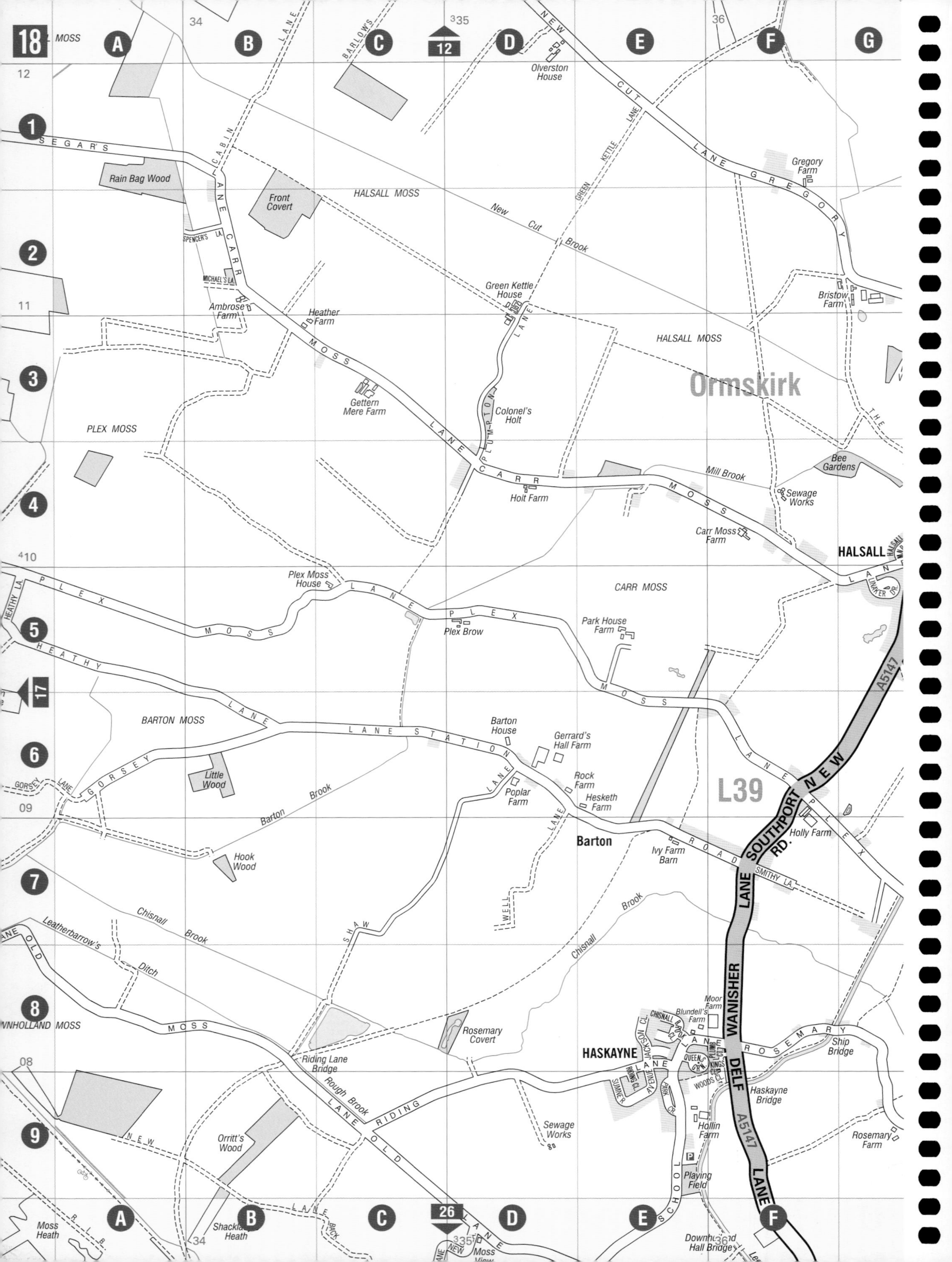

A
B
C
D
E
F
G
1
2
3
4
5
6
7
8
9
12
11
410
09
08
34
335
36
12
17
26
SEGAR'S
Rain Bag Wood
CABIN LANE
CARR
SPENCER'S LA.
MICHAEL'S LA.
Ambrose Farm
Front Covert
HALSALL MOSS
New Cut Brook
BARLOWS LANE
Olverston House
NEW CUT LANE
GREEN KETTLE LANE
Gregory Farm
GREGORY
Green Kettle House
Heather Farm
MOSS LANE
Bristow Farm
HALSALL MOSS
Ormskirk
PLEX MOSS
Gettern Mere Farm
PLUMPTON LANE
Colonel's Holt
CARR
Holt Farm
Mill Brook
Bee Gardens
Sewage Works
MOSS
Carr Moss Farm
HALSALL
LINAKER DR.
CARR MOSS
Plex Moss House
PLEX MOSS LANE
PLEX
Plex Brow
Park House Farm
MOSS LANE
HEATHY LA.
HEATHY LANE
BARTON MOSS
STATION LANE
Barton House
Gerrard's Hall Farm
A5147
GORSEY LANE
GORSEY LANE
Little Wood
Barton Brook
Poplar Farm
Rock Farm
Hesketh Farm
L39
NEW SOUTHPORT RD.
PLEX
Holly Farm
Barton
ROAD
Ivy Farm Barn
SMITHY LA.
Hook Wood
Chisnall Brook
WELL LANE
LANE
OLD LANE
Leatherbarrow's Ditch
SHAW
Chisnall Brook
WANISHER LANE
NHOLLAND MOSS
MOSS
Rosemary Covert
Moor Farm
Blundell's Farm
CHISNALL CL.
HASKAYNE
JACKSON CL.
ROSEMARY LANE
Ship Bridge
Riding Lane Bridge
RIDING CL.
QUEEN'S
KINGS
WOODS CL.
SUMNER
AVENUE
PARK CR.
DELF LANE
Rough Brook
RIDING LANE
Haskayne Bridge
Sewage Works
NEW
Orritt's Wood
OLD
Hollin Farm
Rosemary Farm
A5147
P
Playing Field
SCHOOL LANE
LANE
Moss Heath
Shacklady Heath
BACK LANE
NEW LANE
Moss View
Downholland Hall Bridge

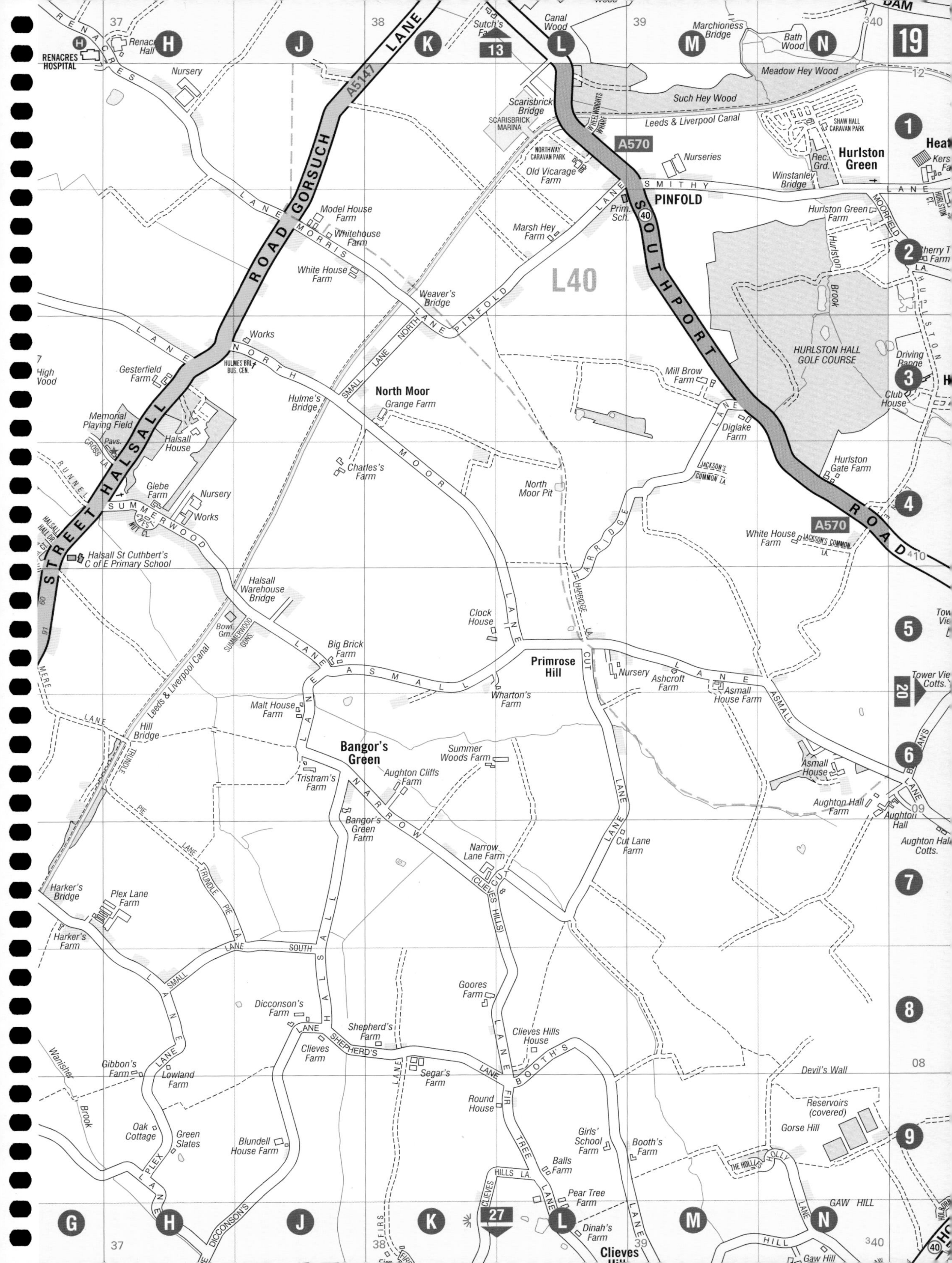
RENACRES HOSPITAL
Renacres Hall
Nursery
Sutch's Farm
13
Canal Wood
Marchioness Bridge
Bath Wood
Meadow Hey Wood
Such Hey Wood
Leeds & Liverpool Canal
Scarisbrick Bridge
SCARISBRICK MARINA
WHEELWRIGHTS WHARF
A570
A5147
GORSUCH LANE
GORSUCH ROAD
NORTHWAY CARAVAN PARK
Old Vicarage Farm
Nurseries
SHAW HALL CARAVAN PARK
Rec. Grd.
Hurlston Green
Winstanley Bridge
SMITHY LANE
PINFOLD
Prim. Sch.
Hurlston Green Farm
MOORFIELD
Model House Farm
Whitehouse Farm
MORRIS LANE
Marsh Hey Farm
White House Farm
L40
SOUTHPORT ROAD
Hurlston Brook
Weaver's Bridge
PINFOLD LANE
NORTH LANE
Works
HULMES BRI. BUS. CEN.
NORTH MOOR LANE
SMALL LANE
North Moor
Grange Farm
Hulme's Bridge
Gesterfield Farm
Mill Brow Farm
HURLSTON HALL GOLF COURSE
Driving Range
Club House
Diglake Farm
Memorial Playing Field
Pavs.
Halsall House
CROSS LA.
RUNNEL
Charles's Farm
North Moor Pit
JACKSON'S COMMON LA.
Hurlston Gate Farm
Glebe Farm
Nursery
Works
SUMMERWOOD
CHEST. NUT CL.
HALSALL HALL DR.
HALSALL STREET
Halsall St Cuthbert's C of E Primary School
ARRIDGE
HARRIDGE LA.
White House Farm
A570
ROAD
Halsall Warehouse Bridge
Clock House
Bowl. Grn.
SUMMERWOOD GDNS.
Big Brick Farm
ASMALL LANE
Primrose Hill
CUT
Nursery
Ashcroft Farm
Asmall House Farm
Wharton's Farm
Malt House Farm
MERE LANE
Hill Bridge
TRUNDLE
Bangor's Green
Summer Woods Farm
Tristram's Farm
Aughton Cliffs Farm
NARROW LANE
Asmall House
Aughton Hall Farm
Aughton Hall
Aughton Hall Cotts.
Bangor's Green Farm
PIE LANE
CUT LANE
Cut Lane Farm
Narrow Lane Farm
CUT & (CLIEVES HILLS)
Harker's Bridge
Plex Lane Farm
TRUNDLE PIE LA
HALSALL LANE
Harker's Farm
SOUTH LANE
SMALL LANE
Goores Farm
Dicconson's Farm
Shepherd's Farm
Clieves Hills House
Clieves Farm
SHEPHERD'S LANE
BOOTH'S LANE
Devil's Wall
Wanisher Brook
Gibbon's Farm
Lowland Farm
Segar's Farm
Round House
FIR TREE LANE
Reservoirs (covered)
Gorse Hill
Oak Cottage
Green Slates
Blundell House Farm
Girls' School Farm
Booth's Farm
Balls Farm
THE HOLLY
HOLLY
PLEX LANE
HILLS LA.
CLIEVES
Pear Tree Farm
GAW HILL LANE
27
Dinah's Farm
Clieves
DICCONSON'S
FIRS
HILL
Gaw Hill
Tower View Cotts.
20
37
38
39
340
G
H
J
K
L
M
N
1
2
3
4
5
6
7
8
9
12
11
410
09
08

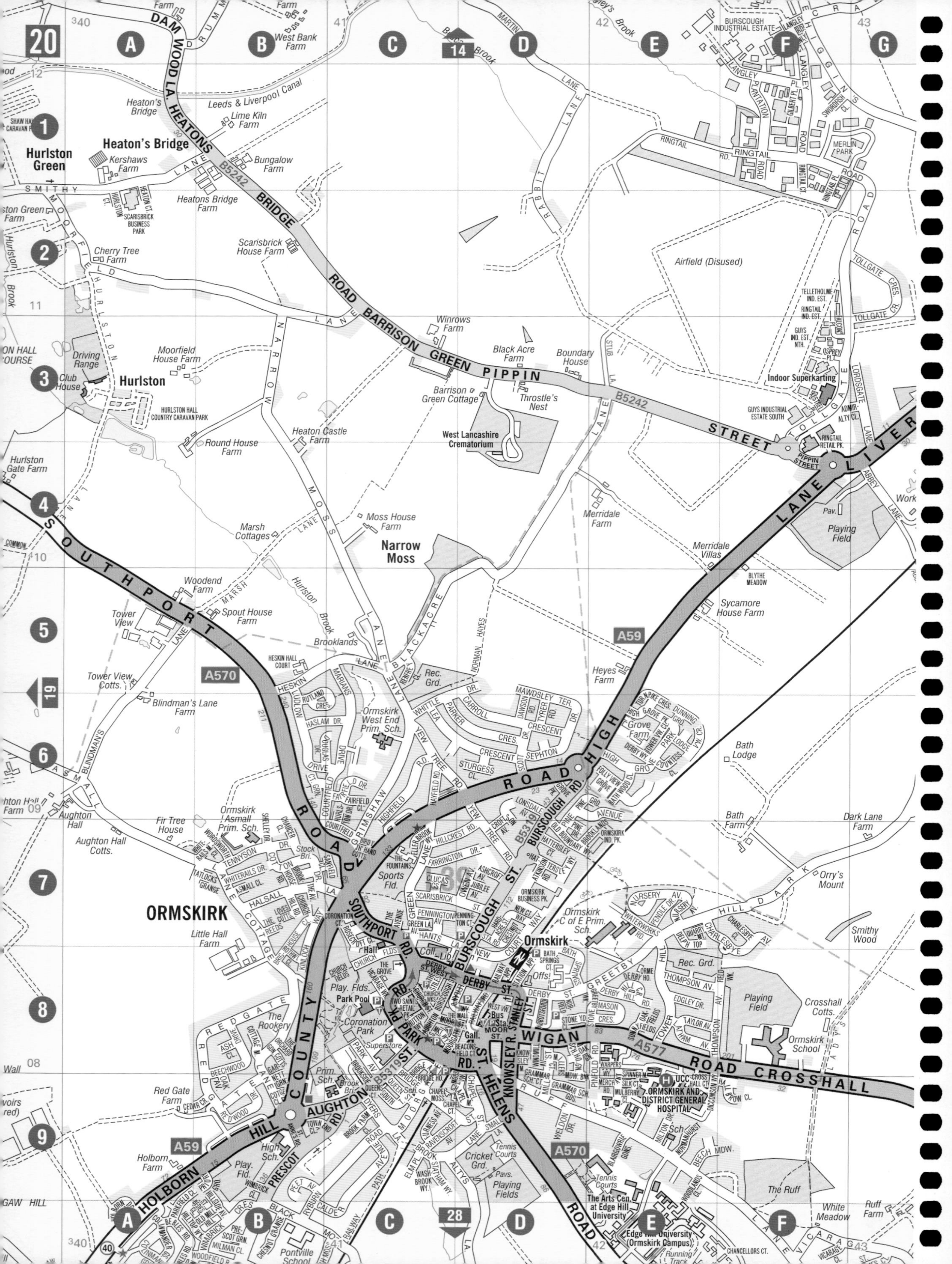

Hurlston Green
Heaton's Bridge
Hurlston
Narrow Moss
ORMSKIRK
Dam Wood La.
Heatons Bridge Road
Barrison Green
Pippin Street
B5242
Southport Road
A570
A59
A577
Liverpool
Wigan Road
Crosshall
Leeds & Liverpool Canal
West Bank Farm
Lime Kiln Farm
Kershaws Farm
Bungalow Farm
Heatons Bridge Farm
Scarisbrick Business Park
Cherry Tree Farm
Scarisbrick House Farm
Winrows Farm
Black Acre Farm
Boundary House
Barrison Green Cottage
Throstle's Nest
West Lancashire Crematorium
Moorfield House Farm
Driving Range
Club House
Hurlston Hall Country Caravan Park
Heaton Castle Farm
Round House Farm
Hurlston Gate Farm
Moss House Farm
Marsh Cottages
Woodend Farm
Spout House Farm
Tower View
Brooklands
Tower View Cotts.
Blindman's Lane Farm
Aughton Hall
Aughton Hall Cotts.
Fir Tree House
Ormskirk Asmall Prim. Sch.
Ormskirk West End Prim. Sch.
Little Hall Farm
Red Gate Farm
Holborn Farm
Airfield (Disused)
Burscough Industrial Estate
Ringtail Rd.
Merlin Park
Tollgate Cres.
Indoor Superkarting
Guys Industrial Estate South
Ringtail Retail Pk.
Merridale Farm
Merridale Villas
Playing Field
Sycamore House Farm
Heyes Farm
Bath Lodge
Bath Farm
Dark Lane Farm
Orry's Mount
Smithy Wood
Ormskirk C of E Prim. Sch.
Ormskirk
Rec. Grd.
Playing Field
Crosshall Cotts.
Ormskirk School
Ormskirk and District General Hospital
Park Pool
Coronation Park
Superstore
Play. Flds.
Sports Fld.
High Sch.
Cricket Grd.
Tennis Courts
Playing Fields
The Arts Cen. at Edge Hill University
Edge Hill University (Ormskirk Campus)
The Ruff
White Meadow
Ruff Farm
Pontville School
Holborn Hill
Aughton St.
County Road
Burscough St.
Burscough Rd.
Derby St.
Moor St.
St. Helens Rd.
Knowsley Rd.
Stanley St.
Prescot Rd.
Redgate
High Lane
Blackacre Lane
Narrow Moss Lane
Rabbit Lane
Stub Lane
Dark Lane
Vicarage

14
19
28

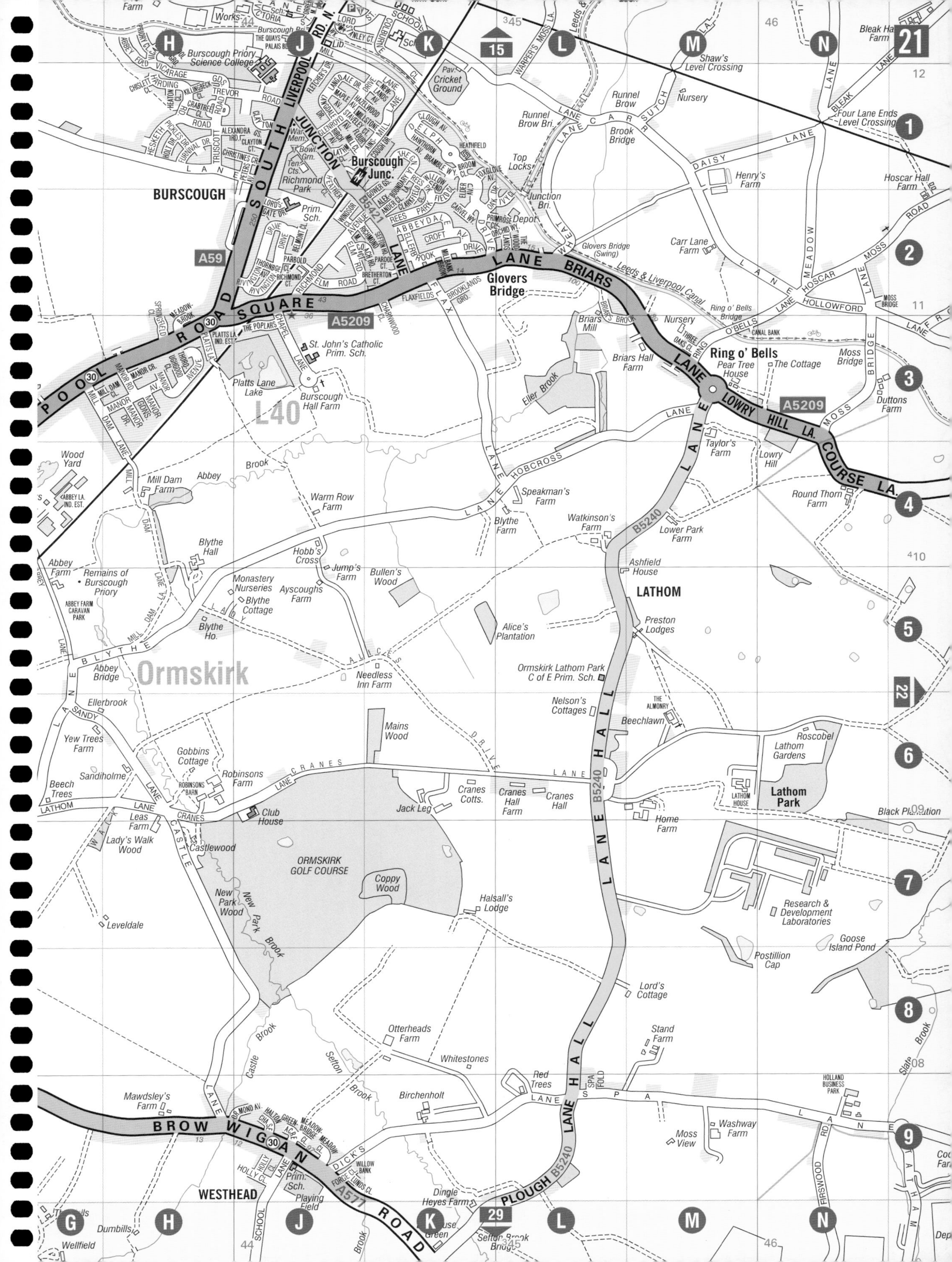

BURSCOUGH
Burscough Junc.
Burscough Priory Science College
Richmond Park
Prim. Sch.
Cricket Ground
Runnel Brow
Runnel Brow Bri.
Brook Bridge
Shaw's Level Crossing
Nursery
Bleak Hall Farm
Four Lane Ends Level Crossing
Top Locks
Junction Bri.
Depot
Henry's Farm
Hoscar Hall Farm
Carr Lane Farm
Glovers Bridge (Swing)
Leeds & Liverpool Canal
Glovers Bridge
Ring o' Bells Bridge
Ring o' Bells
Pear Tree House
The Cottage
Moss Bridge
Duttons Farm
Briars Mill
Briars Hall Farm
Taylor's Farm
Lowry Hill
Round Thorn Farm
St. John's Catholic Prim. Sch.
Platts Lane Lake
Burscough Hall Farm
L40
Wood Yard
Mill Dam Farm
Abbey
Warm Row Farm
Speakman's Farm
Blythe Farm
Watkinson's Farm
Lower Park Farm
Ashfield House
LATHOM
Blythe Hall
Hobb's Cross
Jump's Farm
Bullen's Wood
Abbey Farm
Remains of Burscough Priory
ABBEY FARM CARAVAN PARK
Monastery Nurseries
Blythe Cottage
Ayscoughs Farm
Blythe Ho.
Alice's Plantation
Preston Lodges
Abbey Bridge
Ormskirk
Needless Inn Farm
Ormskirk Lathom Park C of E Prim. Sch.
Ellerbrook
Nelson's Cottages
THE ALMONRY
Beechlawn
Yew Trees Farm
Mains Wood
Roscobel
Lathom Gardens
Gobbins Cottage
Robinsons Farm
ROBINSONS BARN
Sandiholme
Beech Trees
Cranes Cotts.
Cranes Hall Farm
Cranes Hall
Jack Leg
LATHOM HOUSE
Lathom Park
Black Plantation
Leas Farm
Club House
Home Farm
Lady's Walk Wood
Castlewood
ORMSKIRK GOLF COURSE
Coppy Wood
Halsall's Lodge
Research & Development Laboratories
New Park Wood
Leveldale
Postillion Cap
Goose Island Pond
Lord's Cottage
Otterheads Farm
Stand Farm
Whitestones
Red Trees
Mawdsley's Farm
Birchenholt
HOLLAND BUSINESS PARK
Moss View
Washway Farm
WESTHEAD
Prim. Sch.
Playing Field
Dingle Heyes Farm
Dumbills
Wellfield
Sefton Brook Bridge
A59
A5209
B5421
B5240
A577
LIVERPOOL ROAD SOUTH
JUNCTION LANE
POOL ROAD SQUARE
BRIARS LANE
LOWRY HILL LA.
COURSE LA.
HOBCROSS LANE
CRANES LANE
HALL LANE
SPA LANE
PLOUGH LANE
WIGAN ROAD
BROW
DAISY LANE
HOSCAR MOSS ROAD
HOLLOWFORD LANE
BLEAK LANE
CARR LANE
MEADOW LANE
SANDY LANE
LATHOM LANE
BLYTHE LANE
MILL DAM LANE
DICK'S LANE
SCHOOL LANE
FIRSWOOD RD.
CASTLE LANE
Eller Brook
Castle Brook
Sefton Brook
New Park Brook
Slate Brook
15
22
29

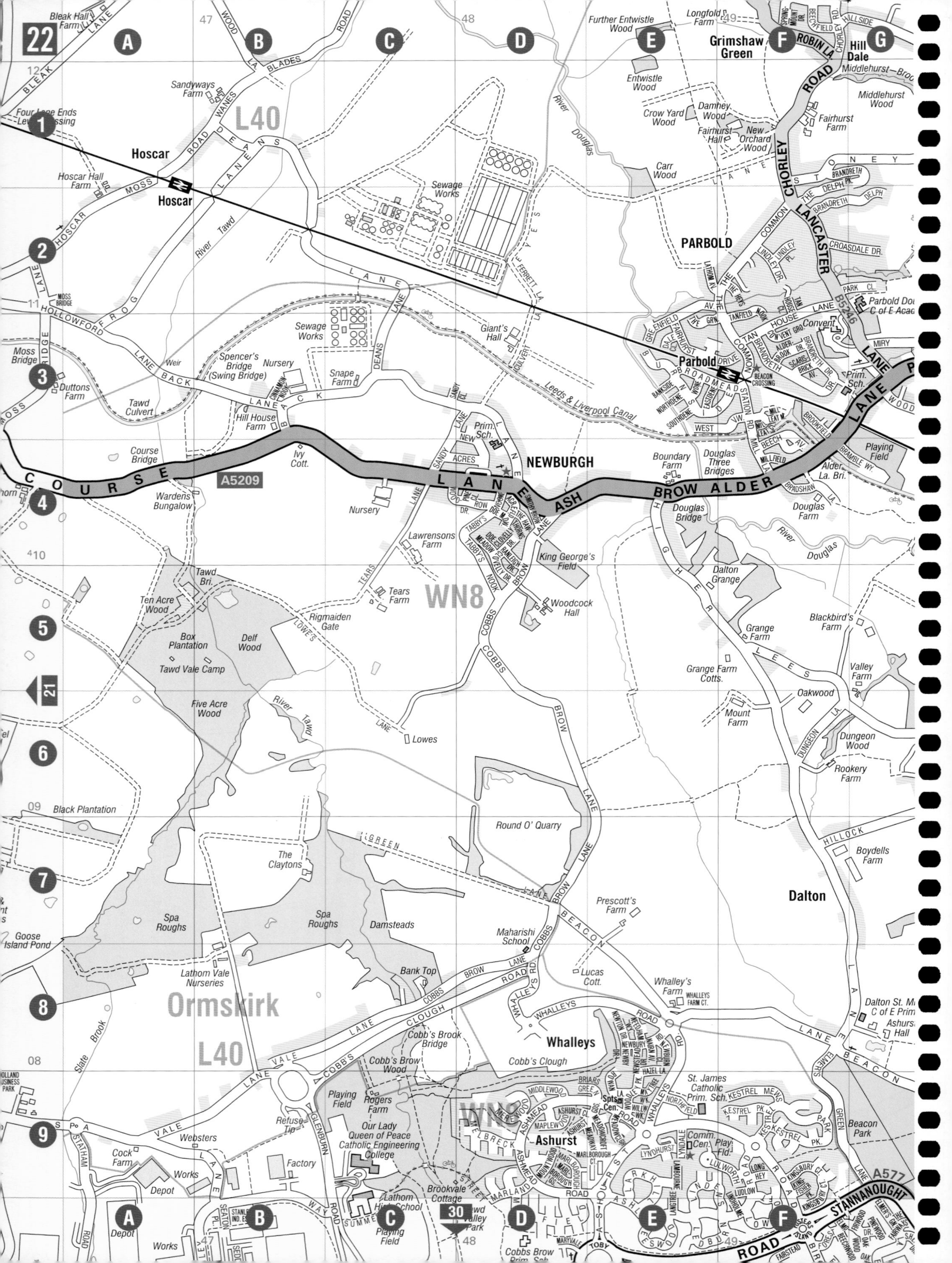

A
B
C
D
E
F
G
1
2
3
4
5
6
7
8
9
Hoscar
Hoscar
L40
PARBOLD
Parbold
NEWBURGH
WN8
Grimshaw Green
Hill Dale
Dalton
Whalleys
Ashurst
Ormskirk
L40
A5209
A577
B5246
COURSE LANE
ASH BROW
ALDER LANE
Leeds & Liverpool Canal
River Douglas
River Tawd
Sewage Works
Sewage Works
Bleak Hall Farm
Sandyways Farm
Hoscar Hall Farm
Moss Bridge
Duttons Farm
Tawd Culvert
Spencer's Bridge (Swing Bridge)
Nursery
Hill House Farm
Course Bridge
Ivy Cott.
Wardens Bungalow
Snape Farm
Giant's Hall
Lawrensons Farm
Tears Farm
Rigmaiden Gate
King George's Field
Woodcock Hall
Tawd Bri.
Ten Acre Wood
Box Plantation
Delf Wood
Tawd Vale Camp
Five Acre Wood
Lowes
Black Plantation
Round O' Quarry
The Claytons
Spa Roughs
Spa Roughs
Damsteads
Goose Island Pond
Lathom Vale Nurseries
Bank Top
Maharishi School
Prescott's Farm
Lucas Cott.
Whalley's Farm
Cobb's Brook Bridge
Cobb's Brow Wood
Cobb's Clough
Playing Field
Rogers Farm
Our Lady Queen of Peace Catholic Engineering College
Refuse Tip
Factory
Websters
Cock Farm
Works
Depot
Lathom High School
Brookvale Cottage
St. James Catholic Prim. Sch.
Further Entwistle Wood
Longfold Farm
Entwistle Wood
Crow Yard Wood
Damhey Wood
Fairhurst Hall
New Orchard Wood
Carr Wood
Middlehurst Wood
Fairhurst Farm
Parbold Douglas C of E Academy
Convent
Prim. Sch.
Boundary Farm
Douglas Three Bridges
Douglas Bridge
Alder La. Bri.
Playing Field
Douglas Farm
Dalton Grange
Grange Farm
Grange Farm Cotts.
Blackbird's Farm
Valley Farm
Oakwood
Mount Farm
Dungeon Wood
Rookery Farm
Boydells Farm
Dalton St. Michael's C of E Prim.
Ashurst Hall
Beacon Park
Cobbs Brow Prim. Sch.
21
30

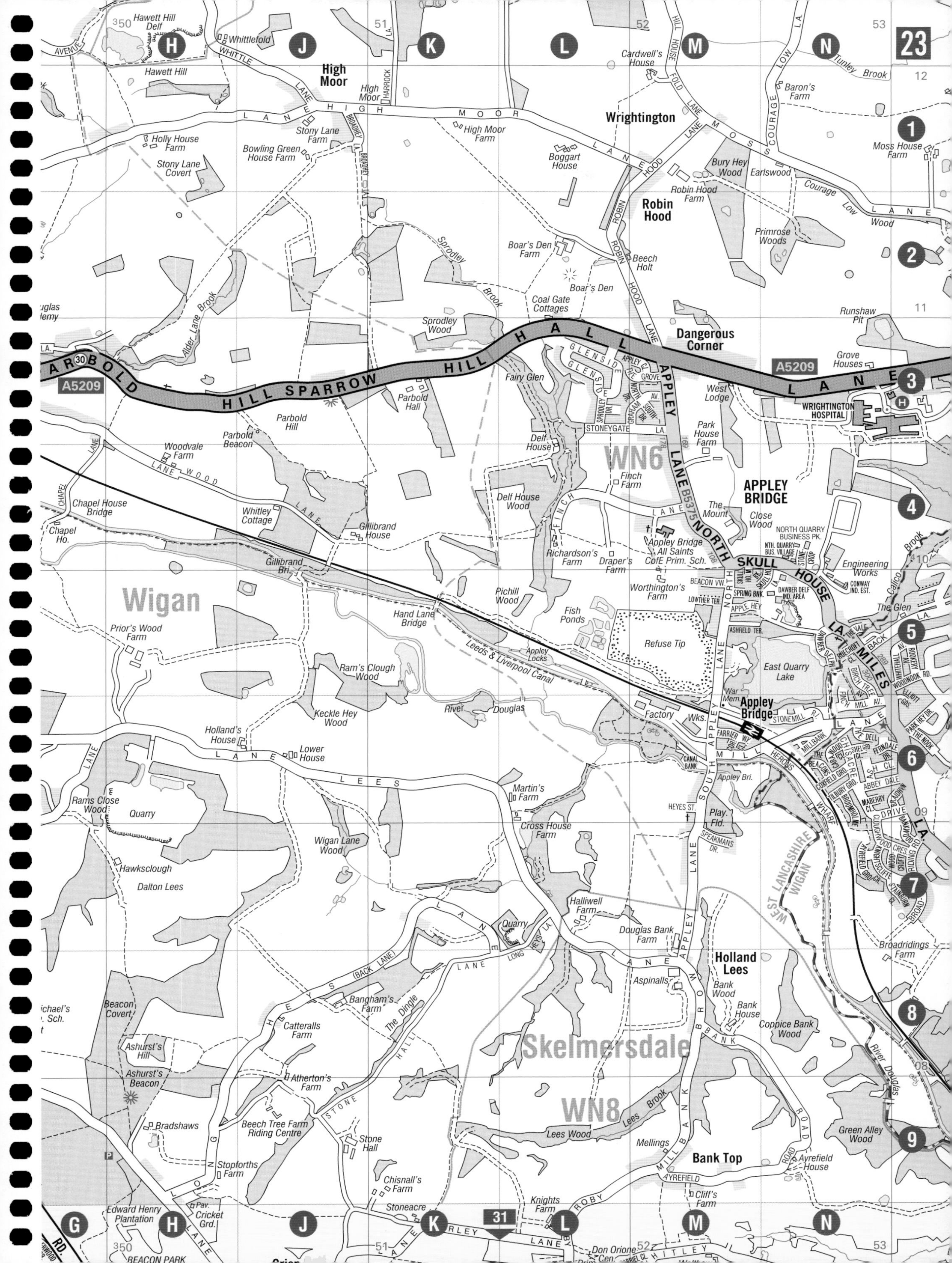

High Moor
Wrightington
Robin Hood
Dangerous Corner
APPLEY BRIDGE
WN6
Wigan
Skelmersdale
WN8
Holland Lees
Bank Top
Appley Bridge
A5209
SPARROW HILL
HALL LANE
HIGH MOOR LANE
Hawett Hill Delf
Whittlefold
Hawett Hill
Holly House Farm
Stony Lane Covert
Bowling Green House Farm
Stony Lane Farm
High Moor Farm
Boggart House
Cardwell's House
Baron's Farm
Moss House Farm
Bury Hey Wood
Earlswood
Robin Hood Farm
Primrose Woods
Boar's Den Farm
Boar's Den
Beech Holt
Coal Gate Cottages
Sprodley Wood
Sprodley Brook
Alder Lane Brook
Runshaw Pit
Grove Houses
WRIGHTINGTON HOSPITAL
West Lodge
Park House Farm
Fairy Glen
Parbold Hall
Parbold Hill
Parbold Beacon
Woodvale Farm
Delf House
Finch Farm
Delf House Wood
Chapel House Bridge
Chapel Ho.
Whitley Cottage
Gillibrand House
Gillibrand Bri.
The Mount
Close Wood
NORTH QUARRY BUSINESS PK.
Engineering Works
Appley Bridge All Saints CofE Prim. Sch.
Richardson's Farm
Draper's Farm
Worthington's Farm
Pichill Wood
Fish Ponds
Refuse Tip
Hand Lane Bridge
Appley Locks
Leeds & Liverpool Canal
Prior's Wood Farm
Ram's Clough Wood
East Quarry Lake
The Glen
River Douglas
Keckle Hey Wood
Holland's House
Lower House
LEES LANE
Factory
Wks.
War Mem.
Appley Bri.
Play. Fld.
Rams Close Wood
Quarry
Martin's Farm
Cross House Farm
Wigan Lane Wood
Hawksclough
Dalton Lees
Halliwell Farm
Douglas Bank Farm
WEST LANCASHIRE
WIGAN
Broadridings Farm
Aspinalls
Bank Wood
Bank House
Coppice Bank Wood
Beacon Covert
Bangham's Farm
The Dingle
Catteralls Farm
Ashurst's Hill
Ashurst's Beacon
Atherton's Farm
Bradshaws
Beech Tree Farm Riding Centre
Stone Hall
Lees Wood
Lees Brook
Mellings
Green Alley Wood
Ayrefield House
Stopforths Farm
Chisnall's Farm
Cliff's Farm
Edward Henry Plantation
Cricket Grd.
Stoneacre
Knights Farm
Don Orione Cen.
BEACON PARK
31

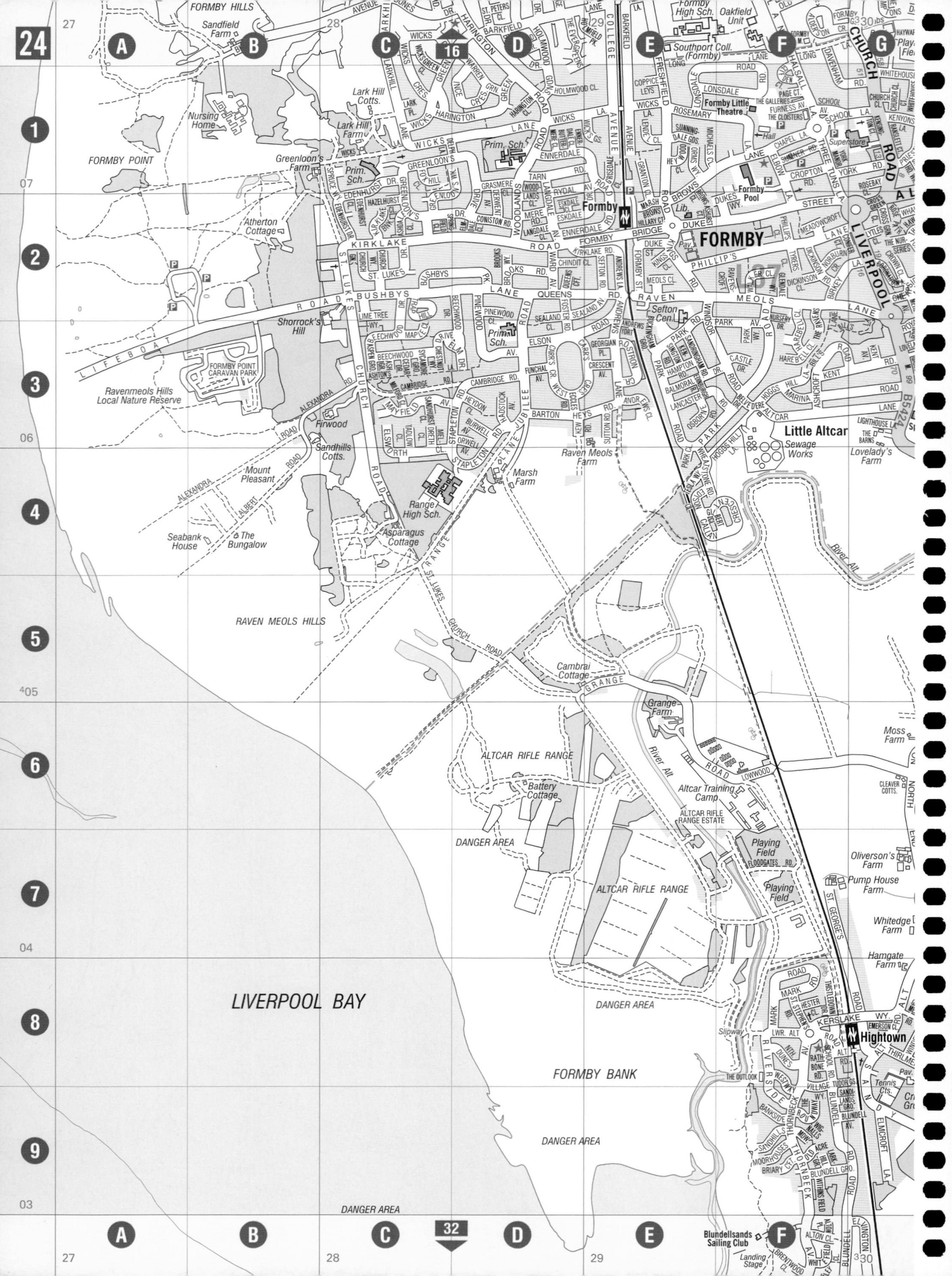
FORMBY HILLS
Sandfield Farm
FORMBY POINT
Nursing Home
Lark Hill Cotts.
Lark Hill Farm
Greenloon's Farm
Prim. Sch.
Atherton Cottage
Shorrock's Hill
FORMBY POINT CARAVAN PARK
Ravenmeols Hills Local Nature Reserve
Firwood
Sandhills Cotts.
Mount Pleasant
Seabank House
The Bungalow
Asparagus Cottage
Range High Sch.
Marsh Farm
Raven Meols Farm
RAVEN MEOLS HILLS
Formby
FORMBY
Formby High Sch.
Oakfield Unit
Southport Coll. (Formby)
Formby Little Theatre
Formby Pool
Lib.
Sefton Cen.
Superstore
Little Altcar
Sewage Works
Lovelady's Farm
River Alt
Cambrai Cottage
Grange Farm
ALTCAR RIFLE RANGE
Battery Cottage
DANGER AREA
Altcar Training Camp
ALTCAR RIFLE RANGE ESTATE
Playing Field
Moss Farm
Cleaver Cotts.
Oliverson's Farm
Pump House Farm
Whitedge Farm
Hamgate Farm
LIVERPOOL BAY
FORMBY BANK
Slipway
Hightown
The Outlook
Tennis Cts.
Blundellsands Sailing Club
Landing Stage
B5424

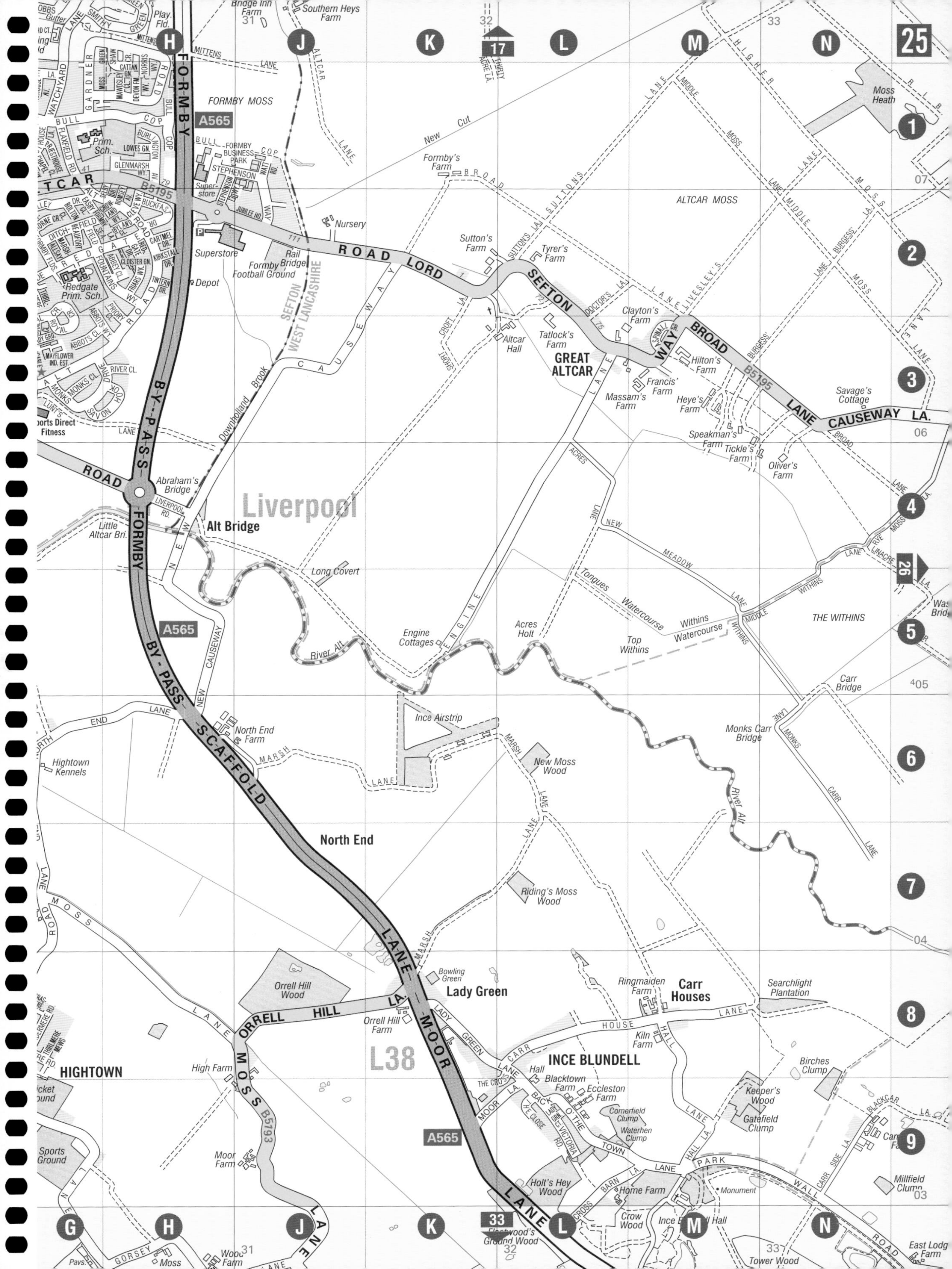
FORMBY MOSS
ALTCAR MOSS
Moss Heath
Formby's Farm
Nursery
Superstore
Depot
Redgate Prim. Sch.
Formby Football Ground
Rail Bridge
SEFTON
WEST LANCASHIRE
Sutton's Farm
Tyrer's Farm
Altcar Hall
Tatlock's Farm
GREAT ALTCAR
Clayton's Farm
Hilton's Farm
Francis' Farm
Massam's Farm
Heye's Farm
Speakman's Farm
Tickle's Farm
Oliver's Farm
Savage's Cottage
ROAD LORD SEFTON WAY
BROAD LANE
CAUSEWAY LA.
FORMBY BY-PASS
A565
B5195
Abraham's Bridge
Liverpool
Alt Bridge
Little Altcar Bri.
Long Covert
Engine Cottages
Acres Holt
Top Withins
THE WITHINS
Withins Watercourse
Tongues Watercourse
Carr Bridge
Monks Carr Bridge
River Alt
Ince Airstrip
North End Farm
Hightown Kennels
New Moss Wood
North End
Riding's Moss Wood
SCAFFOLD LANE
MOOR LANE
Orrell Hill Wood
ORRELL HILL LA.
Orrell Hill Farm
Bowling Green
Lady Green
Ringmaiden Farm
Carr Houses
Searchlight Plantation
Kiln Farm
INCE BLUNDELL
L38
High Farm
HIGHTOWN
Blacktown Farm
Eccleston Farm
Keeper's Wood
Birches Clump
Gatefield Clump
Comerfield Clump
Waterhen Clump
Moor Farm
Sports Ground
Holt's Hey Wood
Home Farm
Crow Wood
Monument
Millfield Clump
Tower Wood
East Lodge Farm
Fleetwood's Ground Wood
HIGHER MOSS LANE
New Cut
Downholland Brook

17
26
33

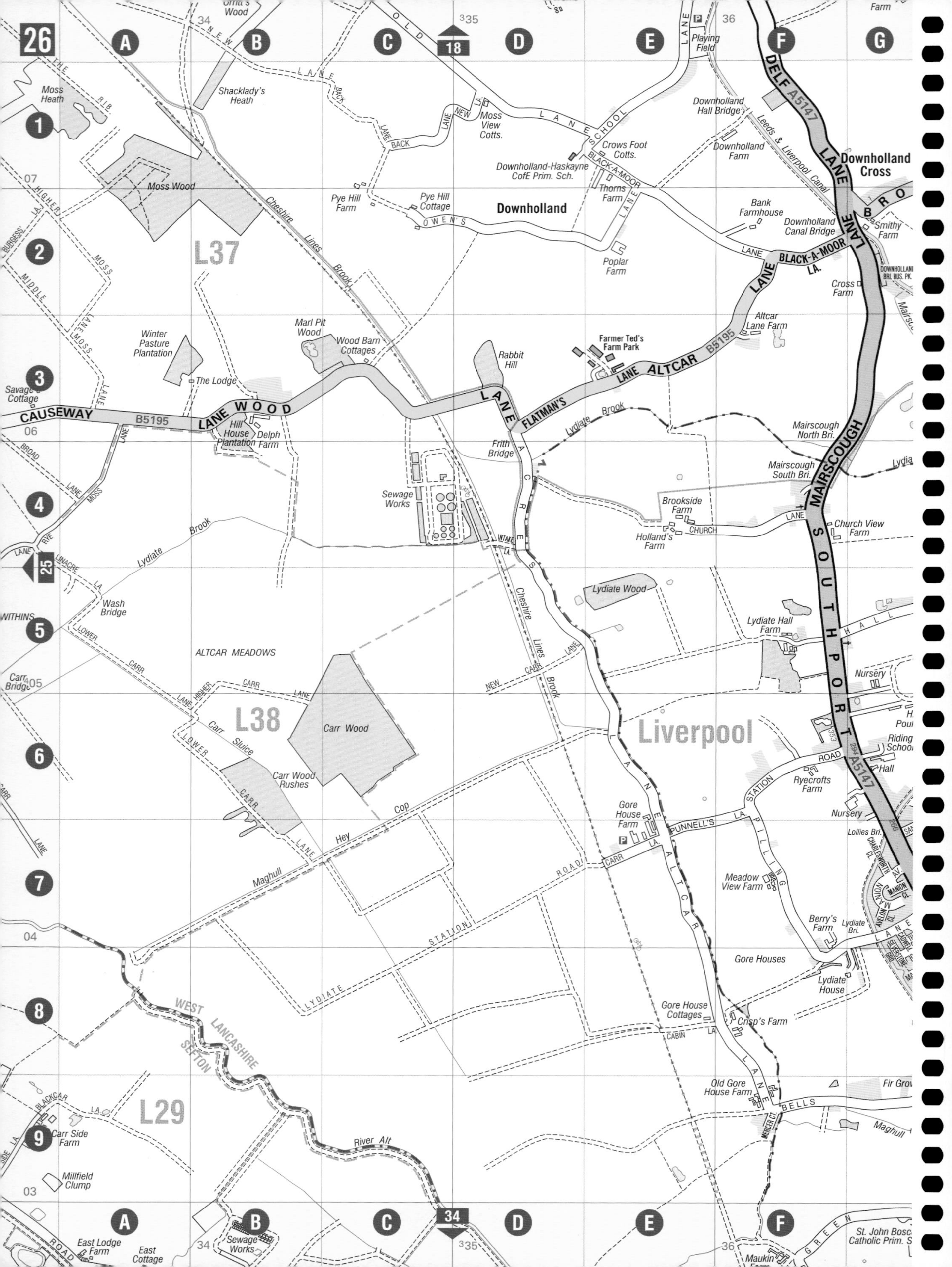
Moss Heath
Shacklady's Heath
Moss Wood
Downholland
Downholland Cross
Downholland-Haskayne CofE Prim. Sch.
Crows Foot Cotts.
Thorns Farm
Poplar Farm
Pye Hill Farm
Pye Hill Cottage
Moss View Cotts.
Downholland Hall Bridge
Downholland Farm
Leeds & Liverpool Canal
Bank Farmhouse
Downholland Canal Bridge
Smithy Farm
Cross Farm
Altcar Lane Farm
Farmer Ted's Farm Park
Rabbit Hill
Marl Pit Wood
Wood Barn Cottages
Winter Pasture Plantation
The Lodge
Savage's Cottage
CAUSEWAY
B5195
WOOD LANE
ALTCAR LANE
FLATMAN'S LANE
BLACK-A-MOOR LA.
DELF LANE
A5147
Hill House Plantation
Delph Farm
Frith Bridge
Sewage Works
Lydiate Brook
Mairscough North Bri.
Mairscough South Bri.
MAIRSCOUGH LANE
SOUTHPORT ROAD
Brookside Farm
Holland's Farm
CHURCH LANE
Church View Farm
Lydiate Wood
Lydiate Hall Farm
Nursery
Wash Bridge
ALTCAR MEADOWS
Carr Bridge
L37
L38
L29
Carr Wood
Carr Sluice
Carr Wood Rushes
Cheshire Lines Brook
Liverpool
Hey Cop
Maghull
Gore House Farm
PUNNELL'S LA.
STATION ROAD
Ryecrofts Farm
PILLING LANE
Meadow View Farm
Berry's Farm
Lydiate Bri.
Gore Houses
Lydiate House
Gore House Cottages
Crisp's Farm
CABIN LA
Old Gore House Farm
BELLS LANE
Fir Grove
WEST LANCASHIRE
SEFTON
River Alt
Carr Side Farm
Millfield Clump
East Lodge Farm
East Cottage
Sewage Works
Maukin
St. John Bosco Catholic Prim. S
Riding School
Hall
Playing Field
18
25
34

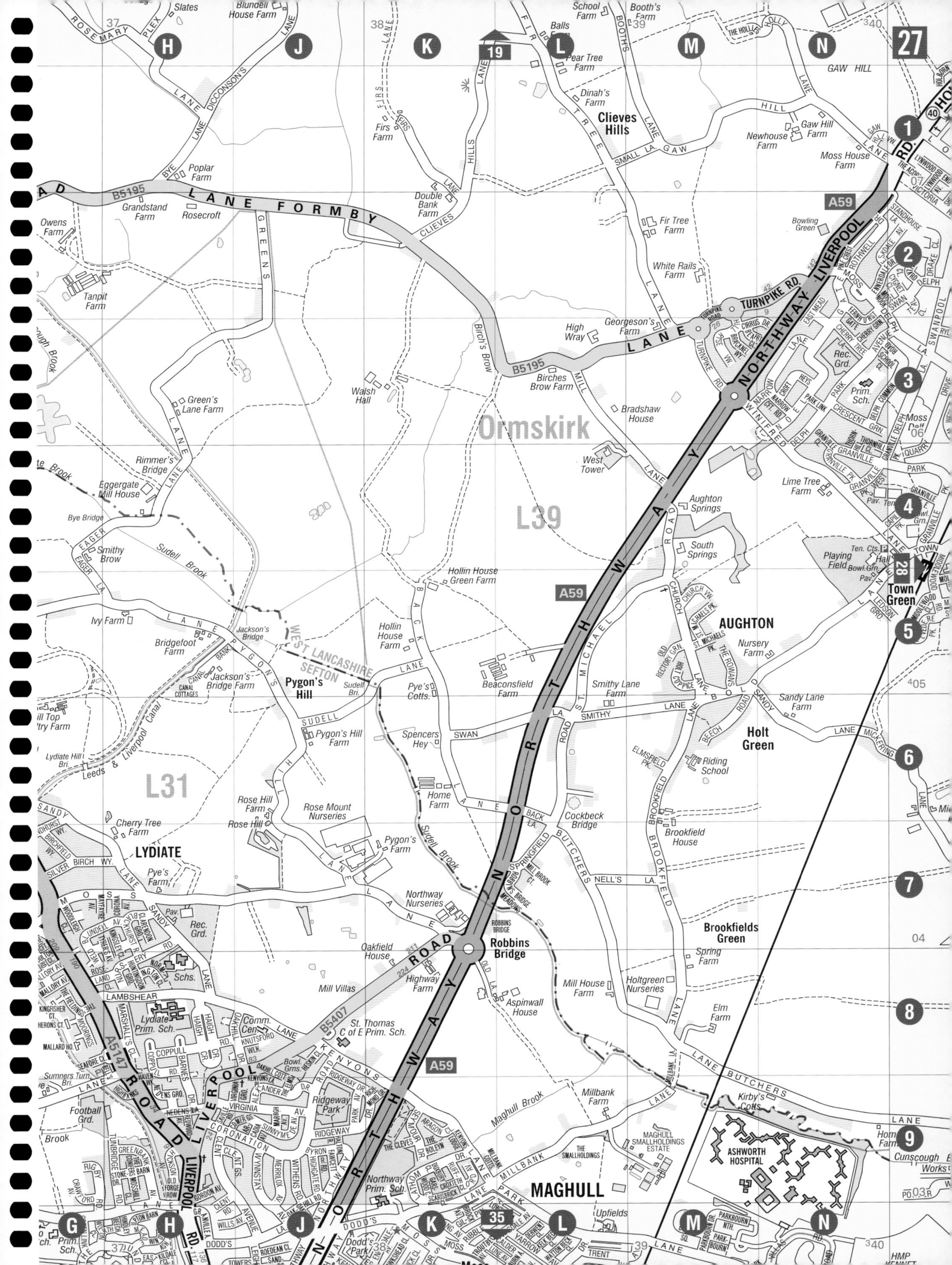

Clieves Hills
Ormskirk
L39
AUGHTON
Holt Green
Pygon's Hill
L31
LYDIATE
Robbins Bridge
Brookfields Green
MAGHULL
ASHWORTH HOSPITAL
Town Green
LANE FORMBY
B5195
A59
NORTHWAY
LIVERPOOL ROAD
A5147
B5407
Leeds & Liverpool Canal
WEST LANCASHIRE
SEFTON
Sudell Brook
Maghull Brook
Grandstand Farm
Rosecroft
Owens Farm
Tanpit Farm
Poplar Farm
Double Bank Farm
Firs Farm
Walsh Hall
Green's Lane Farm
Rimmer's Bridge
Eggergate Mill House
Smithy Brow
Ivy Farm
Bridgefoot Farm
Jackson's Bridge Farm
Pygon's Hill Farm
Hollin House Farm
Hollin House Green Farm
Beaconsfield Farm
Spencers Hey
Home Farm
Rose Hill Farm
Rose Mount Nurseries
Cherry Tree Farm
Pye's Farm
Pygon's Farm
Northway Nurseries
Oakfield House
Mill Villas
Highway Farm
Aspinwall House
Mill House Farm
Holtgreen Nurseries
Elm Farm
Millbank Farm
Kirby's Cotts.
Spring Farm
Brookfield House
Riding School
Cockbeck Bridge
Smithy Lane Farm
Nursery Farm
Sandy Lane Farm
South Springs
Aughton Springs
Lime Tree Farm
West Tower
Bradshaw House
Birches Brow Farm
High Wray
Georgeson's Farm
White Rails Farm
Fir Tree Farm
Dinah's Farm
Pear Tree Farm
School Farm
Booth's Farm
Blundell House Farm
Newhouse Farm
Gaw Hill Farm
Moss House Farm
GAW HILL
Bowling Green
Playing Field
Lydiate Prim. Sch.
St. Thomas C of E Prim. Sch.
Northway Prim. Sch.
MAGHULL SMALLHOLDINGS ESTATE
THE SMALLHOLDINGS
Upfields
Football Grnd.

19
28
35

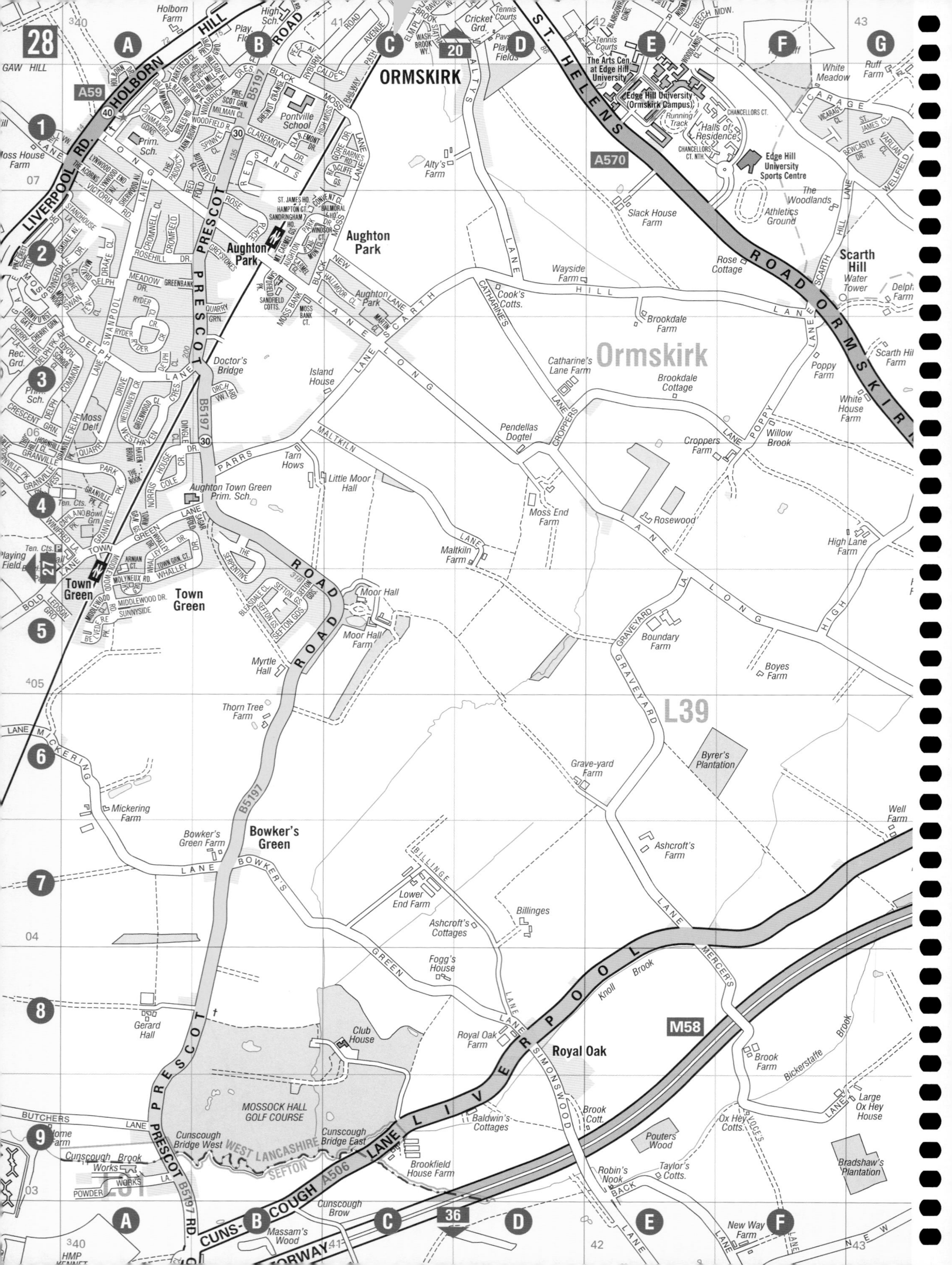

28
ORMSKIRK
Ormskirk
L39
Aughton Park
Town Green
Bowker's Green
Royal Oak
Scarth Hill
Water Tower
Holborn Farm
Play. Fld.
High Sch.
Cricket Grd.
Tennis Courts
Pavs.
Play Fields
20
ST. HELENS ROAD
ORMSKIRK ROAD
A570
A59
HOLBORN HILL
LIVERPOOL RD.
PRESCOT ROAD
B5197
Pontville School
Prim. Sch.
The Arts Cen at Edge Hill University
Edge Hill University (Ormskirk Campus)
Running Track
Halls of Residence
Edge Hill University Sports Centre
The Woodlands
Athletics Ground
Slack House Farm
Alty's Farm
White Meadow
Ruff Farm
Rose Cottage
Delph Farm
Wayside Farm
Cook's Cotts.
Brookdale Farm
Catharine's Lane Farm
Brookdale Cottage
Poppy Farm
Scarth Hill Farm
White House Farm
Willow Brook
Croppers Farm
Pendellas Dogtel
Island House
Doctor's Bridge
Moss Delf
Rec. Grd.
Prim. Sch.
Tarn Hows
Little Moor Hall
Aughton Town Green Prim. Sch.
Moss End Farm
Rosewood
Maltkiln Farm
High Lane Farm
Moor Hall
Moor Hall Farm
Myrtle Hall
Boundary Farm
Boyes Farm
Thorn Tree Farm
Byrer's Plantation
Grave-yard Farm
Mickering Farm
Bowker's Green Farm
Well Farm
Ashcroft's Farm
Lower End Farm
Billinges
Ashcroft's Cottages
Fogg's House
Gerard Hall
Club House
Royal Oak Farm
Knoll Brook
M58
Brook Farm
Bickerstaffe Brook
Large Ox Hey House
MOSSOCK HALL GOLF COURSE
Baldwin's Cottages
Brook Cott.
Ox Hey Cotts.
Pouters Wood
Cunscough Bridge West
Cunscough Bridge East
WEST LANCASHIRE
SEFTON
Brookfield House Farm
Robin's Nook
Taylor's Cotts.
Bradshaw's Plantation
Cunscough Brook
Works
Cunscough Brow
Massam's Wood
New Way Farm
36
27
Playing Field
Ten. Cts.
Bowl. Grn.
Home Farm
Moss House Farm
GAW HILL
LIVERPOOL ROAD
CUNSCOUGH LANE
A506
MOTORWAY
LONG LANE
PARRS LANE
MALTKILN LANE
GRAVEYARD LANE
MERCERS LANE
SIMONSWOOD LANE
BILLINGE LANE
BOWKER'S GREEN LANE
MICKERING LANE
BUTCHERS LANE
BACK LANE
HIGH LANE
POPPY LANE
CROPPERS LANE
CATHARINES LANE
VICARAGE LANE
SCARTH HILL LANE
WAYSIDE HILL LANE
BLACK MOSS LANE
NEW LANE
GREEN LANE
A B C D E F G
1 2 3 4 5 6 7 8 9
340 41 42 43
07 06 405 04 03

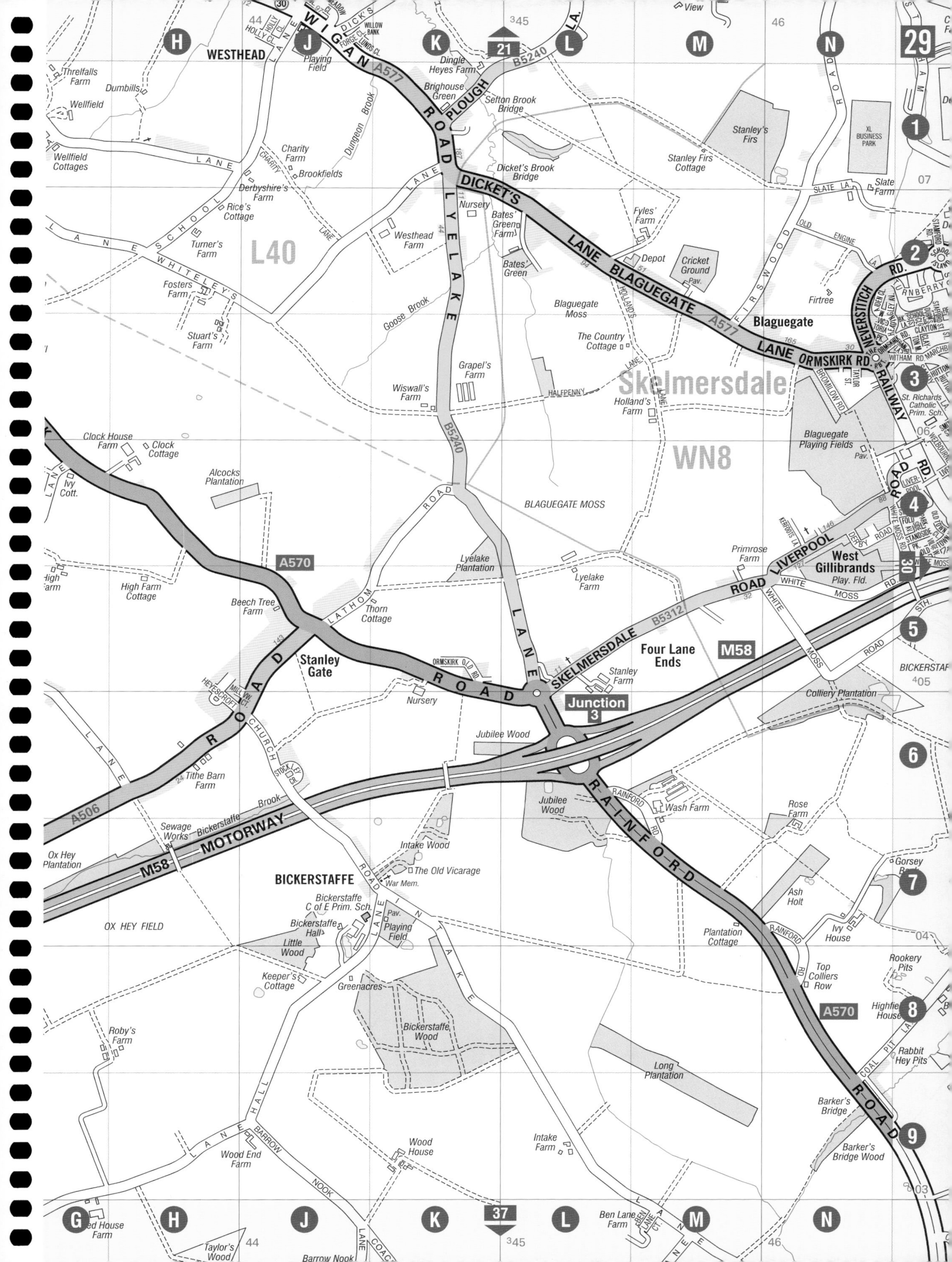
WESTHEAD
Threlfalls Farm
Dumbills
Wellfield
Wellfield Cottages
Playing Field
WIGAN
A577
Dingle Heyes Farm
Brighouse Green
PLOUGH
Sefton Brook Bridge
B5240
21
View
Stanley's Firs
XL BUSINESS PARK
Stanley Firs Cottage
Charity Farm
Brookfields
Dungeon Brook
Derbyshire's Farm
Rice's Cottage
Turner's Farm
L40
Dicket's Brook Bridge
DICKET'S
LANE
Nursery
Bates' Green Farm
Westhead Farm
Fyles' Farm
Depot
Cricket Ground
Pav.
SLATE LA.
Slate Farm
OLD ENGINE
Bates' Green
BLAGUEGATE
FIRSWOOD
Firtree
Fosters Farm
Stuart's Farm
WHITELEY'S
SCHOOL
Goose Brook
LYELAKE
Blaguegate Moss
The Country Cottage
Blaguegate
LANE
ORMSKIRK RD.
NEVERSTITCH RD.
Grapel's Farm
Wiswall's Farm
HALFPENNY
Skelmersdale
Holland's Farm
HOLLANDS
RAILWAY
St. Richards Catholic Prim. Sch.
Blaguegate Playing Fields
WN8
Clock House Farm
Clock Cottage
Alcocks Plantation
Ivy Cott.
B5240
BLAGUEGATE MOSS
LIVERPOOL
ROAD
Primrose Farm
West Gillibrands Play. Fld.
WHITE MOSS RD.
A570
Lyelake Plantation
Lyelake Farm
High Farm Cottage
Beech Tree Farm
Thorn Cottage
LATHOM
B5312
SKELMERSDALE
Four Lane Ends
M58
Stanley Gate
ORMSKIRK OLD RD.
Stanley Farm
Junction 3
Nursery
BICKERSTAFFE
Colliery Plantation
Jubilee Wood
CHURCH
Tithe Barn Farm
Jubilee Wood
RAINFORD RD.
Wash Farm
Rose Farm
A506
Brook
Bickerstaffe
Sewage Works
MOTORWAY
Ox Hey Plantation
M58
Intake Wood
The Old Vicarage
War Mem.
Gorsey Bank
BICKERSTAFFE
Bickerstaffe C of E Prim. Sch.
Ash Holt
Bickerstaffe Hall
Pav.
Playing Field
OX HEY FIELD
Little Wood
Plantation Cottage
Ivy House
Keeper's Cottage
Greenacres
Top Colliers Row
Rookery Pits
A570
Highfield House
Roby's Farm
Bickerstaffe Wood
Rabbit Hey Pits
COAL PIT LA.
Long Plantation
Barker's Bridge
Barker's Bridge Wood
HALL LANE
BARROW NOOK
Wood End Farm
Wood House
Intake Farm
Ben Lane Farm
Taylor's Wood
Barrow Nook
37
G H J K L M N
1 2 3 4 5 6 7 8 9
44 345 46
07 06 405 04 03

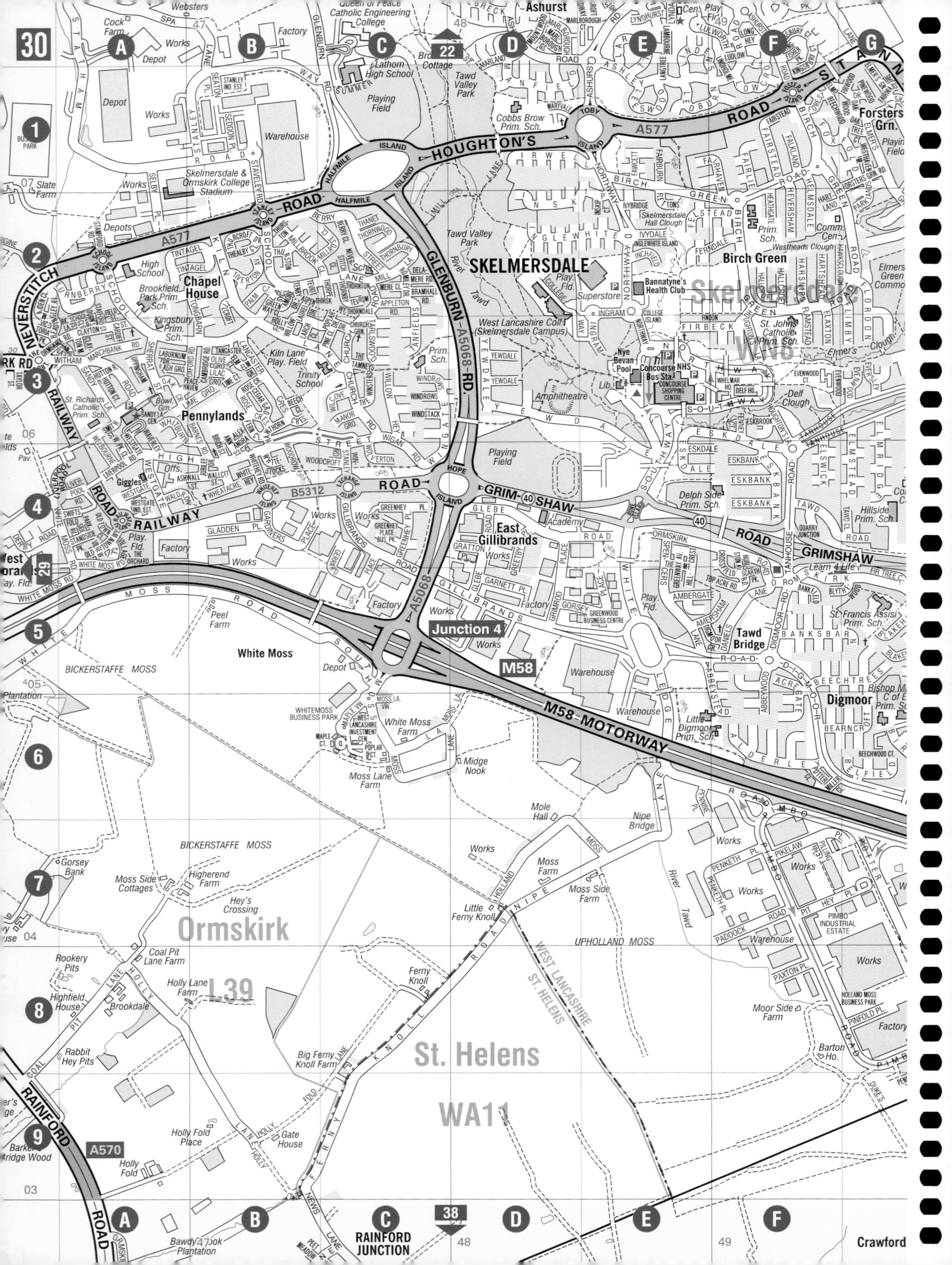
SKELMERSDALE
Skelmersdale
WN8
Chapel House
Pennylands
Birch Green
East Gillibrands
Tawd Bridge
Digmoor
Forsters Grn.
Ashurst
White Moss
BICKERSTAFFE MOSS
UPHOLLAND MOSS
Ormskirk
L39
St. Helens
WA11
HOUGHTON'S ROAD
A577
HALFMILE ISLAND
STANLEY ISLAND
SCHOOL ISLAND
NEVERSTITCH ROAD
GLENBURN ROAD
A5068
GRIMSHAW ROAD
RAILWAY ROAD
B5312
HIGH STREET
WHITE MOSS ROAD
M58 MOTORWAY
M58
Junction 4
PIMBO ROAD
PIMBO INDUSTRIAL ESTATE
HOLLAND MOSS BUSINESS PARK
NIPE LANE
HOLLY LANE
COAL PIT LANE
FERNY KNOLL ROAD
RAINFORD ROAD
A570
WEST LANCASHIRE
ST. HELENS
Skelmersdale & Ormskirk College Stadium
Lathom High School
Cobbs Brow Prim. Sch.
Tawd Valley Park
West Lancashire Coll. (Skelmersdale Campus)
Concourse Bus Sta.
CONCOURSE SHOPPING CENTRE
Nye Bevan Pool
Bannatyne's Health Club
Superstore
Amphitheatre
Trinity School
Kiln Lane Play. Field
High School
Brookfield Park Prim. Sch.
Kingsbury Prim. Sch.
St. Richards Catholic Prim. Sch.
St. John's Catholic Prim. Sch.
Delph Side Prim. Sch.
Hillside Prim. Sch.
St. Francis Assisi Prim. Sch.
Little Digmoor Prim. Sch.
Academy
WHITEMOSS BUSINESS PARK
White Moss Farm
Midge Nook
Moss Lane Farm
Mole Hall
Nipe Bridge
Moss Farm
Moss Side Farm
Little Ferny Knoll
Ferny Knoll
Big Ferny Knoll Farm
Gorsey Bank
Moss Side Cottages
Higherend Farm
Hey's Crossing
Rookery Pits
Coal Pit Lane Farm
Holly Lane Farm
Highfield House
Brookdale
Rabbit Hey Pits
Holly Fold Place
Holly Fold
Gate House
Moor Side Farm
Barton Ho.
Peel Farm
Cock Farm
Websters
RAINFORD JUNCTION
Crawford
22
38
29

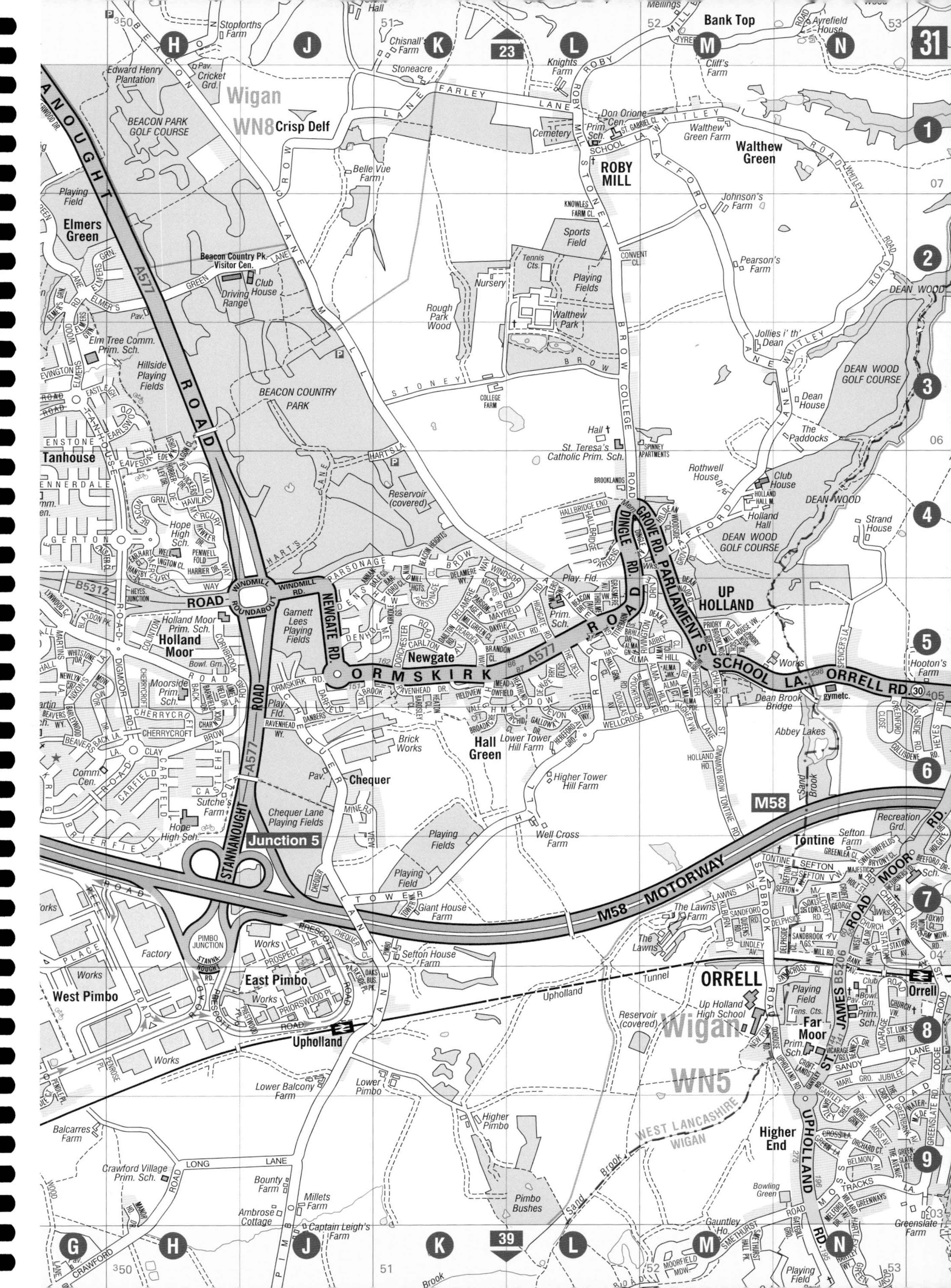
Wigan
WN8
Crisp Delf
Stopforths Farm
Edward Henry Plantation
Cricket Grd.
BEACON PARK GOLF COURSE
Chisnall's Farm
Stoneacre
Knights Farm
Bank Top
Ayrefield House
Cliff's Farm
Mellings
FARLEY LANE
ROBY MILL
Don Orione Cen.
Prim. Sch.
Cemetery
SCHOOL LA.
Walthew Green Farm
Walthew Green
WHITLEY ROAD
Belle Vue Farm
Playing Field
Elmers Green
Johnson's Farm
Pearson's Farm
KNOWLES FARM CL.
Sports Field
CONVENT CL.
Tennis Cts.
Playing Fields
Nursery
Beacon Country Pk. Visitor Cen.
Club House
Driving Range
Rough Park Wood
Walthew Park
Jollies i' th' Dean
DEAN WOOD
DEAN WOOD GOLF COURSE
Elm Tree Comm. Prim. Sch.
Hillside Playing Fields
BEACON COUNTRY PARK
STONEY BROW
COLLEGE FARM
Dean House
The Paddocks
Hall
St. Teresa's Catholic Prim. Sch.
SPINNEY APARTMENTS
Rothwell House
Club House
HOLLAND HALL M.
Holland Hall
Tanhouse
HART'S LA.
Reservoir (covered)
BROOKLANDS
Strand House
DEAN WOOD GOLF COURSE
Hope High Sch.
HALLBRIDGE END
DINGLE RD.
GROVE RD.
PARLIAMENT ST.
B5312
WINDMILL ROUNDABOUT
WINDMILL RD.
PARSONAGE BROW
NEWGATE RD.
Garnett Lees Playing Fields
Prim. Sch.
UP HOLLAND
Holland Moor Prim. Sch.
Holland Moor
Newgate
ORMSKIRK ROAD
A577
SCHOOL LA.
ORRELL RD.
Works
Hooton's Farm
Moorside Prim. Sch.
Dean Brook Bridge
Abbey Lakes
Hall Green
Lower Tower Hill Farm
Brick Works
Higher Tower Hill Farm
HOLLAND HO.
Comm. Cen.
Chequer
Sutche's Farm
Hope High Sch.
M58
Chequer Lane Playing Fields
Playing Fields
Well Cross Farm
Recreation Grd.
Tontine
Sefton Farm
Junction 5
STANNANOUGHT ROAD
M58 MOTORWAY
Playing Field
Giant House Farm
The Lawns Farm
The Lawns
Factory
PIMBO JUNCTION
Works
Sefton House Farm
West Pimbo
East Pimbo
Tunnel
ORRELL
Orrell
Upholland
Reservoir (covered)
Up Holland High School
Wigan
WN5
Far Moor
Prim. Sch.
Lower Balcony Farm
Lower Pimbo
Higher Pimbo
WEST LANCASHIRE
WIGAN
Higher End
UPHOLLAND RD.
Balcarres Farm
LONG LANE
Crawford Village Prim. Sch.
Bounty Farm
Millets Farm
Ambrose Cottage
Captain Leigh's Farm
Pimbo Bushes
Sand Brook
Gauntley Ho.
Bowling Green
Greenslate Farm
Playing Field
CRAWFORD
23
39
07
06
04
03
405
350
51
52
53

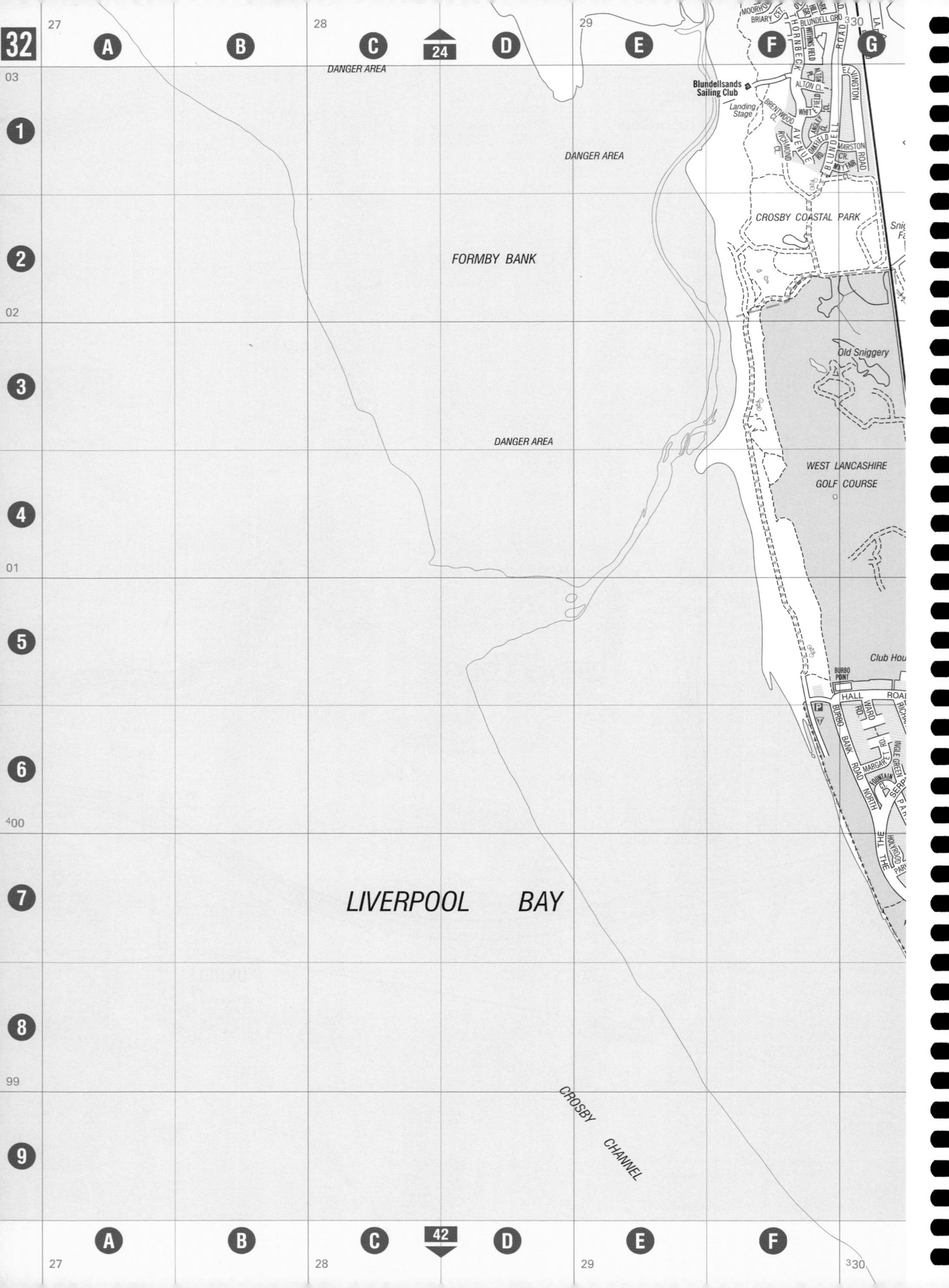

32

27   Ⓐ   Ⓑ   28   Ⓒ   ⬆️24   Ⓓ   29   Ⓔ   Ⓕ   Ⓖ

03

1

DANGER AREA

Blundellsands
Sailing Club

Landing
Stage

DANGER AREA

2

FORMBY BANK

CROSBY COASTAL PARK

02

3

Old Sniggery

DANGER AREA

4

WEST LANCASHIRE
GOLF COURSE

01

5

Club Hou

BURBO
POINT

6

HALL   ROA

BURBO

BANK   ROAD   NORTH

⁴00

7

LIVERPOOL   BAY

99

8

9

CROSBY

CHANNEL

Ⓐ   Ⓑ   Ⓒ   ⬇️42   Ⓓ   Ⓔ   Ⓕ

27   28   29   330

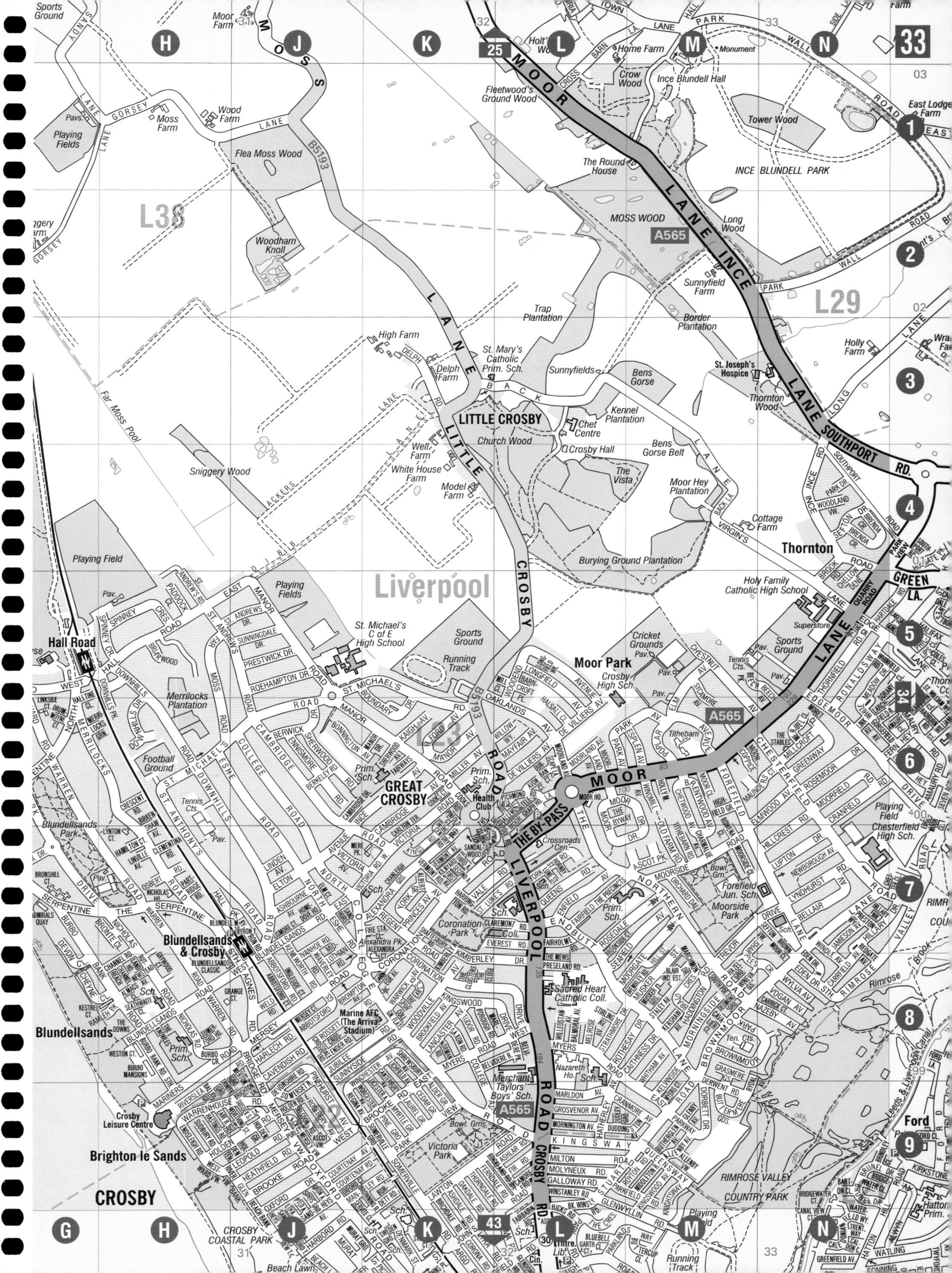
Sports Ground
Moor Farm
Moss Lane
Holt's Wood
Home Farm
Monument
Crow Wood
Ince Blundell Hall
Fleetwood's Ground Wood
Moor Lane
Wood Farm
Moss Farm
Gorsey Lane
Playing Fields
Pavs.
East Lodge Farm
Tower Wood
Flea Moss Wood
B5193
The Round House
Ince Blundell Park
L38
Woodham Knoll
Moss Wood
Long Wood
A565
Park Wall
Sunnyfield Farm
L29
Trap Plantation
Border Plantation
Holly Farm
High Farm
Delph Farm
St. Mary's Catholic Prim. Sch.
Sunnyfields
Bens Gorse
St. Joseph's Hospice
Thornton Wood
Far Moss Pool
Back Lane
Little Crosby
Chet Centre
Kennel Plantation
Church Wood
Crosby Hall
Bens Gorse Belt
Well Farm
White House Farm
Sniggery Wood
Model Farm
The Vista
Moor Hey Plantation
Southport Rd.
Little Crosby Road
Cottage Farm
Thornton
Virgin's Lane
Playing Field
Burying Ground Plantation
Playing Fields
Liverpool
Holy Family Catholic High School
Green La.
Pav.
St. Michael's C of E High School
Sports Ground
Running Track
Cricket Grounds
Superstore
Hall Road
Moor Park
Crosby High Sch.
Sports Ground
Merrilocks Plantation
Manor Road
L23
Tithebarn
Football Ground
Prim. Sch.
Great Crosby
Health Club
Moor Lane
The By-Pass
Playing Field
Chesterfield High Sch.
Blundellsands Park
Tennis Cts.
Crossroads Cen.
Liverpool Road
College Road
Forefield Jun. Sch.
Moorside Park
Coronation Park
Alexandra Pk.
Blundellsands & Crosby
Sacred Heart Catholic Coll.
Marine AFC (The Arriva Stadium)
Blundellsands
Rimrose Brook
Nazareth Ho.
Merchant Taylors Boys' Sch.
Crosby Leisure Centre
Victoria Park
Kingsway
Ford
Leeds & Liverpool Canal
Brighton le Sands
Rimrose Valley Country Park
Crosby
Crosby Coastal Park
Beach Lawn
Running Track
Hatton Prim.
43
25
34
G H J K L M N
1 2 3 4 5 6 7 8 9
31 32 33

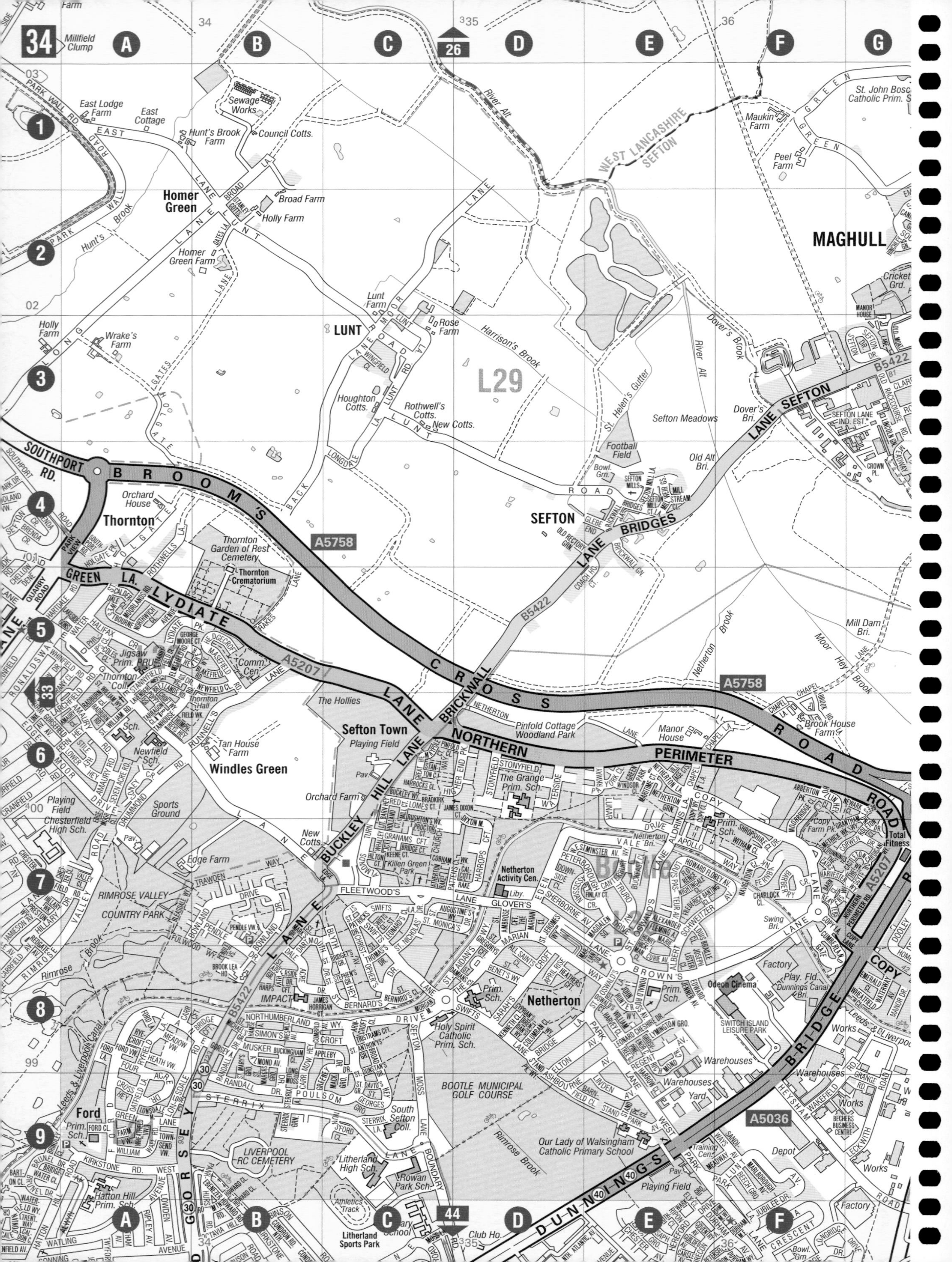
Millfield Clump
26
A B C D E F G
1 2 3 4 5 6 7 8 9
East Lodge Farm
East Cottage
Sewage Works
Hunt's Brook Farm
Council Cotts.
Homer Green
Broad Farm
Holly Farm
Homer Green Farm
Hunt's Brook
River Alt
WEST LANCASHIRE
SEFTON
Maukin Farm
Peel Farm
St. John Bosco Catholic Prim. Sch.
MAGHULL
Cricket Grd.
Holly Farm
Wrake's Farm
Lunt Farm
LUNT
Rose Farm
Harrison's Brook
L29
Dover's Brook
Houghton Cotts.
Rothwell's Cotts.
New Cotts.
St. Helen's Gutter
Sefton Meadows
Dover's Bri.
Football Field
Old Alt Bri.
SEFTON LANE IND. EST.
SOUTHPORT RD.
BROOM'S CROSS ROAD
A5758
Orchard House
Thornton
SEFTON
Thornton Garden of Rest Cemetery
Thornton Crematorium
LYDIATE LANE
A5207
B5422
BRICKWALL LANE
Mill Dam Bri.
Netherton Brook
Moor Hey Brook
Jigsaw Prim. PRU
Thornton Coll.
Comm. Cen.
The Hollies
Sefton Town Playing Field
Pinfold Cottage Woodland Park
Manor House
Brook House Farm
NORTHERN PERIMETER ROAD
33
Tan House Farm
Newfield Sch.
Windles Green
The Grange Prim. Sch.
Playing Field
Chesterfield High Sch.
Sports Ground
Orchard Farm
BUCKLEY HILL LANE
New Cotts.
Edge Farm
Killen Green Park
Netherton Activity Cen.
Liby.
Bootle
Netherton
Prim. Sch.
Copy Farm
Total Fitness
RIMROSE VALLEY COUNTRY PARK
Rimrose Brook
FLEETWOOD'S LANE
GLOVER'S LANE
BROWN'S LANE
COPY LANE
Swing Bri.
Factory
Play. Fld.
Odeon Cinema
Dunnings Canal Bri.
SWITCH ISLAND LEISURE PARK
IMPACT
Holy Spirit Catholic Prim. Sch.
Leeds & Liverpool Canal
Ford
Ford Prim. Sch.
GORSEY LANE
BOOTLE MUNICIPAL GOLF COURSE
Warehouses
Yard
Works
A5036
South Sefton Coll.
LIVERPOOL RC CEMETERY
Litherland High Sch.
Rowan Park Sch.
Our Lady of Walsingham Catholic Primary School
Rimrose Brook
Training Cen.
Depot
Playing Field
DUNNINGS BRIDGE ROAD
Hatton Hill Prim. Sch.
Athletics Track
Litherland Sports Park
Club Ho.
44
Factory
Bowl. Grn.

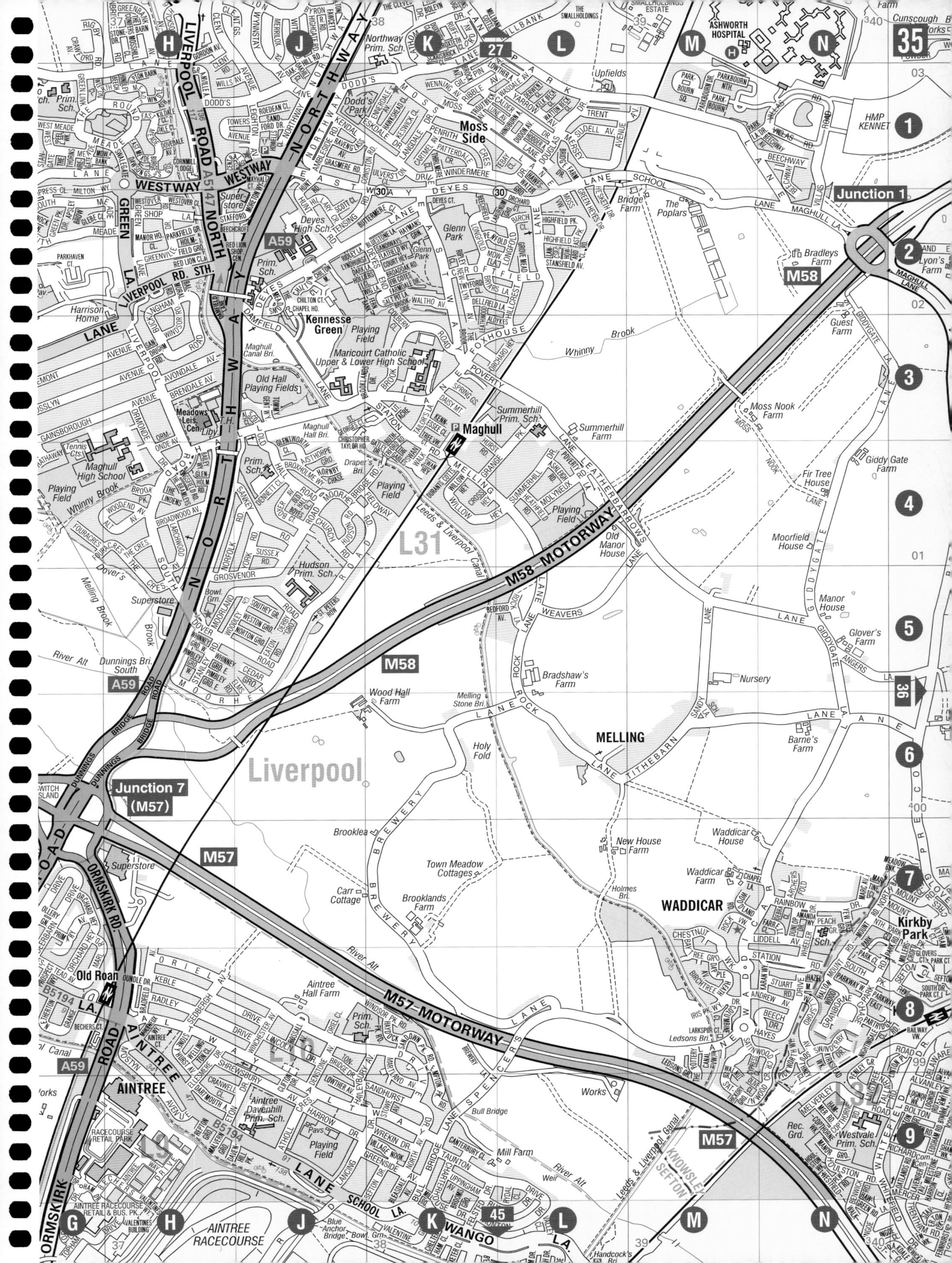

H
J
K
L
M
N
27
ASHWORTH HOSPITAL
Northway Prim. Sch.
Upfields
HMP KENNET
1
Moss Side
Dodd's Park
WESTWAY
NORTHWAY
LIVERPOOL ROAD NORTH
A5147
Junction 1
2
Bradleys Farm
Lyon's Farm
M58
Deyes High Sch.
A59
Glenn Park
Kennesse Green
Maricourt Catholic Upper & Lower High School
Whinny Brook
Guest Farm
3
Old Hall Playing Fields
Meadows Leis. Cen.
Maghull
Summerhill Prim. Sch.
Summerhill Farm
Moss Nook Farm
Giddy Gate Farm
Fir Tree House
Maghull High School
Playing Field
4
L31
M58 MOTORWAY
Old Manor House
Moorfield House
Leeds & Liverpool Canal
Hudson Prim. Sch.
Superstore
Melling Brook
Manor House
5
Glover's Farm
River Alt
Dunnings Bri. South
M58
Bradshaw's Farm
Nursery
Wood Hall Farm
Melling Stone Bri.
36
MELLING
Barne's Farm
6
Holy Fold
Liverpool
Junction 7 (M57)
Brooklea
New House Farm
Waddicar House
M57
Superstore
Town Meadow Cottages
Waddicar Farm
7
Carr Cottage
Brooklands Farm
Holmes Bri.
WADDICAR
Kirkby Park
Old Roan
Aintree Hall Farm
M57 MOTORWAY
8
Ledsons Bri.
L10
A59
AINTREE
Aintree Davenhill Prim. Sch.
Works
Westvale Prim. Sch.
9
RACECOURSE RETAIL PARK
L9
Playing Field
Bull Bridge
Mill Farm
M57
KNOWSLEY
SEFTON
AINTREE RACECOURSE RETAIL & BUS. PK.
G
H
J
K
L
M
N
AINTREE RACECOURSE
45
WANGO LA.
Handcock's Bri.
L33

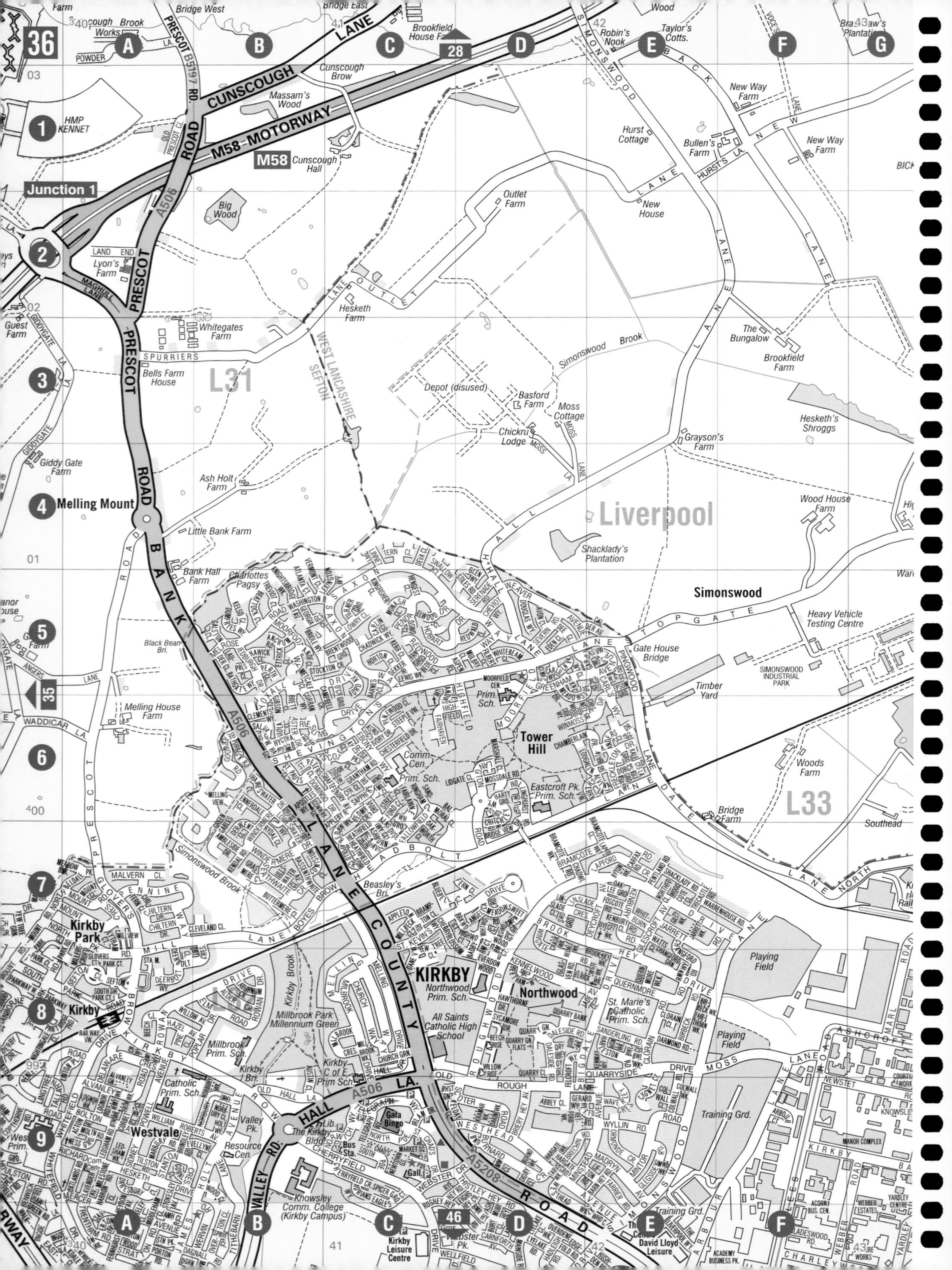

36
A
B
C
D
E
F
G
1
2
3
4
5
6
7
8
9
28
35
46
40
41
42
43
03
02
01
400
99
Bridge West
Bridge East
Cunscough Brook Works
POWDER
Brookfield House Farm
Robin's Nook
Taylor's Cotts.
PRESCOT B5197 RD.
LANE
CUNSCOUGH
Cunscough Brow
Massam's Wood
M58 MOTORWAY
M58
Cunscough Hall
HMP KENNET
Junction 1
Big Wood
LAND END
Lyon's Farm
MAGHULL LANE
PRESCOT
ROAD
A506
OLD PRESCOT CL.
Guest Farm
GIDDYGATE LA.
Whitegates Farm
SPURRIERS
Bells Farm House
L31
WEST LANCASHIRE
SEFTON
Hesketh Farm
OUTLET LANE
Outlet Farm
Hurst Cottage
New Way Farm
Bullen's Farm
HURST'S LA.
NEW LANE
BACK LANE
SIMONSWOOD LANE
New House
The Bungalow
Brookfield Farm
Simonswood Brook
Depot (disused)
Basford Farm
Moss Cottage
MOSS LANE
Chickru Lodge
Grayson's Farm
Hesketh's Shroggs
Giddy Gate Farm
Ash Holt Farm
Melling Mount
Little Bank Farm
Liverpool
Wood House Farm
Shacklady's Plantation
HALL LANE
BANK
Bank Hall Farm
Charlottes Pagsy
Simonswood
TOPGATE
Heavy Vehicle Testing Centre
Gate House Bridge
Timber Yard
SIMONSWOOD INDUSTRIAL PARK
Black Bean Bri.
ANGERS LANE
WADDICAR LA.
Melling House Farm
Tower Hill
MOORFIELD
Prim. Sch.
Comm. Cen.
Eastcroft Pk. Prim. Sch.
SHEVINGTON'S
Woods Farm
L33
Bridge Farm
Southead
DALE LANE
LANE NORTH
Simonswood Brook
Beasley's Bri.
BOYES BROW
LANE
COUNTY
MALVERN CL.
PENNINE WAY
CHILTERN DR.
CLEVELAND CL.
Kirkby Park
Kirkby
KIRKBY
Northwood Prim. Sch.
Northwood
All Saints Catholic High School
St. Marie's Catholic Prim. Sch.
Playing Field
Kirkby Brook
Millbrook Park Millennium Green
Millbrook Prim. Sch.
Catholic Prim. Sch.
Kirkby C of E Prim Sch.
Kirkby Bri.
OLD HALL LA.
HALL LA.
A506
Valley Pk.
Resource Cen.
Westvale
QUARRYSIDE
MOSS LANE
ASHCROFT
Training Grd.
ROUGH LANE
WESTHEAD
Gala Bingo
Bus Sta.
The Kirkby Bldg
CHERRYFIELD
Knowsley Comm. College (Kirkby Campus)
A5208
ROAD
VALLEY RD.
Kirkby Leisure Centre
Webster Pk.
David Lloyd Leisure
KIRKBY
MANOR COMPLEX
ACORN BUS. CEN.
WEBBER ESTATES
YARDLEY CENTRE
ACADEMY BUSINESS PK.
GLADESWOOD RD.
CHARLEY

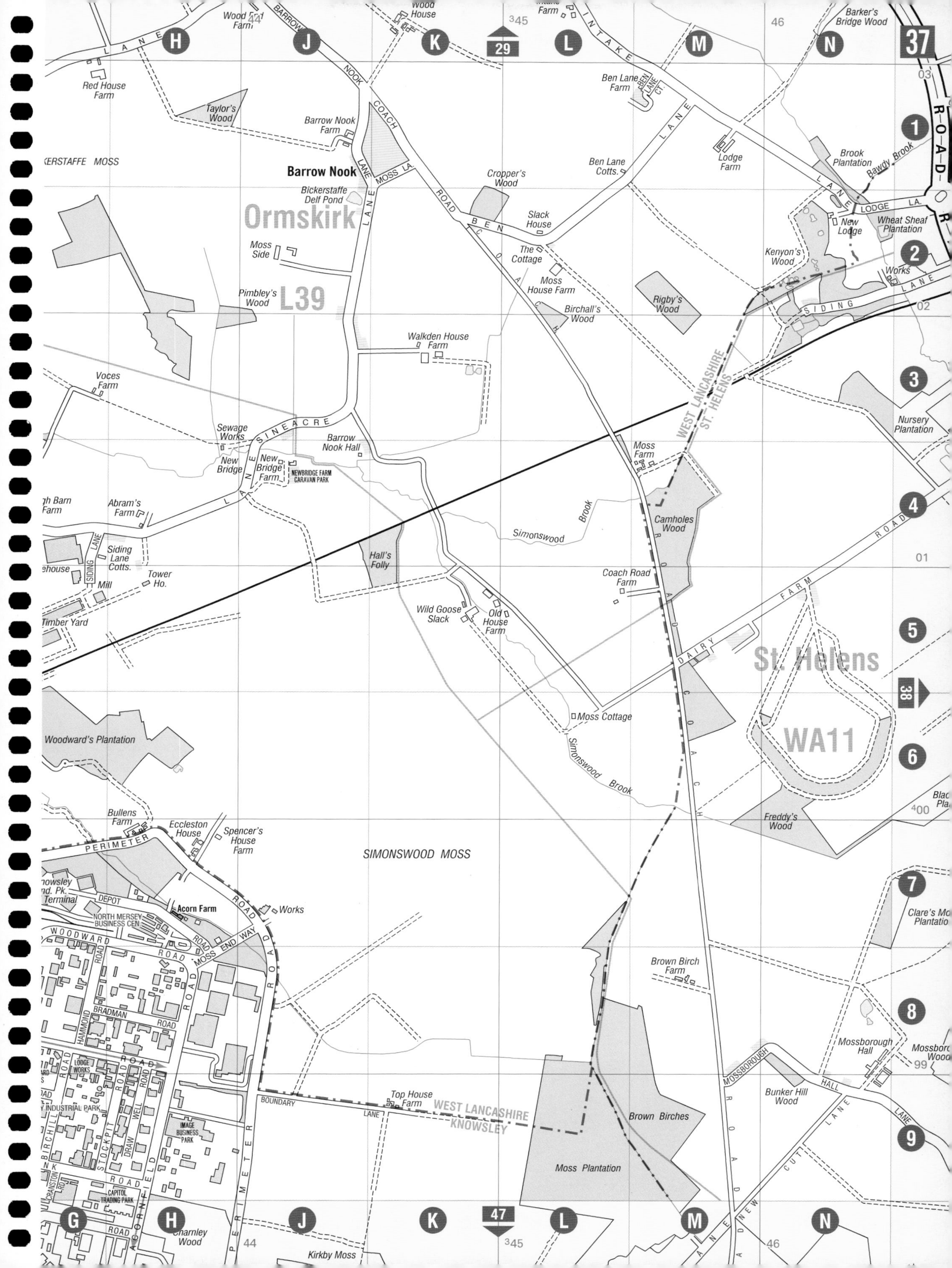
Barrow Nook
Ormskirk
L39
St. Helens
WA11
SIMONSWOOD MOSS
Red House Farm
Taylor's Wood
Barrow Nook Farm
Bickerstaffe Delf Pond
Moss Side
Pimbley's Wood
Walkden House Farm
Voces Farm
Sewage Works
New Bridge
New Bridge Farm
NEWBRIDGE FARM CARAVAN PARK
Barrow Nook Hall
Abram's Farm
Siding Lane Cotts.
Tower Ho.
Mill
Timber Yard
Hall's Folly
Wild Goose Slack
Old House Farm
Moss Cottage
Coach Road Farm
Camholes Wood
Moss Farm
Simonswood Brook
Cropper's Wood
Slack House
The Cottage
Moss House Farm
Birchall's Wood
Rigby's Wood
Ben Lane Farm
Ben Lane Cotts.
Lodge Farm
Brook Plantation
Bawdy Brook
New Lodge
Wheat Sheaf Plantation
Kenyon's Wood
Works
Barker's Bridge Wood
Nursery Plantation
Woodward's Plantation
Bullens Farm
Eccleston House
Spencer's House Farm
Acorn Farm
NORTH MERSEY BUSINESS CEN.
LODGE WORKS
IMAGE BUSINESS PARK
CAPITOL TRADING PARK
Charnley Wood
Kirkby Moss
Top House Farm
WEST LANCASHIRE
KNOWSLEY
ST. HELENS
Brown Birches
Moss Plantation
Brown Birch Farm
Freddy's Wood
Clare's Mo Plantatio
Mossborough Hall
Bunker Hill Wood
BARROW NOOK LANE
COACH ROAD
MOSS LANE
BEN LANE
INTAKE LANE
LODGE LA.
SIDING LANE
SINEACRE LANE
DAIRY FARM ROAD
PERIMETER ROAD
MOSS END WAY
WOODWARD ROAD
BRADMAN ROAD
HAMMOND ROAD
BOUNDARY LANE
MOSSBOROUGH HALL LANE
NEW CUT LANE
STOCKPIT ROAD
DRAW WELL ROAD
ACORNFIELD ROAD
DEPOT
29
38
47
44
345
46
03
02
01
400
99
H J K L M N G
1 2 3 4 5 6 7 8 9

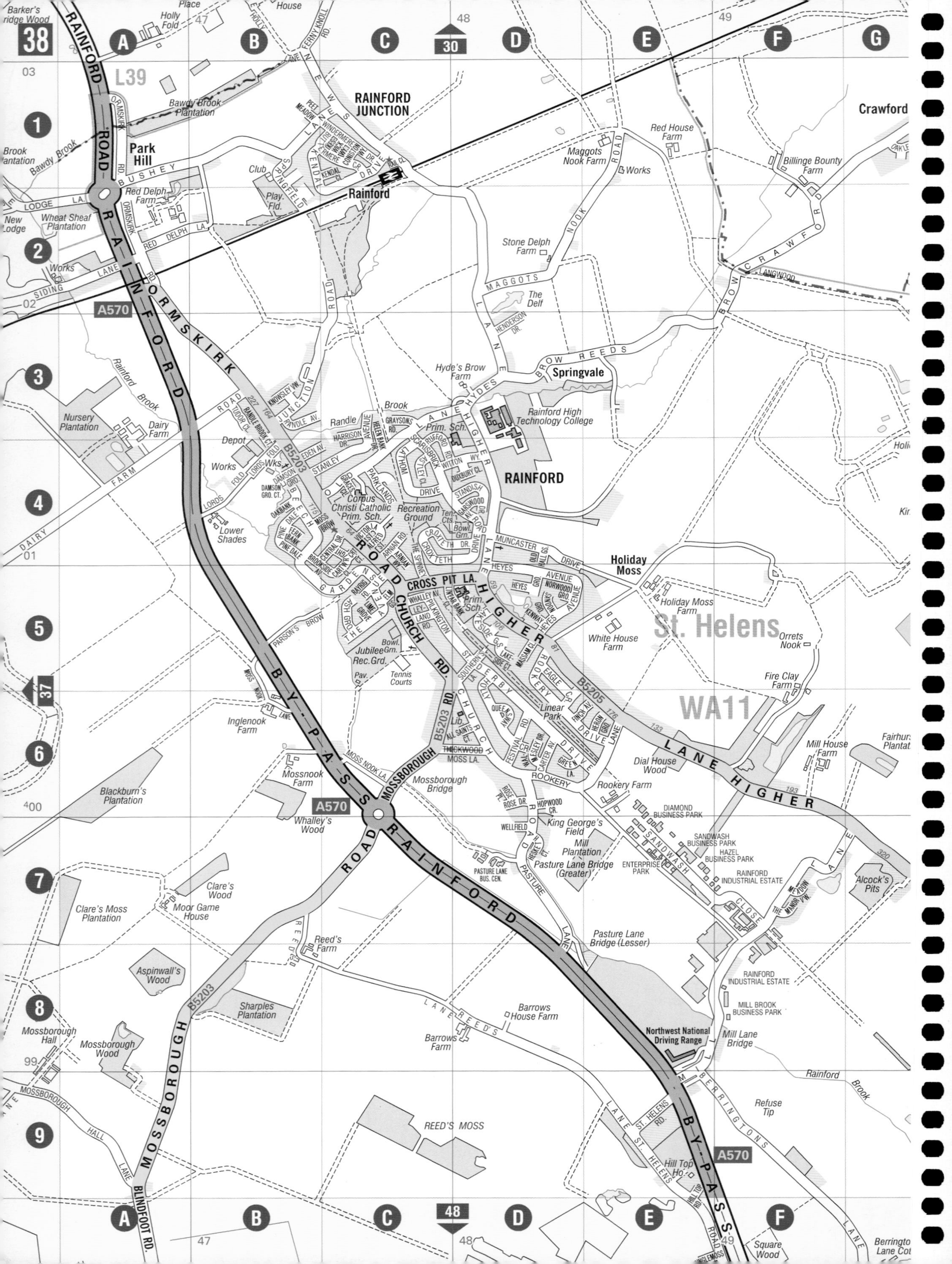

Barker's ridge Wood
Holly Fold
Place
House
L39
Bawdy Brook Plantation
RAINFORD JUNCTION
Crawford
Park Hill
Brook Plantation
Bawdy Brook
Club
Rainford
Red House Farm
Maggots Nook Farm
Works
Billinge Bounty Farm
Red Delph Farm
New Lodge
Wheat Sheaf Plantation
Play Fld.
Stone Delph Farm
Works
The Delf
A570
Springvale
Hyde's Brow Farm
Rainford High Technology College
Rainford Brook
Nursery Plantation
Dairy Farm
Depot
Works
Randle Brook
Prim. Sch.
RAINFORD
Corpus Christi Catholic Prim. Sch.
Recreation Ground
Lower Shades
Holiday Moss
Holiday Moss Farm
St. Helens
White House Farm
Orrets Nook
Jubilee Rec. Grd.
Tennis Courts
Fire Clay Farm
WA11
Inglenook Farm
Linear Park
Mill House Farm
Mossnook Farm
Mossborough Bridge
Dial House Wood
Rookery Farm
Blackburn's Plantation
Whalley's Wood
DIAMOND BUSINESS PARK
King George's Field
SANDWASH BUSINESS PARK
HAZEL BUSINESS PARK
Mill Plantation
ENTERPRISE PARK
RAINFORD INDUSTRIAL ESTATE
Alcock's Pits
Pasture Lane Bridge (Greater)
PASTURE LANE BUS. CEN.
Clare's Wood
Clare's Moss Plantation
Moor Game House
Reed's Farm
Pasture Lane Bridge (Lesser)
Aspinwall's Wood
RAINFORD INDUSTRIAL ESTATE
MILL BROOK BUSINESS PARK
Sharples Plantation
Barrows House Farm
Mossborough Hall
Mossborough Wood
Barrows Farm
Northwest National Driving Range
Mill Lane Bridge
Rainford Brook
Refuse Tip
REED'S MOSS
Hill Top Ho.
Square Wood
Berrington Lane Cot
RAINFORD BY-PASS
ORMSKIRK RD.
MOSSBOROUGH RD.
CHURCH RD.
HIGHER LANE
CROSS PIT LA.
B5203
B5205
30
48
37

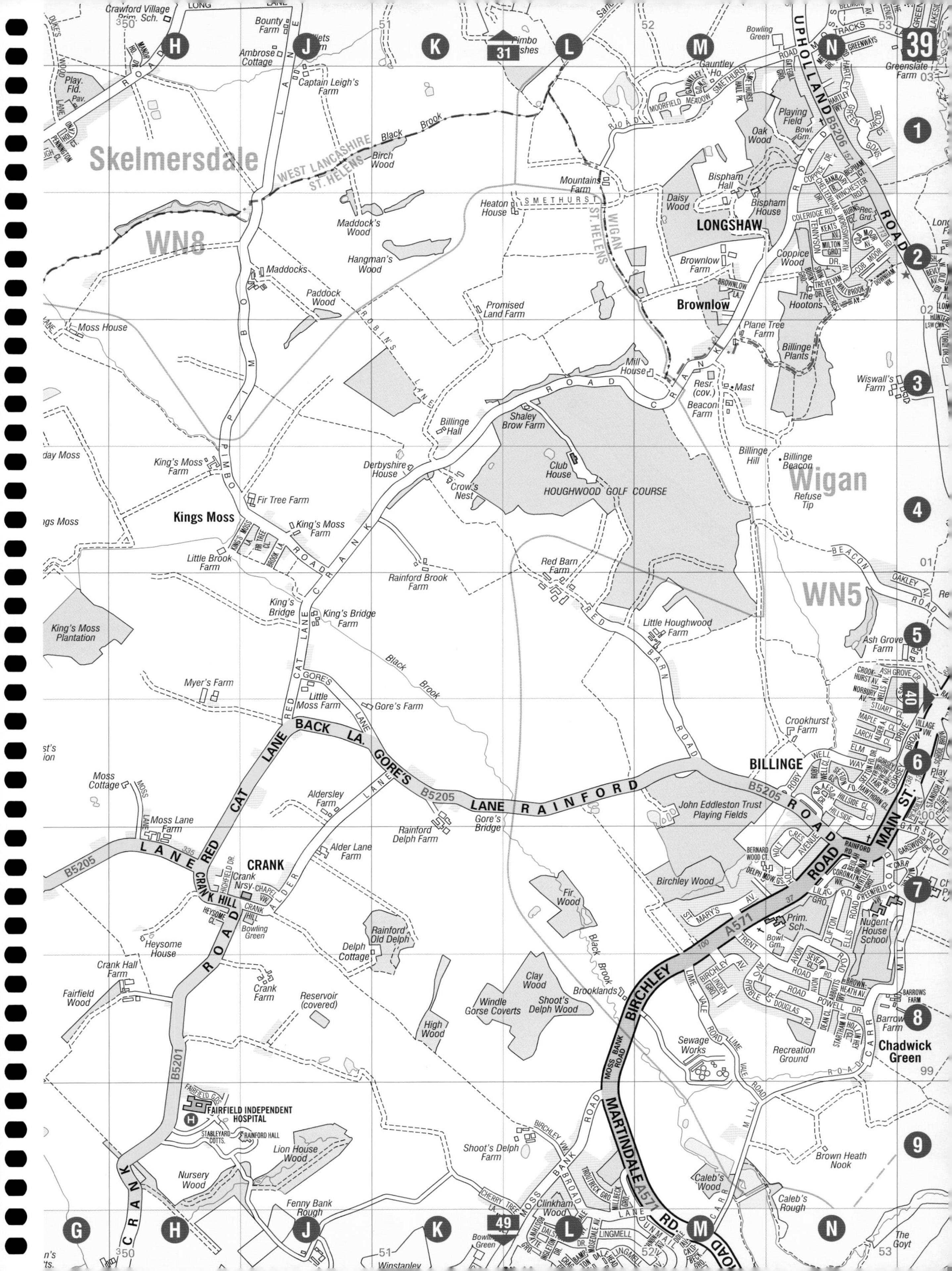
Skelmersdale
WN8
Kings Moss
CRANK
LONGSHAW
Brownlow
Wigan
WN5
BILLINGE
Chadwick Green
HOUGHWOOD GOLF COURSE
FAIRFIELD INDEPENDENT HOSPITAL
John Eddleston Trust Playing Fields
WEST LANCASHIRE
ST. HELENS
WIGAN
RAINFORD
B5205
B5201
B5206
A571
31
49
40
H
J
K
L
M
N
G
1
2
3
4
5
6
7
8
9

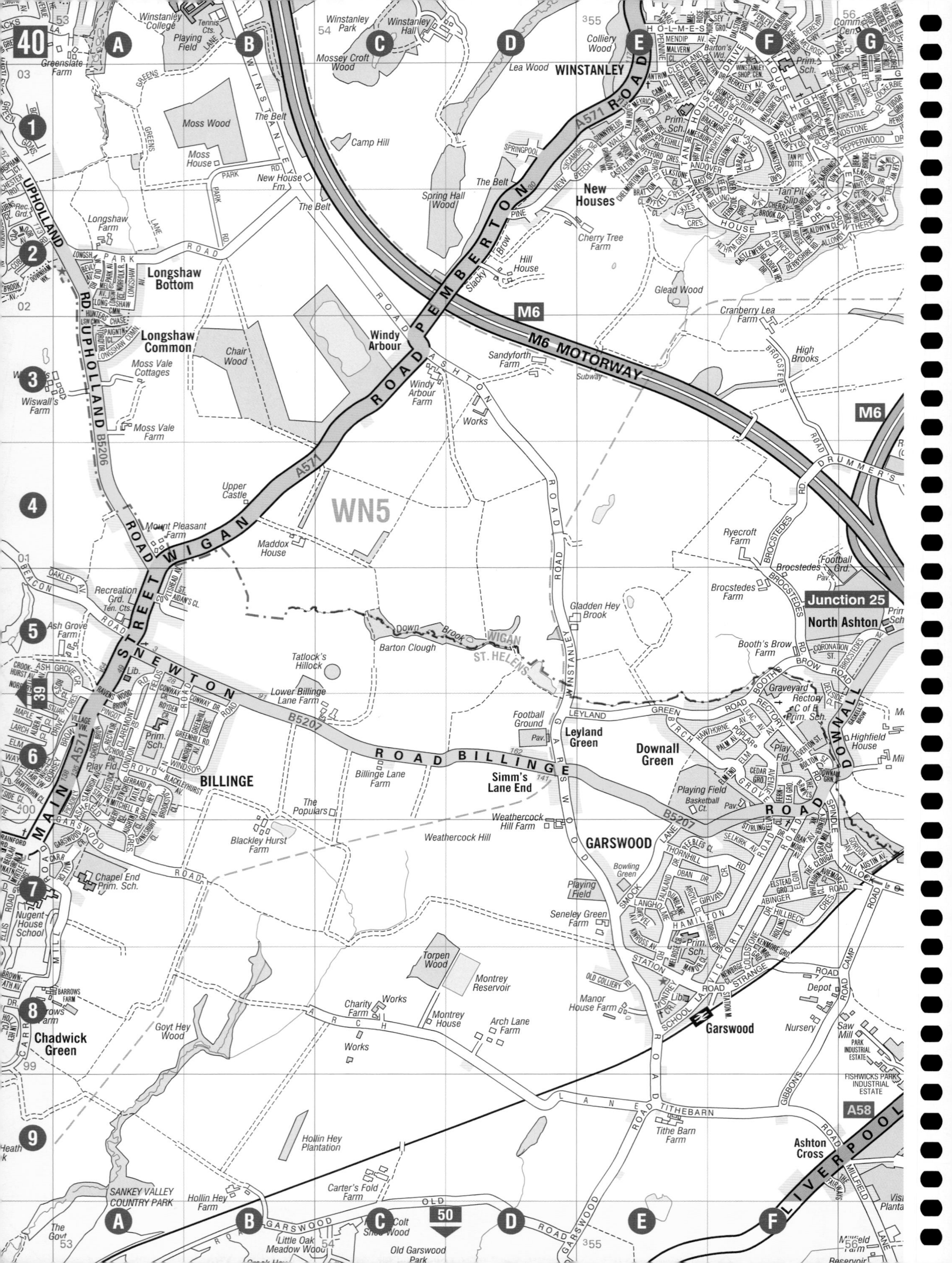
Winstanley College
Playing Field
Tennis Cts.
Greenslate Farm
Winstanley Park
Winstanley Hall
Mossey Croft Wood
Colliery Wood
WINSTANLEY
Lea Wood
Moss Wood
The Belt
Camp Hill
Moss House
New House Fm.
Spring Hall Wood
New Houses
Cherry Tree Farm
Hill House
Glead Wood
Longshaw Farm
Longshaw Bottom
Longshaw Common
Moss Vale Cottages
Moss Vale Farm
Wiswall's Farm
Chair Wood
Windy Arbour
Windy Arbour Farm
Sandyforth Farm
Subway
Works
M6
M6 MOTORWAY
Cranberry Lea Farm
High Brooks
Upper Castle
WN5
Mount Pleasant Farm
Maddox House
Ryecroft Farm
Brocstedes
Brocstedes Farm
Football Grd.
Junction 25
North Ashton
Booth's Brow Farm
Recreation Grd.
Ten. Cts.
Ash Grove Farm
Gladden Hey Brook
Down Brook
Barton Clough
WIGAN
ST. HELENS
Tatlock's Hillock
Lower Billinge Lane Farm
Graveyard
Rectory
C of E Prim. Sch.
Highfield House
Football Ground
Leyland Green
Downall Green
Prim. Sch.
Play Fld.
BILLINGE
Billinge Lane Farm
Simm's Lane End
Playing Field
Basketball Ct.
The Populars
Blackley Hurst Farm
Weathercock Hill Farm
Weathercock Hill
GARSWOOD
Bowling Green
Chapel End Prim. Sch.
Nugent House School
Seneley Green Farm
Torpen Wood
Montrey Reservoir
Manor House Farm
Garswood
Depot
Nursery
Saw Mill
PARK INDUSTRIAL ESTATE
FISHWICKS PARK INDUSTRIAL ESTATE
A58
Charity Farm
Works
Montrey House
Arch Lane Farm
Goyt Hey Wood
Chadwick Green
Tithe Barn Farm
Ashton Cross
Hollin Hey Plantation
SANKEY VALLEY COUNTRY PARK
Hollin Hey Farm
Carter's Fold Farm
Little Oak Meadow Wood
Colt Shoe Wood
Old Garswood Park
50
39
WIGAN ROAD
PEMBERTON ROAD
A571
B5206
B5207
NEWTON ROAD
BILLINGE ROAD
DOWNALL ROAD
UPHOLLAND ROAD
MAIN STREET
WINSTANLEY ROAD
GARSWOOD ROAD
ASHTON ROAD
BROCSTEDES ROAD
DRUMMER'S LANE
LIVERPOOL ROAD
TITHEBARN ROAD
ARCH LANE
OLD GARSWOOD ROAD
LEYLAND GREEN ROAD
SMOCK LANE
STATION ROAD
VICTORIA ROAD
CAMP ROAD
A B C D E F G
1 2 3 4 5 6 7 8 9
53 54 355 56
03 02 01 400 99

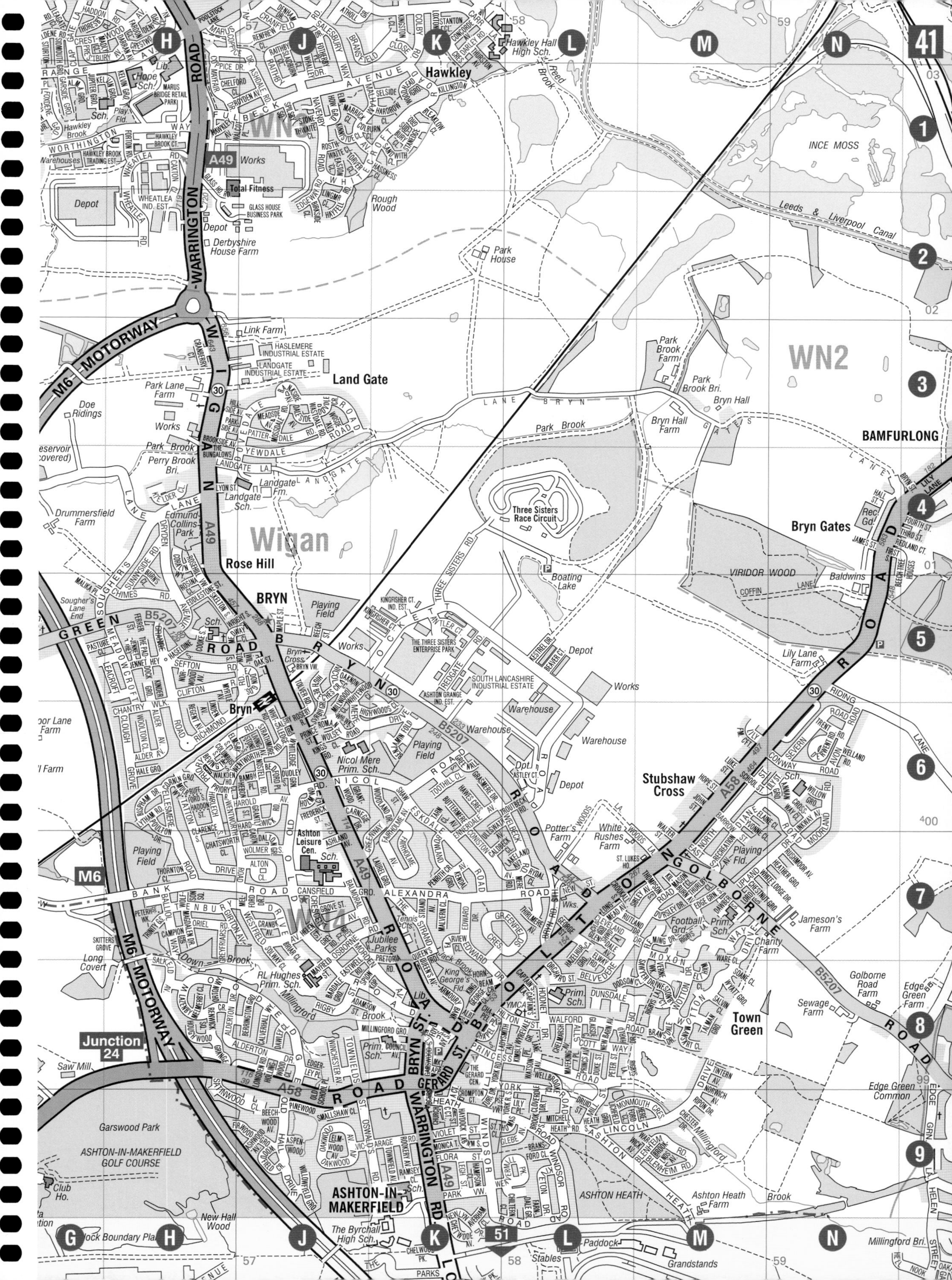
Hawkley
Hawkley Hall High Sch.
WN2
INCE MOSS
Leeds & Liverpool Canal
Park House
Derbyshire House Farm
WARRINGTON ROAD
M6 MOTORWAY
Link Farm
HASLEMERE INDUSTRIAL ESTATE
LANDGATE INDUSTRIAL ESTATE
Land Gate
Park Brook Farm
Park Brook Bri.
Bryn Hall
Bryn Hall Farm
BAMFURLONG
Three Sisters Race Circuit
Bryn Gates
Wigan
Rose Hill
BRYN
Boating Lake
VIRIDOR WOOD
Lily Lane Farm
THE THREE SISTERS ENTERPRISE PARK
SOUTH LANCASHIRE INDUSTRIAL ESTATE
Nicol Mere Prim. Sch.
Stubshaw Cross
Ashton Leisure Cen.
White Rushes Farm
Potter's Farm
Jameson's Farm
Town Green
Golborne Road Farm
Edge Green Farm
Sewage Farm
Edge Green Common
RL Hughes Prim. Sch.
Junction 24
Garswood Park
ASHTON-IN-MAKERFIELD GOLF COURSE
ASHTON-IN-MAKERFIELD
The Byrchall High Sch.
ASHTON HEATH
Ashton Heath Farm
Millingford Bri.
New Hall Wood
Grandstands
Paddock
Stables

51

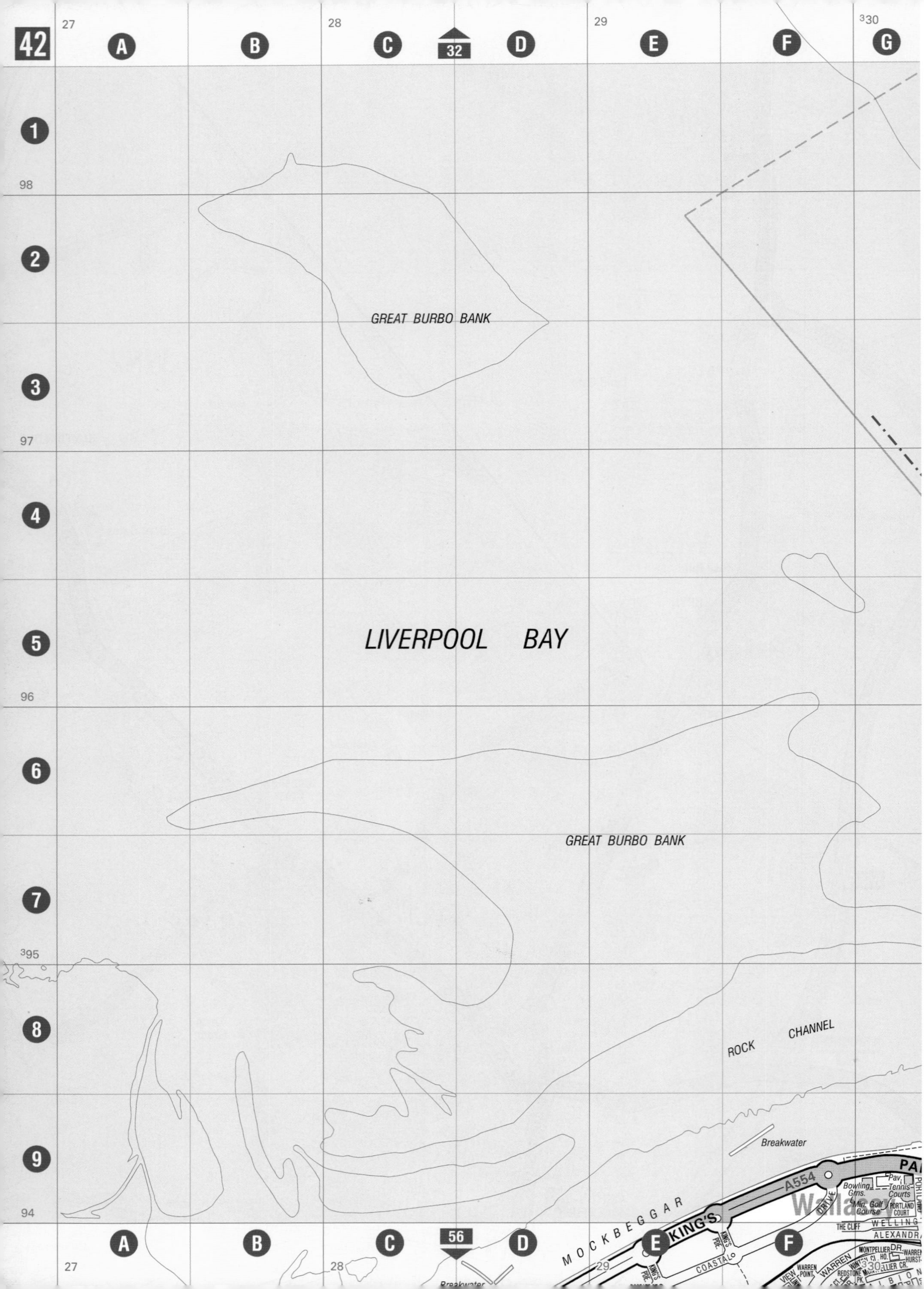

42

27 **A**   **B**   28 **C** ▲ **32** **D** 29 **E** **F** ³30 **G**

1

98

2

GREAT BURBO BANK

3

97

4

LIVERPOOL   BAY

5

96

6

GREAT BURBO BANK

7

³95

ROCK   CHANNEL

8

Breakwater

9

94

A   **B**   **C** **56** **D** **E** KING'S **F**

27   28   29

MOCKBEGGAR

A554

Bowling
Grns. Pav.
Tennis
Courts
Min. Golf
Course PORTLAND
COURT

PA

Wallas

THE CLIFF WELLING

ALEXANDRA

KING'S
FRE.

COASTAL

VIEW
POINT WARREN
DR. WARREN WARREN

REDSTONE WANT
RD. ³30 CULLIER CR. HURST

MONTPELIER DR

ALBION

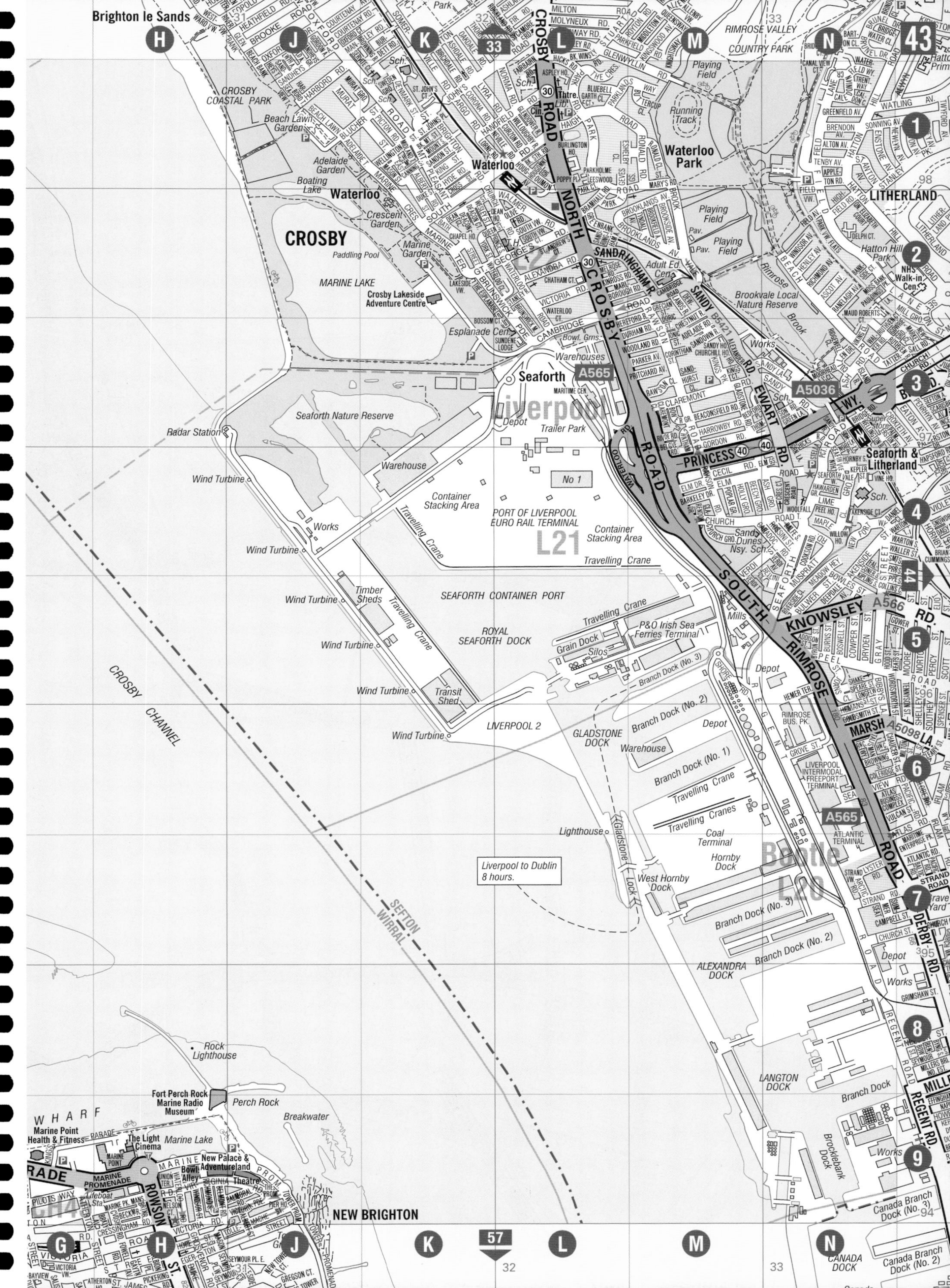
Brighton le Sands
CROSBY COASTAL PARK
Beach Lawn Garden
Adelaide Garden
Boating Lake
Waterloo
Crescent Garden
CROSBY
Paddling Pool
Marine Garden
MARINE LAKE
Crosby Lakeside Adventure Centre
Esplanade Cen.
Seaforth
A565
Liverpool
Seaforth Nature Reserve
Radar Station
Trailer Park
Depot
Warehouse
Wind Turbine
Works
Container Stacking Area
PORT OF LIVERPOOL EURO RAIL TERMINAL
L21
No 1
Travelling Crane
Timber Sheds
SEAFORTH CONTAINER PORT
ROYAL SEAFORTH DOCK
Grain Dock
Silos
P&O Irish Sea Ferries Terminal
Transit Shed
LIVERPOOL 2
GLADSTONE DOCK
Branch Dock (No. 3)
Branch Dock (No. 2)
Branch Dock (No. 1)
Travelling Cranes
Coal Terminal
Hornby Dock
Lighthouse
Gladstone Lock
West Hornby Dock
Liverpool to Dublin 8 hours.
ALEXANDRA DOCK
LANGTON DOCK
Brocklebank Dock
Canada Branch Dock (No. 3)
Canada Branch Dock (No. 2)
CANADA DOCK
Branch Dock
CROSBY CHANNEL
SEFTON WIRRAL
Rock Lighthouse
Fort Perch Rock Marine Radio Museum
Perch Rock
Breakwater
Marine Point Health & Fitness
The Light Cinema
Marine Lake
New Palace & Adventureland
Bowl. Alley
Theatre
NEW BRIGHTON
MARINE PROMENADE
ROWSON ST.
NORTH CROSBY ROAD
SOUTH ROAD
CROSBY ROAD
RIMROSE ROAD
KNOWSLEY RD.
A566
A5036
A5098
MARSH LA.
DERBY RD.
REGENT RD.
PRINCESS WY.
EWART RD.
Waterloo Park
Playing Field
Running Track
RIMROSE VALLEY COUNTRY PARK
LITHERLAND
Hatton Hill Park
NHS Walk-in Cen.
Brookvale Local Nature Reserve
Rimrose Brook
Adult Ed. Cen.
Seaforth & Litherland
LIVERPOOL INTERMODAL FREEPORT TERMINAL
ATLANTIC TERMINAL
RIMROSE BUS. PK.
Bootle
L20
Grave Yard
H J K L M N G
1 2 3 4 5 6 7 8 9
33 44 57

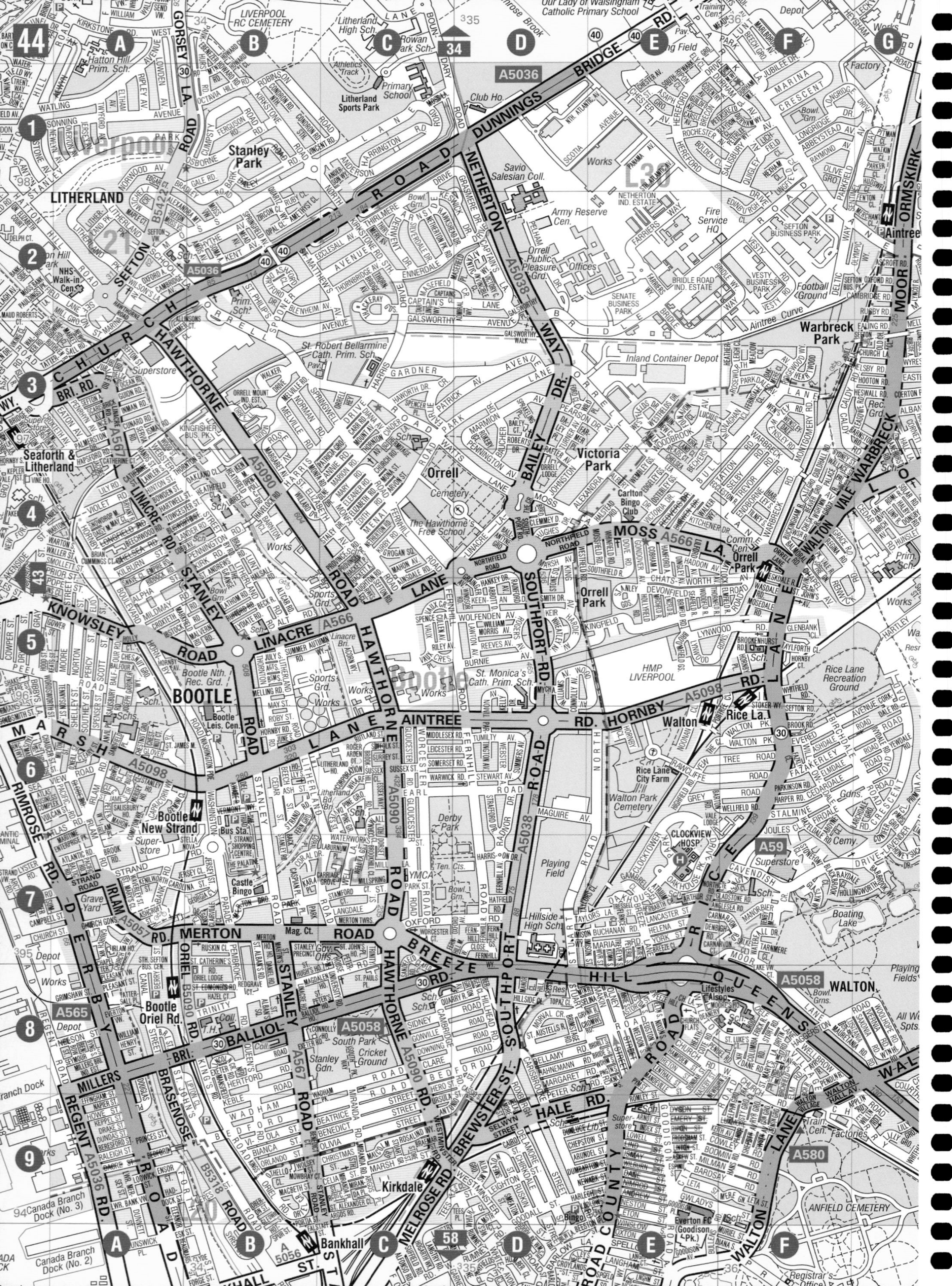
LITHERLAND
Stanley Park
Litherland Sports Park
Seaforth & Litherland
BOOTLE
Bootle New Strand
Bootle Oriel Rd.
Orrell
Orrell Park
Victoria Park
Warbreck Park
HMP LIVERPOOL
Rice Lane Recreation Ground
Walton
WALTON
Kirkdale
Bankhall
ANFIELD CEMETERY
Canada Branch Dock (No. 3)
Canada Branch Dock (No. 2)
Branch Dock
Aintree

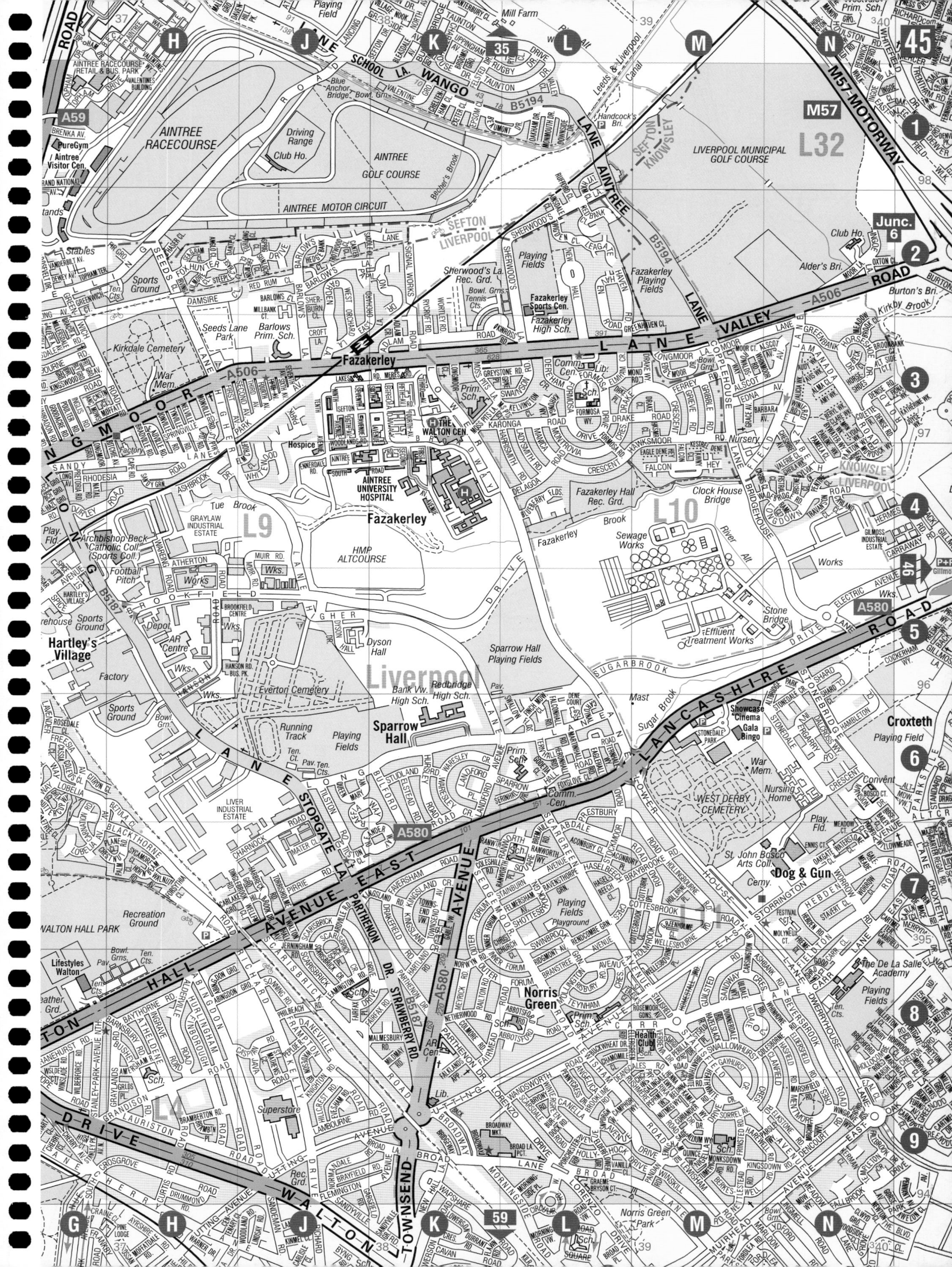
35
AINTREE RACECOURSE
AINTREE GOLF COURSE
AINTREE MOTOR CIRCUIT
Driving Range
Club Ho.
Aintree Visitor Cen.
AINTREE RACECOURSE RETAIL & BUS. PARK
A59
PureGym
SCHOOL LA.
WANGO
B5194
Leeds & Liverpool Canal
Mill Farm
Handcock's Bri.
SEFTON
KNOWSLEY
LIVERPOOL
LIVERPOOL MUNICIPAL GOLF COURSE
L32
M57
M57 MOTORWAY
Junc. 6
Alder's Bri.
Burton's Bri.
Kirkby Brook
A506
VALLEY ROAD
LANE
AINTREE LANE
LONGMOOR LANE
Fazakerley
Fazakerley Sports Cen.
Fazakerley High Sch.
Fazakerley Playing Fields
Sherwood's La. Rec. Grd.
Barlows Prim. Sch.
Seeds Lane Park
Kirkdale Cemetery
War Mem.
Sports Ground
Stables
THE WALTON CEN.
Hospice
AINTREE UNIVERSITY HOSPITAL
L9
L10
Fazakerley Hall Rec. Grd.
Clock House Bridge
Fazakerley Brook
Sewage Works
River Alt
Effluent Treatment Works
Stone Bridge
GILMOSS INDUSTRIAL ESTATE
Works
46
A580
EAST LANCASHIRE ROAD
HMP ALTCOURSE
GRAYLAW INDUSTRIAL ESTATE
Tue Brook
Archbishop Beck Catholic Coll. (Sports Coll.)
Football Pitch
Hartley's Village
Factory
Dyson Hall
Sparrow Hall Playing Fields
Liverpool
Everton Cemetery
Bank Vw. High Sch.
Redbridge High Sch.
Sparrow Hall
Running Track
Playing Fields
Showcase Cinema
Gala Bingo
Mast
Sugar Brook
WEST DERBY CEMETERY
Nursing Home
Convent
Croxteth
Playing Field
St. John Bosco Arts Coll.
Dog & Gun
The De La Salle Academy
LIVER INDUSTRIAL ESTATE
Recreation Ground
WALTON HALL PARK
Lifestyles Walton
WALTON HALL AVENUE
STOPGATE LANE
LONG LANE
PARTHENON DR.
STRAWBERRY RD.
B5187
A580
Norris Green
Health Club
Superstore
L4
WALTON LANE
QUEENS DRIVE
TOWNSEND
BROADWAY
BROADWAY MKT.
Norris Green Park
59
Liverpool
G
H
J
K
L
M
N
1
2
3
4
5
6
7
8
9
37
38
39
340
391
395
94
96
97
98

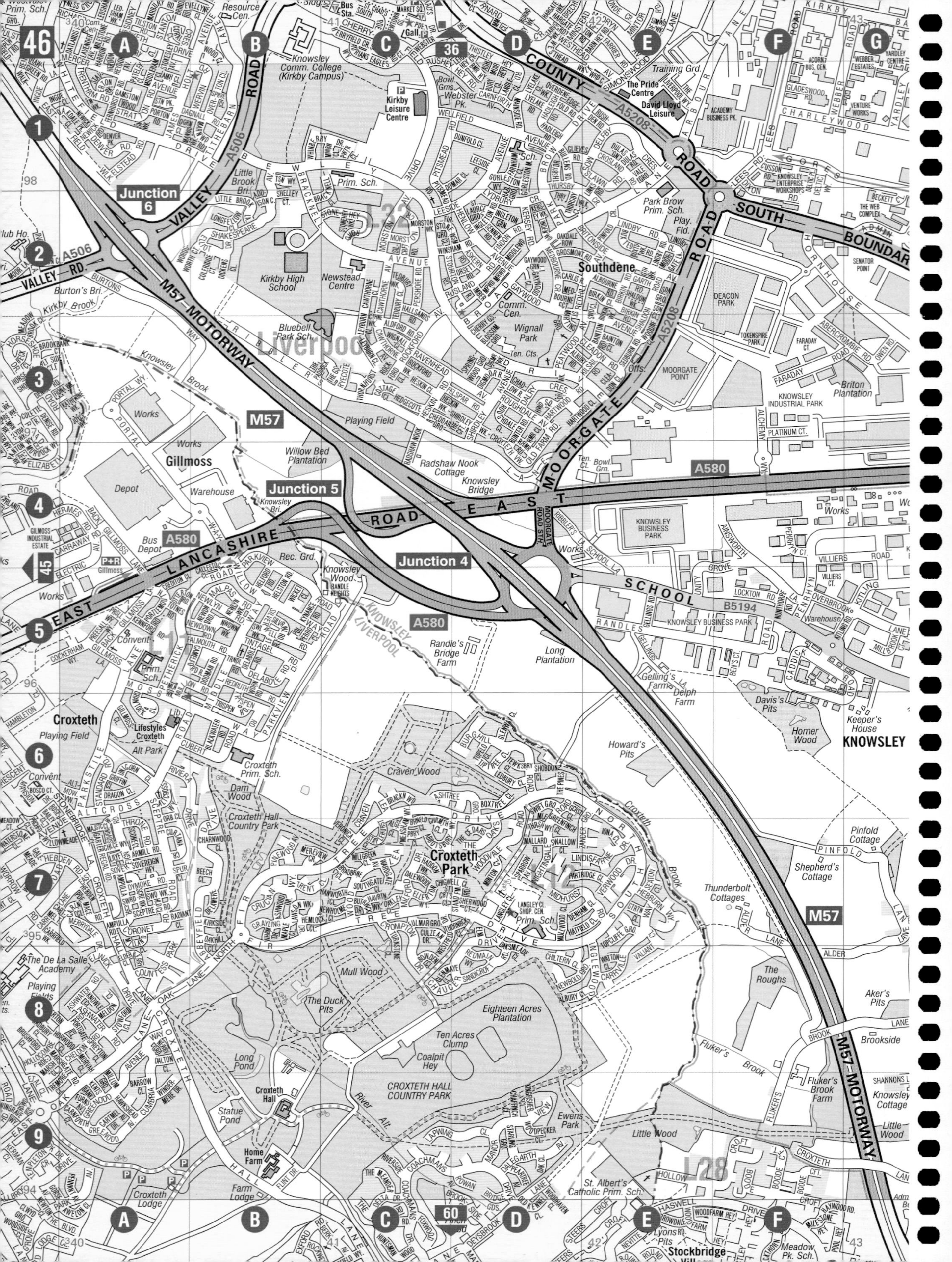
A
B
C
D
E
F
G
1
2
3
4
5
6
7
8
9
36
45
60
Knowsley Comm. College (Kirkby Campus)
Kirkby Leisure Centre
Webster Pk.
COUNTY ROAD
A5208
Training Grd.
The Pride Centre
David Lloyd Leisure
ACADEMY BUSINESS PK.
CHARLEYWOOD
Junction 6
VALLEY ROAD
A506
Little Brook Bri.
Prim. Sch.
Park Brow Prim. Sch.
Play. Fld.
SOUTH BOUNDARY
L32
Kirkby High School
Newstead Centre
Southdene
DEACON PARK
M57 MOTORWAY
Burton's Bri.
Kirkby Brook
Bluebell Park Sch.
Liverpool
Comm. Cen.
Wignall Park
Ten. Cts.
Offs.
MOORGATE POINT
KNOWSLEY INDUSTRIAL PARK
Briton Plantation
Knowsley Brook
Works
M57
Gillmoss
Playing Field
Willow Bed Plantation
Radshaw Nook Cottage
Knowsley Bridge
MOORGATE ROAD
A580
Depot
Warehouse
Junction 5
EAST LANCASHIRE ROAD
KNOWSLEY BUSINESS PARK
Bus Depot
Rec. Grd.
Knowsley Wood
Junction 4
SCHOOL LANE
B5194
A580
Randle's Bridge Farm
Long Plantation
Gelling's Farm
Delph Farm
Davis's Pits
Homer Wood
Keeper's House
KNOWSLEY
Convent
Prim. Sch.
Croxteth
Playing Field
Lifestyles Croxteth
Alt Park
Croxteth Prim. Sch.
Craven Wood
Howard's Pits
Dam Wood
Croxteth Hall Country Park
Croxteth Park
L12
LANGLEY CL. SHOP. CEN.
Prim. Sch.
Pinfold Cottage
Shepherd's Cottage
Thunderbolt Cottages
Croxteth Brook
M57
The De La Salle Academy
Playing Fields
Mull Wood
The Duck Pits
Eighteen Acres Plantation
The Roughs
Aker's Pits
Brookside
Ten Acres Clump
Coalpit Hey
Long Pond
Croxteth Hall
CROXTETH HALL COUNTRY PARK
River Alt
Fluker's Brook
Fluker's Brook Farm
Knowsley Cottage
Statue Pond
Ewens Park
Little Wood
Little Wood
M57 MOTORWAY
Home Farm
L28
Croxteth Lodge
Farm Lodge
St. Albert's Catholic Prim. Sch.
Lyons Pits
Stockbridge
Meadow Pk. Sch.

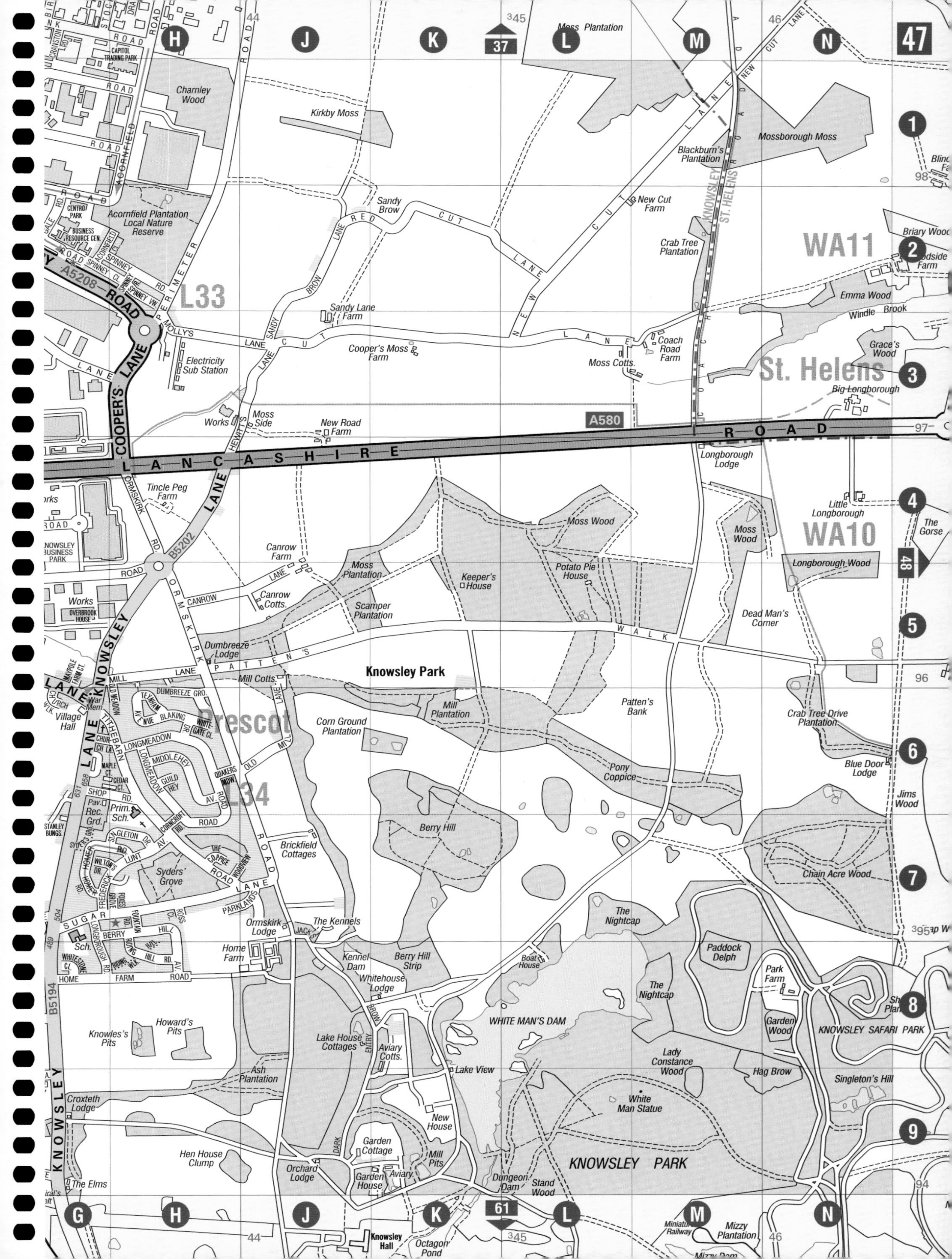
37
61
48
L33
L34
WA11
WA10
St. Helens
Prescot
Knowsley Park
KNOWSLEY PARK
KNOWSLEY SAFARI PARK
LANCASHIRE ROAD
A580
A5208
B5202
B5194
Charnley Wood
Kirkby Moss
Moss Plantation
Mossborough Moss
Blackburn's Plantation
New Cut Farm
Crab Tree Plantation
Sandy Brow
Acornfield Plantation Local Nature Reserve
Sandy Lane Farm
Cooper's Moss Farm
Coach Road Farm
Moss Cotts.
Electricity Sub Station
Emma Wood
Windle Brook
Grace's Wood
Big Longborough
Briary Wood
Works
Moss Side
New Road Farm
Longborough Lodge
Tincle Peg Farm
Little Longborough
The Gorse
Moss Wood
Canrow Farm
Moss Plantation
Keeper's House
Potato Pie House
Longborough Wood
Canrow Cotts.
Scamper Plantation
Dead Man's Corner
Dumbreeze Lodge
Mill Cotts.
Mill Plantation
Patten's Bank
Crab Tree Drive Plantation
Corn Ground Plantation
Blue Door Lodge
Pony Coppice
Jims Wood
Village Hall
Berry Hill
Brickfield Cottages
Syders' Grove
Chain Acre Wood
The Kennels
Ormskirk Lodge
The Nightcap
Paddock Delph
Home Farm
Kennel Dam
Berry Hill Strip
Boat House
Park Farm
Whitehouse Lodge
White Man's Dam
Garden Wood
Howard's Pits
Knowles's Pits
Lake House Cottages
Aviary Cotts.
Lady Constance Wood
Hag Brow
Singleton's Hill
Lake View
Ash Plantation
White Man Statue
Croxteth Lodge
New House
Garden Cottage
Hen House Clump
Mill Pits
Orchard Lodge
Garden House
Aviary
Dungeon Dam
Stand Wood
The Elms
Knowsley Hall
Octagon Pond
Miniature Railway
Mizzy Plantation
Capitol Trading Park
Centro Park
Business Resource Cen.
Knowsley Business Park
Overbrook House
War Mem.
Prim. Sch.
Rec. Grd.
Sch.
Cooper's Lane
Molly's Lane
Perimeter Road
Spinney
Sandy Lane
Red Cut Lane
New Cut Lane
Cut Lane
Knowsley Lane
Ormskirk Road
Canrow Lane
Patten's Lane
Walk
Mill Lane
Old Mill Lane
Dumbreeze Gro.
Longmeadow
Middlehey
Guild Hey
Blakeing Ave
Tithebarn
Sugar Lane
Parklands
Home Farm Road
Berry Hill
Knowsley St. Helens Road
Coach Road
Hewitt's Lane
Acornfield Road
Spinney Cl.
Spinney Vw.
Cranston Rd.
Maypole Farm Ct.
Church Wk.
Maple Ct.
Cedar Ct.
Shop Rd.
Stanley Bungs.
Syders Gro.
Homer Rd.
Wilton's Dr.
Frederick Gro.
Lunt Av.
Gleton Dr.
Corncroft Rd.
The Coppice
Woodview
Quakers Mdw.
Whitegate Cl.
Fountain Rd.
Foxes Gro.
Ross Cl.
Riding Hill Rd.
Whitestone Cl.
Longborough Rd.
Jacks
Dark Entry
Brow
Dungeon
44
345
46
94
95
96
97
98
489
504
631
658
G H J K L M N
1 2 3 4 5 6 7 8 9

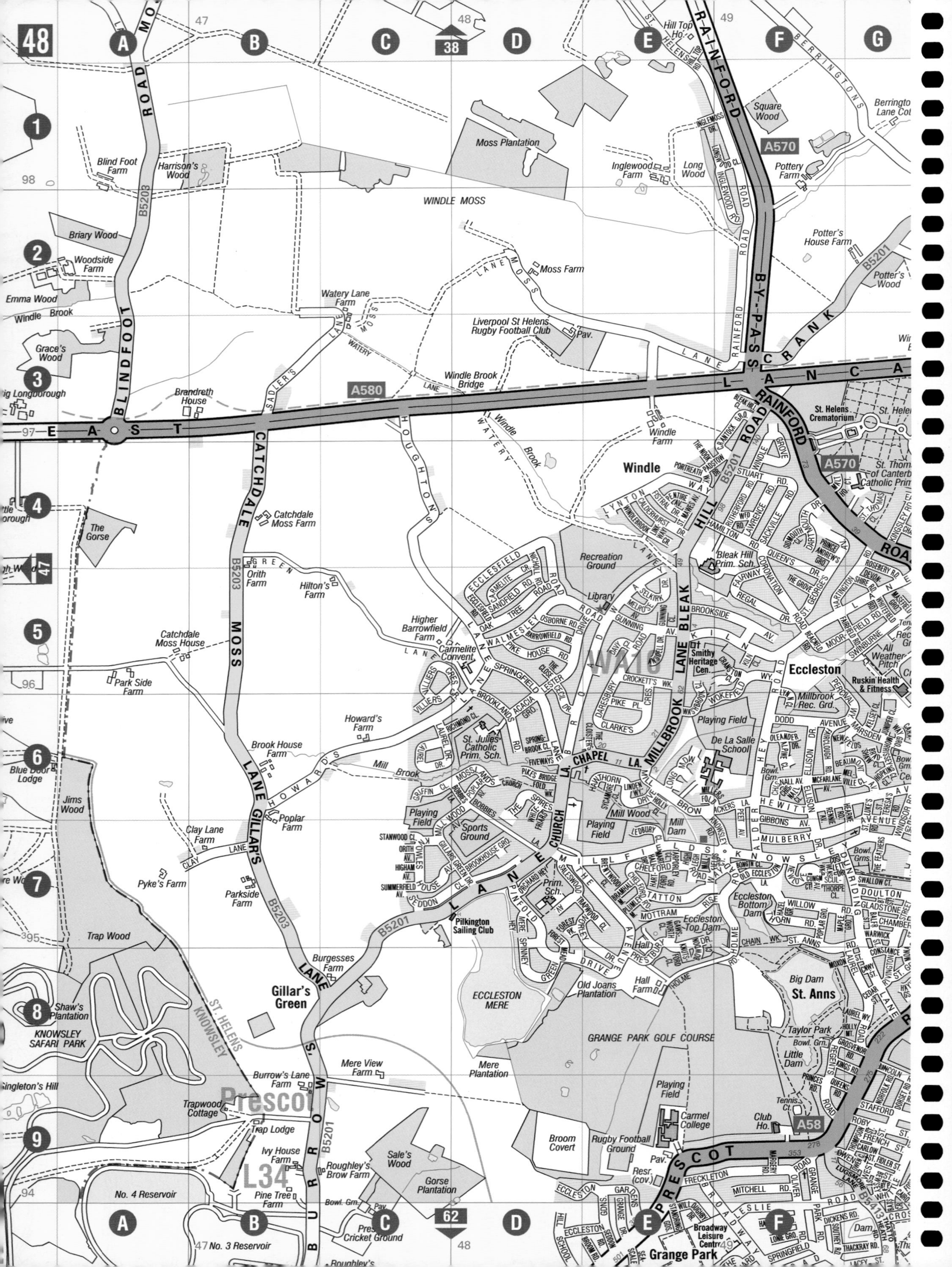
38
47
48
49
A
B
C
D
E
F
G
1
2
3
4
5
6
7
8
9
98
97
96
395
94
Blind Foot Farm
Harrison's Wood
Moss Plantation
WINDLE MOSS
Inglewood Farm
Long Wood
Square Wood
Berrington Lane Cot
Pottery Farm
Hill Top Ho.
BERRINGTONS
A570
Briary Wood
Woodside Farm
Emma Wood
Windle Brook
Grace's Wood
Big Longborough
Watery Lane Farm
Moss Farm
Liverpool St Helens Rugby Football Club
Pav.
Potter's House Farm
Potter's Wood
B5201
Brandreth House
A580
Windle Brook Bridge
EAST LANCASHIRE ROAD
BLINDFOOT ROAD
B5203
RAINFORD BY-PASS
RAINFORD ROAD
CRANK
St. Helens Crematorium
Windle Farm
Windle
A570
The Gorse
Catchdale Moss Farm
CATCHDALE MOSS LANE
47
Orith Farm
Hilton's Farm
Recreation Ground
Bleak Hill Prim. Sch.
Library
Higher Barrowfield Farm
Carmelite Convent
WA10
Catchdale Moss House
Park Side Farm
Smithy Heritage Cen.
Eccleston
Ruskin Health & Fitness
Millbrook Rec. Grd.
Howard's Farm
Brook House Farm
St. Julie's Catholic Prim. Sch.
Playing Field
De La Salle School
Mill Brook
Blue Boar Lodge
Jims Wood
Poplar Farm
Clay Lane Farm
Sports Ground
Mill Wood
Mill Dam
Pyke's Farm
Parkside Farm
GILLAR'S LANE
CHURCH LANE
MILLBROOK LANE
Prim. Sch.
Eccleston Bottom Dam
Eccleston Top Dam
Pilkington Sailing Club
Trap Wood
Burgesses Farm
Gillar's Green
Hall Farm
Old Joans Plantation
ECCLESTON MERE
Big Dam
St. Anns
Taylor Park
Little Dam
Shaw's Plantation
KNOWSLEY SAFARI PARK
ST. HELENS
KNOWSLEY
GRANGE PARK GOLF COURSE
Mere View Farm
Mere Plantation
Burrow's Lane Farm
Singleton's Hill
Prescot
Trapwood Cottage
Trap Lodge
Playing Field
Carmel College
Club Ho.
A58
Broom Covert
Rugby Football Ground
Ivy House Farm
Sale's Wood
Roughley's Brow Farm
Gorse Plantation
L34
Resr. (cov.)
PRESCOT ROAD
BURROW'S LANE
No. 4 Reservoir
No. 3 Reservoir
Pine Tree Farm
Bowl. Grn.
Pav.
Prescot Cricket Ground
62
Broadway Leisure Centre
Grange Park

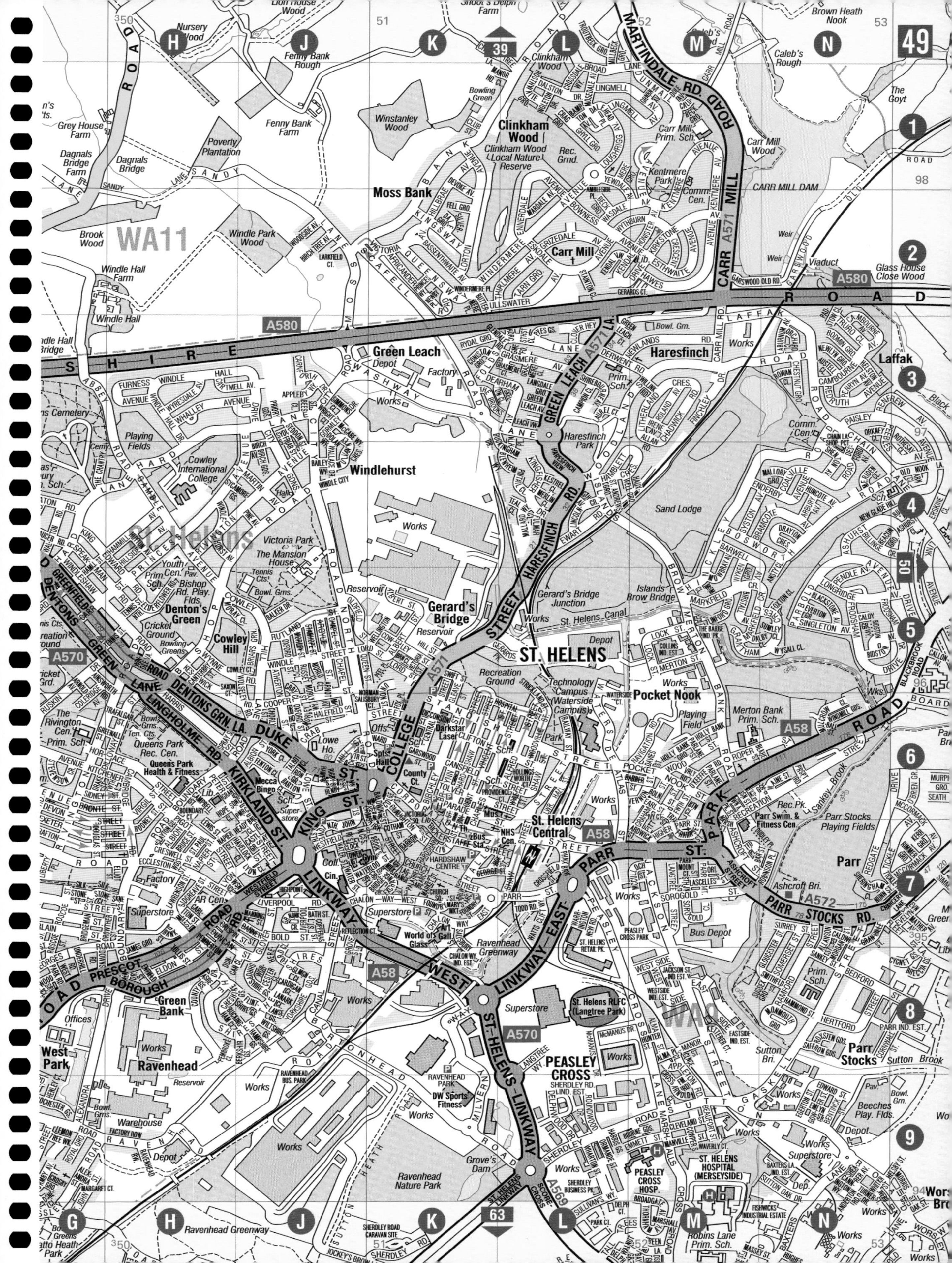

Nursery Wood
Fenny Bank Rough
Fenny Bank Farm
Winstanley Wood
Clinkham Wood
Clinkham Wood Local Nature Reserve
Grey House Farm
Dagnals Bridge Farm
Dagnals Bridge
Poverty Plantation
Moss Bank
Carr Mill Prim. Sch.
Kentmere Park
Carr Mill Wood
Caleb's Rough
Brown Heath Nook
The Goyt
CARR MILL DAM
Brook Wood
WA11
Windle Park Wood
Windle Hall Farm
Windle Hall
Carr Mill
Viaduct
Glass House Close Wood
A580
A571
SHIRE
ROAD
CARR MILL ROAD
MARTINDALE RD.
Green Leach
Depot
Factory
Haresfinch
Laffak
Works
Windlehurst
Cowley International College
Playing Fields
Haresfinch Park
Sand Lodge
St. Helens
Victoria Park
The Mansion House
Reservoir
Gerard's Bridge
Gerard's Bridge Junction
Islands Brow Bridge
St. Helens Canal
Denton's Green
Cowley Hill
Cricket Ground
ST. HELENS
Recreation Ground
Technology Campus (Waterside Campus)
Pocket Nook
Playing Field
Merton Bank Prim. Sch.
A570
A58
Queens Park Rec. Cen.
Queens Park Health & Fitness
Mecca Bingo
County Ct.
Darkstar Laser
St. Helens Central
Parr Swim. & Fitness Cen.
Parr Stocks Playing Fields
Parr
Ashcroft Bri.
A572
Bus Sta.
HARDSHAW CENTRE
World of Glass
Superstore
Ravenhead Greenway
St. Helens RLFC (Langtree Park)
Bus Depot
WA9
Green Bank
Ravenhead
West Park
PEASLEY CROSS
Sutton Bri.
Parr Stocks
Sutton Brook
DW Sports Fitness
Grove's Dam
Ravenhead Nature Park
PEASLEY CROSS HOSP.
ST. HELENS HOSPITAL (MERSEYSIDE)
Robins Lane Prim. Sch.
Beeches Play. Flds.
A569
Ravenhead Greenway
SHERDLEY ROAD CARAVAN SITE
LINKWAY
ST. HELENS LINKWAY
39
63
50

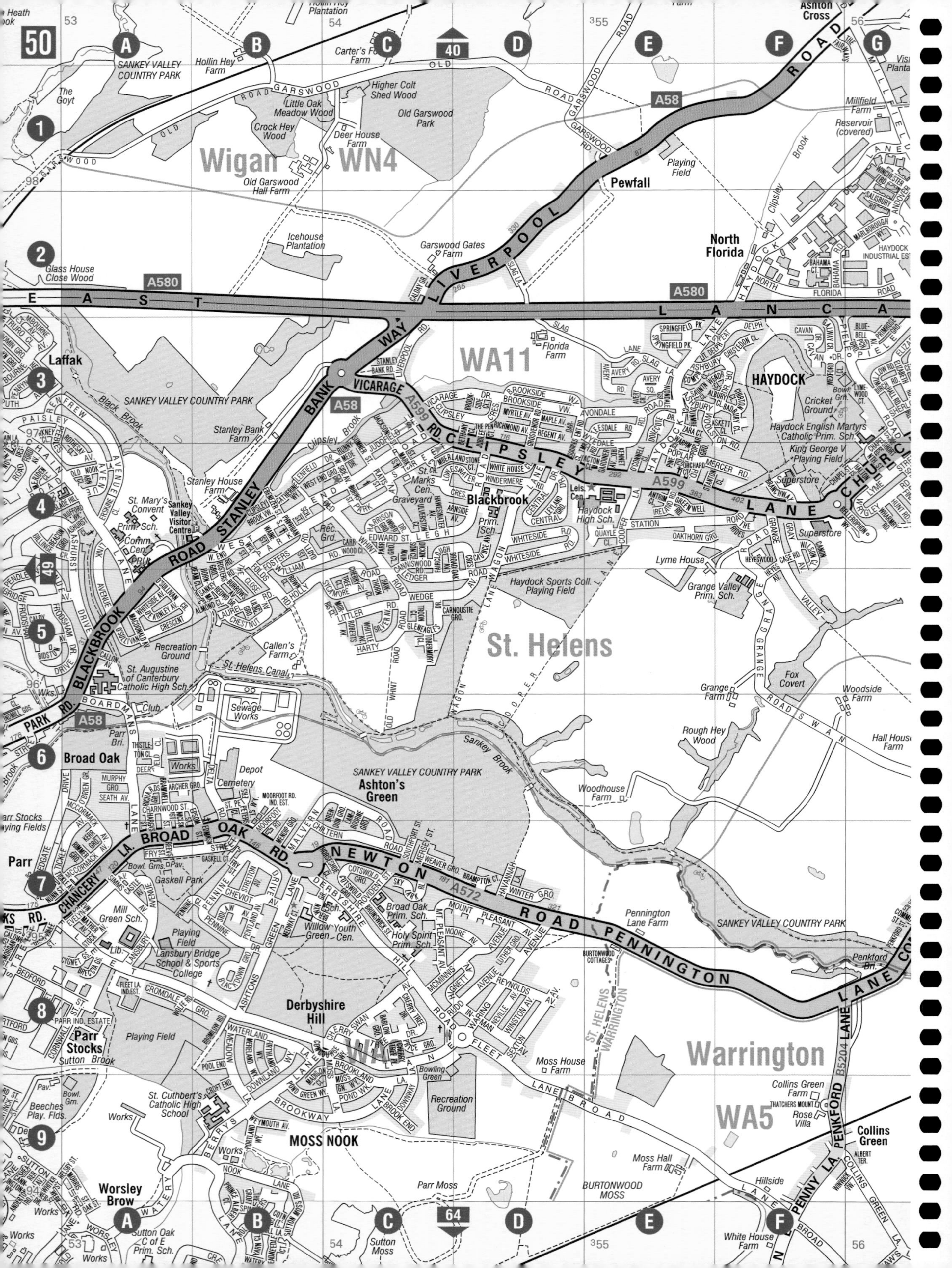

50
40
49
64
Wigan
WN4
WA11
St. Helens
Warrington
WA5
SANKEY VALLEY COUNTRY PARK
The Goyt
Hollin Hey Farm
Carter's Fold Farm
Higher Colt Shed Wood
Little Oak Meadow Wood
Crock Hey Wood
Deer House Farm
Old Garswood Park
Old Garswood Hall Farm
Pewfall
Playing Field
North Florida
HAYDOCK INDUSTRIAL EST.
Millfield Farm
Reservoir (covered)
Icehouse Plantation
Garswood Gates Farm
Glass House Close Wood
A580
A58
A599
A572
B5204
EAST LANCASHIRE ROAD
LIVERPOOL ROAD
OLD GARSWOOD ROAD
Florida Farm
Laffak
HAYDOCK
Cricket Ground
Haydock English Martyrs Catholic Prim. Sch.
King George V Playing Field
Superstore
Black Brook
Stanley Bank Farm
Stanley House Farm
St. Mary's Convent
Sankey Valley Visitor Centre
Blackbrook
Haydock High Sch.
CLIPSLEY LANE
STANLEY BANK WAY
BLACKBROOK ROAD
Lyme House
Grange Valley Prim. Sch.
Haydock Sports Coll. Playing Field
Recreation Ground
Callen's Farm
St. Augustine of Canterbury Catholic High Sch.
St. Helens Canal
Sewage Works
Fox Covert
Grange Farm
Woodside Farm
Rough Hey Wood
Hall House Farm
Broad Oak
Depot
Cemetery
Ashton's Green
Sankey Brook
Woodhouse Farm
Parr
Parr Stocks Playing Fields
BROAD OAK RD.
NEWTON ROAD
PENNINGTON LANE
Gaskell Park
Mill Green Sch.
Playing Field
Lansbury Bridge School & Sports College
Broad Oak Prim. Sch.
Holy Spirit Prim. Sch.
Willow Green Youth Cen.
Pennington Lane Farm
BURTONWOOD COTTAGES
Penkford Bri.
PARR IND. ESTATE
Parr Stocks
Sutton Brook
Derbyshire Hill
Recreation Ground
Bowling Green
Moss House Farm
Collins Green Farm
Rose Villa
Collins Green
Beeches Play. Flds.
St. Cuthbert's Catholic High School
MOSS NOOK
Moss Hall Farm
Parr Moss
BURTONWOOD MOSS
Hillside
Worsley Brow
Sutton Oak C of E Prim. Sch.
Sutton Moss
White House Farm

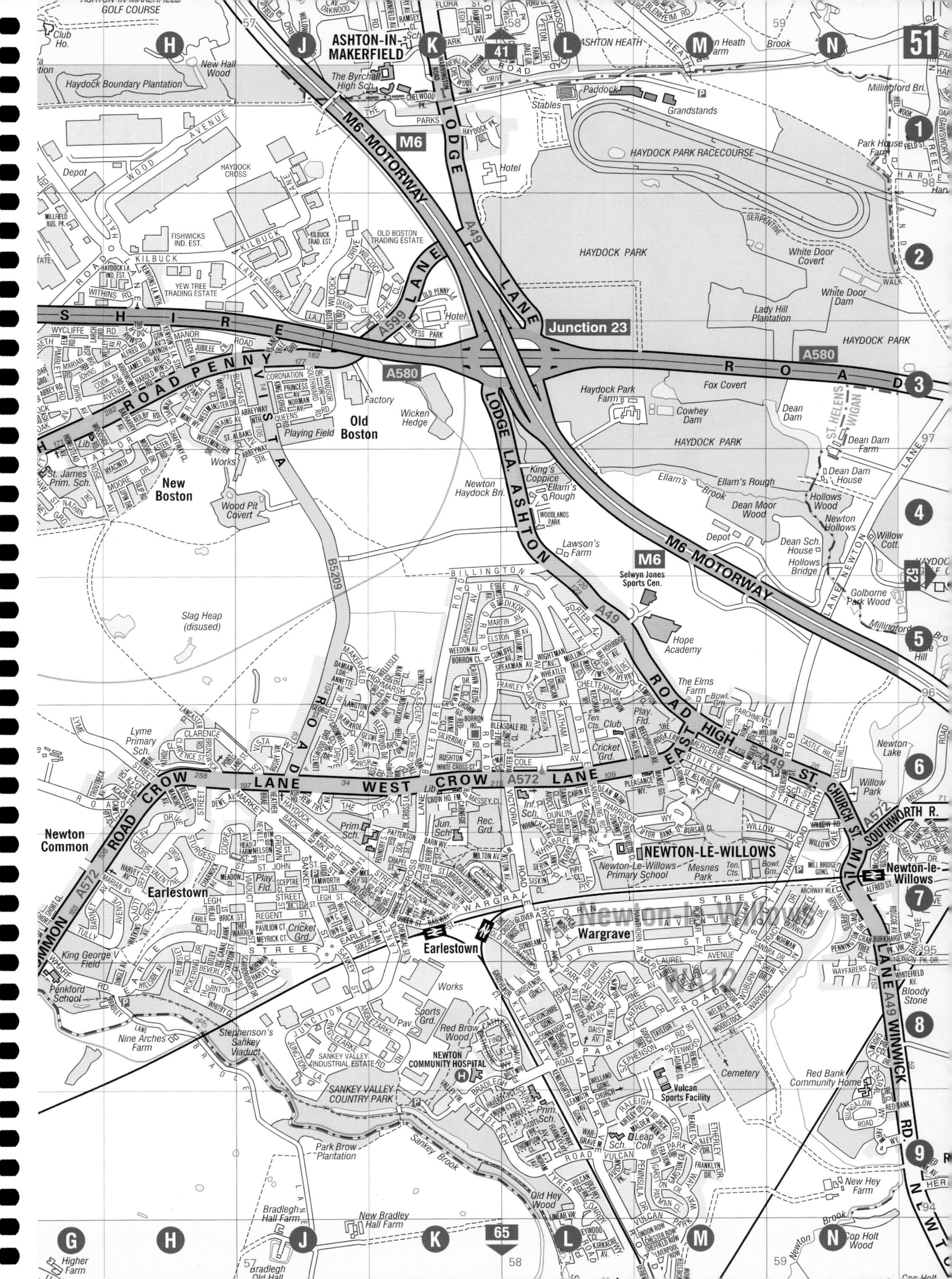
ASHTON-IN-MAKERFIELD
ASHTON HEATH
Haydock Boundary Plantation
New Hall Wood
The Byrchall High Sch.
Paddock
Stables
Grandstands
Millingford Bri.
Park House Farm
HAYDOCK PARK RACECOURSE
M6 MOTORWAY
M6
LODGE LANE
A49
Hotel
HAYDOCK CROSS
Depot
MILLFIELD BUS. PK.
FISHWICKS IND. EST.
KILBUCK TRAD. EST.
OLD BOSTON TRADING ESTATE
HAYDOCK LA. IND. EST.
YEW TREE TRADING ESTATE
HAYDOCK PARK
White Door Covert
White Door Dam
Lady Hill Plantation
Junction 23
A580
A599
EAST LANCASHIRE ROAD
ROAD PENNY
Haydock Park Farm
Fox Covert
Cowhey Dam
Dean Dam
ST. HELENS
WIGAN
Dean Dam Farm
Factory
Old Boston
Playing Field
Wicken Hedge
St. James' Prim. Sch.
New Boston
Works
Wood Pit Covert
King's Coppice
Ellam's Rough
Newton Haydock Bri.
LODGE LA.
ASHTON
WOODLANDS PARK
Lawson's Farm
Ellam's Brook
Ellam's Rough
Dean House
Hollows Wood
Dean Moor Wood
Newton Hollows
Depot
Dean Sch. House
Hollows Bridge
Willow Cott.
Golborne Park Wood
Millingford Brook
B5209
Slag Heap (disused)
Selwyn Jones Sports Cen.
Hope Academy
The Elms Farm
Bowl. Grn.
Play. Fld.
Cricket Grd.
Club
Ten. Cts.
Lyme Primary Sch.
CROW LANE
WEST CROW LANE
A572
HIGH ST.
ROAD
Newton Lake
Willow Park
SOUTHWORTH R.
CHURCH ST.
MILL LANE
Newton Common
Earlestown
Prim. Sch.
Jun. Sch.
Rec. Grd.
Inf. Sch.
Lib.
Play. Fld.
Cricket Grd.
NEWTON-LE-WILLOWS
Newton-le-Willows Primary School
Mesnes Park
Newton-le-Willows
Wargrave
King George V Field
Penkford School
Works
Sports Grd.
Pav.
Red Brow Wood
Nine Arches Farm
Stephenson's Sankey Viaduct
SANKEY VALLEY INDUSTRIAL ESTATE
NEWTON COMMUNITY HOSPITAL
SANKEY VALLEY COUNTRY PARK
Cemetery
Vulcan Sports Facility
Red Bank Community Home
Bloody Stone
WINWICK RD.
Leap Coll.
Sch.
Prim. Sch.
Park Brow Plantation
Sankey Brook
Old Hey Wood
New Hey Farm
Bradlegh Hall Farm
New Bradley Hall Farm
Cop Holt Wood
Higher Farm
Bradlegh Old Hall
Newton Brook
65
41
52
G
H
J
K
L
M
N
1
2
3
4
5
6
7
8
9

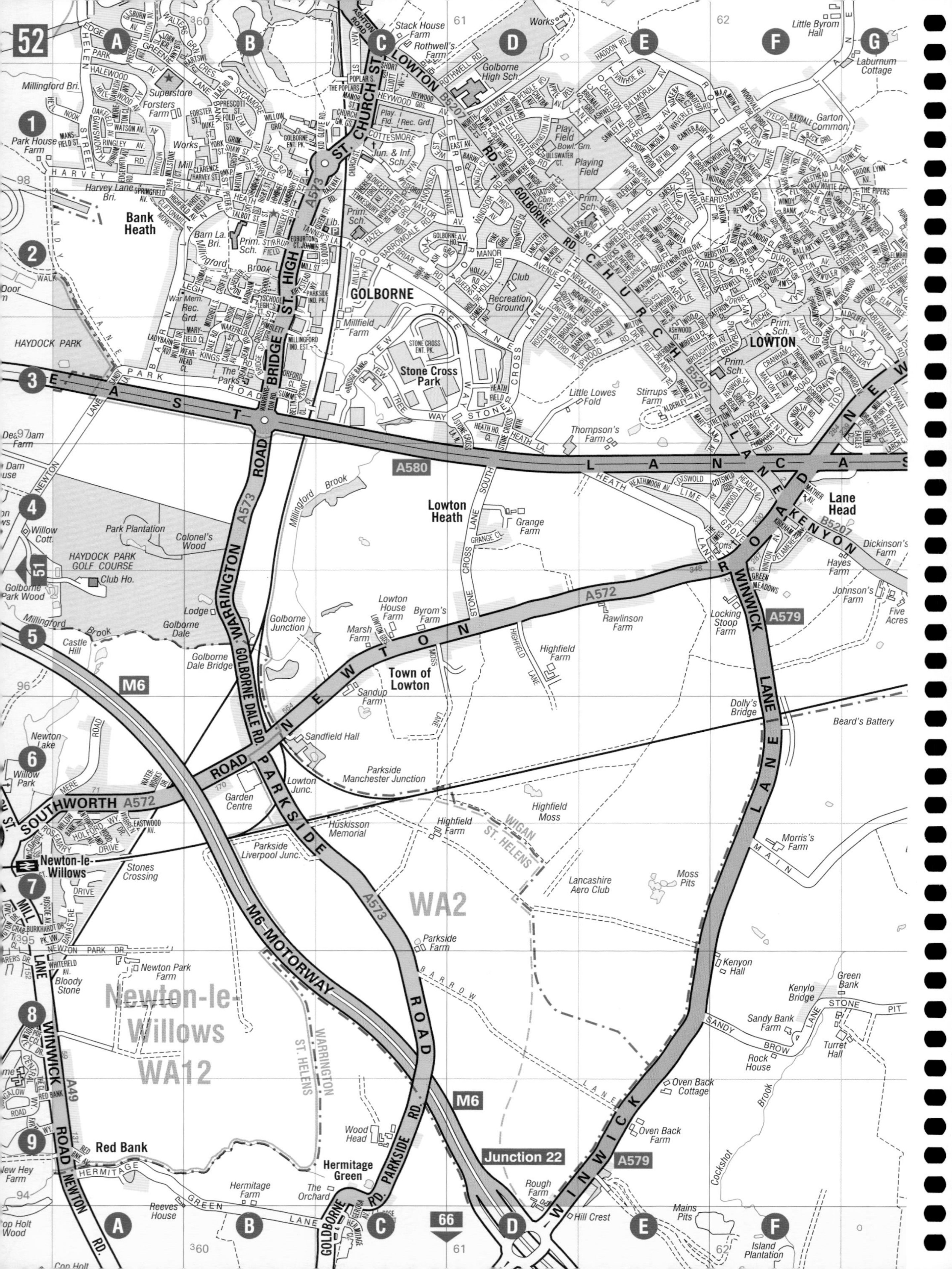
GOLBORNE
LOWTON
Bank Heath
Stone Cross Park
Lowton Heath
Town of Lowton
Lane Head
HAYDOCK PARK
HAYDOCK PARK GOLF COURSE
Club Ho.
Park Plantation
Colonel's Wood
Golborne Park Wood
Golborne Dale
Golborne Dale Bridge
Castle Hill
Golborne Junction
Millingford Brook
Lowton House Farm
Byrom's Farm
Marsh Farm
Rawlinson Farm
Highfield Farm
Locking Stoop Farm
Grange Farm
Little Lowes Fold
Stirrups Farm
Thompson's Farm
Dickinson's Farm
Hayes Farm
Johnson's Farm
Five Acres
Sandup Farm
Sandfield Hall
Dolly's Bridge
Beard's Battery
Parkside Manchester Junction
Lowton Junc.
Garden Centre
Huskisson Memorial
Parkside Liverpool Junc.
Highfield Farm
Highfield Moss
Stones Crossing
Lancashire Aero Club
Moss Pits
Morris's Farm
WA2
Parkside Farm
Kenyon Hall
Kenylo Bridge
Green Bank
Sandy Bank Farm
Turret Hall
Rock House
Oven Back Cottage
Oven Back Farm
Wood Head
Hermitage Green
The Orchard
Hermitage Farm
Reeves House
Rough Farm
Hill Crest
Mains Pits
Island Plantation
Cockshot
Newton-le-Willows
WA12
Newton Park Farm
Bloody Stone
Red Bank
New Hey Farm
Cop Holt Wood
Newton Lake
Willow Park
Millingford Bri.
Park House Farm
Harvey Lane Bri.
Forsters Farm
Superstore
Stack House Farm
Rothwell's Farm
Golborne High Sch.
Little Byrom Hall
Laburnum Cottage
Garton Common
Playing Field
Recreation Ground
A573
A580
A572
A579
A49
B5207
M6
M6 MOTORWAY
Junction 22
EAST LANCASHIRE ROAD
WARRINGTON ROAD
NEWTON ROAD
SOUTHWORTH ROAD
PARKSIDE ROAD
WINWICK LANE
WINWICK ROAD
KENYON LANE
STONE CROSS LANE
HIGH ST.
BRIDGE ST.
CHURCH ST.
GOLBORNE DALE RD.
WIGAN
ST. HELENS
WARRINGTON
51
66
360
61
62
98
96
94

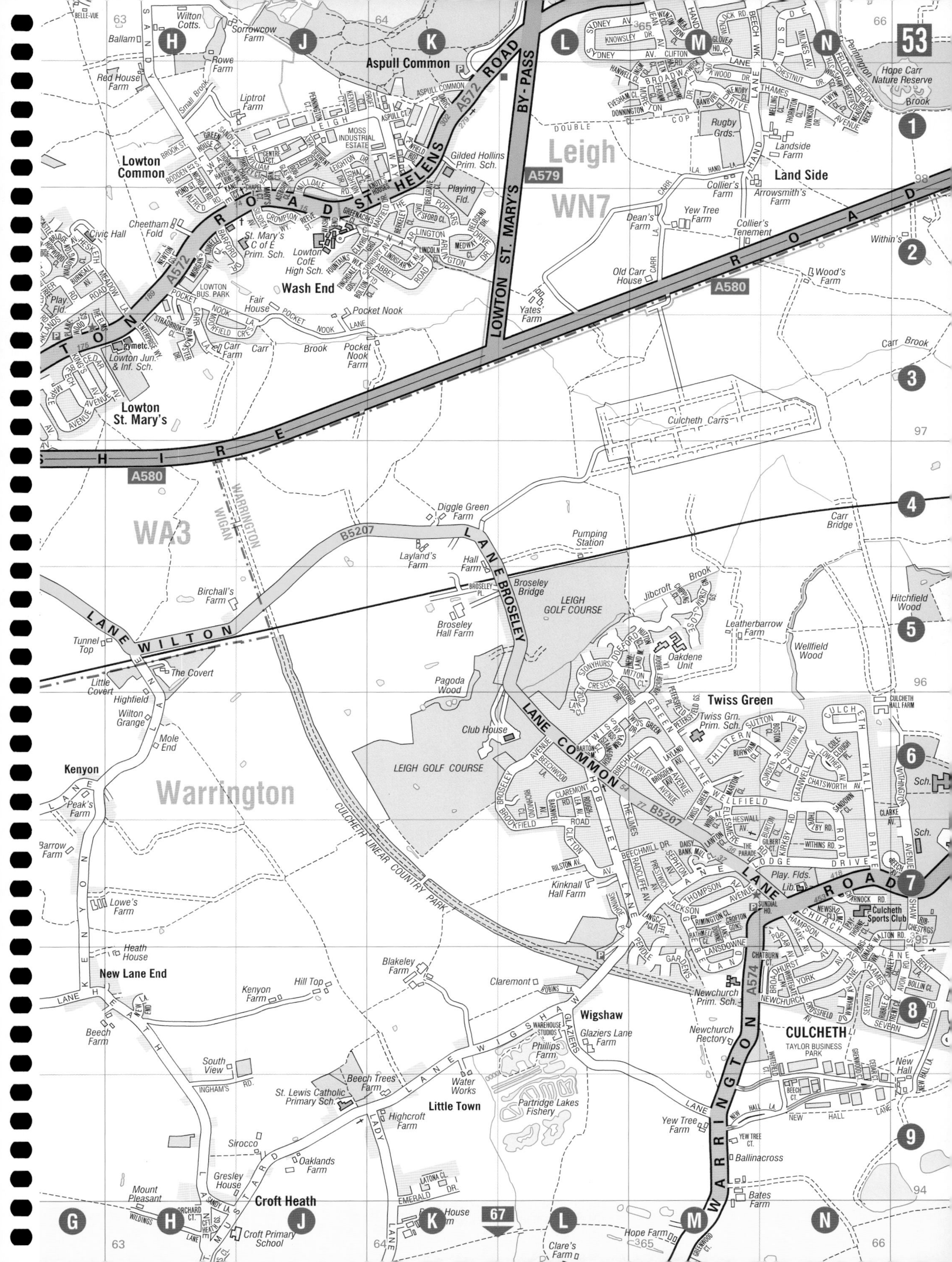

Aspull Common
Lowton Common
Leigh
WN7
A579
A572
A580
Land Side
Wash End
Lowton St. Mary's
WA3
Warrington
Twiss Green
Kenyon
New Lane End
Wigshaw
CULCHETH
Little Town
Croft Heath
LEIGH GOLF COURSE
Culcheth Carrs
Culcheth Linear Country Park
Hope Carr Nature Reserve
Rugby Grds.
Playing Fld.
Taylor Business Park
Culcheth Sports Club
Partridge Lakes Fishery
St. Lewis Catholic Primary Sch.
Croft Primary School
Newchurch Prim. Sch.
Twiss Grn. Prim. Sch.
Lowton CofE High Sch.
St. Mary's C of E Prim. Sch.
Lowton Jun. & Inf. Sch.
Gilded Hollins Prim. Sch.
Moss Industrial Estate
Pumping Station
Lowton St. Mary's By-Pass
St. Helens Road
Wilton Lane
Broseley Lane
Common Lane
Warrington Road
B5207
A574
67

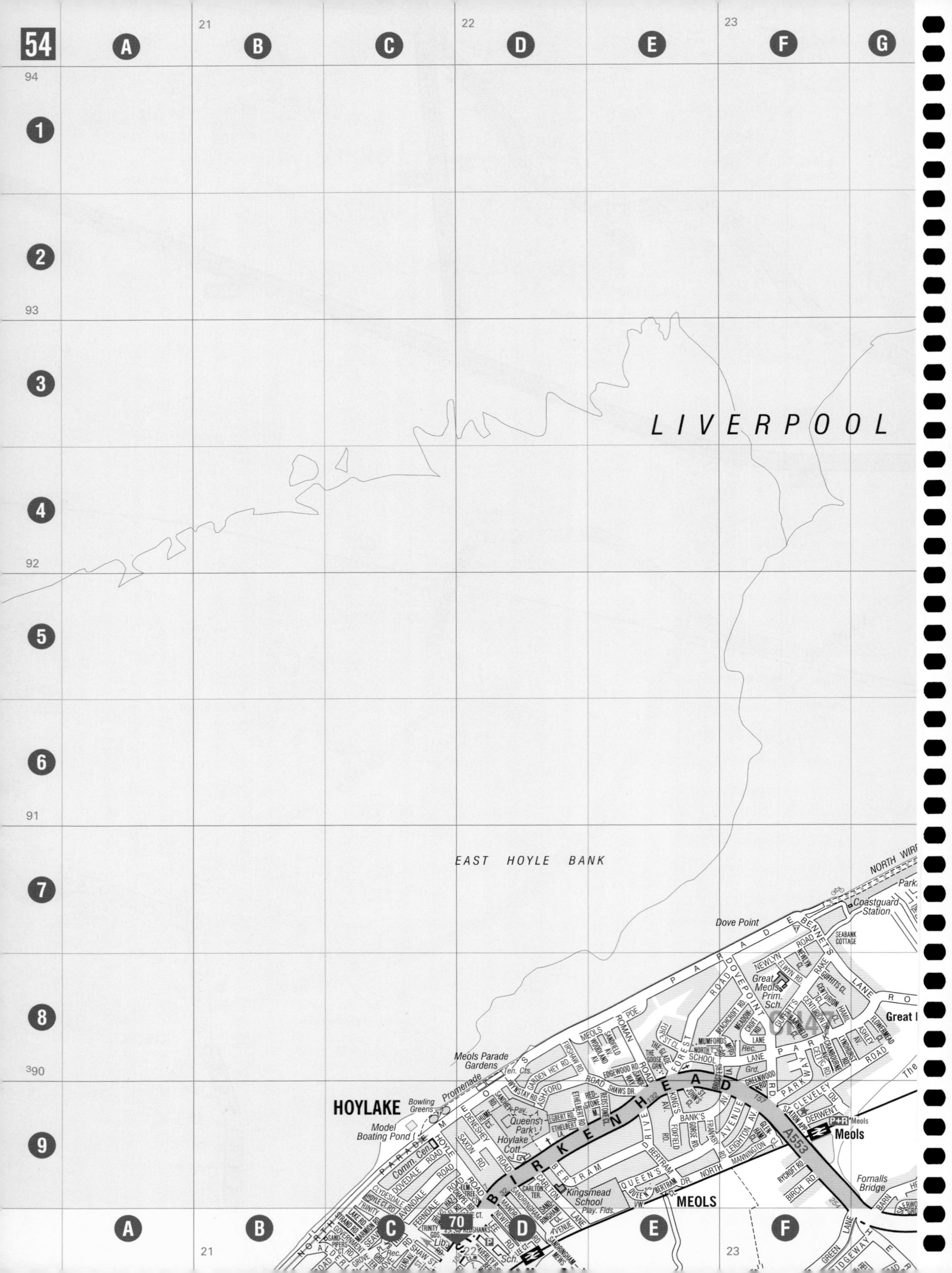

A · B · C · D · E · F · G

94

1

21 · 22 · 23

2

93

3

L I V E R P O O L

4

92

5

6

91

EAST   HOYLE   BANK

7

Coastguard Station

Dove Point

NORTH WIRR

Park

SEABANK COTTAGE

8

390

Great Meols Prim. Sch.

Newlyn Rd

RAKE LANE

Great

MUMFORDS

Meols Parade Gardens

Ten. Cts.

ROMAN

Promenade

Greenwood Rd

9

HOYLAKE

Bowling Greens

Model Boating Pond

Comm. Cen

P+R Meols

Meols

Queens Park

Hoylake Cott.

B I R K E N H E A D

A553

Fornalls Bridge

Kingsmead School Play. Flds.

MEOLS

A · B · C · D · E · F

21 · 23

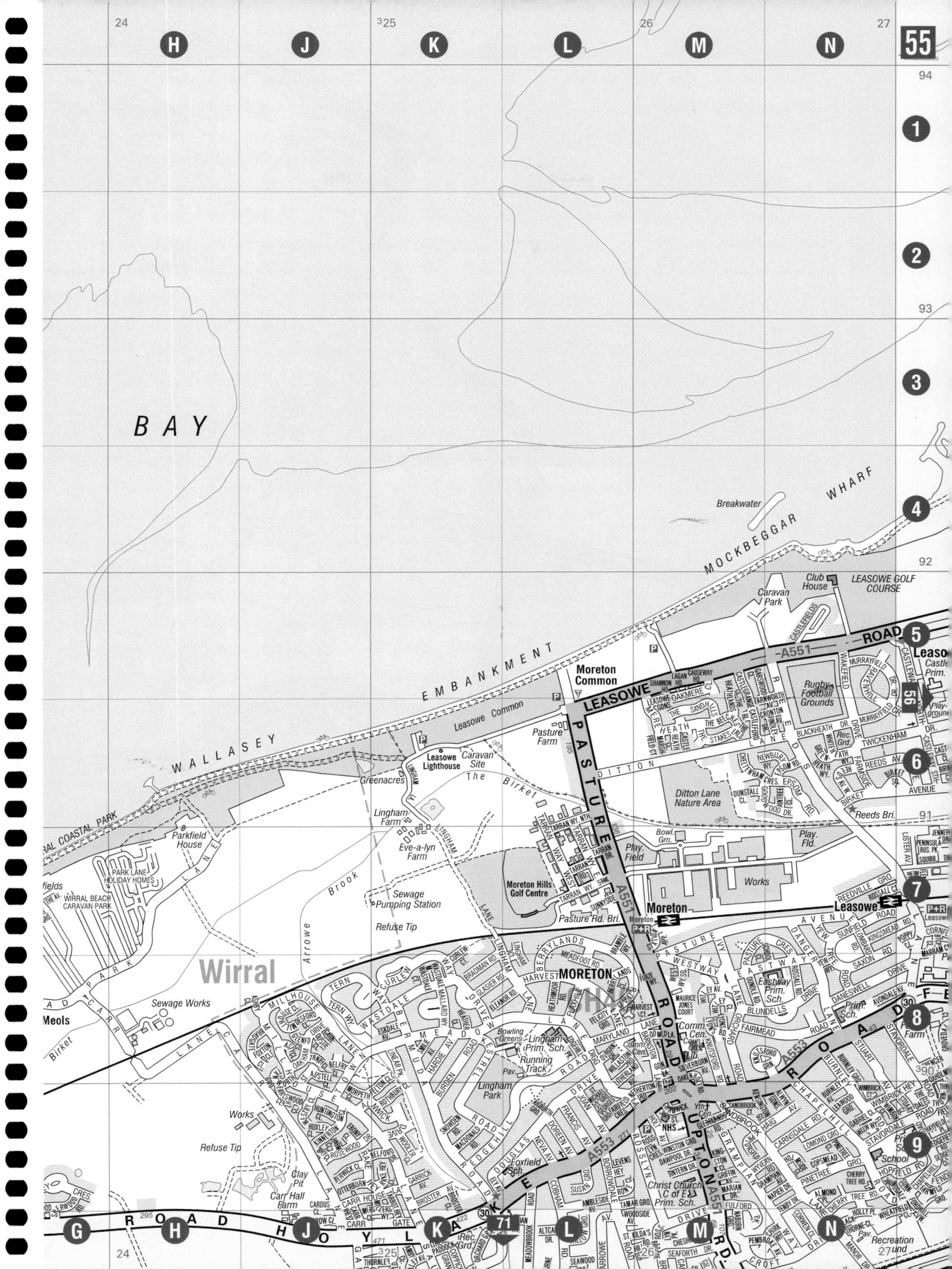
H
J
K
L
M
N
BAY
Breakwater
MOCKBEGGAR WHARF
Club House
LEASOWE GOLF COURSE
Caravan Park
ROAD
A551
Leasowe
Castle Prim.
Moreton Common
LEASOWE
Rugby Football Grounds
EMBANKMENT
WALLASEY
Leasowe Common
Pasture Farm
PASTURE
Leasowe Lighthouse
Caravan Site
The Birket
Greenacres
Lingham Farm
Eve-a-lyn Farm
DITTON
Ditton Lane Nature Area
Reeds Bri.
Bowl. Grn.
Play. Field
Play. Fld.
Works
Parkfield House
PARK LANE HOLIDAY HOMES
WIRRAL BEACH CARAVAN PARK
Moreton Hills Golf Centre
Sewage Pumping Station
Refuse Tip
Moreton
Pasture Rd. Bri.
Wirral
Sewage Works
Meols
MORETON
Eastway Prim. Sch.
Lingham Prim. Sch.
Running Track
Lingham Park
Foxfield Sch.
Christ Church C of E Prim. Sch.
Clay Pit
Carr Hall Farm
Works
Refuse Tip
School
Recreation Ground
A553
UPTON
HOYLAKE ROAD
G
71
56

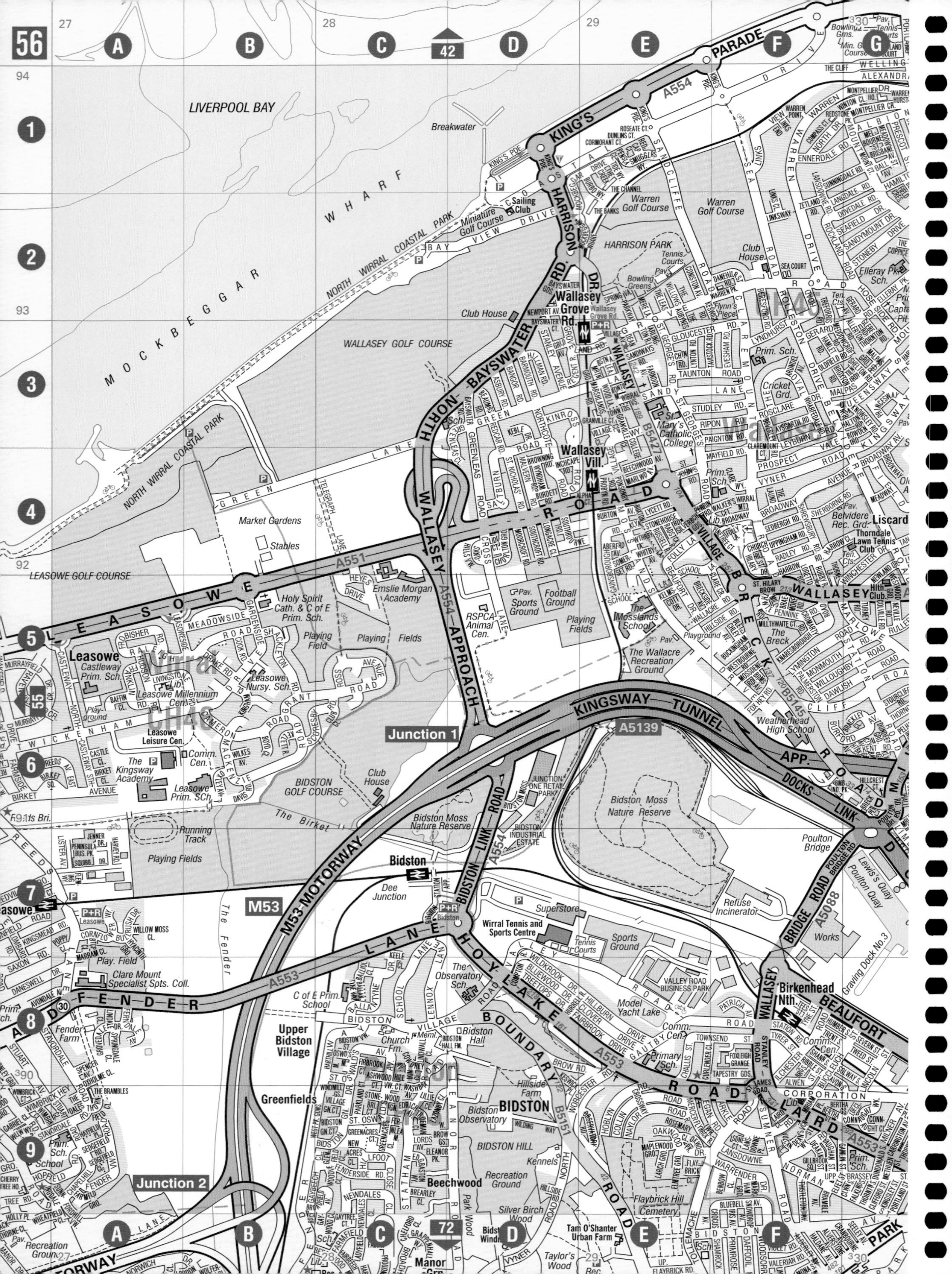
LIVERPOOL BAY
MOCKBEGGAR WHARF
NORTH WIRRAL COASTAL PARK
Breakwater
KING'S PARADE
HARRISON DR.
Sailing Club
Miniature Golf Course
BAY VIEW DRIVE
Warren Golf Course
HARRISON PARK
Club House
WALLASEY GOLF COURSE
Wallasey Grove Rd.
NORTH BAYSWATER RD.
WALLASEY VILLAGE
Wallasey Vill.
St. Mary's Catholic College
Wallasey
CH45
CH46
GREEN LANE
Market Gardens
Stables
LEASOWE GOLF COURSE
LEASOWE ROAD
A551
Holy Spirit Cath. & C of E Prim. Sch.
Emslie Morgan Academy
WALLASEY APPROACH
A554
RSPCA Animal Cen.
Sports Ground
Football Ground
Playing Fields
The Mosslands School
The Wallacre Recreation Ground
The Breck
Belvidere Rec. Grd.
Liscard
Thorndale Lawn Tennis Club
Leasowe
Castleway Prim. Sch.
Leasowe Millennium Cen.
Leasowe Nursy. Sch.
Leasowe Leisure Cen.
The Kingsway Academy
Leasowe Prim. Sch.
Junction 1
KINGSWAY TUNNEL APP.
A5139
DOCKS LINK
Weatherhead High School
BIDSTON GOLF COURSE
Club House
Bidston Moss Nature Reserve
BIDSTON INDUSTRIAL ESTATE
Junction One Retail Park
BIDSTON LINK ROAD
M53 MOTORWAY
Running Track
Playing Fields
Bidston
Dee Junction
Refuse Incinerator
Poulton Bridge
Lewis's Quay
Poulton Quay
BRIDGE ROAD
A5088
Works
Graving Dock No.3
Superstore
Wirral Tennis and Sports Centre
Sports Ground
VALLEY ROAD BUSINESS PARK
Model Yacht Lake
Birkenhead Nth.
BEAUFORT ROAD
M53
FENDER LANE
A553
Play. Field
Clare Mount Specialist Spts. Coll.
Fender Farm
C of E Prim. School
The Observatory Sch.
HOYLAKE ROAD
BOUNDARY ROAD
Upper Bidston Village
Bidston Hall
Church Fm.
Hillside Farm
BIDSTON
Bidston Observatory
BIDSTON HILL
Kennels
Recreation Ground
Silver Birch Wood
Flaybrick Hill Cemetery
Tam O'Shanter Urban Farm
Greenfields
Beechwood
Park Wood
Junction 2
Recreation Ground
Taylor's Wood
LAIRD ST.
CORPORATION RD.
B5151
B5145
42
72
55
27
28
29
330
390
92
93
94

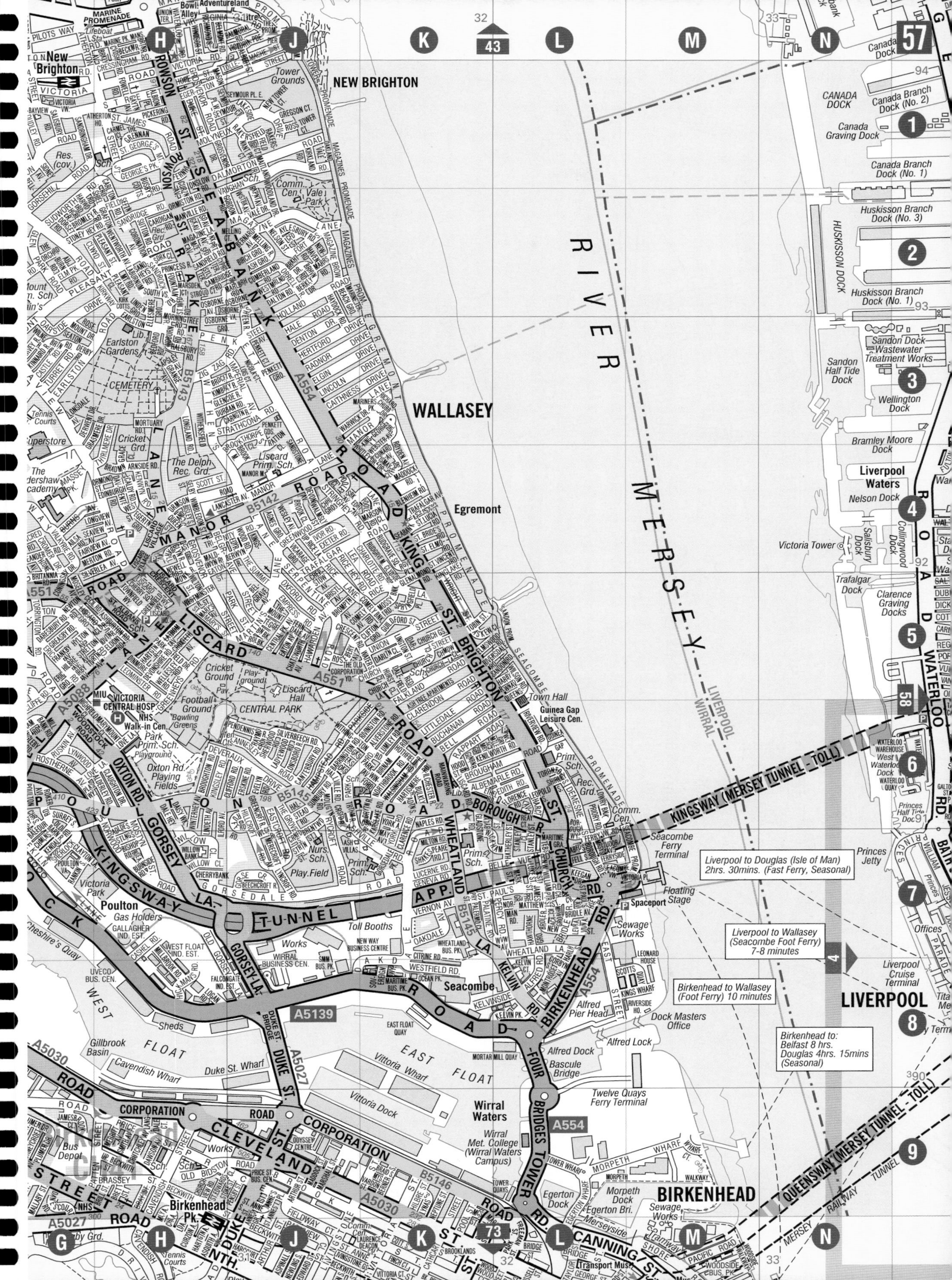

WALLASEY

NEW BRIGHTON

RIVER MERSEY

Egremont

Liverpool Waters

Nelson Dock

Victoria Tower

Liverpool to Douglas (Isle of Man) 2hrs. 30mins. (Fast Ferry, Seasonal)

Liverpool to Wallasey (Seacombe Foot Ferry) 7-8 minutes

Birkenhead to Wallasey (Foot Ferry) 10 minutes

Birkenhead to: Belfast 8 hrs. Douglas 4hrs. 15mins (Seasonal)

LIVERPOOL

Liverpool Cruise Terminal

KINGSWAY (MERSEY TUNNEL - TOLL)

QUEENSWAY (MERSEY TUNNEL - TOLL)

Seacombe

BIRKENHEAD

Wirral Waters

Wirral Met. College (Wirral Waters Campus)

Twelve Quays Ferry Terminal

Poulton

TUNNEL

Birkenhead Pk.

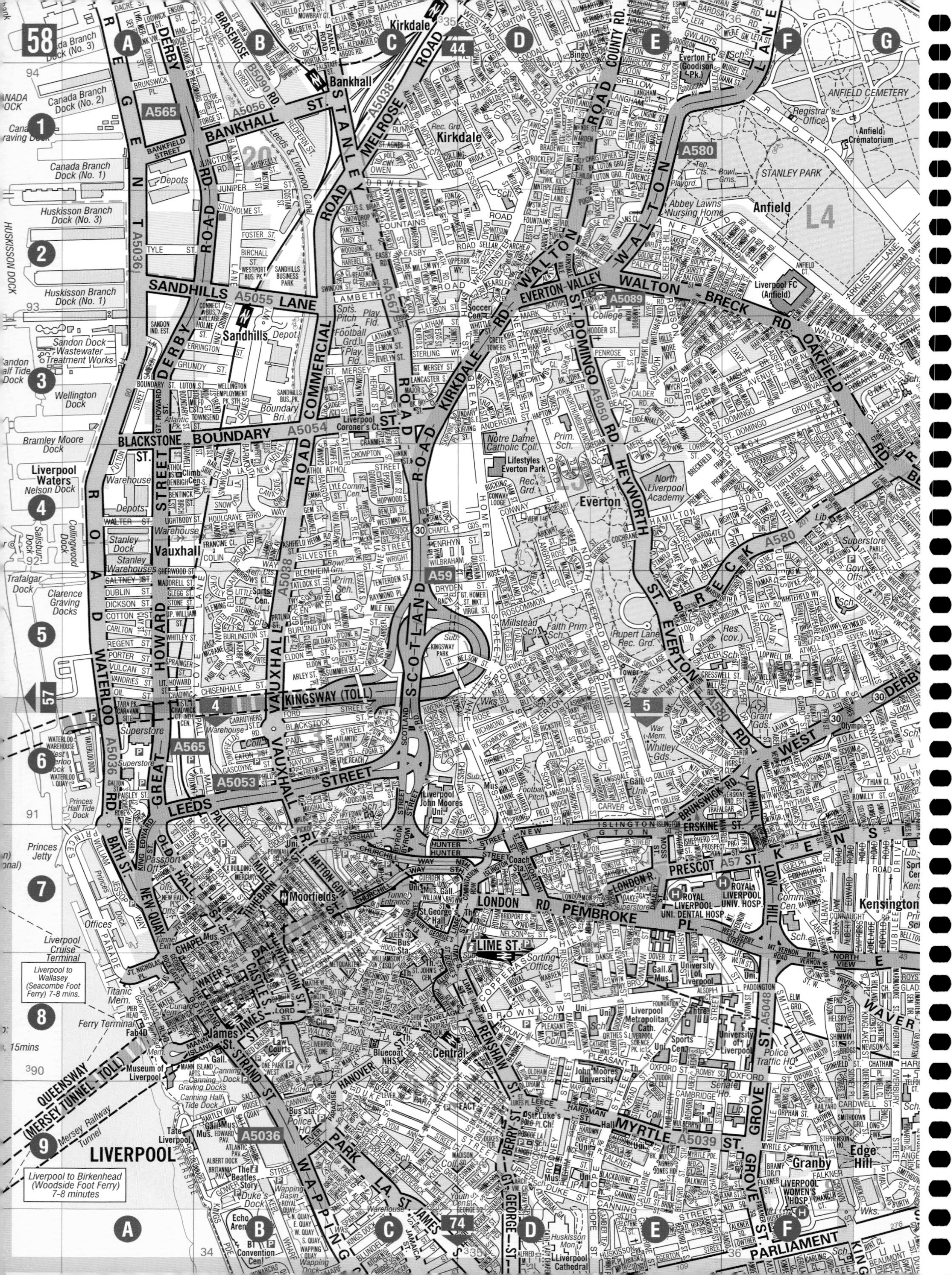

A
B
C
D
E
F
G
1
2
3
4
5
6
7
8
9
Kirkdale
Bankhall
Canada Branch Dock (No. 3)
Canada Branch Dock (No. 2)
Canada Branch Dock (No. 1)
Huskisson Branch Dock (No. 3)
Huskisson Branch Dock (No. 1)
HUSKISSON DOCK
Sandon Dock Wastewater Treatment Works
Wellington Dock
Bramley Moore Dock
Liverpool Waters
Nelson Dock
Salisbury Dock
Collingwood Dock
Stanley Dock
Trafalgar Dock
Clarence Graving Docks
Princes Half Tide Dock
Princes Jetty
Liverpool Cruise Terminal
Liverpool to Wallasey (Seacombe Foot Ferry) 7-8 mins.
Titanic Mem.
Pier Head
Ferry Terminal
Museum of Liverpool
Canning Dock
Canning Graving Docks
Canning Half Tide Dock
Tate Liverpool
Albert Dock
The Beatles Story
Duke's Dock
Wapping Basin
Wapping Dock
Echo Arena
BT Convention Cent.
LIVERPOOL
Liverpool to Birkenhead (Woodside Foot Ferry) 7-8 minutes
QUEENSWAY (MERSEY TUNNEL TOLL)
Mersey Railway Tunnel
REGENT RD.
A5036
WATERLOO RD.
GREAT HOWARD STREET
DERBY RD.
A565
BANKHALL ST.
A5056
SANDHILLS A5055 LANE
Sandhills
BLACKSTONE BOUNDARY A5054 ST.
COMMERCIAL ROAD
STANLEY ROAD
A5038
MELROSE ROAD
A567
Vauxhall
VAUXHALL RD.
KINGSWAY (TOLL)
LEEDS A5053 STREET
SCOTLAND ROAD
A59
KIRKDALE RD.
EVERTON VALLEY
WALTON RD.
COUNTY RD.
A5089
ST. DOMINGO A5050 RD.
HEYWORTH ST.
EVERTON ST.
Everton
Notre Dame Catholic Coll.
Lifestyles Everton Park
North Liverpool Academy
Rupert Lane Rec. Grd.
Prince Rupert's Tower
Everton FC (Goodison Pk.)
ANFIELD CEMETERY
Registrar's Office
Anfield Crematorium
STANLEY PARK
Anfield
L4
Abbey Lawns Nursing Home
WALTON LANE
A580
WALTON BRECK RD.
Liverpool FC (Anfield)
OAKFIELD RD.
BRECK RD.
WEST DERBY RD.
Olympia
Liverpool John Moores Uni.
ISLINGTON
ERSKINE ST.
PRESCOT A57 ST.
KENSINGTON
Kensington
LONDON RD.
PEMBROKE PL.
ROYAL LIVERPOOL UNIV. HOSP.
UNI. DENTAL HOSP.
LIME ST.
St. George's Hall
Moorfields
Central
James St.
STRAND ST.
A5036
WAPPING
PARK LA
HANOVER ST.
RENSHAW ST.
BERRY ST.
MYRTLE A5039 ST.
GROVE ST.
A5048
University of Liverpool
Liverpool Metropolitan Cath.
John Moores University
Liverpool Cathedral
Huskisson Mon.
LIVERPOOL WOMEN'S HOSP.
Granby
Edge Hill
PARLIAMENT
44
57
74
4
5
34
35
36
94
93
92
91
390

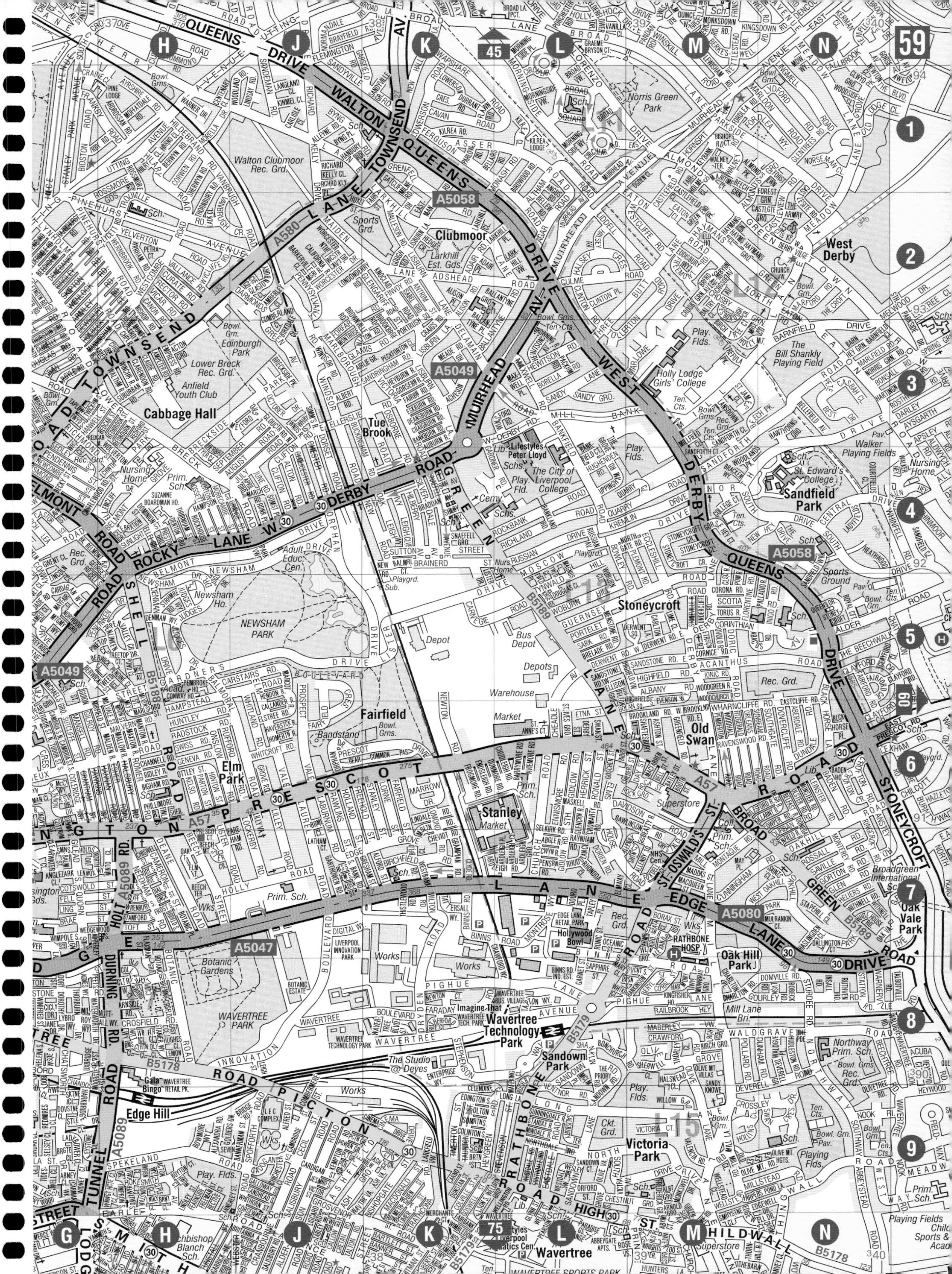

H
J
K
L
M
N
45
QUEENS DRIVE
WALTON
TOWNSEND AV.
QUEENS DRIVE
Norris Green Park
Walton Clubmoor Rec. Grd.
LANE
A580
A5058
Clubmoor
Larkhill Est. Gds.
Sports Grd.
MUIRHEAD AV.
West Derby
WEST DERBY
Edinburgh Park
Lower Breck Rec. Grd.
Anfield Youth Club
Cabbage Hall
A5049
Tue Brook
Holly Lodge Girls' College
The Bill Shankly Playing Field
BARNFIELD DRIVE
Walker Playing Fields
Lifestyles Peter Lloyd
The City of Liverpool College
St. Edward's College
Sandfield Park
BELMONT ROAD
ROCKY LANE W.
DERBY ROAD
GREEN
Adult Educ. Cen.
Newsham Ho.
NEWSHAM PARK
QUEENS DRIVE
A5058
Sports Ground
Stoneycroft
B5189
Depot
Bus Depot
Depots
Warehouse
Market
A5049
Fairfield
Bandstand
Rec. Grd.
Old Swan
Elm Park
PRESCOT ROAD
A57
Stanley Market
Superstore
BROAD GREEN
STONEYCROFT
Broadgreen International Sch.
Oak Vale Park
EDGE LANE
A5080
A5047
Botanic Gardens
WAVERTREE PARK
Liverpool Innovation Park
Works
Hollywood Bowl
RATHBONE HOSP.
Oak Hill Park
DRIVE
Edge Lane Retail Park
Imagine That
Wavertree Technology Park
Mill Lane Bri.
Northway Prim. Sch.
Sandown Park
The Studio @ Deyes
Gala Bingo
Edge Hill
PICTON ROAD
A5089
B5178
Works
Victoria Park
L15
Playing Flds.
Ckt. Grd.
Play. Flds.
RATHBONE ROAD
HIGH ST.
Wavertree
HILDWALL
B5178
Playing Fields
G
H
J
K
L
M
N
75
1
2
3
4
5
6
7
8
9
60

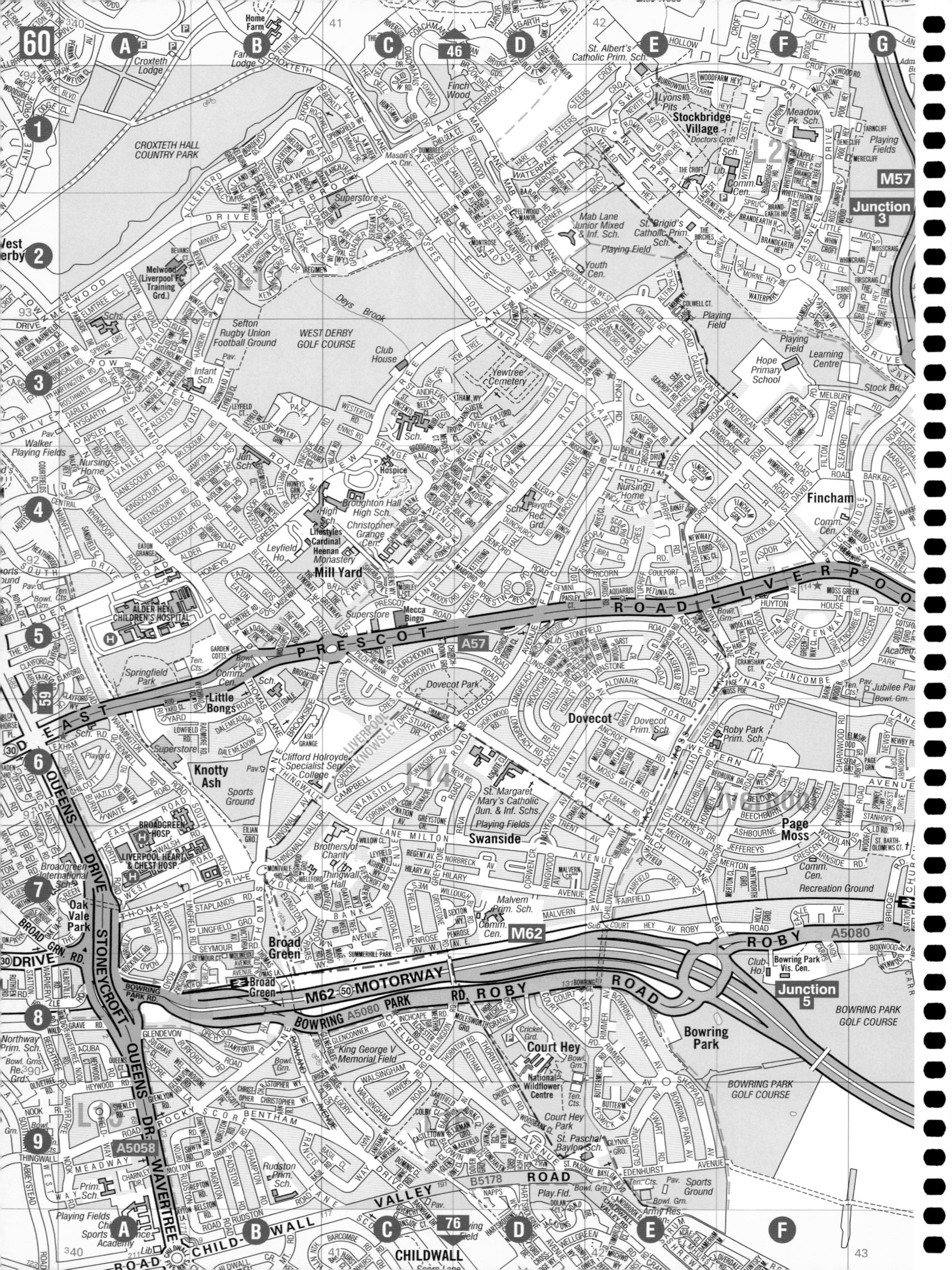
A
B
C
D
E
F
G
1
2
3
4
5
6
7
8
9
46
76
59
Croxteth Lodge
Home Farm
Farm Lodge
CROXTETH HALL COUNTRY PARK
Finch Wood
St. Albert's Catholic Prim. Sch.
Lyons Pits
Stockbridge Village
Doctors Croft
Meadow Pk. Sch.
Playing Fields
M57
Junction 3
Mason's Cnr.
Superstore
Mab Lane Junior Mixed & Inf. Sch.
St. Brigid's Catholic Prim. Sch.
Playing Field
Youth Cen.
West Derby
Melwood (Liverpool FC Training Grd.)
Deys Brook
Sefton Rugby Union Football Ground
WEST DERBY GOLF COURSE
Club House
Yewtree Cemetery
Hope Primary School
Learning Centre
Stock Bri.
Walker Playing Fields
Infant Sch.
Nursing Home
Jun. Sch.
Hospice
Broughton Hall High Sch.
Christopher Grange Cen.
Lifestyles Cardinal Heenan
Monastery
Leyfield Ho.
Mill Yard
Fincham
Comm. Cen.
ALDER HEY CHILDREN'S HOSPITAL
Mecca Bingo
PRESCOT ROAD
LIVERPOOL ROAD
A57
Springfield Park
Little Bongs
Dovecot Park
Dovecot
Dovecot Prim. Sch.
Roby Park Prim. Sch.
Jubilee Park
Knotty Ash
Sports Ground
Superstore
Clifford Holroyde Specialist Sep. College
L14
St. Margaret Mary's Catholic Jun. & Inf. Schs.
Playing Fields
Swanside
Page Moss
Comm. Cen.
Recreation Ground
BROADGREEN HOSP.
LIVERPOOL HEART & CHEST HOSP.
Broadgreen International Sch.
Brothers of Charity
Thingwall Hall
Malvern Prim. Sch.
Oak Vale Park
QUEENS DRIVE
STONEYCROFT
M62
M62 MOTORWAY
Broad Green
BOWRING PARK ROAD
ROBY ROAD
A5080
Bowring Park Vis. Cen.
Junction 5
BOWRING PARK GOLF COURSE
Bowring Park
Court Hey
National Wildflower Centre
King George V Memorial Field
Court Hey Park
St. Paschal Baylon Sch.
Northway Prim. Sch.
A5058
QUEENS DR. WAVERTREE
Rudston Prim. Sch.
B5178
CHILDWALL VALLEY ROAD
Sports Ground
Army Res. Cen.
Playing Fields
Prim. Sch.
CHILDWALL
340
41
42
43

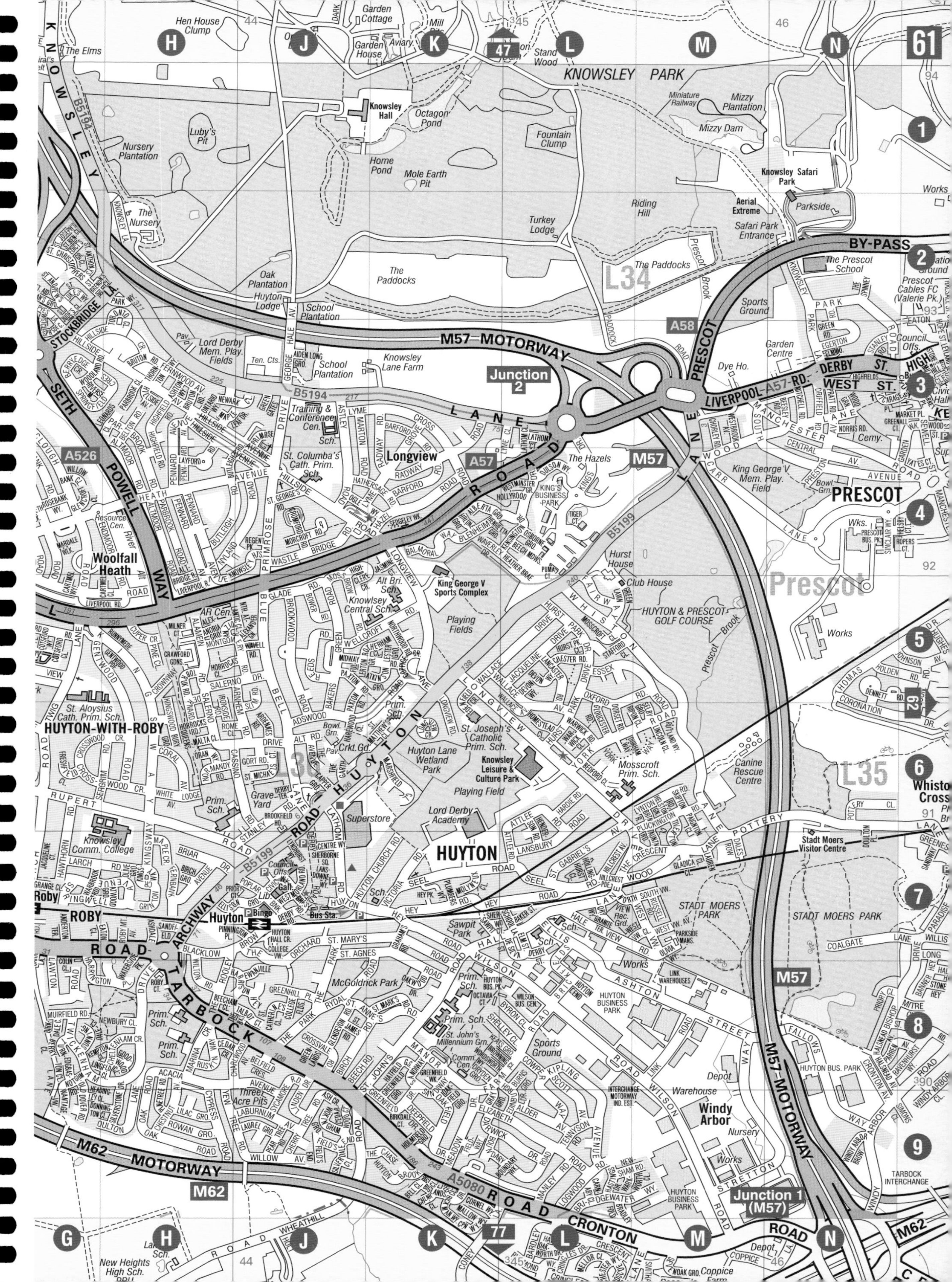
KNOWSLEY PARK
Knowsley Hall
Knowsley Safari Park
Hen House Clump
Garden Cottage
Garden House
Aviary
Mill
Stand Wood
The Elms
Miniature Railway
Mizzy Plantation
Mizzy Dam
Octagon Pond
Fountain Clump
Luby's Pit
Nursery Plantation
Home Pond
Mole Earth Pit
Riding Hill
Aerial Extreme
Parkside
Safari Park Entrance
Turkey Lodge
The Nursery
The Paddocks
Oak Plantation
Huyton Lodge
School Plantation
L34
M57 MOTORWAY
BY-PASS
The Prescot School
Prescot Cables FC (Valerie Pk.)
Sports Ground
A58
PRESCOT
Junction 2
Lord Derby Mem. Play. Fields
Knowsley Lane Farm
B5194
LANE
Training & Conference Cen.
Longview
St. Columba's Cath. Prim. Sch.
A57
M57
The Hazels
King's Business Park
LIVERPOOL A57 RD.
DERBY ST.
WEST ST.
Dye Ho.
Garden Centre
Council Offs.
King George V Mem. Play. Field
PRESCOT
Prescot
A526
POWELL WAY
SETH
Woolfall Heath
Resource Cen.
B5199
Hurst House
Club House
HUYTON & PRESCOT GOLF COURSE
King George V Sports Complex
Playing Fields
Alt Bri. Sch.
Knowlsey Central Sch.
AR Cen.
Works
St. Aloysius Cath. Prim. Sch.
HUYTON-WITH-ROBY
L35
Whiston Cross
Huyton Lane Wetland Park
St. Joseph's Catholic Prim. Sch.
Knowsley Leisure & Culture Park
Playing Field
Mosscroft Prim. Sch.
Canine Rescue Centre
Lord Derby Academy
HUYTON
Superstore
Grave Yard
Knowsley Comm. College
Stadt Moers Visitor Centre
STADT MOERS PARK
Roby
ROBY
Huyton
Bingo
Bus Sta.
Sawpit Park
HUYTON ROAD
ARCHWAY
TARBOCK ROAD
McGoldrick Park
Huyton Business Park
Sports Ground
Interchange Motorway Ind. Est.
Depot
Warehouse
Windy Arbor
Nursery
M57 MOTORWAY
HUYTON BUS. PARK
Three Acre Pits
M62 MOTORWAY
M62
A5080 ROAD
CRONTON ROAD
Junction 1 (M57)
TARBOCK INTERCHANGE
New Heights High Sch.
Coppice Farm
47
77
62
44
345
46
94
93
92
91
390

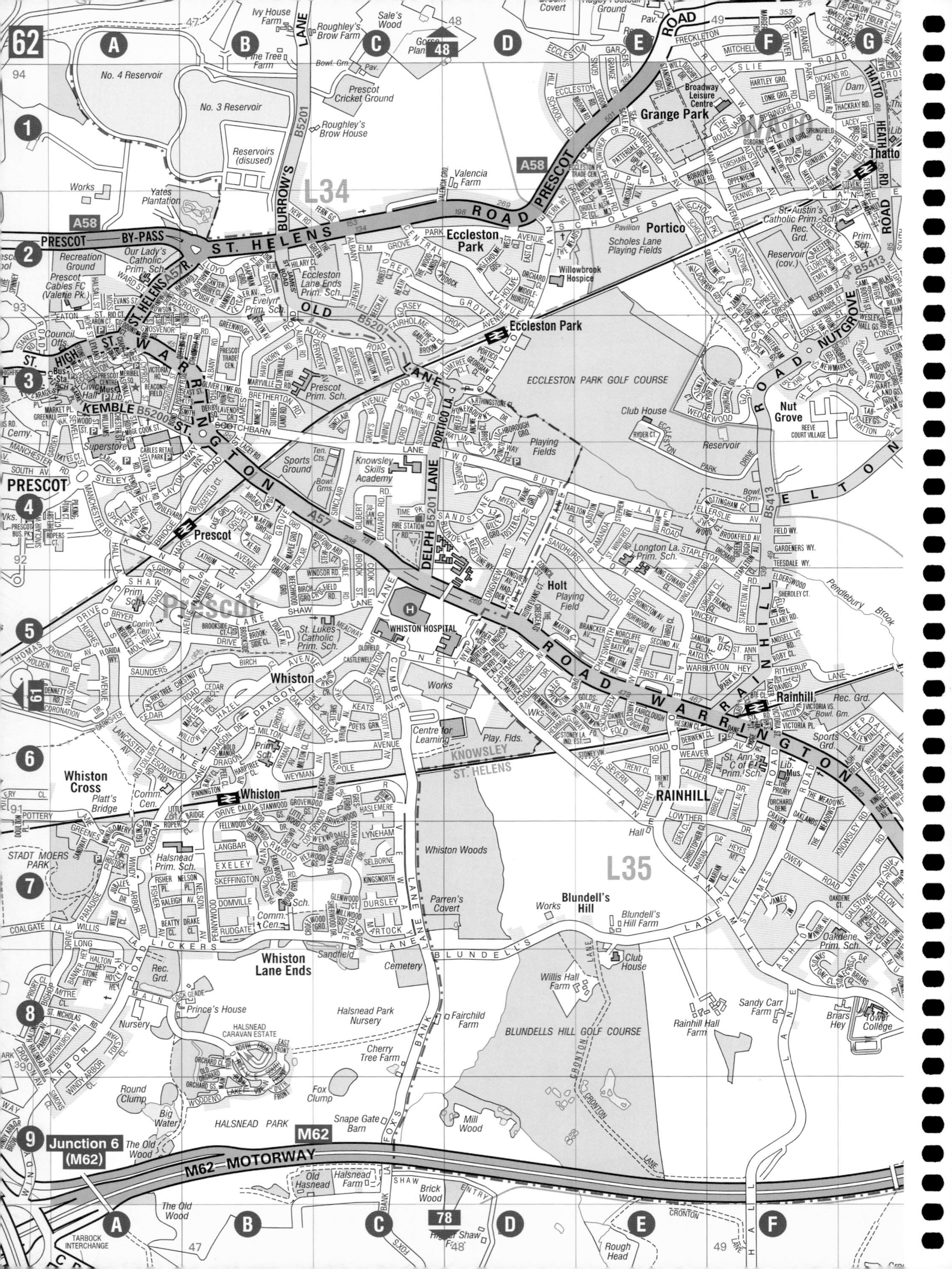
62
A
B
C
D
E
F
G
1
2
3
4
5
6
7
8
9
48
78
L34
L35
A58
M62
B5201
B5200
B5413
A57
No. 4 Reservoir
No. 3 Reservoir
Reservoirs (disused)
Ivy House Farm
Pine Tree Farm
Roughley's Brow Farm
Sale's Wood
Roughley's Brow House
Prescot Cricket Ground
Yates Plantation
Valencia Farm
PRESCOT BY-PASS
ST. HELENS ROAD
PRESCOT ROAD
Eccleston Park
Grange Park
Broadway Leisure Centre
Portico
Scholes Lane Playing Fields
Willowbrook Hospice
Thatto Heath
St. Austin's Catholic Prim. Sch.
Our Lady's Catholic Prim. Sch.
Recreation Ground
Prescot Cables FC (Valerie Pk.)
Evelyn Prim. Sch.
Eccleston Lane Ends Prim. Sch.
OLD LANE
Eccleston Park
ECCLESTON PARK GOLF COURSE
Club House
Reservoir
Nut Grove
NUTGROVE ROAD
Council Offs.
Civic Hall
Superstore
PRESCOT
Prescot
WARRINGTON ROAD
Prescot Prim. Sch.
Sports Ground
Knowsley Skills Academy
Playing Fields
Longton La. Prim. Sch.
Holt
Playing Fields
DELPH LANE
PORTICO LA.
WHISTON HOSPITAL
St. Lukes Catholic Prim. Sch.
Whiston
Works
Centre for Learning
Play. Flds.
KNOWSLEY
ST. HELENS
Rainhill
Rec. Grd.
Sports Grd.
St. Ann's C of E Prim. Sch.
RAINHILL
Whiston Cross
Platt's Bridge
Whiston
Halsnead Prim. Sch.
STADT MOERS PARK
Whiston Woods
Parren's Covert
Blundell's Hill
Blundell's Hill Farm
Oakdene Prim. Sch.
Whiston Lane Ends
Sandfield
Cemetery
Rec. Grd.
Club House
Willis Hall Farm
Sandy Carr Farm
Briars Hey
Tower College
Prince's House
Nursery
Halsnead Park Nursery
Fairchild Farm
BLUNDELLS HILL GOLF COURSE
Rainhill Hall Farm
HALSNEAD CARAVAN ESTATE
Cherry Tree Farm
Round Clump
Fox Clump
Big Water
HALSNEAD PARK
Snape Gate Barn
Mill Wood
Junction 6 (M62)
The Old Wood
M62 MOTORWAY
Old Hasnead
Halsnead Farm
Brick Wood
The Old Wood
TARBOCK INTERCHANGE
Higher Shaw F.
Rough Head
47
49

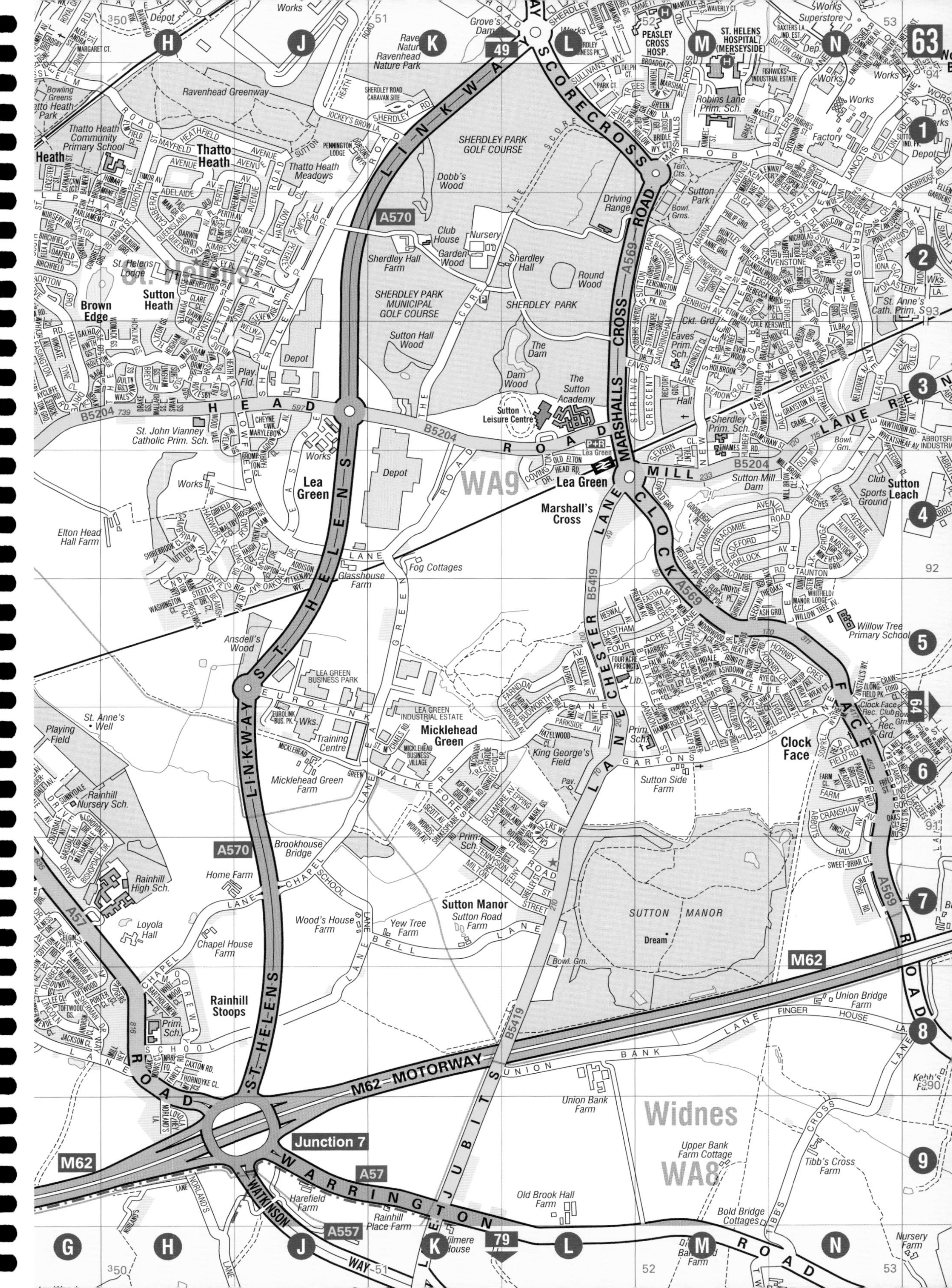
Thatto Heath
St. Helens
Sutton Heath
Brown Edge
Lea Green
Marshall's Cross
Sutton Leach
Clock Face
Micklehead Green
Sutton Manor
Rainhill Stoops
Widnes
WA9
WA8
SHERDLEY PARK GOLF COURSE
SHERDLEY PARK MUNICIPAL GOLF COURSE
SHERDLEY PARK
SUTTON MANOR
ST. HELENS HOSPITAL (MERSEYSIDE)
PEASLEY CROSS HOSP.
LINKWAY
ST. HELENS LINKWAY
SCORECROSS ROAD
MARSHALLS CROSS ROAD
HEAD ROAD
MILL LANE
CLOCK FACE ROAD
CHESTER LANE
JUBITS LANE
WARRINGTON ROAD
M62 MOTORWAY
Junction 7
A570
A569
A57
A557
B5204
B5419
M62
The Sutton Academy
Sutton Leisure Centre
Lea Green Business Park
Lea Green Industrial Estate
Rainhill High Sch.
Ravenhead Greenway
Ravenhead Nature Park
Union Bank Farm
Upper Bank Farm Cottage
Tibb's Cross Farm
Old Brook Hall Farm
Bold Bridge Cottages
Harefield Farm
Rainhill Place Farm
Willow Tree Primary School
St. Anne's Cath. Prim. Sch.
Eaves Prim. Sch.
Sherdley Prim. Sch.
St. John Vianney Catholic Prim. Sch.
Thatto Heath Community Primary School
Robins Lane Prim. Sch.
Rainhill Nursery Sch.
Sutton Park
Sutton Mill Dam
Dream
49
79
64
G H J K L M N
1 2 3 4 5 6 7 8 9

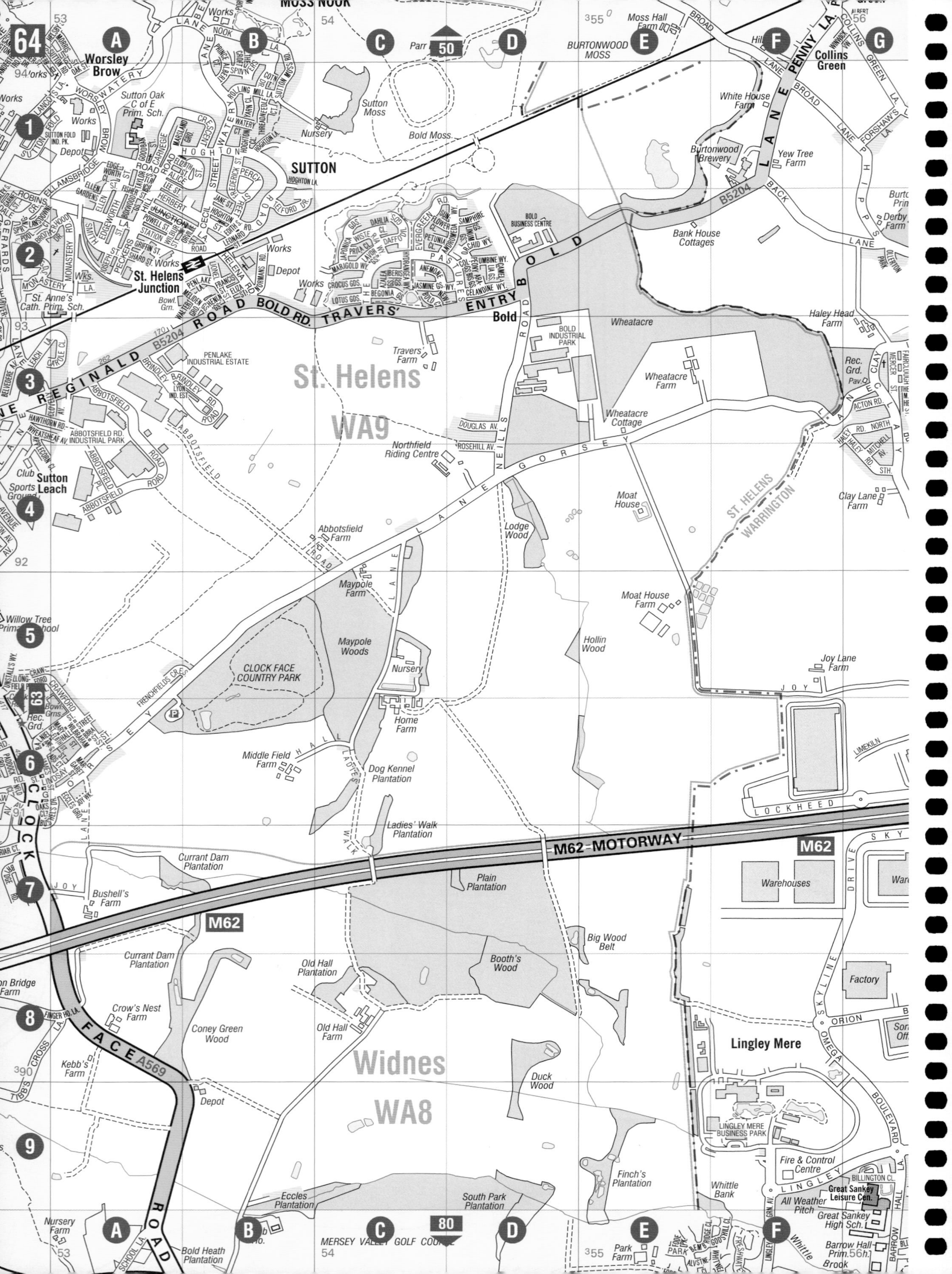
MOSS NOOK
50
Worsley Brow
Sutton Oak C of E Prim. Sch.
SUTTON
Sutton Moss
Bold Moss
Moss Hall Farm
BURTONWOOD MOSS
Collins Green
White House Farm
Burtonwood Brewery
Yew Tree Farm
Bank House Cottages
BOLD BUSINESS CENTRE
St. Helens Junction
St. Anne's Cath. Prim. Sch.
BOLD RD. TRAVERS' ENTRY
Bold
REGINALD ROAD
PENLAKE INDUSTRIAL ESTATE
Travers' Farm
BOLD INDUSTRIAL PARK
Wheatacre
Haley Head Farm
St. Helens
WA9
Wheatacre Farm
Wheatacre Cottage
Northfield Riding Centre
ABBOTSFIELD RD. INDUSTRIAL PARK
Sutton Leach
GORSEY LANE
Moat House
Clay Lane Farm
ST. HELENS
WARRINGTON
Lodge Wood
Abbotsfield Farm
Maypole Farm
Moat House Farm
Willow Tree Primary School
Maypole Woods
Hollin Wood
CLOCK FACE COUNTRY PARK
Nursery
Joy Lane Farm
63
Home Farm
Middle Field Farm
Dog Kennel Plantation
Ladies' Walk Plantation
LOCKHEED
M62-MOTORWAY
M62
Currant Dam Plantation
Plain Plantation
Warehouses
Bushell's Farm
Big Wood Belt
Booth's Wood
Old Hall Plantation
Factory
Crow's Nest Farm
Coney Green Wood
Old Hall Farm
Lingley Mere
Kebb's Farm
Widnes
Duck Wood
CLOCK FACE A569 ROAD
Depot
WA8
LINGLEY MERE BUSINESS PARK
Fire & Control Centre
Finch's Plantation
Whittle Bank
Great Sankey Leisure Cen.
Eccles Plantation
South Park Plantation
All Weather Pitch
Great Sankey High Sch.
Nursery Farm
80
MERSEY VALLEY GOLF COURSE
Park Farm
Barrow Hall Prim. Sch.
Bold Heath Plantation

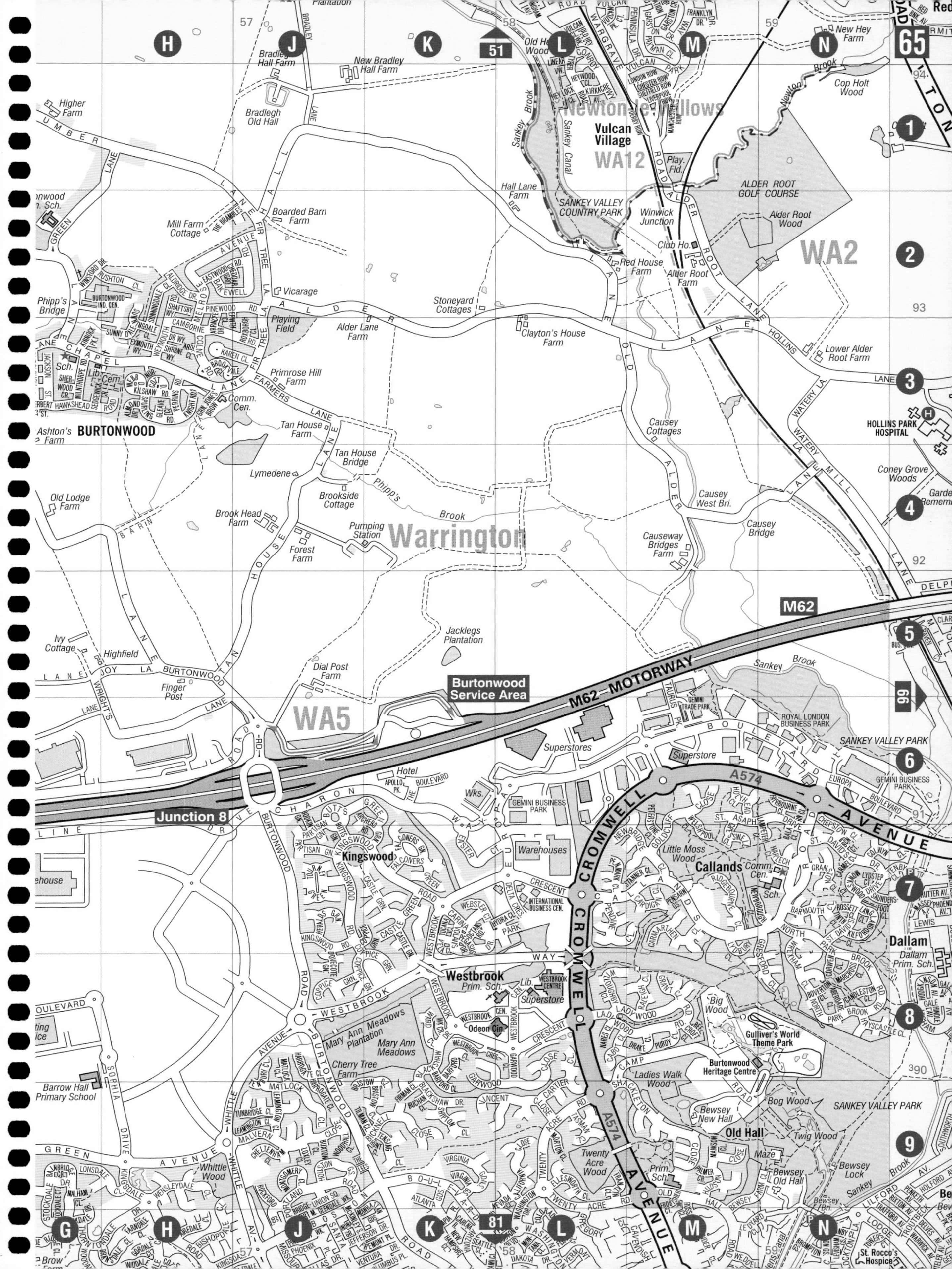

65
Newton-le-Willows
Vulcan Village
WA12
Sankey Valley Country Park
Alder Root Golf Course
WA2
Hollins Park Hospital
Burtonwood
Warrington
M62
M62 Motorway
Burtonwood Service Area
WA5
Junction 8
Kingswood
Westbrook
Callands
Dallam
Old Hall
Cromwell Avenue
A574
Gulliver's World Theme Park
Burtonwood Heritage Centre
Sankey Valley Park
Royal London Business Park
Gemini Business Park
Barrow Hall Primary School
St. Rocco's Hospice
51
81
69

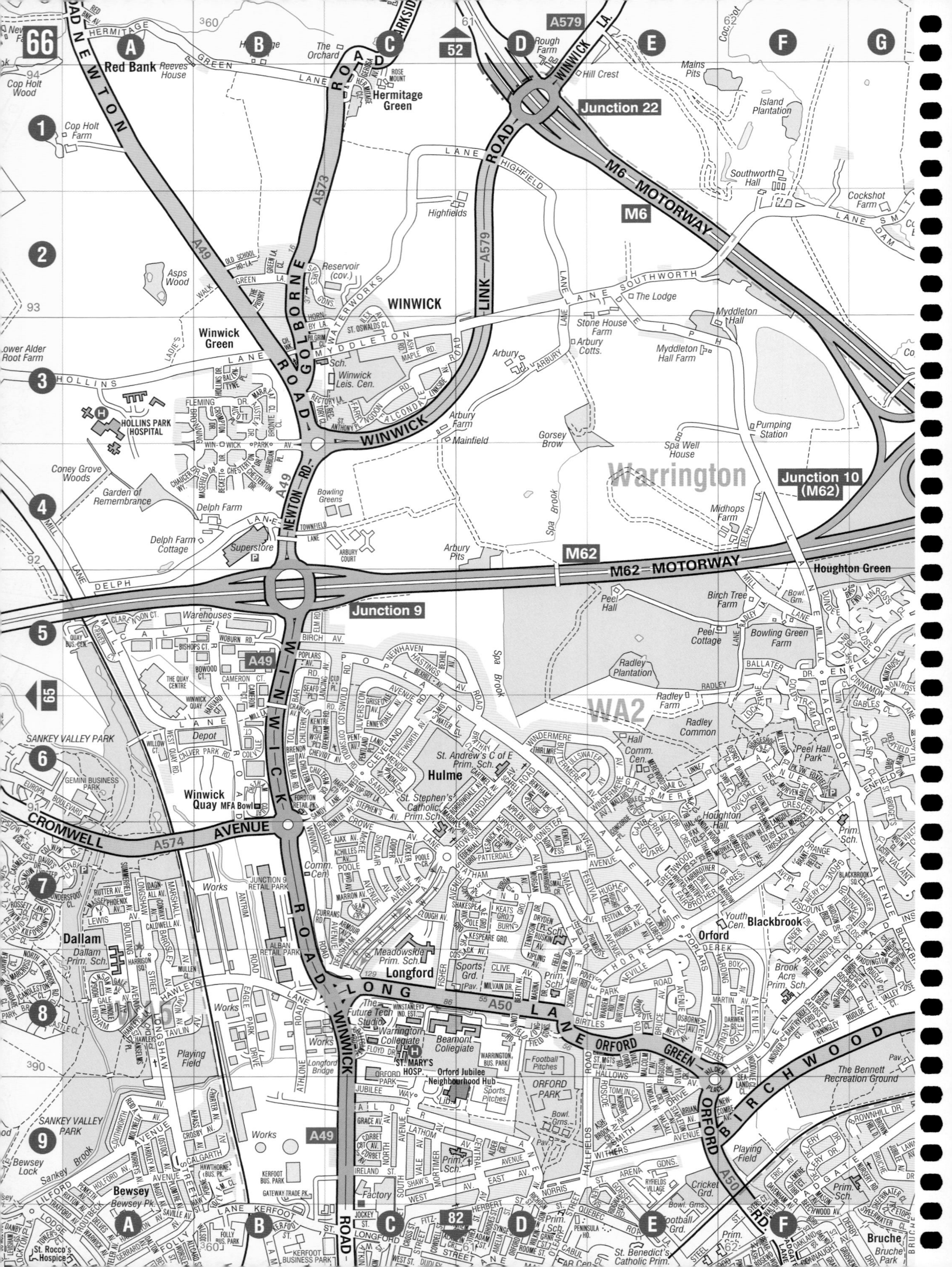
52
65
82
A579
Junction 22
M6 MOTORWAY
M6
Junction 10 (M62)
M62 MOTORWAY
M62
Junction 9
A49
A573
A574
A50
Red Bank
Reeves House
Cop Holt Wood
Cop Holt Farm
The Orchard
Hermitage Green
Rough Farm
Hill Crest
Mains Pits
Island Plantation
Southworth Hall
Cockshot Farm
Highfields
Asps Wood
Reservoir (cov.)
WINWICK
Winwick Green
Lower Alder Root Farm
The Lodge
Stone House Farm
Arbury Cotts.
Myddleton Hall
Myddleton Hall Farm
Arbury
Winwick Leis. Cen.
HOLLINS PARK HOSPITAL
Arbury Farm
Mainfield
Gorsey Brow
Spa Well House
Pumping Station
Warrington
Coney Grove Woods
Garden of Remembrance
Delph Farm
Delph Farm Cottage
Superstore
Bowling Greens
Arbury Pits
Midhops Farm
Houghton Green
Peel Hall
Birch Tree Farm
Warehouses
Peel Cottage
Bowling Green Farm
Radley Plantation
Radley Farm
Radley Common
WA2
SANKEY VALLEY PARK
GEMINI BUSINESS PARK
Depot
Winwick Quay
MFA Bowl
St. Andrew's C of E Prim. Sch.
Hulme
St. Stephen's Catholic Prim. Sch.
Hall Comm. Cen.
Peel Hall Park
Houghton Hall
Comm. Cen.
Works
JUNCTION 9 RETAIL PARK
ALBAN RETAIL PARK
Dallam
Dallam Prim. Sch.
Meadowside Prim. Sch.
Longford
Sports Grd.
Youth Cen.
Blackbrook
Orford
Brook Acre Prim. Sch.
WA5
Playing Field
Future Tech Studio
Warrington Collegiate
Beamont Collegiate
ST. MARY'S HOSP.
Orford Jubilee Neighbourhood Hub
Football Pitches
ORFORD PARK
Sports Pitches
Longford Bridge
The Bennett Recreation Ground
SANKEY VALLEY PARK
Bewsey Lock
Bewsey
Bewsey Pk.
Factory
Prim. Sch.
Cricket Grd.
Playing Field
Bruche
Bruche Park
St. Rocco's Hospice
KERFOOT BUSINESS PARK
St. Benedict's Catholic Prim.
Football Grd.

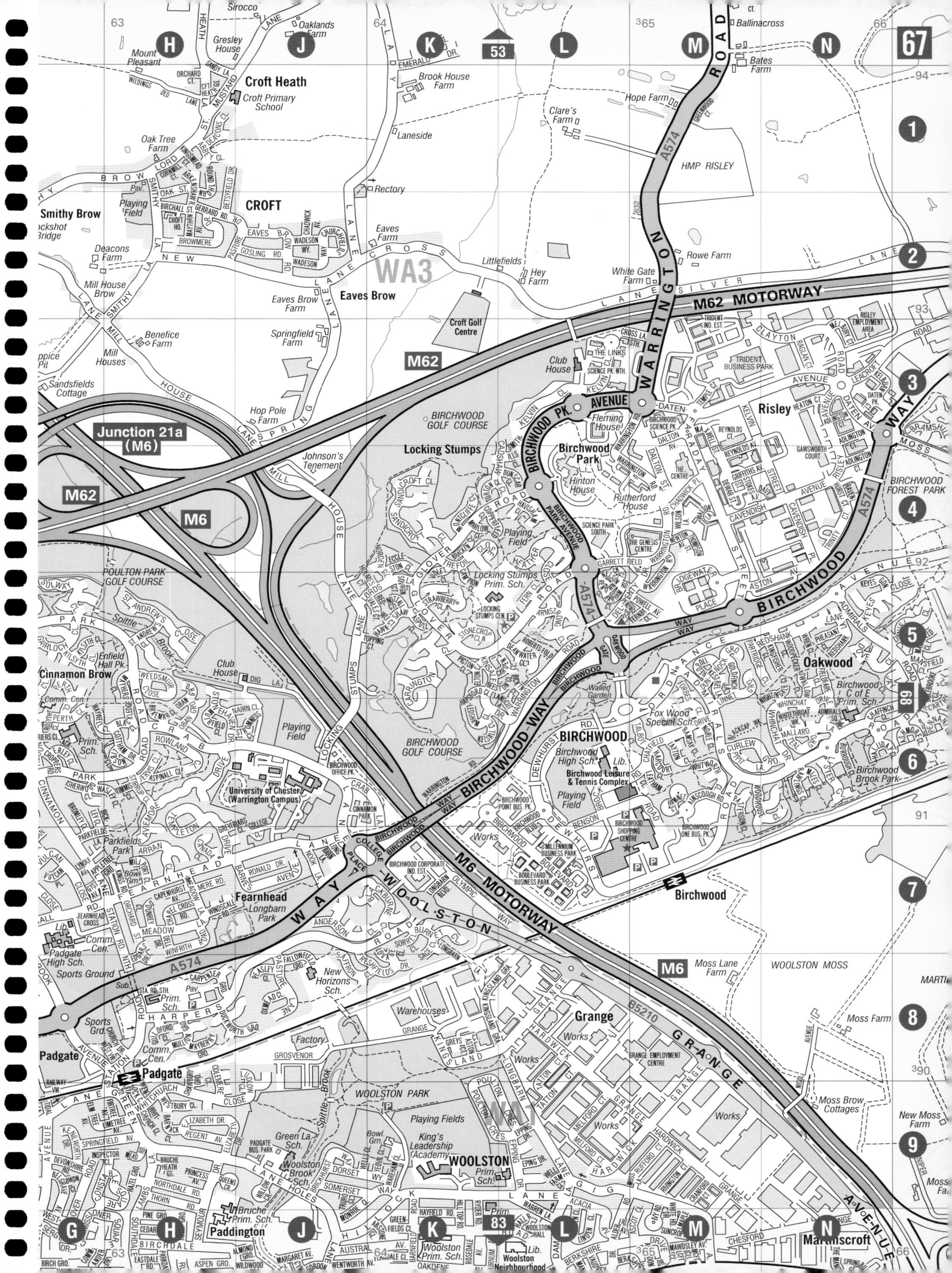

53
Croft Heath
Croft Primary School
Gresley House
Oaklands Farm
Mount Pleasant
Brook House Farm
Ballinacross
Bates Farm
Hope Farm
Clare's Farm
Laneside
Oak Tree Farm
HMP RISLEY
Rectory
Smithy Brow
CROFT
Playing Field
Deacons Farm
Eaves Farm
Rowe Farm
WA3
Littlefields
Hey Farm
White Gate Farm
Mill House Brow
Eaves Brow Farm
Eaves Brow
M62 MOTORWAY
Croft Golf Centre
Springfield Farm
Benefice Farm
Mill Houses
Sandsfields Cottage
M62
Club House
THE LINKS
TRIDENT IND. EST.
TRIDENT BUSINESS PARK
RISLEY EMPLOYMENT AREA
Hop Pole Farm
Junction 21a (M6)
BIRCHWOOD GOLF COURSE
Fleming House
Risley
Locking Stumps
Johnson's Tenement
Birchwood Park
Hinton House
Rutherford House
BIRCHWOOD FOREST PARK
M62
M6
SCIENCE PARK SOUTH
THE GENESIS CENTRE
POULTON PARK GOLF COURSE
Locking Stumps Prim. Sch.
Enfield Hall Pk.
Cinnamon Brow
Club House
Oakwood
Walled Garden
Birchwood C of E Prim. Sch.
Fox Wood Special Sch.
Playing Field
BIRCHWOOD
Birchwood High Sch.
Lib.
Birchwood Leisure & Tennis Complex
BIRCHWOOD GOLF COURSE
Birchwood Brook Park
University of Chester (Warrington Campus)
Playing Field
BIRCHWOOD SHOPPING CENTRE
Works
MILLENNIUM BUSINESS PARK
BOULEVARD BUSINESS PARK
BIRCHWOOD CORPORATE IND. EST.
Parkfields Park
Birchwood
Fearnhead
Longbarn Park
M6 MOTORWAY
Padgate High Sch.
Sports Ground
New Horizons Sch.
Moss Lane Farm
WOOLSTON MOSS
M6
Grange
Warehouses
Moss Farm
Factory
Works
GRANGE EMPLOYMENT CENTRE
Padgate
WOOLSTON PARK
Moss Brow Cottages
Playing Fields
New Moss Farm
Green La. Sch.
King's Leadership Academy
Woolston Brook Sch.
WOOLSTON
Works
Bruche Prim. Sch.
Paddington
83
Woolston Prim. Sch.
Woolston Neighbourhood
Martinscroft

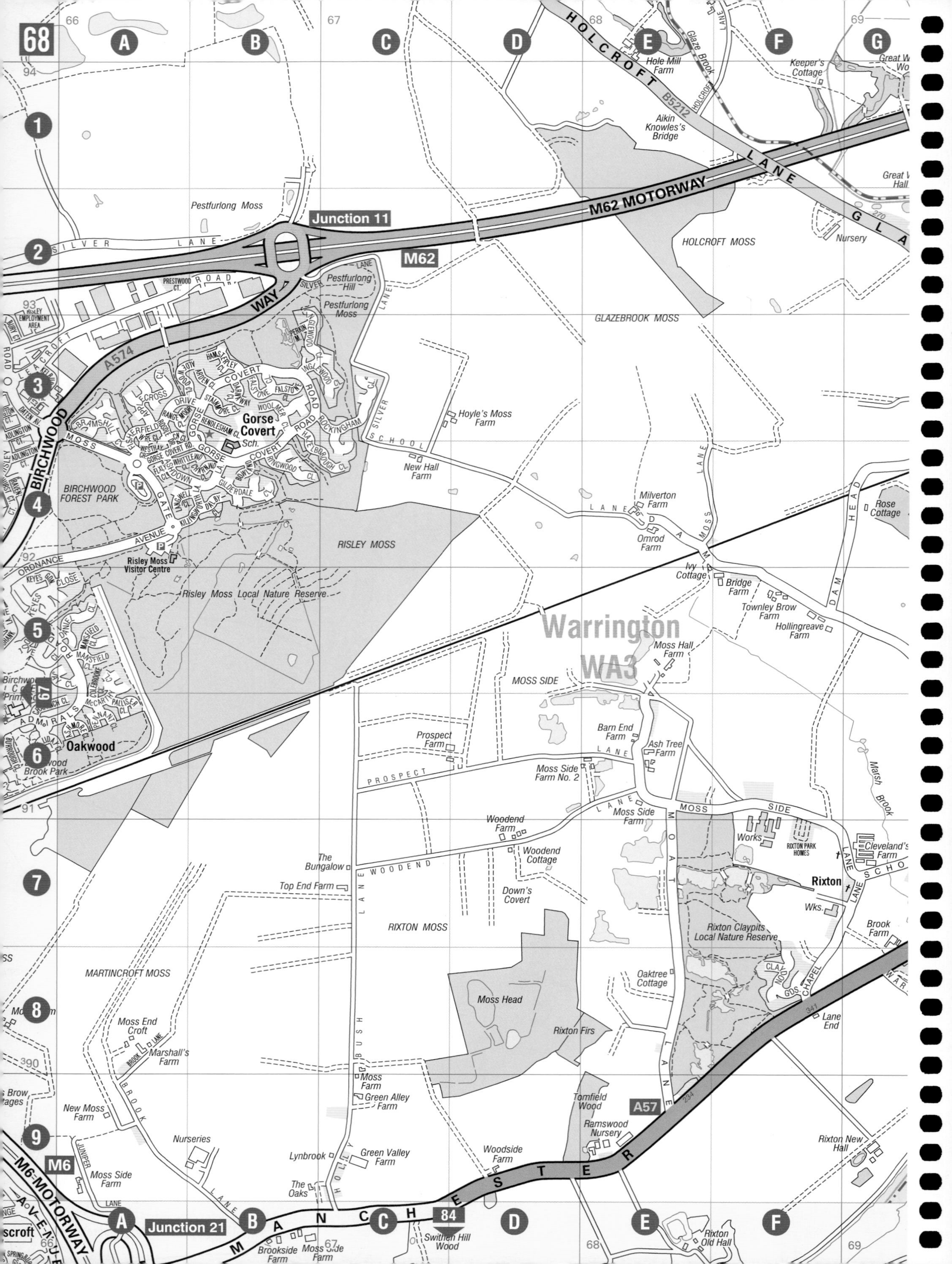

HOLCROFT LANE
Hole Mill Farm
Glaze Brook
Keeper's Cottage
Aikin Knowles's Bridge
B5212
M62 MOTORWAY
Junction 11
M62
Pestfurlong Moss
SILVER LANE
HOLCROFT MOSS
Nursery
GLAZEBROOK MOSS
Pestfurlong Hill
BIRCHWOOD WAY
A574
Gorse Covert
Sch.
Hoyle's Moss Farm
New Hall Farm
SCHOOL LANE
Milverton Farm
Omrod Farm
Rose Cottage
BIRCHWOOD FOREST PARK
RISLEY MOSS
Risley Moss Visitor Centre
Risley Moss Local Nature Reserve
Ivy Cottage
Bridge Farm
Townley Brow Farm
Hollingreave Farm
Warrington WA3
Moss Hall Farm
MOSS SIDE
Oakwood
Barn End Farm
Prospect Farm
Ash Tree Farm
Moss Side Farm No. 2
PROSPECT LANE
Woodend Farm
Moss Side Farm
MOSS SIDE
Works
RIXTON PARK HOMES
Cleveland's Farm
Woodend Cottage
The Bungalow
WOODEND LANE
Top End Farm
Down's Covert
Rixton
Wks.
RIXTON MOSS
Rixton Claypits Local Nature Reserve
Brook Farm
MARTINCROFT MOSS
Oaktree Cottage
Moss Head
Rixton Firs
Lane End
Moss End Croft
Marshall's Farm
Moss Farm
Green Alley Farm
New Moss Farm
Tomfield Wood
A57
Ramswood Nursery
Nurseries
Lynbrook
Green Valley Farm
Woodside Farm
Rixton New Hall
M6
Moss Side Farm
The Oaks
M6 MOTORWAY
Junction 21
MANCHESTER
84
Swithen Hill Wood
Brookside Farm
Moss Side Farm
Rixton Old Hall

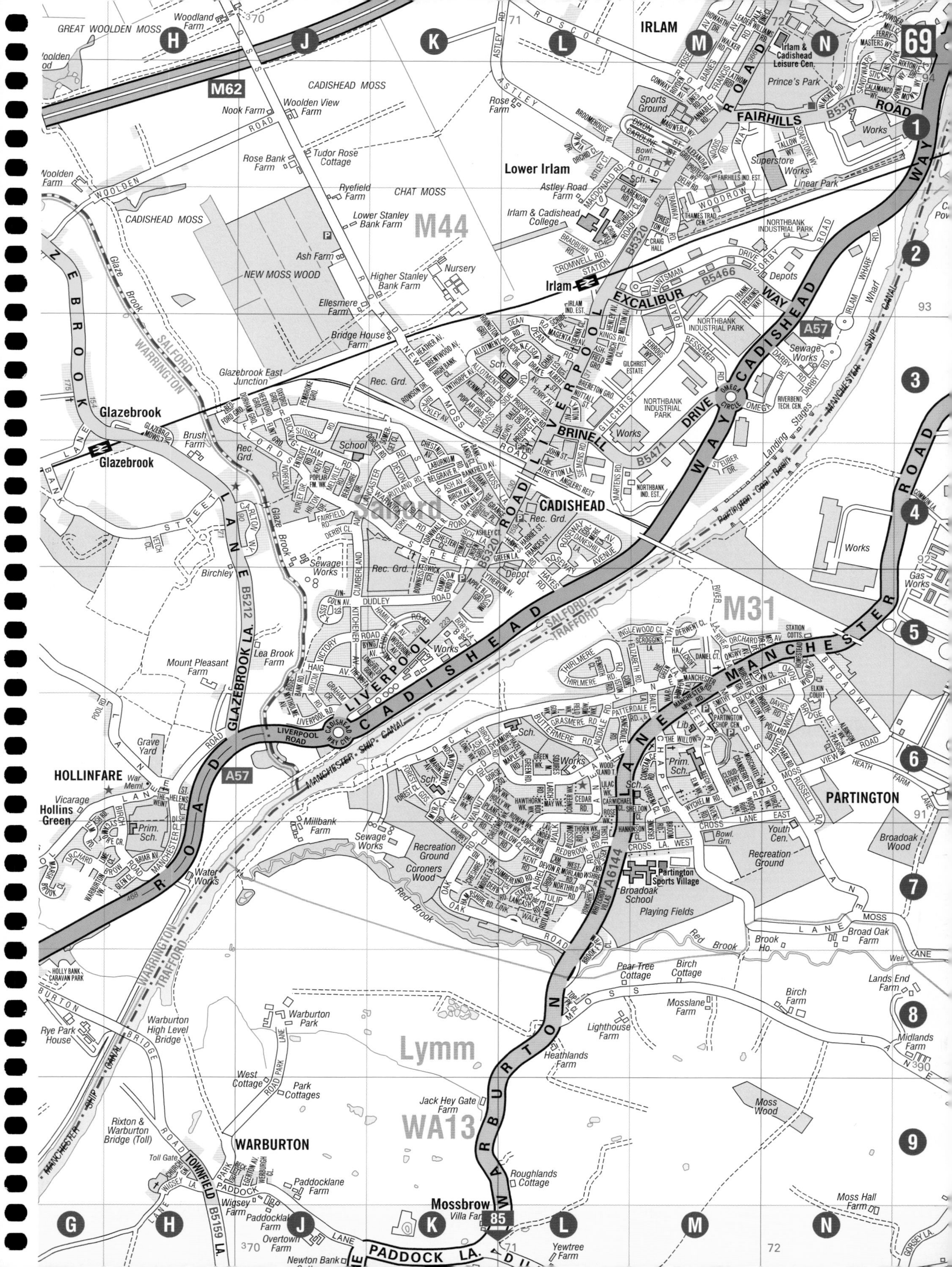
69
IRLAM
Lower Irlam
CADISHEAD MOSS
CHAT MOSS
NEW MOSS WOOD
M44
M62
Irlam
CADISHEAD
Glazebrook
HOLLINFARE
Hollins Green
PARTINGTON
M31
Lymm
WA13
WARBURTON
Mossbrow
MANCHESTER SHIP CANAL
CADISHEAD WAY
LIVERPOOL ROAD
MANCHESTER ROAD
WARBURTON LANE
PADDOCK LA.
A57
A6144
B5320
B5212
B5159
B5311
B5466
B5471
85
G
H
J
K
L
M
N
1
2
3
4
5
6
7
8
9

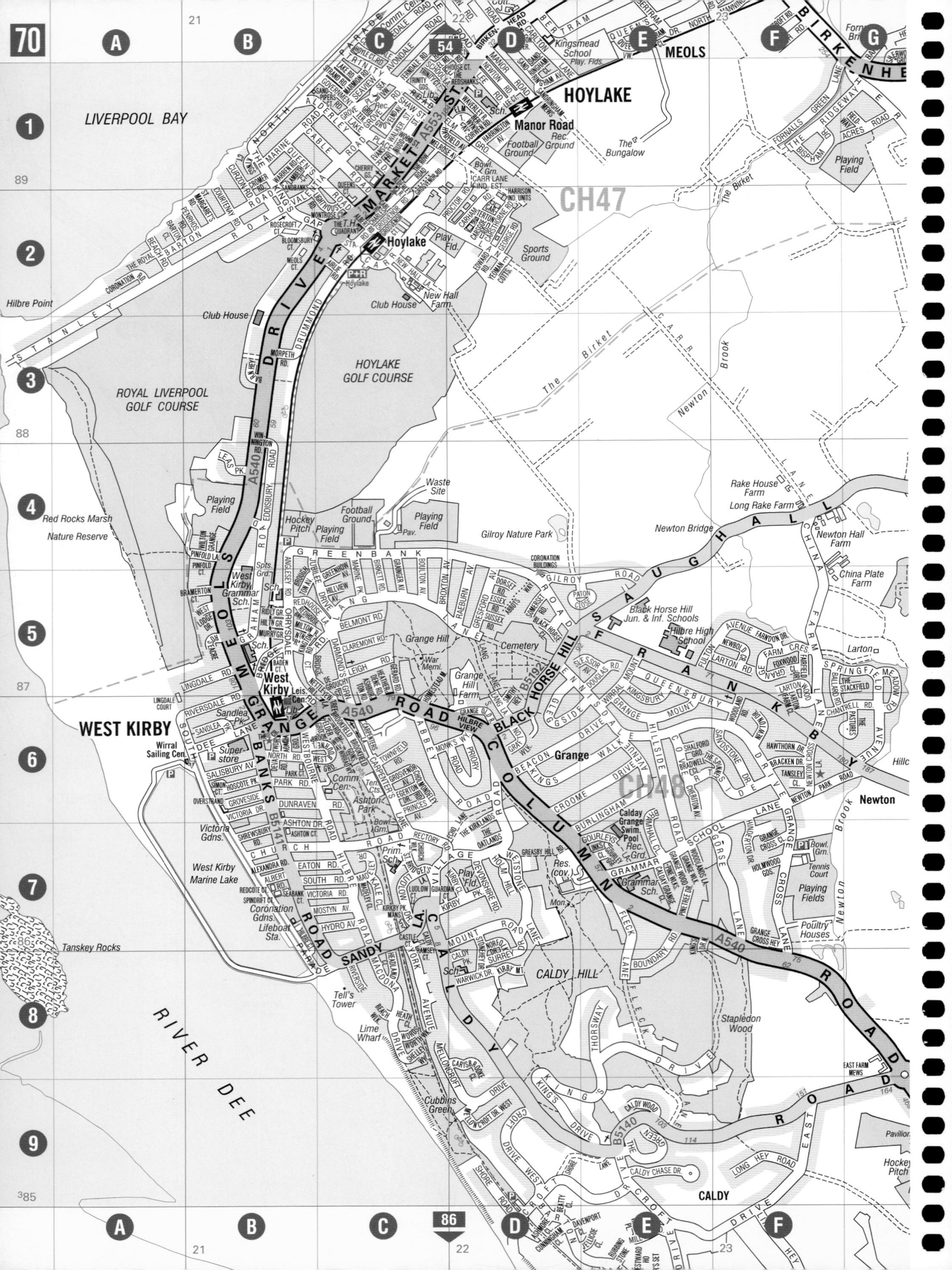

LIVERPOOL BAY
HOYLAKE
MEOLS
Manor Road
Hoylake
CH47
Hilbre Point
ROYAL LIVERPOOL GOLF COURSE
HOYLAKE GOLF COURSE
Red Rocks Marsh Nature Reserve
WEST KIRBY
West Kirby
Grange Hill
Gilroy Nature Park
Newton Bridge
Black Horse Hill Jun. & Inf. Schools
Hilbre High School
Grange
CH48
Newton
Larton
West Kirby Marine Lake
Tanskey Rocks
RIVER DEE
CALDY HILL
Stapledon Wood
CALDY
Caldy Grange Swim. Pool
Tell's Tower
Lime Wharf
Cubbins Green

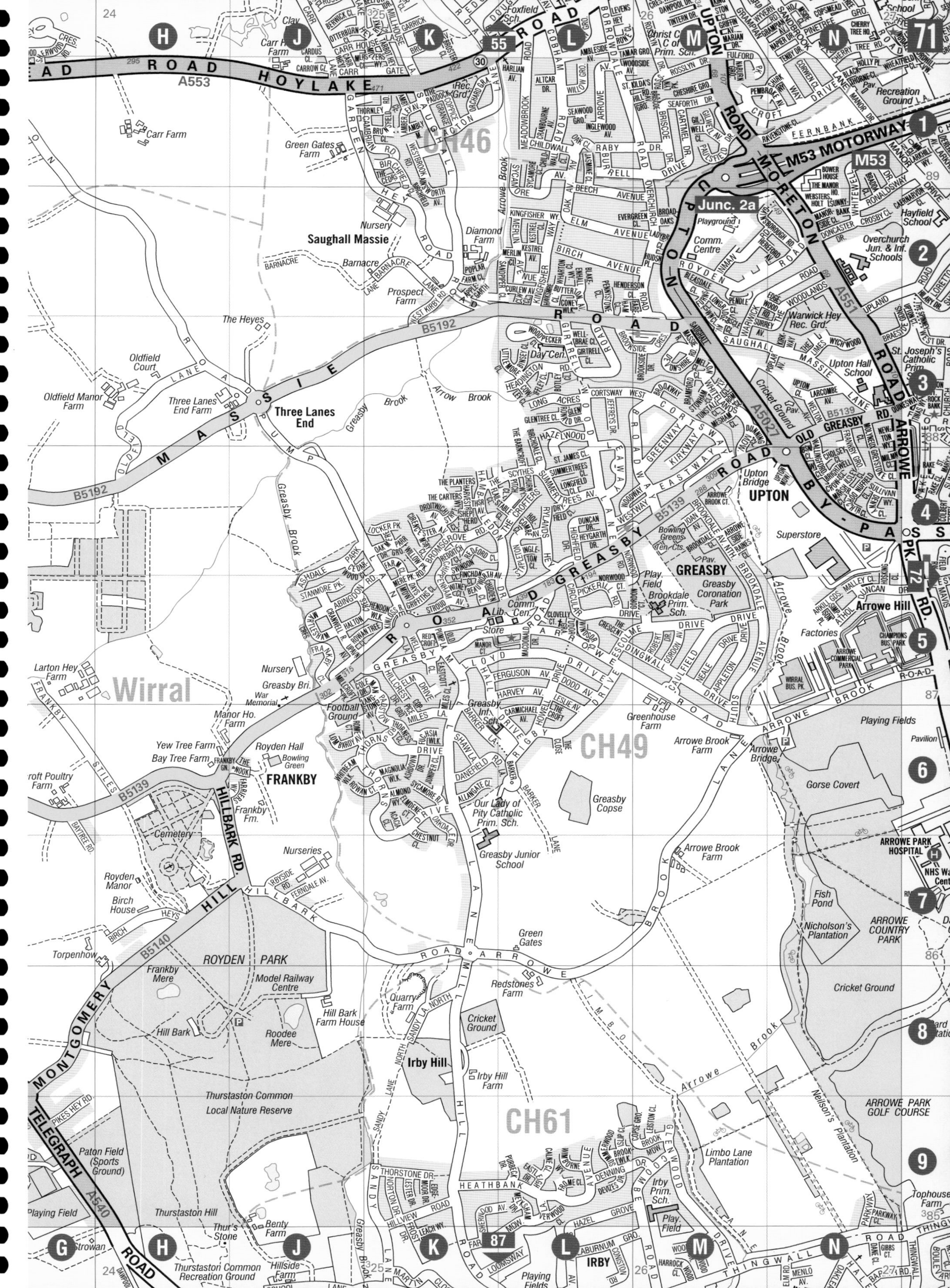
HOYLAKE ROAD
A553
Carr Farm
Green Gates Farm
CH46
Saughall Massie
Nursery
Barnacre
Diamond Farm
Prospect Farm
The Heyes
Oldfield Court
Oldfield Manor Farm
Three Lanes End Farm
Three Lanes End
MASSIE ROAD
B5192
Greasby Brook
Arrow Brook
M53 MOTORWAY
M53
Junc. 2a
Playground
Comm. Centre
Overchurch Jun. & Inf. Schools
Hayfield School
Warwick Hey Rec. Grd.
Upton Hall School
St. Joseph's Catholic Prim.
Cricket Ground
Day Cen.
UPTON
Upton Bridge
A5027
A551
B5139
ARROWE PARK ROAD
MORETON BY-PASS
UPTON ROAD
Superstore
Factories
Arrowe Hill
GREASBY
Greasby Coronation Park
Brookdale Prim. Sch.
Bowling Greens
Play. Field
Comm. Cen.
Lib.
Store
GREASBY ROAD
Wirral
Larton Hey Farm
Nursery
Greasby Bri.
War Memorial
Manor Ho. Farm
Football Ground
Greasby Inf. Sch.
Greenhouse Farm
CH49
Arrowe Brook Farm
Arrowe Bridge
Playing Fields
Pavilion
Yew Tree Farm
Bay Tree Farm
Royden Hall
Bowling Green
FRANKBY
Croft Poultry Farm
Frankby Fm.
Cemetery
B5139
HILLBARK RD.
Our Lady of Pity Catholic Prim. Sch.
Greasby Junior School
Greasby Copse
Gorse Covert
ARROWE PARK HOSPITAL
Nurseries
Royden Manor
Birch House
Arrowe Brook Farm
Fish Pond
Nicholson's Plantation
ARROWE COUNTRY PARK
Torpenhow
B5140
ROYDEN PARK
Frankby Mere
Model Railway Centre
Green Gates
ARROWE ROAD
Redstones Farm
Quarry Farm
Hill Bark Farm House
Cricket Ground
Cricket Ground
Hill Bark
Roodee Mere
Irby Hill
Irby Hill Farm
MONTGOMERY
Thurstaston Common Local Nature Reserve
Arrowe Brook
Arrowe Park Golf Course
CH61
Limbo Lane Plantation
Neilson's Plantation
Paton Field (Sports Ground)
TELEGRAPH ROAD
A540
Playing Field
Thurstaston Hill
Irby Prim. Sch.
Play. Field
Thur's Stone
Benty Farm
Tophouse Farm
Strowan
Hillside Farm
Thurstaston Common Recreation Ground
IRBY
Playing Fields
THINGWALL ROAD
55
87
72
G H J K L M N
1 2 3 4 5 6 7 8 9

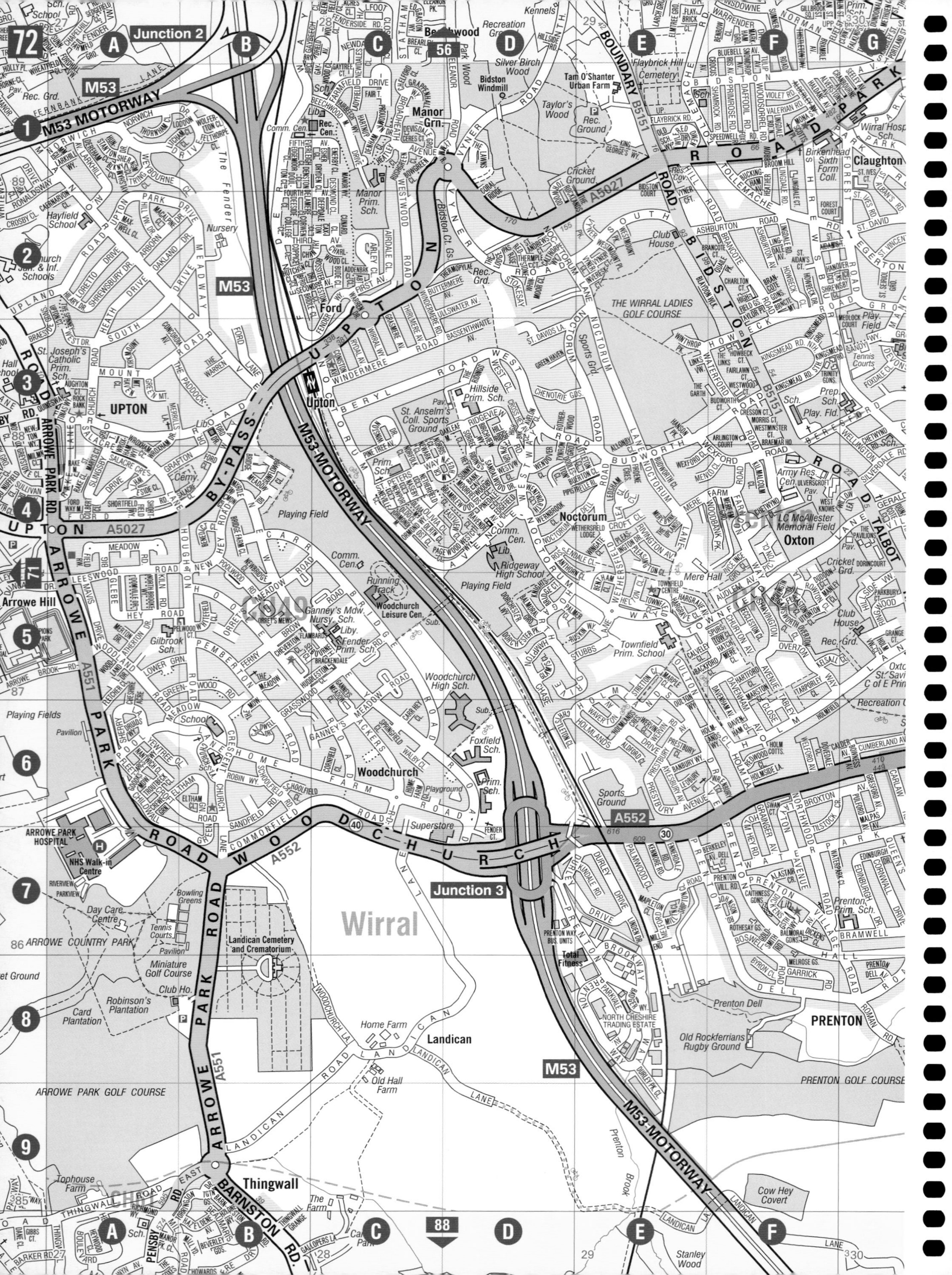
Junction 2
M53 MOTORWAY
Beechwood
56
Manor Grn.
Bidston Windmill
Silver Birch Wood
Tam O'Shanter Urban Farm
Flaybrick Hill Cemetery
Taylor's Wood
BOUNDARY ROAD
BIDSTON ROAD
Claughton
Birkenhead Sixth Form Coll.
Wirral Hosp. Sch.
Hayfield School
Church Jun. & Inf. Schools
Manor Prim. Sch.
THE WIRRAL LADIES GOLF COURSE
Ford
UPTON BY-PASS
St. Joseph's Catholic Prim. Sch.
UPTON
Upton
St. Anselm's Coll. Sports Ground
Hillside Prim. Sch.
Noctorum
Oxton
LC McAllester Memorial Field
Cemy.
Playing Field
Comm. Cen.
Ridgeway High School
Mere Hall
71
Arrowe Hill
Gilbrook Sch.
Woodchurch Leisure Cen.
Fender Prim. Sch.
Townfield Prim. School
Woodchurch High Sch.
Foxfield Sch.
Woodchurch
ARROWE PARK HOSPITAL
NHS Walk-in Centre
WOODCHURCH ROAD
A552
Junction 3
Wirral
ARROWE COUNTRY PARK
Landican Cemetery and Crematorium
Miniature Golf Course
Robinson's Plantation
Card Plantation
Home Farm
Landican
Old Hall Farm
ARROWE PARK GOLF COURSE
Old Rockferrians Rugby Ground
PRENTON
Prenton Dell
PRENTON GOLF COURSE
NORTH CHESHIRE TRADING ESTATE
Total Fitness
M53
Thingwall
Tophouse Farm
Cow Hey Covert
Stanley Wood
Prenton Brook
ARROWE PARK ROAD
BARNSTON RD.

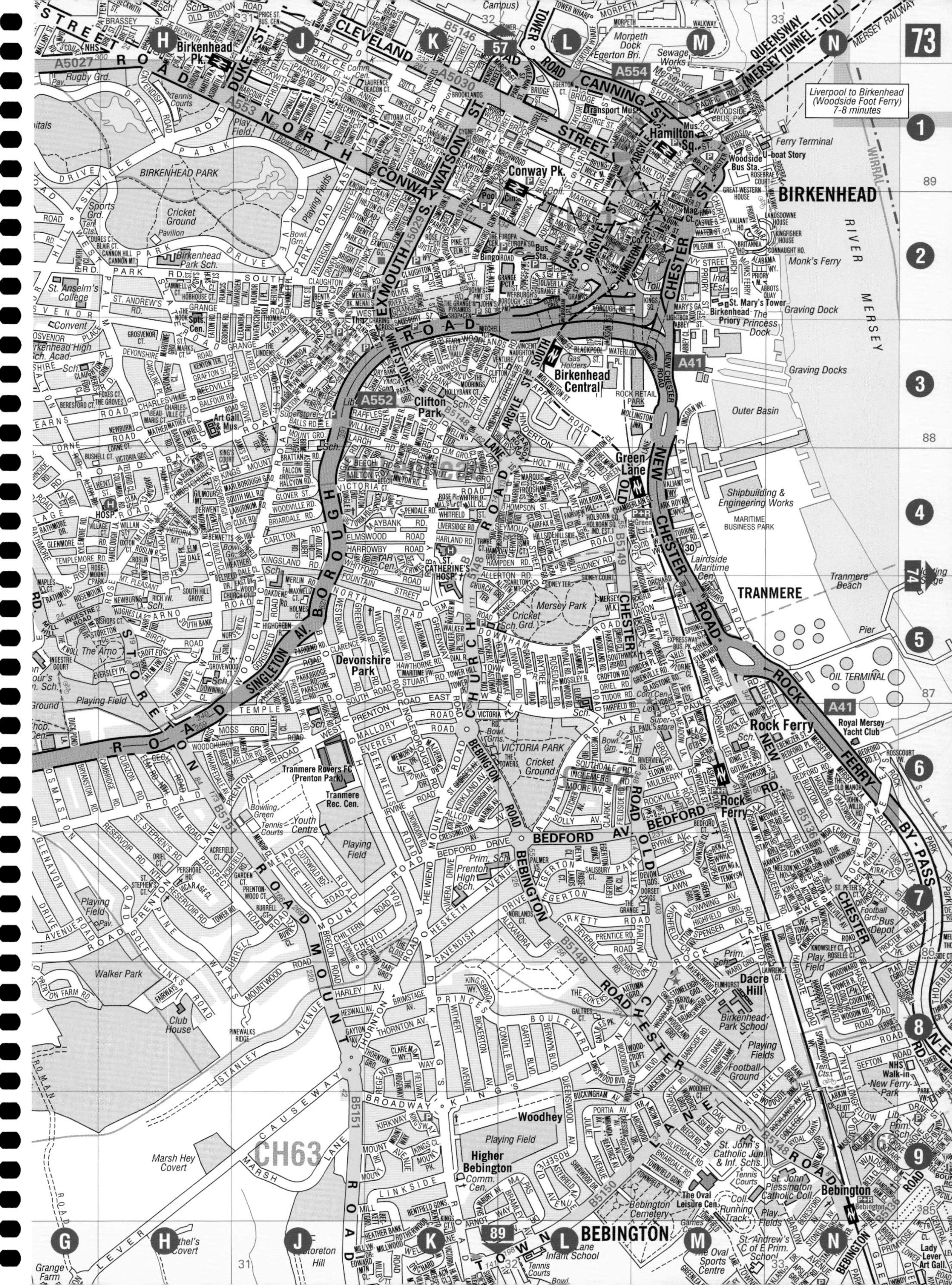
Liverpool to Birkenhead (Woodside Foot Ferry) 7-8 minutes
BIRKENHEAD
RIVER MERSEY
QUEENSWAY MERSEY TUNNEL - TOLL
MERSEY RAILWAY
Birkenhead Pk.
BIRKENHEAD PARK
Cricket Ground
Pavilion
Birkenhead Park Sch.
St. Anselm's College
Convent
Rugby Grd.
Tennis Courts
Sports Grd.
Playing Fields
Play. Field
Bowl. Grns.
Hamilton Sq.
Conway Pk.
Ferry Terminal
U-boat Story
Woodside Bus Sta.
Transport Mus.
Morpeth Dock
Egerton Bri.
Sewage Works
Birkenhead Central
Birkenhead Priory
St. Mary's Tower
Graving Dock
Graving Docks
The Princess Dock
Outer Basin
Monk's Ferry
Rock Retail Park
Green Lane
Shipbuilding & Engineering Works
MARITIME BUSINESS PARK
Lairdside Maritime Cen.
TRANMERE
Tranmere Beach
Landing Stage
Pier
OIL TERMINAL
Royal Mersey Yacht Club
Rock Ferry
Clifton Park
Art Gall. & Mus.
Superstore
St. Catherine's Hosp.
Mersey Park
Cricket Grd.
Devonshire Park
Tranmere Rovers FC (Prenton Park)
Tranmere Rec. Cen.
Bowling Green
Tennis Courts
Youth Centre
Playing Field
VICTORIA PARK
Cricket Ground
The Arno
Prenton High Sch.
Walker Park
Club House
Dacre Hill
Birkenhead Park School
Playing Fields
Football Ground
Bus Depot
NHS Walk-in
New Ferry Park
Woodhey
Playing Field
Higher Bebington
Marsh Hey Covert
CH63
BEBINGTON
Bebington Cemetery
The Oval Leisure Cen.
Running Track
St. John's Catholic Jun. & Inf. Schs.
St. John Plessington Catholic Coll.
St. Andrew's C of E Prim. School
The Oval Sports Centre
Bebington
Lady Lever Art Gall.
Storeton Hill
Grange Farm
A5027
A553
A5030
A554
A5029
A552
A41
B5146
B5148
B5149
B5151
B5150
B5136
CONWAY STREET
NORTH ROAD
CANNING ST.
BOROUGH ROAD
SINGLETON AV.
STORETON ROAD
EXMOUTH ST.
S. WATSON ST.
CHESTER ST.
NEW CHESTER ROAD
OLD CHESTER ROAD
ROCK FERRY BY-PASS
BEDFORD AV.
BEDFORD DRIVE
BEBINGTON ROAD
MOUNT ROAD
KINGS LANE
BROADWAY
TOWN LANE
CHURCH ROAD
CLEVELAND ST.
DUKE ST.
WHETSTONE LA.
CAUSEWAY
LEVER
H
J
K
L
M
N
G
1
2
3
4
5
6
7
8
9
57
74
89
31
32
33
86
87
88
89

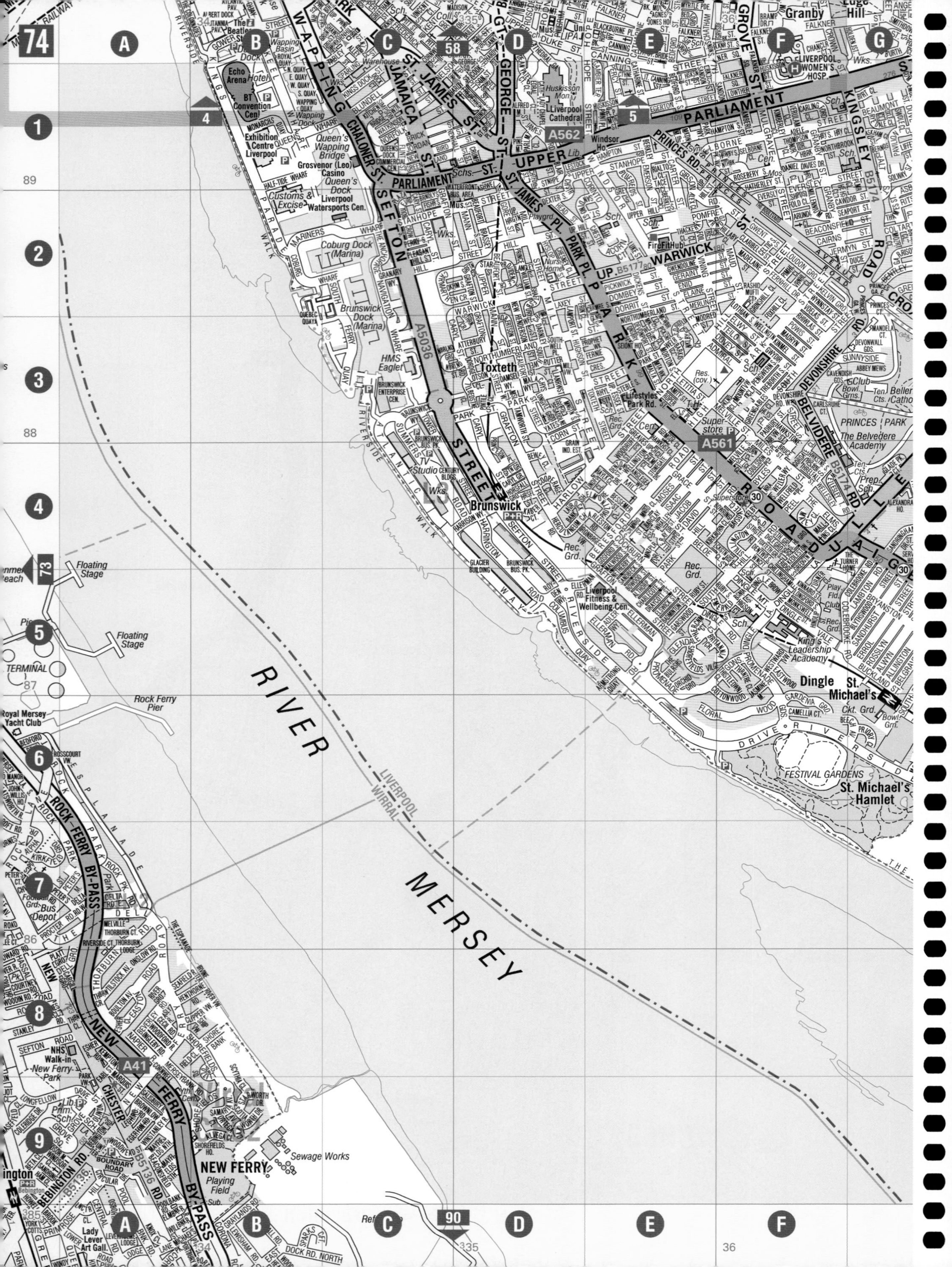

RIVER MERSEY
LIVERPOOL
WIRRAL
Toxteth
Brunswick
Dingle
St. Michael's
St. Michael's Hamlet
FESTIVAL GARDENS
NEW FERRY
Granby
Echo Arena
BT Convention Cen.
Exhibition Centre Liverpool
Queen's Wapping Bridge
Grosvenor (Leo) Casino
Queen's Dock
Customs & Excise
Liverpool Watersports Cen.
Coburg Dock (Marina)
Brunswick Dock (Marina)
HMS Eaglet
Liverpool Cathedral
Liverpool Women's Hosp.
Windsor Ho.
Huskisson Mon.
Lifestyles Park Rd.
Liverpool Fitness & Wellbeing Cen.
King's Leadership Academy
PRINCES PARK
The Belvedere Academy
Glacier Building
Brunswick Bus. Pk.
Rock Ferry Pier
Royal Mersey Yacht Club
Floating Stage
Sewage Works
Playing Field
NHS Walk-in
New Ferry Park
Bus Depot
Lady Lever Art Gall.
PARLIAMENT
UPPER PARLIAMENT ST.
ST. JAMES ST.
PARK RD.
PRINCES RD.
SEFTON ST.
CHALONER ST.
WAPPING
JAMAICA ST.
GEORGE ST.
WARWICK
KINGSLEY RD.
DEVONSHIRE RD.
BELVIDERE RD.
NEW CHESTER RD.
NEW FERRY BY-PASS
ROCK FERRY BY-PASS
BEBINGTON RD.
A562
A5036
A561
A41
B5177
B5174
B5136
58
4
5
73
90

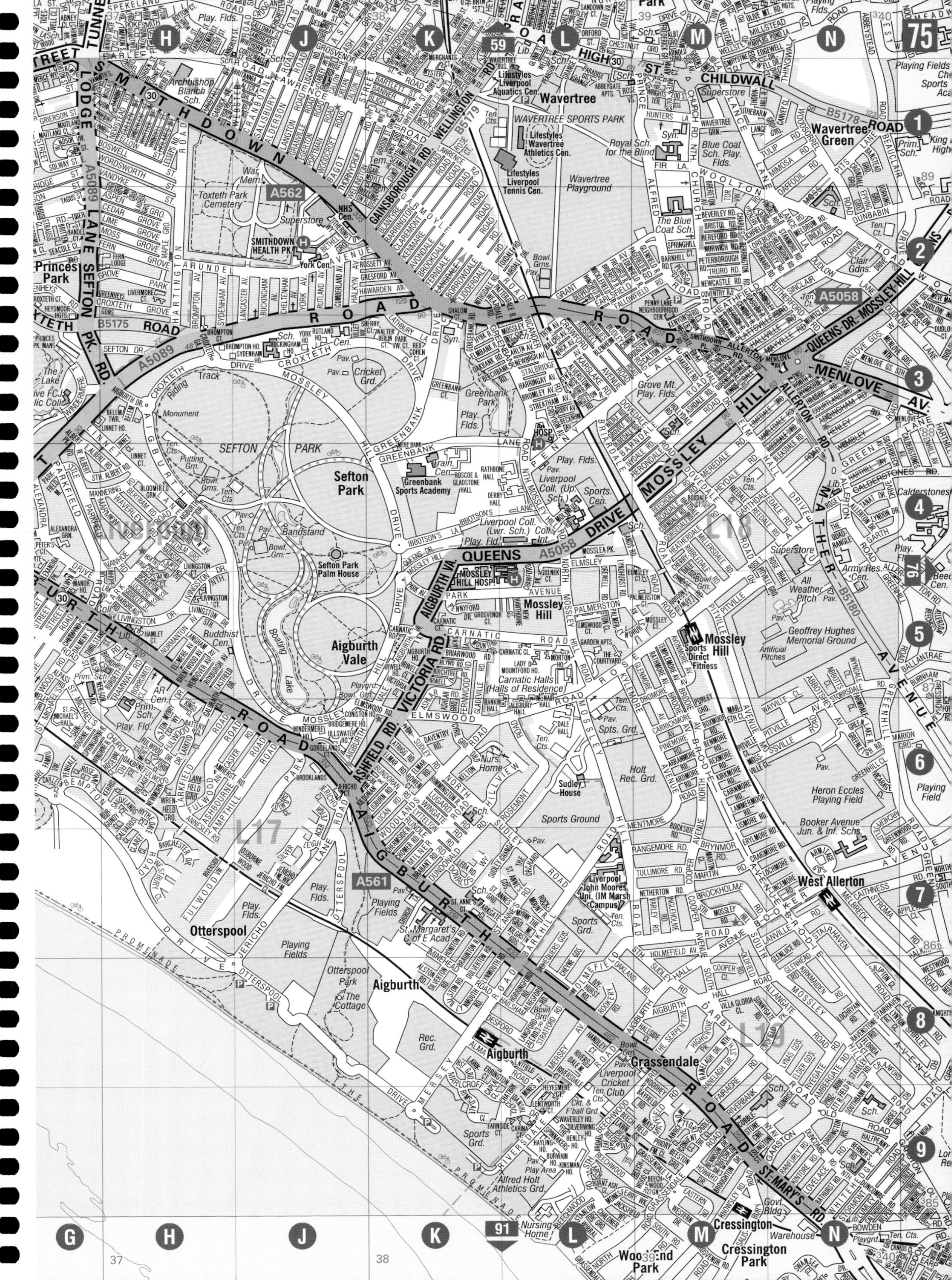

Wavertree
Childwall
Wavertree Green
Princes Park
Sefton Park
Aigburth Vale
Mossley Hill
Otterspool
Aigburth
Grassendale
Cressington
Cressington Park
West Allerton
Calderstones
Liverpool
L17
L18
L19
SMITHDOWN ROAD
AIGBURTH ROAD
QUEENS DRIVE
MOSSLEY HILL
MENLOVE AV.
MATHER AVENUE
A5089
A562
A5058
A561
B5175
B5179
B5178
B5180
59
91
76

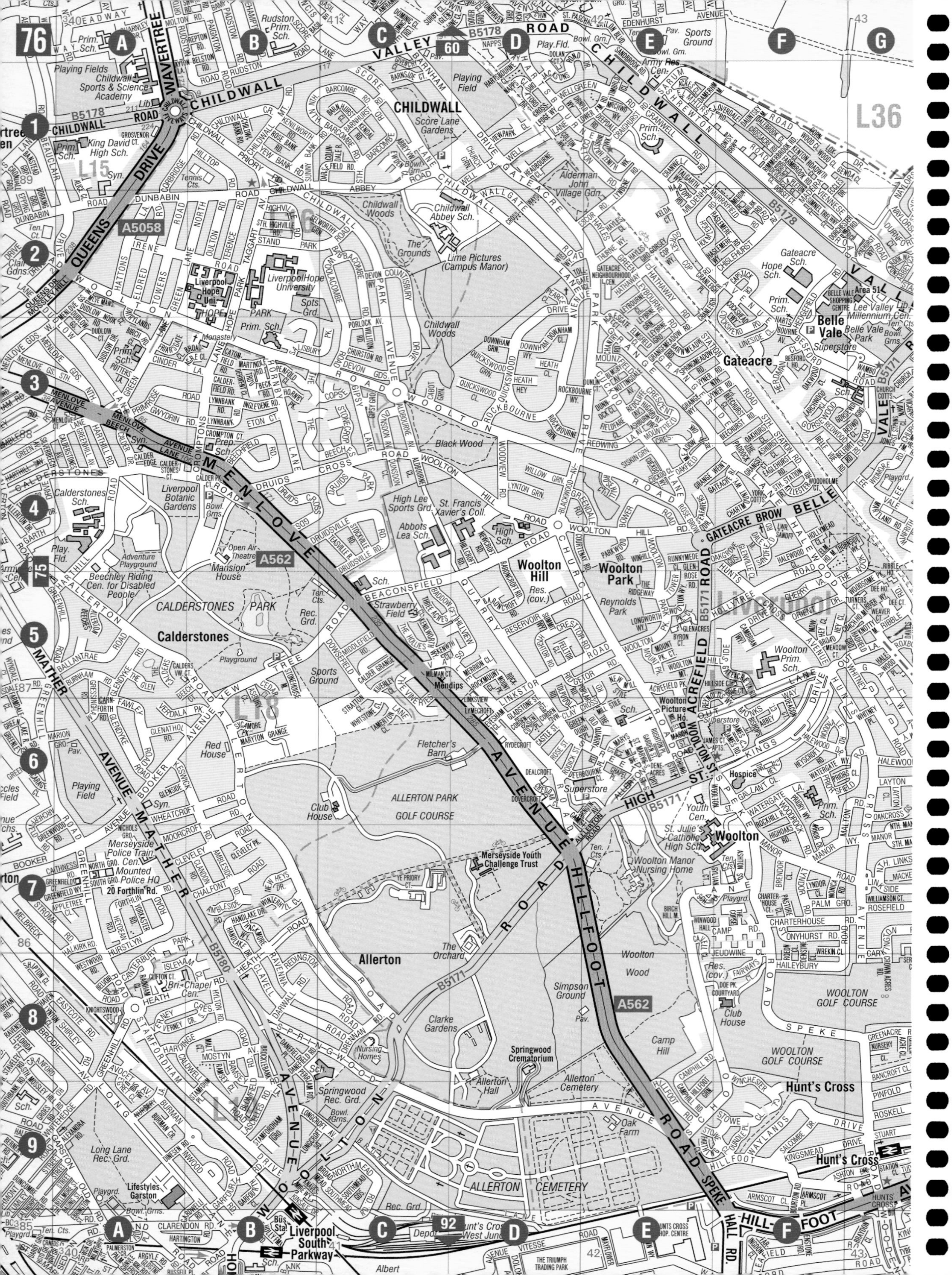

A
B
C
D
E
F
G
1
2
3
4
5
6
7
8
9
60
75
92
L15
L18
L36
B5178
A5058
A562
B5171
B5180
CHILDWALL
Childwall Sports & Science Academy
King David High Sch.
QUEENS DRIVE
WAVERTREE
CHILDWALL ROAD
VALLEY ROAD
Score Lane Gardens
Childwall Woods
Childwall Abbey Sch.
Lime Pictures (Campus Manor)
Liverpool Hope Uni.
Liverpool Hope University
HOPE PARK
Alderman John Village Gdn.
Gateacre Sch.
Hope Sch.
Belle Vale Shopping Centre
Area 51
Lee Valley Millennium Cen.
Belle Vale
Belle Vale Park
Superstore
Gateacre
MENLOVE AVENUE
WOOLTON ROAD
Black Wood
Calderstones Sch.
Liverpool Botanic Gardens
High Lee Sports Grd.
St. Francis Xavier's Coll.
Abbots Lea Sch.
Woolton Hill
Woolton Park
Reynolds Park
Liverpool
Woolton Prim. Sch.
CALDERSTONES PARK
Calderstones
Mansion House
Open Air Theatre
Adventure Playground
Beechley Riding Cen. for Disabled People
Strawberry Field
Sports Ground
Mendips
Woolton Picture Ho.
Fletcher's Barn
Red House
Club House
ALLERTON PARK GOLF COURSE
Merseyside Youth Challenge Trust
Merseyside Police Train. Cen.
Mounted Police HQ
20 Forthlin Rd.
MATHER AVENUE
HILLFOOT ROAD
Hospice
St. Julie's Catholic High Sch.
Woolton
Woolton Manor Nursing Home
Allerton
The Orchard
Woolton Wood
Simpson Ground
Clarke Gardens
Camp Hill
WOOLTON GOLF COURSE
Springwood Crematorium
Allerton Hall
Allerton Cemetery
Springwood Rec. Grd.
Nursing Homes
Hunt's Cross
Oak Farm
ALLERTON CEMETERY
Long Lane Rec. Grd.
Lifestyles Garston
Liverpool South Parkway
Hunt's Cross
HUNTS CROSS SHOP. CENTRE
SPEKE ROAD
HILLFOOT
HALL RD.
THE TRIUMPH TRADING PARK
Albert

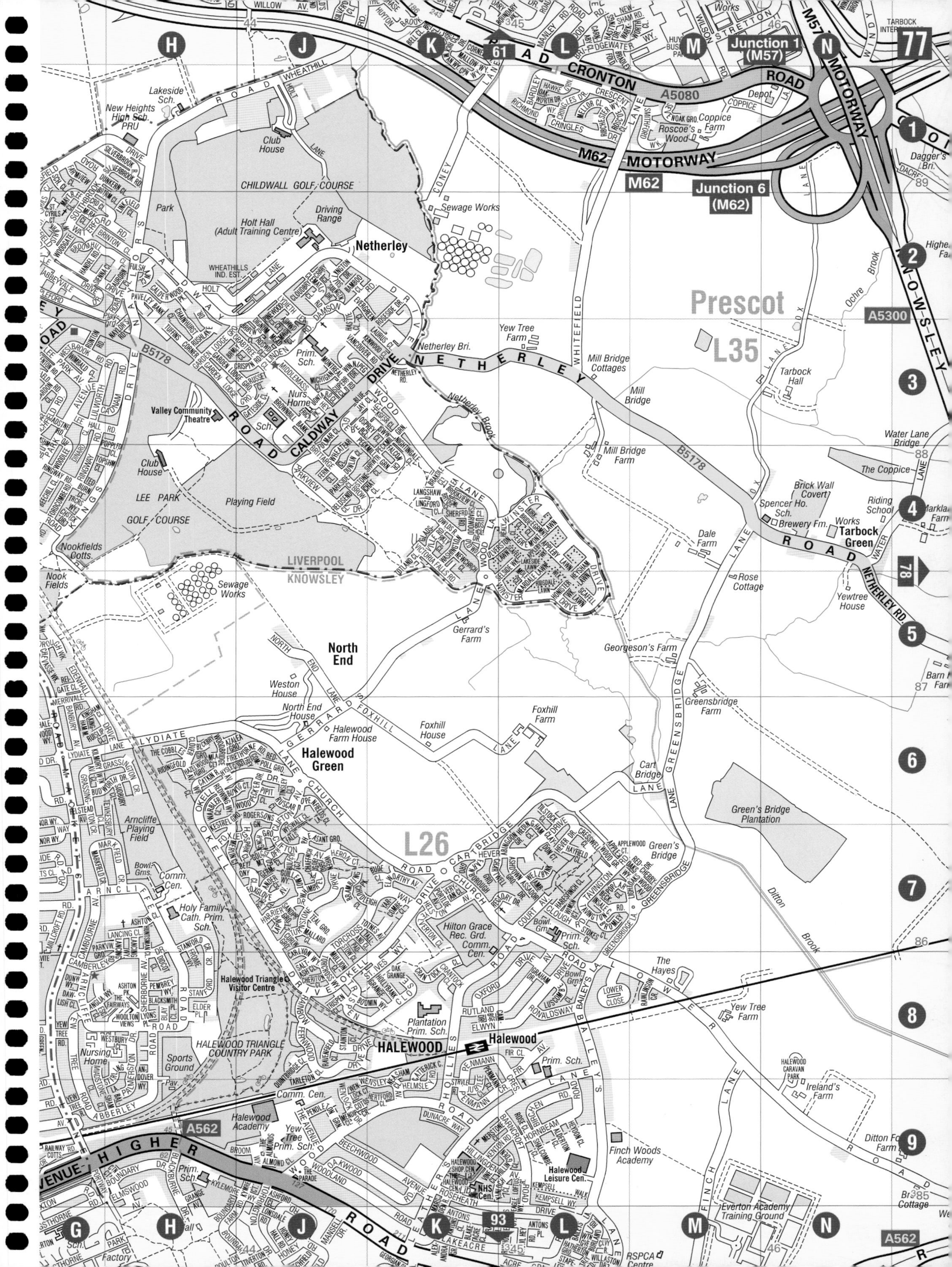
Prescot
L35
L26
Netherley
North End
Halewood Green
Halewood
Tarbock Green
CRONTON ROAD
A5080
M62 MOTORWAY
M57 MOTORWAY
Junction 1 (M57)
Junction 6 (M62)
A5300
B5178
NETHERLEY ROAD
CALDWAY DRIVE
CHILDWALL GOLF COURSE
LEE PARK GOLF COURSE
Holt Hall (Adult Training Centre)
Driving Range
Sewage Works
Yew Tree Farm
Netherley Bri.
Mill Bridge Cottages
Mill Bridge
Mill Bridge Farm
Tarbock Hall
Water Lane Bridge
The Coppice
Brick Wall Covert
Spencer Ho. Sch.
Brewery Fm.
Riding School
Dale Farm
Rose Cottage
Yewtree House
Georgeson's Farm
Greensbridge Farm
Foxhill Farm
Foxhill House
Gerrard's Farm
Weston House
North End House
Halewood Farm House
Cart Bridge
Green's Bridge Plantation
Green's Bridge
Ditton Brook
The Hayes
Yew Tree Farm
Ireland's Farm
Halewood Caravan Park
Ditton Fold Farm
Everton Academy Training Ground
Finch Woods Academy
Halewood Leisure Cen.
Halewood Academy
HALEWOOD TRIANGLE COUNTRY PARK
Halewood Triangle Visitor Centre
Plantation Prim. Sch.
Hilton Grace Rec. Grd. Comm. Cen.
Arncliffe Playing Field
Holy Family Cath. Prim. Sch.
Valley Community Theatre
Playing Field
Nookfields Cotts.
Nook Fields
Lakeside Sch.
New Heights High Sch. PRU
Club House
WHEATHILLS IND. EST.
LIVERPOOL
KNOWSLEY
HIGHER ROAD
A562
RSPCA Centre
61
93
78

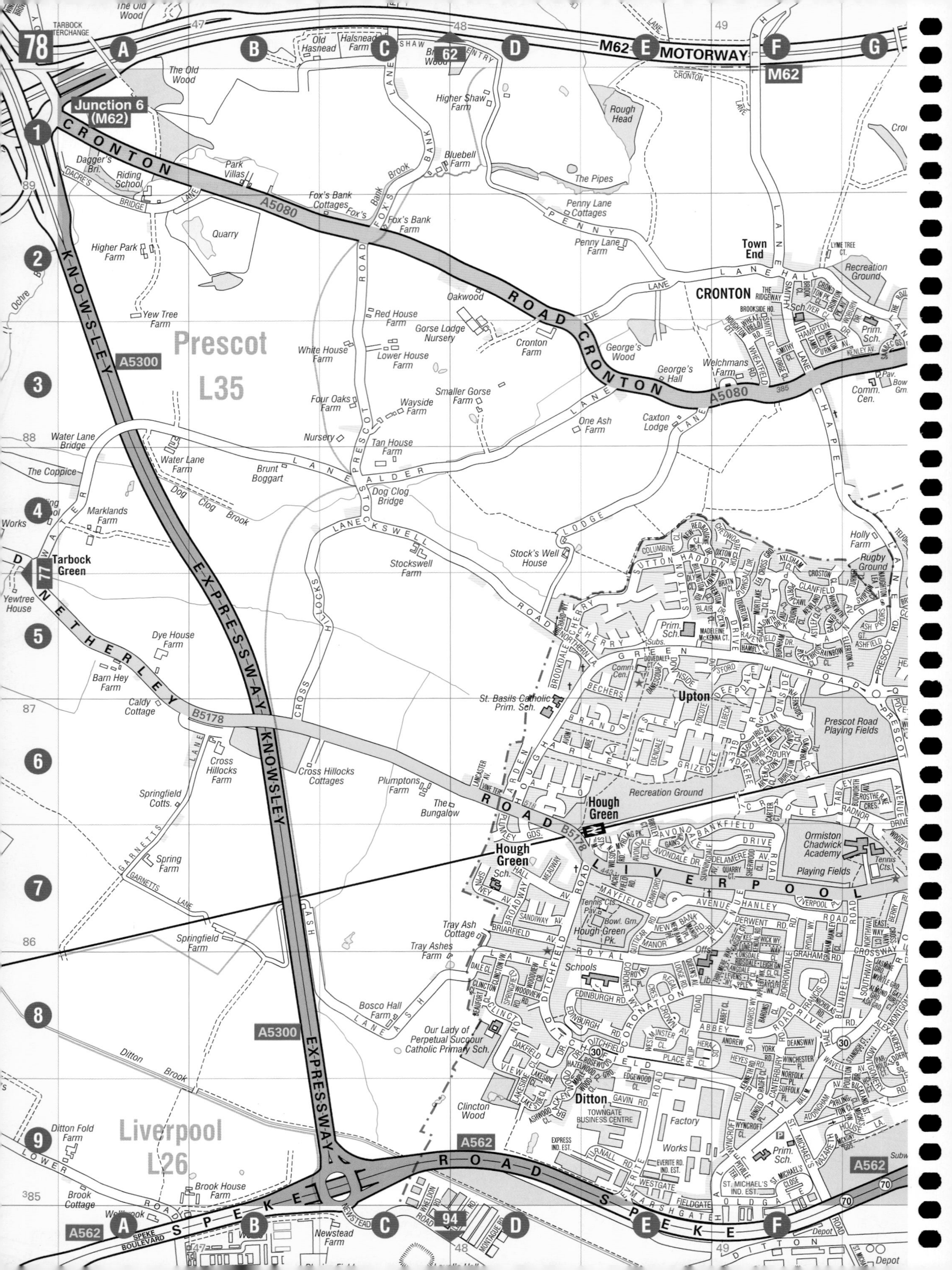

M62 MOTORWAY
Junction 6 (M62)
CRONTON ROAD
A5080
KNOWSLEY EXPRESSWAY
A5300
Prescot
L35
Liverpool
L26
CRONTON
Town End
Upton
Hough Green
Ditton
Tarbock Green
NETHERLEY ROAD
B5178
SPEKE ROAD
A562
SPEKE BOULEVARD
LIVERPOOL ROAD
ALDER LANE
PRESCOT ROAD
Dog Clog Brook
Ditton Brook
Recreation Ground
Prescot Road Playing Fields
Ormiston Chadwick Academy
Quarry
Rough Head
The Pipes
The Old Wood
Old Hasnead
Halsnead Farm
Higher Shaw Farm
Bluebell Farm
Park Villas
Riding School
Dagger's Bri.
Fox's Bank Cottages
Fox's Bank Farm
Higher Park Farm
Yew Tree Farm
Red House Farm
Gorse Lodge Nursery
White House Farm
Lower House Farm
Oakwood
Cronton Farm
George's Wood
George's Hall
Welchmans Farm
Four Oaks Farm
Wayside Farm
Smaller Gorse Farm
Nursery
Tan House Farm
One Ash Farm
Caxton Lodge
Penny Lane Cottages
Penny Lane Farm
Water Lane Bridge
Water Lane Farm
The Coppice
Brunt Boggart
Dog Clog Bridge
Marklands Farm
Stockswell Farm
Stock's Well House
Holly Farm
Rugby Ground
Yewtree House
Dye House Farm
Barn Hey Farm
Caldy Cottage
Cross Hillocks Farm
Cross Hillocks Cottages
Plumptons Farm
The Bungalow
Springfield Cotts.
Spring Farm
Springfield Farm
Tray Ash Cottage
Tray Ashes Farm
Bosco Hall Farm
Our Lady of Perpetual Succour Catholic Primary Sch.
St. Basils Catholic Prim. Sch.
Clincton Wood
Ditton Fold Farm
Brook House Farm
Brook Cottage
Newstead Farm
TOWNGATE BUSINESS CENTRE
EXPRESS IND. EST.
Factory
Works
ST. MICHAEL'S IND. EST.
Hough Green Pk.
Schools
Comm. Cen.
Prim. Sch.

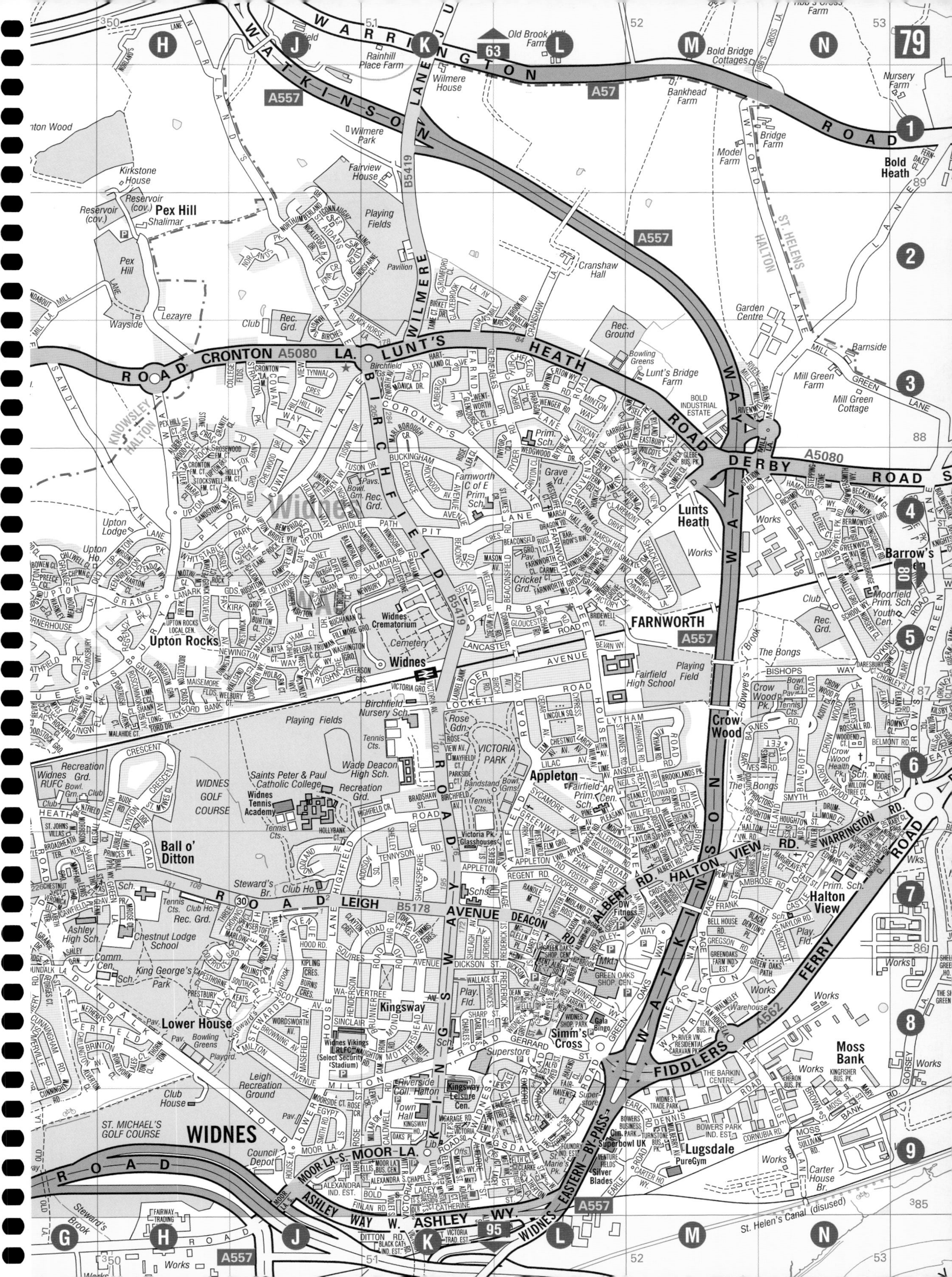

WARRINGTON ROAD
WATKINSON WAY
A557
A57
A5080
B5419
B5178
A562
Pex Hill
Bold Heath
Lunts Heath
Upton Rocks
Widnes
FARNWORTH
Crow Wood
Appleton
Barrow's Green
Ball o' Ditton
Halton View
Lower House
Kingsway
Simm's Cross
Moss Bank
Lugsdale
WIDNES
CRONTON ROAD
LUNT'S HEATH ROAD
DERBY ROAD
BIRCHFIELD ROAD
KINGSWAY
LEIGH AVENUE
DEACON RD.
HALTON VIEW RD.
FIDDLERS FERRY ROAD
WIDNES EASTERN BY-PASS
ASHLEY WAY
MOOR LA.
VICTORIA PARK
WIDNES GOLF COURSE
ST. MICHAEL'S GOLF COURSE
Fairfield High School
Wade Deacon High Sch.
Saints Peter & Paul Catholic College
Widnes Crematorium
Widnes Vikings RLFC (Select Security Stadium)
Riverside Coll. Halton
Kingsway Leisure Cen.
Town Hall
Superstore
Superbowl UK
PureGym
Silver Blades
St. Helen's Canal (disused)
Bold Industrial Estate
Leigh Recreation Ground
King George's Park
Chestnut Lodge School
Ashley High Sch.

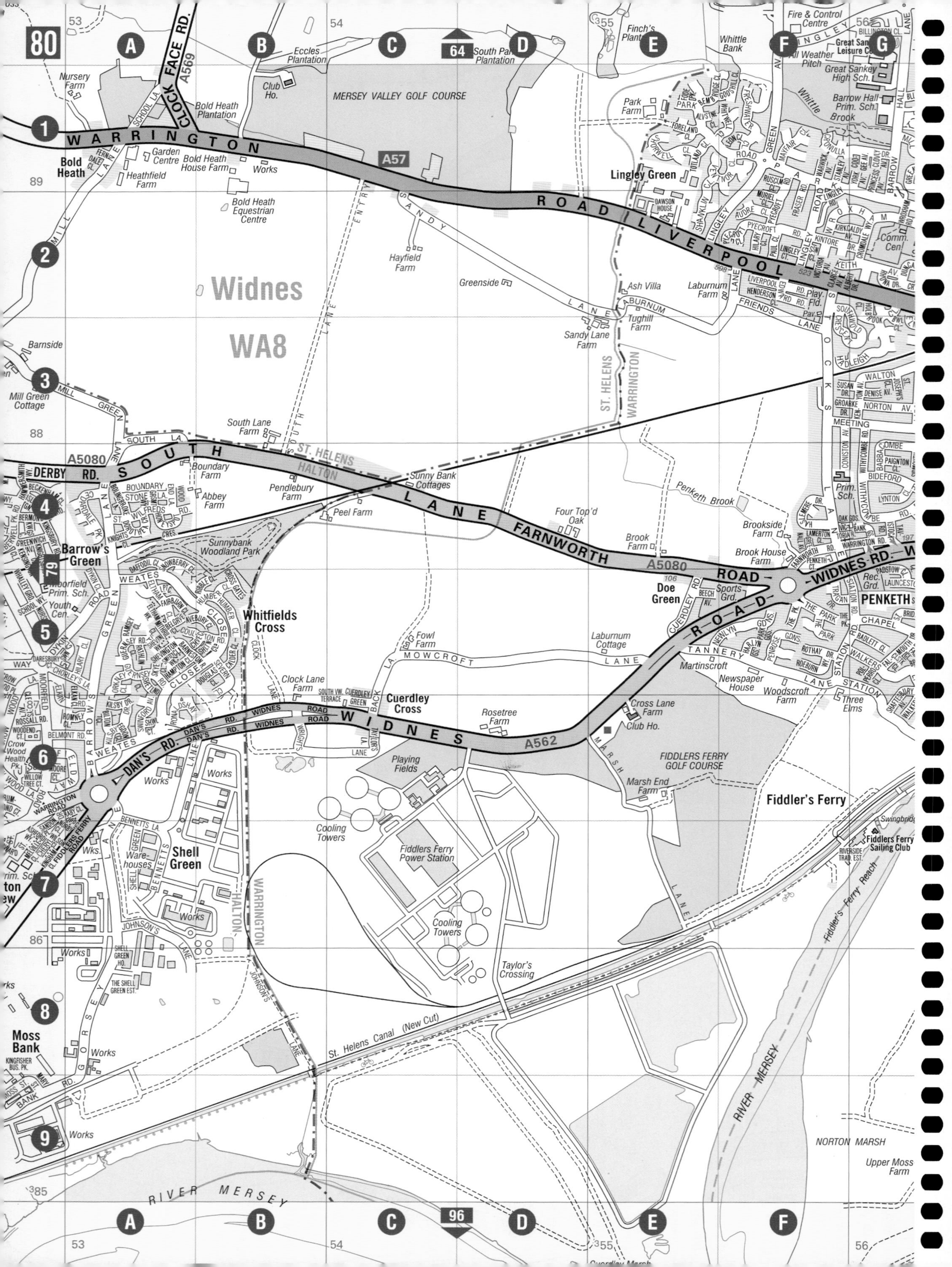

Widnes
WA8
Bold Heath
Lingley Green
Barrow's Green
Whitfields Cross
Cuerdley Cross
Doe Green
PENKETH
Shell Green
Moss Bank
Fiddler's Ferry
WARRINGTON ROAD
LIVERPOOL ROAD
A57
CLOCK FACE RD.
A569
SOUTH LANE
FARNWORTH ROAD
A5080
DERBY RD.
WIDNES ROAD
A562
DAN'S RD.
MERSEY VALLEY GOLF COURSE
FIDDLERS FERRY GOLF COURSE
Fiddlers Ferry Power Station
Cooling Towers
St. Helens Canal (New Cut)
RIVER MERSEY
NORTON MARSH
Fiddler's Ferry Reach
Fiddlers Ferry Sailing Club
Eccles Plantation
South Park Plantation
Bold Heath Plantation
Bold Heath Equestrian Centre
Heathfield Farm
Hayfield Farm
Greenside
Sandy Lane Farm
Tughill Farm
Ash Villa
Laburnum Farm
South Lane Farm
Boundary Farm
Abbey Farm
Pendlebury Farm
Peel Farm
Sunny Bank Cottages
Sunnybank Woodland Park
Four Top'd Oak
Brook Farm
Brookside Farm
Brook House Farm
Penketh Brook
Fowl Farm
Laburnum Cottage
Clock Lane Farm
Rosetree Farm
Cross Lane Farm
Marsh End Farm
Martinscroft
Newspaper House
Woodscroft Farm
Three Elms
Taylor's Crossing
Upper Moss Farm
Whittle Bank
Whittle Brook
Great Sankey High Sch.
Great Sankey Leisure Centre
Barrow Hall Prim. Sch.
Fire & Control Centre
All Weather Pitch
Park Farm
Nursery Farm
Mill Green Cottage
Barnside
Youth Cen.
Moorfield Prim. Sch.
ST. HELENS
HALTON
WARRINGTON
64
79
96

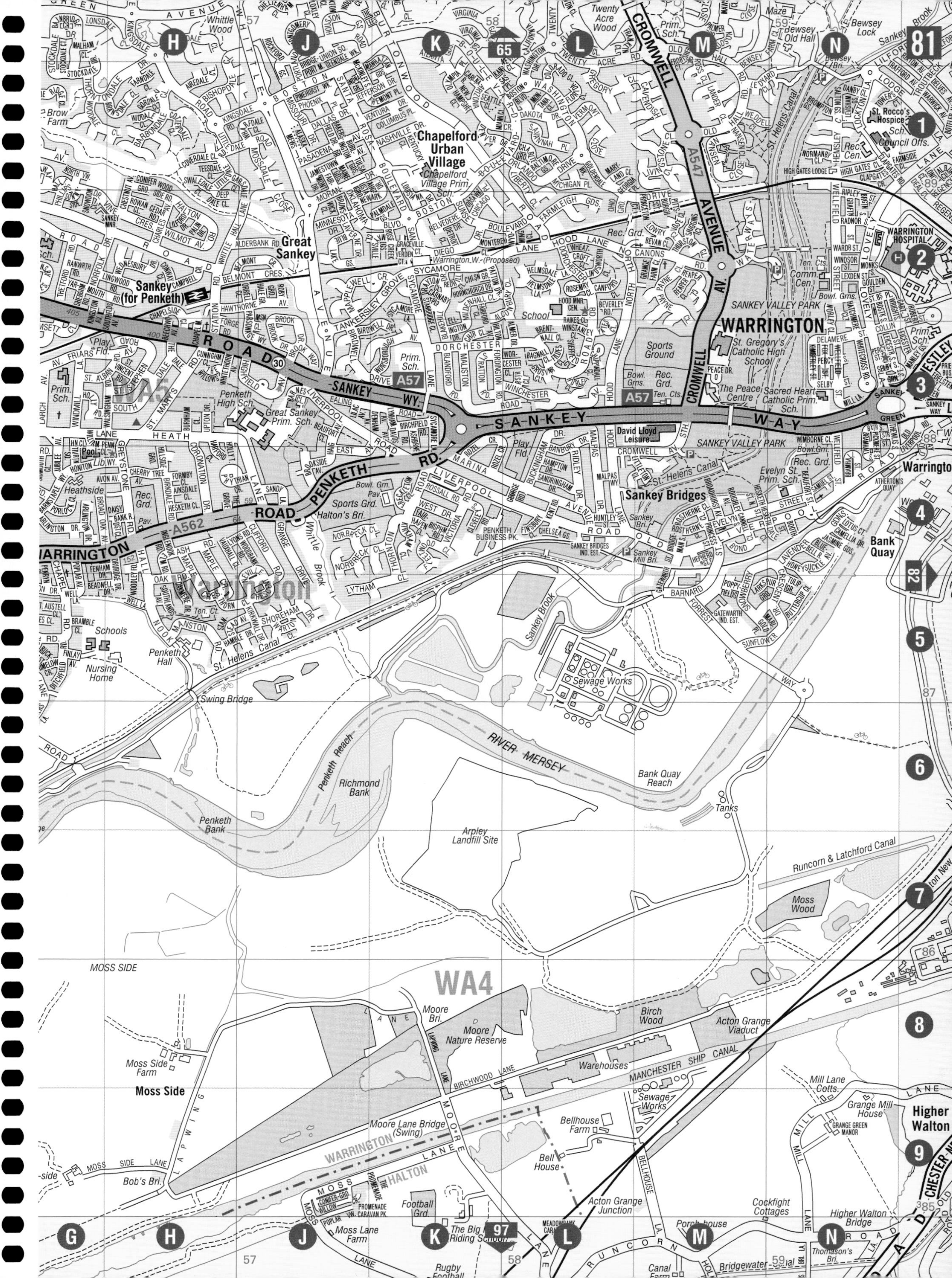

Chapelford Urban Village
Great Sankey
Sankey (for Penketh)
WARRINGTON
Sankey Bridges
Sankey Valley Park
WA5
WA4
Warrington
Bank Quay
Sewage Works
River Mersey
Penketh Reach
Richmond Bank
Penketh Bank
Bank Quay Reach
Arpley Landfill Site
Runcorn & Latchford Canal
Moss Wood
Moss Side
Moore Nature Reserve
Birch Wood
Acton Grange Viaduct
Manchester Ship Canal
Higher Walton
Sankey Way
Cromwell Avenue
Penketh Road
Warrington Road
Liverpool Road
St. Helens Canal
Whittle Wood
Twenty Acre Wood
Bewsey Old Hall
Warrington Hospital
St. Rocco's Hospice
Penketh Hall
Swing Bridge
Moss Side Farm
Moore Lane Bridge (Swing)
Bellhouse Farm
Acton Grange Junction
Higher Walton Bridge
Runcorn Road

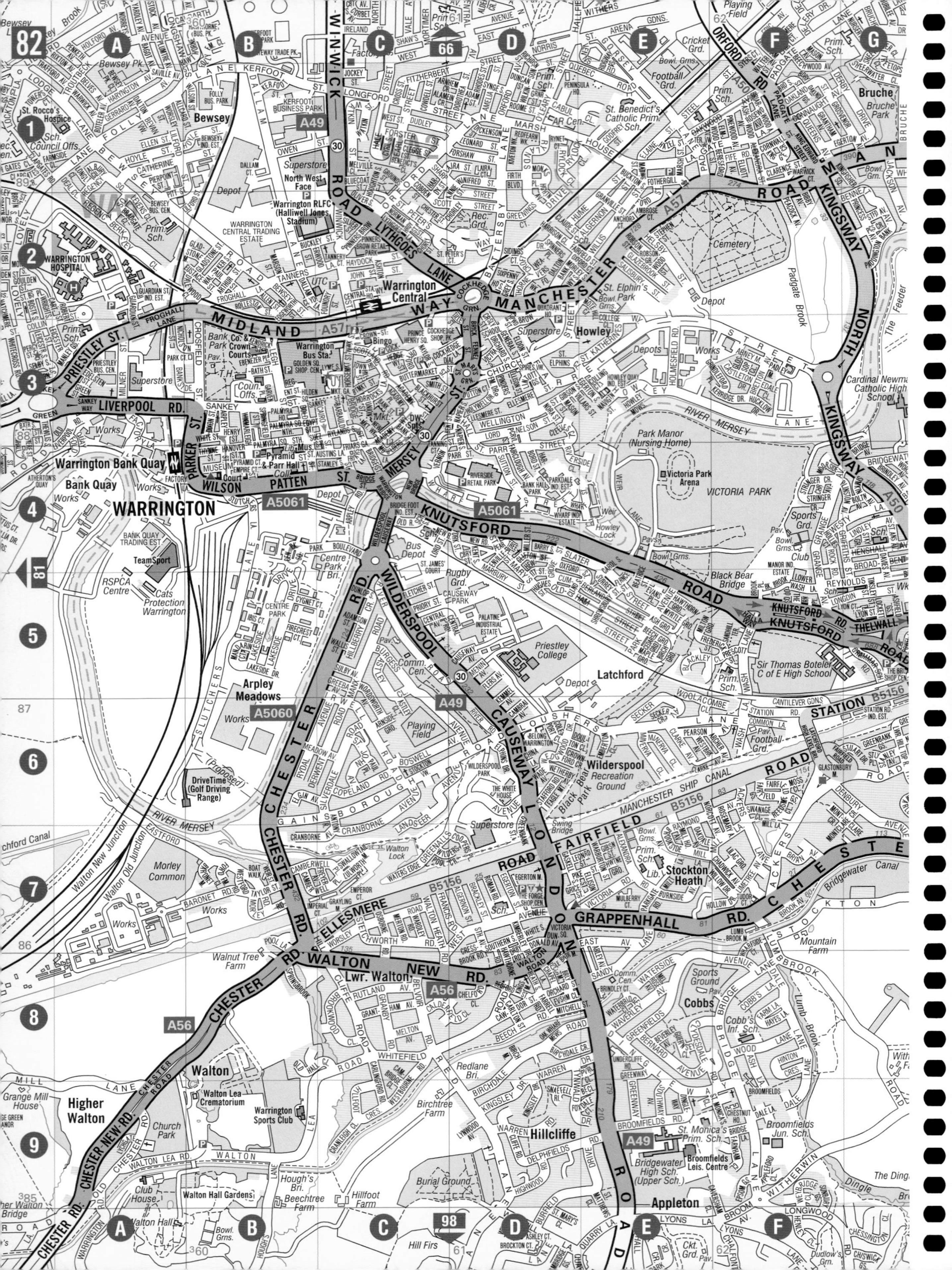

WARRINGTON
Bewsey
Bewsey Pk.
St. Rocco's Hospice
Council Offs.
Warrington Hospital
Warrington RLFC (Halliwell Jones Stadium)
Warrington Central Trading Estate
Warrington Central
Kerfoot Business Park
Folly Bus. Park
Superstore
North West Face
Warrington Bus Sta.
Golden Sq. Shop. Cen.
Warrington Bank Quay
Bank Quay
Bank Quay Trading Est.
TeamSport
RSPCA Centre
Cats Protection Warrington
Centre Park
Arpley Meadows
DriveTime (Golf Driving Range)
Morley Common
Walton New Junction
Walton Old Junction
Walnut Tree Farm
Lwr. Walton
Walton
Higher Walton
Grange Mill House
Walton Lea Crematorium
Warrington Sports Club
Church Park
Club House
Walton Hall Gardens
Walton Hall
Hough's Bri.
Beechtree Farm
Hillfoot Farm
Hill Firs
Burial Ground
Birchtree Farm
Redlane Bri.
Hillcliffe
Appleton
Bridgewater High Sch. (Upper Sch.)
Broomfields Leis. Centre
St. Monica's Prim. Sch.
Broomfields Jun. Sch.
Cobbs
Cobb's Inf. Sch.
Sports Ground
Stockton Heath
Wilderspool Recreation Ground
Black Bear Park
Swing Bridge
Walton Lock
Latchford
Priestley College
Palatine Industrial Estate
Causeway Park
Rugby Grd.
Bus Depot
Riverside Retail Park
Victoria Park
Victoria Park Arena
Park Manor (Nursing Home)
Howley
Howley Lock
Black Bear Bridge
Sir Thomas Boteler C of E High School
Cardinal Newman Catholic High School
Bruche
Bruche Park
Padgate Brook
Cemetery
St. Elphin's Park
St. Benedict's Catholic Prim. Sch.
Cricket Grd.
Football Grd.
Playing Field
Mountain Farm
The Dingle
RIVER MERSEY
MANCHESTER SHIP CANAL
Bridgewater Canal
Lumb Brook
The Feeder
MIDLAND WAY
LIVERPOOL RD.
WILSON PATTEN ST.
KNUTSFORD ROAD
MANCHESTER ROAD
WINWICK ROAD
LYTHGOES LANE
KINGSWAY NORTH
KINGSWAY
CHESTER RD.
WILDERSPOOL CAUSEWAY
LONDON ROAD
FAIRFIELD ROAD
GRAPPENHALL RD.
WALTON NEW RD.
CHESTER NEW RD.
ELLESMERE RD.
STATION ROAD
A49
A50
A56
A57
A5060
A5061
B5156
66
81
98

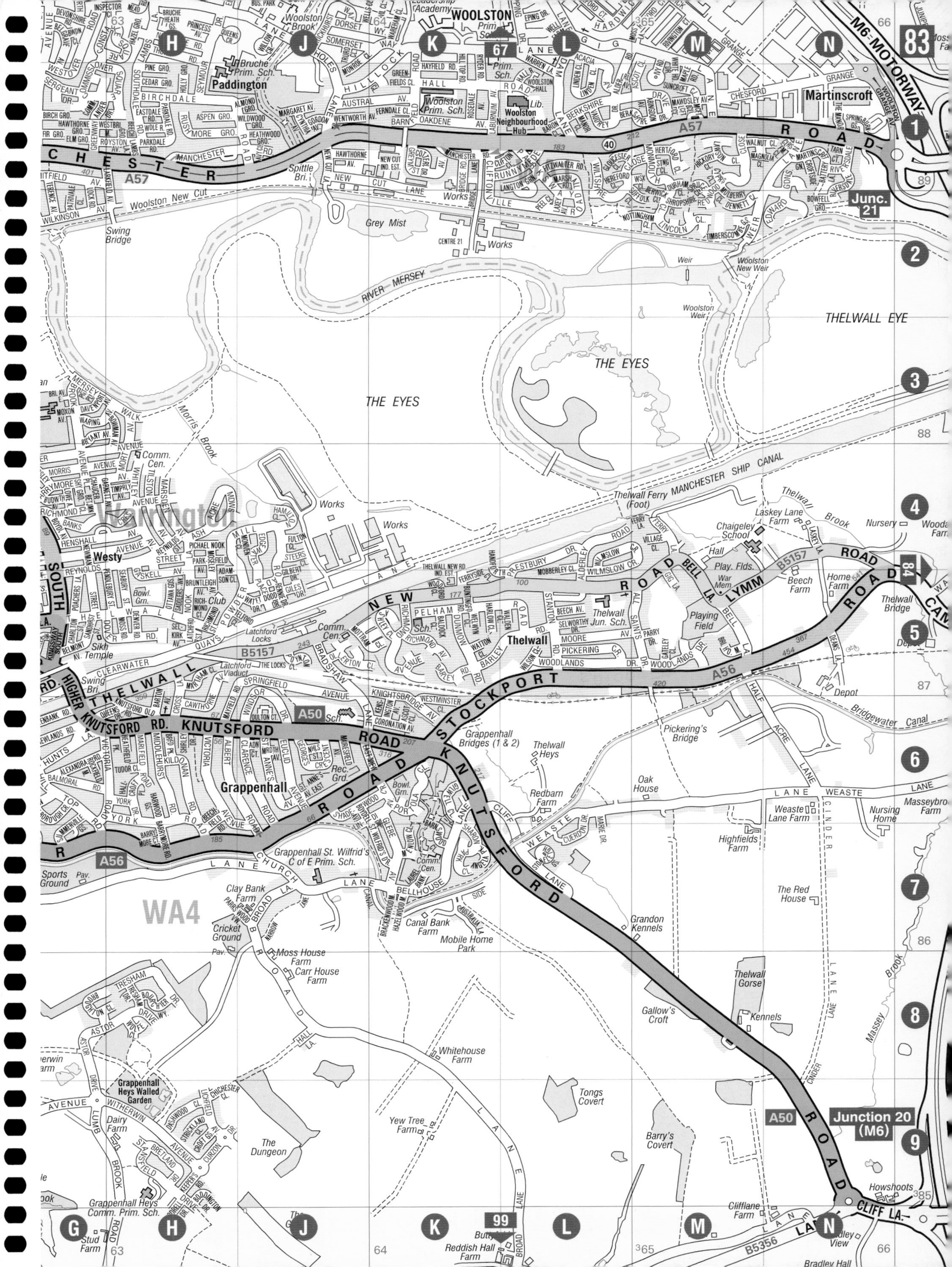
WOOLSTON
Paddington
Martinscroft
M6 MOTORWAY
CHESTER ROAD
A57
Woolston New Cut
RIVER MERSEY
THE EYES
THELWALL EYE
MANCHESTER SHIP CANAL
Warrington
Westy
Thelwall
Grappenhall
KNUTSFORD ROAD
STOCKPORT ROAD
A50
A56
B5157
Bridgewater Canal
WA4
Junc. 21
Junction 20 (M6)
Grappenhall Heys Walled Garden
Thelwall Gorse
Barry's Covert
Tongs Covert
The Dungeon
Yew Tree Farm
Whitehouse Farm
Grandon Kennels
Gallow's Croft
Howshoots
CLIFF LA.
B5356
67
84
99

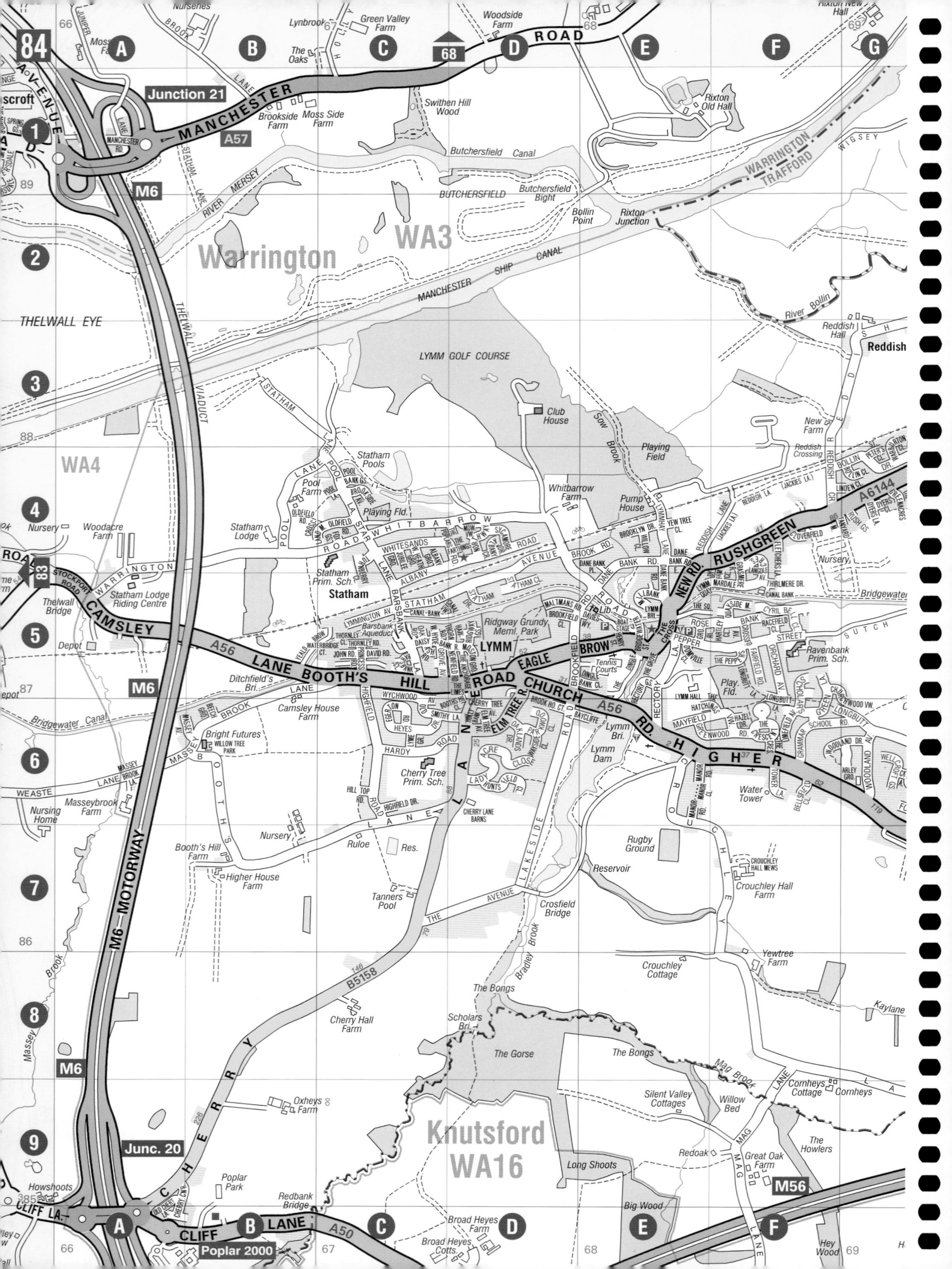
Junction 21
MANCHESTER ROAD
A57
M6
Warrington
WA3
WA4
THELWALL EYE
MANCHESTER SHIP CANAL
Butchersfield Canal
RIVER MERSEY
LYMM GOLF COURSE
Statham
LYMM
Rixton Old Hall
Rixton Junction
Bollin Point
Swithen Hill Wood
Brookside Farm
Moss Side Farm
Green Valley Farm
Woodside Farm
Statham Pools
Pool Farm
Playing Fld.
Statham Lodge
Statham Prim. Sch.
Statham Lodge Riding Centre
Thelwall Bridge
CAMSLEY LANE
BOOTH'S HILL ROAD
CHURCH RD.
EAGLE BROW
HIGHER RD.
A56
RUSHGREEN RD.
A6144
NEW RD.
Reddish Hall
Reddish
Whitbarrow Farm
Pump House
Playing Field
Club House
Ridgway Grundy Meml. Park
Ravenbank Prim. Sch.
Cherry Tree Prim. Sch.
Camsley House Farm
Bright Futures
Masseybrook Farm
Nursing Home
Booth's Hill Farm
Higher House Farm
Tanners Pool
Crosfield Bridge
Reservoir
Rugby Ground
Water Tower
Lymm Dam
Crouchley Hall Farm
Yewtree Farm
Crouchley Cottage
The Bongs
Scholars Bri.
The Gorse
Cherry Hall Farm
Oxheys Farm
Knutsford
WA16
Long Shoots
Big Wood
Silent Valley Cottages
Willow Bed
Cornheys Cottage
Cornheys
Great Oak Farm
The Howlers
Redoak
Broad Heyes Farm
Broad Heyes Cotts
Redbank Bridge
Poplar Park
Poplar 2000
Howshoots
CLIFF LANE
A50
B5158
Junc. 20
M6 MOTORWAY
M56
Hey Wood
Kaylane
Bridgewater Canal
River Bollin

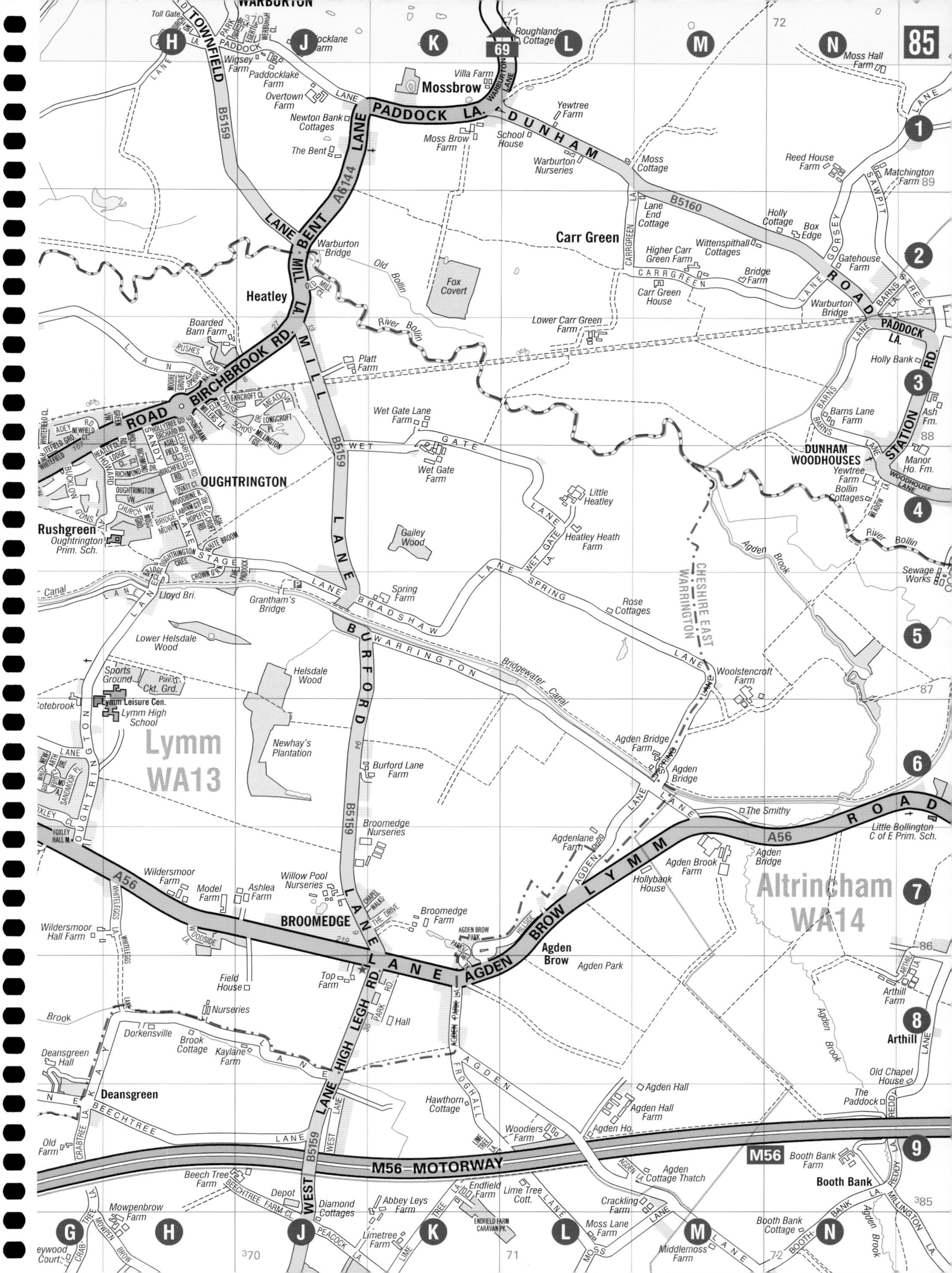

Heatley
Mossbrow
Carr Green
OUGHTRINGTON
Rushgreen
Lymm WA13
Altrincham WA14
DUNHAM WOODHOUSES
BROOMEDGE
Agden Brow
Deansgreen
Booth Bank
Arthill
PADDOCK LA.
DUNHAM ROAD
B5160
BIRCHBROOK RD.
BENT LANE
A6144
MILL LANE
B5159
BURFORD LANE
LYMM ROAD
A56
AGDEN BROW
HIGH LEGH RD.
M56 MOTORWAY
WARRINGTON LANE
BRADSHAW LANE
SPRING LANE
WET GATE LANE
STATION RD.
River Bollin
Bridgewater Canal
Agden Brook
CHESHIRE EAST
WARRINGTON
Fox Covert
Gailey Wood
Helsdale Wood
Lower Helsdale Wood
Newhay's Plantation
Lymm Leisure Cen.
Lymm High School
Oughtrington Prim. Sch.
Little Bollington C of E Prim. Sch.
Sewage Works
Agden Park
The Smithy
Agden Bridge
Warburton Bridge
Grantham's Bridge
Lloyd Bri.
Warburton Nurseries
Broomedge Nurseries
Willow Pool Nurseries
Wet Gate Farm
Little Heatley
Heatley Heath Farm
Rose Cottages
Woolstencroft Farm
Agden Hall
Agden Hall Farm
Booth Bank Farm
Beech Tree Farm
Endfield Farm
Diamond Cottages
Abbey Leys Farm
Middlemoss Farm

385

21

A   B   C   70   D   E   CALDY   F   G

Hockey
Pitch

CH48

1

Caldy Blacks

Club
House

2

CALDY   GOLF   COURSE

84

Dee Sailing
Club

Nature
Reserve

3

Caravan
Park

WIRRA

Caravan
Park

DAWPOOL   BANK

4

83

R I V E R

5

D E E

6

82

7

8

81

9

A   B   C   D   E   F

21   22   23

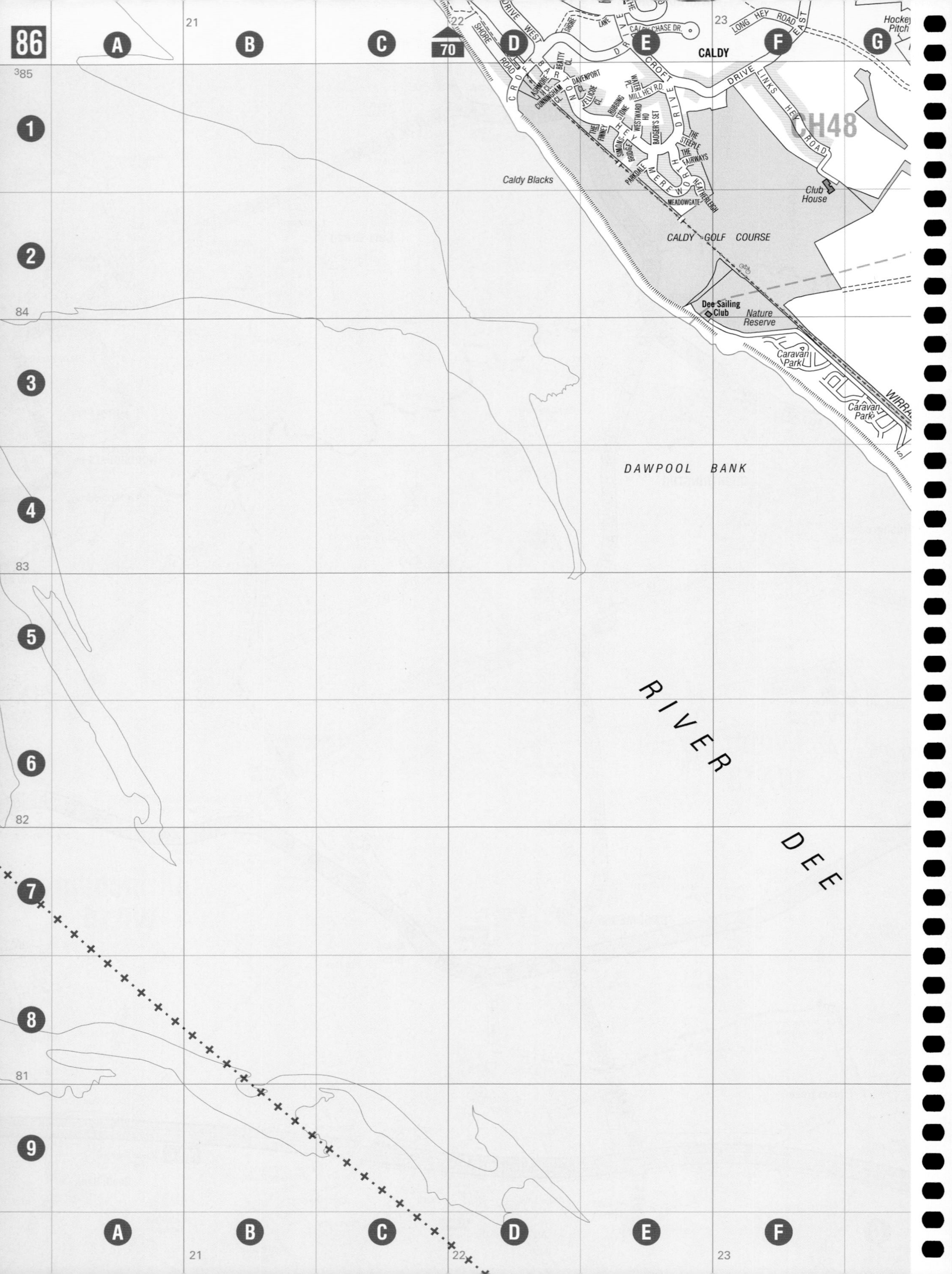

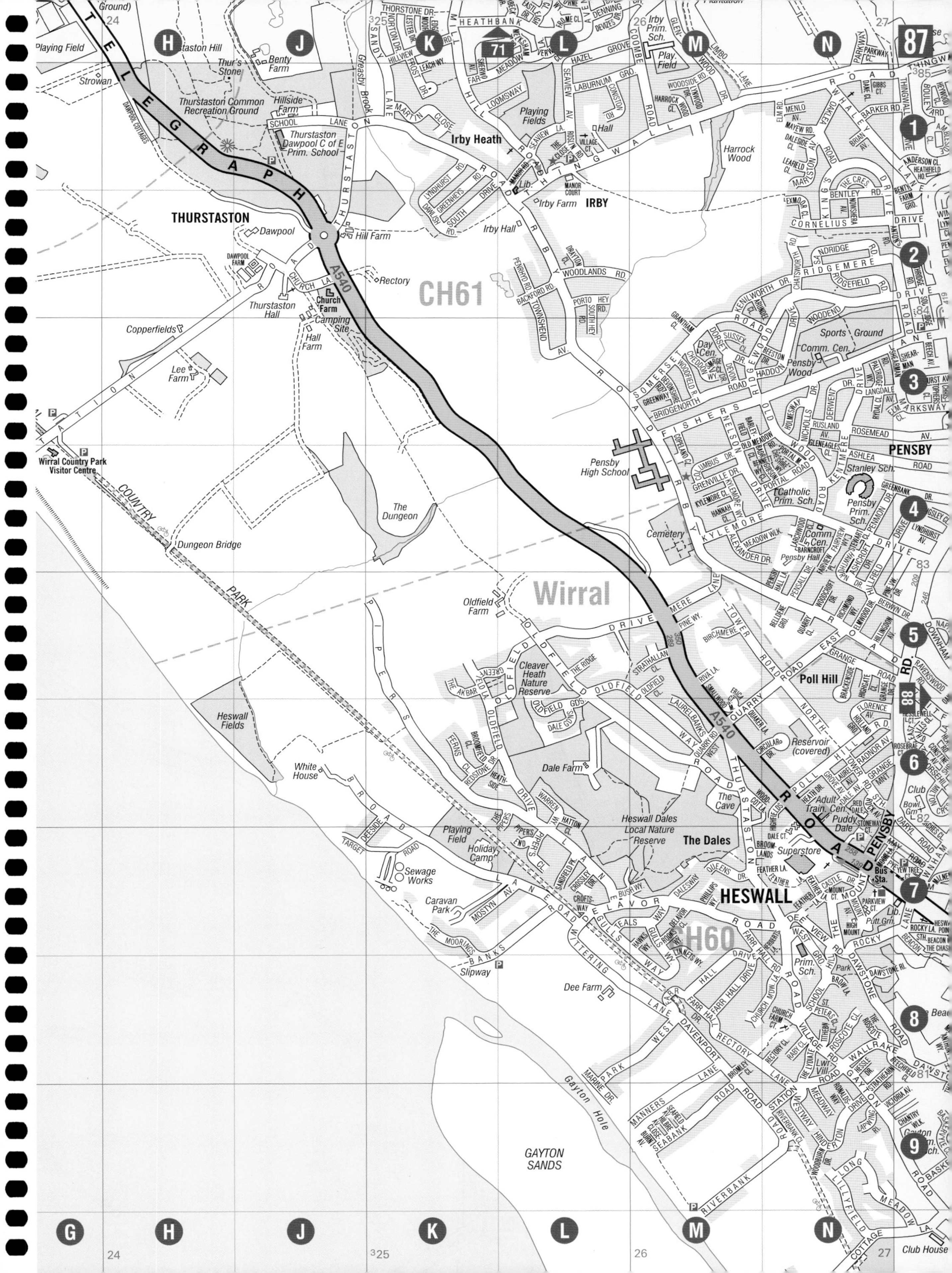
THURSTASTON
Thurstaston Common Recreation Ground
Thurstaston Dawpool C of E Prim. School
Irby Heath
IRBY
CH61
Wirral
Pensby High School
PENSBY
Poll Hill
Wirral Country Park Visitor Centre
Dungeon Bridge
The Dungeon
Heswall Fields
Cleaver Heath Nature Reserve
Heswall Dales Local Nature Reserve
The Dales
HESWALL
CH60
GAYTON SANDS
Gayton Hole
Sewage Works
Caravan Park
Slipway
Dee Farm
Holiday Camp
Superstore
Reservoir (covered)
TELEGRAPH ROAD
A540
COUNTRY PARK
Irby Prim. Sch.
Harrock Wood
Sports Ground
Pensby Wood
Stanley Sch.
Pensby Prim. Sch.
Catholic Prim. Sch.
Cemetery
Dale Farm
White House
Oldfield Farm
Copperfields
Lee Farm
Thurstaston Hall
Church Farm
Camping Site
Hall Farm
Rectory
Dawpool
Hill Farm
Irby Farm
Irby Hall
Benty Farm
Thur's Stone
Hillside Farm
Strowan
Playing Fields
Prim. Sch.
Club House

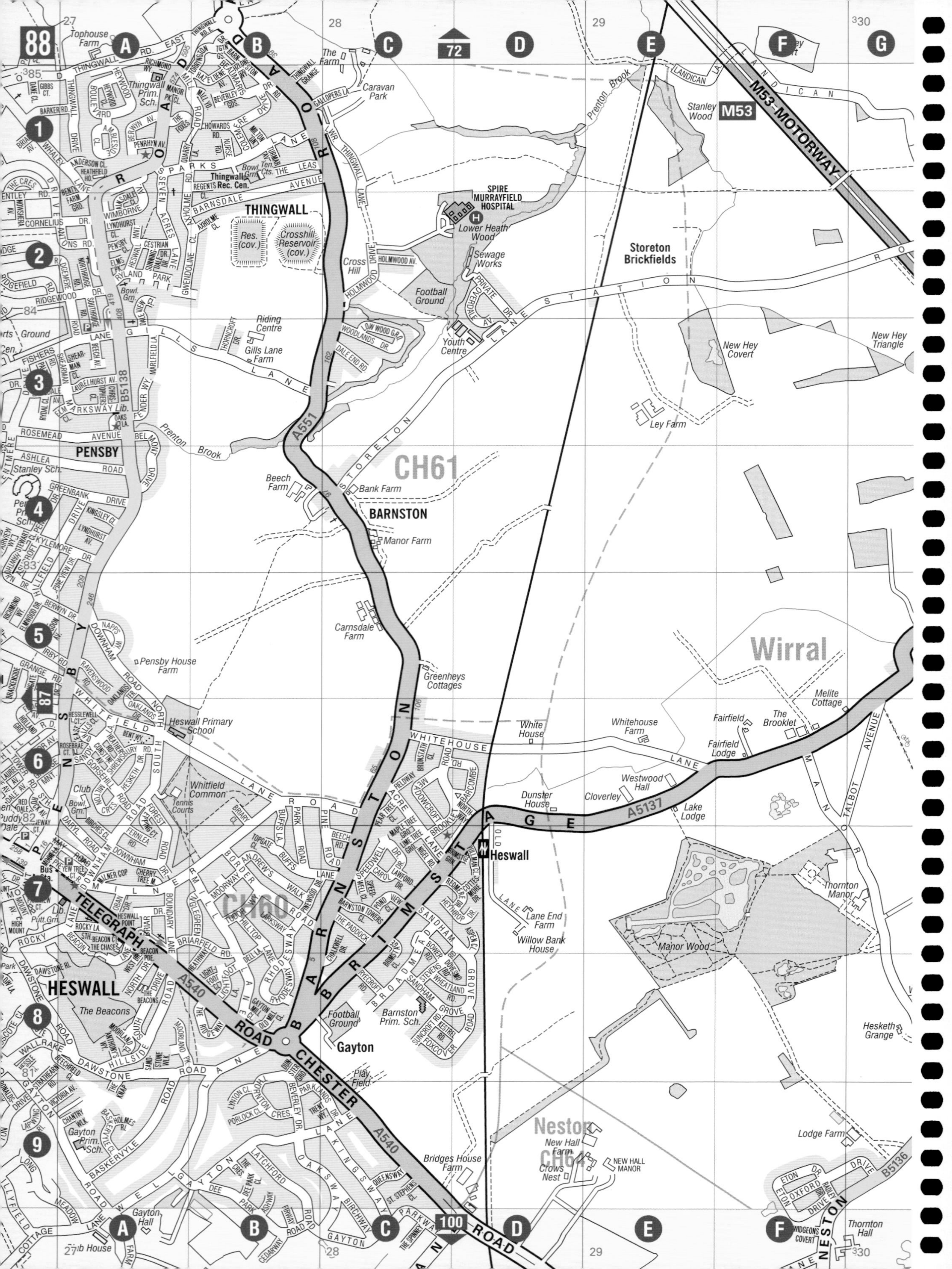
72
100
87
Tophouse Farm
THINGWALL
Thingwall Prim. Sch.
Thingwall Rec. Cen.
Res. (cov.)
Crosshill Reservoir (cov.)
The Farm
Caravan Park
Prenton Brook
LANDICAN LANE
Stanley Wood
M53
M53 MOTORWAY
SPIRE MURRAYFIELD HOSPITAL
Lower Heath Wood
Sewage Works
Cross Hill
Football Ground
Storeton Brickfields
STATION ROAD
Riding Centre
Gills Lane Farm
GILLS LANE
Youth Centre
New Hey Covert
New Hey Triangle
Ley Farm
PENSBY
ROSEMEAD AVENUE
Stanley Sch.
B5138
A551
STORETON LANE
CH61
Beech Farm
Bank Farm
BARNSTON
Manor Farm
Carnsdale Farm
Greenheys Cottages
Pensby House Farm
Wirral
Heswall Primary School
Whitfield Common
Tennis Courts
White House
Whitehouse Farm
WHITEHOUSE LANE
Fairfield
Fairfield Lodge
The Brooklet
Melite Cottage
Westwood Hall
Cloverley
Dunster House
Lake Lodge
A5137
TALBOT AVENUE
Heswall
Thornton Manor
Lane End Farm
Willow Bank House
Manor Wood
CH60
TELEGRAPH ROAD
A540
HESWALL
The Beacons
Football Ground
Barnston Prim. Sch.
Gayton
CHESTER ROAD
Play Field
Hesketh Grange
Gayton Prim. Sch.
Neston
New Hall Farm
CH64
NEW HALL MANOR
Crows Nest
Bridges House Farm
Lodge Farm
B5136
Thornton Hall
Gayton Hall
Club House

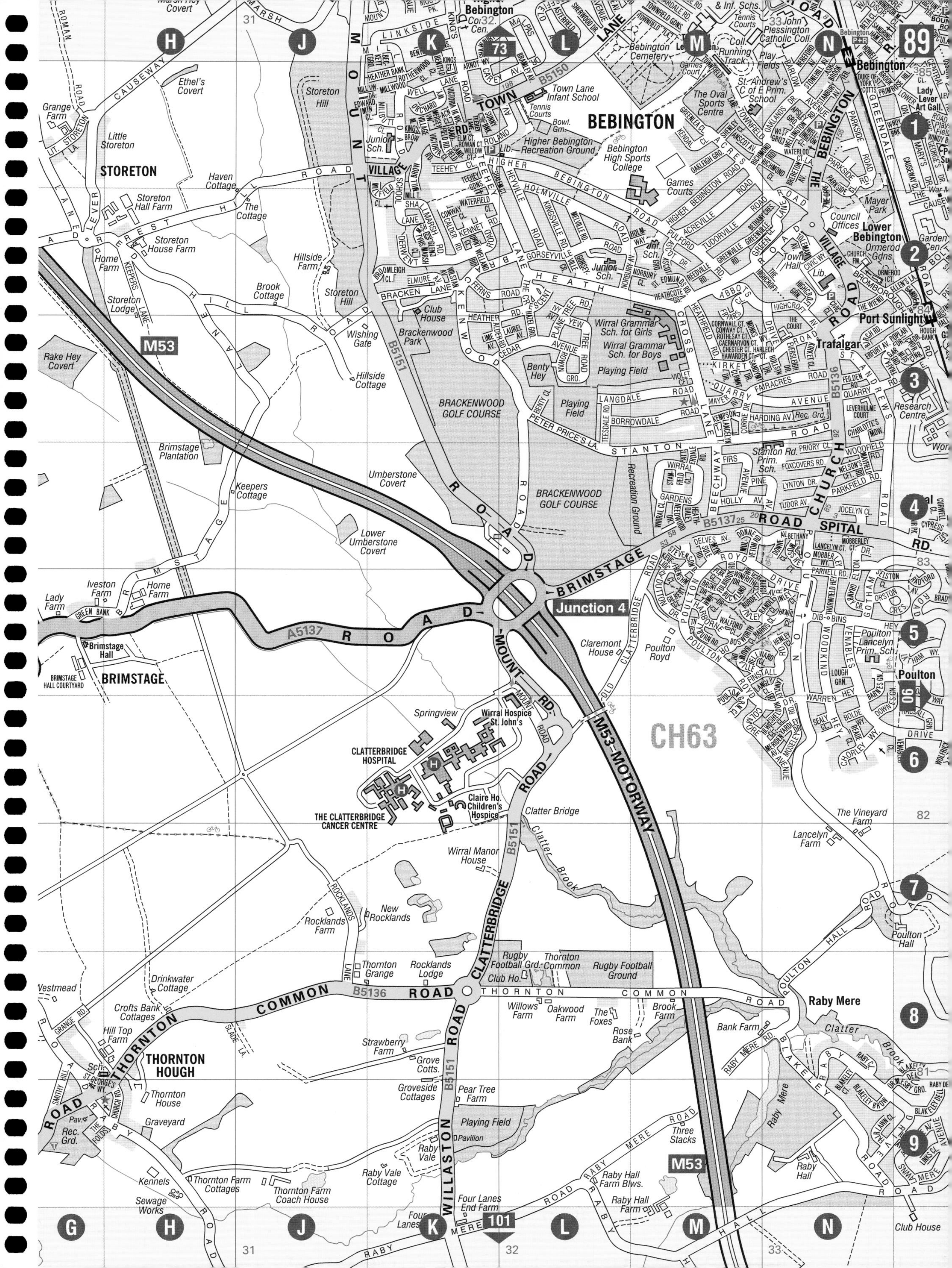

BEBINGTON
Higher Bebington
STORETON
Little Storeton
Storeton Hill
Ethel's Covert
Grange Farm
Storeton Hall Farm
Storeton House Farm
Home Farm
Storeton Lodge
Haven Cottage
The Cottage
Brook Cottage
Hillside Farm
Wishing Gate
Hillside Cottage
Rake Hey Covert
M53
Brackenwood Park
BRACKENWOOD GOLF COURSE
Bebington Cemetery
Bebington High Sports College
Higher Bebington Recreation Ground
Town Lane Infant School
The Oval Sports Centre
St. Andrew's C of E Prim. School
John Plessington Catholic Coll.
Lower Bebington
Council Offices
Mayer Park
Port Sunlight
Trafalgar
Lady Lever Art Gall.
Wirral Grammar Sch. for Girls
Wirral Grammar Sch. for Boys
Playing Field
Benty Hey
Stanton Rd. Prim. Sch.
Research Centre
Recreation Ground
Brimstage Plantation
Keepers Cottage
Umberstone Covert
Lower Umberstone Covert
Iveston Farm
Lady Farm
Home Farm
Brimstage Hall
BRIMSTAGE
BRIMSTAGE HALL COURTYARD
A5137 ROAD
BRIMSTAGE
B5137 ROAD
SPITAL RD.
Junction 4
Claremont House
Poulton Royd
Poulton Lancelyn Prim. Sch.
Poulton
CH63
Springview
Wirral Hospice St. John's
CLATTERBRIDGE HOSPITAL
THE CLATTERBRIDGE CANCER CENTRE
Claire Ho. Children's Hospice
Clatter Bridge
M53-MOTORWAY
The Vineyard Farm
Lancelyn Farm
Wirral Manor House
New Rocklands
Rocklands Farm
Rugby Football Grd.
Club Ho.
Thornton Common
Rugby Football Ground
Thornton Grange
Rocklands Lodge
Drinkwater Cottage
Vestmead
Crofts Bank Cottages
Hill Top Farm
THORNTON HOUGH
Thornton House
Graveyard
Rec. Grd.
Kennels
Sewage Works
Thornton Farm Cottages
Thornton Farm Coach House
Raby Vale Cottage
Raby Vale
Pavilion
Playing Field
Pear Tree Farm
Groveside Cottages
Grove Cotts.
Strawberry Farm
Willows Farm
Oakwood Farm
The Foxes
Rose Bank
Brook Farm
Bank Farm
Raby Mere
Poulton Hall
Three Stacks
Raby Hall Farm Blws.
Raby Hall Farm
Raby Hall
Four Lanes End Farm
Four Lanes
Club House
THORNTON COMMON ROAD
B5136
CLATTERBRIDGE ROAD
WILLASTON ROAD
B5151
RABY MERE ROAD
73
101
90
G H J K L M N
1 2 3 4 5 6 7 8 9
31 32 33

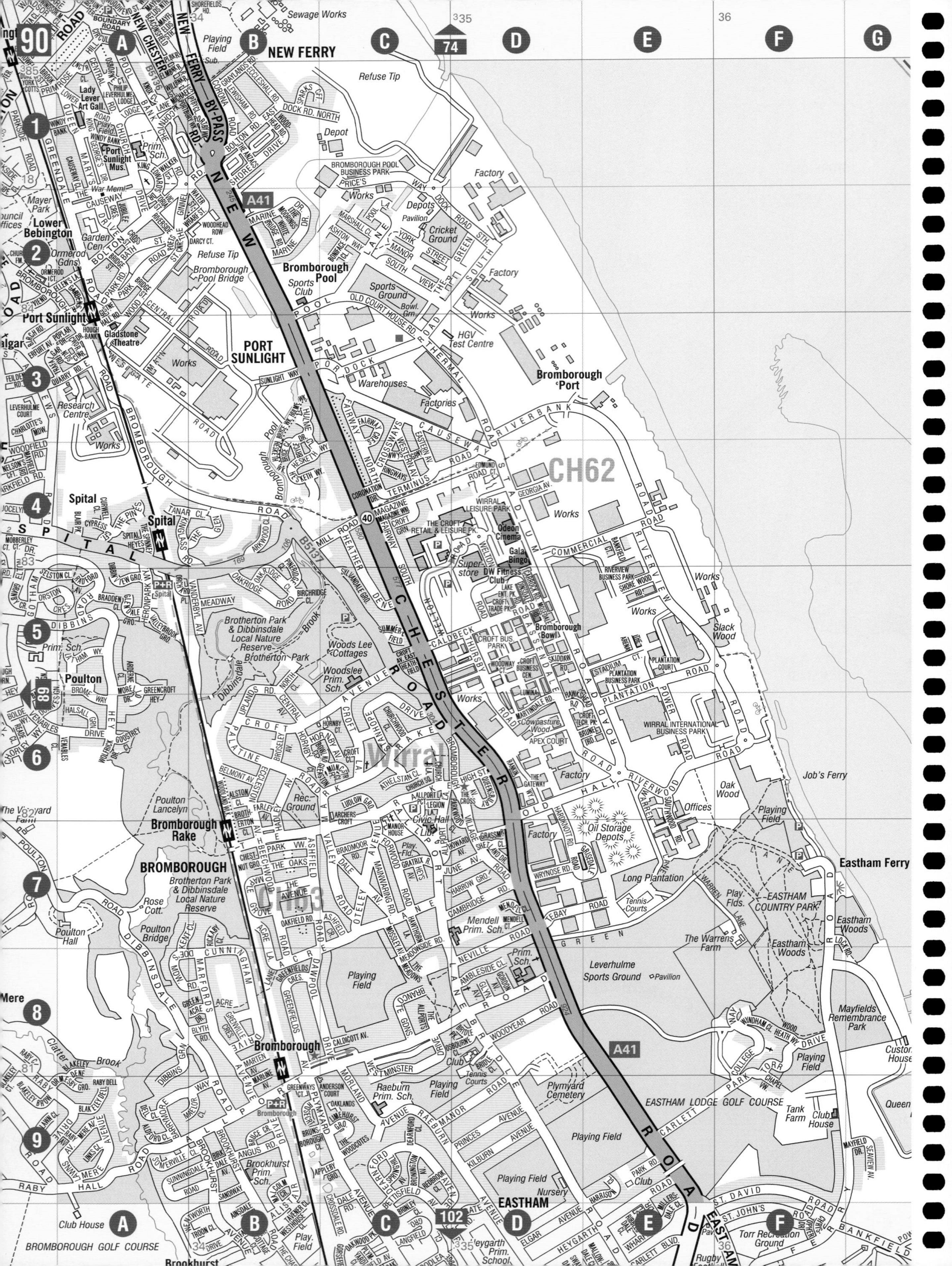

NEW FERRY
74
Sewage Works
Playing Field
Refuse Tip
Lady Lever Art Gall.
Port Sunlight Mus.
Prim. Sch.
War Meml.
Mayer Park
Lower Bebington
Ormerod Gdns.
Garden Cen.
Refuse Tip
Bromborough Pool Bridge
Port Sunlight
Gladstone Theatre
PORT SUNLIGHT
Works
Research Centre
Depot
BROMBOROUGH POOL BUSINESS PARK
Works
Depots
Pavilion
Cricket Ground
Factory
Bromborough Pool
Sports Club
Sports Ground
HGV Test Centre
Warehouses
Factories
Bromborough Port
CH62
Spital
NEW CHESTER ROAD
NEW FERRY BY-PASS
A41
B5137
THE CROFT RETAIL & LEISURE PK.
WIRRAL LEISURE PARK
Odeon Cinema
Gala Bingo
Superstore
DW Fitness Club
Works
Bromborough Bowl
RIVERVIEW BUSINESS PARK
Slack Wood
PLANTATION BUSINESS PARK
WIRRAL INTERNATIONAL BUSINESS PARK
Brotherton Park & Dibbinsdale Local Nature Reserve
Brotherton Park
Woods Lee Cottages
Woodslee Prim. Sch.
Poulton
89
Wirral
Cowpasture Wood
APEX COURT
Factory
Job's Ferry
Oak Wood
Offices
Playing Field
Oil Storage Depots
Poulton Lancelyn
The Vineyard Farm
Bromborough Rake
BROMBOROUGH
Rec. Ground
Civic Hall
Brotherton Park & Dibbinsdale Local Nature Reserve
Rose Cott.
Poulton Hall
Poulton Bridge
CH63
Mendell Prim. Sch.
Long Plantation
Tennis Courts
EASTHAM COUNTRY PARK
Eastham Ferry
Eastham Woods
The Warrens Farm
Leverhulme Sports Ground
Pavilion
Playing Field
Prim. Sch.
Mere
Mayfields Remembrance Park
Bromborough
Clatter Brook
Raeburn Prim. Sch.
Playing Field
Plymyard Cemetery
EASTHAM LODGE GOLF COURSE
Custom House
Playing Field
Tank Farm
Club House
Brookhurst Prim. Sch.
Playing Field
Nursery
Club
EASTHAM
102
Club House
BROMBOROUGH GOLF COURSE
Play. Field
Heygarth Prim. School
Torr Recreation Ground
Brookhurst
A B C D E F G
1 2 3 4 5 6 7 8 9

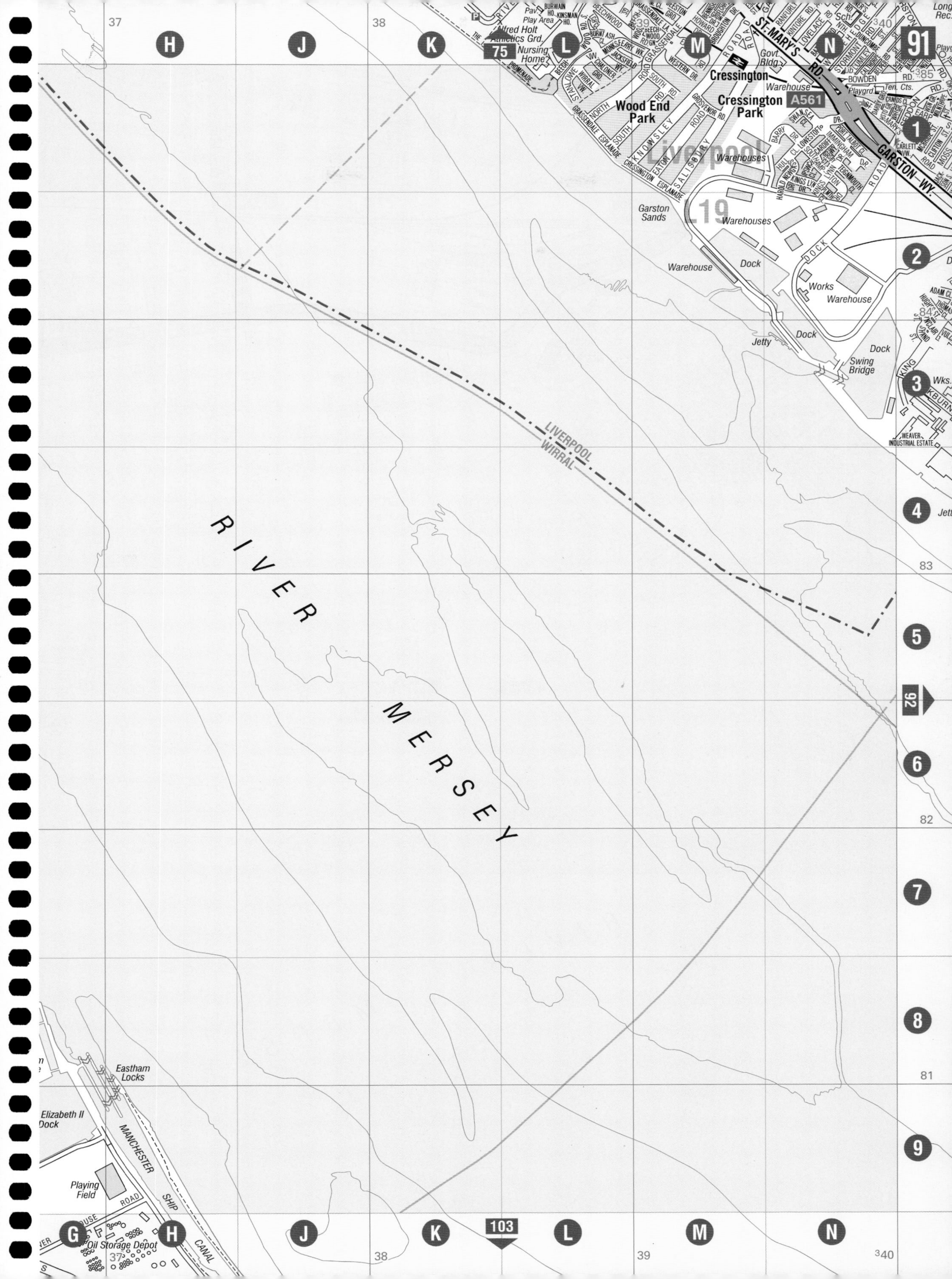
RIVER MERSEY
LIVERPOOL
WIRRAL
Cressington
Cressington Park
Wood End Park
Liverpool
L19
A561
ST. MARY'S RD.
GARSTON WY.
Garston Sands
Warehouses
Warehouse
Dock
Works
Jetty
Swing Bridge
Govt. Bldg.
Alfred Holt Athletics Grd.
Nursing Home
Play Area
WEAVER INDUSTRIAL ESTATE
Eastham Locks
Elizabeth II Dock
MANCHESTER SHIP CANAL
Playing Field
Oil Storage Depot
75
92
103
H J K L M N
G H J K L M N
1 2 3 4 5 6 7 8 9
37 38 39 340
81 82 83 84 385

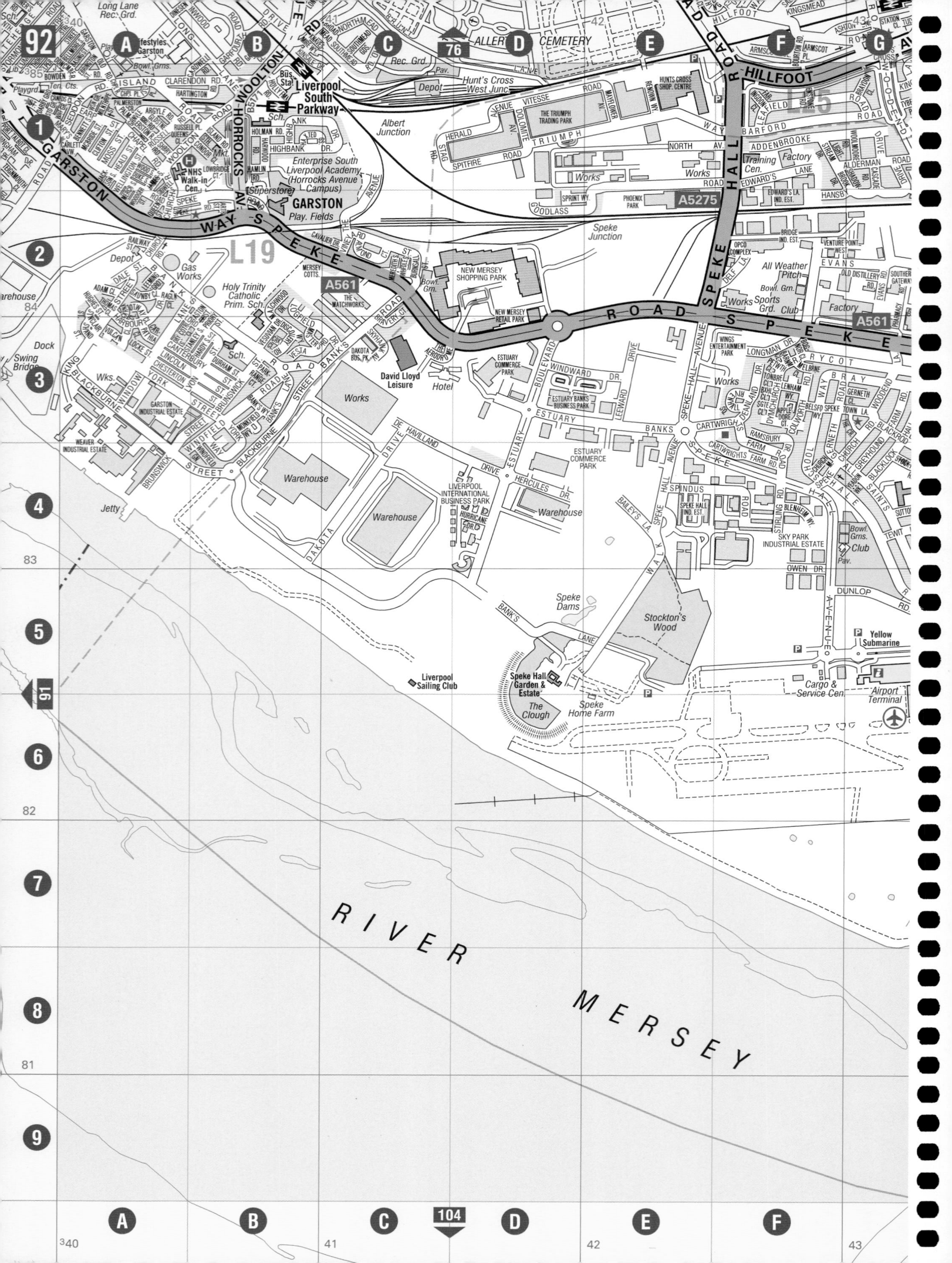

76
104
91
GARSTON
L19
L25
Liverpool South Parkway
Enterprise South Liverpool Academy (Horrocks Avenue Campus)
NHS Walk-in Cen.
Holy Trinity Catholic Prim. Sch.
Gas Works
Garston Industrial Estate
Weaver Industrial Estate
Jetty
Swing Bridge
Dock
Allerton Cemetery
Hunt's Cross West Junc.
Albert Junction
Speke Junction
Hunts Cross Shop. Centre
The Triumph Trading Park
Phoenix Park
A5275
A561
B5171
New Mersey Shopping Park
New Mersey Retail Park
The Matchworks
David Lloyd Leisure
Hotel
Estuary Commerce Park
Estuary Banks Business Park
Liverpool International Business Park
Warehouse
Works
Wings Entertainment Park
All Weather Pitch
Sports Grd.
Training Cen.
Factory
Speke Hall Ind. Est.
Sky Park Industrial Estate
Speke Dams
Stockton's Wood
Speke Hall Garden & Estate
The Clough
Speke Home Farm
Liverpool Sailing Club
Yellow Submarine
Cargo & Service Cen.
Airport Terminal
RIVER MERSEY
GARSTON WAY
SPEKE ROAD
SPEKE HALL ROAD
SPEKE HALL AVENUE
HILLFOOT
WOOLTON RD.
HORROCKS AV.
BANK'S ROAD
BLACKBURNE STREET
ESTUARY BOULEVARD
DE HAVILLAND DRIVE
DAKOTA DRIVE
BANK'S LANE
DUNLOP RD.

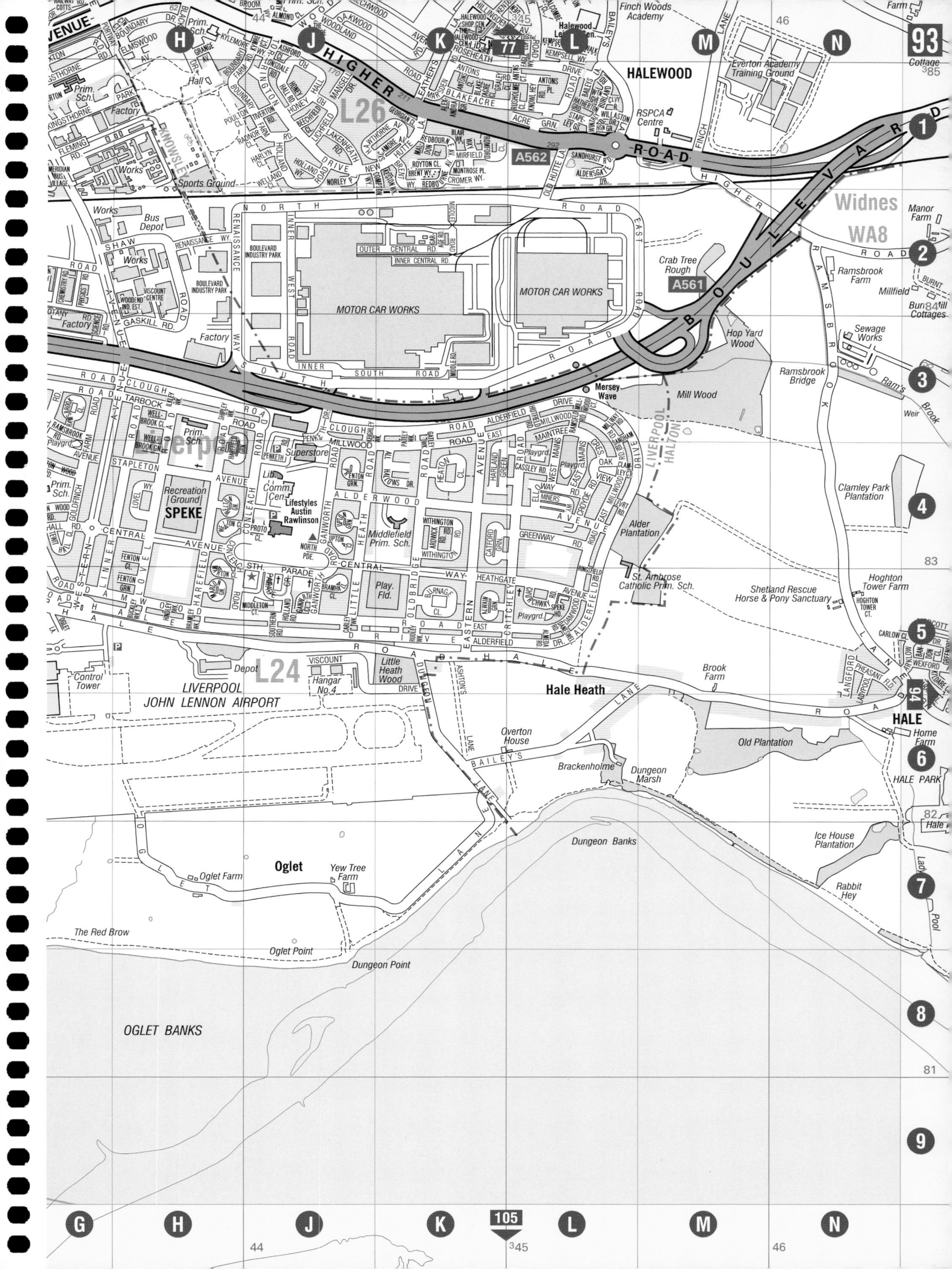
HALEWOOD
Finch Woods Academy
Everton Academy Training Ground
RSPCA Centre
HIGHER ROAD
A562
L26
Halewood Leisure Cen.
Widnes
WA8
Manor Farm
Crab Tree Rough
A561
BOULEVARD
MOTOR CAR WORKS
BOULEVARD INDUSTRY PARK
NORTH ROAD
SOUTH ROAD
INNER CENTRAL RD.
OUTER CENTRAL RD.
EAST ROAD
Bus Depot
Works
Factory
Sports Ground
KNOWSLEY
Ramsbrook Farm
Millfield
Sewage Works
Hop Yard Wood
Ramsbrook Bridge
Mill Wood
Mersey Wave
Rams Brook
Weir
LIVERPOOL
HALTON
Clamley Park Plantation
Alder Plantation
St. Ambrose Catholic Prim. Sch.
Hoghton Tower Farm
Shetland Rescue Horse & Pony Sanctuary
SPEKE
Recreation Ground
Liverpool
Superstore
Lifestyles Austin Rawlinson
Middlefield Prim. Sch.
Play. Fld.
Brook Farm
Hale Heath
HALE ROAD
HALE
Home Farm
Old Plantation
HALE PARK
Overton House
BAILEY'S LANE
DUNGEON LANE
Brackenholme
Dungeon Marsh
Dungeon Banks
Ice House Plantation
Rabbit Hey
Little Heath Wood
Hangar No.4
Control Tower
Depot
L24
LIVERPOOL JOHN LENNON AIRPORT
Oglet
Oglet Farm
Yew Tree Farm
OGLET LANE
The Red Brow
Oglet Point
Dungeon Point
OGLET BANKS
77
94
105

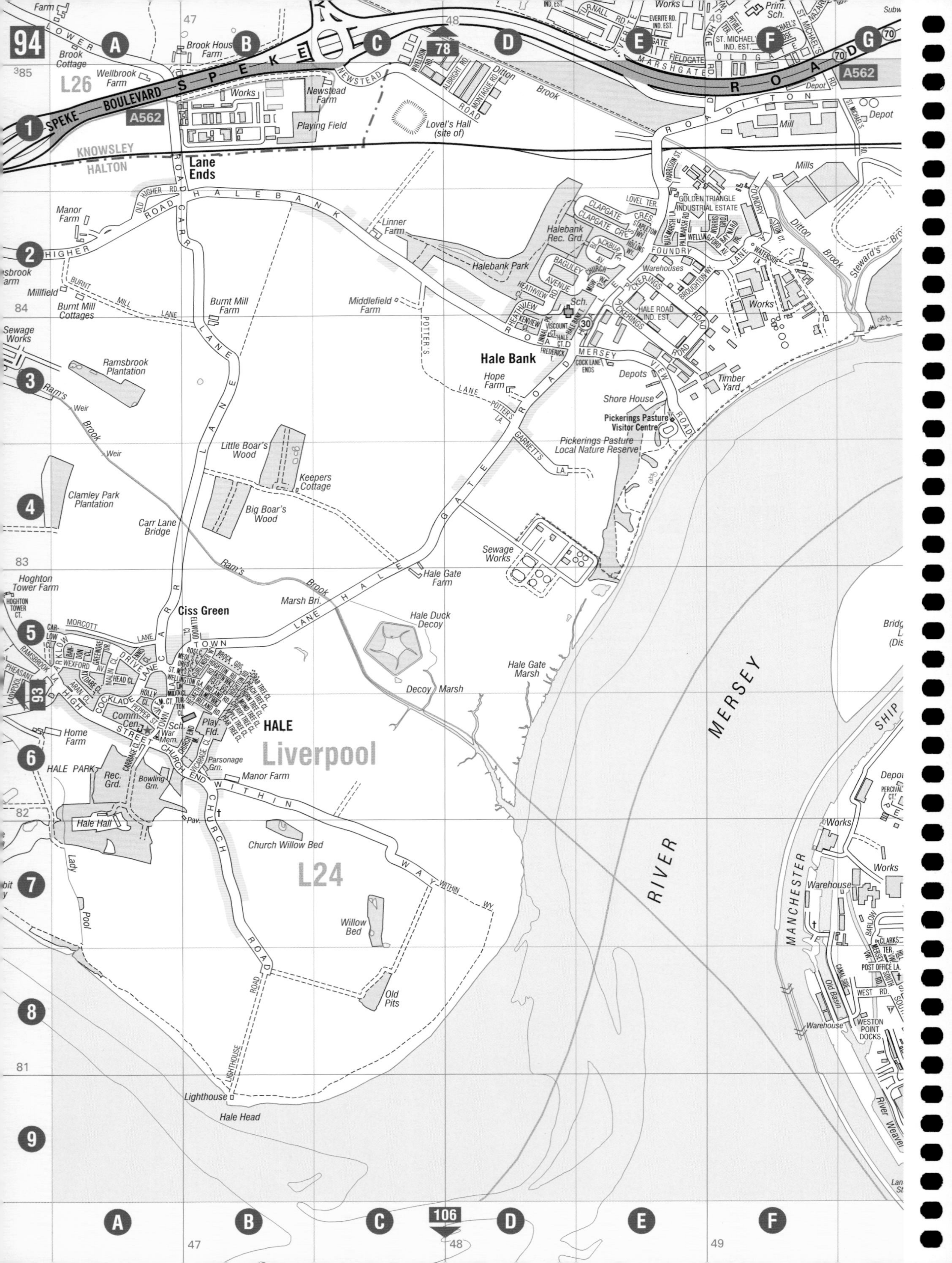
SPEKE BOULEVARD
A562
L26
Lane Ends
KNOWSLEY
HALTON
HALEBANK ROAD
HIGHER ROAD
Manor Farm
Burnt Mill Farm
Ramsbrook Plantation
Little Boar's Wood
Big Boar's Wood
Keepers Cottage
Clamley Park Plantation
Carr Lane Bridge
CARR LANE
Ciss Green
HALE GATE ROAD
Hale Bank
Halebank Park
Halebank Rec. Grd.
GOLDEN TRIANGLE INDUSTRIAL ESTATE
HALE ROAD IND. EST.
Pickerings Pasture Visitor Centre
Pickerings Pasture Local Nature Reserve
Sewage Works
Hale Gate Farm
Hale Duck Decoy
Hale Gate Marsh
Decoy Marsh
Marsh Bri.
HALE
Liverpool
L24
HALE PARK
Hale Hall
Manor Farm
Church Willow Bed
Willow Bed
Old Pits
Lighthouse
Hale Head
RIVER MERSEY
MANCHESTER SHIP CANAL
WESTON POINT DOCKS
River Weaver
DITTON ROAD
Lovel's Hall (site of)
Newstead Farm
Playing Field
Works
Mills
Timber Yard
Depots
Shore House
Hope Farm
Middlefield Farm
Linner Farm
Ditton Brook
Steward's Brook

78
93
106

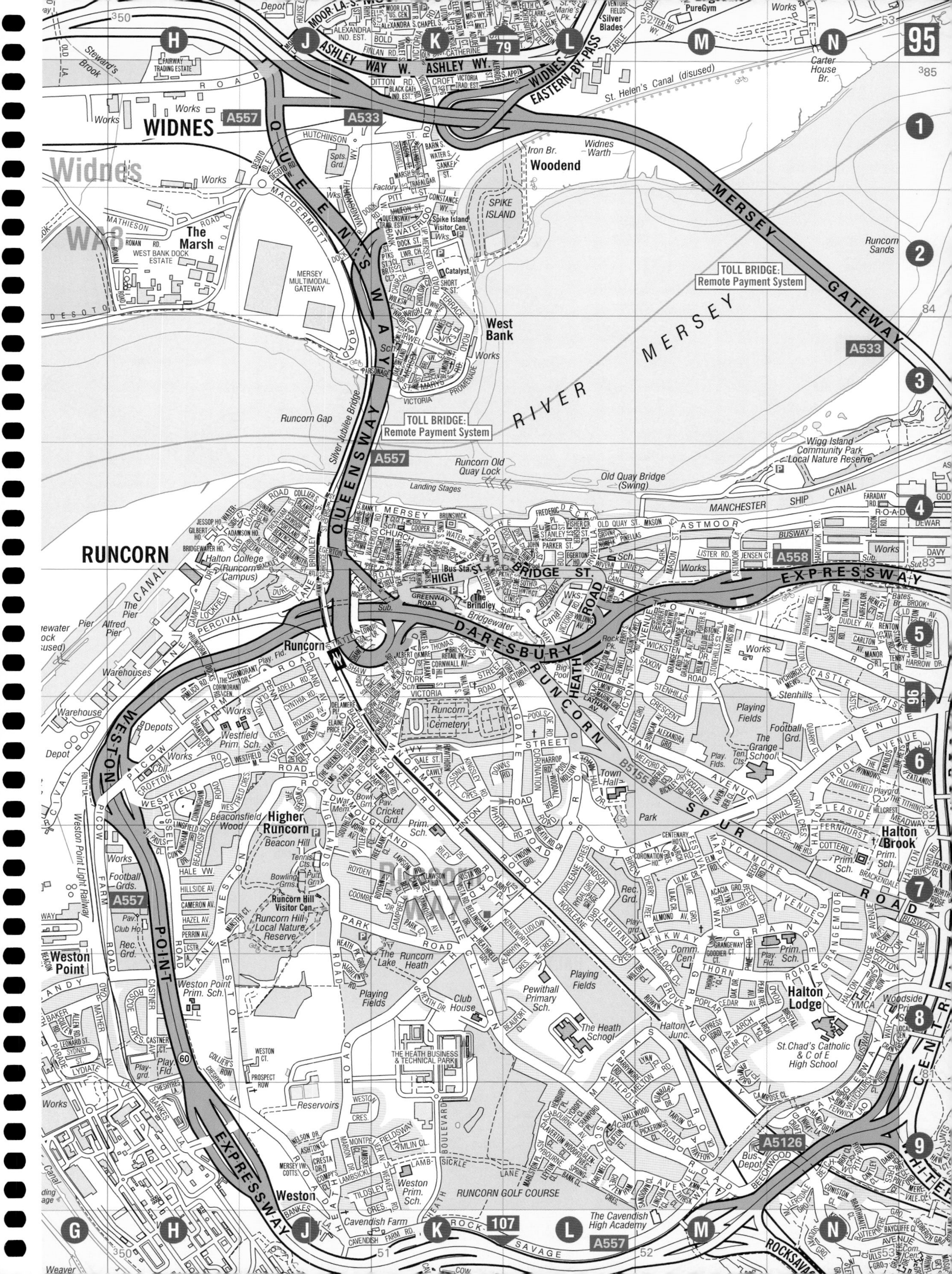
WIDNES
Woodend
The Marsh
West Bank
RIVER MERSEY
MERSEY GATEWAY
TOLL BRIDGE: Remote Payment System
Runcorn Gap
Silver Jubilee Bridge
QUEENSWAY
RUNCORN
MANCHESTER SHIP CANAL
EXPRESSWAY
DARESBURY
Higher Runcorn
Halton Brook
Halton Lodge
Weston Point
Weston
RUNCORN GOLF COURSE
THE HEATH BUSINESS & TECHNICAL PARK
WESTON POINT EXPRESSWAY
A557
A533
A558
A5126
B5155

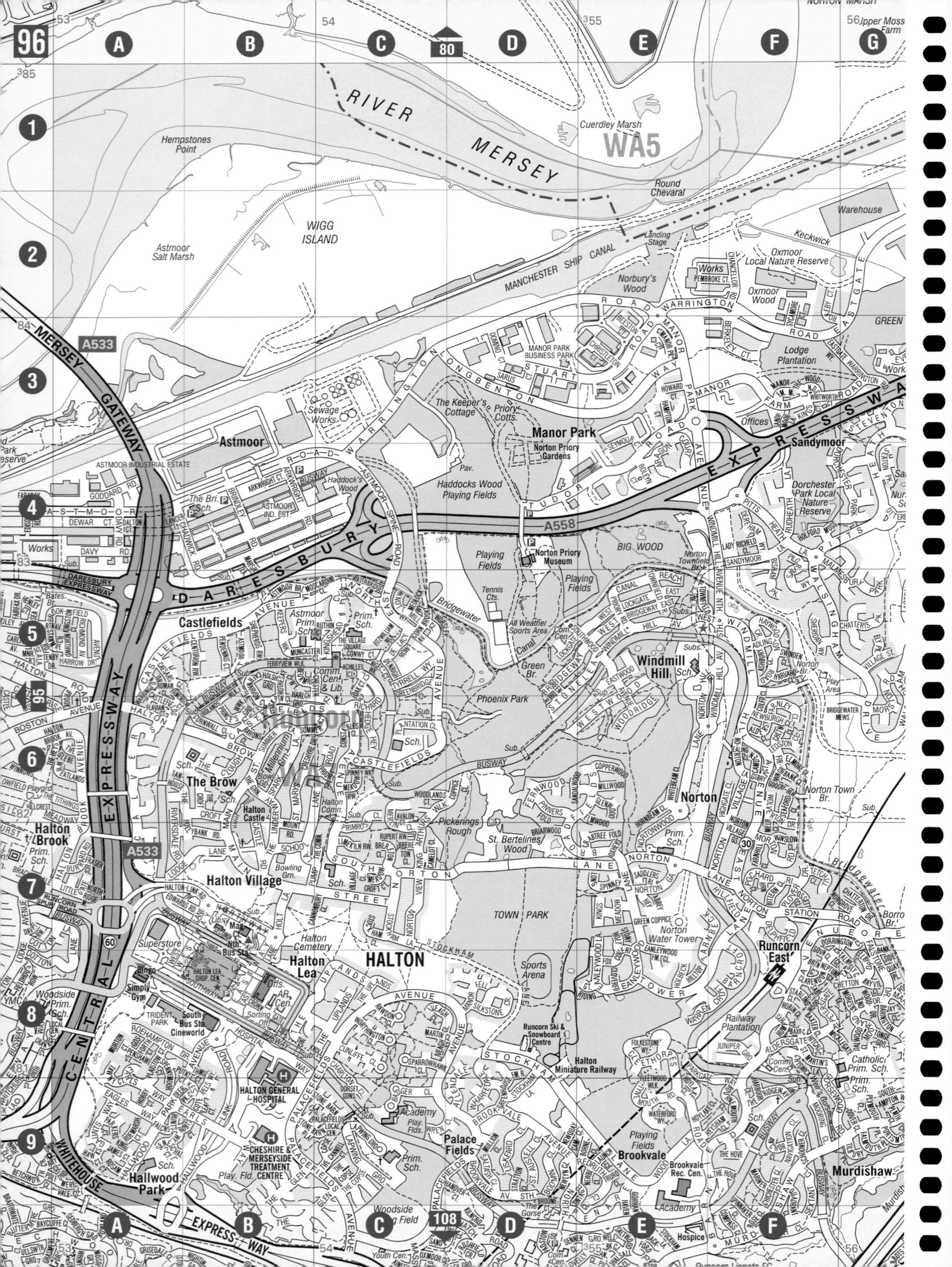
A
B
C
D
E
F
G
80
1
2
3
4
5
6
7
8
9
95
108
RIVER MERSEY
Hempstones Point
Cuerdley Marsh
WA5
Round Chevaral
WIGG ISLAND
Astmoor Salt Marsh
MANCHESTER SHIP CANAL
Landing Stage
Warehouse
Keckwick
Oxmoor Local Nature Reserve
Norbury's Wood
Works
Oxmoor Wood
GREEN
Lodge Plantation
MANOR PARK BUSINESS PARK
A533
MERSEY GATEWAY
Sewage Works
The Keeper's Cottage
Priory Cotts.
Manor Park
Norton Priory Gardens
Offices
Sandymoor
Astmoor
ASTMOOR INDUSTRIAL ESTATE
Haddock's Wood
Haddocks Wood Playing Fields
Dorchester Park Local Nature Reserve
A558
EXPRESSWAY
DARESBURY EXPRESSWAY
Playing Fields
Norton Priory Museum
BIG WOOD
Norton Townfield Br.
Tennis Cts.
All Weather Sports Area
Castlefields
Astmoor Prim. Sch.
Bridgewater Canal
Windmill Hill
Green Br.
Phoenix Park
Runcorn
BUSWAY
Norton Town Br.
The Brow
Halton Castle
Norton
Pickerings Rough
St. Bertelines Wood
Halton Brook
Halton Village
TOWN PARK
Norton Water Tower
Runcorn East
Superstore
Halton Cemetery
Halton Lea
HALTON
Sports Arena
Bingo
Simply Gym
Trident Park
Cineworld
Railway Plantation
Catholic Prim. Sch.
Runcorn Ski & Snowboard Centre
Halton Miniature Railway
HALTON GENERAL HOSPITAL
CENTRAL EXPRESSWAY
Academy
Palace Fields
Playing Fields
Brookvale
Murdishaw
CHESHIRE & MERSEYSIDE TREATMENT CENTRE
Hallwood Park
Brookvale Rec. Cen.
Hospice
WHITEHOUSE EXPRESSWAY
Woodside Playing Field
Youth Cen.

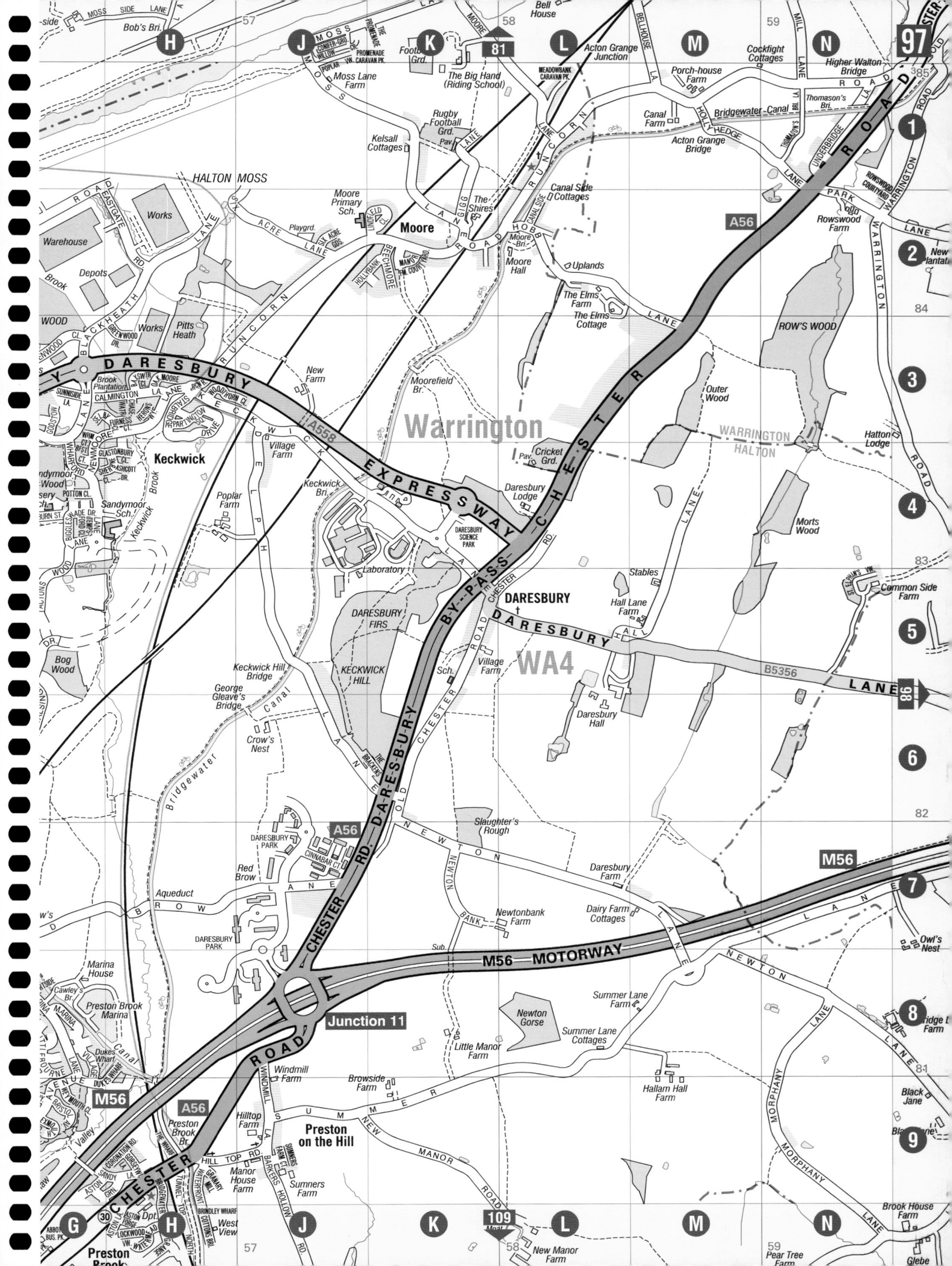

Warrington
WA4
Moore
Keckwick
DARESBURY
Preston on the Hill
HALTON MOSS
DARESBURY EXPRESSWAY
A558
A56
M56
M56 MOTORWAY
Junction 11
CHESTER ROAD
DARESBURY BY-PASS
CHESTER RD.
B5356
DARESBURY LANE
WARRINGTON
HALTON
Bridgewater Canal
Acton Grange Junction
Acton Grange Bridge
Higher Walton Bridge
Cockfight Cottages
Porch-house Farm
The Big Hand (Riding School)
Rugby Football Grd.
Kelsall Cottages
Moore Primary Sch.
Moore Hall
Uplands
The Elms Farm
The Elms Cottage
Rowswood Farm
ROW'S WOOD
Outer Wood
Morts Wood
Hatton Lodge
Cricket Grd.
Daresbury Lodge
DARESBURY SCIENCE PARK
Laboratory
DARESBURY FIRS
KECKWICK HILL
Keckwick Hill Bridge
George Gleave's Bridge
Crow's Nest
Village Farm
Daresbury Hall
Hall Lane Farm
Stables
Common Side Farm
Slaughter's Rough
Daresbury Farm
Newtonbank Farm
Dairy Farm Cottages
Summer Lane Farm
Summer Lane Cottages
Newton Gorse
Little Manor Farm
Hallam Hall Farm
Windmill Farm
Browside Farm
Hilltop Farm
Manor House Farm
Sumners Farm
New Manor Farm
Pear Tree Farm
Brook House Farm
Black Jane
Owl's Nest
Marina House
Preston Brook Marina
Dukes Wharf
Preston Brook Br.
Red Brow
Aqueduct
DARESBURY PARK
Poplar Farm
Sandymoor Sch.
Bog Wood
Pitts Heath
Works
Warehouse
Depots
New Farm
Moorefield Br.
Keckwick Bri.
Moss Lane Farm
Canal Side Cottages
Canal Farm
Thomason's Bri.
Bob's Bri.
Bell House
Preston Brook

81
98
109

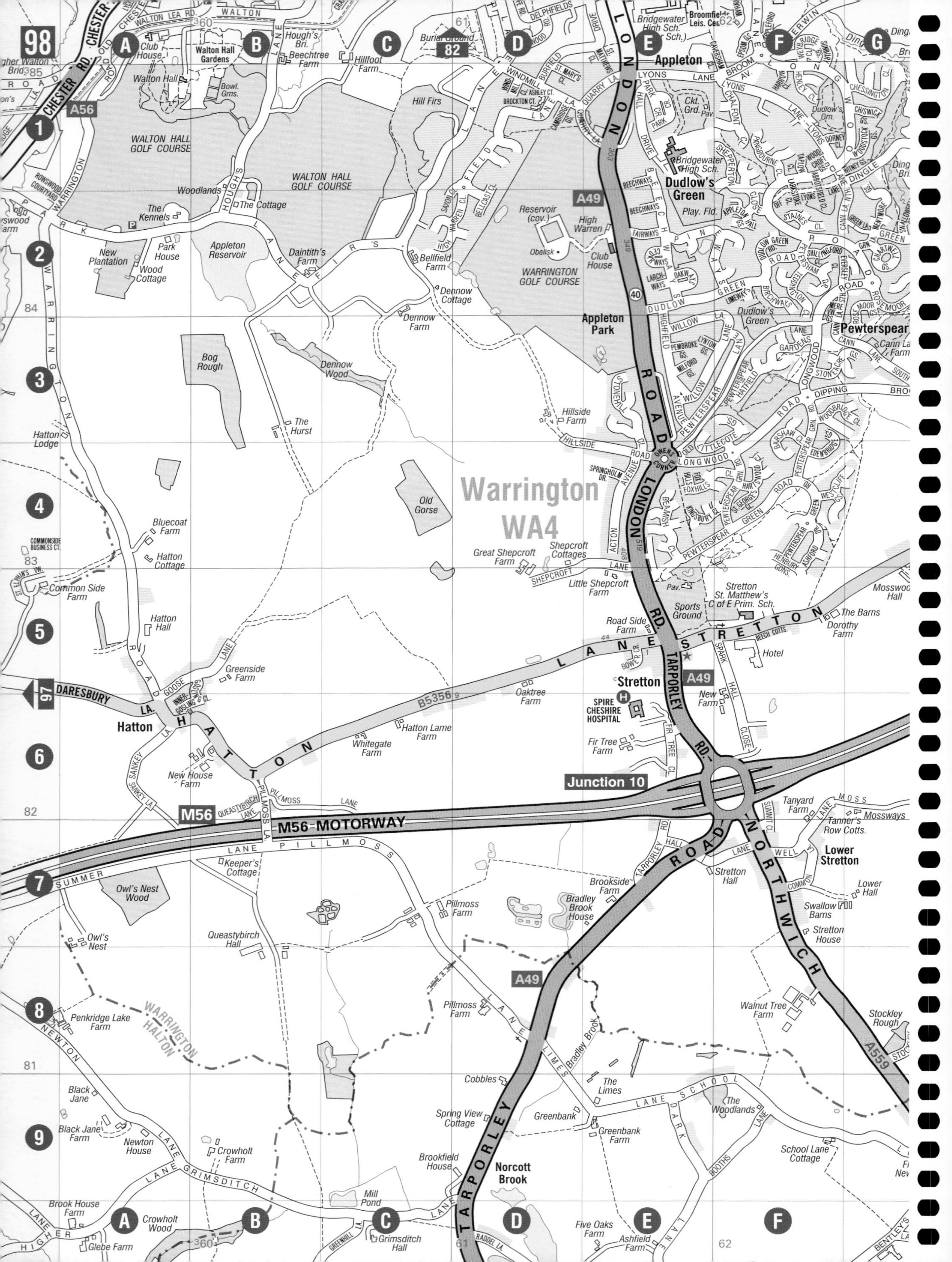

Warrington
WA4
Appleton
Dudlow's Green
Pewterspear
Stretton
Hatton
Lower Stretton
Norcott Brook
Walton Hall Gardens
WALTON HALL GOLF COURSE
WARRINGTON GOLF COURSE
Appleton Park
Appleton Reservoir
Bridgewater High Sch.
SPIRE CHESHIRE HOSPITAL
Stretton St. Matthew's C of E Prim. Sch.
Junction 10
M56 MOTORWAY
LONDON ROAD
TARPORLEY RD.
NORTHWICH ROAD
STRETTON LANE
HATTON LANE
DARESBURY LA.
PILLMOSS LANE
A49
A56
A559
B5356
82
97

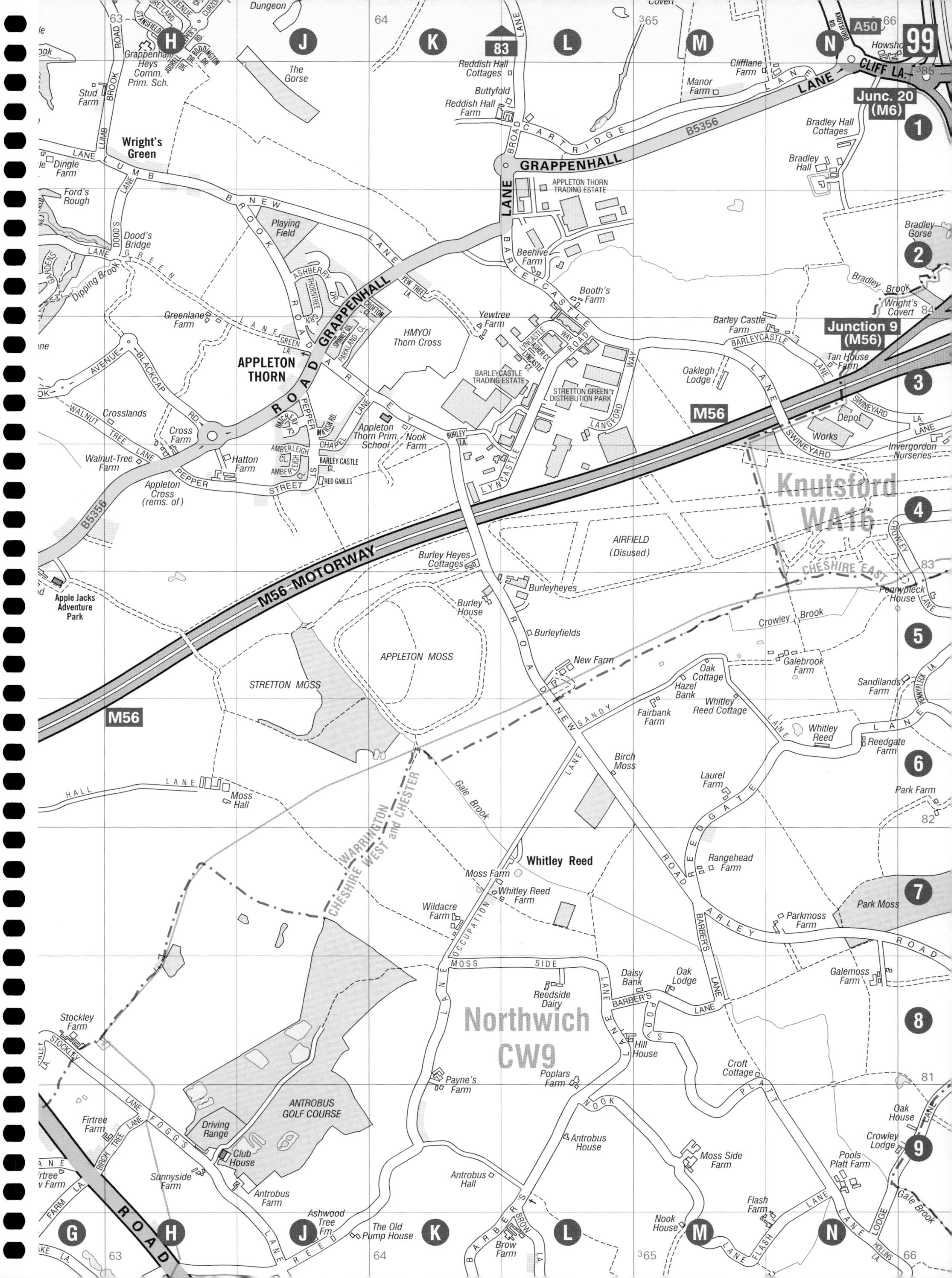

APPLETON THORN
Wright's Green
Whitley Reed
Knutsford WA16
Northwich CW9
M56 MOTORWAY
M56
Junc. 20 (M6)
Junction 9 (M56)
GRAPPENHALL LANE
GRAPPENHALL ROAD
CLIFF LA.
B5356
A50
APPLETON THORN TRADING ESTATE
BARLEYCASTLE TRADING ESTATE
STRETTON GREEN DISTRIBUTION PARK
HMYOI Thorn Cross
Appleton Thorn Prim. School
Grappenhall Heys Comm. Prim. Sch.
Playing Field
The Gorse
Dungeon
Stud Farm
Dingle Farm
Ford's Rough
Dood's Bridge
Dipping Brook
Greenlane Farm
Crosslands
Cross Farm
Walnut-Tree Farm
Appleton Cross (rems. of)
Hatton Farm
Apple Jacks Adventure Park
Reddish Hall Cottages
Buttyfold
Reddish Hall Farm
Manor Farm
Clifflane Farm
Bradley Hall Cottages
Bradley Hall
Bradley Gorse
Bradley Brook
Wright's Covert
Beehive Farm
Booth's Farm
Yewtree Farm
Nook Farm
Barley Castle Farm
Oaklegh Lodge
Tan House Farm
Depot
Works
Invergordon Nurseries
AIRFIELD (Disused)
CHESHIRE EAST
Burley Heyes Cottages
Burleyheyes
Burley House
Burleyfields
New Farm
APPLETON MOSS
STRETTON MOSS
Pennypleck House
Crowley Brook
Galebrook Farm
Oak Cottage
Hazel Bank
Whitley Reed Cottage
Fairbank Farm
Sandilands Farm
Whitley Reed
Reedgate Farm
Birch Moss
Laurel Farm
Park Farm
Moss Hall
Gale Brook
WARRINGTON
CHESHIRE WEST and CHESTER
Rangehead Farm
Moss Farm
Whitley Reed Farm
Wildacre Farm
Parkmoss Farm
Park Moss
Galemoss Farm
Daisy Bank
Oak Lodge
Reedside Dairy
Hill House
Croft Cottage
Stockley Farm
Firtree Farm
ANTROBUS GOLF COURSE
Driving Range
Club House
Sunnyside Farm
Antrobus Farm
Payne's Farm
Poplars Farm
Antrobus House
Antrobus Hall
Moss Side Farm
Oak House
Crowley Lodge
Pools Platt Farm
Flash Farm
Nook House
Ashwood Tree Fm.
The Old Pump House
Brow Farm
LUMB BROOK ROAD
LUMB BROOK LANE
NEW LANE
DOOD'S LANE
GREEN LANE
AVENUE
BLACKCAP RD.
WALNUT TREE LANE
PEPPER STREET
CHAPEL LANE
BARLEY CASTLE CL.
RED GABLES
BARLEY ROAD
BARLEYCASTLE LANE
LYNCASTLE ROAD
LYNCASTLE WAY
LANGFORD WAY
CARTRIDGE LANE
SWINEYARD LANE
CROWLEY LANE
PENNYPLECK LA.
SANDY LANE
NEW ROAD
REEDGATE LANE
ARLEY ROAD
BARBER'S LANE
POOLS PLATT LANE
MOSS SIDE LANE
OCCUPATION LANE
NOOK LANE
HALL LANE
STOCKLEY LANE
FOGG'S LANE
BIRCH TREE LANE
REED LANE
FLASH LANE
LODGE LANE
HOLLINS LA.
BARBER'S BROW
ROAD
H J K L M N
G H J K L M N
1 2 3 4 5 6 7 8 9
63 64 365 66
385 84 83 82 81
83

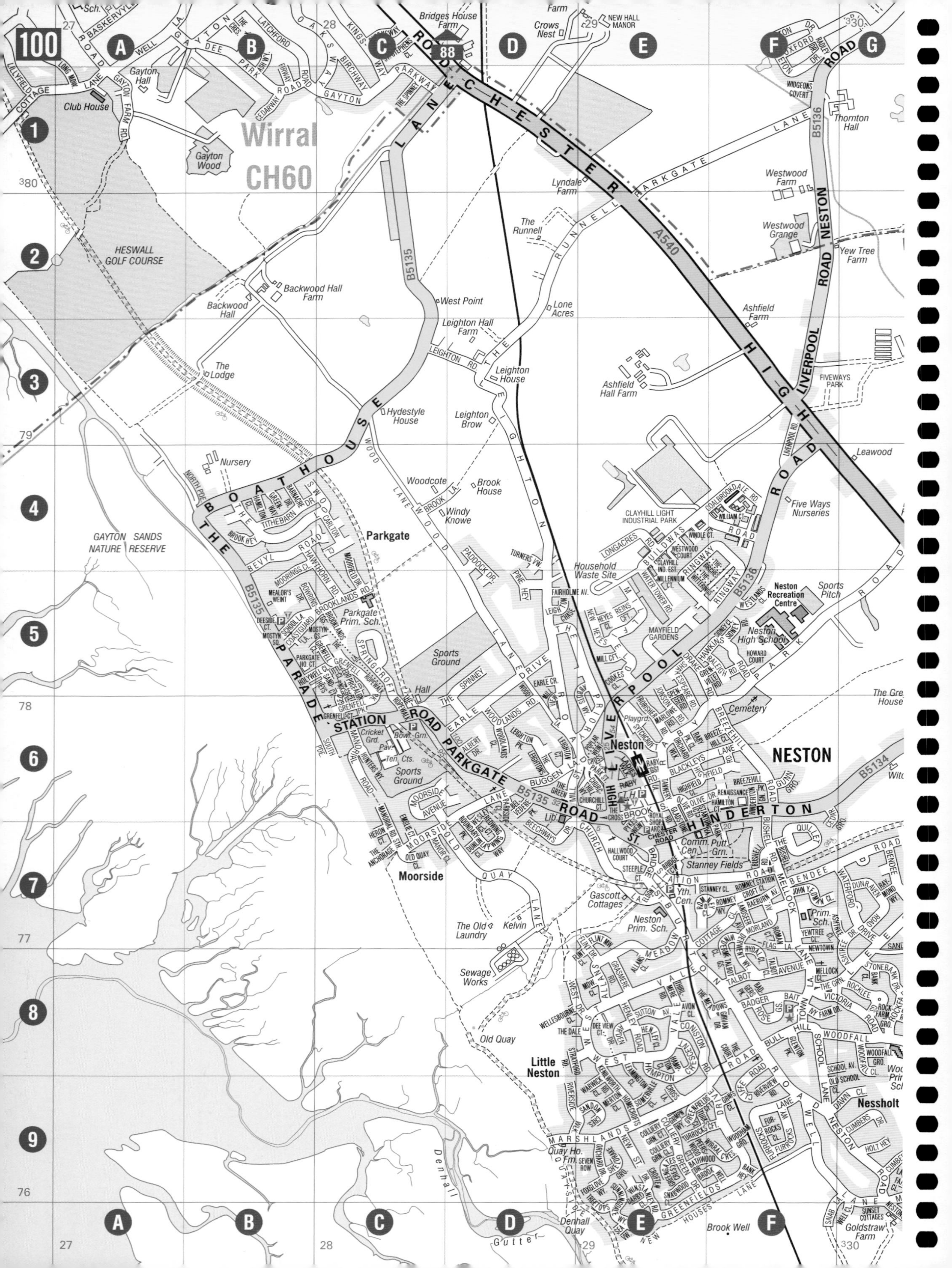
Wirral
CH60
Heswall Golf Course
Gayton Sands Nature Reserve
Parkgate
Neston
NESTON
Little Neston
Moorside
Nessholt
Club House
Gayton Hall
Gayton Wood
Backwood Hall Farm
Backwood Hall
The Lodge
West Point
Leighton Hall Farm
Leighton House
Hydestyle House
Leighton Brow
Woodcote
Brook House
Windy Knowe
Lyndale Farm
The Runnell
Lone Acres
Ashfield Hall Farm
Ashfield Farm
Westwood Farm
Westwood Grange
Yew Tree Farm
Thornton Hall
Bridges House Farm
Crows Nest
NEW HALL MANOR
Fiveways Park
Leawood
Five Ways Nurseries
CLAYHILL LIGHT INDUSTRIAL PARK
Household Waste Site
Neston Recreation Centre
Sports Pitch
Neston High School
Cemetery
Sports Ground
Parkgate Prim. Sch.
Nursery
The Old Laundry
Kelvin
Sewage Works
Old Quay
Gascott Cottages
Neston Prim. Sch.
Stanney Fields
Quay Ho. Fm.
Denhall Quay
Brook Well
Goldstraw Farm
CHESTER HIGH ROAD
A540
LIVERPOOL ROAD
B5136
BOATHOUSE LANE
B5135
THE PARADE
STATION ROAD
PARKGATE ROAD
HINDERTON ROAD
B5134
LEIGHTON ROAD
RUNNELL
PARKGATE LANE
MARSHLANDS
GREENFIELDS
Denhall Gutter

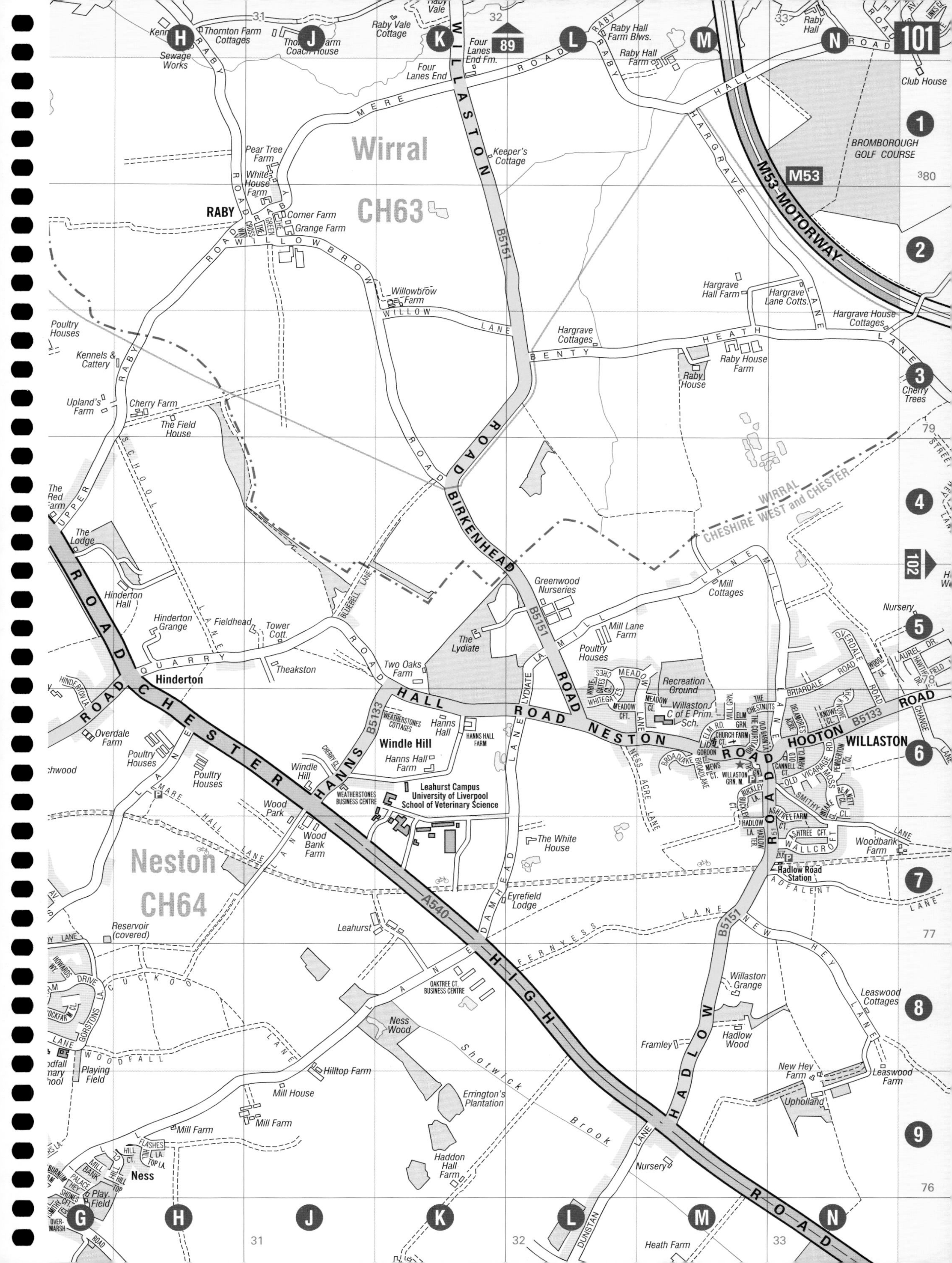

89
102
Wirral
CH63
Neston
CH64
RABY
Hinderton
Windle Hill
WILLASTON
Ness
M53
M53-MOTORWAY
BROMBOROUGH GOLF COURSE
Club House
Raby Vale Cottage
Raby Vale
Thornton Farm Cottages
Sewage Works
Thornton Farm Coach House
Four Lanes End Fm.
Four Lanes End
Raby Hall Farm Blws.
Raby Hall Farm
Raby Hall
Pear Tree Farm
White House Farm
Corner Farm
Grange Farm
Keeper's Cottage
Willowbrow Farm
Hargrave Hall Farm
Hargrave Lane Cotts.
Hargrave House Cottages
Hargrave Cottages
Raby House Farm
Raby House
Cherry Trees
Poultry Houses
Kennels & Cattery
Upland's Farm
Cherry Farm
The Field House
The Red Farm
The Lodge
Hinderton Hall
Hinderton Grange
Fieldhead
Tower Cott.
Theakston
Greenwood Nurseries
Mill Cottages
Nursery
Mill Lane Farm
Poultry Houses
The Lydiate
Two Oaks Farm
Recreation Ground
Willaston C of E Prim. Sch.
Weatherstones Cottages
Hanns Hall
Hanns Hall Farm
Windle Hill
Leahurst Campus University of Liverpool School of Veterinary Science
Weatherstones Business Centre
Overdale Farm
Poultry Houses
Wood Park
Wood Bank Farm
The White House
Woodbank Farm
Hadlow Road Station
Eyrefield Lodge
Reservoir (covered)
Leahurst
Oaktree Ct. Business Centre
Willaston Grange
Leaswood Cottages
Ness Wood
Hadlow Wood
Framley
Playing Field
Hilltop Farm
Mill House
Mill Farm
Errington's Plantation
New Hey Farm
Leaswood Farm
Upholland
Haddon Hall Farm
Nursery
Play. Field
Heath Farm
Shotwick Brook
MERE ROAD
RABY ROAD
RABY HALL ROAD
HARGRAVE LANE
WILLASTON ROAD
B5151
WILLOW BROW
WILLOW LANE
BENTY HEATH LANE
BIRKENHEAD ROAD
UPPER RABY ROAD
SCHOOL LANE
QUARRY ROAD
BLUEBELL LANE
MILL LANE
LYDIATE LANE
HALL ROAD
NESTON ROAD
HOOTON ROAD
B5133
HANNS HALL ROAD
CHESTER HIGH ROAD
A540
MARE HALL LANE
DAMHEAD LANE
HADLOW ROAD
HADLOW LANE
FERNYESS LANE
NEW HEY LANE
ADFALENT LANE
CUCKOO LANE
WOODFALL LANE
DUNSTAN LANE
NESS ACRE LANE
WIRRAL
CHESHIRE WEST and CHESTER
Wood Lane
Hinderton Rd.
Overdale Rd.
Briardale Rd.
Laurel Dr.
Hawthorne Field Dr.
Exchange Rd.
Meadow Cres.
White Gates
Whitegates
Meadow Cl.
Meadow Cft.
Mill Grn.
Elm Grn.
The Chestnuts
The Court
Old Barn La.
Church Farm Ct.
Elm Rd.
Gordon Ct.
Library
Broadoake
Broad Lake
Mews Ct.
Willaston Grn. M.
Buckley La.
Buckley Ct.
Hadlow La.
Hadlow Ter.
Cannell Ct.
Old Vicarage Rd.
Smithy
Ashtree Farm Ct.
Ashtree Cft.
Wallcroft
Delamere
Acre
Knowle Cl.
Pemberton
Bennett Cl.
Weatherstones
Cherry Cl.
Howards Wy.
Drive
Gorstons La.
Ockfar
Cl.
Lane
Hill Ct.
Flashes
Top La.
Mill Bank
Palace Hey
Shones Cft.
Over Marsh
Road
G
H
J
K
L
M
N
1
2
3
4
5
6
7
8
9
31
32
33
380
79
78
77
76

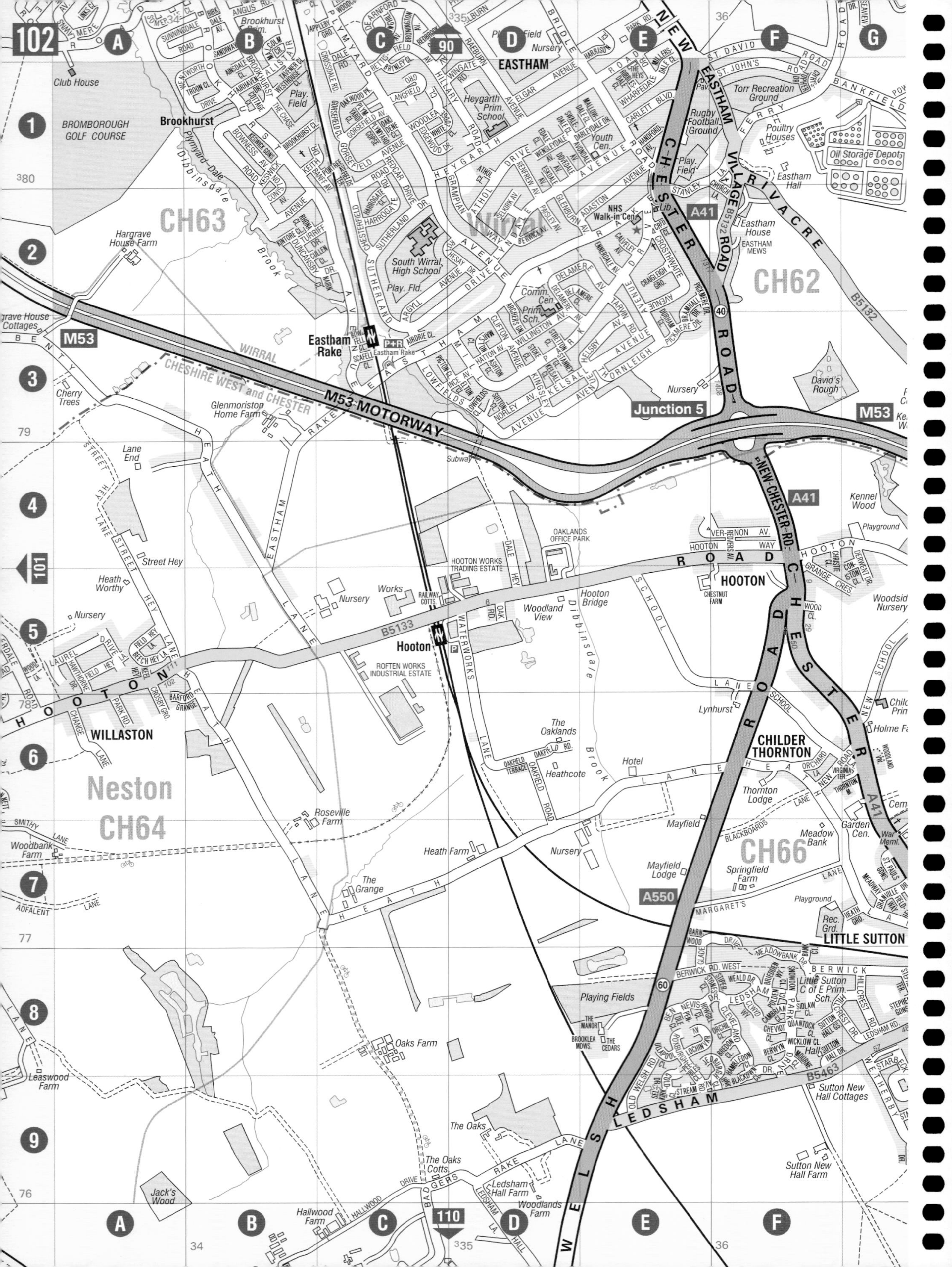

EASTHAM
Brookhurst
BROMBOROUGH GOLF COURSE
Club House
CH63
CH62
CH64
CH66
Neston
Wirral
Hargrave House Farm
M53
M53 MOTORWAY
WIRRAL
CHESHIRE WEST and CHESTER
Eastham Rake
South Wirral High School
Heygarth Prim. School
NHS Walk-in Cen.
Torr Recreation Ground
Rugby Football Ground
Oil Storage Depot
Poultry Houses
Eastham Hall
Eastham House
EASTHAM MEWS
NEW CHESTER ROAD
A41
B5132
B5133
A550
B5463
Junction 5
David's Rough
Kennel Wood
Cherry Trees
Glenmoriston Home Farm
Lane End
Street Hey
Heath Worthy
HOOTON
Hooton
HOOTON WORKS TRADING ESTATE
OAKLANDS OFFICE PARK
ROFTEN WORKS INDUSTRIAL ESTATE
Woodland View
Hooton Bridge
CHESTNUT FARM
WILLASTON
CHILDER THORNTON
Thornton Lodge
The Oaklands
Heathcote
Hotel
Lynhurst
Roseville Farm
Woodbank Farm
Heath Farm
The Grange
Mayfield
Mayfield Lodge
Springfield Farm
Meadow Bank
Garden Cen.
War Meml.
LITTLE SUTTON
Little Sutton C of E Prim. Sch.
Playing Fields
Oaks Farm
Leaswood Farm
The Oaks
The Oaks Cotts
Ledsham Hall Farm
Woodlands Farm
Hallwood Farm
Jack's Wood
Sutton New Hall Cottages
Sutton New Hall Farm
Dibbinsdale Brook
HEATH LANE
HOOTON ROAD
WELSH ROAD
LEDSHAM ROAD
BADGERS RAKE LANE
SCHOOL LANE
WATERWORKS LANE
OAKFIELD ROAD
EASTHAM RAKE
STREET HEY LANE

90
101
110

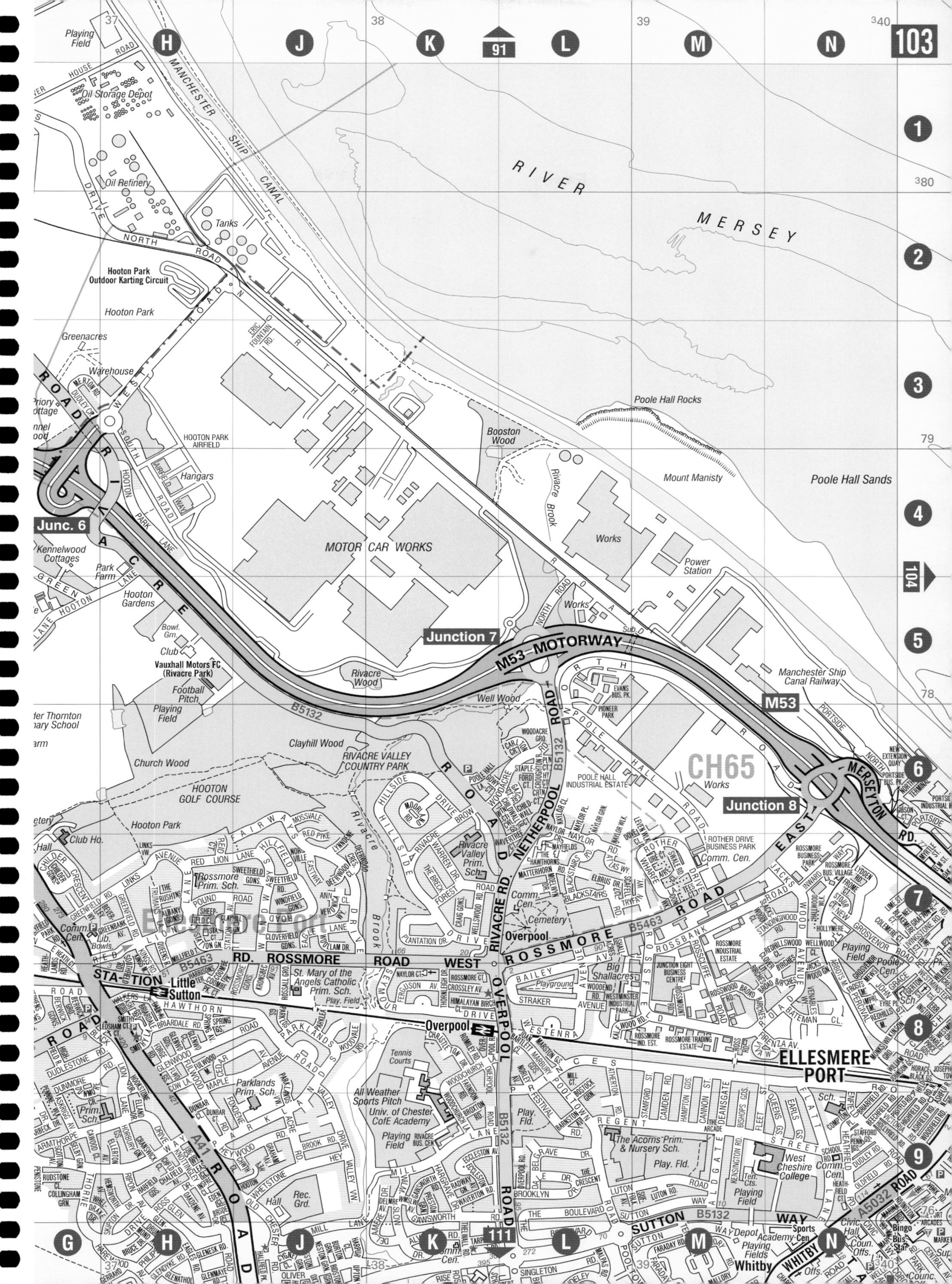

H
J
K
L
M
N
91
1
2
3
4
5
6
7
8
9
104
111
37
38
39
340
380
79
78
77
76
Playing Field
Oil Storage Depot
Oil Refinery
Tanks
MANCHESTER SHIP CANAL
RIVER MERSEY
NORTH ROAD
Hooton Park Outdoor Karting Circuit
Hooton Park
Greenacres
Warehouse
HOOTON PARK AIRFIELD
Hangars
Junc. 6
Kennelwood Cottages
Park Farm
Hooton Gardens
Bowl. Grn.
Club
Vauxhall Motors FC (Rivacre Park)
Football Pitch
Playing Field
Church Wood
HOOTON GOLF COURSE
MOTOR CAR WORKS
Booston Wood
Rivacre Brook
Poole Hall Rocks
Mount Manisty
Poole Hall Sands
Works
Power Station
Junction 7
M53 MOTORWAY
Rivacre Wood
Well Wood
Clayhill Wood
RIVACRE VALLEY COUNTRY PARK
Manchester Ship Canal Railway
M53
CH65
POOLE HALL INDUSTRIAL ESTATE
Junction 8
ROTHER DRIVE BUSINESS PARK
Comm. Cen.
ROSSMORE ROAD EAST
NETHERPOOL ROAD
RIVACRE ROAD
Rivacre Valley Prim. Sch.
Rossmore Prim. Sch.
Ellesmere Port
Cemetery
Overpool
ROSSMORE ROAD WEST
B5463
B5132
Little Sutton
St. Mary of the Angels Catholic Prim. Sch.
Play. Field
Big Shallacres
Playground
STRAKER AVENUE
WESTMINSTER INDUSTRIAL PARK
JUNCTION EIGHT BUSINESS CENTRE
ROSSMORE INDUSTRIAL ESTATE
ROSSMORE TRADING ESTATE
Overpool
OVERPOOL ROAD
Tennis Courts
All Weather Sports Pitch
Univ. of Chester CofE Academy
Playing Field
Parklands Prim. Sch.
ELLESMERE PORT
Play. Fld.
The Acorns Prim. & Nursery Sch.
West Cheshire College
Playing Field
Rec. Grd.
Hall
A41 ROAD
CHESTER ROAD
SUTTON WAY
B5132
Sports Cen.
Academy
Depot
Playing Fields
Whitby
WHITBY ROAD
A5032
Civic Hall
Coun. Offs.
Bingo
Bus Sta.
Grosvenor
Poole Cen.
Sch.
Playing Field
G

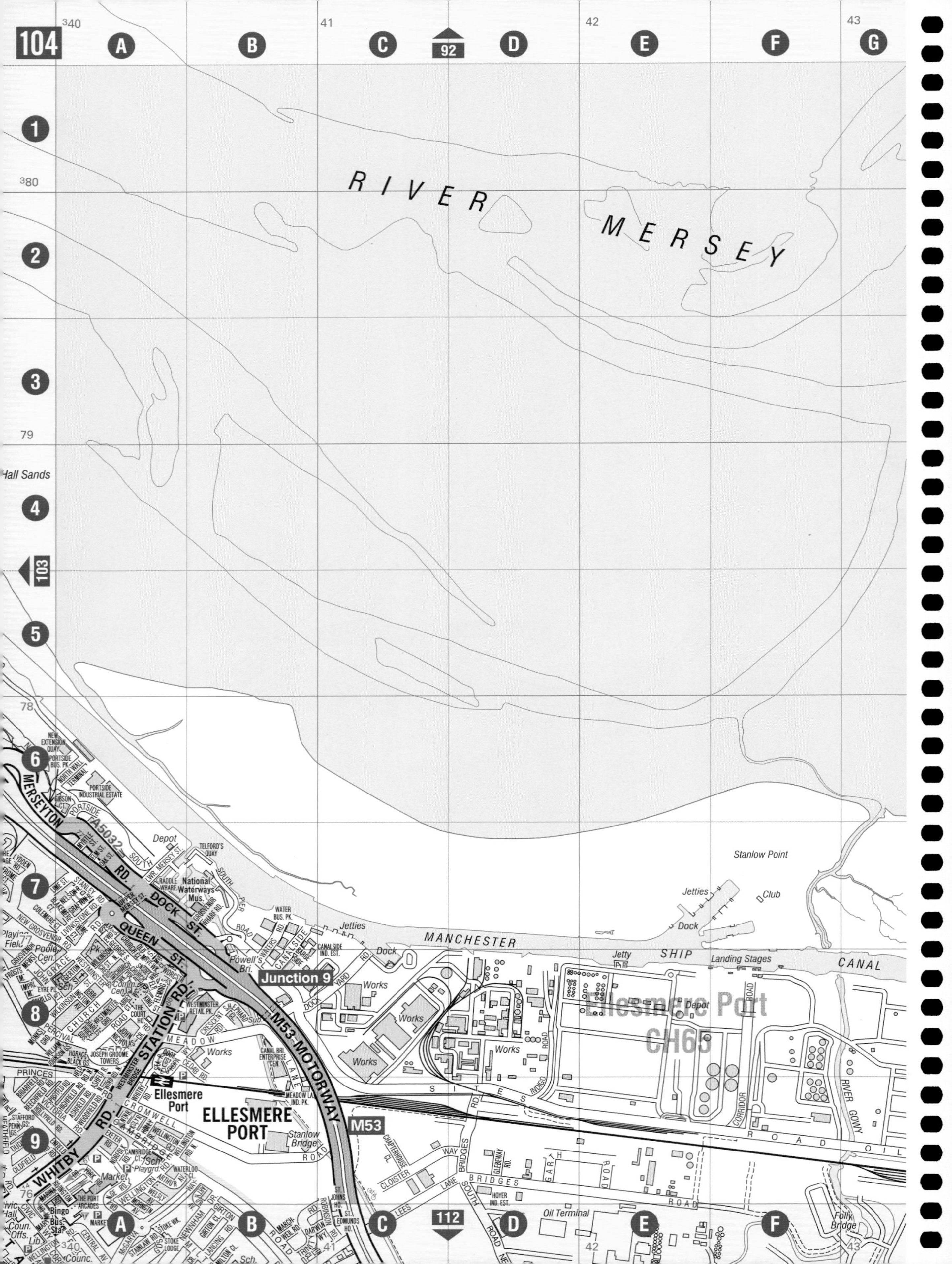

RIVER MERSEY
Hall Sands
MANCHESTER SHIP CANAL
Stanlow Point
Jetties
Club
Dock
Jetty
Landing Stages
Ellesmere Port CH65
ELLESMERE PORT
Ellesmere Port
Junction 9
M53-MOTORWAY
M53
National Waterways Mus.
Depot
Works
Oil Terminal
Folly Bridge
RIVER GOWY
Stanlow Bridge
MERSEYTON RD.
A5032
DOCK ST.
QUEEN ST.
STATION RD.
WHITBY RD.
MEADOW LANE
SITES RD.
OIL SITES ROAD
BRIDGES ROAD
CORRIDOR ROAD
PORTSIDE INDUSTRIAL ESTATE
TELFORD'S QUAY
WESTMINSTER RETAIL PK.
CANALSIDE IND. EST.
HOYER IND. EST.
Market
Bingo
Bus Sta.
92
103
112

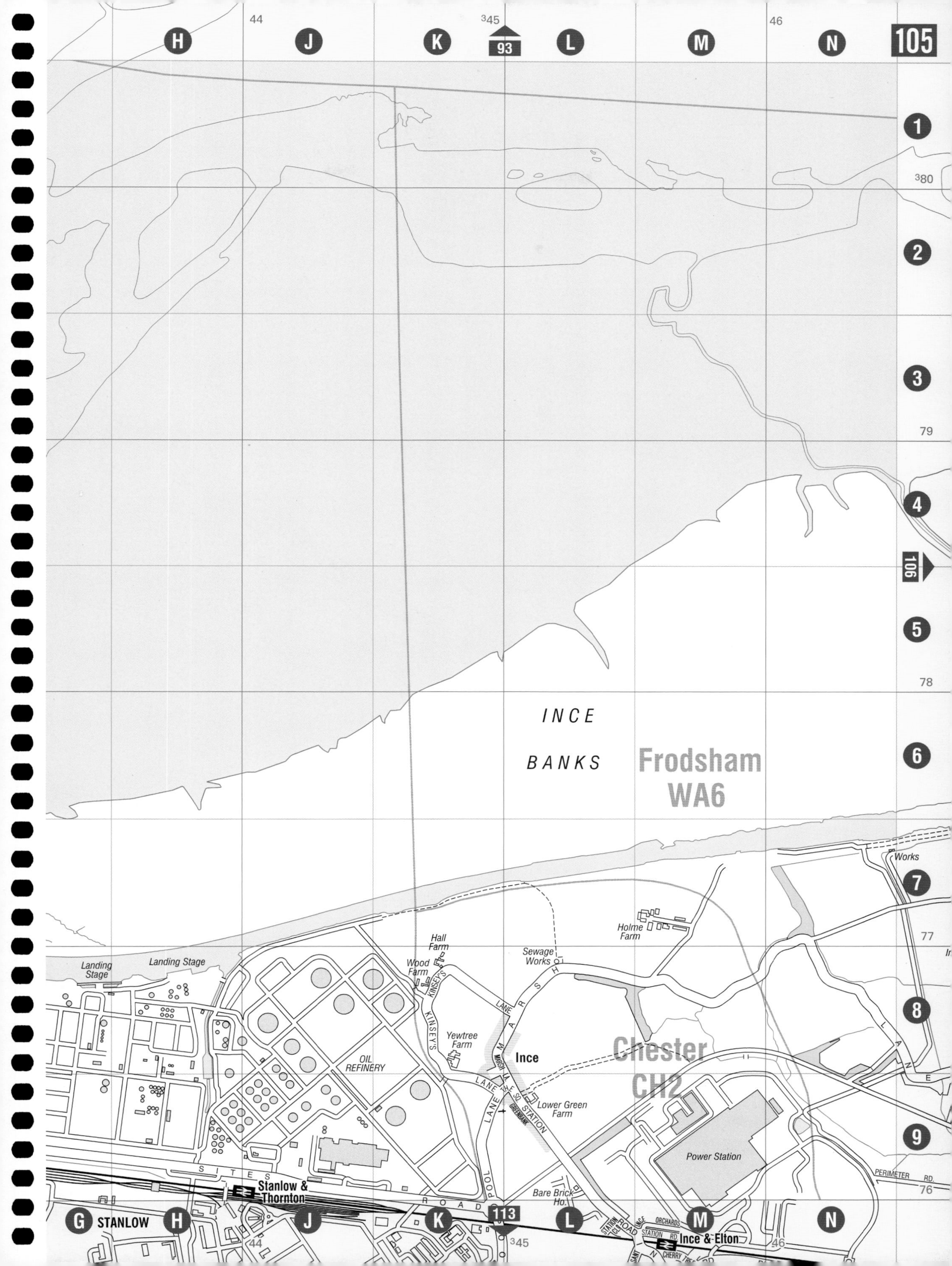

1

380

2

3

79

4

106

5

78

INCE

BANKS

Frodsham
WA6

6

Works

7

77

Hall
Farm
Wood
Farm

Sewage
Works

Holme
Farm

Landing
Stage

Landing Stage

Kinsey's

MARSH LANE

8

OIL
REFINERY

Yewtree
Farm

Ince

Chester
CH2

POOL LANE

STATION ROAD

Lower Green
Farm

Power Station

9

PERIMETER   RD.

76

SITES

Stanlow &
Thornton

ROAD

113

Bare Brick
Ho.

STATION ROAD
ORCHARDS

345

Ince & Elton

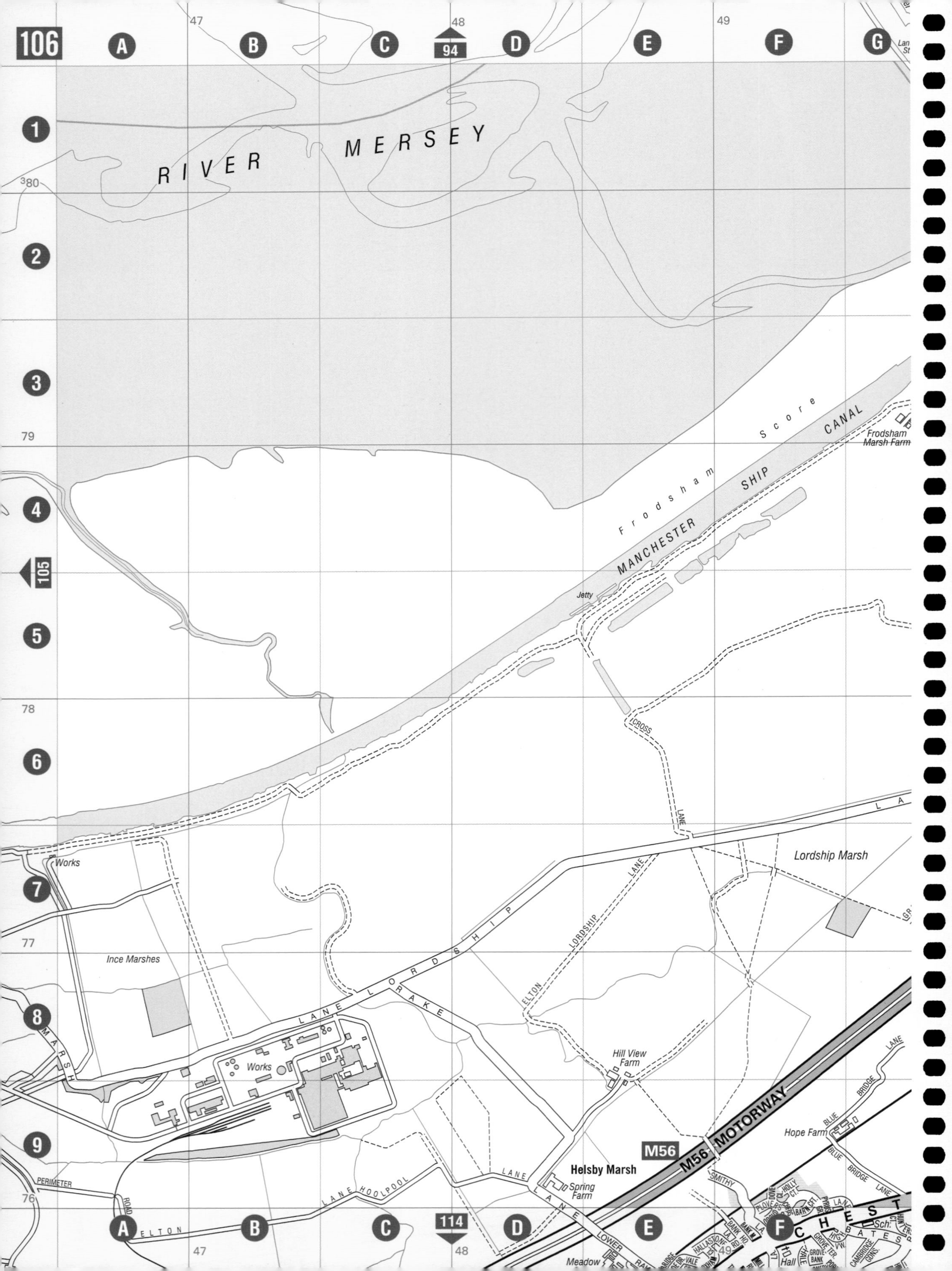

A B C 94 D E F G

1
2
3
4
105
5
6
7
8
9

RIVER MERSEY

³80

79

78

77

76

Frodsham Score

Frodsham
Marsh Farm

MANCHESTER SHIP CANAL

Jetty

CROSS

Lordship Marsh

Works

Ince Marshes

LORDSHIP LANE

DRAKE LANE

LORDSHIP LANE

ELTON LANE

Hill View
Farm

MARSH LANE

Works

PERIMETER ROAD

ELTON

HOOLPOOL LANE

LANE

Helsby Marsh

Spring
Farm

M56 M56 MOTORWAY

Hope Farm

BLUE BRIDGE LANE

SMITHY LANE

LOWER RAKE LANE

CHESTER

A B C 114 D E F

47 48 49

47 48 49

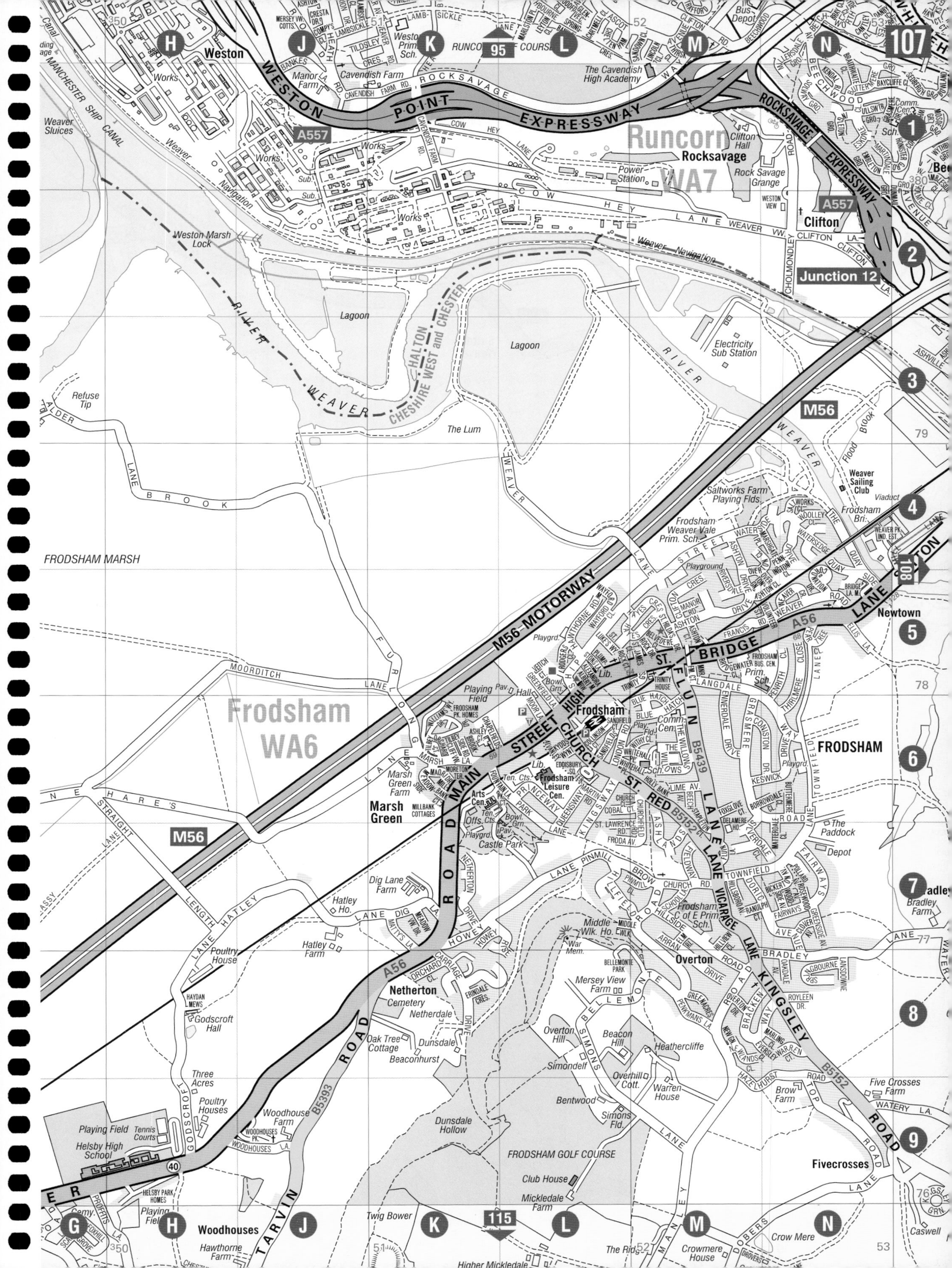

95
115
108
Weston
Runcorn
WA7
Rocksavage
Rock Savage Grange
Clifton
Clifton Hall
Power Station
The Cavendish High Academy
Cavendish Farm
Manor Farm
WESTON POINT EXPRESSWAY
ROCKSAVAGE EXPRESSWAY
A557
Junction 12
COW HEY LANE
WEAVER VW.
CLIFTON LA.
CHOLMONDLEY RD.
MANCHESTER SHIP CANAL
Weaver Navigation
Weaver Sluices
Weston Marsh Lock
RIVER WEAVER
Lagoon
HALTON
CHESHIRE WEST and CHESTER
The Lum
Refuse Tip
ALDER LANE
BROOK
Electricity Sub Station
M56
M56 MOTORWAY
Weaver Sailing Club
Flood Brook
Viaduct
Saltworks Farm Playing Flds.
Frodsham Weaver Vale Prim. Sch.
Frodsham Bri.
WEAVER PK. IND. EST.
Newtown
FRODSHAM MARSH
MOORDITCH LANE
FURLONG
HARE'S LANE
STRAIGHT LANE
LENGTH
Frodsham
WA6
FRODSHAM
Marsh Green
Marsh Green Farm
MILLBANK COTTAGES
Playing Field
BRIDGE LANE
A56
HIGH STREET
MAIN STREET
CHURCH STREET
FLUIN LANE
B5439
RED LANE
B5152
Frodsham Leisure Cen.
Castle Park
Arts Cen.
Comm. Cen.
Lib.
The Paddock
Depot
Bradley Farm
BRADLEY LANE
VICARAGE LANE
KINGSLEY ROAD
Overton
OVERTON DRIVE
Frodsham C of E Prim. Sch.
Middle Wlk. Ho.
War Mem.
BELLEMONTE PARK
Mersey View Farm
Overton Hill
Beacon Hill
Heathercliffe
Simondelf
Overhill Cott.
Warren House
Bentwood
Simons Fld.
Dunsdale Hollow
FRODSHAM GOLF COURSE
Club House
Mickledale Farm
Higher Mickledale
Dig Lane Farm
Hatley Ho.
Hatley Farm
HATLEY LANE
Poultry House
Netherton
Cemetery
Netherdale
Oak Tree Cottage
Dunsdale
Beaconhurst
HAYDAN MEWS
Godscroft Hall
Three Acres
Poultry Houses
GODSCROFT LANE
Woodhouse Farm
WOODHOUSES LA.
Woodhouses
Hawthorne Farm
Playing Field
Tennis Courts
Helsby High School
HELSBY PARK HOMES
Cemy.
TARVIN ROAD
B5393
Twig Bower
The Ridge
Crowmere House
Crow Mere
Caswell
Fivecrosses
Five Crosses Farm
Brow Farm
WATERY LA.
HAZELHURST ROAD
MANLEY LANE
350
51
52
53
76
77
78
79
380
1
2
3
4
5
6
7
8
9
G
H
J
K
L
M
N

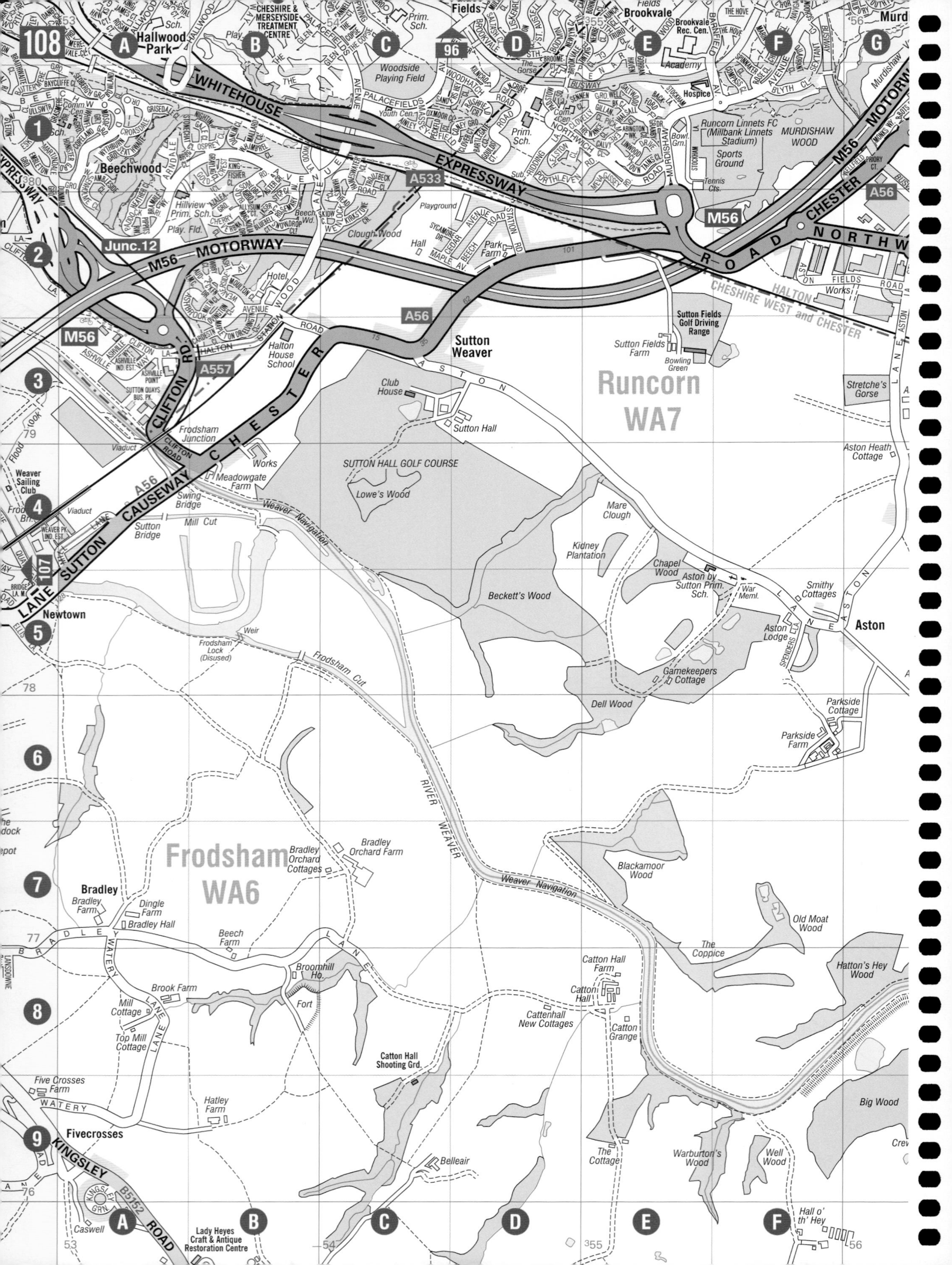
Hallwood Park
CHESHIRE & MERSEYSIDE TREATMENT CENTRE
Prim. Sch.
96
Fields
Brookvale
Brookvale Rec. Cen.
Academy
Hospice
Murdishaw
WHITEHOUSE
EXPRESSWAY
Woodside Playing Field
Youth Cen.
The Gorse
Com. Cen.
Prim. Sch.
Runcorn Linnets FC (Millbank Linnets Stadium)
MURDISHAW WOOD
Sports Ground
Tennis Cts.
Bowl. Grn.
Beechwood
Hillview Prim. Sch.
Play. Fld.
Clough Wood
Playground
A533
M56
Junc.12
M56 MOTORWAY
CHESTER ROAD
NORTHWICH
A56
Hall
Park Farm
Hotel
ASTON FIELDS ROAD
Works
HALTON
CHESHIRE WEST and CHESTER
Sutton Fields Golf Driving Range
Sutton Fields Farm
Bowling Green
Sutton Weaver
Halton House School
A557
CLIFTON RD.
ASHVILLE IND. EST.
SUTTON QUAYS BUS. PK.
Club House
Sutton Hall
ASTON
Runcorn
WA7
Stretche's Gorse
Frodsham Junction
Viaduct
Works
Meadowgate Farm
Weaver Sailing Club
SUTTON HALL GOLF COURSE
Lowe's Wood
Aston Heath Cottage
Swing Bridge
Mill Cut
Sutton Bridge
Weaver Navigation
SUTTON CAUSEWAY
SUTTON LANE
WEAVER PK. IND. EST.
107
Mare Clough
Kidney Plantation
Chapel Wood
Aston by Sutton Prim. Sch.
War Meml.
Smithy Cottages
Beckett's Wood
Newtown
Aston Lodge
ASTON LANE
Aston
Weir
Frodsham Lock (Disused)
Frodsham Cut
Gamekeepers Cottage
Dell Wood
Parkside Cottage
Parkside Farm
RIVER WEAVER
Frodsham
WA6
Bradley Orchard Cottages
Bradley Orchard Farm
Blackamoor Wood
Bradley
Bradley Farm
Dingle Farm
Bradley Hall
Weaver Navigation
Old Moat Wood
Beech Farm
BRADLEY LANE
WATERY LANE
The Coppice
Hatton's Hey Wood
Catton Hall Farm
Broomhill Ho.
Brook Farm
Fort
Catton Hall
Mill Cottage
Cattenhall New Cottages
Catton Grange
Top Mill Cottage
Catton Hall Shooting Grd.
Five Crosses Farm
WATERY LANE
Hatley Farm
Big Wood
Fivecrosses
KINGSLEY ROAD
B5152
The Cottage
Warburton's Wood
Well Wood
Belleair
KINGSLEY GRN.
Caswell
Lady Heyes Craft & Antique Restoration Centre
Hall o' th' Hey
A B C D E F G
1 2 3 4 5 6 7 8 9
53 54 355 56
380 79 78 77 76

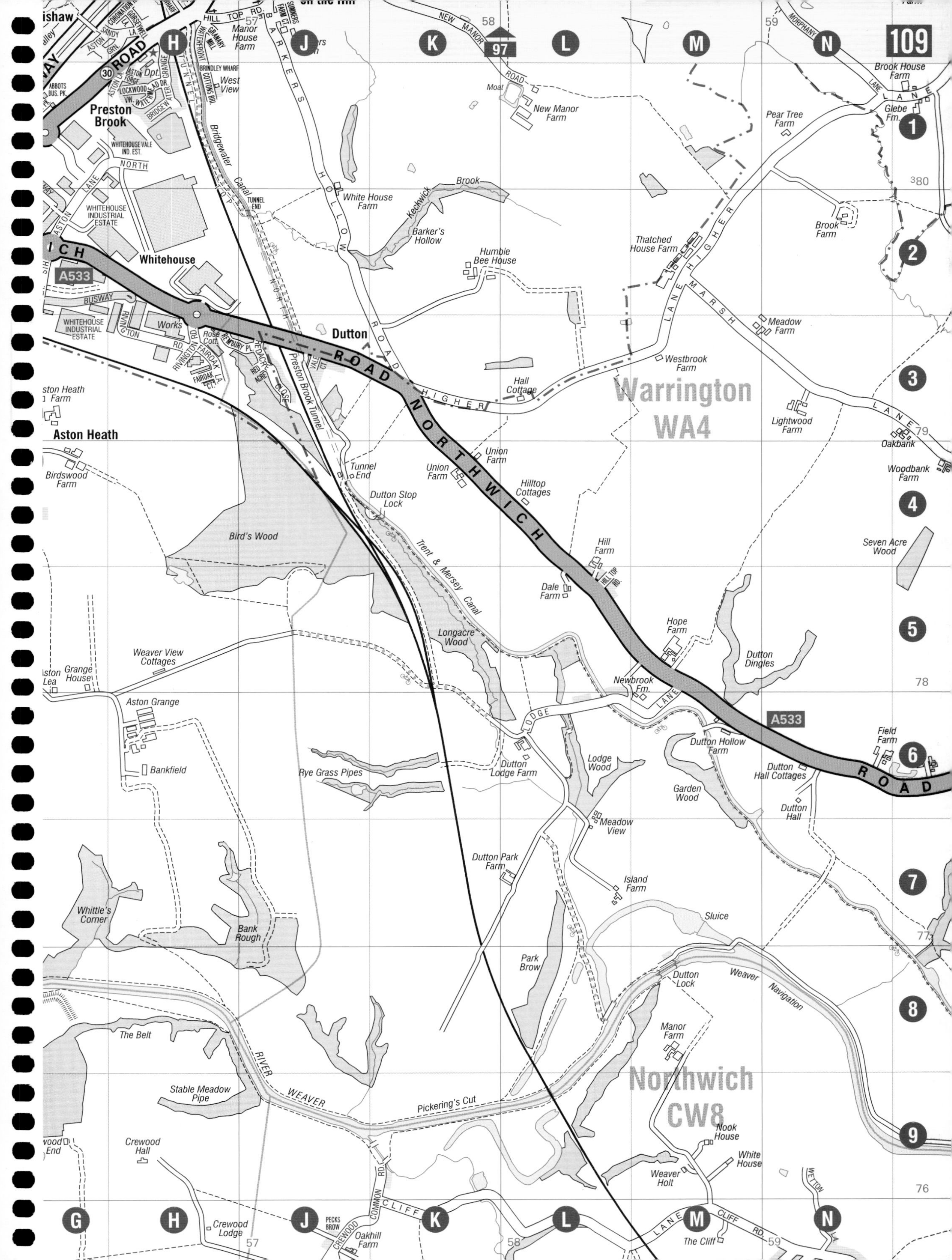

Preston Brook
Whitehouse
WHITEHOUSE INDUSTRIAL ESTATE
WHITEHOUSE VALE IND. EST.
A533
Dutton
Aston Heath
Birdswood Farm
Bird's Wood
Manor House Farm
West View
Bridgewater Canal
TUNNEL END
White House Farm
Keckwick Brook
Barker's Hollow
Humble Bee House
New Manor Farm
Moat
Brook House Farm
Glebe Fm.
Pear Tree Farm
Brook Farm
Thatched House Farm
Meadow Farm
Westbrook Farm
Hall Cottage
Warrington WA4
Lightwood Farm
Oakbank
Woodbank Farm
Union Farm
Hilltop Cottages
Tunnel End
Dutton Stop Lock
Preston Brook Tunnel
Trent & Mersey Canal
Hill Farm
Dale Farm
Seven Acre Wood
Longacre Wood
Hope Farm
Dutton Dingles
Newbrook Fm.
NORTHWICH ROAD
HIGHER ROAD
HOLLOW ROAD
LODGE LANE
HIGHER LANE
MARSH LANE
Weaver View Cottages
Aston Lea
Grange House
Aston Grange
Bankfield
Rye Grass Pipes
Dutton Lodge Farm
Lodge Wood
Dutton Hollow Farm
Field Farm
Dutton Hall Cottages
Garden Wood
Dutton Hall
Meadow View
Dutton Park Farm
Island Farm
Whittle's Corner
Bank Rough
Sluice
Park Brow
Dutton Lock
Weaver Navigation
The Belt
Stable Meadow Pipe
RIVER WEAVER
Pickering's Cut
Manor Farm
Northwich CW8
Nook House
White House
Weaver Holt
Crewood Hall
Crewood Lodge
Oakhill Farm
The Cliff
CLIFF LANE
CLIFF RD.
COMMON RD.
CREWOOD COMMON
WETTON LA.
97
G H J K L M N
1 2 3 4 5 6 7 8 9
57 58 59
76 77 78 79 80

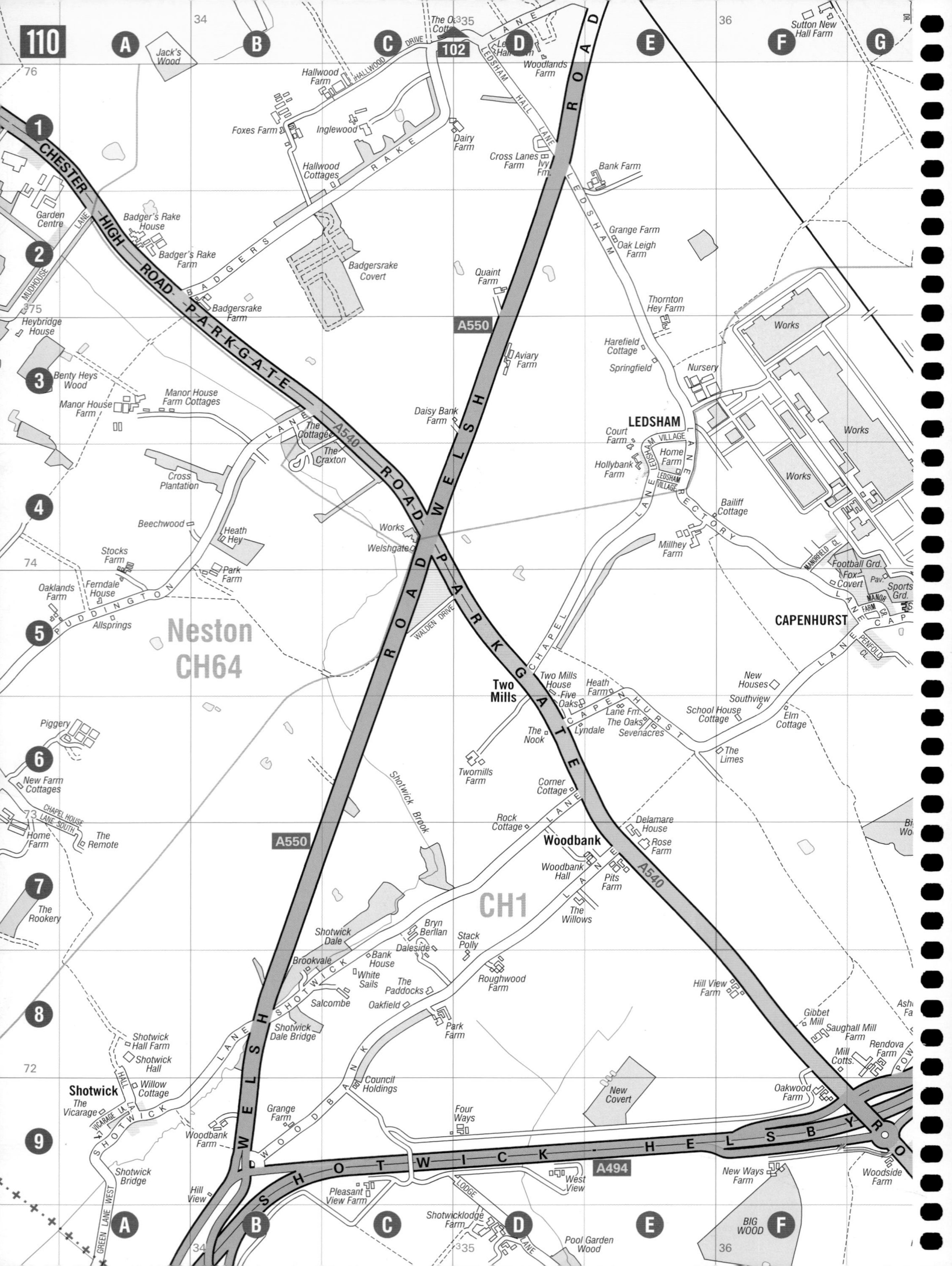

Jack's Wood
Hallwood Farm
Foxes Farm
Inglewood
Dairy Farm
Hallwood Cottages
Cross Lanes Farm
Ivy Fm.
Bank Farm
Woodlands Farm
Sutton New Hall Farm
102
CHESTER HIGH ROAD
PARKGATE ROAD
WELSH ROAD
Garden Centre
Badger's Rake House
Badger's Rake Farm
Badgersrake Covert
Badgersrake Farm
Grange Farm
Oak Leigh Farm
Quaint Farm
Thornton Hey Farm
Heybridge House
A550
Works
Benty Heys Wood
Aviary Farm
Harefield Cottage
Springfield
Nursery
Manor House Farm Cottages
Manor House Farm
Daisy Bank Farm
LEDSHAM
The Cottage
The Craxton
A540
Court Farm
Home Farm
Hollybank Farm
Cross Plantation
Beechwood
Heath Hey
Works
Welshgate
Bailiff Cottage
Millhey Farm
Stocks Farm
Park Farm
Football Grd.
Fox Covert
Sports Grd.
Oaklands Farm
Ferndale House
Allsprings
Neston CH64
WALDEN DRIVE
CAPENHURST
Two Mills
Two Mills House
Five Oaks
Heath Farm
Lane Fm.
The Oaks
Sevenacres
Lyndale
The Nook
New Houses
Southview
School House Cottage
Elm Cottage
The Limes
Piggery
New Farm Cottages
Twomills Farm
Shotwick Brook
Corner Cottage
Rock Cottage
Home Farm
The Remote
Woodbank
Delamare House
Rose Farm
Woodbank Hall
Pits Farm
The Rookery
CH1
The Willows
Shotwick Dale
Bryn Berllan
Stack Polly
Brookvale
Bank House
Daleside
White Sails
The Paddocks
Roughwood Farm
Hill View Farm
Salcombe
Oakfield
Park Farm
Shotwick Dale Bridge
Gibbet Mill
Saughall Mill Farm
Mill Cotts.
Rendova Farm
Shotwick Hall Farm
Shotwick Hall
Shotwick
Willow Cottage
The Vicarage
Council Holdings
New Covert
Oakwood Farm
Grange Farm
Four Ways
Woodbank Farm
SHOTWICK
A494
HELSBY ROAD
Shotwick Bridge
Hill View
Pleasant View Farm
West View
New Ways Farm
Woodside Farm
Shotwicklodge Farm
Pool Garden Wood
BIG WOOD

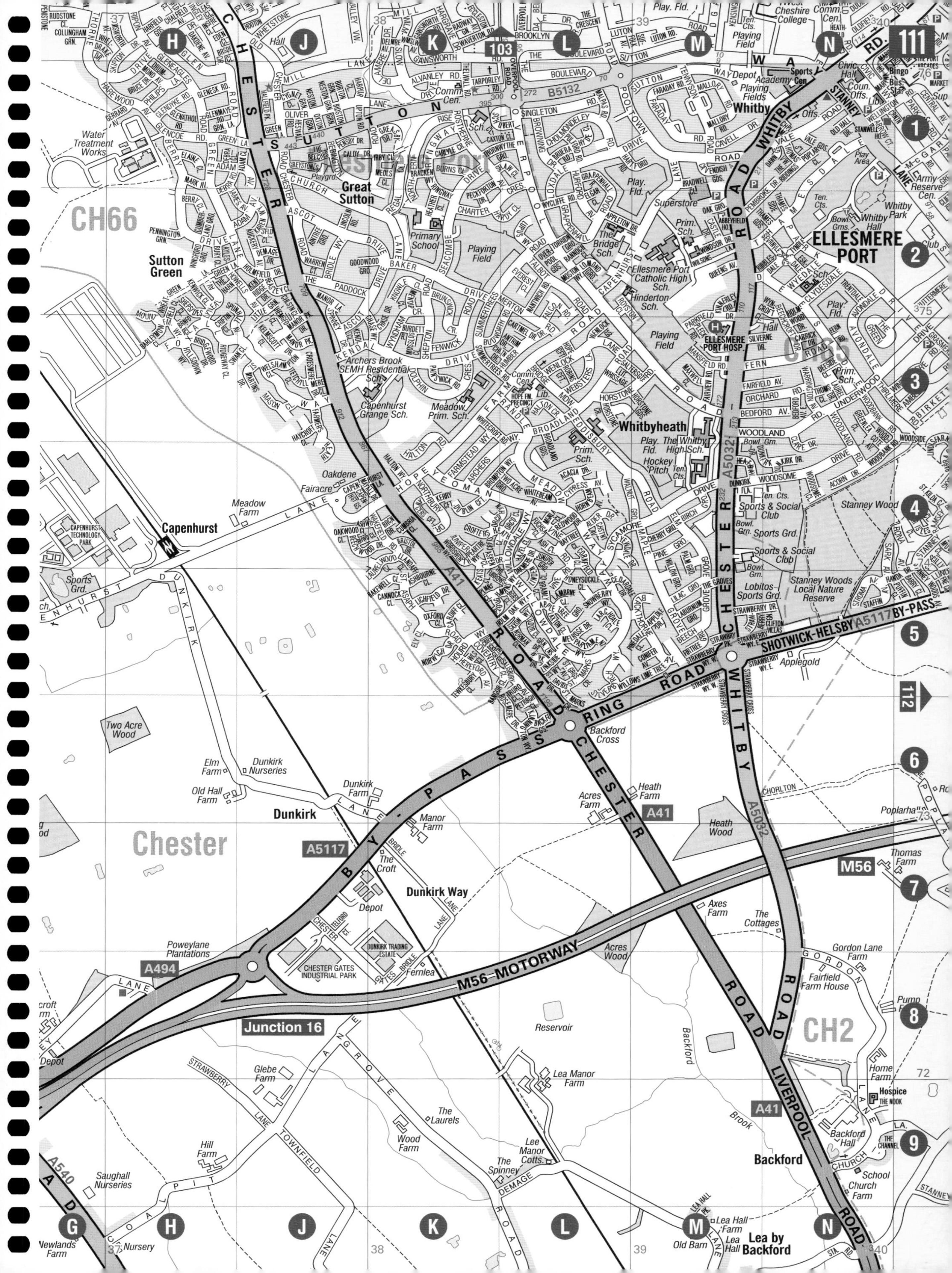

ELLESMERE PORT
Great Sutton
Sutton Green
Whitby
Whitbyheath
Capenhurst
Dunkirk
Chester
Backford
Lea by Backford
CH66
CH65
CH2
Backford Cross
Heath Wood
Stanney Wood
Stanney Woods Local Nature Reserve
Two Acre Wood
Acres Wood
Poweylane Plantations
Junction 16
M56 MOTORWAY
CHESTER GATES INDUSTRIAL PARK
Dunkirk Way
Reservoir
Ellesmere Port Catholic High Sch.
Hinderton Sch.
Ellesmere Port Hosp.
Capenhurst Grange Sch.
Archers Brook SEMH Residential Sch.
Meadow Prim. Sch.
The Whitby High Sch.
The Bridge Sch.
West Cheshire College
Water Treatment Works
CAPENHURST TECHNOLOGY PARK
SUTTON WAY
CHESTER ROAD
WHITBY ROAD
RING ROAD
BY-PASS
SHOTWICK-HELSBY BY-PASS
LIVERPOOL ROAD
A41
A5117
A5032
A494
A540
M56
B5132
103
112
H J K L M N G
1 2 3 4 5 6 7 8 9
37 38 39 40
72 73 74 75 76

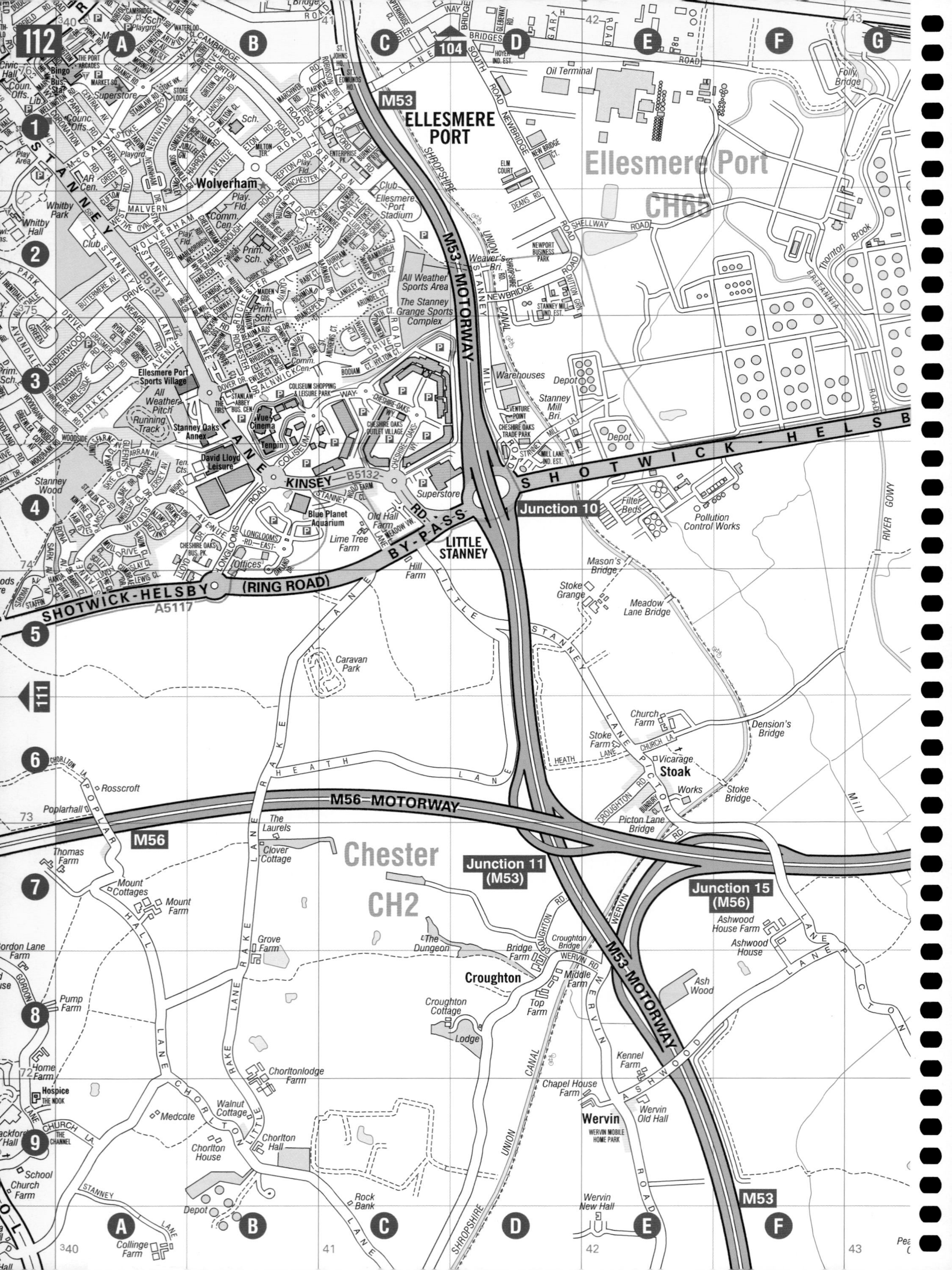
ELLESMERE PORT
Ellesmere Port
CH65
Wolverham
KINSEY
LITTLE STANNEY
Chester
CH2
Croughton
Stoak
Wervin
M53 MOTORWAY
M56 MOTORWAY
SHOTWICK-HELSBY BY-PASS (RING ROAD)
A5117
B5132
Junction 10
Junction 11 (M53)
Junction 15 (M56)
Ellesmere Port Sports Village
Cheshire Oaks Outlet Village
Blue Planet Aquarium
Oil Terminal
Pollution Control Works
SHROPSHIRE UNION CANAL
RIVER GOWY
104
111
A B C D E F G
1 2 3 4 5 6 7 8 9
340 41 42 43
76 75 74 73 72

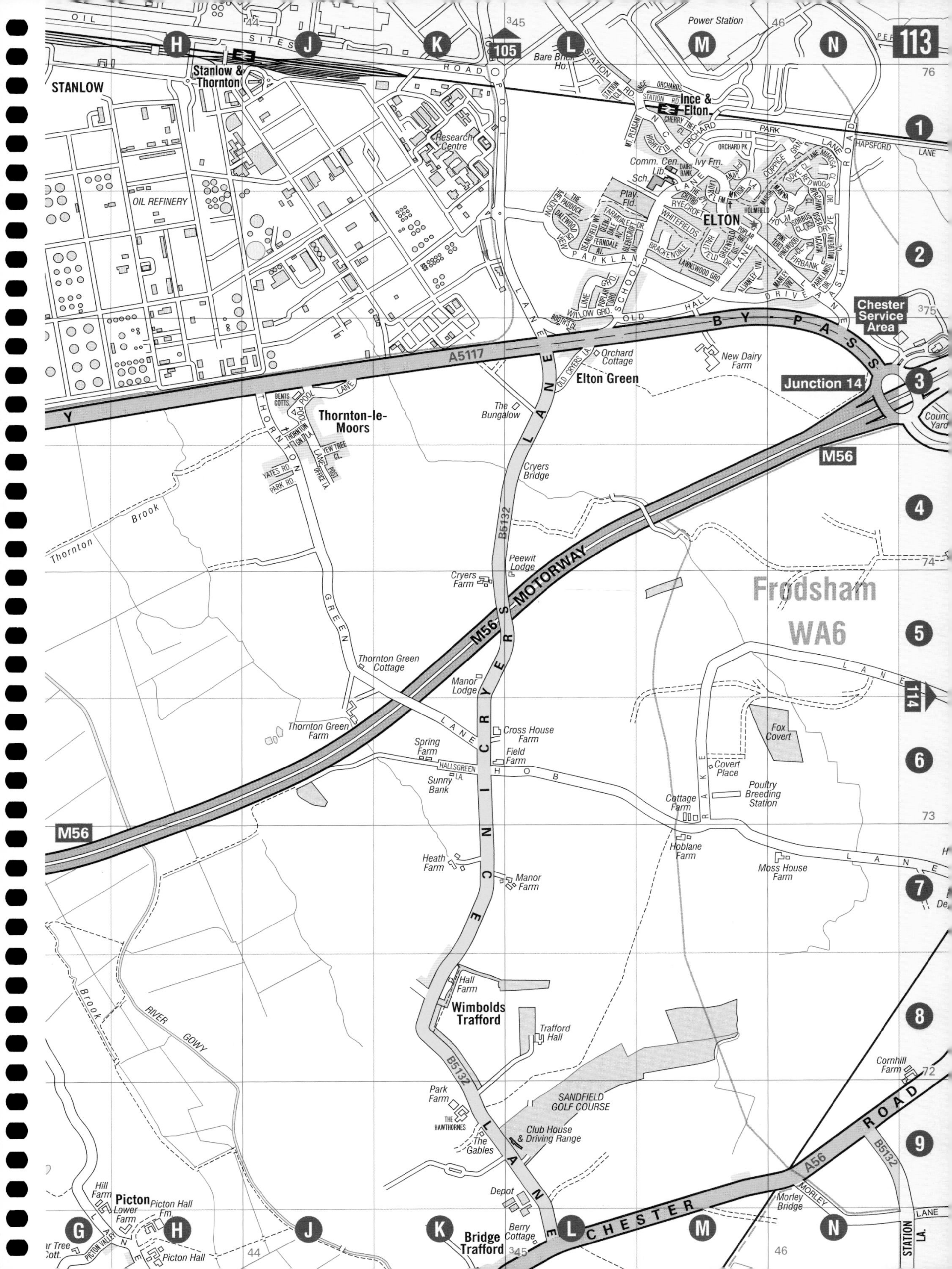
STANLOW
Stanlow & Thornton
OIL SITES ROAD
OIL REFINERY
Research Centre
Power Station
Bare Brick Ho.
Ince & Elton
ELTON
Comm. Cen.
Lib.
Sch.
Ivy Fm.
Play. Fld.
PARKLAND
SCHOOL LANE
OLD HALL DRIVE
ASH LANE
HAPSFORD LANE
PARK LANE
Chester Service Area
Junction 14
A5117
BY-PASS
Orchard Cottage
Elton Green
New Dairy Farm
Thornton-le-Moors
The Bungalow
Cryers Bridge
M56
Thornton Brook
Peewit Lodge
Cryers Farm
M56 MOTORWAY
Frodsham WA6
GREEN LANE
Thornton Green Cottage
Manor Lodge
Thornton Green Farm
Cross House Farm
Spring Farm
Field Farm
HALLSGREEN LA.
HOB LANE
Sunny Bank
Fox Covert
Covert Place
Poultry Breeding Station
Cottage Farm
RAKE LANE
Hoblane Farm
Moss House Farm
Heath Farm
Manor Farm
CRYERS LANE
INCE LANE
B5132
Hall Farm
Wimbolds Trafford
Trafford Hall
RIVER GOWY
Brook
Cornhill Farm
Park Farm
SANDFIELD GOLF COURSE
The Hawthornes
Club House & Driving Range
The Gables
Depot
Berry Cottage
Bridge Trafford
CHESTER ROAD
A56
Morley Bridge
MORLEY
STATION LA.
Hill Farm
Picton
Lower Farm
Picton Hall Fm.
Picton Hall
PICTON VALE
105
114
345
375
44
46
76
74
73
72
H J K L M N
G H J K L M N
1 2 3 4 5 6 7 8 9

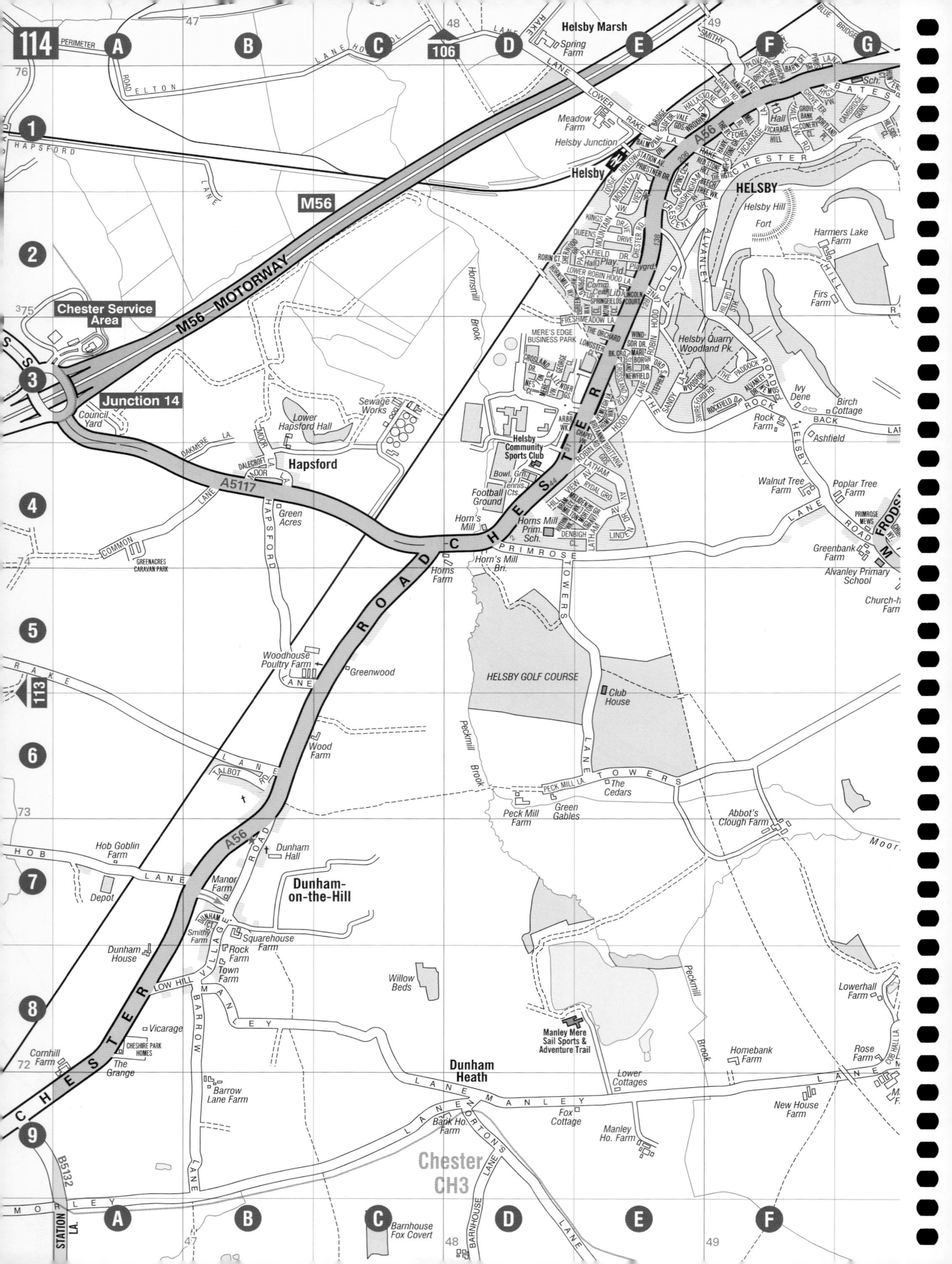

Helsby Marsh
Spring Farm
Meadow Farm
Helsby Junction
Helsby
HELSBY
Helsby Hill Fort
Harmers Lake Farm
Firs Farm
M56
M56 MOTORWAY
Chester Service Area
Junction 14
Council Yard
Lower Hapsford Hall
Sewage Works
Hapsford
A5117
Green Acres
GREENACRES CARAVAN PARK
MERE'S EDGE BUSINESS PARK
Helsby Quarry Woodland Pk.
Helsby Community Sports Club
Football Ground
Horn's Mill
Horns Mill Prim. Sch.
Horn's Mill Bri.
Horns Farm
Ivy Dene
Birch Cottage
Rock Farm
Ashfield
Walnut Tree Farm
Poplar Tree Farm
Greenbank Farm
Alvanley Primary School
CHESTER ROAD
A56
Hornsmill Brook
Woodhouse Poultry Farm
Greenwood
HELSBY GOLF COURSE
Club House
Wood Farm
Peckmill Brook
TOWERS LANE
The Cedars
Peck Mill Farm
Green Gables
Abbot's Clough Farm
Hob Goblin Farm
HOB LANE
Depot
Dunham Hall
Manor Farm
Dunham-on-the-Hill
Smithy Farm
Squarehouse Farm
Dunham House
Rock Farm
Town Farm
Willow Beds
Manley Mere Sail Sports & Adventure Trail
Lowerhall Farm
Vicarage
CHESHIRE PARK HOMES
Cornhill Farm
The Grange
Dunham Heath
Lower Cottages
Homebank Farm
Rose Farm
Barrow Lane Farm
MANLEY LANE
Fox Cottage
New House Farm
Bank Ho. Farm
Manley Ho. Farm
Chester CH3
B5132
MORLEY
STATION LA.
BARNHOUSE LANE
Barnhouse Fox Covert
106
113

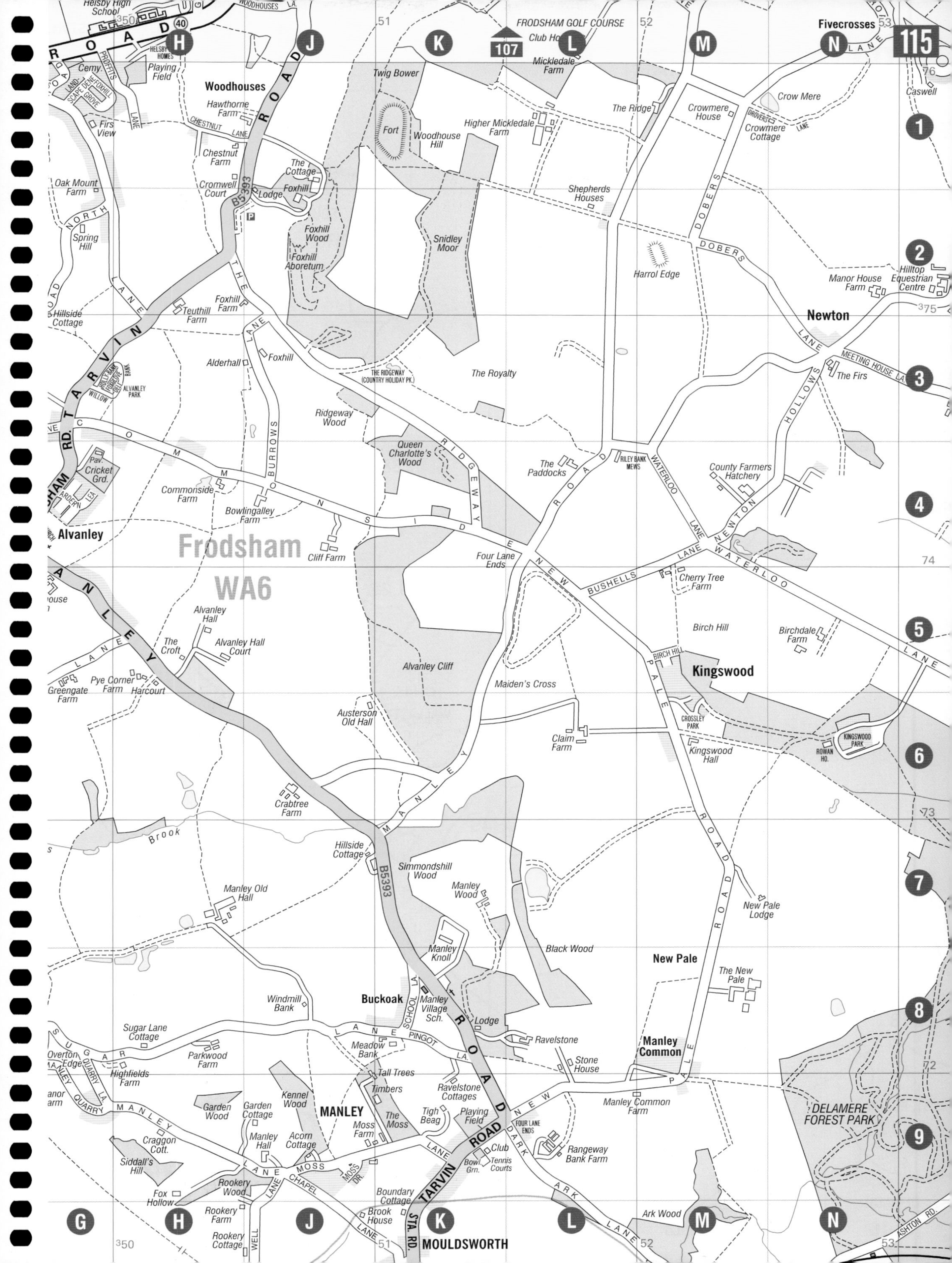
Helsby High School
Woodhouses
FRODSHAM GOLF COURSE
107
Fivecrosses
Cemy.
Playing Field
Woodhouses
Hawthorne Farm
Chestnut Lane
Firs View
Twig Bower
Mickledale Farm
Crow Mere
Caswell
Crowmere House
Crowmere Cottage
The Ridge
Higher Mickledale Farm
Fort
Woodhouse Hill
Chestnut Farm
The Cottage
Foxhill
Lodge
Cromwell Court
Oak Mount Farm
B5393
Shepherds Houses
Spring Hill
Foxhill Wood
Foxhill Aboretum
Snidley Moor
Harrol Edge
Dobers Lane
Manor House Farm
Hilltop Equestrian Centre
Hillside Cottage
Foxhill Farm
Teuthill Farm
Newton
Alderhall
Foxhill
The Ridgeway (Country Holiday Pk.)
The Royalty
Meeting House La.
The Firs
Tarvin Rd.
Alvanley Park
Ridgeway Wood
Queen Charlotte's Wood
Hollows
Commonside
Burrows Lane
Riley Bank Mews
The Paddocks
County Farmers Hatchery
Cricket Grd.
Pav.
Commonside Farm
Bowlingalley Farm
Alvanley
Frodsham
WA6
Cliff Farm
Four Lane Ends
Newton Lane
Waterloo Lane
Bushells Lane
Cherry Tree Farm
New Road
Alvanley Hall
Alvanley Hall Court
The Croft
Birch Hill
Birchdale Farm
Alvanley Cliff
Kingswood
Pye Corner Farm
Harcourt
Greengate Farm
Maiden's Cross
Austerson Old Hall
Claim Farm
Crossley Park
Kingswood Hall
Kingswood Park
Rowan Ho.
Manley Road
Crabtree Farm
Brook
Hillside Cottage
Simmondshill Wood
Manley Wood
Pale Road
New Pale Lodge
Manley Old Hall
Black Wood
Manley Knoll
New Pale
The New Pale
Windmill Bank
Buckoak
Manley Village Sch.
School La.
Lodge
Sugar Lane Cottage
Pingot Lane
Meadow Bank
Ravelstone
Manley Common
Stone House
Overton Edge
Parkwood Farm
Highfields Farm
Quarry La.
Tall Trees
Timbers
Ravelstone Cottages
Manley Common Farm
Kennel Wood
Garden Wood
Garden Cottage
Manley
The Moss
Tigh Beag
Playing Field
Four Lane Ends
Delamere Forest Park
Craggon Cott.
Manley Hall
Moss Farm
Acorn Cottage
Club
Tennis Courts
Bowl Grn.
Rangeway Bank Farm
Siddall's Hill
Moss Lane
Moss Dr.
Dark Lane
Chapel Lane
Rookery Wood
Fox Hollow
Rookery Farm
Rookery Cottage
Boundary Cottage
Brook House
Ark Wood
Ashton Rd.
Sta. Rd.
Mouldsworth
G
H
J
K
L
M
N
1
2
3
4
5
6
7
8
9
350
51
52
53
76
375
74
73
72

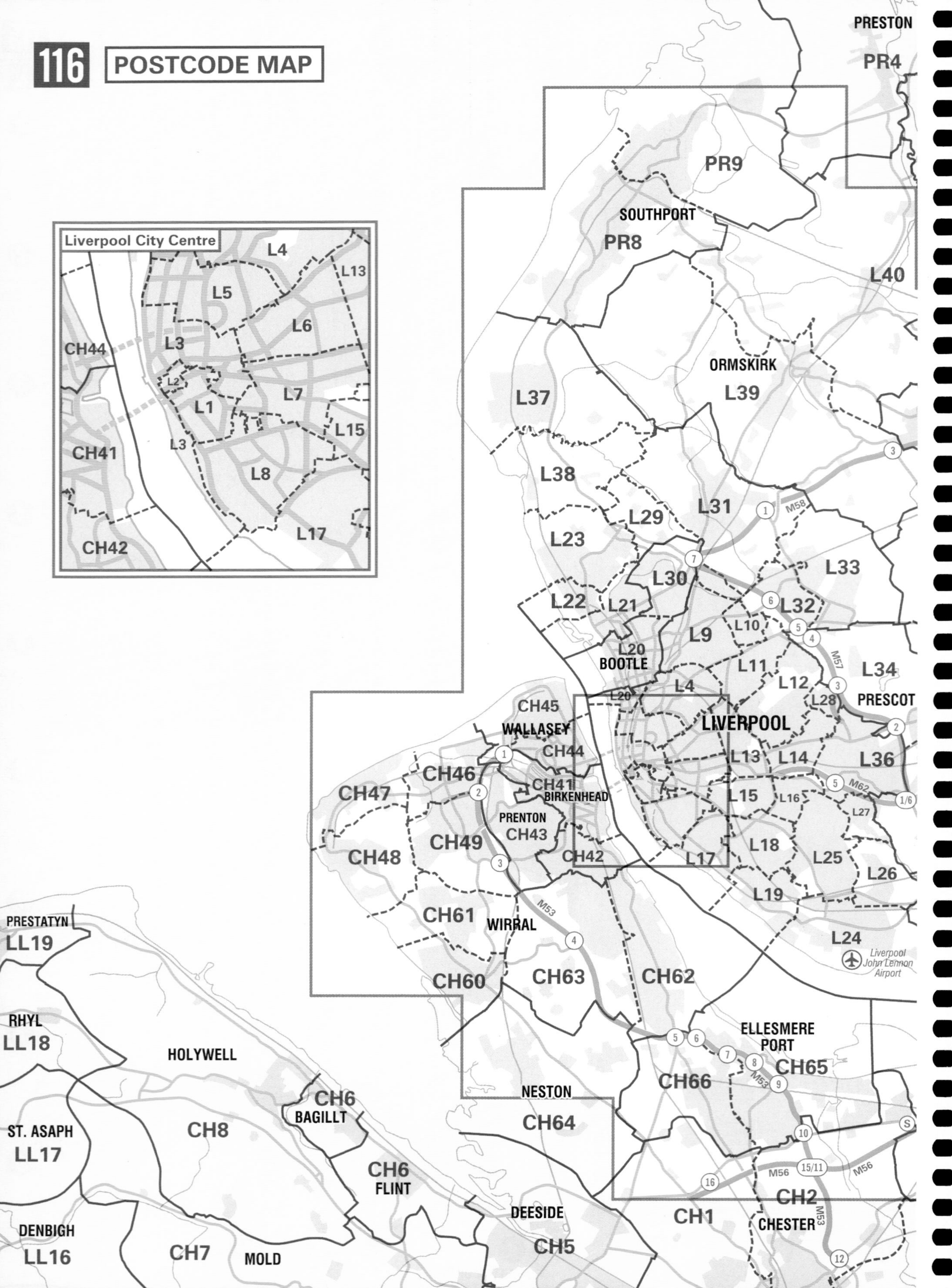

Liverpool City Centre

L4
L13
L5
L6
CH44
L3
L2
L7
L1
L15
CH41
L8
CH42
L17

PRESTON
PR4

PR9

SOUTHPORT
PR8

L40

ORMSKIRK
L39

L37

L38

L31

L29

L23

L30

L22
L21

L33

M58

L32

L9
L10

L20
BOOTLE

L11
L12
L28

L34

PRESCOT

CH45
WALLASEY
CH44

L20
L4

LIVERPOOL

M57

L36

CH46
CH47
CH41
BIRKENHEAD
PRENTON
CH43

L13
L14

L15
L16
L27

M62

CH49
CH48
CH42

L17

L18
L25
L26

L19

CH61
WIRRAL
M53

L24

Liverpool
John Lennon
Airport

CH60
CH63
CH62

PRESTATYN
LL19

RHYL
LL18

HOLYWELL

ELLESMERE
PORT
CH65

CH66
M53

ST. ASAPH
LL17

CH8

CH6
BAGILLT

NESTON

CH64

M56
15/11
M56

CH6
FLINT

CH2
CHESTER
M53

DENBIGH
LL16

CH7

MOLD

DEESIDE

CH5

CH1

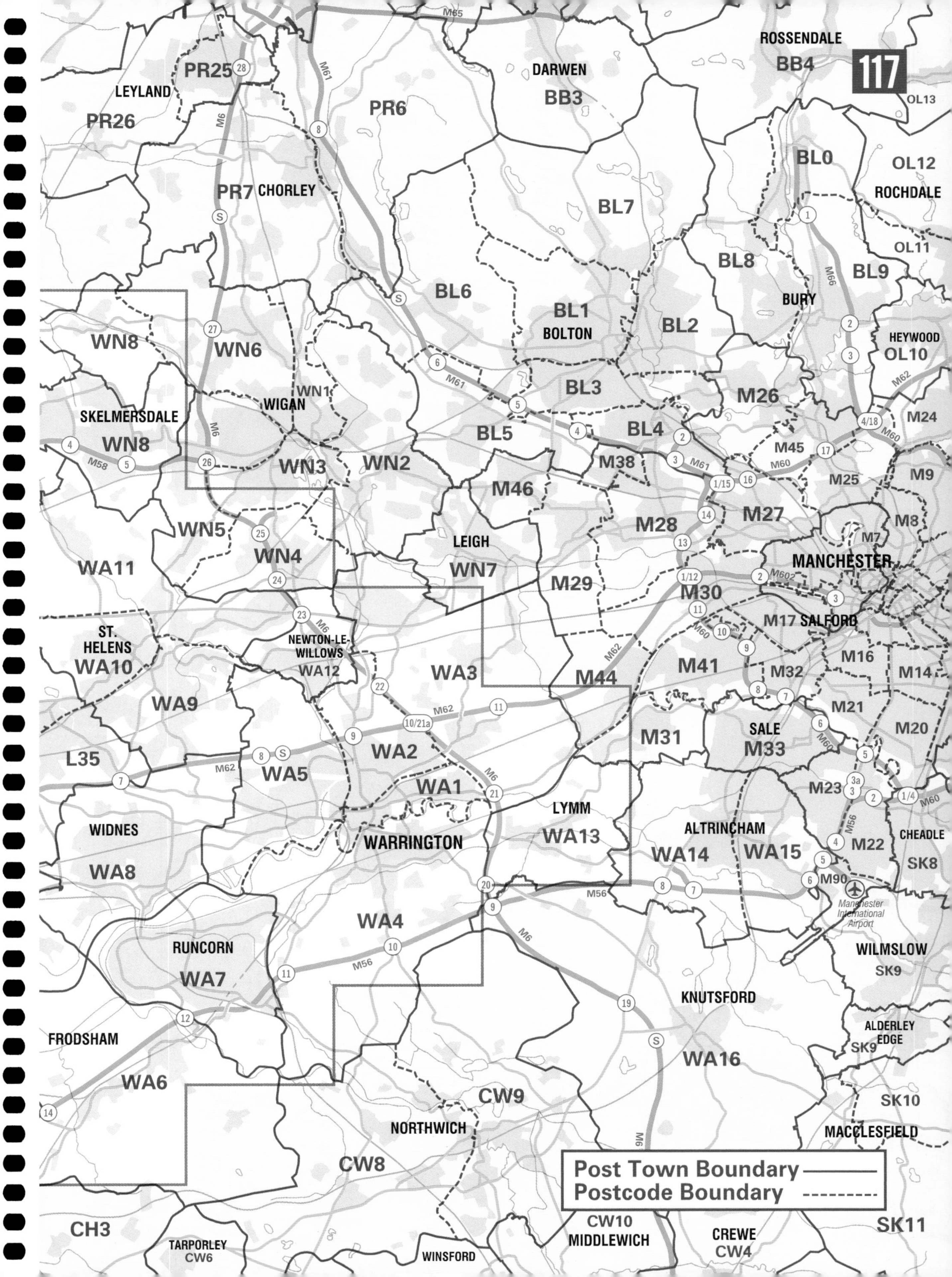
ROSSENDALE
BB4
DARWEN
BB3
PR25
LEYLAND
PR26
PR6
PR7 CHORLEY
BL0
OL12
ROCHDALE
OL13
BL7
OL11
BL8
BL9
BURY
BL6
BL1
BOLTON
BL2
HEYWOOD
OL10
WN8
WN6
WN1
WIGAN
SKELMERSDALE
WN8
WN3
WN2
BL3
BL5
BL4
M26
M24
M45
M25
M9
M38
M46
M28
M27
M8
M7
WN5
WN4
WA11
LEIGH
WN7
M29
MANCHESTER
M30
ST. HELENS
WA10
NEWTON-LE-WILLOWS
WA12
WA3
M17 SALFORD
M41
M16
M32
M14
M44
WA9
M21
M20
WA2
M31
SALE
M33
L35
WA5
WA1
LYMM
WA13
M23
WIDNES
WARRINGTON
ALTRINCHAM
WA14
WA15
M22
CHEADLE
SK8
WA8
Manchester International Airport
WA4
RUNCORN
WA7
WILMSLOW
SK9
KNUTSFORD
FRODSHAM
ALDERLEY EDGE
SK9
WA16
WA6
CW9
SK10
NORTHWICH
MACCLESFIELD
CW8
Post Town Boundary
Postcode Boundary
CH3
CW10
MIDDLEWICH
CREWE
CW4
SK11
TARPORLEY
CW6
WINSFORD

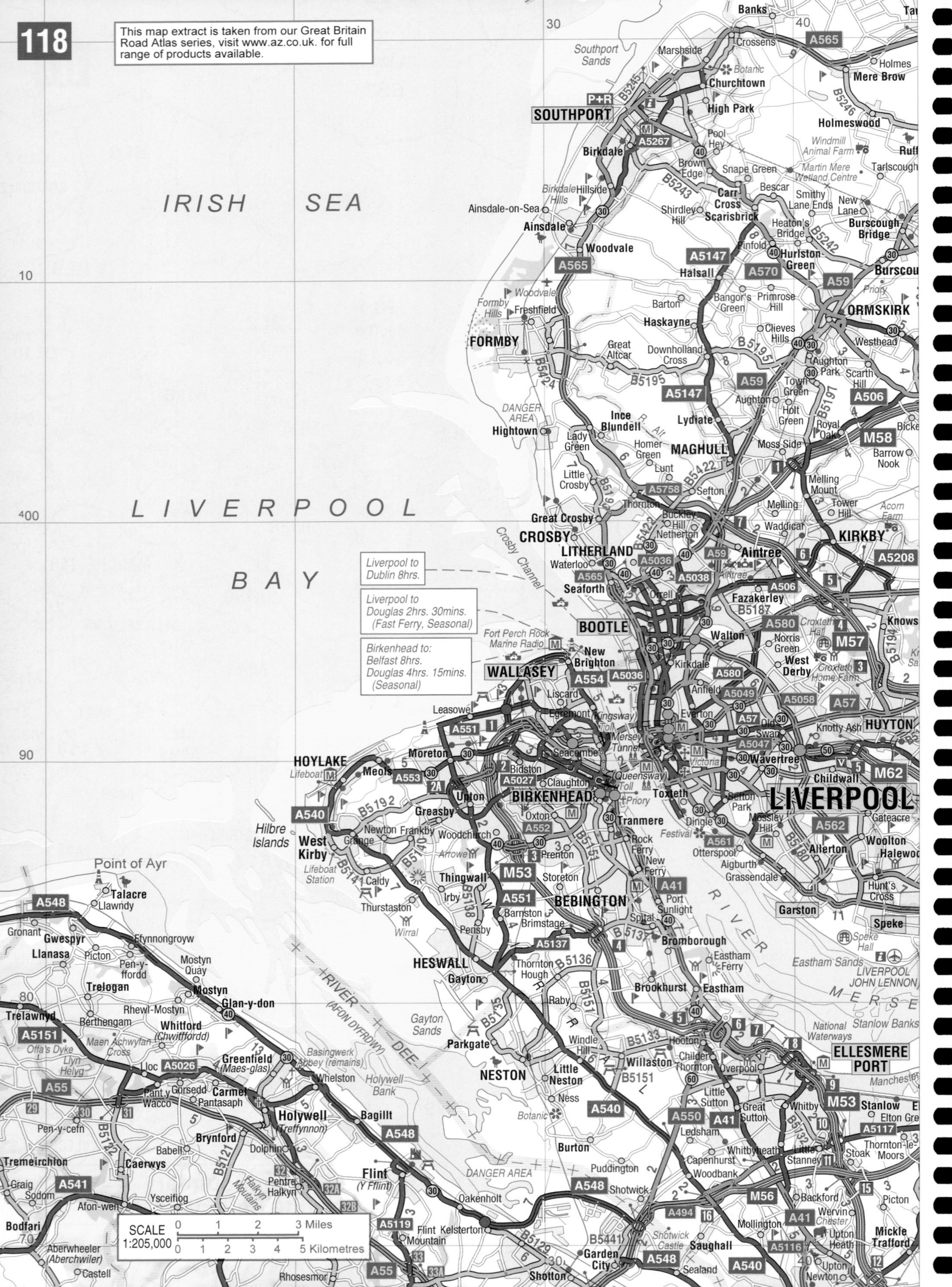
This map extract is taken from our Great Britain Road Atlas series, visit www.az.co.uk. for full range of products available.
IRISH SEA
LIVERPOOL BAY
Liverpool to Dublin 8hrs.
Liverpool to Douglas 2hrs. 30mins. (Fast Ferry, Seasonal)
Birkenhead to: Belfast 8hrs. Douglas 4hrs. 15mins. (Seasonal)
Southport Sands
SOUTHPORT
Banks
Crossens
Marshside
Churchtown
High Park
Mere Brow
Holmeswood
Birkdale
Ainsdale-on-Sea
Ainsdale
Woodvale
Halsall
Scarisbrick
Burscough Bridge
ORMSKIRK
Formby Hills
Freshfield
FORMBY
Haskayne
Great Altcar
Downholland Cross
Hightown
Ince Blundell
Lydiate
MAGHULL
Little Crosby
Great Crosby
CROSBY
LITHERLAND
Waterloo
Seaforth
BOOTLE
Aintree
KIRKBY
Fazakerley
Walton
Knowsley
WALLASEY
New Brighton
Liscard
Egremont
Leasowe
Moreton
HOYLAKE
Meols
BIRKENHEAD
Seacombe
Claughton
Oxton
Tranmere
Upton
Greasby
West Kirby
Hilbre Islands
Point of Ayr
Talacre
Caldy
Thingwall
Irby
Thurstaston
Pensby
BEBINGTON
Port Sunlight
Bromborough
Eastham
HESWALL
Gayton
Parkgate
NESTON
Little Neston
Willaston
Hooton
LIVERPOOL
Wavertree
Toxteth
Anfield
Everton
West Derby
HUYTON
Childwall
Allerton
Woolton
Garston
Speke
LIVERPOOL JOHN LENNON
ELLESMERE PORT
Stanlow Banks
RIVER MERSEY
RIVER DEE (AFON DYFRDWY)
Mostyn
Glan-y-don
Whitford (Chwitffordd)
Greenfield (Maes-glas)
Holywell (Treffynnon)
Bagillt
Flint (Y Fflint)
Oakenholt
Shotwick
Saughall
Garden City
Shotton
Gwespyr
Llanasa
Trelogan
Trelawnyd
Carmel
Brynford
Caerwys
Tremeirchion
Bodfari
A548
A55
A540
A41
A5117
M53
M56
M57
M58
M62
A59
A565
A5147
A570
A506
A580
A57
A562
A561
SCALE 1:205,000
0 1 2 3 Miles
0 1 2 3 4 5 Kilometres

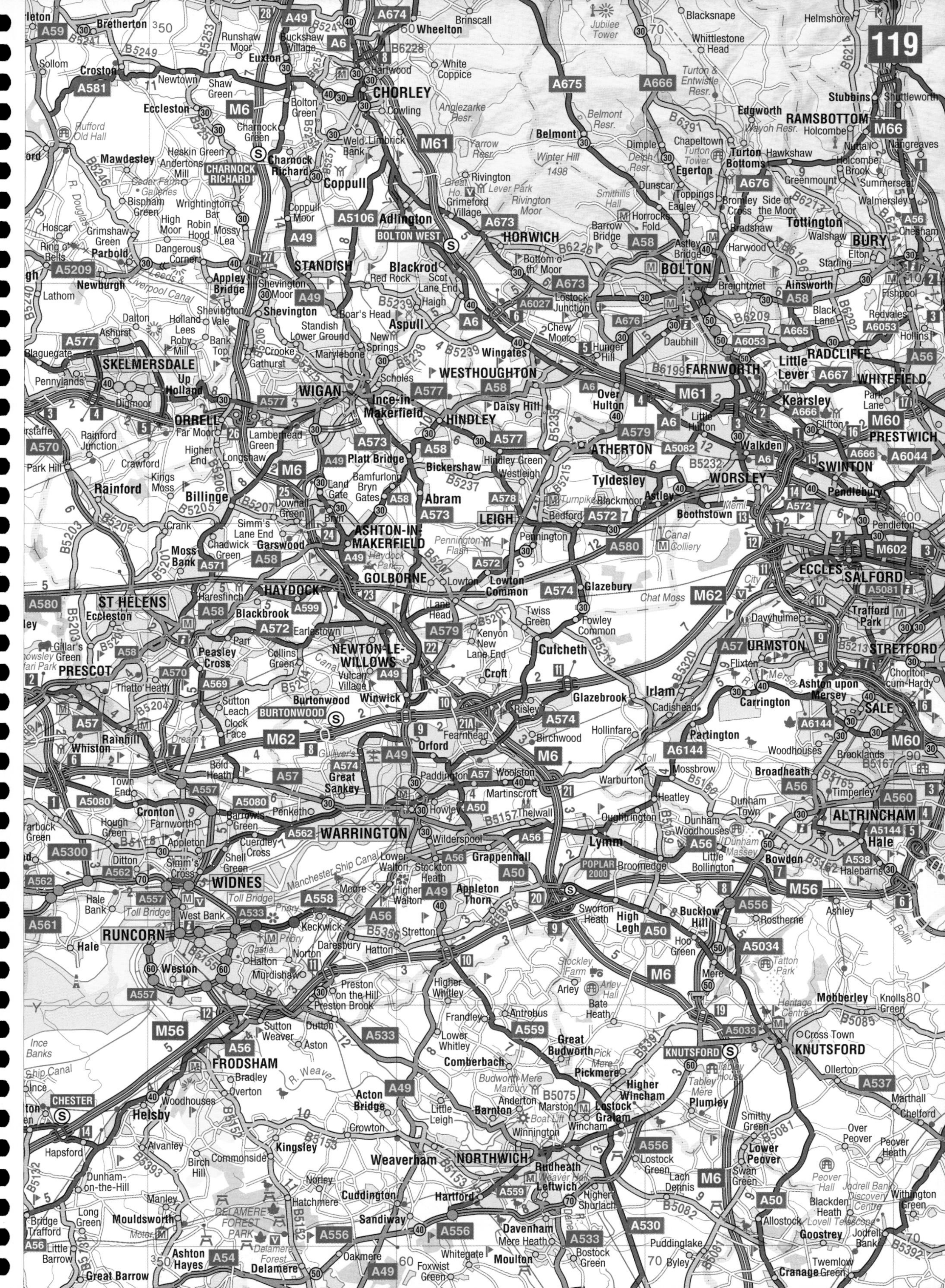

Bretherton
Wheelton
Brinscall
Jubilee Tower
Blacksnape
Helmshore
Whittlestone Head
Runshaw Moor
Buckshaw Village
Euxton
Hartwood
White Coppice
Sollom
Croston
Newtown
Shaw Green
CHORLEY
Cowling
Turton & Entwistle Resr.
Stubbins
Shuttleworth
Eccleston
Bolton Green
Charnock Green
Anglezarke Resr.
Belmont Resr.
Edgworth
RAMSBOTTOM
Wayoh Resr.
Holcombe
Rufford Old Hall
Weld Bank
Limbrick
Yarrow Resr.
Belmont
Dimple
Chapeltown
Turton Tower
Turton Bottoms
Hawkshaw
Nangreaves
Nuttall
Holcombe Brook
Mawdesley
Heskin Green
Andertons Mill
CHARNOCK RICHARD
Charnock Richard
Coppull
Winter Hill
1498
Delph Resr.
Egerton
Rivington
Lever Park
Greenmount
Summerseat
Cedar Farm Galleries
Bispham Green
Wrightington Bar
Coppull Moor
Great House
Grimeford Village
Rivington Moor
Smithills Hall
Dunscar
Toppings
Eagley
Bromley Cross
Side of the Moor
Walmersley
Hoscar
Grimshaw Green
High Moor
Robin Hood
Mossy Lea
Adlington
Horrocks Fold
Barrow Bridge
Tottington
Ring o' Bells
Parbold
Dangerous Corner
BOLTON WEST
HORWICH
Bradshaw
Walshaw
BURY
Chesham
Astley Bridge
Harwood
Elton
Newburgh
Appley Bridge
STANDISH
Blackrod
Bottom o' th' Moor
BOLTON
Starling
Lathom
Leeds & Liverpool Canal
Shevington Moor
Red Rock
Scot Lane End
Brightmet
Ainsworth
Fishpool
Shevington
Haigh
Lostock Junction
Dalton
Holland Lees
Shevington Vale
Boar's Head
Black Lane
Redvales
Ashurst
Standish Lower Ground
Aspull
Chew Moor
Daubhill
Hollins
Roby Mill
Bank Top
New Springs
Wingates
Hunger Hill
Blaguegate
Crooke
Marylebone
RADCLIFFE
Gathurst
Little Lever
SKELMERSDALE
WESTHOUGHTON
FARNWORTH
WHITEFIELD
Pennylands
Up Holland
Scholes
WIGAN
Over Hulton
Park Lane
Digmoor
Ince-in-Makerfield
Daisy Hill
Kearsley
ORRELL
HINDLEY
Little Hulton
Clifton
PRESTWICH
Far Moor
Lamberhead Green
Rainford Junction
ATHERTON
Walkden
SWINTON
Higher End
Platt Bridge
Bickershaw
Hindley Green
Westleigh
Park Hill
Crawford
Longshaw
Tyldesley
WORSLEY
Pendlebury
Kings Moss
Land Gate
Bamfurlong
Bryn Gates
Rainford
Abram
Turnpike
Blackmoor
Astley
Billinge
Downall Green
Bryn
LEIGH
Bedford
Boothstown
Pendleton
Crank
Simm's Lane End
ASHTON-IN-MAKERFIELD
Pennington
Pennington Flash
Canal Colliery
Chadwick Green
Garswood
Moss Bank
Haydock Park
ECCLES
SALFORD
Lowton
Lowton Common
Glazebury
City Airport
Harestinch
HAYDOCK
ST HELENS
GOLBORNE
Chat Moss
Eccleston
Blackbrook
Lane Head
Twiss Green
Fowley Common
Davyhulme
Trafford Park
Earlestown
Kenyon
New Lane End
Gillar's Green
Parr
Peasley Cross
Collins Green
NEWTON-LE-WILLOWS
Culcheth
URMSTON
STRETFORD
PRESCOT
Knowsley Safari Park
Flixton
Chorlton-cum-Hardy
Vulcan Village
Croft
Thatto Heath
Sutton Leach
Burtonwood
Winwick
Glazebrook
Irlam
Cadishead
Ashton upon Mersey
Carrington
BURTONWOOD
Risley
SALE
Clock Face
Rainhill
Fearnhead
Birchwood
Hollinfare
Partington
Whiston
Dream
Gulliver's World
Orford
Woodhouses
Brooklands
Bold Heath
Great Sankey
Toll
Mossbrow
Broadheath
Town End
Paddington
Woolston
Warburton
Timperley
Martinscroft
Heatley
Dunham Town
Cronton
Farnworth
Barrows Green
Penketh
Howley
Thelwall
Oughtrington
ALTRINCHAM
Hough Green
Dunham Woodhouses
Hale
Farbock Green
Appleton
Cuerdley Cross
WARRINGTON
Wilderspool
Lymm
Dunham Massey
Ditton
Shell Green
Grappenhall
Little Bollington
Bowdon
Simm's Cross
Lower Walton
Stockton Heath
POPLAR 2000
Broomedge
Halebarns
WIDNES
Manchester Ship Canal
Hale Bank
Toll Bridge
Moore
Higher Walton
Appleton Thorn
West Bank
Priory
Swineton Heath
High Legh
Bucklow Hill
Ashley
Rostherne
Keckwick
RUNCORN
Stretton
Daresbury
Hatton
Hale
Castle
Halton
Norton
Hoo Green
Tatton Park
Weston
Murdishaw
Stockley Farm
Mere
Preston on the Hill
Preston Brook
Higher Whitley
Arley
Arley Hall
Mobberley
Knolls Green
Heritage Centre
Frandley
Antrobus
Bate Heath
Sutton Weaver
Dutton
Aston
Lower Whitley
Great Budworth
Cross Town
KNUTSFORD
Ince Banks
FRODSHAM
Comberbach
Pick Mere
Ship Canal
Bradley
Budworth Mere
Pickmere
Higher Wincham
Ollerton
Ince
R. Weaver
Overton
Marbury
Tabley House
Tabley Mere
CHESTER
Woodhouses
Acton Bridge
Anderton
Marston
Lostock Gralam
Plumley
Marthall
Chelford
Helsby
Little Leigh
Barnton
Boat Lift
Wincham
Smithy Green
Crowton
Winnington
Over Peover
Peover Heath
Hapsford
Alvanley
Kingsley
Weaverham
NORTHWICH
Lostock Green
Lower Peover
Birch Hill
Commonside
Rudheath
Weaver Hall
Lach Dennis
Swan Green
Dunham-on-the-Hill
Norley
Leftwich
Higher Shurlach
Peover Hall
Jodrell Bank Discovery Centre
Withington Green
Manley
Hatchmere
Cuddington
Hartford
Blackden Heath
Lovell Telescope
Long Green
Mouldsworth
DELAMERE FOREST PARK
Sandiway
Davenham
Allostock
Goostrey
Jodrell Bank
Bridge Trafford
Mere Heath
Little Barrow
Ashton Hayes
Delamere Forest
Oakmere
Whitegate
Moulton
Bostock Green
Puddinglake
Byley
Twemlow Green
Great Barrow
Delamere
Foxwist Green
Cranage
M6
M61
M66
M60
M62
M602
M56
A59
A49
A674
A6
A581
A675
A666
A676
A5106
A673
A56
A5209
A58
A577
A6027
A6053
A665
A667
A570
A579
A5082
A6044
A573
A572
A578
A580
A571
A599
A5081
A57
A574
A6144
A5080
A557
A562
A5300
A561
A558
A560
A5144
A538
A533
A556
A50
A5034
A5033
A559
A537
A54
A530
B5248
B6228
B5249
B5253
B5241
B6391
B6214
B6226
B6209
B6292
B5239
B5238
B6199
B5235
B5237
B5215
B5232
B5207
B5205
B5203
B5201
B5212
B5320
B5213
B5167
B5165
B5204
B5160
B5159
B5157
B5178
B5162
B5356
B5155
B5153
B5152
B5393
B5132
B5075
B5391
B5081
B5082
B5085
B5392

INDEX

Including Streets, Places & Areas, Industrial Estates, Junction Names & Service Areas,
Selected Flats & Walkways, Stations and Selected Places of Interest.

HOW TO USE THIS INDEX

1. Each street name is followed by its Postcode District, then by its Locality abbreviation(s) and then by its map reference;
   e.g. **Abberley Rd.** L25: Hunts X . . . .9H **77** is in the L25 Postcode District and the Hunts Cross Locality and is to be found in square 9H on page **77**.
   The page number is shown in bold type.

2. A strict alphabetical order is followed in which Av., Rd., St., etc. (though abbreviated) are read in full and as part of the street name;
   e.g. **Apple Dell Av.** appears after **Appledale Dr.** but before **Appledore Ct.**

3. Streets and a selection of flats and walkways that cannot be shown on the mapping, appear in the index with the thoroughfare to which they are connected shown in brackets;
   e.g. **Abbotsford M.** L39: Orm . . . .8D **20** (off Abbotsford)

4. Addresses that are in more than one part are referred to as not continuous.

5. Places and areas are shown in the index in BLUE TYPE and the map reference is to the actual map square in which the town centre or area is located and not to the place name shown on the map; e.g. AINTREE 8H 35

6. An example of a selected place of interest is British Lawnmower Mus. 1A 12

7. Examples of stations are: Aigburth Station (Rail) . . .8K 75; Bebington (Park & Ride) . . . . 9N 73; Birkenhead Bus Station 2L 73

8. Junction Names & Service Areas are shown in the index in BOLD CAPITAL TYPE; e.g. BURTONWOOD SERVICE AREA 6K 65

9. Map references for entries that appear on large scale pages **4** & **5** are shown first, with small scale map references shown in brackets; e.g. Bath St. L3: Liv 3B **4** (7A **58**)

GENERAL ABBREVIATIONS

All. : Alley	**Cotts.** : Cottages	**Info.** : Information	**Ri.** : Rise
Apts. : Apartments	**Ct.** : Court	**Intl.** : International	**Rd.** : Road
App. : Approach	**Ctyd.** : Courtyard	**Junc.** : Junction	**Rdbt.** : Roundabout
Arc. : Arcade	**Cres.** : Crescent	**La.** : Lane	**Shop.** : Shopping
Av. : Avenue	**Cft.** : Croft	**Lit.** : Little	**Sth.** : South
Bk. : Back	**Dr.** : Drive	**Lwr.** : Lower	**Sq.** : Square
Blvd. : Boulevard	**E.** : East	**Mnr.** : Manor	**Sta.** : Station
Bri. : Bridge	**Ent.** : Enterprise	**Mans.** : Mansions	**St.** : Street
B'way. : Broadway	**Est.** : Estate	**Mkt.** : Market	**Ter.** : Terrace
Bldg. : Building	**Fld.** : Field	**Mdw.** : Meadow	**Twr.** : Tower
Bldgs. : Buildings	**Flds.** : Fields	**Mdws.** : Meadows	**Trad.** : Trading
Bungs. : Bungalows	**Gdn.** : Garden	**M.** : Mews	**Up.** : Upper
Bus. : Business	**Gdns.** : Gardens	**Mt.** : Mount	**Va.** : Vale
Cvn. : Caravan	**Gth.** : Garth	**Mus.** : Museum	**Vw.** : View
C'way. : Causeway	**Ga.** : Gate	**Nth.** : North	**Vs.** : Villas
Cen. : Centre	**Gt.** : Great	**Pde.** : Parade	**Vis.** : Visitors
Chu. : Church	**Grn.** : Green	**Pk.** : Park	**Wlk.** : Walk
Circ. : Circle	**Gro.** : Grove	**Pas.** : Passage	**W.** : West
Cl. : Close	**Hgts.** : Heights	**Pav.** : Pavilion	**Yd.** : Yard
Comn. : Common	**Ho.** : House	**Pl.** : Place	
Cnr. : Corner	**Ho's.** : Houses	**Pct.** : Precinct	
Cott. : Cottage	**Ind.** : Industrial	**Prom.** : Promenade	

LOCALITY ABBREVIATIONS

Acton Bridge: CW8 . . . . .Act B	**Cronton**: L35,WA8 . . . . .Cron	**Hooton**: CH65,CH66 . . . . .Hoot	**New Brighton**: CH45 . . . . .New B
Aigburth: L17,L19 . . . . .Aig	**Crosby**: L23 . . . . .Crosb	**Hoylake**: CH47 . . . . .Hoy	**Newburgh**: WN8 . . . . .Newb
Ainsdale: L37,PR8 . . . . .Ainsd	**Croughton**: CH2 . . . . .Crou	**Hunts Cross**: L24,L25 . . . . .Hunts X	**New Ferry**: CH62 . . . . .New F
Aintree: L9-10 . . . . .Aintr	**Crowton**: CW8 . . . . .Crowt	**Huyton**: L14,L36 . . . . .Huy	**Newton**: WA6 . . . . .Newt
Allerton: L18,L19,L25 . . . . .Aller	**Croxteth**: L11,L12 . . . . .Crox	**Ince**: CH2 . . . . .Ince	**Newton-le-Willows**: WA11-12 . .Newt W
Alvanley: WA6 . . . . .Alv	**Cuerdley**: WA5 . . . . .Cuerd	**Ince Blundell**: L29,L38 . . . . .Ince B	**Noctorum**: CH43 . . . . .Noct
Antrobus: CW9 . . . . .Ant	**Culcheth**: WA3 . . . . .Cul	**Irby**: CH61 . . . . .Irby	**Norcott Brook**: WA4 . . . . . . .Nor B
Appleton: WA4 . . . . .App	**Dalton**: WN8 . . . . .Dalt	**Irlam**: M44 . . . . .Irlam	**Norley**: WA6 . . . . .Norl
Appleton Thorn: WA4 . . . . . . .App T	**Daresbury**: WA4 . . . . .Dares	**Kingsley**: CW8 . . . . .K'ly	**Norris Green**: L11 . . . . .Norr G
Appley Bridge: WN6 . . . . .App B	**Downholland**: L37,L39 . . . . . . .Down	**Kings Moss**: WA11 . . . . . . .Kings M	**Norton**: WA7 . . . . .Nort
Ashton-in-Makerfield: WN4 . . . . . . .Ash M	**Dunham Massey**: WA14 . . . .Dun M	**Kingswood**: WA6 . . . . .Kgswd	**Old Hall**: WA5 . . . . .Old H
Astmoor: WA7 . . . . .Astm	**Dunham-on-the-Hill**: WA6 . . .Dun H	**Kirkby**: L32,L33,WA11 . . . . . . .Kirkb	**Ormskirk**: L39 . . . . .Orm
Aston: WA7 . . . . .Aston	**Dunkirk**: CH1 . . . . .Dunk	**Kirkdale**: L4-5,L20 . . . . .Kirkd	**Orrell**: WN5 . . . . .Orr
Aughton: L31,L39 . . . . .Augh	**Dutton**: WA4,WA7 . . . . .Dutt	**Knotty Ash**: L12,L14 . . . . . . .Knott A	**Oxton**: CH43 . . . . .Oxton
Backford: CH1,CH2,CH66 . . . .Back	**Eastham**: CH62,CH63 . . . . . . .East	**Knowsley**: L34 . . . . .Know	**Paddington**: WA1 . . . . .Padd
Bamfurlong: WN2 . . . . .Bam	**Eccleston**: WA10 . . . . .Ec'stn	**Knowsley Industrial Park**: L33 . . . .Know I	**Padgate**: WA1,WA2 . . . . .Padg
Banks: PR9 . . . . .Banks	**Eccleston Park**: L34,L35 . . . . .Eccl P	**Knowsley Park**: L34 . . . . . .Know P	**Palace Fields**: WA7 . . . . .Pal F
Barnston: CH61 . . . . .Barns	**Ellesmere Port**: CH65,CH66 . . .Ell P	**Lathom**: L40 . . . . .Lath	**Parbold**: WN8 . . . . .Parb
Barton: L39 . . . . .Bart	**Elton**: CH2 . . . . .Elt	**Lea-by-Backford**: CH1 . . . . . .Lea B	**Parkgate**: CH64 . . . . .P'gte
Bebington: CH63 . . . . .Beb	**Fazakerley**: L9,L10-11,L32 . . . . .Faz	**Leasowe**: CH46 . . . . .Leas	**Partington**: M31 . . . . .Part
Beechwood: WA7 . . . . .Beech	**Fearnhead**: WA2,WA3 . . . . . .Fearn	**Ledsham**: CH66 . . . . .Led	**Penketh**: WA5 . . . . .Penk
Bickerstaffe: L39,WA11 . . . . . . .Bic	**Ford**: L21 . . . . .Ford	**Leigh**: WN7 . . . . .Leigh	**Pensby**: CH61 . . . . .Pens
Bidston: CH43 . . . . .Bid	**Formby**: L37 . . . . .Form	**Litherland**: L21 . . . . .Lith	**Picton**: CH2 . . . . .Pict
Billinge: WN5 . . . . .Bil	**Frankby**: CH48 . . . . .Frank	**Little Barrow**: CH3,WA6 . . . . .L Barr	**Platt Bridge**: WN2 . . . . .Platt B
Birchwood: WA2,WA3 . . . . . .Birchw	**Frodsham**: WA6 . . . . .Frod	**Little Bollington**: WA14 . . . . .L Boll	**Port Sunlight**: CH62 . . . . .Port S
Birkdale: PR8 . . . . .Birkd	**Garston**: L19 . . . . .Garst	**Little Crosby**: L23 . . . . .L Cros	**Prenton**: CH43 . . . . .Pren
Birkenhead: CH41,CH43 . . . . .Birke	**Garswood**: WN4 . . . . .Garsw	**Little Neston**: CH64 . . . . .Lit N	**Prescot**: L34,L35 . . . . .Presc
Blundellsands: L23 . . . . .Blun	**Gateacre**: L25,L27 . . . . .Gate	**Little Stanney**: CH2 . . . . . . .Lit Stan	**Preston Brook**: WA7 . . . . . . .Pres B
Bold: WA9 . . . . .Bold	**Glazebrook**: WA3 . . . . .Glaz	**Little Sutton**: CH66 . . . . .Lit Sut	**Preston on the Hill**: WA4 . . .Pres H
Bold Heath: WA8 . . . . .Bold H	**Glazebury**: WA3 . . . . .G'bury	**Liverpool**: CH41,L1-3,L5-8,L13,L17 . . .Liv	**Puddington**: CH64 . . . . .Pudd
Bootle: L20,L30 . . . . .Boot	**Golborne**: WA3 . . . . .Golb	**Lower Stretton**: WA4 . . . . . . .L Stret	**Raby**: CH63 . . . . .Raby
Bridge Trafford: CH2 . . . . . . .Bri T	**Grappenhall**: WA4 . . . . .Grap	**Lower Whitley**: WA4 . . . . .L Whit	**Raby Mere**: CH63 . . . . .Raby M
Brimstage: CH63 . . . . .Brim	**Grassendale**: L19 . . . . .G'dale	**Lowton**: WA3,WN7 . . . . .Low	**Rainford**: L33,WA11 . . . . .Rainf
Broad Green: L14 . . . . .Brd G	**Greasby**: CH49 . . . . .Grea	**Lydiate**: L31 . . . . .Lydi	**Rainhill**: L35,WA9 . . . . .Rainh
Bromborough: CH62,CH63 . . . .Brom	**Great Altcar**: L31,L37,L38 . . . .Gt Alt	**Lymm**: WA13,WA16 . . . . .Lymm	**Rixton**: WA3 . . . . .Rix
Brookvale: WA7 . . . . .Brook	**Great Sankey**: WA5 . . . . .Gt San	**Maghull**: L31 . . . . .Mag	**Risley**: WA3 . . . . .Ris
Burscough: L39,L40 . . . . .Burs	**Great Sutton**: CH65,CH66 . . . .Gt Sut	**Manley**: WA6 . . . . .Manl	**Roby**: L36 . . . . .Roby
Burton: CH64 . . . . .Burt	**Hale**: L24 . . . . .Hale	**Manley Common**: WA6 . . . . .Manl C	**Roby Mill**: WN8 . . . . .Roby M
Burtonwood: WA5 . . . . .Burtw	**Hale Bank**: WA8 . . . . .Hale B	**Manor Park**: WA7 . . . . .Manor P	**Rock Ferry**: CH42 . . . . .Rock F
Cadishead: M44 . . . . .Cad	**Halewood**: L24,L26 . . . . .Halew	**Melling**: L31 . . . . .Mell	**Rufford**: L40 . . . . .Ruf
Caldy: CH48 . . . . .Caldy	**Halsall**: L39 . . . . .Hals	**Meols**: CH47 . . . . .Meols	**Runcorn**: WA7 . . . . .Run
Callands: WA5 . . . . .Call	**Halton**: WA7 . . . . .Hal	**Mere Brow**: PR4 . . . . .Mere B	**St Helens**: WA9,WA10,WA11 . . .St H
Capenhurst: CH1 . . . . .Cap	**Hapsford**: WA6 . . . . .Haps	**Mickle Trafford**: CH2 . . . . . .Mick T	**Saughall**: CH1 . . . . .Sau
Carrington: M31 . . . . .Carr	**Hatton**: WA4 . . . . .Hatt	**Millington**: WA14 . . . . .M'ton	**Scarisbrick**: L40 . . . . .Scar
Castlefields: WA7 . . . . .Cas	**Haydock**: WA11 . . . . .Hay	**Mollington**: CH1 . . . . .Moll	**Seaforth**: L21 . . . . .Sea
Childer Thornton: CH66 . . . . .Chil T	**Helsby**: WA6 . . . . .Helsb	**Moore**: WA4 . . . . .Moore	**Sefton**: L23,L29 . . . . .Seft
Childwall: L16,L25 . . . . .Child	**Hesketh Bank**: PR4 . . . . . . .Hesk B	**Moreton**: CH46 . . . . .More	**Shevington**: WN6 . . . . .Shev
Chorlton-by-Backford: CH2 . . .Chor B	**Heswall**: CH60,CH61 . . . . . . .Hesw	**Mossley Hill**: L16,L18 . . . . . .Moss H	**Shotwick**: CH1 . . . . .Shot
Claughton: CH43 . . . . .Clau	**Higher Bebington**: CH63 . . . . .H Beb	**Mouldsworth**: CH3 . . . . .Moul	**Simonswood**: L33 . . . . .Simsw
Clifton: WA7 . . . . .Clftn	**Higher Walton**: WA4 . . . . .H Wal	**Murdishaw**: WA7 . . . . .Murd	**Skelmersdale**: WN8 . . . . .Skel
Clock Face: WA8,WA9 . . . . . .Clock F	**Higher Whitley**: WA4 . . . . .H Whi	**Ness**: CH64 . . . . .Ness	**Southport**: L39,PR8,PR9 . . . .South
Collins Green: WA5,WA9 . . . .Coll G	**High Legh**: WA16 . . . . .High L	**Neston**: CH64 . . . . .Nest	**Speke**: L19,L24 . . . . .Speke
Crank: WA11 . . . . .Crank	**Hightown**: L38 . . . . .High	**Netherley**: L27 . . . . .N'ley	**Spital**: CH62,CH63 . . . . .Spit
Croft: WA2,WA3 . . . . .Croft	**Holmeswood**: L40 . . . . .H'wood	**Netherton**: L30 . . . . .Neth	**Stoak**: CH2 . . . . .Stoak

20 Forthlin Road—Albert Gro.

Stockbridge Village: L28 . . . Stockb V
Stockton Heath: WA4 . . . Stockt H
Storeton: CH63 . . . Store
Stretton: WA4 . . . Sttn
Sutton Leach: WA9 . . . Sut L
Sutton Manor: WA9 . . . Sut M
Sutton Weaver: WA7 . . . Sut W
Tarbock Green: L26,L35 . . . Tar G
Tarleton: PR4 . . . Tarl
Thelwall: WA4 . . . Thel
Thingwall: CH61 . . . Thing
Thornton: L23,L29 . . . Thorn
Thornton Hough: CH63 . . . Thorn H
Thornton-le-Moors: CH2 . . . Thorn M
Thurstaston: CH61 . . . Thurs
Tranmere: CH41,CH42 . . . Tran
Upholland: WN8 . . . Uph
Upton: CH2,CH49 . . . Upton
Wallasey: CH41,CH44-45 . . . Wall
Walton: L4,L9,WA4 . . . W'ton
Warburton: M31,WA13,WA14 . . . Warb
Warrington: WA1,WA2,WA4,WA5 . . . Warr
Waterloo: L22 . . . Wloo
Wavertree: L13,L15 . . . Wavtr
Wervin: CH2 . . . Wer
Westbrook: WA5 . . . Westb
West Derby: L12,L13 . . . W Der
Westhead: L40 . . . Westh
West Kirby: CH48 . . . W Kir
Weston: WA7 . . . W'ton
Weston Point: WA7 . . . West P
Westy: WA4 . . . Westy
Whiston: L35 . . . Whis
Whitby: CH65,CH66 . . . Whit
Widnes: WA8 . . . Widnes
Wigan: WN3 . . . Wigan
Willaston: CH64 . . . Will
Wimbolds Trafford: CH2 . . . Wim T
Windle: WA10,WA11 . . . Windle
Windmill Hill: WA7 . . . Wind H
Winstanley: WN3,WN5 . . . Winst
Winwick: WA2,WA3 . . . Winw
Woodbank: CH1 . . . Woodb
Woodchurch: CH49 . . . Wdchu
Woolston: WA1,WA3 . . . Wools
Woolton: L25 . . . Woolt
Wrightington: WN6 . . . Wright

20 Forthlin Road
(Childhood Home of Paul McCartney) . . . 7A 76

A

Abacus Rd. L13: Liv . . . 5M **59**
Abberley Cl. WA10: St H . . . 7J **49**
Abberley Rd. L25: Hunts X . . . 9H **77**
Abberton Pk. L30: Neth . . . 6F **34**
Abbey Cl. CH41: Birke . . . 3M **73**
L33: Kirkb . . . 9D **36**
L37: Form . . . 2H **25**
WA3: Croft . . . 1H **67**
WA8: Widnes . . . 8F **78**
WN8: Uph . . . 5M **31**
Abbey Ct. CH65: Ell P . . . 8A **104**
L25: Woolt . . . 6F **76**
Abbey Dale WN6: App B . . . 6N **23**
Abbeydale L40: Burs . . . 2K **21**
Abbey Farm Cvn. Pk. L40: Lath . . . 5G **21**
Abbeyfield Dr. L12: Crox . . . 8B **46**
Abbeyfield Ho. CH65: Whit . . . 2M **111**
Abbey Fold L40: Burs . . . 9H **15**
Abbey Gdns. PR8: Birkd . . . 2N **11**
Abbeygate Apts. L15: Wavtr . . . 1L **75**
Abbey Hey WA7: Nort . . . 7E **96**
Abbey La. L40: Burs, Lath . . . 4G **20**
Abbey La. Ind. Est. L40: Burs . . . 4G **21**
Abbey M. L8: Liv . . . 3G **74**
Abbeymill Ct. L15: Wavtr . . . 1M **75**
Abbey Rd. CH48: W Kir . . . 6C **70**
L6: Liv . . . 3H **59**
WA3: Low . . . 2K **53**
WA8: Widnes . . . 8E **78**
WA10: St H . . . 3G **49**
WA11: Hay . . . 3G **51**
Abbeystead WN8: Skel . . . 5E **30**
Abbeystead Av. L30: Neth . . . 1F **44**
Abbeystead Rd. L15: Wavtr . . . 9N **59**
Abbey St. CH41: Birke . . . 3M **73**
Abbeyvale Dr. L25: Gate . . . 2G **76**
Abbey Vw. L16: Child . . . 1C **76**
Abbeyway Nth. WA11: Hay . . . 3J **51**
Abbeyway Sth. WA11: Hay . . . 4J **51**
Abbeywood WN8: Skel . . . 6F **30**
Abbeywood Gro. L35: Whis . . . 7C **62**
Abbot Cl. CH43: Bid . . . 2C **72**
Abbotsbury Way L12: Crox . . . 7C **46**
Abbots Bus. Pk. WA7: Pres B . . . 1G **109**
Abbots Cl. L37: Form . . . 3G **25**
Abbots Dr. CH63: Beb . . . 2M **89**
Abbotsfield Cl. WA4: App . . . 1F **98**
Abbotsfield Rd. WA9: Bold, St H . . . 3A **64**
(not continuous)
Abbotsfield Rd. Ind. Est. WA9: St H . . . 3A **64**
Abbotsford L39: Orm . . . 8D **20**
Abbotsford Cl. WA3: Low . . . 1E **52**
Abbotsford Ct. L23: Blun . . . 8J **33**
Abbotsford Gdns. L23: Crosb . . . 8J **33**
Abbotsford M. *L39: Orm . . . 8D 20*
(off Abbotsford)
Abbotsford Rd. L11: Norr G . . . 8L **45**
L23: Blun . . . 8J **33**
Abbotsford St. CH44: Wall . . . 7L **57**
Abbots Hall Av. WA9: Clock F . . . 6N **63**
Abbots M. CH65: Ell P . . . 8N **103**
Abbots Pk. WA7: Pres B . . . 1G **108**
Abbots Quay CH41: Birke . . . 2N **73**
Abbots Way CH48: W Kir . . . 5D **70**
CH64: Nest . . . 5E **100**
L37: Form . . . 3G **25**
WN5: Bil . . . 8N **39**
Abbott Dr. L20: Boot . . . 5D **44**
Abbotts Cl. L18: Moss H . . . 5N **75**
WA7: Run . . . 7K **95**
Abbottshey Av. L18: Moss H . . . 5N **75**
Abdale Rd. L11: Norr G . . . 7L **45**
Abercrombie Rd. L33: Know I . . . 3F **46**
Abercromby Sq. L7: Liv . . . 6L **5** (9E **58**)
Aberdale Rd. L13: Liv . . . 6N **59**
Aberdare Cl. WA5: Call . . . 8N **65**
Aberdeen St. CH41: Birke . . . 1J **73**
Aberford Av. CH45: Wall . . . 4E **56**
Abergele Rd. L13: Liv . . . 7L **59**
Aber St. L6: Liv . . . 1M **5** (6F **58**)
Abingdon Av. WA1: Wools . . . 1M **83**
Abingdon Gro. L4: W'ton . . . 8H **45**
L26: Halew . . . 7L **77**
Abingdon Rd. CH49: Grea . . . 5J **71**
L4: W'ton . . . 8H **45**
Abinger Rd. WN4: Garsw . . . 7F **40**
Abington Dr. PR9: Banks . . . 2E **8**
Abington Wlk. WA7: Brook . . . 1E **108**
Abney Cl. L7: Liv . . . 9G **59**
Abney M. WA1: Warr . . . 3F **82**
Aboyne Cl. L9: W'ton . . . 6F **44**
Abrams Fold PR9: Banks . . . 2D **8**
Abrams Grn. PR9: Banks . . . 2D **8**
Abram St. L5: Liv . . . 4D **58**
Abstone Cl. WA1: Wools . . . 1K **83**
Abyssinia Cl. L15: Wavtr . . . 1K **75**
Acacia Av. L36: Huy . . . 8H **61**
WA1: Wools . . . 9L **67**
WA8: Widnes . . . 5L **79**
Acacia Cl. CH2: Elt . . . 2N **113**
CH49: Grea . . . 6K **71**
Acacia Dr. CH66: Gt Sut . . . 4L **111**
Acacia Gro. CH44: Wall . . . 7L **57**
CH48: W Kir . . . 6B **70**
L9: Aintr . . . 4G **45**
WA7: Run . . . 7M **95**
WA10: Ec'stn . . . 6D **48**
Acacia St. WA12: Newt W . . . 6H **51**
Academy, The *PR9: South . . . 7H 7*
(off Manchester Rd.)
Academy Bus. Pk.
L33: Know I . . . 1F **46**
Academy Pl. WA1: Warr . . . 3C **82**
Academy St. WA1: Warr . . . 3C **82**
Academy Way WA1: Warr . . . 3C **82**
Acanthus Rd. L13: Liv . . . 5M **59**
Access Rd. L12: W Der . . . 2B **60**
Acer Leigh L17: Aig . . . 6J **75**
Acheson Rd. L13: Liv . . . 3K **59**
Achilles Av. WA2: Warr . . . 7C **66**
Achilles Ct. WA7: Cas . . . 5C **96**
Ackerley Cl. WA2: Fearn . . . 6G **67**
Ackers Hall Av. L14: Knott A . . . 5D **60**
Ackers La. L23: L Cros . . . 4J **33**
WA4: Stockt H . . . 6F **82**
WA10: St H . . . 9F **48**
Ackers Rd. CH49: Wdchu . . . 6C **72**
WA4: Stockt H . . . 7F **82**
Ackers St. L34: Presc . . . 3A **62**
Acland Rd. CH44: Wall . . . 5H **57**
Aconbury Cl. L11: Norr G . . . 7L **45**
Aconbury Pl. L11: Norr G . . . 7L **45**
Acorn Bus. Cen. L33: Know I . . . 9F **36**
Acorn Cl. CH63: H Beb . . . 1K **89**
WA9: Clock F . . . 5M **63**
Acorn Ct. L8: Liv . . . 2E **74**
Acorn Dr. CH65: Whit . . . 4N **111**
Acorn Farm . . . 7H **37**
Acornfield Cl. L33: Know I . . . 2G **47**
Acornfield Plantation Local Nature Reserve . . . 2H **47**
Acornfield Rd. L33: Know I . . . 1H **47**
Acorns, The L39: Augh . . . 1A **28**
Acorn St. WA12: Newt W . . . 7L **51**
Acorn Way L20: Boot . . . 5C **44**
A Court WN4: Ash M . . . 9K **41**
Acrefield WN8: Newb . . . 4D **22**
Acrefield Ct. CH42: Tran . . . 7H **73**
Acrefield Pk. L25: Woolt . . . 5E **76**
Acrefield Rd. CH42: Tran . . . 7H **73**
L25: Woolt . . . 5E **76**
WA8: Widnes . . . 7E **78**
Acregate WN8: Skel . . . 5F **30**
Acre Grn. L26: Halew . . . 1L **93**
Acre Gro. PR8: Birkd . . . 2M **11**
Acre La. CH60: Hesw . . . 6C **88**
CH62: Brom . . . 7B **90**
CH63: Brom . . . 8B **90**
Acre Rd. CH66: Gt Sut . . . 9J **103**
Acres Cl. L25: Gate . . . 1E **76**
Acresfield *L13: Liv . . . 7N 59*
(off Broad Grn. Rd.)
Acresgate Ct. L25: Gate . . . 3E **76**
Acres La. L31: Lydi . . . 4D **26**
L37: Gt Alt . . . 4L **25**
L39: Down . . . 4D **26**
Acres Rd. CH47: Meols . . . 1G **70**
CH63: Beb . . . 1M **89**
Acreville Rd. CH63: Beb . . . 2M **89**
Acton Av. WA4: App . . . 4E **98**
Acton Cl. WA11: Hay . . . 4E **50**
Acton Gro. L6: Liv . . . 3H **59**
Acton La. CH46: More . . . 1K **71**
Acton Rake *L30: Neth . . . 6C 34*
(off Higher End Pk.)
Acton Rd. CH42: Rock F . . . 7N **73**
L32: Kirkb . . . 9A **36**
WA5: Burtw . . . 3G **64**
Actons Wood La. WA7: Nort . . . 5G **97**
Acton Way L7: Liv . . . 9H **59**
Acuba Gro. CH42: Tran . . . 4L **73**
Acuba Rd. L15: Wavtr . . . 8A **60**
Adair Pl. L13: Liv . . . 2K **59**
Adair Rd. L13: Liv . . . 2K **59**
Adam Av. CH66: Gt Sut . . . 1H **111**
(not continuous)
Adam Cl. CH66: Gt Sut . . . 1J **111**
L19: Garst . . . 2A **92**
Adams Cl. WA12: Newt W . . . 8M **51**
Adamson Cl. WA4: Westy . . . 5H **83**
Adamson Ct. WA4: Grap . . . 6J **83**
Adamson Ho. WA7: Run . . . 4H **95**
Adamson St. L7: Liv . . . 7J **59**
WA4: Warr . . . 5C **82**
WN4: Ash M . . . 8J **41**
Adam St. L5: Liv . . . 3E **58**
WA2: Warr . . . 1D **82**
Adaston Av. CH62: East . . . 2E **102**
Adcote Cl. L14: Knott A . . . 6D **60**
Adcote Rd. L14: Knott A . . . 6D **60**
Addenbrook Cl. CH43: Bid . . . 2C **72**
Addenbrooke Dr. L24: Speke . . . 1F **92**
Adderley Cl. WA7: Run . . . 6M **95**
Adderley St. L7: Liv . . . 7G **59**
Addingham Av. WA8: Widnes . . . 9F **78**
Addingham Rd. L18: Moss H . . . 3N **75**
Addington St. CH44: Wall . . . 6K **57**
Addison Cl. L32: Kirkb . . . 2B **46**
Addison Sq. WA8: Widnes . . . 7K **79**
Addison St. L3: Liv . . . 2F **4** (6C **58**)
L20: Boot . . . 5N **43**
Addison Way L3: Liv . . . 2F **4** (6C **58**)
WA9: St H . . . 4J **63**
Adelaide Av. WA9: St H . . . 2H **63**
Adelaide Ct. WA8: Widnes . . . 9K **79**
Adelaide Pl. L5: Liv . . . 5D **58**
Adelaide Rd. CH42: Tran . . . 4J **73**
L7: Liv . . . 4N **5** (7G **58**)
(not continuous)
L21: Sea . . . 3M **43**
Adelaide St. CH44: Wall . . . 6H **57**
Adelaide Ter. L22: Wloo . . . 1J **43**
Adela Rd. WA7: Run . . . 5J **95**
Adele Thompson Dr. L8: Liv . . . 9N **5** (1F **74**)
Adelphi St. CH41: Birke . . . 2L **73**
Adey Rd. WA13: Lymm . . . 3G **85**
Adfalent La. CH64: Will . . . 7N **101**
Adlam Cres. L9: Faz . . . 3K **45**
Adlam Rd. L9: Faz . . . 3K **45**
L10: Faz . . . 3K **45**
Adler Way L3: Liv . . . 5E **74**
Adlington Ct. WA3: Ris . . . 3N **67**
(not continuous)
Adlington Ho. L3: Liv . . . 2F **4**
Adlington Rd. WA7: Wind H . . . 5F **96**
Adlington St. L3: Liv . . . 2F **4**
Admin Rd. L33: Know I . . . 2G **46**
Admiral Gro. *L8: Liv . . . 3F 74*
(off High Pk. St.)
Admirals Quay L23: Blun . . . 7G **33**
Admirals Rd. WA3: Birchw . . . 5M **67**
Admirals Sq. WA3: Birchw . . . 6N **67**
Admiral St. L8: Liv . . . 3F **74**
Admiralty Cl. L40: Burs . . . 3F **20**
Admiral Way L30: Boot . . . 2D **44**
Adrian's Way L32: Kirkb . . . 9C **36**
Adshead Rd. L13: Liv . . . 2K **59**
Adstone Rd. L25: Gate . . . 3G **77**
Adswood Rd. L36: Huy . . . 6J **61**
Adwell Cl. WA3: Low . . . 2H **53**
Aerial Extreme
Knowsley . . . 2M **61**
Aerodrome, The L24: Speke . . . 3C **92**
Africander Rd. WA11: St H . . . 2K **49**
Afton WA8: Widnes . . . 6D **78**
Agar Rd. L11: Norr G . . . 2L **59**
Agate St. L5: Liv . . . 4F **58**
AGDEN BROW . . . 7L **85**
Agden Brow WA13: Lymm . . . 8K **85**
Agden Brow Pk. WA13: Lymm . . . 7K **85**
Agden La. WA13: Lymm . . . 8K **85** (7L **85**)
WA14: M'ton . . . 8K **85**
WA16: Lymm . . . 8K **85**
Agden Pk. La. WA13: Lymm . . . 8K **85**
Agincourt Rd. L12: W Der . . . 4A **60**
Agnes Gro. CH44: Wall . . . 4J **57**
Agnes Jones Ho. L8: Liv . . . 8L **5** (9E **58**)
Agnes Rd. CH42: Tran . . . 5L **73**
L23: Blun . . . 8J **33**
Agnes St. WA9: Clock F . . . 6M **63**
Agnes Way L7: Liv . . . 8G **59**
Agulnek Ct. L18: Moss H . . . 5L **75**
Aiden Long Gro. L34: Know P . . . 3J **61**
AIGBURTH . . . 8K **75**
Aigburth Dr. L17: Aig . . . 3H **75**
Aigburth Gro. CH46: More . . . 9L **55**
Aigburth Hall Av. L19: Aig . . . 8L **75**
Aigburth Hall Rd. L19: Aig . . . 8M **75**
Aigburth Ho. L17: Aig . . . 5K **75**
Aigburth Rd. L17: Aig . . . 4G **74**
L19: Aig, G'dale . . . 7K **75**
Aigburth Station (Rail) . . . 8K **75**
Aigburth St. L7: Liv . . . 9G **58**
AIGBURTH VALE . . . 5K **75**
Aigburth Va. L17: Aig . . . 6J **75**
(not continuous)
L18: Moss H . . . 5K **75**
Ailsa Rd. CH45: Wall . . . 4G **57**
Aindow Ct. PR8: Birkd . . . 3M **11**
Ainley Cl. WA7: Brook . . . 1C **108**
Ainscough Dr. L40: Burs . . . 1K **21**
Ainscough Rd. WA3: Birchw . . . 6M **67**
AINSDALE . . . 9J **11**
Ainsdale & Birkdale Hills
Local Nature Reserve . . . 7G **10**
Ainsdale Cl. CH61: Thing . . . 2A **88**
CH63: Brom . . . 1B **102**
L10: Faz . . . 2L **45**
WA5: Penk . . . 4H **81**
Ainsdale Discovery Cen. . . . 8F **10**
AINSDALE-ON-SEA . . . 8F **10**
Ainsdale Rd. L20: Boot . . . 5C **44**
Ainsdale Sand Dunes
National Nature Reserve . . . 2E **16**
Ainsdale Station (Rail) . . . 9J **11**
Ainsworth Av. CH46: More . . . 1K **71**
Ainsworth La. L34: Know . . . 4F **46**
Ainsworth Rd. WA10: St H . . . 5G **49**
Ainsworth St. L3: Liv . . . 5J **5** (8D **58**)
AINTREE . . . 8H **35**
Aintree Cl. CH46: Leas . . . 6N **55**
Aintree Ct. L10: Aintr . . . 8H **35**
Aintree Cres. PR8: South . . . 2E **12**
Aintree Golf Course . . . 1J **45**
Aintree Gro. CH66: Gt Sut . . . 2J **111**
Aintree La. L10: Aintr . . . 8H **35**
L10: Faz . . . 1L **45**
Aintree Motor Circuit . . . 2J **45**
Aintree Racecourse . . . 1H **45**
Aintree Racecourse Retail & Bus. Pk.
L9: Aintr . . . 1G **45**
Aintree Rd. L9: Aintr . . . 4J **45**
L20: Boot . . . 6C **44**
Aintree Station (Rail) . . . 2G **44**
Aintree Vis. Cen. &
Grand National Experience . . . 1G **45**
Aintree Way L9: Aintr . . . 9H **35**
Airdale Cl. CH43: Bid . . . 2C **72**
Airdale Rd. L15: Wavtr . . . 2L **75**
Airdrie Cl. CH62: East . . . 3C **102**
Aire WA8: Widnes . . . 6E **78**
Aire Cl. CH65: Ell P . . . 7M **103**
Airedale Cl. WA5: Gt San . . . 1H **81**
Airegate L31: Mag . . . 1G **35**
Airfield Way CH65: Hoot . . . 4H **103**
Airlie Gro. L13: Liv . . . 3J **59**
Airlie Rd. CH47: Hoy . . . 2C **70**
Aisthorpe Gro. L31: Mag . . . 4J **35**
Aitken Way WA9: St H . . . 5J **63**
Ajax Av. WA2: Warr . . . 7C **66**
Akbar, The CH60: Hesw . . . 5K **87**
A K Bus. Pk. PR9: South . . . 9M **7**
Akenside Ct. L20: Boot . . . 4N **43**
Akenside St. L20: Boot . . . 4N **43**
Alabama Way CH41: Birke . . . 2M **73**
Alamein Cres. WA2: Warr . . . 1C **82**
Alamein Rd. L36: Huy . . . 5H **61**
Alan's Way L33: Kirkb . . . 6C **36**
Alaska M. WA5: Gt San . . . 1J **81**
Alastair Cres. CH43: Pren . . . 7F **72**
Alban Retail Pk. . . . 7B **66**
Alban Rd. L16: Child . . . 9B **60**
Albany, The L3: Liv . . . 4D **4**
Albany Av. L34: Eccl P . . . 2C **62**
Albany Cres. WA13: Lymm . . . 4D **84**
Albany Gdns. CH66: Lit Sut . . . 7H **103**
Albany Gro. WA13: Lymm . . . 4C **84**
Albany Rd. CH42: Rock F . . . 6L **73**
L7: Liv . . . 4N **5** (7F **58**)
L9: Aintr . . . 3G **44**
L13: Liv . . . 5M **59**
L34: Presc . . . 3B **62**
PR9: South . . . 6H **7**
WA13: Lymm . . . 5C **84**
Albany Ter. WA7: Run . . . 5K **95**
Albemarle Rd. CH44: Wall . . . 6K **57**
Alberta Gro. L34: Presc . . . 4K **61**
Albert Ct. PR9: South . . . 6J **7**
WA8: Widnes . . . 7M 79
(off Albert Rd.)
Albert Dock L3: Liv . . . 8D **4** (9B **58**)
Albert Dr. CH64: Nest . . . 6D **100**
L9: W'ton . . . 4E **44**
WA5: Gt San . . . 2F **80**
Albert Edward Rd. L7: Liv . . . 4N **5** (7F **58**)
(not continuous)
Albert Gro. L15: Wavtr . . . 9M **59**
L23: Crosb . . . 7K **33**

Albert Laver Cl. CH41: Birke 1K **73**
Albert Pk. L17: Aig 3G **75**
Albert Pl. PR9: South 7G **6**
Albert Rd. CH42: Tran 4J **73**
CH47: Hoy 2C **70**
CH48: W Kir 7B **70**
L13: Liv 3J **59**
L22: Wloo 1K **43**
L37: Form 4B **24**
L40: Ruf 3L **15**
PR9: South 7H **7**
WA4: Grap 6H **83**
WA8: Widnes 8L **79**
Albert Row WA6: Frod 5L **107**
Albert Schweitzer Av. L30: Neth 8E **34**
Albert Sq. WA8: Widnes 8L **79**
Albert St. CH45: New B 9J **43**
L7: Liv 5N **5** (8F **58**)
M44: Cad 3L **69**
WA7: Run 5K **95**
WA10: St H 5K **49**
WN4: Ash M 8K **41**
Albert Ter. PR8: Birkd 1N **11**
WA5: Coll G 9G **50**
Albinson Wlk. M31: Part 6N **69**
Albion Pl. CH45: New B 1H **57**
Albion St. CH41: Birke 2M **73**
(not continuous)
CH45: New B 1G **56**
L5: Liv 3D **58**
WA10: St H 7H **49**
(not continuous)
Albourne Rd. L32: Kirkb 2E **46**
Albright Rd. WA8: Widnes 1D **94**
Albury Cl. L12: Crox 8D **46**
WA5: Warr 1A **82**
WA11: Hay 3E **50**
Albury Rd. L32: Kirkb 3D **46**
Alcester Rd. L12: W Der 3A **60**
Alchemy Way L33: Know I 3F **46**
Alcock St. WA7: Run 4K **95**
Alconbury Cl. WA5: Gt San 2K **81**
Alcott Pl. WA2: Winw 3B **66**
Aldams Gro. L4: Kirkd 9D **44**
Aldbourne Av. L25: Woolt 3C **76**
Aldbourne Cl. L25: Woolt 4C **76**
Aldcliffe WA3: Low 2G **52**
Alder Av. L36: Huy 9L **61**
WA8: Widnes 5K **79**
WN4: Ash M 6H **41**
WN5: Bil 6N **39**
Alderbank Rd. WA5: Gt San 2J **81**
Alderbrook Dr. WN8: Parb 3F **22**
Alder Cl. L34: Presc 3C **62**
Alder Cres. L32: Kirkb 8B **36**
WA2: Warr 9D **66**
Alderdale Av. PR8: Ainsd 9G **11**
Alder Dr. CH66: Gt Sut 4L **111**
Alderfield Dr. L24: Speke 3K **93**
Alder Gro. L22: Wloo 9K **33**
Alder Hey Rd. WA10: St H 7F **48**
Alder La. L34: Know 7F **46**
(not continuous)
L39: Bart 6L **17**
WA2: Warr 9C **66**
WA5: Burtw 2J **65**
WA6: Frod 3G **107**
WA8: Cron 4C **78**
WA11: Crank 7J **39**
WN8: Parb 4F **22**
Alder Lee Cl. WN3: Winst 1F **40**
Alderlee Pk. PR8: South 4F **12**
Alderley WN8: Skel 6F **30**
Alderley Av. CH41: Birke 1F **72**
WA3: Low 3E **52**
Alderley Cl. WN5: Bil 6A **40**
Alderley Rd. CH44: Wall 6H **57**
CH47: Hoy 1C **70**
WA4: Thel 5L **83**
Alderman Rd. L24: Speke 1G **92**
Alderney Cl. CH65: Ell P 4A **112**
Alderney Rd. L5: Liv 4C **58**
Alder Rd. CH63: H Beb 3K **89**
L12: W Der 5N **59**
L34: Presc 3C **62**
WA1: Wools 1L **83**
WA3: Low 2G **53**
ALDER ROOT GOLF COURSE 2M **65**
Alder Root La. WA2: Winw 2M **65**
Aldersey Cl. WA7: Wind H 6F **96**
Aldersey St. L3: Liv 1G **4** (6C **58**)
Aldersgate CH42: Rock F 6M **73**
Aldersgate Av. WA7: Murd 8F **96**
Aldersgate Dr. L26: Halew 1L **93**
Alderson Cres. L37: Form 9F **16**
Alderson Rd. L15: Wavtr 1J **75**
Alder St. WA12: Newt W 8L **51**
Alderton Cl. L26: Halew 9L **77**
Alderton Dr. WN4: Ash M 8H **41**
Alderville Rd. L4: W'ton 8H **45**
Alderwood Av. L24: Speke 4J **93**
Alderwood Ct. WA8: Widnes 4H **79**
Alderwood Lodge *L24: Speke* *4L* ***93***
(off East Mains)
Aldewood Cl. WA3: Birchw 3B **68**
Aldford Cl. CH43: Oxton 6E **72**
CH63: Brom 9A **90**
Aldford Rd. L32: Kirkb 3C **46**
Aldgate CH65: Ell P 9M **103**
Aldridge Cl. L12: Crox 7C **46**
Aldridge Dr. WA5: Burtw 2H **65**
Aldrins La. L30: Neth 7E **34**
Aldwark Rd. L14: Knott A 5E **60**
Aldwych Rd. L12: W Der 3A **60**
Aldwyn Cl. WN3: Winst 2F **40**
Aldykes L31: Mag 3K **35**
Alexander Cl. L40: Burs 2K **21**
Alexander Dr. CH61: Pens 4M **87**
L31: Lydi 9J **27**
WA8: Widnes 8G **78**
Alexander Fleming Av. L30: Neth 7E **34**
Alexander Grn. L36: Huy 5J **61**
Alexander Ho. L21: Sea 3M **43**
L34: Presc *2A* ***62***
(off Rio Ct.)
Alexander Wlk. *L4: W'ton* *1E* ***58***
(off Florence St.)
Alexander Way *L8: Liv* *4E* ***74***
(off Park Hill Rd.)
Alexander Wharf *L31: Mag* *2H* ***35***
(off Damfield La.)
Alexandra B'way. PR9: South 7J **7**
Alexandra Cl. L6: Liv 6G **58**
WN8: Skel 3B **30**
Alexandra Ct. *CH45: New B* *1G* ***56***
(off Alexandra Rd.)
L23: Crosb 7K **33**
M31: Part *6M* ***69***
(off Bailey La.)
PR9: South 7J **7**
WA9: St H *1G* ***63***
(off Carnarvon St.)
Alexandra Dr. CH42: Rock F 7L **73**
L17: Aig 4G **75**
L20: Boot 4D **44**
WA10: St H 9G **49**
(not continuous)
Alexandra Grn. L17: Aig 4G **75**
Alexandra Gro. L26: Halew 1K **93**
M44: Irlam 1M **69**
WA7: Run 6M **95**
Alexandra Ho. L17: Aig 4G **74**
Alexandra Ind. Est. WA8: Widnes 9J **79**
Alexandra M. *L39: Orm* *7C* ***20***
(off Courtfield)
PR9: South 7H **7**
WA6: Frod 5L **107**
Alexandra Mt. L21: Lith 2A **44**
Alexandra Pk. L17: Aig 5G **75**
Alexandra Rd. CH43: Oxton 3J **73**
CH45: New B 1G **56**
CH48: W Kir 7B **70**
L7: Liv 9H **59**
L13: Liv 7M **59**
L19: Garst 9A **76**
L22: Wloo 2L **43**
L23: Crosb 7K **33**
L37: Form 4A **24**
L40: Burs 1H **21**
PR9: South 6H **7**
WA4: Grap 6G **83**
WA4: Stockt H 7E **82**
WN4: Ash M 7K **41**
Alexandra St. CH65: Ell P 7A **104**
WA1: Warr 1F **82**
WA8: Widnes 9K **79**
WA10: St H 9G **49**
Alexandra Ter. *L8: Liv* *1E* ***74***
(off Princes Rd.)
Alexandra Vs. *L21: Lith* *2A* ***44***
(off Alexandra Mt.)
Alexandria Gro. L36: Huy 5H **61**
Alex Cl. L8: Liv 2E **74**
Alfonso Rd. L4: Kirkd 1C **58**
Alford Av. WA9: Sut M 5L **63**
Alforde St. WA8: Widnes 9K **79**
(not continuous)
Alford St. L7: Liv 7K **59**
Alfred Cl. WA8: Widnes 8L **79**
Alfred M. L1: Liv 9H **5** (1D **74**)
Alfred Rd. CH43: Oxton 3J **73**
CH44: Wall 8L **57**
WA3: Low 2H **53**
WA11: Hay 3H **51**
Alfred Stocks Ct. *L8: Liv* *5F* ***74***
(off Turner Cl.)
Alfred St. L15: Wavtr 9J **59**
M44: Cad *3L* ***69***
(off Dean Rd.)
WA8: Widnes 8L **79**
WA10: St H 6L **49**
WA11: Rainf 4C **38**
WA12: Newt W 7N **51**
Alfriston Rd. L12: W Der 3A **60**
Algernon Cl. CH64: P'gte 5C **100**
Algernon St. WA1: Warr 2E **82**
WA4: Stockt H 7D **82**
WA7: Run 4J **95**
Alice Cl. L15: Wavtr 1A **76**
Alice Ct. WA8: Widnes 3K **95**
Alice St. WA9: St H 1A **64**
Alicia Wlk. L10: Faz 3N **45**
Alison Av. CH42: Rock F 5M **73**
Alison Pl. L13: Liv 2K **59**
Alison Rd. L13: Liv 2K **59**
Alistair Dr. CH63: Brom 1B **102**
Allangate Cl. CH49: Grea 6K **71**
Allangate Rd. L19: G'dale 8N **75**
Allan Rd. WA11: St H 3M **49**
Allans Cl. CH64: Nest 8E **100**
Allans Mdw. CH64: Nest 8E **100**
Allanson St. WA9: St H 7N **49**
Allcard St. WA5: Warr 1A **82**
Allcot Av. CH42: Tran 6K **73**
Allenby Av. L23: Crosb 9M **33**
Allenby Rd. M44: Cad 5K **69**
Allenby Sq. L13: Liv 7M **59**
Allendale WA7: Pal F 9D **96**
Allendale Av. L9: Aintr 3G **45**
L35: Rainh 6G **62**
Allengate L23: Crosb 6L **33**
Allen Rd. WA7: West P 8G **95**
Allen St. WA2: Warr 2B **82**
Allerby Way WA3: Low 2F **52**
Allerford Rd. L12: W Der 2A **60**
ALLERTON 8B **76**
Allerton Beeches L18: Moss H 5A **76**
Allerton Dr. L18: Moss H 4N **75**
Allerton Gro. CH42: Tran 5L **73**
ALLERTON PK. GOLF COURSE 6C **76**
Allerton Rd. CH42: Tran 5K **73**
CH45: Wall 3G **56**
L18: Aller, Moss H 3M **75**
L25: Woolt 7D **76**
PR9: South 6K **7**
WA8: Widnes 7L **79**
Allesley Rd. L14: Knott A 4D **60**
Alleyne Rd. L4: W'ton 1J **59**
All Hallows Dr. L24: Speke 4K **93**
Allington St. L17: Aig 5G **74**
Allinsons Ct. L21: Lith 2A **44**
Allium Way L11: Norr G 9M **45**
Allonby Cl. CH43: Noct 4E **72**
WN3: Winst 2F **40**
Allotment Rd. M44: Cad 3K **69**
Allport La. CH62: Brom 7C **90**
Allport La. Pct. CH62: Brom 6C **90**
Allport Rd. CH62: Brom 9B **90**
CH63: Brom 9B **90**
Allports, The CH62: Brom 8C **90**
All Saints Cl. L30: Neth 8D **34**
All Saints Ct. WA11: Rainf 6D **38**
All Saints Dr. WA4: Thel 5M **83**
All Saints Rd. L24: Speke 4G **92**
Allscott Way WN4: Ash M 8L **41**
Allysum Ct. WA7: Beech 2B **108**
Alma Cl. L10: Faz 3N **45**
WN8: Uph 5M **31**
Alma Ct. PR8: Ainsd 7M **11**
WN8: Uph 5M **31**
Almacs Cl. L23: Blun 8H **33**
Alma Grn. WN8: Uph 5L **31**
Alma Gro. WN3: Wigan 1G **41**
Alma Hill WN8: Uph 5L **31**
Alman Ct. *L17: Aig* *5G* ***75***
(off Bryanston Rd.)
Alma Pde. WN8: Uph 5M **31**
Alma Pl. WA9: St H 8M **49**
Alma Rd. L17: Aig 8K **75**
PR8: Birkd 2N **11**
WN8: Uph 5M **31**
Alma St. CH41: Birke 2L **73**
WA9: St H 8M **49**
WA12: Newt W 7K **51**
Alma Ter. *L15: Wavtr* *9L* ***59***
(off Sandown La.)
Alma Wlk. WN8: Uph 5M **31**
Almeda Rd. L24: Speke 5L **93**
Almer Dr. WA5: Gt San 3L **81**
Almond Av. L30: Neth 8B **34**
L40: Burs 8J **15**
WA7: Run 7M **95**
Almond Brow PR9: Banks 3E **8**
Almond Cl. L26: Halew 9J **77**
WA11: Hay 5B **50**
Almond Ct. L19: Garst 2C **92**
Almond Dr. WA5: Burtw 3H **65**
Almond Gro. WA1: Padd 1J **83**
WA8: Widnes 6B **78**
Almond Pl. CH46: More 9N **55**
Almonds, The L26: Halew 9J **77**
Almond's Grn. L12: W Der 1M **59**
Almond's Gro. L12: W Der 2M **59**
Almond's Pk. L12: W Der 1M **59**
Almonds Turn L30: Neth 7C **34**
Almond Tree Cl. L24: Hale 6B **94**
Almond Wlk. *M31: Part* *6K* ***69***
(off Wood La.)
Almond Way CH49: Grea 6K **71**
Almonry, The L40: Lath 6M **21**
Alness Dr. L35: Rainh 7G **63**
Alnwick Dr. CH46: More 9J **55**
CH65: Ell P 3B **112**
Aloeswood Cl. L6: Liv 4G **58**
Alpass Av. WA5: Warr 9B **66**
Alpass Rd. L17: Aig 5G **75**
Alpha Ct. CH45: Wall 4E **56**
Alpha Dr. CH42: Rock F 7N **73**
Alpha St. L21: Lith 5A **44**
Alpine Cl. WA10: St H 6F **48**
Alpine St. WA12: Newt W 7J **51**
Alresford Rd. L19: Aig 8L **75**
Alroy Rd. L4: W'ton 2F **58**
Alscot Av. L10: Faz 3M **45**
Alscot Cl. L31: Mag 3L **35**
Alsop Ct. L3: Liv 5L **5** (8E **58**)
Alston Cl. CH62: Brom 6B **90**
Alston Ct. PR8: Ainsd 8L **11**
Alstonfield Rd. L14: Knott A 5E **60**
Alston M. WA10: St H 2E **62**
Alston Rd. L17: Aig 8K **75**
Alt WA8: Widnes 6E **78**
Alt Av. L31: Mag 4H **35**
ALT BRIDGE 4H **25**
Altbridge Pk. L11: Crox 6N **45**
(not continuous)
Altbridge Rd. L36: Huy 4H **61**
Altcar Av. L15: Wavtr 1J **75**
Altcar Dr. CH46: More 1L **71**
Altcar La. L31: Lydi 7E **26**
L37: Form 3F **24**
(Belvedere Dr.)
L37: Form 9J **17**
(Downholland Moss La.)
L39: Down 3E **26**
Altcar Rifle Range Est.
L38: Hight 6E **24**
Altcar Rd. L20: Boot 5B **44**
L37: Form, Gt Alt 2G **24**
Altcross Rd. L11: Crox 6A **46**
Altcross Way L11: Crox 6A **46**
Altfield Rd. L14: Knott A 2D **60**
Altfinch Cl. L14: Knott A 2E **60**
Altham Rd. L11: Norr G 2L **59**
PR8: South 4D **12**
Althorpe Dr. PR8: South 3D **12**
Althorp St. L8: Liv 5E **74**
Alt Mdw. Vw. L11: Crox 6A **46**
Altmoor Rd. L36: Huy 3H **61**
Alton Av. L21: Lith 1N **43**
Alton Cl. L38: Hight 1F **32**
WN4: Ash M 7J **41**
Alton Rd. CH43: Oxton 3G **73**
L6: Liv 4J **59**
Alt Rd. L20: Boot 5B **44**
L36: Huy 6J **61**
L37: Form 2G **25**
L38: Hight 8F **24**
(not continuous)
Alt Side Ct. L10: Faz 3N **45**
Alt St. L8: Liv 1G **74**
Altway L10: Aintr 8H **35**
Altway Ct. *L10: Aintr* *8H* ***35***
(off Altway)
Altys La. L39: Orm 9D **20**
Alundale Ct. *L20: Boot* *7B* ***44***
(off Clairville Cl.)
Alundale Rd. L12: W Der 4C **60**
ALVANLEY 4G **115**
Alvanley Dr. WA6: Hel 3F **114**
Alvanley Grn. L32: Kirkb 9A **36**
Alvanley Pk. WA6: Alv 3H **115**
Alvanley Pl. CH43: Oxton 2J **73**
Alvanley Rd. CH66: Gt Sut 1K **111**
L12: W Der 4A **60**
L32: Kirkb 9A **36**
WA6: Hel 2F **114**
Alvanley Ter. WA6: Frod 6L **107**
Alvanley Vw. CH2: Elt 2M **113**
Alvanley Way *CH66: Gt Sut* *1K* ***111***
(off Gawsworth Rd.)
Alva Rd. L35: Rainh 7G **63**
Alvega Cl. CH62: New F 9B **74**
Alverstone Av. CH41: Birke 1F **72**
Alverstone Cl. WA5: Gt San 1E **80**
Alverstone Rd. CH44: Wall 6K **57**
L18: Moss H 3L **75**
Alverton Cl. WA8: Widnes 8G **79**
Alvina La. L4: W'ton 2D **58**
L33: Kirkb 6E **36**
Alwain Grn. L24: Speke 5K **93**
Alwen St. CH41: Birke 8F **56**
Alwyn Av. L21: Lith 1A **44**
Alwyn Cl. L17: Aig 5G **75**
WN7: Leigh 1N **53**
Alwyn Gdns. CH46: More 9N **55**
Alwyn St. L17: Aig 5G **74**
Amanda Rd. L10: Faz 3N **45**
L35: Rainh 4E **62**
Amanda Way L31: Mell 7N **35**
Amaury Cl. L23: Thorn 6A **34**
Amaury Rd. L23: Thorn 6A **34**
Ambassador Dr. L26: Halew 7L **77**
Ambergate WN8: Skel 5E **30**
Ambergate Cl. WA9: St H 2N **63**
Ambergate Rd. L19: G'dale 9N **75**
Amberleigh Cl. WA4: App T 4J **99**
Amberley Av. CH46: More 1K **71**
Amberley Cl. CH46: More 1K **71**
L6: Liv 2J **59**
Amberley St. L8: Liv 9M **5** (1F **74**)
Amber Way L14: Knott A 2E **60**
Ambleside Av. CH46: More 9L **55**
Ambleside Cl. CH61: Thing 1A **88**
CH62: Brom 8D **90**
WA7: Beech 1A **108**
Ambleside Cres. WA2: Warr 6D **66**
Ambleside Dr. L33: Kirkb 7B **36**
Ambleside Pl. WA11: St H 1L **49**
Ambleside Rd. CH65: Ell P 3A **112**
L18: Aller 7B **76**
L31: Mag 1J **35**
Ambrose Ct. WA1: Warr 2E **82**
Amelia Cl. L6: Liv 2L **5** (6E **58**)
WA8: Widnes 4L **79**
Amelia St. WA2: Warr 1D **82**
Amersham WN8: Skel 5E **30**
Amersham Rd. L4: W'ton 8H **45**
(not continuous)
Amery Gro. CH42: Tran 6J **73**
Amesbury Dr. WN3: Winst 1E **40**
Amethyst Cl. L6: Liv 5G **58**
L21: Lith 2B **44**
Amherst Rd. L17: Aig 6H **75**

Amidian Ct.—Ashby Cl.

Amidian Ct. *CH44: Wall* .6H 57
(off Poulton Rd.)
Amis Gro. WA3: Low .2F 52
Amity St. L8: Liv .3E 74
Amos Av. L21: Lith .2B 44
Ampleforth Cl. L32: Kirkb .1A 46
Ampthill Rd. L17: Aig .6H 75
Ampulla Rd. L11: Crox .7A 46
Amy Wlk. L10: Faz .3N 45
Ancaster Rd. L17: Aig .6H 75
Ancholme Cl. L35: Whis .3D 62
Anchorage, The CH64: P'gte .7C 100
L3: Liv .2C 74
WA13: Lymm .5D 84
Anchorage La. L18: Moss H .5K 75
Anchor Cl. WA7: Murd .9F 96
Anchor Ct. PR8: Birkd .1M 11
WA1: Warr .2E 82
Anchor Ctyd. L3: Liv .8D 4
Anchor St. PR9: South .8G 7
Ancient Mdws. L9: Aintr .3G 45
Ancroft Rd. L14: Knott A .6E 60
Ancrum Rd. L33: Kirkb .5B 36
Anders Dr. L33: Kirkb .6E 36
Anderson Cl. CH61: Irby .1A 88
L35: Rainh .8G 63
WA2: Padg .7J 67
Anderson Ct. CH62: Brom .9C 90
Anderson Rd. L21: Lith .1C 44
Anderson St. L5: Liv .3D 58
(not continuous)
Anderson Trad. Est. *WA8: Widnes* .1K 95
(off Croft St.)
Anderson Way L21: Lith .1C 44
Anderton Rd. WA9: St H .1N 63
Anderton Ter. L36: Roby .7G 61
Andover Cl. WA2: Padg .8F 66
Andover Cres. WN3: Winst .1E 40
Andover Rd. WA11: Hay .2G 50
Andover Way L25: Hunts X .8H 77
Andreas Cl. PR8: Birkd .2A 12
Andrew Av. L31: Mell .8N 35
WN5: Bil .6B 40
Andrew Cl. WA8: Widnes .8F 78
Andrew Ho. L8: Liv .9K 5
Andrews Cl. L37: Form .3E 24
Andrews La. L37: Form .2E 24
Andrew St. L4: W'ton .9E 44
Andrew's Wlk. CH60: Hesw .7B 88
Andrews Yort L37: Form .3E 24
Andromeda Way WA9: Bold .2D 64
Anemone Way WA9: Bold .2C 64
ANFIELD .2F 58
Anfield .2F 58
Anfield Ct. L4: W'ton .2F 58
Anfield Crematorium .1G 58
Anfield Rd. L4: W'ton .2E 58
Angela St. L7: Liv .9G 58
Angelica Dr. L11: Norr G .8L 45
Angelica Rd. L32: Kirkb .7D 36
Angers La. L31: Mell .5N 35
Anglers Rest M44: Cad .4L 69
Anglesea Rd. L9: W'ton .7F 44
Anglesea Way L8: Liv .4E 74
Anglesey Cl. CH65: Ell P .4A 112
Anglesey Rd. CH44: Wall .4H 57
CH48: W Kir .4B 70
Anglezark Cl. L7: Liv .7G 59
Anglezarke Rd. WA12: Newt W .8J 51
Anglia Way L25: Hunts X .8G 77
Anglican Ct. *L8: Liv* .1D 74
(off Blair St.)
Anglo Cl. L9: Aintr .2H 45
Angus Rd. CH63: Brom .9B 90
L11: Norr G .1L 59
Annable Rd. M44: Irlam .1M 69
Annandale Cl. L33: Kirkb .5B 36
Annandale Gdns. WN8: Uph .4J 31
Annan Gro. WN4: Ash M .6N 41
Ann Cl. CH66: Lit Sut .7J 103
Ann Conway Ho. *L15: Wavtr* .1K 75
(off Garmoyle Cl.)
Anne Av. PR8: Ainsd .8L 11
Anne Gro. WA9: St H .2M 63
Annerley St. L7: Liv .9H 59
Annesley Rd. CH44: Wall .6J 57
L17: Aig .6H 75
Anne St. WA9: Clock F .6N 63
Annette Av. WA12: Newt W .5J 51
Annexe, The *PR9: South* .7H 7
(off Hoghton Gro.)
Annie Rd. L20: Boot .4C 44
Annie St. WA2: Warr .2D 82
Ann St. WA7: Run .4L 95
WN8: Skel .4B 30
Ann St. W. WA8: Widnes .9L 79
Anscot Av. CH63: Beb .1M 89
Ansdell Dr. WA10: Ec'stn .5E 48
Ansdell Gro. PR9: South .3M 7
Ansdell Rd. WA8: Widnes .6L 79
Ansdell Vs. Rd. L35: Rainh .5F 62
Anson St. L3: Liv .4K 5 (7E 58)
Anstey Cl. CH46: More .8J 55
Anstey Rd. L13: Liv .6N 59
Ansty Cl. WA11: St H .5N 49
Anthony's Way CH60: Hesw .8A 88
Anthorn Cl. CH43: Noct .4D 72
Anthorn Rd. WN3: Wigan .1G 40
Antler Ct. WN4: Ash M .5K 41
Antonio St. L20: Boot .9C 44
Antons Cl. L26: Halew .1K 93
Antons Ct. L26: Halew .1L 93
Antons Rd. CH61: Pens .2A 88
L26: Halew .1K 93
Antony Rd. WA4: Warr .6C 82
Antrim Cl. WA11: Hay .4E 50
WN3: Winst .1E 40
Antrim Dr. CH66: Gt Sut .3L 111
Antrim Rd. WA2: Warr .7B 66
Antrim St. L13: Liv .2K 59
Antrobus Golf Course .9H 99
Anvil Cl. CH2: Elt .1M 113
L20: Boot .6A 44
WN5: Orr .7N 31
Anzacs, The CH62: Port S .1B 90
Anzio Rd. L36: Huy .5H 61
Apartments, The PR9: South .7G 6
Apex Ct. CH62: Brom .6D 90
Apollo Ct. *CH44: Wall* .4K 57
(off Rudgrave Sq.)
Apollo Cres. L33: Kirkb .7C 36
Apollo Pk. WA5: Burtw .6K 65
Apollo Way L6: Liv .4G 58
L30: Neth .7E 34
Apostles Way L33: Kirkb .6B 36
Appin Rd. CH41: Birke .3L 73
Apple Blossom Gro. M44: Cad .5K 69
Appleby Cl. WA8: Widnes .8F 78
Appleby Dr. L30: Neth .8B 34
Appleby Grn. L12: W Der .3B 60
Appleby Gro. CH62: Brom .9C 90
Appleby Lawn L27: N'ley .4L 77
Appleby Rd. L33: Kirkb .7C 36
WA2: Warr .6D 66
Appleby Wlk. L27: N'ley .4L 77
WA8: Widnes .8F 78
Appleby Way WA10: St H .3J 49
Applecorn Cl. WA9: Sut L .3N 63
Apple Ct. *L6: Liv* .6G 59
(off Coleridge St.)
Applecross Cl. WA3: Birchw .3A 68
Appledale Dr. CH66: Whit .5M 111
Apple Dell Av. WA3: Golb .1D 52
Appledore Ct. L24: Speke .3F 92
Appledore Gro. WA9: Sut L .5M 63
Appleford Cl. WA4: App .9F 82
Applegarth CH46: More .2K 71
Apple Hey WN6: App B .5M 23
Apple Jacks Adventure Pk. .5G 99
APPLETON
WA4 .1F 98
WA8 .6L 79
Appleton Dr. CH49: Grea .5M 71
CH65: Whit .2L 111
Appleton Hall Gdns. WA4: App .2F 98
Appleton M. *WA13: Lymm* .4C 84
(off Oldfield Rd.)
APPLETON PARK .3E 98
Appleton Rd. L4: W'ton .9G 44
L21: Lith .1N 43
L32: Kirkb .7C 36
WA8: Widnes .7L 79
WA9: St H .8M 49
WN8: Skel .2C 30
Appleton St. WA8: Widnes .1L 95
APPLETON THORN .3J 99
Appleton Thorn Trad. Est. WA4: App T .1L 99
Appleton Village WA8: Widnes .7K 79
Apple Tree Cl. L24: Hale .6B 94
L28: Stockb V .1F 60
Appletree Cl. L18: Aller .7A 76
Apple Tree Gro. CH66: Gt Sut .5L 111
Appletree Gro. WA2: Fearn .7G 67
Applewood Ct. L26: Halew .7L 77
Applewood Gro. L26: Halew .7L 77
APPLEY BRIDGE .5M 23
Appley Bridge Station (Rail) .6M 23
Appley Cl. WN6: App B .3M 23
Appley La. Nth. WN6: App B .3M 23
Appley La. Sth. WN6: App B .7M 23
WN8: Roby M .7M 23
April Gro. L6: Liv .4J 59
April Ri. L30: Neth .8D 34
Apsley Av. CH45: Wall .3H 57
Apsley Brow L31: Mag .2G 35
Apsley Gro. CH63: Beb .1N 89
Apsley Rd. CH62: New F .8A 74
L12: W Der .3A 60
Aquarius Cl. L14: Knott A .5E 60
Arabis Gdns. WA9: Bold .2D 64
Aragon Cl. L31: Mag .9K 27
Aragon Ct. WA7: Manor P .4E 96
Aran Cl. L24: Hale .5A 94
Arborn Dr. CH49: Upton .2A 72
Arbour Ct. L33: Know I .9F 36
Arbour La. L33: Know I .1E 46
Arbour St. PR8: South .9H 7
Arbour Wlk. WA6: Hel .3D 114
Arbury Av. WA11: St H .4N 49
Arbury Ct. WA2: Winw .4C 66
Arbury La. WA2: Winw .3D 66
Arcade, The CH65: Ell P .9M 103
Arcadia Av. L31: Lydi .9J 27
Archbishop Warlock Ct. L3: Liv .5B 58
Archbrook M. *L13: Liv* .4K 59
(off Sutton St.)
Archer Av. WA4: Warr .6F 82
Archer Cl. L4: Kirkd .2D 58
Archerfield Rd. L18: Aller .6N 75
Archer Gro. WA9: St H .6A 50
Archers Ct. *CH49: Wdchu* .6A 72
(off Childwall Grn.)
Archers Cft. CH62: Brom .6C 90
Archers Fold L31: Mell .7N 35
Archers Grn. CH62: East .2D 102
Archers Grn. Rd. WA5: Westb .6J 65
Archer St. L4: Kirkd .2D 58
Archers Way CH49: Wdchu .6A 72
CH66: Gt Sut .4K 111
Arch La. WN4: Garsw .8C 40
Arch Vw. Cres. L1: Liv .8H 5 (9D 58)
Archway Rd. L36: Huy .7H 61
Archway Wlk. WA12: Newt W .7N 51
Arctic Rd. L20: Boot .7N 43
Arden WA8: Widnes .6D 78
Arden Cl. PR8: Ainsd .9G 11
WA3: Birchw .3B 68
Arden Dr. CH64: Nest .8E 100
Ardennes Rd. L36: Huy .6J 61
Arderne Cl. CH63: Spit .5A 90
Ardern Lea WA6: Alv .4G 115
Ardleigh Av. PR8: South .3D 12
Ardleigh Cl. L13: Liv .7L 59
Ardleigh Gro. L13: Liv .7L 59
Ardleigh Pl. L13: Liv .7L 59
Ardleigh Rd. L13: Liv .7K 59
Ardmore Rd. L18: Moss H .6M 75
Ardrossan Rd. L4: W'ton .1H 59
Ardville Rd. L11: Norr G .7J 45
Ardwick Rd. L24: Speke .4K 93
Ardwick St. WA9: St H .7M 49
Area 51 Laser Quest .2G 76
Arena, The CH62: Brom .5E 90
Arena Gdns. WA2: Warr .9E 66
Argameols Cl. PR8: South .1E 12
Argarmeols Gro. L37: Form .8E 16
Argarmeols Rd. L37: Form .7E 16
Argo Rd. L22: Wloo .1K 43
Argos Pl. L20: Kirkd .9C 44
Argos Rd. L20: Kirkd .9C 44
Argyle Ct. L1: Liv .7F 4
PR9: South .5J 7
Argyle Pk. PR9: South .7J 7
Argyle Rd. L4: W'ton .3G 59
L19: Garst .1A 92
PR9: South .5J 7
Argyle St. CH41: Birke .2L 73
L1: Liv .7F 4 (9C 58)
WA10: St H .5J 49
Argyle St. Sth. CH41: Birke .3L 73
Argyll Av. CH62: East .2C 102
Argyll Cl. WN4: Garsw .7E 40
Ariel Wlk. WA3: Low .2G 52
Aries Cl. L14: Knott A .4E 60
Ariss Gro. L35: Whis .4D 62
Arizona Cres. WA5: Gt San .1K 81
Arkenshaw Rd. WA3: Croft .1H 67
Arkenstone Cl. WA8: Widnes .6F 78
Arkill Gdns. CH49: Upton .5N 71
Arkle Rd. CH43: Bid .9F 56
Arkles La. L4: W'ton .2F 58
Arkles Rd. L4: W'ton .3F 58
Arklow Dr. L24: Hale .5A 94
Ark Royal Way CH41: Tran .4M 73
Arkwood Cl. CH62: Spit .4B 90
Arkwright Ct. WA7: Astm .4B 96
Arkwright Rd. WA7: Astm .4B 96
Arkwright St. L5: Liv .4D 58
Arlescourt Rd. L12: W Der .4A 60
Arley Av. WA4: Stockt H .8E 82
Arley Cl. CH43: Bid .2C 72
Arley Dr. WA8: Widnes .6D 78
Arley Gro. WA13: Lymm .6G 84
Arley Rd. CW9: Ant .7M 99
WA4: App T .3J 99
Arley St. L3: Liv .1E 4 (5B 58)
Arlington Av. L18: Moss H .3L 75
Arlington Cl. PR8: Ainsd .9G 11
Arlington Ct. CH43: Oxton .3F 72
Arlington Dr. WA5: Penk .4G 81
WN7: Leigh .2K 53
Arlington Rd. CH45: Wall .3E 56
Armill Rd. L11: Crox .7A 46
Armitage Gdns. L18: Aller .7N 75
Armley Rd. L4: W'ton .2G 59
Armour Av. WA2: Warr .7C 66
Armour Gro. L13: Liv .7M 59
Armoury, The L12: W Der .2N 59
Armoury Bank WN4: Ash M .8K 41
Armscot Cl. L25: Hunts X .9F 76
Armscot Pl. L25: Hunts X .9F 76
Armstrong Cl. WA3: Birchw .5L 67
Armstrong Quay L3: Liv .5E 74
Armthorpe Dr. CH66: Lit Sut .9G 103
Arncliffe Dr. WA5: Burtw .3H 65
Arncliffe Rd. L25: Hunts X, Woolt .7G 77
Arncroft Cl. L30: Neth .8C 34
Arndale WA7: Beech .1A 108
Arnhem Cres. WA2: Warr .1D 82
Arnhem Rd. L36: Huy .5J 61
Arnian Ct. L39: Augh .4A 28
Arnian Rd. WA11: Rainf .4C 38
Arnian Way WA11: Rainf .4C 38
Arno Ct. CH43: Oxton .5H 73
Arnold Av. WA10: St H .5G 49
Arnold Cl. WA9: St H .9M 49
Arnold Cres. L8: Liv .2F 74
Arnold Gro. L15: Wavtr .9M 59
Arnold Pl. WA8: Widnes .9F 78
Arnold St. CH45: Wall .4H 57
WA1: Warr .2E 82
(off Manchester Rd.)
Arno Rd. CH43: Oxton .5H 73
Arnot Cl. WA10: St H .5J 49
Arnot St. L4: W'ton .9E 44
Arnot Way CH63: H Beb .1K 89
Arnside L21: Lith .2C 44
Arnside Av. L35: Rainh .5D 62
WA11: Hay .4D 50
Arnside Gro. WA4: Warr .6C 82
Arnside Rd. CH43: Oxton .4G 73
CH45: Wall .4H 57
L7: Liv .8H 59
L36: Huy .7F 60
PR9: South .8H 7
Arnside Ter. PR9: South .8H 7
Aron Ct. L34: Presc .3A 62
ARPLEY MEADOWS .5C 82
Arpley Rd. WA1: Warr .4C 82
Arpley St. WA1: Warr .3B 82
Arrad Ho. L7: Liv .6K 5
Arrad St. L7: Liv .7K 5 (9E 58)
Arran Av. CH65: Ell P .4A 112
Arran Cl. WA2: Fearn .7H 67
WA11: St H .4A 50
Arran Dr. WA6: Frod .7M 107
Arranmore Rd. L18: Moss H .6M 75
Arriva Stadium, The .8J 33
Arrivato Plaza *WA10: St H* .7L 49
(off Hall St.)
Arrow Ct. CH65: Ell P .1N 111
Arrowe Av. CH46: More .1L 71
Arrowe Brook Ct. CH49: Grea .4M 71
Arrowe Brook La. CH49: Grea .7L 71
Arrowe Brook Rd. CH49: Wdchu .6N 71
Arrowe Commercial Pk. CH49: Upton .5N 71
Arrowe Country Pk. .7N 71
Arrowe Ct. *CH49: Wdchu* .6A 72
(off Childwall Grn.)
ARROWE HILL .5N 71
Arrowe Pk. Golf Course .8A 72
Arrowe Pk. Rd. CH49: Upton, Wdchu .3A 72
Arrowe Rd. CH49: Grea .5L 71
Arrowe Side CH49: Grea .4M 71
Arrowe Vw. *CH49: Upton* .3A 72
(off Arrowe Pk. Rd.)
Arrowsmith Rd. WA11: Hay .3H 51
ARTHILL .8N 85
Arthill La. WA14: L Boll .8N 85
Art Ho. Sq. L1: Liv .7H 5
Arthur Av. CH65: Ell P .9A 104
(not continuous)
Arthur St. CH41: Birke .1J 73
(not continuous)
L9: W'ton .7E 44
L19: Garst .2B 92
WA2: Warr .2B 82
WA7: Run .5K 95
Arts Cen. at Edge Hill University, The .1E 28
Arundel Av. CH45: Wall .3F 56
L8: Liv .2H 75
L17: Liv .2H 75
Arundel Cl. CH61: Pens .2M 87
L8: Liv .2F 74
Arundel Ct. CH65: Ell P .2C 112
Arundell Cl. WA5: Burtw .3H 65
Arundel Rd. PR8: Birkd .6M 11
Arundel St. L4: W'ton .9D 44
Arvon St. L20: Boot .4C 44
Asbridge St. L8: Liv .2G 74
Asbury Cl. L18: Aller .5B 76
Asbury Rd. CH45: Wall .3D 56
Ascot Av. L21: Lith .2N 43
WA7: Run .9L 95
Ascot Cl. PR8: Birkd .1L 11
WA1: Wools .1M 83
WA4: Grap .6K 83
Ascot Dr. CH63: Beb .2M 89
CH66: Gt Sut .2J 111
L33: Kirkb .6C 36
Ascot Gro. CH63: Beb .2M 89
Ascot Pk. L23: Crosb .7M 33
Ascot Vw. L22: Wloo .9J 33
Ascroft Rd. L9: Aintr .2G 44
Ash Acre Mdws. WA4: Westy .4H 83
Ash Av. M44: Cad .4K 69
WA12: Newt W .8L 51
Ashbank Rd. L11: Norr G .8M 45
Ashberry Dr. WA4: App T .2J 99
Ashbourne Av. L23: Blun .7J 33
L30: Neth .9D 34
WA7: Run .9L 95
Ashbourne Cl. CH66: Gt Sut .5K 111
Ashbourne Cres. L36: Huy .7F 60
Ashbourne Rd. L17: Aig .6H 75
WA5: Gt San .3K 81
Ashbrook Av. WA7: Sut W .2A 108
Ashbrook Cres. WA2: Warr .9E 66
Ashbrook Dr. L9: Aintr .4H 45
Ashbrook Ter. CH63: Beb .1N 89
Ash Brow WN8: Newb .4D 22
Ashburn Av. L25: Gate .3E 76
L33: Kirkb .7C 36
Ashburnham Way L3: Liv .1J 5 (6D 58)
Ashburton Av. CH43: Clau .2F 72
Ashburton Rd. CH43: Clau .2E 72
CH44: Wall .5H 57
CH48: W Kir .5C 70
Ashbury Cl. L14: Knott A .3F 60
WA7: Wind H .5F 96
Ashbury Dr. WA11: Hay .3E 50
Ashbury Rd. L14: Knott A .3F 60
Ashby Cl. CH46: More .8J 55

Ash Cl.—Ayrefield Gro.

Ash Cl. CH66: Gt Sut 4L 111
L15: Wavtr 9K 59
L39: Orm 8B 20
WN6: App B 6N 23
Ashcombe Rd.
L14: Knott A 6A 60
Ash Cres. L36: Huy 9J 61
Ashcroft Av. L39: Orm 7D 20
Ashcroft Dr. CH61: Hesw 4N 87
Ashcroft Rd. L33: Know I 8F 36
L37: Form 3F 24
WA13: Lymm 4H 85
Ashcroft St. L20: Boot 7A 44
WA9: St H 7M 49
(not continuous)
Ashdale L36: Huy 7H 61
Ashdale Cl. L37: Form 2C 24
Ashdale Pk. CH49: Grea 5J 71
Ashdale Rd. L9: W'ton 6F 44
L18: Moss H 3M 75
L22: Wloo 9K 33
WN3: Wigan 1J 41
Ashdown Cl. PR8: South 2D 12
Ashdown Cres. WA9: Clock F 5M 63
Ashdown Dr. CH49: Grea 6K 71
Ashdown Gro. L26: Halew 7L 77
Ashdown La. WA3: Birchw 4A 68
Asher Ct. WA4: App T 3L 99
Ashfarm Ct. L14: Knott A 6D 60
Ashfield L15: Wavtr 9J 59
L35: Rainh 6G 62
Ashfield Cl. WA13: Lymm 4H 85
Ashfield Ct. WA10: St H 7J 49
(off Glover St.)
Ashfield Cres. CH62: Brom 7C 90
WN5: Bil 6A 40
Ashfield Gdns. WA4: Westy 5G 82
Ashfield Gro. M44: Irlam 3L 69
Ashfield Ho. CH64: Nest 6E 100
(off Churchill Way)
Ashfield Rd. CH62: Brom 7B 90
CH65: Ell P 9A 104
L17: Aig 6J 75
Ashfield Rd. Nth. CH65: Ell P 9A 104
Ashfield St. L5: Liv 4B 58
Ashfield Ter. WN6: App B 5M 23
Ashfield Way L14: Brd G 7C 60
Ashford Cl. L21: Lith 2B 44
L26: Halew 9J 77
Ashford Dr. WA4: App 4F 98
Ashford Rd. CH41: Birke 4J 73
CH47: Meols 9D 54
Ashford Way WA8: Widnes 7N 79
Ash Grange L14: Knott A 6B 60
Ash Gro. CH45: New B 2J 57
CH66: Lit Sut 8H 103
L15: Wavtr 9J 59
L21: Sea 4N 43
L35: Presc 5B 62
L37: Form 3C 24
WA3: Golb 2C 52
WA4: Warr 5E 82
WA7: Run 7M 95
WA8: Widnes 8G 78
WA9: Clock F 5M 63
WA11: Rainf 5C 38
WN8: Skel 3A 30
Ash Gro. Cres. WN5: Bil 5N 39
Ash Ho. WA12: Newt W 6J 51
Ashland Av. WN4: Ash M 7J 41
Ashlands WA6: Frod 7M 107
Ash La. WA4: App 8F 82
WA8: Widnes 7B 78
Ashlar Gro. L17: Aig 6K 75
Ashlar Rd. L17: Aig 6K 75
L22: Wloo 9L 33
Ashlea Rd. CH61: Pens 4N 87
Ashleigh Rd. L31: Mag 4L 35
Ashley Av. CH47: Meols 8G 54
Ashley Bus. Cen. L34: Presc 3B 62
(off East St.)
Ashley Cl. L33: Kirkb 6C 36
L35: Rainh 7G 62
WA4: Grap 5K 83
Ashley Ct. M44: Cad 4K 69
WA4: App 1D 98
WA6: Frod 6K 107
Ashley Grn. WA8: Widnes 7G 79
Ashley Rd. PR9: South 8H 7
WA7: Run 5N 95
WN8: Skel 1E 30
Ashley St. CH42: Rock F 6M 73
Ashley Way WA8: Widnes 1K 95
Ashley Way W. WA8: Widnes 9J 79
Ashmead Rd. WN8: Skel 9D 22
Ashmore Cl. CH48: Caldy 1D 86
WA3: Birchw 6A 68
Ashmuir Hey L32: Kirkb 1D 46
Ashover Av. L14: Knott A 5E 60
Ash Priors WA8: Widnes 5G 78
Ashridge St. WA7: Run 4J 95
Ash Rd. CH2: Elt 2N 113
CH42: Tran 4K 73
CH63: H Beb 9M 73
L21: Lith 3N 43
M31: Part 6K 69
WA2: Winw 3C 66
WA3: Rix 7G 69
WA5: Penk 4H 81
WA11: Hay 3G 51
WA13: Lymm 5C 84
Ash St. L20: Boot 6B 44
PR8: South 1B 12
Ashton Av. L35: Rainh 8F 62
Ashton Cl. CH62: East 3D 102
L25: Woolt 7H 77
WA6: Frod 5N 107
WA7: W'ton 9J 95
Ashton Ct. CH48: W Kir 7B 70
WA6: Frod 5M 107
ASHTON CROSS 9F 40
Ashton Dr. CH48: W Kir 7B 70
L25: Hunts X 9F 76
WA6: Frod 4M 107
Ashton Grange Ind. Est. WN4: Ash M 5K 41
Ashton Heath WN4: Ash M 9L 41
ASHTON-IN-MAKERFIELD 8K 41
Ashton-in-Makerfield Golf Course 9G 41
Ashton Leisure Cen.
Ashton-in-Makerfield 7J 41
Ashton Pk. L25: Hunts X 8H 77
Ashton Pl. PR8: South 9G 7
Ashton Rd. PR8: Birkd 5M 11
WA3: Golb 1C 52
WA6: Norl 9N 115
WA12: Newt W 4L 51
WN5: Bil 3C 40
ASHTON'S GREEN 7B 50
Ashtons Grn. Dr. WA9: St H 8B 50
Ashton's La. L24: Hale 5K 93
L37: Form 3C 24
Ashton Sq. L25: Woolt 7F 76
Ashton St. L3: Liv 4L 5 (7E 58)
L13: Liv 6M 59
WA2: Warr 2C 82
Ashton Way CH62: Brom 2C 90
L36: Huy 3H 61
Ash Tree Apts. CH44: Wall 6K 57
Ashtree Cl. CH64: Lit N 7F 100
Ashtree Cft. CH64: Will 7N 101
Ashtree Dr. CH64: Lit N 8G 100
Ashtree Farm Ct. CH64: Will 6N 101
Ashtree Gro. L12: Crox 6C 46
ASHURST 9E 22
Ashurst Cl. L25: Gate 4F 76
WA11: St H 4A 50
WN8: Skel 9D 22
Ashurst Ct. L37: Form 2E 24
Ashurst Dr. WA11: St H 4N 49
Ashurst Gdns. WN8: Skel 9D 22
Ashurst Rd. WN8: Skel 1E 30
Ash Va. L15: Wavtr 9K 59
Ash Vs. CH44: Wall 7J 57
Ashville Ind. Est. WA7: Sut W 3A 108
Ashville Point WA7: Sut W 3A 108
Ashville Rd. CH41: Birke 2G 73
CH43: Clau 2G 73
CH44: Wall 7K 57
Ashville Way WA7: Sut W 3A 108
Ashwall St. WN8: Skel 4A 30
Ashwater Rd. L12: W Der 8A 46
Ashway CH60: Hesw 9B 88
Ashwell Av. WA3: Low 1E 52
Ashwell St. L8: Liv 1D 74
Ashwood WN8: Skel 1F 30
(off Forest Dr.)
Ashwood Av. WA1: Warr 1F 82
WA3: Low 2E 52
WN4: Ash M 9J 41
Ashwood Cl. CH66: Gt Sut 4J 111
L27: N'ley 3J 77
L33: Kirkb 6C 36
WA8: Widnes 9D 78
Ashwood Ct. CH43: Bid 8C 56
WA3: Low 3E 52
Ashwood Dr. L12: Crox 7B 46
Ashwood La. CH2: Wer 9E 112
Askern Rd. L32: Kirkb 2D 46
Askett Cl. WA11: Hay 3F 50
Askew Cl. CH44: Wall 5K 57
Askew St. L4: W'ton 9E 44
Askham Cl. L8: Liv 1G 74
Askrigg Av. CH66: Lit Sut 9G 103
Asland Gdns. PR9: South 3A 8
Asmall Cl. L39: Orm 7B 20
Asmall La. L39: Hals 5K 19
L39: Orm 6N 19
L40: Scar 6N 19
Aspen Cl. CH60: Hesw 7D 88
CH66: Gt Sut 4K 111
L33: Kirkb 5D 36
Aspendale Rd. CH42: Tran 4K 73
Aspen Gdns. PR8: South 9K 7
WA9: St H 3F 62
Aspen Gro. L8: Liv 2H 75
L37: Form 3C 24
WA1: Padd 1H 83
Aspen Way WN8: Skel 2B 30
Aspenwood WN4: Ash M 9J 41
Aspes Rd. L12: W Der 2C 60
Aspinall Cl. WA2: Fearn 6H 67
Aspinall Cres. L37: Gt Alt 3M 25
Aspinall St. CH41: Birke 1J 73
L34: Presc 3A 62
Aspley Ho. L22: Wloo 1L 43
Aspull Cl. WA3: Birchw 5K 67
ASPULL COMMON 1K 53
Aspull Comn. WN7: Leigh 1K 53
Aspull Ct. WN7: Leigh 1K 53
Asquith Av. CH41: Birke 1H 73
Asser Rd. L11: Norr G 1K 59
Asshetton Cl. WA12: Newt W 6K 51
Assheton Wlk. L24: Hale 5B 94
Assissian Cres. L30: Neth 7D 34
Astbury Cl. WA3: Low 2J 53
Aster Cres. WA7: Beech 1B 108
Aster Dr. L33: Kirkb 6B 36
Asterfield Av. CH63: H Beb 9L 73
Aster Rd. WA11: Hay 3H 51
Aster Wlk. M31: Part 7M 69
(off Cross La. W.)
Astley Cl. WA4: Warr 5C 82
WA8: Widnes 5F 78
WA11: Rainf 4C 38
Astley Ct. M44: Irlam 1L 69
WN4: Ash M 6L 41
Astley Rd. L36: Huy 3J 61
M44: Irlam 1K 69
ASTMOOR 4B 96
Astmoor Bri. La. WA7: Cas 5B 96
Astmoor Ind. Est. WA7: Astm 4B 96
(Brindley Rd.)
WA7: Astm 4A 96
(Goddard Rd.)
Astmoor La. WA7: Astm 4M 95
WA7: Cas 5B 96
Astmoor Rd. WA7: Astm 4M 95
Astmoor Spine Rd. WA7: Astm 4C 96
ASTON 5G 108
Aston Av. WA3: Ris 5N 67
Aston Cl. CH43: Oxton 5F 72
Aston Ct. WA1: Wools 8K 67
Aston Flds. Rd. WA7: Pres B 2F 108
Aston Forge WA7: Pres B 1H 109
Aston Grn. WA7: Pres B 9G 97
ASTON HEATH 3G 109
Aston La. WA7: Aston, Sut W 3C 108
WA7: Pres B 1H 109
Aston La. Nth. WA7: Pres B 2G 109
Aston La. Sth. WA7: Pres B 3G 108
Aston St. L19: Garst 2B 92
Astonwood Rd. CH42: Tran 5K 73
Astor Dr. WA4: Grap 8G 83
Astor St. L4: W'ton 8E 44
Atheldene Rd. L4: W'ton 8H 45
Athelstan Cl. CH62: Brom 6C 90
Atherton Cl. L5: Liv 4D 58
Atherton Ct. CH45: New B 1G 57
(off Alexandra Rd.)
Atherton Dr. CH49: Wdchu 5A 72
Atherton Ho. CH45: New B 1H 57
Atherton La. M44: Cad 4L 69
Atherton Rake L30: Neth 7C 34
Atherton Rd. CH65: Ell P 8L 103
L9: Aintr 4H 45
Atherton's Quay WA5: Warr 4N 81
Atherton St. CH45: New B 9G 43
L34: Presc 3A 62
WA10: St H 5J 49
Athlone Rd. WA2: Warr 9B 66
Athol Cl. CH62: East 1D 102
WA12: Newt W 6H 51
Athol Dr. CH62: East 2D 102
Athol Duncan Dr. CH49: Upton 5N 71
Athole Gro. PR9: South 8L 7
Atholl Cres. L10: Aintr 9J 35
Atholl Gro. WN3: Wigan 1J 41
Athol St. CH41: Birke 1L 73
L5: Liv 4B 58
(Bangor St., not continuous)
L5: Liv 4A 58
(Denbigh St., not continuous)
Atkinson, The 8G 6
Atkinson Gro. L36: Huy 5K 61
Atkinson Rd. L39: Orm 7D 20
Atlanta Ct. L33: Kirkb 5B 36
Atlanta Gdns. WA5: Gt San 9K 65
Atlantic Pav. L3: Liv 8D 4 (9B 58)
Atlantic Point L3: Liv 1F 4 (6C 58)
Atlantic Rd. L20: Boot 7A 44
Atlantic Terminal L20: Boot 7N 43
Atlantic Way L3: Liv 3C 74
L30: Boot 2D 44
Atlas Bus. Complex L20: Boot 6N 43
Atlas Rd. L20: Boot 6A 44
Atlas St. WA9: St H 6L 49
Atlas Way CH66: Ell P 7L 103
Atrium Cl. L9: W'ton 7E 44
Atterbury Cl. WA8: Widnes 6F 78
Atterbury St. L8: Liv 3D 74
Attlee Rd. L36: Huy 6L 61
Attwood St. L4: W'ton 2E 58
Atwell St. L6: Liv 5F 58
Atwood Gro. L36: Roby 7H 61
Atworth Ter. CH64: Will 6M 101
(off Neston Rd.)
Aubourn Cl. WA8: Widnes 5F 78
Aubrey Ct. L6: Liv 5F 58
Auburn Rd. CH45: Wall 2G 57
L13: Liv 3K 59
Aubynes, The CH45: Wall 2E 56
Auckery Av. CH66: Gt Sut 2J 111
Auckland Rd. L18: Moss H 3M 75
Audlem Av. CH43: Oxton 5F 72
Audlem Cl. WA7: Sut W 2B 108
Audley St. L3: Liv 3J 5 (7D 58)
Audre Cl. WA5: Gt San 2F 80
Audrey Wlk. L10: Faz 3N 45
AUGHTON 5M 27
Aughton Cl. WN5: Bil 7A 40
Aughton Ct. CH49: Upton 3A 72
Aughton M. PR8: Birkd 1N 11
AUGHTON PARK 2B 28
Aughton Pk. Dr. L39: Augh 2B 28
Aughton Park Station (Rail) 2B 28
Aughton Rd. L20: Boot 5C 44
PR8: Birkd 9E 6
Aughton St. L39: Orm 9B 20
(not continuous)
Augusta Cl. L13: Liv 7M 59
Augusta Gro. WA5: Gt San 1J 81
August Rd. L6: Liv 4J 59
August St. L20: Boot 5B 44
Aukland Gro. WA9: St H 3G 62
Aurorean Cl. L27: N'ley 2H 77
Austell Cl. WA11: St H 3N 49
Austen Dr. WA2: Winw 3B 66
Austin Av. WA10: St H 1F 62
WN4: Garsw 7G 40
Austin Cl. L32: Kirkb 8B 36
Austin St. CH44: Wall 7G 57
Austral Av. WA1: Wools 1J 83
Australia La. WA4: Grap 7K 83
Autumn Gro. CH42: Rock F 8L 73
Autumn Way L20: Boot 5B 44
WA9: Clock F 6M 63
Avalon Ct. WA7: Cas 6C 96
Avalon Ter. L20: Boot 6A 44
(off Tennyson St.)
Avebury Cl. WA3: Low 2F 52
WA8: Widnes 5A 80
Aveley Cl. WA1: Padd 1J 83
Aveling Dr. PR9: Banks 1E 8
Avelon Cl. CH43: Noct 3D 72
L31: Lydi 7G 26
Avenham Cl. PR9: Banks 2F 8
Avens Rd. M31: Part 6M 69
Avenue, The CH47: Meols 7G 55
CH62: Brom 7B 90
L19: Garst 2C 92
L26: Halew 9J 77
L36: Huy 6J 61
L39: Orm 7B 20
(Church Hill Rd.)
L39: Orm 7C 20
(Southport Rd.)
PR8: South 3D 12
PR9: Banks 2D 8
PR9: South 1K 13
WA10: Ec'stn 7E 48
WA11: Rainf 5C 38
WA12: Newt W 6M 51
WA13: Lymm 7C 84
WN5: Bil 9N 31
Averham Cl. WN4: Ash M 1K 51
Avery Cl. WA2: Warr 7F 66
Avery Cres. WA11: Hay 3E 50
Avery Rd. WA11: Hay 3E 50
Avery Sq. WA11: Hay 3E 50
Aviary Ct. L9: W'ton 4E 44
(off Dove Rd.)
Aviemore Cl. WN4: Garsw 7F 40
Aviemore Dr. WA2: Fearn 6H 67
Aviemore Rd. L13: Liv 6L 59
Avington Cl. L12: W Der 2B 60
Avis Wlk. L10: Faz 3N 45
Avocet Av. L19: Garst 8A 76
Avocet Cl. WA2: Warr 6E 66
WA12: Newt W 6L 51
Avolon Rd. L12: W Der 4B 60
Avon WA8: Widnes 6D 78
Avon Av. WA5: Penk 4G 81
Avon Cl. CH64: Nest 8E 100
L4: Kirkd 1D 58
L33: Kirkb 5D 36
Avon Ct. L23: Crosb 6L 33
Avondale CH65: Whit 2N 111
Avondale Av. CH46: More 8N 55
CH62: East 1E 102
L31: Mag 3H 35
Avondale Cl. WA8: Widnes 7E 78
Avondale Dr. WA8: Widnes 7E 78
Avondale Gdns. WA11: Hay 3E 50
Avondale Rd. CH47: Hoy 1C 70
L15: Wavtr 2K 75
PR9: South 7G 7
WA11: Hay 3E 50
Avondale Rd. Nth. PR9: South 6H 7
Avonmore Av. L18: Moss H 5M 75
Avon Rd. WA3: Cul 8N 53
WN4: Ash M 6N 41
WN5: Bil 8M 39
Avon St. CH41: Birke 8F 56
L6: Liv 4G 59
Awelon Cl. L12: W Der 1A 60
Awesome Walls Climbing Cen. 4A 58
Axbridge Av. WA9: Sut L 4N 63
Axholme Cl. CH61: Thing 2B 88
Axholme Rd. CH61: Thing 2A 88
Ayala Cl. L9: W'ton 3E 44
Aycliffe Rd. WA9: St H 3G 63
Aycliffe Wlk. WA8: Widnes 8F 78
Aylesbury Av. CH43: Oxton 6E 72
Aylesbury Cl. CH66: Gt Sut 2H 111
Aylesbury Rd. CH45: New B 2J 57
Aylesford Rd. L13: Liv 6M 59
Aylsham Cl. WA8: Widnes 4F 78
Aylsham Dr. CH49: Upton 1A 72
Aylton Rd. L36: Huy 5F 60
Aylward Pl. L20: Boot 6A 44
(off Glover Pl.)
Aynsley Ct. WA9: St H 3E 62
Ayr Cl. PR8: South 2E 12
Ayrefield Gro. WN6: Shev 7N 23

Ayrefield Rd. WN8: Roby M 9M 23
Ayres Ct. WA9: St H 2H 63
Ayr Rd. L4: W'ton 8F 44
Ayrshire Gdns. WA10: St H 8H 49
Ayrshire Rd. L4: W'ton 1H 59
Ayrton Ho. L8: Liv 1G 75
(off Commerce Way)
Aysgarth Av. L12: W Der 3A 60
Aysgarth Rd. CH45: Wall 3F 56
Ayton La. L16: Child 1A 76
Azalea Gdns. WA9: Bold 2C 64
Azalea Gro. L26: Halew 6H 77
WA7: Beech 2B 108

B

Babbacombe Rd. L16: Child 2C 76
WA5: Penk 4G 80
Bk. Barlow La. L4: Kirkd 1D 58
Bk. Bath St. PR9: South 7G 6
Bk. Bedford St. L7: Liv 7L 5
Bk. Belmont Rd. L6: Liv 4G 59
Bk. Berry St. L1: Liv 7H 5
Bk. Blackfield Ter. L4: Kirkd 2C 58
Bk. Bold St. L1: Liv 6H 5
Bk. Botanic Rd. PR9: South 6M 7
Bk. Boundary Cl. L5: Kirkd 3C 58
Back Bri. Rd. L23: Blun 8J 33
(off Riverslea Rd.)
Back Bri. St. WA12: Newt W 7K 51
Bk. Bridport St. L3: Liv 4H 5
Back Broadway L11: Norr G 9K 45
Bk. Brook Pl. WA4: Westy 5F 82
Back Brow WN8: Uph 5M 31
Bk. Canning St. L8: Liv 8K 5 (9E 58)
Bk. Catharine St. L8: Liv 8K 5
Bk. Chadwick Mt. L5: Liv 2D 58
Bk. Chatham Pl. L7: Liv 8G 58
(off Queensland St.)
Bk. Colquitt St. L1: Liv 7H 5 (9D 58)
Bk. Commutation Row L3: Liv 3H 5
Bk. Compton Rd. PR8: Birkd 3A 12
Bk. Crossland Ter. WA6: Hel 3E 114
Bk. Cross La. WA12: Newt W 6K 51
Bk. Dovecot Pl. L14: Knott A 5D 60
Bk. Egerton St. Nth. L8: Liv 9L 5
Bk. Egerton St. Sth. L8: Liv 9L 5
Bk. Falkner St. Sth. L8: Liv 8M 5 (9F 58)
BACKFORD 9N 111
Backford Cl. CH43: Oxton 5E 72
WA7: Brook 1E 108
Backford Gdns. CH1: Back 6L 111
Backford Rd. CH61: Irby 2L 87
Bk. Forest Rd. PR8: South 9J 7
(not continuous)
Bk. Forshaw St. WA2: Warr 1D 82
(off Forshaw St.)
Bk. Gillmoss La. L11: Crox 4A 46
Bk. Guildford St. L6: Liv 1L 5 (6E 58)
Bk. Hadfield Pl. L25: Woolt 6E 76
(off Church Rd.)
Bk. High St. L25: Woolt 6E 76
(off High St.)
WA7: Run 5K 95
Bk. Holland Pl. L7: Liv 8G 58
(off Wavertree Rd.)
Bk. Hope Pl. L1: Liv 7J 5
Bk. Huskisson St. L8: Liv 9K 5
Bk. Irvine St. L7: Liv 5N 5
Bk. Kelvin Gro. L8: Liv 2F 74
(off Kelvin Gro.)
Bk. Knight St. L1: Liv 8H 5
Back La. L23: L Cros 3L 33
L29: Seft 4B 34
L39: Augh 5K 27
L39: Bic 9E 28
L39: Down 1C 26
L40: Burs 8J 15
WA5: Coll G 2F 64
WA5: Cuerd 6C 80
WA6: Alv 3F 114
WA11: Crank 6J 39
WN6: App B 5N 23
WN8: Dalt 8J 23
WN8: Newb 3A 22
WN8: Skel 5H 31
(Barnfield Dr.)
WN8: Skel 6G 31
(Beavers La.)
Bk. Langham St. L4: W'ton 1E 58
Bk. Leeds St. L3: Liv 2C 4 (6A 58)
Bk. Legh St. WA12: Newt W 7J 51
Bk. Lime St. L1: Liv 5G 5
Bk. Lit. Canning St. L8: Liv 9L 5
Bk. Luton Gro. L4: W'ton 1E 58
Back Mkt. St. WA12: Newt W 6J 51
Bk. Maryland St. L1: Liv 7J 5
Bk. Menai St. CH41: Birke 2J 73
Bk. Mersey Vw. L22: Wloo 9J 33
Bk. Moss La. L40: Burs 7K 15
Bk. Mount St. L22: Wloo 1K 43
Bk. Mulberry St. L7: Liv 8L 5 (9E 58)
Bk. Oliver St. CH41: Birke 2L 73
(off Argyle St.)
Bk. Orford St. L15: Wavtr 9L 59
(off Sandown La.)
Bk. o' the Town La. L38: Ince B 9L 25
Bk. Percy St. L8: Liv 9K 5
Bk. Pickop St. L3: Liv 3E 4
Bk. Price St. CH41: Birke 1K 73
Bk. Renshaw St. L1: Liv 6H 5 (8D 58)
Bk. Rockfield Rd. L4: W'ton 2E 58
(off Blessington Rd.)
Bk. St Bride St. L8: Liv 8L 5
Bk. Sandon St. L8: Liv 9L 5 (1E 74)
Bk. Sandown La. L15: Wavtr 9L 59
(off Sandown La.)
Bk. School La. WN8: Skel 3A 30
WN8: Uph 5M 31
Bk. Seaman Rd. L15: Wavtr 1K 75
(off Seaman Rd.)
Back Seaview CH47: Hoy 1C 70
Bk. Seel St. L1: Liv 7G 5
Bk. Sir Howard St. L8: Liv 8L 5
Bk. Skull Ho. La. WN6: App B 5N 23
Back Sth. Rd. L22: Wloo 1L 43
Bk. Stanley Rd. L20: Boot 7B 44
Bk. Towerlands St. L7: Liv 8G 58
(off Church Mt.)
Bk. Virginia St. PR8: South 9G 7
Bk. Wellesley Rd. L8: Liv 4F 74
(off The Elms)
Bk. Westminster Rd. L4: Kirkd 1D 58
Bk. Windsor Vw. L8: Liv 1G 75
(off Lodge La.)
Bk. Winstanley Rd. L22: Wloo 9L 33
Bk. York Ter. L5: Liv 3D 58
Badbury Cl. WA11: Hay 3F 50
Badby Wood L33: Kirkb 7D 36
Baddow Cft. L25: Woolt 5C 76
Baden Ct. CH48: W Kir 5B 70
Baden Ho. L13: Liv 6N 59
Baden Rd. L13: Liv 6N 59
Bader Cl. CH61: Pens 4M 87
Badger Bait CH64: Lit N 8F 100
Badger Cl. WA7: Pal F 9C 96
Badgers Cl. CH66: Gt Sut 5L 111
L35: Rainh 8H 63
Badgers Pk. CH64: Lit N 8F 100
Badgers Rake L37: Form 8C 16
Badgers Rake La. CH66: Led, Lit Sut 2B 110
Badger's Set CH48: Caldy 1E 86
Badger Way CH43: Pren 8E 72
Badminton St. L8: Liv 5E 74
Baffin Cl. CH46: Leas 5A 56
Bagnall Cl. WA5: Gt San 3L 81
Bagnall St. L4: W'ton 2F 58
Bagot Av. WA5: Warr 9A 66
Bagot St. L15: Wavtr 1J 75
Baguley Av. WA8: Hale B 2D 94
Bahama Cl. WA11: Hay 2F 50
Bahama Rd. WA11: Hay 2F 50
Baildon Grn. CH66: Lit Sut 9G 103
(off Dunmore Rd.)
Bailey Av. CH65: Ell P 8L 103
Bailey Ct. L20: Boot 3D 44
Bailey Dr. L20: Boot 4D 44
Bailey La. M31: Part 6M 69
Baileys Cl. WA8: Widnes 3K 79
Bailey's La. L24: Hale 6K 93
L24: Speke 4E 92
L26: Halew 8L 77
Bailey St. L1: Liv 8H 5 (9D 58)
Bailey Way L31: Mag 4H 35
WA10: St H 4J 49
Bainbridge Av. WA3: Low 2G 52
Bainbridge Cres. WA5: Gt San 9G 65
Baines Av. M44: Irlam 1M 69
Bainton Cl. L32: Kirkb 3E 46
Bainton Rd. L32: Kirkb 3E 46
Baker Dr. CH66: Gt Sut 2K 111
Baker Rd. WA7: West P 8G 95
Bakersfield Dr. WA5: Gt San 1J 81
Bakers Grn. Rd. L36: Huy 5J 61
Bakers La. PR9: South 4L 7
Baker St. L6: Liv 1N 5 (6F 58)
L36: Huy 7L 61
WA9: St H 7M 49
Baker Way L6: Liv 2M 5 (6F 58)
Bakewell Cl. CH66: Gt Sut 5K 111
Bakewell Gro. L9: Aintr 3G 45
Bakewell Rd. WA5: Burtw 2H 65
Bala Cl. WA5: Call 7N 65
Bala Gro. CH44: Wall 6G 56
Bala St. L4: W'ton 3G 58
Balcarres Av. L18: Moss H 3L 75
Baldock Cl. WA4: Thel 5K 83
Baldwin Av. L16: Child 9C 60
Baldwin St. WA10: St H 6K 49
Bales, The L30: Neth 7F 34
Balfe St. L21: Sea 4N 43
Balfour Av. L20: Boot 5A 44
Balfour Rd. CH43: Oxton 3H 73
CH44: Wall 7G 57
L20: Boot 4D 44
PR8: South 1D 12
Balfour St. L4: W'ton 2E 58
WA7: Run 6J 95
WA10: St H 7G 48
Balham Cl. WA8: Widnes 4K 79
Balharry Av. WA11: Hay 3H 51
Balker Dr. WA10: St H 5J 49
Ballantrae Rd. L18: Moss H 5A 76
Ballantyne Dr. CH43: Bid 8C 56
Ballantyne Gro. L13: Liv 2K 59
L20: Boot 4D 44
Ballantyne Pl. L13: Liv 2K 59
WA2: Winw 3B 66
Ballantyne Rd. L13: Liv 3K 59
Ballantyne Wlk. CH43: Bid 8C 56
Ballantyne Way WA3: Low 2F 52
Ballard Rd. CH48: W Kir 5F 70
Ballater Dr. WA2: Warr 5F 66
Ball Av. CH45: New B 1G 56
Balliol Cl. CH43: Bid 8C 56
Balliol Gro. L23: Blun 9H 33
Balliol Ho. L20: Boot 8B 44
Balliol Rd. L20: Boot 8B 44
Balliol Way WN4: Ash M 7H 41
BALL O' DITTON 7H 79
Ball Path WA8: Widnes 7J 79
Ball Path Way WA8: Widnes 7H 79
Balls Pl. PR8: South 8G 6
Ball's Rd. CH43: Oxton 4H 73
Balls Rd. E. CH41: Birke 3J 73
Ball St. WA9: St H 6N 49
Balmer St. WA9: St H 1G 63
Balmoral Av. L23: Crosb 8L 33
WA3: Low 1E 52
WA9: St H 2M 63
Balmoral Cl. L33: Kirkb 6C 36
PR9: South 4N 7
Balmoral Ct. L13: Liv 4K 59
Balmoral Dr. L37: Form 3E 24
PR9: South 5M 7
WA6: Hel 1E 114
Balmoral Gdns. CH43: Pren 7F 72
CH65: Ell P 2B 112
Balmoral Gro. CH43: Noct 5D 72
Balmoral Ho. L39: Augh 2C 28
Balmoral Rd. CH45: New B 9J 43
L6: Liv 5H 59
L9: W'ton 4F 44
L31: Mag 2H 35
WA4: Grap 6G 83
WA8: Widnes 4J 79
WN4: Ash M 7J 41
Balmoral Way L34: Presc 4K 61
Balm St. L7: Liv 7G 59
Balniel St. WA9: Clock F 6N 63
Balsham Cl. L25: Hunts X 9H 77
Baltic Rd. L20: Boot 7A 44
Baltic St. L4: W'ton 2F 58
Baltimore Gdns. WA5: Gt San 1L 81
Baltimore St. L1: Liv 7J 5 (9D 58)
Bamber Gdns. PR9: South 7M 7
Bamboo Cl. L27: N'ley 2J 77
Bamburgh Ct. CH65: Ell P 2C 112
Bamburgh Pl. WN4: Ash M 6J 41
Bamford Cl. WA7: Run 8M 95
Bamford Dr. L6: Liv 1M 5 (5F 58)
BAMFURLONG 4N 41
Bampton Av. WA11: St H 1L 49
Bampton Rd. L16: Child 9B 60
Banastre Dr. WA12: Newt W 7A 52
Banastre Rd. PR8: South 1N 11
Banbury Av. L25: Woolt 6G 77
Banbury Cl. WN7: Leigh 1M 53
Banbury Ct. L20: Boot 6C 44
(off Worcester Rd.)
Banbury Dr. WA5: Gt San 4L 81
Banbury Rd. WN5: Bil 1N 39
Banbury Way CH43: Oxton 6E 72
Bancroft Cl. L25: Hunts X 8G 76
Bancroft Rd. WA8: Widnes 6N 79
Bandon Cl. L24: Hale 5A 94
Banff Av. CH63: East 1C 102
Bangor Cl. CH66: Gt Sut 6K 111
Bangor Rd. CH45: Wall 3D 56
BANGOR'S GREEN 6J 19
Bangor St. L5: Liv 4B 58
Banister House Fishery 7K 9
Bank Av. WN5: Orr 7N 31
Bank Brow WN8: Roby M 9M 23
Bankburn Rd. L13: Liv 3K 59
Bank Cl. CH64: Lit N 8G 100
Bank Dene CH42: Rock F 8N 73
Bankes La. WA7: W'ton 1J 107
WA7: West P 9H 95
Bankfield WN8: Skel 5F 30
Bankfield Av. M44: Cad 4K 69
Bankfield Ct. CH62: Brom 4E 90
L13: Liv 4L 59
Bankfield La. PR9: South 5N 7
Bankfield Rd. L13: Liv 3L 59
WA8: Widnes 7E 78
Bankfields Dr. CH62: East 1G 102
Bankfield St. L20: Kirkd 1A 58
Bank Gdns. WA5: Penk 4G 80
Bankhall La. L20: Kirkd 1B 58
Bank Hall Pk. WA1: Warr 4D 82
Bankhall Station (Rail) 1B 58
Bankhall St. L20: Kirkd 1B 58
BANK HEATH 2A 52
Bank Hey CH64: Lit N 9F 100
Bank Ho. La. WA6: Hel 1F 114
Bankland Rd. L13: Liv 4L 59
Banklands Cl. M44: Cad 4K 69
Bank La. L31: Mell 4A 36
L33: Kirkb 4A 36
Bank M. WA6: Hel 1F 114
Bank Nook PR9: South 4K 7
(not continuous)
Bank Pace PR9: Banks 1B 8
Bank Pas. PR8: South 8G 6
Bank Pl. WA3: Golb 1B 52
BANK QUAY 4N 81
Bank Quay Trad. Est. WA1: Warr 4A 82
Bank Rd. L20: Boot 7A 44
WN8: Roby M 8M 23
BANKS 1E 8
Banks, The CH45: Wall 2E 56
Bank's Av. CH47: Meols 9E 54
Banksbarn WN8: Skel 5F 30
Banks Cres. WA4: Westy 4G 83
Bankside L38: Hight 9F 24
WA1: Warr 3A 82
WA7: Pres B 8G 96
WN8: Parb 3E 22
Bankside Av. WN4: Ash M 3J 41
Bankside Ct. L21: Lith 2N 43
Bankside Rd. CH42: Rock F 8M 73
Banks Ind. Pk. PR9: Banks 4G 9
Bank's La. L19: Garst 3B 92
L24: Speke 5D 92
Banks Leisure Cen. 2F 8
Bank Sq. PR9: South 7G 6
Bank's Rd. L19: Garst 2A 92
Banks Rd. CH48: W Kir 6B 70
CH60: Hesw 8K 87
PR9: Banks, South 2B 8
Bank St. CH41: Birke 2L 73
WA1: Warr 3C 82
WA3: Glaz 4G 69
WA3: Golb 1B 52
WA8: Widnes 3K 95
WA10: St H 7H 49
WA12: Newt W 7H 51
Bank's Way L19: Garst 3B 92
BANK TOP 9M 23
Bankville Rd. CH42: Tran 5L 73
Bankwood WN6: Shev 7N 23
Bannatyne Health Club
Skelmersdale 2E 30
Banner Hey L35: Whis 8A 62
Bannerman St. L7: Liv 9J 59
Banner St. L15: Wavtr 1K 75
WA10: St H 7J 49
Banner Wlk. WA10: St H 7J 49
(off Banner St.)
Banning Cl. CH41: Birke 1K 73
Bannister Way WN3: Winst 1G 40
Banstead Gro. L15: Wavtr 1N 75
Barbara Av. L10: Faz 3M 45
Barbara St. WA9: Clock F 6A 64
Barbauld St. WA1: Warr 3C 82
Barberry Cl. CH46: More 9J 55
Barberry Cres. L30: Neth 7F 34
Barberry Wlk. M31: Part 6M 69
(off Wychelm Rd.)
Barber's La. CW9: Ant 7M 99
Barber St. WA9: St H 6M 49
Barbondale Cl. WA5: Gt San 1H 81
Barbour Dr. L20: Boot 4D 44
Barbrook Way L9: W'ton 7G 44
Barchester Dr. L17: Aig 7H 75
Barclay St. L8: Liv 4E 74
Barcombe Rd. CH60: Hesw 6D 88
Bardale Gro. WN4: Ash M 8J 41
Bardley Cres. L35: Tar G 1L 77
Bardon Cl. L25: Gate 3G 77
Bardsay Rd. L4: W'ton 9E 44
Bardsey Cl. CH65: Ell P 4A 112
Bardsley Av. WA5: Warr 7A 66
Bardsley Cl. WN8: Uph 5K 31
Barford Cl. CH43: Bid 2B 72
PR8: Ainsd 8G 11
WA5: Westb 8K 65
WN8: Uph 5K 31
Barford Dr. WA3: Low 2H 53
Barford Grange CH64: Will 6A 102
Barford Rd. L25: Hunts X 1F 92
L36: Huy 3K 61
Bargate Water WA9: St H 3G 63
Barge Ind. Pk., The WA9: St H 5M 49
Barham Ct. WA3: Ris 5L 67
Barington Dr. WA7: Murd 8G 96
Barkbeth Rd. L36: Huy 4G 60
Barkbeth Wlk. L36: Huy 4G 60
Barkeley Dr. L21: Sea 4M 43
Barker Cl. L36: Huy 9K 61
Barker La. CH49: Grea 6K 71
(not continuous)
Barker Rd. CH61: Irby 1N 87
Barkers Hollow Rd. WA4: Dutt, Pres H 9J 97
Barkerville Cl. L13: Liv 2J 59
Barker Way L6: Liv 4G 58
Barkfield Av. L37: Form 9E 16
Barkfield La. L37: Form 9D 16
Barkhill Rd. L17: Aig 7L 75
Barkin Cen., The WA8: Widnes 8M 79
Barkis Cl. L8: Liv 3E 74
Bark Rd. L21: Lith 1B 44
Barley Castle Cl. WA4: App T 4J 99
Barleycastle La. WA4: App T 2L 99
Barleycastle Trad. Est. WA4: App T 3K 99
Barleyfield CH61: Pens 3M 87
Barley Mere Cl. WA12: Newt W 8L 51
Barleymow Cl. CH66: Gt Sut 3H 111
Barley Rd. WA4: Thel 5K 83
Barlow Av. CH63: Beb 1N 89
Barlow Gro. WA9: St H 8C 50
Barlow La. L4: Kirkd 1D 58
Barlows Cl. L9: Aintr 2J 45
Barlow's La. L9: Aintr 2J 45
L39: Hals 9C 12
Barlow St. L4: Kirkd 1D 58
Barlow Way WA7: West P 7G 94
Barmouth Cl. WA5: Call 7N 65
Barmouth Rd. CH45: Wall 3D 56
Barmouth Way L5: Liv 4B 58
Barnack Cl. WA1: Padg 9H 67
Barnacre Dr. CH64: P'gte 4B 100

Barnacre La.—Beech Gro.

Barnacre La. CH46: More 2J 71
Barnard Dr. CH65: Ell P 2C 112
Barnard Rd. CH43: Oxton 3H 73
Barnard St. WA5: Warr 5M 81
Barn Cl. L30: Neth 7F 34
PR4: Mere B 5L 9
Barn Cft. WA6: Hel 1F 114
Barncroft CH61: Pens 4N 87
WA7: Nort 8F 96
Barncroft, The CH49: Grea 3L 71
Barncroft Pl. L23: Crosb 5L 33
Barncroft Rd. L26: Halew 9L 77
Barndale Rd. L18: Moss H 4L 75
Barnes Av. WA2: Fearn 7J 67
Barnes Cl. L33: Kirkb 5C 36
WA5: Gt San 3J 81
WA8: Widnes 6N 79
Barnes Dr. L31: Lydi 8H 27
Barnes Grn. CH63: Spit 5N 89
Barnes Rd. L39: Augh 1C 28
WA8: Widnes 6M 79
WN8: Skel 3B 30
Barnes St. L6: Liv 4F 58
Barneston Rd.
WA8: Widnes 5A 80
Barnet Cl. L7: Liv 9H 59
Barnett Av. WA12: Newt W 7G 51
Barnfield Av. WA7: Murd 9E 96
Barnfield Cl. CH47: Meols 8F 54
CH66: Gt Sut 3H 111
L12: W Der 3N 59
L30: Neth 9D 34
Barnfield Dr. L12: W Der 3N 59
WN8: Skel 5H 31
Barnfield Rd. WA1: Wools 1K 83
Barnham Cl. L24: Speke 3F 92
WA3: Golb 2B 52
Barnham Dr. L16: Child 1C 76
Barn Hey CH47: Hoy 3B 70
Barn Hey Cres. CH47: Meols 9G 54
Barn Hey Grn. L12: W Der 3N 59
Barn Hey Rd. L33: Kirkb 9E 36
Barnhill Rd. L15: Wavtr 2M 75
Barnhouse La. CH3: L Barr 9D 114
Barnhurst Cl. L16: Child 1C 76
Barnhurst Rd. L16: Child 1C 76
Barn La. WA3: Golb 3A 52
WA5: Burtw 4H 65
Barnmeadow Rd. L25: Gate 3E 76
Barns, The L37: Form 3G 24
Barnsbury Rd. L4: W'ton 8H 45
Barnsdale Av. CH61: Thing 2B 88
Barnside Cl. L16: Child 1C 76
Barns La. WA13: Warb 2N 85
WA14: Dun M, Warb 3N 85
Barnstaple Way WA5: Penk 4G 81
BARNSTON 4C 88
Barnston Av. CH65: Ell P 9L 103
Barnston La. CH46: More 8M 55
Barnston Rd. CH60: Hesw 8B 88
CH61: Barns, Thing 8B 88
L9: Aintr 3G 44
Barnston Towers Cl. CH60: Hesw 7C 88
Barnstream Cl. L27: N'ley 2G 77
Barn St. WA8: Widnes 1K 95
Barnswood Cl. WA4: Grap 7K 83
Barnton Cl. L20: Boot 4B 44
WA3: Low 3E 52
Barn Way WA12: Newt W 7K 51
Barnwell Av. CH44: Wall 4H 57
WA3: Cul 6L 53
Barnwood CH66: Lit Sut 7E 102
Barnwood Rd. L36: Huy 5F 60
Baron Cl. WA1: Wools 1L 83
Baroncroft Rd. L25: Woolt 4D 76
Baronet M. WA4: Warr 7B 82
Baronet Rd. WA4: Warr 7B 82
Barons Cl. WA7: Cas 6B 96
WA8: Widnes 8F 78
Barons Hey L28: Stockb V 1D 60
Barren Gro. CH43: Oxton 4H 73
Barrett Av. PR8: Birkd 4N 11
Barrett Rd. PR8: Birkd 4N 11
Barrington Cl. WN3: Winst 1F 40
Barrington Dr. PR8: Ainsd 9H 11
Barrington Rd. CH44: Wall 6J 57
L15: Wavtr 2K 75
Barrison Grn. L40: Scar 3C 20
Barrow Av. WA2: Warr 7F 66
Barrow Cl. L12: W Der 9A 46
Barrowdale Rd. WA3: Golb 2C 52
Barrowfield Rd. WA10: Ec'stn 5D 48
Barrow Hall La. WA5: Gt San 1G 80
Barrow La. WA2: Croft, Winw 8C 52
WA3: Croft 8C 52
WA6: Dun H 8B 114
BARROW NOOK 1J 37
Barrow Nook La. L39: Bic 9J 29
Barrows Cotts. *L35: Whis* *6B 62*
(off Cross La.)
Barrows Farm WN5: Bil 8A 40
BARROW'S GREEN 4N 79
Barrow's Grn. La. WA8: Widnes 6A 80
Barrow's Row WA8: Widnes 4L 79
Barrow St. WA10: St H 7K 49
WN4: Ash M 6M 41
Barrule Cl. WA4: App 9E 82
Barry Cl. CH65: Ell P 5A 112
Barry Dr. L19: Garst 1N 91
Barrymore Av. WA4: Westy 4G 83
Barrymore Ct. WA4: Grap 7H 83
Barrymore Rd. L13: Liv 6L 59
WA4: Grap 7H 83
WA7: Run 8L 95
Barrymore Way CH63: Brom 9A 90
Barry St. WA4: Warr 4D 82
Barsbank Cl. WA13: Lymm 5C 84
Barsbank La. WA13: Lymm 5C 84
Barshaw Gdns. WA4: App 3F 98
Bartholomew Cl. L35: Rainh 8H 63
Bartlegate Cl. WA7: Brook 1D 108
Bartlett St. L15: Wavtr 1K 75
BARTON 7E 18
Barton Av. WA4: Grap 6H 83
Barton Cl. CH47: Hoy 2A 70
L21: Lith 9N 33
WA7: Murd 8F 96
WA10: St H 6J 49
Barton Clough WN5: Bil 6A 40
Barton Hey Dr. CH48: Caldy 1D 86
Barton Heys Rd. L37: Form 3D 24
Barton M. WA3: Cul 6L 53
Barton Rd. CH47: Hoy 2A 70
L9: W'ton 6E 44
Bartons Cl. PR9: South 2B 8
Barton St. CH41: Birke 2J 73
(not continuous)
WA3: Golb 1B 52
Barwell Av. WA11: St H 4M 49
Barwell Cl. WA3: Golb 1D 52
Basil Cl. L16: Child 9C 60
Basildon Cl. WA9: St H 2J 63
Basil Grange Apts. *L12: W Der* *4M 59*
(off North Dr.)
Basil Rd. L16: Child 9B 60
Basing St. L19: Garst 9A 76
Baskervyle Cl. CH60: Hesw 9A 88
Baskervyle Rd. CH60: Hesw 9A 88
Basnett St. L1: Liv 5F 4 (8C 58)
Bassendale Rd. CH62: Brom 5D 90
Bassenthwaite Av. CH43: Noct 3D 72
L33: Kirkb 7B 36
WA11: St H 2K 49
Bassett Gro. WN3: Winst 1E 40
Bateman Cl. CH65: Ell P 8N 103
Bates Cres. WA10: St H 1G 62
Bates La. WA6: Hel 1G 114
Batey Av. L35: Rainh 5E 62
Batherton Cl. WA8: Widnes 9L 79
Bathgate Way L33: Kirkb 5B 36
Bath Springs L39: Orm 8D 20
Bath Springs Ct. L39: Orm 8D 20
Bath St. CH62: Port S 2A 90
L3: Liv 3B 4 (7A 58)
L22: Wloo 2K 43
PR9: South 7G 6
WA1: Warr 3B 82
WA10: St H 7J 49
Bath St. Nth. PR9: South 7G 7
Bathurst Rd. L19: G'dale 9N 75
Bath Wood Cl. L40: Burs 6E 20
Bathwood Dr. CH64: Lit N 9E 100
Batley St. L13: Liv 6M 59
Battenberg St. L7: Liv 4N 5 (7F 58)
Battersby La. WA2: Warr 2D 82
Battersea Ct. WA8: Widnes 5J 79
Battery Cl. L17: Aig 6H 75
Battery La. WA1: Wools 1N 83
Battle Way *L37: Form* *2H 25*
(off Buckfast Dr.)
Baucher Dr. L20: Boot 3D 44
Baumville Dr. CH63: Spit 5M 89
Bawtry Ct. WA2: Padg 8F 66
Baxter Cl. WA7: Murd 8F 96
(not continuous)
Baxters La. WA9: St H 1N 63
Baxters La. Ind. Est. WA9: St H 9N 49
Baxter St. WA5: Warr 3N 81
Baycliffe WA13: Lymm 6E 84
Baycliffe Cl. WA7: Beech 1N 107
Baycliff Rd. L12: W Der 1C 60
Bayfield Rd. L19: G'dale 9M 75
Bayhorse La. L3: Liv 3K 5 (7E 58)
Baynard Dr. WA8: Hale B 2F 94
Baysdale Cl. L8: Liv 4F 74
Bayswater Cl. WA7: Nort 3H 97
Bayswater Ct. CH45: Wall 3D 56
Bayswater Gdns. CH45: Wall 2D 56
Bayswater Rd. CH45: Wall 3D 56
Baythorne Rd. L4: W'ton 8H 45
Baytree Cl. CH66: Gt Sut 4L 111
PR9: South 2B 8
Bay Tree Gro. WA9: St H 1M 63
Baytree Gro. L31: Mell 8M 35
Baytree Rd. CH42: Tran 5L 73
CH48: Frank 6G 71
Bayview CH45: New B 1G 57
Bay Vw. Dr. CH45: Wall 2C 56
Bayvil Cl. WA7: Murd 8G 96
Beacham Rd. PR8: South 8K 7
Beach Bank L22: Wloo 9J 33
Beachcroft Rd. CH47: Meols 8F 54
Beach Gro. CH45: Wall 2J 57
Beach Lawn L22: Wloo 1J 43
Beach M. PR8: Birkd 9E 6
Beach Priory Gdns. PR8: South 9E 6
Beach Rd. CH47: Hoy 2A 70
L21: Lith 2N 43
PR8: Birkd 9E 6
Beach Wlk. CH48: W Kir 8C 70
Beacon Country Pk. 3J 31
Beacon Country Pk. Vis. Cen. 2H 31
Beacon Ct. CH60: Hesw 7A 88
Beacon Crossing WN8: Parb 3F 22
Beacon Dr. CH48: W Kir 6D 70
Beacon Grn. WN8: Skel 4H 31
Beacon Gro. WA11: St H 4N 49
Beacon Hgts. WN8: Uph 4K 31
Beacon Hill Vw. WA7: West P 8G 95
Beacon Ho. *L5: Liv* *5D 58*
(off Portland Pl.)
Beacon La. CH60: Hesw 7A 88
L5: Liv 3E 58
WN8: Dalt 7D 22
Beacon Pde. CH60: Hesw 7A 88
Beacon Pk. Golf Course 2J 31
Beacon Rd. WN5: Bil 4N 39
Beacons, The CH60: Hesw 8A 88
L37: Form *1F 24*
(off School La.)
WN6: Shev 6N 23
Beaconsfield L34: Presc 3A 62
Beaconsfield Cl. CH42: Tran 5M 73
Beaconsfield Ct. L39: Orm 8D 20
Beaconsfield Cres. WA8: Widnes 4K 79
Beaconsfield Gro. WA8: Widnes 4L 79
Beaconsfield Rd. CH62: New F 9A 74
L21: Sea 3M 43
L25: Woolt 5C 76
PR9: South 9L 7
WA7: Run 7H 95
WA8: Widnes 5L 79
WA10: St H 5F 48
Beaconsfield St. L8: Liv 2F 74
Beaconsfield Ter. *L19: Garst* *1N 91*
(off St Mary's Rd.)
Beacon Sports Hall, The 6K 49
Beacon Vw. WN6: App B 5M 23
Beacon Vw. Dr. WN8: Uph 5L 31
Beadnell Dr. WA5: Penk 5G 81
Beames Cl. L7: Liv 8H 59
Beamish Cl. WA4: App 4E 98
WA9: St H 5H 63
Beamont St. WA8: Widnes 3K 95
Beardsmore Dr. WA3: Low 2F 52
Bearncroft WN8: Skel 6F 30
Bearwood Rd. L33: Kirkb 6B 36
Beasley Cl. CH66: Gt Sut 2J 111
Beatles Story, The 8D 4 (9B 58)
Beatrice Av. CH63: H Beb 9L 73
Beatrice St. L20: Boot 9C 44
WA4: Warr 5E 82
Beattock Cl. L33: Kirkb 5B 36
Beatty Av. WA2: Warr 8D 66
Beatty Cl. CH48: Caldy 1D 86
L35: Whis 7A 62
Beatty Rd. L13: Liv 6M 59
PR8: South 1D 12
Beauclair Dr. L15: Wavtr 1N 75
Beaufort L37: Form 2G 25
Beaufort Cl. L39: Augh 3M 27
WA5: Gt San 3J 81
WA7: Run 8L 95
WA8: Widnes 8D 78
Beaufort Dr. CH44: Wall 4E 56
Beaufort Rd. CH41: Birke 8F 56
Beaufort St. L8: Liv 2D 74
(Hill St.)
L8: Liv 2D 74
(Mann St.)
L8: Liv 3D 74
(Northumberland St.)
WA5: Warr 4N 81
WA9: St H 9M 49
Beaumaris Ct. CH43: Oxton 3H 73
Beaumaris Dr. CH61: Thing 1B 88
CH65: Ell P 3B 112
Beaumaris Rd. CH45: Wall 3D 56
Beaumaris St. L20: Kirkd 1B 58
(not continuous)
Beaumaris Way WA7: Cas 5B 96
Beaumont Av. WA10: St H 6G 48
Beaumont Ct. *WA4: Warr* *6D 82*
(off Elphins Dr.)
Beaumont Cres. L39: Augh 2B 28
Beaumont Dr. L10: Aintr 1K 45
Beaumont St. L8: Liv 1G 74
Beau St. L3: Liv 5D 58
Beauworth Av. CH49: Grea 5K 71
Beaver Ct. WN4: Ash M 5L 41
Beaver Gro. L9: Aintr 4F 44
Beavers La. WN8: Skel 6G 31
Beavers Way WN8: Skel 6G 31
BEBINGTON 1N 89
Bebington (Park & Ride) 9N 73
Bebington Rd. CH42: Rock F, Tran 6K 73
CH62: New F 9A 74
CH63: Beb 1N 89
CH66: Gt Sut 1J 111
Bebington Station (Rail) 9N 73
Bebles Rd. L39: Orm 1A 28
Bechers WA8: Widnes 5E 78
Bechers Bus. Cen. L30: Neth 9F 34
Bechers Ct. L30: Neth 8G 35
Bechers Dr. L9: Aintr 9H 35
Bechers Row L9: W'ton 4E 44
Beck Cl. L10: Faz 3N 45
Beckenham Av. L18: Moss H 3L 75
Beckenham Cl. WA8: Widnes 4N 79
Beckenham Rd. CH45: New B 9H 43
Becket St. L4: Kirkd 2C 58
(not continuous)
Beckett Cl. L33: Know I 2G 46
Beckett Dr. WA2: Winw 4B 66
WA13: Warb 9J 69
Beckett Gro. CH63: H Beb 9K 73
Beckfield Cl. WN7: Leigh 1N 53
Beck Gro. WA11: St H 2L 49
Beckinsale Cl. L26: Halew 7L 77
Beck Rd. L20: Boot 5B 44
Beckwith Ct. *CH41: Birke* *9J 57*
(off Beckwith St.)
Beckwith St. CH41: Birke 9H 57
L1: Liv 8F 4 (9C 58)
Beckwith St. E. CH41: Birke 1K 73
Becky St. L6: Liv 4G 59
Becontree Rd. L12: W Der 5B 60
Bective St. L7: Liv 9H 59
Bedale Cl. WA12: Newt W 9M 51
Bedale Wlk. L33: Kirkb 8D 36
Bedburn Dr. L36: Huy 6F 60
Bede Cl. L33: Kirkb 5C 36
Bedford Av. CH42: Rock F 7L 73
CH65: Whit 3M 111
L31: Mell 5L 35
Bedford Av. E. CH65: Whit 3N 111
Bedford Cl. L7: Liv 8L 5 (9E 58)
L36: Huy 6L 61
Bedford Ct. CH42: Rock F 6M 73
L7: Liv 9L 5
PR8: Birkd 4N 11
Bedford Dr. CH42: Rock F 7K 73
Bedford Gro. M44: Cad 3H 69
Bedford Pl. CH42: Rock F 6N 73
L20: Boot 9A 44
L21: Sea 3M 43
WN4: Ash M 6J 41
Bedford Rd. CH42: Rock F 6M 73
CH45: Wall 3H 57
L4: W'ton 8C 44
L20: Boot 9B 44
PR8: Birkd 4N 11
Bedford Rd. E.
CH42: Rock F 6N 73
Bedford St. WA4: Stockt H 8D 82
WA9: St H 8N 49
Bedford St. Nth. L7: Liv 6L 5 (8E 58)
Bedford St. Sth. L7: Liv 9L 5 (9E 58)
(not continuous)
Bedford Wlk. L7: Liv 8L 5
Bedstone Cl. L8: Liv 3D 74
Beecham Cl. L36: Huy 8H 61
Beech Av. CH49: Upton 2L 71
CH61: Pens 3A 88
L17: Aig 6G 74
L23: Crosb 5N 33
L31: Mell 8N 35
L34: Eccl P 2C 62
WA3: Cul 7N 53
WA3: Low 3G 53
WA4: Thel 5L 83
WA5: Penk 5E 80
WA6: Frod 6M 107
WA9: Clock F 5M 63
WA11: Hay 3H 51
WN8: Parb 4F 22
Beechbank Rd. L18: Moss H 3K 75
Beechburn Cres. L36: Huy 6F 60
Beechburn Rd. L36: Huy 6E 60
Beech Cl. L12: Crox 7B 46
L32: Kirkb 8A 36
L40: Ruf 2N 15
M31: Part 6M 69
WA12: Newt W 8L 51
WN8: Skel 3B 30
Beech Cotts. WA4: Sttn 5F 98
Beech Ct. CH42: Tran 4K 73
L18: Moss H 5A 76
PR9: South 7J 7
WA3: Ris 9N 53
Beechcroft L31: Mag 2H 35
Beechcroft Dr. CH65: Whit 2N 111
Beechcroft Rd. CH44: Wall 7J 57
Beechdale Rd. L18: Moss H 4M 75
Beechdene Rd. L4: W'ton 2G 59
Beech Dr. L37: Form 9D 16
Beeches, The CH42: Rock F 7N 73
CH46: Leas 6M 55
CH66: Gt Sut 1J 111
L18: Moss H 3B 76
PR9: Banks 4H 9
WA6: Hel 1F 114
WA8: Widnes *4N 79*
(off Hampton Ct. Way)
WA9: Sut L 4N 63
Beechfield L31: Mag 2K 35
L36: Roby *7G 60*
(off Church Rd.)
WN8: Parb 1F 22
Beechfield Cl. CH60: Hesw 8A 88
L26: Halew 1J 93
Beechfield Gdns. PR8: South 9E 6
Beechfield M. PR9: South 8G 7
Beechfield Rd. CH65: Ell P 9N 103
L18: Moss H 4B 76
WA4: Grap 6H 83
Beech Gdns. *WA7: Run* *7M 95*
(off Beech Rd.)
WA11: Rainf 4B 38
Beech Grn. L12: W Der 1M 59
Beech Gro. CH66: Whit 5M 111
L9: Aintr 4G 45
L21: Sea 4M 43
L30: Neth 9F 34

Bickerstaffe—Blundellsands Sailing Club

BICKERSTAFFE 7K 29
Bickerstaffe St. L3: Liv 1J 5 (6D 58)
WA10: St H 7K 49
Bickerton Av. CH63: H Beb 8K 73
WA6: Frod 7N 107
Bickerton Cl. WA3: Birchw 5L 67
Bickerton Rd. PR8: Birkd 2M 11
Bickerton St. L17: Aig 5H 75
Bickley Cl. WA2: Fearn 6G 67
WA7: Run 6M 95
Bicknell Cl. WA5: Gt San 9K 65
Bidder St. L3: Liv 1J 5 (6D 58)
Biddleston Cross WA8: Widnes 5H 79
Bideford Av. WA9: Sut L 4M 63
Bideford Rd. WA5: Penk 4G 80
BIDSTON 9D 56
Bidston Av. CH41: Birke 1E 72
CH45: Wall 3E 56
WA11: St H 5N 49
Bidston Ct. CH43: Noct 1E 72
Bidston Golf Course 6C 56
Bidston Grn. CH66: Gt Sut 1J 111
Bidston Grn. Ct. CH43: Bid 9C 56
Bidston Grn. Dr. CH43: Bid 9C 56
Bidston Hall Farm CH43: Bid 8D 56
Bidston Ind. Est. CH44: Wall 6D 56
Bidston Link Rd. CH43: Bid 7D 56
CH44: Wall 7D 56
Bidston Moss CH44: Wall 6D 56
Bidston Moss Nature Reserve 6E 56
Bidston (Park & Ride) 7C 56
Bidston Rd. CH43: Clau, Oxton 2E 72
L4: W'ton 1G 59
Bidston Sta. App. CH43: Bid 7C 56
Bidston Station (Rail) 7C 56
Bidston Vw. CH43: Bid 8C 56
Bidston Village Rd. CH43: Bid 8C 56
Bidston Way WA11: St H 5N 49
Bidston Windmill 1D 72
Bigdale Dr. L33: Kirkb 8D 36
Biggin Ct. WA2: Padg 8F 66
Biggleswade Dr. WA7: Nort 4G 97
Bigham Rd. L6: Liv 6H 59
Biglands Dr. L36: Huy 9K 61
Big Mdw. Rd. CH49: Wdchu 4A 72
BILLINGE 6A 40
Billinge Cres. WA11: St H 4N 49
Billinge La. L39: Bic 7C 28
Billinge Rd. WN4: Garsw 6D 40
WN5: Bil 6D 40
Billingham Rd. WA9: St H 2G 62
Billings Cl. L5: Kirkd 3C 58
Billington Av. WA12: Newt W 4K 51
Billington Cl. WA5: Gt San 9G 64
Billington Rd. WA8: Widnes 4E 78
Bill's La. L37: Form 3F 24
Bilston Rd. L17: Aig 8K 75
Bilton Cl. WA8: Widnes 6A 80
Bingley Rd. L4: W'ton 2G 59
Binns Rd. L7: Liv 7K 59
L13: Liv 7K 59
Binns Rd. Ind. Est. L13: Liv 8L 59
Binsey Cl. CH49: Upton 3L 71
Birbeck Cl. WN3: Winst 2G 40
Birbeck Rd. L33: Kirkb 8E 36
Birbeck Wlk. L33: Kirkb 8E 36
Birchall Av. WA3: Cul 6L 53
Birchall St. L20: Kirkd 2B 58
WA3: Croft 2H 67
Birch Av. CH49: Upton 2L 71
L9: Aintr 4G 44
L40: Burs 1J 21
M44: Cad 4K 69
WA2: Winw 5B 66
WA10: St H 4J 49
Birchbrook Rd. WA13: Lymm 3H 85
Birch Cl. CH43: Oxton 5H 73
L31: Mag 2L 35
L35: Whis 5B 62
Birch Ct. *L8: Liv* *4F 74*
(off Weller Way)
Birch Cres. WA7: Run 7M 95
WA12: Newt W 6H 51
Birchdale Cl. CH49: Grea 3L 71
Birchdale Cres. WA4: App 8D 82
Birchdale Rd. L9: W'ton 6F 44
L22: Wloo 9K 33
WA1: Padd 1H 83
WA4: App 9D 82
Birchen Rd. L26: Halew 9L 77
Birches, The CH44: Wall 7L 57
CH64: Nest 4F 100
L28: Stockb V 2E 60
L37: Form 8E 16
Birches Cl. CH60: Hesw 7A 88
Birchfield CH46: More 1K 71
Birchfield Av. WA8: Widnes 6K 79
Birchfield Cl. CH46: More 2K 71
L7: Liv 7K 59
Birchfield Rd. L4: W'ton 8F 44
L7: Liv 7K 59
WA5: Gt San 3K 81
WA8: Widnes 3K 79
WA13: Lymm 4H 85
Birchfield St. L3: Liv 2J 5 (6D 58)
WA9: St H 2G 63
Birchfield Way L31: Lydi 7G 27
Birch Gdns. WA10: St H 4J 49
BIRCH GREEN 2F 30
Birch Grn. L37: Form 8D 16
Birch Grn. Rd. WN8: Skel 1E 30
Birch Gro. CH45: New B 2J 57
CH66: Whit 4M 111
L15: Wavtr 8M 59
L35: Presc 5B 62
L36: Huy 7H 61
WA1: Padd 1G 83
WA4: Warr 5E 82
WN4: Garsw 6E 40
Birch Heys CH48: Frank 7H 71
Birch Hill WA6: Kgswd 5M 115
Birch Hill M. L25: Woolt 7E 76
Birch Ho. Cl. L18: Moss H 3A 76
Birchill Rd. L33: Know I 9G 37
Birchley Av. WN5: Bil 8M 39
Birchley Rd. WN5: Bil 8M 39
Birchley St. WA10: St H 6K 49
Birchley Vw. WA11: St H 9L 39
Birchmere CH60: Hesw 5M 87
Birchmuir Hey L32: Kirkb 1D 46
Birchridge Cl. CH62: Spit 5B 90
Birch Rd. CH43: Oxton 5H 73
CH47: Meols 9F 54
CH63: Beb 3N 89
L36: Huy 8J 61
M31: Part 6K 69
WA3: Rix 6H 69
WA7: Run 7L 95
WA8: Widnes 5L 79
WA11: Hay 3G 50
Birch St. L5: Liv 4A 58
PR8: South 2A 12
WN8: Skel 3B 30
Birch Tree Av. WA11: St H 2J 49
Birch Tree Ct. L12: W Der 3M 59
Birchtree Dr. L31: Mell 8M 35
Birch Tree La. WA4: H Whi 9G 99
Birch Tree Rd. WA3: Low 2G 52
Birchtree Rd. L17: Aig 5K 75
Birchview Way CH43: Noct 3D 72
Birchway CH60: Hesw 9C 88
Birchways WA4: App 2F 98
BIRCHWOOD 7L 67
Birchwood Av. CH41: Birke 1L 73
Birchwood Blvd. WA3: Birchw 7L 67
Birchwood Cl. CH2: Elt 2N 113
CH41: Birke 1K 73
CH66: Gt Sut 4J 111
WN3: Winst 2F 40
Birchwood Corporate Ind. Est.
WA2: Birchw 7K 67
Birchwood Golf Course 3L 67
Birchwood La. WA4: Moore 8K 81
Birchwood Leisure & Tennis Complex
6L 67
Birchwood Office Pk. WA2: Fearn 6J 67
Birchwood One Bus. Pk.
WA3: Birchw 7M 67
BIRCHWOOD PARK 4M 67
Birchwood Pk. Av. WA3: Birchw, Ris 4L 67
Birchwood Point Bus. Pk.
WA3: Birchw 6L 67
Birchwood Science Pk. WA3: Ris 3M 67
Birchwood Shop. Cen. 6L 67
Birchwood Station (Rail) 7M 67
Birchwood Way L33: Kirkb 6E 36
WA2: Birchw 7K 67
WA2: Padg 9F 66
WA3: Birchw 6K 67
Bird i' th' Hand Cotts. L39: Orm 7C 20
Bird St. L7: Liv 1H 75
Birdwell Dr. WA5: Gt San 3J 81
Birdwood Rd. L11: Norr G 1L 59
BIRKDALE 2N 11
Birkdale Av. CH63: Brom 9B 90
Birkdale Cl. L6: Liv 3J 59
L36: Roby 8G 61
Birkdale Cop PR8: South 4C 12
Birkdale Ct. L36: Huy 9K 61
Birkdale Rd. WA5: Penk 4H 81
WA8: Widnes 3L 79
Birkdale Station (Rail) 2M 11
Birkdale Trad. Est. PR8: Birkd 4M 11
BIRKENHEAD 2M 73
Birkenhead Bus Station 2L 73
Birkenhead Central Station (Rail) 3L 73
Birkenhead North Station (Rail) 8F 56
Birkenhead Park Station (Rail) 9H 57
Birkenhead Priory 2M 73
Birkenhead Rd. CH44: Wall 8L 57
CH47: Hoy, Meols 9D 54
CH64: Will 4K 101
Birkenshaw Av. L23: Blun 6H 33
Birket Av. CH46: Leas 6N 55
Birket Cl. CH46: Leas 6A 56
Birket Dr. WA8: Widnes 2K 79
Birket Sq. CH46: Leas 6N 55
Birkett Av. CH65: Ell P 3A 112
Birkett Rd. CH42: Rock F 7L 73
CH48: W Kir 4C 70
Birkett St. L3: Liv 1H 5 (6D 58)
Birkey La. L37: Form 2F 24
Birkin Cl. L32: Kirkb 2E 46
Birkin Rd. L32: Kirkb 2E 46
Birkin Wlk. L32: Kirkb 2E 46
Birkrig WN8: Skel 6G 30
Birkside Cl. WN3: Wigan 2J 41
Birley Ct. L8: Liv 9K 5
PR8: South 1A 12
Birley St. WA12: Newt W 6M 51
Birleywood WN8: Skel 6G 31
Birnam Dr. L35: Rainh 7G 62
Birnam Rd. CH44: Wall 6K 57
Birstall Av. WA11: St H 5M 49
Birstall Ct. WA7: Run 8N 95
Birstall Rd. L6: Liv 6G 58
Birt Cl. L8: Liv 1G 74
Birtles Rd. WA2: Warr 8D 66
Birtley Ct. WA8: Widnes 7E 78
Bisham Pk. WA7: Nort 4F 96
Bishopdale Cl. WA5: Gt San 1H 81
Bishopdale Dr. L35: Rainh 6G 63
Bishop Dr. L35: Whis 8N 61
Bishopgate St. L15: Wavtr 9K 59
Bishop Reeves Rd. WA11: Hay 3G 51
Bishop Rd. CH44: Wall 7H 57
L6: Liv 2H 59
WA10: St H 5H 49
Bishops Ct. CH43: Oxton 5H 73
L12: W Der 1M 59
L25: Woolt 6F 76
WA2: Winw 5A 66
Bishops Gdns. CH65: Ell P 9M 103
Bishop Sheppard Ct. L3: Liv 1D 4 (5B 58)
Bishops Way WA8: Widnes 5N 79
Bisley St. CH45: Wall 4H 57
L15: Wavtr 1K 75
Bispham Ct. WN5: Bil 1N 39
Bispham Dr. CH47: Meols 1F 70
WN4: Ash M 6H 41
Bispham Ho. L3: Liv 2F 4
Bispham Rd. PR9: South 8L 7
WA5: Gt San 4K 81
Bittern Cl. WA2: Warr 6E 66
WA7: Nort 7F 96
Bixteth St. L3: Liv 3D 4 (7B 58)
Blackacre La. L39: Burs, Orm 5C 20
Black-A-Moor La. L39: Down 1E 26
Blackberry Gro. L26: Halew 6H 77
Blackboards La. CH66: Chil T 7F 102
BLACKBROOK
WA2 7G 66
WA11 4C 50
Blackbrook Av. WA2: Padg, Warr 5F 66
Blackbrook Cl. L9: W'ton 7F 44
WA8: Widnes 5F 78
Blackbrook Rd. WA11: St H 5A 50
Blackbrook Sq. WA2: Padg 7F 66
Blackburn Cl. WA3: Low 2F 52
Blackburne Av. WA8: Hale B 2E 94
Blackburne Cl. WA2: Padg 7K 67
Blackburne Dr. L25: Hunts X 9H 77
WA12: Newt W 6J 51
Blackburne Pl. L8: Liv 8K 5 (9E 58)
Blackburne St. L19: Garst 3A 92
Blackburne Ter. L8: Liv 8K 5
Blackcap Rd. WA4: App 3H 99
Blackcap Wlk. WA3: Birchw 6M 67
Blackcar La. L29: Thorn 9N 25
Black Cat Ind. Est. WA8: Widnes 1K 95
Black Denton's Pl. WA8: Widnes 7M 79
Blackdown Cl. CH66: Lit Sut 9F 102
Blackdown Gro. WA9: St H 8B 50
Blackeys La. CH64: Nest 6E 100
Blackfield St. L5: Kirkd 3C 58
Blackgate La. PR4: Tarl 5M 9
(not continuous)
Blackheath Dr. CH46: Leas 6N 55
Blackheath La. WA7: Manor P 3G 97
Black Horse Cl. CH48: W Kir 5D 70
Black Horse Hill CH48: W Kir 6D 70
Black Horse La. L13: Liv 5N 59
WA8: Widnes 3K 79
Black Horse Pl. L13: Liv 6N 59
Blackhorse St. WA9: St H 6N 49
Blackhurst Rd. L31: Lydi 7H 27
Blackhurst St. WA1: Warr 3C 82
Blackledge Cl. WA2: Fearn 6H 67
Blackley Cl. WA4: Warr 5E 82
Blackley Gro. L33: Kirkb 5E 36
Blackleyhurst Av. WN5: Bil 6A 40
Black Lion La. CH66: Lit Sut 8G 103
Blacklock Hall Rd. L24: Speke 4G 92
Blacklow Brow L36: Huy 7H 61
Blackmoor Dr. L12: W Der 3A 60
Black Moss La. L39: Augh, Orm 1B 28
L40: Scar 7J 13
Blackpool St. CH41: Birke 3L 73
Blackrod Av. L24: Speke 3G 92
Blackshaw Dr. WA5: Gt San, Westb 8K 65
Blacksmith Pl. L25: Hunts X 8H 77
Blackstairs Rd. CH66: Ell P 7L 103
Blackstock Ct. *L30: Neth* *7C 34*
(off Granams Cft.)
Blackstock St. L3: Liv 1E 4 (6B 58)
Blackstone Av. WA11: St H 5N 49
Blackstone St. L5: Liv 3A 58
Blackthorn Cres. L28: Stockb V 1F 60
Blackthorne Av. CH66: Whit 5M 111
Blackthorne Cl. CH46: More 1N 71
Blackthorne Rd. L9: W'ton 7H 45
Blackthorn Wlk. *M31: Part* *7L 69*
(off Wood La.)
Blackwater Rd. L11: Crox 6B 46
Blackwood Av. L25: Woolt 4D 76
Blackwood Ct. *L16: Child* *2A 76*
(off Woolton Rd.)
BLAGUEGATE 3M 29
Blaguegate La. WN8: Skel 2L 29
Blair Ct. CH43: Clau 2H 73
Blair Dr. WA8: Widnes 5E 78
Blairgowrie Gdns. L39: Orm 9E 20
Blair Gro. PR9: South 8L 7
Blair Ind. Est. L23: Crosb 8M 33
Blair Pk. CH63: Spit 4A 90
Blair St. L8: Liv 1D 74
Blair Wlk. L26: Halew 1K 93
Blakeacre Cl. L26: Halew 1K 93
Blakeacre Rd. L26: Halew 1K 93
Blakefield Rd. L23: Thorn 5B 34
Blakehall WN8: Skel 5G 30
(not continuous)
Blakehill Dr. WA5: Gt San 3K 81
Blakeley Brow CH63: Raby M 9N 89
Blakeley Ct. CH63: Raby M 9N 89
Blakeley Dell CH63: Raby M 9A 90
Blakeley Dene CH63: Raby M 8A 90
Blakeley Rd. CH63: Raby M 8N 89
Blakemere Ct. CH65: Ell P 7A 104
Blakeney Cl. CH49: Upton 1A 72
Blakenhall Way CH49: Upton 2L 71
Blaking Dr. L34: Know 6H 47
Blandford Cl. PR8: Birkd 1L 11
Blandford Rd. WA5: Gt San 3K 81
Blantyre Rd. L15: Wavtr 2K 75
Blantyre St. WA7: Run 4J 95
Blay Cl. L25: Hunts X 8H 77
Blaydon Cl. L30: Neth 1F 44
Blaydon Gro. WA9: St H 2G 62
Blaydon Pk. WN8: Skel 5G 31
Blaydon Wlk. CH43: Clau 2E 72
Bleak Hill Cl. WA10: Windle 3F 48
Bleak Hill Rd. WA10: Ec'stn, Windle 5E 48
Bleak La. L40: Lath 1N 21
Bleaklow Cl. WN3: Wigan 1K 41
Bleasdale Av. L10: Aintr 9K 35
Bleasdale Cl. CH49: Upton 2M 71
L39: Augh 5B 28
Bleasdale Rd. L18: Moss H 4N 75
WA12: Newt W 6K 51
Bleasdale Way L21: Ford 7A 34
Blenheim Av. L21: Lith 2B 44
Blenheim Cl. WA2: Padg 7F 66
Blenheim Dr. L34: Presc 4K 61
Blenheim Rd. CH44: Wall 4K 57
L18: Moss H 3L 75
PR8: Ainsd 8H 11
WN4: Ash M 9M 41
Blenheim St. L5: Liv 5B 58
Blenheim Way L24: Speke 4F 92
WA11: St H 4L 49
Blessington Rd. L4: W'ton 2E 58
Bletchley Av. CH44: Wall 5F 56
Bligh St. L15: Wavtr 1K 75
Blindfoot Rd. WA11: Rainf 3A 48
Blindman's La. L39: Orm 6A 20
Blisworth St. L21: Lith 4A 44
Blithedale Ct. *CH42: Rock F* *7N 73*
(off The Hawthornes)
Blomfield Rd. L19: Aller 9B 76
Bloomfield Grn. L17: Aig 4H 75
Bloomsbury Av. L25: Gate 3E 76
Bloomsbury Ct. CH47: Hoy 2B 70
Bloomsbury Way WA8: Widnes 5G 79
Blossom Gro. L32: Kirkb 3D 46
Blossom Rd. M31: Part 7L 69
Blossom St. L20: Boot 5B 44
BLOWICK 9K 7
Blowick Bus. Pk. PR9: South 9M 7
Blowick Ind. Pk. PR9: South 9M 7
Blowick Moss La. PR8: South 3C 12
Blucher St. L22: Wloo 1J 43
Bluebell Av. CH41: Birke 9F 56
WA11: Hay 3G 50
Bluebell Cl. L22: Wloo 1L 43
L32: Kirkb 7C 36
Bluebell Ct. WA7: Beech 2B 108
Blue Bell La. L36: Huy 5J 61
Bluebell La. CH64: Nest 5J 101
Bluebell Rd. WA5: Warr 4N 81
Blueberry Flds. L10: Faz 4L 45
Blue Bri. La. WA6: Hel 9F 106
Bluecoat 6F 4 (8C 58)
Bluecoat Chambers L1: Liv 6F 4
Bluecoat St. WA2: Warr 1C 82
Bluefields St. L8: Liv 1E 74
Blue Hatch WA6: Frod 6M 107
Blue Jay Cl. L27: N'ley 3J 77
Blue Lake Gdns. WA5: Gt San 2J 81
Blue Planet Aquarium 4B 112
Blue Ridge Cl. WA5: Gt San 1G 81
Bluestone La. L31: Mag 2K 35
Bluewood Dr. CH41: Birke 8D 56
Blundell Av. L37: Form 9B 16
L38: Hight 9G 24
PR8: Birkd 4M 11
Blundell Cres. PR8: Birkd 4M 11
Blundell Dr. PR8: Birkd 4M 11
Blundell Gro. L38: Hight 9F 24
Blundell La. PR9: South 4A 8
Blundell Links Ct. PR8: Ainsd 1J 17
Blundell M. L23: Blun 7H 33
Blundell Rd. L35: Whis 4D 62
L38: Hight 9F 24
WA8: Widnes 8F 78
BLUNDELLSANDS 8H 33
Blundellsands & Crosby Station (Rail)
7J 33
Blundellsands Classic L23: Blun 8H 33
Blundellsands Ct. *L23: Blun* *8H 33*
(off Blundellsands Rd. W.)
Blundellsands Rd. E. L23: Blun 7J 33
Blundellsands Rd. W. L23: Blun 8H 33
Blundellsands Sailing Club 1E 32

Blundells Dr.—Bramley Way

Blundells Dr. CH46: More .8M 55
BLUNDELL'S HILL .7E 62
Blundells Hill Golf Course .8E 62
Blundell's La. L35: Rainh .8D 62
Blundell St. L1: Liv .9F 4 (1C 74)
Blyth Cl. WA7: Murd .1F 108
Blythe Av. WA8: Widnes .4L 79
Blythe Ct. PR9: South .5M 7
Blythe La. L40: Lath .5G 21
Blythe Mdw. L40: Burs .5F 20
Blythe M. PR8: Birkd .6N 11
Blythewood WN8: Skel .5F 30
Blyth Hey L30: Neth .7C 34
Blyth Rd. CH63: Brom .8B 90
Blythswood St. L17: Aig .5G 74
BMB Ind. Pk. CH44: Wall .6F 56
Boaler St. L6: Liv .1N 5 (6F 58)
Boaler St. Ind. Est.
L6: Liv .6G 58
(off Boaler St.)
Boardmans La. WA9: St H .6A 50
WA11: St H .6A 50
Boathouse La. CH64: P'gte .4B 100
Boat Stage WA13: Lymm .5E 84
Boat Wlk. WA4: Warr .7B 82
Bobbies La. WA10: Ec'stn .6D 48
Bobbiners La. PR9: Banks .4E 8
Bobby Langton Way
L40: Burs .9J 15
Bob Paisley Ct. L5: Liv .3F 58
(off Hartnup St.)
Bob's La. M44: Cad .5K 69
Bodden St. WA3: Low .1H 53
WA9: Clock F .5N 63
Boddington Dr. WA4: Grap .9H 83
Bodiam Ct. CH65: Ell P .3C 112
Bodkin Grn. WA5: Westb .6J 65
Bodley St. L4: W'ton .2E 58
Bodmin Av. PR9: South .2N 7
Bodmin Cl. WA7: Brook .9D 96
Bodmin Gro. WA11: St H .3N 49
Bodmin Rd. L4: W'ton .9E 44
Bodmin Way L26: Halew .8J 77
Bognor Cl. L24: Speke .3F 92
Bolan St. L13: Liv .6M 59
BOLD .2D 64
Bold Bus. Cen. WA9: Bold .2D 64
Bolden Cl. L30: Neth .1E 44
Bolde Way CH63: Spit .6N 89
BOLD HEATH .1A 80
Bold Ind. Est. WA8: Widnes .3M 79
Bold Ind. Pk. WA9: Bold .3D 64
Bold La. L39: Augh .5M 27
WA5: Coll G .2D 64
WA9: Bold .2D 64
Bold Mnr. L35: Whis .6B 62
Bold Pl. L1: Liv .7J 5 (9D 58)
Bold Rd. WA9: St H .2B 64
Bold St. L1: Liv .6G 5 (8C 58)
PR9: South .7G 6
WA1: Warr .3B 82
WA7: Run .4L 95
WA8: Widnes .9K 79
WA10: St H .7J 49
Boleyn, The L31: Mag .9K 27
Boleyn Ct. WA7: Manor P .4E 96
Bolingbroke La. WA8: Widnes .4A 80
Bollin Cl. WA3: Cul .8N 53
WA13: Lymm .4G 84
Bollin Ct. WA8: Widnes .3L 79
Bollin Dr. WA13: Lymm .4G 84
Bollington Cl. CH43: Oxton .5F 72
Bolton Av. L32: Kirkb .9A 36
WA4: Westy .4G 82
Bolton Cl. L37: Form .2G 25
WA3: Low .2J 53
WA9: St H .6M 49
Bolton Rd. CH62: Port S .2A 90
PR8: Birkd .2N 11
WN2: Bam .8K 41
WN4: Ash M .8K 41
Bolton Rd. E. CH62: Port S .1B 90
Bolton's Cop PR9: Banks .1G 9
Bolton's Meanygate PR4: Tarl .1N 9
Bolton St. L3: Liv .5H 5 (8D 58)
WA9: St H .6M 49
(not continuous)
WN4: Garsw .6F 40
Bolton Wlk. L32: Kirkb .9A 36
Bonchurch Dr. L15: Wavtr .8L 59
Bond Cl. WA5: Warr .4M 81
Bond's La. PR9: Banks .1E 8
Bond St. L3: Liv .5C 58
L34: Presc .3A 62
BONE ISLAND .4E 30
Boniface Cl. CH62: Brom .2C 90
Bonnington Av. L23: Crosb .6J 33
Bonnington Cl. WA10: St H .7F 48
Bonsall Rd. L12: W Der .3N 59
Boode Cft. L28: Stockb V .9F 46
Booker Av. L18: Moss H, Aller .7M 75
BOOTH BANK .9N 85
Boothbank La. WA14: M'ton .9N 85
Booth's Brow Rd.
WN4: Ash M .5F 40
Booth's Cl. CH2: Elt .3L 113
Booths Hill Cl. WA13: Lymm .6C 84
Booth's Hill Rd. WA13: Lymm .5C 84
Booth's La. L39: Augh .8L 19
WA13: Lymm .6B 84
Booths La. WA4: H Whi .9F 98
Booth St. L13: Liv .6M 59
PR9: South .7G 7
WA5: Warr .4N 81
WA9: St H .2G 62
Boothwood Cl. L7: Liv .8G 59
BOOTLE .7B 44
Bootle Leisure Cen. .6B 44
Bootle Municipal Golf Course .1D 44
Bootle New Strand Station (Rail) .6B 44
Bootle Oriel Road Station (Rail) .8A 44
Bootle Strand Bus Station .6B 44
Borax St. L13: Liv .7M 59
Bordehill Gdns. L12: W Der .1B 60
Border Rd. CH60: Hesw .7B 88
Border Way L5: Liv .3D 58
Borella Rd. L13: Liv .3L 59
Borough Pavement CH41: Birke .2L 73
Borough Pl. CH41: Birke .2L 73
(off Grange Rd. E.)
Borough Rd. CH41: Birke .5J 73
CH42: Rock F, Tran .5J 73
CH44: Wall .6K 57
WA10: St H .8H 49
Borough Rd. E. CH41: Birke .2L 73
CH44: Wall .7L 57
Borough Way CH44: Wall .6L 57
Borromeo Cl. L17: Aig .5H 75
Borron Cl. WA12: Newt W .5K 51
Borron Ho. WA12: Newt W .6K 51
Borron Rd. WA12: Newt W .5K 51
Borron Rd. Ind. Est. WA12: Newt W .6K 51
(off Borron Rd.)
Borrowdale L37: Form .8F 16
Borrowdale Av. WA2: Warr .6D 66
Borrowdale Cl. WA6: Frod .6M 107
Borrowdale Rd. CH46: More .9L 55
CH63: Beb .3L 89
L15: Wavtr .2K 75
WA8: Widnes .8F 78
WA10: St H .1E 62
Bosco Ct. L11: Crox .6N 45
Boscow Cres. WA9: St H .2N 63
Bosnia St. L8: Liv .5F 74
Bossom Ct. L22: Wloo .3K 43
Bostock Grn. CH65: Ell P .8L 103
Bostock St. WA5: Warr .2N 81
Boston Av. WA7: Run .7L 95
Boston Blvd. WA5: Gt San .1J 81
Boston Cl. WA3: Cul .6N 53
Boswell Av. WA4: Warr .6C 82
Boswell Rd. CH43: Pren .7F 72
Boswell St. L8: Liv .1H 75
L20: Boot .5N 43
Bosworth Cl. CH63: Spit .5M 89
Bosworth Dr. PR8: Ainsd .1H 17
Bosworth Rd. WA11: St H .4M 49
Botanic Est. L7: Liv .8J 59
Botanic Gdns. .5N 7
Botanic Gro. L7: Liv .8H 59
Botanic Pl. L7: Liv .7H 59
Botanic Rd. L7: Liv .8H 59
PR9: South .6M 7
Botany Rd. L24: Speke .2G 93
Boteler Av. WA5: Warr .1A 82
Boteler Ct. WA4: Warr .6D 82
(off Elphins Dr.)
Botley Cl. CH49: Upton .3L 71
Boulevard L6: Liv .5J 59
Boulevard, The CH65: Gt Sut .9L 103
L8: Liv .2F 74
L12: W Der .1N 59
WA5: Burtw .6K 65
WA10: St H .1F 62
Boulevard Bus. Pk. WA3: Birchw .7L 67
Boulevard Industry Pk. L24: Halew .2H 93
(not continuous)
Boulting Av. WA5: Warr .7A 66
Boulton Av. CH48: W Kir .4C 70
CH62: New F .8A 74
Boundary Ct. WA10: St H .6H 49
Boundary Dr. L23: Crosb .5K 33
L25: Hunts X .9H 77
Boundary Farm Rd. L26: Halew .1H 93
Boundary La. CH60: Hesw .7A 88
L6: Liv .5G 58
L33: Kirkb .9J 37
L40: Burs .1K 21
L40: Burs, Ruf .5J 15
PR4: Hesk B, Tarl .3H 9
Boundary Meanygate PR4: Hesk B .1K 9
Boundary Pk. CH64: P'gte .7D 100
Boundary Rd. CH43: Bid, Noct .8D 56
CH48: W Kir .8E 70
CH62: Port S .9A 74
L21: Lith .9C 34
(not continuous)
L36: Huy .9K 61
WA10: St H .7H 49
Boundary Stone La. WA8: Widnes .4A 80
Boundary St. L5: Liv .3A 58
PR8: South .2A 12
WA1: Warr .1F 82
Boundary St. E. L5: Liv .3D 58
Boundary Wlk. L36: Huy .9L 61
Bourchier Way WA4: Grap .8H 83
Bourne Av. WA3: Low .2E 52
Bourne Gdns. WA9: St H .9M 49
Bournemouth Cl. WA7: Murd .9F 96
Bourne St. L6: Liv .6G 58
Bourton Rd. L25: Hunts X .9F 76
Bousfield St. L4: W'ton .2D 58
Boverton Cl. WA5: Call .8N 65
Bovey Ct. WA1: Warr .4C 82
(off St Austins La.)
Bowden Cl. L12: Crox .8C 46
WA3: Cul .6N 53
Bowden Rd. CH45: Wall .3G 56
L19: Garst .1N 91
WA10: Ec'stn .8E 48
Bowden St. L21: Lith .4A 44
Bowdon Cl. WA1: Padg .9G 67
Bowen Cl. WA8: Widnes .4G 79
Bower Cres. WA4: Sttn .5E 98
Bower Gro. L21: Sea .3M 43
Bower Ho. CH49: Upton .1N 71
Bower Rd. CH60: Hesw .7C 88
L25: Woolt .4E 76
L36: Huy .5J 61
Bowers Bus. Pk. WA8: Widnes .9M 79
Bowers Pk. Ind. Est. WA8: Widnes .9M 79
Bower St. WA8: Widnes .7M 79
Bowfell Cl. CH62: East .3C 102
Bowfell Gro. WA1: Wools .2N 83
Bowfield Rd. L19: G'dale .9N 75
Bowgreen Cl. CH43: Bid .1C 72
BOWKER'S GREEN .7B 28
Bowker's Grn. La. L39: Augh, Bic .7B 28
Bowland Av. L16: Child .8B 60
WA3: Golb .1D 52
WA9: Sut M .6L 63
WN4: Ash M .7K 41
Bowland Cl. CH62: Brom .6C 90
WA3: Birchw .4B 68
WA7: Beech .1A 108
Bowland Ct. PR9: South .7H 7
(off Gordon St.)
Bowland Dr. L21: Ford .7B 34
Bowles St. L20: Boot .5N 43
Bowley Rd. L13: Liv .4L 59
Bowling Grn. Cl. PR8: South .1E 12
Bowman Av. WA4: Westy .3H 83
Bowmore Way L7: Liv .9H 59
Bowness Av. CH43: Pren .6G 72
CH63: Brom .1B 102
M44: Cad .5K 69
PR8: Ainsd .2J 17
WA2: Warr .7D 66
WA11: St H .2L 49
Bowood Ct. WA2: Winw .5B 66
Bowood St. L8: Liv .5E 74
Bowring Ct. L14: Brd G .8D 60
Bowring Dr. CH64: P'gte .5B 100
BOWRING PARK .8E 60
Bowring Pk. Av. L16: Child .8E 60
Bowring Pk. Golf Course .8F 60
Bowring Pk. Rd. L14: Brd G .8A 60
Bowring Pk. Vis. Cen. .8F 60
Bowring St. L8: Liv .4F 74
Bowscale Cl. CH49: Upton .3M 71
Boxdale Ct. L18: Moss H .4M 75
Boxdale Rd. L18: Moss H .4M 75
Boxgrove Cl. WA8: Widnes .5L 79
Boxmoor Rd. L18: Moss H .6M 75
Boxtree Cl. L12: Crox .6D 46
Box Wlk. M31: Part .6L 69
Boxwood Cl. L36: Roby .7G 60
Boxwood Gdns. WA9: St H .2A 64
Boycott St. L5: Liv .3F 58
Boyd Cl. CH46: Leas .6B 56
Boydell Av. WA4: Grap .6J 83
WA4: Westy .4G 83
Boydell Cl. L28: Stockb V .2F 60
Boyer Av. L31: Mag .4J 35
Boyes Brow L33: Kirkb .7B 36
Boyes Ct. L31: Mag .4J 35
Boyle Av. WA2: Warr .8F 66
Boyton Ct. L7: Liv .9H 59
Brabant Rd. L17: Aig .7K 75
Braby Rd. L21: Lith .4B 44
Bracebridge Dr. PR8: South .4E 12
Bracewell Cl. WA9: St H .3M 63
Bracken Cl. WA3: Birchw .4K 67
Bracken Ct. WA9: Clock F .5M 63
Brackendale CH2: Elt .2M 113
CH49: Wdchu .5C 72
WA7: Run .7N 95
Brackendale Av. L9: Aintr .3G 45
Bracken Dr. CH48: W Kir .6F 70
Bracken Gdns. L40: Burs .8J 15
Brackenhurst Dr. CH45: New B .2J 57
Brackenhurst Grn. L33: Kirkb .9C 36
Bracken La. CH63: H Beb .2K 89
Bracken Rd. CH66: Gt Sut .1K 111
Brackens, The WA4: Dares .6K 97
Brackenside CH60: Hesw .5N 87
Bracken Wlk. L32: Kirkb .1B 46
(off Wervin Rd.)
Bracken Way L12: W Der .4M 59
WA6: Frod .8M 107
Brackenway L37: Form .7G 16
Bracken Wood L12: Crox .6C 46
Brackenwood Dr. WA8: Widnes .9D 78
Brackenwood Golf Course .2K 89
Brackenwood Gro. L35: Whis .6C 62
Brackenwood M. WA4: Grap .7K 83
Brackenwood Rd. CH63: H Beb .2K 89
Brackley Av. M44: Cad .3K 69
Brackley Cl. CH44: Wall .6G 56
WA7: Run .4J 95
Brackley St. WA4: Stockt H .7D 82
WA7: Run .4J 95
Bracknell Av. L32: Kirkb .1B 46
Bracknell Cl. L32: Kirkb .2B 46
Bracknel Way L39: Augh .3M 27
Bradbourne Cl. L12: Crox .7C 46
Bradburn Rd. M44: Irlam .2L 69
Bradda Cl. CH49: Upton .1N 71
Braddan Av. L13: Liv .4K 59
Bradden Cl. CH63: Spit .5A 90
Brade St. PR9: South .3A 8
Bradewell Cl. L4: Kirkd .1D 58
Bradewell St. L4: Kirkd .1D 58
Bradfield Av. L10: Aintr .8H 35
Bradfield Rd. L14: Brd G .7C 60
Bradfield St. L7: Liv .7H 59
Bradgate Cl. CH46: More .8J 55
WA5: Warr .2A 82
Bradkirk Ct. L30: Neth .6C 34
Bradlegh Rd. WA12: Newt W .8K 51
BRADLEY .7A 108
Bradley Fold L36: Huy .9L 61
Bradley La. WA5: Burtw .8H 51
WA6: Frod .8N 107
WA12: Newt W .8H 51
Bradley Pl. PR8: South .8G 6
(off Eastbank St.)
Bradley Rd. L21: Lith .1A 44
Bradley St. PR9: South .7H 7
Bradley Way WA8: Widnes .7L 79
Bradman Cl. CH45: Wall .4H 57
Bradman Rd. CH46: More .8K 55
L33: Know I .8G 37
Bradmoor Rd. CH62: Brom .7C 90
Bradshaw Cl. WA10: St H .6G 48
Bradshaw La. WA4: Grap .5J 83
WA13: Lymm .5K 85
WN8: Parb .4F 22
Bradshaw's La. PR8: Ainsd .8K 11
Bradshaw St. WA8: Widnes .6K 79
Bradshaw Wlk. L20: Boot .6A 44
(off St James Dr.)
Bradstone Cl. L10: Faz .4N 45
Bradville Rd. L9: Aintr .3H 45
Bradwall Cl. CH65: Whit .1M 111
Bradwell Cl. CH48: W Kir .6E 70
Bradwell Rd. WA3: Low .3F 52
Braehaven Rd. CH45: New B .2J 57
Braehurst Way L25: Gate .2G 76
Braemar Av. PR9: South .5L 7
(not continuous)
Braemar Cl. L35: Whis .6C 62
WA2: Fearn .6H 67
Braemar Ct. CH65: Ell P .2C 112
Braemar Ho. CH43: Oxton .3F 72
Braemar St. L20: Kirkd .9C 44
Braemore Cl. WN3: Winst .1F 40
Braemore Rd. CH44: Wall .5F 56
Braeside Cl. CH66: Gt Sut .9H 103
Braeside Cres. WN5: Bil .6N 39
Braeside Gdns. CH49: Upton .3N 71
Brae St. L7: Liv .7G 59
Brahms Cl. L8: Liv .2G 74
Braid Cres. L23: Crosb .8M 33
Braidhaven WN6: Shev .6N 23
Braid St. CH41: Birke .9K 57
Braidwood Ct. CH41: Birke .3J 73
(off Mount Gro.)
Brainerd St. L13: Liv .4K 59
Braithwaite Cl. L35: Rainh .6F 62
WA7: Beech .9N 95
Braithwaite Rd. WA3: Low .1E 52
Brakedale Cl. L27: N'ley .4K 77
Bramberton Pl. L4: W'ton .9H 45
Bramberton Rd. L4: W'ton .9H 45
Bramble Av. CH41: Birke .9F 56
Bramble Cl. WA5: Penk .5G 81
Bramblefield Way L14: Knott A .5D 60
Brambles, The CH46: More .9A 56
PR9: Banks .4E 8
WA5: Burtw .2H 65
WN4: Garsw .6F 40
Bramble Way CH46: More .7L 55
L40: Burs .1K 21
WA7: Beech .2A 108
WN8: Parb .4F 22
Bramblewood Cl. CH43: Noct .4D 72
L27: N'ley .3J 77
Brambling Cl. WA7: Beech .1A 108
Brambling Pk. L26: Halew .7J 77
Brambling Way WA3: Low .3F 52
Bramcote Av. WA11: St H .4M 49
Bramcote Cl. L33: Kirkb .7E 36
Bramcote Rd. L33: Kirkb .7D 36
Bramcote Wlk. L33: Kirkb .7D 36
Bramerton Ct. CH48: W Kir .5B 70
Bramford Cl. CH49: Upton .3M 71
Bramhall Cl. CH48: W Kir .6E 70
L24: Speke .5J 93
Bramhall Dr. CH62: East .3E 102
Bramhall M. WA10: Ec'stn .7E 48
Bramhall Rd. L22: Wloo .2L 43
WN8: Skel .2C 30
Bramhall St. WA5: Warr .3N 81
(not continuous)
Bramhope Pk. L12: W Der .2B 60
Bramley Av. CH63: H Beb .9L 73
Bramley Cl. CH66: Gt Sut .5L 111
L27: N'ley .3H 77
Bramley M. WA4: Stockt H .8D 82
Bramleys, The L31: Mag .4H 35
Bramley Wlk. L24: Speke .5H 93
WA6: Hel .4D 114
Bramley Way L32: Kirkb .8A 36

Brampton Cl.—Brock Av.

Brampton Cl. L32: Kirkb 7C 36
Brampton Ct. WA9: St H 7D 50
Brampton Dr. L8: Liv 8M 5 (9F 58)
Bramshill Cl. WA3: Birchw 3A 68
Bramwell Av. CH43: Pren 7G 72
Bramwell St. WA9: St H 6A 50
Brancaster Dr. WA3: Low 3H 53
Brancepeth Ct. CH65: Ell P 2B 112
Branchway WA11: Hay 4F 50
Brancker Av. L35: Rainh 5E 62
Brancote Ct. CH43: Clau 2F 72
Brancote Gdns. CH43: Clau 2F 72
CH62: Brom 8C 90
Brancote Mt. CH43: Clau 2F 72
Brancote Rd. CH43: Clau 2F 72
Brandearth Hey L28: Stockb V 2F 60
Brandearth Ho. L28: Stockb V 2F 60
BRAND HEALD 1J 9
Brandon WA8: Widnes 6E 78
Brandon Cl. WN8: Uph 5K 31
Brandon St. CH41: Birke 2M 73
Brandreth Cl. L35: Rainh 6F 62
Brandreth Delph WN8: Parb 2F 22
Brandreth Dr. WN8: Parb 3F 22
Brandreth Pk. WN8: Parb 1F 22
Brandwood Av. WA2: Warr 7C 66
Brandwood Ho. *WA1: Warr 3D 82*
(off Hall St.)
Branfield Cl. L12: Crox 7C 46
Bransdale Cl. WA5: Gt San 1H 81
Bransdale Dr. WN4: Ash M 8M 41
Bransfield Cl. WN3: Wigan 1J 41
Bransford Cl. WN4: Ash M 9L 41
Branstree Av. L11: Norr G 8L 45
Brantfield Ct. WA2: Warr 7F 66
Branthwaite Cres. L11: Norr G 8M 45
Brasenose Rd.
L20: Boot, Kirkd 8A 44
Brassey St. CH41: Birke 9H 57
L8: Liv 2D 74
Brathay Cl. WA2: Warr 6D 66
Brattan Rd. CH41: Birke 4J 73
Bratton Cl. WN3: Winst 2E 40
Braunton Rd. CH45: Wall 3G 57
L17: Aig 8K 75
Bravery Ct. L19: Speke 3C 92
Braybrooke Rd. L11: Norr G 7M 45
Bray Cl. WA7: Beech 9N 95
Braydon Cl. L25: Hunts X 1G 92
Brayfield Rd. L4: W'ton 9J 45
Bray Rd. L24: Speke 3G 92
Bray St. CH41: Birke 9H 57
Breakout Liverpool 4F 4 (7C 58)
Brearley Cl. CH43: Bid 9C 56
Breccia Gdns. WA9: St H 8A 50
Brechin Rd. L33: Kirkb 9D 36
Breck, The CH66: Ell P 7K 103
Breckfield Pl. L5: Liv 4E 58
Breckfield Rd. Nth. L5: Liv 3E 58
Breckfield Rd. Sth. L6: Liv 4F 58
Breck Pl. CH44: Wall 6G 56
Breck Rd. CH44: Wall 6G 56
L4: W'ton 5E 58
L5: Liv 5E 58
WA8: Widnes 7L 79
Breckside Av. CH44: Wall 5E 56
Breckside Pk. L6: Liv 3H 59
Brecon Av. L30: Neth 1E 44
Brecon Ct. WA5: Call 7N 65
Brecon Dr. CH66: Gt Sut 4K 111
Brecon Rd. CH42: Tran 7J 73
Brecon St. L6: Liv 6G 58
Brecon Wlk. *L30: Neth 1F 44*
(off Durham Av.)
Bredon Cl. CH66: Lit Sut 8F 102
Bredon Ct. L37: Form 9E 16
Breeze Cl. L9: W'ton 7E 44
Breeze Hill L9: W'ton 8E 44
L20: Boot 7C 44
Breezehill Cl. CH64: Nest 6F 100
Breezehill Pk. CH64: Nest 6F 100
Breezehill Rd. CH64: Nest 6F 100
Breeze La. L9: W'ton 7E 44
Breeze Rd. PR8: Birkd 4L 11
Brelade Rd. L13: Liv 5L 59
Bremhill Rd. L11: Norr G 7L 45
Bremner Cl. L7: Liv 8H 59
Brenchley Cl. L14: Knott A 5D 60
Brenda Cres. L23: Thorn 4N 33
Brendale Av. L31: Mag 3H 35
Brendan's Way L30: Neth 8D 34
Brendon Av. L21: Lith 1N 43
WA2: Warr 6B 66
Brendon Gro. WA9: St H 6C 50
Brendor Rd. L25: Woolt 7F 76
Brenig St. CH41: Birke 8F 56
Brenka Av. L9: Aintr 1G 45
Brentfield WA8: Widnes 6G 79
Brentnall Cl. WA5: Gt San 3L 81
Brent Way L26: Halew 1K 93
(not continuous)
Brentwood Av. L17: Aig 5H 75
L23: Crosb 6M 33
M44: Cad 3K 69
Brentwood Cl. L38: Hight 1F 32
WA10: Ec'stn 7E 48
Brentwood Ct. *CH49: Wdchu 6A 72*
(off Childwall Grn.)
PR9: South 6J 7
Brentwood Gro. L33: Kirkb 5C 36
Brentwood St. CH44: Wall 6J 57
Brereton Av. CH63: Beb 1N 89
L15: Wavtr 2M 75
Brereton Cl. WA7: Cas 7C 96
(not continuous)
Brereton Gro. M44: Cad 3L 69
Bretherton Ct. *L35: Rainh 5F 62*
(off Ratcliffe Pl.)
L40: Burs 2K 21
Bretherton Rd. L34: Presc 3B 62
Bretland Dr. WA4: Grap 9H 83
Bretlands Rd. L23: Thorn 5A 34
Brett Cl. L33: Kirkb 6B 36
Bretton Av. WA1: Warr 3F 82
Bretton Fold PR8: South 1E 12
Brett St. CH41: Birke 9H 57
Brewery La. L31: Mell 7K 35
(not continuous)
L37: Form 7F 16
Brewery Pl. PR8: South 2A 12
Brewster St. L4: Kirkd 9D 44
L20: Boot 9D 44
Breydon Gdns. WA9: St H 3H 63
Brian Av. CH61: Irby 1N 87
WA2: Warr 9E 66
WA4: Stockt H 7F 82
Brian Cummings Ct. L21: Lith 4A 44
Briar Av. WA3: Rix 7H 69
Briar Cl. WN4: Ash M 7J 41
Briardale Gdns. CH66: Lit Sut 8H 103
Briardale Rd. CH42: Tran 4J 73
CH44: Wall 7L 57
CH63: H Beb 9M 73
CH64: Will 6N 101
CH66: Lit Sut 8H 103
L18: Moss H 3L 75
Briar Dr. CH60: Hesw 7A 88
L36: Huy 7H 61
Briarfield Av. WA8: Widnes 7D 78
Briarfield Rd. CH60: Hesw 7A 88
CH65: Ell P 9N 103
Briar Rd. PR8: Ainsd 1K 17
WA3: Golb 2C 52
Briars, The PR8: Birkd 5M 11
Briars Brook L40: Lath 2L 21
Briars Cl. L35: Rainh 8G 62
Briars Grn. WA10: St H 5J 49
WN8: Skel 9D 22
Briars La. L31: Mag 2K 35
L40: Lath 2L 21
Briar St. L4: Kirkd 2C 58
Briarswood Cl. CH42: Rock F 8M 73
L35: Whis 6C 62
Briar Wlk. WA3: Golb 2C 52
Briarwood L23: Blun 5H 33
WA7: Nort 7D 96
Briarwood Av. WA1: Warr 1F 82
Briarwood Rd. L17: Aig 5K 75
Briary Cl. CH60: Hesw 6B 88
Briary Cft. L38: Hight 9F 24
Brickfields L36: Huy 8L 61
Brickhurst Way WA1: Wools 9J 67
Brick Kiln La. L40: Ruf 3L 15
Brickmakers Arms Yd. *L39: Orm 7B 20*
(off Whiterails Dr.)
Brick St. L1: Liv 9G 4 (1C 74)
WA1: Warr 3D 82
WA12: Newt W 7H 51
Brickwall Grn. L29: Seft 4E 34
Brickwall La. L29: Seft 6C 34
Bride St. L4: W'ton 8E 44
Bridewell Ct. WA8: Widnes 5L 79
Bridge Av. L39: Orm 8C 20
WA4: Westy 4G 82
Bridge Av. E. WA4: Westy 3G 83
Bridge Bank Cl. WA3: Golb 3C 52
Bridge Cl. M31: Part 6N 69
WA13: Lymm 5H 85
Bridge Ct. CH48: W Kir 5B 70
CH64: Nest 7E 100
L30: Neth 7C 34
Bridge Cft. L21: Ford 8B 34
Bridgecroft Rd. CH45: Wall 3H 57
Bridge Farm Cl. CH49: Wdchu 4B 72
Bridge Farm Dr. L31: Mag 1L 35
Bridgefield Cl. L25: Gate 1F 76
Bridgefield Ct. L34: Presc 4B 62
Bridge Foot Ind. Est. WA4: Warr 4C 82
Bridgeford Av. L12: W Der 2M 59
Bridge Gdns. L12: W Der 9D 46
Bridge Gro. PR8: South 9G 7
Bridgehall Dr. WN8: Uph 5L 31
Bridge Ho. *CH41: Birke 1M 73*
(off Canning St.)
L39: Orm 9C 20
Bridgehouse La. L10: Faz 4M 45
Bridge Ho. M. WA4: Thel 5M 83
Bridge Ind. Est. L24: Speke 2F 92
Bridge La. L30: Neth 8D 34
WA1: Wools 2K 83
WA4: App 8F 82
WA6: Frod 5M 107
Bridge La. M. WA6: Frod 5N 107
Bridgeman St. WA5: Warr 4M 81
WA10: St H 7G 49
(not continuous)
Bridge Mdw. CH66: Gt Sut 3L 111
WA13: Lymm 4H 85
Bridge Mdw. Rd. CH49: Wdchu 4B 72
Bridgemere Cl. L7: Liv 6J 59
Bridgemere Ho. L17: Aig 6J 75
Bridgemill Cl. L27: N'ley 4K 77
Bridgend Cl. WA8: Widnes 5G 79
Bridgend Dr. PR8: Ainsd 1H 17
Bridgenorth Rd. CH61: Pens 3M 87
Bridgeport M. WA5: Gt San 1J 81
Bridge Retail Pk. 5K 95
Bridge Rd. CH48: W Kir 5B 70
L7: Liv 9J 59
L18: Moss H 5M 75
L21: Lith 3N 43
(not continuous)
L23: Blun 8J 33
L31: Mag 4J 35
L34: Presc 4A 62
L36: Roby 7G 60
WA1: Wools 1K 83
WA9: Clock F 7N 63
Bridge Shop. Cen., The 5G 82
Bridgeside Dr. WA6: Hel 1E 114
Bridges La. L29: Seft 4E 34
Bridges Rd. CH65: Ell P 9D 104
Bridge St. CH41: Birke 1L 73
(not continuous)
CH62: Port S 2A 90
(not continuous)
CH64: Nest 7E 100
L20: Boot 8A 44
L39: Orm 9C 20
PR8: South 9G 7
WA1: Warr 3C 82
WA3: Golb 3B 52
WA7: Run 5L 95
WA10: St H 7K 49
WA12: Newt W 7K 51
BRIDGE TRAFFORD 9K 113
Bridge Vw. Cl. WA8: Widnes 3K 95
Bridge Vw. Dr. L33: Kirkb 7D 36
Bridge Wlk. *WA7: Pal F 8B 96*
(within Halton Lea Shop. Cen.)
Bridgewater Av. WA4: Westy 4G 82
Bridgewater Cl. L21: Lith 9N 33
WA6: Frod 5M 107
Bridgewater Ct. L21: Lith 9N 33
Bridgewater Grange WA7: Pres B 1H 109
Bridgewater Ho. WA7: Run 4H 95
Bridgewater M. WA4: Stockt H 8D 82
WA7: Nort 6F 96
Bridgewater Pl. WA3: Ris 5M 67
Bridgewater St. L1: Liv 9F 4 (1C 74)
WA7: Run 4K 95
WA13: Lymm 5E 84
Bridgewater Way L36: Huy 9L 61
Bridgeway L11: Norr G 9K 45
Bridgeway E. WA7: Wind H 5E 96
Bridgeway W. WA7: Wind H 5D 96
Bridge Wills La. PR9: South 2A 8
Bridgewood Dr. CH66: Gt Sut 3H 111
Bridle Av. CH44: Wall 7L 57
Bridle Cl. CH43: Bid 2B 72
CH62: Brom 8D 90
Bridle Ct. WA9: St H 1M 63
Bridle La. CH1: Dunk, Lea B 7K 111
Bridlemere Ct. WA1: Padg 9F 66
Bridle Pk. CH62: Brom 8D 90
Bridle Rd. CH44: Wall 7L 57
CH62: Brom, East 8D 90
L30: Neth 2D 44
Bridle Rd. Ind. Est. L30: Neth 2E 44
Bridle Way CH66: Gt Sut 2J 111
L30: Neth 2E 44
L33: Kirkb 5B 36
Bridport St. L3: Liv 4H 5 (7D 58)
Briedden Way CH66: Lit Sut 8F 102
Brierfield WN8: Skel 6G 31
Brierfield Rd. L15: Wavtr 2L 75
Brierley Cl. *L30: Neth 7G 34*
(off Beeston Dr.)
Brierley Ter. WA8: Widnes 7M 79
Briers Cl. WA2: Fearn 6G 67
Briery Hey Av. L33: Kirkb 9D 36
Brigadier Dr. L12: W Der 2C 60
Brighouse Cl. L39: Orm 8B 20
Brightgate Cl. L7: Liv 9G 59
BRIGHTON LE SANDS 9H 33
Brighton Rd. L22: Wloo 1K 43
L36: Huy 6M 61
PR8: Birkd 3N 11
Brighton St. CH44: Wall 5K 57
WA5: Warr 2N 81
(not continuous)
Brighton Va. L22: Wloo 9J 33
Brightstone Cl. PR9: Banks 2F 8
Bright St. CH41: Birke 2J 73
(not continuous)
L6: Liv 1M 5 (6F 58)
PR9: South 8L 7
Brightwell Cl. CH49: Upton 4N 71
WA5: Gt San 3G 80
Brignall Gro. WA3: Low 1E 52
Brill St. CH41: Birke 9H 57
Brimelow Cres. WA5: Penk 5G 81
BRIMSTAGE 5H 89
Brimstage Av. CH63: H Beb 8K 73
Brimstage Cl. CH60: Hesw 8C 88
Brimstage Grn. CH60: Hesw 7D 88
Brimstage Hall 5G 89
Brimstage Hall Ctyd. CH63: Brim 5G 89
Brimstage La. CH63: Brim, Store 5H 89
Brimstage Rd. CH60: Hesw 8C 88
CH63: Beb, Brim, H Beb 5L 89
L4: W'ton 8D 44
Brimstage St. CH41: Birke 3J 73
Brindley, The 5K 95
Brindley Av. WA4: Westy 4G 82
Brindley Cl. L21: Lith 9N 33
Brindley Ct. WA4: Stockt H 8E 82
Brindley Rd. L32: Kirkb 9A 36
WA7: Astm 4B 96
WA9: St H 3A 64
Brindley St. L8: Liv 2C 74
WA7: Run 4J 95
Brindley Wharf WA4: Pres H 1H 109
Brinell Dr. M44: Irlam 3L 69
Brinklow Cl. PR8: Ainsd 9G 11
Brinley Cl. CH62: Brom 1C 102
Brinton Cl. L27: N'ley 2G 77
WA8: Widnes 8G 79
Brisbane Av. CH45: New B 1G 56
Brisbane St. WA9: St H 2G 63
Briscoe Av. CH46: More 1M 71
Briscoe Dr. CH46: More 1M 71
Bristol Av. CH44: Wall 5J 57
WA7: Murd 9G 97
Bristol Dr. CH66: Gt Sut 4K 111
Bristol Rd. L15: Wavtr 2M 75
Bristow Cl. WA5: Gt San 9K 65
Britannia Av. L15: Wavtr 1J 75
Britannia Cres. L8: Liv 5E 74
Britannia Gdns. WA6: Hel 4E 114
Britannia Ho. CH41: Birke 2M 73
Britannia Pav. L3: Liv 8D 4 (9B 58)
Britannia Rd. CH45: Wall 5G 57
CH65: Ell P 2F 112
WA6: Hel 3E 114
British Lawnmower Mus. 1A 12
British Music Experience 6C 4
Britonside Av. L32: Kirkb 2E 46
Brittarge Brow L27: N'ley 4J 77
Britten Cl. L8: Liv 2G 75
Broadacre WN8: Uph 6K 31
Broadacre Cl. L18: Moss H 3B 76
Broad Arpley La. *WA1: Warr 4C 82*
(off Park Blvd.)
Broadbelt St. L4: W'ton 8E 44
Broadbent Av. WA4: Westy 4G 82
Broad Birches CH65: Ell P 8M 103
Broadfield Av. CH43: Bid 9C 56
Broadfield Cl. CH43: Bid 1B 72
Broadfields WA7: Nort 7E 96
Broadgate Av. WA9: St H 9M 49
BROAD GREEN 8B 60
Broad Grn. Rd. L13: Liv 6M 59
Broad Green Station (Rail) 8B 60
Broadheath Av. CH43: Bid 1C 72
Broadheath Ter. WA8: Widnes 7G 79
Broad Hey L30: Neth 8C 34
Broad Hey Cl. L25: Woolt 5F 76
Broadhey La. WN6: Wright 1J 23
Broadhurst Av. WA3: Cul 8N 53
WA5: Warr 4M 81
Broadhurst St. L17: Aig 5H 75
Broadlake CH64: Will 6M 101
Broadland Gdns. CH66: Gt Sut 3L 111
Broadland Rd. CH66: Gt Sut 3L 111
Broadlands L35: Presc 4B 62
PR8: Birkd 3L 11
Broad La. CH60: Hesw 6J 87
L4: W'ton 9K 45
L11: Norr G 9K 45
L29: Thorn 2B 34
L32: Kirkb 2D 46
L37: Form 6H 17
L37: Gt Alt 1K 25
L39: Down 2G 26
WA4: Grap 7J 83
WA5: Burtw, Coll G 9E 50
WA11: St H 9L 39
Broad La. Pct. L11: Norr G 9L 45
Broadleaf Rd. L19: G'dale 9L 75
Broadley Av. WA3: Low 3D 52
Broadmead CH60: Hesw 8C 88
L19: Aller 9C 76
WN8: Parb 3E 22
BROAD OAK 6B 50
Broad Oak Av. WA5: Penk 4G 81
WA11: Hay 4C 50
Broad Oak Rd. WA9: St H 7A 50
Broadoak Rd. L14: Knott A 5D 60
L31: Mag 2K 35
Broadoaks CH49: Upton 2M 71
Broad Pl. L11: Norr G 1L 59
Broadriding Rd. WN6: Shev 7N 23
Broads, The WA9: St H 3H 63
Broad Sq. L11: Norr G 1L 59
Broadstone Dr. CH63: Spit 5M 89
Broad Vw. L11: Norr G 1L 59
Broadway CH45: Wall 4F 56
CH49: Grea 3M 71
CH63: H Beb 9K 73
L9: Aintr 3K 45
L11: Norr G 9K 45
M31: Part 5N 69
WA8: Widnes 7D 78
WA10: Ec'stn 6D 48
WA10: St H 1F 62
Broadway Av. CH45: Wall 4F 56
Broadway Cl. PR8: Ainsd 9H 11
Broadway Leisure Cen. 1E 62
Broadway Mkt. L11: Norr G 9K 45
Broadwell Dr. WN7: Leigh 1M 53
Broadwood Av. L31: Mag 4H 35
Broadwood St. L15: Wavtr 1K 75
Brock Av. L31: Mag 1K 35

Brockenhurst Rd.—Budworth Rd.

Brockenhurst Rd. L9: W'ton .5F 44
Brock Gdns. L24: Hale .5B 94
Brock Hall Cl. WA9: Clock F .5M 63
Brockhall Cl. L35: Whis .3D 62
Brockholme Rd. L18: Moss H .7M 75
Brocklebank La. L19: Aller .8B 76
Brocklebank Rd. PR9: South .6K 7
Brockley Av. CH45: New B .9H 43
Brock Rd. WA3: Birchw .6L 67
Brock St. L4: Kirkd .1D 58
Brockton Ct. WA4: App .1D 98
Brocstedes Av. WN4: Ash M .5G 40
Brocstedes Rd. WN4: Ash M .3F 40
(not continuous)
Brodie Av. L18: Moss H .5M 75
L19: Aig, Aller .7N 75
Brogden Av. WA3: Cul .6M 53
BROMBOROUGH .6D 90
Bromborough Bowl .5D 90
Bromborough Golf Course .1A 102
Bromborough (Park & Ride) .9B 90
BROMBOROUGH POOL .2C 90
Bromborough Pool Bus. Pk.
CH62: Brom .1C 90
BROMBOROUGH PORT .4D 90
Bromborough Rake Station (Rail) .7B 90
Bromborough Rd. CH63: Beb .2N 89
Bromborough Station (Rail) .8B 90
Bromborough Village Rd.
CH62: Brom .6D 90
Brome Way CH63: Spit .5A 90
Bromilow Rd. WA9: St H .8B 50
WN8: Skel .3N 29
Bromley Av. L18: Moss H .3L 75
WA3: Low .3E 52
Bromley Cl. CH60: Hesw .8M 87
L26: Halew .7L 77
WA2: Fearn .6G 67
Bromley Rd. CH45: New B .2G 57
Brompton Av. CH44: Wall .5J 57
L17: Liv .3H 75
L23: Crosb .8J 33
L33: Kirkb .6E 36
Brompton Cl. WA9: St H .4J 63
Brompton Ct. L17: Liv .3H 75
Brompton Gdns. WA5: Warr .1N 81
Brompton Ho. L17: Aig .3J 75
Brompton Rd. PR8: South .8K 7
Brompton Way CH66: Gt Sut .4K 111
Bromsgrove Rd. CH49: Grea .4K 71
Bromyard Cl. L20: Boot .6A 44
Bronington Av. CH62: Brom .9C 90
Bronshill Ct. L23: Blun .7G 33
Bronte Cl. L23: Blun .7H 33
WA2: Winw .3B 66
Bronte St. L3: Liv .4J 5 (8D 58)
WA10: St H .6G 49
Brook, The L31: Mag .3K 35
Brook Av. WA4: Stockt H .7F 82
WA4: Westy .3G 83
Brookbank Cl. L10: Faz .3N 45
Brookbridge Rd. L13: Liv .3K 59
Brook Cl. CH44: Wall .4J 57
WA8: Cron .2F 78
Brookdale PR8: Ainsd .2K 17
WA8: Widnes .5D 78
Brookdale Av. Nth. CH49: Grea .4M 71
Brookdale Av. Sth. CH49: Grea .4M 71
Brookdale Cl. CH49: Grea .4M 71
Brookdale Rd. L15: Wavtr .2K 75
Brook Dr. WA5: Gt San .3J 81
Brooke Cl. PR9: South .8N 7
Brook End WA9: St H .9C 50
Brooke Rd. E. L22: Wloo .9K 33
Brooke Rd. W. L22: Wloo .9J 33
Brook Farm Cl. L39: Orm .9C 20
M31: Part .8L 69
Brookfield WN8: Parb .3F 22
Brookfield Av. L22: Wloo .2M 43
L23: Crosb .8K 33
L35: Rainh .4F 62
WA7: Run .5A 96
Brookfield Cen. L9: Aintr .5H 45
Brookfield Cl. WA13: Lymm .5D 84
Brookfield Cotts. *WA13: Lymm .5D 84*
(off Elm Tree Rd.)
Brookfield Dr. L9: Aintr, Faz .5H 45
Brookfield Gdns. CH48: W Kir .6C 70
Brookfield Ho. L36: Huy .6J 61
Brookfield La. L39: Augh .6M 27
Brookfield Pk. WA4: Grap .6H 83
Brookfield Rd. CH48: W Kir .6C 70
WA3: Cul .7L 53
WA13: Lymm .5D 84
WN8: Uph .5L 31
BROOKFIELDS GREEN .7M 27
Brookfield St. WA12: Newt W .7K 51
Brook Furlong WA6: Frod .4H 107
Brook Hey CH64: P'gte .4B 100
Brook Hey Dr. L33: Kirkb .7D 36
Brook Hey Wlk. L33: Kirkb .8E 36
Brookhill Cl. L20: Boot .7C 44
Brookhill Rd. L20: Boot .6C 44
Brook Ho. PR8: South .1B 12
Brook Ho. Ct. WA13: Lymm .6D 84
Brookhouse Gro. WA10: Ec'stn .7D 48
Brook Ho. La. L30: Neth .6F 34
Brookhouse Rd. L39: Orm .7B 20
BROOKHURST .1B 102
Brookhurst Av. CH62: East .9B 90
CH63: Brom, East .9B 90
Brookhurst Cl. CH63: Brom .1B 102
Brookhurst Rd. CH63: Brom .9B 90
Brookland La. WA9: St H .8C 50
Brookland Rd. CH41: Birke .3K 73
Brookland Rd. E. L13: Liv .6M 59
Brookland Rd. W. L13: Liv .6M 59
Brooklands CH41: Birke .1K 73
L17: Aig .6J 75
L39: Orm .7E 20
WN8: Uph .4L 31
Brooklands, The L36: Huy .8J 61
Brooklands Av. L22: Wloo .2M 43
WN4: Ash M .9M 41
Brooklands Dr. L31: Mag .3J 35
WN5: Orr .7N 31
Brooklands Gdns. CH64: P'gte .5C 100
Brooklands Gro. L40: Lath .2K 21
Brooklands Pk. WA8: Widnes .6M 79
Brooklands Rd. CH64: P'gte .5C 100
WA10: Ec'stn .6D 48
WN8: Uph .5M 31
Brookland St. WA1: Warr .1F 82
Brook La. CH64: P'gte .4C 100
L39: Orm .9C 20
WA3: Rix .8A 68
WA11: Kings M .4J 39
Brook Lea Ho. L21: Ford .8B 34
Brooklea Mdws. CH66: Lit Sut .8E 102
Brooklet Rd. CH60: Hesw .7C 88
Brooklime Rd. L11: Norr G .9L 45
Brooklyn Cvn. Pk. PR9: Banks .3D 8
Brooklyn Dr. CH65: Gt Sut .9L 103
WA13: Lymm .4E 84
Brook Lynn Av. WA3: Low .1G 52
Brook Mdw. CH61: Irby .9M 71
Brook Pk. L31: Mag .4H 35
Brook Pl. WA4: Westy .5F 82
Brook Rd. CH66: Gt Sut .9J 103
L9: W'ton .6F 44
L20: Boot .7A 44
L23: Thorn .5N 33
L31: Mag .3K 35
WA13: Lymm .4E 84
Brooks, The WA11: St H .3K 49
Brooks All. L1: Liv .6F 4 (8C 58)
Brookside L12: W Der .1D 60
L31: Mag .2K 35
L39: Orm .8C 20
Brookside Av. L14: Knott A .6B 60
L22: Wloo .2M 43
WA4: Stockt H .7E 82
WA5: Gt San .4J 81
WA10: Ec'stn .5E 48
WA11: Rainf .4B 38
WA13: Lymm .4C 84
WN4: Ash M .3H 41
Brookside Cl. L35: Presc .5B 62
WA11: Hay .3D 50
WN5: Bil .6A 40
Brookside Ct. L23: Crosb .7L 33
L35: Presc .5B 62
Brookside Cres. CH49: Upton .3L 71
Brookside Dr. CH49: Upton .3M 71
Brookside Rd. L35: Presc .5B 62
PR8: South .5B 12
WA6: Frod .6K 107
Brookside Vw. WA11: Hay .3D 50
Brookside Way WA11: Hay .3D 50
Brooks Rd. L37: Form .2D 24
Brook St. CH41: Birke .9J 57
CH62: Port S .1N 89
CH64: Nest .6E 100
L3: Liv .3C 4 (7A 58)
L35: Whis .4C 62
PR9: South .3B 8
WA3: Golb .2B 52
WA3: Low .1H 53
WA7: Run .5K 95
(not continuous)
WA8: Widnes .8L 79
WA10: St H .7K 49
WN4: Ash M .9L 41
Brook St. E. CH41: Birke .1L 73
Brooks Way L37: Form .2D 24
Brook Ter. CH48: W Kir .6C 70
WA7: Run .6A 96
Brookthorpe Cl. CH45: Wall .3J 57
BROOKVALE .9E 96
Brook Va. L22: Wloo .2M 43
Brookvale Av. Nth. WA7: Brook .9D 96
Brookvale Av. Sth. WA7: Brook .9D 96
Brookvale Cl. WA5: Burtw .3H 65
Brookvale Local Nature Reserve .2M 43
Brookvale Recreation Cen. .9E 96
Brookview Cl. L27: N'ley .4K 77
Brook Wlk. CH61: Irby .9L 71
Brookward Ct. L32: Kirkb .7D 36
Brook Way WA5: Gt San .3J 81
Brookway CH43: Pren .7E 72
CH45: Wall .4G 56
CH49: Grea .3M 71
Brookway La. WA9: St H .9B 50
Brook Well CH64: Lit N .9E 100
Brookwood Cl. WA4: W'ton .8C 82
Brookwood Rd. L36: Huy .5J 61
Broom Av. WA4: App .1F 98
Broom Cl. L34: Eccl P .3C 62
L40: Burs .1K 21
Broome Cl. PR8: Birkd .3A 12
Broome Ct. WA7: Brook .9D 96
BROOMEDGE .8J 85
Broomehouse Av. M44: Irlam .1L 69
Broome Rd. PR8: Birkd .3A 12
Broomfield Cl. CH60: Hesw .6K 87
Broomfield Gdns. L9: W'ton .5E 44
Broomfield Rd. L9: W'ton .5E 44
(not continuous)
Broomfields WA4: App .9F 82
Broomfields Leisure Cen. .9E 82
Broomfields Rd. WA4: App .9E 82
Broom Hill CH43: Clau .1F 72
Broomhill Cl. L27: N'ley .2G 77
Broomholme WN6: Shev .6N 23
Broomlands CH60: Hesw .7N 87
Broomleigh Cl. CH63: H Beb .2K 89
Broom Rd. M31: Part .7M 69
WA10: St H .1E 62
Brooms Cross Rd. L29: Thorn .4A 34
L30: Neth .4A 34
Brooms Gro. L10: Aintr .9K 35
Broom Way L26: Halew .9J 77
Broseley Av. CH62: Brom .6B 90
WA3: Cul .6L 53
Broseley La. WA3: Cul .5L 53
Broseley Pl. WA3: Cul .5K 53
Broster Av. CH46: More .9K 55
Broster Cl. CH46: More .9K 55
Brosters La. CH47: Meols .9E 54
Brotherhood Dr. WA9: St H .2N 63
Brotherton Cl. CH62: Brom .6B 90
Brotherton Pk. & Dibbinsdale
Local Nature Reserve .5B 90
Brotherton Way
WA12: Newt W .6K 51
Brougham Av. CH41: Tran .5M 73
Brougham Rd. CH44: Wall .6K 57
Brougham Ter. L6: Liv .1M 5
Broughton Av. CH48: W Kir .5B 70
PR8: South .2C 12
WA3: Low .3E 52
Broughton Cl. WA4: Grap .8G 83
Broughton Dr. L19: G'dale .9M 75
Broughton Hall Rd. L12: W Der .4C 60
Broughton Rd. CH44: Wall .6H 57
Broughton Way WA8: Hale B .2E 94
BROW, THE .6B 96
Brow La. CH60: Hesw .8N 87
CW9: Ant .9L 99
Browmere Dr. WA3: Croft .2H 67
Brownbill Bank L27: N'ley .3J 77
BROWN EDGE
PR8 .4F 12
WA9 .2G 62
Brown Edge Cl. PR8: South .4F 12
Brownheath Av. WN5: Bil .8N 39
Brownhill Dr. WA1: Padg .9G 66
Browning Av. CH42: Rock F .7M 73
WA8: Widnes .8J 79
Browning Cl. L36: Huy .8K 61
Browning Dr. CH65: Gt Sut .1L 111
WA2: Winw .3B 66
Browning Grn. *CH65: Gt Sut .1L 111*
(off Browning Dr.)
Browning Rd. CH45: Wall .4D 56
L13: Liv .3L 59
L22: Wloo .9K 33
Browning St. L20: Boot .6N 43
BROWNLOW .2M 39
Brownlow Arc. WA10: St H .7K 49
Brownlow Hill L3: Liv .5H 5 (8D 58)
Brownlow La. WN5: Bil .2M 39
Brownlow Rd. CH62: New F .9A 74
Brownlow St. L3: Liv .5K 5 (8E 58)
Brownmoor Cl. L23: Crosb .7N 33
Brownmoor La. L23: Crosb .8M 33
Brownmoor Pk. L23: Crosb .8M 33
Brown's La. L30: Neth .8E 34
Brown St. WA8: Widnes .9N 79
Brownville Rd. L13: Liv .2J 59
Brow Rd. CH43: Bid .8D 56
Brows Cl. L37: Form .2E 24
Brow Side L5: Liv .5E 58
Brows La. L37: Form .2E 24
Broxholme Way L31: Mag .4J 35
Broxton Av. CH43: Pren .6F 72
CH48: W Kir .5C 70
Broxton Cl. WA8: Widnes .5F 78
Broxton Rd. CH45: Wall .3F 56
CH66: Ell P .9K 103
Broxton St. L15: Wavtr .9K 59
Bruce Av. WA2: Warr .8E 66
Bruce Cres. CH63: Brom .9B 90
Bruce Dr. CH66: Gt Sut .1H 111
Bruce St. L8: Liv .4F 74
WA10: St H .7H 49
BRUCHE .1E 82
Bruche Av. WA1: Padd, Padg .1G 82
Bruche Dr. WA1: Padg .9G 66
Bruche Heath Gdns. WA1: Padg .9H 67
Bruera Rd. CH65: Gt Sut .1L 111
Brunel Dr. L21: Lith .9N 33
Brunel M. L6: Liv .4F 58
Brunel Rd. CH62: Brom .6E 90
Brunner Rd. WA8: Widnes .8K 79
Brunsborough Cl. CH62: Brom .9B 90
Brunsfield Cl. CH46: More .1K 71
Brunstath Cl. CH60: Hesw .6C 88
Brunswick WA7: Run .4K 95
Brunswick Bus. Pk. L3: Liv .3C 74
(not continuous)
Brunswick Cl. L4: Kirkd .1D 58
WA5: Gt San .2J 81
Brunswick Ct. *CH41: Birke .1L 73*
(off Brunswick M.)
Brunswick Cres. CH66: Gt Sut .2K 111
Brunswick Ent. Cen. L3: Liv .3C 74
Brunswick M. CH41: Birke .1L 73
L22: Wloo .2L 43
Brunswick Pde. L22: Wloo .2K 43
Brunswick (Park & Ride) .4D 74
Brunswick Pl. L20: Kirkd .1A 58
Brunswick Rd. L6: Liv .2L 5 (6E 58)
WA12: Newt W .6H 51
Brunswick Station (Rail) .4D 74
Brunswick St. L2: Liv .6C 4 (8B 58)
L3: Liv .6C 4 (8A 58)
L19: Garst .4A 92
(not continuous)
WA9: St H .7C 50
Brunswick Way L3: Liv .3C 74
Brunt La. L19: Aller .9C 76
Bruntleigh Av. WA4: Westy .5H 83
Brushford Cl. L12: W Der .8N 45
Bruton Rd. L36: Huy .3H 61
(not continuous)
Bryanston Rd. CH42: Tran .6G 73
L17: Aig .5G 74
Bryant Av. WA4: Westy .3G 83
Bryant Rd. L21: Lith .4A 44
Bryce Cl. CH62: Brom .4B 90
Bryce Dr. CH62: Brom .4B 90
Bryce Wlk. CH62: Brom .3B 90
Bryceway, The L12: Knott A .5B 60
Brydges St. L7: Liv .6N 5 (8F 58)
Bryer Rd. L35: Presc .5A 62
BRYN .5J 41
Bryn Bank CH44: Wall .5J 57
BRYN GATES .4N 41
Bryn Gates La. WN2: Bam .3L 41
Brynmor Rd. L18: Moss H .7M 75
Brynmoss Av. CH44: Wall .5F 56
Brynn St. WA8: Widnes .8L 79
WA10: St H .6K 49
Bryn Rd. WN4: Ash M .5J 41
Bryn Rd. Sth. WN4: Ash M .7L 41
Bryn Station (Rail) .6J 41
Bryn St. WN2: Bam .4N 41
WN4: Ash M .8K 41
Bryn Vw. WN4: Ash M .5J 41
Bryony Cl. WN5: Orr .7N 31
Bryony Rd. L11: Norr G .9L 45
Bryony Way CH42: Rock F .8M 73
Brythen St. L1: Liv .5G 4 (8C 58)
BT Convention Cen. .9D 4 (1B 74)
Buccleuch St. CH41: Birke .8F 56
Buchanan Cl. WA8: Widnes .5J 79
Buchanan Rd. CH44: Wall .6K 57
L9: W'ton .7E 44
Buchan Cl. WA5: Gt San .9K 65
Buckfast Av. WA11: Hay .3J 51
Buckfast Cl. L30: Neth .7E 34
WA5: Penk .5G 81
Buckfast Ct. WA7: Nort .4G 97
Buckfast Dr. L37: Form .2H 25
Buckingham Av. CH43: Clau .1F 72
CH63: H Beb .9L 73
L17: Liv .2J 75
WA8: Widnes .4K 79
Buckingham Cl. L30: Neth .8B 34
WA10: St H .8H 49
Buckingham Ct. L33: Kirkb .8D 36
L39: Augh .2C 28
(off Aughton Pk. Dr.)
Buckingham Dr. WA5: Gt San .4L 81
WA11: St H .3K 49
Buckingham Gdns. CH65: Ell P .3B 112
Buckingham Gro. L37: Form .3E 24
Buckingham Ho. L17: Aig .3J 75
Buckingham Rd. CH44: Wall .5F 56
L9: W'ton .4F 44
L13: Liv .3J 59
L31: Mag .3H 35
M44: Cad .3J 69
Buckingham St. L5: Liv .4D 58
Buckland Cl. WA8: Widnes .9G 78
Buckland Dr. CH63: Spit .5M 89
Buckland St. L17: Aig .5G 74
Buckley Ct. CH64: Will .6M 101
Buckley Hill La. L29: Seft .7C 34
Buckley La. CH64: Will .6M 101
Buckley St. WA2: Warr .2B 82
Buckley Wlk. L24: Speke .5H 93
Buckley Way L30: Neth .6C 34
Bucklow Av. M31: Part .6M 69
Bucklow Gdns. WA13: Lymm .4G 85
BUCKOAK .8K 115
Buckthorn Cl. L28: Stockb V .2F 60
Buckthorn Gdns. WA9: St H .3F 62
Buckton St. WA1: Warr .1E 82
Buckwheat Dr. L11: Norr G .8L 45
Bude Cl. CH43: Bid .2C 72
Bude Ho. *CH43: Bid .2C 72*
(off Bude Cl.)
Bude Rd. WA8: Widnes .6H 79
Budworth Av. WA4: Westy .4G 83
WA8: Widnes .6G 78
WA9: Sut M .6L 63
Budworth Cl. CH43: Oxton .4E 72
WA7: Run .8N 95
Budworth Ct. CH43: Oxton .3F 72
Budworth Dr. L25: Woolt .6G 77
Budworth Rd. CH43: Noct, Oxton .4E 72
CH66: Gt Sut .3K 111

Buerton Cl.—Cambridge Dr.

Buerton Cl. CH43: Noct 4E 72
Buffs La. CH60: Hesw 6B 88
Buggen La. CH64: Nest 6D 100
Buildwas Rd. CH64: Nest 4E 100
Bulford Rd. L9: Faz 6K 45
Bulkeley Rd. CH44: Wall 6K 57
Bull Bri. La. L10: Aintr 9K 35
Bull Cop L37: Form 1G 25
(not continuous)
Bullens La. L40: Scar 7J 13
Bullens Rd. L4: W'ton 1E 58
L32: Kirkb 1D 46
Bullfinch Ct. L26: Halew 7J 77
Bull Hill CH64: Lit N 8F 100
Bull La. L9: Aintr 3G 44
L9: W'ton 4E 44
Bullrush Dr. CH46: More 7A 56
Bulrushes, The L17: Aig 5E 74
Bulwer St. CH42: Rock F 6M 73
L5: Liv 4F 58
L20: Boot 5N 43
Bunbury Cl. CH2: Stoak 6E 112
Bunbury Dr. WA7: Run 9M 95
Bunbury Grn. CH65: Ell P 3B 112
Bundoran Rd. L17: Aig 6K 75
Bungalow Rd. WA12: Newt W 9N 51
Bungalows, The WN4: Ash M 4H 41
Bunter Rd. L32: Kirkb 3D 46
Bunting Cl. WA3: Low 2F 52
Bunting Ct. L26: Halew 6H 77
Buntingford Rd. WA4: Thel 5K 83
Burbank Cl. WN3: Winst 2G 40
Burbo Bank Rd. L23: Blun 7G 33
Burbo Bank Rd. Nth. L23: Blun 6F 32
Burbo Bank Rd. Sth. L23: Blun 8H 33
Burbo Cres. L23: Blun 8H 33
Burbo Mans. L23: Blun 8H 33
Burbo Point L23: Blun 5G 32
Burbo Way CH45: Wall 1E 56
Burden Rd. CH46: More 9K 55
Burdett Av. CH63: Spit 5M 89
Burdett Cl. CH63: Spit 5N 89
Burdett Rd. CH45: Wall 4D 56
CH66: Gt Sut 3K 111
L22: Wloo 9K 33
Burdett St. L17: Aig 5H 75
Burdock Rd. L11: Norr G 9L 45
Burfield Dr. WA4: App 1D 98
Burford Av. CH44: Wall 6F 56
Burford La. WA13: Lymm 5J 85
Burford Rd. L16: Child 8A 60
Burgess Av. WA4: Warr 5C 82
Burgess Gdns. L31: Mag 1H 35
Burgess' La. L37: Gt Alt 3M 25
Burgess St. L3: Liv 3J 5 (7D 58)
Burghill Rd. L12: Crox 6D 46
Burgundy Cl. L17: Aig 6H 75
Burkhardt Dr. WA12: Newt W 7N 51
Burland Cl. WA7: Run 6J 95
Burland Rd. L26: Halew 1L 93
Burleigh M. *L5: Liv 3E 58*
(off Burleigh Rd. Sth.)
Burleigh Rd. Nth. L5: Liv 3E 58
Burleigh Rd. Sth. L5: Liv 3E 58
Burley Av. WA3: Low 1E 52
Burley Cl. L32: Kirkb 1D 46
Burley Cres. WN3: Winst 1E 40
Burley La. WA4: App T 3K 99
Burlingham Av. CH48: W Kir 7E 70
Burlington Av. L37: Form 1H 25
Burlington Dr. WA5: Gt San 1J 81
Burlington Ho. L22: Wloo 1L 43
Burlington Rd. CH45: New B 9H 43
PR8: Birkd 3M 11
Burlington St. CH41: Birke 2L 73
L3: Liv 5B 58
Burman Cres. L19: Garst 9A 76
Burman Rd. L19: Garst 9A 76
Burmarsh La. WA8: Hale B 2E 94
Burnage Av. WA9: Clock F 5M 63
Burnage Cl. L24: Speke 5K 93
Burnand St. L4: W'ton 2E 58
Burnard Cl. L33: Kirkb 9D 36
Burnard Cres. L33: Kirkb 9D 36
Burnard Wlk. L33: Kirkb 9D 36
Burnell Cl. WA10: St H 7J 49
Burnell Rd. CH65: Ell P 1C 112
Burnet Cl. WA2: Padg 7K 67
Burnet Rd. L5: Liv 3F 58
Burnfell WA3: Low 3F 52
Burnham Cl. WA3: Cul 6M 53
WA5: Penk 3H 81
WA8: Widnes 5F 78
Burnham Rd. L18: Moss H 5A 76
Burnie Av. L20: Boot 5D 44
Burnley Av. CH46: More 9N 55
PR8: Ainsd 9K 11
Burnley Cl. L6: Liv 5F 58
Burnley Gro. CH46: More 8N 55
Burnley Rd. CH46: More 8N 55
PR8: Ainsd 9J 11
Burnsall Av. WA3: Low 2G 53
Burnsall Dr. WA8: Widnes 5F 78
Burnsall St. L19: Garst 2C 92
Burns Av. CH45: Wall 4G 57
Burns Cl. CH66: Gt Sut 1K 111
L16: Child 9D 60
L35: Whis 6B 62
WN4: Ash M 5H 41
WN5: Bil 2N 39
Burns Cres. WA8: Widnes 8J 79
Burns Gro. L36: Huy 8L 61
WA2: Warr 7D 66
Burnside WN8: Parb 3E 22
Burnside Av. CH44: Wall 7H 57
WA4: Stockt H 7E 82
Burnside Rd. CH44: Wall 7H 57
Burns Rd. WA9: Sut M 6K 63
Burns St. L20: Boot 5N 43
Burnt Ash Cl. L19: G'dale 9L 75
Burnthwaite Rd. L14: Knott A 6A 60
Burnt Mill La. WA8: Hale B 2A 94
Burnvale WN3: Winst 1F 40
Burrard Rd. WA7: Run 7A 96
Burrell Cl. CH42: Tran 7J 73
Burrell Ct. CH42: Tran 7J 73
Burrell Dr. CH46: More 1L 71
Burrell Rd. CH42: Tran 7J 73
Burrell St. L4: W'ton 1E 58
Burrough Cl. WA3: Birchw 6N 67
Burroughs Gdns. L3: Liv 5C 58
Burrowdale Rd. L28: Stockb V 1E 60
Burrow's Av. WA11: Hay 5B 50
Burrows Ct. L3: Liv 5B 58
WA9: St H 7A 50
(off Chancery La.)
Burrow's La. L34: Eccl P 2B 62
WA10: Ec'stn 2B 62
Burrows La. WA6: Alv 4J 115
Burrows St. WA11: Hay 4C 50
Bursar Cl. WA12: Newt W 6M 51
BURSCOUGH 9J 15
BURSCOUGH BRIDGE 9H 15
Burscough Bridge Station (Rail) 9J 15
Burscough Fitness & Racquets Leisure Cen. 9J 15
Burscough Ind. Est. L40: Burs 9F 14
Burscough Junction Station (Rail) 1J 21
Burscough Rd. L39: Orm 7D 20
Burscough St. L39: Orm 8C 20
Burscough Wharf *L40: Burs 9J 15*
(off Liverpool Rd. Nth.)
Burton Av. CH45: Wall 4E 56
L35: Rainh 5D 62
Burton Cl. L1: Liv 8F 4 (9C 58)
L35: Rainh 5D 62
WA3: Cul 7N 53
WA8: Widnes 5J 79
Burton Grn. CH66: Gt Sut 1J 111
Burtonhead Ct. *WA9: St H 9L 49*
(off Harris Gdns.)
Burtonhead Rd. WA9: St H 8J 49
WA10: St H 8J 49
Burton Rd. CH64: Lit N, Ness 7E 100
WA2: Warr 8E 66
Burton St. L5: Kirkd 3B 58
Burtons Way L32: Kirkb 4E 46
BURTONWOOD 3G 65
Burtonwood Cotts. WA9: St H 8E 50
Burtonwood Ind. Cen. WA5: Burtw 2H 65
Burtonwood Rd.
WA5: Burtw, Gt San, Westb 5H 65
BURTONWOOD SERVICE AREA 6K 65
Burtree Rd. L14: Knott A 3E 60
Burwain Ho. L19: Aig 9L 75
Burwell Av. L37: Form 3D 24
Burwell Cl. L33: Kirkb 8E 36
Burwell Wlk. L33: Kirkb 8E 36
Burwen Dr. L9: W'ton 4E 44
Bury Rd. PR8: Birkd 3A 12
Busby's Cotts. CH45: New B 1H 57
Bushbys La. L37: Form 2C 24
Bushbys Pk. L37: Form 2C 24
Bushell Cl. CH64: Nest 7F 100
Bushell Ct. CH43: Oxton 4G 73
Bushell Rd. CH64: Nest 7F 100
Bushells La. WA6: Kgswd 5L 115
Bushel's Dr. WA9: Clock F 6N 63
Bushey La. WA11: Rainf 1A 38
Bushey Rd. L4: W'ton 8H 45
Bushley Cl. L20: Boot 6A 44
Bush Way CH60: Hesw 7L 87
Bus. Resource Cen. L33: Know I 2G 47
Butchers La. L39: Augh 7L 27
WN4: Ash M 9K 41
Bute St. L5: Liv 1H 5 (6D 58)
(not continuous)
Butleigh Rd. L36: Huy 4H 61
Butler Cres. L6: Liv 6G 58
Butler St. L6: Liv 5G 58
Buttercup Cl. CH46: More 7A 56
L22: Wloo 1M 43
WA5: Warr 5N 81
Buttercup Way L9: W'ton 6G 45
Butterfield Gdns. L39: Augh 1B 28
Butterfield St. L4: W'ton 2E 58
Buttermarket St. WA1: Warr 3C 82
(not continuous)
Buttermere Av. CH43: Noct 2C 72
CH65: Ell P 2A 112
WA2: Warr 6D 66
WA11: St H 2K 49
WN4: Ash M 6K 41
Buttermere Cl. L31: Mag 2K 35
L33: Kirkb 7B 36
L37: Form 1D 24
WA6: Frod 6N 107
Buttermere Ct. *CH41: Birke 3J 73*
(off Penrith St.)
Buttermere Cres. *WA2: Warr 6D 66*
(off Buttermere Av.)
WA11: Rainf 1C 38
Buttermere Gdns. L23: Crosb 9M 33
Buttermere Gro. WA7: Beech 1N 107
Buttermere Rd. L16: Child 9E 60
M31: Part 6L 69
Buttermere St. L8: Liv 1G 75
Butterton Av. CH49: Upton 2L 71
Butterwick Dr. L12: Crox 7C 46
Button St. L2: Liv 5F 4 (8C 58)
Butts Grn. WA5: Westb 6J 65
Butts La. PR8: South 1E 12
Buxted Rd. L32: Kirkb 2E 46
Buxted Wlk. L32: Kirkb 2E 46
Buxton Cl. WA5: Gt San 9J 65
Buxton La. CH44: Wall 4E 56
Buxton Rd. CH42: Rock F 6N 73
Bye La. L39: Down 1H 27
Byerley St. CH44: Wall 6K 57
Byfleet Cl. WN3: Winst 2E 40
Byland Cl. L37: Form 2H 25
WA8: Widnes 3M 79
Byles St. L8: Liv 4F 74
Byng Av. M44: Cad 5K 69
Byng Pl. L4: W'ton 1J 59
Byng Rd. L4: W'ton 1J 59
Byng St. L20: Boot 8A 44
By-Pass, The L23: Crosb 7L 33
Byrne Av. CH42: Rock F 7M 73
Byrom St. L3: Liv 3G 4 (7C 58)
PR9: South 8L 7
Byron Av. L12: W Der 2M 59
L35: Whis 6C 62
Byron Cl. CH43: Pren 8F 72
L36: Huy 8L 61
L37: Form 9F 16
WA10: St H 5K 49
Byron Ct. L25: Woolt 5E 76
WA2: Warr 7D 66
Byron Rd. L23: Blun 7J 33
L31: Lydi 9J 27
Byron St. L20: Boot 5N 43
WA7: Run 6K 95
Byron Ter. L23: Blun 7J 33
Byton Wlk. L33: Kirkb 7E 36
Bywater Way L10: Faz 3N 45
Byway, The L23: Crosb 6L 33

C

CABBAGE HALL 3G 59
Cabes Cl. L14: Knott A 2E 60
Cabin La. L31: Lydi 8E 26
L39: Hals 1B 18
L40: H'wood 9L 9
PR9: South 4C 8
Cablehouse L2: Liv 3E 4
Cable M. *PR9: South 8G 6*
(off Cable St.)
Cable Rd. CH47: Hoy 1B 70
L35: Presc 4C 62
Cables Retail Pk. 4A 62
Cable St. L37: Form 9G 16
PR9: South 8G 6
Cable Yd., The *L2: Liv 3E 4*
(off Cheapside)
Cabot Cl. WA5: Old H 8L 65
Cabot Grn. L25: Woolt 3C 76
Cabul Cl. WA2: Warr 1D 82
Cadbury Cl. L12: W Der 8N 45
Caddick Rd. L34: Know 5F 46
Cadet Way L12: W Der 2C 60
CADISHEAD 4L 69
Cadishead Way M44: Cad, Irlam 6K 69
Cadishead Way Circ. M44: Cad 6J 69
Cadnam Rd. L25: Gate 3H 77
Cadogan Dr. WN3: Winst 1F 40
Cadogan St. L15: Wavtr 9J 59
Cadshaw Cl. WA3: Birchw 4L 67
Cadwell Rd. L31: Lydi 7G 26
Caernarvon Cl. CH49: Upton 2A 72
WA7: Cas 5B 96
Caernarvon Ct. CH63: Beb 3M 89
CH65: Ell P 3B 112
Caerwys Gro. CH42: Tran 4L 73
Caesars Cl. WA7: Cas 5A 96
Cainfield Wlk. *L4: Kirkd 2C 58*
(off Upperbrook St.)
Cains Brewery 2D 74
Caird St. L6: Liv 1N 5 (6F 58)
Cairn Brae WA12: Newt W 6L 51
Cairn Ct. WA9: St H 1G 63
Cairnmore Rd. L18: Moss H 6M 75
Cairns St. L8: Liv 2F 74
Cairo St. L4: Kirkd 9D 44
WA1: Warr 3C 82
WA10: St H 9G 48
Caister Cl. WN8: Skel 4G 31
Caithness Ct. WA7: Run 5L 95
Caithness Dr. CH45: Wall 3J 57
L23: Crosb 8M 33
Caithness Gdns. CH43: Pren 7F 72
Caithness Rd. L18: Aller 7N 75
Calamanco Way M44: Irlam 1N 69
Calcott Rake L30: Neth 7D 34
(not continuous)
Calday Grange Cl. CH48: W Kir 7E 70
Calday Grange Swimming Pool 6E 70
Calday Gro. WA11: Hay 2C 50
Caldbeck Av. WA2: Warr 7E 66
Caldbeck Cl. WN4: Ash M 7K 41
Caldbeck Gro. WA11: St H 1M 49
Caldbeck Rd. CH62: Brom 5C 90
Calder Av. CH43: Pren 6G 72
L39: Orm 1B 28
Calder Cl. L33: Kirkb 5E 36
WA8: Widnes 5B 80
Calderdale Cl. L23: Thorn 5A 34
Calder Dr. L18: Moss H 3A 76
L31: Mag 1L 35
L35: Rainh 6E 62
Calder Edge L18: Moss H 4A 76
Calderfield Cl. WA4: Stockt H 8C 82
Calderfield Rd. L18: Moss H 3B 76
Calder Grange L18: Aller 5C 76
Calderhurst Dr. WA10: Windle 4E 48
Calder Pk. Ct. L18: Moss H 4B 76
Calder Rd. CH63: H Beb 2K 89
L5: Liv 3E 58
Calders, The L18: Moss H 5A 76
CALDERSTONES 5A 76
Calderstones Av. L18: Moss H 3A 76
Calderstones Ct. L18: Moss H 4A 76
Calderstones Park 5A 76
Calderstones Rd. L18: Moss H 4N 75
Calders Vw. Ct. L18: Moss H 5A 76
Calder Way CH66: Gt Sut 9H 103
Calderwood Pk. L27: N'ley 2H 77
Caldicott Av. CH62: Brom 8C 90
Caldon Cl. L21: Lith 1N 43
Caldway Dr. L27: N'ley 2H 77
Caldwell Av. WA5: Warr 7A 66
Caldwell Dr. CH49: Wdchu 6B 72
Caldwell Rd. L19: Aller 8A 76
WA8: Widnes 9K 79
Caldwell St. WA9: St H 7N 49
CALDY 9E 70
Caldy Chase Dr. CH48: Caldy 9E 70
Caldy Ct. CH48: W Kir 7C 70
Caldy Dr. CH66: Gt Sut 1J 111
Caldy Golf Course 2F 86
Caldy Gro. WA11: St H 5N 49
Caldy Pk. CH48: W Kir 8D 70
Caldy Rd. CH45: Wall 4H 57
CH48: Caldy, W Kir 7C 70
L9: Aintr 3F 44
Caldy Wood CH48: Caldy 9E 70
Caldywood Dr. L35: Whis 6B 62
Caledonian Cres. L21: Lith 1N 43
Caledonia St. L7: Liv 7K 5 (9E 58)
Calgarth Av. WA5: Warr 9B 66
Calgarth Rd. L36: Huy 4G 60
Calgary Way L36: Huy 4G 60
California Cl. WA5: Gt San 9L 65
California Rd. L13: Liv 2J 59
Callaghan Cl. L5: Liv 4C 58
Callan Cres. L37: Form 4E 24
Callander Rd. L6: Liv 6J 59
CALLANDS 7N 65
Callands Rd. WA5: Call 7L 65
Callard Cl. L27: N'ley 2G 77
Callender Gdns. WA6: Hel 3D 114
Callestock Cl. L11: Crox 5B 46
Callington Cl. L14: Knott A 3E 60
Callon Av. WA11: St H 5A 50
Callow Rd. L15: Wavtr 1J 75
Calmet Cl. L5: Liv 3D 58
Calmington La. WA7: Nort 3H 97
Calne Cl. CH61: Irby 9L 71
Calstock Cl. WA5: Penk 5G 80
Calthorpe St. L19: Garst 1N 91
Calthorpe Way CH43: Noct 2D 72
Calton Av. L18: Moss H 3M 75
Calvados Cl. L17: Aig 7H 75
Calveley Av. CH62: East 2E 102
Calveley Cl. CH43: Oxton 5E 72
Calveley Gro. L26: Halew 1L 93
Calverhall Way WN4: Ash M 8J 41
Calverley Cl. WA7: Brook 1E 108
Calver Pk. Rd. WA2: Winw 6A 66
Calver Rd. WA2: Winw 5A 66
Calvers WA7: Hal 6A 96
Camberley Cl. PR8: Birkd 1L 11
Camberley Dr. L25: Hunts X 8G 77
Camberwell Dr. WA4: Warr 7B 82
Camberwell Pk. Rd. WA8: Widnes 4N 79
Camborne Av. L25: Woolt 7G 77
Camborne Cl. WA7: Brook 9E 96
Camborne Rd. WA5: Burtw 3H 65
Cambourne Av. WA11: St H 3N 49
Cambrai Av. WA4: Warr 6D 82
Cambrian Cl. *CH46: More 1J 71*
(off Cambrian Rd.)
CH66: Lit Sut 8F 102
Cambrian Ct. PR9: South 7J 7
Cambrian Cres. WN3: Winst 1E 40
Cambrian Rd. CH46: More 1K 71
Cambrian Way L25: Woolt 5F 76
WA9: St H 4H 63
Cambria St. Nth. L6: Liv 6G 59
Cambria St. Sth. L6: Liv 6G 59
Cambridge Arc. *PR8: South 8G 6*
(off Chapel St.)
Cambridge Av. L21: Lith 2A 44
L23: Crosb 7K 33
PR9: South 5L 7
Cambridge Cl. WA4: Stockt H 8C 82
Cambridge Ct. CH65: Ell P 9A 104
L7: Liv 6K 5 (9E 58)
PR9: South 5L 7
(off Cambridge Rd.)
Cambridge Dr. L23: Crosb 6J 33
L26: Halew 8K 77

Cambridge Gdns.—Cassville Rd.

Cambridge Gdns. PR9: South 5L 7
WA4: App 1D 98
WA6: Hel 1G 114
Cambridge Rd. CH42: Tran 6H 73
CH45: New B 2H 57
CH62: Brom 7D 90
CH65: Ell P 9A 104
L9: Aintr 2G 44
L20: Boot 8C 44
L21: Sea 2M 43
L22: Wloo 3L 43
L23: Crosb 6J 33
L37: Form 3C 24
PR9: South 6K 7
WA10: St H 6H 49
WN8: Skel 3B 30
Cambridge St. L7: Liv 7L 5 (9E 58)
(not continuous)
L15: Wavtr 9J 59
(not continuous)
L34: Presc 3A 62
WA7: Run 5M 95
WA8: Widnes 9L 79
Cambridge Walks *PR8: South 8G 6*
(off Eastbank St. Sq.)
Camdale Cl. L28: Stockb V 2F 60
Camden Cl. CH49: Wdchu 4B 72
Camden Ct. WA7: Nort 6F 96
Camden Pl. CH41: Birke 2L 73
Camden Rd. CH65: Ell P 9M 103
Camden St. L3: Liv 3H 5 (7D 58)
Camelford Rd. L11: Crox 5B 46
Camellia Ct. L17: Aig 6F 74
Camellia Dr. WA5: Warr 4N 81
Camellia Gdns. WA9: Bold 2D 64
Camelot Cl. WA12: Newt W 6H 51
Camelot Ter. *L20: Boot 6A 44*
(off Tennyson St.)
Camelot Way WA7: Cas 7C 96
Cameo Cl. L6: Liv 5G 59
Cameron Av. WA7: Run 7H 95
Cameron Ct. WA2: Winw 5B 66
Cameron Rd. CH46: Leas 6B 56
WA8: Widnes 8K 79
Cameron St. L7: Liv 7H 59
Cammell Ct. CH43: Clau 2H 73
Camomile Wlk. *M31: Part 6M 69*
(off Wychelm Rd.)
Campbell Av. WA7: Run 7K 95
Campbell Cl. WA7: Run 7K 95
Campbell Cres. L33: Kirkb 5B 36
WA5: Gt San 2H 81
Campbell Dr. L14: Brd G 6C 60
Campbell Sq. L1: Liv 7F 4
Campbell St. L1: Liv 7F 4 (9C 58)
L20: Boot 7N 43
WA10: St H 6H 49
Campbeltown Rd. CH41: Tran 4M 73
Camperdown St. CH41: Birke 2M 73
Camphill Rd. L25: Woolt 8E 76
Camphor Way L11: Norr G 9L 45
Campion Cl. WA3: Birchw 5K 67
WA11: St H 3L 49
Campion Gro. L32: Kirkb 7D 36
WN4: Ash M 7H 41
Campion Way L36: Huy 1K 77
Camp Rd. L25: Woolt 7F 76
WA5: Old H 8M 65
WN4: Garsw 8G 40
Campsey Ash WA8: Widnes 4J 79
Campus Dr. WA7: Run 5H 95
Camrose Cl. WA7: Run 9M 95
Camsley La. WA13: Lymm 5A 84
Cam St. L25: Woolt 6D 76
Canaan WA3: Low 2K 53
WN7: Low 2K 53
Canada Blvd. L3: Liv 5C 4 (8A 58)
Canada Cl. WA2: Fearn 7H 67
Canal Bank L31: Lydi 5H 27
L40: Burs 8F 14
L40: Lath 3N 21
WA13: Lymm 5C 84
(Statham Av.)
WA13: Lymm 5F 84
(Thirlmere Dr.)
WN6: App B 6M 23
Canal Bri. Ent. Cen. CH65: Ell P 8B 104
Canal Cotts. L31: Lydi 5H 27
Canal Reach WA7: Wind H 5E 96
Canal Side WA4: Grap 7J 83
WA4: Moore 2L 97
WA7: West P 8G 94
Canalside CH65: Ell P 8B 104
Canalside Gro. L5: Liv 4B 58
Canalside Ind. Est. CH65: Ell P 7C 104
Canal St. L20: Boot 8A 44
WA7: Run 5L 95
WA10: St H 8J 49
WA12: Newt W 7H 51
Canal Vw. L31: Mell 8M 35
WA13: Lymm 5D 84
Canal Vw. Ct. L21: Lith 1N 43
Canberra Av. *WA2: Warr 6E 66*
(off Canberra Sq.)
WA9: St H 2H 63
Canberra Sq. WA2: Warr 7E 66
Candia Towers *L5: Liv 3D 58*
(off Jason St.)
Candleston Cl. WA5: Call 8N 65
Canella Av. L11: Norr G 9L 45
Canford Cl. WA5: Gt San 2L 81
Cannell Ct. CH64: Will 6N 101
WA7: Pal F 9C 96
Cannell St. WA5: Warr 4M 81
Canning Pl. L1: Liv 7E 4 (9B 58)
Canning Rd. PR9: South 8M 7
Canning St. CH41: Birke 1L 73
L8: Liv 8K 5 (9E 58)
L22: Wloo 1K 43
Cannington Way WA9: St H 9N 49
Canniswood Rd. WA11: Hay 4C 50
Cann La. Nth. WA4: App 2F 98
Cann La. Sth. WA4: App 3F 98
Cannock Cl. CH66: Gt Sut 5K 111
Cannock Grn. L31: Mag 2G 34
Cannonbury Cl. WA7: Hal 7C 96
Cannon Hill CH43: Clau 2H 73
Cannon Mt. CH43: Clau 2H 73
Cannon St. CH65: Ell P 9M 103
WA9: Clock F 6M 63
Canon Rd. L6: Liv 2H 59
Canons Rd. WA5: Gt San 2M 81
Canon St. WA7: Run 4K 95
Canon Wilson Cl. WA11: Hay 4F 50
Canova Cl. *L27: N'ley 4K 77*
(off Victoria Falls Rd.)
Canrow La. L34: Know 5H 47
Cansfield Gro. WN4: Ash M 7J 41
Cansfield St. WA10: St H 6K 49
Canterbury Av. L22: Wloo 8K 33
WA3: Low 1E 52
Canterbury Cl. CH66: Gt Sut 5K 111
L10: Aintr 9K 35
L34: Presc 2B 62
L37: Form 8F 16
PR8: Birkd 2M 11
Canterbury Pk. L18: Aller 8A 76
Canterbury Rd. CH42: Rock F 7N 73
CH44: Wall 6J 57
WA8: Widnes 9F 78
Canterbury St. L3: Liv 2J 5 (6D 58)
L19: Garst 3A 92
WA4: Warr 4D 82
WA10: St H 5H 49
Canterbury Way L3: Liv 2K 5 (6E 58)
L30: Neth 7E 34
Canter Cl. L9: Aintr 2J 45
Cantilever Gdns. WA4: Warr 6F 82
Cantley Cl. WA7: Beech 9N 95
Cantlow Fold PR8: Ainsd 1G 17
Canvey Cl. L15: Wavtr 1N 75
Capella Cl. L17: Aig 9K 75
CAPENHURST 5G 110
Capenhurst Av. WA2: Fearn 7H 67
Capenhurst Gdns. CH66: Gt Sut 4J 111
Capenhurst La. CH1: Cap 6D 110
CH65: Whit 2L 111
CH66: Gt Sut 4J 111
Capenhurst Station (Rail) 4H 111
Capenhurst Technology Pk.
CH1: Cap 4G 111
Cape Rd. L9: Aintr 4H 45
Capesthorne Cl. WA8: Widnes 8H 79
Capesthorne Rd. WA2: Warr 8E 66
Capilano Pk. L39: Augh 4A 28
Capital Ga. L3: Liv 3K 5 (7E 58)
Capitol Trad. Pk. L33: Know I 9H 37
Caplin Cl. L33: Kirkb 5C 36
Capper Gro. L36: Huy 6J 61
Capricorn Cres. L14: Knott A 4D 60
Capricorn Way L20: Boot 6A 44
Capstick Cres. L25: Gate 2F 76
Captain Charles Jones Wlk.
CH44: Wall 3K 57
(off Webster Av.)
Captains Cl. L30: Boot 2C 44
Captain's La. L30: Boot 2D 44
WN4: Ash M 8L 41
Caradoc Rd. L21: Sea 4N 43
Caraway Cl. *L23: Thorn 6A 34*
(off Tanhouse Rd.)
Caraway Gro. WA10: St H 6G 48
Carawood Cl. WN6: Shev 6N 23
Carbis Cl. L10: Faz 4M 45
Carden Cl. L4: Kirkd 2D 58
WA3: Birchw 5L 67
Cardeston Cl. WA7: Sut W 3B 108
Cardiff Cl. CH66: Gt Sut 5K 111
Cardiff St. WN8: Skel 3A 30
Cardiff Way L19: Garst 1N 91
Cardigan Av. CH41: Birke 2K 73
Cardigan Cl. WA5: Call 7M 65
WA10: St H 8J 49
Cardigan Rd. CH45: New B 2H 57
PR8: Birkd 5M 11
Cardigan St. L15: Wavtr 9J 59
Cardigan Way L6: Liv 5G 59
L30: Neth 7G 34
Cardinal Gdns. L9: Faz 6L 45
Cardinal Way WA12: Newt W 6M 51
Cardus Cl. CH46: More 9J 55
Cardwell Rd. L19: Garst 1B 92
Cardwell St. L7: Liv 7N 5 (9F 58)
Carey Av. CH63: H Beb 1K 89
Carey Cl. WN3: Winst 1F 40
Carey St. WA8: Widnes 7L 79
Carfax Rd. L33: Kirkb 7E 36
Carfield WN8: Skel 6H 31
Cargill Gro. CH42: Rock F 8A 74
Carham Rd. CH47: Hoy 2D 70
Carillion Cl. L11: Crox 7A 46
Carina Ct. L17: Aig 9L 75
Carina Pk. WA5: Westb 7K 65
Carisbrooke Cl. CH48: Caldy 8D 70
Carisbrooke Dr. PR9: South 6L 7
Carisbrooke Pl. L4: Kirkd 9E 44
Carisbrooke Rd. L4: Kirkd, W'ton 8D 44
L20: Boot 8D 44
Carkington Rd. L25: Woolt 7G 76
Carlake Gro. L9: Aintr 7H 45
Carland Cl. L10: Faz 4N 45
Carlaw Rd. CH42: Tran 6G 72
Carleen Cl. L17: Aig 6G 75
Carlett Blvd. CH62: East 1E 102
Carlett Pk. CH62: East 9E 90
Carlett Vw. L19: Garst 1A 92
Carley Wlk. L24: Speke 5J 93
Carlile Way L33: Kirkb 5D 36
Carlingford Cl. L8: Liv 9N 5 (1F 74)
Carlingford Rd. WA4: Stockt H 8C 82
Carlisle Av. L30: Neth 1E 44
Carlisle Cl. L4: W'ton 1J 59
Carlisle M. CH43: Oxton 3J 73
Carlisle Rd. PR8: Birkd 4N 11
Carlisle St. WA4: Stockt H 8D 82
Carlis Rd. L32: Kirkb 2D 46
Carlow Cl. L24: Hale 5N 93
Carlow St. WA10: St H 9G 48
Carlsruhe Ct. L8: Liv 3F 74
Carl's Way L33: Kirkb 5E 36
Carlton Av. WA7: Run 5N 95
WN8: Uph 5K 31
Carlton Bingo Club 4E 44
Carlton Cl. CH64: P'gte 4C 100
WN4: Ash M 7J 41
Carlton Cres. CH66: Ell P 6L 103
Carlton La. CH47: Meols 9D 54
L13: Liv 5M 59
Carlton Mt. CH42: Tran 5L 73
Carlton Rd. CH42: Tran 4J 73
CH45: New B 1H 57
CH63: Beb 3A 90
PR8: Ainsd 8J 11
WA3: Low 1E 52
WA13: Lymm 3H 85
(not continuous)
Carlton St. L3: Liv 5A 58
L34: Presc 3A 62
WA4: Stockt H 8D 82
WA8: Widnes 8K 79
WA10: St H 7H 49
Carlton Ter. CH47: Meols 9D 54
L23: Crosb 7K 33
Carlton Way WA3: Glaz 4J 69
Carlye St. L8: Liv 2C 74
Carlyle Cres. CH66: Gt Sut 1K 111
Carlyon Way L26: Halew 8J 77
Carman Wlk. L7: Liv 9G 59
Carmarthen Cl. WA5: Call 7M 65
Carmarthen Cres. L8: Liv 2C 74
Carmel Cl. CH45: New B 1H 57
L39: Augh 2B 28
WA5: Call 7N 65
Carmel Ct. WA8: Widnes 4L 79
Carmelite Cres. WA10: Ec'stn 5D 48
Carmichael Av. CH49: Grea 6L 71
Carmichael Cl. M31: Part 6L 69
Carnaby Cl. L36: Huy 9L 61
Carnaby Pl. WA5: Gt San 2K 81
Carnarvon Ct. L9: W'ton 7E 44
Carnarvon Rd. L9: W'ton 7E 44
PR8: Birkd 5M 11
Carnarvon St. WA9: St H 1G 63
Carnatic Cl. L18: Moss H 5L 75
Carnatic Ct. L18: Moss H 5K 75
Carnatic Rd. L18: Moss H 5K 75
Carnation Rd. L9: W'ton 7G 45
Carneghie Ct. PR8: Birkd 2M 11
Carnegie Av. L23: Crosb 8K 33
Carnegie Cl. WA12: Newt W 6K 51
Carnegie Cres. WA9: St H 1A 64
Carnegie Dr. WN4: Ash M 6J 41
Carnegie Rd. L13: Liv 5K 59
Carnforth Av. L32: Kirkb 1D 46
Carnforth Cl. CH41: Birke 3J 73
L12: W Der 9A 46
Carnforth Dr. WA10: St H 3J 49
Carnforth Rd. L18: Moss H 6A 76
Carno St. L15: Wavtr 9K 59
Carnoustie Cl. CH46: More 8J 55
L12: W Der 3D 60
PR8: Birkd 2M 11
Carnoustie Gro. WA11: Hay 5C 50
Carnsdale Rd. CH46: More 9N 55
Carol Dr. CH60: Hesw 7C 88
Carole Cl. WA9: Sut L 3A 64
Carolina Rd. WA5: Gt San 1K 81
Carolina St. L20: Boot 7A 44
Caroline Pl. CH43: Oxton 3H 73
Caroline St. M44: Irlam 1M 69
WA8: Widnes 9L 79
Carol St. WA4: Warr 4E 82
Caronia St. L19: Garst 2A 92
Carpathia Cl. L19: Garst 3A 92
Carpenter Gro. WA2: Padg 8H 67
Carpenter's La. CH48: W Kir 6C 70
Carpenters Row L1: Liv 8F 4 (9C 58)
Carraway Rd. L11: Crox 4A 46
Carr Bri. Rd. CH49: Wdchu 4B 72
Carr Cl. L11: Norr G 8N 45
Carr Cft. L21: Ford 8A 34
CARR CROSS 6J 13
Carrfield Av. L23: Crosb 8N 33
Carrfield Wlk. L11: Norr G 7N 45
Carr Ga. CH46: More 1J 71
CARR GREEN 2L 85
Carrgreen La. WA13: Warb 2L 85
Carr Hey CH46: More 1J 71
Carr Hey Cl. CH49: Wdchu 6C 72
Carr Ho. La. CH46: More 9J 55
L38: Ince B 8L 25
CARR HOUSES 8M 25
Carriage Cl. L24: Hale 6A 94
Carriage Dr. WA6: Frod 8K 107
Carriage Gro. L20: Boot 7C 44
Carrick Ct. L23: Crosb 8N 33
Carrick Dr. CH65: Whit 3N 111
Carrickmore Av. L18: Moss H 6M 75
Carrington Av. CH41: Birke 9G 56
Carrington Cl. WA3: Birchw 5K 67
Carrington Rd. CH45: Wall 3J 57
Carr La. CH46: More 8H 55
CH47: Hoy 2C 70
CH47: Meols 8G 55
CH48: W Kir 3E 70
L11: Norr G 8L 45
L24: Hale 5A 94
L31: Lydi 7E 26
L34: Presc 4M 61
L36: Roby 8G 60
L40: Lath 1L 21
PR8: Ainsd, Birkd 7M 11
(not continuous)
WA3: Low 3H 53
WA8: Hale B 2B 94
WN3: Wigan 1K 41
WN7: Leigh 2M 53
Carr La. E. L11: Norr G 8N 45
Carr La. Ind. Est. CH47: Hoy 1D 70
Carr Mdw. Hey L30: Neth 9B 34
CARR MILL 2L 49
Carr Mill Cres. WN5: Bil 7A 40
Carr Mill Rd. WA11: St H 3M 49
WN5: Bil 8N 39
Carr Moss La. L39: Hals 2B 18
Carrock Rd. CH62: Brom 5D 90
Carroll Cres. L39: Orm 6D 20
Carrow Cl. CH46: More 1J 71
Carr Rd. L20: Boot 3C 44
Carr's Cres. L37: Form 3D 24
Carr's Cres. W. L37: Form 3D 24
Carr Side La. L29: Thorn 9N 25
Carrs Ter. L35: Whis 6A 62
Carr St. WA10: St H 5G 49
Carruthers St. L3: Liv 1D 4 (6B 58)
Carrville Way L12: Crox 8E 46
Carrwood Cl. WA11: Hay 4C 50
Carrwood Pk. PR8: South 3A 12
Carsdale Rd. L18: Moss H 3M 75
Carsgoe Rd. CH47: Hoy 2D 70
Carsington Rd. L11: Norr G 8M 45
Carstairs Rd. L6: Liv 5J 59
Carsthorne Rd. CH47: Hoy 2D 70
Cartbridge La. L26: Halew 7K 77
Carter Av. WA11: Rainf 6D 38
Carter Ho. Way WA8: Widnes 9M 79
Carters, The CH49: Grea 4K 71
L30: Neth 7F 34
Carter St. L8: Liv 1E 74
Carterton Rd. CH47: Hoy 2D 70
Cartier Cl. WA5: Old H 9L 65
Cartmel Av. L31: Mag 1K 35
WA2: Warr 6D 66
Cartmel Cl. CH41: Birke 3J 73
L36: Huy 5H 61
PR8: South 3E 12
Cartmel Dr. CH46: More 1M 71
CH66: Gt Sut 3L 111
L12: W Der 9A 46
L35: Rainh 5D 62
L37: Form 2H 25
Cartmell Av. WA10: St H 3H 49
Cartmell Cl. WA7: Run 9L 95
Cartmel Rd. L36: Huy 4G 60
Cartmel Ter. L11: Norr G 7N 45
Cartmel Way L36: Huy 5G 61
Cartridge La. WA4: Grap 1L 99
Cartwright Cl. WA11: Rainf 5C 38
Cartwright Ct. WA11: Rainf 4C 38
Cartwrights Farm Rd. L24: Speke 3E 92
Cartwright St. WA5: Warr 2N 81
WA7: Run 5M 95
Carvel Way L40: Burs 2K 21
Carver St. L3: Liv 2K 5 (6E 58)
Caryl Gro. L8: Liv 4D 74
Caryl St. L8: Liv 3D 74
(Atterbury St.)
L8: Liv 3D 74
(Park St.)
L8: Liv 2C 74
(Stanhope St.)
Casbah Cl. L12: W Der 3N 59
Cascade Rd. L24: Speke 1G 92
Case Gro. L35: Presc 4B 62
Case Rd. WA11: Hay 4F 50
Cases St. L1: Liv 5G 5 (8C 58)
Cashel Rd. CH41: Birke 7H 57
Caspian Pl. L20: Boot 7B 44
Caspian Rd. L4: W'ton 8J 45
Cassia Cl. L9: W'ton 6G 45
Cassino Rd. L36: Huy 6J 61
Cassio St. L20: Boot 8D 44
Cassley Rd. L24: Speke 4L 93
Cassville Rd. L18: Moss H 2M 75

Castell Gro.—Charlesville

Castell Gro. WA10: St H .7J 49
Castle Av. WA9: St H .7A 50
Castle Bingo
Bootle .7B 44
Castlebridge Ct. CH42: Rock F .7M 73
(off Old Chester Rd.)
Castle Cl. CH46: Leas .6A 56
Castle Ct. CH48: W Kir .7C 70
Castle Dr. CH60: Hesw .7N 87
CH65: Whit .2M 111
L37: Form .3F 24
Castlefield Cl. L12: W Der .2M 59
Castlefield Rd. L12: W Der .2M 59
CASTLEFIELDS .5C 96
Castlefields CH46: Leas .5N 55
WA7: Cas .6A 96
Castlefields Av. E. WA7: Cas .6C 96
Castlefields Av. Nth. WA7: Cas .5A 96
Castlefields Av. Sth. WA7: Cas .6B 96
Castleford Ri. CH46: Leas .6M 55
Castleford St. L15: Wavtr .1M 75
Castlegate Gro. L12: W Der .2N 59
Castlegrange Cl. CH46: Leas .5M 55
Castle Grn. WA5: Westb .7K 65
Castleheath Cl. CH46: Leas .6M 55
Castlehey WN8: Skel .6H 31
Castle Hill L2: Liv .5D 4
WA12: Newt W .6N 51
Castle Keep L12: W Der .2N 59
Castle La. L40: Lath, Westh .7H 21
Castlemere Cl. WN3: Winst .2F 40
Castle Mt. CH60: Hesw .7N 87
(off The Mount)
Castle Pk.
Frodsham .7K 107
Castle Pk. Arts Cen. .6K 107
Castle Ri. WA7: Run .5N 95
Castle Rd. CH45: Wall .3G 57
WA7: Hal .7B 96
Castlesite Rd. L12: W Der .1N 59
Castle St. CH41: Birke .2M 73
L2: Liv .5D 4 (8B 58)
L25: Woolt .6D 76
PR9: South .7G 7
WA8: Widnes .7N 79
Castleton Dr. L30: Neth .7G 34
WA1: Warr .3F 82
Castleton Way WN3: Winst .1E 40
Castletown Cl. L16: Child .9C 60
Castleview Rd. L12: W Der .2N 59
Castle Wlk. PR8: South .9F 6
Castleway Nth. CH46: Leas .5A 56
Castleway Sth. CH46: Leas .6A 56
Castlewell L35: Whis .5C 62
Castlewood Rd. L6: Liv .4G 59
Castner Av. WA7: West P .8H 95
Castner Ct. WA7: West P .8H 95
Castor St. L6: Liv .4G 59
Catalyst Science Discovery Cen. .2K 95
Catchdale Moss La. WA10: Ec'stn .4B 48
Catford Cl. WA8: Widnes .6F 78
Catford Grn. L24: Speke .4K 93
Catfoss Cl. WA2: Padg .8F 66
Catharine's La. L39: Bic .2D 28
Catharine St. L8: Liv .8K 5 (9E 58)
Cathcart St. CH41: Birke .1K 73
Cathedral Cl. L1: Liv .9J 5 (1D 74)
Cathedral Ct. L1: Liv .9K 5
Cathedral Ga. L1: Liv .8J 5 (9D 58)
Cathedral Rd. L6: Liv .3H 59
Cathedral Wlk. L3: Liv .6J 5 (8E 58)
Catherine Ct. L21: Lith .4A 44
Catherine St. CH41: Birke .2K 73
L21: Lith .4A 44
WA5: Warr .1A 82
(not continuous)
WA8: Widnes .9K 79
Catherine Way WA11: Hay .4B 50
WA12: Newt W .8K 51
Catkin Rd. L26: Halew .6H 77
Caton Cl. PR9: South .3L 7
Catonfield Rd. L18: Moss H .3B 76
Cat Tail La. PR8: South .5K 13
Cattan Grn. L37: Form .1H 25
Catterall Av. WA2: Warr .7E 66
WA9: Sut L .3N 63
Catterick Cl. L26: Halew .8K 77
Catterick Fold PR8: South .3E 12
Catton Hall Shooting Ground .8C 108
Caulfield Dr. CH49: Grea .5M 71
Caunce Av. PR9: Banks .1E 8
WA3: Golb .3B 52
WA11: Hay .4D 50
WA12: Newt W .9L 51
Caunce's Rd. PR9: South .2N 13
Causeway, The CH62: Port S .2A 90
L12: W Der .5B 60
PR9: South .2A 8
Causeway Av. WA4: Warr .5D 82
Causeway Cl. CH62: Port S .1A 90
Causeway Ho. CH46: Leas .5M 55
Causeway La. L37: Gt Alt .3N 25
L40: Ruf .5M 15
Causeway Pk. WA4: Warr .5D 82
Cavalier Cl. L23: Crosb .8M 33
Cavalier Dr. L19: Garst .2B 92
Cavalry Cl. L12: W Der .2C 60
Cavan Dr. WA11: Hay .3F 50
Cavan Rd. L11: Norr G .1K 59
Cavell Cl. L25: Woolt .7E 76
Cavell Dr. CH65: Whit .1M 111
Cavendish Av. WA3: Ris .4M 67
Cavendish Cl. WA5: Old H .1M 81
Cavendish Ct. PR9: South .6K 7
Cavendish Dr. CH42: Rock F .7K 73
L9: W'ton .7F 44
WN3: Winst .1F 40
Cavendish Farm Rd.
WA7: W'ton .1J 107
(not continuous)
Cavendish Gdns. CH65: Whit .1M 111
L8: Liv .3F 74
Cavendish Pl. WA3: Ris .4N 67
Cavendish Rd. CH41: Birke .1H 73
CH45: New B .9H 43
L23: Blun .8J 33
PR8: Birkd .3M 11
Cavendish St. CH41: Birke .9H 57
WA7: Run .5J 95
(not continuous)
Cavern Club, The .5E 4
Cavern Ct. L6: Liv .6G 59
(off Coleridge St.)
Cavern Quarter .5E 4
Cavern Walks L2: Liv .5E 4
Caversham Cl. WA4: App .9F 82
Cawdor St. L8: Liv .2F 74
WA4: Stockt H .8D 82
WA7: Run .4J 95
Cawfield Av. WA8: Widnes .7G 79
Cawley Av. WA3: Cul .6M 53
Cawley St. WA7: Run .6K 95
Cawood Cl. CH66: Lit Sut .9G 103
Cawthorne Av. L32: Kirkb .2C 46
WA4: Grap .6H 83
Cawthorne Cl. L32: Kirkb .2C 46
Cawthorne Wlk. L32: Kirkb .3C 46
Caxton Cl. CH43: Bid .2C 72
CH66: Gt Sut .1K 111
WA8: Widnes .5F 78
WN3: Wigan .1H 41
Caxton Rd. L35: Rainh .8H 63
Cazneau St. L3: Liv .1G 5 (6C 58)
C Court WN4: Ash M .9K 41
Cearns Rd. CH43: Oxton .3G 73
Cecil Dr. WA10: Ec'stn .5D 48
Cecil Rd. CH42: Tran .6H 73
CH45: Wall .5G 57
CH62: New F .8A 74
L21: Sea .4M 43
Cecil St. L15: Wavtr .9J 59
WA9: St H .2B 64
Cedab Rd. CH65: Ell P .8B 104
Cedar Av. CH63: H Beb .3L 89
CH66: Lit Sut .8H 103
WA3: Low .3G 53
WA7: Run .8M 95
WA7: Sut W .2D 108
WA8: Widnes .6L 79
Cedar Cl. L18: Aller .5B 76
L35: Whis .5B 62
Cedar Ct. L34: Know .6H 47
WA3: Ris .8N 53
Cedar Cres. L36: Huy .8H 61
L39: Orm .9A 20
Cedardale Dr. CH66: Whit .5L 111
Cedardale Pk. WA8: Widnes .4A 80
Cedardale Rd. L9: W'ton .6F 44
Cedar Dr. L37: Form .3C 24
Cedarfield Rd. WA13: Lymm .3H 85
Cedar Gdns. WA12: Newt W .8M 51
Cedar Gro. CH64: Nest .6F 100
L8: Liv .2H 75
L22: Wloo .9K 33
L31: Mag .5J 35
WA1: Padd .1H 83
WA4: Warr .5E 82
WA11: Hay .3G 51
WN4: Garsw .6F 40
WN8: Skel .3B 30
Cedar Rd. L9: Aintr .4G 44
L35: Whis .6A 62
M31: Part .6L 69
WA5: Gt San .2H 81
Cedars, The CH46: More .1K 71
CH66: Lit Sut .8E 102
L12: Crox .7D 46
Cedar St. CH41: Birke .3K 73
L20: Boot .6B 44
PR8: South .2B 12
WA10: St H .8G 48
WA12: Newt W .8L 51
Cedar Ter. L8: Liv .2H 75
(off Cedar Gro.)
Cedarway CH60: Hesw .1B 100
Cedarways WA4: App .2E 98
Cedarwood Cl.
CH49: Grea .4J 71
Cedarwood Ct. L36: Huy .9J 61
Celandine Way WA9: Bold .2D 64
Celebration Dr. L6: Liv .4H 59
Celendine Cl. L15: Wavtr .9K 59
Celia St. L20: Kirkd .9C 44
Celtic Rd. CH47: Meols .8F 54
Celtic St. L8: Liv .2F 74
Celt St. L6: Liv .5G 59
Cemeas Cl. L5: Liv .4B 58
Cemetery Rd. PR8: South .2A 12
Centenary Cl. L4: W'ton .1H 59
Centenary Ho.
WA7: Run .7M 95
Central 12 Retail Pk. .9H 7
Central Av. CH62: Brom .6B 90
CH65: Ell P .1A 112
L24: Speke .4H 93
L34: Eccl P .2C 62
L34: Presc .3N 61
PR8: Birkd .6M 11
WA2: Warr .9D 66
WA4: Warr .5C 82
Central Bldgs. L23: Crosb .7L 33
(off Church Rd.)
Central Dr. L12: W Der .4N 59
WA11: Hay .4D 50
WA11: Rainf .4C 38
Central Expressway WA7: Run .8A 96
Central Gdns. L1: Liv .6H 5
Central Pk. Av. CH44: Wall .5J 57
Central Rd. CH62: Port S .1A 90
(Osborne Ct.)
CH62: Port S .2A 90
(Wood St.)
M31: Part .6M 69
WA4: Warr .5D 82
Central Shop. Cen. .6G 5 (8C 58)
Central Sq. L31: Mag .1H 35
Central Station (Rail) .6G 5 (8C 58)
Central St. WA10: St H .6K 49
Central Way L24: Speke .4J 93
WA2: Warr .2C 82
WA12: Newt W .8N 51
Centre, The WA3: Ris .4M 67
Centre 21 WA1: Wools .2K 83
Centre Ct. WN7: Leigh .1J 53
Centre Pk. WA1: Warr .5B 82
Centre Pk. Sq. WA1: Warr .4B 82
Centreville Rd. L18: Moss H .2M 75
Centre Way L36: Huy .7J 61
Centro Pk. L33: Know I .2G 47
Centurion Cl. CH47: Meols .8F 54
WA3: Ris .4L 67
Centurion Dr. CH47: Meols .8F 54
Centurion Row WA7: Cas .5B 96
Century Bldgs. L3: Liv .4C 74
Century Rd. L23: Crosb .7K 33
Ceres Ct. CH43: Bid .1C 72
Ceres St. L20: Kirkd .9B 44
Cestrian Dr. CH61: Thing .2A 88
Chadlow Rd. L32: Kirkb .3D 46
Chadwell Rd. L33: Kirkb .7D 36
Chadwick Av. WA3: Croft .2J 67
WA4: Stockt H .7F 82
Chadwick Ct. Ind. Cen. L3: Liv .1C 4 (6A 58)
CHADWICK GREEN .8N 39
Chadwick La. WA8: Widnes .5M 79
Chadwick Pl. WA3: Ris .4M 67
Chadwick Rd. WA7: Astm .4B 96
WA11: St H .3M 49
Chadwick St. CH46: More .9M 55
L3: Liv .1C 4 (5A 58)
Chadwick Way L33: Kirkb .5C 36
Chaffinch Cl. L12: W Der .9D 46
WA3: Birchw .6N 67
Chaffinch Glade L26: Halew .7J 77
Chainhurst Cl. L27: N'ley .2H 77
Chain La. WA11: St H .3N 49
Chain La. Shop. Pct. .3N 49
Chain Wlk. WA10: St H .7F 48
Chaise Mdw. WA13: Lymm .3H 85
Chalfield Av. CH66: Gt Sut .9H 103
Chalfield Cl. CH66: Gt Sut .9H 103
Chalfont Cl. WA4: App .1F 98
Chalfont Rd. L18: Aller .7B 76
Chalfont Way L28: Stockb V .2F 60
Chalgrave Cl. WA8: Widnes .5B 80
Chalice Way L11: Crox .7A 46
Chalkley Cl. CH42: Tran .6J 73
Chalkwell Dr. CH60: Hesw .8C 88
Challis St. CH41: Birke .8E 56
Challoner Cl. L36: Huy .9K 61
Chaloner Gro. L19: G'dale .1L 91
Chaloner St. L3: Liv .1C 74
Chalon Way E. WA10: St H .7K 49
Chalon Way Ind. Est. WA10: St H .8K 49
Chalon Way W. WA10: St H .7J 49
Chamberlain Dr. L33: Kirkb .6D 36
Chamberlain St. CH41: Tran .4L 73
CH44: Wall .7G 57
WA10: St H .7G 48
Chambres Rd. PR8: South .1C 12
Chambres Rd. Nth. PR8: South .9J 7
Chamomile Cl. L11: Norr G .8L 45
Champions Bus. Pk. CH49: Upton .5N 71
Chancellor Ct. L8: Liv .8N 5 (9F 58)
Chancellor Rd. WA7: Manor P .2F 96
Chancellors Ct. L39: Orm .1F 28
Chancellors Ct. Nth. L39: Orm .1E 28
Chancel St. L4: Kirkd .2C 58
Chancery La. WA9: St H .7A 50
Chandlers Ct. WA7: Run .6H 95
Chandlers Edge CH65: Ell P .7B 104
(off Grosvenor Wharf Rd.)
Chandlers Way WA9: Sut M .6L 63
Chandler Way WA3: Low .2F 52
Chandley Cl. PR8: Ainsd .9G 11
Chandos St. L7: Liv .8G 59
Change La. CH64: Will .6A 102
Changford Grn. L33: Kirkb .8E 36
Changford Rd. L33: Kirkb .7E 36
Channel, The CH2: Back .9N 111
CH45: Wall .1E 56
Channell Rd. L6: Liv .6H 59
Channel Reach L23: Blun .8H 33
Channel Rd. L23: Blun .8H 33
Chantler Av. WA4: Westy .4F 82
Chantrell Rd. CH48: W Kir .6F 70
Chantry, The WA10: St H .4G 49
Chantry Cl. CH43: Bid .2B 72
Chantry Rd. L25: Gate .3E 76
Chantry Wlk. CH60: Hesw .9A 88
WN4: Ash M .6H 41
Chapel Av. L9: W'ton .4F 44
Chapel Cl. CH65: Ell P .7A 104
(off Grace Rd.)
PR9: Banks .1F 8
Chapel Ct. L39: Orm .9C 20
Chapelcroft Ct. L12: W Der .3A 60
Chapel Cross Rd. WA2: Fearn .7H 67
Chapelfields WA6: Frod .6K 107
CHAPELFORD URBAN VILLAGE .1K 81
Chapel Gallery, The .8D 20
Chapel Gdns. L5: Liv .4C 58
Chapelhill Rd. CH46: More .9N 55
CHAPEL HOUSE .3A 30
Chapel Ho. L22: Wloo .2K 43
L31: Mag .2J 35
Chapel Ho. La. Sth. CH64: Pudd .6A 110
Chapel Ho. M. WA3: Low .2D 52
Chapel Ho. Wlk. L37: Form .1G 25
Chapel La. CH1: Cap, Woodb .5D 110
CH3: Moul .9J 115
CH66: Led .5D 110
L30: Neth .6E 34
L31: Mell .7M 35
L35: Rainh .8H 63
L37: Form .1F 24
L40: Burs .3J 21
L40: H'wood .1F 14
M31: Part .6M 69
PR9: Banks .1F 8
WA3: Rix .8F 68
WA4: App T .4J 99
WA4: Stockt H .8D 82
WA5: Burtw .3G 65
WA6: Manl .9J 115
WA8: Cron, Widnes .3F 78
WA10: Ec'stn .6E 48
WA13: Warb .6M 69
WN8: Parb .4G 23
Chapel M. CH2: Elt .2M 113
(off Marsh La.)
CH65: Whit .1N 111
L39: Orm .9D 20
WA5: Gt San .3H 81
Chapel Moss L39: Orm .9C 20
Chapel Pl. L19: Garst .1A 92
L25: Woolt .6E 76
WN4: Ash M .8K 41
Chapel Rd. CH47: Hoy .9D 54
L6: Liv .3H 59
L19: Garst .1A 92
(not continuous)
WA5: Penk .5G 80
Chapelside Cl. WA5: Gt San .2H 81
Chapel St. L3: Liv .4C 4 (7A 58)
L34: Presc .3A 62
L39: Orm .9D 20
PR8: South .8G 6
WA8: Widnes .9K 79
WA10: St H .5J 49
WA11: Hay .4F 50
(not continuous)
WA12: Newt W .7K 51
WN4: Ash M .8K 41
Chapel Ter. L20: Boot .7A 44
WA3: Low .1J 53
Chapel Vw. CH62: East .9F 90
WA6: Hel .3E 114
WA11: Crank .7J 39
Chapel Wlk. WA3: Low .1J 53
Chapel Walks WA13: Lymm .7K 85
Chapel Yd. L15: Wavtr .1M 75
(off Waterloo St.)
WA2: Warr .2B 82
Chapman Cl. L8: Liv .3D 74
WA8: Widnes .4G 79
Chapman Gro. L34: Presc .2B 62
Chapterhouse Cl. CH65: Ell P .9C 104
Chardstock Dr. L25: Gate .4G 77
Charing Cross CH41: Birke .3K 73
Charity La. L40: Westh .1J 29
Charlcombe St. CH42: Tran .4K 73
Charlecote St. L8: Liv .5E 74
Charles Av. PR8: Ainsd .8L 11
WA5: Gt San .2H 81
Charles Berrington Rd. L15: Wavtr .2M 75
Charles Best Grn. L30: Neth .7E 34
(off Alexander Fleming Av.)
Charlesbye Av. L39: Orm .7E 20
Charlesbye Cl. L39: Orm .7F 20
Charles Ct. PR9: South .8H 7
Charles Forbes Ct. WA1: Warr .3C 82
(off Mersey St.)
Charles Price Gdns. CH65: Ell P .8A 104
Charles Rd. CH47: Hoy .2C 70
Charles St. CH41: Birke .1K 73
M44: Cad .3L 69
WA3: Golb .1B 52
WA8: Widnes .8K 79
WA10: St H .6K 49
Charleston Cl. CH66: Gt Sut .2J 111
Charleston Gro. WA5: Gt San .2K 81
Charleston Rd. L8: Liv .4E 74
Charlesville CH43: Oxton .3H 73

Charlesville Ct.—Christie Cl.

Charlesville Ct. CH43: Oxton 3H 73
Charles Wlk. L14: Brd G 6D 60
Charlesworth Cl. L31: Lydi 7G 26
Charleywood Rd.
L33: Know I 1F 46
Charlock Cl. L30: Neth 7F 34
Charlock Wlk. *M31: Part 6M 69*
(off Central Rd.)
Charlotte Gro. WA5: Gt San 1L 81
Charlotte Rd. CH44: Wall 4K 57
Charlotte's Mdw. CH63: Beb 3N 89
Charlotte Wlk. WA8: Widnes 9L 79
Charlotte Way L1: Liv 5G 5
Charlton Cl. WA7: Pal F 8C 96
Charlton Ct. CH43: Clau 2F 72
L25: Hunts X 9H 77
Charlton Pl. L13: Liv 8M 59
Charlton Rd. L13: Liv 8M 59
Charlton St. WA4: Westy 5G 83
Charlwood Av. L36: Huy 8J 61
Charlwood Cl. CH43: Bid 2C 72
Charmalue Av. L23: Crosb 7M 33
Charminster Cl. WA5: Gt San 3K 81
Charmouth Cl. L12: Crox 7C 46
WA12: Newt W 6K 51
Charnley Dr. L15: Wavtr 9A 60
Charnley's La. PR9: Banks 1E 8
Charnock WN8: Skel 6H 31
Charnock Av. WA12: Newt W 7H 51
Charnock Rd. L9: Aintr 7J 45
WA3: Cul 7N 53
Charnwood Cl. L12: Crox 7B 46
L40: Burs 2K 21
WA3: Birchw 4B 68
Charnwood Rd. L36: Huy 6F 60
Charnwood St. WA9: St H 6A 50
Charon Way WA5: Westb 6J 65
Charter Av. WA5: Warr 9B 66
Charter Cres. CH66: Gt Sut 2K 111
Charter Ho. *CH44: Wall 5K 57*
(off Church St.)
Charterhouse Cl. L25: Woolt 7F 76
Charterhouse Dr. L10: Aintr 9K 35
Charterhouse Rd. L25: Woolt 7F 76
Chartmount Way L25: Gate 4F 76
Chartwell Gdns. WA4: App 2G 98
Chartwell Gro. L26: Halew 7K 77
Chartwell Rd. PR8: Ainsd 8H 11
Chase, The CH60: Hesw 7A 88
CH63: Brom 1B 102
L36: Huy 9K 61
Chase Cl. PR8: Birkd 2M 11
Chase Dr. CH66: Gt Sut 3K 111
Chase Heys PR9: South 6M 7
Chaser Cl. L9: Aintr 2H 45
Chasewater WA7: Nort 3H 97
Chase Way CH66: Gt Sut 3K 111
L5: Liv 5D 58
Chatbrook Cl. L17: Aig 9L 75
Chatburn Av. WA3: Golb 1D 52
Chatburn Ct. WA3: Cul 8N 53
Chater Cl. *L35: Whis 3D 62*
(off Watling Way)
Chatfield Dr. WA3: Birchw 6M 67
Chatham Cl. L21: Sea 3M 43
Chatham Ct. L22: Wloo 2L 43
Chatham Pl. L7: Liv 8G 58
Chatham Rd. CH42: Rock F 6N 73
Chatham St. L7: Liv 8L 5 (9E 58)
L8: Liv 8L 5 (9E 58)
Chatsworth Av. CH44: Wall 5J 57
L9: W'ton 5E 44
WA3: Cul 6N 53
Chatsworth Cl. CH66: Gt Sut 9J 103
WN4: Ash M 7H 41
Chatsworth Dr. L7: Liv 8G 59
WA8: Widnes 5F 78
Chatsworth Rd. CH42: Rock F 6N 73
CH61: Pens 2N 87
L35: Rainh 5E 62
PR8: Ainsd 8G 11
Chatteris Ct. *WA10: St H 9G 48*
(off Bewsey St.)
Chatteris Pk. WA7: Nort 5G 96
Chatterton Dr. WA7: Murd 7G 96
Chatterton Rd. L14: Knott A 5A 60
Chaucer Dr. L12: Crox 8C 46
Chaucer Pl. WA4: Westy 4G 83
Chaucer Rd. WA10: St H 4G 48
Chaucer St. L3: Liv 1G 5 (6C 58)
L20: Boot 6N 43
WA7: Run 6K 95
Cheadle Av. L13: Liv 6L 59
Cheapside L2: Liv 3E 4 (7B 58)
L37: Form 2G 24
Cheapside All. L2: Liv 4E 4
Cheddar Cl. L25: Woolt 6D 76
Cheddar Gro. L32: Kirkb 3C 46
WA5: Burtw 2H 65
Cheddon Way CH61: Pens 3M 87
Chedworth Dr. WA8: Widnes 4F 78
Chedworth Rd. L14: Knott A 5C 60
Cheldon Rd. L12: W Der 8A 46
Chelford Av. WA3: Low 3E 52
Chelford Cl. CH43: Bid 1C 72
WA4: Stockt H 8D 82
WN3: Wigan 1H 41
Chelford Rd. WA10: Ec'stn 7E 48
Chellow Dene L23: Thorn 5N 33
Chelmarsh Av. WN4: Ash M 8L 41
Chelmorton Gro. WN3: Winst 2E 40
Chelmsford Cl. *L4: Kirkd 2C 58*
(off Harcourt St.)
Chelsea Ct. L12: W Der 1C 60
Chelsea Gdns. WA5: Gt San 4L 81
Chelsea Lea L9: W'ton 4E 44
Chelsea Rd. L9: W'ton 4F 44
L21: Lith 4A 44
Cheltenham Av. L17: Liv 2J 75
Cheltenham Cl. L10: Aintr 1K 45
WA5: Gt San 9J 65
Cheltenham Cres. CH46: Leas 6M 55
L36: Roby 8H 61
WA7: Run 9L 95
Cheltenham Dr. WA12: Newt W 5L 51
WN5: Bil 1N 39
Cheltenham Rd. CH45: Wall 3E 56
CH65: Ell P 2B 112
Cheltenham Way PR8: South 2E 12
Chelwood Av. L16: Child 8C 60
Chelwood Pk. WN4: Ash M 1K 51
Chemical St. WA12: Newt W 7K 51
Chemistry Rd. L24: Speke 2G 93
Chenotrie Gdns. CH43: Noct 3D 72
Chepstow Av. CH44: Wall 5J 57
Chepstow Cl. WA5: Call 6N 65
Chepstow St. L4: W'ton 9D 44
CHEQUER 6J 31
Chequer Cl. WN8: Uph 7J 31
Chequer La. WN8: Uph 6J 31
Chequers Gdns. L19: Aig 8L 75
Cheriton Av. CH48: W Kir 6E 70
Cheriton Cl. L26: Halew 8J 77
Cheriton Pk. PR8: South 3D 12
Chermside Rd. L17: Aig 7K 75
Cherry Av. L4: W'ton 9G 45
Cherrybank CH44: Wall 7H 57
Cherry Blossom Rd. WA7: Beech 2B 108
Cherry Blossom Way L33: Kirkb 7C 36
Cherrybrook Dr. WN3: Winst 2F 40
Cherry Brow Ter. *CH64: Will 6M 101*
(off Hadlow Rd.)
Cherry Cl. CH64: Nest 6J 101
L4: W'ton 9G 45
WA12: Newt W 6H 51
Cherry Cnr. WA13: Lymm 9A 84
Cherry Ct. *WA1: Warr 3D 82*
(off Orchard St.)
Cherrycroft WN8: Skel 5H 31
Cherrydale Rd. L18: Moss H 4M 75
Cherryfield Cres. L32: Kirkb 9C 36
Cherryfield Dr. L32: Kirkb 9C 36
Cherry Gdns. CH47: Hoy 1C 70
L32: Kirkb 3D 46
Cherry Grn. L39: Augh 3N 27
Cherry Gro. CH66: Whit 4M 111
L40: Burs 8J 15
Cherry La. L4: W'ton 9G 44
WA13: Lymm 9B 84
Cherry La. Barns WA13: Lymm 6D 84
Cherry Rd. PR8: Ainsd 3K 17
Cherry Sq. CH44: Wall 5H 57
Cherry Sutton WA8: Widnes 5D 78
Cherry Tree Av. WA5: Penk 4H 81
WA7: Run 7M 95
WA13: Lymm 6D 84
Cherry Tree Cl. CH2: Elt 1M 113
L24: Hale 6B 94
L35: Whis 6A 62
WA11: Hay 5C 50
Cherry Tree Dr. WA9: St H 8C 50
Cherry Tree Ho. CH46: More 9N 55
Cherry Tree La. L39: Augh 3N 27
WA11: St H 9K 39
Cherry Tree M. CH60: Hesw 7A 88
Cherry Tree Pl. WA9: St H 8C 50
Cherry Tree Rd. CH46: More 9N 55
L36: Huy 9J 61
PR9: Banks 5H 9
WA3: Low 2G 52
Cherry Va. L25: Woolt 5F 76
Cherry Vw. L33: Kirkb 6E 36
Cherry Wlk. M31: Part 7K 69
Cherrywood Av. L26: Halew 7M 77
Cherwell Cl. WA2: Warr 7E 66
Cheryl Dr. WA8: Widnes 7N 79
Chesford Grange WA1: Wools 1M 83
Chesham Ct. CH65: Ell P 1B 112
Cheshire Acre CH49: Wdchu 5A 72
Cheshire Av. L10: Faz 3N 45
Cheshire Cl. WA12: Newt W 7N 51
Cheshire Gdns. WA10: St H 8H 49
Cheshire Gro. CH46: More 1M 71
Cheshire Oaks Bus. Pk. CH65: Ell P 4B 112
Cheshire Oaks Outlet Village
CH65: Ell P 3C 112
Cheshire Oaks Trade Pk.
CH2: Lit Stan 3D 112
Cheshire Oaks Way CH65: Ell P 3C 112
Cheshire Pk. Homes WA6: Dun H 8A 114
Cheshire Rd. M31: Part 7K 69
Cheshire Way CH61: Pens 4N 87
Cheshyre Dr. WA7: Hal 6B 96
Cheshyres La. *WA1: Warr 3C 82*
(off Horsemarket St.)
WA7: W'ton, West P 9H 95
(not continuous)
Chesnell Gro. L33: Kirkb 6E 36
Chesney Cl. L8: Liv 2D 74
Chesnut Gro. CH42: Tran 4K 73
L20: Boot 5A 44
(not continuous)
Chesnut Rd. L21: Sea 3M 43
Chessington Cl. WA4: App 1G 98
Chester Av. L30: Neth 1E 44
PR9: South 7K 7
WA3: Low 2E 52
Chester Cl. L23: Crosb 7A 34
M44: Cad 4K 69
WA7: Cas 5C 96
Chester Ct. CH63: Beb 3M 89
Chester Dr. WN4: Ash M 9M 41
Chesterfield Cl. PR8: Ainsd 1J 17
Chesterfield Dr. L33: Kirkb 6C 36
Chesterfield Rd. CH62: East 2C 102
L23: Crosb 6N 33
PR8: Ainsd 1H 17
Chesterfield St. L8: Liv 1D 74
Chester Gates CH1: Dunk 7J 111
Chester Gates Ind. Pk. CH1: Dunk 8J 111
Chester High Rd.
CH64: Burt, Nest 1D 100 (1A 110)
CH66: Led 1A 110
Chester La. WA9: Sut M, St H 5L 63
Chester New Rd. WA4: H Walt 9A 82
Chester Rd. CH1: Back 6L 111
CH2: Bri T 9L 113
CH60: Hesw 8B 88
CH64: Nest 7E 100
CH65: Whit 5M 111
CH66: Chil T, Gt Sut, Hoot, Lit Sut
.... 5F 102
CH66: Whit 5M 111
L6: Liv 4J 59
L36: Huy 5L 61
PR9: South 7L 7
WA4: Dares, H Walt 5K 97
(not continuous)
WA4: Dares, Pres H 7J 97
WA4: Grap, Stockt H 7F 82
WA4: H Walt, W'ton, Warr 6B 82
WA6: Dun H, Frod, Hel 4D 114
WA7: Sut W, Pres B 4B 108
Chester Row WA12: Newt W 1M 65
CHESTER SERVICE AREA 3A 114
Chester St. CH41: Birke 2M 73
CH44: Wall 6G 57
L8: Liv 1D 74
L34: Presc 3A 62
WA2: Warr 2C 82
WA8: Widnes 7L 79
Chesterton Dr. WA2: Winw 4B 66
Chesterton St. L19: Garst 3A 92
Chester Wlk. *L36: Huy 5L 61*
(off Chester Rd.)
Chestnut Av. CH66: Gt Sut 4L 111
L23: Crosb 5M 33
L36: Huy 9H 61
M44: Cad 4K 69
PR9: Banks 4H 9
(off Main Av.)
WA5: Gt San 2H 81
WA8: Widnes 6L 79
WA11: Hay 5B 50
Chestnut Cl. CH49: Grea 7K 71
L35: Whis 5B 62
L39: Hals 4H 19
Chestnut Ct. L20: Boot 6A 44
L39: Orm 7D 20
PR9: South 7H 7
WA8: Widnes 7G 79
Chestnut Dr. Sth. WN7: Leigh 1N 53
Chestnut Farm CH66: Hoot 5F 102
Chestnut Grange L39: Orm 1B 28
Chestnut Gro. CH62: Brom 7B 90
L15: Wavtr 9L 59
WA3: Low 2G 52
WA11: Hay 3N 49
WN4: Ash M 7M 41
Chestnut Ho. *L20: Boot 6A 44*
(off St James Dr.)
WA4: App 9F 82
Chestnut La. WA6: Frod 1H 115
Chestnut Rd. L9: W'ton 7G 45
Chestnuts, The CH64: Will 6M 101
Chestnut St. PR8: South 2B 12
Chestnut Wlk. L31: Mell 7M 35
M31: Part 7K 69
Chestnut Way L37: Form 3C 24
Cheswood Cl. L35: Whis 7B 62
Cheswood Ct. *CH49: Wdchu 6A 72*
(off Childwall Grn.)
Chetham Ct. WA2: Winw 6B 66
Chetton Dr. WA7: Murd 8G 96
Chetwode Av. WN4: Ash M 1K 51
Chetwood Av. L23: Crosb 6M 33
Chetwood Cl. WA12: Newt W 5K 51
Chetwood Dr. WA8: Widnes 4J 79
Chetwynd Cl. CH43: Oxton 4F 72
Chetwynd Rd. CH43: Oxton 3G 72
Chetwynd St. L17: Aig 5G 75
Chevasse Wlk. L25: Woolt 5G 77
Cheverton Cl. CH49: Wdchu 5B 72
Chevin Rd. L9: W'ton 5F 44
Cheviot Av. WA2: Warr 6B 66
WA9: St H 7B 50
Cheviot Cl. CH42: Tran 7K 73
CH66: Lit Sut 8F 102
WN3: Winst 1E 40
Cheviot Rd. CH42: Tran 7J 73
L7: Liv 7K 59
Cheviot Way L33: Kirkb 5D 36
Cheyne Cl. L23: Blun 8G 33
Cheyne Gdns. L19: Aig 8L 75
Cheyne Wlk. WA9: St H 3J 63
Chicago Pl. WA5: Gt San 2K 81
Chichester Cl. L15: Wavtr 9J 59
WA4: Grap 9H 83
WA7: Murd 9F 96
Chicory Way L11: Norr G 9M 45
Chidden Cl. CH49: Grea 5K 71
Chidlow Cl. WA8: Widnes 2K 95
Chigwell Cl. L12: Crox 7C 46
Chilcott Rd. L14: Knott A 6A 60
Childer Cres. CH66: Lit Sut 7G 103
Childer Gdns. CH66: Lit Sut 7G 103
Childers St. L13: Liv 6M 59
CHILDER THORNTON 6F 102
CHILDWALL 1C 76
Childwall Abbey Rd. L16: Child 2B 76
Childwall Av. CH46: More 1L 71
L15: Wavtr 1J 75
Childwall Bank Rd. L16: Child 1B 76
Childwall Cl. CH46: More 1L 71
Childwall Ct. CH66: Ell P 6L 103
Childwall Cres. L16: Child 1B 76
Childwall Fiveways L15: Wavtr 1A 76
Childwall Gdns. CH66: Ell P 6L 103
Childwall Golf Course 1J 77
Childwall Grn. CH49: Wdchu 6A 72
Childwall La. L14: Brd G 7E 60
L16: Child 2D 76
L25: Child 2D 76
Childwall Mt. Rd. L16: Child 1B 76
Childwall Pde. L14: Brd G 7E 60
Childwall Pk. Av. L16: Child 2B 76
Childwall Priory Rd. L16: Child 1B 76
Childwall Rd. CH66: Ell P 6L 103
L15: Wavtr 1M 75
Childwall Valley Rd. L16: Child 1B 76
L25: Gate 9E 60
L27: N'ley 9E 60
Chilhem Cl. L8: Liv 4E 74
Chilington Av. WA8: Widnes 8G 79
Chillerton Rd. L12: W Der 1B 60
Chillingham St. L8: Liv 5F 74
Chilmark Rd. L5: Liv 3F 58
Chiltern Cl. L12: Crox 8D 46
L32: Kirkb 7A 36
WN4: Ash M 9L 41
Chiltern Cres. WA2: Warr 6B 66
Chiltern Dr. L32: Kirkb 7A 36
WN3: Winst 1F 40
Chiltern Pl. *WA2: Warr 6B 66*
(off Chiltern Rd.)
Chiltern Rd. CH42: Tran 7J 73
PR8: Ainsd 8G 11
WA2: Warr 6B 66
WA3: Cul 6M 53
WA9: St H 7B 50
Chilton Cl. L31: Mag 2J 35
Chilton Ct. L31: Mag 2J 35
Chilton Dr. CH66: Gt Sut 3K 111
Chilton M. L31: Mag 2J 35
Chilwell Cl. WA8: Widnes 4G 79
Chimes Rd. WN4: Ash M 5H 41
China Farm La. CH48: W Kir 4F 70
China La. WA4: Warr 6D 82
Chindit Cl. L37: Form 2D 24
Chippenham Av. CH49: Grea 4K 71
Chippindall Cl. WA5: Gt San 3L 81
Chipping Av. PR8: Ainsd 9G 11
Chipping Cl. WA3: Cul 5M 53
Chipping Mnr. PR9: Banks 1E 8
Chirkdale St. L4: Kirkd 9D 44
(not continuous)
Chirk Gdns. CH65: Ell P 2B 112
Chirk Way CH46: More 1N 71
Chirton Cl. WA11: Hay 3F 50
Chisacre Dr. WN6: Shev 6N 23
Chisenhale St. L3: Liv 1D 4 (5B 58)
Chisledon Cl. WA11: Hay 3F 50
Chislehurst Av. L25: Gate 2F 76
Chislet Ct. WA8: Widnes 4H 79
Chislett Cl. L40: Burs 1H 21
Chisnall Av. WA10: St H 6F 48
Chisnall Brook Cl. L39: Down 8E 18
Chisnall Cl. WA10: St H 6F 48
Chiswell St. L7: Liv 7H 59
Chiswick Cl. WA7: Murd 8F 96
Chiswick Gdns. WA4: App 1G 98
Cholmley Dr. WA12: Newt W 8N 51
Cholmondeley Rd. CH48: W Kir 6C 70
CH65: Gt Sut 1L 111
WA7: Clftn 2N 107
Cholmondeley St. WA8: Widnes 3K 95
Cholsey Cl. CH49: Upton 4N 71
Chorley Cl. PR9: Banks 2C 8
Chorley Rd. L34: Presc 3M 61
WN8: Parb 1F 22
Chorley's La. WA8: Widnes 5N 79
Chorley St. WA2: Warr 2C 82
(not continuous)
WA10: St H 6J 49
Chorley Way CH63: Spit 6N 89
Chorlton Cl. L16: Child 9D 60
WA7: Wind H 6F 96
Chorlton Gro. CH45: Wall 4D 56
Chorlton La. CH2: Chor B 6N 111
(not continuous)
Christchurch Cl. L11: Norr G 7L 45
Christchurch Rd. CH43: Oxton 4H 73
Christian St. L3: Liv 2G 5 (6D 58)
Christie Cl. CH66: Hoot 4F 102

Christie St.—Clifton Cl.

Christie St. WA8: Widnes 7N 79
Christines Cres. L40: Burs 1H 21
Christleton Cl. CH43: Oxton 6D 72
Christleton Ct. WA7: Manor P 3E 96
Christleton Dr. CH66: Ell P 8K 103
Christmas St. L20: Kirkd 9C 44
Christopher Cl. L16: Child 9B 60
L35: Rainh 7E 62
Christopher Dr. CH62: East 1F 102
Christophers Cl. CH61: Pens 3A 88
Christopher St. L4: W'ton 1E 58
Christopher Taylor Ho. L31: Mag 3J 35
Christopher Way L16: Child 9B 60
Christowe Wlk. *L11: Crox 5A 46*
(off Kennford Rd.)
Chrisward Cl. L7: Liv 8H 59
Chromolyte Ind. Est.
PR8: South 1A 12
Chudleigh Cl. L26: Halew 7J 77
Chudleigh Rd. L13: Liv 6L 59
Chung Hok Ho. L1: Liv 9H 5
Church All. L1: Liv 6F 4 (8C 58)
Church Av. L9: Aintr 3G 44
Church Cl. CH44: Wall 5K 57
L37: Form 1G 24
PR9: Banks 1E 8
PR9: South 7M 7
WA6: Frod 6L 107
Church Cl. Ct. L37: Form 1G 24
Church Cotts. L25: Gate 3G 76
Church Cres. CH44: Wall 7L 57
Churchdown Cl. L14: Knott A 5D 60
Churchdown Gro. L14: Knott A 5C 60
Churchdown Rd. L14: Knott A 5C 60
Church Dr. CH62: Port S 1A 90
WA2: Padg 8H 67
WA12: Newt W 9L 51
WN5: Orr 7N 31
Church End L24: Hale 6A 94
Church End M. L24: Hale 6B 94
Church Farm 2J 87
Church Farm CH63: Beb 2N 89
Church Farm Ct. CH60: Hesw 8N 87
CH64: Will 6M 101
Churchfield Ct. *L25: Gate 4G 77*
(off Jones Farm Rd.)
Churchfield Rd. L25: Gate 3G 76
WA6: Frod 6M 107
Church Flds. L39: Orm 8C 20
Churchfields L40: Scar 7L 13
PR8: Birkd 3M 11
WA3: Croft 2J 67
WA6: Hel 1F 114
WA8: Widnes 3L 79
WA9: Clock F 5M 63
Church Flats L4: W'ton 8E 44
Church Gdns. CH44: Wall 5K 57
L20: Boot 7A 44
Churchgate PR9: South 6L 7
(not continuous)
Churchgate M. PR9: South 6M 7
Church Grn. L16: Child 1D 76
L32: Kirkb 8C 36
L37: Form 2C 24
WA13: Warb 9H 69
WN8: Skel 3C 30
Church Grn. Gdns. WA3: Golb 1C 52
Church Gro. L21: Sea 4M 43
Church Hill CH45: Wall 4F 56
Church Hill Rd. L39: Orm 7B 20
Churchill Av. CH41: Birke 1H 73
PR9: South 5K 7
Churchill Ct. CH64: Nest 6E 100
Churchill Gdns. WA9: St H 3F 62
Churchill Gro. CH44: Wall 4J 57
Churchill Ho. L21: Sea 3M 43
Churchill Mans. *WA7: Run 4K 95*
(off Cooper St.)
Churchill Way CH64: Nest 6E 100
Churchill Way Nth. L3: Liv 3F 4 (7C 58)
Churchill Way Sth. L3: Liv 4F 4 (7C 58)
Churchlands *CH44: Wall 7L 57*
(off Bridle Rd.)
Church La. CH2: Back 9N 111
CH2: Stoak 6E 112
CH44: Wall 5K 57
(not continuous)
CH49: Wdchu 6B 72
CH61: Thurs 2J 87
CH62: Brom 6C 90
CH62: East 2F 102
CH64: Nest 7E 100
CH66: Gt Sut 1J 111
L4: W'ton 8E 44
L17: Aig 7K 75
L31: Lydi 4E 26
L34: Know 6G 47
L39: Augh 5M 27
WA3: Cul 7N 53
WA3: Low 2E 52
WA4: Grap 7J 83
WA10: Ec'stn 7D 48
Churchmeadow Cl. CH44: Wall 5K 57
Church Mdw. La. CH60: Hesw 8M 87
Church Mdw. Wlk. WA8: Hale B 2E 94
Church M. CH42: Rock F 7N 73
L24: Speke 4F 92
PR9: South 8M 7
Church Mt. L7: Liv 8G 58
Church Pde. CH65: Ell P 8A 104
Church Path L37: Form 8F 16
Church Rd. CH42: Tran 5K 73
CH44: Wall 7L 57
CH48: W Kir 7B 70
CH49: Upton 3A 72
CH63: Beb 4N 89
CH63: Thorn H 9H 89
L4: W'ton 8F 44
L13: Liv 7L 59
L15: Wavtr 2M 75
L19: Garst 2A 92
L20: Boot 4C 44
L21: Lith 3A 44
(not continuous)
L21: Sea 4M 43
L22: Wloo 2K 43
L23: Crosb 7K 33
L24: Hale 6B 94
L25: Woolt 4D 76
L26: Halew 6J 77
L31: Mag 4J 35
L36: Roby 7G 60
L37: Form 9G 16
L39: Bic 6J 29
L40: Ruf 2N 15
PR9: Banks 1E 8
WA6: Frod 7M 107
WA11: Hay 4G 50
WA11: Rainf 5C 38
WA13: Lymm 5D 84
WN8: Skel 3C 30
Church Rd. Nth. L15: Wavtr 1M 75
Church Rd. Sth. L25: Woolt 6E 76
Church Rd. W. L4: W'ton 8E 44
Church Sq. CH62: Brom 6C 90
WA10: St H 7K 49
Church St. CH41: Birke 2M 73
(not continuous)
CH44: Wall 5K 57
CH65: Ell P 8A 104
L1: Liv 5F 4 (8C 58)
L20: Boot 7N 43
L34: Presc 3A 62
L39: Orm 8C 20
PR9: South 8H 7
WA1: Warr 3D 82
WA3: Golb 1C 52
WA6: Frod 6L 107
WA7: Run 4K 95
WA8: Widnes 2K 95
WA10: St H 7K 49
WA12: Newt W 6N 51
WN5: Orr 7N 31
WN8: Uph 5M 31
Church Ter. CH42: Tran 5K 73
WN4: Ash M 9K 41
CHURCHTOWN 6M 7
Churchtown Ct. PR9: South 5M 7
Churchtown Gdns. PR9: South 5M 7
Church Vw. L12: W Der 2N 59
L20: Boot 7A 44
L39: Augh 5M 27
WA13: Lymm 4H 85
Church Vw. Ct. *L39: Orm 8C 20*
(off Burscough St.)
Churchview Rd. CH41: Birke 9H 57
Church Wlk. CH48: W Kir 7C 70
CH65: Ell P 8A 104
L20: Boot 7A 44
L34: Know 6G 47
WA2: Winw 3B 66
WA10: Ec'stn 6D 48
Church Walks L39: Orm 8C 20
Churchward Ct. *L25: Woolt 6E 76*
(off Garden St.)
Church Way L30: Neth 7C 34
L32: Kirkb 8C 36
L37: Form 2C 24
WA6: Alv 4G 114
Churchway Rd. L24: Speke 5L 93
Churchwood Cl. CH62: Brom 6C 90
Churchwood Ct. *CH49: Wdchu 7B 72*
(off Childwall Grn.)
Churchwood Vw. WA13: Lymm 5F 84
Churnet St. L4: Kirkd 1D 58
Churn Way CH49: Grea 4L 71
Churston Rd. L16: Child 3C 76
Churton Av. CH43: Oxton 5F 72
Churton Ct. L6: Liv 1M 5 (6F 58)
Ciaran Cl. L12: W Der 1B 60
Cicely Dr. L7: Liv 8G 59
Cinder La. L18: Moss H 3A 76
L20: Boot 3C 44
PR4: Mere B 5K 9
WA4: Thel 6N 83
Cinema Dr. L15: Wavtr 9K 59
Cineworld Cinema
Halton Lea 8A 96
St Helens 7J 49
Cinnabar Ct. WA4: Dares 7J 97
CINNAMON BROW 6G 66
Cinnamon Brow WN8: Uph 6M 31
Cinnamon Bldg., The L1: Liv 7G 4
Cinnamon La. WA2: Fearn 6G 67
Cinnamon La. Nth. WA2: Fearn 5G 66
Cinnamon Nook WN8: Newb 3B 22
Cinnamon Pk. WA2: Fearn 6J 67
Circle 109 L1: Liv 8G 5
Circular Dr. CH49: Grea 5L 71
CH60: Hesw 6N 87
CH62: Port S 9A 74
Circular Rd. CH41: Birke 3K 73
Circular Rd. E. L11: Norr G 1L 59
Circular Rd. W. L11: Norr G 1L 59
Cirencester Av. CH49: Grea 4K 71
Cirrus Dr. L39: Augh 3M 27
CISS GREEN 5A 94
Citadel, The
St Helens 7K 49
(off Waterloo St.)
Citrine Rd. CH44: Wall 7K 57
Citron Cl. L9: W'ton 6G 45
City Gdns. WA10: St H 3J 49
City Lofts L3: Liv 2B 4
(Waterloo Rd.)
L3: Liv 3B 4
(William Jessop Way)
City Rd. L4: W'ton 9E 44
WA10: St H 3J 49
City Sq. L2: Liv 4E 4
Civic Cl. CH63: Beb 2N 89
Civic Way CH63: Beb 2N 89
CH65: Ell P 1N 111
L36: Huy 7J 61
Clairville PR8: Birkd 1M 11
Clairville Cl. L20: Boot 7B 44
Clairville Ct. *L20: Boot 7B 44*
(off Clairville Cl.)
Clairville Way L13: Liv 4K 59
Clamley Ct. L24: Speke 4L 93
Clamley Gdns. L24: Hale 5B 94
Clanbrook Av. WA13: Lymm 6G 84
Clandon Rd. L18: Aller 7B 76
Clanfield Av. WA8: Widnes 5F 78
Clanfield Rd. L11: Norr G 8N 45
Clanwood Cl. WN3: Winst 1G 40
Clapgate Cres. WA8: Hale B 2E 94
Clap Ga. La. WN3: Wigan 1G 41
Clapgates Cres. WA5: Warr 1N 81
Clapgates Rd. WA5: Warr 1N 81
Clapham Rd. L4: W'ton 3G 58
Clare Cl. WA9: St H 2H 63
Clare Cres. CH44: Wall 5F 56
Clare Dr. CH65: Whit 3N 111
Claremont Av. L31: Mag 3G 34
PR8: Birkd 2N 11
WA8: Widnes 4M 79
Claremont Cl. L21: Sea 3M 43
Claremont Ct. CH45: Wall 3F 56
Claremont Dr. L39: Augh 1B 28
WA8: Widnes 4L 79
Claremont Gdns. PR8: Birkd 2N 11
Claremont Rd. CH48: W Kir 5C 70
L15: Wavtr 2K 75
L21: Sea 3M 43
L23: Crosb 7L 33
PR8: Birkd 2N 11
WA3: Cul 6L 53
WA7: Run 5L 95
WN5: Bil 6A 40
Claremont Way CH63: H Beb 8K 73
Claremount Dr. CH63: Beb 3M 89
Claremount Rd. CH44: Wall 2F 56
CH45: Wall 2F 56
Clarence Av. WA5: Gt San 2F 80
WA8: Widnes 4K 79
Clarence Cl. WA9: St H 8M 49
Clarence Ct. PR8: Birkd 2N 11
Clarence Rd. CH42: Tran 5J 73
CH44: Wall 7K 57
PR8: Birkd 2N 11
WA4: Grap 6J 83
Clarence St. L3: Liv 5J 5 (8D 58)
WA1: Warr 1F 82
WA3: Golb 1B 52
WA7: Run 4J 95
WA12: Newt W 6H 51
WN4: Ash M 6H 41
Clarence Ter. WA7: Run 4K 95
Clarendon Cl. CH43: Oxton 3J 73
WA7: Murd 8F 96
Clarendon Ct. WA2: Winw 5A 66
Clarendon Gro. L31: Lydi 7H 27
Clarendon Rd. CH44: Wall 6K 57
L6: Liv 3H 59
L19: Garst 1A 92
L21: Sea 4M 43
M44: Irlam 2L 69
Clare Rd. L20: Boot 8C 44
Clares Farm Cl. WA1: Wools 1N 83
Claret Cl. L17: Aig 7H 75
Clare Wlk. L10: Faz 3N 45
Clare Way CH45: Wall 4F 56
Claribel St. L8: Liv 2F 74
Claridge Ct. PR9: South 7L 7
Clarke Av. CH42: Rock F 6L 73
WA3: Cul 6N 53
WA4: Warr 6E 82
Clarke Gdns. WA8: Widnes 9L 79
Clarke's Cres. WA10: Ec'stn 6E 48
Clarkfield Cl. L40: Burs 2K 21
Clarks Ter. WA7: West P 7G 94
Classic Rd. L13: Liv 5M 59
Clatterbridge Rd. CH63: Spit 8K 89
Claude Rd. L6: Liv 3H 59
Claude St. WA1: Warr 2D 82
CLAUGHTON 1F 72
Claughton Cl. L7: Liv 8H 59
Claughton Dr. CH44: Wall 6H 57
Claughton Firs CH43: Oxton 4H 73
Claughton Grn. CH43: Oxton 3G 73
Claughton Pl. CH41: Birke 2J 73
Claughton Rd. CH41: Birke 2J 73
Claughton St. WA10: St H 6K 49
Clavell Rd. L19: Aller 8B 76
Claverton Cl. WA7: Run 9L 95
Clay Brow Rd. WN8: Skel 6H 31
Clay Cross Rd. L25: Woolt 6D 76
Claydon Ct. L26: Halew 7L 77
Claydon Gdns. WA3: Rix 8F 68
Clayfield Cl. L20: Boot 8C 44
Clayford Cres. L14: Knott A 5N 59
Clayford Pl. L14: Knott A 5N 59
Clayford Rd. L14: Knott A 5A 60
Clayford Way L14: Knott A 5A 60
Clayhill Grn. CH66: Lit Sut 7H 103
Clayhill Gro. WA3: Low 2J 53
Clayhill Ind. Est. CH64: Nest 4E 100
Clayhill Light Ind. Pk.
CH64: Nest 4E 100
Clay La. WA5: Burtw 3G 64
WA10: Ec'stn 7B 48
Claypole Cl. L7: Liv 9H 59
Clay St. L3: Liv 5A 58
Clayton Av. WA3: Low 2F 52
Clayton Cl. WA10: St H 7H 49
Clayton Cres. WA7: Run 6J 95
WA8: Widnes 7J 79
Clayton Gdns. L40: Burs 1J 21
Clayton La. CH44: Wall 7G 57
Clayton M. WN8: Skel 3A 30
Clayton Pl. CH41: Birke 3J 73
Clayton Rd. WA3: Ris 3N 67
Clayton Sq. L1: Liv 5G 5
Clayton Sq. Shop. Cen. 5G 4 (8C 58)
Clayton St. CH41: Birke 3J 73
WN8: Skel 3A 30
Cleadon Cl. L32: Kirkb 3E 46
Cleadon Rd. L32: Kirkb 3E 46
Cleadon Way WA8: Widnes 4H 79
Clearwater Cl. L7: Liv 7G 59
Clearwater Quays WA4: Westy 5H 83
Cleary St. L20: Boot 6A 44
Cleaver Cotts. L38: Hight 6G 24
Cleaver Heath Nature Reserve 5L 87
Clee Hill Rd. CH42: Tran 7J 73
Cleethorpes Rd. WA7: Murd 8E 96
Cleeves Cl. WA1: Warr 3D 82
Clegge St. WA2: Warr 1C 82
Clegg St. L5: Liv 5D 58
WN8: Skel 3A 30
Clelland St. WA4: Warr 5D 82
Clematis Rd. L27: N'ley 2J 77
Clement Gdns. L3: Liv 5B 58
Clementina Rd. L23: Blun 7H 33
Clements Way L33: Kirkb 6B 36
Clemmey Dr. L20: Boot 4D 44
Clengers Brow PR9: South 5L 7
Clent Av. L31: Lydi, Mag 9H 27
Clent Gdns. L31: Lydi 9H 27
Clent Rd. L31: Mag 9H 27
Cleopas St. L8: Liv 4E 74
Cleveland Av. WN3: Winst 1E 40
Cleveland Cl. L32: Kirkb 7B 36
Cleveland Dr. CH66: Lit Sut 8F 102
WA3: Low 2E 52
WN4: Ash M 7L 41
Cleveland Gdns. WN4: Ash M 7L 41
Cleveland Rd. WA2: Warr 6C 66
Cleveland Sq. L1: Liv 7F 4 (9C 58)
Cleveland St. CH41: Birke 9H 57
WA9: St H 9M 49
Cleveley Pk. L18: Aller 7B 76
Cleveley Rd. CH47: Meols 9F 54
L18: Aller 7A 76
Cleveleys Av. PR9: South 3M 7
WA8: Widnes 6N 79
Cleveleys Rd. PR9: South 4M 7
WA5: Gt San 4K 81
Cleves, The L31: Mag 9K 27
Cleve Way L37: Form 2H 25
CLIEVES HILLS 1L 27
Clieves Hills L39: Hals 7K 19
Clieves Hills La. L39: Augh 2K 27
Clieves Rd. L32: Kirkb 1D 46
Clifden Ct. L37: Form 1F 24
Cliff, The CH45: New B 1F 56
Cliff Dr. CH44: Wall 4K 57
Cliffe Rd. CH64: Lit N 9F 100
WA4: App 9D 82
Cliffe St. WA8: Widnes 7M 79
Cliff La. CW8: Act B, Crowt 9K 109
WA4: Grap 1N 99
(Grappenhall La.)
WA4: Grap 6L 83
(Knutsford Rd.)
WA13: Lymm 9B 84
Clifford Rd. CH44: Wall 6J 57
PR8: Birkd 4N 11
WA5: Penk 4J 81
Clifford St. CH41: Birke 9G 56
L3: Liv 3J 5 (7D 58)
Cliff Rd. CH44: Wall 6F 56
CW8: Act B 9M 109
PR9: South 5J 7
Cliff St. L7: Liv 7H 59
Cliff Vw. WA6: Frod 6K 107
CLIFTON 2N 107
Clifton Av. CH62: East 3D 102
L23: Crosb 6L 33
(off Liverpool Rd.)
L26: Halew 6J 77
WA3: Cul 7L 53
Clifton Cl. WA1: Wools 1L 83

Clifton Ct.—Connolly Ho.

Clifton Ct. CH41: Birke 3K 73
L19: Aller 8A 76
WA7: Run 9L 95
Clifton Cres. CH41: Birke 2L 73
WA6: Frod 5M 107
Clifton Dr. L10: Aintr 9J 35
Clifton Gdns. CH65: Ell P 2A 112
Clifton Ga. *CH41: Birke* 3L 73
(off Clifton Rd.)
Clifton Gro. CH44: Wall 5K 57
L5: Liv 5D 58
Clifton La. WA7: Clftn 2N 107
WA7: Sut W 3A 108
Cliftonmill Mdws.
WA3: Golb 2A 52
CLIFTON PARK 3K 73
Clifton Rd. CH41: Birke 3K 73
L6: Liv 4J 59
L37: Form 8G 17
PR8: South 9L 7
WA7: Run 8K 95
WA7: Sut W 3A 108
WN4: Ash M 5H 41
WN5: Bil 7N 39
WN7: Leigh 1M 53
Clifton Rd. E. L6: Liv 4J 59
Clifton St. L19: Garst 1A 92
WA4: Warr 4D 82
WA10: St H 6K 49
Clifton Vs. CH1: Back 5N 111
Cliftonville Rd. L34: Presc 3B 62
WA1: Wools 1K 83
Clincton Cl. WA8: Widnes 8D 78
Clincton Vw. WA8: Widnes 8D 78
CLINKHAM WOOD 1L 49
Clinkham Wood Local Nature Reserve
1K 49
Clinning Rd. PR8: Birkd 4N 11
Clinton Pl. L12: W Der 2L 59
Clinton Rd. L12: W Der 2L 59
Clint Rd. L7: Liv 8H 59
Clint Rd. W. L7: Liv 8H 59
Clint Way *L7: Liv* 8H 59
(off Clint Rd.)
Clipper Vw. CH62: New F 8B 74
Clipsley Brook Vw. WA11: Hay 4B 50
Clipsley Cres. WA11: Hay 3C 50
Clipsley La. WA11: Hay 4D 50
Clive Av. WA2: Warr 8D 66
Clive Lodge PR8: Birkd 4M 11
Clive Rd. CH43: Oxton 4J 73
PR8: Birkd 4M 11
CLOCK FACE 6N 63
Clock Face Country Pk. 5B 64
Clock Face Pde. WA9: Sut L 5M 63
Clock Face Rd. WA8: Bold H, Clock F 4M 63
WA9: Clock F 4M 63
Clock La. WA5: Cuerd 5B 80
Clocktower, The *WA4: Warr* 6D 82
(off Elphins Dr.)
Clocktower Dr. L9: W'ton 7E 44
Clock Twr. St. WA10: St H 7J 49
Cloister Grn. L37: Form 2H 25
Cloisters, The L23: Crosb 8K 33
L37: Form 1F 24
PR9: Banks 4H 9
PR9: South 7H 7
(off Hoghton Gro.)
WA10: Ec'stn 6E 48
Cloister Way CH65: Ell P 9C 104
Clorain Cl. L33: Kirkb 8E 36
Clorain Rd. L33: Kirkb 8E 36
Clore Natural History Cen. 3G 4
Close, The CH49: Grea 6L 71
CH61: Irby 1L 87
CH63: H Beb 7K 73
L9: W'ton 6E 44
L23: Crosb 8K 33
L28: Stockb V 2G 60
L38: Ince B 9L 25
PR9: Banks 2E 8
WA10: Ec'stn 5D 48
WA11: Hay 5B 50
WA12: Newt W 9N 51
Closeburn Av. CH60: Hesw 9M 87
Close St. WA9: St H 2H 63
Cloudberry Cl. L27: N'ley 2J 77
Cloudberry Wlk. M31: Part 6M 69
Clough, The WA7: Hal 6B 96
WN4: Garsw 7F 40
Clough Av. L40: Burs 1K 21
WA2: Warr 7C 66
Clough Gro. WN4: Ash M 6H 41
Clough Rd. L24: Speke 3H 93
(not continuous)
L26: Halew 7L 77
Cloughwood Cres. WN6: Shev 7N 23
Clovelly Av. WA5: Gt San 1G 80
WA9: St H 3A 64
Clovelly Ct. CH49: Grea 5L 71
Clovelly Dr. PR8: Birkd 6L 11
WN8: Newb 4D 22
Clovelly Gro. WA7: Brook 1D 108
Clovelly Rd. L4: W'ton 3G 59
Clover Av. L26: Halew 6H 77
WA6: Frod 7N 107
Clover Birches CH65: Ell P 7N 103
Clover Ct. WA7: Brook 1D 108
Cloverdale Dr. WN4: Ash M 9L 41
Cloverdale Rd. L25: Gate 1F 76
Clover Dr. CH41: Birke 8E 56
Cloverfield WA7: Nort 8E 96
WA13: Lymm 4F 84
Cloverfield Gdns. CH66: Lit Sut 7J 103
Clover Hey WA11: St H 3L 49
Club 2000 Bingo
Halton Lea 8A 96
Club 3000 Bingo
Huyton 7J 61
Stanley Park 9D 44
CLUBMOOR 2K 59
Club St. WA11: St H 1K 49
Clucas Gdns. L39: Orm 7C 20
Clwyd Gro. L12: W Der 1N 59
Clwyd St. CH41: Birke 2K 73
CH45: New B 2G 57
Clwyd Way CH66: Lit Sut 8F 102
Clyde Rd. L7: Liv 7K 59
Clydesdale CH65: Whit 2N 111
Clydesdale Rd. CH44: Wall 4K 57
CH47: Hoy 9C 54
WA4: App 8E 82
Clyde St. CH42: Rock F 6M 73
L20: Kirkd 1B 58
Clyffes Farm Cl. L40: Scar 7M 13
Coach Ho. Ct. L29: Seft 5D 34
L40: Burs 2J 21
Coach Ho. M. L22: Wloo 1K 43
L25: Woolt 5G 76
Coachmans Dr. L12: W Der 9C 46
Coach Rd. L39: Bic 1K 37
WA11: Rainf, Kirkb 6M 37
Coadys Way WA8: Widnes 6M 79
Coalbrookdale Rd. CH64: Nest 4F 100
Coalgate La. L35: Whis 7N 61
Coal Pit La. L39: Bic 8N 29
Coalpit La. CH1: Dunk, Lea B, Moll 9H 111
Coalport Wlk. WA9: St H 3F 62
Coal St. L3: Liv 4H 5 (7D 58)
Coalville Rd. WA11: St H 4N 49
Coastal Dr. CH45: Wall 2D 56
Coastal Point *CH46: Leas* 5M 55
(off Leasowe Rd.)
Coastal Rd. PR8: Ainsd, Birkd 8G 10
Coastguard La. CH64: P'gte 5B 100
Coastline M. PR9: South 3M 7
Cobal Ct. WA6: Frod 6L 107
Cobb Av. L21: Lith 4A 44
Cobbles, The L26: Halew 6H 77
Cobblestone Cnr. L19: G'dale 9M 75
COBBS 8F 82
Cobbs Brow La. L40: Lath 8C 22
WN8: Newb 5D 22
Cobb's Clough Rd. L40: Lath 8C 22
Cobbs La. WA4: App 8F 82
Cobden Av. CH42: Tran 5M 73
Cobden Ct. CH42: Tran 5M 73
Cobden Pl. CH42: Tran 5M 73
L25: Woolt 6D 76
Cobden Rd. PR9: South 9L 7
Cobden St. L6: Liv 1L 5 (6E 58)
L25: Woolt 6D 76
(not continuous)
WA2: Warr 1C 82
WA12: Newt W 6M 51
Cobden Vw. L25: Woolt 6D 76
Cob Hall La. WA6: Manl 8G 114
Cobham Av. L9: W'ton 4E 44
Cobham Rd. CH46: More 9L 55
Cobham Wlk. L30: Neth 7C 34
Cob Moor Av. WN5: Bil 2N 39
Cob Moor Rd. WN5: Bil 2N 39
Coburg St. CH41: Birke 2K 73
Coburg Wharf L3: Liv 2B 74
Cochrane St. L5: Liv 4E 58
Cockburn St. L8: Liv 4E 74
Cockerell Cl. L4: W'ton 2E 58
Cockerham Way L11: Crox 5N 45
Cock Glade L35: Whis 8A 62
Cockhedge Grn. WA1: Warr 2D 82
WA2: Warr 2D 82
Cockhedge La. WA1: Warr 3C 82
Cockhedge Shop. Pk. 3C 82
Cockhedge Way WA1: Warr 3C 82
Cocklade La. L24: Hale 6A 94
Cock La. Ends WA8: Hale B 3E 94
Cockle Dick's La. PR9: South 5K 7
Cockshead Rd. L25: Gate 3F 76
Cockshead Way L25: Gate 2F 76
Cockspur St. L3: Liv 3E 4 (7B 58)
Cockspur St. W. L3: Liv 3D 4 (7B 58)
Coerton Rd. L9: Aintr 3G 44
Coffin La. WN2: Bam 5M 41
Cokers, The CH42: Rock F 8L 73
Colbern Cl. L31: Mag 3K 35
Colbert Cl. CH49: Upton 4A 72
Colburn Cl. WN3: Wigan 1J 41
Colburne Cl. L40: Burs 9K 15
Colby Cl. L16: Child 9C 60
Colby Rd. WN3: Wigan 1K 41
Colchester Rd. PR8: South 4E 12
Colden Cl. L12: W Der 2C 60
Coldstone Dr. WN4: Garsw 8F 40
Coldstream Cl. WA2: Warr 5F 66
Coldstream Dr. CH66: Lit Sut 9E 102
Cole Av. WA12: Newt W 6L 51
Colebrooke Cl. WA3: Birchw 5A 68
Colebrooke Rd. L17: Aig 5G 74
Coleclough Pl. WA3: Cul 6N 53
Cole Cres. L39: Augh 4A 28
Coleman Dr. CH49: Grea 5J 71
Colemere Cl. WA1: Padg 8H 67
Colemere Ct. CH65: Ell P 7N 103
Colemere Dr. CH61: Thing 1B 88
Coleport Cl. WA4: Warr 6D 82
Coleridge Av. WA10: St H 6G 49
Coleridge Ct. L32: Kirkb 2B 46
Coleridge Dr. CH62: New F 9N 73
Coleridge Gro. WA8: Widnes 7H 79
Coleridge Rd. WN5: Bil 2N 39
Coleridge St. L6: Liv 6G 59
L20: Boot 6N 43
Colerne Way WN3: Winst 1F 40
Colesborne Rd. L11: Norr G 8N 45
Coles Cres. L23: Thorn 5A 34
Coleshill Ri. WN3: Winst 1E 40
Coleshill Rd. L11: Norr G 7K 45
Cole St. CH43: Oxton 2J 73
Colette Rd. L10: Faz 3N 45
Coleus Cl. L9: W'ton 6G 45
Colin Cl. L36: Roby 8G 61
Colindale Rd. L16: Child 1C 76
Colin Dr. L3: Liv 4B 58
Colinmander Gdns. L39: Orm 1A 28
Colinton WN8: Skel 5H 31
Colinton St. L15: Wavtr 9K 59
Coliseum Shop. & Leisure Pk. 3B 112
Coliseum Way CH65: Ell P 4B 112
College Av. L23: Crosb 8K 33
L37: Form 8E 16
College Cl. CH43: Bid 2B 72
CH45: Wall 3E 56
L37: Form 9D 16
PR8: Birkd 3N 11
WA1: Warr 3E 82
WA2: Fearn 6J 67
College Ct. L12: W Der 4M 59
College Dr. CH63: Beb 9N 73
College Farm WN8: Roby M 3K 31
College Flds. L36: Huy 8J 61
WA8: Widnes 3J 79
College Grn. Flats L23: Crosb 8K 33
COLLEGE ISLAND 2E 30
College La. L1: Liv 6F 4 (8C 58)
College Path L37: Form 8D 16
College Pl. WA2: Padg 7K 67
College Rd. L23: Crosb 7J 33
WN8: Uph 3L 31
College Rd. Nth. L23: Blun 6J 33
College St. WA10: St H 6K 49
(not continuous)
College St. Nth. L6: Liv 2K 5 (6E 58)
College St. Sth. L6: Liv 2L 5 (6E 58)
College Vw. L36: Huy 7J 61
College Way CH62: East 8F 90
WN8: Skel 2D 30
Collegiate, The L6: Liv 2L 5
Collegiate Rd. WA2: Warr 8C 66
Collier's Row WA7: W'ton 8H 95
Collier St. WA7: Run 4J 95
Colliery Grn. Cl. CH64: Lit N 9E 100
Colliery Grn. Ct. CH64: Lit N 9E 100
Colliery Grn. Dr. CH64: Lit N 9E 100
Colliford Way L6: Liv 5F 58
Colling Ct. WA1: Warr 3E 82
Collingham Grn. CH66: Lit Sut 9G 103
Collingwood Cl. L4: Kirkd 1C 58
Collingwood Rd. CH63: Beb 3A 90
WA12: Newt W 7K 51
Collin Rd. CH43: Bid 9E 56
Collins Cl. L20: Boot 5N 43
COLLINS GREEN 9F 50
Collins Grn. La. WA5: Coll G 9G 50
Collins Ind. Est. WA9: St H 5M 49
Collinson Ct. WA6: Frod 6L 107
Collin St. WA5: Warr 3N 81
Collisdene Rd. WN5: Orr 6N 31
Colmere La. M44: Cad 4L 69
Colmoor Cl. L33: Kirkb 5D 36
Colmore Av. CH63: Spit 6M 89
Colmore Rd. L11: Norr G 8K 45
Colne Dr. WA9: St H 2N 63
Colne Rd. WA5: Burtw 3H 65
Colonel Dr. L12: W Der 2B 60
Colonnades, The L3: Liv 8D 4 (9A 58)
Colorado Cl. WA5: Gt San 1L 81
Colquitt St. L1: Liv 7H 5 (9D 58)
Coltart Rd. L8: Liv 2G 74
Colton Rd. L25: Gate 1E 76
Colton Wlk. L25: Gate 1D 76
Columban Cl. L30: Neth 8D 34
Columbia Hall *WA8: Widnes* 7L 79
(off Frederick St.)
Columbia La. CH43: Oxton 4H 73
Columbia Rd. CH43: Oxton 4H 73
L4: W'ton 8F 44
L34: Presc 3B 62
Columbine Cl. L31: Mell 8M 35
WA8: Widnes 4E 78
Columbine Wlk. *M31: Part* 6M 69
(off Central Rd.)
Columbine Way WA9: Bold 2D 64
Columbus Dr. CH61: Pens 4M 87
Columbus Pl. WA5: Gt San 1K 81
Columbus Quay L3: Liv 5D 74
Columbus St. WN4: Ash M 6H 41
Columbus Way *L21: Lith* 3A 44
(off Bridge Rd.)
Column Rd. CH48: Caldy, W Kir 6D 70
Colvend Way WA8: Widnes 5H 79
Colville Ct. WA2: Winw 6B 66
Colville Rd. CH44: Wall 5G 56
Colville St. L15: Wavtr 9K 59
Colwall Cl. L33: Kirkb 9E 36
Colwall Rd. L33: Kirkb 9E 36
Colwall Wlk. L33: Kirkb 9E 36
Colwell Cl. L14: Knott A 2E 60
Colwell Ct. L14: Knott A 2E 60
Colwell Rd. L14: Knott A 3E 60
Colworth Rd. L24: Speke 3F 92
Colwyn Cl. CH65: Ell P 2B 112
WA5: Call 7N 65
Colwyn Rd. L13: Liv 7L 59
Colwyn St. CH41: Birke 9G 56
Colyton Av. WA9: Sut L 4N 63
Combermere St. L8: Liv 2E 74
L15: Wavtr 9J 59
Comely Av. CH44: Wall 5J 57
Comely Bank Rd. CH44: Wall 5K 57
Comer Gdns. L31: Lydi 9J 27
Comfrey Gro. L26: Halew 6J 77
Comley Bank PR9: South 6J 7
Commander Dr. WA1: Padd 1G 83
Commerce Way L8: Liv 1G 74
Commercial Rd. CH62: Brom 4D 90
L5: Kirkd 3B 58
Commissioner Sq. WA1: Padd 1G 83
Common, The WA7: Hal 7C 96
WN8: Parb 2F 22
Commonfield Rd. CH49: Wdchu 7B 72
Common La. M31: Carr 4N 69
(not continuous)
PR9: Banks, South 5F 8
WA3: Cul 6L 53
WA4: L Stret 7F 98
WA4: Warr 6F 82
WA6: Haps 4A 114
Common Rd. WA12: Newt W 7G 51
Commonside WA6: Alv 3G 115
Common St. WA9: St H 2G 63
WA12: Newt W 7G 50
Commutation Row L3: Liv 3H 5 (7D 58)
Company's Cl. WA7: W'ton 9J 95
Compass Cl. WA7: Murd 1F 108
Compass Ct. CH45: Wall 1F 56
Compton Ct. WA11: Hay 3E 50
Compton Pl. CH65: Ell P 9N 103
Compton Rd. CH41: Birke 8D 56
L6: Liv 5F 58
PR8: Birkd 3A 12
Compton Wlk. L20: Boot 6A 44
Compton Way L26: Halew 1K 93
Comus St. L3: Liv 1G 5 (6C 58)
Concert Sq. L1: Liv 6G 5
Concert St. L1: Liv 6G 5 (8C 58)
Concorde Av. WN3: Wigan 1K 41
Concorde Pl. WA2: Warr 7E 66
Concordia Av. CH49: Upton 3A 72
Concourse Shop. Cen. 3E 30
Concourse Way WA9: St H 8B 50
Condor Cl. L19: Garst 1B 92
Condron Rd. Nth. L21: Lith 1B 44
Condron Rd. Sth. L21: Lith 1B 44
Conery Cl. WA6: Hel 1F 114
Coney Cres. L23: Thorn 6A 34
Coney Gro. WA7: Brook 1D 108
Coney La. L35: Tar G 1K 77
L36: Huy 1K 77
Coney Wlk. CH49: Upton 2L 71
Congress Gdns. WA9: St H 2G 63
Conifer Cl. CH66: Whit 5M 111
L9: W'ton 7G 44
L33: Kirkb 6C 36
Conifer Ct. L37: Form 2F 24
Conifer Gro. WA4: Moore 9J 81
WA5: Gt San 1H 81
Conifers, The L31: Mag 9H 27
Conifer Wlk. M31: Part 6L 69
Coningsby Dr. CH45: Wall 5G 57
Coningsby Gdns. WA3: Low 2F 52
Coningsby Rd. L4: W'ton 2F 58
Coniston Av. CH43: Noct 3C 72
CH45: Wall 2E 56
CH63: East 2B 102
L34: Presc 3C 62
WA5: Penk 4F 80
WN4: Ash M 7K 41
Coniston Cl. CH66: Hoot 5G 102
L9: Aintr 3G 45
L33: Kirkb 7B 36
WA7: Beech 9N 95
Coniston Ct. PR8: Ainsd 2J 17
Coniston Dr. WA6: Frod 6N 107
Coniston Gro. WA11: St H 3K 49
Coniston Ho. L17: Aig 6J 75
Coniston Rd. CH61: Irby 1L 87
CH64: Nest 8E 100
L31: Mag 1K 35
L37: Form 2D 24
M31: Part 5L 69
Coniston St. L5: Liv 3F 58
Coniston Way WA11: Rainf 1C 38
Conleach Rd. L24: Speke 4J 93
Connaught Av. WA1: Warr 1F 82
Connaught Cl. CH41: Birke 9G 56
Connaught Cres. WA8: Widnes 2J 79
Connaught Dr. WA12: Newt W 8L 51
Connaught Ho. CH41: Birke 2N 73
Connaught Rd. L7: Liv 4N 5 (7F 58)
(not continuous)
Connaught Way CH41: Birke 9G 56
Connect Bus. Village L5: Kirkd 2B 58
Connolly Av. L20: Boot 5D 44
Connolly Ho. L20: Boot 8C 44

Conroy Way—Cranwell Wlk.

Conroy Way WA12: Newt W ... 9L **51**
Consett Rd. WA9: St H ... 3G **62**
Constables Cl. WA7: Cas ... 6C **96**
Constable Sq. WA1: Padd ... 9G **67**
Constance Rd. M31: Part ... 6M **69**
Constance St. L3: Liv ... 3K **5** (7E **58**)
WA10: St H ... 8G **48**
Constance Way WA8: Widnes ... 2K **95**
Constantine Av. CH60: Hesw ... 6A **88**
Convent Cl. CH42: Tran ... 4K **73**
L19: G'dale ... 9M **75**
L39: Augh ... 2B **28**
WN8: Roby M ... 2L **31**
Convent Gro. WN8: Parb ... 3F **22**
Conville Blvd. CH63: H Beb ... 8L **73**
Conway Av. M44: Irlam ... 1M **69**
WA5: Warr ... 7A **66**
Conway Cl. CH63: H Beb ... 2K **89**
L33: Kirkb ... 6B **36**
WA5: Gt San ... 2H **81**
Conway Ct. CH63: Beb ... 3M **89**
CH65: Ell P ... 2B **112**
Conway Cres. WN5: Bil ... 5A **40**
Conway Dr. CH41: Birke ... 2K **73**
WA12: Newt W ... 7N **51**
WN5: Bil ... 6B **40**
Conway Ho. L6: Liv ... 5H **59**
Conway Ind. Est. WN6: App B ... 5N **23**
Conway Lodge L5: Liv ... 4D **58**
Conway Park Station (Rail) ... 1L **73**
Conway Rd. WN4: Ash M ... 6N **41**
Conway St. CH41: Birke ... 1K **73**
(not continuous)
L5: Liv ... 4D **58**
WA10: St H ... 8G **48**
Conwy Ct. WA7: Cas ... 5C **96**
Conwy Dr. L6: Liv ... 4G **59**
Conyers Av. PR8: Birkd ... 3M **11**
Coogee Av. WA5: Gt San ... 1G **80**
Cook Av. WA11: Hay ... 3G **51**
Cookes Cl. CH64: Nest ... 5E **100**
Cooke St. WN4: Ash M ... 5H **41**
Cook Rd. CH46: Leas ... 5B **56**
Cooks Ct. L23: Crosb ... 6K **33**
Cookson Rd. L21: Sea ... 4N **43**
Cookson St. L1: Liv ... 9H **5** (1D **74**)
Cooks Rd. L23: Crosb ... 6K **33**
Cook St. CH41: Birke ... 3K **73**
CH65: Ell P ... 8A **104**
L2: Liv ... 5E **4** (8B **58**)
L34: Presc ... 3A **62**
L35: Whis ... 5C **62**
Coombe Dr. WA7: Run ... 7J **95**
Coombe Pk. CH66: Lit Sut ... 8H **103**
Coombe Pk. Ct. CH66: Lit Sut ... 8H **103**
Coombe Rd. CH61: Irby ... 9M **71**
Cooperage Cl. L8: Liv ... 4D **74**
Cooper Av. WA2: Warr ... 7C **66**
WA12: Newt W ... 7H **51**
Cooper Av. Nth. L18: Moss H ... 7M **75**
Cooper Av. Sth. L19: Aig ... 7M **75**
Cooper Cl. L19: Aig ... 8M **75**
Cooper La. WA11: Hay ... 6D **50**
Cooper's La. L33: Know I ... 4H **47**
Coopers Pl. WA4: Warr ... 7D **82**
Coopers Row *L22: Wloo ... 2L 43*
(off Brunswick Pde.)
Cooper St. WA7: Run ... 4K **95**
WA8: Widnes ... 7L **79**
WA10: St H ... 6J **49**
Copeland Cl. CH61: Pens ... 3M **87**
Copeland Gro. WA7: Beech ... 1A **108**
Copeland Rd. WA4: Warr ... 6C **82**
Copperas Hill L3: Liv ... 5H **5** (8D **58**)
Copperas St. WA10: St H ... 7J **49**
Copperfield Cl. L8: Liv ... 3E **74**
WA3: Birchw ... 4K **67**
Copperwood WA7: Nort ... 6E **96**
Copperwood Dr. L35: Whis ... 7B **62**
Coppice, The CH45: Wall ... 2G **56**
L4: W'ton ... 3H **59**
L34: Know ... 7H **47**
Coppice Cl. CH43: Bid ... 2B **72**
WA7: Cas ... 6D **96**
Coppice Cres. L36: Huy ... 5K **61**
Coppice Dr. WN3: Wigan ... 1H **41**
WN5: Bil ... 1N **39**
Coppice Grange CH46: More ... 1K **71**
Coppice Grn. CH2: Elt ... 1N **113**
WA5: Westb ... 8J **65**
Coppice Gro. CH49: Grea ... 6K **71**
Coppice La. L35: Tar G ... 1M **77**
Coppice Leys L37: Form ... 1E **24**
Coppicewood Cl. M31: Part ... 7L **69**
Coppins, The WA2: Warr ... 7D **66**
Coppins Cl. WA6: Hel ... 1E **114**
Copplehouse Ct. *L10: Faz ... 3M 45*
(off Copplehouse La.)
Copplehouse La. L10: Faz ... 3M **45**
Coppull Rd. L31: Lydi ... 8H **27**
Copse, The L18: Moss H ... 3B **76**
L25: Woolt ... 7F **76**
L37: Form ... 9E **16**
WA7: Pal F ... 9C **96**
(not continuous)
WA12: Newt W ... 6J **51**
Copse Gro. CH61: Irby ... 9M **71**
Copsmead CH46: More ... 9N **55**
Copthorne Rd. L32: Kirkb ... 9N **35**
Copthorne Wlk. L32: Kirkb ... 9N **35**
Copy Cl. L30: Neth ... 6E **34**
Copy La. L30: Neth ... 6E **34**
Copy Way L30: Neth ... 6E **34**
Coral Av. L36: Huy ... 6H **61**
WA9: St H ... 2J **63**
Coral Cl. L32: Kirkb ... 9A **36**
Coral Dr. L20: Boot ... 7B **44**
Coralin Way WN4: Ash M ... 4H **41**
Coral Ridge CH43: Bid ... 1D **72**
Coral St. L13: Liv ... 8M **59**
Corbet Av. WA2: Warr ... 9C **66**
Corbet Cl. L32: Kirkb ... 9A **36**
Corbet St. WA2: Warr ... 9C **66**
Corbet Wlk. L32: Kirkb ... 9A **36**
Corbridge Rd. L16: Child ... 1A **76**
Corbyn St. CH44: Wall ... 8L **57**
Corfu St. CH41: Birke ... 2J **73**
Coriander Rd. L11: Norr G ... 9M **45**
Corinthian Av. L13: Liv ... 5M **59**
Corinthian St. CH42: Rock F ... 6M **73**
L21: Sea ... 3M **43**
Corinth Twr. *L5: Liv ... 3D 58*
(off Anderson St.)
Corinto St. L8: Liv ... 1E **74**
Corkdale Rd. L9: W'ton ... 5G **44**
Cormorant Cen., The WA7: Run ... 5H **95**
Cormorant Ct. CH45: Wall ... 1E **56**
Cormorant Dr. WA7: Run ... 5H **95**
Cornbrook WN8: Skel ... 5H **31**
Cornbrook Av. WA7: Cas ... 5C **96**
Corncroft Rd. L34: Know ... 7H **47**
Corndale Rd. L18: Moss H ... 4M **75**
Cornelian Gro. WN4: Ash M ... 6H **41**
Cornelius Dr. CH61: Pens ... 2N **87**
Cornel Way L36: Huy ... 9K **61**
Corner Brook L28: Stockb V ... 2D **60**
Cornerhouse La. WA8: Widnes ... 5G **79**
Cornerstone Gallery, The ... 2K **5** (6E **58**)
Cornett Rd. L9: Aintr ... 3G **44**
Corney St. L7: Liv ... 1H **75**
Cornfield Cl. CH49: Wdchu ... 6C **72**
CH66: Gt Sut ... 4L **111**
Cornfields Cl. L19: Garst ... 1N **91**
Cornflower Way CH46: More ... 7A **56**
Cornforth Way WA8: Widnes ... 5J **79**
Cornhill L1: Liv ... 8F **4** (9C **58**)
Cornice Rd. L13: Liv ... 5M **59**
Corniche Rd. CH62: Port S ... 1A **90**
Corn Mill Cl. WN4: Garsw ... 7F **40**
Cornmill Ct. WA3: Croft ... 1H **67**
Cornmill Lodge L31: Mag ... 1H **35**
Corn St. L8: Liv ... 3D **74**
Cornubia Rd. WA8: Widnes ... 9M **79**
Cornwall Av. WA7: Run ... 5K **95**
Cornwall Cl. WA7: Cas ... 6B **96**
Cornwall Ct. CH63: Beb ... 3M **89**
Cornwall Dr. CH43: Pren ... 7G **72**
Cornwallis St. L1: Liv ... 9G **4** (9C **58**)
(not continuous)
Cornwall Rd. L20: Boot ... 6C **44**
M44: Cad ... 4K **69**
WA8: Widnes ... 5L **79**
Cornwall St. WA1: Warr ... 1F **82**
WA9: St H ... 8N **49**
Cornwall Way PR8: Ainsd ... 2H **17**
Cornwell Cl. CH62: New F ... 8A **74**
Cornwood Cl. L25: Gate ... 1F **76**
Corona Av. L31: Lydi ... 7H **27**
Corona Rd. CH62: Port S ... 1B **90**
L13: Liv ... 5M **59**
L22: Wloo ... 1K **43**
Coronation Av. CH45: New B ... 2H **57**
L14: Brd G ... 6C **60**
L37: Form ... 2G **24**
WA4: Grap ... 6K **83**
Coronation Bldgs. *CH45: Wall ... 4H 57*
(off Wallasey Rd.)
CH48: W Kir ... 4D **70**
Coronation Ct. L39: Orm ... 7C **20**
Coronation Dr. CH62: Brom ... 4C **90**
L14: Brd G ... 6C **60**
L23: Crosb ... 8K **33**
L35: Presc ... 5N **61**
WA5: Penk ... 4H **81**
WA6: Frod ... 5N **107**
WA8: Widnes ... 8E **78**
WA11: Hay ... 3J **51**
Coronation Ho. WA7: Run ... 7M **95**
Coronation Rd. CH47: Hoy ... 2A **70**
CH65: Ell P ... 1A **112**
L23: Crosb ... 8K **33**
L31: Lydi ... 9H **27**
WA7: Pres B ... 9H **97**
WA7: Run ... 6L **95**
WA10: Windle ... 5F **48**
Coronation St. WN4: Ash M ... 5F **40**
Coronation Wlk. PR8: South ... 8F **6**
WN5: Bil ... 7N **39**
Coroner's Court
Liverpool ... 3C **58**
Coroner's La. WA8: Widnes ... 3K **79**
Coronet Cl. WN6: App B ... 6M **23**
Coronet Rd. L11: Crox ... 7A **46**
Coronet Way WA8: Widnes ... 8E **78**
Corporal Way L12: W Der ... 2C **60**
Corporation Rd. CH41: Birke ... 9F **56**
Corporation St. PR8: South ... 8G **6**
WA9: St H ... 6K **49**
WA10: St H ... 6K **49**
(not continuous)
Corporation Wharf L20: Boot ... 6C **44**
Corridor Rd. CH65: Ell P ... 9F **104**
Corrie Dr. CH63: Beb ... 3M **89**
Corsewall St. L7: Liv ... 9J **59**
Corsican Gdns. WA9: St H ... 2F **62**
Cortsway CH49: Grea ... 3M **71**
Cortsway W. CH49: Grea ... 3L **71**
Corwen Cl. CH43: Bid ... 2B **72**
CH46: More ... 1N **71**
WA5: Call ... 8N **65**
Corwen Cres. L14: Brd G ... 7D **60**
Corwen Dr. L30: Neth ... 7G **34**
Corwen Rd. CH47: Hoy ... 1D **70**
L4: W'ton ... 1H **59**
Cosgrove Cl. L6: Liv ... 2J **59**
Coslett Dr. WA10: St H ... 7F **48**
Cossack Av. WA2: Warr ... 8D **66**
Costain St. L20: Kirkd ... 2B **58**
Cote Lea Ct. WA7: Pal F ... 9B **96**
Cotham St. WA10: St H ... 7K **49**
Coton Way L32: Kirkb ... 8A **36**
Cotsford Cl. L36: Huy ... 5G **61**
Cotsford Pl. L36: Huy ... 5G **60**
Cotsford Rd. L36: Huy ... 5G **60**
Cotsford Way L36: Huy ... 5G **61**
Cotswold Av. WA3: Low ... 4E **52**
Cotswold Gdns. WA3: Low ... 4F **52**
Cotswold Gro. WA9: St H ... 7C **50**
Cotswold Pl. WA2: Warr ... 5C **66**
Cotswold Rd. CH42: Tran ... 7J **73**
WA2: Warr ... 6C **66**
Cotswolds Cres. L26: Halew ... 9J **77**
Cotswold St. L7: Liv ... 7G **59**
Cottage Cl. CH63: Brom ... 1B **102**
CH64: Lit N ... 7E **100**
L32: Kirkb ... 3C **46**
L39: Orm ... 9B **20**
Cottage La. CH60: Hesw ... 9N **87**
L39: Orm ... 7B **20**
Cottage M. L39: Orm ... 8B **20**
Cottage Pl. WA9: Clock F ... 5M **63**
Cottage St. CH41: Birke ... 1K **73**
Cottenham St. L6: Liv ... 6G **59**
Cotterdale Cl. WA5: Gt San ... 1H **81**
WA9: St H ... 3M **63**
Cotterill WA7: Run ... 7N **95**
Cotterill Dr. WA1: Wools ... 1K **83**
Cottesbrook Cl. L11: Norr G ... 7M **45**
Cottesbrook Pl. L11: Norr G ... 7M **45**
Cottesbrook Rd. L11: Norr G ... 7M **45**
Cottesmore Dr. CH60: Hesw ... 7D **88**
Cottesmore Way WA3: Golb ... 1C **52**
Cottham Dr. WA2: Fearn ... 6H **67**
Cotton Dr. L39: Orm ... 7B **20**
Cotton Exchange Bldg.
L3: Liv ... 4D **4**
Cotton La. WA7: Run ... 7N **95**
Cottons Bri. WA4: Pres H ... 1H **109**
Cotton St. L3: Liv ... 5A **58**
Cotton Ter. WA9: St H ... 1B **64**
Cottonwood L17: Aig ... 6F **74**
Cottrell Cl. L19: Garst ... 3A **92**
Cottys Brow PR9: South ... 4L **7**
Coudray Rd. PR9: South ... 6K **7**
Coulport Cl. L14: Knott A ... 5E **60**
Coulsdon Pl. L8: Liv ... 4F **74**
Coulthard Rd. CH42: Rock F ... 8N **73**
Coulton Rd. WA8: Widnes ... 5A **80**
Coultshead Av. WN5: Bil ... 5A **40**
Council Av. WN4: Ash M ... 8K **41**
Council St. L35: Rainh ... 5D **62**
Countess Cl. L40: Burs ... 6E **20**
Countess Pk. L11: Crox ... 8A **46**
Countisbury Dr. L16: Child ... 2C **76**
County & Family Courts
Birkenhead ... 2M **73**
Warrington ... 3B **82**
County Court
St Helens ... 6K **49**
County Dr. WA10: St H ... 8H **49**
County Rd. L4: W'ton ... 9E **44**
L32: Kirkb ... 7C **36**
L39: Orm ... 9B **20**
Courage Low La. WN6: Wright ... 1N **23**
Course La. WN8: Newb ... 4N **21**
Court, The CH63: Beb ... 3N **89**
CH64: Lit N ... 8F **100**
L28: Stockb V ... 2G **60**
PR9: South ... 7G **7**
Court Av. L26: Halew ... 7L **77**
Courtenay Av. L22: Wloo ... 9J **33**
Courtenay Rd. CH47: Hoy ... 2B **70**
L22: Wloo ... 9J **33**
L25: Woolt ... 4D **76**
Courtfield L39: Orm ... 6C **20**
Courtfields Cl. L12: W Der ... 4N **59**
Court Grn. L39: Orm ... 6B **20**
COURT HEY ... 8D **60**
Court Hey L31: Mag ... 2K **35**
Court Hey Av. L36: Roby ... 7E **60**
Court Hey Dr. L16: Child ... 8D **60**
Court Hey Pk. ... 9D **60**
Court Hey Rd. L16: Child ... 8D **60**
Courthope Rd. L4: W'ton ... 8G **44**
Court Ho., The
CH65: Ell P ... 8A **104**
Courtier Cl. L5: Liv ... 5D **58**
Courtland Rd. L18: Moss H ... 3N **75**
Court M. PR9: South ... 6M **7**
Courtney Av.
CH44: Wall ... 6G **56**
Courtney Rd. CH42: Rock F ... 8N **73**
Court Rd. PR9: South ... 7H **7**
Courtyard, The CH2: Elt ... 2M **113**
CH64: Will ... 6M **101**
L18: Moss H ... 5L **75**
PR8: South ... 8G 6
(off Lord St.)
WA12: Newt W ... 6N 51
(off Golborne St.)
Courtyard Works L33: Know I ... 8G **36**
Cousin's La. L40: Ruf ... 3L **15**
Covent Gdn. L2: Liv ... 4D **4** (8B **58**)
Coventry Av. CH66: Gt Sut ... 5K **111**
L30: Neth ... 1E **44**
Coventry Rd. L15: Wavtr ... 2M **75**
Coventry St. CH41: Birke ... 2K **73**
Coverdale Av. L35: Rainh ... 6G **63**
Coverdale Cl. WA5: Gt San ... 1H **81**
Covert Cl. PR8: South ... 4F **12**
Covertside CH48: W Kir ... 6E **70**
Covertside Rd. PR8: South ... 4F **12**
Covington Dr. WA9: St H ... 4L **63**
Cowan Dr. L6: Liv ... 5F **58**
Cowan Way WA8: Widnes ... 3J **79**
Cowdell St. WA2: Warr ... 1C **82**
Cowdrey Av. CH43: Bid ... 8C **56**
Cow Hey La. WA7: Clftn ... 1K **107**
(not continuous)
Cow La. CH66: Lit Sut ... 8H **103**
Cowley Cl. CH49: Upton ... 3L **71**
Cowley Ct. WA10: St H ... 5H **49**
COWLEY HILL ... 5J **49**
Cowley Hill La. WA10: St H ... 5J **49**
Cowley Rd. L4: W'ton ... 9E **44**
Cowley St. WA10: St H ... 5K **49**
Cowper Rd. L13: Liv ... 6N **59**
Cowper St. L20: Boot ... 5N **43**
WA9: St H ... 9M **49**
Cowper Way L36: Huy ... 8L **61**
Coxfield Gro. WN6: Shev ... 6N **23**
Coxheath CH42: Rock F ... 7N **73**
Coyford Dr. PR9: South ... 3M **7**
Coylton Av. L35: Rainh ... 7G **63**
Crab La. WA2: Fearn ... 6H **67**
Crab St. WA10: St H ... 6J **49**
Crab Tree Cl. L24: Hale ... 5B **94**
Crabtree Cl. L27: N'ley ... 3J **77**
L40: Burs ... 1H **21**
WA12: Newt W ... 7N **51**
Crabtree Fold WA7: Nort ... 7E **96**
Crabtree La. L40: Burs ... 9F **14**
WA13: Lymm ... 9G **85**
WA16: High L ... 9G **85**
Cradley WA8: Widnes ... 6F **78**
Crag Gro. WA11: St H ... 1L **49**
Craigburn Rd. L13: Liv ... 3K **59**
Craig Gdns. CH66: Ell P ... 7K **103**
Craig Hall M44: Irlam ... 2M **69**
Craighurst Rd. L25: Gate ... 1E **76**
Craigleigh Gro. CH62: East ... 2E **102**
Craigmore Rd. L18: Moss H ... 7M **75**
Craigside Av. L12: W Der ... 2M **59**
Craigs Rd. L13: Liv ... 3K **59**
Craigwood Way L36: Huy ... 6F **60**
Craine Cl. L4: W'ton ... 1G **59**
Cramond Av. L18: Moss H ... 3L **75**
Cranage Cl. WA7: Run ... 8N **95**
Cranberry Cl. L27: N'ley ... 2J **77**
WA10: St H ... 5J **49**
Cranberry Ct. WN4: Ash M ... 3H **41**
Cranberry Rd. M31: Part ... 6M **69**
Cranborne Av. WA4: Warr ... 7B **82**
Cranborne Rd. L15: Wavtr ... 1J **75**
Cranbourne Av. CH41: Birke ... 1G **72**
CH46: More ... 1L **71**
CH47: Meols ... 8F **54**
Cranbrook Av. WN4: Ash M ... 7J **41**
Crane Av. WA9: Sut L ... 3N **63**
Cranehurst Rd. L4: W'ton ... 8G **45**
Cranes La. L40: Lath ... 6H **21**
Cranfield Rd. L23: Crosb ... 6N **33**
WN3: Wigan ... 1J **41**
Cranford Cl. CH62: East ... 2E **102**
Cranford Ct. WA1: Wools ... 9M **67**
Cranford Rd. L19: G'dale ... 8N **75**
Cranford St. CH44: Wall ... 7J **57**
Cranham Av. WA3: Low ... 3F **52**
CRANK ... 7H **39**
Crank Hill WA11: Crank ... 7H **39**
Crank Rd. WA11: Crank, St H ... 3F **48**
WA11: Kings M ... 5J **39**
WN5: Bil ... 3M **39**
Cranleigh Cl. WA4: Stockt H ... 9C **82**
Cranleigh Gdns. L23: Crosb ... 7K **33**
Cranleigh Pl. L25: Gate ... 2E **76**
Cranleigh Rd. L25: Gate ... 2E **76**
Cranmer St. L5: Liv ... 4B **58**
(not continuous)
Cranmore Av. L23: Crosb ... 9L **33**
Cranshaw Av. WA9: Clock F ... 6N **63**
Cranshaw La. WA8: Widnes ... 3L **79**
Cranston Cl. WA10: St H ... 5F **48**
Cranston Rd. L33: Know I ... 9G **37**
Cranswick Grn. CH66: Lit Sut ... 9H **103**
Crantock Cl. L11: Crox ... 6A **46**
L26: Halew ... 8K **77**
Crantock Gro. WA10: Windle ... 3F **48**
Cranwell Av. WA3: Cul ... 6N **53**
Cranwell Cl. L10: Aintr ... 9H **35**
Cranwell Rd. CH49: Grea ... 5J **71**
L25: Gate ... 1E **76**
Cranwell Wlk. *L25: Gate ... 1E 76*
(off Cranwell Rd.)

Crask Wlk.—Cumberland Gro.

Crask Wlk. L33: Kirkb 7D 36
Craven Av. WA3: Low 3F 52
Craven Cl. CH41: Birke 2K 73
Craven Ct. WA2: Winw 5A 66
Craven Lea L12: Crox 7C 46
Craven Rd. L12: W Der 2A 60
L35: Rainh 6F 62
Craven St. CH41: Birke 2J 73
L3: Liv 3J 5 (7D 58)
CRAWFORD 1G 38
Crawford Av. L18: Moss H 3L 75
L31: Mag 9G 27
WA8: Widnes 7E 78
Crawford Cl. L12: W Der 2B 60
WA9: Clock F 5N 63
Crawford Dr. L15: Wavtr 8M 59
Crawford Gdns. L36: Huy 5H 61
Crawford Pk. L18: Moss H 5L 75
Crawford Pl. WA7: Run 9L 95
Crawford Rd. WN8: Skel 2F 38
Crawford St. WA9: Clock F 5A 64
Crawford Way L7: Liv 7L 59
Crawley Av. WA2: Warr 6B 66
Crawshaw Ct. L36: Huy 5F 60
Crediton Av. PR9: South 2N 7
Crediton Cl. L11: Crox 5A 46
Creek, The CH45: Wall 1E 56
Cremona Cnr. L22: Wloo 1L 43
(off South Rd.)
Cremorne Hey L28: Stockb V 2F 60
Creola Ct. WA5: Gt San 2K 81
(off Louisiana Dr.)
Crescent, The CH48: W Kir 6B 70
CH49: Grea 5L 71
CH60: Hesw 9B 88
CH61: Pens 1N 87
CH63: H Beb 2L 89
CH65: Gt Sut 9L 103
L20: Boot 4D 44
L22: Wloo 1L 43
L23: Thorn 5N 33
L24: Speke 3G 92
L31: Mag 4H 35
L35: Whis 5C 62
L36: Huy 7L 61
PR9: South 4A 8
WA13: Lymm 6F 84
Crescent Av. L37: Form 3E 24
WN4: Ash M 7J 41
Crescent Ct. L21: Sea 4N 43
Crescent Dr. WA6: Hel 2E 114
Crescent Grn. L39: Augh 3N 27
Crescent Rd. CH44: Wall 5J 57
CH65: Ell P 8B 104
L9: W'ton 6G 44
L21: Sea 4N 43
L23: Blun 6H 33
PR8: Birkd 3M 11
Crescent Row WA7: Run 5J 95
(off Hankey St.)
Crescents, The L35: Rainh 5D 62
Crescent Wlk. CH48: W Kir 6B 70
(off The Crescent)
Cressbrook Rd. WA4: Stockt H 7D 82
Cressida Av. CH63: H Beb 9L 73
Cressingham Rd. CH45: New B 1H 57
Cressington Av. CH42: Tran 7K 73
Cressington Esplanade L19: G'dale 1M 91
Cressington Gdns. CH65: Ell P 8A 104
CRESSINGTON PARK 9M 75
Cressington Station (Rail) 9M 75
Cresson Ct. CH43: Oxton 3F 72
Cresswell Cl. L26: Halew 7L 77
WA5: Call 7M 65
Cresswell St. L6: Liv 1L 5 (5E 58)
(not continuous)
Cresta Dr. WA7: W'ton 9J 95
Cresttor Rd. L25: Woolt 5D 76
Crestwood Av. WN3: Wigan 1G 41
Creswell St. WA10: St H 7H 49
Cretan Rd. L15: Wavtr 1J 75
Crete Towers L5: Kirkd 3D 58
Crewe Grn. CH49: Wdchu 6A 72
Crewood Comn. Rd. CW8: K'ly 9J 109
Criccieth Ct. CH65: Ell P 3B 112
Cricket Cl. L19: Garst 3B 92
Cricket Path L37: Form 8F 16
PR8: Birkd 3M 11
Cricklade Cl. L20: Boot 6A 44
Criftin Cl. CH66: Gt Sut 3H 111
Cringles Dr. L35: Tar G 1L 77
CRISP DELF 1J 31
Crispin Rd. L27: N'ley 3J 77
Crispin St. WA10: St H 7H 49
Critchley Rd. L24: Speke 5L 93
Critchley Way L33: Kirkb 7D 36
Croasdale Dr. WA7: Beech 1A 108
WN8: Parb 2F 22
Crockett's Wlk. WA10: Ec'stn 5E 48
Crockleford Av. PR8: South 3D 12
Crocus Av. CH41: Birke 1F 72
Crocus Gdns. WA9: Bold 2C 64
Crocus St. L5: Kirkd 2C 58
Croesmere Dr. CH66: Gt Sut 3J 111
CROFT 2H 67
Croft, The CH49: Grea 6L 71
L12: W Der 2N 59
L28: Stockb V 1E 60
L31: Lydi 7G 27
L32: Kirkb 3D 46
WA7: Hal 6B 96
Croft, The WA9: St H 9B 50
WN5: Bil 8N 31
Croft Av. CH62: Brom 6B 90
L40: Burs 2K 21
WN5: Orr 7N 31
Croft Av. E. CH62: Brom 5C 90
Croft Bus. Cen. CH62: Brom 5D 90
Croft Bus. Pk. CH62: Brom 5D 90
Croft Cl. CH43: Noct 4E 72
CH62: Brom 6C 90
Croft Cotts. CH66: Chil T 6F 102
(off School La.)
Croft Ct. CH65: Ell P 2C 112
WN7: Leigh 1K 53
Croft Dr. CH46: More 1M 71
CH48: Caldy 1D 86
Croft Dr. E. CH48: Caldy 9E 70
Croft Dr. W. CH48: Caldy 9D 70
Croft Edge CH43: Oxton 5H 73
Croft End WA9: St H 9B 50
Croften Dr. CH64: Lit N 9E 100
Crofters, The CH49: Grea 4L 71
Crofters Cl. CH66: Gt Sut 4K 111
Crofters Heath CH66: Gt Sut 4K 111
Crofters La. L33: Kirkb 6E 36
Croftfield L31: Mag 2K 35
Croft Gdns. WA4: Grap 9H 83
Croft Golf Cen. 3K 67
Croft Grn. CH62: Brom 4C 90
CROFT HEATH 1H 67
Croft Heath Gdns. WA3: Croft 1H 67
Croft Hey L40: Ruf 2M 15
Croft Heys L39: Augh 3N 27
Croft Ho. WA3: Croft 2H 67
Croftlands WN5: Orr 8N 31
Croft La. CH62: Brom 6C 90
L9: Aintr 3J 45
Crofton Cl. WA4: App T 2K 99
Crofton Cres. L13: Liv 6N 59
Crofton Gdns. WA3: Cul 7M 53
Crofton Rd. CH42: Tran 5L 73
L13: Liv 6N 59
WA7: Run 6H 95
Croft Retail & Leisure Pk. 4C 90
Croftside WA1: Wools 1N 83
Croftson Av. L39: Orm 7D 20
Croft St. WA3: Golb 2B 52
WA8: Widnes 1K 95
Croftsway CH60: Hesw 7L 87
Croft Technology Pk. CH62: Brom 6E 90
Croft Trade Pk. CH62: Brom 5D 90
Croft Way L23: Thorn 6A 34
Croftwood Gro. L35: Whis 7B 62
Cromarty Rd. CH44: Wall 5F 56
L13: Liv 6L 59
Cromdale Gro. WA9: St H 8A 50
Cromdale Way WA5: Gt San 2G 80
Cromer Dr. CH45: Wall 4G 57
Cromer Rd. CH47: Hoy 1B 70
L17: Aig 7K 75
PR8: Birkd 4L 11
Cromer Way L26: Halew 1K 93
Cromfield L39: Augh 2A 28
Cromford Rd. L36: Huy 4J 61
Crompton Ct. L3: Liv 1K 5
L18: Moss H 3B 76
WN4: Ash M 9K 41
Crompton Dr. L12: Crox 7C 46
WA2: Winw 3B 66
Cromptons La. L18: Moss H 4B 76
Crompton St. L5: Liv 4C 58
Crompton Way WA3: Low 2J 53
Cromwell Av. WA2: Warr 7L 65
WA5: Gt San, Old H, Westb 7L 65
Cromwell Av. Sth. WA5: Gt San 4L 81
Cromwell Cl. L39: Augh 2A 28
WA12: Newt W 6J 51
Cromwell Ct. M44: Irlam 2L 69
WA1: Warr 3B 82
(off Dixon St.)
Cromwell Rd. CH65: Ell P 9A 104
L4: W'ton 8E 44
M44: Irlam 2L 69
Cromwell St. WA8: Widnes 1K 95
Crondall Gro. L15: Wavtr 1N 75
CRONTON 3F 78
Cronton Av. CH46: Leas 6N 55
L35: Whis 8N 61
Cronton Farm Ct. WA8: Widnes 4H 79
Cronton La. L35: Rainh 8E 62
WA8: Cron 1E 78
WA8: Widnes 3H 79
Cronton La. M. WA8: Widnes 3J 79
Cronton Pk. Av. WA8: Cron 2F 78
Cronton Pk. Cl. WA8: Cron 2F 78
Cronton Rd. L15: Wavtr 3M 75
L35: Tar G 1L 77
WA8: Cron, Widnes 3E 78
Cronulla Dr. WA5: Gt San 1F 80
Crookall St. WN4: Ash M 7L 41
Crookhurst Av. WN5: Bil 5N 39
Croome Dr. CH48: W Kir 6D 70
Croppers Hill Ct. WA10: St H 8H 49
(off Prescot Rd.)
Croppers La. L39: Bic 3D 28
Croppers Rd. WA2: Fearn 6G 67
Cropper St. L1: Liv 6H 5 (8D 58)
Cropton Rd. L37: Form 1F 24
CROSBY 2L 43
Crosby Av. WA5: Warr 9A 66
Crosby Civic Hall (Theatre) 1L 43
Crosby Cl. CH49: Upton 2N 71
Crosby Coastal Pk. 1J 43 (2F 32)
Crosby Grn. L12: W Der 2M 59
Crosby Gro. CH64: Will 5A 102
WA10: St H 9G 49
Crosby Lakeside Adventure Cen. 2K 43
Crosby Leisure Cen. 9H 33
Crosby Rd. PR8: Birkd 3M 11
Crosby Rd. Nth. L22: Wloo 9L 33
Crosby Rd. Sth. L21: Sea 2L 43
L22: Wloo 2L 43
Crosender Rd. L23: Crosb 8J 33
Crosfield Cl. L7: Liv 8H 59
Crosfield Rd. CH44: Wall 6J 57
L7: Liv 8H 59
L35: Presc 5C 62
Crosfield St. WA1: Warr 3B 82
Crosfield Wlk. L7: Liv 8H 59
(off Crosfield Cl.)
Crosgrove Rd. L4: W'ton 9H 45
Crosland Dr. WA6: Hel 3D 114
Crosland Rd. L32: Kirkb 1E 46
Cross, The CH62: Brom 6D 90
CH64: Nest 6E 100
L38: Ince B 9K 25
WA13: Lymm 5E 84
Crossacre Rd. L25: Gate 1F 76
Cross Barn La. L38: Ince B 1L 33
Crossdale Rd. CH62: Brom 9C 90
L23: Crosb 8J 33
Crossdale Way WA11: St H 1L 49
CROSSENS 3A 8
Crossens Way PR9: South 1A 8
Cross Farm Rd. WA9: St H 9M 49
Crossfield Av. WA3: Cul 8N 53
WA13: Lymm 5F 84
Crossfield Rd. WN8: Skel 4F 30
Crossfield St. WA9: St H 7L 49
Crossford Rd. L14: Knott A 3E 60
Cross Gates WA8: Widnes 5B 80
Cross Grn. L37: Form 2G 24
Cross Grn. Cl. L37: Form 2G 24
Crosshall Brow L39: Orm 8F 20
L40: Westh 8F 20
Cross Hall Ct. L39: Orm 9E 20
Crosshall St. L1: Liv 4F 4 (7C 58)
Cross Hey L21: Ford 9A 34
L31: Mag 4K 35
Cross Hey Av. CH43: Noct 3D 72
Cross Hillocks La. WA8: Widnes 6B 78
Crossings, The WA12: Newt W 7L 51
Crossland M. WA13: Lymm 4B 84
Crossland Ter. WA6: Hel 3E 114
Cross La. CH45: Wall 4D 56
CH63: Beb 3M 89
CH64: Lit N 9E 100
L35: Presc, Whis 5A 62
L39: Hals 4G 19
WA3: Croft 2K 67
WA4: Grap 6H 83
WA6: Frod 6E 106
WA12: Newt W 7K 51
WN5: Bil 9N 31
Cross La. E. M31: Part 7M 69
Cross La. Sth. WA3: Ris 3M 67
Cross La. W. M31: Part 7M 69
Crossledge Way L25: Gate 1D 76
Crossley Av. CH66: Ell P 8K 103
Crossley Dr. CH60: Hesw 7L 87
L15: Wavtr 9M 59
Crossley Pk. WA6: Kgswd 6M 115
Crossley Rd. WA10: St H 1G 62
Crossley St. WA1: Warr 3D 82
Cross Mdw. Ct. WA9: St H 8M 49
(off Appleton Rd.)
Cross Meanygate L40: H'wood 1F 14
Cross Pit La. WA11: Rainf 5C 38
Cross St. CH41: Birke 2M 73
CH62: Port S 2A 90
CH64: Nest 6E 100
L22: Wloo 1K 43
L34: Presc 2B 62
PR8: South 9G 6
WA2: Warr 1C 82
WA3: Golb 3B 52
WA7: Run 4K 95
WA8: Widnes 7L 79
(not continuous)
WA10: St H 7K 49
Crossvale Rd. L36: Huy 8J 61
Crossway CH43: Bid 9E 56
WA8: Widnes 8G 78
Crossway, The CH63: Raby 2J 101
Crossway Cl. WN4: Ash M 6N 41
Crossway Ct. WA8: Widnes 7G 78
Crossways CH62: Brom 4C 90
L25: Gate 2D 76
Crosswood Cres. L36: Huy 6G 61
Crosthwaite Av. CH62: East 2E 102
Croston Av. L35: Rainh 4E 62
Croston Cl. WA8: Widnes 5F 78
Croston's Brow PR9: South 4L 7
Crouchley Hall M. WA13: Lymm 7F 84
Crouchley La. WA13: Lymm 6E 84
Crouch St. L5: Liv 3F 58
WA9: St H 1N 63
CROUGHTON 8D 112
Croughton Ct. CH66: Ell P 6L 103
Croughton Rd. CH2: Crou, Stoak 7D 112
(not continuous)
CH66: Ell P 6L 103
Crowe Av. WA2: Warr 7C 66
Crow Ho Farm Dr. WA12: Newt W 6K 51
Crowland Cl. PR9: South 9M 7
Crowland St. PR9: South 1E 12
Crowland St. Ind. Est. PR9: South 9M 7
Crowland Way L37: Form 2H 25
Crow La. WN8: Dalt 1J 31
Crow La. E. WA12: Newt W 6K 51
Crow La. W. WA12: Newt W 6H 51
Crowley La. CW9: Ant 4N 99
WA16: High L 4N 99
Crowmarsh Cl. CH49: Upton 4N 71
Crown Acres Rd. L25: Woolt 8G 76
Crown Av. WA8: Widnes 8E 78
Crown Cl. L37: Form 2G 24
Crown Court
Liverpool 6E 4
Warrington 3B 82
Crown Flds. Cl. WA12: Newt W 5K 51
Crownford Cres. WA4: Warr 6D 82
Crown Gdns. WA12: Newt W 6K 51
Crown Ga. WA7: Pal F 8B 96
Crown Grn. WA13: Lymm 5H 85
Crown Pk. Dr. WA12: Newt W 5K 51
Crown Rd. L12: W Der 2A 60
Crown Sta. Pl. L7: Liv 7N 5 (9F 58)
Crown St. L7: Liv 4L 5 (7E 58)
(Elizabeth St., not continuous)
L7: Liv 7N 5 (9F 58)
(Oxford St. E.)
L8: Liv 7N 5 (9F 58)
WA1: Warr 3C 82
WA9: St H 2G 63
WA12: Newt W 7J 51
Crownway L36: Huy 5H 61
Crown Wood Ct. WN2: Bam 4N 41
(off Fourth St.)
Crow St. L8: Liv 2C 74
Crowther Dr. WN3: Winst 2G 40
Crowther St. WA10: St H 7H 49
CROW WOOD 6N 79
Crow Wood La. WA8: Widnes 6N 79
Crow Wood Pl. WA8: Widnes 5N 79
Crow Wood Rd. WA3: Low 1E 52
Croxdale Rd. L14: Knott A 2E 60
Croxdale Rd. W. L14: Knott A 2D 60
CROXTETH 6A 46
Croxteth Av. CH44: Wall 5H 57
L21: Lith 3N 43
Croxteth Cl. L31: Mag 9K 27
Croxteth Ct. L8: Liv 2G 75
Croxteth Dr. L17: Aig 3H 75
WA11: Rainf 4C 38
Croxteth Ga. L17: Aig 3H 75
Croxteth Gro. L8: Liv 2H 75
Croxteth Hall 9B 46
Croxteth Hall Country Pk. 9C 46
Croxteth Hall La. L11: Crox 7A 46
L12: Crox, W Der 8A 46
Croxteth La. L34: Know 9F 46
CROXTETH PARK 7D 46
Croxteth Rd. L8: Liv 2G 74
L20: Boot 5A 44
Croxteth Vw. L32: Kirkb 3D 46
Croxton Ct. PR9: South 6K 7
Croyde Cl. PR9: South 2N 7
Croyde Pl. WA9: Sut L 5M 63
Croyde Rd. L24: Speke 4L 93
Croydon Av. L18: Moss H 3L 75
Croylands St. L4: Kirkd 1D 58
Crucian Way L12: Crox 7B 46
Crump St. L1: Liv 1D 74
Crutchley Av. CH41: Birke 9H 57
Cryers La. CH2: Thorn M 6K 113
Crystal Cl. L13: Liv 7M 59
Cubbin Cres. L5: Kirkd 3C 58
Cubert Rd. L11: Crox 6A 46
Cuckoo Cl. L25: Gate 4E 76
Cuckoo La. CH64: Lit N, Nest 8H 101
L25: Gate 3E 76
Cuckoo Way L25: Gate 4E 76
Cuerden St. L3: Liv 3G 4 (7C 58)
CUERDLEY CROSS 6C 80
Cuerdley Grn. WA5: Cuerd 5C 80
Cuerdley Rd. WA5: Penk 5E 80
Cuerdon Dr. WA4: Thel 7L 83
Culbin Cl. WA3: Birchw 3A 68
CULCHETH 7N 53
Culcheth Hall Dr. WA3: Cul 6N 53
Culcheth Hall Farm WA3: Cul 6N 53
Culcheth Linear Country Pk. 6J 53
Culcheth Sports Club 7N 53
Culford Cl. WA7: Wind H 6F 96
Cullen Av. L20: Boot 5C 44
Cullen Cl. CH63: East 2C 102
Cullen Dr. L21: Lith 3N 43
Cullen Rd. WA7: West P 8G 95
Cullen St. L8: Liv 1H 75
Culme Rd. L12: W Der 2L 59
Culshaw Way L40: Scar 7L 13
Culvert La. WN8: Newb 3D 22
Culzean Cl. L12: Crox 7C 46
Cumberland Av. CH43: Pren 6G 72
L17: Liv 2J 75
L30: Neth 8B 34
M44: Cad 5J 69
WA10: St H 1E 62
Cumberland Cl. L6: Liv 2J 59
Cumberland Cres. WA11: Hay 4C 50
Cumberland Ga. L30: Neth 7F 34
Cumberland Gro. CH66: Gt Sut 2H 111

Cumberland Rd.—Deansgreen

Cumberland Rd. CH45: New B ... 2J 57
M31: Part ... 7L 69
PR8: South ... 1C 12
Cumberland St. L1: Liv ... 4E 4 (7B 58)
WA4: Warr ... 5D 82
Cumber La. L35: Whis ... 5C 62
Cumbers Dr. CH64: Ness ... 9G 100
Cumbers La. CH64: Ness ... 9G 100
Cumbrae Dr. CH65: Ell P ... 5A 112
Cumbria Cl. CH66: Gt Sut ... 4K 111
Cumbria Way L12: W Der ... 9A 46
Cummings St. L1: Liv ... 8H 5 (9D 58)
Cummins Av. L37: Form ... 8E 16
Cumpsty Rd. L21: Lith ... 1B 44
Cunard Av. CH44: Wall ... 4K 57
Cunard Cl. CH43: Bid ... 2C 72
Cunard Rd. L21: Lith ... 3A 44
Cunliffe Av. WA12: Newt W ... 5K 51
Cunliffe Cl. WA7: Pal F ... 8C 96
Cunliffe St. L2: Liv ... 3E 4 (7B 58)
Cunningham Cl. CH48: Caldy ... 1D 86
WA5: Gt San ... 3H 81
Cunningham Ct. WA10: St H ... 7F 48
Cunningham Dr. CH63: Brom ... 8B 90
WA7: Run ... 7H 95
(not continuous)
Cunningham Rd. L13: Liv ... 7M 59
WA8: Widnes ... 8G 79
Cunscough La. L31: Mag ... 1B 36
Cuper Cres. L36: Huy ... 5H 61
Curate Rd. L6: Liv ... 2H 59
Curlender Cl. CH41: Birke ... 8E 56
Curlender Way L24: Hale ... 5B 94
Curlew Av. CH49: Upton ... 2L 71
Curlew Cl. CH49: Upton ... 2L 71
WA3: Low ... 2E 52
Curlew Ct. CH46: More ... 8K 55
Curlew Gro. L26: Halew ... 7J 77
WA3: Birchw ... 6M 67
Curlew La. L40: Burs, Ruf ... 6H 15
Curlew Way CH46: More ... 8K 55
Currans Rd. WA2: Warr ... 7C 66
Curran Way L33: Kirkb ... 6B 36
Curtana Cres. L11: Crox ... 7A 46
Curtis Rd. L4: W'ton ... 9H 45
Curwell Cl. CH63: Spit ... 4A 90
Curzon Av. CH41: Birke ... 1H 73
CH45: New B ... 1H 57
Curzon Dr. WA4: Grap ... 9H 83
Curzon Pl. *WA12: Newt W* ... *7K 51*
(off King St.)
Curzon Rd. CH42: Tran ... 6H 73
CH47: Hoy ... 1B 70
L22: Wloo ... 1L 43
PR8: South ... 1C 12
Curzon St. WA7: Run ... 6J 95
Cusson Rd. L33: Know I ... 1F 46
Custley Hey L28: Stockb V ... 1F 60
Custom Ho. Pl. L1: Liv ... 7E 4 (9B 58)
Cut La. L33: Kirkb ... 3J 47
L39: Hals ... 5L 19
Cygnet Cl. CH66: Gt Sut ... 1J 111
L39: Augh ... 2A 28
Cygnet Ct. CH41: Birke ... 1K 73
L33: Kirkb ... 9E 36
WA1: Warr ... 5B 82
Cygnet Gdns. WA9: St H ... 8A 50
Cynthia Av. WA1: Wools ... 1J 83
Cynthia Rd. WA7: Run ... 6J 95
Cypress Av. CH66: Gt Sut ... 4L 111
WA8: Widnes ... 5L 79
Cypress Cl. L31: Mell ... 8M 35
WA1: Wools ... 1M 83
Cypress Cft. CH63: Spit ... 4A 90
Cypress Gdns. WA9: St H ... 2F 62
Cypress Gro. WA7: Run ... 8M 95
Cypress Rd. L36: Huy ... 9H 61
PR8: South ... 9K 7
Cyprian's Way L30: Neth ... 8D 34
Cyprus Gro. L8: Liv ... 4F 74
Cyprus St. L34: Presc ... 3A 62
Cyprus Ter. CH45: New B ... 2H 57
Cyril Bell Cl. WA13: Lymm ... 5F 84
Cyril Gro. L17: Aig ... 6K 75
Cyril St. WA2: Warr ... 1C 82

D

DACRE HILL ... 8M 73
Dacre's Bri. La. L35: Tar G ... 1A 78
Dacre St. CH41: Birke ... 2L 73
L20: Boot ... 9A 44
Dacy Rd. L5: Liv ... 4F 58
Daffodil Cl. WA8: Widnes ... 4A 80
Daffodil Gdns. WA9: Bold ... 2C 64
Daffodil Rd. CH41: Birke ... 1F 72
L15: Wavtr ... 2N 75
Dagnall Av. WA5: Warr ... 7A 66
Dagnall Rd. L32: Kirkb ... 1A 46
Dahlia Cl. L9: W'ton ... 6G 45
WA9: Bold ... 2C 64
Dailton Rd. WN8: Uph ... 5K 31
Dairy Bank CH2: Elt ... 1M 113
Dairy Farm Cl. WA13: Lymm ... 5F 84
Dairy Farm Rd. WA11: Rainf ... 5M 37
Dairylands Cl. L16: Moss H ... 2A 76
Daisy Av. WA12: Newt W ... 8L 51
Daisy Bank Mill Cl. WA3: Cul ... 7M 53
Daisy Bank Rd. WA5: Penk ... 4H 81
WA13: Lymm ... 5C 84
Daisy Cl. PR9: Banks ... 3E 8
Daisy Gro. *L7: Liv* ... *8G 59*
(off Dorothy Dr.)
Daisy La. L40: Lath ... 1M 21
Daisy M. L21: Lith ... 4A 44
Daisy Mt. L31: Mag ... 3K 35
Daisy St. L5: Kirkd ... 2C 58
Daisy Wlk. CH44: Wall ... 6H 57
PR8: South ... *8K 7*
(off Beacham Rd.)
Daisy Way PR8: South ... 4B 12
Dakin Wlk. L33: Kirkb ... 9D 36
Dakota Bus. Pk. L19: Speke ... 3C 92
Dakota Dr. L24: Speke ... 4B 92
WA5: Gt San ... 1L 81
Dalby Cl. WA3: Birchw ... 4B 68
WA11: St H ... 5M 49
Dalcross Way L11: Crox ... 6N 45
Dale, The CH64: Nest ... 8D 100
WA5: Gt San, Penk ... 3H 81
Dale Acre Dr. L30: Neth ... 8B 34
Dale Av. CH60: Hesw ... 6N 87
CH62: Brom ... 7C 90
CH66: Lit Sut ... 8H 103
Dalebrook Cl. L25: Gate ... 1F 76
Dale Cl. L31: Mag ... 1H 35
WA5: Warr ... 4N 81
WA8: Widnes ... 8D 78
WN8: Parb ... 3E 22
Dale Ct. CH60: Hesw ... 7N 87
Dale Cres. WA9: Sut L ... 3N 63
Dalecrest WN5: Bil ... 2N 39
Dale Cft. WA6: Haps ... 4B 114
Dale Dr. CH65: Gt Sut ... 9L 103
Dale End Rd. CH61: Barns ... 3C 88
Dale Gdns. CH60: Hesw ... 6L 87
CH65: Whit ... 2N 111
Dalegarth Av. L12: W Der ... 9D 46
Dale Gro. M44: Cad ... 3L 69
Dale Hall L18: Moss H ... 6L 75
Dalehead Pl. WA11: St H ... 1L 49
Dale Hey CH44: Wall ... 6H 57
CH66: Hoot ... 4D 102
Dalehurst Cl. CH44: Wall ... 5K 57
Dale La. L33: Kirkb ... 6E 36
WA4: App ... 8F 82
(not continuous)
Dalemeadow Rd. L14: Knott A ... 6B 60
Dale M. L25: Gate ... 4F 76
Dale Rd. CH62: Brom ... 9C 90
WA3: Golb ... 3B 52
DALES, THE ... 7M 87
Dales, The CH46: More ... 9A 56
Dalesford Cl. WN7: Leigh ... 2K 53
Daleside Av. WN4: Ash M ... 3J 41
Daleside Cl. CH61: Irby ... 1N 87
Daleside Rd. L33: Kirkb ... 8D 36
Daleside Wlk. L33: Kirkb ... 8D 36
Dales Row L36: Huy ... 7M 61
Dale St. L2: Liv ... 4E 4 (7B 58)
L19: Garst ... 2A 92
WA7: Run ... 6K 95
Dales Wlk. L37: Form ... 7G 16
Dalesway CH60: Hesw ... 7M 87
Dale Vw. WA12: Newt W ... 6N 51
Dale Vw. Cl. CH61: Pens ... 2A 88
Dalewood L12: Crox ... 7C 46
Dalewood Cl. WA2: Warr ... 2B 82
Dalewood Cres. CH2: Elt ... 2L 113
Dalewood Gdns. L35: Whis ... 7C 62
Daley Pl. L20: Boot ... 3D 44
Daley Rd. L21: Lith ... 1B 44
DALLAM ... 7A 66
Dallam Ct. WA2: Warr ... 1B 82
Dallam La. WA2: Warr ... 1B 82
Dallas Dr. WA5: Gt San ... 1J 81
Dallas Gro. L9: Aintr ... 4F 44
Dallington Ct. L13: Liv ... 7N 59
Dalmeny St. L17: Aig ... 5G 75
Dalmorton Rd. CH45: New B ... 1H 57
Dalry Cres. L32: Kirkb ... 3D 46
Dalry Wlk. L32: Kirkb ... 3D 46
Dalston Dr. WA11: St H ... 1L 49
Dalston Gro. WN3: Winst ... 1F 40
DALTON ... 7F 22
Dalton Av. WA3: Ris ... 3M 67
WA5: Warr ... 1A 82
Dalton Bank WA1: Warr ... 2D 82
Dalton Cl. L12: W Der ... 8A 46
Dalton Ct. WA7: Astm ... 4A 96
Dalton Dr. WN3: Winst ... 1G 40
Dalton Gro. WN4: Ash M ... 7J 41
Dalton Rd. CH45: New B ... 2J 57
Dalton St. WA3: Ris ... 4M 67
WA7: Run ... 5N 95
Daltry Cl. L12: W Der ... 2M 59
Dalwood Cl. WA7: Murd ... 8G 96
Damerham M. L25: Gate ... 1E 76
Damfield La. L31: Mag ... 2H 35
Dam Head La. WA3: Glaz, Rix ... 5F 68
Damhead La. CH64: Will ... 7K 101
Damian Dr. WA12: Newt W ... 5J 51
Dam La. L40: Scar ... 8N 13
WA1: Wools ... 1L 83
WA3: Croft ... 2G 66
WA3: Rix ... 4E 68
Damsel Way L8: Liv ... 3D 74
Damsire Cl. L9: Aintr ... 2H 45
Damson Gro. WA11: Rainf ... 4B 38
Damson Gro. Ct. WA11: Rainf ... 4B 38
Damson Rd. L27: N'ley ... 2J 77
Damson Wlk. *M31: Part* ... *6K 69*
(off Wood La.)
Dam Wood La. L40: Scar ... 9A 14
Damwood Rd. L24: Speke ... 5G 93
Danbers WN8: Uph ... 6J 31
Danby Cl. L5: Liv ... 4E 58
WA5: Warr ... 1N 81
WA7: Beech ... 9N 95
Danby Fold L35: Rainh ... 6E 62
Dandy's Meanygate PR4: Tarl ... 1M 9
Dane Av. M31: Part ... 5M 69
Dane Bank Rd. WA13: Lymm ... 5E 84
Dane Bank Rd. E. WA13: Lymm ... 4E 84
Dane Cl. CH61: Irby ... 1N 87
Dane Ct. L35: Rainh ... 6F 62
Danefield Pl. L19: Aller ... 8B 76
Danefield Rd. CH49: Grea ... 6K 71
L19: Aller ... 8B 76
Danefield Ter. *L19: Aller* ... *9B 76*
(off Mather Av.)
Danehurst Rd. CH45: Wall ... 2F 56
L9: Aintr ... 3G 44
Danesbury Cl. WN5: Bil ... 7A 40
Danescourt Rd. CH41: Birke ... 9G 57
L12: W Der ... 4A 60
Danescroft WA8: Widnes ... 5E 78
Daneshill Cl. L17: Aig ... 9L 75
Daneshill La. M44: Cad ... 4L 69
Danesmead Cl. L14: Knott A ... 5D 60
Dane St. L4: W'ton ... 9E 44
Daneswell Dr. CH46: More ... 8N 55
Daneswell Rd. L24: Speke ... 5L 93
Dane Vw. L33: Kirkb ... 8C 36
Daneville Rd. L4: W'ton ... 8J 45
Daneway PR8: Ainsd ... 8H 11
Danger La. CH46: More ... 7N 55
DANGEROUS CORNER ... 3M 23
Daniel Adamson Av. M31: Part ... 6K 69
Daniel Cl. L20: Boot ... 4N 43
WA3: Birchw ... 5A 68
Daniel Ct. M31: Part ... 5M 69
Daniel Davies Dr. L8: Liv ... 1F 74
Daniel Ho. L20: Boot ... 8B 44
Daniels La. WN8: Skel ... 5F 30
Dannette Hey L28: Stockb V ... 3G 60
Dansie St. L3: Liv ... 5K 5 (8E 58)
Dan's Rd. WA8: Widnes ... 6A 80
Dante Cl. L9: Aintr ... 2H 45
Danube St. L8: Liv ... 1H 75
Dapple Heath Av.
L31: Mell ... 8M 35
Darby Cl. CH64: Lit N ... 9E 100
Darby Gro. L19: Garst ... 1N 91
Darby Rd. L19: G'dale ... 8M 75
M44: Irlam ... 3N 69
Darcy Ct. CH62: Port S ... 2B 90
Darent Rd. WA11: Hay ... 3D 50
DARESBURY ... 5L 97
Daresbury Av. PR8: Ainsd ... 9G 11
Daresbury By-Pass ... 6K 97
Daresbury Cl. L32: Kirkb ... 9A 36
Daresbury Ct. WA8: Widnes ... 5N 79
Daresbury Expressway ... 5K 95
Daresbury La.
WA4: Dares, Hatt ... 5L 97
Daresbury Pk. WA4: Dares ... 7J 97
(not continuous)
Daresbury Rd. CH44: Wall ... 5G 57
WA10: Ec'stn ... 6E 48
Daresbury Science Pk. WA4: Dares ... 4K 97
Darfield WN8: Uph ... 5J 31
Daric Cl. WN7: Leigh ... 1K 53
Dark Ark La. WA6: Manl ... 9L 115
Dark Entry L34: Know P ... 9J 47
Dark La. L31: Mag ... 2J 35
L40: Lath ... 7F 20
WA4: H Whi ... 9E 98
Darkstar Ultimate Laser Arena
St Helens ... 6K 49
Darley Av. WA2: Warr ... 6F 66
Darley Cl. WA8: Widnes ... 5E 78
Darleydale Dr. CH62: East ... 1E 102
Darley Dr. L12: W Der ... 3A 60
Darley Rd. WN3: Wigan ... 1K 41
Darlington Cl. CH44: Wall ... 5K 57
Darlington Ct. WA8: Widnes ... 9K 79
Darlington St. CH44: Wall ... 5K 57
Darmond Rd. L33: Kirkb ... 8E 36
Darmond's Grn. CH48: W Kir ... 5C 70
Darmonds Grn. Av. L6: Liv ... 2J 59
Darnaway Cl. WA3: Birchw ... 3B 68
Darnley St. L8: Liv ... 3D 74
Darran Av. WN3: Wigan ... 1H 41
Darrel Dr. L7: Liv ... 1H 75
Darsefield Rd. L16: Child ... 1C 76
Dartford Cl. L14: Knott A ... 3D 60
Dartford Dr. L21: Lith ... 2B 44
Dartington Rd. L16: Child ... 9B 60
Dartmouth Av. L10: Aintr ... 9H 35
Dartmouth Dr. L30: Neth ... 7B 34
WA10: Windle ... 4F 48
Darvel Av. WN4: Garsw ... 7E 40
Darwall Rd. L19: Aller ... 8B 76
Darwen Gdns. WA2: Warr ... 8F 66
Darwen St. L5: Liv ... 4B 58
Darwick Dr. L36: Huy ... 9K 61
Darwin Ct. PR9: South ... 6K 7
Darwin Gro. WA9: St H ... 2H 63
Darwin Way CH65: Ell P ... 1B 112
Daryl Rd. CH60: Hesw ... 6A 88
Dashwood Cl. WA4: Grap ... 9H 83
Daten Av. WA3: Ris ... 3M 67
Daten Pk. WA3: Ris ... 3N 67
Daulby St. L3: Liv ... 4K 5 (7E 58)
Dauntsey Brow L25: Gate ... 1F 76
Dauntsey M. L25: Gate ... 1F 76
Davenham Av. CH43: Oxton ... 5F 72
WA1: Padg ... 9F 66
Davenham Cl. CH43: Oxton ... 6F 72
Davenham Ct. L15: Wavtr ... 1N 75
Davenham Rd. L37: Form ... 9F 16
Davenhill Pk. L10: Aintr ... 9H 35
Davenport Av. WA4: Westy ... 3G 83
Davenport Cl. CH48: Caldy ... 1D 86
Davenport Gro. L33: Kirkb ... 7C 36
Davenport Rd. CH60: Hesw ... 8M 87
Davenport Row WA7: Run ... 7N 95
Daventree Rd. CH45: Wall ... 4H 57
Daventry Rd. L17: Aig ... 6K 75
David Lewis St. L1: Liv ... 6F 4 (8C 58)
David Lloyd Leisure
Ellesmere Port ... 4B 112
Liverpool ... 1E 46
Speke ... 3C 92
Warrington ... 3L 81
David Rd. WA13: Lymm ... 5C 84
David's Av. WA5: Gt San ... 3K 81
Davidson Rd. L13: Liv ... 6L 59
David St. L8: Liv ... 4E 74
Davids Wlk. L25: Woolt ... 5G 76
Davies Av. WA4: Westy ... 4G 82
WA12: Newt W ... 5L 51
Davies Cl. WA8: Widnes ... 3K 95
Davies Rd. M31: Part ... 6N 69
Davies St. L1: Liv ... 4E 4 (7B 58)
L20: Boot ... 6C 44
WA9: St H ... 6M 49
Davies Way WA13: Lymm ... 5E 84
Davis Rd. CH46: Leas ... 6B 56
Davy Av. WA3: Ris ... 4N 67
Davy Cl. WA10: Ec'stn ... 5E 48
Davy Rd. WA7: Astm ... 4A 96
Davy St. L5: Liv ... 3F 58
Dawber Cl. L6: Liv ... 5F 58
Dawber Delf Ind. Area
WN6: App B ... 5N 23
Dawber Delph WN6: App B ... 5N 23
Dawber St. WN4: Ash M ... 7M 41
Dawley Cl. WN4: Ash M ... 8J 41
Dawlish Cl. L25: Hunts X ... 8G 77
WA3: Rix ... 6H 69
Dawlish Dr. PR9: South ... 2M 7
Dawlish Rd. CH44: Wall ... 5F 56
CH61: Irby ... 2K 87
Dawlish Way WA3: Golb ... 1A 52
Dawn Cl. CH64: Ness ... 9G 100
WA9: St H ... 2H 63
Dawn Gdns. CH65: Whit ... 1N 111
Dawn Wlk. *L10: Faz* ... *4N 45*
(off Panton Way)
Dawpool Cotts. CH48: Caldy ... 1H 87
Dawpool Dr. CH46: More ... 9M 55
CH62: Brom ... 8B 90
Dawpool Farm CH61: Thurs ... 2J 87
Dawson Av. CH41: Birke ... 9H 57
PR9: South ... 2A 8
WA9: St H ... 2N 63
Dawson Gdns. L31: Mag ... 1H 35
Dawson Ho. WA5: Gt San ... 2E 80
Dawson Rd. L39: Orm ... 6D 20
Dawson St. L1: Liv ... 5F 4 (8C 58)
Dawson Way L1: Liv ... 5G 4
Dawstone Ri. CH60: Hesw ... 8N 87
Dawstone Rd. CH60: Hesw ... 8N 87
Daybrook WN8: Uph ... 5J 31
Dayfield WN8: Uph ... 5K 31
Days Mdw. CH49: Grea ... 5K 71
Day St. L13: Liv ... 6M 59
Deacon Cl. L22: Wloo ... 2K 43
Deacon Ct. L22: Wloo ... 2K 43
L25: Woolt ... 6F 76
Deacon Pk. L33: Know I ... 2F 46
Deacon Rd. WA8: Widnes ... 7L 79
Deacons Cl. WA3: Croft ... 1H 67
Deakin St. CH41: Birke ... 9F 56
Deal Cl. WA5: Warr ... 1A 82
Dealcroft L25: Woolt ... 6D 76
Dean Av. CH45: Wall ... 3E 56
Dean Cl. M31: Part ... 5M 69
WA8: Widnes ... 8L 79
WN5: Bil ... 8N 39
WN8: Uph ... 5M 31
Dean Ct. WA3: Golb ... 3B 52
Dean Cres. WA2: Warr ... 7C 66
Dean Dillistone Ct. L1: Liv ... 9H 5
Deane Rd. L7: Liv ... 7H 59
Deanery Cl. L4: W'ton ... 8E 44
Dean Ho. L22: Wloo ... 2L 43
Deanland Dr. L24: Speke ... 3F 92
Dean Mdw. WA12: Newt W ... 6L 51
Dean Patey Ct.
L1: Liv ... 8H 5 (9D 58)
Dean Rd. M44: Cad ... 3L 69
WA3: Golb ... 3B 52
Deansburn Rd. L13: Liv ... 3K 59
Deanscales Rd. L11: Norr G ... 8L 45
Deans Ct. L37: Form ... 8F 16
Deansfield Way CH2: Elt ... 2L 113
Deansgate CH65: Ell P ... 9M 103
Deansgate La. L37: Form ... 8H 17
Deansgate La. Nth. L37: Form ... 7G 17
DEANSGREEN ... 9H 85

Deans La. L40: Lath 1B 22
WA4: Thel 5N 83
WN8: Newb 3C 22
Deans Rd. CH65: Ell P 2D 112
Dean St. L22: Wloo 2K 43
WA8: Widnes 8L 79
Deans Way CH41: Birke 9F 56
Deansway WA8: Widnes 8F 78
Deanwater Cl. WA3: Birchw 5L 67
Dean Wood Cl. WN8: Uph 5M 31
Deanwood Cl. L35: Whis 7C 62
Dean Wood Golf Course 4M 31
Dearden Way WN8: Uph 5K 31
Dearham Av. WA11: St H 3K 49
Dearne Cl. L12: W Der 4C 60
Dearnford Av. CH62: Brom 9C 90
Dearnford Cl. CH62: Brom 9C 90
Dearnley Av. WA11: St H 3A 50
Deauville Rd. L9: Aintr 3H 45
Debra Cl. CH66: Gt Sut 1H 111
L31: Mell 7N 35
Debra Rd. CH66: Gt Sut 2H 111
Decks, The WA7: Run 4K 95
Dee Cl. L33: Kirkb 5D 36
Dee Ct. L25: Gate 5G 76
Dee Ho. L25: Gate 5G 76
Dee La. CH48: W Kir 6B 70
Deeley Cl. L7: Liv 8H 59
Dee Pk. Cl. CH60: Hesw 9B 88
Dee Pk. Rd. CH60: Hesw 9B 88
Deepdale WA8: Widnes 5F 78
Deepdale Av. L20: Boot 5N 43
WA11: St H 1M 49
Deepdale Cl. CH43: Bid 2C 72
WA5: Gt San 2H 81
Deepdale Dr. L35: Rainh 6G 62
Deepdale Rd. L25: Gate 1E 76
Deepfield Dr. L36: Huy 9K 61
Deepfield Rd. L15: Wavtr 2L 75
Deepwood Gro. L35: Whis 7B 62
Deerbarn Dr. L30: Neth 7G 35
Deerbolt Cl. L32: Kirkb 8A 36
Deerbolt Cres. L32: Kirkb 8A 36
Deerbolt Way L32: Kirkb 8A 36
Deerbourne Cl. L25: Woolt 6D 76
Deerfield Cl. WA9: St H 6A 50
Dee Rd. L35: Rainh 6E 62
Deer Pk. Ct. WA7: Pal F 9A 96
Deerwood Cl. CH66: Lit Sut 7J 103
Deerwood Cres. CH66: Lit Sut 7J 103
Dee Sailing Club 2E 86
Deeside CH60: Hesw 7K 87
CH65: Whit 2N 111
Deeside Cl. CH43: Bid 2B 72
CH65: Whit 3N 111
Deeside Ct. CH64: P'gte 5B 100
Dee Vw. Ct. CH64: Nest 8E 100
Dee Vw. Rd. CH60: Hesw 7N 87
De Grouchy St. CH48: W Kir 5C 70
De-Haviland Way WN8: Skel 4H 31
De Havilland Dr. L24: Speke 3C 92
Deirdre Av. WA8: Widnes 7K 79
Dekker Rd. L33: Kirkb 5C 36
Delabole Rd. L11: Crox 5B 46
De Lacy Row WA7: Cas 5C 96
Delafield Cl. WA2: Fearn 6G 66
Delagoa Rd. L10: Faz 4L 45
Delamain Rd. L13: Liv 3K 59
Delamere Av. CH62: East 2D 102
CH66: Gt Sut 9K 103
WA3: Low 4F 52
WA8: Widnes 7F 78
WA9: Sut M 6K 63
Delamere Cl. CH43: Bid 2B 72
CH62: East 2D 102
L12: Crox 7B 46
Delamere Dr. CH66: Gt Sut 1K 111
Delamere Forest Pk. 9N 115
Delamere Grn. *CH66: Gt Sut* *1K 111*
(off Delamere Dr.)
Delamere Gro. *CH44: Wall* *7L 57*
(off Tudor Av.)
Delamere Ho. WA6: Frod 6M 107
Delamere Pl. WA7: Run 6J 95
Delamere Rd. PR8: Ainsd 9H 11
WN8: Skel 2C 30
Delamere St. WA5: Warr 3N 81
Delamere Way WN8: Uph 5K 31
Delamore Pl. L4: Kirkd 9D 44
Delamore's Acre CH64: Will 6N 101
Delamore St. L4: Kirkd 9D 44
Delavor Cl. CH60: Hesw 7M 87
Delavor Rd. CH60: Hesw 7L 87
Delaware Cres. L32: Kirkb 8A 36
Delaware Rd. L20: Boot 6B 44
Delenty Dr. WA3: Ris 5L 67
Delery Dr. WA1: Padg 9F 66
Delfby Cres. L32: Kirkb 1E 46
Delf Ho. WN8: Skel 3F 30
Delf La. L4: W'ton 8F 44
L24: Speke 2F 92
L39: Down 8F 18
Delhi Rd. M44: Irlam 1M 69
Dell, The CH42: Rock F 7A 74
L12: W Der 1C 60
WN6: App B 6N 23
WN8: Uph 5L 31
Della Robbia Ho. *CH41: Birke* *3K 73*
(off Clifton Rd.)
Dell Cl. CH63: Brom 9A 90
Dell Ct. CH43: Pren 7F 72

Dell Dr. WA2: Fearn 7H 67
Dellfield La. L31: Mag 2K 35
Dell Gro. CH42: Rock F 8A 74
Dell La. CH60: Hesw 8B 88
Dellside Cl. WN4: Ash M 5F 40
Dellside Gro. WA9: St H 1M 63
Dell St. L7: Liv 7H 59
Delph, The WN8: Parb 2F 22
Delph Cl. L39: Augh 3A 28
Delph Comn. Rd. L39: Augh 3N 27
Delph Ct. L21: Lith 2N 43
WA9: St H 1L 63
Delph Dr. L40: Burs 1K 21
Delphfield WA7: Nort 7F 96
Delphfields Rd. WA4: App 9D 82
Delph Hollow Way
WA9: St H 1L 63
Delph La. L35: Whis 4C 62
L37: Form 1C 24
L39: Augh 3A 28
WA2: Warr 3E 66
WA2: Winw 5A 66
WA4: Dares 4J 97
Delph Mdw. Gdns. WN5: Bil 7M 39
Delph Pk. Av. L39: Augh 3N 27
Delph Rd. L23: L Cros 3K 33
Delphside Cl. WN5: Orr 7N 31
Delphside Rd. WN5: Orr 7N 31
Delph Top L39: Orm 7E 20
Delphwood Dr. WA9: St H 9L 49
Delta Cres. WA5: Westb 7L 65
Delta Dr. L12: W Der 1C 60
Delta Rd. L21: Lith 3A 44
WA9: St H 6B 50
Delta Rd. E. CH42: Rock F 7A 74
Delta Rd. W. CH42: Rock F 7A 74
Deltic Pl. L33: Know I 1F 46
Deltic Way L30: Neth 2F 44
L33: Know I 2F 46
Delves Av. CH63: Spit 4M 89
WA5: Warr 1A 82
Delyn Cl. CH42: Rock F 7L 73
Demage Dr. CH66: Gt Sut 2J 111
Demage La. CH1: Lea B 9L 111
Demesne St. CH44: Wall 6L 57
Denbigh Av. PR9: South 4L 7
WA9: St H 2M 63
Denbigh Cl. WA6: Hel 4D 114
Denbigh Ct. CH65: Ell P 2B 112
WA7: Cas 5C 96
Denbigh Gdns. CH65: Ell P 2A 112
Denbigh Rd. CH44: Wall 6K 57
L9: W'ton 7E 44
Denbigh St. L5: Liv 4A 58
Denbury Av. WA4: Stockt H 6G 82
Dencourt Rd. L11: Norr G 9N 45
Deneacres L25: Woolt 6E 76
Dene Av. WA12: Newt W 6H 51
Denebank Rd. L4: W'ton 2G 59
Denecliff L28: Stockb V 1F 60
Dene Ct. L9: Faz 6L 45
Denefield Ho. PR8: South 9G 6
Denehurst Cl. WA5: Penk 4H 81
Deneshey Rd. CH47: Meols 9D 54
Denes Way L28: Stockb V 2E 60
Denford Cl. WN3: Wigan 1H 41
Denford Rd. L14: Knott A 4D 60
Denham Av. WA5: Gt San 3K 81
Denham Cl. CH43: Bid 1C 72
L12: Crox 7D 46
Denham Dr. WN3: Wigan 1J 41
Denholme WN8: Uph 5J 31
Denise Av. WA5: Penk 3G 80
Denise Rd. L10: Faz 3N 45
Denison Gro. WA9: St H 2H 63
Denison St. L3: Liv 2C 4 (6A 58)
Denman Dr. L6: Liv 5H 59
Denman Gro. *CH44: Wall* *7L 57*
(off Tudor Av.)
Denman St. L6: Liv 6G 59
Denman Way L6: Liv 5H 59
Denmark Rd. PR9: South 5M 7
Denmark St. L22: Wloo 1K 43
Dennett Cl. L31: Mag 4J 35
WA1: Wools 2M 83
Dennett Rd. L35: Presc 5N 61
Denning Dr. CH61: Irby 9L 71
Dennis Av. WA10: St H 2F 62
Dennis Rd. WA8: Widnes 9M 79
Denny Cl. CH49: Upton 4N 71
Densham Av. WA2: Warr 8C 66
Denshaw WN8: Uph 5J 31
Denston Cl. CH43: Bid 1B 72
Denstone Av. L10: Aintr 9J 35
Denstone Cl. L25: Woolt 8F 76
Dentdale Dr. L5: Liv 5D 58
Denton Dr. CH45: Wall 3J 57
Denton Gro. L6: Liv 4H 59
DENTON'S GREEN 5H 49
Dentons Grn. La. WA10: St H 5G 49
Denton St. L8: Liv 4E 74
WA8: Widnes 7M 79
Dentwood St. L8: Liv 4F 74
Denver Dr. WA5: Gt San 1K 81
Denver Pk. L32: Kirkb 1A 46
Denver Rd. L32: Kirkb 1A 46
WA4: Westy 5H 83
Denwall Ho. *CH64: Nest* *6E 100*
(off Churchill Way)
Depot Rd. L33: Know I 7H 37
Derby Bldgs. L7: Liv 5N 5

Derby Cl. M44: Cad 4J 69
WA12: Newt W 7K 51
Derby Ct. L37: Form 9E 16
Derby Dr. WA1: Warr 1F 82
WA11: Rainf 5D 38
Derby Gro. L31: Mag 5J 35
Derby Hall L17: Aig 4K 75
Derby Hill Cres. L39: Orm 8E 20
Derby Hill Rd. L39: Orm 8E 20
Derby Ho. *L39: Orm* *8D 20*
(off Derby St.)
Derby La. L13: Liv 5M 59
Derby Rd. CH42: Tran 5K 73
CH45: Wall 3G 57
L5: Kirkd 3A 58
L20: Boot, Kirkd 7A 44
L36: Huy 7J 61
(not continuous)
L37: Form 8E 16
PR9: South 8H 7
WA3: Golb 1D 52
WA4: Stockt H 7D 82
WA8: Widnes 5K 79
WN8: Skel 4N 29
Derby Row WA12: Newt W 1M 65
DERBYSHIRE HILL 8C 50
Derbyshire Hill Rd. WA9: St H 7C 50
Derbyshire Rd. M31: Part 7K 69
WN3: Winst 2F 40
Derby Sq. L2: Liv 6E 4 (8B 58)
L34: Presc 3B 62
Derby St. L13: Liv 6L 59
L19: Garst 3A 92
L34: Presc 3N 61
L36: Huy 7L 61
L39: Orm 8D 20
WA12: Newt W 7K 51
Derby St. W. L39: Orm 8C 20
Derby Ter. L36: Huy 6J 61
Derby Way L40: Burs 6E 20
Dereham Av. CH49: Upton 1A 72
Dereham Cres. L10: Faz 3L 45
Dereham Way WA7: Nort 4F 96
WN3: Winst 1F 40
Derek Av. WA2: Warr 7E 66
Derna Rd. L36: Huy 5H 61
Derringstone Cl. WA10: St H 9G 49
Derwent Av. L34: Presc 3C 62
L37: Form 2D 24
PR9: South 6L 7
WA3: Golb 1D 52
Derwent Cl. CH63: H Beb 2K 89
L31: Mag 1L 35
L33: Kirkb 7B 36
L35: Rainh 6E 62
M31: Part 5M 69
Derwent Ct. L18: Moss H 3B 76
Derwent Dr. CH45: Wall 3G 57
CH61: Pens 3N 87
CH66: Hoot 4G 102
L21: Lith 2C 44
Derwent Rd. CH43: Oxton 4H 73
CH47: Meols 9F 54
CH63: H Beb 2K 89
L23: Crosb 9M 33
WA4: Warr 6B 82
WA8: Widnes 7F 78
WA11: St H 3L 49
WN4: Ash M 6N 41
Derwent Rd. E. L13: Liv 5M 59
Derwent Rd. W. L13: Liv 5L 59
Derwent Sq. L13: Liv 5M 59
Derwent Way CH64: Lit N 7F 100
L14: Brd G 7C 60
WN7: Leigh 1J 53
Desborough Cres. L12: W Der 2M 59
Desford Av. WA11: St H 4N 49
Desford Cl. CH46: More 8J 55
Desford Rd. L19: Aig 8K 75
De Silva St. L36: Huy 7L 61
Desmond Cl. CH43: Bid 1C 72
Desmond Gro. L23: Crosb 8M 33
Desoto Rd. WA8: Widnes 3G 95
Desoto Rd. E. WA8: Widnes 1J 95
(not continuous)
Desoto Rd. W. WA8: Widnes 1J 95
Detroit Cl. WA5: Gt San 2K 81
Deva Cl. L33: Kirkb 4C 36
Deva Rd. CH48: W Kir 6B 70
Deveraux Dr. CH44: Wall 6H 57
Deverell Gro. L15: Wavtr 8N 59
Deverell Rd. L15: Wavtr 9M 59
Deverill Rd. CH42: Rock F 7L 73
Devilla Cl. L14: Knott A 4E 60
De Villiers Av. L23: Crosb 6L 33
Devisdale Gro. CH43: Bid 1C 72
Devizes Cl. L25: Gate 1F 76
Devizes Dr. CH61: Irby 9L 71
Devoke Av. WA11: St H 1K 49
Devon Av. CH45: Wall 4J 57
WN8: Uph 6L 31
Devon Cl. L23: Blun 7G 33
Devon Ct. *L5: Liv* *4F 58*
(off Tynemouth Cl.)
Devondale Rd. L18: Moss H 3M 75
Devon Dr. CH61: Pens 3M 87
Devon Farm Way L37: Form 1H 25
Devonfield Rd. L9: W'ton 5E 44
Devon Gdns. CH42: Rock F 7M 73
L16: Child 3C 76
Devon Pl. WA8: Widnes 5K 79

Devonport St. L8: Liv 3E 74
Devon Rd. M31: Part 7L 69
M44: Cad 4K 69
Devonshire Cl. CH43: Oxton 3H 73
L33: Kirkb 7C 36
Devonshire Gdns. WA12: Newt W 8L 51
Devonshire M. *L8: Liv* *3G 74*
(off Devonshire Rd.)
DEVONSHIRE PARK 5J 73
Devonshire Pl. CH43: Oxton 3G 72
L5: Liv 3D 58
(not continuous)
WA7: Run 5K 95
Devonshire Rd. CH43: Oxton 3H 73
CH44: Wall 5H 57
(not continuous)
CH48: W Kir 7D 70
CH49: Upton 3M 71
CH61: Pens 3M 87
L8: Liv 3F 74
L22: Wloo 9J 33
PR9: South 7M 7
WA1: Padg 9G 67
WA10: St H 5G 48
Devonshire Rd. W. L8: Liv 3F 74
Devon St. L3: Liv 3J 5 (7D 58)
WA10: St H 6G 49
Devonwall Gdns. L8: Liv 3G 74
Devon Way L16: Child 2C 76
L36: Huy 5L 61
(not continuous)
Dewar Ct. WA7: Astm 4A 96
Dewar St. WA3: Ris 4M 67
Dewberry Cl. CH42: Tran 4K 73
Dewberry Flds. WN8: Uph 5L 31
Dewey Av. L9: Aintr 2G 45
Dewhurst Rd. WA3: Birchw 6L 67
Dewlands Rd. L21: Sea 2M 43
Dewsbury Rd. L4: W'ton 3G 59
Dexter St. L8: Liv 2D 74
Dexter Way WN8: Uph 6L 31
Deycroft Av. L33: Kirkb 7E 36
Deycroft Wlk. L33: Kirkb 7E 36
Deyes Ct. L31: Mag 2K 35
Deyes End L31: Mag 2K 35
Deyes La. L31: Mag 2J 35
(not continuous)
Deysbrook La. L12: W Der 3A 60
Deysbrook Side L12: W Der 3A 60
Deysbrook Way L12: W Der 1B 60
Dial Rd. CH42: Tran 5K 73
Dial St. L7: Liv 7H 59
WA1: Warr 3D 82
Diamond Bus. Pk. WA11: Rainf 6E 38
Diamond Jubilee Rd. L40: Ruf 2N 15
Diamond St. L5: Liv 5C 58
Diana Rd. L20: Boot 3C 44
Diana St. L4: W'ton 1F 58
Diane Ho. L8: Liv 9K 5
Diane Rd. WN4: Ash M 6M 41
Dibbinsdale Rd. CH63: Brom 7A 90
Dibbins Grn. CH63: Brom 9A 90
Dibbins Hey CH63: Spit 5N 89
Dibbinview Gro. CH63: Spit 5A 90
Dibb La. L23: L Cros 4J 33
Dicconson's La. L39: Hals 1H 27
Dicconson St. WA10: St H 6K 49
Dicconson Way L39: Orm 9E 20
Dickens Av. CH43: Pren 7F 72
Dickens Cl. CH43: Pren 7F 72
L32: Kirkb 2B 46
Dickenson St. L1: Liv 8F 4 (9C 58)
WA2: Warr 1D 82
Dickens Rd. WA10: St H 1F 62
Dickens St. L8: Liv 2E 74
Dicket's La. WN8: Skel 1K 29
Dickinson Cl. L37: Form 2F 24
WA11: Hay 4C 50
Dickinson Ct. PR8: Birkd 4N 11
Dickinson Rd. L37: Form 2F 24
Dick's La. L40: Westh 9J 21
Dickson Cl. WA8: Widnes 8L 79
Dickson St. L3: Liv 5A 58
WA8: Widnes 8K 79
(not continuous)
Didcot Cl. L25: Hunts X 8H 77
Didsbury Cl. L33: Kirkb 9D 36
Digg La. CH46: More 8L 55
Digital Way L7: Liv 7J 59
Dig La. WA2: Fearn 5J 67
WA6: Frod 7K 107
DIGMOOR 6G 31
Digmoor Dr. WN8: Skel 5E 30
Digmoor Rd. L32: Kirkb 3D 46
WN8: Skel 5F 30
Digmoor Wlk. L32: Kirkb 3D 46
Dignum Mead L27: N'ley 3J 77
Dilloway St. WA10: St H 6H 49
Dinaro Cl. L25: Gate 4G 77
Dinas La. L36: Huy 5E 60
Dinas La. Pde. L14: Huy 5E 60
Dinesen Rd. L19: Garst 9A 76
DINGLE 5E 74
Dingle, The WA13: Lymm 5E 84
Dingle Av. WA12: Newt W 8H 51
WN8: Uph 4L 31
Dingle Bank Cl.
WA13: Lymm 5E 84
Dinglebrook Rd. L9: Aintr 7H 45
Dingle Brow L8: Liv 5F 74
Dingle Cl. L39: Augh 3A 28

Dingle Grange—Dunfold Cl.

Dingle Grange *L8: Liv* 5F *74*
(off Dingle Brow)
Dingle Gro. L8: Liv 4F **74**
Dingle La. L8: Liv 5F **74**
WA4: App 1G **98**
Dingle Mt. L8: Liv 5F **74**
Dingle Rd. CH42: Tran 4J **73**
L8: Liv 5E **74**
WN8: Uph 4L **31**
Dingle Va. L8: Liv 5F **74**
Dingleway WA4: App 8E **82**
Dingley Av. L9: W'ton 4E **44**
Dingwall Dr. CH49: Grea 5L **71**
Dinmore Rd. CH44: Wall 5H **57**
Dinnington Ct. WA8: Widnes 5H **79**
Dinorben Av. WA9: St H 2M **63**
Dinorwic Rd. L4: W'ton 3F **58**
PR8: Birkd 3N **11**
Dinsdale Rd. CH62: Brom 5D **90**
Dipping Brook Av. WA4: App 3F **98**
Discovery Rd. L19: Garst 3B **92**
Ditchfield L37: Form 2G **25**
Ditchfield Pl. WA8: Widnes 8E **78**
Ditchfield Rd. WA5: Penk 5G **81**
WA8: Widnes 8D **78**
DITTON 9E 78
Ditton Ct. WA8: Hale B 2F **94**
Ditton La. CH46: Leas 6L **55**
Ditton Rd. WA8: Widnes 1F **94**
(not continuous)
Dixon Av. WA12: Newt W 5L **51**
Dixon Cl. WA11: Hay 2J **51**
Dixon M. L30: Neth 7D **34**
Dixon Rd. L33: Know I 1F **46**
Dixon St. M44: Irlam 1M **69**
WA1: Warr 3B **82**
Dobbs Dr. L37: Form 9G **17**
Dobers La. WA6: Frod, Newt 2M **115**
Dobson St. L6: Liv 5F **58**
Dobsons Way WA9: St H 1J **63**
Dock Rd. CH41: Birke 7G **57**
L19: Garst 2N **91**
WA8: Widnes 2J **95**
(not continuous)
Dock Rd. Nth. CH62: Port S 1B **90**
Dock Rd. Sth. CH62: Brom 3C **90**
Docks Link CH44: Wall 6F **56**
Dock St. CH65: Ell P 7A **104**
WA8: Widnes 2K **95**
Dock Yd. Rd. CH65: Ell P 8B **104**
Doctor's La. L37: Gt Alt 2L **25**
Dodd Av. CH49: Grea 5L **71**
WA10: St H 6F **48**
Dodd Dr. WA4: Westy 5J **83**
Doddridge Rd. L8: Liv 3D **74**
Dodd's La. L31: Mag 1H **35**
Dodleston Cl. CH43: Noct 4D **72**
Dodman Rd. L11: Crox 5B **46**
Dodson Cl. WN4: Ash M 8L **41**
Dodworth Av. PR8: South 1D **12**
Doeford Cl. WA3: Cul 5L **53**
DOE GREEN 5F 80
Doe Mdw. WN8: Newb 4D **22**
(not continuous)
Doe Pk. Ctyd. L25: Woolt 8F **76**
Doe's Mdw. Rd. CH63: Brom 8A **90**
DOG & GUN 7N 45
Dolan Ct. L25: Gate 9D **60**
Dolan Way WA10: St H 3J **49**
Dolly's La. PR9: South 7B **8**
(not continuous)
Dolmans La. *WA1: Warr* 3C *82*
(off Bridge St.)
Dolomite Av. L24: Speke 1D **92**
Dolphin Cres. CH66: Gt Sut 3K **111**
Domar Cl. L32: Kirkb 1D **46**
Dombey Pl. *L8: Liv* 2E *74*
(off Dombey St.)
Dombey St. L8: Liv 2E **74**
Domingo Dr. L33: Kirkb 6B **36**
Dominic Cl. L16: Child 9C **60**
Dominic Rd. L16: Child 9C **60**
Dominion St. L6: Liv 4H **59**
Domino Ct. WA7: Manor P 3D **96**
Domville L35: Whis 7B **62**
Domville Cl. WA13: Lymm 5E **84**
Domville Dr. CH49: Wdchu 5A **72**
Domville Rd. L13: Liv 8N **59**
Donaldson Ct. L5: Liv 3F **58**
Donaldson St. L5: Liv 3F **58**
Donalds Way L17: Aig 7K **75**
Doncaster Dr. CH49: Upton 2N **71**
Donegal Rd. L13: Liv 6N **59**
Donne Av. CH63: Spit 4M **89**
Donne Cl. CH63: Spit 4N **89**
Donnington Cl. L36: Roby 9H **61**
WN7: Leigh 1L **53**
Donnington Lodge PR8: South 9E **6**
Donsby Rd. L9: Aintr 4G **44**
Don Wlk. CH65: Ell P 7M **103**
Dood's La. WA4: App 2H **99**
Dooley Dr. L30: Neth 7G **34**
Doon Cl. L4: Kirkd 1D **58**
Dorans La. L2: Liv 5E **4** (8B **58**)
Dorbett Dr. L23: Crosb 9M **33**
Dorchester Cl. CH49: Upton 4N **71**
Dorchester Dr. L33: Kirkb 6E **36**
Dorchester Pk. CH43: Noct 5D **72**
WA7: Nort 4F **96**
Dorchester Pk. Local Nature Reserve 4F 96
Dorchester Rd. L25: Gate 2F **76**
WA5: Gt San 3K **81**
WN8: Uph 5K **31**
Dorchester Way CH43: Noct 5D **72**
WA5: Burtw 3H **65**
Doreen Av. CH46: More 9L **55**
Dorgan Cl. L35: Rainh 5E **62**
Doric Av. WA6: Frod 7M **107**
Doric Grn. WN5: Bil 9N **31**
Doric Rd. L13: Liv 5M **59**
Doric St. CH42: Rock F 6M **73**
L21: Sea 3M **43**
Dorien Rd. L13: Liv 7L **59**
Dorincourt CH43: Oxton 4G **72**
Dorking Gro. L15: Wavtr 2N **75**
Dorney Cl. WA4: App 1F **98**
Dorney Ct. L12: W Der 1B **60**
Dorothea Cres. WA8: Widnes 4A **80**
Dorothea St. WA2: Warr 1D **82**
Dorothy Dr. L7: Liv 8G **59**
Dorothy St. L7: Liv 8G **59**
WA9: St H 2H **63**
Dorringo Dr. L11: Norr G 8M **45**
Dorrington Cl. WA7: Murd 7F **96**
Dorrington Wlk. *L5: Liv* 5D *58*
(off Roscommon St.)
Dorrit St. L8: Liv 2E **74**
Dorset Av. L15: Wavtr 1J **75**
PR8: Ainsd 3J **17**
Dorset Cl. L20: Boot 7C **44**
Dorset Ct. L25: Gate 2F **76**
Dorset Dr. CH61: Pens 3M **87**
Dorset Gdns. CH42: Rock F 7M **73**
WA7: Pal F 9C **96**
Dorset Rd. CH45: New B 2G **57**
CH48: W Kir 5D **70**
L6: Liv 3J **59**
L36: Huy 6L **61**
M44: Cad 4K **69**
WA10: St H 9G **48**
Dorset Way WA1: Wools 9J **67**
Double Cop WN7: Leigh 1L **53**
Dougals Way WN7: Leigh 1J **53**
Doughton Grn. WA8: Widnes 5H **79**
Douglas Av. WA9: Bold 3D **64**
WN5: Bil 8N **39**
WN8: Uph 5L **31**
Douglas Cl. L13: Liv 5L **59**
L40: Ruf 3N **15**
WA8: Widnes 5B **80**
Douglas Dr. CH46: More 9L **55**
L31: Mag 1L **35**
L39: Orm 6B **20**
Douglas Pl. L20: Boot 8A **44**
Douglas Rd. CH48: W Kir 5E **70**
L4: W'ton 3G **59**
PR9: South 3A **8**
Douglas St. CH41: Birke 2L **73**
WA10: St H 7G **49**
Douglas Way L33: Kirkb 5D **36**
Doulton Cl. CH43: Bid 1B **72**
WA4: Warr 6D **82**
Doulton Pl. L35: Whis 7N **61**
Doulton St. WA10: St H 7G **48**
Doune Ct. CH65: Ell P 2B **112**
Dounrey Cl. WA2: Fearn 7H **67**
Douro Pl. L13: Liv 7L **59**
Douro St. L5: Liv 1H **5** (5D **58**)
Dove Cl. CH2: Elt 1N **113**
CH66: Ell P 7M **103**
WA3: Birchw 5N **67**
WA6: Hel 9F **106**
DOVECOT 5D 60
Dovecot Av. L14: Knott A 6D **60**
Dovecote Dr. WA11: Hay 3E **50**
Dovecote Grn. WA5: Westb 8J **65**
Dovecot Pl. *L14: Knott A* 5D *60*
(off Dovecot Av.)
Dove Ct. L25: Woolt 5F **76**
Dovedale Av. CH62: East 1D **102**
L31: Mag 1H **35**
Dovedale Cl. CH43: Pren 6F **72**
WA2: Warr 6F **66**
Dovedale Ct. WA8: Widnes 5E **78**
Dovedale Cres. WN4: Ash M 3J **41**
Dovedale Rd. CH45: Wall 2G **56**
CH47: Hoy 9C **54**
L18: Moss H 3L **75**
WN4: Ash M 4J **41**
Dovepoint Rd. CH47: Meols 8F **54**
Dovercliffe Rd. L13: Liv 6N **59**
Dover Cl. CH41: Birke 1K **73**
WA7: Murd 9G **96**
Dover Ct. CH65: Ell P 3B **112**
Dovercroft L25: Woolt 6D **76**
Dover Dr. CH65: Ell P 3B **112**
Dover Gro. L16: Child 9D **60**
Dove Rd. L9: W'ton 4E **44**
Dover Rd. L31: Mag 5H **35**
PR8: Birkd 4L **11**
WA4: Westy 5H **83**
Dover St. L3: Liv 5K **5** (8E **58**)
WA7: Run 4L **95**
Dovesmead Rd. CH60: Hesw 8C **88**
Dovestone Cl. L7: Liv 9G **59**
Dove St. L8: Liv 1G **74**
Dovey St. L8: Liv 3F **74**
Doward St. WA8: Widnes 6M **79**
Dowhills Dr. L23: Blun 6H **33**
Dowhills Pk. L23: Blun 6H **33**
Dowhills Rd. L23: Blun 5H **33**
DOWNALL GREEN 7F 40
Downall Grn. WN4: Garsw 6F **40**
Downall Grn. Rd. WN4: Ash M 6G **40**
Downbrook Way *WN4: Ash M* 6M *41*
(off North St.)
Downes Grn. CH63: Spit 6N **89**
Downgreen Cl. L32: Kirkb 1A **46**
Downham Av. WA3: Cul 8N **53**
Downham Cl. L25: Woolt 3D **76**
Downham Dr. CH60: Hesw 7A **88**
Downham Grn. L25: Woolt 3D **76**
Downham Rd. CH42: Tran 5K **73**
Downham Rd. Nth. CH61: Hesw 5A **88**
Downham Rd. Sth. CH60: Hesw 7A **88**
Downham Wlk. WN5: Bil 2N **39**
Downham Way L25: Woolt 3D **76**
DOWNHOLLAND 2D 26
Downholland Bri. Bus. Pk.
L39: Down 2G **26**
DOWNHOLLAND CROSS 2G 26
Downholland Moss La.
L37: Form 9H **17**
Downing Cl. CH43: Oxton 5H **73**
Downing Rd. L20: Boot 8C **44**
Downing St. L5: Liv 4F **58**
Downlands Rd. L27: N'ley 4K **77**
Downland Way WA9: St H 9B **50**
Downs, The L23: Blun 8H **33**
Downside WA8: Widnes 5E **78**
Downside Cl. L30: Neth 7D **34**
Downside Dr. L10: Aintr 1L **45**
Downs Rd. WA7: Run 6K **95**
WA10: St H 8G **49**
Downway La. WA9: St H 9C **50**
Dowsefield La. L18: Aller 5C **76**
Dragon Cl. L11: Crox 6A **46**
WN8: Skel 4H **31**
Dragon Cres. L35: Whis 5C **62**
Dragon Dr. L35: Whis 6B **62**
Dragon La. L35: Whis 7A **62**
Dragon Wlk. *L11: Crox* 6A *46*
(off Dragon Cl.)
Dragon Yd. WA8: Widnes 4L **79**
Drake Av. M44: Cad 3L **69**
Drake Cl. L10: Faz 3M **45**
L35: Whis 7B **62**
L39: Augh 2A **28**
WA5: Old H 8M **65**
Drake Cres. L10: Faz 3L **45**
Drakefield Rd. L11: Norr G 7K **45**
Drake Gdns. WA9: St H 3H **63**
Drake Pl. L10: Faz 3L **45**
Drake Rd. CH46: Leas 5B **56**
CH64: Nest 5E **100**
L10: Faz 3L **45**
Drake St. L20: Boot 9A **44**
WA10: St H 6G **49**
Drake Way L10: Faz 3M **45**
Drapers Ct. WA3: Low 3G **52**
Draw Well Rd. L33: Know I 9H **37**
Draycott St. L8: Liv 5E **74**
Drayton Cl. CH61: Irby 2L **87**
WA5: Gt San 2K **81**
WA7: Run 6J **95**
Drayton Cres. WA11: St H 4N **49**
Drayton Rd. CH44: Wall 6K **57**
L4: W'ton 8F **44**
Dream 7M 63
Drennan Rd. L19: Aller 8C **76**
Drewell Rd. L18: Moss H 5L **75**
Drewitt Cres. PR9: South 3B **8**
Driffield Rd. L34: Presc 3N **61**
Drill at Grange Road West 3H 73
Drinkwater Gdns. L3: Liv 1H **5** (6D **58**)
Drive, The L12: W Der 4N **59**
WA13: Lymm 7K **85**
DriveTime (Golf Driving Range) 6B 82
Driveway L35: Whis 6C **62**
Droitwich Av. CH49: Grea 4K **71**
Dromore Av. L18: Moss H 5M **75**
Dronfield Way L25: Gate 1D **76**
(not continuous)
Drovers La. WA6: Frod 1M **115**
Droxford Dr. L25: Gate 1D **76**
Druids Cross Gdns. L18: Moss H 4B **76**
Druids Cross Rd. L18: Moss H 4B **76**
Druids Pk. L18: Moss H 4C **76**
Druid St. WN4: Ash M 9L **41**
Druidsville Rd. L18: Moss H 4C **76**
Druids Way CH49: Wdchu 6A **72**
Drum Cl. L14: Knott A 4E **60**
DRUMMERSDALE 7A 14
Drummersdale La. L40: Scar 5M **13**
Drummer's La. WN4: Ash M 4F **40**
Drummond Av. CH66: Gt Sut 1H **111**
Drummond Ct. WA8: Widnes 6N **79**
Drummond Rd. CH47: Hoy 3B **70**
L4: W'ton 9H **45**
L23: Thorn 6A **34**
Drummoyne Ct. L23: Blun 6G **33**
Druridge Dr. WA5: Penk 4H **81**
Drury La. L2: Liv 5D **4** (8B **58**)
Drybeck Gro. WA9: St H 3N **63**
Dryburgh Way *L4: Kirkd* 1D *58*
(off Bradwell St.)
Dryden Av. WN4: Ash M 4H **41**
Dryden Cl. CH43: Bid 1C **72**
L35: Whis 6B **62**
Dryden Gro. L36: Huy 8K **61**
Dryden Pl. WA2: Warr 7D **66**
Dryden Rd. L7: Liv 8K **59**
Dryden St. L5: Liv 5C **58**
L20: Boot 5N **43**
Dryfield Cl. CH49: Grea 4L **71**
Dublin Cft. CH66: Gt Sut 4K **111**
Dublin St. L3: Liv 5A **58**
Ducie St. L8: Liv 2G **74**
Duckinfield St. L3: Liv 6K **5** (8E **58**)
Duck Pond La. CH42: Tran 6G **73**
Duckworth Gro. WA2: Padg 8H **67**
Duddingston Av.
L18: Moss H 3M **75**
L23: Crosb 9L **33**
Duddon Av. L31: Mag 1L **35**
Duddon Cl. CH43: Oxton 5F **72**
Dudleston Rd. CH66: Lit Sut 8G **103**
Dudley Av. WA7: Run 5N **95**
Dudley Cl. CH43: Oxton 4H **73**
Dudley Cres. CH65: Hoot 3G **103**
Dudley Gro. L23: Crosb 9L **33**
Dudley Pl. WA9: St H 7N **49**
Dudley Rd. CH45: New B 1G **57**
CH65: Ell P 9N **103**
L18: Moss H 3L **75**
M44: Cad 5K **69**
Dudley St. WA2: Warr 1C **82**
WN4: Ash M 6J **41**
Dudlow Ct. L18: Moss H 3A **76**
Dudlow Dr. L18: Moss H 3A **76**
Dudlow Gdns. L18: Moss H 3A **76**
Dudlow Grn. Rd. WA4: App 2E **98**
Dudlow La. L18: Moss H 2N **75**
Dudlow Nook Rd. L18: Moss H 2A **76**
DUDLOW'S GREEN 2F 98
Dugdale Cl. L19: G'dale 9M **75**
Duke Av. PR8: South 2B **12**
Duke Cl. WA7: Run 5J **95**
Duke of York Cotts. CH62: Port S 1N **89**
Dukesbridge Ct. *WA13: Lymm* 5E *84*
(off New Rd.)
Dukes Rd. L5: Liv 3D **58**
Dukes Ter. L1: Liv 7H **5** (9D **58**)
Duke St. CH41: Birke 8J **57**
CH45: New B 1H **57**
L1: Liv 7F **4** (9C **58**)
L19: Garst 1A **92**
L22: Wloo 2K **43**
L34: Presc 3A **62**
L37: Form 2E **24**
(not continuous)
PR8: South 9F **6**
WA3: Golb 1B **52**
WA10: St H 6J **49**
WA12: Newt W 7K **51**
WN4: Ash M 8L **41**
Duke St. Bri. CH41: Birke 8J **57**
Duke St. La. L1: Liv 7F **4** (9C **58**)
Dukes Way L37: Form 2F **24**
Dukes Wharf WA7: Pres B 9G **97**
Duke's Wood La. WN8: Skel 9G **30**
Dulas Grn. L32: Kirkb 1E **46**
Dulas Rd. L15: Wavtr 2N **75**
L32: Kirkb 1E **46**
Dulson Way L34: Presc 4L **61**
Dulverton Rd. L17: Aig 8K **75**
Dumbarton St. L4: W'ton 9D **44**
Dumbrees Gdns. L12: W Der 1C **60**
Dumbrees Rd. L12: W Der 1C **60**
Dumbreeze Gro. L34: Know 6H **47**
Dumfries Way L33: Kirkb 5B **36**
Dunacre Way L26: Halew 9K **77**
Dunbabin Rd. L15: Wavtr 2N **75**
L16: Child 2A **76**
Dunbar Cl. CH66: Lit Sut 9H **103**
Dunbar Ct. CH66: Lit Sut 9H **103**
Dunbar Cres. PR8: Birkd 6M **11**
Dunbar Rd. PR8: Birkd 4L **11**
Dunbar St. L4: W'ton 8E **44**
Dunbeath Av. L35: Rainh 8G **63**
Dunbeath Cl. L35: Rainh 8G **63**
Dunblane Cl. WN4: Garsw 7E **40**
Duncan Av. WA7: Run 6M **95**
WA12: Newt W 5L **51**
Duncan Cl. WA10: St H 8H **49**
Duncan Dr. CH49: Grea 4L **71**
Duncansby Cres. WA5: Gt San 2G **80**
Duncansby Dr. CH63: East 2B **102**
Duncan St. CH41: Birke 2M **73**
L1: Liv 9H **5** (1D **74**)
WA2: Warr 1D **82**
WA10: St H 7H **49**
Dunchurch Rd. L14: Knott A 4D **60**
Duncombe Rd. Nth. L19: G'dale 9N **75**
Duncombe Rd. Sth. L19: Garst 9N **75**
Duncote Cl. CH43: Oxton 4G **72**
L35: Whis 4D **62**
Dundale Rd. L13: Liv 6N **59**
Dundalk La. WA8: Widnes 8G **79**
Dundalk Rd. WA8: Widnes 8G **79**
Dundas St. L20: Boot 9A **44**
Dundee Cl. WA2: Fearn 5F **66**
Dundee Ct. CH65: Ell P 2C **112**
Dundee Gro. CH44: Wall 6G **56**
Dundonald Av. WA4: Stockt H 7D **82**
Dundonald Rd. L17: Aig 7K **75**
Dundonald St. CH41: Birke 9G **56**
Dunedin St. WA9: St H 2H **63**
Dunes Cl. PR8: Ainsd 9H **11**
Dunes Dr. L37: Form 9C **16**
Dunes Splash World 8E 6
Dunes Way L5: Kirkd 3B **58**
Dunfold Cl. L32: Kirkb 1D **46**

Edinburgh Rd.—Enerby Cl.

Edinburgh Rd. CH45: Wall 4H 57
L7: Liv 3N 5 (7F 58)
(not continuous)
L37: Form 3E 24
WA8: Widnes 8E 78
Edington St. L15: Wavtr 9K 59
Edison Cl. L37: Form 4E 24
Edison Rd. WA7: Astm 4N 95
Edith Rd. CH44: Wall 6L 57
L4: W'ton 3F 58
L20: Boot 4C 44
Edith St. WA7: Run 4J 95
WA9: St H 2B 64
Edmondson St. WA9: St H 7B 50
Edmonton Cl. L5: Kirkd 3C 58
Edmund Ct. CH62: Brom 4D 90
Edmund St. L3: Liv 4D 4 (7B 58)
Edna Av. L10: Faz 3M 45
Edrich Av. CH43: Bid 9C 56
Edward Dr. WN4: Ash M 7K 41
Edward Gdns. WA1: Wools 2N 83
Edward Jenner Av. L30: Neth 8E 34
Edward Manton Cl. CH63: H Beb 1J 89
Edward Pav. L3: Liv 7D 4 (9B 58)
Edward Price Cl. CH64: P'gte 5C 100
Edward Rd. CH47: Hoy 2D 70
L35: Whis 4C 62
WA5: Gt San 2F 80
Edward's La. L24: Speke 1F 92
Edward's La. Ind. Est. L24: Speke 2F 92
Edwards Rd. WA7: Pal F 7A 96
Edward St. CH65: Ell P 7A 104
WA8: Widnes 7N 79
WA9: St H 9N 49
WA11: Hay 4C 50
Edwards Way WA8: Widnes 8F 78
Edwin St. WA8: Widnes 7M 79
Effingham St. L20: Boot 9A 44
Egan Ct. *CH41: Birke 1L 73*
(off Lord St.)
Egan Rd. CH43: Bid 9E 56
Egbert Rd. CH47: Meols 9D 54
Egdon Cl. WA8: Widnes 6A 80
Egerton WN8: Skel 4G 31
Egerton Av. WA1: Warr 1F 82
(not continuous)
WA13: Warb 9J 69
Egerton Ct. CH41: Birke 1L 73
Egerton Dr. CH48: W Kir 6C 70
Egerton Gdns. CH42: Rock F 7L 73
Egerton Gro. CH45: Wall 4H 57
Egerton Ho. WA7: Run 4L 95
Egerton M. WA4: Stockt H 7D 82
Egerton Pk. CH42: Rock F 7L 73
Egerton Pk. Cl. CH42: Rock F 7L 73
Egerton Rd. CH43: Clau 2G 72
CH62: New F 9A 74
L15: Wavtr 1J 75
L34: Presc 3N 61
WA13: Lymm 6C 84
Egerton St. CH45: New B 1H 57
CH65: Ell P 8A 104
L8: Liv 9L 5 (1E 74)
WA1: Warr 3E 82
WA4: Stockt H 7D 82
WA7: Run 4J 95
WA9: St H 9N 49
Egerton Wharf CH41: Birke 9L 57
Eglington Av. L35: Whis 7A 62
EGREMONT 4K 57
Egremont Cl. L27: N'ley 4L 77
Egremont Lawn L27: N'ley 4L 77
Egremont Prom. CH44: Wall 3K 57
CH45: Wall 3K 57
Egret Cl. L19: Garst 9A 76
Egypt St. WA1: Warr 3B 82
WA8: Widnes 9J 79
Eight Acre La. L37: Form 7G 17
(not continuous)
Eighth Av. L9: Aintr 3J 45
Eilian Gro. L14: Knott A 7B 60
Elaine Cl. CH66: Gt Sut 1H 111
WA8: Widnes 6M 79
WN4: Ash M 6M 41
Elaine Norris Sports Cen. 5B 58
Elaine Price Ct. WA7: Run 6J 95
Elaine St. L8: Liv 2E 74
WA1: Warr 1E 82
Elbow La. L37: Form 1F 24
Elbrus Dr. CH66: Ell P 7L 103
Elcombe Av. WA3: Low 3F 52
Elder Av. L40: Burs 2K 21
Elderberry Cl. L11: Crox 8A 46
Elderberry Wlk. *M31: Part 6L 69*
(off Wood La.)
Elderdale Rd. L4: W'ton 2G 59
Elderflower Dr. L11: Norr G 9L 45
Elderflower Rd. WA10: St H 5H 49
Elder Gdns. L19: G'dale 8N 75
Elder Gro. CH48: W Kir 6C 70
Elder Pl. L25: Hunts X 8H 77
Eldersfield Rd. L11: Norr G 8N 45
Elderswood L35: Rainh 5F 62
Elderwood Rd. CH42: Tran 5L 73
Eldon Cl. *WA10: St H 8H 49*
(off Eldon St.)
Eldon Gdns. WN4: Ash M 5J 41
Eldon Gro. *L3: Liv 5C 58*
(off Limekiln La.)
Eldonian Way L3: Liv 5B 58
Eldon Pl. L3: Liv 5B 58
Eldon Rd. CH42: Rock F 6M 73
CH44: Wall 5H 57
Eldons Cft. PR8: Ainsd 9K 11
Eldon St. L3: Liv 5B 58
WA1: Warr 3D 82
WA10: St H 8H 49
Eldon Ter. CH64: Nest 7E 100
Eldred Rd. L16: Child 2A 76
Eleanor Pk. CH43: Bid 9C 56
Eleanor Rd. CH43: Bid 8D 56
CH46: More 8K 55
L20: Boot 4C 44
Eleanor St. CH65: Ell P 8A 104
L20: Kirkd 9A 44
WA8: Widnes 9K 79
Electric Av. L10: Faz 5N 45
L11: Crox 5A 46
Elephant La. WA9: St H 2G 63
Elfet St. CH41: Birke 9F 56
Elgar Av. CH62: East 1D 102
Elgar Cl. CH65: Gt Sut 2L 111
Elgar Rd. L14: Knott A 4D 60
Elgin Av. WA4: Warr 6B 82
WN4: Garsw 7F 40
Elgin Ct. L35: Rainh 7G 63
Elgin Dr. CH45: Wall 3J 57
Elgin Way CH41: Birke 1L 73
Eliot Cl. CH62: New F 9N 73
Eliot St. L20: Boot 5A 44
Elizabeth Av. PR8: Ainsd 8L 11
Elizabeth Ct. WA8: Widnes 9L 79
Elizabeth Dr. WA1: Padg 9H 67
Elizabeth Rd. L10: Faz 3N 45
L20: Boot 4C 44
L36: Huy 9K 61
M31: Part 5M 69
WA11: Hay 3G 50
Elizabeth St. L3: Liv 4L 5 (7E 58)
WA9: Clock F 6A 64
WA9: St H 1A 64
Elizabeth Ter. WA8: Widnes 7G 79
Eliza St. WA9: St H 2B 64
Elkan Cl. WA8: Widnes 5A 80
Elkan Rd. WA8: Widnes 5N 79
Elkin Ct. M31: Part 5N 69
Elkstone Cl. WN3: Winst 1E 40
Elkstone Rd. L11: Norr G 9N 45
Ellaby M. L35: Rainh 5F 62
Ellaby Rd. L35: Rainh 5F 62
Ellamsbridge Rd. WA9: St H 1A 64
Elland Dr. CH66: Lit Sut 9H 103
Ellel Gro. L6: Liv 4H 59
Ellencliff Dr. L6: Liv 4H 59
Ellen Gdns. WA9: St H 1A 64
Ellens Cl. L6: Liv 3M 5 (7F 58)
Ellen's La. CH63: Beb 2A 90
Ellen St. WA5: Warr 1A 82
WA9: St H 2A 64
Elleray Dr. L8: Liv 4E 74
Elleray Pk. Rd. CH45: Wall 2G 56
Ellerbrook Dr. L40: Burs 2K 21
Ellerbrook Way L39: Orm 7C 20
Ellerby Cl. WA7: Murd 8G 96
Ellergreen Rd. L11: Norr G 8L 45
Ellerman Rd. L3: Liv 5D 74
(not continuous)
Ellerslie Av. L35: Rainh 4E 62
Ellerslie Rd. L13: Liv 3J 59
Ellerton Av. CH66: Lit Sut 9H 103
Ellerton Cl. WA8: Widnes 5G 78
Ellerton Way L12: Crox 7C 46
Ellesmere Dr. L10: Aintr 9H 35
Ellesmere Gro. CH45: Wall 3H 57
ELLESMERE PORT 9A 104
Ellesmere Port Bus Station 1N 111
Ellesmere Port Sports Village 3A 112
Ellesmere Port Station (Rail) 9A 104
Ellesmere Rd. WA3: Cul 6M 53
WA4: Stockt H, W'ton 7C 82
WN4: Ash M 6H 41
Ellesmere St. WA1: Warr 3D 82
(not continuous)
WA7: Run 5L 95
Ellesworth Cl. WA5: Old H 9L 65
Ellington Dr. WA5: Gt San 3K 81
Ellington Way WA9: St H 4J 63
Elliot Dr. L32: Kirkb 2B 46
Elliot St. L1: Liv 5G 5 (8C 58)
WA8: Widnes 8L 79
WA10: St H 7H 49
Elliott Av. WA1: Warr 1F 82
WA3: Golb 1C 52
Elliott Gdns. WN6: App B 6N 23
Ellis Ashton St. L36: Huy 7L 61
Ellis La. WA6: Frod 5N 107
Ellison Dr. WA10: St H 6F 48
Ellison Gro. L36: Huy 7H 61
Ellison St. L13: Liv 5L 59
WA1: Warr 3D 82
WA4: Stockt H 7E 82
Ellis Pl. L8: Liv 3E 74
Ellis Rd. WN5: Bil 7N 39
Ellis St. WA8: Widnes 9K 79
Ellon Av. L35: Rainh 7G 62
Elloway Rd. L24: Speke 4L 93
Ellwood Cl. L24: Hale 5B 94
Elmar Rd. L17: Aig 6K 75
(not continuous)
Elm Av. CH49: Upton 2L 71
L23: Crosb 6M 33
WA3: Golb 1B 52
Elm Av. WA8: Widnes 6L 79
WA12: Newt W 8L 51
WN4: Garsw 6F 40
Elm Bank *L4: W'ton 2E 58*
(off Walton Breck Rd.)
Elmbank Rd. CH62: New F 1A 90
L18: Moss H 3K 75
Elmbank St. CH44: Wall 6J 57
Elmbridge Ct. WA3: Low 2G 52
Elm Cl. CH61: Pens 3A 88
L12: Crox 7D 46
M31: Part 6M 69
Elm Ct. CH63: H Beb 1K 89
CH65: Ell P 1D 112
L23: Blun 7J 33
WN8: Skel 3B 30
Elmcroft Cl. L9: Aintr 4J 45
Elmcroft La. L38: Hight 9G 24
Elmdale Cl. L37: Form 2D 24
Elmdale Rd. L9: W'ton 6F 44
Elmdene Ct. CH49: Grea 6K 71
Elm Dr. CH49: Grea 5K 71
L21: Sea 4M 43
L37: Form 3D 24
WN5: Bil 6N 39
ELMERS GREEN 2G 31
Elmers Grn. WN8: Skel 2G 31
(not continuous)
Elmer's Grn. La.
WN8: Dalt, Skel 8F 22
(not continuous)
Elmers Wood Rd.
WN8: Skel 3G 31
Elmfield Cl. WA9: St H 1H 63
Elmfield Rd. L9: W'ton 5F 44
Elm Gdns. L21: Sea 4N 43
WA11: Rainf 5C 38
Elm Grn. CH64: Will 6M 101
Elm Gro. CH42: Tran 4K 73
CH47: Hoy 1D 70
CH66: Whit 4M 111
L7: Liv 5N 5 (8F 58)
L34: Eccl P 2C 62
WA1: Padd 1G 83
WA8: Widnes 7L 79
WN8: Skel 3B 30
Elm Hall Dr.
L18: Moss H 3M 75
Elmham Cres. L10: Faz 3L 45
Elm Ho. *L22: Wloo 1L 43*
(off Lorne Rd.)
L34: Presc 3N 61
Elm Ho. M. L25: Gate 4F 76
Elmhow Gro. WN3: Wigan 1J 41
Elmhurst CH42: Rock F 8M 73
Elmhurst Rd. L25: Gate 1E 76
Elmore Cl. L5: Liv 4E 58
WA7: Wind H 6F 96
ELM PARK 6H 59
Elm Pk. Dr. PR8: Ainsd 9L 11
Elm Pk. Rd. CH45: Wall 2G 57
Elm Pl. L39: Orm 9C 20
Elmridge WN8: Skel 3G 30
Elm Ri. WA6: Frod 7M 107
Elm Rd. CH42: Tran 6H 73
(Elm Rd. Nth.)
CH42: Tran 5K 73
(Walker M.)
CH61: Irby 1N 87
CH63: H Beb 9M 73
CH64: Will 6M 101
L4: W'ton 8F 44
L21: Sea 4M 43
L32: Kirkb 8B 36
L40: Burs 2J 21
PR8: South 2A 12
WA2: Winw 5B 66
WA3: Rix 7G 69
WA5: Penk 4H 81
WA7: Run 7M 95
WA9: St H 1G 63
WA10: St H 1G 63
WA11: Hay 3G 51
Elm Rd. Nth. CH42: Tran 6H 73
Elms, The L8: Liv 4F 74
L31: Lydi 9J 27
PR8: South 1B 12
(Ash St.)
PR8: South 9E 6
(Beach Priory Gdns.)
WA3: Low 3G 53
WA7: Run 6J 95
Elmsbury St. WN4: Ash M 6H 41
Elmsdale Rd. L18: Moss H 3M 75
Elmsett Cl. WA5: Gt San 3G 80
Elmsfield Cl. L25: Gate 3E 76
Elmsfield Pk. L39: Augh 6M 27
Elmsfield Rd. L23: Thorn 5A 34
Elms Ho. Rd. L13: Liv 6L 59
Elmsley Ct. L18: Moss H 5M 75
Elmsley Rd. L18: Moss H 4L 75
Elms Pk. CH61: Thing 2A 88
Elms Rd. L31: Mag 5J 35
Elmstead WN8: Skel 4G 30
Elm St. CH41: Birke 2K 73
CH65: Ell P 7A 104
L36: Huy 7L 61
Elmswood Av. L25: Hunts X 9H 77
L35: Rainh 8G 63
Elmswood Ct. L18: Moss H 5L 75
Elmswood Gro. L36: Huy 6G 60
Elmswood Rd. CH42: Tran 4J 73
CH44: Wall 5K 57
L17: Aig 6J 75
L18: Moss H 6K 75
Elm Ter. CH47: Hoy 1D 70
L7: Liv 7H 59
Elm Tree Av. WA1: Padg 9G 67
WA13: Lymm 6D 84
Elmtree Cl. L12: W Der 2A 60
Elm Tree Ct. CH47: Hoy 9D 54
Elmtree Gro. CH43: Bid 9E 56
Elm Tree Rd. WA3: Low 2G 52
WA13: Lymm 6D 84
Elmure Av. CH63: H Beb 2K 89
Elm Va. L6: Liv 5J 59
Elmway Cl. L13: Liv 7L 59
Elmwood WA7: Nort 6E 96
WN8: Skel 1F 30
Elmwood Av. L23: Crosb 6N 33
WA1: Warr 1F 82
WN4: Ash M 9J 41
Elmwood Dr. CH61: Hesw 5N 87
Elphin Gro. L4: W'ton 9F 44
Elphins Dr. WA4: Warr 6D 82
Elric Wlk. L33: Kirkb 8D 36
Elsbeck Gro. WA9: St H 3N 63
Elsie Rd. L4: W'ton 3G 58
Elsmere Av. L17: Aig 5H 75
Elson Rd. L37: Form 3D 24
Elstead Gro. WN4: Garsw 7F 40
Elstead Rd. L9: Faz 6K 45
L32: Kirkb 1A 46
Elston Av. WA12: Newt W 5K 51
Elstow St. L5: Kirkd 2C 58
Elstree Ct. WA8: Widnes 4N 79
Elstree Rd. L6: Liv 6J 59
Elswick WN8: Skel 4F 30
Elswick Grn. PR9: South 2M 7
Elswick Rd. PR9: South 3L 7
Elswick St. L8: Liv 5E 74
Elsworth Cl. L37: Form 3C 24
Eltham Av. L21: Lith 1A 44
Eltham Cl. CH49: Wdchu 6B 72
WA8: Widnes 5A 80
WN4: Ash M 8M 41
Eltham Grn. CH49: Wdchu 6B 72
Eltham St. L7: Liv 7J 59
Eltham Wlk. WA8: Widnes 5A 80
ELTON 2M 113
Elton Av. L23: Blun 7J 33
L30: Neth 8D 34
Elton Cl. CH62: East 3D 102
WA3: Birchw 5K 67
WA3: Low 3F 52
Elton Dr. CH63: Spit 5N 89
ELTON GREEN 3L 113
Elton Head Rd. WA9: St H 4F 62
Elton La. WA6: Hel 1A 114
Elton Lordship La. WA6: Frod 8D 106
Elton St. L4: W'ton 8E 44
Elvington Cl. WA7: Sut W 3B 108
Elvington Rd. L38: Hight 1G 32
Elway Rd. WN4: Ash M 7L 41
Elwick Dr. L11: Crox 8A 46
Elwood Cl. L33: Kirkb 5C 36
Elworth Av. WA8: Widnes 3K 79
Elworthy Av. L26: Halew 7K 77
Elwyn Dr. L26: Halew 8K 77
Elwyn Rd. CH47: Meols 8F 54
Elwy St. L8: Liv 3F 74
Ely Av. CH46: More 9K 55
Ely Cl. CH66: Gt Sut 5K 111
L30: Neth 1E 44
Ely M. PR9: South 5M 7
Ely Pk. WA7: Nort 5G 96
Ember Cres. L6: Liv 5E 58
Emberton Cl. WA4: Warr 6E 82
Embledon St. L8: Liv 1G 74
Embleton Gro. WA7: Beech 1N 107
Emerald Cl. L30: Neth 8G 34
Emerald Dr. WA3: Croft 1K 67
Emerald St. L8: Liv 5F 74
Emerson Cl. L38: Hight 8G 24
Emerson St. L8: Liv 1E 74
Emery St. L4: W'ton 9E 44
Emily St. WA8: Widnes 9K 79
WA9: St H 2F 62
Emlyn St. WA9: St H 9N 49
Emmanuel Rd. PR9: South 5L 7
Emmett St. WA9: St H 9M 49
Emperor Cl. WA4: Warr 7C 82
Empire Ct. WA1: Warr 4B 82
Empire Rd. L21: Lith 4A 44
Empress Cl. L31: Mag 2G 35
Empress Pk. WA11: Hay 3K 51
Empress Rd. CH44: Wall 5J 57
L6: Liv 3H 59
L7: Liv 4N 5 (7G 58)
(not continuous)
Emslie Ct. CH64: P'gte 7C 100
Emstrey Wlk. L32: Kirkb 9A 36
Endborne Rd. L9: W'ton 4F 44
Endbrook Way L25: Gate 2G 76
Endbutt La. L23: Crosb 7L 33
Enderby Av. WA11: St H 4N 49
Endfield Farm Cvn. Pk. WA16: High L 9K 85
Endfield Pk. L19: G'dale 8N 75
Endmoor Rd. L36: Huy 4H 61
Endsleigh Rd. L13: Liv 6K 59
L22: Wloo 9H 33
Enerby Cl. CH43: Bid 1C 72

Enfield Av.—Falstone Dr.

Enfield Av. L23: Crosb 7L **33**
Enfield Pk. Rd.
WA2: Fearn 5G **66**
Enfield Rd. CH65: Ell P 9N **103**
L13: Liv 7N **59**
Enfield St. WA10: St H 8H **49**
Enfield Ter. CH43: Oxton 3H **73**
Enford Dr. WA9: St H 2N **63**
Engine La. L37: Gt Alt 5K **25**
Enid St. L8: Liv 2E **74**
Ennerdale WN8: Skel 4G **31**
Ennerdale Av.
CH62: East 2E **102**
L31: Mag 1K **35**
WA2: Warr 6C **66**
WA11: St H 2L **49**
WN4: Ash M 6K **41**
Ennerdale Cl. L33: Kirkb 6B **36**
L37: Form 1D **24**
Ennerdale Dr. L21: Lith 2C **44**
L39: Augh 2N **27**
WA6: Frod 6M **107**
Ennerdale Rd. CH43: Pren 7E **72**
CH45: Wall 1F **56**
L9: Aintr 4J **45**
L37: Form 1D **24**
M31: Part 6L **69**
Ennerdale St. L3: Liv 5C **58**
Ennis Cl. L24: Hale 5A **94**
Ennis Ct. L11: Norr G 7N **45**
Ennisdale Dr. CH48: W Kir 5D **70**
Ennismore Rd. L13: Liv 6L **59**
L23: Crosb 6J **33**
Ennis Rd. L12: W Der 3C **60**
Ensor St. L20: Boot 9A **44**
Enstone WN8: Skel 3G **31**
Enstone Av. L21: Lith 1N **43**
Enstone Rd. L25: Hunts X 1F **92**
Ensworth Rd. L18: Moss H 3N **75**
Enterprise Pk.
CH65: Ell P 1C **112**
WA11: Rainf 7E **38**
Enterprise Way L13: Wavtr 8K **59**
WA3: Low 3H **53**
Enticott Rd. M44: Cad 4J **69**
Enville St. WA4: Warr 4D **82**
Epping Av. WA9: Sut M 6L **63**
Epping Cl. L35: Rainh 7G **62**
Epping Ct. CH60: Hesw 6A **88**
Epping Dr. WA1: Wools 9L **67**
Epping Gro. L15: Wavtr 2N **75**
Epsom Cl. L10: Aintr 1K **45**
Epsom Gdns. WA4: App 9F **82**
Epsom Gro. L33: Kirkb 5E **36**
Epsom Rd. CH46: Leas 6N **55**
Epsom St. WA9: St H 6B **50**
Epsom Way L5: Liv 4C **58**
Epstein Ct. *L6: Liv 6G 59*
(off Coleridge St.)
Epstein Theatre, The 6G 4 (8C 58)
Epworth Cl. CH43: Clau 2G **73**
WA5: Burtw 3H **65**
Epworth Grange
CH43: Clau 2G 73
(off Epworth Cl.)
Epworth St. L6: Liv 3L **5** (7E **58**)
Eremon Cl. L9: Aintr 2J **45**
Erfurt Av. CH63: Beb 3N **89**
Erica Ct. CH60: Hesw 5M **87**
Erica Pk. L27: N'ley 3J **77**
Eric Av. WA1: Padg 9F **66**
Eric Fountain Rd. CH65: Ell P 3J **103**
Eric Gro. CH44: Wall 5G **57**
Eric Rd. CH44: Wall 5G **57**
Ericson Dr. PR8: South 1A **12**
Ericsson Dr. L14: Brd G 8A **60**
Eric St. WA8: Widnes 6M **79**
Eridge St. L8: Liv 4F **74**
Erin Cl. L8: Liv 2D **74**
Erindale Cres. WA6: Frod 8K **107**
Erl St. L9: Aintr 4F **44**
Ermine Cres. L5: Liv 4E **58**
Erradale Cres. WN3: Winst 1F **40**
Errington Av. CH65: Ell P 8A **104**
Errington Ct. L17: Aig 8K **75**
Errington St. L5: Kirkd 3B **58**
Errol St. L17: Aig 5G **74**
Erskine Cl. WA11: St H 4A **50**
Erskine Ind. Est. L6: Liv 2L **5** (6F **58**)
Erskine Rd. CH44: Wall 6J **57**
M31: Part 7M **69**
Erskine St. L6: Liv 3L **5** (7E **58**)
Erskine St. Ind. Est. L6: Liv 3M **5**
Erwood St. WA2: Warr 2C **82**
Erylmore Rd. L18: Moss H 7M **75**
Escolme Dr. CH49: Grea 5L **71**
Escor Rd. L25: Gate 2E **76**
Escort Cl. L25: Hunts X 8G **77**
Eshelby Cl. L22: Wloo 1L **43**
Esher Cl. CH43: Bid 1C **72**
CH62: New F 8A **74**
Eshe Rd. L23: Blun 7J **33**
Eshe Rd. Nth. L23: Blun 6H **33**
Esher Rd.
CH62: New F 8A **74**
L6: Liv 6H **59**
Eskbank WN8: Skel 4F **30**
Eskbrook WN8: Skel 3F **30**
Eskburn Rd. L13: Liv 3K **59**
Eskdale CH65: Whit 2N **111**
WN8: Skel 4E **30**
Eskdale Av. CH46: More 8K **55**
CH62: East 1D **102**
L39: Augh 2N **27**
WA2: Warr 6D 66
(off Bentham Av.)
WA11: St H 2L **49**
Eskdale Cl. L37: Form 2D **24**
WA7: Beech 1N **107**
Eskdale Dr. L31: Mag 1K **35**
L37: Form 2D **24**
Eskdale Rd. L9: W'ton 5F **44**
WN4: Ash M 6K **41**
Esk St. L20: Kirkd 1A **58**
Eslington St. L19: G'dale 9M **75**
Esmond St. L6: Liv 4G **59**
Esonwood Rd. L35: Whis 6A **62**
Espin St. L4: W'ton 9E **44**
Esplanade CH42: Rock F 6A **74**
PR8: South 1L **11**
Esplanade, The CH62: New F 7A **74**
L20: Boot 7B 44
(off Strand Shop. Cen.)
L22: Wloo 2K **43**
Esplanade (Park & Ride) 8E 6
Esplen Av. L23: Crosb 6M **33**
Essex Gdns. M44: Cad 5J **69**
Essex Rd. CH48: W Kir 5D **70**
L36: Huy 5L **61**
PR8: Birkd 6N **11**
Essex Way L20: Boot 6C **44**
Esthwaite Av. WA11: St H 2M **49**
Estuary Banks L24: Speke 3D **92**
Estuary Banks Bus. Pk. L24: Speke 3D **92**
Estuary Blvd. L24: Speke 4D **92**
Estuary Commerce Pk. L24: Speke 3D **92**
(not continuous)
Etal Cl. L11: Norr G 9N **45**
Ethelbert La. CH47: Meols 9D **54**
Ethelbert Rd. CH47: Meols 9D **54**
Ethel Rd. CH44: Wall 6K **57**
Etherley Dr. WA12: Newt W 9M **51**
Etna St. L13: Liv 6L **59**
Eton Ct. L18: Moss H 3B **76**
PR9: South 6H **7**
Eton Dr. CH63: Thorn H 9F **88**
L10: Aintr 9H **35**
Eton Hall Dr. WA9: St H 2M **63**
Eton Rd. CH65: Ell P 1B **112**
Eton St. L4: W'ton 9E **44**
Etruscan Rd. L13: Liv 5M **59**
Ettington Dr. PR8: Ainsd 9G **11**
Ettington Rd. L4: W'ton 2G **59**
Ettrick Cl. L33: Kirkb 5B **36**
Euclid Av. WA4: Grap 6J **83**
(not continuous)
Eurolink WA9: St H 5J **63**
Eurolink Bus. Pk. WA9: St H 6J **63**
Europa Blvd. CH41: Birke 2L **73**
WA5: Westb 7L **65**
Europa Cen., The CH41: Birke 2K **73**
Europa Pools Leisure Cen. 2K 73
Europa Sq. CH41: Birke 2L **73**
Europa Way CH65: Ell P 8A **104**
Eustace St. WA2: Warr 2B **82**
Euston Gro. CH43: Oxton 3H **73**
Euston St. L4: W'ton 8E **44**
Evans Bus. Pk. CH65: Ell P 5L **103**
Evans Cl. WA11: Hay 3H **51**
Evans Pl. WA4: Warr 5E **82**
Evans Rd. CH47: Hoy 1C **70**
L24: Speke 2F **92**
Evans St. L34: Presc 2A **62**
Evellynne Cl. L32: Kirkb 9B **36**
Evelyn Av. L34: Presc 3B **62**
WA9: St H 7A **50**
Evelyn Rd. CH44: Wall 6J **57**
Evelyn St. L5: Kirkd 3C **58**
WA5: Warr 4M **81**
WA9: St H 7A **50**
Evenson Way L13: Liv 5M **59**
Evenwood WA9: St H 3M **63**
WN8: Skel 3G **30**
Evenwood Cl. WA7: Manor P 3G **97**
Evenwood Ct. WN8: Skel 3F **30**
Everard Cl. L40: Scar 7L **13**
Everard Rd. PR8: South 2C **12**
Evercroft Rd. L14: Brd G 7C **60**
Everdon Wood L33: Kirkb 8D **36**
Evered Av. L9: W'ton 6F **44**
Everest Cl. CH66: Gt Sut 2L **111**
Everest Rd. CH42: Tran 6K **73**
L23: Crosb 7L **33**
Evergreen Cl. CH49: Upton 2L **71**
L27: N'ley 2J **77**
Evergreens, The L37: Form 9D **16**
Evergreen Way WA9: Bold 2C **64**
Everite Rd. WA8: Widnes 9E **78**
Everite Rd. Ind. Est. WA8: Widnes 9E **78**
Everleigh Cl. CH43: Bid 1B **72**
Eversham Cl. PR9: Banks 2E **8**
Eversleigh Dr. CH63: Beb 3N **89**
Eversley WA8: Widnes 6E **78**
WN8: Skel 3G **30**
Eversley Cl. WA4: App 2F **98**
WA6: Frod 8N **107**
Eversley Pk. CH43: Oxton 5H **73**
Eversley St. L8: Liv 2F **74**
(not continuous)
EVERTON 4D 58
Everton Brow L3: Liv 1J **5** (6D **58**)
Everton FC 9E 44
Everton Gro. WA11: St H 5N **49**
Everton Rd. L6: Liv 1L **5** (5E **58**)
PR8: Birkd 2N **11**
Everton St. WN4: Garsw 6F **40**
Everton Valley L4: W'ton 2D **58**
Everton Vw. L20: Boot 8A **44**
Every St. L6: Liv 5G **59**
Evesham Cl. L25: Woolt 6D **76**
WA4: Stockt H 8D **82**
WN7: Leigh 1L **53**
Evesham Rd. CH45: Wall 3F **56**
L4: W'ton 9J **45**
Evington WN8: Skel 3G **31**
Evington Dr. L14: Brd G 7B **60**
Ewanville L36: Huy 8J **61**
Ewart Rd. L16: Child 9E **60**
L21: Sea 3N **43**
WA11: St H 4L **49**
Ewden Cl. L16: Child 1C **76**
Ewloe Ct. CH65: Ell P 3B **112**
Excalibur Way M44: Irlam 2L **69**
Exchange Flags L2: Liv 4D **4**
EXCHANGE ISLAND 4C **30**
Exchange Pas. E. L2: Liv 4D **4** (7B **58**)
Exchange Pas. W. L2: Liv 4D **4** (7B **58**)
Exchange Pl. L35: Rainh 6F **62**
Exchange St. WA10: St H 7K **49**
Exchange St. E. L2: Liv 4D **4** (7B **58**)
Exchange St. W.
L2: Liv 5D **4** (8B **58**)
Exeley L35: Whis 7B **62**
Exeter Cl. L10: Aintr 1K **45**
Exeter Rd. CH44: Wall 4J **57**
CH65: Ell P 9A **104**
L20: Boot 8B **44**
Exeter St. WA10: St H 7G **49**
Exford Rd. L12: W Der 1B **60**
Exhibition Cen. Liverpool 9D **4** (1B **74**)
Exmoor Cl. CH61: Pens 2N **87**
PR9: South 1N **7**
Exmouth Cl. CH41: Birke 2K **73**
Exmouth Cres. WA7: Murd 9G **97**
Exmouth Gdns. CH41: Birke 2K **73**
Exmouth St. CH41: Birke 2K **73**
Exmouth Way CH41: Birke 2K **73**
WA5: Burtw 3H **65**
Express Ind. Est. WA8: Widnes 9D **78**
Expressway Bus. Pk. CH42: Tran 5M **73**
Extension Vw. WA9: St H 1N **63**
Eyes La. WN8: Parb 2D **22**
Eyre Pl. CH65: Ell P 8N **103**

F

Fab4D 6C 4 (8A 58)
FACT 7H 5 (9D 58)
Factory La. WA1: Warr 4A **82**
WA5: Warr 3A **82**
WA8: Widnes 5L **79**
Factory Row WA10: St H 9H **49**
Fairacre Rd. L19: G'dale 9M **75**
Fairacres Rd. CH63: Beb 3N **89**
Fairbairn Rd. L22: Wloo 1L **43**
Fairbank St. L15: Wavtr 1K **75**
Fairbeech M. CH43: Bid 1C **72**
Fairbourne Cl. WA5: Call 6N **65**
Fairbrook Dr. CH41: Birke 8E **56**
Fairbrother Cres. WA2: Warr 7E **66**
Fairburn WN8: Skel 1E **30**
Fairburn Cl. WA8: Widnes 5A **80**
Fairburn Rd. L13: Liv 3K **59**
Fairclough Av. WA1: Warr 4D **82**
Fairclough Cl. L35: Rainh 6E **62**
Fairclough Cres. WA11: Hay 4C **50**
Fairclough La. CH43: Oxton 4H **73**
Fairclough Rd. L35: Rainh 6E **62**
L36: Huy 3G **60**
WA10: St H 6F **48**
Fairclough St. L1: Liv 6G **5** (8C **58**)
WA5: Burtw 3G **64**
WA12: Newt W 7K **51**
Fairfax Dr. WA7: Run 5N **95**
Fairfax Pl. L11: Norr G 8J **45**
Fairfax Rd. CH41: Tran 4L **73**
L11: Norr G 8K **45**
FAIRFIELD 6J **59**
Fairfield L23: Crosb 7L **33**
Fairfield Av. CH65: Whit 3M **111**
L36: Huy 7E **60**
Fairfield Cl. L36: Huy 7E **60**
L39: Orm 6C **20**
Fairfield Cres. CH46: More 9L **55**
L6: Liv 6J **59**
L36: Huy 7E **60**
Fairfield Dr. CH48: W Kir 5F **70**
L39: Orm 6C **20**
Fairfield Gdns. WA4: Stockt H 6F **82**
WA11: Crank 9H **39**
Fairfield Rd. CH42: Tran 6L **73**
M44: Cad 4J **69**
PR8: Ainsd 9J **11**
WA4: Stockt H 7D **82**
WA8: Widnes 7L **79**
WA10: St H 5F **48**
WA13: Lymm 5F **84**
Fairfield St. L7: Liv 6K **59**
WA1: Warr 2D **82**
Fairford Cl. WA5: Gt San 2K **81**
Fairford Cres. L14: Knott A 5N **59**
Fairford Rd. L14: Knott A 5N **59**
Fairhaven L33: Kirkb 6C **36**
WN8: Skel 1F **30**
Fairhaven Cl. CH42: Rock F 6M **73**
WA5: Gt San 4K **81**
Fairhaven Dr. CH63: Brom 1B **102**
Fairhaven Ho. *L19: Aig 9L 75*
(off The Spinnakers)
Fairhaven Rd. PR9: South 3N **7**
WA8: Widnes 6M **79**
Fairhavens Ct. WA8: Widnes 8L **79**
Fairhills Ind. Est. M44: Irlam 1M **69**
Fairhills Rd. M44: Irlam 1M **69**
Fairholme Av. CH64: Nest 5D **100**
L34: Eccl P 3C **62**
WN4: Ash M 7K **41**
Fairholme Cl. L12: W Der 1M **59**
Fairholme M. *L23: Crosb 7L 33*
(off Fairholme Rd.)
Fairholme Rd. L23: Crosb 7L **33**
Fairhurst Dr. WN8: Parb 3E **22**
Fairhurst Ter. *L34: Presc 3B 62*
(off Scotchbarn La.)
Fair Isles Cl. CH65: Ell P 4A **112**
Fairlawn Cl. CH63: Raby M 9N **89**
Fairlawn Ct. CH43: Oxton 3F **72**
Fairlawne Cl. L33: Kirkb 6C **36**
Fairlie WN8: Skel 1F **30**
Fairlie Cres. L20: Boot 3C **44**
Fairlie Dr. L35: Rainh 7G **62**
Fairmead Rd. CH46: More 8M **55**
L11: Norr G 8K **45**
Fairmont Dr. WA5: Gt San 1J **81**
Fair Oak Ct. WA7: Pres B 3H **109**
Fairoak La. WA7: Pres B 3H **109**
Fairstead WN8: Skel 1F **30**
Fairthorn Wlk. L33: Kirkb 8E **36**
Fair Vw. WN5: Bil 6N **39**
Fairview CH41: Tran 4L **73**
Fair Vw. Av. WN5: Bil 6N **39**
Fairview Av. CH45: Wall 4G **57**
Fairview Cl. CH43: Oxton 5H **73**
WN4: Ash M 7K **41**
Fairview Pl. CH61: Pens 4N **87**
L8: Liv 3F **74**
Fairview Rd. CH43: Oxton 6H **73**
CH65: Whit 3M **111**
Fairview Way CH61: Pens 4N **87**
Fairway L36: Huy 5L **61**
WA10: Windle 5F **48**
Fairway, The L12: Knott A 5B **60**
Fairway Cres. CH62: Brom 3C **90**
Fairway Nth. CH62: Brom 3C **90**
Fairways CH42: Tran 8H **73**
L23: Crosb 6K **33**
PR9: South 5H **7**
WA4: App 2E **98**
WA6: Frod 7N **107**
Fairways, The CH48: Caldy 1E **86**
L25: Hunts X 8H **77**
WN4: Ash M 9G **40**
WN8: Skel 1G **30**
Fairways Cl. L25: Woolt 8F **76**
Fairways Ct. L37: Form 8C **16**
Fairways Dr. CH66: Lit Sut 6J **103**
Fairway Sth. CH62: Brom 4C **90**
Fairways (Park & Ride) 5H 7
Fairway Trad. Est. WA8: Widnes 9H **79**
Falcon Cres. L27: N'ley 4K **77**
Falcondale Rd. WA2: Winw 3C **66**
Falconers Grn. WA5: Westb 7K **65**
Falconer St. L20: Boot 4N **43**
Falcongate Ind. Est. CH44: Wall 8J **57**
Falconhall Rd. L9: Faz 6L **45**
Falcon Hey L10: Faz 4M **45**
Falcon Pl. L40: Burs 3F **20**
Falcon Rd. CH41: Birke 4J **73**
CH66: Gt Sut 2L **111**
Falcons Way WA7: Pal F 9A **96**
Falkirk Av. WA8: Widnes 5H **79**
Falkland WN8: Skel 1F **30**
Falkland Dr. WN4: Garsw 7E **40**
Falkland Rd. CH44: Wall 5K **57**
PR8: South 2C **12**
Falklands App. L11: Norr G 8K **45**
Falkland St. CH41: Birke 9G **56**
L3: Liv 3K **5** (7E **58**)
(not continuous)
Falkner Sq. L7: Liv 9F **58**
L8: Liv 9L **5** (1E **74**)
Falkner St. L7: Liv 8N **5** (9F **58**)
L8: Liv 8K **5** (9E **58**)
(not continuous)
Falkner Ter. L8: Liv 9M **5**
Fallbrook Dr. L12: W Der 9N **45**
Fallow Cl. WA9: Clock F 5M **63**
Fallowfield L33: Kirkb 7C **36**
WA7: Run 6N **95**
Fallowfield Cl. L37: Form 9H **17**
Fallowfield Gro.
WA2: Padg 8J **67**
Fallowfield Rd. L15: Wavtr 2L **75**
Fallows Way L35: Whis 8N **61**
Falls La. L26: Halew 7J **77**
Falmouth Dr. WA5: Penk 5G **80**
Falmouth Pl.
WA7: Murd 9G **96**
Falmouth Rd. L11: Crox 5B **46**
Falstaff St. L20: Kirkd 1B **58**
Falstone Cl. WA3: Birchw 3B **68**
WN3: Winst 1F **40**
Falstone Dr. WA7: Murd 7G **96**

Faraday Rd.—Fiveways Pk.

Faraday Rd. CH65: Whit 1M **111**
L13: Wavtr 8K **59**
L33: Know I 3F **46**
WA7: Astm 4N **95**
Faraday St. L5: Liv 4F **58**
WA3: Ris 3M **67**
Farcroft Cl. WA13: Lymm 3J **85**
Fardon Cl. WN3: Wigan 1H **41**
Fareham Cl. CH49: Upton 2M **71**
Fareham Dr. PR9: Banks 2E **8**
Fareham Rd. L7: Liv 7J **59**
Faringdon Cl. L25: Hunts X 1F **92**
Farley Av. CH62: Brom 6B **90**
Farley La. WN8: Roby M 1K **31**
Farlow Rd. CH42: Rock F 7M **73**
Farmbrook Rd. L25: Gate 1F **76**
Farm Cl. CH49: Grea 4K **71**
PR9: South 7M **7**
WA9: Clock F 6N **63**
Farmdale Cl. L18: Moss H 6N **75**
Farmdale Dr. CH2: Elt 2L **113**
L31: Mag 2K **35**
Far Mdw. La. CH61: Irby 1K **87**
Farmer Pl. L20: Boot 3D **44**
Farmers Heath CH66: Gt Sut 3J **111**
Farmers La. WA5: Burtw 3J **65**
Farmer Ted's Farm Pk. 3E **26**
Farmfield Dr. CH43: Bid 1C **72**
Farmfield Gro. CH46: More 9A **56**
Farm La. WA4: App 8F **82**
Farmleigh Gdns. WA5: Gt San 2L **81**
Farm Mdw. Rd. WN5: Orr 7N **31**
FAR MOOR 8N **31**
Far Moss Rd. L23: Blun 5H **33**
Farm Rd. WA9: Clock F 6N **63**
Farmside CH46: Leas 6N **55**
Farmside Cl. WA5: Warr 1N **81**
Farmstead Way CH66: Gt Sut 4K **111**
Farm Vw. L21: Ford 9A **34**
Farmview Cl. L27: N'ley 1G **77**
Farm Way WA12: Newt W 9N **51**
Farnborough Gro. L26: Halew 7K **77**
Farnborough Rd. PR8: Birkd 6M **11**
Farndale WA8: Widnes 3K **79**
Farndale Cl. WA5: Gt San 1H **81**
Farndale Gro. WN4: Ash M 9L **41**
Farndon Av. CH45: Wall 3E **56**
WA9: Sut M 5L **63**
Farndon Dr. CH48: W Kir 5F **70**
Farndon Rd. CH66: Ell P 8K **103**
Farndon Way CH43: Oxton 4F **72**
Farne Cl. CH65: Ell P 5A **112**
Farnham Cl. L32: Kirkb 1D **46**
WA4: App 9F **82**
Farnhill Cl. WA7: Nort 7F **96**
Farnley Cl. WA7: Wind H 6F **96**
Farnside Ct. L17: Aig 9K **75**
FARNWORTH 5L **79**
Farnworth Av. CH46: Leas 6M **55**
Farnworth Cl. WA8: Widnes 4L **79**
Farnworth Gro. L33: Kirkb 6C **36**
Farnworth M. WA8: Widnes 5L **79**
Farnworth Rd. WA5: Penk 4D **80**
Farnworth St. L6: Liv 1N **5** (6G **58**)
WA8: Widnes 4L **79**
WA9: St H 6M **49**
Farrant St. WA8: Widnes 8L **79**
Farrar St. L13: Liv 2K **59**
Farrell Cl. L31: Mell 7N **35**
Farrell Rd. WA4: Stockt H 8D **82**
Farrell St. WA1: Warr 3D **82**
Farr Hall Dr. CH60: Hesw 8M **87**
Farr Hall Rd. CH60: Hesw 7M **87**
Farrier Rd. L33: Kirkb 9E **36**
Farriers Wlk. WA9: Clock F 5M **63**
Farriers Way CH48: Frank 6J **71**
L30: Neth 2E **44**
Farrier Way WN6: App B 6M **23**
Farringdon Cl. WA9: St H 4J **63**
Farringdon Rd. WA2: Winw 3C **66**
Farrington Dr. L39: Orm 7C **20**
Farthing Cl. L25: Hunts X 9E **76**
Farthings, The WA13: Lymm 4D **84**
Farthingstone Cl. L35: Whis 3D **62**
Fatherside Dr. L30: Neth 8B **34**
Faulkner Cl. PR8: Ainsd 9J **11**
Faulkner Gdns. PR8: Ainsd 8J **11**
Faversham Rd. L11: Norr G 7K **45**
Faversham Way CH42: Rock F 6M **73**
Fawcett WN8: Skel 1E **30**
Fawcett Rd. L31: Lydi 9J **27**
Fawley Rd. L18: Moss H 6A **76**
L35: Rainh 8H **63**
FAZAKERLEY 3L **45**
Fazakerley Cl. L9: W'ton 6F **44**
Fazakerley Rd. L9: W'ton 6F **44**
L35: Presc 5B **62**
Fazakerley Sports Cen. 2L **45**
Fazakerley Station (Rail) 3J **45**
Fazakerley St. L3: Liv 4C **4** (7A **58**)
Fearnham Cl. WN7: Leigh 1M **53**
FEARNHEAD 7H **67**
Fearnhead Cross WA2: Fearn 7G **67**
Fearnhead La. WA2: Fearn 7H **67**
Fearnley Hall CH41: Birke 3K **73**
Fearnley Rd. CH41: Birke 3K **73**
Fearnley Way WA12: Newt W 9L **51**
Fearnside St. L7: Liv 9H **59**
Feather La. CH60: Hesw 7N **87**
Feathers, The WA10: St H 7G **48**
Feeny St. WA9: Sut M 7L **63**
Feilden Rd. CH63: Beb 3N **89**
Felcroft Way L33: Kirkb 9D **36**
Felicity Gro. CH46: More 8L **55**
Fell Gro. WA11: St H 2K **49**
Fellow Brook WN7: Leigh 1N **53**
Fell St. CH44: Wall 7L **57**
L7: Liv 7G **59**
Felltor Cl. L25: Woolt 5D **76**
Fell Vw. PR9: South 1B **8**
Fellwood Gro. L35: Whis 7B **62**
Felmersham Av. L11: Norr G 7L **45**
Felspar Rd. L32: Kirkb 3D **46**
Felstead WN8: Skel 2E **30**
Felstead Av. L25: Woolt 6G **77**
Felsted Dr. L10: Aintr 1K **45**
Felthorpe Cl. CH49: Upton 1B **72**
Felton Cl. CH46: More 9K **55**
Felton Ct. *L17: Aig 5H 75*
(off Lark La.)
Felton Gro. L13: Liv 5L **59**
Feltons WN8: Skel 2E **30**
Feltwell Rd. L4: W'ton 3G **58**
Feltwood Cl. L12: W Der 2D **60**
Feltwood Mnr. L12: W Der 2D **60**
Feltwood Rd. L12: W Der 1D **60**
Feltwood Wlk. L12: W Der 2D **60**
Fendale Av. CH46: More 8A **56**
Fender Ct. CH49: Wdchu 7D **72**
Fender La. CH43: Bid 8A **56**
CH46: More 8A **56**
Fenderside Rd. CH43: Bid 9C **56**
Fender Vw. Rd. CH46: More 9A **56**
Fender Way CH43: Bid 2B **72**
CH61: Pens 3A **88**
Fenham Dr. WA5: Penk 4G **81**
Fennel St. WA1: Warr 3D **82**
Fenney Ct. WN8: Skel 3F **30**
Fenton Cl. L24: Speke 4H **93**
L30: Neth 2G **44**
WA8: Widnes 5F **78**
WA10: St H 6J **49**
Fenton Grn. L24: Speke 5H **93**
Fenwick La. WA7: Run 9N **95**
Fenwick Rd. CH66: Gt Sut 3K **111**
Fenwick St. L2: Liv 5D **4** (8B **58**)
Ferguson Av. CH49: Grea 5L **71**
CH66: Ell P 8K **103**
Ferguson Dr. WA2: Warr 8E **66**
Ferguson Rd. L11: Norr G 1K **59**
L21: Lith 1B **44**
Fern Bank L31: Mag 2K **35**
WA11: Rainf 4B **38**
Fernbank Av. L36: Huy 7H **61**
Fernbank Cl. WA3: Ris 5M **67**
Fernbank Dr. L30: Neth 7F **34**
Fernbank La. CH49: Upton 1N **71**
Fern Cl. L27: N'ley 4J **77**
L32: Kirkb 7D **36**
WA3: Birchw 5L **67**
WN8: Skel 3B **30**
Ferndale WN8: Skel 2E **30**
Ferndale Av. CH2: Elt 2L **113**
CH44: Wall 5J **57**
CH48: Frank 7J **71**
Ferndale Cl. L9: W'ton 3F **44**
WA1: Wools 1K **83**
WA8: Bold H 1A **80**
Ferndale Dr. WN6: App B 6N **23**
Ferndale Rd. CH47: Hoy 1C **70**
L15: Wavtr 2K **75**
L22: Wloo 9K **33**
Fern End PR9: Banks 3E **8**
Fern Gdns. L34: Eccl P 2C **62**
Fern Gro. CH43: Noct 4D **72**
L8: Liv 2H **75**
L20: Boot 6B **44**
Fern Hey L23: Thorn 6A **34**
Fernhill CH45: New B 1H **57**
Fernhill Av. L20: Boot 7D **44**
Fernhill Cl. L20: Boot 7D **44**
(not continuous)
Fernhill Dr. L8: Liv 2F **74**
Fernhill Gdns. L20: Boot 7D **44**
Fernhill M. E. *L20: Boot 7D 44*
(off Fernhill Rd.)
Fernhill M. W. L20: Boot 7D **44**
Fernhill Rd. L20: Boot 4C **44**
Fernhill Wlk. WA9: Clock F 6M **63**
Fernhill Way L20: Boot 7D **44**
Fernhurst WA7: Run 7N **95**
Fernhurst Ga. L39: Augh 2N **27**
Fernhurst Rd. L32: Kirkb 1A **46**
Fernie Cres. L8: Liv 3E **74**
Fernlea Av. WA9: St H 2G **63**
Fernlea Gro. WN4: Garsw 6F **40**
Fernlea M. CH43: Bid 9C **56**
Fernlea Rd. CH60: Hesw 7A **88**
Fernleigh Rd. L13: Liv 6N **59**
Fernley Rd. PR8: South 1N **11**
Fern Lodge L8: Liv 2H **75**
Fern Rd. CH65: Whit 3M **111**
Ferns Cl. CH60: Hesw 6K **87**
Fernside Gro. WN3: Winst 2F **40**
Ferns Rd. CH63: H Beb 2K **89**
Fernwood WA7: Nort 6D **96**
Fernwood Av. L36: Huy 3H **61**
Fernwood Dr. L26: Halew 8J **77**
Fernwood Rd. L17: Aig 6K **75**
Ferny Brow Rd. CH49: Wdchu 5B **72**
Fernyess La. CH64: Will 8L **101**
Ferny Knoll Rd. WA11: Rainf 9B **30**
Ferrer St. WN4: Ash M 5H **41**
Ferrett La. WN8: Parb 2D **22**
Ferrey Rd. L10: Faz 3M **45**
Ferries Cl. CH42: Rock F 8N **73**
Ferrous Way M44: Irlam 3M **69**
Ferry La. WA4: Thel 4M **83**
Ferrymasters Way M44: Irlam 1N **69**
Ferry Rd. CH62: East 1F **102**
Ferryside CH44: Wall 7L **57**
WA4: Thel 5K **83**
Ferryside La. PR9: South 2A **8**
Ferry Vw. Rd. CH44: Wall 7L **57**
Ferryview Wlk. WA7: Cas 5B **96**
Festival Av. WA2: Warr 7E **66**
Festival Ct. L11: Norr G 7N **45**
Festival Cres. WA2: Warr 7E **66**
Festival Gdns. 6F **74**
Festival Rd. CH65: Ell P 9L **103**
WA11: Rainf 6D **38**
Festival Ter. *WA7: Run 7M 95*
(off Festival Way)
Festival Way WA7: Run 7M **95**
Ffrancon Dr. CH63: H Beb 9M **73**
FIDDLER'S FERRY
PR9 1A **8**
WA5 7F **80**
Fiddlers Ferry Golf Course 6E **80**
Fiddlers Ferry Rd. WA8: Widnes 8M **79**
Fiddlers Ferry Sailing Club 7G **80**
Fidler St. WA10: St H 9G **48**
Field Av. L21: Lith 2N **43**
Field Cl. CH62: New F 8A **74**
L40: Burs 2K **21**
WA9: Clock F 6N **63**
Fieldfare Cl. L25: Gate 3E **76**
WA3: Birchw 5N **67**
WA3: Low 2E **52**
Fieldgate WA8: Widnes 9E **78**
Field Hey La. CH64: Will 5A **102**
(not continuous)
Field Ho. L12: W Der 2M **59**
Fieldhouse Row WA7: Run 8N **95**
Fieldings, The L31: Lydi 8G **27**
Fielding St. L6: Liv 2N **5** (6F **58**)
Fieldlands PR8: South 4F **12**
Field La. L10: Faz 4M **45**
L21: Lith 1N **43**
WA4: App 1D **98**
Field Rd. CH45: New B 2H **57**
WA9: Clock F 6N **63**
Field's End L36: Huy 9J **61**
Fieldsend Cl. L27: N'ley 4J **77**
Fieldsend Dr. WN7: Leigh 2K **53**
Fieldside Rd. CH42: Rock F 6L **73**
Field St. L3: Liv 1J **5** (6D **58**)
(not continuous)
WN8: Skel 2A **30**
Fieldsway WA7: W'ton 9K **95**
Fieldton Rd. L11: Norr G 8N **45**
Field Vw. L21: Lith 2N **43**
Fieldview WN8: Uph 5K **31**
Fieldview Dr. WA2: Warr 8D **66**
Field Wlk. L23: Thorn 6A **34**
L39: Orm 8F **20**
M31: Part 6L **69**
Field Way L35: Rainh 4F **62**
Fieldway CH45: Wall 4G **56**
CH47: Meols 1G **70**
CH60: Hesw 6C **88**
CH63: H Beb 8K **73**
CH66: Lit Sut 7G **102**
L15: Wavtr 9A **60**
L31: Mag 4K **35**
L36: Huy 9K **61**
WA6: Frod 7M **107**
WA8: Widnes 6A **80**
Fieldway Ct. CH41: Birke 9J **57**
Fife Rd. WA1: Warr 1F **82**
Fifth Av. CH43: Bid 1B **72**
L9: Aintr 3K **45**
(Broadway)
L9: Aintr 3J **45**
(Sixth Av.)
WA7: Pal F 8B **96**
Filbert Cl. L33: Kirkb 5D **36**
Filby Gdns. WA9: St H 3H **63**
Fildes Cl. WA5: Gt San 3L **81**
Fillmore Gro. WA8: Widnes 5J **79**
Filton Rd. L14: Knott A 4F **60**
Finborough Rd. L4: W'ton 8H **45**
FINCHAM 4G **60**
Fincham Grn. L14: Knott A 4F **60**
Fincham Rd. L14: Knott A 4E **60**
Fincham Sq. L14: Knott A 4E **60**
Finch Av. WA11: Rainf 6D **38**
Finch Cl. WA9: Clock F 6N **63**
Finch Ct. CH41: Birke 1K **73**
Finchdale Gdns. WA3: Low 2J **53**
Finchdean Cl. CH49: Grea 4K **71**
Finch Dene L14: Knott A 3D **60**
Finch La. L14: Knott A 3D **60**
L26: Halew 1M **93**
WN6: App B 4L **23**
Finch Lea Dr. L14: Knott A 4E **60**
Finchley Dr. WA11: St H 3M **49**
Finchley Rd. L4: W'ton 2G **58**
Finch Mdw. Cl. L9: Faz 6L **45**
Finch Mill Av. WN6: App B 6N **23**
Finch Pl. L3: Liv 3K **5** (7E **58**)
Finch Rd. L14: Knott A 3E **60**
Finch Way L14: Knott A 4D **60**
Findlay Cl. WA12: Newt W 8K **51**
(not continuous)
Findley Dr. CH46: Leas 6N **55**
Findon WN8: Skel 3E **30**
Findon Rd. L32: Kirkb 2D **46**
Fine Jane's Way PR9: South 7N **7**
Fingall Rd. L15: Wavtr 2N **75**
Finger Ho. La. WA8: Bold H 8N **63**
Fingland Rd. L15: Wavtr 1K **75**
Finlan Rd. WA8: Widnes 9J **79**
Finlay Av. WA5: Penk 5G **81**
Finlay Ct. L30: Neth 7E **34**
Finlay St. L6: Liv 6H **59**
Finney, The CH48: Caldy 1E **86**
Finney Gro. WA11: Hay 4G **50**
Finningley Ct. WA2: Padg 8F **66**
Finsbury Cl. WA5: Gt San 4L **81**
Finsbury Pk. WA8: Widnes 3M **79**
Finstall Rd. CH63: Spit 5M **89**
Finvoy Rd. L13: Liv 2K **59**
Fiona Wlk. L10: Faz 3N **45**
Fir Av. L26: Halew 8L **77**
Firbank CH2: Elt 2N **113**
Firbank Cl. WA7: Wind H 6F **96**
Firbeck WN8: Skel 3E **30**
Firbrook Ct. CH43: Bid 8C **56**
Fir Cl. L26: Halew 8L **77**
Fir Cotes L31: Mag 2K **35**
Firdale Rd. L9: W'ton 6F **44**
Firdene Cres. CH43: Noct 4E **72**
Firecrest Ct. WA1: Warr 5B **82**
FireFitHub 2E **74**
Firenza Av. CH65: Ell P 8M **103**
Fire Station Cl. L23: Crosb 7K **33**
Fire Station Rd. L35: Whis 4C **62**
Firethorne Rd. L26: Halew 6H **77**
Fir Gro. L9: Aintr 2H **45**
WA1: Padd 1G **83**
Fir La. L15: Wavtr 1M **75**
Firman Cl. WA5: Gt San 9K **65**
Fir Pk. WA8: Widnes 5H **79**
Fir Rd. L22: Wloo 9L **33**
Firs, The CH65: Ell P 3B **112**
Firs Av. CH63: Beb 4M **89**
Firs Cl. L37: Form 8D **16**
Firscraig L28: Stockb V 2G **60**
Firs Cres. L37: Form 8D **16**
Firshaw Rd. CH47: Meols 8D **54**
Firs La. L39: Augh, Hals 1K **27**
WA4: App 2C **98**
Firs Link L37: Form 9D **16**
First Av. CH43: Bid 2C **72**
L9: Aintr 3H **45**
(Higher La.)
L9: Aintr 4K **45**
(Second Av.)
L23: Crosb 7K **33**
L35: Rainh 5E **62**
Firstone Gro. L32: Kirkb 2C **46**
Fir St. M44: Cad 3J **69**
PR8: South 9K **7**
WA8: Widnes 6M **79**
WA10: St H 1G **62**
First St. WN2: Bam 4N **41**
Firswood Rd. WN8: Skel 2M **29**
Firth Blvd. WA2: Warr 1D **82**
Firthland Way WA9: St H 8B **50**
Fir Tree Av. WA3: Low 2G **52**
Firtree Av. WA1: Padg 9H **67**
Fir Tree Cl. WA4: Sttn 6E **98**
WA11: Kings M 4J **39**
WN8: Skel 5G **30**
Fir Tree Dr. Nth. L12: Crox 7B **46**
Fir Tree Dr. Sth. L12: Crox 7B **46**
Firtree Gro. CH66: Whit 5M **111**
Fir Tree La. L39: Augh, Hals 9L **19**
WA5: Burtw 2J **65**
Fir Tree Wlk. WA3: Low 2G **52**
Firway CH60: Hesw 1B **100**
Firwood WN8: Skel 1G **30**
Firwood Gro. WN4: Ash M 9J **41**
Fisher Av. L35: Whis 7A **62**
WA2: Warr 8C **66**
Fisher Ct. WA7: Run 4L **95**
Fisher Dr. PR9: South 8L **7**
Fisherfield Dr. WA3: Birchw 3A **68**
Fishermans Cl. L37: Form 7E **16**
Fisherman's Path L37: Form 5C **16**
Fisher Pl. L35: Whis 7A **62**
Fishers La. CH61: Pens 3M **87**
Fisher St. L8: Liv 2C **74**
WA7: Run 4L **95**
WA9: St H 1A **64**
Fishguard Cl. L6: Liv 5E **58**
Fish La. L40: Burs, H'wood 2F **14**
Fishwicks Ind. Est. WA9: St H 1M **63**
WA11: Hay 2H **51**
Fishwicks Pk. Ind. Est. WN4: Ash M 9G **40**
Fistral Cl. L10: Faz 4N **45**
Fistral Dr. WA10: Windle 4E **48**
Fitzclarence Wlk. L6: Liv 1L **5**
Fitzclarence Way L6: Liv 1L **5** (5E **58**)
Fitzgerald Rd. L13: Liv 6M **59**
Fitzherbert St. WA2: Warr 1C **82**
Fitzpatrick Ct. L3: Liv 5B **58**
Fitzroy Way L6: Liv 2M **5** (6F **58**)
Fitzwalter Rd. WA1: Wools 1L **83**
Fitzwilliam Wlk. WA7: Cas 5C **96**
FIVECROSSES 9N **107**
Fiveways WA10: Ec'stn 6D **48**
Fiveways Pk. CH64: Nest 3F **100**

Flag La.—Frodsham Station (Rail)

Flag La. CH64: Lit N 7F 100
Flail Cl. CH49: Grea 4K 71
Flambards CH49: Wdchu 5B 72
Flamstead WN8: Skel 3F 30
Flander Cl. WA8: Widnes 6F 78
Flashes La. CH64: Ness 9H 101
Flash La. CW9: Ant 9M 99
L40: Ruf 2N 15
Flatfield Way L31: Mag 2K 35
Flatman's La. L39: Down 3D 26
Flatt La. CH43: Oxton 5F 72
CH65: Ell P 9N 103
Flavian Ct. WA7: Cas 6A 96
Flawn Rd. L11: Norr G 1K 59
Flaxfield Rd. L37: Form 1G 25
Flaxfields L40: Lath 2K 21
Flaxhill CH46: More 8L 55
Flax La. L40: Lath 2K 21
Flaxley Cl. WA3: Birchw 4A 68
Flaxman Ct. L7: Liv 7H 59
(off Botanic Gro.)
Flaxman St. L7: Liv 7H 59
Flaxton WN8: Skel 3F 30
Flaybrick Cl. CH43: Bid 9E 56
Fleck La. CH48: Caldy, W Kir 7E 70
Fleetcroft Rd. CH49: Wdchu 6A 72
Fleet La. WA9: St H 7A 50
Fleet La. Ind. Est. WA9: St H 8A 50
Fleet St. CH65: Ell P 9M 103
L1: Liv 6G 4 (8C 58)
Fleetwood Cl. PR9: South 4L 7
WA5: Gt San 4K 81
Fleetwood Ct. PR9: South 6J 7
(off Park Rd.)
Fleetwood Cres. PR9: Banks 1E 8
Fleetwood Dr. PR9: Banks 1E 8
WA12: Newt W 6K 51
Fleetwood Gdns. L33: Kirkb 6D 36
(not continuous)
Fleetwood Pl. L25: Woolt 6D 76
(off Castle St.)
Fleetwood Rd. PR9: South 6H 7
(not continuous)
Fleetwoods La. L30: Neth 7C 34
Fleetwood Wlk. WA7: Murd 8E 96
Fleming Ct. L3: Liv 5B 58
Fleming Dr. WA2: Winw 3B 66
WN4: Ash M 7M 41
Fleming Rd. L24: Speke 1G 93
Fleming St. CH65: Ell P 8A 104
Flemington Av. L4: W'ton 9J 45
Fleming Way CH46: Leas 7A 56
Flers Av. WA4: Warr 5D 82
Fletcher Av. CH42: Rock F 6L 73
L34: Presc 2B 62
Fletcher Cl. CH49: Wdchu 5A 72
Fletcher Dr. L19: G'dale 9M 75
Fletcher's Dr. L40: Burs 1J 21
Fletchers La. WA13: Lymm 4F 84
Fletchers Row WA7: Hal 6B 96
(off Spark La.)
Fletcher St. WA4: Warr 5C 82
Flimby WN8: Skel 3G 30
Flint Cl. CH64: Nest 8E 100
Flint Ct. CH65: Ell P 3B 112
Flint Dr. CH64: Nest 7E 100
L12: Crox 9B 46
Flint Gro. M44: Cad 3J 69
Flint Mdw. CH64: Nest 7E 100
Flintshire Gdns. WA10: St H 8J 49
Flint St. L1: Liv 9G 4 (1C 74)
Flixton Gdns. WA9: St H 3H 63
Floodgates Rd. L38: Hight 7F 24
Floral Pavilion Theatre 9J 43
Floral Wood L17: Aig 6E 74
Flora St. WN4: Ash M 9K 41
Flordon WN8: Skel 2G 30
Florence Av. CH60: Hesw 6N 87
Florence Cl. L9: W'ton 7E 44
Florence Ct. L9: W'ton 7E 44
(off Buchanan Rd.)
Florence Nightingale Cl. L30: Neth 7E 34
Florence Rd. CH44: Wall 6L 57
Florence St. CH41: Birke 2K 73
L4: W'ton 1E 58
WA4: Warr 5E 82
WA9: St H 2F 62
Florentine Rd. L13: Liv 5M 59
Florida Cl. WA5: Gt San 1L 81
Florida Ct. L19: G'dale 8N 75
Florida Way L35: Presc 5A 62
Flour Mill Cl. L40: Burs 1J 21
Flowermead Cl. CH47: Meols 8G 54
Floyd Dr. WA2: Warr 8C 66
Fluin La. WA6: Frod 5M 107
Fluker's Brook La. L34: Know 9F 46
(not continuous)
Focus Bldg., The L3: Liv 3F 4
(off Crosshall St.)
Fogg's La. CW9: Ant 9H 99
Foinavon Cl. L9: W'ton 3E 44
Folds, The CH63: Thorn H 9G 89
Folds La. WA11: St H 3K 49
Folds Rd. WA11: Hay 5B 50
Fold St. WA3: Golb 1B 52
Foley Cl. L4: Kirkd 2D 58
Foley St. L4: Kirkd 2D 58
Foley St. Nth. L4: Kirkd 2D 58
Folkestone Rd. PR8: South 3D 12
Folkestone Way WA7: Murd 8E 96
Folly Farm Cl. WA5: Warr 1B 82
Folly La. CH44: Wall 4E 56
(not continuous)
WA5: Warr 1A 82
WA7: Run 6G 95
Folly Vw. Gro. L40: Burs 6E 20
Fontenoy St. L3: Liv 3F 4 (7C 58)
Fonthill Cl. L4: Kirkd 2C 58
Fonthill Rd. L4: Kirkd 1C 58
Forbes Cl. WA3: Birchw 5M 67
FORD
CH43 2C 72
L21 9A 34
Ford Av. L33: Kirkb 5C 36
Ford Cl. CH49: Upton 4B 72
L20: Boot 3D 44
L21: Ford 9A 34
Fordcombe Rd. L25: Gate 4G 77
Ford Dr. CH49: Upton 3B 72
Ford Farm Cl. WA4: Warr 7B 82
Fordham Cl. PR8: South 3D 12
Fordham St. L4: Kirkd 1D 58
Fordhill Vw. CH46: More 9A 56
Fordington Rd. WA5: Gt San 3K 81
Fordland Cl. WA3: Low 1F 52
Ford La. CH49: Upton 3B 72
L21: Ford 9A 34
Fordlea Rd. L12: W Der 1M 59
Fordlea Way L12: W Der 1M 59
Ford Rd. CH49: Upton 3A 72
L35: Presc 3C 62
Ford St. L3: Liv 1E 4 (6B 58)
WA1: Warr 2E 82
Fordton Retail Pk. 6B 66
Ford Vw. L21: Ford 8A 34
Ford Way CH49: Upton 4A 72
Ford Way M. CH49: Upton 4A 72
Forefield La. L23: Crosb 6M 33
Foreland Cl. WA5: Gt San 1E 80
Forest Cl. CH47: Meols 8E 54
L34: Eccl P 2C 62
Forest Ct. CH43: Clau 2F 72
Forest Dr. L36: Huy 6G 60
WN8: Skel 1F 30
Forest Gdns. M31: Part 6K 69
Forest Grn. L12: W Der 1N 59
Forest Gro. L34: Eccl P 2C 62
Forest Lawn L12: W Der 1N 59
Forest Mead WA10: Ec'stn 7D 48
Forest Rd. CH43: Clau 1G 72
CH47: Meols 8E 54
CH60: Hesw 6A 88
CH66: Ell P 7K 103
PR8: South 9J 7
WA9: Sut M 6K 63
Forest Wlk. WA7: Pal F 8B 96
(within Halton Lea Shop. Cen.)
Forfar Rd. L13: Liv 3J 59
Forge Cl. L40: Westh 9J 21
WA8: Cron 3F 78
Forge Cotts. L17: Aig 4H 75
Forge Rd. CH66: Lit Sut 8H 103
WA5: Gt San 3H 81
Forge Shop. Cen., The 7D 82
Forge St. L20: Kirkd 1B 58
FORMBY 1F 24
Formby Av. WA10: St H 9G 49
Formby Bri. L37: Form 2E 24
Formby Bus. Pk. L37: Form 1H 25
Formby By-Pass 7H 17
Formby Cl. WA5: Penk 4H 81
Formby Flds. L37: Form 2G 25
Formby Gdns. L37: Form 9F 16
Formby Golf Course 8D 16
Formby Hall Golf Course 5J 17
Formby La. L37: Form 2G 25
L39: Augh 2J 27
Formby Little Theatre 1F 24
Formby M. L37: Form 9F 16
Formby Nature Reserve 8B 16
Formby Point Cvn. Pk. L37: Form 3B 24
Formby Pool 1F 24
Formby Station (Rail) 2E 24
Formby St. L37: Form 2E 24
Formosa Dr. L10: Faz 3L 45
Formosa Rd. L10: Faz 3L 45
Formosa Way L10: Faz 3L 45
Fornalls Grn. La. CH47: Meols 1F 70
Forres Gro. WN4: Garsw 7F 40
Forrester Av. WA9: St H 2F 62
Forrest St. L1: Liv 8F 4 (9C 58)
Forrest Way WA4: Warr 5M 81
WA5: Warr 5M 81
Forshaw Av. WA10: St H 1F 62
Forshaw's La. WA5: Burtw 1G 64
Forshaw St. WA2: Warr 1D 82
FORSTERS GREEN 1G 30
Forsters Grn. Rd. WN8: Skel 1G 30
Forster St. WA2: Warr 1C 82
WA3: Golb 1B 52
Forsythia Cl. L9: W'ton 7H 45
Forsythia Wlk. M31: Part 7L 69
(off Blossom Rd.)
Forthlin Rd. L18: Aller 7A 76
(not continuous)
Forth St. L20: Kirkd 9B 44
Forton Lodge Flats L23: Blun 7J 33
(off Blundellsands Rd. E.)
Forton Rd. WN3: Wigan 1H 41
Fort Perch Rock Marine Radio Mus. 8H 43
Fort St. CH45: New B 2J 57
Forum Ct. PR8: South 8F 6
Forwood Rd. CH62: Brom 7C 90
Foscote Rd. L33: Kirkb 7E 36
Foster Cl. L35: Whis 4D 62
Foster Rd. L37: Form 2D 24
Fosters Cl. PR9: South 7N 7
Fosters Gro. WA11: Hay 4B 50
FOSTERS ISLAND 1F 30
Fosters Rd. WA11: Hay 4B 50
Foster St. L20: Kirkd 2B 58
WA8: Widnes 7L 79
Fotherby Pl. WN3: Wigan 1J 41
Fothergill St. WA1: Warr 1E 82
Fotheringay Ct. CH65: Ell P 3B 112
(off Rochester Dr.)
Foul La. PR8: South 2F 12
(not continuous)
PR9: South 1F 12
Foundation, The L3: Liv 5L 5 (8E 58)
Foundry, The L1: Liv 7G 4
Foundry Ind. Est. WA8: Widnes 9L 79
Foundry La. WA8: Hale B 2E 94
Foundry St. WA2: Warr 2C 82
WA10: St H 7K 49
(not continuous)
WA12: Newt W 7K 51
Fountain Ct. L23: Blun 6G 32
Fountain La. WA6: Frod 6K 107
Fountain Rd. CH45: New B 2H 57
L34: Know 7H 47
Fountains, The L39: Orm 7C 20
Fountains Av. WA11: Hay 3H 51
Fountains Cl. L4: W'ton 2E 58
WA7: Brook 1E 108
Fountains Ct. L4: Kirkd 2C 58
(off Stanley Cl.)
Fountains Rd. L4: Kirkd, W'ton 2C 58
(not continuous)
Fountain St. CH42: Tran 5J 73
WA9: St H 3F 62
Fountains Wlk. WA3: Low 2J 53
Fountains Way L37: Form 2G 25
Four Acre Dr. L21: Ford 8A 34
Four Acre La. WA9: Clock F 5L 63
Four Acre Pct. WA9: Clock F 5L 63
Fouracres L31: Mag 4G 35
Four Bridges CH41: Birke 8L 57
FOUR LANE ENDS 5L 29
Four La. Ends WA6: Manl 9L 115
Fourth Av. CH43: Bid 2B 72
L9: Aintr 3K 45
(Broadway)
L9: Aintr 3J 45
(Fifth Av.)
WA7: Pal F 8B 96
Fourth St. WN2: Bam 4N 41
Fowell Rd. CH45: New B 1H 57
Fowler Cl. L7: Liv 8H 59
Foxall Way CH66: Gt Sut 3H 111
Fox Bank Cl. WA8: Widnes 4J 79
Foxcote WA8: Widnes 6E 78
Foxcover Rd. CH60: Hesw 8C 88
Foxcovers Rd. CH63: Beb 4N 89
Fox Covert WA7: Nort 8E 96
Foxdale Cl. CH43: Oxton 3G 72
PR8: South 3D 12
Foxdale Ct. WA4: App 9E 82
Foxdale Rd. L15: Wavtr 2L 75
Foxdell Cl. L13: Liv 7M 59
Foxdene CH66: Lit Sut 9H 103
Foxdene Gro. WN3: Winst 1G 41
Foxes, The CH61: Thing 1A 88
Foxes Ct. CH43: Oxton 3H 73
Foxes Gro. L34: Know 7H 47
Foxfield Cl. WA2: Warr 6F 66
Foxfield Rd. CH47: Meols 9E 54
WA9: St H 5H 63
Foxfold WN8: Skel 1F 30
Fox Gdns. WA13: Lymm 4C 84
Foxglove Av. L26: Halew 7J 77
L40: Burs 1K 21
Foxglove Cl. L9: Faz 6L 45
WA3: Low 2E 52
Foxglove Ct. WA6: Frod 6M 107
Foxglove Dell WA6: Alv 3G 115
Foxglove Rd. CH41: Birke 1F 72
Foxglove Wlk. M31: Part 7M 69
(off Cross La. W.)
Foxglove Way CH64: Lit N 9E 100
Fox Hey Rd. CH44: Wall 6F 56
Foxhill Cl. L8: Liv 2F 74
L37: Form 1C 24
Foxhill Gro. WA6: Hel 1G 115
Foxhill La. L26: Halew 6J 77
Foxhills Cl. WA4: App 4E 98
Foxhouse La. L31: Mag 3K 35
Foxhunter Dr. L9: Aintr 2H 45
Foxleigh L26: Halew 7H 77
Foxleigh Grange CH41: Birke 8F 56
Foxley Cl. WA13: Lymm 6G 85
Foxley Hall M. WA13: Lymm 7G 85
Foxley Heath WA8: Widnes 8H 79
Fox Pl. WA10: St H 6K 49
Fox's Bank La. L35: Whis 2C 78
(not continuous)
Foxshaw Cl. L35: Whis 8A 62
Fox St. CH41: Birke 2J 73
L3: Liv 1H 5 (5D 58)
WA5: Warr 3N 81
WA7: Run 6K 95
Foxton Cl. CH46: More 8J 55
WA11: St H 5N 49
Foxwood L12: W Der 1C 60
WA9: St H 2F 62
Foxwood Cl. CH48: W Kir 5F 70
WN5: Orr 7N 31
Foy St. WN4: Ash M 8K 41
Frailey Cl. PR8: Ainsd 1J 17
Framlington Ct. WA7: Cas 5A 96
Frampton Rd. L4: W'ton 8J 45
Francine Cl. L3: Liv 4B 58
Francis Av. CH43: Clau 2H 73
CH46: More 9L 55
Francis Cl. L35: Rainh 5F 62
WA8: Widnes 8F 78
Francis Rd. M44: Irlam 1M 69
WA4: Stockt H 7C 82
WA6: Frod 5M 107
Francis St. M44: Cad 4L 69
WA9: St H 2B 64
Francis Way L16: Child 9B 60
FRANKBY 6J 71
Frankby Av. CH44: Wall 5G 57
Frankby Cl. CH49: Grea 5J 71
Frankby Grn. CH48: Frank 6H 71
Frankby Gro. CH49: Upton 3N 71
Frankby Rd. CH47: Meols 9E 54
CH48: Frank, W Kir 5E 70
CH49: Grea 5E 70
L4: W'ton 1G 59
Frankby Stiles CH48: Frank 5G 71
Franklin Cl. WA5: Old H 9L 65
Franklin Gro. L33: Kirkb 5C 36
Franklin Pl. L6: Liv 4G 58
Franklin Rd. CH46: Leas 5A 56
Franklyn Dr. WA12: Newt W 9M 51
Frank Perkins Way M44: Irlam 2M 69
Frank St. WA8: Widnes 7M 79
Franton Wlk. L32: Kirkb 9A 36
Fraser Cl. WA7: Run 7A 96
Fraser Rd. WA5: Gt San 2F 80
Fraser St. L3: Liv 3H 5 (7D 58)
Frawley Av. WA12: Newt W 5L 51
Freckleton Cl. WA5: Gt San 4K 81
Freckleton Dr. L33: Kirkb 6E 36
Freckleton Rd. PR9: South 3L 7
WA10: St H 9E 48
Freda Av. WA9: St H 3M 63
Frederick Banting Cl. L30: Neth 7E 34
Frederick Gro. L15: Wavtr 9M 59
Frederick Lunt Av. L34: Know 7G 47
Frederick St. WA4: Warr 5E 82
WA8: Widnes 7L 79
(not continuous)
WA9: St H 1B 64
WN4: Ash M 6J 41
Frederick Ter. WA8: Hale B 3D 94
Frederic Pl. WA7: Run 4L 95
Freedom Cl. L7: Liv 7N 5 (9F 58)
Freehold St. L7: Liv 6J 59
Freeland St. L4: Kirkd 2D 58
Freeman St. CH41: Birke 1L 73
L7: Liv 9H 59
Freemantle Av. WA9: St H 2H 63
Freemason's Row L3: Liv 2E 4 (6B 58)
Freemont Rd. L12: W Der 2M 59
Freeport Gro. L9: Aintr 3G 45
Freesia Av. L9: W'ton 6G 45
Freme Cl. L11: Norr G 7N 45
Fremont Pl. WA5: Gt San 1K 81
Frenchfields Cres. WA9: Clock F 5A 64
Frenchfield St. WA9: Clock F 6N 63
French St. WA8: Widnes 7N 79
WA10: St H 9G 48
Frensham Cl. CH63: Spit 5M 89
FRESHFIELD 8E 16
Freshfield Cvn. Pk. L37: Form 7B 16
Freshfield Cl. L36: Huy 6G 61
Freshfield Ct. L37: Form 9E 16
Freshfield Rd. L15: Wavtr 2L 75
L37: Form 8E 16
Freshfields Dr. WA2: Padg 8J 67
Freshfield Station (Rail) 8E 16
Freshford WA9: St H 3N 63
Freshmeadow La. WA6: Hel 3D 114
Freshwater Cl. WA5: Gt San 1F 80
Freyer Av. WA4: Warr 7C 82
Friars Av. WA5: Gt San 3G 81
Friars Cl. CH63: Beb 2M 89
Friars Ga. WA1: Warr 4C 82
Friarsgate Cl. L18: Moss H 3A 76
Friars La. WA1: Warr 4C 82
Friar St. L5: Liv 4E 58
WA10: St H 4J 49
Friars Wlk. L37: Form 2H 25
Friars Way L14: Brd G 7B 60
Friends La. WA5: Gt San 2F 80
Frinsted Rd. L11: Norr G 9M 45
Frith Ct. L35: Rainh 5F 62
(off Ratcliffe Pl.)
Frobisher Ct. WA5: Old H 9M 65
Frobisher Rd. CH46: Leas 5A 56
CH64: Nest 6E 100
Froda Av. WA6: Frod 7L 107
FRODSHAM 6L 107
Frodsham Bus. Cen. WA6: Frod 5M 107
Frodsham Dr. WA11: St H 5N 49
Frodsham Golf Course 9L 107
Frodsham Leisure Cen. 6L 107
Frodsham Pk. Homes
WA6: Frod 6K 107
Frodsham Rd. WA6: Alv 4G 114
Frodsham Station (Rail) 6L 107

Frodsham St.—Girvan Dr.

Frodsham St. CH41: Tran 4L 73
(not continuous)
L4: W'ton 9E 44
Froghall La. WA1: Warr 2A 82
WA2: Warr 2B 82
WA13: Lymm 8K 85
(not continuous)
WA16: High L 8K 85
Frog La. L40: Lath 3A 22
Frogmore Rd. L13: Liv 6K 59
Frome Cl. CH61: Irby 9L 71
Frome Ct. CH65: Ell P 7N 103
Frome Way L25: Hunts X 8H 77
Frontfield Ct. *WA9: St H 8M 49*
(off Appleton Rd.)
Frost Dr. CH61: Irby 1K 87
Frosts M. CH65: Ell P 8N 103
Frost St. L7: Liv 7H 59
Fryer St. WA7: Run 4K 95
Fry St. WA9: St H 7A 50
(not continuous)
Fuchsia Cl. CH66: Gt Sut 4L 111
Fuchsia Wlk. CH49: Grea 6K 71
Fulbeck WA8: Widnes 6F 78
Fulbeck Av. WN3: Wigan 1H 41
Fulbrook Cl. CH63: Spit 5M 89
Fulbrook Rd. CH63: Spit 5M 89
Fulford Cl. L12: W Der 3D 60
Fulford Pk. CH46: More 9M 55
Fullerton Gro. L36: Huy 5J 61
Fulmar Cl. L27: N'ley 3J 77
WA11: St H 4L 49
Fulmar Gro. L12: Crox 7C 46
Fulshaw Cl. L27: N'ley 2H 77
Fulton Av. CH48: W Kir 5E 70
Fulton Cl. WA4: Westy 4J 83
Fulton St. L5: Liv 4A 58
Fulwood Av. PR8: South 2C 12
Fulwood Cl. L17: Aig 6J 75
Fulwood Dr. L17: Aig 6H 75
Fulwood Gdns. CH66: Lit Sut 8H 103
Fulwood M. CH66: Lit Sut 8H 103
Fulwood Pk. L17: Aig 7H 75
Fulwood Rd. CH66: Lit Sut 8H 103
L17: Aig 6H 75
WA3: Low 3F 52
Fulwood Way L21: Ford 7A 34
Funchal Av. L37: Form 3D 24
Furlong Cl. L9: Aintr 2J 45
Furness Av. L12: W Der 9A 46
L37: Form 1F 24
L39: Orm 9C 20
WA10: St H 3H 49
Furness Cl. CH49: Upton 2M 71
PR8: Ainsd 2H 17
Furness Ct. WA7: Nort 3H 97
Furness St. L4: W'ton 2D 58
Furnival Dr. L40: Burs 1H 21
Furrocks Cl. CH64: Ness 9F 100
Furrocks La. CH64: Ness 9F 100
Furrocks Way CH64: Ness 9F 100
Furrows, The CH66: Gt Sut 5K 111
Furze Wlk. M31: Part 6N 69
Furze Way CH46: More 8M 55
Fylde Rd. PR9: South 3L 7
Fylde Rd. Ind. Est. PR9: South 3M 7

G

Gable Ct. L11: Norr G 7K 45
Gable M. L37: Form 3G 24
Gables, The L31: Mag 4K 35
L34: Eccl P 3C 62
Gables Cl. WA2: Fearn 6G 66
Gable St. WA12: Newt W 7J 51
Gable Vw. L11: Norr G 7K 45
Gabriel Cl. CH46: More 9N 55
Gainford Cl. WA8: Widnes 5F 78
Gainford Rd. L14: Knott A 3E 60
Gainsborough Av. L31: Mag 3G 35
Gainsborough Cl. L12: W Der 4C 60
Gainsborough Ct. WA8: Widnes 7E 78
Gainsborough Rd. CH45: Wall 5E 56
CH49: Upton 2M 71
L15: Wavtr 2K 75
PR8: Birkd 3L 11
WA4: Warr 6B 82
Gairloch Cl. WA2: Fearn 5G 67
Gaisgill Ct. WA8: Widnes 7F 78
Gala Bingo
Bromborough 4D 90
Kirkby 9C 36
Liverpool -
East Lancashire Road 6M 45
Wavertree Road 8H 59
Warrington 3C 82
Widnes 8L 79
Gala Cl. L14: Knott A 5C 60
Galbraith Cl. L17: Aig 6H 75
Gale Av. WA5: Warr 8A 66
Galemeade L11: Norr G 7N 45
Gale Rd. L21: Lith 1B 44
L33: Know I 2G 47
Galingale Rd. L11: Norr G 9M 45
Galion Way WA8: Widnes 4J 79
Gallagher Ind. Est. CH44: Wall 7H 57
Gallant Cl. L25: Woolt 6F 76
Galleries, The L37: Form 1F 24
Gallopers La. CH61: Thing 1B 88
Galloway Dr. WN8: Uph 6L 31
Galloway Rd. L22: Wloo 9L 33
Galloway St. L7: Liv 9J 59
Galston Av. L35: Rainh 7G 62
Galston Cl. L33: Kirkb 5B 36
Galsworthy Av. L30: Boot 2C 44
Galsworthy Pl. L30: Boot 2D 44
Galsworthy Wlk. L30: Boot 3D 44
Galton St. L3: Liv 2B 4 (6A 58)
Galtres Ct. CH63: H Beb 8L 73
Galtres Pk. CH63: H Beb 8L 73
Galway Av. WA8: Widnes 5H 79
Galway Cres. WA11: Hay 3F 50
Gambier Ter. L1: Liv 9K 5 (1E 74)
Gamble Av. WA10: St H 4H 49
Gambrel Cl. L9: W'ton 7E 44
Gamlin St. CH41: Birke 9F 56
Gamston Wood L32: Kirkb 1A 46
Ganneys Mdw. Cl. CH49: Wdchu 5C 72
Ganney's Mdw. Rd.
CH49: Wdchu 6C 72
Gannock St. L7: Liv 7H 59
Gantley Av. WN5: Bil 8N 31
Gantley Cres. WN5: Bil 9N 31
Gantley Rd. WN5: Bil 8N 31
Ganton Cl. PR8: South 3D 12
WA8: Widnes 4L 79
Ganworth Cl. L24: Speke 5J 93
Ganworth Rd. L24: Speke 5J 93
Garage Rd. L24: Halew 2K 93
Garden Apts. L18: Moss H 5L 75
Garden Cotts. L12: W Der 5B 60
L39: Orm 8B 20
Garden Ct. CH42: Tran 7J 73
Gardeners Vw. L33: Kirkb 5E 36
Gardeners Way L35: Rainh 4F 62
Gdn. Hey Rd. CH46: More 1J 71
CH47: Meols 9D 54
Gardenia Gro. L17: Aig 6F 74
Garden La. CH46: More 8M 55
L5: Liv 5E 58
L9: Aintr 2J 45
Gdn. Lodge Gro. L27: N'ley 3H 77
Gardenside CH46: Leas 5B 56
Gardenside St. L6: Liv 1L 5 (6E 58)
Gardens Rd. CH63: Beb 2A 90
Garden St. L25: Woolt 6E 76
Garden Wlk. L34: Presc 4A 62
M31: Part 6L 69
Gardiner Av. WA11: Hay 4E 50
Gardiners Pl. WN8: Skel 4B 30
Gardner Av. L20: Boot 3C 44
Gardner Rd. L13: Liv 4K 59
L37: Form 1G 25
Gardner's Dr. L6: Liv 5H 59
Gardner's Row L3: Liv 1F 4 (6C 58)
Gareth Av. WA11: St H 4L 49
Garfield Ter. CH49: Upton 3A 72
Garfourth Cl. L19: Garst 9B 76
Garfourth Rd. L19: Garst 9B 76
Garmoyle Cl. L15: Wavtr 1K 75
Garmoyle Rd. L15: Wavtr 1K 75
Garner St. WA2: Warr 1D 82
Garnet St. L13: Liv 8L 59
WA9: St H 2N 63
Garnett Av. L4: Kirkd 1D 58
WA4: Westy 4H 83
Garnett Grn. L39: Orm 8B 20
Garnett Pl. WN8: Skel 5D 30
Garnett's La. WA8: Hale B 3D 94
Garnetts La. L35: Tar G 7A 78
Garrett Fld. WA3: Ris 4L 67
Garrick Av. CH46: More 9K 55
Garrick Pde. PR8: South 9F 6
Garrick Rd. CH43: Pren 8F 72
Garrick St. L7: Liv 1H 75
Garrigill Cl. WA8: Widnes 3L 79
Garrison Cl. L8: Liv 2G 74
Garrowby Dr. L36: Huy 6G 60
Garsdale Av. L35: Rainh 7G 63
Garsdale Cl. WA5: Gt San 1H 81
Garsfield Rd. L4: W'ton 9J 45
Garside Av. WA3: Low 3E 52
Garside Gro. WN3: Wigan 1G 41
Garstang Rd. PR9: South 3L 7
GARSTON 1A 92
Garston Cres. WA12: Newt W 9M 51
Garston Ind. Est. L19: Garst 3A 92
Garston Old Rd. L19: Garst, G'dale 9N 75
Garston Way L19: Garst 1N 91
GARSWOOD 8E 40
Garswood Av. WA11: Rainf 4D 38
Garswood Cl. CH46: Leas 5M 55
L31: Mag 9K 27
Garswood Cres. WN5: Bil 7A 40
Garswood Old Rd. WA11: St H 2M 49
WN4: Garsw 1B 50
Garswood Rd. WA11: Hay 1D 50
WN4: Garsw 6D 40
WN5: Bil 7A 40
Garswood Station (Rail) 8E 40
Garswood St. L8: Liv 5E 74
WA10: St H 6K 49
WN4: Ash M 8K 41
Garter Cl. L11: Crox 7A 46
Garth, The CH43: Oxton 3E 72
L36: Huy 6J 61
Garth Blvd. CH63: H Beb 8L 73
Garth Ct. L22: Wloo 1L 43
Garthdale Rd. L18: Moss H 4M 75
Garth Dr. L18: Moss H 4N 75
Garthowen Rd. L7: Liv 7J 59
Garth Rd. CH65: Ell P 9D 104
L32: Kirkb 2E 46
Garth Wlk. L32: Kirkb 2E 46
Garton Dr. WA3: Low 1F 52
Gartons La.
WA9: Clock F, Sut M 6M 63
Garven Pl. WA1: Warr 3B 82
Garway L25: Woolt 5G 76
Garwood Cl. WA5: Westb 8L 65
Gascoyne St. L3: Liv 2D 4 (6B 58)
Gaskell Av. WA4: Westy 5H 83
Gaskell Ct. WA9: St H 7B 50
Gaskell Rake *L30: Neth 6C 34*
(off Higher End Pk.)
Gaskell's Brow WN4: Ash M 6G 40
Gaskell St. WA4: Stockt H 7D 82
WA9: St H 9N 49
Gaskill Rd. L24: Speke 3H 93
Gatclif Rd. L13: Liv 1K 59
GATEACRE 3F 76
Gateacre Brow L25: Gate 4F 76
Gateacre Ct. CH66: Ell P 6L 103
L25: Gate 1D 76
(off Headbourne Cl.)
Gateacre Neighbourhood Cen.
L25: Gate 2E 76
Gateacre Pk. Dr. L25: Gate 1D 76
Gateacre Ri. L25: Gate 4F 76
Gateacre Va. Rd. L25: Woolt 5F 76
Gategill Gro. WN5: Bil 9N 31
Gateley Cl. WA4: Thel 5M 83
Gateside Cl. L27: N'ley 3J 77
Gates La. L29: Thorn 3A 34
Gatewarth Ind. Est. WA5: Warr 5M 81
Gatewarth St. WA5: Warr 5M 81
Gateway, The CH62: Brom 6D 90
Gateway Trade Pk. WA2: Warr 9B 66
Gathurst Ct. WA8: Widnes 8G 78
Gatley Dr. L31: Mag 4K 35
Gatley Wlk. L24: Speke 3K 93
Gauntley Gdns. WN5: Bil 1M 39
Gaunts Way WA7: Pal F 9A 96
Gautby Rd. CH41: Birke 8E 56
Gavin Rd. WA8: Widnes 9E 78
Gaw Hill La. L39: Augh 1M 27
Gaw Hill Vw. L39: Augh 1N 27
Gawsworth Cl. CH43: Oxton 5F 72
WA10: Ec'stn 7E 48
Gawsworth Ct. WA3: Ris 4N 67
Gawsworth Rd. CH66: Gt Sut 9K 103
WA3: Golb 1A 52
Gaybeech Cl. CH43: Bid 9B 56
Gayhurst Av. WA2: Fearn 7G 67
Gayhurst Cres. L11: Norr G 8M 45
Gaynor Av. WA11: Hay 3H 51
GAYTON 8B 88
Gayton Av. CH45: New B 1H 57
CH63: H Beb 8J 73
Gayton Farm Rd. CH60: Hesw 1A 100
Gayton La. CH60: Hesw 9B 88
Gayton Mill Cl. CH60: Hesw 8B 88
Gayton Parkway CH60: Hesw 1C 100
Gayton Rd. CH60: Hesw 9N 87
Gayton Sands Nature Reserve 4A 100
Gaytree Ct. CH43: Bid 1C 72
Gaywood Av. L32: Kirkb 2D 46
Gaywood Cl. CH43: Bid 1C 72
L32: Kirkb 2D 46
Gaywood Ct. L23: Blun 8H 33
Gaywood Grn. L32: Kirkb 2D 46
Gellings La. L34: Know 5E 46
Gellings Rd. L34: Know 5E 46
Gelling St. L8: Liv 3E 74
Gemini Bus. Pk. PR9: South 1E 12
WA5: Westb 6L 65
(not continuous)
Gemini Cl. L20: Boot 6A 44
Gemini Dr. L14: Knott A 5D 60
Gemini Trade Pk. WA5: Westb 6M 65
Gem St. L5: Liv 4B 58
General Dr. L12: W Der 2B 60
General St. WA1: Warr 3D 82
Genesis Cen., The WA3: Ris 4M 67
Geneva Cl. *L36: Huy 5J 61*
(off Salerno Dr.)
Geneva Rd. CH44: Wall 7K 57
L6: Liv 6H 59
Genista Cl. L9: W'ton 7F 44
Genoa Cl. L25: Gate 1F 76
Gentwood Pde. L36: Huy 5H 61
Gentwood Rd. L36: Huy 5G 61
George Cl. WA6: Hel 3D 114
George Dr. CH64: P'gte 6C 100
PR8: Ainsd 9L 11
George Hale Av. L34: Know P 3J 61
George Harrison Cl. L6: Liv 6G 58
George Moore Ct. L23: Thorn 5A 34
George Rd. CH47: Hoy 2D 70
WA5: Gt San 4L 81
Georges Cres. WA4: Grap 6J 83
George's Dock Gates L3: Liv 5C 4 (8A 58)
Georges Dock Way L3: Liv 6D 4 (8A 58)
George's La. PR9: Banks 1E 8
George's Rd. L6: Liv 4G 59
George St. CH41: Birke 1L 73
CH65: Ell P 7A 104
L3: Liv 4D 4 (7B 58)
WA10: St H 7K 49
WA12: Newt W 6J 51
WN4: Ash M 7L 41
George Ter. WN5: Orr 7N 31
Georgia Av. CH62: Brom 4D 90
L33: Kirkb 5B 36
Georgia Cl. L20: Boot 7B 44
Georgian Cl. L26: Halew 1K 93
L35: Eccl P 3D 62
Georgian Pl. L37: Form 3E 24
Georgia Pl. WA5: Gt San 1L 81
Geraint St. L8: Liv 2E 74
Gerald Rd. CH43: Oxton 4G 72
Gerard Av. CH45: Wall 2G 56
Gerard Cen., The WN4: Ash M 8K 41
Gerard Rd. CH45: Wall 3F 56
CH48: W Kir 5C 70
GERARD'S BRIDGE 5K 49
Gerards Ct. WA11: St H 2L 49
Gerards La. WA9: St H, Sut L 2N 63
Gerards Pk. WA10: St H 5L 49
Gerard St. L3: Liv 3G 5 (7D 58)
WN4: Ash M 8K 41
Gerard Way L33: Kirkb 9D 36
Germander Cl. L26: Halew 7J 77
German's La. L40: Burs 7L 15
Gerneth Cl. L24: Speke 3G 92
Gerneth Rd. L24: Speke 4F 92
Gerosa Av. WA2: Winw 1C 66
Gerrard Av. CH66: Gt Sut 1H 111
WA5: Warr 1A 82
Gerrard Pl. WN8: Skel 4C 30
Gerrard Rd. WA3: Croft 2H 67
WN5: Bil 6A 40
Gerrard's La. L26: Halew 6J 77
Gerrard St. WA8: Widnes 8L 79
Gertrude Rd. L4: W'ton 3G 58
Gertrude St. CH41: Birke 2M 73
WA9: St H 2F 62
Geves Gdns. L22: Wloo 1L 43
Ghyll Gro. WA11: St H 1L 49
Gibbons Av. WA10: St H 7F 48
Gibbon's Rd. WN4: Garsw 9F 40
Gibbs Ct. CH61: Irby 1N 87
Gibfield Rd. WA9: St H 4H 63
Gibraltar Row L3: Liv 3C 4 (7A 58)
Gibson Cl. CH61: Pens 4N 87
L33: Kirkb 6B 36
Gibson Ct. CH65: Ell P 6A 104
Gibson Rd. L8: Liv 1E 74
Gibson Sq. *WA3: Golb 2B 52*
(off Turton St.)
Gibson St. WA1: Warr 3D 82
WA4: Stockt H 7E 82
Gibson Ter. *CH44: Wall 4K 57*
(off Royden Av.)
Giddygate La. L31: Mag, Mell 3N 35
Gidlow Rd. L13: Liv 6L 59
Gidlow Rd. Sth. L13: Liv 7L 59
Gigg La. WA4: Moore 2K 97
Giggles Fun Cen. 4A 30
Gig La. WA1: Wools 9L 67
WA4: Thel 5M 83
Gilbert Cl. CH63: Spit 5M 89
L37: Form 4E 24
Gilbert Ct. WA3: Cul 7N 53
Gilbert Dr. WA4: Westy 5J 83
Gilbert Ho. WA7: Run 4H 95
Gilbert Pl. L40: Burs 1F 20
Gilbert Rd. L35: Whis 4C 62
Gilbert St. L1: Liv 7F 4 (9C 58)
Gilchrist Rd. M44: Irlam 3L 69
Gildarts Gdns. L3: Liv 5B 58
Gildart St. L3: Liv 3K 5 (7E 58)
Gilderdale Cl. WA3: Birchw 4B 68
Gilead St. L7: Liv 7G 59
Gilescroft Av. L33: Kirkb 7E 36
Gilescroft Wlk. L33: Kirkb 7E 36
Giles Dr. WA4: Westy 5J 83
Gillan Cl. WA7: Brook 1E 108
GILLAR'S GREEN 8B 48
Gillars Grn. Dr. WA10: Ec'stn 7C 48
Gillar's La. WA10: Ec'stn 7B 48
Gillbrook Sq. CH41: Birke 9F 56
Gilleney Gro. L35: Whis 4D 62
Gillibrands Rd. WN8: Skel 4C 30
GILLMOSS 5B 46
Gillmoss Cl. L11: Crox 6A 46
Gillmoss Ind. Est. L10: Faz 4N 45
Gillmoss La. L11: Crox 5A 46
Gillmoss (Park & Ride) 4A 46
Gills La. CH61: Barns, Pens 3A 88
Gill St. L3: Liv 4K 5 (7E 58)
Gilman St. L4: W'ton 2F 58
Gilmartin Gro. L6: Liv 3M 5 (6F 58)
Gilmour Mt. CH43: Oxton 4H 73
Gilpin Av. L31: Mag 1K 35
Gilroy Nature Pk. 4D 70
Gilroy Rd. CH48: W Kir 5D 70
L6: Liv 6G 59
Giltbrook Cl. WA8: Widnes 5J 79
Gilwell Av. CH46: More 1M 71
Gilwell Cl. CH46: More 1M 71
WA4: Grap 6K 83
Ginnel, The CH62: Port S 2A 90
Gipsy Gro. L18: Moss H 3C 76
Gipsy La. L18: Moss H 3C 76
Girton Av. L20: Boot 8D 44
WN4: Ash M 7H 41
Girton Cl. CH65: Ell P 1B 112
Girton Rd. CH65: Ell P 1B 112
Girtrell Cl. CH49: Upton 3L 71
Girtrell Rd. CH49: Upton 3L 71
Girvan Cres. WN4: Garsw 7F 40
Girvan Dr. CH64: Lit N 8F 100

Gisburn Av.—Grampian Av.

Gisburn Av. WA3: Golb 1A 52
Givenchy Cl. L16: Child 9C 60
Glacier Bldg. L3: Liv 4D 74
Gladden Hey Dr. WN3: Winst 2F 40
Gladden Pl. WN8: Skel 4B 30
Glade, The CH47: Meols 8E 54
Glade Dr. CH66: Lit Sut 8E 102
Glade Pk. Ct. L8: Liv 4G 74
Glade Rd. L36: Huy 5J 61
Gladeswood Rd. L33: Know I 1F 46
Gladeville Rd. L17: Aig 6K 75
Gladica Cl. L36: Huy 7M 61
Gladstone Av. L16: Child 9E 60
L21: Sea 3M 43
(off Gladstone Rd.)
Gladstone Cl. CH41: Birke 2K 73
Gladstone Ct. L8: Liv 9L 5
Gladstone Hall Rd. CH62: Port S 2A 90
Gladstone M. WA2: Warr 2B 82
Gladstone Rd. CH42: Rock F 5M 73
CH44: Wall 6K 57
CH64: Nest 6E 100
L7: Liv 8G 58
L9: W'ton 7F 44
L19: Garst 1A 92
L21: Sea 3M 43
PR9: South 9L 7
Gladstone St. L3: Liv 2E 4 (6B 58)
L25: Woolt 6D 76
WA2: Warr 2B 82
WA8: Widnes 8L 79
WA10: St H 7G 48
Gladstone Ter. CH64: Will 6M 101
(off Neston Rd.)
Gladstone Theatre 3A 90
Gladstone Way WA12: Newt W 6J 51
Gladsville Rd. L27: N'ley 4K 77
Glaisdale Cl. WN4: Ash M 8L 41
Glaisdale Dr. PR8: South 3E 12
Glaisher St. L5: Liv 3F 58
Glamis Cl. CH43: Noct 5D 72
Glamis Dr. PR9: South 4N 7
Glamis Gro. WA9: St H 2M 63
Glamis Rd. L13: Liv 3J 59
Glamorgan Cl. WA10: St H 8J 49
Glan Aber Pk. L12: W Der 1C 60
Glasier Rd. CH46: More 8K 55
Glaslyn Way L9: W'ton 7F 44
Glass Ho. Bus. Pk. WN3: Wigan 2J 41
Glass Ho. Rd. WN3: Wigan 1H 41
Glastonbury Av. WA3: Low 2K 53
Glastonbury Cl. L6: Liv 2J 59
WA7: Nort 4H 97
Glastonbury M. WA4: Stockt H 6F 82
Glasven Rd. L33: Kirkb 8D 36
GLAZEBROOK 3G 69
Glazebrook La. WA3: Glaz 2G 68
WA8: Widnes 2K 79
Glazebrook Mdws. WA3: Glaz 3H 69
Glazebrook Station (Rail) 4G 69
Glazebrook St. WA1: Warr 2E 82
Glaziers La. WA3: Cul 8L 53
Gleadmere WA8: Widnes 6F 78
Gleaner Cl. WA7: Run 4J 95
Gleaston Cl. CH62: Brom 6C 90
Gleave Cl. WA5: Burtw 3H 65
Gleave Cres. L6: Liv 1L 5 (5F 58)
Gleave St. WA10: St H 6K 49
Glebe, The WA7: Run 6A 96
Glebe Av. WA4: Grap 7K 83
WN4: Ash M 9L 41
Glebe Bus. Pk. WA8: Widnes 4M 79
Glebe Cl. L31: Mag 2G 35
Glebecroft Av. CH2: Elt 2L 113
Glebe End L29: Seft 4E 34
Glebe Hey L27: N'ley 3J 77
Glebe Hey Rd. CH49: Wdchu 5A 72
Glebeland WA3: Cul 7M 53
Glebelands Rd. CH46: More 9M 55
Glebe La. PR9: Banks 1E 8
WA8: Widnes 3K 79
Glebe Pl. PR9: South 8G 6
Glebe Rd. CH45: Wall 3G 56
WN8: Skel 4D 30
Glebeway Way CH65: Ell P 9D 104
Gleggside CH48: W Kir 6D 70
Glegg St. L3: Liv 5A 58
Glegside Rd. L33: Kirkb 9E 36
Glen, The CH63: Spit 4B 90
L18: Moss H 5A 76
WA7: Pal F 9B 96
Glenacres L25: Woolt 5E 76
Glenalmond Rd. CH44: Wall 5K 57
Glenathol Rd. CH66: Gt Sut 1H 111
L18: Moss H 6A 76
Glenavon Rd. CH43: Pren 7G 73
L16: Child 9A 60
Glen Bank L22: Wloo 9J 33
Glenbank Cl. L9: W'ton 5F 44
Glenburn Av. CH62: East 2D 102
Glenburn Rd. CH44: Wall 6K 57
WN8: Skel 9B 22
Glenby Av. L23: Crosb 9M 33
Glencairn Rd. L13: Liv 6L 59
Glen Cl. WA3: Rix 7H 69
Glencoe Rd. CH45: Wall 3H 57
CH66: Gt Sut 1H 111
Glenconner Rd. L16: Child 8C 60
Glencourse Rd. WA8: Widnes 3K 79
Glencoyne Dr. PR9: South 1N 7
Glencroft Cl. L36: Huy 4G 61
Glendale Av. CH2: Elt 2L 113
WN4: Ash M 7L 41
Glendale Cl. L8: Liv 5E 74
Glendale Gro. CH63: Spit 5A 90
L33: Kirkb 6E 36
Glendale Rd. WA11: St H 3K 49
Glendale Wlk. WA5: Gt San 9J 65
Glendale Way L37: Form 2F 24
Glendevon Rd. L16: Child 8A 60
L36: Huy 8J 61
Glendower Rd. L22: Wloo 1L 43
Glendower St. L20: Boot 9B 44
Glendyke Rd. CH66: Gt Sut 1H 111
L18: Moss H 6A 76
Gleneagles Cl. CH61: Pens 3N 87
L33: Kirkb 5B 36
WA3: Low 3G 52
Gleneagles Dr. PR8: Ainsd 2H 17
WA8: Widnes 3K 79
WA11: Hay 5C 50
Gleneagles Rd. CH66: Gt Sut 9H 103
L16: Child 8C 60
Glenesk Rd. CH66: Gt Sut 1H 111
Glenfield Cl. CH43: Bid 9C 56
CH46: More 8J 55
Glenfield Rd. L15: Wavtr 2M 75
Glengariff St. L13: Liv 2K 59
Glenham Cl. CH47: Meols 9F 54
Glenhead Rd. L19: Aller 8N 75
Glenholm Rd. L31: Mag 4H 35
Glenluce Rd. L19: Aig 8N 75
Glenlyon Rd. L16: Child 9A 60
Glenmarsh Cl. CH63: H Beb 2K 89
L12: W Der 3A 60
Glenmarsh Way L37: Form 1H 25
Glenmaye Cl. L12: Crox 8C 46
Glenmaye Rd. CH66: Gt Sut 1H 111
Glenmore Av. L18: Moss H 5M 75
Glenmore Rd. CH43: Oxton 4G 73
Glenn Pl. WA8: Widnes 7H 79
Glenpark Dr. PR9: South 3N 7
Glen Pk. Rd. CH45: Wall 2G 57
Glen Rd. CH66: Gt Sut 9H 103
L13: Liv 7N 59
Glen Ronald Dr. CH49: Grea 3L 71
Glenrose Rd. L25: Woolt 4E 76
Glenrose Ter. PR8: Birkd 1N 11
Glenroyd Dr. L40: Burs 1J 21
Glenside L18: Aller 6A 76
WN6: App B 3L 23
Glenton Pk. CH64: Lit N 8F 100
Glentree Cl. CH49: Grea 3L 71
Glentrees Rd. L12: W Der 1N 59
Glentworth Cl. L31: Mag 4J 35
Glenville Cl. L25: Woolt 4F 76
WA7: Run 9L 95
Glenvine Cl. L16: Child 9C 60
Glen Way L33: Kirkb 5D 36
Glenway Cl. L12: Crox 6D 46
Glenwood WA7: Nort 6E 96
Glenwood Cl. CH66: Lit Sut 8H 103
L35: Whis 7C 62
Glenwood Dr. CH61: Irby 9M 71
Glenwood Gdns. CH66: Lit Sut 8H 103
Glenwood Rd. CH66: Lit Sut 8H 103
Glenwyllin Rd. L22: Wloo 9L 33
Globe Rd. L20: Boot 6A 44
Globe St. L4: W'ton 2D 58
Glossop Cl. WA1: Warr 3F 82
Gloucester Av. WA3: Golb 1C 52
Gloucester Cl. CH66: Gt Sut 5K 111
WA1: Wools 1L 83
Gloucester Ct. L6: Liv 2N 5 (6F 58)
Gloucester Pl. L6: Liv 2M 5
Gloucester Rd. CH45: Wall 3E 56
L6: Liv 4J 59
L20: Boot 6C 44
L36: Huy 6L 61
PR8: Birkd 1M 11
WA8: Widnes 5L 79
Gloucester Rd. Nth. L6: Liv 3J 59
Gloucester St. WA9: St H 8N 49
Glover Ho. Cl. WN7: Leigh 1M 53
Glover Pl. L20: Boot 6A 44
Glover Rd. WA3: Birchw 5K 67
GLOVERS BRIDGE 2K 21
Glover's Brow L32: Kirkb 7A 36
Glovers Ct. L32: Kirkb 8A 36
Glover's La. L30: Neth 7D 34
Glover St. CH42: Tran 4J 73
WA10: St H 8J 49
WA12: Newt W 7L 51
Glyn Av. CH62: Brom 8D 90
Glynne Dr. L20: Boot 4C 44
Glynne Gro. L16: Child 9E 60
Glynn St. L15: Wavtr 1L 75
Glyn Rd. CH44: Wall 4H 57
Goddard Rd. WA7: Astm 4A 96
Godetia Cl. L9: Faz 6L 45
Godfrey Pilkington Art Gallery 7K 49
Godfrey St. WA2: Warr 1E 82
Godscroft La. WA6: Frod 9H 107
Godshill Cl. WA5: Gt San 1F 80
Godstow WA7: Nort 3G 97
GOLBORNE 2B 52
Golborne Dale Rd. WA12: Newt W 5B 52
Golborne Ent. Pk. WA3: Golb 1B 52
Golborne Ho. WA3: Golb 2C 52
Golborne Rd. WA2: Winw 3B 66
WA3: Low 2D 52
WN4: Ash M 7M 41
Golborne St. WA12: Newt W 6N 51
Goldcliff Cl. WA5: Call 7M 65
Goldcrest Cl. L12: Crox 6D 46
WA7: Beech 1B 108
Goldcrest M. L26: Halew 7J 77
Goldendale Wlk. WA5: Gt San 1L 81
Golden Gro. L4: W'ton 9F 44
Golden Sq. Shop. Cen. 3B 82
Golden Triangle Ind. Est.
WA8: Hale B 2E 94
Golders Grn. L7: Liv 9H 59
Goldfinch Cl. L26: Halew 7J 77
Goldfinch Farm Rd. L24: Speke 4G 93
Goldfinch La. WA3: Birchw 5M 67
Goldie St. L4: W'ton 2E 58
Goldsmith Rd. CH43: Pren 7F 72
Goldsmith St. L6: Liv 6G 58
L20: Boot 6N 43
Goldsmith Way CH43: Pren 7F 72
Goldsworth Fold L35: Rainh 6E 62
Golf Links Rd. CH42: Tran 7H 73
Golf Rd. L37: Form 8E 16
Gondover Av. L9: W'ton 4E 44
Gonville Rd. L20: Boot 8C 44
Gooch Dr. WA12: Newt W 8M 51
Goodacre Rd. L9: Aintr 3G 45
Goodakers Ct. CH49: Wdchu 6A 72
(off Childwall Grn.)
Goodakers Mdw. CH49: Wdchu 6A 72
Goodall Pl. L4: Kirkd 1D 58
Goodall St. L4: Kirkd 9D 44
Goodban St. WA9: St H 1A 64
Goodier Ct. WA7: Run 7M 95
Goodison Av. L4: W'ton 1E 58
Goodison Pk. 1E 58
Goodison Pl. L4: W'ton 9E 44
Goodison Rd. L4: W'ton 9E 44
Goodlass Rd. L24: Speke 2D 92
Goodleigh Pl. WA9: Sut L 4M 63
Good Shepherd Cl. L11: Norr G 8N 45
Goodwood Cl. L36: Roby 8H 61
Goodwood Ct. WA9: St H 3G 62
Goodwood Dr. CH46: Leas 6N 55
Goodwood Gro. CH66: Gt Sut 2J 111
Goodwood St. L5: Liv 4C 58
Gooseberry Hollow WA7: Wind H 6F 96
Gooseberry La. WA7: Nort 6F 96
Goose Grn., The CH47: Meols 8E 54
Goose La. WA4: Hatt 5A 98
Goostrey Cl. CH63: Spit 6A 90
Gordale Cl. L8: Liv 4F 74
WA5: Gt San 1H 81
Gordon Av. CH49: Grea 5M 71
CH62: Brom 8D 90
L22: Wloo 9J 33
L31: Mag 9H 27
PR9: South 6H 7
WA1: Wools 1J 83
WA11: Hay 3H 51
WN4: Garsw 7G 40
Gordon Ct. CH49: Grea 5M 71
Gordon Dr. L14: Brd G 6C 60
L19: G'dale 9M 75
Gordon La. CH2: Back 8N 111
Gordon M. PR9: South 6H 7
Gordon Pl. L18: Moss H 5M 75
Gordon Rd. CH45: New B 2J 57
L21: Sea 3M 43
Gordon St. CH41: Birke 2J 73
L15: Wavtr 1K 75
PR9: South 7G 7
Gordon Ter. CH64: Will 6M 101
Gordon Way PR9: South 7H 7
(off Gordon St.)
Gore Dr. L39: Augh 1C 28
Goree L2: Liv 5C 4 (8B 58)
Goree Piazza L2: Liv 5D 4
(off The Strand)
Gore's La. WA11: Crank 5J 39
Gores La. L37: Form 8E 16
Gores Rd. L33: Know I 1F 46
Gore St. L8: Liv 2D 74
Gorleston M. L32: Kirkb 1D 46
Gorleston Way L32: Kirkb 1D 46
Gormley Dr. WA10: St H 3J 49
Gorran Haven WA7: Brook 9E 96
Gorse Av. L12: W Der 9N 45
Gorsebank Rd. L18: Moss H 3K 75
Gorsebank St. CH44: Wall 6J 57
Gorseburn Rd. L13: Liv 3K 59
GORSE COVERT 3B 68
Gorse Covert Rd. WA3: Birchw 4A 68
Gorse Cres. CH44: Wall 7J 57
Gorsedale Pk. CH44: Wall 7K 57
Gorsedale Rd. CH44: Wall 7H 57
L18: Moss H 4M 75
Gorsefield L37: Form 7G 17
WA9: St H 2G 63
Gorsefield Av. CH62: Brom 1C 102
L23: Thorn 6N 33
Gorsefield Cl. CH62: Brom 1C 102
Gorsefield Rd. CH42: Tran 5J 73
Gorse Hey Ct. L13: W Der 4M 59
Gorsehill Rd. CH45: New B 2G 57
CH60: Hesw 6A 88
Gorselands Ct. L17: Aig 6J 75
Gorse La. CH48: W Kir 7F 70
PR4: Tarl 2M 9
Gorse Rd. CH47: Meols 9E 54
Gorse Sq. M31: Part 6K 69
Gorse Way L37: Form 9C 16
Gorsewood Cl. L25: Gate 3G 76
(off Gorsewood Rd.)
Gorsewood Gro. L25: Gate 3F 76
Gorsewood Rd. L25: Gate 3F 76
WA7: Murd 9F 96
Gorsey Av. L30: Neth 8B 34
Gorsey Brow WN5: Bil 6N 39
Gorsey Brow Cl. WN5: Bil 6N 39
Gorsey Cop Rd. L25: Gate 2E 76
Gorsey Cop Way L25: Gate 2E 76
Gorsey Cft. L34: Eccl P 2C 62
Gorsey La. CH44: Wall 7H 57
L21: Ford 1A 44
L30: Neth 1A 44
L38: Hight 2G 33
L39: Bart 6M 17
PR9: Banks 1F 8
WA1: Warr 9E 66
WA2: Warr 9E 66
WA5: Burtw 4D 64
WA8: Widnes 8A 80
WA9: Bold, Clock F 6A 64
WA13: Warb 2N 85
Gorsey Pl. WN8: Skel 5D 30
Gorseyville Cres. CH63: H Beb 2L 89
Gorseyville Rd. CH63: H Beb 2L 89
Gorseywell La. WA7: Pres B 9H 97
Gorst La. L40: Burs 9D 14
Gorstons La. CH64: Lit N 8G 101
Gorst St. L4: W'ton 2E 58
Gorsuch La. L40: Scar 2J 19
Gorton Rd. L13: Liv 7N 59
Gort Rd. L36: Huy 6J 61
Goschen St. L5: Liv 2E 58
L13: Liv 6L 59
Gosford St. L8: Liv 4E 74
Gosforth Ct. WA7: Pal F 8A 96
Gosforth Rd. PR9: South 7L 7
Gosling Cl. WA4: Hatt 5B 98
Gosling Rd. WA3: Croft 2J 67
Gosport Cl. WA2: Padg 8F 66
Goswell St. L15: Wavtr 9K 59
Gotham Rd. CH63: Spit 5N 89
Gothic St. CH42: Rock F 6M 73
Gough Av. WA2: Warr 7B 66
Gough Rd. L13: Liv 2K 59
Goulden St. WA5: Warr 2N 81
Goulders Ct. WA7: Brook 1D 108
Gourley Grange CH48: W Kir 7E 70
Gourley Rd. L13: Liv 8N 59
Gourleys La. CH48: W Kir 7E 70
Government Rd. CH47: Hoy 1C 70
Govett Rd. WA9: St H 2F 62
Gower Gdns. L40: Burs 2K 21
Gower St. L3: Liv 8D 4 (9B 58)
L20: Boot 5A 44
WA9: St H 9N 49
Gowery, The L37: Form 1G 24
(off Church Rd.)
Gowrie Gro. L21: Lith 3A 44
Gowy Ct. CH66: Ell P 6K 103
Goyt Hey Av. WN5: Bil 6A 40
Graburn Rd. L37: Form 9F 16
Grace Av. L10: Faz 3M 45
WA2: Warr 9C 66
Grace Cl. CH45: Wall 4H 57
Grace Rd. CH65: Ell P 8N 103
L9: W'ton 4F 44
Graces Cl. WA11: Rainf 4C 38
Grace St. L8: Liv 4E 74
WA9: St H 1M 63
Graceville Ct. WA5: Gt San 2K 81
Gradwell St. L1: Liv 6F 4 (8C 58)
Graeme Bryson Ct. L11: Norr G 9L 45
Grafton Cres. L8: Liv 2D 74
Grafton Dr. CH49: Upton 4A 72
PR8: Ainsd 9G 11
Grafton Gro. L8: Liv 4D 74
Grafton Rd. CH45: New B 2H 57
CH65: Ell P 7A 104
Grafton St. CH43: Oxton 3H 73
L8: Liv 5E 74
(Beresford Rd.)
L8: Liv 2C 74
(Stanhope St., not continuous)
WA5: Warr 2N 81
WA10: St H 7G 49
WA12: Newt W 7K 51
Grafton Wlk. CH48: W Kir 6D 70
Graham Av. CH66: Gt Sut 9J 103
WN6: App B 3M 23
Graham Cl. WA8: Widnes 7F 78
Graham Cres. M44: Cad 5J 69
Graham Dr. L26: Halew 8L 77
Graham Rd. CH48: W Kir 5B 70
WA8: Widnes 8F 78
Graham's Rd. L36: Huy 7K 61
Graham St. WA9: St H 6M 49
Grainger Av. CH43: Pren 6F 72
CH48: W Kir 4C 70
L20: Boot 5D 44
Grain Ind. Est. L8: Liv 4D 74
Graley Cl. L26: Halew 1K 93
Grammar School Ct. L39: Orm 8D 20
WA4: Warr 5G 82
(off Grammar School Rd.)
Grammar School Gdns. L39: Orm 9D 20
Grammar School La. CH48: W Kir 7E 70
Grammar School Rd. WA4: Warr 5G 82
WA13: Lymm 6F 84
Grampian Av. CH46: More 9N 55

Grampian Rd. L7: Liv .7K 59
Grampian Way CH46: More .9M 55
CH62: East .2D 102
CH64: Lit N .9E 100
WA3: Low .1E 52
Granams Cft. L30: Neth .7C 34
Granard Rd. L15: Wavtr .2M 75
Granary Mill WA4: Pres H .9H 97
Granary Way L3: Liv .2C 74
Granborne Chase L32: Kirkb .8N 35
GRANBY .9N 5 (1F 74)
Granby Cl. PR9: South .4L 7
WA7: Brook .1E 108
Granby Cres. CH63: Spit .5N 89
Granby Rd. WA4: W'ton .8C 82
Granby St. L8: Liv .9N 5 (1F 74)
Grand Central L3: Liv .5H 5
Grandison Rd. L4: W'ton .9H 45
Grand National Av. L9: Aintr .1G 45
GRANGE
CH48 .6D 70
WA1 .8L 67
Grange, The CH42: Rock F .7M 73
CH44: Wall .5J 57
L20: Boot .4B 44
PR9: South .4A 8
Grange & Pyramids Shop. Cen., The .2K 73
Grange Av. CH45: Wall .3H 57
L12: W Der .4C 60
L25: Hunts X .9H 77
PR9: South .7K 7
WA4: Westy .4F 82
Grange Av. Nth. L12: W Der .4C 60
Grange Cl. L36: Roby .7G 61
PR9: Banks .2E 8
WA3: Low .4D 52
Grange Ct. CH43: Oxton .5G 72
L15: Wavtr .1L 75
(off Grange Ter.)
L23: Blun .8J 33
Grange Cres. CH66: Hoot .5F 102
Grange Cross Cl. CH48: W Kir .7F 70
Grange Cross Hey CH48: W Kir .7F 70
Grange Cross La. CH48: W Kir .7F 70
Grange Dr. CH60: Hesw .5N 87
CH63: Thorn H .8G 89
WA5: Penk .4J 81
WA8: Widnes .7G 79
WA10: St H .1E 62
Grange Employment Cen.
WA1: Wools .8M 67
Grange Farm Cl. WA5: Gt San .2M 81
Grange Farm Cres. CH48: W Kir .5F 70
Grange Grn. Mnr. WA4: H Walt .9N 81
Grangehurst Ct. L25: Gate .4F 76
Grange La. L25: Gate .3E 76
L37: Form .8E 16
Grangemeadow Rd. L25: Gate .3E 76
Grangemoor WA7: Run .7N 95
Grange Mt. CH43: Oxton .3J 73
CH48: W Kir .6E 70
CH60: Hesw .6N 87
Grange Old Rd. CH48: W Kir .6D 70
GRANGE PARK .1E 62
Grange Pk. L31: Mag .4K 35
Grange Pk. Av. WA7: Run .5M 95
Grange Pk. Golf Course
St Helens .9F 48
Grange Pk. Rd. WA10: St H .9F 48
Grange Pl. CH41: Birke .2J 73
M44: Cad .4K 69
Grange Pct. CH41: Birke .2L 73
Grange Rd. CH41: Birke .2K 73
(not continuous)
CH48: W Kir .6B 70
CH60: Hesw .5N 87
CH65: Ell P .9A 104
L30: Neth .9G 34
L38: Hight .5E 24
PR9: South .8K 7
WA7: Run .5M 95
WA11: Hay, Newt W .5F 50
WN4: Ash M .5H 41
Grange Rd. E. CH41: Birke .2L 73
Grange Rd. Nth. WA7: Run .5M 95
Grange Rd. W. CH41: Birke .2H 73
CH43: Oxton .2H 73
Grangeside L25: Gate .3E 76
Grange St. L6: Liv .4J 59
Grange Ter. L15: Wavtr .1L 75
Grange Valley WA11: Hay .4F 50
Grange Vw. CH43: Oxton .3J 73
Grange Wlk. CH48: W Kir .7E 70
Grange Way L25: Gate .3E 76
Grangeway WA7: Run .7M 95
Grangeway Ct. WA7: Run .7M 95
Grange Weint L25: Gate .4E 76
Grange Wood CH48: W Kir .7E 70
Grangewood L16: Child .8D 60
Granite Ter. L36: Huy .7L 61
Granston Cl. WA5: Call .7N 65
Grant Av. L15: Wavtr .2L 75
Grant Cl. L14: Knott A .6E 60
WA5: Old H .8M 65
WA10: St H .6H 49
Grant Ct. *L20: Boot .7B 44*
(off Clairville Cl.)
Grantham Av. WA1: Warr .1F 82
WA4: W'ton .8C 82
Grantham Cl. CH61: Pens .3M 87
PR8: Birkd .5N 11
Grantham Cres. WA11: St H .5M 49
Grantham Rd. L33: Kirkb .6C 36
PR8: Birkd .5N 11
Grantham St. L6: Liv .6G 59
Grantham Way L30: Neth .7G 34
Grantley Rd. L15: Wavtr .2N 75
Grantley St. WN4: Ash M .6J 41
Granton Cl. L37: Form .1E 24
Grant Rd. CH46: Leas .6B 56
L14: Knott A .6D 60
Grantwood WN4: Ash M .6J 41
Granville Av. L31: Mag .1H 35
Granville Cl. CH45: Wall .3E 56
L39: Augh .3N 27
Granville Ct. CH45: Wall .3E 56
PR9: South .6J 7
Granville Dr. CH66: Lit Sut .7G 102
Granville Pk. L39: Augh .4N 27
Granville Pk. W. L39: Augh .4N 27
Granville Rd. L15: Wavtr .1J 75
L19: Garst .1A 92
PR8: Birkd .3K 11
Granville St. WA1: Warr .2E 82
WA7: Run .4K 95
WA9: St H .7N 49
GRAPPENHALL .6H 83
Grappenhall Heys Walled Garden .9H 83
Grappenhall La. WA4: App T, Grap .3J 99
Grappenhall Rd. CH65: Gt Sut .1L 111
WA4: Stockt H .7E 82
Grappenhall Way CH43: Bid .1C 72
Grasmere Av. CH43: Noct .3C 72
L34: Presc .3C 62
WA2: Warr .6E 66
WA11: St H .3L 49
WN8: Uph .5L 31
Grasmere Cl. L33: Kirkb .7B 36
WA11: St H .3L 49
Grasmere Ct. *CH41: Birke .3J 73*
(off Penrith St.)
WA11: St H .3L 49
Grasmere Dr. CH45: Wall .3H 57
L21: Lith .1D 44
WA7: Beech .1N 107
WN4: Ash M .6K 41
Grasmere Fold WA11: St H .3L 49
Grasmere Gdns. L23: Crosb .8M 33
Grasmere Ho. *L17: Aig .6J 75*
(off Mossley Hill Dr.)
Grasmere Rd. CH64: Nest .8E 100
CH65: Ell P .3A 112
L31: Mag .1J 35
L37: Form .1D 24
L38: Hight .8G 24
M31: Part .6L 69
WA6: Frod .6M 107
WA13: Lymm .4F 84
Grasmere St. L5: Liv .4G 58
GRASSENDALE .8M 75
Grassendale Ct. *L19: G'dale .9M 75*
(off Grassendale Rd.)
Grassendale Esplanade L19: G'dale .1L 91
Grassendale La. L19: G'dale .9M 75
Grassendale Rd. L19: G'dale .9M 75
Grassington Cres. L25: Woolt .6G 77
Grassmoor Cl. CH62: Brom .7D 90
Grasswood Rd. CH49: Wdchu .6B 72
Grassy La. WA6: Frod .7G 107
Grasville Rd. CH42: Tran .5L 73
Gratrix Rd. CH62: Brom .7C 90
Gratton Pl. WN8: Skel .4D 30
Gravel, The PR4: Mere B .5J 9
Gravel Cl. PR9: Banks .2D 8
Gravel La. PR9: Banks .2D 8
(not continuous)
Graveyard La. L39: Bic .5E 28
Gray Av. WA11: Hay .4F 50
Gray Gro. L36: Huy .9K 61
Graylag Cl. WA7: Beech .1B 108
Graylands Pl. L4: W'ton .9H 45
Graylands Rd. CH62: Port S .1B 90
L4: W'ton .9H 45
Graylaw Ind. Est. L9: Aintr .4H 45
Grayling Dr. L12: Crox .7B 46
Grayling M. WA4: Warr .7C 82
Gray's Av. L35: Presc .3C 62
Grayson M. *CH41: Birke .1M 73*
(off John St.)
Graysons Rd. WA11: Rainf .3C 38
Grayson St. L1: Liv .8F 4 (9C 58)
Grayston Av. WA9: Sut L .3N 63
Gray St. L20: Boot .5N 43
GREASBY .5L 71
Greasby Dr. CH66: Gt Sut .1K 111
Greasby Hill Rd. CH48: W Kir .7D 70
Greasby Rd. CH44: Wall .5G 57
CH49: Grea .5K 71
GREAT ALTCAR .3L 25
Great Ashfield WA8: Widnes .5G 78
Gt. Charlotte St. L1: Liv .5G 5 (8C 58)
GREAT CROSBY .6L 33
Gt. Crosshall St. L3: Liv .3E 4 (7C 58)
Great Delph WA11: Hay .3F 50
Gt. Eastern Vw. *CH62: New F .8A 74*
(off New Ferry Rd.)
Gt. George Pl. L1: Liv .1D 74
Gt. George Sq. L1: Liv .9H 5 (9D 58)
Gt. George's Rd. L22: Wloo .2K 43
Gt. George's Sq. L1: Liv .8H 5
Gt. George St. L1: Liv .9H 5 (9D 58)
Gt. Heath Rd. L4: Kirkd .2C 58
Great Hey L30: Neth .6C 34
Gt. Homer St. L5: Liv .3D 58
Gt. Homer St. Mkt. L5: Liv .5D 58
Gt. Howard St. L3: Liv .2C 4 (6A 58)
L5: Liv .3A 58
GREAT MEOLS .8F 54
Gt. Mersey St. L5: Kirkd .3C 58
(not continuous)
Gt. Nelson St. L3: Liv .5C 58
Gt. Newton St. L3: Liv .4K 5 (7E 58)
Gt. Orford St. L3: Liv .6K 5 (8E 58)
Gt. Richmond St. L3: Liv .1G 5 (6D 58)
Great Riding WA7: Nort .8E 96
GREAT SANKEY .2H 81
Great Sankey Leisure Cen. .9F 64
GREAT SUTTON .1J 111
Gt. Western Ho. CH41: Birke .1M 73
Greaves Cl. PR9: Banks .1E 8
Greaves Hall Av. PR9: Banks .2E 8
Greaves Hall Ind. Est.
PR9: Banks .2F 8
Greaves St. L8: Liv .3E 74
Grebe Av. WA10: St H .1D 62
Grecian St. L21: Sea .2M 43
Grecian Ter. L5: Liv .4E 58
Gredington St. L8: Liv .4F 74
Greeba Av. WA4: Warr .5C 82
Greek St. L3: Liv .4J 5 (7D 58)
WA7: Run .4J 95
Green, The CH48: Caldy .9E 70
CH62: Brom .2C 90
CH63: Raby .2J 101
CH64: Lit N .8F 100
CH64: Nest .6D 100
CH64: Will .6M 101
CH65: Whit .3N 111
L13: Liv .7A 60
L23: Crosb .7K 33
L34: Eccl P .2C 62
M31: Part .5M 69
WA7: Hal .6B 96
WN8: Parb .3E 22
Greenacre L40: Westh .9J 21
Greenacre Cl. L25: Hunts X .8G 76
Greenacre Dr. CH63: Brom .8B 90
Greenacre Rd. L25: Hunts X .8G 76
Greenacres WA6: Frod .8M 107
Greenacres, The WA13: Lymm .4G 84
Greenacres Cvn. Pk. WA6: Haps .4A 114
Greenacres Cl. CH43: Bid .9C 56
WN7: Leigh .2J 53
Greenacres Ct. CH43: Bid .9C 56
Greenall Av. WA5: Penk .4F 80
Greenall Ct. L34: Presc .3N 61
Greenalls Av. WA4: Warr .7C 82
Greenall St. WA10: St H .6H 49
WN4: Ash M .6K 41
GREEN BANK .8H 49
Green Bank CH63: Brim .5G 89
Greenbank CH2: Ince .9L 105
L22: Wloo .2L 43
L39: Augh .2A 28
Greenbank Av. CH45: New B .2H 57
CH66: Lit Sut .7H 103
L31: Mag .9H 27
WN5: Bil .9N 31
Greenbank Ct. L17: Aig .3K 75
Greenbank Cres. WA10: St H .7J 49
Greenbank Dr. CH61: Pens .4N 87
L10: Faz .3N 45
L17: Aig .4K 75
PR8: Birkd .4L 11
Greenbank Gdns. WA4: Stockt H .6G 82
Greenbank La. L17: Aig .4K 75
Greenbank Rd. CH42: Tran .5J 73
CH48: W Kir .4C 70
L18: Moss H .3K 75
WA4: Stockt H .6G 82
Greenbank Sports Academy .4K 75
Greenbank St. WA4: Warr .7D 82
Greenbridge Cl. WA7: Cas .5C 96
Greenbridge Rd. WA7: Wind H .5D 96
Greenburn Av. WA11: St H .1M 49
Green Coppice WA7: Nort .7E 96
Green Ct. WN7: Leigh .1J 53
Greencroft Hey CH63: Spit .5A 90
Greencroft Rd. CH44: Wall .6J 57
Greendale Rd. CH62: Port S .1N 89
L25: Woolt .4D 76
Grn. End. La. WA9: St H .1M 63
Grn. End Pk. L12: W Der .2M 59
Greenes Rd. L35: Whis .7A 62
Greenfield Av. WN8: Parb .3E 22
Greenfield Cl. PR9: South .4M 7
Greenfield Ct. L18: Aller .7A 76
Greenfield Dr. L36: Huy .9K 61
Greenfield Gdns. CH2: Elt .2M 113
Greenfield Gro. L36: Huy .8K 61
Greenfield La. CH60: Hesw .5K 87
L21: Lith .1N 43
WA6: Frod .5L 107
Greenfield Rd. CH66: Lit Sut .7G 103
L13: Liv .6M 59
PR8: South .5H 13
WA10: St H .5G 49
GREENFIELDS .9C 56
Greenfields Av. CH62: Brom .8B 90
WA4: App .8E 82
Greenfields Cl. CH64: Lit N .9F 100
WA1: Wools .1K 83
WA12: Newt W .6L 51
Greenfields Cres. CH62: Brom .8B 90
WN4: Ash M .7L 41
Greenfields Cft. CH64: Lit N .9E 100
Greenfields Dr. CH64: Lit N .9E 100
Greenfield Vw. WN5: Bil .7N 39
Greenfield Wlk. L36: Huy .8K 61
Greenfield Way CH44: Wall .5H 57
L18: Aller .7A 76
Greenfinch Cl. L12: Crox .7D 46
Greenfinch Gro. L26: Halew .7J 77
Greenford Cl. WN5: Orr .6N 31
Greenford Rd. PR8: Ainsd .1J 17
Green Gables L33: Kirkb .7B 36
Greengables Cl. L8: Liv .3F 74
Green Gates L36: Huy .3J 61
Greengates Cres. CH64: Lit N .9E 100
Greenham Av. L33: Kirkb .5D 36
Green Haven CH43: Noct .3D 72
Greenhaven *WN8: Uph .5L 31*
(off Tower Hill Rd.)
Greenhaven Cl. L10: Faz .3M 45
Greenheath Way CH46: Leas .6N 55
Greenhey Dr. L30: Neth .9B 34
Greenhey Pl. WN8: Skel .4C 30
Greenhey Pl. Bus. Pk. WN8: Skel .4C 30
Grn. Heys Dr. L31: Mag .2L 35
Greenheys Gdns. L8: Liv .2H 75
Greenheys Rd. CH44: Wall .6H 57
CH61: Irby .2K 87
L8: Liv .2G 74
Greenhill Av. L18: Moss H .3A 76
Greenhill Cl. L18: Moss H .6N 75
Greenhill Cres. WN5: Bil .6B 40
Greenhill La. WA4: L Whit .9C 98
Greenhill Pl. L36: Huy .8J 61
Greenhill Rd. L18: Aller, Moss H .5N 75
L19: Aller .8A 76
WN5: Bil .6B 40
Greenholme Cl. L11: Norr G .7M 45
Green Ho. Cl. WA3: Low .1H 53
Greenhouse Farm Rd. WA7: Pal F .9D 96
Greenhow Av. CH48: W Kir .5C 70
Greenings Ct. WA2: Warr .2D 82
Greenings La. PR9: South .3A 14
Grn. Jones Brow WA5: Burtw .3H 65
Grn. Kettle La. L39: Hals .2E 18
Greenlake Rd. L18: Moss H .6N 75
Greenlands L36: Huy .8J 61
Greenland St. L1: Liv .9H 5 (1C 74)
Green La. CH41: Tran .4L 73
CH45: Wall .3D 56
(Redcar Rd.)
CH45: Wall .4B 56
(Telegraph La.)
CH62: East .7E 90
CH63: Beb .2M 89
CH65: Ell P .1A 112
CH66: Gt Sut .1H 111
(not continuous)
L3: Liv .6J 5 (8D 58)
L13: Liv .4K 59
L18: Moss H .4N 75
(not continuous)
L21: Ford .9A 34
L21: Sea .3N 43
(not continuous)
L22: Wloo .9J 33
L23: Thorn .5A 34
L31: Mag .1F 34
(not continuous)
L37: Form .8F 16
L39: Orm .7C 20
L40: Lath .7C 22
M44: Cad .4L 69
PR4: Tarl .5M 9
(Blackgate La.)
PR4: Tarl .3M 9
(Gorse La.)
PR9: Banks .3F 8
WA1: Padg .9H 67
WA2: Winw .2B 66
WA4: App, App T .2G 98
WA5: Burtw .2G 65
WA8: Widnes .7H 79
WA10: Ec'stn .4B 48
WA11: Rainf .6D 38
WN5: Bil .9N 31
Green La., The L40: Burs .1K 21
Green La. Av. L39: Orm .7C 20
Green La. Cl. WA2: Winw .2B 66
Green La. Nth. L16: Child .2A 76
Green Lane (Park & Ride) .4M 73
Green Lane Station (Rail) .4M 73
Green La. W. CH1: Shot .9A 110
Green Lawn CH42: Rock F .7M 73
L36: Huy .5L 61
Grn. Lawn Gro. CH42: Rock F .7M 73
Grn. Lawns Dr. CH66: Gt Sut .5L 111
GREEN LEACH .3K 49
Grn. Leach Av. WA11: St H .3L 49
Grn. Leach Ct. WA11: St H .3L 49
Grn. Leach La. WA11: St H .3L 49
Greenlea Cl. CH63: Beb .1M 89
CH65: Whit .3N 111
WN5: Orr .7N 31
Greenleaf St. L8: Liv .1H 75
Greenleas Cl. CH45: Wall .3D 56
Greenleas Rd. CH45: Wall .3D 56
Greenleigh Rd. L18: Moss H .6N 75
Green Link L31: Mag .1G 35
Greenloon's Dr. L37: Form .1C 24

Greenloon's Wlk.—Halewood Green

Greenloon's Wlk. L37: Form 2C 24
Green Mdws. WA3: Low 5F 52
Green Mt. CH49: Upton 3A 72
Greenoaks Farm Ind. Est.
WA8: Widnes 7M 79
Grn. Oaks Path WA8: Widnes 8N 79
Grn. Oaks Shop. Cen.
Deacon Rd. 7L 79
Green Oaks Way 8L 79
Grn. Oaks Way WA8: Widnes 8L 79
Greenock M. WA8: Widnes 5H 79
Greenock St. L3: Liv 2B 4 (6A 58)
Greenodd Av. L12: W Der 9A 46
Greenore Dr. L24: Hale 5A 94
Greenough Av. L35: Rainh 4F 62
Greenough St. L25: Woolt 6D 76
Green Pk. L30: Neth 6E 34
Green Pk. Dr. L31: Mag 2G 35
Green Rd. L34: Presc 3N 61
M31: Part 6L 69
Greensbridge La. L26: Halew, Tar G 7L 77
L35: Tar G 6M 77
Greenshank Cl. WA12: Newt W 6L 51
Greenside L6: Liv 2L 5 (6E 58)
Greenside Av. L10: Aintr 9K 35
L15: Wavtr 9M 59
WA6: Frod 7N 107
Greenside Cl. L33: Kirkb 5E 36
Greens La. L31: Lydi 2J 27
WN5: Bil 1A 40
Greenslate Ct. WN5: Bil 9N 31
Greenslate Rd. WN5: Bil 9N 31
Green St. L5: Liv 5B 58
WA5: Warr 3N 81
(not continuous)
Greens Wlk. *L17: Aig* *5K 75*
(off Aigburth Va.)
Green Vw. WA13: Lymm 3H 85
Greenville Cl. CH63: Beb 2M 89
Greenville Dr. L31: Mag 2H 35
Greenville Rd. CH63: Beb 2M 89
Green Wlk. M31: Part 6L 69
PR8: Ainsd 9K 11
Greenway CH49: Grea 4M 71
CH61: Pens 3M 87
CH62: Brom 4C 90
CH64: P'gte 4B 100
L23: Crosb 6N 33
L36: Huy 5F 60
WA1: Padd 1G 83
WA4: App 8E 82
WA5: Gt San 1G 80
WN4: Ash M 7J 41
Greenway, The L12: Knott A 5C 60
Greenway Av. WN8: Skel 5E 30
Greenway Cl. L36: Huy 5F 60
WA6: Hel 2E 114
WN8: Skel 2B 30
Greenway Rd. CH42: Tran 5K 73
L24: Speke 4L 93
WA7: Run 5K 95
WA8: Widnes 6L 79
Greenways WN5: Bil 9N 31
Greenways Ct. CH62: Brom 9B 90
Greenwell Rd. WA11: Hay 4E 50
Greenwich Av. WA8: Widnes 4N 79
Greenwich Ct. L9: Aintr 2G 45
Greenwich Rd. L9: Aintr 2G 45
Greenwood Bus. Cen. WN8: Skel 5E 30
Greenwood Cl. L34: Presc 3B 62
L39: Augh 3A 28
Greenwood Ct. WA3: Ris 8N 53
(Cedar Ct.)
WA3: Ris 1M 67
(Warrington Rd.)
WA9: Clock F 5M 63
Greenwood Cres. WA2: Warr 7E 66
Greenwood Dr. WA7: Manor P 3H 97
WA12: Newt W 8M 51
Greenwood Gdns. PR8: Birkd 1N 11
Greenwood La. CH44: Wall 4J 57
Greenwood Rd. CH47: Meols 9F 54
CH49: Wdchu 5A 72
L18: Aller 7N 75
WA13: Lymm 6E 84
Greetby Hill L39: Orm 8E 20
Greetby Pl. WN8: Skel 4D 30
Greetby Wlk. L39: Orm 8E 20
Greetham St. L1: Liv 8F 4 (9C 58)
Gregory Cl. L16: Child 9C 60
WA5: Old H 1L 81
Gregory La. L39: Hals 1F 18
Gregory Row *WA3: Low* *1H 53*
(off Sandy La.)
Gregory Way L16: Child 9C 60
Gregson Ct. CH45: New B 1J 57
Gregson Rd. L35: Presc 5A 62
WA8: Widnes 7M 79
Gregsons Av. L37: Form 8E 16
Gregson St. L6: Liv 1L 5 (6E 58)
Grenadier Dr. L12: W Der 2C 60
Grenfell Cl. CH64: P'gte 5C 100
Grenfell Ct. CH64: P'gte 6C 100
Grenfell Pk. CH64: P'gte 5C 100
Grenfell Rd. L13: Liv 1K 59
Grenfell St. WA8: Widnes 8L 79
Grennan, The CH45: New B 1H 57
Grennan Ct. *CH45: New B* *1H 57*
(off The Grennan)
Grenville Cres. CH63: Brom 8B 90
Grenville Dr. CH61: Pens 4M 87
Grenville Rd. CH42: Tran 5M 73
CH64: Nest 5E 100
Grenville St. Sth. L1: Liv 8G 5 (9C 58)
Grenville Way CH42: Tran 5M 73
Gresford Av. CH43: Pren 6G 72
CH48: W Kir 5D 70
L17: Liv 2K 75
Gresford Cl. L35: Whis 6C 62
WA5: Call 7N 65
Gresham St. L7: Liv 7K 59
Gresley Cl. L7: Liv 8H 59
Gressingham Rd. L18: Moss H 5A 76
Gretton Rd. L14: Knott A 4F 60
Greyfriars WN4: Ash M 7H 41
Greyfriars Cl. WA2: Fearn 7H 67
Greyfriars Rd. PR8: Ainsd 8H 11
Greyhound Farm Rd.
L24: Speke 4G 92
Greymist Av. WA1: Wools 1K 83
Grey Rd. L9: W'ton 6E 44
WN4: Ash M 7J 41
Greys Ct. WA1: Wools 8K 67
Greystoke Cl. CH49: Upton 4N 71
Greystokes L39: Augh 2B 28
Greystone Cres. L14: Brd G 6C 60
Greystone Pl. L10: Faz 3L 45
Greystone Rd. L10: Faz 3K 45
L14: Brd G 7C 60
WA5: Penk 4H 81
Greystones CH66: Gt Sut 1J 111
Grey St. L8: Liv 2E 74
WA1: Warr 2D 82
Gribble Rd. L10: Faz 3M 45
Grice St. WA4: Stockt H 7D 82
Grierson St. L8: Liv 1G 75
Grieve Rd. L10: Faz 3M 45
Griffin Av. CH46: More 9M 55
Griffin Cl. L11: Crox 6A 46
WA10: Ec'stn 6C 48
Griffin M. WA8: Widnes 5L 79
Griffin St. WA9: St H 2A 64
Griffiths Av. WA3: Ris 4M 67
Griffiths Cl. CH49: Grea 5K 71
Griffiths Dr. PR9: South 7L 7
Griffiths Rd. L36: Huy 7J 61
Griffiths St. L1: Liv 8H 5 (9D 58)
WA4: Westy 4G 82
Griffon Ho. *PR9: South* *5L 7*
(off Cambridge Rd.)
Grimrod Pl. WN8: Skel 5D 30
Grimsby Ct. L19: Garst 1N 91
Grimsditch La. WA4: L Whit, Nor B 9B 98
Grimshaw Ct. WA3: Golb 1B 52
GRIMSHAW GREEN 1F 22
Grimshaw La. L39: Orm 7C 20
Grimshaw Rd. WN8: Skel 4D 30
Grimshaw St. L20: Boot 8A 44
WA3: Golb 1B 52
WA9: Sut L 3M 63
Grindleford Pl. WA1: Warr 3F 82
Grindley Gdns. CH65: Ell P 3A 112
Grindlow Wlk. WN3: Winst 1E 40
Grinfield St. L7: Liv 6N 5 (8F 58)
Grinshill Cl. L8: Liv 2F 74
Grinstead Cl. PR8: Birkd 5M 11
Grinton Cres. L36: Roby 7H 61
Grisedale Av. WA2: Warr 6C 66
Grisedale Cl. L37: Form 1E 24
WA7: Beech 1A 108
Grisedale Rd. CH62: Brom 7E 90
Grizedale WA8: Widnes 6E 78
Grizedale Av. WA11: St H 2L 49
Groarke Dr. WA5: Penk 3F 80
Groes Rd. L19: G'dale 9N 75
Grogan Sq. L20: Boot 4C 44
Gronow Pl. *L20: Boot* *4D 44*
(off Hughes Dr.)
Grosmont Rd. L32: Kirkb 2D 46
Grosmont Way WA8: Widnes 4A 80
Grosvenor Av. CH48: W Kir 6C 70
L23: Crosb 9L 33
WA1: Warr 1F 82
WA3: Low 2E 52
Grosvenor Cl. L30: Neth 8E 34
PR8: Birkd 3L 11
WA5: Gt San 3L 81
Grosvenor Ct. CH43: Oxton 3H 73
CH47: Hoy 2C 70
L15: Wavtr 1A 76
L18: Moss H 5K 75
L34: Presc *3A 62*
(off Grosvenor Rd.)
WA12: Newt W 8K 51
Grosvenor Dr. CH45: New B 1H 57
Grosvenor Gdns. PR8: Birkd 3M 11
WA12: Newt W 8L 51
Grosvenor Grange WA1: Wools 8J 67
Grosvenor (Leo) Casino
Liverpool 9F 4 (1C 74)
Grosvenor M. CH65: Ell P 8N 103
Grosvenor Pl. CH43: Oxton 3G 73
PR8: Birkd 3M 11
Grosvenor Rd. CH43: Oxton 2G 72
CH45: New B 1H 57
CH47: Hoy 2C 70
L4: W'ton 8E 44
L15: Wavtr 9J 59
L19: G'dale 1M 91
L31: Mag 5H 35
L34: Presc 3A 62
PR8: Birkd 2K 11
Grosvenor Rd. WA8: Widnes 4L 79
WA10: St H 8G 48
WA11: Hay 3D 50
Grosvenor St. CH44: Wall 4H 57
L3: Liv 1G 5 (6C 58)
WA7: Run 4L 95
Grosvenor Ter. *L8: Liv* *4G 74*
(off Wellesley Rd.)
Grosvenor Wharf Rd. CH65: Ell P 7B 104
Grounds St. WA2: Warr 1C 82
Grove, The CH43: Oxton 5H 73
CH44: Wall 6J 57
CH47: Meols 7G 54
CH63: Beb 2N 89
L13: Liv 3L 59
L28: Stockb V 2G 60
L39: Augh 5A 28
L39: Orm 8C 20
L40: Ruf 3L 15
WA3: Low 1E 52
WA5: Penk 4H 81
WA10: Windle 5F 48
WA13: Lymm 5E 84
WN6: App B 3M 23
Grove Av. CH60: Hesw 6N 87
WA13: Lymm 5C 84
Grove Bank WA6: Hel 1F 114
Grove Cl. WN8: Uph 4M 31
Grovedale Dr. CH46: More 8A 56
Grovedale Rd. L18: Moss H 3L 75
Grove Ho. Ct. WA8: Widnes 5L 79
Grovehurst Av. L14: Knott A 5D 60
Groveland Av. CH45: Wall 3D 56
CH47: Hoy 1C 70
Groveland Rd. CH45: Wall 3D 56
Grovelands L7: Liv 8M 5
Grove Mead L31: Mag 2L 35
Grove Pk. L8: Liv 2H 75
L39: Orm 6D 20
PR9: South 7L 7
Grove Pk. Av. L12: W Der 1N 59
Grove Pl. CH47: Hoy 1C 70
Grove Ri. WA13: Lymm 5E 84
Grove Rd. CH1: Moll 8J 111
CH42: Rock F 6M 73
CH45: Wall 3E 56
CH47: Hoy 1C 70
L6: Liv 6J 59
WN8: Uph 4M 31
Groves, The CH43: Oxton 3H 73
CH66: Whit 5M 111
L7: Liv 7M 5
L32: Kirkb 3C 46
Groveside CH48: W Kir 6B 70
L7: Liv 8M 5 (9F 58)
Grove Sq. CH62: New F 9N 73
Grove St. CH62: New F 9A 74
L7: Liv 8M 5 (9F 58)
L15: Wavtr 9L 59
L20: Boot 6N 43
PR8: South 2N 11
WA4: Warr 5D 82
WA7: Run 4J 95
WA10: St H 7J 49
WN4: Ash M 7J 41
Grove Ter. CH47: Hoy 1C 70
PR8: Birkd 1N 11
WA6: Hel 1F 114
Grove Way L7: Liv 8M 5 (9F 58)
Grovewood PR8: Birkd 1L 11
Grovewood Ct. CH43: Oxton 5H 73
Grovewood Gdns. L35: Whis 6B 62
Grundy Cl. PR8: South 1D 12
WA8: Widnes 5J 79
Grundy Homes PR8: South 1D 12
Grundy St. L5: Kirkd 3A 58
WA3: Golb 3B 52
Guardian Ct. CH48: W Kir 7C 70
PR8: Birkd 1M 11
Guardian St. WA5: Warr 2A 82
Guardian St. Ind. Est. WA5: Warr 2A 82
Guelph Pl. L7: Liv 3N 5
Guelph St. L7: Liv 3M 5 (7F 58)
Guernsey Cl. WA4: App 8E 82
Guernsey Dr. CH65: Ell P 4A 112
Guernsey Rd. L13: Liv 5L 59
WA8: Widnes 5A 80
Guest St. WA8: Widnes 9K 79
Guffitts Cl. CH47: Meols 8F 54
Guffitt's Rake CH47: Meols 8F 54
Guildford Av. L30: Neth 1E 44
Guildford Cl. WA2: Padg 8H 67
Guildford Rd. PR8: Birkd 7M 11
Guildford St. CH44: Wall 5K 57
Guildhall Rd. L9: Aintr 4F 44
Guild Hey L34: Know 6H 47
Guillemot Way L26: Halew 7J 77
Guilsted Rd. L11: Norr G 8M 45
Guinea Gap CH44: Wall 6L 57
Guinea Gap Leisure Cen. 6L 57
Guinea Hall Cl. PR9: Banks 2E 8
Guinea Hall La. PR9: Banks 1E 8
Guinea Hall M. PR9: Banks 2E 8
Guion Rd. L21: Lith 3A 44
Guion St. L6: Liv 5G 59
Gulliver's World Theme Pk. 8N 65
Gulls Way CH60: Hesw 7L 87
Gunn Gro. CH64: Nest 6F 100
Gunning Av. WA10: Ec'stn 5E 48
Gunning Cl. WA10: Ec'stn 5E 48
Gurnall St. L4: W'ton 2E 58
Gutticar Rd. WA8: Widnes 7E 78
Guy Cl. CH41: Tran 4L 73
Guys Ind. Est. Nth. L40: Burs 3F 20
Guys Ind. Est. Sth. L40: Burs 3F 20
Gwendoline Cl. CH61: Thing 2A 88
Gwendoline St. L8: Liv 2E 74
Gwenfron Rd. L6: Liv 6G 58
Gwent Cl. L6: Liv 4G 59
Gwent St. L8: Liv 2F 74
Gwladys St. L4: W'ton 9E 44
Gwydir St. L8: Liv 3F 74
Gwydrin Rd. L18: Moss H 3A 76
Gym, The
Liverpool 6E 4
gymetc.
Lowton 3H 53
Orrell 5N 31
Gym Health & Fitness, The
St Helens 7J 49

H

Hackett Av. L20: Boot 4C 44
Hackett Pl. L20: Boot 4C 44
Hackins Hey L2: Liv 4D 4 (7B 58)
Hackthorpe St. L5: Liv 2D 58
Hackworth Cl. L14: Brd G 8A 60
Hadassah Gro. L17: Aig 4H 75
Hadden Cl. L35: Rainh 5D 62
Haddington Rd. L23: Crosb 8M 33
Haddock St. L20: Kirkd 9A 44
Haddon Av. L9: W'ton 4E 44
Haddon Dr. CH61: Pens 3N 87
WA8: Widnes 4E 78
Haddon Ho. *CH64: Nest* *6E 100*
(off Churchill Way)
Haddon Rd. CH42: Rock F 6N 73
WA3: Low 1E 52
WN3: Wigan 1G 41
Haddon St. WN4: Ash M 6H 41
Haddon Wlk. L12: Crox 7C 46
Hadfield Av. CH47: Hoy 1D 70
Hadfield Cl. WA8: Widnes 7A 80
Hadfield Gro. L25: Woolt 5G 76
Hadleigh Cl. WA5: Gt San 3F 80
Hadleigh Gro. WA7: Cas 5B 96
Hadleigh Rd. L32: Kirkb 1D 46
Hadley Av. CH62: Brom 6B 90
Hadlow La. CH64: Will 7M 101
Hadlow Rd. CH64: Will 9M 101
Hadlow Road Station 7N 101
Hadlow Ter. CH64: Will 7M 101
Hadlow Way L14: Knott A 5D 60
Hadstock Av. L37: Form 3D 24
Haggerston Rd. L4: W'ton 8F 44
Hague Bush Cl. WA3: Low 1F 52
Hahnemann Rd. L4: W'ton 8D 44
Haig Av. CH46: More 9N 55
M44: Cad 5J 69
PR8: South 1D 12
WA5: Gt San 4J 81
Haigh Cl. WA9: St H 4J 63
Haigh Ct. PR8: South 9L 7
Haigh Cres. L31: Lydi 8H 27
Haigh Rd. L22: Wloo 1L 43
Haigh St. L3: Liv 1K 5 (5E 58)
(not continuous)
Haig Rd. WA8: Widnes 7K 79
Haileybury Av. L10: Aintr 9J 35
Haileybury Rd. L25: Woolt 8F 76
Hailsham Rd. L19: Aig 8L 75
Halby Rd. L9: Aintr 4G 44
Halcombe Rd. L12: W Der 1B 60
Halcyon Rd. CH41: Birke 4J 73
Haldane Av. CH41: Birke 1F 72
Haldane Rd. L4: W'ton 8F 44
HALE 6A 94
HALE BANK 2E 94
Halebank Rd. WA8: Hale B 2B 94
Hale Bank Ter. WA8: Hale B 3D 94
Hale Ct. WA8: Hale B 3D 94
Hale Dr. L24: Hale, Speke 5H 93
Halefield St. WA10: St H 6J 49
(not continuous)
Hale Ga. Rd. WA8: Hale B 5C 94
Hale Gro. WA5: Gt San 2J 81
WN4: Ash M 6H 41
HALE HEATH 5L 93
Hale M. WA8: Widnes 9F 78
Hale Rd. CH45: Wall 3J 57
L4: W'ton 9D 44
L24: Hale, Speke 4F 92
(not continuous)
WA8: Hale B, Widnes 3E 94
Hale Rd. Ind. Est. WA8: Hale B 2E 94
Hale St. L2: Liv 4E 4 (7B 58)
WA2: Warr 1C 82
Hale Vw. WA7: Run 7H 95
Hale Vw. Rd. L36: Huy 7L 61
WA6: Hel 1F 114
HALEWOOD 9K 77
Halewood Av. WA3: Golb 1A 52
Halewood Cvn. Pk. L26: Halew 8N 77
Halewood Cen., The L26: Halew 9K 77
Halewood Cl. L25: Gate 4F 76
Halewood Dr. L25: Woolt 6F 76
(Kings Dr.)
L25: Woolt 6G 76
(Layton Rd.)
HALEWOOD GREEN 6J 77

Harron Cl.—Heather Gro.

Harron Cl. L32: Kirkb .9A 36
Harrop Rd. WA7: Run .6L 95
Harrops Cft. L30: Neth .7D 34
Harrowby Cl. L8: Liv .9N 5 (1F 74)
Harrowby Rd. CH42: Tran .4J 73
CH44: Wall .5L 57
L21: Sea .3M 43
Harrowby Rd. Sth. CH42: Tran .4J 73
Harrowby St. L8: Liv .9N 5 (1F 74)
(Granby St.)
L8: Liv .1F 74
(Park Way)
Harrow Cl. CH44: Wall .4F 56
L30: Neth .9E 34
WA4: App .1F 98
Harrow Dr. L10: Aintr .9J 35
WA7: Run .5A 96
Harrow Gro. CH62: Brom .7D 90
Harrow Rd. CH44: Wall .4F 56
CH65: Ell P .1B 112
L4: W'ton .3G 58
Harsnips WN8: Skel .2F 30
Hartdale Rd. L18: Moss H .4M 75
L23: Thorn .5N 33
Hartford Cl. CH43: Oxton .5F 72
Hartford Dr. CH65: Whit .1L 111
Hartford Rd. WA10: Ec'stn .7E 48
Harthill Av. L18: Moss H .4N 75
Harthill M. CH43: Bid .8C 56
Harthill Rd. L18: Moss H .3A 76
Hartington Av. CH41: Birke .1H 73
Hartington Rd. CH44: Wall .5H 57
L8: Liv .2H 75
L12: W Der .3N 59
L19: Garst .1A 92
WA10: St H .5F 48
Hartington Ter. *L19: Garst* .*1N 91*
(off St Mary's Rd.)
Hartismere Rd. CH44: Wall .6K 57
Hartland WN8: Skel .2F 30
Hartland Av. PR9: South .2N 7
Hartland Cl. WA8: Widnes .3K 79
Hartland Gdns. WA9: St H .3G 62
Hartland Rd. L11: Norr G .8K 45
Hartley Av. L9: Aintr .5G 44
Hartley Cl. L4: W'ton .2E 58
WA13: Lymm .5F 84
Hartley Cres. PR8: Birkd .4M 11
Hartley Grn. Gdns. WN5: Bil .1N 39
Hartley Gro. L33: Kirkb .6D 36
WA10: St H .1F 62
Hartley Quay L3: Liv .7D 4 (9B 58)
Hartley Rd. PR8: Birkd .4M 11
HARTLEY'S VILLAGE .5G 45
Hartley's Village L9: Aintr .5G 45
Hartley Way WN5: Bil .1N 39
Hartnup St. L5: Liv .3F 58
(Glaisher St.)
L5: Liv .3E 58
(Mycroft Cl.)
Hartnup Way CH43: Bid .1C 72
Harton Cl. WA8: Widnes .5H 79
Hartopp Rd. L25: Gate .2E 76
Hartopp Wlk. *L25: Gate* .*1E 76*
(off Hartopp Rd.)
Hartor Cl. L5: Liv .3D 58
(not continuous)
Hartsbourne Av. L25: Gate .9D 60
(not continuous)
Hartsbourne Cl. L25: Gate .1D 76
Hartsbourne Wlk. L25: Gate .1E 76
Hartshead WN8: Skel .2F 30
Hart's La. WN8: Uph .4J 31
Hart St. L3: Liv .4J 5 (7D 58)
PR8: South .9J 7
Hart St. Bri. *PR8: South* .*9J 7*
(off Hart St.)
Hartswell Cl. WA3: Golb .1B 52
Hartswood Cl. WA4: App .4F 98
Hartwell St. L21: Lith .4A 44
Hartwood Cl. L32: Kirkb .3D 46
Hartwood Rd. L32: Kirkb .3D 46
PR9: South .8J 7
Hartwood Sq. L32: Kirkb .3D 46
Harty Rd. WA11: Hay .5C 50
Harvard Cl. WA7: Wind H .5F 96
Harvard Ct. WA2: Winw .6B 66
Harvard Gro. L34: Presc .2B 62
Harvest Ct. CH46: More .8M 55
Harvester Way CH49: Grea .4K 71
L30: Neth .7F 34
Harvest La. CH46: More .8L 55
Harvest Way WA9: Clock F .5M 63
Harvey Av. CH49: Grea .5L 71
WA12: Newt W .7H 51
Harvey Ct. WA2: Warr .6C 66
WA3: Golb .1B 52
WN7: Leigh .1J 53
Harvey La. WA3: Golb .1A 52
Harvey Rd. CH45: Wall .3G 56
CH46: Leas .7A 56
Harvington Dr. PR8: Ainsd .9G 11
Harwich Gro. L16: Child .9D 60
Harwood Gdns. WA4: Grap .6H 83
Harwood Rd. L19: Garst .1B 92
Harworth Rd. WA9: St H .4H 63
Haryngton Av. WA5: Warr .1A 82
Haselbeech Cl. L11: Norr G .7L 45
Haselbeech Cres. L11: Norr G .7L 45
Haseldine St. WN4: Ash M .5H 41
Hasfield Rd. L11: Norr G .8N 45
HASKAYNE .8E 18
Haslam Dr. L39: Orm .6B 20
Haslemere L35: Whis .6C 62
Haslemere Dr. WA5: Penk .4F 80
Haslemere Ind. Est.
WN4: Ash M .3J 41
Haslemere Rd. L25: Gate .2F 76
Haslemere Way L25: Gate .2E 76
Haslingden Cl. L13: Liv .7N 59
Haslington Gro. L26: Halew .1L 93
Hassal Rd. CH42: Rock F .8N 73
Hassness Cl. WN3: Wigan .1K 41
Hastie Cl. L27: N'ley .3J 77
Hastings Av. WA2: Warr .5C 66
Hastings Dr. L36: Huy .9L 61
Hastings Rd. L22: Wloo .9H 33
PR8: Birkd .4L 11
Haswell Dr. L28: Stockb V .1E 60
Hatchery Cl. WA4: App T .3J 99
Hatchings, The WA13: Lymm .6E 84
Hatchmere Cl. CH43: Oxton .5F 72
WA5: Warr .2N 81
Hatfield Cl. L12: Crox .7D 46
WA9: St H .2J 63
Hatfield Gdns. L36: Huy .8K 61
WA4: App .3F 98
Hatfield Rd. L20: Boot .7D 44
PR8: Ainsd .8J 11
Hathaway L31: Mag .4G 35
Hathaway Cl. L25: Gate .2E 76
Hathaway Rd. L25: Gate .2E 76
Hatherley Av. L23: Crosb .9L 33
Hatherley Cl. L8: Liv .1F 74
(not continuous)
Hatherley St. CH44: Wall .7L 57
L8: Liv .1F 74
Hathersage Rd. L36: Huy .4J 61
Hatherton Gro. L26: Halew .1L 93
Hatley La. WA6: Frod .7H 107
Hattersley Ct. L39: Orm .7D 20
Hattersley Way L39: Orm .7D 20
Hatters Row *WA1: Warr* .*3C 82*
(off Horsemarket St.)
HATTON .6A 98
Hatton Av. CH62: East .3D 102
Hatton Cl. CH60: Hesw .6L 87
Hatton Gdn. L3: Liv .3E 4 (7B 58)
Hatton Gdn. Ind. Est. L3: Liv .3F 4
Hatton Hill Rd. L21: Lith .1N 43
Hatton La. WA4: Hatt, Sttn .6B 98
Hattons La. L16: Child .2A 76
Hauxwell Gro. WA11: St H .4M 49
Havannah La. WA9: St H .7D 50
Havelock Cl. WA10: St H .7J 49
Havelock Rd. L20: Boot .4B 44
Haven Brow L39: Augh .4A 28
Haven Rd. L10: Faz .2L 45
Haven Wlk. L31: Lydi .8H 27
Havercroft Cl. WN3: Wigan .1G 40
Havergal St. WA7: Run .6J 95
Haverstock Rd. L6: Liv .6J 59
Haverton Wlk. L12: Crox .7C 46
(not continuous)
Haverty Pct. WA12: Newt W .9K 51
Havisham Cl. WA3: Birchw .4L 67
Hawarde Cl. WA12: Newt W .6J 51
Hawarden Av. CH43: Oxton .2J 73
CH44: Wall .5J 57
L17: Liv .2K 75
Hawarden Ct. CH63: Beb .3M 89
Hawarden Gdns. CH65: Ell P .3B 112
Hawarden Gro. L21: Sea .4N 43
Hawdon Ct. L7: Liv .9H 59
Hawes Av. WA11: St H .2M 49
Hawes Cres. WN4: Ash M .6K 41
Hawesside St. PR9: South .8H 7
Haweswater Av. WA11: Hay .4C 50
Haweswater Cl. L33: Kirkb .6B 36
WA7: Beech .1C 108
Haweswater Gro. L31: Mag .1L 35
Hawgreen Rd. L32: Kirkb .9N 35
Hawick Cl. CH66: Lit Sut .9F 102
L33: Kirkb .5B 36
Hawke Grn. L35: Tar G .1L 77
Hawker Dr. WN8: Skel .4H 31
Hawke St. L3: Liv .5H 5 (8D 58)
Hawkesworth St. L4: W'ton .3F 58
Hawkhurst Cl. L8: Liv .4E 74
Hawkhurst Dr. CH42: Rock F .7N 73
Hawkins Rd. CH64: Nest .5E 100
Hawkins St. L6: Liv .6G 59
HAWKLEY .1K 41
Hawkley Av. WN3: Wigan .1H 41
Hawkley Brook Ct. WN3: Wigan .1H 41
Hawksclough WN8: Skel .2G 30
Hawks Ct. WA7: Pal F .9A 96
Hawkshaw Cl. WA3: Birchw .5K 67
Hawkshead Av. L12: W Der .9A 46
Hawkshead Cl. L31: Mag .1K 35
WA7: Beech .1C 108
Hawkshead Dr. L21: Lith .2C 44
Hawkshead Rd. CH62: Brom .6D 90
WA5: Burtw .3G 65
Hawkshead St. PR8: South .8J 7
PR9: South .7H 7
Hawksmoor Cl. L10: Faz .3M 45
Hawksmoor Rd. L10: Faz .4M 45
Hawksmore Cl. CH49: Upton .2L 71
Hawkstone Gro. WA6: Hel .1F 114
Hawkstone St. L8: Liv .3F 74
(not continuous)
Hawkstone Wlk. *L8: Liv* .*4F 74*
(off Hawkstone St.)
Hawks Way CH60: Hesw .7M 87
Hawksworth Cl. L37: Form .7G 17
Hawksworth Dr. L37: Form .7G 17
Hawley Brook Trad. Est. WN3: Wigan .1G 41
Hawleys Cl. WA5: Warr .8A 66
Hawleys La. WA2: Warr .8A 66
WA5: Warr .8A 66
Haworth Dr. L20: Boot .3C 44
Hawthorn Av. L40: Burs .1K 21
WA7: Run .6K 95
WA8: Widnes .6L 79
WA12: Newt W .7M 51
WN4: Garsw .6E 40
Hawthorn Cl. WA11: Hay .5C 50
WN5: Bil .6N 39
Hawthorn Cres. WN8: Skel .3B 30
Hawthorn Dr. CH48: W Kir .6F 70
CH61: Hesw .4N 87
M44: Cad .4K 69
WA10: Ec'stn .6E 48
Hawthorne Av. L26: Halew .1J 93
WA1: Wools .1J 83
WA5: Gt San .2H 81
Hawthorne Bus. Pk. WA5: Warr .9B 66
Hawthorne Ct. *L21: Lith* .*2A 44*
(off Sefton Rd.)
Hawthorne Cres. L37: Form .2G 24
Hawthorne Dr. CH64: Will .5A 102
L33: Kirkb .8D 36
PR9: Banks .5H 9
Hawthorne Gro. CH44: Wall .7L 57
PR9: South .8L 7
WA1: Padd .1G 83
WA4: Stockt H .7E 82
Hawthorne Rd. CH42: Tran .5K 73
L20: Boot .5C 44
L21: Lith .2A 44
WA4: Stockt H .8D 82
WA6: Frod .5L 107
Hawthornes, The CH2: Wim T .9K 113
CH42: Rock F .7N 73
L40: Ruf .3M 15
Hawthorne St. WA5: Warr .9B 66
Hawthorn Gro. WA4: Warr .5E 82
Hawthorn La. CH62: Brom .7C 90
Hawthorn Rd. CH64: P'gte .4B 100
CH66: Lit Sut .8H 103
L34: Presc .3B 62
L36: Roby .7G 61
WA9: Sut L .3N 63
WA13: Lymm .5D 84
Hawthorns, The CH66: Ell P .7L 103
WN8: Newb .4D 22
Hawthorns Gro. L12: W Der .3N 59
Hawthorn Wlk. M31: Part .6L 69
Haxted Gdns. L19: Garst .1B 92
Haycroft Cl. CH66: Gt Sut .3J 111
Haydan M. WA6: Frod .8H 107
Haydn Rd. L14: Knott A .3D 60
HAYDOCK .4E 50
Haydock Cross WA11: Hay .1H 51
Haydock Ind. Est. WA11: Hay .2G 50
Haydock La. WA11: Hay .4E 50
(not continuous)
Haydock La. Ind. Est. WA11: Hay .2H 51
Haydock Leisure Cen. .4D 50
Haydock Pk. Gdns. WA12: Newt W .1K 51
Haydock Pk. Golf Course .5A 52
Haydock Pk. Racecourse .1M 51
Haydock Pk. Rd. L10: Aintr .8K 35
Haydock Rd. CH45: Wall .2J 57
Haydock St. WA2: Warr .2C 82
WA10: St H .7K 49
WA12: Newt W .6J 51
WN4: Ash M .9K 41
Hayes Av. L35: Presc .4B 62
Hayes Cres. WA6: Frod .5M 107
Hayes Dr. L31: Mell .8N 35
Hayes La. WA4: App .8F 82
Haye's Rd. M44: Cad .4L 69
(not continuous)
Hayes Row WA3: Low .1H 53
Hayes St. WA10: St H .1F 62
Hayfell Rd. WN3: Wigan .2J 41
Hayfield Cl. L26: Halew .7L 77
Hayfield Pl. CH46: More .9A 56
Hayfield Rd. L39: Orm .6C 20
WA1: Wools .1K 83
Hayfield St. L4: W'ton .2E 58
Hayfield Way WA9: Clock F .5M 63
Haylemere Ct. PR8: Birkd .1L 11
Hayles Cl. L25: Gate .2E 76
Hayles Grn. L25: Gate .2E 76
Hayles Gro. L25: Gate .2E 76
Hayles Hey L19: Aig .9L 75
Haylock Cl. L8: Liv .4E 74
Haymans Cl. L12: W Der .2M 59
Haymans Grn. L12: W Der .2M 59
L31: Mag .2K 35
Haymans Gro. L12: W Der .2M 59
Hayscastle Cl. WA5: Call .8N 65
Hayward Ct. L37: Form .9G 16
Haywood Cl. WA3: Low .1F 52
Haywood Cres. WA7: Wind H .5F 96
Haywood Gdns. WA10: St H .8G 48
Haywood Rd. L28: Stockb V .1F 60
Hazel Av. L32: Kirkb .8A 36
L35: Whis .6B 62
WA7: Run .7H 95
Hazelbank Gdns. L37: Form .8E 16
Hazelborough Cl. WA3: Birchw .4B 68
Hazel Bus. Pk. WA11: Rainf .7F 38
Hazel Cl. CH66: Gt Sut .4L 111
Hazel Ct. *L8: Liv* .*4F 74*
(off Byles St.)
L20: Boot .8B 44
Hazeldale Rd. L9: W'ton .6F 44
Hazeldene Av. CH45: Wall .4G 57
CH61: Thing .1B 88
Hazeldene Way CH61: Thing .1B 88
Hazel Dr. WA13: Lymm .6F 84
Hazelfield Ct. WA9: Clock F .5M 63
Hazel Gro. CH61: Irby .9L 71
CH63: H Beb .3L 89
L9: Aintr .4G 45
L23: Crosb .8M 33
L32: Kirkb .2D 46
PR8: South .8K 7
WA1: Padd .9H 67
WA3: Golb .2C 52
WA10: St H .7F 48
Hazelhurst Cl. L37: Form .2C 24
Hazelhurst Gro. WN4: Ash M .7L 41
Hazelhurst Rd. L4: W'ton .2G 59
Hazel La. WN8: Skel .9E 22
Hazelmere Ho. *L17: Aig* .*6J 75*
(off Mossley Hill Dr.)
Hazel M. L31: Mell .8N 35
Hazel Rd. CH41: Birke .3K 73
CH47: Hoy .9C 54
L36: Huy .4K 61
Hazelslack Rd. L11: Norr G .8M 45
Hazel St. WA1: Warr .1E 82
Hazelton Cl. WN7: Leigh .1M 53
Hazel Wlk. M31: Part .6L 69
Hazelwood CH49: Grea .3L 71
Hazelwood Av. L40: Burs .1J 21
Hazelwood Cl. WA8: Widnes .8D 78
WA9: Sut M .6L 63
Hazelwood Gro. L26: Halew .6H 77
Hazelwood M. WA4: Grap .7K 83
Hazlehurst Rd. WA6: Frod .9M 107
Hazleton Rd. L14: Knott A .6A 60
Headbolt La. L33: Kirkb .7C 36
PR8: Ainsd .1N 17
PR8: Birkd .8N 11
Headbourne Cl. L25: Gate .1D 76
Headbourne Ct. *L25: Gate* .*1D 76*
(off Headbourne Cl.)
Head Farm Ct. WA12: Newt W .7J 51
Headingley Cl. L36: Roby .9G 61
WA9: St H .3M 63
Headingly Av. WN8: Skel .3N 29
Headington Rd. CH49: Upton .3L 71
Headland Cl. CH48: W Kir .8C 70
WA3: Low .4F 52
Headley Cl. WA10: St H .7J 49
Head St. L8: Liv .2D 74
Heald St. L19: Garst .1A 92
WA12: Newt W .7H 51
Healy Cl. L27: N'ley .4L 77
Heanor Dr. PR8: South .3E 12
Heap Ct. PR9: South .7K 7
Hearne Rd. WA10: St H .6G 48
Hearts Health Club
Great Crosby .6K 33
Hearts Ladies Health Club
Wallasey .5G 56
Heartwood Cl. L9: W'ton .3F 44
Heath Av. CH65: Whit .4M 111
Heathbank Av. CH44: Wall .6G 56
CH61: Irby .9K 71
Heathbank Rd. CH42: Tran .5K 73
Heath Blvd. WA7: W'ton .9K 95
Heath Bus. & Technical Pk., The
WA7: W'ton .8K 95
Heath Cl. CH48: W Kir .8C 70
L25: Woolt .3D 76
L34: Eccl P .2C 62
Heathcote Cl. L7: Liv .9H 59
Heathcote Gdns. CH63: Beb .2M 89
Heathcote Rd. L4: W'ton .8E 44
Heath Ct. CH66: Lit Sut .7G 103
Heathdale CH63: Beb .4M 89
Heath Dr. CH49: Upton .3A 72
CH60: Hesw .6N 87
WA7: W'ton .8K 95
Heather Av. M44: Cad .3K 69
Heather Bank CH63: H Beb .1K 89
Heather Brae L34: Presc .4L 61
WA12: Newt W .6J 51
Heather Brow CH43: Clau .1F 72
Heather Cl. CH46: More .8K 55
CH66: Gt Sut .2K 111
L4: W'ton .1E 58
L33: Kirkb .*7C 36*
(off Heathfield Dr.)
L37: Form .8H 17
L40: Burs .1J 21
PR8: Ainsd .3K 17
WA3: Birchw .4L 67
WA7: Beech .2A 108
Heatherdale Cl. CH42: Tran .4J 73
Heatherdale Rd. L18: Moss H .4M 75
Heather Dene CH62: Brom .4C 90
Heatherdene Rd. CH48: W Kir .5C 70
Heatherfield Ct. *CH42: Tran* .*4J 73*
(off Victoria Flds.)
Heathergreen Ct. L4: W'ton .9G 45
Heather Gro. WN4: Ash M .7N 41

Heatherlea Cl.—Highfield Pk.

Heatherlea Cl. WN8: Uph 5M 31
Heatherleigh CH48: Caldy 1E 86
WA9: St H 3F 62
Heatherleigh Cl. L9: W'ton 3F 44
Heather Rd. CH60: Hesw 6A 88
CH63: H Beb 3K 89
Heathers Cft. L30: Neth 8D 34
Heather Wlk. *M31: Part* *6L 69*
(off Gorse Sq.)
Heather Way L23: Thorn 5A 34
Heatherways L37: Form 7G 16
Heathey La. L39: Hals, South 6F 12
Heath Farm La. M31: Part 6N 69
Heathfield CH62: Brom 5C 90
L40: Burs 1K 21
Heathfield Av. WA9: St H 1H 63
Heath Fld. Cl. WA3: Low 3D 52
Heathfield Cl. L21: Lith 4B 44
L37: Form 7G 16
Heathfield Ct. CH65: Ell P 9N 103
Heathfield Dr. L20: Boot 4B 44
L33: Kirkb 7C 36
Heathfield Gdns. WA7: Run 7K 95
Heathfield Ho. CH61: Thing 1A 88
Heathfield Pk. WA4: Grap 6H 83
WA8: Widnes 5G 79
Heathfield Rd. CH43: Oxton 4J 73
CH63: Beb 2M 89
CH65: Ell P 9N 103
L15: Wavtr 2M 75
L22: Wloo 9J 33
L31: Mag 4L 35
PR8: Ainsd 8L 11
Heathfield St. L1: Liv 6H 5 (8D 58)
(not continuous)
Heathgate WN8: Skel 2F 30
Heathgate Av. L24: Speke 5K 93
Heath Gro. CH66: Lit Sut 7G 102
Heath Hey L25: Woolt 3D 76
Heath Ho. Cl. WA3: Low 3D 52
Heathland WN8: Uph 5L 31
Heathland Rd. WA9: Clock F 5M 63
Heathlands, The CH46: Leas 5M 55
Heathlands Rd. CH66: Lit Sut 8G 103
Heath La. CH2: Lit Stan, Stoak 6B 112
(not continuous)
CH64: Will 5B 102
CH66: Chil T, Lit Sut 7C 102
WA3: Croft 8H 53
WA3: Low 3D 52
(not continuous)
Heathmoor Av. WA3: Low 4E 52
Heathmoor Rd. CH46: More 8L 55
Heath Pk. Gro. WA7: Run 7J 95
Heath Rd. CH63: Beb, H Beb 2L 89
L19: Aller 8A 76
L36: Huy 4G 60
WA5: Penk 3H 81
WA7: Run 7K 95
WA8: Widnes 6G 79
WN4: Ash M 9K 41
Heath Rd. Cres. WA7: Run 7L 95
Heath Rd. Sth. WA7: Run, W'ton 1J 107
Heathside CH60: Hesw 6K 87
Heath St. WA3: Golb 2B 52
WA4: Stockt H 8D 82
WA9: St H 2G 62
WN4: Ash M 9L 41
Heath Vw. L21: Ford 8A 34
Heathview Cl. WA8: Hale B 2D 94
Heathview Rd. WA8: Hale B 3D 94
Heathwaite Cres. L11: Norr G 9M 45
Heathway CH60: Hesw 8B 88
Heathwood L12: W Der 4N 59
Heathwood Gro. WA1: Padd 1J 83
Heathy La. L39: Bart 5N 17
HEATLEY 2J 85
Heatley Cl. CH43: Bid 1C 72
WA13: Lymm 4G 85
Heaton Cl. L24: Speke 4K 93
L40: Burs 1H 21
WN8: Uph 5K 31
Heaton Ct. L40: Scar 2A 20
WA3: Ris 3N 67
HEATON'S BRIDGE 1A 20
Heatons Bri. Rd. L40: Scar 1A 20
Hebburn Way L12: Crox 7E 46
Hebden Pde. L11: Norr G 7A 46
Hebden Rd. L11: Norr G 7N 45
Hebdon Cl. WN4: Ash M 6J 41
Hedgebank Cl. L9: Aintr 2J 45
Hedgecote L32: Kirkb 3C 46
Hedgecroft L23: Thorn 5B 34
Hedgefield Rd. L25: Gate 3F 76
Hedge Hey WA7: Cas 6C 96
Hedgerows, The WA11: Hay 3H 51
Hedges Cres. L13: Liv 2K 59
Hedingham Cl. L26: Halew 7L 77
Hedworth Gdns. WA9: St H 3G 62
Heigham Gdns. WA9: St H 3H 63
Heights, The WA6: Hel 1F 114
Helena Rd. WA9: St H 2B 64
Helena St. CH41: Birke 3L 73
L7: Liv 8G 59
L9: W'ton 7E 44
Helen Bank Dr. WA11: Rainf 3C 38
Helen Ho. L8: Liv 9K 5
Helen St. WA3: Golb 9N 41
WN4: Ash M 7J 41
Helford Cl. L35: Whis 3D 62
Helford Rd. L11: Crox 5B 46
Heliers Rd. L13: Liv 7N 59
Hell Nook WA3: Golb 1N 51
Helmingham Gro. CH41: Tran 4L 73
Helmsdale WN8: Skel 2F 30
Helmsdale La. WA5: Gt San 2L 81
Helmsley Cl. WA5: Warr 1N 81
WA12: Newt W 8H 51
Helmsley Rd. L26: Halew 9K 77
HELSBY 2E 114
Helsby Av. CH62: East 3E 102
Helsby Community Sports Club 3D 114
Helsby Ct. L34: Presc 4A 62
Helsby Golf Course 5E 114
HELSBY MARSH 9D 106
Helsby Pk. Homes WA6: Frod 9H 107
Helsby Rd. L9: Aintr 3G 44
WA6: Alv 3F 114
Helsby Station (Rail) 1E 114
Helsby St. L7: Liv 6N 5 (8F 58)
WA1: Warr 2E 82
WA9: St H 9A 50
Helsby Way WN3: Winst 1E 40
Helston Av. L26: Halew 7K 77
WA11: St H 3N 49
Helston Cl. PR9: South 2N 7
WA5: Penk 3G 81
WA7: Brook 1D 108
Helston Grn. L36: Huy 6M 61
Helston Rd. L11: Crox 5B 46
Helton Cl. CH43: Noct 5E 72
Hemans St. L20: Boot 6N 43
Hemer Ter. L20: Boot 5N 43
Hemingford Cl. CH66: Gt Sut 2J 111
Hemingford St. CH41: Birke 2K 73
Hemlegh Va. WA6: Hel 3E 114
Hemlock Cl. L12: Crox 7B 46
WA7: Run 8M 95
Hemmingsway L35: Rainh 6D 62
Hempstead Cl. WA9: St H 2J 63
Hemsworth Av.
CH66: Lit Sut 9H 103
Henbury Gdns. WA4: App 4F 98
Henbury Pl. WA7: Run 9L 95
Henderson Cl. CH49: Upton 2L 71
WA5: Gt San 2F 80
Henderson Dr. WA11: Rainf 3D 38
Henderson Rd. L36: Huy 6L 61
WA8: Widnes 8J 79
Hendon Rd. L6: Liv 5J 59
Hendon Wlk. CH49: Grea 5K 71
Hengest Cl. L33: Kirkb 5C 36
Henglers Cl. L6: Liv 2M 5 (6F 58)
Henley Av. L21: Lith 2N 43
M44: Irlam 3L 69
Henley Cl. CH63: Spit 5N 89
CH64: Nest 8E 100
WA4: App 1F 98
Henley Ct. PR9: South 6K 7
WA7: Run 5N 95
WA10: St H 9G 49
Henley Dr. PR9: South 6K 7
Henley Ho. L19: Aig 9L 75
Henley Rd. CH64: Nest 8E 100
L18: Moss H 3N 75
Henllan Gdns. WA9: St H 2B 64
Henlow Av. L32: Kirkb 2D 46
Henna Way L11: Norr G 9M 45
Hennawood Cl. L6: Liv 4G 58
Henrietta Gro. L34: Presc 4K 61
Henry Edward St. L3: Liv 2F 4 (6C 58)
Henry Hickman Cl. L30: Neth 7E 34
Henry St. CH41: Birke 2L 73
L1: Liv 7F 4 (9C 58)
WA1: Warr 3B 82
WA8: Widnes 7M 79
WA10: St H 6J 49
WA13: Lymm 5E 84
Henshall Av. WA4: Westy 4G 82
Henthorne Rd. CH62: New F 8A 74
Henthorne St. CH43: Oxton 3J 73
Hepherd St. WA5: Warr 4M 81
Herald Av. L24: Speke 1D 92
Herald Cl. L11: Crox 7A 46
Heralds Cl. WA8: Widnes 8E 78
Heralds Grn. WA5: Westb 7J 65
Herbarth Cl. L9: W'ton 7E 44
Herberts La. CH60: Hesw 7N 87
Herbert St. WA5: Burtw 3G 65
WA9: St H 2A 64
Herbert Taylor Cl. L6: Liv 4H 59
Herbie Higgins Cl. L8: Liv 2F 74
Herculaneum Ct. L8: Liv 5E 74
Herculaneum Rd. L8: Liv 4D 74
Hercules Dr. L24: Speke 4D 92
Herdman Cl. L25: Gate 3F 76
Hereford Av. CH49: Upton 2M 71
CH66: Gt Sut 5K 111
WA3: Golb 1C 52
Hereford Cl. WA1: Wools 1L 83
WA10: St H 8J 49
WN4: Ash M 9M 41
Hereford Dr. L30: Neth 1E 44
Hereford Gro. WN8: Uph 6L 31
Hereford Rd. L15: Wavtr 2M 75
L21: Sea 3L 43
PR9: South 8L 7
Heriot St. L5: Kirkd 3C 58
(not continuous)
Hermes Cl. *L30: Boot* *2D 44*
(off Atlantic Way)
Hermes Rd. L11: Crox 4N 45
Hermitage, The *CH60: Hesw* *8N 87*
(off School Hill)
Hermitage Cl. WA2: Winw 1C 66
HERMITAGE GREEN 1C 66
Hermitage Grn. La. WA2: Winw 9A 52
Hermitage Gro. L20: Boot 3C 44
Herm Rd. L5: Liv 4B 58
Heron Bus. Pk. WA8: Widnes 8N 79
Heron Cl. WA7: Nort 7F 96
Heron Ct. CH64: P'gte 7C 100
L26: Halew 7J 77
Herondale Rd. L18: Moss H 4M 75
Heron Dr. WN3: Winst 1G 40
Heron Gro. WA11: Rainf 6E 38
Heronhall Rd. L9: Faz 6L 45
Heronpark Way CH63: Spit 5A 90
Heron Rd. CH47: Meols 1G 70
CH48: W Kir 1G 70
Herons Ct. L31: Lydi 8G 27
Herons Way WA7: Nort 3H 97
Herons Wharf WN6: App B 6N 23
Hero St. L20: Boot 8C 44
Herrick St. L13: Liv 6L 59
Hertford Cl. L26: Halew 9K 77
WA1: Wools 1M 83
Hertford Dr. CH45: Wall 3J 57
Hertford Gro. M44: Cad 3J 69
Hertford Rd. L20: Boot 8B 44
Hertford St. WA9: St H 8N 49
Hesketh Av. CH42: Rock F 7K 73
PR9: Banks 1E 8
Hesketh Cl. WA5: Penk 4H 81
Hesketh Ct. WA11: Rainf 7D 38
Hesketh Dr. CH60: Hesw 6A 88
L31: Mag 2L 35
L40: Ruf 3L 15
PR9: South 5K 7
Hesketh Golf Course 5K 7
Hesketh Grn. L40: Ruf 3M 15
Hesketh Hall *CH62: Port S* *9A 74*
(off Boundary Rd.)
Hesketh Links Ct. PR9: South 5K 7
Hesketh Mnr. PR9: South 5K 7
Hesketh Mdw. La. WA3: Low 2G 53
Hesketh Rd. L24: Hale 6B 94
L40: Burs 1H 21
PR9: South 4J 7
Hesketh St. L17: Aig 4H 75
WA5: Warr 4M 81
Hesketh St. Nth. WA5: Warr 4M 81
Hesketh Vw. *PR9: South* *6K 7*
(off Park Cres.)
Hesketh Wlk. CH62: Brom 4B 90
Hesketh Way CH62: Brom 4B 90
Heskin Cl. L31: Lydi 8J 27
L32: Kirkb 3C 46
L35: Rainh 6E 62
Heskin Hall Ct. L39: Orm 5B 20
Heskin La. L39: Orm 5B 20
L40: Scar 5B 20
Heskin Rd. L32: Kirkb 3C 46
Heskin Wlk. L32: Kirkb 3C 46
Hessle Dr. CH60: Hesw 8N 87
Hesslewell Ct. CH60: Hesw 6A 88
Hester Cl. L38: Hight 8F 24
HESWALL 7A 88
Heswall Av. CH63: H Beb 8J 73
WA3: Cul 7M 53
WA9: Clock F 5L 63
Heswall Bus Station 7N 87
Heswall Dales Local Nature Reserve
6M 87
Heswall Golf Course 1A 100
Heswall Mt. CH61: Thing 2A 88
Heswall Point CH60: Hesw 7A 88
Heswall Rd. CH66: Gt Sut 1J 111
L9: Aintr 3G 44
Heswall Station (Rail) 7D 88
Hever Dr. L26: Halew 7K 77
Heversham WN8: Skel 2F 30
Heward Av. WA9: St H 3M 63
Hewitson Av. L13: Liv 3L 59
Hewitson Rd. L13: Liv 3L 59
Hewitt Av. WA10: St H 6F 48
Hewitt's La. L33: Kirkb 4H 47
L34: Know 4H 47
Hewitts Pl. *L2: Liv* *4E 4*
(off Vernon St.)
Hewitt St. WA4: Warr 4D 82
Hexagon, The *L20: Boot* *7B 44*
(off Strand Shop. Cen.)
Hexham Cl. L30: Neth 1F 44
WA9: St H 3G 63
Heyburn Rd. L13: Liv 3K 59
Heydale Rd. L18: Moss H 4M 75
Heydean Rd. L18: Aller 7A 76
Heydean Wlk. *L18: Aller* *7A 76*
(off Heydean Rd.)
Heydon Av. L32: Kirkb 1A 46
Heydon Cl. L26: Halew 9L 77
L37: Form 3D 24
Heyes, The L25: Woolt 6F 76
Heyes Av. WA11: Hay 5F 50
WA11: Rainf 5D 38
Heyescroft L39: Bic 5H 29
Heyes Dr. CH45: Wall 5C 56
WA13: Lymm 6C 84
Heyes Gro. WA11: Rainf 5D 38
HEYES JUNC. 5H 31
Heyesmere Ct. L17: Aig 9L 75
Heyes Mt. L35: Rainh 7F 62
Heyes Rd. WA8: Widnes 8F 78
WN5: Orr 6N 31
Heyes St. L5: Liv 4F 58
WN6: App B 6M 23
Heyeswood WA11: Hay 4F 50
Heyfield Pk. Rd. CH66: Lit Sut 7G 103
Heygarth Dr. CH49: Grea 4L 71
Heygarth Rd. CH62: East 1D 102
Heygreen Rd. L15: Wavtr 9K 59
Hey Lock Cl. WA12: Newt W 1L 65
Hey Pk. L36: Huy 7K 61
Hey Rd. L36: Huy 7K 61
Heys, The CH62: East 1E 102
PR8: Birkd 2K 11
WA7: Run 6A 96
WN8: Parb 2F 22
Heys Av. CH62: Brom 7C 90
Heyscroft Rd. L25: Woolt 6F 76
Heysham Cl. WA7: Murd 9F 96
Heysham Lawn L27: N'ley 5L 77
Heysham Rd. L30: Neth 9F 34
PR9: South 8L 7
Heysmoor Hgts. L8: Liv 2G 75
Heysome Cl. WA11: Crank 7H 39
Heythrop Dr. CH60: Hesw 7C 88
Heyville Rd. CH63: H Beb 1L 89
Heywood Av. WA3: Golb 1C 52
Heywood Blvd. CH61: Thing 1A 88
Heywood Cl. CH61: Thing 1A 88
L37: Form 1E 24
WA12: Newt W 1L 65
Heywood Ct. L15: Wavtr 8A 60
Heywood Gdns. L35: Whis 7B 62
WA3: Golb 1C 52
Heywood Rd. CH66: Gt Sut 9H 103
L15: Wavtr 9A 60
Heyworth St. L5: Liv 4E 58
Hibbert St. WA8: Widnes 8L 79
Hickling Gdns. WA9: St H 3H 63
Hickmans Rd. CH41: Birke 8H 57
Hickory Cl. WA1: Wools 1M 83
WA12: Newt W 8L 51
Hickory Gro. L31: Mell 9M 35
Hickson Av. L31: Mag 9H 27
Hicks Rd. L21: Sea 3N 43
L22: Wloo 9L 33
Higgins La. L40: Burs 9F 14
Highacre Rd. CH45: New B 2G 57
Higham Av. WA5: Warr 8A 66
WA10: Ec'stn 7C 48
Higham Sq. L5: Liv 5D 58
High Bank Cl. CH43: Noct 3D 72
M44: Cad 3K 69
Highbank Dr. L19: Garst 1B 92
Highbanks L31: Lydi 9H 27
High Beeches L16: Child 8D 60
High Beeches Cres. WN4: Ash M 5J 41
Highbury Dr. L25: Gate 3E 76
High Carrs L36: Roby 7F 60
Highclere Cres. L36: Huy 4J 61
Highcroft, The CH63: Beb 2N 89
Highcroft Av. CH63: Beb 2N 89
Highcroft Grn. CH63: Beb 2N 89
Highcross *WA11: Rainf* *4C 38*
(off Victoria St.)
Higher Ashton WA8: Widnes 5J 79
HIGHER BEBINGTON 9K 73
Higher Bebington Rd. CH63: H Beb 1K 89
Higher Carr La. L38: Gt Alt 6B 26
HIGHER END 9N 31
Higher End Pk. L30: Neth 6C 34
Higher Knutsford Rd. WA4: Stockt H 5G 83
Higher La. L9: Aintr, Faz 3H 45
(not continuous)
PR4: Tarl 5N 9
WA4: Dutt, L Whit 3K 109
WA11: Crank, Rainf 3D 38
WA13: Lymm 6E 84
WN8: Dalt 4E 22
WN8: Uph 5M 31
Higher Moss La. L37: Gt Alt 9M 17
Higher Parr St. WA9: St H 7M 49
Higher Rd. L25: Hunts X 9H 77
L26: Halew 1M 93
WA8: Hale B 1M 93
HIGHER RUNCORN 6J 95
Higher Vw. WN8: Uph 6M 31
HIGHER WALTON 9A 82
Highfield CH2: Elt 1M 113
L33: Kirkb 6C 36
Highfield Av. WA3: Golb 2A 52
WA4: App 3E 98
WA5: Gt San 3J 81
Highfield Cl. CH44: Wall 6G 57
CH64: Nest 6E 100
Highfield Cres.
CH42: Rock F 7M 73
WA8: Widnes 6K 79
Highfield Dr. CH49: Grea 4L 71
WA11: Crank 7H 39
WA13: Lymm 6C 84
Highfield Gdns. CH43: Clau 2F 72
Highfield Grange Av.
WN3: Wigan, Winst 1F 40
Highfield Gro.
CH42: Rock F 7M 73
L23: Crosb 6M 33
Highfield La. L40: Scar 7A 14
WA2: Winw 1D 66
WA3: Low 5D 52
Highfield Pk. L31: Mag 2L 35

Highfield Rd.—Hollyrood

Highfield Rd. CH42: Rock F 6M 73
CH64: Nest 6E 100
CH65: Ell P 9A 104
CH66: Lit Sut 8G 103
L9: W'ton 6E 44
L13: Liv 5M 59
L21: Lith 2N 43
L36: Huy 3H 61
L39: Orm 6C 20
PR9: South 4N 7
WA8: Widnes 7J 79
WA13: Lymm 5C 84
Highfield Rd. Nth. CH65: Ell P 8A 104
Highfields CH60: Hesw 6N 87
L34: Presc 3N 61
Highfield Sth. CH42: Rock F 9M 73
Highfield Sq. L13: Liv 5M 59
Highfield St. L3: Liv 2D 4 (6B 58)
(not continuous)
WA9: St H 1N 63
Highfield Vw. L13: Liv 5M 59
Highgate Cl. CH60: Hesw 5N 87
WA7: Nort 6F 96
Highgate Ct. L7: Liv 6N 5
Highgate Rd. L31: Lydi 9J 27
WN8: Uph 5L 31
High Gates Cl. WA5: Warr 1N 81
High Gates Lodge WA5: Warr 1N 81
Highgate St. L7: Liv 5N 5 (8F 58)
Highgreen Rd. CH42: Tran 5J 73
High Gro. Pk. L40: Burs 6E 20
Highgrove Pk. L19: G'dale 8M 75
Highlands Rd. WA7: Run 6J 95
High La. L39: Bic 5F 28
L40: Burs 6E 20
High Legh WA10: Ec'stn 7E 48
High Legh Rd. WA13: Lymm 8J 85
Highmarsh Cres. WA12: Newt W 5K 51
Highmeadow WN8: Uph 5K 31
HIGH MOOR 1J 23
High Moor La. WN6: Wright 1J 23
High Moss L39: Orm 1B 28
High Mt. CH60: Hesw 7N 87
Highoaks Rd. L25: Woolt 7F 76
HIGH PARK 7M 7
High Pk. Pl. PR9: South 7M 7
High Pk. Rd. PR9: South 7M 7
Highpark Rd. CH42: Tran 5J 73
High Pk. St. L8: Liv 3E 74
Highpoint WA10: St H 7J 49
Highsands Av. L40: Ruf 3L 15
High St. CH62: Brom 6D 90
CH64: Nest 6E 100
L2: Liv 4D 4 (7B 58)
L15: Wavtr 9L 59
L24: Hale 6A 94
L25: Woolt 6E 76
L34: Presc 3A 62
WA3: Golb 2B 52
WA6: Frod 6L 107
WA7: Run 5J 95
WA12: Newt W 6M 51
WN8: Skel 4A 30
Hightor Rd. L25: Woolt 5D 76
HIGHTOWN 8F 24
Hightown Station (Rail) 8G 24
High Vw. WA6: Hel 1F 114
Highville Rd. L16: Child 2B 76
High Warren Cl. WA4: App 2C 98
Highwood Ct. L33: Kirkb 7D 36
Highwood Rd. WA4: App 9D 82
Highwoods Cl. WN4: Ash M 6J 41
Hignett Av. WA9: St H 8C 50
Higson Ct. L8: Liv 5F 74
Hilary Av. L14: Brd G 7C 60
WA3: Low 1E 52
Hilary Cl. L4: W'ton 1H 59
L34: Eccl P 2B 62
WA5: Gt San 2F 80
WA8: Widnes 5A 80
Hilary Dr. CH49: Upton 2A 72
Hilary Mans. *CH44: Wall 5G 56*
(off Colville Rd.)
Hilary Rd. L4: W'ton 1H 59
Hilberry Av. L13: Liv 4K 59
Hilbre Av. CH44: Wall 5G 57
CH60: Hesw 9M 87
Hilbre Ct. PR9: South 6L 7
Hilbre Cl. CH48: W Kir 7B 70
Hilbre Dr. CH65: Ell P 4A 112
PR9: South 6L 7
Hilbre Rd. CH48: W Kir 7C 70
Hilbre St. CH41: Birke 9K 57
L3: Liv 5H 5 (8D 58)
Hilbre Vw. CH48: W Kir 6D 70
Hilda Rd. L12: W Der 4C 60
Hildebrand Cl. L4: W'ton 1H 59
Hildebrand Rd. L4: W'ton 1H 59
Hilden Pl. WA2: Warr 8E 66
Hilden Rd. WA2: Padg 8F 66
Hilden Sq. WA1: Warr 3B 82
Hillaby Cl. L8: Liv 2F 74
Hillam Rd. CH45: Wall 3D 56
Hillary Ct. L37: Form 2E 24
Hillary Cres. L31: Mag 2J 35
Hillary Dr. L23: Crosb 7N 33
Hillary Rd. CH62: East 1C 102
Hillary Wlk. L23: Crosb 7N 33
Hillbark Rd. CH48: Frank 6H 71
Hillbeck Cres. WN4: Garsw 7F 40
Hillberry Cres. WA4: Warr 5C 82
Hillbrae Av. WA11: St H 2K 49
Hillbrook Dr. L9: Aintr 7J 45
Hillburn Dr. CH41: Birke 8E 56
HILLCLIFFE 9D 82
Hill Cliffe Rd. WA4: W'ton 7C 82
Hill Cl. CH64: Ness 9H 101
Hill Ct. CH64: Ness 9H 101
Hill Crest L20: Boot 8D 44
Hillcrest L31: Mag 2L 35
WA7: Run 6N 95
WN8: Skel 5E 30
Hillcrest Av. L36: Huy 7L 61
Hillcrest Ct. CH44: Wall 6G 56
Hillcrest Dr. CH49: Grea 5K 71
CH66: Lit Sut 8F 102
L40: Scar 6L 13
Hillcrest Pde. L36: Huy 7L 61
Hillcrest Rd. CH66: Lit Sut 8G 102
L4: W'ton 9J 45
L23: Crosb 7N 33
L39: Orm 7C 20
Hillcroft Rd. CH44: Wall 6J 57
L25: Woolt 4D 76
HILL DALE 1G 22
Hilldean WN8: Uph 4M 31
Hillerton Cl. L12: W Der 8N 45
Hillfield WA6: Frod 7L 107
WA7: Nort 7F 96
Hillfield Dr. CH61: Hesw, Pens 5N 87
Hillfield Rd. CH66: Lit Sut 7J 103
Hillfoot Av. L25: Hunts X 1F 92
Hillfoot Cl. CH43: Bid 9C 56
Hillfoot Cres. WA4: Stockt H 9C 82
Hillfoot Grn. L25: Woolt 9E 76
Hillfoot Rd. L25: Hunts X, Woolt 7D 76
Hill Gro. CH46: More 1M 71
Hillhead Rd. L20: Boot 8D 44
Hill Ho. Fold La. WN6: Wright 1M 23
Hillingden Av. L26: Halew 9K 77
Hillingden Cl. L26: Halew 9L 77
Hillingdon Av. CH61: Hesw 5N 87
Hillingdon Rd. L15: Wavtr 2N 75
Hillock Cl. L40: Scar 7M 13
Hillock La. L40: Scar 7M 13
WA1: Wools 1J 83
WN8: Dalt 7F 22
Hill Ridge CH43: Noct 3D 72
Hill Ri. Vw. L39: Augh 3M 27
Hill Rd. CH43: Clau 1E 72
Hill Rd. Nth. WA6: Hel 2F 114
Hill Rd. Sth. WA6: Hel 2F 114
Hillsboro Av. WA6: Frod 7M 107
Hill School Rd. WA10: St H 1D 62
Hillsdown Way CH66: Gt Sut 3H 111
HILLSIDE 5L 11
Hillside WA13: Lymm 7L 85
Hillside Av. L36: Huy 3G 61
L39: Orm 9B 20
WA7: Run 7H 95
WA10: St H 4H 49
WA12: Newt W 8H 51
WN4: Ash M 3H 41
WN8: Parb 1G 22
Hillside Cl. CH41: Tran 4L 73
L20: Boot 8D 44
WA6: Hel 1G 114
WN5: Bil 6N 39
Hillside Ct. CH41: Tran 4L 73
L25: Woolt 5E 76
Hillside Cres. L36: Huy 3G 61
Hillside Dr. CH66: Ell P 6K 103
L25: Woolt 5F 76
Hillside Golf Course 5L 11
Hillside Gro. WA5: Penk 4H 81
Hillside Rd. CH41: Tran 4L 73
CH43: Bid 9D 56
CH44: Wall 5E 56
CH48: W Kir 6E 70
CH60: Hesw 8A 88
L18: Moss H 3N 75
L36: Huy 4J 61
PR8: Birkd 5L 11
WA4: App 4D 98
WA6: Frod 7M 107
Hillside Station (Rail) 5L 11
Hillside St. L6: Liv 1L 5 (6E 58)
Hillside Vw. CH43: Oxton 5G 72
Hillsmore Way L5: Liv 3E 58
Hills Pl. L15: Wavtr 1M 75
Hill St. L8: Liv 2C 74
(not continuous)
L23: Crosb 8M 33
L34: Presc 3A 62
PR9: South 8G 7
WA1: Warr 3C 82
WA7: Run 5K 95
WA10: St H 5K 49
Hill St. Bus. Cen. *L8: Liv 2C 74*
(off Hill St.)
Hillsview Rd. PR8: Ainsd 1J 17
Hilltop WA7: Nort 8E 96
Hill Top La. CH64: Ness 9H 101
Hilltop La. CH60: Hesw 7B 88
Hill Top Rd. WA1: Wools 9K 67
WA4: Dutt 5L 109
WA4: Pres H 9H 97
WA4: Stockt H 6G 83
WA11: Rainf 9E 38
WA13: Lymm 6C 84
Hilltop Rd. L16: Child 1B 76
Hilltop Wlk. L39: Orm 1A 28
Hill Vw. WA8: Widnes 3J 79
Hillview L17: Aig 6K 75
Hill Vw. Av. WA6: Hel 4D 114
Hillview Av. CH48: W Kir 5C 70
Hillview Cl. WA6: Frod 7M 107
Hillview Ct. CH43: Bid 8C 56
Hill Vw. Dr. CH49: Upton 2A 72
Hillview Gdns. L25: Woolt 5D 76
Hillview Rd. CH61: Irby 9K 71
Hillwood Cl. CH63: Spit 6N 89
Hilton Av. WA5: Gt San 3K 81
Hilton Cl. CH41: Birke 2J 73
Hilton Ct. L30: Neth 7C 34
Hilton Dr. M44: Cad 4J 69
Hilton Gro. CH48: W Kir 5B 70
Hilton St. WN4: Ash M 8L 41
Himalayan Birch Cl. CH66: Ell P 8K 103
Hinchley Grn. L31: Mag 2G 34
Hinckley Rd. WA11: St H 5M 49
Hindburn Av. L31: Mag 1L 35
HINDERTON 5H 101
Hinderton Cl. CH41: Birke 4L 73
Hinderton Dr. CH48: W Kir 7F 70
CH60: Hesw 9N 87
Hinderton Grn. CH64: Nest 6F 100
Hinderton La. CH64: Nest 5G 101
Hinderton Rd. CH41: Birke 3L 73
CH64: Nest 6F 100
Hindle Av. WA5: Warr 8A 66
Hindley Beech L31: Mag 1H 35
Hindley Wlk. L24: Speke 5H 93
Hindlip St. L8: Liv 5F 74
Hind St. CH41: Birke 3L 73
Hinson St. CH41: Birke 2L 73
Hinton Cres. WA4: App 8F 82
Hinton Rd. WA7: Run 7K 95
Hinton St. L6: Liv 6H 59
L21: Lith 4A 44
Hitchens Cl. WA7: Murd 8F 96
HMP Altcourse 4J 45
HMP Kennet 1A 36
HMP Liverpool 5E 44
HMP Risley 1M 67
HMYOI Thorn Cross 3K 99
Hobart Dr. L33: Kirkb 5C 36
Hobart St. WA9: St H 1H 63
Hobberley Dr. WN8: Skel 4H 31
Hobb La. WA4: Dares, Moore 2L 97
Hobby Ct. WA7: Pal F 9A 96
Hobcross La. L40: Lath 4L 21
Hob Hey La. WA3: Cul 6L 53
Hobhouse Ct. CH43: Clau 2H 73
Hob La. CH2: Wim T 6L 113
WA6: Dun H 6L 113
Hoblyn Rd. CH43: Bid 9E 56
Hockenhall All. L2: Liv 4E 4 (7B 58)
Hockenhull Cl. CH63: Spit 5N 89
Hodder Av. L31: Mag 1L 35
Hodder Cl. WA11: St H 3L 49
Hodder Rd. L5: Liv 3E 58
Hodder St. L5: Liv 3E 58
Hodge St. PR8: South 8G 6
Hodgkinson Av. WA5: Warr 8A 66
Hodnet Dr. WN4: Ash M 8L 41
Hodson Pl. L6: Liv 5F 58
Hodson St. PR8: South 9H 7
Hogarth Dr. CH43: Noct 5D 72
Hogarth St. *L21: Sea 4N 43*
(off Seaforth Va. Nth.)
Hogarth Wlk. L4: Kirkd 1C 58
Hoggs Hill La. L37: Form 4E 24
Hoghton Cl. WA9: St H 1B 64
Hoghton Gro. PR9: South 7H 7
Hoghton La. WA9: St H 1B 64
(not continuous)
Hoghton Pl. PR9: South 8G 7
Hoghton Rd. L24: Hale 5B 94
WA9: St H 1B 64
Hoghton St. PR9: South 8G 7
Hoghton Twr. Ct. L24: Hale 5N 93
Holbeck WA7: Nort 8E 96
Holbeck St. L4: W'ton 3G 59
Holborn Ct. WA8: Widnes 5J 79
Holborn Dr. L39: Orm 1A 28
Holborn Hill CH41: Tran 4L 73
L39: Orm 1A 28
Holborn Sq. CH41: Tran 4L 73
Holborn Sq. Ind. Est. CH41: Tran 4L 73
Holborn St. L6: Liv 3M 5 (7F 58)
Holbrook Cl. WA5: Gt San 2G 80
WA9: St H 3M 63
Holcombe Av. WA3: Golb 2D 52
Holcombe Cl. CH49: Grea 4L 71
Holcroft La. WA3: Cul 1E 68
Holden Gro. L22: Wloo 9J 33
Holden Rd. L22: Wloo 9H 33
L35: Presc 5N 61
Holden Rd. E. L22: Wloo 9J 33
Holden St. L8: Liv 8N 5 (9G 58)
Holden Ter. L22: Wloo 9J 33
Holdsworth Dr. L7: Liv 7G 59
Holes La. WA1: Wools 9J 67
Holford Av. WA5: Warr 9A 66
Holford Moss WA7: Nort 4F 96
Holford Way WA12: Newt W 7A 52
Holgate L23: Thorn 3A 34
Holgate Dr. WN5: Orr 7N 31
Holgate Pk. L23: Thorn 4A 34
HOLIDAY MOSS 5E 38
Holingsworth Ct. WA10: St H 6L 49
Holkham Cl. WA8: Widnes 7J 79
Holkham Gdns. WA9: St H 3G 62
Holland Bus. Pk. L40: Lath 9N 21
Holland Cl. PR8: South 9H 7
Holland Ct. L30: Neth 7C 34
WN8: Skel 1G 39
Holland Gro. CH60: Hesw 6N 87
Holland Hall M. WN8: Uph 4M 31
Holland Ho. WN8: Uph 6M 31
HOLLAND LEES 8M 23
HOLLAND MOOR 5H 31
Holland Moss WN8: Skel 7D 30
Holland Moss Bus. Pk. WN8: Skel 8G 30
Holland Pl. L7: Liv 5N 5 (8G 58)
Holland Rd. CH45: Wall 2J 57
L24: Speke 5J 93
L26: Halew 1J 93
Holland's La. WN8: Skel 2L 29
Holland St. L7: Liv 6J 59
Holland Way L26: Halew 1J 93
Holley Ct. *L35: Rainh 6F 62*
(off Rainhill Rd.)
Holliers Cl. L31: Mag 2J 35
Hollies, The L25: Woolt 5C 76
L39: Augh 9M 19
PR8: South 9E 6
(off Beechfield Gdns.)
WA7: Run 7N 95
Hollies Ct. WA4: Westy 4F 82
Hollies Rd. L26: Halew 9K 77
HOLLINFARE 6H 69
Hollingbourne Pl. L11: Norr G 7M 45
Hollingbourne Rd. L11: Norr G 7M 45
Hollinghurst Cl. L36: Huy 7L 61
Hollinghurst Rd. L33: Kirkb 6D 36
Hollington Way WN3: Winst 1E 40
Hollingwood Cl. WN4: Ash M 8J 41
Hollingworth Cl. L9: W'ton 7F 44
Hollin Hey Cl. WN5: Bil 8N 39
Hollinhey Cl. L30: Neth 6F 34
Hollins Cl. L15: Wavtr 9M 59
WN4: Garsw 7F 40
Hollins Dr. WA2: Winw 3B 66
HOLLINS GREEN 7G 69
Hollins La. CW9: Ant 9N 99
WA2: Winw 3N 65
Hollins Way WA8: Hale B 2E 94
Hollocombe Rd. L12: W Der 8N 45
Holloway WA7: Run 6J 95
Hollow Cft. L28: Stockb V 9E 46
Hollow Dr. WA4: Stockt H 7F 82
Hollowford La. L40: Lath 2N 21
Holly Av. CH63: Beb 4M 89
WA12: Newt W 7M 51
Holly Bank WA6: Alv 3G 115
WA6: Frod 6M 107
WA13: Lymm 6D 84
Hollybank WA4: Moore 2J 97
Holly Bank Av. L14: Brd G 7B 60
Holly Bank Cvn. Pk. WA3: Rix 8G 69
Holly Bank Cotts. *M31: Part 5M 69*
(off Manchester Rd.)
Hollybank Ct. CH41: Birke 3K 73
WA8: Widnes 6J 79
Hollybank Grange L26: Halew 8K 77
Holly Bank Gro. WA9: St H 6M 49
Hollybank Rd. CH41: Birke 3K 73
L18: Moss H 3K 75
WA7: Hal 7B 96
Holly Bank St. WA9: St H 6M 49
Hollybrook Rd. PR8: South 1N 11
Holly Bush La. WA3: Rix 9C 68
Holly Bush Sq. WA3: Low 1F 52
Holly Cl. L24: Hale 5A 94
L40: Westh 9J 21
WA10: Ec'stn 6E 48
WN8: Skel 3B 30
Holly Ct. L20: Boot 5A 44
WA6: Hel 9F 106
Holly Cres. WA11: Rainf 5D 38
Hollydale Rd. L18: Moss H 3M 75
Holly Farm Ct. WA8: Widnes 4J 79
Holly Farm Rd. L19: Garst 1B 92
Hollyfield Rd. CH65: Ell P 9N 103
L9: W'ton 5E 44
Holly Fold La. L39: Bic 9B 30
WA11: Bic 9B 30
Holly Gro. CH42: Tran 4L 73
L21: Sea 4M 43
L36: Roby 7F 60
PR9: Banks 3E 8
WA1: Padd 1H 83
Hollyhedge La. WA4: H Walt 1M 97
Holly Hey L35: Whis 8A 62
Hollyhock Dr. L11: Norr G 9L 45
Hollyhurst Cl. L8: Liv 3F 74
Holly La. L39: Augh 9N 19
L39: Bic 8A 30
L40: Ruf 3N 15
Hollymead Cl. L25: Gate 4F 76
Hollymere CH65: Ell P 7N 103
Holly M. L23: Crosb 6M 33
Holly Mt. L12: W Der 3M 59
WA10: St H 8G 48
Holly Pl. CH46: More 1N 71
Holly Rd. CH65: Ell P 9A 104
L7: Liv 7J 59
WA3: Golb 2D 52
WA5: Penk 3G 81
WA11: Hay 5B 50
WA13: Lymm 3H 85
Hollyrood L34: Presc 4L 61

Holly St.—Hurst Grn. Gdns.

Holly St. L20: Boot 6B 44
Holly Ter. WA5: Penk 4H 81
Hollytree Gdns. WA13: Lymm 3H 85
Hollytree Rd. L25: Woolt 5F 76
Holly Wlk. M31: Part 6K 69
Hollywood Bowl
Liverpool 7L 59
Hollywood Rd. L17: Aig 5K 75
Holman Rd. L19: Garst 1B 92
Holm Cotts. CH43: Oxton 6F 72
Holmdale Av. PR9: South 3N 7
Holm Dr. CH2: Elt 2N 113
Holme Cl. L34: Eccl P 2D 62
Holmefield Av. L19: Aig 7M 75
Holmefield Rd. L19: Aig 8L 75
Holme Rd. WA10: St H 8E 48
HOLMES 4M 9
Holmes Ct. CH42: Tran 5J 73
WA3: Birchw 5K 67
Holmesfield Rd. WA1: Warr 3E 82
Holmes Ho. Av. WN3: Winst 1E 40
Holmes La. L21: Lith 3N 43
(off Bridge Rd.)
Holmes St. L8: Liv 1H 75
Holme St. L5: Kirkd 3B 58
Holmesway CH61: Pens 3N 87
HOLMESWOOD 9N 9
Holmes Wood Cl. WN3: Winst 2F 40
Holmeswood Rd.
L40: H'wood, Ruf 1H 15 (8M 9)
Holmfield CH2: Elt 2M 113
CH43: Oxton 6F 72
Holmfield Av. WA7: Run 5M 95
Holmfield Dr. CH66: Gt Sut 2J 111
Holmfield Gro. L31: Mag 2H 35
L36: Huy 9K 61
Holmfield Pk. L37: Form 9E 16
Holm Hey Rd. CH43: Pren 6F 72
Holm Hill CH48: W Kir 7D 70
Holmlands Cres. CH43: Oxton 6E 72
Holmlands Dr. CH43: Oxton 6E 72
Holmlands Way CH43: Oxton 6F 72
Holm La. CH43: Oxton 6F 72
Holmleigh Rd. L25: Gate 2E 76
Holm Oak Way CH66: Gt Sut 5L 111
Holmrook Rd. L11: Norr G 8M 45
Holmside Cl. CH46: More 9N 55
Holmside La. CH43: Oxton 6F 72
Holm Vw. Cl. CH43: Oxton 5G 72
Holmville Rd. CH63: H Beb 2L 89
Holmway CH63: H Beb 2M 89
Holmwood Av. CH61: Thing 2C 88
Holmwood Cl. L37: Form 1D 24
WN4: Ash M 6J 41
Holmwood Dr. CH61: Thing 2C 88
CH65: Whit 2N 111
L37: Form 9D 16
Holmwood Gdns. CH48: W Kir 7F 70
L37: Form 9D 16
HOLT 5D 62
Holt Av. CH46: More 9M 55
WN5: Bil 7N 39
Holt Coppice L39: Augh 5M 27
Holt Cres. WN5: Bil 7N 39
Holt Dr. L40: Burs 1H 21
HOLT GREEN 6M 27
Holt Hey CH64: Ness 9G 100
Holt Hill CH41: Birke 4L 73
Holt Hill Ter. CH42: Tran 3L 73
Holt La. L27: N'ley 1J 77
(not continuous)
L35: Rainh 5D 62
WA7: Hal 7B 96
Holton Way WN3: Winst 2G 40
Holt Rd. CH41: Tran 4L 73
L7: Liv 7H 59
Holt St. WN5: Orr 7N 31
Holtswell Cl. WA3: Low 1F 52
Holt Way L32: Kirkb 9B 36
Holy Cross Cl. L3: Liv 2F 4 (6C 58)
Holyhead Cl. WA5: Call 6M 65
Holyrood L23: Blun 7G 32
Holyrood Av. WA8: Widnes 4K 79
Holywell Cl. CH64: P'gte 5B 100
WA9: St H 3N 63
Holywell Dr. WA1: Warr 3D 82
Holywell Gdns. PR8: Birkd 3N 11
Homechase Ho. PR8: Birkd 2M 11
(off Chase Cl.)
Homecrofts CH64: Lit N 9E 100
Homedove Ho. L23: Blun 7J 33
Home Farm 9B 46
Home Farm Cl. CH49: Wdchu 6C 72
Home Farm Rd. CH49: Wdchu 6B 72
L34: Know 8G 47
Homeport Ho. PR9: South 7H 7
(off Hoghton St.)
HOMER GREEN 2B 34
Homer Rd. L34: Know 7G 47
Homerton Cl. CH65: Ell P 1B 112
Homerton Rd. L6: Liv 6J 59
Homesands Ho. PR9: South 7J 7
Homestall Rd. L11: Norr G 8M 45
Homestead Av. L30: Neth 8G 34
WA11: Hay 3G 51
Homestead Cl. L36: Huy 6L 61
M31: Part 5N 69
Homestead M. CH48: W Kir 6C 70
Homeway WA6: Hel 3E 114
Honeybourne Dr. L35: Whis 7A 62
Honey Hall Rd. L26: Halew 1J 93
Honeys Grn. Cl. L12: W Der 4B 60
Honeys Grn. La. L12: W Der 4B 60
Honeys Grn. Pct. L12: W Der 4B 60
Honeyspot Gro. WA8: Widnes 4A 80
Honey St. WA9: St H 2F 62
Honeysuckle Av. PR9: Banks 5H 9
WA5: Warr 4N 81
Honeysuckle Cl. CH66: Gt Sut 5L 111
L26: Halew 6H 77
WA8: Widnes 4L 79
Honeysuckle Dr. L9: W'ton 7G 44
Honister Av. WA2: Warr 7D 66
WA11: St H 2M 49
Honister Gro. WA7: Beech 1A 108
Honister Wlk. L27: N'ley 5L 77
Honiston Av. L35: Rainh 5E 62
Honiton Rd. L17: Aig 7K 75
Honiton Way WA5: Penk 4G 81
Hood La. WA5: Gt San 3L 81
Hood La. Nth. WA5: Gt San 2L 81
Hood Mnr. Cen. WA5: Gt San 2L 81
Hood Rd. WA8: Widnes 7J 79
Hood St. CH44: Wall 6K 57
L1: Liv 4F 4 (7C 58)
L20: Boot 5N 43
Hookstone Dr. CH66: Lit Sut 8H 103
Hoole La. PR9: Banks 1E 8
Hoole Rd. CH49: Wdchu 5B 72
Hoolpool La. WA6: Hel 9C 106
Hoose Ct. CH47: Hoy 1D 70
HOOTON 5F 102
Hooton Golf Course 7G 103
Hooton Grn. CH66: Hoot 4F 102
Hooton Hey CH66: Gt Sut 9J 103
Hooton La. CH66: Hoot 5G 103
Hooton Pk. Airfield CH65: Hoot 3H 103
Hooton Pk. La. CH65: Hoot 4H 103
Hooton Pk. Outdoor Karting Circuit 2H 103
Hooton Rd. CH64: Will 6N 101
CH66: Hoot 6N 101
L9: Aintr 3G 44
Hooton Station (Rail) 5C 102
Hooton Way CH66: Hoot 4E 102
Hooton Works Trad. Est. CH66: Hoot 4D 102
Hope Carr Nature Reserve 1N 53
Hope Cl. WA10: St H 6H 49
Hope Cotts. CH66: Chil T 6F 102
(off New Rd.)
Hope Cft. CH66: Gt Sut 3L 111
Hope Farm Pct. CH66: Gt Sut 3L 111
Hope Farm Rd. CH66: Gt Sut 4K 111
Hopefield Rd. WA13: Lymm 4H 85
HOPE ISLAND 4D 30
Hope Pk. L16: Child 3B 76
Hope Pl. L1: Liv 7J 5 (9D 58)
Hope Sq. PR9: South 8H 7
Hope St. CH41: Birke 1K 73
CH45: New B 1H 57
L1: Liv 8K 5 (9E 58)
L34: Presc 3A 62
PR9: South 8H 7
WA12: Newt W 7K 51
WN4: Ash M 6M 41
Hope Way L8: Liv 8K 5 (9E 58)
Hopfield Rd. CH46: More 9N 55
Hopkins Cl. WA10: St H 6G 48
Hopwood Cl. WA3: Low 2G 53
Hopwood Cres. WA11: Rainf 6D 38
Hopwood St. L5: Liv 4C 58
WA1: Warr 2D 82
(not continuous)
Horace Black Gdns. CH65: Ell P 8A 104
Horace St. WA10: St H 6G 49
Horatio St. CH41: Birke 2K 73
Horbury Gdns. CH66: Lit Sut 9H 103
Hornbeam Av. CH66: Gt Sut 4L 111
Hornbeam Cl. CH46: More 9J 55
WA7: Wind H 6E 96
WA11: Hay 5B 50
Hornbeam Cres. WN4: Ash M 8K 41
Hornbeam Rd. L9: W'ton 7H 45
L26: Halew 9L 77
Hornby Av. CH62: Brom 6B 90
L20: Boot 5A 44
Hornby Blvd. L20: Boot 4A 44
L21: Lith 4A 44
Hornby Chase L31: Mag 4J 35
Hornby Cl. L9: W'ton 6E 44
Hornby Ct. CH62: Brom 6C 90
L9: W'ton 5F 44
Hornby Cres. WA9: Clock F 5N 63
Hornby Flats L21: Lith 4A 44
(off Linacre Rd.)
Hornby La. L18: Moss H 3B 76
WA2: Winw 3B 66
Hornby Pk. L18: Moss H 3B 76
Hornby Pl. L9: W'ton 5F 44
Hornby Rd. CH62: Brom 6B 90
L9: W'ton 6E 44
L20: Boot 5A 44
(Hornby Av.)
L20: Boot 6B 44
(Roby St.)
PR9: South 2M 7
Hornby St. CH41: Birke 2M 73
L21: Sea 4N 43
L23: Crosb 7L 33
Hornby Wlk. L5: Liv 5B 58
Horncastle Cl. WA3: Low 2G 52
Hornchurch Dr. WA5: Gt San 2K 81
Horne St. L6: Liv 5G 58
Hornet Cl. L6: Liv 4F 58
Hornhouse La. L33: Know I 2F 46
Hornsey Gro. WN3: Winst 1F 40
Hornsey Rd. L4: W'ton 3G 58
Hornsmill Av. WA8: Widnes 3K 79
Hornsmill Way WA6: Hel 2D 114
Hornspit La. L12: W Der 1M 59
Horridge Av. WA12: Newt W 5L 51
Horringford Rd. L19: Aig 8L 75
Horrocks Av. L19: Garst 1B 92
Horrocks Cl. L36: Huy 5H 61
Horrocks La. WA1: Warr 3C 82
Horrocks Rd. L36: Huy 6H 61
Horseman Pl. CH44: Wall 7L 57
Horsemarket St. WA1: Warr 3C 82
Horseshoe Cl. WA9: St H 7C 50
Horseshoe Cres. WA2: Warr 6F 66
Horseshoe Dr. L10: Faz 3N 45
Horsey Mere Gdns. WA9: St H 3H 63
Horsfall Gro. L8: Liv 4D 74
Horsfall St. L8: Liv 4D 74
Horstone Cres. CH66: Gt Sut 3L 111
Horstone Gdns. CH66: Gt Sut 3M 111
Horstone Rd. CH66: Gt Sut 3L 111
Horton Cl. L33: Kirkb 5C 36
Horwood Av. L35: Rainh 5E 62
Horwood Cl. L12: W Der 8A 46
HOSCAR 1A 22
Hoscar Ct. WA8: Widnes 9G 78
Hoscar Moss Rd. L40: Lath 2N 21
Hoscar Station (Rail) 1A 22
Hoscote Pk. CH48: W Kir 6B 70
Hose Side Rd. CH45: Wall 2G 56
Hosking Cl. CH49: Upton 5N 71
Hospital St. WA10: St H 6L 49
Hospital Way WA7: Pal F 8B 96
Hosta Cl. L33: Kirkb 6B 36
Hostock Cl. L35: Whis 7A 62
Hotel St. WA12: Newt W 7K 51
Hotham St. L3: Liv 4H 5 (7D 58)
Hothfield Rd. CH44: Wall 6K 57
Hotspur St. L20: Boot 1B 58
Hough Bank CH63: Beb 3A 90
HOUGH GREEN 7D 78
Hough Grn. Rd. WA8: Widnes 6D 78
Hough Green Station (Rail) 7E 78
Hough's La. WA4: H Walt 2B 98
Houghton Av. WA2: Warr 2D 82
Houghton Cl. WA8: Widnes 6M 79
WA12: Newt W 7K 51
Houghton Cft. WA8: Cron 3F 78
HOUGHTON GREEN 5F 66
Houghton La. L1: Liv 5G 4 (8C 58)
Houghton Rd. CH49: Wdchu 4B 72
L24: Hale 5B 94
Houghton's La. WA10: Ec'stn 4C 48
WN8: Skel 3F 30
(not continuous)
Houghton's Rd. WN8: Skel 1C 30
Houghton St. L1: Liv 5G 4 (8C 58)
L34: Presc 3A 62
L35: Rainh 6F 62
WA2: Warr 1C 82
WA8: Widnes 6N 79
WA12: Newt W 7K 51
Houghton Way L1: Liv 5G 4
Houghwood Golf Course 4L 39
Houghwood Grange WN4: Ash M 8H 41
Hougoumont Av. L22: Wloo 1L 43
Hougoumont Gro. L22: Wloo 1L 43
Houlding St. L4: W'ton 3F 58
Houlgrave Rd. L5: Liv 4B 58
Houlston Rd. L32: Kirkb 9N 35
Houlston Wlk. L32: Kirkb 9N 35
Hourd Way CH66: Gt Sut 5K 111
House La. WA8: Widnes 9J 79
Houston Gdns. WA5: Gt San 9J 65
Hove, The WA7: Murd 9F 96
(not continuous)
Hoveton Gdns. WA9: St H 3G 63
Howard Av. CH62: Brom 7D 90
WA13: Lymm 4H 85
Howard Cl. L21: Ford 9B 34
(not continuous)
L31: Mag 2L 35
Howard Ct. CH64: Nest 5F 100
PR9: South 6J 7
WA7: Manor P 3E 96
Howard Dr. L19: G'dale 9M 75
Howard Florey Av. L30: Neth 7E 34
Howard's La. WA10: Ec'stn 6B 48
Howards Rd. CH61: Thing 1B 88
Howard St. WA10: St H 1G 62
Howards Way CH64: Lit N 8G 101
Howarth Ct. WA7: Run 5L 95
Howarth Dr. M44: Irlam 1M 69
Howbeck Cl. CH43: Clau 2F 72
Howbeck Ct. CH43: Oxton 3F 72
Howbeck Dr. CH43: Clau 2F 72
Howbeck Rd. CH43: Oxton 3F 72
Howden Dr. L36: Huy 6E 60
Howell Dr. CH49: Grea 6L 71
Howell Rd. CH62: New F 9N 73
Howells Av. CH66: Gt Sut 2H 111
Howells Cl. L31: Mag 1J 35
Howe St. L20: Boot 9A 44
Howey La. WA6: Frod 7K 107
Howey Ri. WA6: Frod 7K 107
Howgill Cl. CH66: Lit Sut 8E 102
HOWLEY 3D 82
Howley La. WA1: Warr 3E 82
Howley Mdws. WA1: Warr 3E 82
Howley Quay Ind. Est. WA1: Warr 3E 82
Howson Rd. WA2: Warr 7D 66
Howson St. CH42: Rock F 6M 73
Hoyer Ind. Est. CH65: Ell P 9D 104
HOYLAKE 2C 70
Hoylake Cl. WA7: Murd 9E 96
(not continuous)
Hoylake Golf Course 2C 70
Hoylake Gro. WA9: Clock F 5M 63
Hoylake (Park & Ride) 2C 70
Hoylake Rd. CH41: Birke 7D 56
CH46: More 1J 71
Hoylake Station (Rail) 2C 70
Hoyle Ct. Rd. CH47: Hoy 9C 54
Hoyle Rd. CH47: Hoy 9C 54
Hoyle St. WA5: Warr 1A 82
Hucklow Dr. WA1: Warr 3F 82
Huddleston Cl. CH49: Wdchu 5B 72
Hudleston Rd. L15: Wavtr 8N 59
Hudson Cl. WA5: Old H 9M 65
Hudson Gro. WA3: Low 2F 52
Hudson Pl. CH49: Upton 2M 71
Hudson Rd. CH46: Leas 5A 56
L31: Mag 4J 35
WA2: Padg 7F 66
Hudswell Cl. L30: Neth 1G 44
Hughenden Rd. L13: Liv 4L 59
Hughes Av. L35: Presc 5A 62
WA2: Warr 7E 66
Hughes Cl. L7: Liv 8H 59
Hughes Dr. L20: Boot 4D 44
Hughes La. CH43: Oxton 5H 73
Hughes Pl. WA2: Warr 7E 66
Hughes St. L6: Liv 1N 5 (5F 58)
(not continuous)
L19: Garst 2A 92
WA4: Warr 5D 82
WA9: St H 1N 63
Hughestead Gro. L19: Garst 1N 91
Hughson St. L8: Liv 3D 74
Hull Cl. L19: Garst 1N 91
HULME 6C 66
Hulme Cl. CH62: Brom 3B 90
Hulmes Bri. Bus. Cen. L39: Hals 3H 19
Hulme St. PR8: South 8F 6
Hulme Wlk. CH62: Brom 3B 90
Hulmewood CH63: Beb 9N 73
Hulton Av. L35: Whis 5C 62
Humber Cl. L4: Kirkd 1D 58
WA8: Widnes 5B 80
Humber Cres. WA9: Sut L 3M 63
Humber Rd. CH66: Gt Sut 3L 111
WA2: Warr 7F 66
Humber St. CH41: Birke 8F 56
Hume Ct. CH47: Meols 9D 54
Hume St. WA1: Warr 2E 82
Humphrey's Cl. WA7: Murd 8F 96
Humphreys Hey L23: Thorn 6A 34
Huncote Av. WA11: St H 4N 49
Hunslet Rd. L9: Aintr 4G 44
Hunstanton Cl. CH49: Upton 1A 72
Hunt Cl. WA5: Gt San 9K 65
Hunter Av. WA2: Warr 6C 66
Hunter Ct. L34: Presc 3B 62
Hunters Chase WN5: Bil 2A 40
Hunters Ct. WA6: Hel 1G 114
WA7: Pal F 9A 96
Hunter's La. PR4: Tarl 4L 9
Hunters La. L15: Wavtr 1M 75
Hunter St. L3: Liv 3G 4 (7C 58)
WA9: St H 8M 49
Hunters Way CH64: P'gte 6C 100
Huntingdon Ct. PR9: South 5M 7
Huntingdon Gro. L31: Lydi 8H 27
Huntington Cl. CH46: More 9J 55
Huntley Av. WA9: St H 2M 63
Huntley Gro. WA9: St H 2M 63
Huntley Rd. L6: Liv 6H 59
Huntley St. WA5: Gt San 4L 81
Hunt Rd. L31: Mag 1J 35
WA11: Hay 4G 50
Hunts Cotts. PR9: South 6M 7
HUNT'S CROSS 9F 76
Hunts Cross L25: Hunts X 9G 76
Hunts Cross Av. L25: Woolt 5F 76
(not continuous)
Hunts Cross Shop. Pk. 1E 92
Hunt's Cross Station (Rail) 9G 76
Hunts Fld. Cl. WA13: Lymm 6D 84
Hunts La. WA4: Stockt H 6G 83
Huntsman Cl. L25: Hunts X 7H 77
Huntsman Dr. M44: Irlam 2M 69
Huntsman Wood L12: W Der 1C 60
Hurford Av. CH65: Gt Sut 1L 111
Hurley Cl. WA5: Gt San 3L 81
Hurlingham Rd. L4: W'ton 8H 45
HURLSTON 3A 20
Hurlston Av. WN8: Skel 4F 30
Hurlston Cl. L40: Scar 2A 20
Hurlston Dr. L39: Orm 6C 20
HURLSTON GREEN 1N 19
Hurlston Hall Country Cvn. Pk.
L40: Scar 3A 20
Hurlston Hall Golf Course 3A 20
Hurlston La. L40: Scar 2A 20
Hurrell Rd. CH41: Birke 8D 56
Hurricane Dr. L24: Speke 4D 92
Hursley Rd. L9: Faz 6K 45
Hurst Bank CH42: Rock F 8M 73
Hurst Grn. Gdns. WA3: Cul 5M 53

Hurstlyn Rd. L18: Aller 7A 76
Hurst Pk. Cl. L36: Huy 5L 61
Hurst Pk. Dr. L36: Huy 5L 61
Hurst Rd. L31: Mag 4K 35
Hurst's La. L39: Bic 1E 36
Hurst St. L1: Liv 8F 4 (9C 58)
WA8: Widnes 3K 95
Hurstwood L37: Form 8E 16
Huskisson St. L8: Liv 9K 5 (1E 74)
Huskisson Way WA12: Newt W 6K 51
Hutchinson Cl. CH43: Bid 2B 72
Hutchinson St. L6: Liv 2N 5 (6F 58)
WA8: Widnes 1J 95
Hutchinson Wlk. L6: Liv 2N 5 (6F 58)
Hutfield Rd. L24: Speke 3L 93
Hutton Cl. WA3: Cul 5M 53
Hutton Ct. WN8: Skel 3A 30
Hutton Rd. WN8: Skel 3A 30
Hutton Way L39: Orm 8C 20
Huxley Cl. CH46: More 9J 55
Huxley Ct. CH66: Ell P 6L 103
Huxley St. L13: Liv 2J 59
HUYTON 7J 61
Huyton & Prescot Golf Course 5L 61
Huyton Av. WA10: St H 4H 49
Huyton Brook L36: Huy 9K 61
Huyton Bus. Pk. L35: Whis 8N 61
L36: Huy 8L 61 (Brickfields)
L36: Huy 8K 61 (Octavia Ct.)
L36: Huy 9M 61 (Stretton Way)
Huyton Bus Station 7J 61
Huyton Chu. Rd. L36: Huy 7J 61
Huyton Gallery 7J 61
Huyton Hall Cres. L36: Huy 7J 61
Huyton Hey Rd. L36: Huy 7J 61
Huyton Ho. Rd. L36: Huy 5F 60
Huyton La. L34: Presc 6J 61
L36: Huy 6J 61
Huyton Lane Wetland Pk. 6K 61
Huyton Station (Rail) 7J 61
HUYTON-WITH-ROBY 6G 61
Hyacinth Av. L33: Kirkb 6B 36
Hyacinth Cl. WA11: Hay 4H 51
Hyacinth Gro. CH46: More 7A 56
Hyacinth Wlk. *M31: Part* 7L 69 (off Redbrook Rd.)
Hyde Cl. CH65: Gt Sut 1L 111
WA7: Beech 9N 95
Hyde Rd. L22: Wloo 1K 43
Hyde's Brow WA11: Rainf 3D 38
Hydra Cl. WA5: Westb 7L 65
Hydrangea Way WA9: Bold 2C 64
Hydro Av. CH48: W Kir 7C 70
Hygeia St. L6: Liv 5F 58
Hylton Av. CH44: Wall 5G 57
Hylton Ct. CH65: Ell P 3C 112
Hylton Rd. L19: Aller 8B 76
Hyslop St. L8: Liv 2D 74
Hythe Av. L21: Lith 2B 44
Hythe Cl. PR8: South 3D 12
Hythedale Cl. L17: Aig 6H 75

I

Ibbotson's La. L17: Aig 4K 75
Iberis Gdns. WA9: Bold 2C 64
Ibis Ct. WA1: Warr 5B 82
Ibis Way L19: Garst 9A 76
Ibstock Rd. L20: Boot 5A 44
Idaho Wlk. *WA5: Gt San* 2L 81 (off Washington Dr.)
Iffley Cl. CH49: Upton 3L 71
Ikin Cl. CH43: Bid 8C 56
Ilchester Rd. CH41: Birke 8F 56
CH44: Wall 6K 57
L16: Child 8C 60
Ilex Av. WA2: Winw 3C 66
Ilford Av. CH44: Wall 7H 57
L23: Crosb 6K 33
Ilford St. L3: Liv 3K 5 (7E 58)
Ilfracombe Rd. WA9: Sut L 4M 63
Iliad St. L5: Liv 5D 58
Ilkley Av. PR9: South 1A 8
Ilkley Wlk. L24: Speke 3H 93
Ilsley Cl. CH49: Upton 4N 71
Image Bus. Pk. L33: Know I 9H 37
Imagine That! 8K
Imber Rd. L32: Kirkb 2D 46
Imison St. L9: W'ton 7E 44
Imison Way L9: W'ton 7D 44
Immingham Dr. L19: Garst 1N 91
Imperial Av. CH45: Wall 3J 57
Imperial Chambers L1: Liv 4E 4
Imperial Ct. L2: Liv 4D 4
WA4: Warr 7B 82
Imperial M. CH65: Ell P 8N 103
Imrie St. L4: W'ton 8E 44
INCE 8L 105
Ince & Elton Station (Rail) 1M 113
Ince Av. CH62: East 3D 102
L4: W'ton 1G 59
L21: Lith 3A 44
L23: Crosb 6J 33
INCE BLUNDELL 9L 25
Ince Cl. CH43: Oxton 4F 72
Ince Cres. L37: Form 1D 24
Ince Gro. CH43: Oxton 4F 72
Ince La. CH2: Elt 1M 113
CH2: Wim T 6K 113
L23: Thorn 2M 33
Incemore Rd. L18: Moss H 7N 75
Ince Orchards CH2: Elt 1M 113
Ince Rd. L23: Thorn 4N 33
Inchcape Rd. CH45: Wall 4D 56
L16: Child 8C 60
Inchfield WN8: Skel 2E 30
Index St. L4: W'ton 9E 44
Indiana Gro. WA5: Gt San 1J 81
Indigo Rd. CH65: Ell P 9D 104
Indoor Superkarting
Burscough 3F 20
Ingestre Ct. CH43: Oxton 5G 73
Ingestre Rd. CH43: Oxton 5G 73
Ingham Av. WA12: Newt W 9L 51
Ingham Rd. WA8: Widnes 4J 79
Ingham's Rd. WA3: Croft 9H 53
Ingleborough Rd. CH42: Tran 6K 73
Ingleby Rd. CH44: Wall 6G 57
CH62: New F 8A 74
Ingledene Rd. L18: Moss H 3B 76
Inglefield Ct. *CH42: Rock F* 7N 73 (off The Hawthornes)
Ingle Grn. L23: Blun 6G 32
Inglegreen CH60: Hesw 7B 88
Ingleholme Gdns. L34: Eccl P 2D 62
Ingleholme Rd. L19: Aig 7M 75
Inglemere Rd. CH42: Rock F 6L 73
Inglemoss Dr. WA11: Rainf 1E 48
Inglenook Rd. WA5: Penk 4H 81
Inglesham Cl. WN7: Leigh 1M 53
Ingleside Ct. L23: Blun 8J 33
Inglestone Cl. WA12: Newt W 6K 51
Ingleton Cl. CH49: Grea 4L 71
Ingleton Dr. WA11: St H 1L 49
Ingleton Grn. L32: Kirkb 2D 46
Ingleton Gro. WA7: Beech 1N 107
Ingleton Rd. L18: Moss H 3L 75
L32: Kirkb 2D 46
PR8: South 3D 12
Inglewhite WN8: Skel 2D 30
INGLEWHITE ISLAND 2E 30
Inglewood L12: Crox 8E 46
Inglewood Av. CH46: More 1L 71
Inglewood Cl. M31: Part 5L 69
WA3: Birchw 3B 68
Inglewood Rd. WA11: Rainf 1F 48
Inglis Rd. L9: Aintr 3G 45
Ingoe Cl. L32: Kirkb 1N 45
Ingoe La. L32: Kirkb 1N 45 (not continuous)
Ingram WN8: Skel 3E 30
Ingrave Rd. L4: W'ton 8H 45
Ingrow Rd. L6: Liv 6G 59
Inigo Rd. L13: Liv 5N 59
Inley Cl. CH63: Spit 5N 89
Inley Rd. CH63: Spit 5M 89
Inman Av. WA9: St H 8D 50
Inman Rd. CH49: Upton 2M 71
L21: Lith 3A 44
Inner Central Rd. L24: Halew 2K 93
Inner Forum L11: Norr G 7K 45
Inner Gosling Cl. WA4: Hatt 6A 98
Inner Sth. Rd. L24: Halew 3J 93
Inner W. Rd. L24: Halew 2J 93
Innisfree Cl. CH66: Gt Sut 9H 103
Innovation Blvd. L7: Liv 8J 59
Insall Rd. L13: Liv 8N 59
WA2: Padg 7G 66
Inskip WN8: Skel 2D 30
Inskip Ct. WN8: Skel 2E 30
Inskip Rd. PR9: South 3M 7
Inspector Cl. WA1: Padg 9G 67
Intake Cl. CH64: Will 6N 101
Intake La. L37: Down 4D 26
L39: Bic 7K 29
Interchange Motorway Ind. Est.
L36: Huy 8L 61
International Bus. Cen. WA5: Westb 7L 65
International Slavery Mus. 7D 4 (9B 58)
Inveresk Ct. CH43: Noct 2E 72
Invergarry Rd. L11: Crox 6N 45
Invincible Cl. L30: Boot 2D 44
Inward Way CH65: Ell P 7N 103
Inwood Rd. L19: Garst 9B 76
Iona Cl. L12: Crox 7E 46
Iona Cres. WA8: Widnes 2J 79
Iona Gdns. WA9: St H 2N 63
Ionic Rd. L13: Liv 5M 59
Ionic St. CH42: Rock F 6M 73
L21: Sea 3M 43
Ipswich Cl. L19: Garst 1N 91
IRBY 1L 87
Irby Av. CH44: Wall 5G 57
Irby Cl. CH66: Gt Sut 1K 111
IRBY HEATH 1K 87
IRBY HILL 8K 71
Irby Rd. CH61: Hesw, Irby, Pens 2L 87
L4: W'ton 1G 59
Irbyside Rd. CH48: Frank 7J 71
Ireland Rd. L24: Hale 5B 94 (not continuous)
WA11: Hay 4E 50
Ireland St. WA2: Warr 9C 66
WA8: Widnes 7N 79
Irene Av. WA11: St H 3M 49
Irene Rd. L16: Child 2A 76
Ireton St. L4: W'ton 8E 44
Iris Av. CH41: Birke 1F 72
Iris Cl. WA8: Widnes 6F 78
Iris Gro. L33: Kirkb 6B 36
Iris Pk. Wlk. L31: Mell 8M 35
Iris Wlk. *M31: Part* 7M 69 (off Cross La. W.)
IRLAM 1N 69
Irlam & Cadishead Leisure Cen. 1N 69
Irlam Dr. L32: Kirkb 9C 36
Irlam Ho. L20: Boot 7A 44
Irlam Ind. Est. M44: Irlam 2L 69
Irlam Pl. L20: Boot 6A 44
Irlam Rd. L20: Boot 6A 44
Irlam Station (Rail) 2L 69
Irlam Wharf Rd.
M44: Irlam 2N 69
Ironbridge Vw. L8: Liv 4E 74
Ironside Rd. L36: Huy 5H 61
Irton Rd. PR9: South 7K 7
Irvin Av. PR9: South 2A 8
Irvine Rd. CH42: Tran 6K 73
Irvine St. L7: Liv 5N 5 (8F 58)
Irvine St. W. L7: Liv 5N 5 (8F 58)
Irvine Ter. CH62: New F 8B 74
Irving Cl. L9: Aintr 2H 45
Irving St. PR9: South 6G 7
Irwell WN8: Skel 1D 30
Irwell Chambers L3: Liv 4D 4
Irwell Cl. L17: Aig 5K 75
Irwell Ho. L17: Aig 5K 75
Irwell La. L17: Aig 5K 75
WA7: Run 4L 95
Irwell Rd. WA4: Warr 6C 82
Irwell St. WA8: Widnes 3K 95
Irwin Rd. WA9: St H 2M 63
Isaac St. L8: Liv 4E 74
Isabel Gro. L13: Liv 2K 59
Isherwood Cl. WA2: Fearn 6G 67
Island Pl. L19: Garst 1A 92
Island Rd. L19: Garst 1A 92
L21: Lith 3N 43
Island Rd. Sth. L19: Garst 1B 92
Islands Brow WA11: St H 4L 49
Isla Sq. L5: Liv 3E 58
Islay Cl. CH65: Ell P 4A 112
Isleham Cl. L19: Aller 8A 76
Islington L3: Liv 3H 5 (7D 58)
L23: Crosb 7K 33
Islington Grn.
WA8: Widnes 4N 79
Islington Sq. L3: Liv 3L 5 (6E 58)
Islip Cl. CH61: Irby 9L 71
Ismay Dr. CH44: Wall 4K 57
Ismay Rd. L21: Lith 3A 44
Ismay St. L4: W'ton 9E 44
Ivanhoe Av. WA3: Low 1E 52
Ivanhoe Rd. L17: Aig 4H 75
L23: Blun 7J 33
Ivatt Way L7: Liv 8H 59
Iveagh Cl. WA7: Pal F 8C 96
Iver Cl. WA8: Cron 2F 78
Ivernia Rd. L4: W'ton 8G 44
Ivor Rd. CH44: Wall 4J 57
Ivory Dr. L33: Kirkb 6C 36
Ivy Av. CH63: H Beb 2L 89
L19: G'dale 9N 75
L35: Whis 5D 62
WA12: Newt W 8L 51
Ivybridge WN8: Skel 2E 30
Ivychurch M. WA7: Run 5N 95
Ivy Cl. L40: Burs 2L 21
Ivy Ct. WA9: St H 6M 49
Ivydale WN8: Skel 2E 30
Ivydale Rd. CH42: Tran 5L 73
L9: W'ton 6G 44
L18: Moss H 4M 75
Ivy Farm Ct. L24: Hale 6A 94
Ivy Farm Dr. CH64: Lit N 8F 100
Ivy Farm Gdns. WA3: Cul 6L 53
Ivy Farm Rd. L35: Rainh 5E 62
Ivy Ho. Rd. WA3: Low 1E 52
Ivyhurst Cl. L19: Aig 8L 75
Ivy La. CH46: More 7M 55
Ivy Leigh L13: Liv 4K 59
Ivy Rd. WA1: Wools 1M 83
WA3: Golb 2C 52
Ivy St. CH41: Birke 2M 73
PR8: South 9J 7
WA7: Run 6K 95
WN4: Ash M 8K 41
Ivy Wlk. M31: Part 6K 69

J

Jackies La. WA13: Lymm 4F 84
Jack McBane Ct. L3: Liv 5B 58
Jackman Cl. WA12: Newt W 9M 51
Jack's Brow L34: Know P 7J 47
Jacksfield Way
L19: G'dale 9L 75
Jacksmere La. L40: Scar 6F 12
PR8: South 6F 12
Jackson Av. WA1: Padd 1G 82
WA3: Cul 7M 53
Jackson Cl. CH63: H Beb 8M 73
L35: Rainh 8G 63
L39: Down 8E 18
Jackson's Comn. La.
L40: Scar 4M 19 (not continuous)
Jacksons Pond Dr. L25: Gate 1D 76
Jackson St. CH41: Birke 3L 73
L19: Garst 1A 92
WA5: Burtw 3G 65
WA9: St H 7M 49
WA11: Hay 3C 50
Jackson St. Ind. Est. WA9: St H 8M 49
Jacks Wood Av. CH65: Ell P 7N 103
Jacks Wood Grn. CH65: Ell P 8N 103
Jacob Ct. WN5: Bil 1N 39
Jacobs Cl. L21: Lith 4A 44
Jacob St. L8: Liv 4E 74
Jacqueline Ct. L36: Roby 7G 61
Jacqueline Dr. L36: Huy 5L 61
Jade Cl. L33: Kirkb 8E 36
Jade Rd. L6: Liv 5G 59
Jamaica St. L1: Liv 9G 4 (1C 74)
James Av. CH66: Gt Sut 2H 111
Jamesbrook Cl. CH41: Birke 9G 57
James Clarke St. L5: Liv 5B 58
James Cl. WA8: Widnes 3K 95
James Ct. L25: Woolt 6F 76
James Ct. Apts. L25: Woolt 6E 76
James Dixon Ct. L30: Neth 6C 34
James Dunne Av. L5: Liv 4B 58
James Gro. WA10: St H 8H 49
James Holt Av. L32: Kirkb 1A 46
James Hopkins Way L4: Kirkd 2C 58
James Horrigan Ct. L30: Neth 8B 34
James Larkin Way L4: Kirkd 2C 58
James Rd. L25: Woolt 6F 76
WA11: Hay 3H 51
James Simpson Way *L30: Neth* 7E 34 (off Alexander Fleming Av.)
James St. CH43: Oxton 4J 73
CH44: Wall 7L 57
L2: Liv 6D 4 (8B 58)
L19: Garst 1A 92
WA1: Warr 3C 82 (off Buttermarket St.)
WA9: Clock F 6N 63
WN2: Bam 4N 41
James Street Station (Rail) 6D 4 (8B 58)
Jamestown Av. WA5: Gt San 1J 81
Jamieson Av. L23: Crosb 7N 33
Jamieson Rd. L15: Wavtr 1K 75
Jane's Brook Rd. PR8: South 2C 12
Jane St. WA9: St H 2B 64
Janet Dr. L7: Liv 8G 59
Japonica Gdns. WA9: Bold 2C 64
Jardin M. *L17: Aig* 4G 75 (off Parkfield M.)
Jarrett Rd. L33: Kirkb 7E 36
Jarrett Wlk. L33: Kirkb 7E 36
Jarrow Cl. CH43: Oxton 4H 73
Jasmine Cl. CH49: Upton 1L 71
L5: Liv 5E 58
Jasmine Ct. L36: Huy 4K 61
Jasmine Gdns. WA5: Warr 4N 81
WA9: Bold 2C 64
Jasmine Gro. WA8: Widnes 8G 78
Jasmine M. L17: Aig 5F 74
Jasmine Wlk. *M31: Part* 7M 69 (off Erskine Wlk.)
Jason St. L5: Liv 3D 58
Jason Wlk. L5: Liv 3D 58
Java Rd. L4: W'ton 8J 45
Jay Cl. WA3: Birchw 5N 67
Jay's Cl. WA7: Murd 8G 96
Jean Av. WN7: Leigh 1M 53
Jean Wlk. L10: Faz 4N 45
Jedburgh Av. CH66: Lit Sut 8E 102
Jedburgh Dr. L33: Kirkb 5B 36
Jeffereys Cres. L36: Huy 7F 60
Jeffereys Dr. L36: Huy 6E 60
Jefferson Dr. WA5: Gt San 1J 81
Jefferson Gdns. WA8: Widnes 5J 79
Jeffreys Dr. CH49: Grea 3L 71
Jellicoe Av. M44: Cad 3L 69
Jellicoe Cl. CH48: Caldy 1E 86
Jenkinson St. L3: Liv 1J 5 (6D 58)
Jenner Dr. CH46: Leas 7A 56
Jennet Hey WN4: Ash M 5H 41
Jensen Ct. WA7: Astm 4M 95
Jericho Cl. L17: Aig 6J 75
Jericho Ct. L17: Aig 6J 75
Jericho Farm Cl. L17: Aig 7J 75
Jericho Farm Wlk. L17: Aig 7J 75
Jericho La. L17: Aig 7J 75
Jermyn St. L8: Liv 2F 74
Jerningham Rd. L11: Norr G 7J 45
Jersey Av. CH65: Ell P 4A 112
L21: Lith 1A 44
Jersey Cl. L20: Boot 7B 44
Jersey St. L20: Boot 7B 44
WA9: Clock F 6M 63
Jervis Cl. WA2: Fearn 6H 67
Jesmond St. L15: Wavtr 9J 59
Jessamine Rd. CH42: Tran 5L 73
Jessop Ct. *CH66: Lit Sut* 8H 103 (off Black Lion La.)
Jessop Ho. WA7: Run 4H 95
Jet Cl. L6: Liv 5G 59
Jeudwine Cl. L25: Woolt 7F 76
Jibcroft Brook La. WA3: Cul 5M 53
Joan Av. CH46: More 9L 55
CH49: Grea 4M 71
Joan Bartlett Cl. CH65: Ell P 8L 103
Jocelyn Cl. CH63: Spit 4N 89
Jockey's Brow La. WA9: St H 1J 63
Jockey St. WA2: Warr 1C 82
Jodrell Dr. WA4: Grap 1H 99

John Bagot Cl.—Kilburn St.

John Bagot Cl. L5: Liv 4D 58
John Hunter Way L30: Neth 8E 34
John Lennon Dr. L6: Liv 6G 59
John Lennon Statue *5E 4*
(off Mathew St., above The Cavern Club)
John Lloyd Ct. *M44: Irlam 1M 69*
(off Alexandra Gro.)
John Middleton Cl. L24: Hale 5A 94
John Moores Cl. L7: Liv 7M 5 (9F 58)
John Moores University
Hope Pl. 9E 58
John Morris Ho. *WA1: Warr 3D 82*
(off Mersey St.)
John Nicholas Cres. CH65: Ell P 8A 104
John Rd. WA13: Lymm 5C 84
Johns Av. WA7: Run 7J 95
WA11: Hay 3G 51
Johnson Av. L35: Presc 5A 62
WA12: Newt W 5K 51
Johnson Gro. L12: W Der 4C 60
Johnson Rd. CH43: Pren 7F 72
Johnson's La. WA8: Widnes 7A 80
Johnson St. L3: Liv 3F 4 (7C 58)
PR9: South 7G 7
WA9: St H 6M 49
Johnson Wlk. *L7: Liv 8H 59*
(off Claughton Cl.)
Johnston Av. L20: Boot 4D 44
John St. CH41: Birke 1M 73
CH65: Ell P 8N 103
L3: Liv 1J 5 (6D 58)
M44: Cad 4L 69
WA2: Warr 2C 82
WA3: Golb 2B 52
WN4: Ash M 6M 41
John Willis Ho. CH42: Rock F 6N 73
John Yeoman Cl. CH64: Lit N 7F 100
Jones Farm Rd. L25: Gate 3G 76
Jonson Rd. CH64: Nest 5E 100
Jonville Rd. L9: Aintr 3H 45
Jordan St. L1: Liv 9G 4 (1C 74)
Joseph Gardner Way L20: Boot 5A 44
Joseph Groome Towers CH65: Ell P 8A 104
Josephine Butler Sq. L6: Liv 2K 5
Joseph Lister Cl. L30: Neth 8E 34
Joseph St. WA8: Widnes 6M 79
WA9: St H 2A 64
Joshua Cl. L5: Liv 3D 58
Joules Cl. L9: W'ton 6F 44
Joyce Wlk. L10: Faz 3A 46
Joy La. WA5: Burtw 5F 64
WA8: Clock F 7A 64
WA9: Clock F 7A 64
Joy Wlk. WA9: Clock F 6A 64
Jubilee Av. L14: Brd G 8B 60
L39: Orm 7D 20
WA1: Padg 9G 66
WA5: Penk 4G 81
WN5: Orr 8N 31
Jubilee Cl. L26: Halew 9K 77
Jubilee Ct. *PR9: South 7M 7*
(off Church Cl.)
WA3: Golb 1B 52
(off Grimshaw St.)
WA11: Hay 3D 50
Jubilee Cres. CH62: Port S 2A 90
WA11: Hay 3H 51
Jubilee Dr. CH48: W Kir 4B 70
L7: Liv 7G 58
(not continuous)
L30: Neth 1F 44
L35: Whis 7A 62
WN8: Skel 4B 30
Jubilee Gdns. WA9: St H 2G 63
Jubilee Grn. CH65: Ell P 1A 112
Jubilee Gro. WA13: Lymm 4C 84
Jubilee Ho. L37: Form 2J 25
Jubilee Rd. L21: Lith 3A 44
L23: Crosb 8J 33
L37: Form 3D 24
Jubilee Sports Bank 7G 58
Jubilee Way WA2: Warr 9C 66
WA8: Widnes 7H 79
Jubits La. WA8: Bold H 9K 63
WA9: Sut M 9K 63
Juddfield St. WA11: Hay 4C 50
Judges Dr. L6: Liv 5H 59
Judges Way L6: Liv 5H 59
Jugglers Yd. *L3: Liv 2E 4*
(off Midghall St.)
Julian Way WA8: Widnes 4J 79
Julie Gro. L12: W Der 4D 60
Juliet Av. CH63: H Beb 9L 73
July Rd. L6: Liv 4J 59
July St. L20: Boot 5B 44
Junction 9 Retail Pk. 7B 66
Junction Eight Bus. Cen.
CH65: Ell P 8M 103
Junction La. L40: Burs 1J 21
WA9: St H 2A 64
WA12: Newt W 8J 51
Junction One Retail Pk. 6D 56
Junction Rd. L20: Kirkd 1B 58
WA11: Rainf 3B 38
June Av. CH62: Brom 7D 90
June Rd. L6: Liv 4J 59
June St. L20: Boot 6B 44
Juniper Cl. CH49: Grea 6K 71
L28: Stockb V 2F 60
WA10: St H 6G 48
Juniper Dr. CH66: Gt Sut 4K 111
Juniper Gdns. L23: Thorn 5A 34
Juniper Gro. CH66: Gt Sut 4L 111
WA7: Murd 8F 96
Juniper La. WA3: Wools 9A 68
Juniper St. L20: Kirkd 1B 58
Juniper Way PR9: Banks 3E 8
Jupiter Gro. WN3: Wigan 1G 41
Jurby Ct. WA2: Padg 8G 66
Justan Way L35: Rainh 4E 62
Juvenal Pl. L3: Liv 1H 5 (5D 58)
Juvenal St. L3: Liv 1G 5 (6C 58)

K

Kaber Ct. L8: Liv 4D 74
Kaigh Av. L23: Crosb 6K 33
Kale Cl. CH48: W Kir 7C 70
Kale Gro. L33: Kirkb 6E 36
Kalewood Rd. CH65: Ell P 8L 103
Kamala Way L11: Norr G 9M 45
Kane Ct. WA3: Low 2H 53
Kansas Pl. WA5: Gt San 1K 81
Kara Cl. L20: Boot 7B 44
Karan Way L31: Mell 8N 35
Karen Cl. WA5: Burtw 3H 65
Karen Way CH66: Gt Sut 2J 111
Karonga Rd. L10: Faz 3K 45
Karonga Way L10: Faz 3L 45
Karslake Rd. CH44: Wall 6K 57
L18: Moss H 3L 75
Katherine Wlk. L10: Faz 3A 46
Kaye Av. WA3: Cul 7N 53
Kay La. WA13: Lymm 8G 85
Kearsley Cl. L4: W'ton 2D 58
Kearsley St. L4: W'ton 2D 58
Keats Av. L35: Whis 6C 62
WN5: Bil 2N 39
Keats Cl. CH66: Gt Sut 5K 111
WA8: Widnes 8J 79
Keats Gro. L36: Huy 8K 61
WA2: Warr 7D 66
Keats St. L20: Boot 5A 44
Keats Ter. PR8: South 9L 7
Keble Dr. CH45: Wall 3D 56
L10: Aintr 8H 35
Keble Rd. L20: Boot 9B 44
Keble St. L6: Liv 2N 5 (6F 58)
WA8: Widnes 9L 79
KECKWICK 3H 97
Keckwick La. WA4: Dares 3H 97
Kedleston St. L8: Liv 4F 74
Keegan Dr. CH44: Wall 7L 57
Keele Cl. CH43: Bid 7C 56
Keel Hey CH64: Will 5A 102
Keel Wharf L3: Liv 8E 4 (9B 58)
Keenan Dr. L20: Boot 5D 44
Keene Ct. L30: Neth 7C 34
Keepers La. CH63: Store 2H 89
Keeper's Rd. WA4: Grap 9H 83
Keepers Wlk. WA7: Cas 5B 96
Keighley Av. CH45: Wall 4E 56
Keightley St. CH41: Birke 1K 73
Keir Hardie Av. L20: Boot 5D 44
Keith Av. L4: W'ton 9E 44
WA5: Gt San 2F 80
Keith Dr. CH63: East 1B 102
Keithley Wlk. L24: Speke 3J 93
Kelbrook Cl. WA9: St H 3N 63
Kelburn Ct. WA3: Ris 3N 67
Kelburn Gro. L12: W Der 1B 60
Kelby Cl. L8: Liv 4F 74
Kelda Ct. L25: Gate 2E 76
Kelday Cl. L33: Kirkb 9C 36
Kelk Beck Cl. L31: Mag 1L 35
Kellet's Pl. CH42: Rock F 5M 73
Kellett Rd. CH46: Leas 6B 56
Kellitt Rd. L15: Wavtr 1K 75
Kelly Dr. L20: Boot 5D 44
Kelly St. L34: Presc 3B 62
Kelmscott Cl. CH66: Gt Sut 3J 111
Kelmscott Dr. CH44: Wall 5E 56
Kelsall Av. CH62: East 3D 102
WA9: Sut M 5L 63
Kelsall Cl. CH43: Oxton 5F 72
CH62: East 3D 102
WA3: Birchw 6K 67
WA8: Widnes 7G 79
Kelsey Cl. WA10: St H 6G 48
Kelso Cl. L33: Kirkb 5B 36
Kelso Rd. L6: Liv 6H 59
Kelton Gro. L17: Aig 6K 75
Kelvin Cl. WA3: Birchw 3L 67
WN4: Garsw 7F 40
Kelvin Ct. CH44: Wall 8L 57
Kelvin Gro. L8: Liv 2F 74
WN3: Wigan 1G 41
(not continuous)
Kelvington Cl. L10: Faz 3L 45
Kelvin Pk. CH41: Birke 8L 57
Kelvin Rd. CH41: Tran 4L 73
CH44: Wall 8L 57
Kelvinside CH44: Wall 8K 57
L23: Crosb 9M 33
Kelvin St. WA3: Ris 3M 67
Kemberton Dr. WA8: Widnes 3K 79
Kemble St. L6: Liv 6G 58
L34: Presc 3A 62
Kemlyn Rd. L4: W'ton 2F 58
Kemmel Av. WA4: Warr 6D 82
Kemp Av. L5: Liv 3E 58
Kempsell Wlk. L26: Halew 9L 77
Kempsell Way L26: Halew 9L 77
Kempsey Gro. WA9: St H 2H 63
Kempson Ter. CH63: Beb 3M 89
Kempston St. L3: Liv 3J 5 (7D 58)
Kempton Cl. L36: Roby 8G 61
WA7: Run 9M 95
WA12: Newt W 5M 51
Kempton Pk. Fold PR8: South 3E 12
Kempton Pk. Rd. L10: Aintr 8K 35
Kempton Rd. CH62: New F 8A 74
L15: Wavtr 9J 59
Kemsley Rd. L14: Knott A 6D 60
Kenbury Cl. L33: Kirkb 7E 36
Kenbury Rd. L33: Kirkb 7E 36
Kendal Av. WA2: Warr 7D 66
Kendal Cl. CH63: Beb 1M 89
CH66: Gt Sut 3J 111
WA11: Rainf 1C 38
Kendal Dr. CH66: Gt Sut 3J 111
L31: Mag 1J 35
L35: Rainh 6D 62
WA11: Rainf 1B 38
WA11: St H 2L 49
Kendal Gro. WN4: Ash M 7K 41
Kendal M. *L33: Kirkb 7B 36*
(off Windermere Dr.)
Kendal Pk. L12: W Der 3B 60
Kendal Ri. WA7: Beech 1N 107
Kendal Rd. CH44: Wall 7G 57
L16: Child 1C 76
L33: Kirkb 7B 36
WA8: Widnes 7F 78
Kendal St. CH41: Birke 2L 73
Kendal Vw. WA11: St H 2L 49
Kendal Way PR8: Ainsd 2H 17
Kendricks Fold L35: Rainh 6E 62
Kendrick St. WA1: Warr 3B 82
Kenford Dr. WN3: Winst 1G 40
Kenilworth Av. WA7: Run 7L 95
Kenilworth Cl. L25: Woolt 5C 76
Kenilworth Ct. CH65: Ell P 3C 112
Kenilworth Dr. CH61: Pens 2M 87
WA1: Padg 9G 67
Kenilworth Gdns. WA12: Newt W 8L 51
Kenilworth Rd. CH44: Wall 6K 57
CH64: Nest 8E 100
L16: Child 1B 76
L23: Blun 7J 33
PR8: Ainsd 9H 11
WA3: Low 3F 52
Kenilworth St. L20: Boot 7A 44
Kenilworth Way L25: Woolt 5C 76
Kenley Av. WA8: Cron 3G 78
Kenmare Rd. L15: Wavtr 2K 75
Kenmay Wlk. L33: Kirkb 8E 36
Ken M. L20: Boot 4B 44
Kenmore Gro. M44: Cad 3K 69
WN4: Garsw 7F 40
Kenmore Rd. CH43: Pren 7E 72
Kennelwood Av. L33: Kirkb 8D 36
Kennessee Cl. L31: Mag 3K 35
KENNESSE GREEN 3J 35
Kenneth Cl. L30: Neth 8D 34
L34: Presc 4A 62
Kenneth Rd. WA8: Widnes 9F 78
Kennet Rd. CH63: H Beb 2K 89
WA11: Hay 4E 50
Kennford Rd. L11: Crox 5A 46
Kennington Pk. WA8: Widnes 5H 79
KENSINGTON 7G 59
Kensington L7: Liv 3N 5 (7F 58)
Kensington Av. WA4: Grap 6K 83
WA9: St H 2M 63
Kensington Cl. WA8: Widnes 4N 79
Kensington Ct. L37: Form 1G 24
Kensington Dr. L34: Presc 4L 61
Kensington Gdns. CH46: More 9M 55
Kensington Ind. Est. PR9: South 9H 7
Kensington Rd. CH65: Ell P 9M 103
L37: Form 3E 24
PR9: South 8H 7
Kensington St. L6: Liv 3N 5 (7F 58)
Kent Av. L21: Lith 2B 44
L37: Form 3G 24
Kent Cl. CH63: Brom 7A 90
L20: Boot 6C 44
(off Brookhill Rd.)
Kent Gro. WA7: Run 6L 95
Kentmere Av. WA11: St H 2M 49
Kentmere Dr. CH61: Pens 4N 87
Kentmere Pl. WA2: Warr 6B 66
Kent M. *CH43: Oxton 4H 73*
(off Kent St.)
Kenton Cl. L25: Gate 1F 76
L37: Form 7F 16
Kenton Rd. L26: Halew 9K 77
Kentridge Dr. CH66: Gt Sut 2J 111
Kent Rd. CH44: Wall 6G 56
L37: Form 3F 24
M31: Part 7L 69
M44: Cad 4J 69
PR8: Birkd 2N 11
WA5: Gt San 4L 81
WA9: St H 1M 63
Kents Bank L12: W Der 9A 46
Kent St. CH43: Oxton 4H 73
L1: Liv 8G 5 (9C 58)
WA4: Warr 4D 82
WA8: Widnes 7L 79
Kentucky Cl. WA5: Gt San 1K 81
Kentway WA12: Newt W 9L 51
Kentwell Gro. L12: W Der 2B 60
Kenview Cl. WA8: Hale B 3D 94
Kenway WA11: Rainf 5D 38
Kenwick Cl. CH66: Gt Sut 2H 111
Kenwood Cl. L27: N'ley 3K 77
Kenworthys Flats PR9: South 7G 7
Kenwright Cres. WA9: St H 1M 63
Kenwyn Rd. CH45: Wall 4H 57
KENYON 6G 53
Kenyon Av. WA5: Penk 3G 80
Kenyon Cl. L33: Kirkb 5D 36
Kenyon Ct. *L8: Liv 2E 74*
(off Park Rd.)
WN7: Leigh 1J 53
Kenyon La. WA3: Croft 8G 53
WA3: Cul, Low 4F 52
Kenyon Rd. L15: Wavtr 3M 75
Kenyons La. L31: Lydi, Mag 8J 27
L37: Form 1G 24
Kenyons La. Nth. WA11: Hay 2H 51
Kenyons La. Sth. WA11: Hay 3H 51
Kenyons Lodge L31: Mag 9K 27
Kenyons Pl. L31: Lydi 9J 27
Kenyons Steps L1: Liv 6F 4
Kenyon Ter. CH43: Oxton 3H 73
Kepler St. L21: Sea 4N 43
Keppel St. L20: Boot 9A 44
Kerfoot Bus. Pk. WA2: Warr 9B 66
(not continuous)
Kerfoots La. WN8: Skel 4N 29
Kerfoot St. WA2: Warr 1B 82
Kerman Cl. L12: W Der 9N 45
Kerr Cl. L33: Kirkb 5C 36
Kerr Gro. WA9: St H 7A 50
Kerridge Dr. WA1: Warr 3F 82
Kerris Cl. L17: Aig 6H 75
Kerry Cft. CH66: Gt Sut 4K 111
Kerry La. PR9: Banks 3E 8
Kerrysdale Cl. WA9: St H 2N 63
Kersey Rd. L32: Kirkb 2D 46
Kersey Wlk. L32: Kirkb 2D 46
Kershaw Av. L23: Crosb 8M 33
Kershaw St. WA8: Widnes 7G 79
Kershaw Way WA12: Newt W 5L 51
Kerslake Way L38: Hight 8F 24
Kerswell Cl. WA9: St H 3N 63
Kerton Row PR8: Birkd 2M 11
Keston Wlk. L26: Halew 1K 93
Kestrel Av. CH49: Upton 2L 71
Kestrel Cl. CH49: Upton 2L 71
WA11: St H 4L 49
Kestrel Ct. L23: Blun 8G 33
PR9: South 8J 7
Kestrel Dene L10: Faz 4M 45
Kestrel Dr. WN4: Ash M 5L 41
Kestrel Gro. L26: Halew 7H 77
Kestrel La. WA3: Birchw 5M 67
Kestrel M. WN8: Skel 9F 22
Kestrel Pk. WN8: Skel 9F 22
Kestrel Pl. L40: Burs 3F 20
Kestrel Rd. CH46: More 8K 55
CH60: Hesw 8C 88
Kestrels Way WA7: Pal F 9B 96
Keswick Av. CH63: East 1B 102
WA2: Warr 7D 66
Keswick Cl. L31: Mag 1K 35
M44: Cad 5K 69
PR8: Ainsd 2J 17
WA8: Widnes 7F 78
Keswick Cres. WA2: Warr 7D 66
Keswick Dr. L21: Lith 2C 44
WA6: Frod 6M 107
Keswick Gdns. CH63: Brom 1B 102
Keswick Pl. CH43: Bid 8D 56
Keswick Rd. CH45: Wall 2E 56
L18: Aller 6A 76
WA10: St H 5H 49
Keswick Vs. *L16: Child 9E 60*
(off Buttermere Rd.)
Keswick Way L16: Child 9E 60
WA11: Rainf 1C 38
Ketterer Ct. WA9: St H 8M 49
Kettering Cl. L14: Knott A 4D 60
Kettering Rd. PR8: Ainsd 9H 11
Kevelioc Cl. CH63: Spit 4M 89
KEW 3D 12
Kew Gdns. Cl. WA8: Widnes 4N 79
Kew Ho. Dr. PR8: South 4F 12
Kew (Park & Ride) 1F 12
Kew Retail Pk. 3F 12
Kew Rd. L37: Form 3D 24
PR8: Birkd 3N 11
Kew St. L5: Liv 4C 58
Keybank Rd. L12: W Der 1M 59
Keyes Cl. WA3: Birchw 5N 67
Keyes Gdn. WA3: Birchw 5N 67
Keyhouse Gdns. L13: Liv 5L 59
Keys Ct. L1: Liv 6F 4 (8C 58)
Keystone Cl. L7: Liv 9G 59
Kiddman St. L9: W'ton 7E 44
Kid Glove Rd. WA3: Golb 1C 52
Kidstone Cl. WA9: St H 2N 63
Kielder Cl. WN4: Ash M 4H 41
Kilbuck La. WA11: Hay 2H 51
Kilburn Av. CH62: East 9D 90
WN4: Ash M 7M 41
Kilburn Gro. WA9: St H 2H 63
WN3: Winst 1F 40
Kilburn Rd. WN5: Orr 7M 31
Kilburn St. L21: Lith 4A 44

Kildale Cl.—Kylemore Rd.

Kildale Cl. L31: Mag 1H 35
Kildare Cl. L24: Hale 5A 94
Kildonan Rd. L17: Aig 6J 75
WA4: Grap 6H 83
Kilford Cl. WA5: Call 7N 65
Kilgraston Gdns. L17: Aig 7L 75
Killarney Gro. CH44: Wall 6G 56
Killarney Rd. L13: Liv 6N 59
Killester Rd. L25: Gate 4F 76
Killingbeck Cl. L40: Burs 1H 21
Killington Cl. WN3: Wigan 1K 41
Killington Way L4: Kirkd 1D 58
Killingworth La.
WA3: Birchw 4A 68
Kilmalcolm Cl. CH43: Oxton 4F 72
Kilmore Cl. L9: Aintr 2H 45
Kilmory Av. L25: Woolt 6G 77
Kiln Cl. WA10: Ec'stn 5F 48
Kilncroft WA7: Brook 1D 108
(not continuous)
Kiln Hey L12: W Der 4A 60
Kiln La. WA10: Ec'stn, St H 5E 48
WN8: Skel 2B 30
Kiln Rd. CH49: Wdchu 5A 72
Kilnyard Rd. L23: Crosb 7K 33
Kilrea Cl. L11: Norr G 1L 59
Kilrea Lodge L11: Norr G 1L 59
Kilrea Rd. L11: Norr G 1K 59
Kilsail Rd. L32: Kirkb 3E 46
Kilsby Dr. WA8: Widnes 6A 80
Kilshaw Rd. WA5: Burtw 3H 65
Kilshaw St. L6: Liv 1N 5 (5F 58)
(not continuous)
Kilsyth Cl. WA2: Fearn 5G 67
Kimberley Av. L23: Crosb 8K 33
WA9: St H 2H 63
Kimberley Cl. L8: Liv 9M 5 (1F 74)
Kimberley Dr. L23: Crosb 8K 33
WA4: Stockt H 7D 82
Kimberley Pl. WN4: Ash M 8L 41
Kimberley Rd. CH45: Wall 3H 57
Kimberley St. WA5: Warr 3N 81
Kindale Rd. CH43: Pren 7E 72
Kinder Gro. WN4: Ash M 5H 41
Kinder St. L6: Liv 2L 5 (6E 58)
King Arthurs Wlk. WA7: Cas 7C 96
King Av. L20: Boot 4D 44
King Edward Cl. L35: Rainh 5E 62
King Edward Dr. CH62: Port S 1A 90
King Edward Ind. Est. L3: Liv 3B 4
King Edward Pde. L3: Liv 3C 4
King Edward Rd. L35: Rainh 5E 62
WA10: St H 4G 49
King Edward St. L3: Liv 3C 4 (7A 58)
WA1: Warr 1F 82
Kingfield Rd. L9: W'ton 5E 44
Kingfisher Bus. Pk. L20: Boot 3B 44
WA8: Widnes 8N 79
Kingfisher Cl. L27: N'ley 3K 77
L33: Kirkb 5C 36
WA3: Birchw 5N 67
WA7: Beech 1B 108
Kingfisher Ct. L31: Lydi 8G 27
PR9: South 7J 7
WN4: Ash M 5K 41
Kingfisher Ct. Ind. Est. WN4: Ash M 5K 41
Kingfisher Dr. WA11: St H 4L 49
Kingfisher Gro. L12: W Der 9D 46
Kingfisher Ho. CH41: Birke 2N 73
L13: Liv 8M 59
Kingfisher Pk. WN8: Skel 9F 22
Kingfisher Sq. WA1: Warr 1G 82
Kingfisher Way CH49: Upton 2L 71
King George V Sports Complex 5K 61
King George Cl. WN4: Ash M 8K 41
King George Cres. WA1: Warr 1F 82
King George Dr. CH44: Wall 3K 57
King George Rd. WA11: Hay 3J 51
King George's Dr. CH62: Port S 1A 90
King George's Way CH43: Bid 1E 72
Kingham Cl. CH46: Leas 6B 56
L25: Woolt 6G 77
WA8: Widnes 7N 79
Kingham M. L25: Woolt 6G 77
King James Ct. WA7: Pal F 9A 96
Kinglake Rd. CH44: Wall 5K 57
Kinglake St. L7: Liv 5N 5 (8G 58)
Kinglass Rd. CH63: Spit 4A 90
King Oswald Cres. WA8: Widnes 2J 79
King's Av. CH47: Meols 9E 54
WA3: Low 3G 53
Kingsbrook Way CH63: H Beb 8K 73
King's Brow CH63: H Beb 1K 89
Kingsbury CH48: W Kir 5E 70
Kingsbury Cl. PR8: Ainsd 1H 17
WA4: App 4E 98
Kingsbury Ct. WN8: Skel 9F 22
Kingsbury Rd. WA8: Widnes 4N 79
King's Bus. Pk. L34: Presc 4L 61
Kings Cl. CH63: H Beb 9K 73
L17: Aig 6H 75
L37: Form 2E 24
L39: Down 8F 18
King's Ct. CH43: Oxton 4H 73
Kings Ct. CH47: Hoy 1B 70
CH63: H Beb 9K 73
L21: Sea 3M 43
WA7: Manor P 3F 96
Kingscourt Rd. L12: W Der 4A 60
Kingsdale Av. CH42: Tran 6K 73
L35: Rainh 6G 62
Kingsdale Rd. L18: Moss H 3M 75
WA5: Gt San 9H 65
Kings Dock St. L1: Liv 9F 4 (1C 74)
Kingsdown Rd. L11: Norr G 9M 45
Kingsdown St. CH41: Tran 4L 73
King's Dr. CH48: Caldy 9D 70
CH61: Pens 2N 87
Kings Dr. L25: Gate 4G 77
L25: Woolt 6F 76
L34: Presc 4L 61
WA6: Hel 2E 114
King's Dr. Nth. CH48: W Kir 7E 70
Kingsfield Rd. L31: Mag 4H 35
King's Gap, The CH47: Hoy 1B 70
Kingshead Cl. WA7: Cas 5C 96
Kingsheath Av. L14: Knott A 5C 60
Kings Hey Dr. PR9: South 6L 7
Kingsland Cres. L11: Norr G 7K 45
Kingsland Grange WA1: Wools 8K 67
Kingsland Rd. CH42: Tran 4J 73
L11: Norr G 7K 45
King's La. CH63: H Beb 9K 73
Kingsley Av. CH62: East 3D 102
Kingsley Cl. CH61: Pens 4A 88
L31: Lydi 7H 27
Kingsley Cres. WA7: Run 6K 95
Kingsley Dr. WA4: App 9D 82
Kingsley Grn. WA6: Frod 9A 108
Kingsley Rd. CH44: Wall 6H 57
CH65: Ell P 9A 104
L8: Liv 9N 5 (1G 74)
WA6: Frod, Newt 8N 107
WA7: Run 6K 95
WA10: St H 4G 48
Kingsley St. CH41: Birke 9G 56
Kings Lynn Dr. L19: Garst 1N 91
Kingsmead Ct. WA3: Croft 1H 67
Kingsmead Dr. L25: Hunts X 9F 76
Kingsmead Gro. CH43: Oxton 3F 72
Kings Mdw. PR8: Ainsd 2K 17
WA7: Nort 7E 96
Kingsmead Rd. CH43: Oxton 3F 72
CH46: More 7N 55
Kingsmead Rd. Nth. CH43: Oxton 3F 72
Kingsmead Rd. Sth. CH43: Oxton 3F 72
Kings M. CH66: Lit Sut 7H 103
WA4: Stockt H 8D 82
KINGS MOSS 4J 39
Kings Moss La. WA11: Kings M 4H 39
Kings Mt. CH43: Oxton 4H 73
Kingsnorth L35: Whis 7C 62
King's Pde. CH45: Wall, New B 1D 56
Kings Pde. L3: Liv 8D 4 (1B 74)
Kings Pk. L21: Sea 3M 43
King's Rd. CH63: H Beb 8K 73
L20: Boot 8B 44
Kings Rd. CH66: Lit Sut 7H 103
L23: Crosb 7K 33
L37: Form 2E 24
M44: Irlam 3L 69
WA2: Fearn 7H 67
WA3: Golb 3B 52
WA10: St H 8F 48
WN4: Ash M 6J 41
Kings Sq. CH41: Birke 2M 73
Kings Ter. L20: Boot 9B 44
Kingsthorne Pk. L25: Hunts X 1G 93
Kingsthorne Rd. L25: Hunts X 1G 92
Kingston Av. WA5: Gt San 2G 81
Kingston Cl. CH46: More 9M 55
L12: W Der 4C 60
WA7: Run 5A 96
WN3: Wigan 1K 41
Kingston Cres. PR9: South 2A 8
King St. CH42: Rock F 7N 73
CH44: Wall 4K 57
CH65: Ell P 8A 104
L19: Garst 3A 92
L22: Wloo 1K 43
PR8: South 9F 6
WA7: Run 4K 95
WA10: St H 7J 49
WA12: Newt W 7K 51
Kingsville Rd. CH63: H Beb 2L 89
Kings Wlk. CH42: Rock F 7N 73
CH48: W Kir 6D 70
KINGSWAY 8K 79
Kingsway CH45: Wall 3G 56
CH60: Hesw 9C 88
CH63: H Beb 9K 73
L3: Liv 1D 4 (6B 58)
L22: Wloo 9L 33
L35: Presc 4A 62
L36: Huy, Roby 5H 61
PR8: South 8F 6
WA6: Frod 6L 107
WA8: Widnes 9K 79
WA11: St H 2K 49
WA12: Newt W 8L 51
Kingsway Ct. L3: Liv 5C 58
Kingsway Ho. *WA4: Westy 4G 82*
(off Kingsway Sth.)
WA8: Widnes 9K 79
Kingsway Leisure Cen. 8K 79
Kingsway Nth. WA1: Warr 2F 82
Kingsway Pde. *L36: Huy 5G 61*
(off Kingsway)
Kingsway Pk. L3: Liv 5C 58
Kingsway Sth. WA4: Westy 3F 82
Kingsway Tunnel App. CH44: Wall 6E 56
Kingswell Cl. L7: Liv 9G 58
Kings Wharf CH41: Birke 8M 57
KINGSWOOD
WA5 7J 65
WA6 5M 115
Kingswood L36: Huy 6H 61
Kingswood Av. L9: Aintr 3G 45
L22: Wloo 9M 33
Kingswood Blvd. CH63: H Beb 8L 73
Kingswood Ct. L33: Kirkb 7D 36
Kingswood Dr. L23: Crosb 8K 33
Kingswood Ho. PR8: Birkd 1M 11
Kingswood Pk. PR8: Birkd 1M 11
WA6: Kgswd 6N 115
Kingswood Pk. M. PR8: Birkd 9E 6
Kingswood Rd. CH44: Wall 4J 57
WA5: Westb 7J 65
Kington Rd. CH48: W Kir 5B 70
Kinley Gdns. *L20: Boot 5D 44*
(off Wheatley Av.)
Kinloch Cl. L26: Halew 9L 77
Kinloch Way L39: Orm 8B 20
Kinloss Rd. CH49: Grea 5K 71
Kinmel Cl. CH41: Birke 1K 73
L4: W'ton 1J 59
Kinmel St. L8: Liv 3F 74
WA9: St H 1M 63
Kinnaird Rd. CH45: Wall 3G 57
Kinnaird St. L8: Liv 5F 74
Kinnerley Rd. CH65: Whit 2M 111
Kinnerton Cl. CH46: More 9J 55
Kinnington Way CH1: Back 6L 111
Kinniside Rd. WN3: Wigan 1J 41
Kinnock Pk. WA5: Burtw 3G 65
Kinross Av. WN4: Garsw 7E 40
Kinross Cl. WA2: Fearn 5G 66
Kinross Rd. CH45: Wall 3D 56
L10: Faz 3L 45
L22: Wloo 2L 43
Kinsale Dr. L19: Aller 9B 76
WA3: Birchw 5K 67
Kinsey Rd. CH65: Ell P 4B 112
Kinsey's La. CH2: Ince 8K 105
Kinsman Ho. L19: G'dale 9L 75
Kintore Cl. CH63: East 2B 102
Kintore Dr. WA5: Gt San 2F 80
Kintore Rd. L19: G'dale 9N 75
Kintyre Cl. CH65: Ell P 4A 112
Kipling Av. CH42: Rock F 7M 73
L36: Huy 8L 61
WA2: Warr 8D 66
Kipling Cres. WA8: Widnes 8J 79
Kipling Gro. WA9: Sut M 6K 63
Kipling St. L20: Boot 5N 43
Kirby Cl. CH48: W Kir 7D 70
Kirby Mt. CH48: W Kir 8D 70
Kirby Pk. CH48: W Kir 7D 70
Kirby Pk. Mans. CH48: W Kir 7C 70
Kirby Rd. L20: Boot 4C 44
Kirkacre Av. WA12: Newt W 1L 65
Kirkbride Cl. L27: N'ley 4L 77
Kirkbride Lawn *L27: N'ley 4L 77*
(off Kirkbride Cl.)
Kirkbride Wlk. *L27: N'ley 4L 77*
(off Kirkbride Cl.)
Kirkburn Cl. L8: Liv 4E 74
KIRKBY 9C 36
Kirkby Bank Rd. L33: Know I 9F 36
Kirkby Bus Station 9C 36
Kirkby Gallery 9C 36
Kirkby Leisure Cen. 1C 46
KIRKBY PARK 8A 36
Kirkby Rd. WA3: Cul 7N 53
Kirkby Row L32: Kirkb 8A 36
Kirkby Station (Rail) 8A 36
Kirkcaldy Av. WA5: Gt San 2F 80
Kirk Cotts. CH45: Wall 2H 57
KIRKDALE 1D 58
Kirkdale Gdns. WN8: Uph 5K 31
Kirkdale Rd. L5: Kirkd 3C 58
Kirkdale Station (Rail) 9C 44
Kirkdale Va. L4: W'ton 2D 58
Kirket Cl. CH63: Beb 3N 89
Kirket La. CH63: Beb 3M 89
Kirkfield Gro. CH42: Rock F 7N 73
Kirkham Av. WA3: Low 4F 52
Kirkham Cl. WA5: Gt San 4K 81
Kirkham Rd. PR9: South 3M 7
WA8: Widnes 6M 79
Kirklake Bank L37: Form 2C 24
Kirklake Rd. L37: Form 2C 24
Kirkland Av. CH42: Tran 6K 73
Kirkland Cl. L9: W'ton 3E 44
Kirkland Rd. CH45: New B 1J 57
Kirklands, The CH48: W Kir 7D 70
Kirkland St. WA10: St H 6J 49
Kirklees Rd. PR8: Birkd 5M 11
Kirkmaiden Rd. L19: Aller 8N 75
Kirkman Fold L35: Rainh 6E 62
Kirkmore Rd. L18: Moss H 6M 75
Kirkmount CH49: Upton 3A 72
Kirk Rd. L21: Lith 4B 44
Kirkside Cl. L12: Crox 7B 46
Kirkstall Dr. L37: Form 2H 25
Kirkstall Rd. PR8: Birkd 4M 11
Kirkstead Wlk. L31: Mell 8N 35
Kirkstead Way WA3: Golb 2B 52
Kirkstile Cres. WN3: Winst 1G 40
Kirkstone Av. WA2: Warr 7D 66
WA11: St H 2M 49
Kirkstone Cres. WA7: Beech 2C 108
Kirkstone Rd. Nth. L21: Lith 1B 44
Kirkstone Rd. Sth. L21: Lith 2C 44
Kirkstone Rd. W. L21: Ford, Lith 9A 34
Kirk St. L5: Liv 3D 58
Kirkwall Dr. WA5: Penk 5J 81
Kirkway CH45: Wall 2H 57
CH49: Grea 4M 71
CH49: Upton 3N 71
CH63: H Beb 9K 73
Kirtley Dr. WA12: Newt W 9L 51
Kitchener Av. M44: Cad 5J 69
Kitchener Dr. L9: W'ton 4E 44
Kitchener St. WA10: St H 6G 49
Kitchen St. L1: Liv 9F 4 (1C 74)
Kitling Rd. L34: Know 5F 46
Kiverley Cl. L18: Aller 5C 76
Kiveton Dr. WN4: Ash M 9L 41
Kiveton Wlk. WA2: Warr 1D 82
Knap, The CH60: Hesw 9A 88
Knaresborough Rd. CH44: Wall 5F 56
Knavesmire Way L19: Aller 9B 76
Knebworth Cl. L12: W Der 2B 60
Knighton Rd. L4: W'ton 9J 45
Knight Rd. WA5: Burtw 3H 65
Knightsbridge Av. WA4: Grap 5K 83
Knightsbridge Cl. WA8: Widnes 4N 79
Knightsbridge Ct. CH43: Noct 5D 72
WA1: Warr 3B 82
(off Palmyra Sq. Nth.)
Knightsbridge Wlk. L33: Kirkb 5B 36
Knightscliffe Cres. WN6: Shev 7N 23
Knights Cl. WA8: Widnes 4A 80
Knights Grange WA9: St H 6M 49
Knight St. L1: Liv 8H 5 (9D 58)
Knightsway L22: Wloo 9M 33
Knightswood Ct. L18: Aller 8A 76
Knob Hall Gdns. PR9: South 4L 7
Knob Hall La. PR9: South 4L 7
Knoclaid Rd. L13: Liv 2K 59
Knoll, The CH43: Oxton 5G 73
WA7: Pal F 8B 96
Knottingley Dr. CH66: Gt Sut 9H 103
Knott Mill Way WA7: Cas 5C 96
Knott's Ho's. WN7: Leigh 1K 53
KNOTTY ASH 6A 60
Knotty M. L25: Woolt 5G 76
Knowe, The CH64: Will 6N 101
Knowle Av. PR8: Ainsd 8J 11
Knowle Cl. CH66: Gt Sut 2K 111
L12: W Der 8A 46
Knowles, The L23: Blun 8H 33
Knowles Farm Cl.
WN8: Roby M 2L 31
Knowles Ho. Av. WA10: Ec'stn 7C 48
Knowles St. CH41: Birke 1J 73
WA8: Widnes 6M 79
Knowl Hey Rd. L26: Halew 1L 93
KNOWSLEY 6H 47
Knowsley Av. WA3: Golb 2C 52
Knowsley Bus. Pk. L34: Know 4E 46
(School La., not continuous)
L34: Know 4G 47
(Villiers Rd.)
Knowsley Cl. CH42: Rock F 7N 73
Knowsley Ct. CH42: Rock F 7N 73
Knowsley Dr. WN7: Leigh 1L 53
Knowsley Ent. Workshops
L33: Know I 1F 46
Knowsley Expressway 2A 78
Knowsley Hall 1K 61
Knowsley Hgts. L36: Huy 4J 61
Knowsley Ind. Pk. L33: Know I 3F 46
(Faraday Rd.)
L33: Know I 9G 36
(Manor Complex)
Knowsley La. L34: Know, Know P 9G 47
L36: Huy 9G 47
Knowsley Leisure & Culture Pk. 6K 61
Knowsley M. L39: Orm 8D 20
KNOWSLEY PARK 5K 47
Knowsley Pk. La. L34: Presc 2N 61
Knowsley Rd. CH42: Rock F 7N 73
CH45: Wall 3G 56
L19: G'dale 1M 91
L20: Boot 5N 43
L35: Rainh 7G 62
L39: Orm 9D 20
PR9: South 6G 7
WA10: St H 7F 48
Knowsley Safari Pk. 1N 61
Knowsley St. L4: W'ton 8E 44
Knowsley Vw.
WA11: Rainf 3B 38
Knox Cl. CH62: Port S 1A 90
Knox St. CH41: Birke 2M 73
Knutsford Cl. WA10: Ec'stn 8E 48
Knutsford Grn. CH46: More 8M 55
Knutsford Old Rd.
WA4: Grap 6H 83
Knutsford Rd. CH46: More 8M 55
WA4: Grap 6H 83
WA4: Warr 4C 82
Knutsford Wlk. L31: Lydi 8J 27
Kramar Wlk. L33: Kirkb 9D 36
Kremlin Dr. L13: Liv 4L 59
Kronsbec Av. CH66: Lit Sut 8J 103
Kydds Wynt WA6: Frod 6L 107
Kylemore Av. L18: Moss H 5L 75
Kylemore Cl. CH61: Pens 4M 87
Kylemore Ct. L26: Halew 9J 77
Kylemore Dr. CH61: Pens 4M 87
Kylemore Rd. CH43: Oxton 4G 73

Kylemore Way—Laurel Ct.

Kylemore Way CH61: Pens ... 4M **87**
(not continuous)
L26: Halew ... 9H **77**
Kynance Rd. L11: Crox ... 5B **46**

L

Laburnam St. WN4: Ash M ... 9K **41**
Laburnum Av. L36: Huy ... 9J **61**
WA1: Wools ... 1K **83**
WA11: St H ... 3N **49**
Laburnum Ct. *L8: Liv ... 4F 74*
(off Weller Way)
WA13: Lymm ... 4H **85**
Laburnum Cres. L32: Kirkb ... 8B **36**
Laburnum Dr. WN8: Skel ... 3A **30**
Laburnum Farm Cl.
CH64: Ness ... 9G **101**
Laburnum Gro. CH61: Irby ... 1L **87**
CH66: Whit ... 5M **111**
L15: Wavtr ... 9M 59
(off Chestnut Gro.)
L31: Mag ... 2L **35**
L40: Burs ... 8K **15**
PR8: South ... 8L **7**
WA7: Run ... 7L **95**
Laburnum La. WA5: Gt San ... 2E **80**
Laburnum Pl. L20: Boot ... 7C **44**
Laburnum Rd.
CH43: Oxton ... 4J **73**
CH45: New B ... 2H **57**
L7: Liv ... 6J **59**
M44: Cad ... 4K **69**
WA3: Low ... 3G **52**
Laburnum Ter.
L19: Garst ... 1A 92
(off Chapel Rd.)
Lace St. L3: Liv ... 3F **4** (7C **58**)
Lacey Ct. WA8: Widnes ... 9L **79**
Lacey Rd. L34: Presc ... 4B **62**
Lacey St. WA8: Widnes ... 9K **79**
WA10: St H ... 1G **62**
Laddock Cl. L4: W'ton ... 2H **59**
Ladies Wlk. CH64: Nest ... 6E **100**
Ladies' Wlk. WA2: Winw ... 3A **66**
WA9: Bold ... 6C **64**
Lady Acre Cl. WA13: Lymm ... 6D **84**
Lady Alice's Dr. L40: Lath ... 5H **21**
Lady Anne Cl. L40: Scar ... 7N **13**
Ladybarn Av. WA3: Golb ... 3A **52**
Ladybower Cl. CH49: Upton ... 2M **71**
L7: Liv ... 9G **59**
Lady Chapel Cl. L1: Liv ... 9J **5** (1D **74**)
Lady Chapel Sq. L1: Liv ... 9J **5**
Ladycroft Cl. WA1: Wools ... 1M **83**
Ladyewood Rd. CH44: Wall ... 6J **57**
Ladyfield CH43: Bid ... 1C **72**
Ladyfields L12: W Der ... 4N **59**
LADY GREEN ... 8K 25
Lady Grn. Ct. L38: Ince B ... 9L **25**
Lady Grn. La. L38: Ince B ... 8K **25**
Lady Heyes Craft & Antique Restoration Cen. ... 9B 108
Lady La. WA3: Croft ... 9K **53**
Lady Lever Art Gallery ... 1A 90
Lady Mountford Ho. L18: Moss H ... 5L **75**
Ladypool L24: Hale ... 6N **93**
Lady Richeld Cl. WA7: Nort ... 4F **96**
Ladysmith Av. WN4: Ash M ... 8L **41**
Ladysmith Rd. L10: Faz ... 3L **45**
Lady's Wlk. L40: Lath, Westh ... 8F **20**
Ladywood Rd. WA5: Old H ... 8L **65**
LAFFAK ... 3N 49
Laffak Rd. WA11: St H ... 3M **49**
Lafford La. WN8: Roby M, Uph ... 1M **31**
Lagan Ho. CH46: Leas ... 5M **55**
Laggan St. L7: Liv ... 7G **59**
Lagrange Arc. WA10: St H ... 7K **49**
Laira Ct. WA2: Warr ... 1D **82**
Laira St. WA2: Warr ... 1D **82**
Laird Cl. CH41: Birke ... 9F **56**
Lairds Pl. L3: Liv ... 5C **58**
Laird St. CH41: Birke ... 9F **56**
Laithwaite Cl. WA9: Sut M ... 6L **63**
Lake Ent. Pk. CH62: Brom ... 5D **90**
Lakeland Av. WN4: Ash M ... 7L **41**
Lakeland Cl. L1: Liv ... 7F **4** (9C **58**)
Lake La. WA4: H Whi ... 9G **99**
Lakemoor Cl. WA9: St H ... 2N **63**
Lakenheath Rd. L26: Halew ... 1J **93**
Lake Pl. CH47: Hoy ... 1C **70**
Lake Rd. CH47: Hoy ... 1C **70**
L15: Wavtr ... 1M **75**
Lakeside Cl. WA8: Widnes ... 9D **78**
Lakeside Ct. CH45: New B ... 1J **57**
WA11: Rainf ... 5D **38**
Lakeside Dr. WA1: Warr ... 5B **82**
Lakeside Gdns. L23: Thorn ... 5A **34**
WA11: Rainf ... 5D **38**
Lakeside Lawn L27: N'ley ... 4L **77**
Lakeside Miniature Railway ... 8E 6
Lakeside Rd. WA13: Lymm ... 7D **84**
Lakeside Vw. L22: Wloo ... 2K **43**
Lakes Rd. L9: Aintr ... 3J **45**
Lake Vw. L35: Whis ... 9B **62**
Lake Vw. Cl. PR8: South ... 2E **12**
Lake Vw. Ct. L4: W'ton ... 8F **44**
Lakeview Ct. *PR9: South ... 7G 6*
(off Promenade)
Laleston Cl. WA8: Widnes ... 8H **79**
Lambert St. L3: Liv ... 3J **5** (7D **58**)
(Kempston St.)
L3: Liv ... 3J **5**
(Lambert Way)
Lambert Way L3: Liv ... 3J **5** (7D **58**)
Lambeth Ct. CH47: Hoy ... 1B **70**
Lambeth Rd. L4: Kirkd ... 2C **58**
L5: Kirkd ... 2C **58**
Lambourn Av. WA8: Cron ... 3F **78**
Lambourne WN8: Skel ... 9E **22**
Lambourne Cl. CH66: Gt Sut ... 5L **111**
Lambourne Gro. WA9: St H ... 7C **50**
Lambourne Rd. L4: W'ton ... 9J **45**
Lambrigg Row L5: Liv ... 2E **58**
Lambshear La. L31: Lydi ... 8H **27**
Lambsickle Cl. WA7: W'ton ... 9J **95**
Lambsickle La. WA7: Run, W'ton ... 9J **95**
Lambs La. WA1: Padd ... 1H **83**
WA1: Padd, Padg ... 9H **67**
Lambton Rd. L17: Aig ... 5G **74**
Lamerton Cl. WA5: Penk ... 4F **80**
Lammermoor Rd. L18: Moss H ... 6M **75**
Lampeter Cl. WA5: Call ... 7N **65**
Lampeter Rd. L6: Liv ... 3H **59**
Lamport Cl. WA8: Widnes ... 5A **80**
Lamport St. L8: Liv ... 2D **74**
Lanark Cl. WA10: St H ... 8J **49**
Lanark Gdns. WA8: Widnes ... 5H **79**
Lancashire Gdns. WA10: St H ... 8J **49**
Lancashire Rd. M31: Part ... 7L **69**
Lancaster Av. CH45: Wall ... 4H **57**
L17: Liv ... 2J **75**
L23: Crosb ... 8K **33**
L35: Whis ... 6A **62**
WA3: Golb ... 2D **52**
WA7: Run ... 7H **95**
WA8: Widnes ... 6D **78**
Lancaster Cl. CH62: Port S ... 1A **90**
L5: Kirkd ... 3C **58**
L31: Mag ... 2L **35**
PR8: Birkd ... 2L **11**
WA2: Padg ... 7G **66**
WA12: Newt W ... 6H **51**
Lancaster Ct. *WA4: Stockt H ... 7F 82*
(off Lime Tree Av.)
Lancaster Cres. WN8: Skel ... 3B **30**
Lancaster Dr. PR9: Banks ... 2C **8**
Lancaster Gdns. CH65: Ell P ... 2B **112**
PR8: Birkd ... 2L **11**
Lancaster Ga. PR9: Banks ... 2D **8**
Lancaster La. WN8: Parb ... 2F **22**
Lancaster Rd. L36: Huy ... 5L **61**
L37: Form ... 3E **24**
M44: Cad ... 4J **69**
PR8: Birkd ... 3K **11**
WA8: Widnes ... 5K **79**
Lancaster St. L5: Kirkd ... 3C **58**
L9: W'ton ... 7E **44**
WA5: Warr ... 3N **81**
Lancaster Wlk. *L36: Huy ... 5L 61*
(off Lancaster Rd.)
Lance Cl. L5: Liv ... 4E **58**
Lancefield Rd. L9: W'ton ... 5E **44**
Lance Gro. L15: Wavtr ... 1M **75**
Lance La. L15: Wavtr ... 1M **75**
Lancelots Hey L3: Liv ... 4C **4**
Lancelyn Ct. CH63: Spit ... 4N **89**
Lancelyn Pct. *CH63: Spit ... 4N 89*
(off Spital Rd.)
Lancelyn Ter. CH63: Beb ... 3M **89**
Lancer Ct. WA7: Astm ... 4A **96**
Lancers Cft. CH66: Gt Sut ... 4K **111**
Lancer Way L12: W Der ... 2C **60**
Lancing Av. WA2: Warr ... 5B **66**
Lancing Cl. L25: Hunts X ... 7H **77**
Lancing Dr. L10: Aintr ... 9J **35**
Lancing Rd. CH65: Ell P ... 1B **112**
L25: Hunts X ... 7H **77**
Lancing Way L25: Hunts X ... 7H **77**
Lancots La. WA9: St H ... 1N **63**
Landcut La. WA3: Birchw ... 6L **67**
Land End L31: Mag ... 2A **36**
Lander Cl. WA5: Old H ... 1M **81**
Lander Rd. L21: Lith ... 4A **44**
Landford Av. L9: Faz ... 6K **45**
Landford Pl. L9: Faz ... 6K **45**
LAND GATE ... 3J 41
Landgate Ind. Est. WN4: Ash M ... 3J **41**
Landgate La. WN4: Ash M ... 4H **41**
LANDICAN ... 8C 72
Landican Cemetery & Crematorium ... 7B **72**
Landican La. CH49: Wdchu ... 8C **72**
CH63: Store ... 1E **88**
Landican Rd. CH49: Wdchu ... 9B **72**
Land La. PR9: South ... 3B **8**
Landor Cl. L5: Liv ... 4B **58**
WA3: Low ... 2F **52**
Landscape Dene WA6: Hel ... 1G **115**
Landsdowne Ho. CH41: Birke ... 2N **73**
Landseer Av. CH64: Lit N ... 7F **100**
WA4: Warr ... 7C **82**
Landseer Rd. L5: Liv ... 4E **58**
LAND SIDE ... 1N 53
Landside WN7: Leigh ... 1N **53**
LANE ENDS ... 1B 94
LANE HEAD ... 4F 52
Lane Head Av. WA3: Low ... 1F **52**
Lanfranc Cl. L16: Child ... 9C **60**
Lanfranc Way L16: Child ... 9C **60**
Langbar L35: Whis ... 7B **62**
Langcliffe Cl. WA3: Cul ... 7M **53**
Langdale Av. CH61: Pens ... 3N **87**
L37: Form ... 1D **24**
WA3: Golb ... 1D **52**
WA13: Lymm ... 4F **84**
Langdale Cl. L32: Kirkb ... 1D **46**
L37: Form ... 2D **24**
WA2: Warr ... 6F **66**
WA8: Widnes ... 8F **78**
Langdale Ct. CH41: Birke ... 9H **57**
Langdale Dr. L31: Mag ... 1K **35**
L40: Burs ... 1J **21**
Langdale Gdns. PR8: Birkd ... 5M **11**
Langdale Gro. WA11: St H ... 3L **49**
Langdale Rd. CH45: Wall ... 2F **56**
CH63: Beb ... 3L **89**
L15: Wavtr ... 2K **75**
M31: Part ... 6L **69**
WA7: Run ... 6L **95**
Langdale St. L20: Boot ... 7C **44**
Langdale Way WA6: Frod ... 5M **107**
Langden Cl. WA3: Cul ... 6L **53**
Langfield WA3: Low ... 3F **52**
Langfield Gro. CH62: Brom ... 1C **102**
Langford L24: Hale ... 5N **93**
Langford Rd. L19: Aig ... 8L **75**
Langford Way WA4: App T ... 3L **99**
Langham Av. L17: Aig ... 5H **75**
Langham Ct. L4: W'ton ... 1E **58**
Langham St. L4: W'ton ... 1E **58**
Langham St. Ind. Est. *L4: W'ton ... 1E 58*
(off Langham St.)
Langholm Cl. WN3: Winst ... 1G **40**
Langholm Rd. WN4: Garsw ... 7E **40**
Langland Cl. L4: W'ton ... 1J **59**
WA5: Call ... 7N **65**
Lang La. CH48: W Kir ... 5C **70**
Lang La. Sth. CH48: W Kir ... 6D **70**
Langley Av. WA12: Newt W ... 9L **51**
Langley Beck WA8: Widnes ... 4M **79**
Langley Cl. CH63: Spit ... 5N **89**
L12: Crox ... 7D **46**
L38: Hight ... 1F **32**
WA3: Golb ... 1D **52**
Langley Cl. Shop. Cen. ... 7D **46**
Langley Ct. CH65: Ell P ... 2C **112**
L40: Burs ... 9F **14**
Langley Pl. L40: Burs ... 1F **20**
Langley Rd. CH63: Spit ... 5N **89**
L40: Burs ... 9F **14**
Langley St. L8: Liv ... 2D **74**
Langrove St. L5: Liv ... 4D **58**
Langsdale St. L3: Liv ... 2J **5** (6D **58**)
(not continuous)
Langshaw Lea L27: N'ley ... 4K **77**
Langstone Av. CH49: Grea ... 5K **71**
Langton Cl. WA8: Widnes ... 5E **78**
WA12: Newt W ... 6J **51**
Langton Grn. WA1: Wools ... 1L **83**
Langton Rd. L15: Wavtr ... 1J **75**
L33: Kirkb ... 6D **36**
Langtree WN8: Skel ... 1E **30**
Langtree Pk. ... 8L 49
Langtree St. WA9: St H ... 7M **49**
Langtree Way WA9: St H ... 8L **49**
Langtry Cl. L4: Kirkd ... 1C **58**
Langtry Rd. L4: Kirkd ... 1C **58**
Langwell Cl. WA3: Birchw ... 4A **68**
Langwood La. WA11: Rainf ... 2F **38**
Lansbury Av. WA9: St H ... 8A **50**
Lansbury Rd. L36: Huy ... 7L **61**
Lansdown L12: W Der ... 3M **59**
Lansdowne WA3: Cul ... 8M **53**
WA6: Frod ... 8N **107**
Lansdowne Cl. CH41: Birke ... 9G **56**
Lansdowne Ct. CH43: Bid ... 9F **56**
WA9: St H ... 2N **63**
Lansdowne Pl. CH43: Bid ... 9F **56**
L5: Liv ... 3E **58**
Lansdowne Rd. CH41: Birke ... 9F **56**
CH43: Bid ... 9F **56**
CH45: Wall ... 1F **56**
PR8: South ... 9K **7**
Lansdowne Way L36: Huy ... 7J **61**
Lanville Rd. L19: Aig ... 7N **75**
Lanyard Way L6: Liv ... 5G **58**
Lanyork Rd. L3: Liv ... 2C **4** (6A **58**)
Lapford Cres. L33: Kirkb ... 7E **36**
Lapford Wlk. L33: Kirkb ... 7E **36**
Lapwing Cl. L12: W Der ... 9C **46**
WA3: Low ... 2E **52**
WA12: Newt W ... 6L **51**
Lapwing Ct. L26: Halew ... 7J **77**
Lapwing Gro. WA7: Pal F ... 9C **96**
Lapwing La. WA4: Moore ... 9H **81**
Lapwing Ri. CH60: Hesw ... 9N **87**
Lapwing Way CH64: P'gte ... 7D **100**
Lapworth Cl. CH46: More ... 9J **55**
Lapworth St. L5: Kirkd ... 3C **58**
Larch Av. WA5: Penk ... 3G **81**
WA8: Widnes ... 6L **79**
WA12: Newt W ... 8L **51**
Larch Cl. L19: G'dale ... 9L **75**
WA3: Low ... 4G **52**
WA7: Run ... 8M **95**
WN5: Bil ... 6N **39**
WN8: Skel ... 3B **30**
Larch Ct. *L8: Liv ... 4F 74*
(off Weller Way)
Larchdale Cl. CH66: Whit ... 5L **111**
Larchdale Gro. L9: W'ton ... 6G **44**
Larchfield Rd. L23: Thorn ... 6N **33**
Larch Gro. CH43: Bid ... 9E **56**
L15: Wavtr ... 8M **59**
Larch Ho. L7: Liv ... 7L **5**
Larch Lea L6: Liv ... 4G **58**
(not continuous)
Larch Rd. CH42: Tran ... 3J **73**
L36: Roby ... 7G **61**
M31: Part ... 6L **69**
WA7: Run ... 8M **95**
WA11: Hay ... 3G **51**
Larch St. PR8: South ... 1D **12**
Larchtree M. L12: W Der ... 1C **60**
Larch Way L37: Form ... 9D **16**
Larchways WA4: App ... 2E **98**
Larchwood Av. L31: Mag ... 4H **35**
Larchwood Cl. CH61: Pens ... 4N **87**
L25: Gate ... 3F **76**
Larchwood Dr. CH63: H Beb ... 9M **73**
Larcombe Av. CH49: Upton ... 3N **71**
Larkfield Av. WA1: Padd ... 1H **83**
Larkfield Cl. L17: Aig ... 6H **75**
Larkfield Ct. PR9: South ... 4M **7**
WA11: St H ... 2J **49**
Larkfield Gro. L17: Aig ... 6H **75**
Larkfield La. PR9: South ... 4M **7**
Larkfield Rd. L17: Aig ... 6H **75**
Larkfield Vw. L15: Wavtr ... 9K **59**
Larkhill WN8: Skel ... 9E **22**
Larkhill Av.
CH49: Upton ... 1A **72**
Larkhill Cl. L13: Liv ... 2K **59**
Larkhill Gro. L38: Hight ... 9F **24**
Larkhill La. L13: Liv ... 2K **59**
L37: Form ... 9C **16**
Larkhill Pl. L13: Liv ... 2L **59**
Larkhill Vw. L13: Liv ... 2L **59**
Larkhill Way CH49: Upton ... 1A **72**
Larkin Cl. CH62: New F ... 9N **73**
Lark La. L17: Aig ... 5H **75**
Larkspur Cl.
PR8: South ... 9J **7**
WA7: Beech ... 2B **108**
Larkspur Ct. L31: Mell ... 8M **35**
Larkspur Gro. WA5: Warr ... 5M **81**
Larkstoke Cl. WA4: App ... 1F **98**
Larksway CH60: Hesw ... 7B **88**
Lark Way L17: Aig ... 5H **75**
Larne Ct. WA8: Widnes ... 6H **79**
Larton Farm Cl. CH48: W Kir ... 6F **70**
Larton Rd. CH48: W Kir ... 5F **70**
Lartonwood CH48: W Kir ... 5F **70**
Lascelles Rd. L19: Aller ... 9B **76**
Lascelles St. WA9: St H ... 7M **49**
Laskey La. WA4: Thel ... 4N **83**
LATCHFORD ... 5E 82
Latchford High Level Bri. WA4: Warr ... 6F **82**
Latchford Rd. CH60: Hesw ... 9B **88**
Latchford St. WA4: Westy ... 5H **83**
Late Moffatt Rd. W. *L9: Aintr ... 3G 45*
(off Moffatt Rd.)
Latham Av. L39: Orm ... 8E **20**
WA6: Hel ... 4E **114**
WA7: Run ... 6L **95**
WA12: Newt W ... 6L **51**
Latham Ct. L7: Liv ... 7J **59**
Latham St. L5: Kirkd ... 3C **58**
(not continuous)
Latham Way CH63: Spit ... 5A **90**
Lathbury La. L17: Aig ... 3K **75**
LATHOM ... 5M 21
Lathom Av. CH44: Wall ... 5H **57**
L21: Sea ... 4M 43
(off Chatham Cl.)
WA2: Warr ... 9C **66**
WN8: Parb ... 2E **22**
Lathom Cl. *L21: Sea ... 4M 43*
(off Chatham Cl.)
L36: Huy ... 3L **61**
L40: Burs ... 1J **21**
Lathom Ct. L36: Huy ... 3L **61**
Lathom Dr. L31: Mag ... 9K **27**
WA11: Rainf ... 4C **38**
Lathom Ho. L40: Lath ... 6M **21**
Lathom La. L40: Lath ... 6G **21**
LATHOM PARK ... 6N 21
Lathom Rd. L20: Boot ... 5B **44**
L36: Huy ... 6J **61**
L39: Bic ... 5J **29**
M44: Irlam ... 1M **69**
PR9: South ... 6G **7**
Lathum Cl. L35: Presc ... 4B **62**
Latimer Cl. WA8: Widnes ... 4M **79**
Latimer St. L5: Liv ... 3C **58**
Latona Cl. WA3: Croft ... 9K **53**
Latrigg Rd. L17: Aig ... 6K **75**
Lauder Cl. L33: Kirkb ... 5B **36**
Launceston Cl. WA7: Brook ... 9E **96**
Launceston Dr. WA5: Penk ... 5G **80**
Laund, The CH45: Wall ... 4F **56**
Laurel Av. CH60: Hesw ... 6N **87**
CH63: H Beb ... 3L **89**
L40: Burs ... 8J **15**
WA1: Wools ... 1L **83**
WA12: Newt W ... 8M **51**
(not continuous)
Laurel Bank WA4: Grap ... 7K **83**
WA8: Widnes ... 5K **79**
Laurelbanks CH60: Hesw ... 6M **87**
Laurel Ct. *L7: Liv ... 6J 59*
(off Laurel Rd.)
WA11: St H ... 3L **49**

Laurel Dr.—Lily Pl.

Laurel Dr. CH64: Will 5A 102
CH65: Whit 3N 111
WA10: Ec'stn 6C 48
WN8: Skel 2B 30
Laurel Farm Ct. CH2: Elt 1M 113
Laurel Gro. L8: Liv 2H 75
L22: Wloo 9K 33
L36: Huy 9J 61
PR8: South 8K 7
WA3: Low 2E 52
WN4: Ash M 7K 41
Laurelhurst Av. CH61: Pens 3A 88
Laurel Rd. CH42: Tran 4K 73
L7: Liv 6J 59
L34: Presc 3B 62
WA10: St H 8G 48
WA11: Hay 5B 50
Laurels, The CH46: Leas 6M 55
Laurel Wlk. M31: Part 7L 69
Laurel Way WA10: St H 8G 48
Laurelwood Dr. CH66: Gt Sut 5K 111
Laurence Deacon Ct. CH41: Birke 1K 73
Lauren Cl. L36: Huy 7M 61
Lauriston Rd. L4: W'ton 9H 45
Laurus Cl. L27: N'ley 3K 77
Lavan Cl. L6: Liv 1M 5 (6F 58)
Lavan St. L6: Liv 1N 5 (6F 58)
Lavender Av. L32: Kirkb 9A 36
Lavender Cl. WA7: Run 6M 95
Lavender Cres. L34: Presc 3B 62
Lavender Gdns. L23: Thorn 6A 34
WA5: Warr 4N 81
WA9: Bold 2C 64
Lavender Wlk. M31: Part 7L 69
WN4: Garsw 6F 40
Lavender Way L9: W'ton 6G 45
Laverne Dr. WA5: Gt San 2J 81
Lavrock Bank L8: Liv 4D 74
Lawford Dr. CH60: Hesw 7C 88
Lawler Gro. L34: Presc 2B 62
Lawler St. L21: Lith 4A 44
Lawn Av. WA1: Padg 9G 66
Lawnhurst Gro. L17: Aig 8K 75
Lawns, The CH43: Bid 1D 72
PR9: South 5L 7
Lawns Av. CH63: Raby M 9A 90
WN5: Orr 7M 31
Lawnside Cl. CH42: Rock F 7M 73
Lawnswood Gro. CH2: Elt 2M 113
Lawrence Cl. L19: G'dale 9M 75
Lawrence Ct. CH42: Rock F 8N 73
Lawrence Gro. L15: Wavtr 1K 75
Lawrence Rd. L15: Wavtr 1J 75
WA10: Windle 4F 48
Lawrenson St. WA10: St H 7H 49
Lawson Cl. WA1: Wools 1M 83
Lawson Ho. WA7: Run 7K 95
Lawson Rd. WA7: Run 7K 95
Lawson St. PR9: South 8M 7
Lawson Wlk. L12: Crox 7B 46
Lawswood L37: Form 8E 16
Lawton Av. L20: Boot 5D 44
Lawton Cl. WA3: Cul 7M 53
Lawton Rd. L22: Wloo 9K 33
L35: Rainh 7G 62
L36: Roby 8G 61
Lawton St. L1: Liv 6H 5 (8D 58)
Laxey Av. WA1: Wools 2L 83
Laxey St. L8: Liv 2D 74
Laxton Cl. CH66: Gt Sut 5L 111
Laxton Rd. L25: Hunts X 9G 77
Layford Rd. L36: Huy 4H 61
Layland Av. WA3: Cul 6M 53
Layton Av. CH43: Pren 6F 72
Layton Cl. L25: Woolt 6G 76
WA3: Birchw 6M 67
Layton Rd. L25: Woolt 6G 76
Layton Way L34: Presc 4A 62
Lazenby Cres. WN4: Ash M 8H 41
Lazonby Cl. CH43: Bid 9C 56
LEA BY BACKFORD 9M 111
Leach Cft. L28: Stockb V 2E 60
Leach La. WA9: Sut L 5N 63
Leach St. WA10: St H 6J 49
Leach Vw. WA11: St H 3L 49
Leach Way CH61: Irby 1K 87
Lea Cl. CH43: Noct 4E 72
Lea Cres. L39: Orm 6C 20
Leacroft WN4: Ash M 5H 41
Leacroft Rd. WA3: Ris 3N 67
Lea Cross Gro. WA8: Widnes 5F 78
Leadenhall Cl. L5: Liv 3E 58
Leader Williams Rd. M44: Irlam 1M 69
Leafield Cl. CH61: Irby 1N 87
Leafield Rd. L25: Hunts X 1F 92
Leagate L10: Faz 2L 45
Leagate Cl. WN3: Wigan 1G 41
LEA GREEN 4J 63
Lea Grn. Bus. Pk. WA9: St H 5J 63
Lea Grn. Ind. Est. WA9: St H 6K 63
Lea Green (Park & Ride) 3L 63
Lea Grn. Rd. WA9: St H 6J 63
Lea Green Station (Rail) 4L 63
Lea Hall Pk. CH1: Lea B 9M 111
Leamington Av. PR8: Ainsd 9K 11
WA12: Newt W 9L 51
Leamington Cl. CH64: Nest 8E 100
WA5: Gt San 9J 65
Leamington Rd. L11: Norr G 8J 45
PR8: Ainsd 9J 11
Leamoore Cl. L12: Knott A 3D 60
Leander Rd. CH45: Wall 4G 57
Lea Rd. CH44: Wall 4J 57
Leas, The CH45: Wall 2E 56
CH61: Thing 1B 88
Leas Cl. CH66: Gt Sut 9H 103
Leaside WA7: Run 6N 95
WA9: St H 4J 63
LEASOWE 5B 56
Leasowe Av. CH45: Wall 3E 56
Leasowe Gdns.
CH46: Leas 6M 55
Leasowe Golf Course 5N 55
Leasowe Leisure Cen. 6A 56
Leasowe Lighthouse 6K 55
Leasowe (Park & Ride) 7A 56
Leasowe Rd. CH44: Wall 6L 55
CH45: Wall 6L 55
CH46: Leas 6L 55
L9: Aintr 3G 44
Leasoweside CH46: Leas 5A 56
Leasowe Station (Rail) 7N 55
Leas Pk. CH47: Hoy 4B 70
Leatham Cl. WA3: Birchw 6M 67
Leatherbarrows La.
L31: Mag, Mell 4L 35
Leather La. L2: Liv 4E 4
Leather's La. L26: Halew 1K 93
Leathwood L31: Mag 3K 35
Leaway CH49: Grea 4L 71
Leawood Gro. CH46: More 9N 55
L E C Complex L15: Wavtr 9J 59
Leckwith Rd. L30: Neth 9G 34
Leda Gro. *L17: Aig 4H 75*
(off Hesketh St.)
Ledburn WN8: Skel 1E 30
Ledbury Cl. CH43: Oxton 6E 72
L12: Crox 6D 46
WA10: Ec'stn 7E 48
Ledger Rd. WA11: Hay 5C 50
Ledmore Gro. WN4: Garsw 8F 40
LEDSHAM 4E 110
Ledsham Cl. CH43: Noct 4E 72
WA3: Birchw 6K 67
Ledsham Ct. CH66: Lit Sut 8H 103
Ledsham Hall La. CH66: Led 9D 102
Ledsham La. CH66: Led 1D 110
Ledsham Pk. Dr. CH66: Lit Sut 8F 102
Ledsham Rd. CH66: Lit Sut 9E 102
L32: Kirkb 9A 36
Ledsham Village CH66: Led 4E 110
Ledsham Wlk. L32: Kirkb 9A 36
Ledson Gro. L39: Augh 5N 27
Ledson Pk. L33: Kirkb 5D 36
Ledsons Gro. L31: Mell 8M 35
Ledston Cl. WA7: Wind H 6F 96
Ledyard Cl. WA5: Old H 1M 81
Leece St. L1: Liv 7J 5 (9D 58)
Lee Cl. L35: Rainh 8G 63
Lee Ct. CH47: Hoy 1D 70
WA2: Warr 7D 66
Leecourt Cl. L12: W Der 4B 60
Leeds St. L3: Liv 2C 4 (6A 58)
Lee Hall Rd. L25: Gate 3G 77
Leeming Gro. L19: Garst 2A 92
Lee Pk. Av. L25: Gate 3G 77
Lee Pk. Golf Course 4H 77
Lee Rd. CH47: Hoy 1D 70
Lees, The WA5: Gt San 9J 65
(not continuous)
Lees Av. CH42: Rock F 6M 73
Leeside Av. L32: Kirkb 2C 46
Leeside Cl. L32: Kirkb 1D 46
Lees La. CH64: Lit N, Nest 8G 100
CH65: Ell P 1C 112
L12: W Der 2B 60
WN8: Dalt, Roby M 5F 22
Lees Rd. L33: Know I 1F 46
Lee St. WA9: St H 1A 64
Leeswood L22: Wloo 1L 43
WN8: Skel 1E 30
Leeswood Rd. CH49: Wdchu 5A 72
Lee Va. Rd. L25: Gate 4G 76
Lee Valley Millennium Cen. 2G 76
Leeward Dr. L24: Speke 3E 92
Legh Ct. WA3: Golb 2B 52
Legh La. PR4: Tarl 4L 9
Legh Rd. CH62: New F 9A 74
WA11: Hay 4C 50
Legh St. WA1: Warr 3B 82
WA3: Golb 2B 52
WA12: Newt W 7H 51
(not continuous)
WA13: Lymm 5E 84
(off Bridgewater St.)
WN4: Ash M 9K 41
Legion La. CH62: Brom 6C 90
Legion Rd. WA10: St H 1G 62
Leicester Av. L22: Wloo 9K 33
Leicester Rd. L20: Boot 6C 44
Leicester St. PR9: South 6G 7
WA5: Warr 3N 81
(not continuous)
WA9: St H 1G 63
Leigh Av. WA8: Widnes 7J 79
Leigh Bri. Way *L5: Liv 4B 58*
(off New Hedley Gro.)
Leigh Golf Course 6K 53
Leigh Grn. Cl. WA8: Widnes 8F 78
Leigh Pl. L1: Liv 5G 4
Leigh Rd. CH48: W Kir 5C 70
Leighs Hey Cres. L32: Kirkb 9D 36
Leigh St. L1: Liv 5F 4 (8C 58)
(not continuous)
L7: Liv 8J 59
Leighton Av. CH47: Meols 9F 54
L31: Mag 1J 35
Leighton Chase CH64: Nest 5D 100
Leighton Ct. CH64: Nest 6D 100
Leighton Dr. WA9: St H 2M 63
WN7: Leigh 1J 53
Leighton Pk. CH64: Nest 6D 100
Leighton Rd. CH41: Tran 4L 73
CH64: Nest 3C 100
Leightons, The CH64: Nest 6D 100
Leighton St. L4: Kirkd 9D 44
Leinster Gdns. WA7: Run 4J 95
Leinster Rd. L13: Liv 6N 59
Leinster St. WA7: Run 4J 95
Leiria Way WA7: Run 5K 95
Leison St. L4: Kirkd 2C 58
L5: Kirkd 3C 58
Leiston Cl. CH61: Irby 9M 71
Leisure Lakes Cvn. Pk. PR4: Mere B 6H 9
Leisure Lakes Outdoor Pursuits & Watersports Cen. 7H 9
Lemon Cl. L7: Liv 8H 59
Lemon Gro. L8: Liv 2H 75
Lemon St. L5: Kirkd 3C 58
Lemon Tree Wlk. WA10: St H 9G 49
Lendel Cl. L37: Form 1E 24
Lenfield Dr. WA11: Hay 4B 50
Lenham Way L24: Speke 3F 92
Lennox Av. CH45: New B 2H 57
Lennox La. CH43: Bid 8C 56
Lennox Way L7: Liv 7G 59
Lenthall St. L4: W'ton 8E 44
Lenton Av. L37: Form 9D 16
Lenton Rd. L25: Gate 3G 77
Lentworth Ct. L17: Aig 9L 75
Leo Cl. L14: Knott A 5D 60
Leominster Rd. CH44: Wall 5H 57
Leonard Cheshire Dr. L30: Neth 8E 34
Leonard Ho. CH41: Birke 7M 57
Leonards Cl. L36: Huy 3H 61
Leonard St. WA2: Warr 1D 82
WA4: Stockt H 7E 82
WA7: West P 8G 95
WA9: St H 2B 64
Leon Cl. WA5: Gt San 1F 80
Leonora St. L8: Liv 4F 74
Leopold Gro. WA9: Sut L 4M 63
Leopold Rd. L7: Liv 7G 58
(not continuous)
L22: Wloo 9J 33
Leopold St. CH44: Wall 6L 57
Lesley Rd. PR8: South 8K 7
Leslie Av. CH49: Grea 5L 71
Leslie Rd. WA10: St H 1F 62
Lesseps Rd. L8: Liv 1H 75
Lessingham Rd. WA8: Widnes 5J 79
Lester Cl. L4: Kirkd 2D 58
Lester Dr. CH61: Irby 9K 71
WA10: Ec'stn 5D 48
Lester Gro. L36: Huy 5K 61
Lestock St. L8: Liv 1D 74
Leta St. L4: W'ton 9E 44
(not continuous)
Letchworth St. L6: Liv 4H 59
Lethbridge Cl. L5: Kirkd 3B 58
Lethbridge Rd. PR8: South 1C 12
Letitia St. L8: Liv 3E 74
Levens Cl. PR9: Banks 2E 8
WA5: Warr 2A 82
Levens Hey CH46: More 9L 55
Leven St. L4: Kirkd 1D 58
Levens Way WA8: Widnes 8F 78
Leven Wlk. CH66: Ell P 6M 103
Lever Av. CH44: Wall 7L 57
Lever C'way. CH63: H Beb, Store 2G 89
Lever Ct. L1: Liv 7F 4 (9C 58)
Leveret Rd. L24: Speke 4L 93
Leverhulme Ct. CH63: Beb 3N 89
Lever St. WA9: Clock F 6N 63
Lever Ter. *CH42: Tran 5L 73*
(off Summerford Cl.)
Leveson Rd. L13: Liv 8N 59
Levisham Gdns. WA5: Warr 1N 81
Lewis Av. WA5: Warr 7A 66
Lewis Cl. CH65: Ell P 5A 112
Lewis Cres. WA8: Widnes 9K 79
Lewis Gro. WA8: Widnes 7G 79
Lewisham Rd. CH62: Port S 1B 90
L11: Norr G 8L 45
Lewis St. WA10: St H 7H 49
Lewis Wlk. L33: Kirkb 5C 36
Lexden St. WA5: Warr 2N 81
Lexham Rd. L14: Knott A 6A 60
Lexington Wlk. *WA5: Gt San 1L 81*
(off Boston Blvd.)
Lexington Way L33: Kirkb 5C 36
Lexton Dr. PR9: South 4N 7
Leybourne Av. PR8: Ainsd 7M 11
Leybourne Cl. L25: Gate 2E 76
Leybourne Grn. L25: Gate 3E 76
Leybourne Gro. L25: Gate 3E 76
Leybourne Rd. L25: Gate 2E 76
Leyburn Cl. L32: Kirkb 3C 46
(not continuous)
Leyburn Rd. CH45: Wall 3F 56
Ley Cl. WA9: Clock F 5M 63
Leyfield Cl. L12: W Der 3B 60
Leyfield Ct. L12: W Der 3B 60
Leyfield Rd. L12: W Der 3A 60
Leyfield Wlk. L12: W Der 3B 60
Leyfield Way L14: Brd G 7C 60
Leyland Cl. PR9: Banks 2C 8
LEYLAND GREEN 6D 40
Leyland Grn. Rd. WN4: Garsw 6E 40
Leyland Gro. WA11: Hay 4D 50
Leyland Mans. PR9: South 7J 7
Leyland Rd. PR9: South 6H 7
WA11: Rainf 5C 38
Leyland St. L34: Presc 3A 62
Leyland Way L39: Orm 8D 20
Leyton Cl. WA7: Run 9L 95
Liberation Rd. WA12: Newt W 9M 51
Liberton Ct. *L5: Liv 3F 58*
(off St Domingo Va.)
Liberty Cl. WA5: Gt San 1L 81
Liberty Pl. WA10: St H 7G 49
Liberty St. L15: Wavtr 1K 75
Libra Cl. L14: Knott A 4E 60
Library St. WA10: St H 7K 49
Librex Cl. L20: Boot 4B 44
Libson Cl. WA2: Fearn 6H 67
Lichfield Av. L22: Wloo 8K 33
WA3: Low 2E 52
WA4: Grap 9H 83
Lichfield Cl. L30: Neth 1F 44
Lichfield Dr. CH66: Gt Sut 5K 111
Lichfield Gro. WN4: Ash M 9L 41
Lichfield Rd. L15: Wavtr 2M 75
L26: Halew 1J 93
Lichfield St. CH45: New B 2J 57
Lickers La. L35: Whis 7A 62
Liddell Av. L31: Mell 7N 35
Liddell Ct. CH45: Wall 4D 56
Liddell Rd. L12: W Der 2L 59
Lidderdale Ct. *L15: Wavtr 2K 75*
(off Lidderdale Rd.)
Lidderdale Rd. L15: Wavtr 2K 75
Lidgate Cl. L33: Kirkb 6C 36
Liebig Ct. WA8: Widnes 8L 79
Liege Ho. *CH49: Upton 2N 71*
(off Manorside Cl.)
Lifeboat Rd. L37: Form 3A 24
Lifestyles
Alsop 8E 44
Croxteth 6A 46
Everton Pk. 4D 58
Garston 9A 76
Liverpool Aquatics Cen. 1L 75
Liverpool -
Millennium 4F 4
Peter Lloyd 3L 59
Liverpool Tennis Cen. 1L 75
Mill Yard - Cardinal Heenan 4B 60
Norris Green - Ellergreen 8M 45
Speke - Austin Rawlinson 4J 93
Toxteth - Park Road 3E 74
Walton 8G 45
Wavertree Athletics Cen. 1L 75
Liffey Ct. L3: Liv 3K 5
Liffey St. L8: Liv 1G 74
Lifton Rd. L33: Kirkb 9E 36
Lighbox CH41: Birke 2M 73
Lightbody St. L5: Liv 4A 58
Lightbound Rd. CH41: Tran 4L 73
Lightburn St. WA7: Run 6J 95
Light Cinema, The 9H 43
Lightfoot Cl. CH60: Hesw 8B 88
Lightfoot La. CH60: Hesw 8B 88
Lighthorne Dr. PR8: Ainsd 1G 17
Lighthouse La. L37: Form 3G 24
Lighthouse Rd. CH47: Hoy 2C 70
L24: Hale 9B 94
Lightoaks Dr. L26: Halew 7M 77
Lightstream Dr. L24: Speke 1F 92
Lightwood Dr. L7: Liv 9H 59
Lightwood St. L7: Liv 9H 59
Lilac Av. PR8: Ainsd 3K 17
WA5: Gt San 3J 81
WA8: Widnes 6L 79
WN4: Garsw 6F 40
Lilac Cres. WA7: Run 7M 95
Lilac Gro. CH66: Whit 5M 111
L36: Huy 9H 61
WA4: Stockt H 7F 82
WA11: Hay 5B 50
WN5: Bil 7N 39
WN8: Skel 3B 30
Lilac Rd. WA3: Golb 1B 52
Lilac Wlk. M31: Part 6L 69
Lilford Av. L9: W'ton 4E 44
WA5: Warr 9N 65
Lilford Dr. WA5: Gt San 2H 81
Lilford St. WA5: Warr 1A 82
(not continuous)
Lilley Rd. L7: Liv 6J 59
Lillian Rd. L4: W'ton 3G 58
Lille Cl. CH43: Bid 9C 56
Lillyfield CH60: Hesw 9N 87
Lilly Grn. *L4: W'ton 9G 44*
(off Lilly Gro.)
Lilly Gro. L4: W'ton 9G 44
(not continuous)
Lilly Va. L7: Liv 6J 59
Lily Farm Cft. WN4: Ash M 6M 41
Lilyfont Cl. L11: Crox 7A 46
Lily Gro *L7: Liv 8G 59*
(off Dorothy Dr.)
Lily La. WN2: Bam, Platt B 4N 41
Lily Pl. WN4: Ash M 9L 41

Lock Rd.—Lyle St.

Lock Rd. CH62: East 7F **90**
WA1: Padd 2G **83**
Locks, The WA4: Grap 5J **83**
Lock St. WA9: St H 5M **49**
Lockton La. WA5: Warr 1N **81**
Lockton Rd. L34: Know 5F **46**
Lockwood Vw. WA7: Pres B 1H **109**
Loddon Cl. CH49: Upton 1B **72**
Lodge, The CH43: Noct 2D **72**
Lodge Cl. WA13: Lymm 4H **85**
Lodge Dr. WA3: Cul 7N **53**
Lodge Hollow WA6: Hel 1E **114**
Lodge La. CH1: Sau 9D **110**
CH62: Port S 1A **90**
CW9: Ant 9N **99**
L8: Liv 1G **75**
L39: Bic 2N **37**
WA4: Dutt 6L **109**
WA5: Warr 1N **81**
WA7: Hal 7A **96**
WA8: Cron 4D **78**
WA12: Newt W 1K **51**
(not continuous)
Lodge Pl. WA8: Widnes 7G **79**
Lodge Rd. WA8: Widnes 8E **78**
WN5: Orr 8N **31**
Lodge Vw. Cres. L40: Burs 6E **20**
Lodge Works L33: Know I 8G **37**
Lodwick St. L20: Kirkd 9A **44**
Lofthouse Ga. WA8: Widnes 5J **79**
Loftus Rd. L26: Halew 9L **77**
Logan Rd. CH41: Birke 8H **57**
Logfield Dr. L19: Garst 2B **92**
Lognor Rd. L32: Kirkb 9A **36**
Lognor Wlk. L32: Kirkb 9A **36**
Logwood Rd. L36: Huy 9L **61**
Lois Ct. CH45: Wall 3J **57**
Lombard Rd. CH46: More 7N **55**
Lombardy Av. CH49: Grea 6J **71**
Lomond Gro. CH46: More 9N **55**
CH66: Gt Sut 2L **111**
Lomond Rd. L7: Liv 6K **59**
Londonderry Rd. L13: Liv 2J **59**
London Flds. WN5: Bil 6A **40**
London La. PR8: South 7B **12**
London Rd. L3: Liv 4H **5** (7D **58**)
WA4: App, Stockt H, Sttn 7D **82**
WA6: Frod 6L **107**
London Row WA12: Newt W 1M **65**
London Sq. PR9: South 8G **6**
London St. PR9: South 8G **7**
Longacre PR9: South 4L **7**
Longacre Cl. CH45: Wall 4D **56**
Long Acres CH49: Grea 3L **71**
Longacres Rd. CH64: Nest 4E **100**
Long Av. L9: Aintr 4G **45**
Longbarn Blvd. WA2: Birchw 7K **67**
Long Barn La. WA2: Fearn 7J **67**
Longbarn La. WA1: Wools 8L **67**
WA2: Padg 7K **67**
Longbenton Way WA7: Manor P 3D **96**
Longborough Rd. L34: Know 7G **47**
Longbutt La. WA13: Lymm 5F **84**
(not continuous)
Longcliffe Dr. PR8: Ainsd 1H **17**
Longcroft Av. L19: Aller 9B **76**
Longcroft Pl. WA13: Lymm 3J **85**
Longcroft Sq. L19: Aller 9B **76**
Longdale La. L29: Seft 4C **34**
Longden Rd. WN4: Ash M 8J **41**
Longdin St. WA4: Westy 5F **82**
Longdown Rd. L10: Faz 4N **45**
Longfellow Cl. L32: Kirkb 2B **46**
Longfellow Dr. CH62: New F 9N **73**
Longfellow St. L8: Liv 1H **75**
(not continuous)
L20: Boot 5N **43**
Longfield L37: Form 8H **17**
Longfield Av. L23: Crosb 5L **33**
Longfield Cl. CH49: Grea 4L **71**
Longfield Gdns. M44: Cad 5K **69**
WA2: Warr 8D **66**
Longfield Pk. WA9: Clock F 5N **63**
Longfield Rd. L21: Lith 4A **44**
WA2: Warr 8D **66**
Longfield Wlk. L23: Crosb 5L **33**
Longfold L31: Mag 2K **35**
PR4: Mere B 5L **9**
LONGFORD 8C **66**
Longford Dr. WA8: Widnes 6H **79**
Longford Rd. PR8: Birkd 4N **11**
Longford St. L8: Liv 5F **74**
WA2: Warr 1C **82**
Long Hey L35: Whis 7A **62**
WN8: Skel 9F **22**
Long Hey Rd. CH48: Caldy 9F **70**
Long Heys La. WN8: Dalt 9H **23**
Longland Rd. CH45: Wall 3H **57**
Long La. L9: Aintr, Faz 4G **45**
L15: Wavtr 9L **59**
L19: Garst 9A **76**
L29: Thorn 3N **33**
L37: Form 9E **16**
L39: Augh, Bic 1A **28**
PR9: Banks 1F **8**
WA2: Warr 8C **66**
WN8: Uph 9H **31**
Longleat Cl. WA5: Warr 1A **82**
Longlooms Rd. CH65: Ell P 4B **112**
Longlooms Rd. E. CH65: Ell P 4B **112**
Longman Dr. L24: Speke 3F **92**
Longmead Av. WN4: Ash M 7L **41**
Long Mdw. CH60: Hesw 9N **87**
WA10: Ec'stn 6E **48**
Longmeadow Rd. L34: Know 6H **47**
Long Meanygate PR9: South 6D **8**
Longmoor Cl. L10: Faz 3K **45**
Longmoor Gro. L9: Aintr 4G **45**
Longmoor La. L9: Aintr 4G **44**
L10: Faz 3M **45**
Long Moss L30: Neth 8B **34**
Longreach Rd. L14: Knott A 5D **60**
Longridge Av. CH49: Upton 2M **71**
WA11: St H 5N **49**
Longridge Dr. L30: Neth 1F **44**
Longridge Wlk. L4: Kirkd 1D **58**
LONGSHAW 2N **39**
Longshaw Av. WN5: Bil 2A **40**
LONGSHAW BOTTOM 2A **40**
Longshaw Cl. L40: Ruf 1L **15**
WN5: Bil 2A **40**
LONGSHAW COMMON 3A **40**
Longshaw Comn. WN5: Bil 2A **40**
(not continuous)
Longshaw Old Rd. WN5: Bil 2A **40**
Longshaw St. WA5: Warr 7A **66**
Long Spinney WA7: Nort 7E **96**
Longster Cl. WA6: Hel 3E **114**
Longstone Wlk. L7: Liv 9G **58**
Longton Av. WA3: Low 2D **52**
Longton Ct. PR9: South 7J **7**
Longton Dr. L37: Form 7G **17**
Longton La. L35: Rainh 4E **62**
LONGVIEW 4K **61**
Longview Av. CH45: Wall 4G **57**
L35: Rainh 5D **62**
Longview Cres. L36: Huy 6K **61**
Longview Dr. L36: Huy 5K **61**
Longview La. L36: Huy 4K **61**
Longview Rd. L35: Rainh 5D **62**
L36: Huy 6K **61**
Longville St. L8: Liv 3D **74**
Long Wlk. M31: Part 6K **69**
Longwood Cl. WA11: Rainf 1F **48**
Longwood Rd. WA4: App 1F **98**
Longworth Way L25: Woolt 5E **76**
Lonie Gro. WA10: St H 1F **62**
Lonmore Cl. PR9: Banks 2E **8**
Lonsboro Rd. CH44: Wall 6J **57**
Lonsdale Av. CH45: Wall 3G **57**
L39: Orm 6D **20**
WA10: St H 2E **62**
Lonsdale Cl. L21: Ford 9A **34**
WA5: Gt San 9G **65**
WA8: Widnes 8F **78**
Lonsdale M. L21: Ford 9A **34**
Lonsdale Rd. L21: Ford 9A **34**
L26: Halew 1J **93**
L37: Form 1E **24**
PR8: South 2C **12**
Lonsdale Vs. *CH45: Wall* *3G* ***57***
(off Seaview Rd.)
Looe Cl. WA8: Widnes 6H **79**
Looe Rd. L11: Crox 5B **46**
Looms, The CH64: P'gte 4B **100**
Loomsway CH61: Irby 1K **87**
Lopwell Dr. L6: Liv 5F **58**
Loraine St. L5: Liv 4E **58**
Lordens Cl. L14: Knott A 4E **60**
Lordens Rd. L14: Knott A 4E **60**
(not continuous)
Lord Nelson St. L1: Liv 4H **5** (7D **58**)
L3: Liv 4H **5** (7D **58**)
WA1: Warr 3D **82**
Lords Av. CH43: Bid 9C **56**
Lord Sefton Way L37: Gt Alt 2K **25**
Lords Fold WA11: Rainf 4B **38**
Lordsgate Dr. L40: Burs 2J **21**
Lordsgate La. L40: Burs 3G **20**
Lordship La. WA6: Frod 8C **106**
Lords La. WA3: Birchw 5K **67**
Lords St. M44: Cad 4J **69**
Lord St. CH41: Birke 1L **73**
L2: Liv 5E **4** (8B **58**)
L19: Garst 3B **92**
L40: Burs 9J **15**
PR8: South 9F **6**
PR9: South 9F **6**
WA3: Croft 1H **67**
WA4: Warr 4C **82**
WA7: Run 4J **95**
WA10: St H 5J **49**
(not continuous)
WA12: Newt W 7J **51**
WN4: Ash M 7M **41**
Lord St. W. PR8: South 9F **6**
Loreburn Rd. L15: Wavtr 2M **75**
Lorenzo Dr. L11: Norr G 9K **45**
Loretto Dr. CH49: Upton 2A **72**
Loretto Rd. CH44: Wall 4F **56**
Lorna Way M44: Irlam 1N **69**
Lorn Ct. CH41: Birke 2L **73**
Lorne Ct. CH43: Oxton 4H **73**
Lorne Rd. CH43: Oxton 4G **73**
L22: Wloo 1K **43**
Lorne St. L7: Liv 6K **59**
Lorn St. CH41: Birke 2L **73**
Lorton Av. WA11: St H 2K **49**
Lorton St. L8: Liv 1G **75**
Lostock Av. WA5: Warr 9A **66**
Lostock Cl. WN5: Bil 6A **40**
Lothian St. L8: Liv 2F **74**
Lotus Ct. WA5: Warr 4N **81**
Lotus Gdns. WA9: Bold 2C **64**
Loudon Gro. L8: Liv 2F **74**
Lough Grn. CH63: Spit 5N **89**
Loughlin Dr. L33: Kirkb 6D **36**
Loughrigg Av. WA11: St H 1L **49**
Louis Braille Cl. L30: Neth 7E **34**
Louisiana Dr. WA5: Gt San 2K **81**
Louis Pasteur Av. L30: Neth 7E **34**
Loushers La. WA4: Warr 6D **82**
Lovage Cl. WA2: Padg 7K **67**
Lovatt Ct. WA13: Lymm 4H **85**
Lovelace Rd. L19: G'dale 9N **75**
Lovelady Gro. L37: Form 3G **24**
Love La. CH44: Wall 6G **57**
L3: Liv 5B **58**
Lovel Rd. L24: Speke 5H **93**
Lovel Ter. WA8: Hale B 2E **94**
Lovel Way L24: Speke 4H **93**
Lovely La. WA5: Warr 2N **81**
Loves Cotts. L39: Orm 7B **20**
Lovett Dr. L35: Presc 4B **62**
Low Bank Rd. WN4: Ash M 7G **40**
Lowbridge Ct. L19: Garst 1B **92**
Lowcroft WN8: Skel 1F **30**
Lowden Av. L21: Lith 1A **44**
Lowe Av. WA4: Westy 4G **83**
Lowell St. L4: W'ton 9E **44**
Lwr. Alt Rd. L38: Hight 8F **24**
Lwr. Appleton Rd. WA8: Widnes 7L **79**
Lwr. Bank Vw. L20: Kirkd 9A **44**
LOWER BEBINGTON 2N **89**
Lwr. Breck Rd. L6: Liv 3H **59**
Lowerbrook Way L4: Kirkd 2C **58**
Lwr. Carr La. L38: Gt Alt 5A **26**
Lwr. Castle St. L2: Liv 5D **4** (8B **58**)
Lwr. Church St. WA8: Widnes 2K **95**
Lower Cl. L26: Halew 8L **77**
Lwr. Farm Rd. L25: Gate 1E **76**
Lowerfield Gdns. WA3: Golb 1D **52**
Lwr. Flaybrick Rd. CH43: Bid 9E **56**
Lwr. Gill St. L3: Liv 4K **5** (7E **58**)
Lower Grn. CH49: Wdchu 5A **72**
Lwr. Hall St. WA10: St H 6L **49**
Lower Hey L23: Thorn 6A **34**
Lwr. Hill Top Rd. WA4: Stockt H 6G **82**
LOWER HOUSE 8H **79**
Lower Ho. La. L11: Norr G 6M **45**
WA8: Widnes 9J **79**
LOWER IRLAM 1M **69**
Lower La. L9: Faz 3K **45**
Lwr. Mersey St. CH65: Ell P 7A **104**
Lwr. Mersey Vw. L20: Kirkd 9A **44**
Lwr. New Hall Pl. L3: Liv 4C **4**
Lower Promenade PR8: South 8F **6**
PR9: South 7G **6**
Lwr. Rake La. WA6: Hel 1E **114**
Lower Rd. CH62: Port S 1A **90**
L26: Halew 8M **77**
WA8: Hale B 8M **77**
Lwr. Robin Hood La. WA6: Hel 2E **114**
Lower Sandfield L25: Gate 4F **76**
Lowerson Cres. L11: Norr G 1K **59**
Lowerson Rd. L11: Norr G 1K **59**
LOWER STRETTON 7F **98**
Lwr. Thingwall La. CH61: Thing 1C **88**
LOWER WALTON 8C **82**
Lwr. Wash La. WA4: Westy 5F **82**
Lowes Grn. L37: Form 1H **25**
Lowe's La. WN8: Newb 5B **22**
Lowestoft Dr. L19: Garst 1N **91**
Lowe St. WA3: Golb 2B **52**
WA10: St H 6J **49**
Lowe St. Sth. WA10: St H 7J **49**
Loweswater Cl. WA2: Warr 6C **66**
Loweswater Cres. WA11: Hay 4C **50**
Loweswater Way L33: Kirkb 6B **36**
Lowfield La. WA9: St H 3J **63**
Lowfield Rd. L14: Knott A 6A **60**
Lowfields Av. CH62: East 3C **102**
Lowfields Cl. CH62: East 3D **102**
Low Hill L6: Liv 2M **5** (6F **58**)
L7: Liv 4M **5** (7F **58**)
WA6: Dun H 8A **114**
Lowlands Rd. WA7: Run 5J **95**
Lowndes Rd. L6: Liv 3J **59**
Lowry Bank CH44: Wall 6L **57**
Lowry Cl. L33: Kirkb 5C **36**
WA5: Gt San 2M **81**
Lowry Hill La. L40: Lath 3M **21**
Lowther Av. L10: Aintr 9J **35**
L31: Mag 1K **35**
WA3: Cul 6N **53**
Lowther Cres. WA10: St H 1E **62**
Lowther Dr. L35: Rainh 6E **62**
Lowther St. L8: Liv 9M **5** (1F **74**)
Lowther Ter. WN6: App B 5M **23**
LOWTON 3G **53**
Lowton Bus. Pk. WA3: Low 2H **53**
LOWTON COMMON 1H **53**
Lowton Gdns. WA3: Low 5C **52**
LOWTON HEATH 4D **52**
Lowton Rd. WA3: Golb 1C **52**
LOWTON ST MARY'S 3H **53**
Lowton St Mary's By-Pass 3K **53**
Low Wood L38: Hight 6F **24**
Low Wood Gro. CH61: Barns 3C **88**
Lowwood Gro. CH41: Birke 3K **73**
Lowwood Rd. CH41: Birke 3K **73**
Low Wood St. L6: Liv 3M **5** (6F **58**)
Loxdale Cl. L8: Liv 4F **74**
Loxdale Dr. CH65: Gt Sut 2L **111**
Loxley Cl. WA5: Gt San 9J **65**
Loxley Rd. PR8: South 2C **12**
Loxton Cres. WN3: Wigan 1K **41**
Loxwood Cl. L25: Gate 1F **76**
Loyola Hey L35: Rainh 9H **63**
Lucan Rd. L17: Aig 6K **75**
Lucas Ct. *L35: Rainh* *5F* ***62***
(off Ratcliffe Pl.)
Lucerne Rd. CH44: Wall 7K **57**
Lucerne St. L17: Aig 5H **75**
Lucius Cl. L9: W'ton 3E **44**
Lucknow St. L17: Aig 4H **75**
Ludlow WN8: Skel 9F **22**
Ludlow Cl. WA1: Padg 8J **67**
Ludlow Ct. CH48: W Kir 7C **70**
Ludlow Cres. WA7: Run 7L **95**
Ludlow Dr. CH48: W Kir 7C **70**
CH65: Ell P 2C **112**
L39: Orm 6B **20**
Ludlow Gro. CH62: Brom 6C **90**
Ludlow St. L4: Kirkd 9E **44**
Ludwig Rd. L4: W'ton 3G **58**
Lugard Rd. L17: Aig 6K **75**
LUGSDALE 9M **79**
Lugsdale Rd. WA8: Widnes 9K **79**
Lugsmore La. WA10: St H 9G **48**
Luke St. CH44: Wall 7L **57**
L8: Liv 2E **74**
WN4: Ash M 6M **41**
Lulworth WN8: Skel 9E **22**
Lulworth Av. L22: Wloo 9J **33**
Lulworth Lodge PR8: Birkd 1M **11**
Lulworth Pl. WA4: Warr 7C **82**
Lulworth Rd. L25: Gate 3G **77**
PR8: Birkd 2M **11**
Lulworth Vw. PR8: Birkd 2L **11**
Lumb Brook M. WA4: Stockt H 7F **82**
Lumb Brook Rd. WA4: App, App T 9G **83**
Lumbbrook Rd. WA4: App 7F **82**
Lumber La. WA5: Burtw 1G **65**
Lumina CH62: Brom 5D **90**
Lumley Rd. CH44: Wall 6K **57**
Lumley St. L19: Garst 9N **75**
Lumley Wlk. L24: Hale 6B **94**
Lunar Dr. L30: Neth 6E **34**
Lunar Rd. L9: Aintr 4G **44**
Lunds Cl. L40: Westh 9J **21**
Lundy Dr. CH65: Ell P 5A **112**
Lune Av. L31: Mag 1K **35**
Lunehurst WA3: Low 2F **52**
Lunesdale Av. L9: Aintr 3G **44**
Lune St. L23: Crosb 7L **33**
Lune Way WA8: Widnes 7F **78**
Lunsford Rd. L14: Knott A 5D **60**
LUNT 3C **34**
Lunt Av. L30: Neth 9F **34**
L35: Whis 6B **62**
Lunt La. L29: Seft 3C **34**
Lunt Rd. L20: Boot 4B **44**
L29: Seft, Thorn 2B **34**
LUNTS HEATH 4L **79**
Lunt's Heath Rd. WA8: Widnes 3K **79**
Lunt's La. L37: Form 3G **25**
Luntswood Gro. WA12: Newt W 6J **51**
Lupin Dr. WA11: Hay 4H **51**
Lupton Dr. L23: Crosb 7N **33**
Lupus Way CH66: Gt Sut 2L **111**
Luscombe Cl. L26: Halew 8L **77**
Lusitania Rd. L4: W'ton 8F **44**
Luther Gro. WA9: St H 8D **50**
Luton Gro. L4: W'ton 1E **58**
Luton Rd. CH65: Ell P 9L **103**
Luton St. L5: Kirkd 3A **58**
WA8: Widnes 9K **79**
Lutyens Cl. L4: W'ton 1E **58**
Luxmore Rd. L4: W'ton 9F **44**
Lybro Way L7: Liv 8G **59**
Lycett Rd. CH44: Wall 4E **56**
L4: W'ton 2H **59**
Lyceum Pl. L1: Liv 6G **5**
Lychgate WA4: H Walt 9A **82**
Lycroft Cl. WA7: Run 9L **95**
Lydbrook Cl. CH42: Rock F 5M **73**
Lydbury Cl. WA5: Call 7M **65**
Lydbury Cres. L32: Kirkb 2D **46**
Lydden Rd. CH65: Ell P 7N **103**
Lydford Rd. L12: W Der 1N **59**
Lydia Ann St. L1: Liv 7F **4** (9C **58**)
LYDIATE 7G **27**
Lydiate, The CH60: Hesw 8N **87**
Lydiate La. CH64: Will 6L **101**
L23: Seft, Thorn 5A **34**
L25: Woolt 6G **77**
L26: Halew 6H **77**
L29: Thorn 5A **34**
WA7: West P 8G **95**
Lydiate Pk. L23: Thorn 5A **34**
Lydiate Rd. L20: Boot 5B **44**
Lydiate Sta. Rd. L31: Lydi 8B **26**
Lydia Wlk. L10: Faz 3N **45**
Lydieth Lea L27: N'ley 2J **77**
Lydney Rd. L36: Huy 5F **60**
Lydstep Ct. WA5: Call 7N **65**
Lyelake Cl. L32: Kirkb 1D **46**
Lyelake Gdns. *L32: Kirkb* *1D* ***46***
(off Lyelake Rd.)
Lyelake La. L39: Bic 2K **29**
L40: Westh 2K **29**
Lyelake Rd. L32: Kirkb 1D **46**
Lyle St. L5: Liv 4C **58**

Lyme Cl.—Manorfield Cl.

Lyme Cl. L36: Huy 3L 61
Lymecroft L25: Woolt 6D 76
Lyme Cross Rd. L36: Huy 3J 61
Lyme Gro. L36: Huy 4J 61
WA13: Lymm 6C 84
Lyme St. WA1: Warr 3C 82
WA11: Hay 4G 50
WA12: Newt W 6G 51
Lyme Tree Ct. WA8: Cron 2F 78
Lymewood Ct. WA11: Hay 3G 50
Lymington Gro. L30: Neth 8E 34
Lymington Rd. CH44: Wall 5F 56
LYMM 5E 84
Lymm Bri. WA13: Lymm 5E 84
Lymm Golf Course 3D 84
Lymm Hall WA13: Lymm 5E 84
Lymmhay La. WA13: Lymm 4E 84
Lymmington Av.
WA13: Lymm 5C 84
Lymm Leisure Cen. 6H 85
Lymm Quay WA13: Lymm 5E 84
Lymm Rd. CH43: Bid 1D 72
WA4: Thel 5M 83
WA13: Lymm 7L 85
WA14: L Boll 7L 85
Lynas Gdns. L19: G'dale 8N 75
Lynas St. CH41: Birke 9K 57
Lyncastle Rd. WA4: App T 4K 99
Lyncastle Way WA4: App T 3L 99
Lyncot Rd. L9: Aintr 2G 44
Lyncroft Rd. CH44: Wall 7J 57
Lyndale WA7: Run 7M 95
WN8: Skel 9E 22
Lyndale Av. CH62: East 2D 102
WA2: Fearn 7G 67
WA2: Warr 9E 66
Lyndene Rd. L25: Gate 2E 76
Lyndhurst L31: Mag 2J 35
WN8: Skel 9E 22
Lyndhurst Av. CH61: Pens 4A 88
L18: Moss H 5L 75
Lyndhurst Cl. CH61: Thing 2A 88
Lyndhurst Rd. CH45: Wall 3F 56
CH47: Meols 8F 54
CH61: Irby 2K 87
L18: Moss H 4L 75
L23: Crosb 7N 33
PR8: Birkd 4N 11
Lyndhurst Way L36: Huy 7J 61
Lyndon Dr. L18: Moss H 4N 75
Lyndon Gro. WA7: Run 7L 95
Lyndor Cl. L25: Woolt 7F 76
Lyndor Rd. L25: Woolt 7F 76
Lyneal Av. CH66: Gt Sut 2H 111
Lyneham L35: Whis 7C 62
Lynham Av. WA5: Gt San 3K 81
Lynholme Rd. L4: W'ton 2G 59
Lynmouth Rd. L17: Aig 8K 75
Lynnbank CH43: Oxton 4H 73
Lynnbank Rd. L18: Moss H 3B 76
Lynn Cl. WA7: Run 8M 95
WA10: St H 6F 48
Lynndene CH66: Lit Sut 7J 103
Lynscott Pl. L16: Child 9B 60
Lynsted Rd. L14: Knott A 5D 60
Lynthorpe Av. M44: Cad 3K 69
Lynton Av. M44: Cad 3L 69
Lynton Cl. CH60: Hesw 9B 88
L19: Aller 8N 75
WA5: Penk 4G 80
Lynton Ct. L23: Blun 7H 33
Lynton Cres. WA8: Widnes 6H 79
Lynton Dr. CH63: Beb 4N 89
PR8: Birkd 5L 11
Lynton Gdns. WA4: App 3E 98
Lynton Grn. L25: Woolt 4D 76
Lynton Gro. WA9: Sut L 4M 63
Lynton Rd. CH45: Wall 3E 56
L36: Huy 6M 61
PR8: Birkd 6L 11
Lynton Way WA10: Windle 4E 48
Lynwood Av. CH44: Wall 6G 57
L39: Augh 1A 28
WA3: Low 4F 52
WA4: App 9D 82
Lynwood Cl. WN8: Skel 5G 31
Lynwood Dr. CH61: Irby 1M 87
Lynwood End L39: Augh 1A 28
Lynwood Gdns. L9: W'ton 5E 44
Lynwood Rd. L9: W'ton 5E 44
Lynxway, The L12: Knott A 5B 60
Lyon Cl. WA10: St H 7J 49
Lyon Ct. WA4: Warr 5G 82
Lyon Ind. Est. WA9: St H 3A 64
Lyon Rd. L4: W'ton 3G 58
Lyons Cl. CH46: More 8M 55
Lyons La. WA4: App 1E 98
(not continuous)
Lyons Pl. L25: Hunts X 8H 77
Lyons Rd. CH46: More 8M 55
PR8: Birkd 1N 11
WA5: Penk 4H 81
Lyon St. L19: Garst 3A 92
WA4: Warr 5G 82
WA10: St H 7H 49
WN4: Ash M 4H 41
Lyra Rd. L22: Wloo 1K 43
Lysander Cl. L6: Liv 5F 58
Lysander Dr. WA2: Padg 7F 66
Lyster Cl. WA3: Birchw 6N 67
Lyster Rd. L20: Boot 7N 43
Lytham Cl. L10: Faz 1L 45
WA5: Gt San 5J 81
Lytham Ct. L32: Kirkb 7A 36
Lytham Rd. PR9: South 3M 7
WA8: Widnes 6L 79
WN4: Ash M 6H 41
Lytham Way L12: W Der 3D 60
Lytherton Av. M44: Cad 5K 69
Lythgoes La. WA2: Warr 2C 82
(not continuous)
Lytles Cl. L37: Form 2G 24
Lyttelton Rd. L17: Aig 6K 75
Lytton Av. CH42: Rock F 7M 73
Lytton Gro. *L21: Sea* *4N 43*
(off Ash Gro.)
Lytton St. L6: Liv 1L 5 (6E 58)

M

Maberley Vw. L15: Wavtr 8M 59
Maberry Cl. WN6: Shev 6N 23
Mab La. L12: W Der 1D 60
McAllester Lodge *CH43: Oxton* *4F 72*
(off Bidston Rd.)
Macalpine Cl. CH49: Upton 2A 72
Macbeth St. L20: Kirkd 9B 44
McBride St. L19: Garst 1A 92
McCabe Way WA10: St H 3J 49
McCarthy Cl. WA3: Birchw 6A 68
McClellan Pl. WA8: Widnes 7L 79
McCormack Av. WA9: St H 6A 50
McCorquodale Gdns.
WA12: Newt W 7N 51
McCulloch St. WA9: St H 7M 49
Macdermott Rd. WA8: Widnes 2J 95
Macdona Dr. CH48: W Kir 8C 70
Macdonald Av. WA11: St H 5A 50
Macdonald Dr. CH49: Grea 5L 71
Macdonald Rd. CH46: More 9K 55
M44: Irlam 2L 69
Macdonald St. L15: Wavtr 9K 59
Mace Rd. L11: Crox 7A 46
McFarlane Av. WA10: St H 6F 48
Macfarren St. L13: Liv 6M 59
McGarva Way CH65: Ell P 1A 112
McGill Ct. *CH41: Birke* *1K 73*
(off Cathcart St.)
McGough Cl. WA9: Sut M 6K 63
McKeagney Gdns. WA8: Widnes 9G 78
McKee Av. WA2: Warr 7C 66
Mackenzie Rd. CH46: Leas 6B 56
McKeown Cl. L5: Liv 4C 58
Mackets Cl. L25: Woolt 7G 76
Macket's La. L25: Woolt, Hunts X 6G 77
Mack Gro. L30: Neth 9C 34
McKinley St. WA5: Gt San 1J 81
McKinley Way WA8: Widnes 5J 79
McManus Dr. WA9: St H 8L 49
McMinnis Av. WA9: St H 8C 50
McNair Hall L18: Moss H 5L 75
Macqueen St. L13: Liv 7M 59
McVinnie Rd. L35: Presc 3C 62
Maddock Rd. CH44: Wall 4K 57
Maddocks St. L13: Liv 7M 59
Maddock St. CH41: Birke 9J 57
Maddrell St. L3: Liv 5A 58
Madeira Dr. L25: Gate 2F 76
Madelaine St. L8: Liv 2F 74
Madeleine McKenna Ct. WA8: Widnes 5E 78
Madeley Cl. CH48: W Kir 7C 70
WN3: Wigan 1G 41
Madeley Dr. CH48: W Kir 7C 70
WA9: St H 4J 63
Madeley St. L6: Liv 6H 59
Madingley Ct. PR9: South 5L 7
Madison Cl. WA9: St H 9B 50
Madison Sq. L1: Liv 8H 5 (9D 58)
Madryn Av. L33: Kirkb 9E 36
Madryn St. L8: Liv 3F 74
Maelor Cl. CH63: Brom 9B 90
Maesbrook Cl. PR9: Banks 2F 8
Mafeking Cl. L15: Wavtr 8L 59
Mafeking Pl. WN4: Ash M 8L 41
Magazine Av. CH45: New B 2H 57
Magazine Brow CH45: New B 2J 57
Magazine La. CH45: New B 2H 57
Magazine Rd. CH62: Brom 4C 90
Magazines Prom. CH45: New B 1J 57
Magazine Wlk. CH62: Brom 4C 90
Magdala St. L8: Liv 1H 75
Magdalen Dr. WN4: Ash M 7H 41
Magdalene Wlk. *CH65: Ell P* *1C 112*
(off Robinson Rd.)
Magdalen Ho. L20: Boot 8B 44
Magdalen Sq. L30: Neth 7E 34
Magenta Av. M44: Irlam 3L 69
Maggots Nook Rd. WA11: Rainf 2D 38
MAGHULL 1J 35
Maghull La. L31: Mag 2N 35
Maghull Smallholdings Est.
L31: Mag 9M 27
Maghull Station (Rail) 4K 35
Magistrates' Court
Liverpool 6E 4
Runcorn (Halton) 7B 96
Sefton 7B 44
Warrington 4B 82
Wirral 2M 73
Mag La. WA13: Lymm 9F 84
WA16: High L 9F 84
Magnolia Cl. CH66: Gt Sut 4L 111
L26: Halew 6H 77
M31: Part *7L 69*
(off Redbrook Rd.)
WA1: Wools 1M 83
WA11: Hay 5B 50
Magnolia Dr. WA7: Beech 2B 108
Magnolia Wlk. CH49: Grea 6K 71
Magnus Cl. L13: Liv 4L 59
Maguire Av. L20: Boot 6D 44
Mahon Av. L20: Boot 4C 44
Mahon Ct. L8: Liv 9K 5
Maiden Cl. WN8: Skel 2N 29
Maiden Gdns. CH65: Ell P 2B 112
Maiden La. L13: Liv 2J 59
Maidford Rd. L14: Knott A 4D 60
Maidstone Cl. L25: Hunts X 8G 77
Maidstone Dr. L12: W Der 4D 60
Main Av. PR9: Banks 4H 9
WA10: St H 1F 62
Main Cl. WA11: Hay 4C 50
Main Dr. L35: Whis 8A 62
Maine Gdns. WA5: Gt San 1J 81
Main Front L35: Whis 9B 62
Main La. WA3: Croft 7F 52
Main Rd. CH62: Port S 3A 90
Mainsail Cl. L3: Liv 5B 58
Mainside Rd. L32: Kirkb 1D 46
Main St. WA6: Frod 6K 107
WA7: Hal 6B 96
WN5: Bil 7N 39
Maintree Cres. L24: Speke 3L 93
Mainwaring Rd. CH44: Wall 6K 57
CH62: Brom 7C 90
Mairesfield Av. WA4: Grap 6J 83
Mairscough La. L31: Lydi 4F 26
L39: Down 4F 26
Maisemore Flds. WA8: Widnes 5H 79
Maitland Cl. L8: Liv 1G 75
Maitland Rd. CH45: New B 1J 57
Maitland St. L8: Liv 1G 75
Majestic Cl. L11: Crox 7A 46
Majestic M. WN5: Orr 7N 31
Major Cross St. WA8: Widnes 9K 79
Major St. L5: Kirkd 3C 58
Makepeace Wlk. *L8: Liv* *2E 74*
(off Thackeray Cl.)
Makerfield Dr. WA12: Newt W 5J 51
Makin St. L4: W'ton 8E 44
Malachys Way L8: Liv 3D 74
Malahide Ct. WA8: Widnes 6H 79
Malcolm Av. WA2: Warr 8E 66
Malcolm Cres. CH63: Brom 9B 90
Malcolm Gro. L20: Kirkd 9C 44
Malcolm Pl. L15: Wavtr 8L 59
Malcolm St. WA7: Run 5L 95
Malden Rd. L6: Liv 6H 59
WA12: Newt W 9M 51
Maldon Cl. L26: Halew 1K 93
Maldwyn Rd. CH44: Wall 4H 57
Maley Cl. L8: Liv 4F 74
Malham Av. WN3: Wigan 1J 41
Malham Cl. PR8: South 3D 12
WA5: Gt San 9G 65
Malhamdale Av. L35: Rainh 7G 63
Malika Pl. WN4: Ash M 5G 41
Malin Cl. L24: Hale 5A 94
Maliston Rd. WA5: Gt San 3K 81
Mall, The L5: Liv 4F 58
L39: Orm 8C 20
WA1: Warr *3C 82*
(within Golden Sq. Shop. Cen.)
Mallaby Ct. *CH41: Birke* *9G 57*
(off Mallaby St.)
Mallaby St. CH41: Birke 9G 57
Mallard Cl. L12: Crox 7D 46
L26: Halew 7J 77
L39: Augh 2A 28
WA2: Warr 6E 66
WA7: Beech 1B 108
Mallard Gdns. WA9: St H 3H 63
Mallard Ho. L31: Lydi 8G 27
Mallard La. WA3: Birchw 6N 67
Mallards, The PR9: South 4A 8
Mallard Way CH46: More 8K 55
WA11: St H 4L 49
Mallee Av. PR9: South 4M 7
Mallee Cres. PR9: South 4M 7
Malleson Rd. L13: Liv 2K 59
Malley Cl. CH49: Upton 5N 71
Mallins Cl. L8: Liv 4F 74
Mallory Av. L31: Lydi 8G 27
Mallory Gro. WA11: St H 4N 49
Mallory Rd. CH42: Tran 6K 73
CH65: Whit 1M 111
Mallowdale Cl. CH62: East 1E 102
Mallow Rd. L6: Liv 6H 59
Mallow Wlk. *M31: Part* *7M 69*
(off Broom Rd.)
Mallow Way L36: Huy 9K 61
Malmesbury Cl. CH49: Grea 4K 71
Malmesbury Pk. WA7: Nort 4F 96
Malmesbury Rd. L11: Norr G 8K 45
Malpas Av. CH43: Pren 6G 72
Malpas Dr. CH63: H Beb 9L 73
WA5: Gt San 3L 81
Malpas Gro. CH45: Wall 3G 56
Malpas Rd. CH45: Wall 3F 56
CH65: Gt Sut 1L 111
L11: Crox 5B 46
WA7: Run 8L 95
Malpas Way WA5: Gt San 4L 81
Malta Cl. L36: Huy 6H 61
Malta St. L8: Liv 3E 74
Malta Wlk. L8: Liv 3E 74
Maltby Cl. WA9: St H 4H 63
Malt Ho. Ct. WA10: Windle 4F 48
Maltkiln La. L39: Augh 3B 28
Maltmans Rd. WA13: Lymm 5D 84
Malton Av. WA3: Low 3F 52
Malton Cl. WA8: Cron 3F 78
Malton Rd. L25: Woolt 7F 76
Malt St. L7: Liv 9G 58
Malvern Av. CH65: Ell P 2A 112
L14: Brd G 7D 60
Malvern Cl. L32: Kirkb 7A 36
WA5: Gt San 9J 65
WN3: Winst 1E 40
WN4: Ash M 7K 41
Malvern Ct. PR8: South 9F 6
Malvern Cres. L14: Brd G 7D 60
Malvern Gdns. PR8: South 9F 6
Malvern Gro. CH42: Tran 6K 73
L10: Aintr 9H 35
Malvern Rd. CH45: Wall 4D 56
L6: Liv 6H 59
L20: Boot 5B 44
WA9: St H 7B 50
Malwood St. L8: Liv 4E 74
Manchester New Rd. M31: Part 6M 69
Manchester Rd. L34: Presc 3M 61
M31: Carr, Part 5M 69
PR9: South 7H 7
WA1: Padd, Warr, Wools 2D 82
WA3: Rix, Wools 1A 84
Manchester Row WA12: Newt W 1M 65
Mancroft Cl. WA1: Wools 1M 83
Mandarin Ct. WA1: Warr 5B 82
Mandela Ct. L8: Liv 3G 74
Manderston Dr. L12: W Der 2B 60
Manderville Cl. WN3: Winst 1F 40
Mandeville Rd. PR8: Ainsd 9H 11
Mandeville St. L4: W'ton 8E 44
Manesty's La. L1: Liv 6F 4 (8C 58)
Manfield WN8: Skel 1D 30
Manfred St. L6: Liv 3M 5 (7F 58)
Manhattan Gdns. WA5: Gt San 9K 65
Manica Cres. L10: Faz 3L 45
Manion Av. L31: Lydi 7G 26
Manion Cl. L31: Lydi 7G 26
MANLEY 9J 115
Manley Cl. CH43: Oxton 5F 72
MANLEY COMMON 8M 115
Manley Gdns. WA5: Warr 3A 82
Manley La. WA6: Dun H, Manl 8B 114
(not continuous)
Manley Mere Sail Sports & Adventure Trail
8D 114
Manley Pl. WA9: St H 2H 63
Manley Quarry WA6: Manl 8G 115
Manley Rd. L22: Wloo 9J 33
L36: Huy 9L 61
WA6: Alv, Frod 6K 115
WA6: Alv, Manl 5G 115
Manley Vw. CH2: Elt 2N 113
Manna Dr. CH2: Elt 2N 113
Mannering Ct. *L17: Aig* *4H 75*
(off Mannering Rd.)
Mannering Rd. L17: Aig 4G 75
Manners La. CH60: Hesw 9M 87
Manningham Rd. L4: W'ton 3G 59
Manning Rd. PR8: South 9K 7
Manning St. WA10: St H 7J 49
Mannington Cl. CH47: Meols 9F 54
Mann Island L3: Liv 6C 4 (8B 58)
Mann Island Apts. L3: Liv 6D 4 (8A 58)
Mann St. L8: Liv 2D 74
Manor, The CH66: Lit Sut 8E 102
WA1: Wools 1N 83
WA11: Rainf 7F 38
Manor Av. L23: Crosb 6K 33
L35: Rainh 7F 62
L40: Burs 3H 21
WA3: Golb 2D 52
WA12: Newt W 6H 51
Manorbier Cres. L9: W'ton 7F 44
Manor Cl. CH64: P'gte 7C 100
L20: Boot 8D 44
WA1: Wools 1L 83
WA13: Lymm 6E 84
WN4: Garsw 8E 40
Manor Complex L33: Know I 9G 36
Manor Ct. *CH48: W Kir* *5B 70*
(off Bridge Rd.)
CH49: Grea 5K 71
CH61: Irby 1L 87
WA3: Golb 2D 52
WA9: Sut L 5N 63
Manor Cres. L25: Woolt 7F 76
L40: Burs 3H 21
Manor Dr. CH49: Upton 1N 71
L23: Crosb 6K 33
L30: Neth 8G 34
L40: Burs 3H 21
Mnr. Farm Ct. WA6: Frod 5M 107
Mnr. Farm Ctyd. WA4: Moore 2K 97
Mnr. Farm Cres. CH1: Cap 5G 110
Mnr. Farm M. WA7: Manor P 3F 96
Mnr. Farm Rd. L36: Huy 8K 61
WA7: Manor P 3E 96
Manor Fell WA7: Pal F 8D 96
Manorfield Cl. CH1: Cap 4F 110

Manor Gdns.—Martin Gro.

Manor Gdns. L40: Burs 3H 21
MANOR GREEN 1C 72
Manor Gro. L32: Kirkb 9N 35
WN8: Skel 3C 30
Manor Hill CH43: Clau, Oxton 2G 72
Manor Ho. CH62: Brom 7C 90
CH66: Gt Sut 3J 111
(off Kelmscott Cl.)
L17: Aig 5G 75
L31: Mag 2G 34
Manor Ho., The CH49: Upton 1N 71
Manor Ho. Cl. L31: Mag 2H 35
L40: Ruf 2N 15
WA11: St H 1K 49
Manor Ho. Dr. WN8: Skel 9H 31
Manorial Rd. CH64: P'gte 6C 100
Manorial Rd. Sth. CH64: P'gte 6C 100
Manor Ind. Est. WA4: Westy 4F 82
Manor La. CH42: Rock F 6N 73
CH45: Wall 4J 57
CH66: Gt Sut 2J 111
Manor Lodge L37: Form 9E 16
Manor M. CH45: Wall 4J 57
MANOR PARK 3E 96
Manor Pk. Av. WA7: Manor P 3E 96
Manor Pk. Bus. Pk. WA7: Manor P 3D 96
Manor Pk. Cl. CH61: Thing 1A 88
Manor Pk. Ct. WA7: Manor P 3E 96
Manor Pk. Dr. CH66: Gt Sut 3J 111
Manor Pl. CH62: Brom 2C 90
WA8: Widnes 7E 78
Manor Rd. CH44: Wall 4H 57
CH45: Wall 4H 57
CH47: Hoy 9D 54
CH61: Irby 1L 87
CH62: East 9C 90
CH63: Brim, Thorn H 6F 88
L23: Blun, Crosb 5J 33
L25: Woolt 7F 76
L40: Burs 3H 21
PR9: South 5M 7
WA6: Frod 5M 107
WA7: Run 5N 95
WA8: Widnes 7E 78
WA11: Hay 3H 51
WA13: Lymm 6E 84
(not continuous)
Manor Road Station (Rail) 1D 70
Manorside Cl. CH49: Upton 2N 71
Manor St. WA3: Golb 1C 52
WA9: St H 8M 49
Manor Vw. L12: W Der 9D 46
Manor Way CH43: Bid 1C 72
L25: Woolt 7F 76
(not continuous)
Manorwood Dr. L35: Whis 7B 62
Mansart Cl. WN4: Ash M 8M 41
Manse Gdns. WA12: Newt W 6M 51
Mansell Cl. WA8: Widnes 3M 79
Mansell Dr. L26: Halew 1J 93
Mansell Rd. L6: Liv 6G 59
Mansfield Cl. WA3: Birchw 5A 68
Mansfield Rd. CH65: Whit 3M 111
L20: Boot 8B 44
Mansfield St. L3: Liv 2H 5 (6D 58)
WA3: Golb 1A 52
Mansion Dr. L11: Crox 6N 45
Manston Rd. WA5: Penk 5H 81
Manton Rd. L6: Liv 6H 59
Manton Way WA9: St H 5H 63
Manvers Rd. L16: Child 9C 60
Manville Rd. CH45: New B 2H 57
Manville St. WA9: St H 9M 49
Manx Jane's La. PR9: South 3M 7
Manx Rd. WA4: Warr 5C 82
Maori Dr. WA6: Frod 6K 107
Maple Av. CH66: Lit Sut 8H 103
L40: Burs 1J 21
WA3: Low 3G 53
WA7: Run 7M 95
WA7: Sut W 2C 108
WA8: Widnes 7L 79
WA11: Hay 3D 50
WA12: Newt W 8M 51
Maple Cl. L12: Crox 7B 46
L21: Sea 4N 43
L35: Whis 6B 62
L37: Form 3C 24
WN5: Bil 6N 39
Maple Ct. L21: Lith 2A 44
L34: Know 6G 47
WN8: Skel 6C 30
Maple Cres. L36: Roby 7H 61
WA5: Penk 4H 81
Mapledale Rd. L18: Moss H 3N 75
Maple Gro. CH62: Brom 7B 90
CH66: Whit 4M 111
L8: Liv 2H 75
L35: Presc 4B 62
WA4: Warr 5E 82
WA10: St H 7F 48
Maple Leaf Dr. L36: Huy 3H 61
Maple Rd. M31: Part 6L 69
WA1: Wools 1M 83
WA2: Winw 3C 66
Maples Ct. CH43: Oxton 5G 73
Maple St. CH41: Birke 3K 73
PR8: South 9J 7
WN4: Ash M 5J 41
Mapleton Cl. CH43: Pren 7E 72
Mapleton Dr. WA7: Sut W 3B 108
Maple Tree Gro. CH60: Hesw 7C 88
Maple Vw. WN8: Skel 6C 30
Maplewood L32: Kirkb 2D 46
PR9: South 5L 7
WN8: Skel 9D 22
Maplewood Cl. L27: N'ley 3J 77
WA8: Widnes 9D 78
Maplewood Gro. CH43: Bid 9E 56
Mapplewell Cres.
WA5: Gt San 2J 81
Marathon Cl. L6: Liv 5E 58
Marble Pl. Shop. Cen. 8G 6
Marbury Gdns. CH65: Ell P 8L 103
Marbury Rd. L32: Kirkb 9A 36
Marbury St. WA4: Warr 5D 82
Marc Av. L31: Mell 7N 35
Marcham Way L11: Norr G 9N 45
Marchbank Rd. WN8: Skel 3A 30
Marchfield Rd. L9: W'ton 5E 44
Marchmont Dr. L23: Crosb 8M 33
March Rd. L6: Liv 4J 59
Marchweil Rd. CH65: Ell P 1B 112
Marchwood Way L25: Gate 1E 76
Marcien Way WA8: Widnes 5J 79
Marcot Rd. L6: Liv 5J 59
Marcross Cl. WA5: Call 8N 65
Marcus Ct. L36: Huy 5L 61
(off Mosscroft Cl.)
Marcus St. CH41: Birke 9K 57
(not continuous)
Mardale Av. WA2: Warr 6C 66
WA11: St H 2L 49
Mardale Cl. L27: N'ley 5L 77
PR8: Ainsd 1H 17
Mardale Cres.
WA13: Lymm 5F 84
Mardale Lawn L27: N'ley 5L 77
Mardale Rd. L36: Huy 4G 60
Mardale Wlk. L27: N'ley 5L 77
(off Mardale Cl.)
L36: Huy 4G 61
Maregreen Rd. L4: Kirkd 2C 58
Mare Hall La. CH64: Nest 6H 101
Mareth Cl. L18: Moss H 6M 75
Marford Rd. L12: W Der 2N 59
Marfords Av. CH63: Brom 8B 90
Margaret Av. L20: Boot 4B 44
WA1: Wools 1J 83
WA9: St H 1M 63
Margaret Ct. WA8: Widnes 9L 79
WA10: St H 9G 49
Margaret Rd. L4: W'ton 8D 44
L23: Blun 6G 32
Margaret's La. CH66: Chil T 7E 102
Margaret St. L6: Liv 1M 5 (5F 58)
WA9: Clock F 6A 64
Margery Rd. WA10: St H 9F 48
Marian Av. WA12: Newt W 7H 51
Marian Cl. L35: Rainh 7F 62
Marian Cl., The L30: Neth 7D 34
Marian Dr. CH46: More 9M 55
L35: Rainh 7E 62
Marian Rd. WA11: Hay 3G 51
Marians Dr. L39: Orm 5C 20
Marian Sq. L30: Neth 8E 34
Marian Way, The L30: Neth 8D 34
Maria Rd. L9: W'ton 7E 44
Marie Curie Av. L30: Neth 7E 34
(not continuous)
Marie Dr. WA4: Thel 7L 83
Marigold Pl. WA5: Warr 5N 81
Marigold Way WA9: Bold 2C 64
Marina Av. L21: Lith 3A 44
WA5: Gt San 4K 81
WA9: St H 2M 63
Marina Cres. L30: Neth 1F 44
L36: Huy 8H 61
Marina Dr. CH65: Ell P 1N 111
WA2: Warr 8D 66
Marina Gro. WA7: Run 5L 95
Marina La. WA7: Murd 8G 96
Marina Rd. L37: Form 3F 24
Marina Village WA7: Pres B 8G 97
Marina Wlk. CH65: Ell P 9N 103
(within The Port Arcades)
Marine AFC 8J 33
Marine Av. M31: Part 6K 69
Marine Cres. L22: Wloo 1K 43
Marine Dr. CH60: Hesw 8L 87
CH62: Port S 2B 90
PR8: South 8E 6
PR9: South 4H 7
Marine Ga. Mans. PR9: South 7G 7
Marine Lake 8F 6
Marine Pde. PR8: South 7F 6
Marine Pk. CH48: W Kir 4C 70
Marine Pk. Mans. CH45: New B 9H 43
Marine Point CH45: New B 9H 43
Marine Point Health & Fitness 9G 43
Marine Prom. CH45: New B 9H 43
Mariner Cl. WA7: Murd 9F 96
Mariner Ct. PR9: South 6H 7
Marine Rd. CH47: Hoy 1B 70
PR8: South 9D 6
Mariners Ho. L1: Liv 9G 4
Mariners Pk. CH45: Wall 3K 57
Mariners Rd. CH45: New B 2J 57
L23: Blun 9H 33
Mariners Way L20: Boot 7B 44
(off Strand Shop. Cen.)
M44: Irlam 1M 69
Mariners Wharf CH65: Ell P 7B 104
(off Grosvenor Wharf Rd.)
L3: Liv 2B 74
Marine Ter. CH45: Wall 2J 57
L22: Wloo 2K 43
Marion Dr. WA7: W'ton 9J 95
Marion Gro. L18: Moss H 6A 76
Marion Rd. L20: Boot 4C 44
Marion St. CH41: Birke 2L 73
Maritime Bus. Pk. CH41: Birke 8K 57
CH41: Tran 4M 73
Maritime Cen. L21: Sea 3L 43
Maritime Cl. WA12: Newt W 5L 51
Maritime Ct. CH49: Wdchu 7B 72
(off Childwall Grn.)
L12: W Der 1M 59
L30: Neth 6E 34
PR8: South 8F 6
Maritime Ent. Pk. L20: Boot 7A 44
Maritime Grange CH44: Wall 7L 57
Maritime Gro. CH43: Oxton 3H 73
Maritime Lodge L5: Liv 3E 58
(off Towson St.)
Maritime Pk. CH43: Oxton 3J 73
Maritime Pl. L3: Liv 2J 5 (6D 58)
Maritime Vw. CH42: Tran 5K 73
Maritime Way L1: Liv 7F 4 (9C 58)
Marius Cl. L4: W'ton 1E 58
Mark Av. CH66: Gt Sut 1H 111
Markden M. L8: Liv 1E 74
Market App. WN4: Ash M 8K 41
Market Ga. WA1: Warr 3C 82
Market Hall PR8: South 8G 6
Market Pl. L34: Presc 3A 62
WA8: Widnes 9K 79
WA12: Newt W 7J 51
Market Pl. Sth. CH41: Birke 2M 73
Market Sq. CH65: Ell P 1A 112
L1: Liv 5G 4
L32: Kirkb 9C 36
Market St. CH41: Birke 2L 73
CH47: Hoy 2C 70
PR8: South 8F 6
WA8: Widnes 9K 79
WA10: St H 7K 49
WA12: Newt W 6J 51
Market Way L1: Liv 5G 5
L39: Orm 8C 20
Markfield Cres. L25: Woolt 7G 77
WA11: St H 5M 49
Markfield Rd. L20: Boot 5A 44
Markham Dr. PR8: South 4D 12
Markham Gro. CH43: Bid 9F 56
Mark Rake CH62: Brom 6C 90
Mark Rd. L38: Hight 8F 24
Mark St. CH44: Wall 7L 57
L5: Liv 2D 58
Marksway CH61: Pens 3A 88
Marland WN8: Skel 9D 22
Marlborough WN8: Skel 9D 22
Marlborough Av. L30: Neth 9F 34
L31: Lydi 9J 27
Marlborough Ct. L17: Aig 6K 75
(off Aigburth Va.)
PR9: South 8H 7
WN8: Skel 9D 22
Marlborough Cres. WA4: Stockt H 6G 83
WA8: Widnes 3K 79
Marlborough Dr. WA6: Hel 3E 114
Marlborough Gdns. PR9: South 7H 7
WN8: Skel 9D 22
Marlborough Gro. CH43: Oxton 4J 73
Marlborough Pl. L3: Liv 2E 4 (6B 58)
Marlborough Rd. CH45: New B 2J 57
CH65: Ell P 2B 112
L13: Liv 3J 59
L22: Wloo 2L 43
L23: Crosb 8K 33
L34: Presc 2B 62
PR9: South 8H 7
Marlborough St. L3: Liv 2E 4 (6B 58)
Marlborough Ter. PR9: South 8H 7
(off Marlborough Rd.)
Marlborough Wlk. CH65: Ell P 2B 112
Marlborough Way WA11: Hay 2G 50
Marlbrook Rd. L25: Gate 2F 76
Marlcroft Dr. L17: Aig 8K 75
Marldon Av. L23: Crosb 9L 33
Marldon Rd. L12: W Der 1M 59
Marled Hey L28: Stockb V 1E 60
Marley Cl. L35: Rainh 8H 63
Marlfield Av. WA13: Lymm 6G 85
Marlfield La. CH61: Pens 3A 88
Marlfield Rd. L12: W Der 3N 59
WA4: Grap 6H 83
Marl Gro. WN5: Orr 8N 31
Marline Av. CH63: Brom 9B 90
Marling Cl. WA6: Frod 8N 107
Marling Pk. WA8: Widnes 7E 78
Marlow Cl. WA3: Birchw 4K 67
Marlowe Cl. WA8: Widnes 7J 79
Marlowe Dr. L12: W Der 3M 59
Marlowe Rd. CH44: Wall 5G 56
CH64: Nest 6E 100
Marl Rd. L30: Neth 8G 35
L33: Know I 8G 36
Marlsford St. L6: Liv 6H 59
Marlston Av. CH61: Irby 1N 87
Marlston Pl. WA7: Run 9L 95
Marlwood Av. CH45: Wall 4E 56
Marmaduke St. L7: Liv 8G 58
Marmion Av. L20: Boot 3D 44
Marmion Cl. WA3: Low 1F 52
Marmion Rd. CH47: Hoy 1C 70
L17: Aig 4H 75
Marmonde St. L4: W'ton 1D 58
Marnell Cl. L5: Liv 4B 58
Marnwood Rd. L32: Kirkb 1B 46
Marnwood Wlk. L32: Kirkb 1A 46
Marple Cl. CH43: Oxton 5E 72
Marquis St. CH41: Tran 4L 73
CH62: New F 9A 74
L3: Liv 4J 5 (7D 58)
Marram Cl. CH46: More 7A 56
Marrick Cl. WN3: Wigan 1J 41
Marron Av. WA2: Warr 7C 66
Marrow Dr. L7: Liv 6K 59
Marryat Cl. WA2: Winw 3B 66
Marsden Av. WA4: Westy 4H 83
WA10: St H 6G 48
Marsden Cl. CH44: Wall 4K 57
Marsden Ct. CH45: New B 2H 57
WA8: Widnes 4H 79
Marsden Rd. L26: Halew 1K 93
PR9: South 8K 7
Marsden St. L6: Liv 2M 5 (6F 58)
Marsden Way L6: Liv 2M 5 (6F 58)
MARSH, THE 2H 95
Marshall Av. WA5: Warr 7A 66
WA9: St H 1M 63
Marshall Cl. CH62: Brom 2C 90
L33: Kirkb 6D 36
Marshall Pl. L3: Liv 1E 4 (5B 58)
Marshall Rd. WA1: Wools 1L 83
Marshallsay L37: Form 2G 25
Marshall's Cl. L31: Lydi 8H 27
MARSHALL'S CROSS 4L 63
Marshalls Cross Rd. WA9: St H 3L 63
Marshall St. CH41: Birke 9J 57
Marsham Cl. CH49: Upton 1A 72
Marsham Rd. L25: Gate 3G 77
Marsh Av. L20: Boot 4D 44
Marsh Brook Cl. WA3: Rix 7G 69
Marsh Brook Rd. WA8: Widnes 3L 79
Marsh Brows L37: Form 2E 24
Marshes La., The PR4: Mere B 5K 9
Marshfield Cl. L36: Huy 6K 61
Marshfield Ct. CH46: Leas 6M 55
Marshfield Rd. L11: Norr G 9N 45
(not continuous)
Marshgate WA8: Widnes 9E 78
Marshgate Pl. WA6: Frod 4N 107
Marshgate Rd. L12: W Der 8N 45
MARSH GREEN 6K 107
Marsh Hall Pad WA8: Widnes 4L 79
Marsh Hall Rd. WA8: Widnes 4L 79
Marsh Ho. La. WA1: Warr 1D 82
WA2: Warr 1D 82
Marshlands Rd. CH45: Wall 3E 56
CH64: Lit N 9D 100
Marsh La. CH2: Elt 1M 113
(not continuous)
CH2: Ince 8K 105
CH63: H Beb 9J 73
L20: Boot 6N 43
L38: Ince B 6J 25
L40: Scar 5B 20
WA4: Dutt, L Whit 2M 109
WA5: Cuerd 6E 80
WA6: Frod 6K 107
WA6: Hel 8K 105
WA7: Astm 4B 96
Marsh Moss La. L40: Burs 7F 14
Marsh Rd. WA4: App T 3J 99
MARSHSIDE 4M 7
Marshside Cl. L8: Liv 3E 74
Marshside Nature Reserve 1L 7
Marshside Rd. PR9: South 2K 7
Marsh St. L20: Kirkd 9C 44
WA1: Warr 1E 82
WA8: Widnes 1K 95
WA9: St H 7M 49
Marsh Vista Cvn. Club L40: Burs 5G 14
Marshway Dr. WA12: Newt W 6K 51
Marsland Gro. WA9: St H 1A 64
Marson St. WA2: Warr 2B 82
Marston Cl. CH43: Oxton 5F 72
CH62: East 3D 102
Marston Cres. L38: Hight 1G 32
Marston Gdns. CH65: Ell P 8L 103
Marsworth Dr. L6: Liv 5E 58
Marten Av. CH63: Brom 8B 90
Martensen Dr. L7: Liv 8G 58
Martens Rd. M44: Irlam 4L 69
Marthall Dr. WA10: Ec'stn 7E 48
Martham Cl. WA4: Grap 5H 83
Martham Gdns. WA9: St H 3H 63
Martin Av. WA2: Warr 8F 66
WA10: St H 4J 49
WA12: Newt W 5K 51
Martin Cl. CH61: Irby 1K 87
L18: Moss H 7M 75
L35: Rainh 5D 62
L39: Augh 3C 28
WA7: Pal F 8C 96
Martindale Gro. WA7: Beech 1N 107
Martindale Rd. CH62: Brom 6D 90
L18: Moss H 3B 76
WA11: St H 9L 39
Martine Cl. L31: Mell 7N 35
Martinette Cl. L5: Liv 3F 58
Martin Gro. L35: Presc 4B 62

Martinhall Rd.—Menlove Gdns. W.

Martinhall Rd. L9: Faz 6L 45
Martin La. L40: Burs 6C 14
Martin Mere Vis. Cen. 5F 14
Martin Mere Wetland Cen. 5F 14
Martin Rd. L18: Moss H 7M 75
WA6: Frod 6L 107
MARTINSCROFT 1M 83
Martinscroft Grn. WA1: Wools 1N 83
Martin's La. CH44: Wall 5J 57
Martins La. WN8: Skel 5G 31
Martinsville Ct. WA8: Widnes 9K 79
Martland Av. L10: Aintr 8K 35
WA3: Low 3E 52
Martland Rd. L25: Gate 4G 76
Mart La. L40: Burs 9J 15
Martlesham Cres. CH49: Grea 5J 71
Martlett Rd. L12: W Der 4B 60
Martock L35: Whis 7C 62
Marton Cl. L24: Speke 5H 93
WA3: Cul 6M 53
Marton Grn. L24: Speke 5H 93
Marton Rd. L36: Huy 3J 61
Marus Av. WN3: Wigan 1H 41
Marus Bri. Retail Pk. 1H 41
Marvin St. L6: Liv 2N 5 (6F 58)
Marwood Rd. L14: Brd G 8C 60
Marwood Towers *L5: Liv 3D 58*
(off Boundary St. E.)
Mary Av. PR8: Ainsd 8L 11
Marybone L3: Liv 3E 4 (7C 58)
Marybone Apts. *L3: Liv 2F 4*
(off Marybone)
Marybone Student Village *L3: Liv 3F 4*
(off Marybone)
Maryfield Cl. WA3: Golb 3B 52
Maryhill Rd. WA7: Run 7K 95
Maryland Cl. WA5: Gt San 1L 81
Maryland Ho. *L20: Boot 7B 44*
(off Georgia Cl.)
Maryland La. CH46: More 8L 55
Maryland St. L1: Liv 7J 5 (9D 58)
Marylebone Av. WA9: St H 3J 63
Marymount Cl. CH44: Wall 6H 57
Maryport Cl. L5: Liv 3E 58
Mary Rd. L20: Boot 4C 44
Mary Stockton Ct. *L21: Sea 4N 43*
(off Seaforth Va. W.)
Mary St. WA8: Widnes 9N 79
WA9: Clock F 6A 64
Maryton Grange L18: Aller 6B 76
Maryvale WN8: Skel 1D 30
Maryville Cl. CH65: Ell P 8A 104
Maryville Rd. L34: Presc 3B 62
Maryville Wlk. CH65: Ell P 8A 104
Marywell Cl. WA9: St H 2N 63
Marzhan Way WA8: Widnes 7M 79
Masefield Av. WA8: Widnes 8J 79
Masefield Cl. CH62: New F 9N 73
Masefield Cres. L30: Boot 2C 44
Masefield Dr. WA2: Winw 4B 66
Masefield Gro. L16: Child 9D 60
WA10: St H 5G 48
Masefield Pl. L30: Boot 2D 44
Masefield Rd. L23: Thorn 5B 34
Maskell Rd. L13: Liv 6L 59
Maslin Dr. L5: Liv 3F 58
Mason Av. WA1: Padg 9F 66
WA8: Widnes 4L 79
Mason Cl. CH66: Gt Sut 3J 111
WN4: Ash M 7M 41
Mason St. CH45: New B 1H 57
L7: Liv 5N 5 (8F 58)
L22: Wloo 1K 43
L25: Woolt 6E 76
WA1: Warr 3D 82
WA7: Run 4M 95
Massam Cl. WA11: Rainf 5D 38
Massam's La. L37: Form 7E 16
Massey Av. WA5: Warr 7A 66
WA13: Lymm 6A 84
Massey Brook La. WA13: Lymm 6A 84
Massey Cl. WA12: Newt W 6K 51
Masseyfield Rd. WA7: Brook 1C 108
Massey Pk. CH45: Wall 4G 57
Massey St. CH41: Birke 9K 57
WA9: St H 1M 63
Master's Way L19: Garst 3B 92
Matchwood Cl. L19: Garst 2B 92
Matchworks, The L19: Garst 2C 92
Mater Cl. L9: Aintr 7J 45
Mather Av. L18: Aller, Moss H 4N 75
L19: Aller 7A 76
WA3: Low 4F 52
WA7: West P 8G 95
WA9: St H 7A 50
Mather Ct. CH43: Oxton 3H 73
Mather Rd. CH43: Oxton 3H 73
Mathers Cl. WA2: Fearn 5H 67
Mathew St. L2: Liv 5E 4 (8B 58)
Mathieson Rd. WA8: Widnes 2H 95
Matlock Av. L9: W'ton 4F 44
PR8: Birkd 2A 12
Matlock Cl. PR8: Birkd 2A 12
WA5: Gt San 3J 65
Matlock Cres. PR8: Birkd 2A 12
Matlock Rd. PR8: Birkd 3A 12
Matterdale Cl. WA6: Frod 7N 107
Matterhorn Rd. CH66: Ell P 7L 103
Matthew Cl. CH44: Wall 7L 57
Matthews St. WA1: Warr 1E 82
Matthew St. CH44: Wall 7L 57
Matty's La. WA6: Frod 7K 107
Maud Roberts Ct. L21: Lith 2N 43
Maud St. L8: Liv 2F 74
Maunders Ct. L23: Crosb 6M 33
Maureen Wlk. L10: Faz 3N 45
Mauretania Rd. L4: W'ton 8F 44
Maurice Jones Ct.
CH46: More 8M 55
Mavis Dr. CH49: Wdchu 5A 72
Mawdsley Av. WA1: Wools 1M 83
Mawdsley Cl. L37: Form 1H 25
Mawdsley Ter. L39: Orm 5D 20
Mawson Cl. WA5: Old H 9M 65
Max Rd. L14: Knott A 4D 60
Maxton Rd. L6: Liv 6H 59
Maxwell Cl. CH49: Upton 2A 72
CH65: Whit 3M 111
Maxwell Ct. CH42: Tran 5J 73
Maxwell Pl. L13: Liv 3L 59
Maxwell Rd. L13: Liv 3L 59
Maxwell St. WA3: Ris 3M 67
WA10: St H 7H 49
Mayall Dr. CH66: Gt Sut 4J 111
May Av. CH44: Wall 7K 57
Maybank Cl. PR9: South 6M 7
Maybank Gro. L17: Aig 7L 75
Maybank Rd. CH42: Tran 4K 73
Mayberry Gro. WA2: Padg 8H 67
Maybrook Pl. *WA4: Warr 5G 82*
(off Knutsford Rd.)
Maybury Way L17: Aig 6H 75
May Cl. L21: Lith 4A 44
Mayer Av. CH63: Beb 3M 89
Mayew Rd. CH61: Irby 1N 87
Mayfair Av. L14: Brd G 7D 60
L23: Crosb 6L 33
Mayfair Cl. L6: Liv 5G 59
L38: Hight 1G 32
WA5: Gt San 1F 80
Mayfair Ct. *CH43: Oxton 5H 73*
(off The Grove)
Mayfair Dr. WN3: Wigan 1H 41
Mayfair Gro. WA8: Widnes 7G 79
Mayfayre Av. L31: Lydi 7G 27
Mayfield Av. L37: Form 3C 24
WA8: Widnes 7E 78
WA9: St H 1H 63
Mayfield Cl. L12: W Der 3A 60
Mayfield Ct. L37: Form 8E 16
WA8: Widnes 6K 79
Mayfield Dr. CH62: East 9G 90
WN7: Leigh 2K 53
Mayfield Gdns. CH64: Nest 5E 100
L19: G'dale 9M 75
Mayfield Rd. CH45: Wall 4F 56
CH63: Beb 4N 89
L19: G'dale 9M 75
WA4: Grap 6H 83
WN8: Uph 5K 31
Mayfields CH66: Ell P 7L 103
L4: Kirkd 1D 58
Mayfields Ho. *CH62: New F 9A 74*
(off Mayfields Nth.)
Mayfields Nth. CH62: New F 9A 74
Mayfields Sth. CH62: New F 9A 74
Mayfield St. WN4: Ash M 8J 41
Mayfield Vw. WA13: Lymm 6E 84
Mayflower Av. L24: Speke 1E 92
Mayflower Ind. Est. L37: Form 3G 25
Mayford Cl. L25: Gate 2G 76
Mayhall Ct. L31: Mag 1J 35
May Pl. L13: Liv 7M 59
Maypole Ct. L30: Neth 6C 34
Maypole Farm Ct. L34: Know 5G 47
May Rd. CH60: Hesw 7A 88
May St. L3: Liv 6J 5 (8D 58)
L20: Boot 5B 44
WA3: Golb 1C 52
Maysville Cl. WA5: Gt San 2K 81
Maythorn Av. WA3: Croft 2H 67
Maytree Cl. L27: N'ley 2G 77
Maytree Wlk. WN8: Skel 9E 22
Mayville Rd. L18: Moss H 3N 75
May Wlk. M31: Part 6L 69
Mazenod Ct. L3: Liv 2F 4
Mazzini Cl. L5: Liv 4D 58
Mead Av. L21: Lith 2B 44
Meade Cl. L35: Rainh 8G 63
Meade Rd. L13: Liv 3K 59
Meadfoot Rd. CH46: More 8L 55
Meadow, The CH49: Wdchu 5B 72
(not continuous)
Meadow Av. PR8: South 2B 12
WA4: Warr 6B 82
WA9: Clock F 6N 63
Meadow Bank L31: Mag 1G 35
L32: Kirkb 7A 36
L39: Orm 9D 20
Meadowbank Cvn. Pk. WA4: Moore 1L 97
Meadowbank Cl. L12: W Der 4C 60
Meadowbank Dr. CH66: Lit Sut 8F 102
Meadowbarn Cl. L32: Kirkb 1C 46
Meadow Beck WN7: Leigh 1N 53
Meadowbridge Cl. L40: Westh 9J 21
Meadowbrook L40: Burs 2H 21
Meadow Brook Cl. L10: Faz 3N 45
Meadowbrook Rd. CH46: More 1L 71
Meadow Brow PR9: South 2B 8
Meadow Cl. CH64: Nest 8E 100
CH64: Will 6M 101
L40: Westh 9J 21
Meadow Cl. WA6: Hel 2E 114
WA8: Widnes 5G 79
WA12: Newt W 7H 51
WN7: Leigh 1M 53
WN8: Skel 5G 31
Meadowclough WN8: Skel 9E 22
Meadow Ct. L11: Norr G 7N 45
L25: Woolt 5F 76
Meadow Cres. CH49: Wdchu 6A 72
Meadow Cft. CH64: Will 6L 101
Meadowcroft CH60: Hesw 6C 88
L37: Form 2F 24
WA9: St H 3M 63
WN4: Ash M 5H 41
WN8: Skel 9E 22
Meadowcroft Ct. WA7: Cas 7C 96
Meadowcroft Pk. L12: W Der 5B 60
Meadowcroft Rd. CH47: Meols 8F 54
Meadow Dr. L36: Huy 9K 61
L39: Augh 2A 28
Meadowfield WN8: Uph 5K 31
Meadowfield Cl. CH42: Rock F 6M 73
L9: W'ton 3F 44
Meadow Gdns. WN5: Orr 7N 31
Meadowgate CH48: Caldy 2E 86
Meadow Hey L20: Boot 5N 43
Meadow Hey Cl. L25: Woolt 5F 76
Meadow La. CH42: Rock F 6M 73
CH64: Will 5L 101
CH65: Ell P 8A 104
L12: W Der 9N 45
L31: Mag 2K 35
L40: Burs, Lath 6M 15
PR8: Ainsd 2J 17
WA2: Fearn 7H 67
WA9: St H 8B 50
WA14: Dun M 4N 85
Meadow La. Ind. Pk. CH65: Ell P 9B 104
Meadow Oak Dr. L25: Gate 4E 76
Meadow Pk. CH42: Rock F 6M 73
Meadow Rd. CH48: W Kir 5G 70
Meadow Row WA7: Cas 6C 96
Meadows, The *CH41: Birke 1K 73*
(off Conway St.)
CH62: Brom 8C 90
CH64: Lit N 8F 100
L31: Mag 2J 35
L35: Rainh 6F 62
M44: Cad 3K 69
Meadowside CH46: Leas 5B 56
WA6: Frod 6K 107
Meadowside Av. WN4: Ash M 3J 41
Meadowside Dr. L33: Kirkb 5D 36
Meadowside Rd. CH62: Brom 8C 90
Meadows Leisure Cen. 3H 35
Meadow St. CH45: New B 1G 56
Meadowsweet Rd. L32: Kirkb 7D 36
Meadow Vw. CH2: Elt 2L 113
CH65: Ell P 4C 112
L21: Ford 8A 34
PR8: South 2C 12
WA11: Rainf 7F 38
WA13: Lymm 4D 84
Meadow Vw. Dr. WA6: Frod 7K 107
Meadow Wlk. CH61: Pens 4M 87
M31: Part 6L 69
WA7: Pal F 8B 96
(within Halton Lea Shop. Cen.)
Meadow Way L12: W Der 9N 45
PR9: Banks 3E 8
Mead Rd. WA1: Padg 9H 67
Meads, The L34: Eccl P 2D 62
Meadway CH45: Wall 4G 56
CH49: Upton 2B 72
CH60: Hesw 9N 87
CH62: Spit 5B 90
CH66: Lit Sut 7G 102
L15: Wavtr 9A 60
L30: Neth 9F 34
L31: Mag 4G 34
L35: Whis 5C 62
WA3: Low 2E 52
WA7: Run 6A 96
WA8: Widnes 7D 78
WN8: Skel 9E 22
Mealor's Weint CH64: P'gte 5B 100
Meander, The L12: W Der 9C 46
Meanygate PR9: Banks 1F 8
Measham Cl. WA11: St H 5M 49
Measham Way L12: Crox 7C 46
Mecca Bingo
Birkenhead 2K 73
Ellesmere Port 1N 111
Knotty Ash 5C 60
St Helens 6J 49
Southport 8F 6
Medbourne Ct. L32: Kirkb 2D 46
Medbourne Cres. L32: Kirkb 2D 46
Meddowcroft Rd. CH45: Wall 3F 56
Medea Cl. L5: Liv 3D 58
Medlar Way WN4: Ash M 6H 41
Medlock Ct. CH43: Oxton 3G 72
Medlock St. L4: Kirkd 1D 58
Medlock Way WA7: Cas 5C 96
Medway *L20: Boot 7B 44*
(off Strand Shop. Cen.)
Medway Cl. WA2: Warr 7F 66
WN4: Ash M 5H 41
WN7: Leigh 2K 53
Medway Ct. WA9: St H 7B 50
Medway Rd. CH42: Rock F 6N 73
Meerbrook Gro. *L33: Kirkb 6D 36*
(off Langton Rd.)
Meeting Ho. La. WA6: Frod, Newt 3N 115
Meeting La. WA5: Penk 3F 80
Melbourne Cl. L24: Speke 3F 92
Melbourne St. CH45: New B 1G 56
WA9: St H 2H 63
Melbreck WN8: Skel 9D 22
Melbreck Rd. L18: Aller 7N 75
Melbury Ct. WA3: Ris 3N 67
Melbury Rd. L14: Knott A 3F 60
Melda Cl. L6: Liv 2L 5 (6E 58)
Meldon Cl. L12: W Der 8A 46
Meldreth Cl. L37: Form 3C 24
Meldrum Rd. L15: Wavtr 2N 75
Melford Ct. WA1: Wools 9L 67
Melford Dr. CH43: Pren 7E 72
WA7: Run 6M 95
WN4: Ash M 7J 41
WN5: Bil 9N 31
Melford Gro. L6: Liv 3J 59
Meliden Gdns. WA9: St H 2B 64
Meliden Gro. WA6: Hel 4E 114
Melksham Dr. CH61: Irby 9L 71
MELLING 6L 35
Melling Av. L9: Aintr 3G 44
Melling Cl. WN7: Leigh 1N 53
Melling Ct. CH45: New B 2J 57
Melling Dr. L32: Kirkb 8C 36
Melling La. L31: Mag 4K 35
MELLING MOUNT 4A 36
Melling Rd. CH45: New B 2J 57
L9: Aintr 2G 45
L10: Aintr 2G 45
L20: Boot 5B 44
PR9: South 7K 7
Mellings Av. WN5: Bil 2A 40
Melling Vw. L33: Kirkb 6B 36
Melling Way L32: Kirkb 8C 36
WN3: Winst 2F 40
Mellock Cl. CH64: Lit N 8F 100
Mellock La. CH64: Lit N 7F 100
Melloncroft Dr. CH48: Caldy 8C 70
Melloncroft Dr. W. CH48: Caldy 9D 70
Mellor Cl. L35: Tar G 1L 77
WA7: Wind H 7F 96
Mellor Rd. CH42: Tran 6J 73
Mellors Cl. PR8: South 1E 12
Melly Rd. L17: Aig 5G 75
Melmerby Cl. WN4: Ash M 8H 41
Melrose Av. CH47: Hoy 1C 70
L23: Crosb 8L 33
PR9: South 2N 7
WA4: App 8E 82
WA5: Burtw 2H 65
WA10: Ec'stn 5E 48
Melrose Cres. WN4: Garsw 8E 40
Melrose Dr. CH66: Gt Sut 5L 111
WN3: Winst 1E 40 (1F 40)
Melrose Gdns. CH43: Pren 8F 72
Melrose Pk. *L22: Wloo 2L 43*
(off Melrose Rd.)
Melrose Rd. L4: Kirkd 1C 58
L22: Wloo 2L 43
L33: Kirkb 5B 36
Melton Av. WA4: W'ton 8C 82
Melton Cl. CH49: Upton 3M 71
Melton Rd. WA7: Run 9M 95
Melverley Rd. L32: Kirkb 9N 35
Melville CH62: New F 7A 74
Melville Av. CH42: Rock F 7N 73
Melville Cl. WA2: Warr 1C 82
WA8: Widnes 7N 79
WA10: St H 6G 48
Melville Pl. L7: Liv 7M 5 (9F 58)
Melville Rd. CH63: H Beb 2L 89
L20: Boot 3B 44
M44: Cad 4J 69
Melville St. L8: Liv 3F 74
Melvin Ho. PR9: South 7G 7
Melwood Dr. L12: W Der 2A 60
Melwood
(Liverpool FC Training Ground) 2A 60
Memorial Dr. CH42: Tran 6K 73
Menai M. *L34: Presc 3B 62*
(off St James' Rd.)
Menai Rd. L20: Boot 4C 44
Menai St. CH41: Birke 2J 73
Mendell Cl. CH62: Brom 7D 90
Mendell Ct. CH62: Brom 7D 90
Mendip Av. WA2: Warr 6C 66
WN3: Winst 1E 40
Mendip Cl. CH42: Tran 7J 73
CH66: Gt Sut 2K 111
L26: Halew 9J 77
Mendip Gro. WA9: St H 7B 50
Mendip Rd. CH42: Tran 7J 73
L15: Wavtr 2M 75
Mendips
(Childhood Home of John Lennon)
5C 76
Menin Av. WA4: Warr 5D 82
Menivale Cl. PR9: South 1N 7
Menlo Av. CH61: Irby 1N 87
Menlo Cl. CH43: Oxton 4E 72
Menlove Av. L18: Aller, Moss H 3N 75
L25: Woolt 4B 76
Menlove Ct. L18: Moss H 3A 76
Menlove Gdns. Nth. L18: Moss H 3N 75
Menlove Gdns. Sth. L18: Moss H 3N 75
Menlove Gdns. W. L18: Moss H 3N 75

Menlove Mans.—Mill Rd.

Menlove Mans. L18: Moss H 2A 76
Menlow Cl. WA4: Grap 7K 83
Menstone Rd. L13: Liv 5L 59
Mentmore Cres. L11: Norr G 9N 45
Mentmore Gdns. WA4: App 2G 98
Mentmore Rd. L18: Moss H 6M 75
MEOLS 9F 54
Meol's Cl. L24: Hale 5B 94
Meols Cl. CH66: Gt Sut 1K 111
L37: Form 2E 24
MEOLS COP 1E 12
Meols Cop Retail Pk. 2F 12
Meols Cop Rd. PR8: South 1E 12
Meols Cop Station (Rail) 8L 7
Meols Ct. CH47: Hoy 2B 70
PR9: Banks 1E 8
Meols Dr. CH47: Hoy 5B 70
CH48: W Kir 5B 70
Meols Pde. CH47: Meols 9C 54
Meols (Park & Ride) 9F 54
Meols Station (Rail) 9F 54
Meols Vw. Cl. PR8: South 3F 12
Meols Wood PR9: South 6N 7
Mercer Av. L32: Kirkb 9A 36
Mercer Ct. L12: W Der 3C 60
L20: Boot 7B 44
(off Clairville Cl.)
L31: Lydi 9F 26
Mercer Dr. L4: Kirkd 2D 58
Mercer Rd. CH43: Bid 9E 56
WA11: Hay 4F 50
Mercer's La. L39: Bic 8E 28
Mercer St. L19: Garst 2A 92
WA5: Burtw 3G 64
WA12: Newt W 6M 51
Mercer Wlk. *CH65: Ell P 1A 112*
(within The Port Arcades)
Merchant Cl. L30: Neth 2G 44
Merchant Rd. L39: Orm 9E 20
Merchants Ct. L2: Liv 6E 4
L15: Wavtr 9K 59
L40: Burs 8K 15
Merchants Cres. WA3: Low 1F 52
Mercury Ct. L2: Liv 3D 4 (7B 58)
Mercury Way WN8: Skel 4H 31
Mere Av. CH63: Raby M 9A 90
L40: Burs 8J 15
Mere Bank L17: Aig 4K 75
Merebank CH43: Oxton 4E 72
MERE BROW 5K 9
Mere Brow La. PR4: Mere B 5K 9
Merecliff L28: Stockb V 1G 60
Mere Cl. CH66: Gt Sut 3J 111
WN8: Skel 2C 30
Mere Ct. L40: Burs 8J 15
Merecroft Av. CH44: Wall 7J 57
Meredale Rd. L18: Moss H 4M 75
Meredith Av. WA4: Grap 6J 83
Meredith St. L19: Garst 2C 92
Mere Farm Gro. CH43: Oxton 4F 72
Mere Farm Rd. CH43: Oxton 4E 72
Mere Grn. L4: W'ton 9F 44
Mere Gro. WA11: St H 1L 49
Mereheath CH46: Leas 6M 55
Mereheath Gdns. *CH46: Leas 6M 55*
(off Mereheath)
Mere Hey WA10: Ec'stn 7D 48
Mereland Way WA9: St H 8B 50
Mere La. CH45: Wall 2E 56
CH60: Hesw 5M 87
L5: Liv 4E 58
L39: Hals 5G 19
L40: Ruf 3H 15
PR4: Mere B 7K 9
PR9: Banks 4E 8
Mere Meanygate PR4: Mere B 6J 9
Mere Pk. L23: Blun 7J 33
Merepark Dr. PR9: South 3N 7
Mere Pk. Rd. CH49: Grea 5K 71
Mere Rd. L37: Form 2D 24
WA2: Fearn 7H 67
WA12: Newt W 6A 52
WN4: Ash M 7L 41
Mere Sands Wood Nature Reserve 2K 15
Mere Sands Wood Nature Reserve Vis. Cen. 2K 15
Mere's Edge Bus. Pk. WA6: Hel 3D 114
MERE SIDE 1G 14
Meres Rd. L9: Aintr 3K 45
Meres Way PR8: South 4A 12
Merevale Cl. WA7: Beech 9A 96
Mere Vw. PR9: Banks 4H 9
WA6: Hel 3D 114
Mereview Cres. L12: Crox 7B 46
Mere Vw. Gdns. WA4: App 2F 98
Merewood L32: Kirkb 2D 46
WN8: Skel 9D 22
Merewood Cl. WA2: Warr 6E 66
Mereworth CH48: Caldy 1E 86
Meribel Cl. L23: Crosb 6N 33
Meribel Sq. L34: Presc 3A 62
Meriden Av. CH63: Spit 6N 89
Meriden Cl. PR8: Ainsd 9H 11
WA11: St H 4N 49
Meriden Rd. L25: Gate 2F 76
Meridian Bus. Village L24: Speke 1G 93
Merlewood Av. PR9: South 4N 7
Merlin Av. CH49: Upton 2L 71
Merlin Cl. CH49: Upton 2L 71
WA7: Cas 6C 96
WA11: St H 4L 49
Merlin Ct. L26: Halew 7H 77
Merlin Pk. L40: Burs 1F 20
Merlin Rd. CH42: Tran 5J 73
Merlin St. L8: Liv 2E 74
Merrick Cl. WA2: Warr 6F 66
Merrills La. CH49: Upton 3A 72
Merrilocks Grn. L23: Blun 6G 33
Merrilocks Rd. L23: Blun 6G 33
Merrilox Av. L31: Lydi 9J 27
Merrion Cl. L25: Woolt 5D 76
Merritt Av. CH41: Birke 9H 57
Merrivale Rd. L25: Woolt 6G 77
Merrydale Dr. L11: Crox 7A 46
Merscar La. L40: Scar 8B 14
Mersey Av. L19: Aig 8L 75
L31: Mag 1L 35
L37: Form 7E 16
Merseybank Ho. *CH62: New F 8A 74*
(off New Ferry Rd.)
Merseybank Rd. CH62: New F 8A 74
Mersey Cotts. L19: Garst 2B 92
Mersey Ct. *CH44: Wall 7L 57*
(off Borough Rd. E.)
L23: Crosb 8J 33
Mersey Dr. M31: Part 5N 69
Mersey Gateway 2M 95
Mersey Ho. L20: Boot 6A 44
Mersey La. Sth. CH42: Rock F 6N 73
Mersey Multimodal Gateway
WA8: Widnes 2J 95
Merseyrail Community Stadium 1D 12
Mersey Rd. CH42: Rock F 6N 73
L17: Aig 9K 75
L23: Blun, Crosb 8J 33
WA7: Run 4J 95
(not continuous)
WA8: Widnes 3K 95
Merseyside Maritime Mus. 7D 4 (9B 58)
Merseyside Tramway 1L 73
Merseyside Youth Challenge Trust 7D 76
Mersey St. CH44: Wall 7L 57
WA1: Warr 4C 82
WA9: St H 7C 50
Mersey Ter. *CH65: Ell P 7A 104*
(off Lwr. Mersey St.)
Merseyton Rd. CH65: Ell P 6N 103
Merseyton Rd. Workshops
CH65: Ell P 7A 104
(off Merseyton Rd.)
Mersey Tunnel - Toll 1A 4 (6M 57)
(not continuous)
Mersey Valley Golf Course 1B 80
Mersey Vw. *CH41: Tran 4L 73*
(off Marquis St.)
CH63: H Beb 1K 89
L22: Wloo 9J 33
WA7: West P 8G 94
Mersey Vw. Cotts. WA7: W'ton 9J 95
Mersey Vw. Rd. WA8: Hale B 3E 94
Mersey Wlk. CH42: Tran 5L 73
WA4: Westy 3G 83
Mersey Wave 3L 93
Mersham Ct. WA8: Widnes 4J 79
Merstone Cl. L26: Halew 9K 77
Merthyr Gro. L16: Child 8C 60
Merton Bank Rd. WA9: St H 5M 49
Merton Cl. CH64: Nest 9E 100
L36: Huy 7F 60
Merton Cres. L36: Huy 7F 60
Merton Dr. CH49: Wdchu 5A 72
L36: Huy 7E 60
Merton Gro. L20: Boot 7B 44
L23: Blun 8J 33
Merton Ho. L20: Boot 7B 44
Merton Pl. CH43: Oxton 2J 73
Merton Rd. CH45: Wall 4G 57
CH65: Hoot 3G 103
CH66: Gt Sut 2L 111
L20: Boot 7B 44
Merton St. WA9: St H 5M 49
Merton Towers L20: Boot 7C 44
Mertoun Rd. WA4: W'ton 7C 82
Mesham Cl. CH49: Upton 3M 71
Metcalf Cl. L33: Kirkb 5B 36
Meteor Cres. WA2: Warr 6E 66
Methuen St. CH41: Birke 9G 56
L15: Wavtr 9K 59
Metquarter L1: Liv 5F 4 (8C 58)
Mevagissey Rd. WA7: Brook 1E 108
Mews, The L17: Aig 7L 75
L23: Crosb 8L 33
L28: Stockb V 2G 60
PR8: South 1N 11
WA5: Burtw 3G 64
WA9: Clock F 6N 63
Mews Ct. CH64: Will 6M 101
Meyrick Cl. WN3: Winst 1E 40
Meyrick Ct. WA12: Newt W 7J 51
Meyrick Rd. L11: Norr G 8K 45
MFA Bowl
Warrington 6B 66
Miami Cl. WA5: Gt San 1K 81
Micawber Cl. L8: Liv 3E 74
Michael Dragonette Ct. L3: Liv 5B 58
Michaels Cl. L37: Form 1E 24
Michael's La. L39: Hals 2B 18
Michigan Cl. L27: N'ley 3J 77
Michigan Pl. WA5: Gt San 1L 81
Mickering La. L39: Augh 6N 27
Micklefield Rd. L15: Wavtr 2L 75
Micklegate WA7: Murd 8F 96
Micklehead Bus. Village WA9: St H 6K 63
MICKLEHEAD GREEN 6K 63
Micklehead Grn. WA9: St H 6J 63
Mickleton Dr. PR8: Ainsd 9G 11
Middlefield Rd. L18: Aller 5C 76
Middleham Cl. L32: Kirkb 1A 46
Middlehey Av. L34: Know 6H 47
Middlehurst Av. WA10: St H 6J 49
Middlehurst Cl. L34: Eccl P 2D 62
Middlehurst Rd. WA4: Grap 6H 83
Middle La. M31: Part 7K 69
Middlemass Hey L27: N'ley 3J 77
Middle Meanygate PR4: Tarl 1L 9
Middle Moss La. L37: Gt Alt 1M 25
Middle Rd. L24: Halew 2K 93
(not continuous)
Middlesex Rd. L20: Boot 6C 44
Middleton Ct. L24: Speke 5J 93
Middleton Rd. L7: Liv 7K 59
L22: Wloo 9M 33
Middle Wlk. WA6: Frod 7L 107
Middle Way L11: Crox 6B 46
Middle Withins La. L38: Gt Alt 5M 25
Middlewood L32: Kirkb 2D 46
WA3: Low 2F 52
WN8: Skel 9D 22
Middlewood Cl. L39: Augh 5A 28
Middlewood Dr. L39: Augh 5A 28
Middlewood Rd. L39: Augh 4A 28
Midge Hall La. PR9: South 2N 13
Midghall St. L3: Liv 2E 4 (6B 58)
Midhurst Dr. PR8: Ainsd 1H 17
Midhurst Rd. L12: Crox 7D 46
Midland St. CH43: Oxton 3J 73
WA8: Widnes 7L 79
Midland Ter. L22: Wloo 1K 43
Midland Way WA1: Warr 3B 82
WA2: Warr 3B 82
Midlothian Dr. L23: Blun 8J 33
Midway Rd. L36: Huy 5J 61
Midwood St. WA8: Widnes 8L 79
Milbrook Cres. L32: Kirkb 8C 36
Milbrook Dr. L32: Kirkb 8C 36
Milbrook Wlk. L32: Kirkb 8C 36
Mildenhall Cl. WA5: Gt San 2K 81
Mildenhall Rd. L25: Gate 2E 76
Mildenhall Way *L25: Gate 2F 76*
(off Mildenhall Rd.)
Mildmay Rd. L11: Norr G 8K 45
L20: Boot 5A 44
Mile End L5: Liv 5C 58
Miles Cl. CH49: Grea 5K 71
WA3: Birchw 6N 67
Miles La. CH49: Grea 6K 71
WN6: App B, Shev 5N 23
(not continuous)
Miles St. L8: Liv 4F 74
Milestone Hey L28: Stockb V 1F 60
Milestone Rd. L32: Kirkb 9A 36
Milford Cl. L37: Form 3C 24
Milford Dr. L12: Crox 7C 46
Milford Gdns. WA4: App 3E 98
Milford St. L5: Kirkd 3B 58
Milk St. WA10: St H 7K 49
Millachip Ct. *L6: Liv 5G 58*
(off White Rock St.)
Milland Cl. L11: Crox 7A 46
Millar Cres. WA8: Widnes 9K 79
Millar's Pace PR9: South 2N 7
Mill Av. WA5: Gt San 1G 80
Mill Bank CH64: Ness 9G 101
L13: Liv 3L 59
Millbank WA13: Lymm 5E 84
WN6: App B 6N 23
Millbank Brow L40: Burs 2K 21
Millbank Cotts. L31: Mag 9K 27
WA6: Frod 6K 107
Millbank Ct. L9: Aintr 2J 45
WA6: Frod 6K 107
Millbank La. L31: Augh, Mag 9L 27
L39: Augh 9M 27
Mill Bank Rd. CH44: Wall 6G 57
Millbeck Cl. L32: Kirkb 7C 36
Millbeck Gro. WA11: St H 9L 39
Mill Bri. Gdns. WA12: Newt W 7N 51
Millbrook PR8: South 2A 12
Mill Brook Bus. Pk. WA11: Rainf 8F 38
Millbrook Cl. WN8: Skel 2B 30
Mill Brook Ct. L39: Augh 7L 27
Millbrook Ct. L34: Know 5G 46
Millbrook La. WA10: Ec'stn 6E 48
Millbrook Rd. CH41: Birke 7H 57
Mill Brow CH63: H Beb 1K 89
WA8: Widnes 6M 79
WA9: Sut L 4N 63
WA10: Ec'stn 6E 48
Mill Brow Cl. WA9: Sut L 4N 63
Millbutt Cl. CH63: H Beb 1K 89
Mill Cl. CH42: Tran 4K 73
L23: Crosb 5L 33
WA2: Fearn 6F 66
Mill Ct. CH65: Ell P 8L 103
L30: Neth 6C 34
Mill Cft. CH64: Nest 5E 100
Millcroft L23: Crosb 6N 33
Millcroft Av. WN5: Orr 7N 31
Millcroft Pk. CH49: Grea 5J 71
Millcroft Rd. L25: Woolt 7G 77
Milldale Rd. WN7: Leigh 1J 53
Mill Dam Cl. L40: Burs 3H 21
Mill Dam La. L40: Burs, Lath 3G 21
Millennium Bus. Pk. WA3: Birchw 7L 67
Millennium Ct. CH64: Nest 5E 100
Millennium Rd. L8: Liv 2F 74
Millennium Wlk. *WA5: Gt San 1K 81*
(off Arizona Cres.)
Miller Av. L23: Crosb 6K 33
Miller Cl. WN8: Skel 6F 30
Millers Bri. L20: Boot 8A 44
Millers Bri. Ind. Est. L20: Boot 8A 44
Millers Cl. CH46: More 1J 71
Millers Ct. L39: Orm 8D 20
Millerscroft L32: Kirkb 8A 36
Millersdale WA9: Clock F 5M 63
Millersdale Av. L9: Aintr 3G 45
Millersdale Cl. CH62: East 1E 102
Millersdale Gro. WA7: Beech 9N 95
Millersdale Rd. L18: Moss H 4M 75
Millers Fold WA10: Ec'stn 6E 48
Millers La. WA13: Lymm 3H 85
Millers Nook WN8: Uph 5L 31
Millerstoll Way L8: Liv 3D 74
Miller St. WA4: Warr 4D 82
Millers Way CH46: More 9K 55
Mill Farm Cl. WA2: Warr 6F 66
Millfield CH64: Nest 5E 100
WN8: Parb 4F 22
Millfield Bus. Pk. WA11: Hay 2G 51
Millfield Cl. CH63: H Beb 2K 89
L13: W Der 3M 59
Millfield La. WA11: Hay 9G 40
WN4: Ash M 9G 40
Millfield Pk. WA3: Golb 2C 52
Millfield Rd. WA8: Widnes 6M 79
Millfields WA10: Ec'stn 7D 48
Millfields Ct. WA10: Ec'stn 7E 48
Millfield Ter. CH66: Lit Sut 7H 103
Mill Grn. CH64: Will 6M 101
Millgreen Cl. L12: Crox 7C 46
WN8: Uph 5K 31
Mill Grn. La. WA8: Widnes 3N 79
Mill Gro. L21: Lith 2A 44
Mill Hey L35: Rainh 8H 63
Mill Hey La. L40: Ruf 3N 15
Mill Hey Rd. CH48: Caldy 1E 86
Mill Hill CH43: Oxton 5G 73
Mill Hill Rd. CH61: Irby 8K 71
Mill Ho. Av. WA4: Stockt H 7E 82
Millhouse Cl. CH46: More 8J 55
Millhouse Ct. L12: W Der 3M 59
Mill Ho. La. WA3: Birchw, Croft 3H 67
Millhouse La. CH46: More 8J 55
Mill Ho. Lodge PR8: Ainsd 9K 11
Mill Ho. Vw. WN8: Uph 5M 31
Millingford Gro. WN4: Ash M 8K 41
Millingford Ind. Est. WA3: Golb 3B 52
Millington Cl. CH43: Pren 7E 72
WA7: Sut W 2B 108
WA8: Widnes 8J 79
Millington Gdns. WA13: Lymm 3J 85
Millington La. WA14: M'ton 9N 85
Mill La. CH44: Wall 6G 56
CH49: Grea 5K 71
CH60: Hesw 7B 88
CH64: Ness 9G 101
CH64: Will 5L 101
CH66: Ell P, Gt Sut 1J 111
(not continuous)
L3: Liv 3G 5 (7C 58)
L12: W Der 3M 59
L13: Liv 7M 59
L15: Wavtr 7M 59
L20: Boot 7C 44
L32: Kirkb 7A 36
L34: Know 5H 47
L35: Rainh 7F 62
L39: Augh 3L 27
L40: Burs 9J 15
(not continuous)
PR9: South 6M 7
WA2: Warr 5F 66
WA2: Winw 4N 65
WA4: H Walt 9N 81
WA4: Stockt H 7E 82
(not continuous)
WA5: Warr 3N 81
WA6: Frod 4A 108
WA8: Cron 3G 79
WA8: Widnes, Bold H 3N 79
WA9: Sut L 4M 63
WA11: Rainf 8E 38
WA12: Newt W 7N 51
WA13: Lymm 2J 85
WN6: App B 6M 23
WN8: Dalt, Uph 2J 31
WN8: Parb 4F 22
WN8: Skel 2C 30
(not continuous)
Mill La. Cres. PR9: South 6M 7
Mill La. Ind. Est. CH2: Lit Stan 4D 112
Mill Leat Cl. WN8: Parb 3F 22
Mill Leat M. WN8: Parb 3F 22
Mill Mdw. WA12: Newt W 7N 51
Millom Av. L35: Rainh 5E 62
Millom Gro. L12: W Der 9A 46
WA10: St H 1F 62
Mill Pk. Dr. CH62: East 3D 102
Millport Cl. WA2: Fearn 7H 67
Mill Ri. WA6: Hel 1F 114
Mill Rd. CH61: Thing 1A 88
CH62: Brom 4C 90
CH63: H Beb 9K 73

A-Z Merseyside Atlas 167

Mill Rd.—Morston Rd.

Mill Rd. L6: Liv 1L **5** (5E **58**)
(not continuous)
PR8: Ainsd 9K **11**
WN5: Orr 7N **31**
Millrose Cl. WN8: Skel 2C **30**
Mill Spring Ct. L20: Boot 7C **44**
Mill Sq. L10: Aintr 9K **35**
Millstead Rd. L15: Wavtr 9M **59**
Millstead Wlk. *L15: Wavtr 9M **59***
(off Millstead Rd.)
Mill Stile L25: Woolt 6E **76**
Millstone Ct. L40: Burs 1K **21**
WA3: Golb .1A **52**
Mill Stream Cl. L29: Seft 4E **34**
Millstream Way L4: Kirkd 2C **58**
Mill St. CH42: Tran 4K **73**
CH64: Nest 6D **100**
L8: Liv 2D **74**
L25: Woolt .6E **76**
L34: Presc .3A **62**
L39: Orm 9D **20**
PR8: South .9H **7**
WA3: Golb .2B **52**
WA10: St H .6J **49**
WN4: Ash M 9L **41**
Mill Ter. CH63: H Beb 2K **89**
Millthwaite Ct. CH44: Wall 5F **56**
Millthwaite Rd. CH44: Wall 5F **56**
Millvale St. L6: Liv 6H **59**
Mill Vw. CH64: Nest 5D **100**
L8: Liv 3D **74**
Millview L32: Kirkb 7A **36**
Mill Vw. Ct. L39: Bic 5H **29**
Mill Vw. Dr. CH63: H Beb 1J **89**
Millway Rd. L24: Speke 3L **93**
Mill Weir Gdns. L29: Seft 4E **34**
Millwood CH63: H Beb 1K **89**
WA7: Nort .6E **96**
Millwood Av. WA10: Ec'stn 7C **48**
Millwood Cl. WN4: Ash M 6J **41**
Millwood Ct. L24: Speke 3L **93**
Millwood Gdns. L35: Whis 7C **62**
Millwood Rd. L24: Speke 4J **93**
MILL YARD 5B **60**
Mill Yd. CH61: Thing 1B **88**
Milman Cl. CH49: Upton 4N **71**
L39: Orm 1B **28**
Milman Ct. L25: Woolt 5C **76**
Milman Rd. L4: W'ton 9E **44**
Milner Av. CH41: Birke 9G **56**
Milner Cop CH60: Hesw 7A **88**
Milner Ct. L36: Huy 5H **61**
Milne Rd. L13: Liv 1K **59**
Milner Rd. CH60: Hesw 7A **88**
L17: Aig 7K **75**
Milner St. WA5: Warr 3A **82**
Milnes Av. WN7: Leigh 1N **53**
Milnthorpe Cl. L4: Kirkd 1D **58**
Milnthorpe Rd. WA5: Burtw 3G **65**
Milnthorpe St. L19: Garst 1A **92**
Milroy Way L7: Liv 8G **59**
Milton Av. L14: Brd G 7C **60**
L35: Whis .6B **62**
M44: Irlam .3L **69**
WA8: Widnes 8J **79**
WA12: Newt W 7K **51**
Milton Cl. CH65: Ell P 1B **112**
L35: Whis .6B **62**
Milton Cres. CH60: Hesw 6A **88**
Milton Dr. L39: Orm 9E **20**
Milton Grn. CH61: Thing 1B **88**
Milton Gro. WA4: Warr 5E **82**
WA6: Hel .4D **114**
WN5: Bil 2N **39**
Milton Pavement CH41: Birke 2K **73**
Milton Rd. CH42: Tran 4J **73**
CH44: Wall .7K **57**
CH48: W Kir 5B **70**
CH65: Ell P 1B **112**
L4: W'ton .8D **44**
L7: Liv 7K **59**
L22: Wloo .9L **33**
WA3: Low 3E **52**
WA8: Widnes 8J **79**
Milton Rd. E. CH42: Tran 4K **73**
Milton St. L20: Boot 6A **44**
PR9: South .8L **7**
WA8: Widnes 2K **95**
WA9: Sut M 7K **63**
Milton Ter. CH65: Ell P 1B **112**
Milton Way L31: Mag 2G **35**
Milvain Dr. WA2: Warr 8D **66**
Milverny Way WA9: St H 9K **49**
Milverton St. L6: Liv 5H **59**
Mimosa Cl. CH2: Elt 1N **113**
Mimosa Rd. L15: Wavtr 1N **75**
Mindale Rd. L15: Wavtr 9L **59**
Minehead Gro. WA9: Sut L 4N **63**
Minehead Rd. L17: Aig 7K **75**
Miners Vw. WN8: Uph 6J **31**
Miners Way L24: Speke 4L **93**
WA8: Widnes 9K **79**
Minerva Cl. WA4: Warr 6E **82**
Mine's Av. L34: Presc 3B **62**
Mines Av. L17: Aig 9L **75**
Mine Way WA11: Hay 3H **51**
Minnesota Dr. WA5: Gt San 2J **81**
Minstead Av. L33: Kirkb 9D **36**
Minster Ct. L7: Liv 7M **5** (9F **58**)
WA7: Run 7H **95**
Minto Cl. L7: Liv 7H **59**
Minton Cl. L12: Crox 7D **46**
Minton Way WA8: Widnes 3L **79**
Mintor Rd. L33: Kirkb 9E **36**
Minver Rd. L12: W Der 2B **60**
Miranda Av. CH63: H Beb 9L **73**
Miranda Pl. L20: Kirkd 9C **44**
Miranda Rd. L20: Boot 9C **44**
Miranda Rd. Sth.
L20: Kirkd 9C **44**
Mirfield Cl. L26: Halew 1K **93**
WA3: Low 3E **52**
Mirfield St. L6: Liv 6G **59**
Miriam Pl. CH41: Birke 9F **56**
Miriam Rd. L4: W'ton 3F **58**
Miry La. WN8: Parb 3G **22**
Miskelly St. L20: Kirkd 1B **58**
Missouri Dr. WA5: Gt San 1J **81**
Missouri Rd. L13: Liv 2J **59**
Mistle Thrush Way
L12: Crox .7D **46**
Miston St. L20: Kirkd 1B **58**
Misty Cl. WA8: Widnes 6F **78**
Mitchell Av. WA5: Burtw 4G **64**
Mitchell Ct. CH41: Birke 3K **73**
Mitchell Cres. L21: Lith 2A **44**
Mitchell Pl. L1: Liv 5H **5** (8C **58**)
Mitchell Rd. L34: Presc 3N **61**
WA10: St H .9F **48**
WN5: Bil 6A **40**
Mitchell St. WA3: Golb 3B **52**
WA4: Stockt H 8D **82**
WN4: Ash M 9L **41**
Mithril Cl. WA8: Widnes 5A **80**
Mitre Cl. L35: Whis 8A **62**
Mittens La. L37: Form 9H **17**
Mitton Cl. WA3: Cul 5M **53**
Mitylene St. L5: Liv 3D **58**
Moat La. WA3: Rix 7E **68**
Mobberley Cl. WA4: Thel 5L **83**
Mobberley Ct. CH63: Spit 4N **89**
Mobberley Way CH63: Spit 4N **89**
Mockbeggar Dr. CH45: Wall 2D **56**
Mockbeggar Wharf CH45: Wall 2E **56**
Modred St. L8: Liv 3E **74**
Moel Famau Vw. L17: Aig 6G **75**
Moelwyn Dr. CH66: Ell P 7L **103**
Moffatdale Rd. L4: W'ton 1H **59**
Moffatt Rd. L9: Aintr 3H **45**
Moira Sephton Ct. *CH43: Noct 4D **72***
(off Sandalwood Dr.)
Moira St. L6: Liv 3L **5** (7E **58**)
Molesworth Gro. L16: Child 8D **60**
Molineux Av. L14: Brd G 8B **60**
Molland Cl. L12: W Der 1B **60**
Mollington Av. L11: Norr G 8L **45**
Mollington Link CH41: Birke 3L **73**
Mollington Rd. CH44: Wall 6J **57**
L32: Kirkb .9A **36**
Mollington St. CH41: Birke 3L **73**
Molly's La. L33: Kirkb 3H **47**
Molton Rd. L16: Child 9A **60**
Molyneux Av. WA5: Warr 9A **66**
Molyneux Cl. CH49: Upton 3N **71**
L35: Presc .5A **62**
L36: Huy 7K **61**
Molyneux Ct. L11: Norr G 7N **45**
*L14: Brd G 8B **60***
(off Molineux Av.)
Molyneux Dr. CH45: New B 1H **57**
L35: Presc .5A **62**
Molyneux Rd. L6: Liv 6G **58**
L18: Moss H 4L **75**
L22: Wloo .9L **33**
L31: Mag 4L **35**
L39: Augh .5A **28**
Molyneux Way L10: Aintr 8H **35**
Monaghan Cl. L9: W'ton 3F **44**
Monarch Cl. M44: Irlam 3L **69**
Monarchs Quay L3: Liv 9E **4** (1B **74**)
Monash Cl. L33: Kirkb 5C **36**
Monash Rd. L11: Norr G 1L **59**
Monastery La. WA9: St H 2N **63**
Monastery Rd. L6: Liv 3H **59**
WA9: St H .2A **64**
Mona St. CH41: Birke 1F **72**
L20: Boot .4C **44**
WA10: St H .8G **48**
Mona Way M44: Irlam 1N **69**
Mond Rd. L10: Faz 3M **45**
WA8: Widnes 8K **79**
Monfa Rd. L20: Boot 4B **44**
Monica Dr. WA8: Widnes 3K **79**
Monica Rd. L25: Woolt 7F **76**
Monica Ter. WN4: Ash M 9K **41**
Moniven Cl. WA4: Westy 4J **83**
Monkfield Way L19: Garst 3B **92**
Monk Rd. CH44: Wall 5H **57**
Monks Carr La. L38: Gt Alt 6N **25**
Monks Cl. L37: Form 3G **25**
Monksdown Rd. L11: Norr G 9M **45**
Monks Dr. L37: Form 3G **25**
Monks Ferry CH41: Birke 2M **73**
Monksferry Wlk. L19: G'dale 9L **75**
Monks Gro. CH65: Ell P 8N **103**
Monk's La. L40: Burs 8H **15**
Monks Pl. WA2: Warr 1D **82**
Monks St. WA5: Warr 2N **81**
Monk St. *CH41: Birke 2M **73***
(off Cross St.)
L5: Liv 3E **58**
Monk's Way CH48: W Kir 6C **70**
Monks Way CH63: Beb 3M **89**
L25: Woolt .6F **76**
WA7: Pres B 1G **108**
Monkswell Dr. L15: Wavtr 9M **59**
Monkswell St. L8: Liv 5F **74**
Monkswood Cl. WA5: Call 7N **65**
Monmouth Cl. WA1: Wools 1M **83**
Monmouth Cres. WN4: Ash M 9L **41**
Monmouth Dr. L10: Aintr 1L **45**
Monmouth Gro. WA9: St H 8N **49**
Monmouth Rd. CH44: Wall 5F **56**
Monro Cl. L8: Liv 4E **74**
Monroe Cl. WA1: Wools 1J **83**
Monro St. L8: Liv 4E **74**
Mons Sq. *L20: Boot 7B **44***
(off Strand Shop. Cen.)
Montague Rd. L13: Liv 7M **59**
WA8: Widnes 1D **94**
Montagu M. L37: Form 8E **16**
Montagu Rd. L37: Form 7E **16**
Montana Cl. WA5: Gt San 1L **81**
Montclair Dr. L18: Moss H 2N **75**
Montclare Cres. WA4: Stockt H 7F **82**
Montcliffe Cl. WA3: Birchw 4K **67**
Monterey Cl. WA5: Gt San 2K **81**
Monterey Rd. L13: Liv 7N **59**
Montfort Dr. L19: G'dale 9M **75**
Montgomery Av. PR9: South 9M **7**
Montgomery Cl. L35: Whis 7A **62**
WA5: Gt San 9J **65**
Montgomery Hill CH48: Caldy, Frank 8G **71**
Montgomery Rd. L9: W'ton 4F **44**
L36: Huy 5H **61**
WA8: Widnes 8G **78**
Montgomery Way L6: Liv 5G **59**
Montpelier Av. WA7: W'ton 9J **95**
Montpelier Dr. L8: Liv 4E **74**
Montpellier Ct. *CH45: New B 1G **56***
(off Montpellier Cres.)
Montpellier Cres. CH45: New B 1G **56**
Montpellier Ho. CH45: New B 1G **56**
Montreal Rd. L27: N'ley 3J **77**
Montrey Cres. WN4: Garsw 8E **40**
Montrose Av. CH44: Wall 8L **57**
Montrose Bus. Pk. *L7: Liv 7K **59***
(off Tattersall Way)
Montrose Cl. WA2: Fearn 5G **66**
Montrose Ct. CH47: Hoy 2C **70**
L12: W Der .2D **60**
Montrose Dr. PR9: South 6L **7**
Montrose Pl. L26: Halew 1K **93**
Montrose Rd. L13: Liv 3J **59**
Montrose Way L13: Liv 7L **59**
Montrovia Cres. L10: Faz 3L **45**
Montvale Ho. L14: Brd G 7B **60**
Monument Pl. L3: Liv 4J **5** (7D **58**)
Monville Rd. L9: Aintr 3H **45**
Moorbridge Cl. L30: Neth 7F **34**
Moor Cl. L23: Crosb 6M **33**
PR8: Ainsd .3J **17**
Moor Coppice L23: Crosb 6M **33**
Moor Ct. L10: Faz 3M **45**
Moorcroft Rd. CH45: Wall 4D **56**
L18: Aller .7A **76**
Moorditch La. WA6: Frod 5J **107**
Moor Dr. L23: Crosb 6L **33**
WN8: Skel .5G **31**
MOORE 2K **97**
Moore Av. CH42: Rock F 6L **73**
WA4: Thel 5L **83**
WA9: St H .7D **50**
Moore Cl. WA8: Widnes 6N **79**
Moore Dr. WA11: Hay 3H **51**
Moore Gro. WA13: Lymm 3H **85**
Moore La. WA4: Moore 9K **81**
Moore Nature Reserve 8K **81**
Moore's Ho. L4: W'ton 8E **44**
Moore St. L20: Boot 5A **44**
Mooreway L35: Rainh 8B **63**
Moorfield L33: Kirkb 6D **36**
Moorfield Cen. L33: Kirkb 5D **36**
Moorfield Cres. WA3: Low 3H **53**
Moorfield Dr. CH64: P'gte 4C **100**
Moorfield La. L40: Scar 2N **19**
Moorfield Mdw. WN5: Bil 1M **39**
Moorfield Rd. L23: Crosb 6N **33**
WA8: Widnes 4N **79**
WA10: St H .5F **48**
Moorfields L2: Liv 4E **4** (7B **58**)
Moorfields Av. CH43: Noct 4D **72**
Moorfields Station (Rail) 4E **4** (7B **58**)
Moorfoot Rd. WA9: St H 7B **50**
Moorfoot Rd. Ind. Est. WA9: St H 6B **50**
Moorfoot Way L33: Kirkb 5B **36**
Moorgate L39: Orm 9C **20**
Moorgate Av. L23: Crosb 8M **33**
Moorgate La. L32: Kirkb 2E **46**
Moorgate Point L33: Know I 3E **46**
Moorgate Rd. L33: Kirkb 4D **46**
Moorgate Rd. Sth. L34: Know 4D **46**
Moorgate St. L7: Liv 8G **59**
Moorhead Cl. L21: Lith 3N **43**
Moorhey Rd. L31: Mag 4J **35**
Moor Ho. L23: Crosb 6L **33**
Moorhouses L38: Hight 9F **24**
Mooring Cl. WA7: Murd 9F **96**
Moorings, The CH41: Birke 3K **73**
CH60: Hesw 7K **87**
CH62: Port S 2B **90**
L31: Lydi 8G **27**
Moorings Cl. CH64: P'gte 5B **100**
Moorland Av. L23: Crosb 6L **33**
Moorland Cl. CH60: Hesw 8A **88**
Moorland Dr. WA7: Murd 8G **96**
Moorland Pk. CH60: Hesw 8A **88**
Moorland Rd. CH42: Tran 5L **73**
CH66: Ell P 6K **103**
L31: Mag 5H **35**
WN4: Ash M 7N **41**
Moorlands Rd. L23: Thorn 5A **34**
Moor La. CH60: Hesw 7N **87**
L4: W'ton .7F **44**
L10: Faz 3M **45**
L23: Crosb .6L **33**
L23: Crosb, Thorn 6L **33**
L29: Seft 3C **34**
L32: Kirkb .2N **45**
L38: Ince B .8K **25**
PR8: Ainsd .3J **17**
WA6: Frod .6L **107**
WA6: Haps .3B **114**
WA8: Widnes 9J **79**
(not continuous)
Moor La. Bus. Cen. WA8: Widnes 9K **79**
Moor La. Sth. WA8: Widnes 9J **79**
MOOR PARK 5L **33**
Moor Pl. L3: Liv 4J **5** (7D **58**)
Moor Rd. WN5: Orr 7N **31**
MOORSIDE 7C **100**
Moorside WA4: Westy 4F **82**
Moorside Av. CH64: P'gte 6C **100**
Moorside Cl. L23: Crosb 7M **33**
Moorside Ct. WA8: Widnes 9J **79**
Moorside La. CH64: P'gte 7C **100**
Moorside Rd. L23: Crosb 7M **33**
Moor St. L2: Liv 5D **4** (8B **58**)
L39: Orm 8C **20**
Moorway CH60: Hesw 7B **88**
Moorwood Cres. WA9: Clock F 5M **63**
Moran Dr. WA5: Gt San 2J **81**
Moray Cl. WA10: St H 5H **49**
Morcott La. L24: Hale 5A **94**
Morcroft Rd. L36: Huy 4J **61**
Morden Av. WN4: Ash M 7J **41**
Morden St. L6: Liv 6H **59**
Morecambe St. L6: Liv 4H **59**
Morecroft Rd. CH42: Rock F 7N **73**
Moreland Dr. PR8: South 1C **12**
Morella Rd. L4: W'ton 1H **59**
Morello Cl. WA10: St H 5J **49**
Morello Dr. CH63: Spit 5A **90**
Moresby Cl. WA7: Murd 8G **96**
Moret Cl. L23: Crosb 6N **33**
MORETON 9M **55**
Moreton Av. WA9: Clock F 5M **63**
Moreton Cl. WA3: Golb 1A **52**
WN3: Winst .1E **40**
MORETON COMMON 5L **55**
Moreton Dr. WN7: Leigh 1M **53**
Moreton Gro. CH45: Wall 3E **56**
Moreton Hills Golf Cen. 7L **55**
Moreton (Park & Ride) 7M **55**
Moreton Rd. CH49: Upton 1N **71**
Moreton Station (Rail) 7M **55**
Moreton Ter. WA6: Frod 6K **107**
Morgan Av. WA2: Warr 7D **66**
Morgan M. L30: Neth 8C **34**
Morgan St. WA9: St H 8N **49**
Morgans Way WA3: Low 2H **53**
Morland Av. CH62: Brom 9C **90**
CH64: Lit N 7F **100**
Morley Av. CH41: Birke 9H **57**
Morley Ct. L14: Knott A 5C **60**
Morley La. CH3: L Barr 9N **113**
WA6: L Barr 9N **113**
Morley Rd. CH44: Wall 6G **56**
PR9: South .6K **7**
WA4: Warr .7B **82**
WA7: Run 6K **95**
Morley St. L4: W'ton 2D **58**
WA1: Warr .2D **82**
WA10: St H .5J **49**
(not continuous)
Morley Way WA10: St H 6J **49**
Morningside L23: Crosb 8M **33**
Morningside Pl. L11: Norr G 9L **45**
Morningside Rd. L11: Norr G 9L **45**
Morningside Vw. L11: Norr G 1L **59**
Morningside Way L11: Norr G 1L **59**
Mornington Av. CH65: Ell P 9A **104**
L23: Crosb .9L **33**
Mornington Rd. CH45: New B 3H **57**
PR9: South .8H **7**
Mornington St. L8: Liv 3D **74**
Morpeth Cl. CH46: More 9J **55**
Morpeth Rd. CH47: Hoy 3B **70**
Morpeth St. L8: Liv 9K **5** (1E **74**)
Morpeth Walkway CH41: Birke 9L **57**
Morpeth Wharf CH41: Birke 9L **57**
Morphany La. WA4: Dares 9N **97**
Morris Av. WA4: Westy 4G **83**
Morris Cl. WA11: Hay 5C **50**
Morris Ct. CH43: Oxton 3F **72**
Morris La. L34: Hals 2J **19**
Morrison Cl. WA5: Gt San 3J **81**
Morrison M. WA8: Widnes 6G **79**
Morris Rd. WN8: Uph 5K **31**
Morrissey Cl. WA10: St H 6G **48**
Morris St. WA9: St H 9A **50**
Morston Av. L32: Kirkb 2C **46**
Morston Cres. L32: Kirkb 2C **46**
Morston Rd. WA7: Nort 6G **96**

Morston Wlk.—Nelson Ho.

Morston Wlk. L32: Kirkb 2C **46**
Mortar Mill Quay CH41: Birke 8K **57**
Mort Av. WA4: Westy 4H **83**
Mortimer Av. WA2: Warr 9C **66**
Mortimer St. CH41: Birke 2M **73**
Mortlake Cl. WA8: Widnes 5F **78**
Morton Av. WA6: Hel 4E **114**
Morton Cl. WA5: Old H 9L **65**
Morton Ho. L18: Moss H 5L **75**
Morton Rd. WA7: Nort 7F **96**
Morton St. L8: Liv 3E **74**
(not continuous)
Mortuary Rd. CH45: Wall 3H **57**
Morvah Cl. L12: W Der 8A **46**
Morval Cres. L4: W'ton 8D **44**
WA7: Run 6N **95**
Morven Cl. WA2: Warr 6F **66**
Morven Gro. PR8: South 8K **7**
Moscardini Cl. WA7: Cas 5C **96**
Moschatel Wlk. M31: Part 6M **69**
Moscow Dr. L13: Liv 4L **59**
Mosedale Av. WA11: St H 1L **49**
Mosedale Gro. WA7: Beech 1A **108**
Mosedale Rd. CH62: Brom 5D **90**
L9: W'ton 5F **44**
Moseley Av. CH45: Wall 5G **57**
WA4: Westy 4H **83**
Moseley Rd. CH63: Spit 6N **89**
Moses St. L8: Liv 4E **74**
Mosley St. PR8: South 2A **12**
Moss Av. WN5: Bil 9N **31**
MOSS BANK
WA8 9N **79**
WA11 2K **49**
Moss Bank L39: Augh 2B **28**
Moss Bank Ct. L39: Augh 2B **28**
Moss Bank Pk. L21: Lith 2N **43**
Moss Bank Rd. WA8: Widnes 9N **79**
WA11: St H 2J **49**
Mossborough Hall La.
WA11: Rainf 9M **37**
Mossborough Rd. WA11: Rainf 9A **38**
Moss Bri. L40: Lath 2A **22**
Moss Bri. La. L40: Lath 3N **21**
MOSSBROW 1K **85**
Moss Brow WA11: Rainf 4C **38**
Mossbrow Rd. L36: Huy 5J **61**
Moss Cl. CH64: Will 6N **101**
WA4: Stockt H 6F **82**
Mosscraig L28: Stockb V 2G **60**
Mosscroft Cl. L36: Huy 5L **61**
Mossdale Cl. WA5: Gt San 1J **81**
Mossdale Dr. L35: Rainh 6G **62**
Mossdale Rd. L33: Kirkb 6D **36**
WN4: Ash M 3J **41**
Moss Delph La. L39: Augh 2N **27**
Mossdene Rd. CH44: Wall 5F **56**
Moss Dr. WA6: Manl 9J **115**
Moss End Way L33: Know I 8H **37**
Mossfield Rd. L9: W'ton 4E **44**
Moss Gdns. PR8: South 4B **12**
Moss Ga. WA3: Birchw 3A **68**
Moss Ga. Gro. L14: Knott A 6E **60**
Moss Ga. Rd. L14: Knott A 6E **60**
Mossgiel Av. PR8: Ainsd 1H **17**
Moss Grn. L37: Form 1G **25**
Moss Grn. Cl. L36: Huy 5F **60**
Moss Grn. Way WA9: St H 9C **50**
Moss Gro. CH42: Tran 6H **73**
L8: Liv 2H **75**
WA13: Lymm 4H **85**
Moss Hall La. WA4: L Stret 6G **98**
Mosshey Ct. CH63: Spit 4N **89**
Moss Hey La. PR4: Mere B 4L **9**
Mosshill Cl. L31: Mag 9H **27**
Moss Ind. Est. WN7: Leigh 1J **53**
Mosslake Way L4: Kirkd 2C **58**
Mosslands WA10: Ec'stn 6D **48**
Mosslands Cl. CH66: Gt Sut 3K **111**
Mosslands Dr. CH44: Wall 4E **56**
CH45: Wall 4E **56**
Moss La. CH42: Tran 6H **73**
L9: W'ton 4E **44**
L20: Boot 4D **44**
L21: Lith 2A **44**
L23: L Cros 9J **25**
L31: Lydi 7G **27**
L31: Mag 1K **35**
(not continuous)
L33: Kirkb 8F **36**
L33: Simsw 3D **36**
L38: Hight 7G **25**
L39: Bic 1K **37**
L39: Down 8M **17**
L40: Burs 8K **15**
M31: Part, Warb 6M **69**
M44: Cad 4K **69**
PR9: Banks 1G **8**
PR9: South 7M **7**
WA1: Wools 9M **67**
WA3: Low 5C **52**
WA3: Rix 4E **68**
WA4: Moore 9J **81**
WA6: Manl 9J **115**
WA9: St H 8C **50**
WA11: Crank 6H **39**
WA11: Windle 3C **48**
WA13: Warb 8L **69**
WA16: High L 9L **85**
WN6: Wright 1M **23**
WN8: Skel 6C **30**
Moss La. Vw. WN8: Skel 6C **30**
Mosslawn Rd. L32: Kirkb 1E **46**
Mosslea Pk. L18: Moss H 4L **75**
Mossley Av. CH62: Brom 7C **90**
L18: Moss H 3L **75**
Mossley Ct. L18: Moss H 5M **75**
MOSSLEY HILL 5L **75**
Mossley Hill Dr. L17: Aig 3J **75**
(not continuous)
Mossley Hill Rd. L18: Moss H 6L **75**
L19: Aig 6L **75**
Mossley Hill Station (Rail) 5M **75**
Mossley Rd. CH42: Tran 5L **73**
MOSS NOOK 9B **50**
Moss Nook L39: Augh 2N **27**
L40: Burs 8J **15**
Moss Nook La.
L31: Mag, Mell 3M **35**
WA11: Rainf 5B **38**
(not continuous)
Mossock Hall Golf Course 8C **28**
Moss Pits Cl. L10: Faz 3L **45**
Moss Pits La. L10: Faz 3K **45**
L15: Wavtr 2N **75**
Moss Rd. M44: Cad 1J **69**
PR8: South 4A **12**
WA4: Westy 5H **83**
WN5: Bil 9N **31**
MOSS SIDE
L31 1K **35**
WA4 9H **81**
Moss Side L14: Knott A 6E **60**
L37: Form 9H **17**
Moss Side La. CW9: Ant 8K **99**
PR4: Mere B 3J **9**
WA3: Rix 6E **68**
WA4: Moore 9G **81**
Moss Side Rd. M44: Cad 3K **69**
Moss St. L6: Liv 3L **5** (7E **58**)
L19: Garst 1A **92**
L34: Presc 2A **62**
WA8: Widnes 9N **79**
Mossvale CH66: Lit Sut 6J **103**
Moss Vw. L21: Lith 2B **44**
L31: Mag 2L **35**
L39: Orm 9D **20**
Moss Vw. Rd. M31: Part 6N **69**
Mossville Cl. L18: Moss H 6M **75**
Mossville Rd. L18: Moss H 6N **75**
Moss Way L11: Crox 5A **46**
Mossy Bank Rd. CH44: Wall 5K **57**
Moston Gro. WA13: Lymm 5D **84**
Moston Way CH66: Gt Sut 2L **111**
Mostyn Av. CH48: W Kir 7C **70**
CH60: Hesw 7K **87**
L10: Aintr 8H **35**
L19: Aller 8B **76**
Mostyn Cl. L4: Kirkd 2D **58**
Mostyn Gdns. CH64: P'gte 5B **100**
Mostyn Sq. CH64: P'gte 5B **100**
Mostyn St. CH44: Wall 6H **57**
Mote Hill Ct. WA1: Warr 2E **82**
Motherwell Cl. WA8: Widnes 5H **79**
Motherwell Cres. PR8: South 3E **12**
Mottershead Cl. WA8: Widnes 8K **79**
Mottershead Rd. WA8: Widnes 8K **79**
Mottram Cl. L33: Kirkb 9D **36**
WA4: Grap 5J **83**
Mottram Ri. WA10: Ec'stn 7E **48**
Moughland La. WA7: Run 6J **95**
Moulders La. WA1: Warr 4C **82**
MOULDSWORTH 9K **115**
Moulton Cl. WA7: Sut W 2B **108**
Mounsey Rd. CH42: Tran 3K **73**
Mount, The CH44: Wall 5J **57**
CH60: Hesw 7N **87**
WN8: Skel 4E **30**
Mountain Vw. WA6: Hel 2E **114**
Mount Av. CH60: Hesw 7N **87**
CH63: H Beb 9K **73**
L20: Boot 3C **44**
Mt. Carmel Gdns. L39: Augh 2B **28**
Mount Cl. L32: Kirkb 7A **36**
Mount Ct. CH45: Wall 1G **56**
CH60: Hesw 7N **87**
Mount Cres. L32: Kirkb 7A **36**
Mount Dr. CH63: H Beb 9K **73**
Mt. Farm Way CH66: Gt Sut 3H **111**
Mountfield Cres. L25: Gate 3E **76**
Mountford Gdns. L18: Moss H 5K **75**
Mount Gro. CH41: Birke 3J **73**
Mount Gro. Pl. *CH41: Birke 3J 73*
(off Mount Gro.)
Mt. Haven Cl. CH49: Upton 3A **72**
Mounthouse Cl. L37: Form 8H **17**
Mount Ho. Rd. L37: Form 8H **17**
Mount Olive CH43: Oxton 5G **73**
Mount Pk. CH63: H Beb 9K **73**
L25: Woolt 5E **76**
Mount Pk. Ct. L25: Woolt 5E **76**
Mt. Pleasant CH2: Elt 1L **113**
CH43: Oxton 5H **73**
L3: Liv 6H **5** (8D **58**)
L22: Wloo 1K **43**
WA8: Widnes 6L **79**
Mt. Pleasant Av. WA9: St H 7C **50**
Mt. Pleasant Cl. CH45: New B 2H **57**
Mt. Pleasant Rd. CH45: New B, Wall 3G **56**
Mount Rd. CH42: Tran 7J **73**
CH45: Wall 1G **56**
CH48: W Kir 7D **70**
Mount Rd. CH49: Upton 3A **72**
CH63: H Beb, Spit 5L **89**
L32: Kirkb 8N **35**
(not continuous)
WA7: Hal 7B **96**
Mount St. L1: Liv 8J **5** (9D **58**)
L22: Wloo 1K **43**
L25: Woolt 6E **76**
PR9: South 8J **7**
WA8: Widnes 6L **79**
Mount Ter. PR9: South 8J **7**
Mount Vernon L7: Liv 5N **5** (8F **58**)
Mt. Vernon Grn. L7: Liv 4N **5** (7F **58**)
Mt. Vernon Rd. L7: Liv 4M **5** (7F **58**)
Mt. Vernon St. L7: Liv 4M **5** (7F **58**)
Mountview Cl. L8: Liv 3F **74**
Mount Way CH63: H Beb 9K **73**
Mountwood WN8: Skel 9D **22**
Mountwood Lodge PR8: Ainsd 9J **11**
Mountwood Rd. CH42: Tran 8J **73**
Mourne Cl. CH66: Lit Sut 8F **102**
Mowbray Av. WA11: St H 5M **49**
Mowbray Ct. L20: Kirkd 9B **44**
Mowbray Gro. L13: Liv 8M **59**
Mowcroft La. WA5: Cuerd 5C **80**
Mowpen Brow WA16: High L 9H **85**
Moxon Av. WA4: Westy 3G **83**
Moxon St. WA10: St H 8F **48**
Moxon Way WN4: Ash M 7M **41**
Moyles Cl. WA8: Widnes 6G **79**
Mozart Cl. L8: Liv 2G **74**
Mr Hardman's Home Photographic Studio
8J **5** (9D **58**)
Mudhouse La. CH64: Burt 2A **110**
Muirfield Cl. L12: W Der 3C **60**
WA2: Fearn 6H **67**
Muirfield Dr. PR8: Ainsd 1J **17**
Muirfield Rd. L36: Roby 8G **61**
Muirhead Av. L6: Liv 5H **59**
L13: Liv, W Der 3K **59**
Muirhead Av. E. L11: Norr G 1M **59**
Muir Rd. L9: Aintr 4J **45**
Mulberry Av. WA3: Low 3G **52**
WA8: Widnes 9M **79**
WA10: St H 7F **48**
Mulberry Cl. CH2: Elt 2N **113**
CH42: Rock F 6M **73**
L33: Kirkb 5D **36**
L39: Orm 9E **20**
WA1: Wools 2M **83**
Mulberry Ct. L7: Liv 7L **5**
WA4: Stockt H 7E **82**
Mulberry Gro. CH44: Wall 6K **57**
Mulberry Pl. L7: Liv 7L **5** (9E **58**)
Mulberry Rd. CH42: Rock F 6M **73**
Mulberry St. L7: Liv 7L **5** (9E **58**)
Mulcrow Cl. WA9: St H 6N **49**
Mulgrave St. L8: Liv 9M **5** (1F **74**)
Mull Cl. CH65: Ell P 4A **112**
Mullein Cl. WA3: Low 2E **52**
Mullen Cl. WA5: Warr 8A **66**
Mullins Av. WA12: Newt W 5L **51**
Mullion Cl. L26: Halew 8J **77**
PR9: South 2N **7**
WA7: Brook 9D **96**
Mullion Gro. WA2: Padg 8H **67**
Mullion Rd. L11: Crox 5A **46**
Mullion Wlk. L11: Crox 5A **46**
Mullrea Cl. L27: N'ley 2G **77**
Mullwood Cl. L12: Crox 7D **46**
Mulrankin Ct. L13: Liv 7N **59**
Mulvanney Cres. WA10: St H 4J **49**
Mulveton Rd. CH63: Spit 4M **89**
Mumfords Gro. CH47: Meols 8F **54**
Mumfords La. CH47: Meols 8E **54**
(not continuous)
Muncaster Cl. CH62: Brom 6C **90**
Muncaster Ct. WA7: Cas 5B **96**
Muncaster Dr. WA11: Rainf 4D **38**
Munster Rd. L13: Liv 6N **59**
Murat Gro. L22: Wloo 1J **43**
Murat St. L22: Wloo 1J **43**
Murcote Rd. L14: Knott A 4D **60**
MURDISHAW 9F **96**
Murdishaw Av. WA7: Brook, Murd 1E **108**
Murdock Way L10: Faz 4N **45**
Muriel Cl. WA5: Gt San 2F **80**
Muriel St. L4: W'ton 1F **58**
Murphy Gro. WA9: St H 6A **50**
Murrayfield Dr. CH46: Leas 5N **55**
Murrayfield Rd. L25: Gate 2F **76**
Murrayfield Wlk. *L25: Gate 1F 76*
(off Murrayfield Rd.)
Murray Gro. CH48: W Kir 5B **70**
Mus. of Liverpool 6C **4** (8A **58**)
Museum St. WA1: Warr 4B **82**
Musker Dr. L30: Neth 8B **34**
Musker Gdns. L23: Crosb 8M **33**
Musker St. L23: Crosb 8M **33**
Muspratt Rd. L21: Sea 5N **43**
Mustard La. WA3: Croft 1H **67**
Muttocks Rake *L30: Neth 6C 34*
(off Great Hey)
Mycroft Cl. L5: Liv 3E **58**
Myddleton La. WA2: Winw 3C **66**
Myers Av. L35: Whis 4D **62**
Myerscough Av. L20: Boot 5D **44**
Myers Ct. L23: Crosb 9M **33**
Myers Rd. E. L23: Crosb 8L **33**
Myers Rd. W. L23: Crosb 8K **33**
Mylia Cl. L14: Knott A 6E **60**
Mynsule Rd. CH63: Spit 4M **89**
Myrtle Av. WA11: Hay 3D **50**
WN4: Ash M 5H **41**
Myrtle Ct. L7: Liv 9F **58**
L8: Liv 8N **5** (9F **58**)
Myrtle Gro. CH44: Wall 6L **57**
L22: Wloo 9K **33**
PR8: South 9K **7**
WA4: Warr 5E **82**
WA8: Widnes 8G **78**
WN5: Bil 7N **39**
Myrtle Pde. L7: Liv 8L **5** (9E **58**)
Myrtle Rd. M31: Part 6K **69**
Myrtle St. CH65: Ell P 7A **104**
L7: Liv 7K **5** (9E **58**)
Myrtle Way CH49: Wdchu 4B **72**
Mystery Cl. L15: Wavtr 1K **75**
Mystic M. *L39: Orm 8C 20*
(off Burscough St.)
Mytholme Av. M44: Cad 6J **69**

N

Naburn Gro. CH46: More 1M **71**
Nairn Av. WN8: Skel 8E **22**
Nairn Cl. CH63: East 2C **102**
WA2: Fearn 6J **67**
Nansen Cl. WA5: Old H 1M **81**
Nansen Gro. L4: W'ton 9F **44**
Nant Pk. Ct. CH45: New B 1J **57**
Nantwich Cl. CH49: Wdchu 6A **72**
Nantwich Rd. CH66: Gt Sut 2L **111**
Napier Cl. WA10: St H 7H **49**
Napier Dr. CH46: More 9N **55**
Napier Rd. CH62: New F 8A **74**
Napier St. L20: Boot 9A **44**
WA1: Warr 3D **82**
(not continuous)
WA10: St H 7H **49**
Napier Ter. PR8: Birkd 1N **11**
Naples Rd. CH44: Wall 6K **57**
Napps Cl. L25: Gate 1D **76**
Napps Wlk. *L25: Gate 1D 76*
(off Napps Cl.)
Napps Way CH61: Hesw 5A **88**
L25: Gate 9D **60**
Nares Cl. WA5: Old H 8L **65**
Narrow Cft. Rd. L39: Augh 3N **27**
Narrow La. L39: Augh 3N **27**
L39: Hals 6K **19**
WA4: Grap 7J **83**
NARROW MOSS 4C **20**
Narrow Moss La. L40: Scar 3B **20**
Naseby Cl. CH43: Noct 4C **72**
Naseby St. L4: W'ton 8E **44**
Nashville Dr. WA5: Gt San 1K **81**
Natal Rd. L9: Aintr 4G **45**
Nathan Dr. WA11: Hay 4G **51**
Nathan Gro. L33: Kirkb 7D **36**
National Waterways Mus. 7B **104**
National Wildflower Cen. 8D **60**
Naughton Lea WA8: Widnes 5G **78**
Naughton Rd. WA8: Widnes 8K **79**
Navenby Rd. WN3: Wigan 1J **41**
Navigation Cl. L30: Neth 7F **34**
WA7: Murd 9F **96**
Navigation Rd. WA9: St H 6M **49**
Navigation St. WA1: Warr 3E **82**
Navigation Wharf L3: Liv 2C **74**
Naylor Av. WA3: Golb 2C **52**
Naylor Cl. CH66: Ell P 6L **103**
Naylor Ct. CH66: Ell P 8K **103**
Naylor Cres. CH66: Ell P 6L **103**
Naylor Grn. CH66: Ell P 6L **103**
Naylor Pl. CH66: Ell P 6L **103**
Naylor Rd. CH43: Bid 9E **56**
CH66: Ell P 7L **103**
WA8: Widnes 7N **79**
Naylorsfield Dr. L27: N'ley 2G **76**
Naylor's Rd. L25: Gate 3H **77**
L27: N'ley 2H **77**
Naylor St. L3: Liv 2E **4** (6B **58**)
WA1: Warr 3C **82**
Naylor Wlk. CH66: Ell P 7L **103**
Nazareth Ho. La.
WA8: Widnes 9F **78**
Nazeby Av. L23: Crosb 8N **33**
Neale Dr. CH49: Grea 5M **71**
Neales Fold PR9: South 2B **8**
Neasham Cl. L26: Halew 8K **77**
Nedens Gro. L31: Lydi 9H **27**
Nedens La. L31: Lydi 9H **27**
Needham Cl. WA7: Run 5N **95**
Needham Cres. CH43: Noct 4D **72**
Needham Rd. L7: Liv 7H **59**
Needham Way WN8: Skel 8E **22**
Needwood Dr. CH63: Beb 4M **89**
Neills Rd. WA9: Bold 4D **64**
Neilson Rd. L17: Aig 5G **75**
Neilson St. L17: Aig 5G **75**
Neil St. WA8: Widnes 6M **79**
Nell's La. L39: Augh 7L **27**
Nelson Av. L35: Whis 7B **62**
Nelson Ct. CH42: Rock F 7N **73**
CH45: New B 9H **43**
PR8: Birkd 2M **11**
Nelson Dr. CH61: Pens 3M **87**
M44: Cad 3L **69**
WA7: W'ton 9J **95**
Nelson Ho. CH42: Rock F 7N **73**

Nelson Memorial—Norbury Wlk.

Nelson Memorial 4D 4
(off Exchange Pas. E.)
Nelson Pl. L35: Whis 7B 62
Nelson Rd. CH42: Rock F 7N 73
CH65: Ell P .7A 104
L7: Liv 8G 58
L21: Lith .3A 44
(off Bridge Rd.)
WA3: Ris 5L 67
Nelson's Cft. CH63: Beb 4N 89
Nelson St. CH45: New B 2J 57
L1: Liv 9G 5 (1C 74)
(not continuous)
L15: Wavtr .9K 59
L20: Boot 8A 44
PR8: South .9F 6
WA7: Run 5K 95
WA8: Widnes 1K 95
WA12: Newt W 7J 51
(not continuous)
Nelville Rd. L9: Aintr 3H 45
Nemos Cl. WA6: Hel 3F 114
Neptune Cl. WA7: Murd 8F 96
Neptune St. CH41: Birke 9K 57
NESS 9G 101
Ness Acre La. CH64: Will 6L 101
Nesse Ho. CH64: Nest 6E 100
(off Churchill Way)
Ness Gro. L32: Kirkb 9A 36
NESSHOLT 9F 100
NESTON 6E 100
Neston Av. WA9: Clock F 5L 63
Neston Cl. WA6: Hel 3D 114
Neston Gdns. CH41: Birke 9H 57
(off Churchview Rd.)
Neston Grn.
CH66: Gt Sut 1J 111
(not continuous)
Neston Recreation Cen. 5F 100
Neston Rd. CH63: Thorn H 2F 100
CH64: Burt, Ness 9F 100
CH64: Nest .2F 100
CH64: Will 6L 101
Neston Station (Rail) 6E 100
Neston St. L4: W'ton 9E 44
Netherby St. L8: Liv 5E 74
Netherfield WA8: Widnes 8G 79
Netherfield Cl. CH43: Noct 4C 72
Netherfield Rd. Nth. L5: Liv 3D 58
Netherfield Rd. Sth. L5: Liv 5D 58
NETHERLEY 3J 77
Netherley Rd. L27: N'ley 3K 77
L35: Tar G 3K 77
WA8: Widnes 5N 77
Netherpool Rd. CH66: Ell P 7L 103
NETHERTON
L30 . . . . .8E 34
WA6 . . . . .7K 107
Netherton Activity Cen. 7D 34
Netherton Dr. WA6: Frod 7K 107
Netherton Grange L30: Neth 8G 35
Netherton Grn. L30: Neth 6E 34
Netherton Ind. Est. L30: Neth 2E 44
Netherton La. L30: Neth 6D 34
(not continuous)
Netherton Pk. Rd. L21: Lith 2C 44
Netherton Rd. CH46: More 9M 55
L18: Moss H 7M 75
L20: Boot 4C 44
Netherton Way L30: Boot 2D 44
(off Captain's La.)
L30: Neth 1D 44
Netherwood Gro. WN3: Winst 2G 40
Netherwood Rd. L11: Norr G 8K 45
Netley St. L4: Kirkd 1D 58
Nettle Hill CH48: W Kir 5B 70
Nettlestead Rd. L11: Norr G 1M 59
Neva Av. CH46: More 9L 55
Nevada Cl. WA5: Gt San 9L 65
Neverstitch Cl. WN8: Skel 2C 30
Neverstitch Rd. WN8: Skel 3N 29
Neville Av. WA2: Warr 8E 66
WA9: St H 8D 50
Neville Cl. CH43: Noct 4C 72
Neville Cres. WA5: Penk 5J 81
Neville Rd. CH44: Wall 5G 56
CH62: Brom .8D 90
L22: Wloo 1L 43
Neville St. WA12: Newt W 6J 51
Nevill St. PR9: South 7G 6
Nevin St. L6: Liv 2M 5 (6F 58)
Nevison St. L7: Liv 8G 58
Nevitte Cl. L28: Stockb V 1E 60
New Acres WN8: Newb 3D 22
New Acres Cl. CH43: Bid 9C 56
New Albert Ter. WA7: Run 4L 95
(off Frederic Pl.)
Newark Cl. CH43: Noct 4C 72
L30: Neth 6G 34
L36: Huy 3H 61
Newark Dr. WA5: Gt San 2J 81
Newark St. L4: W'ton 9E 44
Newarth Dr. WA13: Lymm 6G 85
New Bank Pl. WA8: Widnes 7E 78
New Bank Rd. WA8: Widnes 7E 78
New Barn Av. WN4: Ash M 8L 41
New Barnet WA8: Widnes 5J 79
New Bird St. L1: Liv 9H 5 (1C 74)
New Bold Ct. WA9: Bold 2C 64
Newbold Cres. CH48: W Kir 5F 70
Newbold Gro. L12: Crox 8D 46
Newborough Av. L18: Moss H 3L 75
L23: Crosb .7N 33
Newborough Cl. WA5: Call 7M 65
NEW BOSTON .4G 51
New Bridge WA1: Warr 4C 82
WA4: Warr 4C 82
Newbridge Cl. CH49: Wdchu 4B 72
WA5: Call 7L 65
WA7: Brook .9E 96
WN4: Garsw .8F 40
New Bri. Ct. CH65: Ell P 1D 112
Newbridge Farm Cvn. Pk. L33: Simsw . . .4J 37
Newbridge Rd. CH2: Lit Stan 2D 112
CH65: Ell P .1D 112
NEW BRIGHTON 9H 43
New Brighton Station (Rail) 1G 57
NEWBURGH 4D 22
Newburgh Cl. WA7: Wind H 6F 96
Newburn CH43: Oxton 3H 73
Newburn Cl. WN8: Skel 8E 22
Newburns La. CH43: Oxton 5H 73
Newburn St. L4: W'ton 8E 44
Newbury Cl. L36: Roby 8H 61
WA8: Widnes 5K 79
Newbury Rd. WN8: Skel 8E 22
Newbury Way CH46: Leas 6N 55
L12: W Der .4C 60
Newby Av. L35: Rainh 5D 62
Newby Cl. PR8: Ainsd 2H 17
Newby Dr. L36: Huy 6G 60
WN8: Skel 8E 22
Newby Gro. L12: W Der 8A 46
Newby Pl. WA11: St H 2K 49
Newby St. L4: W'ton 1E 58
New Carr La. L31: Gt Alt 5D 26
Newcastle Rd. L15: Wavtr 2M 75
New Causeway L37: Gt Alt 4H 25
L38: Ince B .6H 25
New Charlotte Way L1: Liv 5G 4 (8C 58)
New Chester Rd. CH41: Birke, Tran 3M 73
CH42: Rock F, Tran 6N 73
CH62: Brom, East, New F, Port S 1B 90
CH66: Hoot .4F 102
Newchurch Cl. L27: N'ley 4K 77
Newchurch La. WA3: Cul 8N 53
Newcombe Av. WA2: Warr 9F 66
Newcombe St. L6: Liv 4G 59
New Ct. Way L39: Orm 8D 20
Newcroft Rd. L25: Woolt 4D 76
New Cross St. L34: Presc 2A 62
WA10: St H .6J 49
(Henry St.)
WA10: St H .7J 49
(Westfield St.)
New Cross St. Sth. WA10: St H 7J 49
(off Nth. John St.)
New Cut Cl. PR8: Birkd 6N 11
New Cut Ind. Est. WA1: Wools 1K 83
New Cut La. L33: Kirkb, Rainf 3L 47
L39: Hals 8C 12
PR8: Birkd 6N 11
WA1: Wools .1J 83
WA11: Rainf 1M 47
Newdales Cl. CH43: Bid 9C 56
Newdown Rd. L11: Crox 5B 46
Newdown Wlk. L11: Crox 5B 46
Newell Rd. CH44: Wall 4H 57
Newenham Cres. L14: Knott A 5C 60
New Extension Quay CH65: Ell P 6N 103
NEW FERRY 9A 74
New Ferry By-Pass 8A 74
New Ferry Rd. CH62: New F 9A 74
Newfield Cl. L23: Thorn 5B 34
Newfield Ct. WA13: Lymm 3G 85
Newfield Rd. WA13: Lymm 5D 84
Newfields WA10: St H 6F 48
Newfield Ter. WA6: Hel 3E 114
New Fold WN5: Orr 8M 31
New Fort Way L20: Boot 4N 43
New Foul La. PR8: South 2F 12
NEWGATE 5K 31
Newgate Rd. WN8: Uph 5J 31
New Glade Hill WA11: St H 4N 49
New Grey Rock Cl. L6: Liv 5G 58
New Grosvenor Rd. CH65: Ell P 7N 103
New Hall L10: Faz 2L 45
New Hall Dr. PR8: South 5H 13
New Hall La. CH47: Hoy 2C 70
L11: Norr G .1K 59
WA3: Cul, Ris 9M 53
(not continuous)
New Hall Mnr. CH64: Nest 9E 88
New Hall Pl. L3: Liv 4C 4 (7A 58)
Newhall St. L1: Liv 9H 5 (1C 74)
New Hampshire Cl. WA5: Gt San 1K 81
Newhaven Rd. CH45: New B 2J 57
WA2: Warr 5C 66
New Hawthorne Gdns. L18: Moss H 5L 75
New Hedley Gro. L5: Liv 4B 58
New Henderson St. L8: Liv 2D 74
New Hey L12: W Der 4M 59
New Heyes CH64: Nest 5E 100
New Hey La. CH64: Will 7M 101
New Hey Rd. CH49: Wdchu 4B 72
New Heys Dr. L18: Aller 7B 76
Newholme Cl. L12: Crox 7C 46
Newhope Rd. CH41: Birke 1J 73
Newhouse Dr. WN3: Winst 2F 40
Newhouse Rd. L15: Wavtr 1J 75
NEW HOUSES 1E 40
New Houses La. CH64: Lit N 9E 100
New Hutte La. L26: Halew 1J 93
Newick Pk. L32: Kirkb 1A 46
Newick Rd. L32: Kirkb 1A 46
Newington L1: Liv 6H 5 (8D 58)
Newington Way WA8: Widnes 5J 79
New Islington L3: Liv 3H 5 (7D 58)
Newland Cl. WA8: Widnes 5F 78
Newland Ct. L17: Aig 5H 75
Newland Dr. CH44: Wall 5G 56
Newland M. WA3: Cul 5M 53
Newlands Av. L40: Burs 1K 21
Newlands Cl. WA6: Frod 8M 107
Newlands Dr. WA3: Low 2E 52
Newlands Rd. CH63: Beb 3A 90
WA4: Stockt H 6G 83
WA11: St H .3M 49
NEW LANE 8F 14
New La. L39: Augh 2C 28
L39: Down 1D 26
(Back La.)
L39: Down 9A 18
(Old Moss La.)
L40: Burs 7F 14
PR9: South .3B 8
WA3: Croft .2H 67
WA4: App T .2J 99
NEW LANE END .8H 53
New La. End WA3: Croft 8H 53
New La. Pace PR9: Banks 1F 8
New Lane Station (Rail) 7F 14
Newling St. CH41: Birke 1J 73
Newlove Av. WA10: St H 7F 48
Newlyn Av. L21: Lith 1N 43
L31: Mag 2K 35
Newlyn Cl. CH47: Meols 8F 54
WA7: Brook .9D 96
Newlyn Dr. WN4: Ash M 9K 41
WN8: Skel 5G 31
Newlyn Gdns. WA5: Penk 5F 80
Newlyn Gro. WA11: St H 3N 49
Newlyn Rd. CH47: Meols 8F 54
L11: Crox 5B 46
Newlyn Wlk. L11: Crox 5B 46
New Mnr. Rd. WA4: Pres H 9K 97
Newman St. L4: Kirkd 2C 58
WA4: Westy .4G 83
New Mkt. Cl. L21: Lith 3A 44
Newmarket Gdns. WA9: St H 3F 62
New Mkt. Hall WA7: Run 4K 95
(off Granville St.)
New Mkt. Wlk. WA1: Warr 3C 82
New Mdw. La. L37: Gt Alt 4L 25
New Mersey Retail Pk. 2D 92
New Mersey Shop. Pk. 2D 92
New Mill Stile L25: Woolt 5E 76
Newmoore La. WA7: Nort 4G 97
Newmorn Ct. L17: Aig 6H 75
New Moss Rd. M44: Cad 3K 69
Newnham Dr. CH65: Ell P 1A 112
New Palace & Adventureland 9H 43
NEW PALE 8M 115
New Pale Rd. WA6: Kgswd, Manl C 4L 115
Newport Av. CH45: Wall 2D 56
Newport Bus. Pk. CH65: Ell P 2D 112
Newport Cl. CH43: Noct 4C 72
Newport Ct. L5: Liv 4B 58
New Quay L3: Liv 4C 4 (7A 58)
Newquay Cl. WA7: Brook 9D 96
New Quay Ter. L3: Liv 4C 4
New Red Rock Vw. L6: Liv 5G 58
New Rd. CH66: Chil T 6F 102
CW9: Ant 6L 99
L13: Liv 4K 59
L34: Eccl P .2B 62
L37: Form 8G 16
L40: Ruf 3M 15
WA4: Warr 4C 82
(not continuous)
WA13: Lymm .5E 84
New Rd. Ct. L13: Liv 4K 59
(off Oak Leigh)
New School La. CH66: Chil T 6G 102
Newsham Cl. WA8: Widnes 4E 78
Newsham Dr. L6: Liv 5H 59
(not continuous)
Newsham Rd. L36: Huy 9L 61
Newsham St. L5: Liv 4C 58
Newsholme Cl. WA3: Cul 7N 53
News La. WA11: Rainf 1C 38
Newstead Av. L23: Blun 8H 33
Newstead Dr. WN8: Skel 8E 22
Newstead Rd. L8: Liv 1H 75
WA8: Widnes 1C 94
Newstet Rd. L33: Know I 9F 36
New St. CH44: Wall 7L 57
CH64: Lit N 9E 100
L39: Hals 6F 18
WA7: Run 5K 95
WA8: Widnes 8L 79
WA9: St H, Sut L 4M 63
WN4: Ash M .7L 41
NEWTON
CH48 . . . . .6F 70
WA6 . . . . .3N 115
Newton Av. WA3: Ris 4M 67
Newton Bank WA4: Dares 7K 97
Newton Cl. L12: W Der 1N 59
NEWTON COMMON 7G 51
Newton Ct. CH42: Rock F 7N 73
(off New Chester Rd.)
L13: Wavtr 8K 59
Newton Cross La. CH48: W Kir 6F 70
Newton Dr. CH48: W Kir 6F 70
WN8: Skel 8E 22
Newton Gdns. WA3: Low 2H 53
Newton Gro. WA2: Fearn 6G 66
Newton Hollows WA6: Frod 4M 115
Newton La. WA4: Dares, L Whit 7K 97
(not continuous)
WA12: Newt W 4N 51
NEWTON-LE-WILLOWS 6M 51
Newton-le-Willows Station (Rail) 7N 51
Newton Pk. Dr. WA12: Newt W 7A 52
Newton Pk. Rd. CH48: W Kir 6F 70
Newton Rd. CH44: Wall 5G 57
CH47: Hoy 1D 70
CH65: Ell P .9A 104
L13: Liv 5K 59
WA2: Winw .9A 52
WA3: Low 6B 52
WA9: St H 7C 50
WN5: Bil 5A 40
Newton St. CH41: Birke 1K 73
PR9: South 8L 7
Newton Wlk. L20: Boot 6A 44
(off Capricorn Way)
Newton Way CH49: Upton 3N 71
L3: Liv 5K 5 (8E 58)
New Twr. Ct. CH45: New B 1J 57
NEWTOWN 5N 107
Newtown CH64: Lit N 8F 100
Newtown Gdns. L32: Kirkb 9C 36
New Va. PR9: Banks 4E 8
New Way L39: Bic 1F 36
Newway L14: Knott A 4E 60
New Way Bus. Cen. CH44: Wall 7K 57
New William Cl. M31: Part 5M 69
(off Moss La.)
Nicander Rd. L18: Moss H 3L 75
Nicholas Ho. L23: Blun 7H 33
Nicholas Rd. L23: Blun 7H 33
WA8: Widnes 8F 78
Nicholas St. L3: Liv 1F 4 (6C 58)
Nicholl Rd. WA10: Ec'stn 4D 48
Nicholls Dr. CH61: Pens 3N 87
Nicholls St. WA4: Grap 6J 83
Nichols Gro. L18: Aller 7A 76
Nicholson St. WA1: Warr 3A 82
WA9: St H 6A 50
Nickleby Cl. L8: Liv 3E 74
Nickleford Hall Dr. WA8: Widnes 2J 79
Nicola Ct. CH45: Wall 3J 57
Nicol Av. WA3: Wools 9N 67
Nicol Mere Dr. WN4: Ash M 5J 41
Nicol Rd. WN4: Ash M 6J 41
Nidderdale Av. L35: Rainh 6G 62
Nigella Dr. L11: Norr G 9M 45
Nigel Rd. CH60: Hesw 7C 88
Nigel Wlk. WA7: Cas 5C 96
Nightingale Cl. L27: N'ley 3K 77
L32: Kirkb .8N 35
WA3: Birchw 5N 67
WA7: Beech 1B 108
Nightingale Rd. L12: Crox 7D 46
Nimrod St. L4: W'ton 9E 44
Ninth Av. L9: Aintr 3J 45
Nipe La. WN8: Skel 7D 30
Nithsdale Rd. L15: Wavtr 2K 75
Nixon's La. PR8: Ainsd 7L 11
Nixons La. WN8: Skel 5G 31
Nixon St. L4: W'ton 8E 44
Noble Cl. WA3: Birchw 6M 67
NOCTORUM 4D 72
Noctorum Av. CH43: Noct 3C 72
Noctorum Dell CH43: Noct 4D 72
Noctorum La. CH43: Noct, Oxton 2D 72
Noctorum Rd. CH43: Noct 3D 72
Noctorum Way CH43: Noct 4D 72
Noel Ga. L39: Augh 3N 27
Noel St. L8: Liv 1H 75
Nolan St. PR8: South 1B 12
Nook, The CH2: Back 9N 111
CH43: Oxton 2H 73
CH48: Frank .6J 71
L25: Gate 5F 76
L39: Augh 4A 28
WA10: Windle 4E 48
WN6: App B .6N 23
Nook La. CW9: Ant 9L 99
WA2: Fearn .7J 67
WA3: Golb 2C 52
WA4: Westy .5H 83
WA9: St H 9B 50
Nook Ri. L15: Wavtr 9N 59
Noonan Cl. L9: W'ton 6E 44
Noon Ct. WA12: Newt W 9K 51
Noon La. L40: Ruf 4J 15
Nora St. WA1: Warr 3D 82
Norbreck Av. L14: Brd G 7D 60
Norbreck Cl. WA5: Gt San 4J 81
Norburn Cres. L37: Form 2F 24
Norbury Av. CH63: H Beb 2L 89
L18: Moss H 3L 75
WA2: Warr 9E 66
WN5: Bil 5N 39
Norbury Cl. CH63: H Beb 2M 89
L32: Kirkb 9B 36
PR9: South 2A 8
WA8: Widnes 7N 79
Norbury Fold L35: Rainh 8H 63
Norbury Rd. L32: Kirkb 9B 36
Norbury Wlk. L32: Kirkb 9B 36

Norcliffe Rd.—Oak Tree Ct.

Norcliffe Rd. L35: Rainh .5E 62
Norcott Av. WA4: Stockt H .6E 82
NORCOTT BROOK .9D 98
Norcott Dr. WA5: Burtw .3H 65
Norden Cl. WA3: Birchw .4K 67
Norfield L39: Orm .8D 20
Norfolk Cl. CH43: Noct .4C 72
L20: Boot .6C 44
(off Brookhill Rd.)
M44: Cad .4J 69
Norfolk Dr. CH48: W Kir .7D 70
WA5: Gt San .2G 81
Norfolk Gro. PR8: Birkd .5M 11
Norfolk Pl. L21: Sea .3N 43
WA8: Widnes .8F 78
Norfolk Rd. CH65: Ell P .9A 104
L31: Mag .4H 35
PR8: Birkd .5M 11
WA10: St H .9G 48
WN5: Bil .2A 40
Norfolk St. L1: Liv .9F 4 (1C 74)
WA7: Run .4L 95
Norgate St. L4: W'ton .2E 58
Norgrove Cl. WA7: Murd .7F 96
Norlands Ct. CH42: Rock F .7L 73
Norland's La. L35: Rainh .9H 63
WA8: Cron, Widnes .9H 63
Norlands Pk. WA8: Widnes .2J 79
Norland St. WA8: Widnes .7N 79
Norleane Cres. WA7: Run .7L 95
Norley Av. CH62: East .3D 102
CH65: Ell P .8L 103
Norley Cl. WA5: Warr .2N 81
Norley Dr. WA10: Ec'stn .7D 48
Norley Pl. L26: Halew .1J 93
Norman Av. WA11: Hay .3J 51
WA12: Newt W .7N 51
Normanby Cl. WA5: Warr .1N 81
Norman Cl. CH66: Gt Sut .5L 111
Normandale Rd. L4: W'ton .9J 45
Normandy Rd. L36: Huy .6H 61
Norman Harvey VC Cl. WA12: Newt W .8J 51
Norman Hayes L39: Orm .5D 20
Normanhurst L39: Orm .9E 20
Norman Rd. CH44: Wall .7L 57
L20: Boot .3B 44
L23: Crosb .8K 33
WA7: Run .6K 95
Norman Salisbury Ct. WA10: St H .5K 49
Normans Rd. WA9: St H .2B 64
Normanston Cl. CH43: Oxton .4H 73
Normanston Rd. CH43: Oxton .4H 73
Norman St. CH41: Birke .9F 56
L3: Liv .3K 5
WA2: Warr .2C 82
Normanton Av. L17: Aig .5K 75
Norma Rd. L22: Wloo .1L 43
Normington Cl. L31: Lydi .8H 27
Norreys Av. WA5: Warr .9A 66
Norris Cl. CH43: Noct .4C 72
NORRIS GREEN .8L 45
Norris Grn. Rd. L12: W Der .3N 59
Norris Gro. WA8: Hale B .2F 94
Norris Ho. Dr. L39: Augh .4A 28
Norris Rd. L34: Presc .3N 61
Norris St. WA2: Warr .9D 66
Norris Way L37: Form .1H 25
Norseman Cl. L12: W Der .1N 59
Northam Cl. PR9: South .2M 7
NORTH ASHTON .5F 40
Nth. Atlantic Av. L30: Neth .1D 44
Nth. Atlantic Cl. L36: Huy .5J 61
North Av. L10: Aintr .9K 35
L24: Speke .1E 92
WA2: Warr .9C 66
Northbank Ind. Est. M44: Irlam .4M 69
Northbank Ind. Pk. M44: Irlam .2N 69
(not continuous)
Nth. Barcombe Rd. L16: Child .1B 76
Northbrook Cl. L8: Liv .1F 74
Nth. Brooke Way CH49: Wdchu .5A 72
Northbrook Rd. CH44: Wall .6K 57
Northbrook St. L8: Liv .9N 5 (1F 74)
(Granby St.)
L8: Liv .1F 74
(Rosebery St.)
Northbury Rd. CH66: Gt Sut .4K 111
Nth. Cantril Av. L12: W Der .1C 60
Nth. Cheshire Trad. Est. CH43: Pren .8E 72
North Cl. CH62: Brom .5B 90
Northcote Cl. L5: Liv .5E 58
Northcote Rd. CH45: Wall .3D 56
L9: W'ton .7E 44
Northdale Rd. L15: Wavtr .9L 59
WA1: Padd .9H 67
Northdene WN8: Parb .3E 22
North Dingle L4: Kirkd .1C 58
(not continuous)
North Dr. CH45: Wall .1F 56
CH60: Hesw .8A 88
L12: W Der .4M 59
L15: Wavtr .9L 59
WN6: App B .3M 23
North Dunes L38: Hight .8F 24
NORTH END
L26 .5J 77
L38 .7J 25
Nth. End La. L26: Halew .5J 77
L38: Hight .6G 25
Northern La. WA8: Widnes .5D 78
Northern Perimeter Rd. L30: Neth .6D 34
Northern Ri. CH66: Gt Sut .2K 111
Northern Rd., The L23: Crosb .6L 33
Northfield WN8: Skel .9E 22
Northfield Cl. L33: Kirkb .7E 36
WA9: Clock F .6N 63
Northfield Ct. WA3: Golb .1D 52
Northfield Rd. L9: W'ton .4D 44
L20: Boot .4D 44
NORTH FLORIDA .2F 50
Nth. Florida Rd. WA11: Hay .2F 50
North Front L35: Whis .8B 62
Northgate Rd. L13: Liv .4M 59
North Gro. L18: Aller .7A 76
Nth. Hill St. L8: Liv .3E 74
Nth. John St. L2: Liv .4E 4 (8B 58)
WA10: St H .7J 49
(not continuous)
Northleach Dr. PR8: Ainsd .9G 11
Nth. Linkside Rd. L25: Woolt .7G 76
North Mnr. Way L25: Woolt .7G 76
North Meade L31: Mag .1H 35
Northmead Rd. L19: Aller .9C 76
Nth. Mersey Bus. Cen. L33: Know I .7G 37
NORTH MOOR .3K 19
Nth. Moor La. L39: Hals .3J 19
Nth. Moss La. L37: Form .7J 17
Nth. Mossley Hill Rd. L18: Moss H .4L 75
North Mt. Rd. L32: Kirkb .7N 35
Northolt Ct. WA2: Padg .8F 66
Northop Rd. CH45: Wall .3F 56
North Pde. CH47: Hoy .1B 70
CH64: P'gte .4B 100
L24: Speke .4J 93
L32: Kirkb .9C 36
North Pk. Brook Rd. WA5: Call .7N 65
North Pk. Ct. CH44: Wall .6L 57
(off Demesne St.)
North Pk. Rd. L32: Kirkb .7N 35
Nth. Parkside Wlk. L12: W Der .1M 59
(off Parkside Dr.)
Nth. Perimeter Rd. L33: Know I .7F 36
Nth. Quarry Bus. Pk. WN6: App B .4N 23
Nth. Quarry Bus. Village WN6: App B .4N 23
North Quay L3: Liv .9E 4 (1B 74)
Northridge M. WA7: Run .7A 96
Northridge Rd. CH61: Pens .2A 88
North Rd. CH42: Tran .5J 73
CH48: W Kir .6B 70
CH65: Ell P .2H 103
(not continuous)
L14: Brd G .7A 60
L19: G'dale .1L 91
L24: Halew .2J 93
PR9: South .3N 7
WA10: St H .5J 49
North St. L3: Liv .3F 4 (7C 58)
PR9: South .7H 7
WA11: Hay .4G 50
WA12: Newt W .6H 51
WN4: Ash M .7M 41
Nth. Sudley Rd. L17: Aig .6K 75
North Ter. CH47: Meols .8E 54
Northumberland Gro. L8: Liv .3C 74
Northumberland Rd. M31: Part .7L 69
WA8: Widnes .2J 79
Northumberland St. L8: Liv .3D 74
Northumberland Ter. L5: Liv .3D 58
Northumberland Way L30: Neth .8B 34
North Vw. CH66: Lit Sut .8H 103
(off Station Rd.)
L7: Liv .5N 5 (8F 58)
L36: Huy .7L 61
WA5: Gt San .1G 81
Nth. Wallasey App. CH45: Wall .3C 56
Nth. Wall Terminal CH65: Ell P .6A 104
Northway CH60: Hesw .6D 88
L15: Wavtr .8N 59
L31: Augh, Lydi, Mag .4H 35
(not continuous)
L39: Augh .6L 27
WA2: Warr .8C 66
WA7: Pal F .7B 96
WA8: Widnes .7G 78
WA13: Lymm .4D 84
WN8: Skel .1E 30
Northway Cvn. Pk. L40: Scar .1L 19
Northways CH62: Brom .4C 90
North West Face Indoor Climbing Cen.
.1B 82
North West Mus. of Road Transport .6K 49
Northwest National Driving Range .8E 38
Northwich Cl. L23: Thorn .5A 34
Northwich Rd. WA4: Dutt, L Whit .3K 109
WA4: H Whi, L Stret .7F 98
WA7: Brook .1D 108
WA7: Dutt, Pres B .2F 108
Nth. William St. CH44: Wall .7L 57
North Wirral Coastal Pk. .7G 54
NORTHWOOD .9D 36
Northwood Av. WA12: Newt W .6A 52
Northwood Rd. CH43: Pren .6F 72
L36: Huy .5K 61
WA7: Run .5A 96
NORTON .7F 96
Norton Av. WA5: Penk .3G 80
Norton Ct. CH44: Wall .6L 57
(off Borough Rd.)
Norton Dr. CH61: Irby .9K 71
Norton Ga. WA7: Nort .7E 96
Norton Gro. L31: Mag .5J 35
WA9: St H .2G 63
Norton Hill WA7: Wind H .6E 96
Norton La. WA7: Hal, Nort .7C 96
(not continuous)
WA7: Nort .6F 96
Norton Priory Gdns. .4D 96
Norton Priory Mus. .4D 96
Norton Rd. CH48: W Kir .5B 70
Norton's La. CH3: L Barr, Moul .9D 114
Norton Sta. Rd. WA7: Murd, Nort .7F 96
Norton St. L3: Liv .3H 5 (7D 58)
L20: Boot .5A 44
Norton Vw. WA7: Hal .7C 96
Norton Village WA7: Nort .7F 96
Norton Village Gdns.
WA7: Nort .7F 96
Nortonwood La. WA7: Wind H .7E 96
Norville CH66: Lit Sut .7J 103
Norville Rd. L14: Brd G .7A 60
Norwich Av. WA3: Low .2E 52
WN4: Ash M .9M 41
Norwich Dr. CH49: Upton .1A 72
CH66: Gt Sut .5K 111
Norwich Rd. L15: Wavtr .2M 75
Norwich Way L32: Kirkb .9C 36
Norwood Av. L21: Lith .1A 44
PR9: South .7K 7
WA3: Low .3G 52
WN4: Ash M .5H 41
Norwood Ct. CH49: Grea .5L 71
Norwood Cres. PR9: South .7K 7
Norwood Gdns. PR9: South .8L 7
Norwood Gro. L6: Liv .5G 59
WA11: Rainf .5D 38
Norwood Rd. CH44: Wall .7H 57
CH49: Grea .4L 71
PR8: South .8L 7
Norwyn Rd. L11: Norr G .8K 45
Nostell Rd. WN4: Ash M .6J 41
Nottingdale Av. L25: Gate .3E 76
Nottingham Cl. L35: Rainh .4F 62
WA1: Wools .2L 83
Nottingham Rd. L36: Roby .8G 61
Nowshera Av. CH61: Pens .2N 87
Nuffield Cl. CH49: Upton .4N 71
Nuffield Rd. L20: Boot .8B 44
Nun Cl. CH43: Oxton .5H 73
Nunn St. WA9: St H .7N 49
Nunsford Cl. L21: Lith .9C 34
Nunthorpe Av. L34: Know .5F 46
Nurseries, The L37: Form .2G 24
Nurse Rd. CH61: Thing .1B 88
Nursery Av. L39: Orm .7E 20
Nursery Cl. CH43: Oxton .5H 73
L25: Hunts X .8G 76
WA8: Widnes .5N 79
Nursery Dr. L37: Form .2F 24
Nursery Gro. M31: Part .5M 69
Nursery La. L19: Garst .9A 76
Nursery Rd. L31: Lydi .8B 76
WA1: Padg .9G 66
WA9: St H .2G 63
NUT GROVE .3F 62
Nutgrove Av. WA9: St H .2G 62
Nutgrove Hall Dr. WA9: St H .2G 62
Nutgrove Rd. WA9: St H .3F 62
Nuthall Rd. PR8: South .3E 12
Nutmeg Way L11: Norr G .9M 45
Nut St. WA9: St H .2G 62
Nuttall Ct. WA3: Birchw .5K 67
Nuttall St. M44: Cad .3L 69
Nuttall Way L7: Liv .8H 59
Nye Bevan Pool .3E 30
Nyland Rd. L36: Huy .4H 61

O

Oak Av. CH49: Upton .2L 71
L9: Aintr .4G 44
L39: Orm .9B 20
M44: Cad .4K 69
PR9: Banks .5H 9
WA3: Golb .2C 52
WA11: Hay .3G 51
WA12: Newt W .7L 51
Oak Bank CH41: Birke .3J 73
Oakbank Rd. L18: Moss H .3K 75
Oakbank St. CH44: Wall .6J 57
Oakbourne Cl. L17: Aig .6H 75
Oak Cl. CH46: More .1L 71
L12: W Der .9D 46
L35: Whis .6B 62
Oak Ct. L8: Liv .4F 74
(off Weller Way)
WA7: Cas .5C 96
Oak Cres. WN8: Skel .3A 30
Oakcross Gdns. L25: Woolt .6G 76
Oakdale Av. CH44: Wall .7K 57
WA4: Stockt H .7E 82
WA6: Frod .8N 107
Oakdale Cl. L32: Kirkb .1A 46
Oakdale Dr. CH49: Grea .6K 71
WA9: St H .5J 63
Oakdale Rd. CH44: Wall .7K 57
L18: Moss H .3M 75
L22: Wloo .9K 33
Oakdale Row L32: Kirkb .2D 46
Oakdene Av. CH66: Gt Sut .9H 103
WA1: Wools .1K 83
Oakdene Cl. CH62: Brom .1C 102
Oakdene Ct. L35: Rainh .7G 62
Oakdene Rd. CH42: Tran .5J 73
L4: W'ton .2G 58
Oak Dr. L40: Burs .2K 21
WA7: Run .8M 95
Oakenden Cl. WN4: Ash M .5J 41
Oakenholt Rd. CH46: More .8M 55
Oakes St. L3: Liv .4K 5 (7E 58)
Oakfield L4: W'ton .3G 58
Oakfield Av. L25: Gate .4E 76
WA3: Golb .1A 52
Oakfield Cl. WA9: St H .2G 63
Oakfield Dr. L36: Huy .9K 61
L37: Form .9D 16
WA8: Widnes .8D 78
Oakfield Gro. L36: Huy .9K 61
Oakfield Rd. CH62: Brom .7B 90
CH66: Chil T .6D 102
L4: W'ton .3F 58
L38: Hight .1F 32
Oakfields L39: Orm .8E 20
Oakfield Ter. CH66: Chil T .6D 102
Oakford Cl. PR9: Banks .2F 8
Oak Gdns. WA5: Penk .4F 80
Oakgate Cl. L11: Norr G .7N 45
Oak Grange L26: Halew .8K 77
Oak Grn. L39: Orm .8D 20
Oak Gro. CH65: Whit .2M 111
Oakgrove Gdns. L25: Woolt .4F 76
Oakham Ct. PR9: South .7H 7
Oakham Dr. CH46: More .8J 55
L10: Aintr .1L 45
Oakham St. L8: Liv .2C 74
Oakhill Cl. L12: Crox .7B 46
L31: Mag .1J 35
Oakhill Cott. La. L31: Lydi .8J 27
Oakhill Dr. L31: Lydi .8J 27
OAK HILL PARK .7N 59
Oakhill Pk. L13: Liv .7N 59
Oakhill Rd. L13: Liv .7N 59
L31: Mag .1J 35
Oakhouse Pk. L9: W'ton .7E 44
Oakhurst Cl. L25: Gate .3F 76
Oakland Cl. L21: Lith .4B 44
Oakland Dr. CH49: Upton .2A 72
CH65: Ell P .4B 112
Oakland Gdns. WA1: Warr .1F 82
Oakland Rd. L19: Aig .8L 75
Oaklands CH62: Brom .9C 90
L35: Rainh .6F 62
Oaklands Av. L23: Crosb .6L 33
Oaklands Ct. WA9: Clock F .5M 63
Oaklands Dr. CH61: Hesw .6A 88
CH63: Beb .1N 89
WA13: Lymm .6D 84
Oaklands Office Pk. CH66: Hoot .4D 102
Oaklands Rd. WA3: Low .3G 53
Oaklands Ter. CH61: Hesw .5A 88
Oakland St. WA1: Warr .1F 82
WA8: Widnes .3K 95
Oakland Va. CH45: New B .1J 57
Oak La. L12: W Der .9A 46
Oak La. Nth. L12: Crox .8A 46
Oakleaf M. CH43: Noct .3D 72
Oaklea Rd. CH61: Irby .1N 87
Oaklee Gro. L33: Kirkb .7E 36
Oak Leigh L13: Liv .4K 59
Oakleigh WN8: Skel .1G 38
Oakleigh Gro. CH63: Beb .1M 89
Oakley Av. WN5: Bil .5A 40
Oakley Cl. L12: Crox .7C 46
Oakley Ct. CH65: Ell P .1A 112
Oak Mdws. Cl. L35: Rainh .8H 63
Oakmere Cl. CH46: Leas .5M 55
L9: W'ton .3F 44
Oakmere Dr. CH49: Grea .4K 71
CH66: Gt Sut .4L 111
WA5: Penk .5H 81
Oakmere La. WA6: Haps .4B 114
Oakmere St. WA7: Run .5K 95
Oakmoore WA7: Nort .3H 97
Oakridge Cl. CH62: Spit .5B 90
Oakridge Rd. CH62: Spit .5B 90
Oak Rd. CH63: H Beb .9M 73
CH66: Hoot .5D 102
L35: Whis .6B 62
L36: Huy .9H 61
M31: Part .7K 69
WA5: Penk .5H 81
WA13: Lymm .5C 84
Oaks, The CH62: Brom .7B 90
L12: Crox .7D 46
WA8: Widnes .4N 79
(off Hampton Ct. Way)
WA9: Sut L .5N 63
Oaks Bus. Pk. WN8: Uph .8J 31
Oaks Cl. WA9: Clock F .6N 63
Oaks La. CH61: Pens .3A 88
Oaksmeade Cl. L12: Crox .8D 46
Oaks Pl. WA8: Widnes .9K 79
Oakston Av. L35: Rainh .7G 62
Oak St. CH65: Ell P .7A 104
L20: Boot .6B 44
(off Holly St.)
PR8: South .9K 7
WA3: Croft .2H 67
WA9: St H .1A 64
WN4: Ash M .5J 41
Oaksway CH60: Hesw .9B 88
Oak Ter. L7: Liv .7H 59
Oakthorn Gro. WA11: Hay .4E 50
Oak Tree Ct. WN8: Skel .1G 30

Oaktree Ct. Bus. Cen.—Ormskirk Rd.

Oaktree Ct. Bus. Cen. CH64: Ness 8K **101**
Oaktree Gdns. *L9: Faz* *6L 45*
(off Ternhall Way)
Oaktree Pl. CH42: Rock F 5M **73**
Oak Tree Rd. WA10: Ec'stn 5D **48**
Oak Va. L13: Liv .7N **59**
OAK VALE PARK 7N 59
Oakvale Rd. L14: Brd G 7C **60**
Oak Vw. L24: Speke 4L **93**
Oakways WA4: App 2E **98**
Oak Wharf M. WA4: App 8D **82**
OAKWOOD 6N 67
Oakwood WN8: Skel 1G **30**
Oakwood Av. PR8: Ainsd 8L **11**
WA1: Warr .1E **82**
WN4: Ash M 9J **41**
Oakwood Cl. CH66: Gt Sut 4J **111**
L25: Gate 3F **76**
Oakwood Dr. CH43: Bid 9E **56**
L36: Huy 8K **61**
PR8: Ainsd .9L **11**
WN7: Leigh .1M **53**
Oakwood Ga. WA3: Birchw 5L **67**
Oakwood Pk. CH43: Bid 9E **56**
CH62: Brom 1C **102**
Oakwood Rd. L26: Halew 9J **77**
Oakworth Cl. L33: Kirkb 7C **36**
Oakworth Dr. CH62: New F 9B **74**
L35: Tar G .1L **77**
Oarside Dr. CH45: Wall 3G **57**
Oasis Cl. L40: Ruf 3M **15**
Oatfield La. L21: Ford 9A **34**
Oatlands, The CH48: W Kir 7D **70**
Oatlands Rd. L32: Kirkb 9A **36**
Oban Dr. CH60: Hesw 7A **88**
WN4: Garsw 7E **40**
Oban Gro. WA2: Fearn 6H **67**
Oban Rd. L4: W'ton 3G **59**
Oberon St. L20: Boot 9B **44**
O'Brien Gro. WA9: St H 6A **50**
Observatory Rd. CH43: Bid 9E **56**
Occupation La. CW9: Ant 7K **99**
Oceanic Rd. L13: Liv 7L **59**
Ocean Pk. CH41: Wall 8K **57**
Ocean Plaza PR8: South 7F **6**
(not continuous)
Ocean Rd. L21: Lith 3A **44**
O'Connell Cl. WA11: Hay 4E **50**
O'Connell Rd. L3: Liv 5C **58**
O'Connor Gro. L33: Kirkb 5C **36**
Octans Rd. WA5: Westb 7K **65**
Octavia Ct. L36: Huy 8K **61**
Octavia Hill Rd. L21: Ford 1B **44**
October Dr. L6: Liv 3J **59**
Oddfellows Arms Yd. *L25: Woolt* *6E 76*
(off Allerton Rd.)
Odeon Cinema
Bootle 8F 34
Bromborough 4D 90
Liverpool 6E 4 (8B 58)
Warrington 8K 65
Odessa Wlk. WA5: Gt San 2K **81**
Odsey St. L7: Liv 7H **59**
Odyssey Cen. CH41: Birke 9J **57**
Off Botanic Rd. PR9: South 6M **7**
Off Lyons La. WA4: App 2F **98**
Ogden Cl. L13: W Der 1M **59**
Ogle Cl. L35: Presc 4B **62**
OGLET 7J 93
Oglet La. L24: Hale 7H **93**
L24: Speke .5G **93**
Ogle Way L36: Huy 4J **61**
Ohio Gro. WA5: Gt San 2L **81**
Oil Sites Rd. CH65: Ell P 7B **104**
Oil St. L3: Liv 1B **4** (5A **58**)
O'Keeffe Rd. WA9: St H 6M **49**
Okehampton Rd. L16: Child 9B **60**
Okell Dr. L26: Halew 6H **77**
Okell St. WA7: Run 5K **95**
Oklahoma Blvd. WA5: Gt San 2J **81**
Old Acre L38: Hight 9F **24**
Old Albert Ter. *WA7: Run* *4L 95*
(off Thomas St.)
Old Alder La. WA5: Burtw 3M **65**
Old Barn La. CH64: Will 6M **101**
Old Barn Rd. CH44: Wall 6G **57**
L4: W'ton 3G **58**
Old Bidston Rd. CH41: Birke 9H **57**
OLD BOSTON 3H 51
Old Boston WA11: Hay 2J **51**
Old Boston Trad. Est. WA11: Hay 2K **51**
Old Boundary Way L39: Orm 7D **20**
Oldbridge Rd. L24: Speke 5K **93**
Old Cherry La. WA13: Lymm 9A **84**
Old Chester Rd. CH41: Tran 4L **73**
CH42: Rock F, Tran 7M **73**
CH63: Beb, H Beb 7M **73**
CH66: Gt Sut 9J **103**
WA4: Dares .6K **97**
WA4: H Walt 9A **82**
WA6: Hel 2E **114**
Old Church Cl. CH65: Ell P 7A **104**
L9: Aintr 3G **44**
Old Churchyard L2: Liv 5D **4** (8A **58**)
Old Clatterbridge Rd. CH63: Spit 5L **89**
Old Coach Rd. WA7: Run 4J **95**
Old College Pl. L7: Liv 8H **59**
Old Colliery Rd. L35: Whis 6A **62**
Old Colliery Yd. WN4: Garsw 8E **40**
Old Corporation Yd., The CH44: Wall 5J **57**
Old Court Ho. Rd. CH62: Brom 2C **90**
Old Cryers La. CH2: Elt 3L **113**
Old Distillery Rd. L24: Speke 2G **92**
Old Dover Rd. L36: Roby 9G **61**
Old Eccleston La. WA10: St H 7F **48**
Old Elton Head Rd. WA9: St H 4L **63**
Old Engine La. WN8: Skel 2N **29**
Old Farm Cl. CH64: Will 6N **101**
Old Farm Rd. L23: Crosb 7M **33**
L32: Kirkb .4D **46**
Oldfield L35: Whis 5C **62**
Oldfield Cl. CH60: Hesw 5M **87**
Oldfield Dr. CH60: Hesw 5L **87**
Oldfield Gdns. CH60: Hesw 6L **87**
Oldfield La. CH48: W Kir 4H **71**
Oldfield Rd. CH45: Wall 3F **56**
CH60: Hesw 5L **87**
CH65: Ell P 9N **103**
L19: Aig 8M **75**
WA13: Lymm 4B **84**
Oldfield St. WA10: St H 5J **49**
Oldfield Way CH60: Hesw 5L **87**
Old Forge Row L31: Mag 9H **27**
Oldgate WA8: Widnes 9F **78**
Old Gorsey La. CH44: Wall 7H **57**
Old Greasby Rd. CH49: Upton 3N **71**
OLD HALL 9M 65
Old Hall L35: Whis 9B **62**
Old Hall Cl. L31: Mag 4J **35**
WA4: H Walt 8B **82**
Old Hall Dr. CH65: Whit 1N **111**
WN4: Ash M 9J **41**
Old Hall Farm Bus. Pk. PR9: South 1F **12**
Old Hall Gdns. WA11: Rainf 4D **38**
Old Hall La. CH2: Elt 3L **113**
L32: Kirkb .9B **36**
Old Hall Rd. CH62: Brom 6D **90**
L31: Mag 3J **35**
WA5: Old H 9M **65**
Old Hall St. L3: Liv 3C **4** (7A **58**)
Oldham Pl. L1: Liv 6J **5** (8D **58**)
Oldham St. L1: Liv 7H **5** (9D **58**)
WA4: Warr .5D **82**
Old Haymarket L1: Liv 4F **4** (7C **58**)
(not continuous)
Old Hey Wlk. WA12: Newt W 9L **51**
Old Higher Rd. WA8: Hale B 2A **94**
Old Hutte La. L24: Halew 2L **93**
L26: Halew .2L **93**
Old Kennel Cl. L12: W Der 1D **60**
Old La. CH60: Hesw 7D **88**
L31: Lydi 8K **27**
L34: Eccl P .2C **62**
L35: Eccl P .2C **62**
L35: Rainh .6E **62**
L37: Form 7F **16**
L39: Down .9C **18**
WA8: Widnes 9G **79**
WA11: Rainf 4C **38**
Old Leeds St. L3: Liv 3C **4** (7A **58**)
Old Links Cl. PR9: South 7N **7**
Old Liverpool Rd. WA5: Warr 4M **81**
Old Lodge Cl. L12: W Der 1N **59**
Old Mnr., The CH42: Rock F 6N **73**
Old Mkt. Pl. *WA1: Warr* *3C 82*
(off Lyme St.)
Old Maryland La. CH46: More 8M **55**
Old Mdw. L34: Know 6H **47**
Old Mdw. Rd. CH61: Pens 3M **87**
Old Mill, The *CH66: Lit Sut* *7H 103*
(off Station Rd.)
Old Mill Av. WA9: Sut L 4N **63**
Old Mill Cl. CH60: Hesw 8B **88**
L15: Wavtr .9M **59**
WA13: Lymm 2J **85**
Old Mill Hill L39: Orm 1B **28**
Old Mill La. L15: Wavtr 9M **59**
L34: Know .6J **47**
L37: Form 9F **16**
Old Moat La. L31: Mag 3G **34**
Old Moss La. L39: Down 7N **17**
Old Nook La. WA11: St H 4A **50**
Old Orchard L35: Whis 8B **62**
Old Pk. La. PR9: South 8M **7**
Old Penny La. WA11: Hay 2K **51**
Old Pewterspear La. WA4: App 4E **98**
Old Post Office Pl. L1: Liv 6F **4**
Old Prescot Cl. L31: Mag 1A **36**
Old Pump La. CH49: Grea 5K **71**
Old Quarry, The L25: Woolt 6E **76**
Old Quay Cl. CH64: P'gte 7C **100**
Old Quay La. CH64: P'gte 7D **100**
Old Quays, The WA4: Westy 5F **82**
Old Quay St. WA7: Run 4L **95**
Old Racecourse Rd. L31: Mag 3G **34**
Old Rectory Grn. L29: Seft 4D **34**
L39: Augh .5M **27**
Old Riding L14: Knott A 4D **60**
Old Rd. WA4: Warr 4C **82**
WN4: Ash M 7J **41**
Old Roan Station (Rail) 8H 35
Old Ropery L2: Liv 5D **4**
Old Rough La. L33: Kirkb 8C **36**
Old School Cl. CH64: Lit N 9F **100**
PR9: Banks .1D **8**
Old School Ho., The *CH43: Oxton* *3G 72*
(off Beresford Rd.)
Old School Ho. La. WA2: Winw 2B **66**
Old School Pl. WN4: Ash M 9J **41**
Old School Way CH41: Birke 1E **72**
Old Smithy La. WA13: Lymm 6C **84**
Old Stableyard, The L7: Liv 6N **5** (8F **58**)
OLD SWAN 6M 59
Old Thomas La. L14: Brd G 8B **60**
Old Town Cl. WN8: Skel 4A **30**
Old Town Ct. L37: Form 9E **16**
Old Town La. L37: Form 9E **16**
Old Town Way WN8: Skel 4A **30**
Old Upton La. WA8: Widnes 4H **79**
Old Vicarage Rd. CH64: Will 6N **101**
Old Wargrave Rd. WA12: Newt W 7K **51**
Old Welsh Rd. CH66: Lit Sut 9E **102**
Old Whint Rd. WA11: Hay 4C **50**
(Edward St.)
WA11: Hay .6C **50**
(Harty Rd.)
Old Wood La. L27: N'ley 4K **77**
Old Wood Rd. CH61: Pens 3N **87**
Oleander Dr. WA10: St H 6F **48**
Oleander Way L9: Faz 7J **45**
O'Leary St. WA2: Warr 1D **82**
Olga Rd. WA9: St H 2M **63**
Olinda St. CH62: New F 9A **74**
Olive Cl. L31: Mell 9M **35**
Olive Cres. CH41: Tran 4L **73**
Olivedale Rd. L18: Moss H 3L **75**
Olive Dr. CH64: Nest 6E **100**
Olive Gro. L15: Wavtr 8M **59**
L30: Neth 1F **44**
L36: Roby .7H **61**
PR8: South .8K **7**
WN8: Skel .3B **30**
Olive La. L15: Wavtr 8M **59**
Olive Mt. CH41: Tran 4L **73**
Olive Mt. Hgts. L15: Wavtr 9N **59**
Olive Mt. Rd. L15: Wavtr 9M **59**
Olive Mt. Vs. L15: Wavtr 8M **59**
Olive Mt. Wlk. *L15: Wavtr* *9N 59*
(off Olive Mt. Rd.)
Oliver Ho. *CH66: Gt Sut* *1J 111*
(off Oliver La.)
Oliver La. CH41: Birke 2L **73**
CH66: Gt Sut 1J **111**
Oliver Lyme Ho. *L34: Presc* *3B 62*
(off Lavender Cres.)
Oliver Lyme Rd. L34: Presc 3B **62**
Olive Rd. CH64: Nest 6E **100**
L22: Wloo .2L **43**
Oliver Rd. WA10: St H 9F **48**
Oliver St. CH41: Birke 2K **73**
WA2: Warr .2C **82**
Oliver St. E. CH41: Birke 2L **73**
Olivetree Rd. L15: Wavtr 9N **59**
Olive Va. L15: Wavtr 9L **59**
Olivia Cl. CH43: Noct 4C **72**
Olivia M. CH43: Noct 4C **72**
Olivia St. L20: Boot 9C **44**
Olivia Way L36: Huy 7M **61**
Ollerton Cl. CH43: Noct 4C **72**
WA4: Grap .5J **83**
Ollerton Pk. WA5: Burtw 2G **64**
Ollery Grn. L30: Neth 7G **35**
Ollier St. WA8: Widnes 9K **79**
Olney St. L4: W'ton 8E **44**
Olton St. L15: Wavtr 9K **59**
Olympia Pl. WA5: Gt San 1K **81**
Olympia St. L6: Liv 1N **5** (6F **58**)
Olympic Way L30: Neth 2G **44**
WA2: Birchw 7K **67**
Omega Blvd. WA5: Gt San 8F **64**
Omega Circ. M44: Irlam 3M **69**
Omega Dr. M44: Irlam 3M **69**
O'Neill St. L20: Boot 6A **44**
One Pk. W. L1: Liv 6E **4** (8B **58**)
Onslow Cres. PR8: Birkd 4N **11**
Onslow Rd. CH45: New B 1H **57**
CH62: New F 8A **74**
L6: Liv 6H **59**
Ontario Cl. L27: N'ley 3J **77**
Ontario Way L36: Huy 3H **61**
Opal Cl. L6: Liv 5G **58**
L21: Lith 2B **44**
Opal Ct. L3: Liv 3K **5**
Opco Complex L24: Speke 2F **92**
Open Eye Gallery 6D 4 (8B 58)
Openfields Cl. L26: Halew 6J **77**
Openshaw La. *M44: Cad* *3L 69*
(off Prospect Av.)
Ophelia Ct. L5: Liv 3D **58**
Oppenheim Av. WA10: St H 1F **62**
Orange Gro. L8: Liv 2H **75**
WA2: Warr .7F **66**
Orange Tree Cl. L28: Stockb V 1F **60**
Oran Way L36: Huy 6H **61**
Orb Cl. L11: Crox 7A **46**
Orb Wlk. *L11: Crox* *7A 46*
(off Sceptre Rd.)
Orchard, The CH45: Wall 2G **57**
L17: Aig 7L **75**
L35: Rainh .4F **62**
L36: Huy 7J **61**
L39: Orm 8B **20**
WA6: Hel 3E **114**
WN8: Skel .4A **30**
Orchard Av. L14: Brd G 8B **60**
M31: Part .5M **69**
WA13: Lymm 5F **84**
Orchard Brow WA3: Rix 7G **69**
Orchard Cl. CH66: Gt Sut 4L **111**
L34: Eccl P .2D **62**
L35: Whis .8B **62**
WA6: Frod .8K **107**
WA11: St H 3N **49**
Orchard Ct. CH41: Tran 5M **73**
L31: Mag 2L **35**
WA3: Croft .1H **67**
WA6: Frod .6K **107**
WA11: Hay .4E **50**
WN5: Bil 9N **31**
Orchard Dale L23: Crosb 7M **33**
Orchard Dene L35: Rainh 6F **62**
Orchard Dr. CH64: Lit N 9E **100**
Orchard Farm Cl. PR4: Mere B 5K **9**
Orchard Gdns. L35: Whis 9B **62**
Orchard Grange CH46: More 1K **71**
Orchard Haven CH66: Gt Sut 4K **111**
Orchard Hey L30: Neth 7G **35**
L31: Mag 3L **35**
WA10: Ec'stn 7D **48**
Orchard La. CH66: Chil T 6F **102**
PR8: Ainsd .1K **17**
Orchard Pk. CH2: Elt 1M **113**
Orchard Pk. La. CH2: Elt 1M **113**
Orchard Pl. CH62: Spit 5A **90**
WA6: Hel 1F **114**
Orchard Rd. CH46: More 8M **55**
CH65: Whit 3M **111**
WA13: Lymm 3H **85**
Orchards, The PR8: Ainsd 1K **17**
Orchard St. WA1: Warr 3D **82**
WA2: Fearn 7H **67**
WA4: Stockt H 8D **82**
WN4: Ash M 8L **41**
Orchard Vw. L39: Augh 3B **28**
Orchard Wlk. CH64: Nest 6E **100**
WA7: Pal F *8B 96*
(within Halton Lea Shop. Cen.)
Orchard Way CH63: H Beb 1K **89**
WA8: Widnes 5D **78**
Orchid Cl. M44: Irlam 1L **69**
WN8: Uph 6L **31**
Orchid Gro. L17: Aig 5E **74**
Orchid Way L40: Burs 2L **21**
WA9: Bold .2D **64**
Orchil Cl. CH66: Lit Sut 8F **102**
Ordnance Av. WA3: Birchw 5M **67**
Oregon Cl. L20: Boot 7B **44**
O'Reilly Ct. L3: Liv 5B **58**
ORFORD 7E 66
Orford Av. WA2: Warr 1D **82**
Orford Cl. L24: Hale 5B **94**
WA3: Golb .3B **52**
Orford Grn. WA2: Warr 8E **66**
Orford Jubilee Neighbourhood Hub 9C 66
Orford La. WA2: Warr 2C **82**
Orford Pk. WA2: Warr 8C **66**
Orford Rd. WA1: Warr 9E **66**
WA2: Warr .9E **66**
Orford St. L15: Wavtr 9L **59**
WA1: Warr .3C **82**
Oriel Cl. L2: Liv 5D **4**
L10: Aintr .8J **35**
Oriel Ct. CH42: Tran 7H **73**
Oriel Cres. L20: Kirkd 9B **44**
Oriel Dr. L10: Aintr 8H **35**
Oriel Lodge L20: Boot 8B **44**
Oriel Rd. CH42: Tran 5L **73**
L20: Boot .7A **44**
L20: Kirkd .9B **44**
WN4: Ash M 7H **41**
Oriel St. L3: Liv 1E **4** (6B **58**)
Orient Dr. L25: Woolt 5F **76**
Origen Rd. L16: Child 8B **60**
Oriole Cl. WA10: St H 2E **62**
Orion Blvd. WA5: Gt San 8G **64**
Orith Av. WA10: Ec'stn 7C **48**
Orkney Cl. CH65: Ell P 4A **112**
WA8: Widnes 5A **80**
WA11: St H 3N **49**
Orlando Cl. CH43: Noct 4C **72**
Orlando Dr. WA5: Gt San 1L **81**
Orlando St. L20: Boot 9B **44**
Orleans Ct. *WA5: Gt San* *2K 81*
(off Louisiana Dr.)
Orleans Rd. L13: Liv 6M **59**
Ormande St. WA9: St H 9L **49**
Orme Ho. L39: Orm 8E **20**
Ormerod Ct. CH63: Beb 2N **89**
Ormesby Gdns. WA9: St H 3H **63**
Ormesby Gro. CH63: Raby M 9A **90**
Ormiston Rd. CH45: New B 2H **57**
Ormond Av. L40: Westh 9J **21**
Ormond Cl. WA8: Widnes 6F **78**
Ormonde Av. L31: Mag 4H **35**
Ormonde Cres. L33: Kirkb 9E **36**
Ormonde Dr. L31: Mag 3H **35**
Ormond M. CH43: Noct 4C **72**
Ormond St. CH45: Wall 4H **57**
L3: Liv 4D **4** (7B **58**)
Ormond Way CH43: Noct 4C **72**
Ormsby St. L15: Wavtr 1K **75**
Ormside Gro. WA9: St H 2N **63**
ORMSKIRK 8C 20
Ormskirk Bus. Pk.
L39: Orm 7D **20**
Ormskirk Bus Station 8D 20
Ormskirk Civic Hall 8C 20
Ormskirk Golf Course 6J 21
Ormskirk Ind. Pk. L39: Orm 7E **20**
Ormskirk Old Rd. L39: Bic 5K **29**
Ormskirk Rd. L9: Aintr 2G **44**
L10: Aintr .7G **35**
L34: Know .4H **47**
L39: Bic 3F **28**

Ormskirk Rd.—Park Ct.

Ormskirk Rd. WA11: Bic, Rainf 1A 38
(not continuous)
WA11: Rainf 2A 38
WN8: Skel 3N 29
(Bromilow Rd.)
WN8: Skel 4E 30
(Spencers La.)
WN8: Uph 5J 31
Ormskirk Station (Rail) 8D 20
Ormskirk St. WA10: St H 6K 49
Orms Way L37: Form 1E 24
Orphan Dr. L6: Liv 4J 59
(not continuous)
Orphan St. L7: Liv 7M 5 (9F 58)
ORRELL
L20 3C 44
WN5 7N 31
Orrell Cl. WA5: Gt San 2J 81
Orrell Hey L20: Boot 3C 44
Orrell Hill La. L38: Ince B 8J 25
Orrell La. L9: W'ton 4F 44
L20: Boot 3D 44
L40: Burs 9H 15
Orrell Lodge L20: Boot 4D 44
Orrell M. L40: Burs 9J 15
Orrell Mt. L20: Boot 3B 44
Orrell Mt. Ind. Est. L20: Boot 3B 44
ORRELL PARK 4E 44
Orrell Park Station (Rail) 4F 44
Orrell Rd. CH45: New B 2J 57
L20: Boot 2B 44
L21: Lith 2B 44
WN5: Orr 5N 31
Orrell Station (Rail) 8N 31
Orrell St. WA9: St H 7M 49
Orret's Mdw. Rd.
CH49: Wdchu 5B 72
Orret's M. CH49: Wdchu 5B 72
Orrysdale Rd. CH48: W Kir 5B 70
Orry St. L5: Liv 4C 58
Orsett Rd. L32: Kirkb 2D 46
Orston Cres. CH63: Spit 5N 89
Ortega Cl. CH62: New F 9B 74
Orthes St. L3: Liv 6K 5 (8E 58)
Orton Rd. L16: Child 9A 60
Orton Way WN4: Ash M 8H 41
Orville St. WA9: St H 2B 64
Orwell Cl. L37: Form 3D 24
WA9: Sut M 6K 63
Orwell Rd. L4: Kirkd 1C 58
Osbert Rd. L23: Blun 7H 33
Osborne Av.
CH45: New B 2H 57
WA2: Warr 8E 66
Osborne Ct. *CH43: Oxton 2H 73*
(off Osborne Rd.)
CH62: Port S 1A 90
WA10: St H 1F 62
Osborne Gro. CH45: New B 3H 57
L34: Presc 4L 61
Osborne Rd. CH43: Oxton 3H 73
CH45: New B 2J 57
L13: Liv 3K 59
L21: Lith 1B 44
(not continuous)
L37: Form 3E 24
PR8: Ainsd 9H 11
WA3: Low 3F 52
WA4: W'ton 7C 82
WA10: Ec'stn 5D 48
WN4: Ash M 7J 41
Osborne Va. CH45: New B 2H 57
Osborne Wood L17: Aig 7J 75
Osbourne Cl. CH62: Brom 8D 90
Osier Cl. CH2: Elt 2N 113
Osmaston Rd. CH42: Tran 6G 73
Osprey Cl. L27: N'ley 3J 77
WA2: Warr 6F 66
WA7: Beech 1B 108
Osprey Pl. L40: Burs 3F 20
Ossett Cl. CH43: Noct 4C 72
WA7: Nort 7F 96
Osterley Gdns. L9: W'ton 4E 44
O'Sullivan Cres. WA11: St H 5A 50
Oswald Cl. L33: Kirkb 5C 36
Oteley Av. CH62: Brom 7C 90
Othello Cl. L20: Kirkd 9B 44
Otley Cl. WA12: Newt W 7H 51
Ottawa Gdns. WA4: Westy 5H 83
Otterburn Cl. CH46: More 9J 55
Otterburn St. WA7: Nort 4G 96
OTTERSPOOL 7H 75
Otterspool Dr. L17: Aig 8J 75
Otterspool Rd. L17: Aig 7J 75
Otterstye Vw. PR8: South 5G 13
Otterton Rd. L11: Crox 5A 46
Ottery Cl. PR9: South 2M 7
Ottley St. L6: Liv 6H 59
Otway Cl. L19: Garst 2A 92
OUGHTRINGTON 4H 85
Oughtrington Cres.
WA13: Lymm 4H 85
Oughtrington La. WA13: Lymm 6G 85
Oughtrington Vw.
WA13: Lymm 4H 85
Oulton Cl. CH43: Oxton 5E 72
L31: Lydi 8G 27
Oulton Ct. WA4: Grap 6J 83
Oulton Gdns. WA9: St H 3H 63
Oulton La. L36: Roby 9H 61
Oulton Rd. L16: Child 2B 76
Oulton Way CH43: Oxton 6E 72
Oundle Dr. L10: Aintr 8H 35
Oundle Pl. L25: Hunts X 9F 76
Oundle Rd. CH46: More 8M 55
Outer Central Rd.
L24: Halew 2J 93
Outer Forum L11: Norr G 7K 45
Out La. L25: Woolt 6E 76
Outlet La. L31: Mell 2C 36
L39: Bic 2C 36
Outlook, The L38: Hight 8F 24
Oval, The CH45: Wall 3F 56
CH65: Ell P 2A 112
PR9: Banks 3E 8
Oval Leisure Cen., The 9M 73
Overbrook Ho. L34: Know 5G 47
Overbrook La. L34: Know 5F 46
Overbury St. L7: Liv 8G 58
Overchurch Rd.
CH49: Upton 2M 71
Overdale Av. CH61: Barns 2D 88
Overdale Rd. CH64: Will 5N 101
Overdene Wlk. L32: Kirkb 1D 46
Overgreen Gro. CH46: More 8L 55
Overmarsh CH64: Ness 9G 101
OVERPOOL 8K 103
Overpool Gdns.
CH66: Gt Sut 2L 111
Overpool Rd.
CH66: Ell P, Gt Sut, Whit 8L 103
(not continuous)
Overpool Station (Rail) 8K 103
Overstrand CH48: W Kir 6B 70
OVERTON 8M 107
Overton Av. L21: Lith 1A 44
Overton Cl. CH43: Oxton 5F 72
L32: Kirkb 1B 46
WA6: Frod 5M 107
Overton Dr. WA6: Frod 8M 107
Overton Grn. WA6: Frod 5N 107
Overton Rd. CH44: Wall 5H 57
Overton St. L7: Liv 8G 58
Overton Way CH43: Oxton 5F 72
Ovington Cl. WA7: Sut W 3B 108
Ovington Dr. PR8: South 3D 12
Ovolo Rd. L13: Liv 5M 59
Owen Av. L39: Orm 7D 20
Owen Cl. WA10: St H 9G 48
Owen Dr. L24: Speke 4F 92
Owen Rd. L4: Kirkd 1C 58
L33: Know I 3G 46
L35: Rainh 7F 62
Owens Cnr. WA4: App 4E 98
Owen's La. L39: Down 2C 26
Owen St. WA2: Warr 1B 82
WA10: St H 9G 48
Owlsfield WA12: Newt W 7N 51
Oxborough Cl.
WA8: Widnes 4J 79
Oxbow Rd. L12: W Der 1C 60
Oxendale Cl. L8: Liv 1G 74
Oxenham Rd. WA2: Warr 6C 66
Oxford Av. L20: Boot 7D 44
L21: Lith 2A 44
Oxford Cl. CH66: Gt Sut 5K 111
L17: Aig 6H 75
Oxford Ct. L22: Wloo 9J 33
PR8: Birkd 2M 11
WA1: Warr 2E 82
Oxford Dr. CH63: Thorn H 9F 88
L22: Wloo 9J 33
L26: Halew 8K 77
Oxford Gdns. PR8: Birkd 2L 11
Oxford Gro. M44: Cad 3J 69
Oxford Ho. *L20: Boot 7D 44*
(off Fernhill Rd.)
Oxford Rd. CH44: Wall 5J 57
L9: Aintr 2G 44
L20: Boot 7C 44
L22: Wloo 9J 33
L36: Huy 5L 61
PR8: Birkd 1L 11
WA7: Run 6K 95
WN8: Skel 3B 30
Oxford St. *CH65: Ell P 8A 104*
(off Worcester St.)
L7: Liv 6K 5 (8E 58)
(not continuous)
WA4: Warr 4D 82
WA8: Widnes 8L 79
WA10: St H 6J 49
(Cooper St.)
WA10: St H 5J 49
(Rutland St.)
WA12: Newt W 7J 51
Oxford St. E. L7: Liv 6N 5 (8F 58)
Oxheys WA7: Nort 7E 96
Oxholme Cl. CH46: More 8A 56
Oxhouse Rd. WN5: Orr 8N 31
Ox La. L35: Tar G 4M 77
Oxley Av. CH46: Leas 6B 56
Oxley St. WA9: St H 2N 63
Oxmead Cl. WA2: Padg 8J 67
Oxmoor Cl. WA7: Brook 1C 108
Oxmoor Local Nature Reserve 2F 96
OXTON 4F 72
Oxton Cl. L17: Aig 6H 75
L32: Kirkb 2N 45
WA8: Widnes 4F 78
Oxton Ct. CH43: Oxton 4H 73
Oxton Grn. CH66: Gt Sut 1J 111
Oxton Rd. CH41: Birke 3J 73
CH44: Wall 6H 57
Oxton St. L4: W'ton 1E 58

P

Pacific Rd. CH41: Birke 1M 73
L20: Boot 7A 44
(Atlantic Rd.)
L20: Boot 6A 44
(Globe Rd.)
Packenham Rd. L13: Liv 3L 59
Padbury St. L8: Liv 3F 74
PADDINGTON 9G 67
Paddington L7: Liv 5M 5 (8F 58)
(not continuous)
Paddington Bank WA1: Warr 2G 82
Paddock, The CH2: Elt 2L 113
CH46: More 1K 71
CH49: Upton 3B 72
CH60: Hesw 7C 88
CH66: Gt Sut 2J 111
L25: Gate 4F 76
L32: Kirkb 3B 46
L34: Eccl P 2D 62
L37: Form 8G 16
L39: Augh 1A 28
L40: Ruf 2N 15
PR8: Ainsd 1H 17
WA6: Hel 3F 114
WA13: Lymm 5J 85
WN4: Ash M 5H 41
Paddock Cl. L23: Blun 5H 33
Paddock Dr. CH64: P'gte 4D 100
Paddock Gro. WA9: Clock F 6N 63
Paddock La. WA13: Warb 9H 69
WA14: Dun M 3N 85
Paddock Ri. WA7: Beech 2A 108
Paddock Rd. L34: Presc 3L 61
WN8: Skel 7F 30
Padeswood Cl. WA9: St H 3M 63
PADGATE 8G 67
Padgate Bus. Pk. WA1: Padg 9J 67
Padgate La. WA1: Padg, Warr 1E 82
(not continuous)
Padgate Station (Rail) 8H 67
Padley M. WA1: Warr 3F 82
Padstow Cl. L26: Halew 7J 77
PR9: South 2N 7
WA5: Penk 5G 80
Padstow Dr. WA10: Windle 4E 48
Padstow Rd. CH49: Grea 5K 71
L16: Child 9B 60
Padstow Sq. WA7: Brook 1D 108
Pagebank Rd. L14: Knott A 6E 60
Page Ct. L37: Form 1F 24
Pagefield Rd. L15: Wavtr 2M 75
Page Grn. L36: Huy 6G 60
Page La. WA8: Widnes 7M 79
PAGE MOSS 6F 60
Page Moss Av. L36: Huy 5F 60
Page Moss La. L14: Knott A 6E 60
Page Moss Pde. L36: Huy 5F 60
Page Wlk. L3: Liv 2J 5 (6D 58)
(not continuous)
Pagewood Cl. CH43: Noct 4C 72
Paignton Cl. L36: Huy 6M 61
WA5: Penk 4G 80
WN5: Bil 3A 40
Paignton Rd. CH45: Wall 3F 56
L16: Child 9B 60
Painswick Rd. CH66: Gt Sut 3K 111
Paisley Av. CH62: East 2D 102
WA11: St H 3N 49
Paisley Ct. L14: Knott A 5D 60
Paisley St. L3: Liv 2B 4 (6A 58)
Palace Arc. *WN4: Ash M 8K 41*
(off Foy St.)
PALACE FIELDS 9C 96
Palacefields Av. WA7: Pal F 9B 96
Palacefields Local Cen. WA7: Pal F 9C 96
Palace Hey CH64: Ness 9G 101
Palace Rd. L9: Aintr 4F 44
PR8: Birkd 1L 11
Palais Bldgs. L40: Burs 9J 15
Palatine, The L20: Boot 7B 44
Palatine Arc. WA10: St H 7K 49
Palatine Cl. M44: Irlam 1M 69
Palatine Ind. Est. WA4: Warr 5D 82
Palatine Rd. CH44: Wall 7K 57
CH62: Brom 6B 90
PR8: Birkd 1M 11
Palermo Cl. CH44: Wall 7K 57
Paley Cl. L4: W'ton 2E 58
Palin Dr. WA5: Gt San 2H 81
Palladio Rd. L13: Liv 5N 59
Palliser Cl. WA3: Birchw 6A 68
Pall Mall L3: Liv 1D 4 (6B 58)
Palmarsh Rd. WA8: Hale B 2E 94
Palm Av. WN4: Garsw 6F 40
Palm Cl. L9: W'ton 7H 45
Palm Ct. *L8: Liv 4F 74*
(off Weller Way)
WN8: Skel 2B 30
Palmdale Gdns. WA5: Gt San 2K 81
Palmer Cl. CH43: Noct 5D 72
WA10: St H 6J 49
Palmer Cres. WA5: Old H 9M 65
Palmerston Av. L21: Lith 3N 43
Palmerston Cl. L18: Moss H 5L 75
Palmerston Ct. L18: Moss H 5M 75
Palmerston Cres. L19: Garst 1A 92
Palmerston Dr. L21: Lith 3A 44
L25: Hunts X 9H 77
Palmerston Rd. CH44: Wall 5F 56
L18: Moss H 5L 75
L19: Garst 1A 92
PR9: South 9L 7
Palmerston St. CH42: Rock F 6M 73
Palmer Vs. CH42: Rock F 7L 73
Palm Gro. CH43: Oxton 2H 73
CH66: Whit 4M 111
L25: Woolt 7F 76
PR8: South 9K 7
Palm Hill CH43: Oxton 4H 73
Palmwood Av. L35: Rainh 7G 63
Palmwood Cl. CH43: Pren 7E 72
Palmyra Ho. WA1: Warr 3B 82
Palmyra Sq. Nth. WA1: Warr 3B 82
Palmyra Sq. Sth. WA1: Warr 3B 82
Palomar Cl. L18: Liv 1G 74
Paltridge Way CH61: Pens 3N 87
Pamela Cl. L10: Faz 4N 45
Pampas Gro. L9: W'ton 6G 44
Panama Av. L30: Neth 1E 44
Pandan Rd. L11: Norr G 9M 45
Pangbourne Cl. WA4: App 1F 98
Pankhurst Rd. L21: Ford 9B 34
Pansy St. L5: Kirkd 2C 58
Panton Way L10: Faz 4N 45
Papillon Dr. L9: Aintr 2J 45
Paprika Dr. L11: Norr G 8M 45
Parade, The CH64: P'gte 4B 100
L15: Wavtr 8N 59
L26: Halew 9J 77
WA3: Cul 7M 53
Parade Cres. L24: Speke 5J 93
Parade St. WA10: St H 6K 49
Paradise Gdns. L15: Wavtr 1L 75
Paradise La. L35: Whis 7A 62
L37: Form 7F 16
Paradise Pl. L1: Liv 6F 4
Paradise St. L1: Liv 7F 4 (9C 58)
Paragon Cl. WA8: Widnes 3L 79
PARBOLD 3F 22
Parbold Av. WA11: St H 5N 49
Parbold Cl. L40: Burs 2J 21
Parbold Ct. WA8: Widnes 8G 78
Parbold Hill WN8: Parb 3G 23
Parbold Station (Rail) 3F 22
Parbrook Cl. L36: Huy 3H 61
Parbrook Rd. L36: Huy 3H 61
Parchments, The WA12: Newt W 6M 51
Pardoe Ct. L40: Burs 2K 21
Paris Av. WN3: Winst 1E 40
Parish M. L14: Knott A 5C 60
Park, The L36: Huy 8J 61
WA5: Penk 5F 80
(not continuous)
Park & Ride
Bebington 9N 73
Bidston 7C 56
Bromborough 9B 90
Brunswick 4D 74
Eastham Rake 3C 102
Esplanade 8E 6
Fairways 5H 7
Gillmoss 4A 46
Green Lane 4M 73
Hoylake 2C 70
Kew 1F 12
Lea Green 3L 63
Leasowe 7A 56
Meols 9F 54
Moreton 7M 55
Rock Ferry 6M 73
Spital 5A 90
Wallasey Grove Road 3E 56
Park Av. CH44: Wall 6K 57
L9: Aintr 3J 45
L18: Moss H 5K 75
L23: Crosb 6L 33
L31: Lydi 9J 27
L34: Eccl P 2C 62
L35: Rainh 5F 62
L37: Form 3F 24
L39: Orm 8C 20
PR9: South 6K 7
WA3: Golb 1A 52
WA4: Warr 5E 82
WA8: Widnes 6L 79
WA11: Hay 4C 50
WN5: Bil 2A 40
Park Av. Nth. WA12: Newt W 8L 51
Park Av. Sth. WA12: Newt W 8L 51
Park Blvd. WA1: Warr 4C 82
Parkbourn L31: Mag 1M 35
Parkbourn Dr. L31: Mag 1M 35
Parkbourn Nth. L31: Mag 1M 35
Parkbourn Sq. L31: Mag 1M 35
Parkbridge Rd. CH42: Tran 5J 73
Park Brow Dr. L32: Kirkb 2D 46
Parkbury Ct. CH43: Oxton 5G 72
Park Cl. CH41: Birke 2J 73
L32: Kirkb 7N 35
L37: Form 4E 24
WN8: Parb 2G 22
Park Ct. CH48: W Kir 6B 70
L22: Wloo 2L 43
L32: Kirkb 8A 36
PR9: South 7J 7

Pendennis St.—Pinfold Cottage Woodland Pk.

Pendennis St. L6: Liv 4G 59
Pendine Cl. L6: Liv 5H 59
WA5: Call 7L 65
Pendle Av. WA11: St H 5N 49
Pendlebury St. WA4: Westy 5H 83
WA9: Clock F 6M 63
Pendle Cl. CH49: Upton 2M 71
CH66: Lit Sut 8E 102
Pendle Ct. WN8: Skel 9G 30
Pendle Dr. L21: Ford 7B 34
L39: Orm 7E 20
Pendle Gdns. WA3: Cul 8M 53
Pendle Pl. WN8: Skel 8G 31
Pendle Rd. WA3: Golb 1D 52
Pendleton Ct. L34: Presc 4A 62
Pendleton Grn. L26: Halew 9J 77
Pendleton Rd. L4: W'ton 8F 44
Pendle Vw. L21: Ford 7B 34
Pendle Vs. L21: Ford 8B 34
Penfield Rd. WN7: Leigh 1K 53
Penfold L31: Mag 2K 35
Penfold Cl. CH1: Cap 5G 110
L18: Moss H 3B 76
Penfolds WA7: Run 6N 95
Pengwern Gro. L15: Wavtr 9J 59
Pengwern St. L8: Liv 3F 74
Pengwern Ter. *CH45: Wall 2J 57*
(off Holland Rd.)
Penhale Cl. L17: Aig 6G 75
Penhurst Way WA9: St H 2N 63
Peninsula Bus. Pk. CH46: Leas 7A 56
Peninsula Cl. CH45: Wall 1E 56
Peninsula Dr. WA12: Newt W 9M 51
Peninsula Ho. WA2: Warr 1D 82
Penistone Dr. CH66: Lit Sut 9G 103
PENKETH 4H 81
Penketh Av. WA5: Warr 9A 66
Penketh Bus. Pk. WA5: Gt San 4K 81
Penketh Ct. WA5: Penk 4F 80
WA7: Run 5L 95
Penketh Dr. L24: Speke 3J 93
Penketh Parish Swimming Pool 4G 81
Penketh Pl. WN8: Skel 7F 30
Penketh Rd. L24: Speke 4J 93
WA5: Gt San 4J 81
Penketh's La. WA7: Run 4K 95
Penkett Ct. CH45: Wall 3J 57
Penkett Gdns. CH45: Wall 3J 57
Penkett Gro. CH45: Wall 3J 57
Penkett Rd. CH45: Wall 3H 57
Penkford La. WA5: Coll G 9F 50
Penkford St. WA12: Newt W 7G 50
Penkmans La. WA6: Frod 8M 107
Penlake La. WA9: St H 2B 64
Penley Cres. L32: Kirkb 9N 35
Penlinken Dr. L6: Liv 5G 59
Penmann Cl. L26: Halew 8K 77
Penmann Cres. L26: Halew 8K 77
Penmark Cl. WA5: Call 7L 65
Penmon Dr. CH61: Pens 4N 87
Pennant Av. L12: W Der 9A 46
Pennant Cl. WA3: Birchw 6A 68
Pennard Av. L36: Huy 4H 61
(not continuous)
Penn Gdns. CH65: Ell P 9N 103
Pennine Av. WN3: Winst 1E 40
Pennine Cl. WA9: St H 7A 50
Pennine Dr. WA9: St H 7B 50
Pennine La. WA3: Golb 1D 52
Pennine Pl. WN8: Skel 6E 30
Pennine Rd. CH42: Tran 7J 73
CH44: Wall 5F 56
WA2: Warr 7F 66
Pennine Wlk. CH66: Lit Sut 8G 103
Pennine Way L32: Kirkb 7A 36
Pennington Av. L20: Boot 3D 44
L39: Orm 7C 20
Pennington Cl. WA6: Frod 4N 107
WN8: Skel 1G 39
Pennington Ct. L39: Orm 7D 20
WN7: Leigh 1J 53
Pennington Dr. WA12: Newt W 7N 51
Pennington Gdns. *L34: Presc 3A 62*
(off Houghton St.)
Pennington Grn. CH66: Gt Sut 2H 111
Pennington La. WA9: Coll G, St H 7E 50
Pennington Lodge WA9: St H 1J 63
Pennington Rd. L21: Lith 4B 44
Pennington St. L4: W'ton 8E 44
Penn La. WA7: Run 5J 95
Pennsylvania Rd. L13: Liv 2J 59
Pennybutts Cl. WA3: Golb 1A 52
Pennycress Dr. L11: Norr G 8L 45
Pennyford Dr. L18: Moss H 5K 75
PENNYLANDS 3A 30
Penny La. L18: Moss H 4L 75
WA5: Coll G 1F 64
WA8: Cron 2D 78
WA11: Hay 3H 51
Penny La. Neighbourhood Cen.
L15: Wavtr 2M 75
Pennypleck La. CW9: Ant 5N 99
Pennystone Cl. CH49: Upton 2L 71
Pennywood Dr. L35: Whis 7B 62
Penpoll Cl. L20: Boot 4B 44
Penrhos Rd. CH47: Hoy 2B 70
Penrhyd Rd. CH61: Irby 2L 87
Penrhyn Av. CH61: Thing 1A 88
L21: Lith 3A 44
Penrhyn Ct. L34: Know 4F 46
Penrhyn Cres. WA7: Run 8L 95
Penrhyn Rd. L34: Know 5F 46
Penrhyn St. L5: Liv 4C 58
Penrith Av. PR8: Ainsd 2J 17
WA2: Warr 7D 66
Penrith Cl. M31: Part 5L 69
WA6: Frod 5N 107
Penrith Cres. L31: Mag 1K 35
WN4: Ash M 7K 41
Penrith Rd. WA10: St H 1E 62
Penrith St. CH41: Birke 3J 73
Penrose Av. E. L14: Brd G 7D 60
Penrose Av. W. L14: Brd G 7C 60
Penrose Gdns. WA5: Penk 5F 80
Penrose Pl. WN8: Skel 8H 31
Penrose St. L5: Liv 3E 58
Penry Av. M44: Cad 3L 69
Penryn Av. WA11: St H 3N 49
Penryn Cl. WA5: Penk 5G 81
Pensall Dr. CH61: Hesw 5N 87
Pensarn Gdns. WA5: Call 7M 65
Pensarn Rd. L13: Liv 7L 59
PENSBY 3A 88
Pensby Cl. CH61: Thing 2A 88
Pensby Dr. CH66: Gt Sut 1J 111
Pensby Hall La. CH61: Hesw 5N 87
Pensby Rd. CH60: Hesw 7N 87
CH61: Hesw, Irby, Pens 7N 87
Pensby St. CH41: Birke 9J 57
Penshaw Cl. L14: Knott A 3E 60
Penshaw Ct. WA7: Pal F 8A 96
Pentire Av. WA10: Windle 4E 48
Pentire Cl. L10: Faz 4N 45
Pentland Av. L4: W'ton 9F 44
WA2: Warr 6C 66
WA9: St H 7B 50
Pentland Pl. WA2: Warr 6C 66
Pentland Rd. L33: Kirkb 7E 36
Penty Pl. PR8: South 9G 6
Penuel Rd. L4: W'ton 8E 44
Penvalley Cres. L6: Liv 5H 59
Penwell Fold WN8: Skel 4H 31
Penzance Cl. WA3: Ris 5L 67
Peony Gdns. WA9: Bold 2D 64
Peover St. L3: Liv 1G 5 (6C 58)
Peploe Rd. L4: W'ton 8J 45
Peplow Rd. L32: Kirkb 9N 35
Peppermint Way L11: Norr G 9M 45
Peppers, The WA13: Lymm 5F 84
Pepper St. L24: Hale 6A 94
WA4: App T 4H 99
WA13: Lymm 5E 84
Pepperwood Dr. WN3: Winst 1G 40
Pera Cl. L6: Liv 2N 5 (6F 58)
Perch Pool La. L40: Scar 3L 13
PR9: South 2L 13
Percival Ct. *PR8: South 9F 6*
(off Lord St.)
WA7: Run 6G 94
Percival La. WA7: Run 6G 94
Percival Rd. CH65: Ell P 8N 103
Percival St. WA1: Warr 3D 82
Percival Way WA10: St H 5F 48
Percy Rd. CH44: Wall 7L 57
Percy St. L8: Liv 9K 5 (1E 74)
L20: Boot 5A 44
WA5: Warr 3N 81
(not continuous)
WA9: St H 1B 64
Percy Vs. *L9: W'ton 6F 44*
(off Cedardale Rd.)
Perilla Dr. L11: Norr G 8M 45
Perimeter Rd. L33: Know I 2H 47
WA6: Hel 9N 105
Perriam Rd. L19: Aller 8B 76
Perrin Av. WA7: Run 7H 95
Perrin Rd. CH45: Wall 4E 56
Perrins Rd. WA5: Burtw 3H 65
Perrybrook Wlk. *WN4: Ash M 7M 41*
(off North St.)
Perrygate Cl. L7: Liv 9G 58
Perry St. L8: Liv 2C 74
WA7: Run 5L 95
Pershore Gro. PR8: Ainsd 1G 17
Pershore Ho. CH42: Tran 7H 73
Pershore Rd. L32: Kirkb 2C 46
Perth Av. WA9: St H 2H 63
Perth Cl. L33: Kirkb 5B 36
WA2: Fearn 5G 67
Perth St. L6: Liv 1N 5 (6F 58)
Pete Best Dr. L12: W Der 3N 59
Peterborough Cl. CH66: Gt Sut 6L 111
Peterborough Dr. L30: Neth 7D 34
Peterborough Rd. L15: Wavtr 2M 75
Peter Ho. L2: Liv 3E 4
Peterhouse M. L20: Boot 7C 44
Peterhouse Wlk. WN4: Ash M 7H 41
Peter Kane Sq. *WA3: Golb 2B 52*
(off Heath St.)
Peterlee Cl. WA9: St H 2J 63
Peterlee Way L30: Neth 1F 44
Peter Mahon Way L20: Boot 6A 44
Peter Price's La. CH63: H Beb 3L 89
Peter Rd. L4: W'ton 8D 44
(not continuous)
Peters Arc. L1: Liv 6F 4
Peters Av. L40: Burs 1J 21
Petersfield Cl. L30: Neth 1E 44
Petersfield Gdns. WA3: Cul 6M 53
Petersgate WA7: Murd 8F 96
Petersham Dr. WA4: App 2F 98
Peter's La. L1: Liv 6F 4 (8C 58)
Peterstone Cl. WA5: Call 6M 65
Peter St. CH44: Wall 7L 57
L1: Liv 4F 4 (7C 58)
WA3: Golb 2B 52
WA10: St H 6H 49
WN4: Ash M 8L 41
Peterwood CH42: Rock F 7N 73
Petham Ct. WA8: Widnes 4H 79
Petherick Rd. L11: Crox 5A 46
Petra Ct. L4: W'ton 2H 59
Petunia Cl. L14: Knott A 5E 60
WA9: Bold 2C 64
Petworth Av. WA2: Warr 6C 66
WN3: Winst 1F 40
Petworth Cl. L24: Speke 3F 92
Petworth Rd. PR8: Ainsd 8H 11
Peveril Cl. WA4: App 8E 82
Peveril St. L9: W'ton 7E 44
PEWFALL 1E 50
PEWTERSPEAR 3G 98
Pewterspear Grn. Rd. WA4: App 4E 98
Pewterspear La. WA4: App 3E 98
PEX HILL 2H 79
Pex Hill Ct. WA8: Widnes 3H 79
Pharmacy Rd. L24: Speke 3G 92
Pheasant Cl. WA3: Birchw 5N 67
Pheasant Fld. L24: Hale 5N 93
Pheasant Gro. L26: Halew 7J 77
Philbeach Rd. L4: W'ton 8J 45
L11: Norr G 8J 45
Philharmonic Ct. L8: Liv 8K 5
Philip Dr. PR8: Ainsd 8M 11
Philip Gro. WA9: St H 2M 63
Philip Leverhulme Lodge
CH62: Port S 1A 90
Philip Rd. WA8: Widnes 8E 78
Philips La. CH66: Gt Sut 1H 111
Phillimore Rd. L6: Liv 6H 59
Phillip Gro. L12: W Der 4D 60
Phillips Cl. L23: Thorn 5A 34
L37: Form 2F 24
Phillips Dr. WA5: Gt San 2G 81
Phillip's La. L37: Form 2E 24
Phillips St. L3: Liv 2E 4 (6B 58)
Phillips Way CH60: Hesw 7M 87
Phipps La. WA5: Burtw 1G 64
Phoenix Av. WA5: Warr 7A 66
Phoenix Brow WA9: St H 7L 49
Phoenix Ct. CH64: P'gte 5C 100
Phoenix Dr. L14: Knott A 5E 60
Phoenix Pk. L24: Speke 2E 92
Phoenix Pl. WA5: Gt San 1J 81
Physics Rd. L24: Speke 2G 93
Phythian Cl. L6: Liv 2N 5 (6G 58)
Phythian Cres. WA5: Penk 4H 81
Phythian St. L6: Liv 2M 5 (6F 58)
WA11: Hay 4B 50
Picadilly WN5: Bil 6A 40
Pichael Nook WA4: Westy 4H 83
Pickerill Rd. CH49: Grea 5L 71
Pickering Cres. WA4: Thel 5L 83
Pickering Dr. WA12: Newt W 8H 51
Pickering Rake *L30: Neth 6C 34*
(off Red Lomes)
Pickering Rd. CH45: New B 1H 57
Pickerings Cl. WA7: Run 9M 95
Pickerings Pasture Local Nature Reserve
3D 94
Pickerings Pasture Vis. Cen. 3E 94
Pickerings Rd. WA8: Hale B 2E 94
Pickering St. L6: Liv 4F 58
Pickles Dr. L40: Burs 1H 21
Pickmere Dr. CH62: East 3E 102
(not continuous)
WA7: Brook 1E 108
Pickmere St. WA5: Warr 3N 81
Pickop St. L3: Liv 2E 4 (7B 58)
Pickwick St. L8: Liv 2E 74
Pickworth Way L31: Mell 9N 35
Picow Farm Rd. WA7: Run, West P 6H 95
Picow St. WA7: Run 6J 95
PICTON 9H 113
Picton Av. WA7: Run 6L 95
Picton Cl. CH43: Oxton 4F 72
CH62: East 3C 102
WA3: Birchw 5K 67
Picton Cres. L15: Wavtr 9K 59
Picton Gro. L15: Wavtr 9J 59
Picton La.
CH2: Mick T, Pict, Stoak, Wer 6E 112
Picton Rd. L15: Wavtr 9J 59
L22: Wloo 1K 43
Picton Valley CH2: Pict 9G 113
Piele Rd. WA11: Hay 3F 50
Piercefield Ct. L37: Form 8F 16
Piercefield Rd. L37: Form 9F 16
Pier Head L3: Liv 6B 4 (8A 58)
Pier Ho. CH45: New B 9J 43
Pierpoint St. WA5: Warr 1A 82
Pighue La. L7: Liv 8K 59
L13: Liv 8M 59
Pigot Pl. WA4: Westy 3G 83
Pigot St. WA10: St H 7H 49
Pigotts Rake *L30: Neth 6C 34*
(off Higher End Pk.)
Pike Ho. Rd. WA10: Ec'stn 5D 48
Pike La. L40: Burs 5G 15
Pikelaw Pl. WN8: Skel 7F 30
Pike Pl. WA10: Ec'stn 6E 48
Pikes Bri. Fold WA10: Ec'stn 6D 48
Pikes Hey Rd. CH48: Caldy 9G 71
Pike St. WA4: Stockt H 7D 82
Pilch Bank Rd. L14: Knott A 5C 60
Pilch La. L14: Knott A 5C 60
Pilch La. E. L36: Huy, Roby 7E 60
Pilgrim Cl. WA2: Winw 3B 66
Pilgrim St. CH41: Birke 2M 73
L1: Liv 8J 5 (9D 58)
Pilgrims Way WA7: Nort 4F 96
Pilkington Ct. L34: Presc 4A 62
Pilkington Rd. PR8: South 1C 12
Pilkington Sailing Club 7D 48
Pilkington St. WA11: Rainf 5C 38
Pilling Cl. PR9: South 2L 7
Pilling La. L31: Lydi 7F 26
Pilling Pl. WN8: Skel 7F 30
Pillmoss La. WA4: Hatt, L Whit 6B 98
Pilot Gro. L15: Wavtr 9J 59
Pilots Way CH45: New B 9G 43
Pimblett Rd. WA11: Hay 3G 51
Pimblett St. WA3: Golb 3B 52
Pimbley Gro. E. L31: Mag 5H 35
Pimbley Gro. W. L31: Mag 5H 35
Pimbo Ind. Est. WN8: Skel 7F 30
(not continuous)
PIMBO JUNC. 7H 31
Pimbo La. WN8: Uph 3J 39
Pimbo Rd. WA11: Kings M 4H 39
WN8: Skel 6F 30
Pimhill Cl. L8: Liv 2F 74
Pimlico Rd. WA7: Run 5H 95
Pincroft Way *L4: Kirkd 2C 58*
(off Fountains Rd.)
Pinders Farm Dr. WA1: Warr 3D 82
Pine Av. CH63: Beb 4M 89
L39: Orm 7D 20
WA8: Widnes 6L 79
WA10: St H 4J 49
WA12: Newt W 8L 51
Pine Cl. L32: Kirkb 8A 36
L35: Whis 6B 62
L36: Huy 5H 61
WA11: Hay 4E 50
WN8: Newb 4D 22
WN8: Skel 3C 30
Pine Ct. CH41: Birke 2K 73
L8: Liv 4F 74
(off Byles St.)
PR9: South 6H 7
Pine Crest L39: Augh 2N 27
Pine Dale WA11: Rainf 4B 38
Pinedale Cl. CH43: Noct 4D 72
CH66: Whit 5M 111
Pine Dr. L39: Orm 7D 20
Pinefield Cl. L5: Liv 3E 58
Pine Gro. CH66: Whit 4M 111
L20: Boot 6C 44
L22: Wloo 9K 33
L39: Orm 6D 20
PR9: South 8J 7
WA1: Padd 1H 83
WA3: Golb 2D 52
Pine Hey CH64: Nest 5D 100
Pinehurst Av. L4: W'ton 2G 59
L22: Wloo 8J 33
Pinehurst Rd. L4: W'ton 2G 59
Pinehurst Wlk. WA5: Gt San 1J 81
Pinellas WA7: Run 4L 95
Pine Lodge L4: W'ton 1H 59
Pine M. L1: Liv 9H 5 (1D 74)
Pinemore Rd. L18: Moss H 6M 75
Pineridge Cl. CH62: Spit 4B 90
Pine Rd. CH60: Hesw 6C 88
WA7: Run 8M 95
Pines, The CH63: Spit 4A 90
L12: Crox 6D 46
WA8: Widnes 4N 79
(off Hampton Ct. Way)
Pinetop Cl. L6: Liv 5G 59
Pine Tree Av. CH43: Noct 4C 72
Pinetree Cl. CH46: More 9N 55
L30: Neth 8E 34
Pinetree Ct. CH44: Wall 4F 56
Pinetree Dr. CH48: W Kir 7E 70
Pinetree Gro. CH46: More 9N 55
Pinetree Rd. L36: Huy 9H 61
Pine Vw. WN3: Winst 2D 40
Pine Vw. Dr. CH61: Hesw 5N 87
Pine Wlk. *M31: Part 6L 69*
(off Wood La.)
Pine Walks CH42: Tran 7H 73
CH48: W Kir 7E 70
Pinewalks Ridge CH42: Tran 8J 73
Pine Way CH60: Hesw 5M 87
Pineways WA4: App 2E 98
Pinewood WN4: Ash M 9J 41
WN8: Skel 1G 30
Pinewood Av. L12: Crox 7B 46
L37: Form 2D 24
WA1: Warr 1F 82
Pinewood Cl. CH2: Elt 2N 113
L27: N'ley 2J 77
L37: Form 2D 24
PR8: South 5H 13
Pinewood Dr. CH60: Hesw 7B 88
Pinewood Gdns.
L33: Kirkb 6C 36
Pinewood Rd. WA5: Burtw 2H 65
PINFOLD 2M 19
Pinfold Cl. L30: Neth 6C 34
PR8: Ainsd 2H 17
Pinfold Cottage Woodland Pk. 6D 34

Pinfold Ct.—Prescott St.

Pinfold Ct. CH48: W Kir 4B 70
L23: Crosb 6K 33
Pinfold Cres. L32: Kirkb 2E 46
Pinfold Dr. WA10: Ec'stn 7D 48
Pinfold La. CH48: W Kir 4B 70
L34: Know 7F 46
L40: Scar 3K 19
PR8: Ainsd 2G 17
(not continuous)
Pinfold Pl. WN8: Skel 8G 30
Pinfold Rd. L25: Hunts X 9G 76
L39: Orm 9E 20
Pingot La. WA6: Manl 8K 115
Pingot Rd. WN5: Bil 6A 40
Pingwood La. L33: Kirkb 5E 36
Pinmill Brow WA6: Frod 7L 107
Pinmill Cl. WA6: Frod 7M 107
Pinners Brow WA2: Warr 2C 82
Pinners Brow Retail Pk. 2C 82
Pinners Fold WA7: Nort 6D 96
Pinnington Pl. L36: Huy 7H 61
Pinnington Rd. L35: Whis 6B 62
Pintail Cl. WA11: St H 4L 49
Pintail Way PR9: Banks 2E 8
Pintile Cl. L8: Liv 3D 74
Pioneer Pk. CH65: Ell P 6L 103
Pipers, The CH60: Hesw 6L 87
WA3: Low 2G 52
Piper's Cl. CH60: Hesw 7L 87
Piper's End CH60: Hesw 7L 87
Pipers La. CH60: Hesw 5K 87
Pipistrelle Ri. CH43: Noct 4D 72
Pipit Av. WA12: Newt W 7L 51
Pipit Cl. L26: Halew 6J 77
Pipit La. WA3: Birchw 6M 67
Pippin St. L40: Burs 3D 20
Pippits Row WA7: Beech 2A 108
Pirrie Rd. L9: Aintr 7J 45
Pitch Cl. CH49: Grea 4L 71
Pit Hey Pl. WN8: Skel 7F 30
Pit La. WA8: Widnes 4K 79
Pit Pl. L25: Woolt 6E 76
Pitsford Way L6: Liv 1M 5 (5F 58)
Pitsmead Rd. L32: Kirkb 1C 46
Pittsburgh Ct. WA5: Gt San 2M 81
Pitts Heath La. WA7: Nort 4F 96
Pitts Ho. La. PR9: South 7N 7
Pitt St. L1: Liv 8G 4 (9C 58)
PR9: South 9L 7
WA5: Warr 2A 82
WA8: Widnes 2K 95
WA9: St H 7M 49
Pitville Av. L18: Moss H 5M 75
Pitville Cl. L18: Moss H 6M 75
Pitville Gro. L18: Moss H 5N 75
Pitville Rd. L18: Moss H 5M 75
Pitville Ter. WA8: Widnes 9F 78
Plaistow Ct. WA7: Pal F 8A 96
Plane Cl. L9: W'ton 7H 45
Plane Tree Gro. WA11: Hay 3J 51
Plane Tree Rd. CH63: H Beb 3L 89
Planetree Rd. L12: W Der 2D 60
M31: Part 6K 69
Planewood Gdns. WA3: Low 3G 53
Plantation Bus. Pk. CH62: Brom 5E 90
Plantation Cl. WA7: Cas 6C 96
Plantation Ct. CH62: Brom 5E 90
Plantation Dr. CH66: Ell P 7K 103
Plantation Rd. CH62: Brom 6E 90
L40: Burs 1F 20
Planters, The CH49: Grea 4K 71
L30: Neth 7F 34
(off Harvester Way)
Platinum Ct. L33: Know I 3F 46
Platt Gro. CH42: Rock F 8N 73
Platts La. L40: Burs 3H 21
Platts La. Ind. Est. L40: Burs 3H 21
Platts St. WA11: Hay 4C 50
Plattsville Rd. L18: Moss H 3M 75
Playfield Rd. L12: W Der 2D 60
Playfield Wlk. L12: W Der 2D 60
Plaza Blvd. L8: Liv 2C 74
Plaza Cinema
Waterloo 1L 43
Pleasance Way WA12: Newt W 6L 51
Pleasant Hill St. L8: Liv 2C 74
Pleasant St. CH45: New B 2H 57
L3: Liv 6J 5 (8D 58)
L20: Boot 8A 44
Pleasant Vw. L20: Boot 8A 44
Pleasington Cl. CH43: Noct 4E 72
Pleasington Dr. CH43: Noct 4E 72
Pleck Rd. CH65: Whit 3M 111
Plemont Rd. L13: Liv 4M 59
Plemston Ct. CH66: Ell P 6L 103
Plex La. L39: Hals 6F 18
Plex Moss La. L39: Hals 4K 17
Plex Moss La. Cvn. Pk. PR8: Ainsd 4K 17
Plinston Av. WA4: Westy 4G 82
Plough La. L40: Lath 1K 29
Ploughmans Cl. CH66: Gt Sut 5K 111
PR9: South 2B 8
Ploughmans Way CH66: Gt Sut 5K 111
Plover Cl. PR9: Banks 2E 8
WA12: Newt W 7L 51
Plover Dr. WA7: Nort 7F 96
Plovers La. WA6: Hel 9F 106
Plover Way WA3: Low 2F 52
Pluckington Rd. L36: Huy 6M 61
Plumb Ct. L39: Down 8F 18
Plumbers Way L36: Huy 7K 61
Plumer Dr. CH41: Birke 9G 57
Plumer St. L15: Wavtr 1K 75
Plumley Gdns. WA8: Widnes 6D 78
Plumley M. WA10: Ec'stn 7E 48
Plumpstons La. WA6: Frod 5L 107
Plumpton La. L39: Hals 4D 18
Plumpton M. WA8: Widnes 7M 79
Plumpton St. L6: Liv 5E 58
Plumtre Av. WA5: Warr 9A 66
Plum Tree Cl. L28: Stockb V 1F 60
Plumtree Cl. L35: Eccl P 3D 62
Plymouth Cl. L19: Garst 2N 91
WA7: Murd 9G 96
(not continuous)
Plymyard Av. CH62: Brom, East 9C 90
Plymyard Cl. CH62: Brom 1C 102
Plymyard Copse CH62: Brom 1C 102
Plymyard Ct. *CH62: Brom 9B 90*
(off Plymyard Av.)
Poachers La. WA4: Westy 5G 83
Pochard Ri. WA7: Nort 7F 96
POCKET NOOK 7M 49
Pocket Nook La. WA3: Low 2H 53
Pocket Nook St. WA9: St H 6M 49
Pocklington Ct. WA2: Padg 8G 66
Podium Rd. L13: Liv 5M 59
Poets Cnr. CH62: Port S 2A 90
Poets Grn. L35: Whis 6C 62
(not continuous)
Polden Cl. CH66: Lit Sut 8F 102
Poleacre Dr. WA8: Widnes 6G 78
Polinda Gdns. WA10: St H 1F 62
Pollard Av. WA6: Frod 7N 107
Pollard Rd. L15: Wavtr 8M 59
Pollard Sq. M31: Part 6N 69
POLL HILL 5N 87
Poll Hill Rd. CH60: Hesw 6N 87
Pollitt Cres. WA9: Clock F 6M 63
Pollitt Sq. CH62: New F 8B 74
Pollitt St. WA9: Clock F 6M 63
Polperro Cl. L11: Crox 5B 46
WA5: Penk 5G 80
Pomfret St. L8: Liv 2E 74
Pomona St. L3: Liv 6J 5 (8D 58)
Pond Cl. L6: Liv 5H 59
Pond Grn. Way WA9: St H 9B 50
Pond St. WA3: Low 2H 53
Pond Vw. Cl. CH60: Hesw 7C 88
Pond Wlk. WA9: St H 9C 50
Pondwater Cl. L32: Kirkb 1C 46
Ponsonby Rd. CH45: Wall 4E 56
Pontins Southport Cen. PR8: Ainsd 8F 10
Pool Bank CH62: Port S 9A 74
Pool Bank Gdns. WA13: Lymm 4C 84
Poolbank Rd. CH62: New F 9A 74
Poole Av. WA2: Warr 7C 66
Poole Cres. WA2: Warr 7C 66
Poole Hall Ind. Est. CH66: Ell P 6L 103
Poole Hall La. CH66: Ell P 6K 103
Poole Hall Rd. CH65: Ell P 6L 103
Pool End WA9: St H 8B 50
Poole Rd. CH44: Wall 4K 57
Pooley Cl. CH44: Wall 4J 57
POOL HEY 3G 13
Pool Hey L28: Stockb V 1F 60
(not continuous)
Pool Hey Cvn. Pk. PR9: South 2H 13
Pool Hey La. PR8: South 3F 12
PR9: South 3F 12
Pool Hollow WA7: Run 6L 95
Pool La. CH2: Elt, Ince 9K 105
CH2: Thorn M 3J 113
CH49: Wdchu 6A 72
CH62: Brom 2B 90
WA4: W'ton 7B 82
WA7: Run 4L 95
WA13: Lymm 4B 84
Pool Rd. WA3: Rix 6G 69
Poolside Rd. WA7: Run 6L 95
Poolside Wlk. PR9: South 3A 8
Pools Platt La. CW9: Ant 8M 99
Poolstock La. WN3: Wigan 1H 41
Pool St. CH41: Birke 1K 73
PR9: South 2A 8
WA8: Widnes 9L 79
Pooltown Rd. CH65: Ell P, Whit 8L 103
Poolwood Rd. CH49: Wdchu 4B 72
Pope St. L20: Boot 5A 44
POPLAR 2000 SERVICE AREA 9A 84
Poplar Av. CH49: Upton 3N 71
L23: Crosb 6M 33
WA3: Cul 7N 53
WA5: Penk 4G 81
WA7: Run 8M 95
WA10: Ec'stn 6D 48
WA12: Newt W 7M 51
WN4: Garsw 6F 40
Poplar Bank L36: Huy 7J 61
PR9: South 6J 7
Poplar Cl. CH65: Whit 1N 111
L26: Halew 7L 77
WA7: Run 8M 95
Poplar Ct. *L8: Liv 4F 74*
(off Byles St.)
WN8: Skel 6C 30
Poplar Dr. CH63: Beb 3A 90
L5: Liv 4F 58
L32: Kirkb 8B 36
WN8: Skel 3C 30
Poplar Farm Cl. CH46: More 2K 71
Poplar Farm Wlk. M44: Cad 4J 69
Poplar Gro. CH2: Elt 2L 113
CH42: Tran 4K 73
(off Ash Rd.)
L21: Sea 4M 43
L35: Presc 4B 62
M44: Cad 3K 69
WA10: St H 7F 48
WA11: Hay 4E 50
Poplar Hall La. CH2: Chor B 6A 112
Poplar Rd. CH43: Oxton 4H 73
L25: Woolt 5E 76
WA11: Hay 4E 50
Poplar Row CH2: Elt 2M 113
Poplars, The L40: Burs 3J 21
WA3: Golb 1C 52
WA13: Lymm 4D 84
WN7: Leigh 2K 53
Poplars Av. WA2: Warr 5B 66
(not continuous)
Poplars Pl. *WA2: Warr 7E 66*
(off Hughes Av.)
Poplar St. PR8: South 1D 12
WA3: Golb 1C 52
Poplar Ter. CH45: New B 2H 57
Poplar Vw. WA4: Moore 1J 97
Poplar Wlk. *M31: Part 6K 69*
(off Long Wlk.)
Poplar Way L4: Kirkd 1C 58
Poplar Weint CH64: Nest 6E 100
Poppleford Cl. L25: Gate 4H 77
Poppy Cl. CH46: More 7A 56
PR8: South 4A 12
Poppyfields WA5: Warr 5M 81
Poppy La. L39: Bic 3F 28
Poppy Nook PR9: Banks 3E 8
Poppy Pl. L22: Wloo 1L 43
Poppy Rd. L23: Thorn 6A 34
Porchester Rd. L11: Norr G 9L 45
Porchfield Cl. L11: Norr G 7N 45
Porlock Av. L16: Child 3C 76
WA9: Sut L 4M 63
Porlock Cl. CH60: Hesw 9B 88
WA5: Penk 4G 81
Portal M. CH61: Pens 4N 87
Portal Rd. CH61: Pens 4N 87
Portal Way L11: Crox 3A 46
Port Arcades, The CH65: Ell P 9A 104
Portbury Cl. CH62: Port S 1B 90
Portbury Wlk. CH62: Port S 1A 90
Portbury Way CH62: Port S 1B 90
Port Causeway CH62: Brom 3C 90
Portelet Rd. L13: Liv 5L 59
Porter Av. WA12: Newt W 5L 51
Porter Cl. L35: Rainh 8G 63
Porter St. L3: Liv 5A 58
WA7: Run 5M 95
Portgate Cl. L12: W Der 8A 46
Porthcawl Cl. WA8: Widnes 5F 78
Porthleven Rd. WA7: Brook 1D 108
Portia Av. CH63: H Beb 9L 73
Portia St. L20: Kirkd 9B 44
PORTICO 2E 62
Portico Av. L35: Eccl P 3D 62
Portico Ct. *L35: Eccl P 3D 62*
(off Portico La.)
Portico La. L34: Eccl P 3D 62
L35: Eccl P 3D 62
L35: Presc, Eccl P 3C 62
Portland Av. L22: Wloo 9J 33
Portland Ct. CH45: New B 9G 42
Portland Gdns. *L5: Liv 5B 58*
(off Green St.)
Portland Ga. *CH62: Port S 1B 90*
(off Portbury Cl.)
Portland Pl. L5: Liv 5D 58
WA6: Hel 1F 114
Portland Rd. WA5: Gt San 1J 81
Portland St. CH41: Birke 9G 56
CH45: New B 9G 42
L5: Liv 5B 58
PR8: South 9F 6
WA7: Run 4J 95
WA12: Newt W 6H 51
Portland Way WA9: St H 9B 50
Portlemouth Rd. L11: Crox 5A 46
Portloe Av. L26: Halew 7K 77
Portman Rd. L15: Wavtr 1J 75
Porto Hey Rd. CH61: Irby 2L 87
Portola Cl. WA4: Grap 6K 83
Porton Rd. L32: Kirkb 1A 46
Portreath Way WA10: Windle 4E 48
Portree Av. CH63: East 1C 102
Portree Cl. L9: W'ton 6E 44
Portrush Cl. WA8: Widnes 5H 79
Portrush St. L13: Liv 3K 59
Portside WA7: Pres B 8G 97
Portside Bus. Pk. CH65: Ell P 6N 103
Portside Ind. Est. CH65: Ell P 6A 104
Portside Nth. CH65: Ell P 6N 103
Portside Sth. CH65: Ell P 6A 104
Portsmouth Pl. WA7: Murd 9G 96
PORT SUNLIGHT 1A 90
Port Sunlight Mus. 1A 90
Port Sunlight Station (Rail) 2A 90
Port Talbot Cl. L19: Garst 1N 91
Portway L25: Hunts X 9G 77
Portwood Cl. L7: Liv 9G 59
Post Office Av. *PR9: South 8G 7*
(off Anchor St.)
Post Office La. CH2: Thorn M 4J 113
WA7: West P 8G 94
Potter Cl. WN8: Skel 6F 30
Potter Pl. WN8: Skel 7G 30
Potter's La. WA8: Hale B 3C 94
Potters La. L18: Moss H 3A 76
Pottery, The L31: Mell 9M 35
Pottery Cl. L35: Whis 6N 61
Pottery Flds. L34: Presc 3A 62
Pottery La. L35: Whis 6M 61
L36: Huy 6M 61
Potton Cl. WA7: Nort 4G 97
Poulevara Ho. *L13: Liv 7N 59*
(off W. Oakhill Pk.)
Poulsom Dr. L30: Neth 9B 34
Poulter Rd. L9: Aintr 3G 45
POULTON
CH44 7G 57
CH63 5N 89
Poulton Bri. Rd. CH41: Birke 7F 56
CH44: Wall 6G 56
Poulton Cl. L26: Halew 1H 93
Poulton Ct. PR9: South 8L 7
Poulton Cres. WA1: Wools 9K 67
Poulton Dr. WA8: Widnes 9G 78
WN4: Ash M 6H 41
Poulton Grn. Cl. CH63: Spit 6M 89
Poulton Hall Rd. CH44: Wall 6G 57
CH63: Raby M 8N 89
Poulton Pk. Golf Course 5H 67
Poulton Rd. CH44: Wall 6G 57
CH63: Spit 4N 89
PR9: South 8L 7
Poulton Royd Dr. CH63: Spit 5M 89
Poulton Va. CH44: Wall 7G 57
Pound Rd. CH66: Lit Sut 7H 103
Poverty La. L31: Mag 3K 35
(not continuous)
Povey Rd. WA2: Warr 8D 66
Powder Mill Cl. M44: Irlam 1N 69
Powder Mill Rd. WA4: Westy 5H 83
Powder Works La. L31: Mag 9A 28
Powell Av. WA3: Ris 5M 67
Powell Dr. WN5: Bil 8N 39
Powell St. WA4: Warr 5G 82
WA9: St H 2A 64
Powerhouse *L8: Liv 1G 75*
(off Commerce Way)
Power Ho. Rd. CH62: East 1G 102
Powerleague
Liverpool 2D 58
Power Rd. CH42: Rock F 8N 73
CH62: Brom 6E 90
Powey La. CH1: Moll 8G 110
Powis St. L8: Liv 3F 74
Pownall Sq. L3: Liv 3E 4 (7B 58)
Pownall St. L1: Liv 7E 4 (9B 58)
Powys St. *WA5: Warr 3A 82*
(off Old Liverpool Rd.)
Poynter St. WA9: St H 2H 63
Poynton Cl. WA4: Grap 5J 83
Pratt Rd. L34: Presc 3N 61
Precincts, The L23: Crosb 7L 33
Preece Cl. WA8: Widnes 5G 79
Preesall Cl. PR9: South 2L 7
Preesall Way L11: Crox 5A 46
(not continuous)
Premier Bowl & Laser 7E 6
Premier St. L5: Liv 4E 58
(not continuous)
Prentice Rd. CH42: Rock F 7L 73
PRENTON 7F 72
Prenton Av. WA9: Clock F 5M 63
Prenton Dell Av. CH43: Pren 8G 72
Prenton Dell Rd. CH43: Pren 7E 72
Prenton Farm Rd. CH43: Pren 8G 73
Prenton Golf Course 8H 73
Prenton Grn. L24: Speke 4J 93
Prenton Hall Rd. CH43: Pren 7F 72
Prenton La. CH42: Tran 7H 73
Prenton Pk. 6J 73
Prenton Pk. Rd. CH42: Tran 5J 73
Prenton Rd. E. CH42: Tran 6J 73
Prenton Rd. W. CH42: Tran 6J 73
Prenton Village Rd. CH43: Pren 7F 72
Prenton Way CH43: Pren 7D 72
Prenton Way Bus. Units CH43: Pren 7D 72
Prentonwood Ct. CH42: Tran 7J 73
PRESCOT 3A 62
Prescot Bus. Pk. L34: Presc 4N 61
Prescot Bus Station 3A 62
Prescot By-Pass L34: Presc 3M 61
Prescot Cen. L34: Presc 3A 62
Prescot Ct. L7: Liv 7H 59
Prescot Dr. L6: Liv 6J 59
Prescot Grn. L39: Orm 1B 28
Prescot Mus. 3A 62
Prescot Rd. L7: Liv 6J 59
L13: Liv 6J 59
L31: Mag, Mell 2A 36
L39: Augh, Orm 2B 28
WA8: Cron 4C 78
WA8: Widnes 5G 78
WA10: St H 1D 62
Prescot Station (Rail) 4B 62
Prescot St. CH45: New B 1G 56
L7: Liv 3L 5 (7E 58)
Prescott Av. L40: Ruf 3L 15
WA3: Golb 1A 52
Prescot Trade Cen. L34: Presc 3B 62
Prescott Rd. WN8: Skel 7J 31
Prescott St. WA3: Golb 1B 52
WA4: Warr 5F 82

Preseland Rd.—Quince Way

Preseland Rd. L23: Crosb ... 8L 33
Prestbury Av. CH43: Oxton ... 6E 72
PR8: Ainsd ... 9H 11
WN3: Wigan ... 1G 41
Prestbury Cl. CH43: Oxton ... 6E 72
WA8: Widnes ... 8H 79
Prestbury Dr. WA4: Thel ... 4L 83
WA10: Ec'stn ... 8E 48
Prestbury Rd. L11: Norr G ... 6L 45
Prescot Av. L34: Presc ... 4N 61
M44: Irlam ... 2M 69
PRESTON BROOK ... 9H 97
Preston Gro. L6: Liv ... 4H 59
Preston New Rd. PR9: South ... 5M 7
PRESTON ON THE HILL ... 9J 97
Preston Rd. PR9: South ... 7K 7
Preston St. L1: Liv ... 4F 4 (7C 58)
WA9: Sut M ... 7K 63
Preston Way L23: Crosb ... 7N 33
Prestwich Av. WA3: Cul ... 7M 53
Prestwick Cl. WA8: Widnes ... 5J 79
WA9: St H ... 5H 63
Prestwick Dr. L23: Blun ... 5J 33
Prestwood Ct. WA3: Ris ... 2A 68
Prestwood Cres. L14: Knott A ... 5D 60
Prestwood Pl. WN8: Skel ... 8J 31
Prestwood Rd. L14: Knott A ... 5D 60
Pretoria Rd. L9: Aintr ... 4G 45
WN4: Ash M ... 7K 41
Price Gro. WA9: St H ... 8C 50
Price's La. CH43: Oxton ... 4H 73
Price St. CH41: Birke ... 9H 57
L1: Liv ... 7F 4 (9B 58)
Price St. Bus. Cen. CH41: Birke ... 9J 57
Price's Way CH62: Brom ... 1C 90
Pride Cen., The ... 1E 46
Pride Cl. WA12: Newt W ... 8N 51
Priestfield Rd. CH65: Ell P ... 9N 103
Priesthouse Cl. L37: Form ... 1G 25
Priesthouse La. L37: Form ... 1G 24
Priestley Bus. Cen. WA5: Warr ... 3A 82
Priestley Ct. *WA4: Warr ... 6D 82*
(off Elphins Dr.)
Priestley St. WA5: Warr ... 3A 82
Priestner Dr. WA6: Hel ... 1E 114
Primary Av. L30: Neth ... 7G 35
Primary Cl. M44: Cad ... 4K 69
Primrose Cl. L37: Form ... 8H 17
L40: Burs ... 2K 21
PR9: South ... 1A 8
WA2: Warr ... 7E 66
WA7: Cas ... 7C 96
WA8: Widnes ... 7H 79
Primrose Ct. *CH45: New B ... 1H 57*
(off Egerton St.)
L36: Huy ... 3J 61
Primrose Dr. L36: Huy ... 4J 61
Primrose Gro. CH44: Wall ... 7L 57
WA11: Hay ... 3G 50
PRIMROSE HILL ... 5L 19
Primrose Hill CH62: Port S ... 1N 89
L3: Liv ... 3F 4 (7C 58)
Primrose La. WA6: Alv, Hel ... 4D 114
Primrose M. WA6: Alv ... 4G 114
Primrose Pl. *WN4: Ash M ... 9K 41*
(off Haydock St.)
Primrose Rd. CH41: Birke ... 1F 72
L18: Moss H ... 3A 76
Primrose St. L4: Kirkd ... 2C 58
Primrose Vw. WN4: Ash M ... 9K 41
Primula Cl. WA9: Bold ... 2C 64
Primula Dr. L9: W'ton ... 6G 44
WA3: Low ... 2E 52
Prince Albert Ct. WA9: St H ... 9B 50
Prince Albert M. L1: Liv ... 9H 5
Prince Alfred Rd. L15: Wavtr ... 1M 75
Prince Andrew's Gro. WA10: Windle ... 4F 48
Prince Charles Gdns. PR8: Birkd ... 1M 11
Prince Edward St. CH41: Birke ... 1J 73
Prince Edwin St. L5: Liv ... 5D 58
Prince Henry Sq. WA1: Warr ... 3C 82
Prince Rupert's Tower ... 5E 58
Princes Av. CH48: W Kir ... 6C 70
CH62: East ... 9D 90
L8: Liv ... 1E 74
L23: Crosb ... 7K 33
Princes Blvd. CH63: H Beb ... 8K 73
Prince's Cl. WA7: Cas ... 6B 96
Princes Ct. L8: Liv ... 2G 74
Princes Gdns. L3: Liv ... 2D 4 (6B 58)
PR8: South ... 9K 7
Princes Ga. E. L8: Liv ... 2G 74
Princes Ga. Ho. *L8: Liv ... 2G 74*
(off Kingsley Rd.)
Princes Ga. W. L8: Liv ... 2G 74
Princes Pde. L3: Liv ... 3B 4 (7A 58)
PRINCES PARK ... 2G 74
Princes Pk. Mans. L8: Liv ... 3G 75
Princes Pavement CH41: Birke ... 2L 73
Princes Pl. WA8: Widnes ... 7H 79
Princes Rd. CH65: Ell P ... 8L 103
L8: Liv ... 9L 5 (1E 74)
WA10: St H ... 9F 48
Princess Av. WA1: Padg ... 9H 67
WA1: Warr ... 2G 82
WA5: Gt San ... 1G 80
WA10: St H ... 5H 49
WA11: Hay ... 3J 51
WN4: Ash M ... 8L 41
Princess Ct. PR9: South ... 7J 7
Princess Cres. WA1: Warr ... 2G 82
Princess Dr. L12: W Der ... 1C 60
L14: Knott A ... 1C 60
Princess Rd. CH45: New B ... 2H 57
WA13: Lymm ... 5C 84
WN4: Ash M ... 8K 41
Princess St. WA5: Warr ... 4M 81
WA7: Run ... 4K 95
Princess Ter. CH43: Oxton ... 3J 73
Princes St. L2: Liv ... 4E 4 (7B 58)
L20: Boot ... 9A 44
PR8: South ... 9F 6
WA8: Widnes ... 8K 79
WA12: Newt W ... 7K 51
Princess Way L21: Lith, Sea ... 4M 43
Prince St. L22: Wloo ... 2L 43
WN4: Ash M ... 6J 41
Princes Way WA11: St H ... 2K 49
Princesway CH45: Wall ... 3G 56
Princeton Ct. WA5: Gt San ... 2M 81
Princeton Pl. L8: Liv ... 4D 74
Princeway WA6: Frod ... 6L 107
Prince William St. L8: Liv ... 2D 74
Priors Cl. L25: Woolt ... 6F 76
Priorsfield CH46: More ... 9M 55
Priorsfield Rd. L25: Woolt ... 6F 76
Prior St. L20: Boot ... 4N 43
Priorswood Gro. L14: Brd G ... 7B 60
Priorswood Pl. WN8: Skel ... 8J 31
Priory, The CH64: Nest ... 5D 100
L15: Wavtr ... 8L 59
L35: Rainh ... 6F 62
WA2: Winw ... 2B 66
Priory Cl. CH63: Beb ... 4N 89
L17: Aig ... 6G 74
L35: Whis ... 8N 61
L37: Form ... 2H 25
L40: Burs ... 9H 15
WA7: Hal ... 6C 96
Priory Ct. L36: Huy ... 7H 61
PR8: South ... 9E 6
WA7: Pres B ... 1G 108
Priory Farm Cl. L19: G'dale ... 9M 75
Priory Gdns. PR8: Birkd ... 2M 11
WA10: St H ... 3J 49
Priory Grange PR8: Birkd ... 2N 11
Priory Gro. L39: Orm ... 9B 20
Priory M. CH41: Birke ... 2M 73
PR8: South ... 9E 6
Priory Nook WN8: Uph ... 5M 31
Priory Rd. CH44: Wall ... 6L 57
CH48: W Kir ... 6D 70
L4: W'ton ... 1F 58
WA7: Wind H ... 5E 96
WN4: Ash M ... 6H 41
WN8: Uph ... 5M 31
Priory St. CH41: Birke ... 2M 73
L19: Garst ... 3B 92
WA4: Warr ... 5C 82
Priory Way L25: Woolt ... 6F 76
Priory Wharf CH41: Birke ... 2M 73
Pritchard Av. L21: Sea ... 3M 43
Pritt St. L3: Liv ... 1H 5 (6D 58)
Private Dr. CH61: Barns ... 2D 88
Prizett Rd. L19: G'dale ... 9N 75
Probyn Rd. CH45: Wall ... 4E 56
Procter Rd. CH42: Rock F ... 7N 73
Proctor Ct. L30: Neth ... 7C 34
Proctor Rd. CH47: Hoy ... 2D 70
L37: Form ... 9C 16
Proctors Cl. WA8: Widnes ... 6M 79
Proffits La. WA6: Hel ... 9G 107
Progress Pl. L1: Liv ... 4E 4
Promenade PR8: Ainsd ... 8F 10
PR8: South ... 8F 6
PR9: South ... 6G 7
Promenade, The CH45: New B ... 9J 43
L17: Aig ... 7G 74
L19: Aig ... 9J 75
WA4: Moore ... 9K 81
Promenade Cvn. Pk. WA4: Moore ... 9J 81
Promenade Gdns. L17: Aig ... 5E 74
Prophet Wlk. L8: Liv ... 3E 74
Prospect Av. M44: Cad ... 3L 69
Prospect Ct. *L6: Liv ... 6J 59*
(off Prospect Va.)
Prospect La. WA3: Rix ... 6C 68
Prospect Pl. WN8: Skel ... 7J 31
Prospect Point L6: Liv ... 3L 5 (7E 58)
Prospect Rd. CH42: Tran ... 7H 73
M44: Cad ... 3L 69
WA9: St H ... 6N 49
Prospect Row WA7: W'ton ... 8J 95
Prospect St. L6: Liv ... 3M 5 (7F 58)
Prospect Va. CH45: Wall ... 4F 56
L6: Liv ... 5J 59
Prospect Way L30: Neth ... 8G 35
Protector Way M44: Irlam ... 1M 69
Proto Cl. L24: Speke ... 4J 93
Proudman Dr. CH43: Bid ... 1C 72
Providence Ct. WA10: St H ... 6K 49
Providence Cres. L8: Liv ... 2D 74
Provident St. WA9: St H ... 7C 50
Province Pl. L20: Boot ... 4C 44
Province Rd. L20: Boot ... 4C 44
Prussia St. L3: Liv ... 3D 4 (7B 58)
(not continuous)
Public Hall St. WA7: Run ... 4K 95
Puddington La. CH64: Burt, Pudd ... 5A 110
Pudsey St. L1: Liv ... 4H 5 (7D 58)
Puffin Cl. CH65: Ell P ... 5A 112
Pugin St. L4: W'ton ... 2D 58
Pulford Av. CH43: Pren ... 6G 72
Pulford Cl. WA7: Beech ... 9A 96
Pulford Rd. CH63: Beb ... 2M 89
CH65: Gt Sut ... 1L 111
Pulford St. L4: W'ton ... 2E 58
Pullman Cl. CH60: Hesw ... 7D 88
Puma Ct. L34: Presc ... 4L 61
Pumpfields Rd. L3: Liv ... 1D 4 (6B 58)
Pump La. CH49: Grea ... 3J 71
WA7: Hal ... 7B 96
Punnell's La. L31: Lydi ... 7E 26
Purbeck Dr. CH61: Irby ... 9L 71
Purbeck Rd. L33: Kirkb ... 6B 36
Purdy Cl. WA5: Old H ... 8M 65
PureGym
Aintree ... 1G 45
Widnes ... 9M 79
Purley Dr. M44: Cad ... 4J 69
Purley Gro. L18: Moss H ... 6M 75
Purley Rd. L22: Wloo ... 9J 33
Purser Gro. L15: Wavtr ... 9J 59
Putney Ct. WA7: Pal F ... 8A 96
Pye Cl. WA11: Hay ... 2K 51
Pyecroft Cl. WA5: Gt San ... 2F 80
Pyecroft Rd. WA5: Gt San ... 2F 80
Pye Rd. CH60: Hesw ... 7N 87
Pyes Gdns. WA11: St H ... 3L 49
Pyes La. L36: Huy ... 2G 61
Pye St. L15: Wavtr ... 1M 75
PYGON'S HILL ... 5J 27
Pygon's Hill La. L31: Lydi ... 5J 27
Pykes Weint CH64: Nest ... 7E 100
Pym St. L4: W'ton ... 8E 44
Pyramid & Parr Hall ... 4B 82
Pyramid Ct. WA1: Warr ... 4B 82
Pyrus Gro. WA6: Hel ... 9F 106

Q

Quadrangle, The L18: Moss H ... 4N 75
Quadrant, The CH47: Hoy ... 2C 70
WA3: Ris ... 3M 67
(off Faraday St.)
Quadrant Cl. WA7: Murd ... 9F 96
Quadrant Ho. WA1: Warr ... 2D 82
Quail Cl. WA2: Warr ... 6E 66
Quaile Pk. CH43: Clau ... 2F 72
Quaker La. CH60: Hesw ... 6M 87
Quakers All. L2: Liv ... 4E 4
Quakers Mdw. L34: Know ... 6H 47
Quantock Cl. CH66: Lit Sut ... 8F 102
WN3: Winst ... 1E 40
Quarry Av. CH63: Beb ... 3M 89
Quarry Bank CH41: Birke ... 3K 73
L33: Kirkb ... 8D 36
Quarry Bank Flats *CH41: Birke ... 3K 73*
(off Quarry Bank)
Quarrybank St. CH41: Birke ... 3J 73
Quarrybank Workshops *CH41: Birke ... 3J 73*
(off Quarrybank St.)
Quarry Cl. CH61: Hesw ... 5N 87
L13: Liv ... 4M 59
L33: Kirkb ... 8D 36
WA7: Run ... 6N 95
Quarry Ct. WA8: Widnes ... 7F 78
Quarry Dale L33: Kirkb ... 8D 36
Quarry Dr. L39: Augh ... 4A 28
Quarry Grn. L33: Kirkb ... 8D 36
L39: Augh ... 2B 28
Quarry Grn. Flats L33: Kirkb ... 8D 36
Quarry Hey L33: Kirkb ... 8D 36
QUARRY JUNC. ... 4F 30
Quarry La. CH61: Thing ... 1A 88
WA4: App ... 1E 98
WA6: Manl ... 8G 115
Quarry Mt. L39: Orm ... 7E 20
Quarry Pk. *L35: Rainh ... 8G 63*
(off Lincoln Way)
Quarry Pl. *L25: Woolt ... 6D 76*
(off Quarry St.)
Quarry Rd. CH64: Nest ... 5H 101
L13: Liv ... 4L 59
L20: Boot ... 8C 44
L23: Thorn ... 5N 33
Quarry Rd. E. CH60: Hesw ... 6M 87
CH61: Hesw ... 6M 87
CH63: Beb ... 3N 89
Quarry Rd. W. CH60: Hesw ... 6M 87
Quarryside Dr. L33: Kirkb ... 8E 36
Quarry St. L25: Woolt ... 5D 76
Quarry St. Sth. L25: Woolt ... 6E 76
Quarry Way L36: Huy ... 7L 61
Quartz Way L21: Lith ... 2B 44
Quatrain Cl. L5: Liv ... 4D 58
Quay, The WA6: Frod ... 4N 107
Quay Bus. Cen. WA2: Winw ... 5A 66
Quay Cen., The WA2: Winw ... 5A 66
Quay Fold WA5: Warr ... 3A 82
Quayle Cl. WA11: Hay ... 4E 50
Quay Pl. WA7: Pres B ... 8G 96
Quays, The L40: Burs ... 9J 15
Quay Side WA6: Frod ... 4N 107
Quayside CH64: Lit N ... 9D 100
CH65: Ell P ... 7B 104
(off Grosvenor Wharf Rd.)
Quayside M. WA13: Lymm ... 5F 84
Queastybirch La. WA4: Hatt ... 6B 98
Quebec Quay L3: Liv ... 2B 74
Quebec Rd. WA2: Warr ... 1E 82
Queen Anne Pde. L3: Liv ... 4C 4
Queen Anne St. L3: Liv ... 2H 5 (6D 58)
PR8: South ... 8G 6
(off Market St.)
Queen Av. L2: Liv ... 5E 4
Queen Charlotte Vs. *PR8: Ainsd ... 9J 11*
(off Station Rd.)
Queen Elizabeth II Law Courts
Liverpool ... 6E 4 (8B 58)
Queen Elizabeth Ct. L21: Lith ... 2N 43
Queen Mary's Dr. CH62: Port S ... 1A 90
Queen Mary Way L9: Faz ... 6J 45
Queen's Av. CH47: Meols ... 9E 54
WA8: Widnes ... 8E 78
WN4: Ash M ... 8K 41
Queens Av. CH65: Whit ... 2M 111
L37: Form ... 8E 16
WA1: Warr ... 1F 82
Queensberry St. L8: Liv ... 3E 74
Queensbury CH48: W Kir ... 5E 70
Queensbury Av. CH62: Brom ... 6D 90
Queensbury Gro. L36: Huy ... 6H 61
Queensbury Way WA8: Widnes ... 5G 79
Queens Cl. L19: Garst ... 1A 92
WA7: Run ... 6J 95
Queens Ct. CH47: Hoy ... 1C 70
L6: Liv ... 4F 58
L15: Wavtr ... 8A 60
L39: Orm ... 9C 20
Queenscourt Rd. L12: W Der ... 4A 60
Queens Cres. WA1: Padg ... 9H 67
Queens Cft. L37: Form ... 2D 24
Queensdale Rd. L18: Moss H ... 3M 75
Queens Dock Commercial Cen.
L1: Liv ... 9F 4 (1C 74)
Queen's Dr. CH43: Pren ... 7G 72
WA10: Windle ... 4F 48
Queens Dr. CH60: Hesw ... 7M 87
L12: W Der ... 5N 59
WA3: Golb ... 2D 52
WA4: Grap ... 6H 83
WA6: Hel ... 2E 114
WA12: Newt W ... 5K 51
Queens Dr. Mossley Hill L18: Moss H ... 4K 75
Queens Dr. Stoneycroft L13: Liv ... 4M 59
L15: Wavtr ... 4M 59
Queens Dr. Walton L4: W'ton ... 8F 44
Queens Dr. Wavertree L15: Wavtr ... 8A 60
Queens Dr. W. Derby L13: W Der ... 1K 59
Queens Gdns. CH65: Ell P ... 9N 103
Queens Grn. L39: Down ... 8E 18
Queen's Hotel Ct. *PR9: South ... 7G 6*
(off Promenade)
Queensland Av. WA9: St H ... 2H 63
Queensland Pl. WA9: St H ... 2H 63
Queensland St. L7: Liv ... 7N 5 (8G 58)
Queens M. L6: Liv ... 5F 58
Queens Pk. Health & Fitness ... 6H 49
Queen Sq. L1: Liv ... 4G 4 (7C 58)
Queen Square Bus Station ... 4G 4 (7C 58)
Queen's Rd. CH47: Hoy ... 1B 70
L20: Boot ... 8B 44
PR9: South ... 7H 7
WA7: Run ... 6J 95
WN4: Ash M ... 7K 41
Queens Rd. CH42: Rock F ... 7N 73
CH44: Wall ... 5L 57
CH66: Lit Sut ... 7H 103
L6: Liv ... 1N 5 (4F 58)
L23: Crosb ... 7L 33
L34: Presc ... 3B 62
L37: Form ... 2D 24
WA10: St H ... 9F 48
WA11: Hay ... 3J 51
WN5: Orr ... 7M 31
Queen St. CH41: Tran ... 4L 73
CH45: Wall ... 4H 57
CH65: Ell P ... 7A 104
L19: Garst ... 2A 92
L22: Wloo ... 2K 43
L39: Orm ... 9C 20
WA3: Golb ... 2C 52
WA7: Run ... 4K 95
WA10: St H ... 5J 49
WA12: Newt W ... 7K 51
Queen's Wlk. L1: Liv ... 9J 5
Queensway CH41: Birke, Liv ... 9N 57
CH45: Wall ... 3G 56
CH60: Hesw ... 9C 88
L3: Liv ... 7A 4 (9N 57)
L22: Wloo ... 9M 33
M31: Part ... 5M 69
WA6: Frod ... 6L 107
WA7: Run ... 4J 95
WA8: Widnes ... 1J 95
WA11: Rainf ... 6D 38
WA11: St H ... 2K 49
Queensway Trad. Est. WA8: Widnes ... 2K 95
Queens Wharf L3: Liv ... 9E 4 (1B 74)
Queenswood Av. CH63: H Beb ... 8L 73
Quernmore Rd. L33: Kirkb ... 8E 36
Quernmore Wlk. L33: Kirkb ... 8E 36
Quickswood Cl. L25: Woolt ... 3D 76
Quickswood Dr. L25: Woolt ... 3D 76
Quickswood Grn. L25: Woolt ... 3D 76
Quickthorn Cres. L28: Stockb V ... 2F 60
Quigley Av. L30: Neth ... 1F 44
Quigley St. CH41: Tran ... 4M 73
Quill Ct. *M44: Irlam ... 3L 69*
(off Magenta Av.)
Quillet, The CH64: Nest ... 7F 100
Quince Way L11: Norr G ... 9M 45

Quincey Row—Redwood Gro.

Quincey Row PR9: Banks 3E 8
Quinesway CH49: Upton 3N 71
Quinn St. WA8: Widnes 9L 79
Quintbridge Cl. L26: Halew 9J 77
Quinton Cl. PR8: Ainsd 1G 17
Quorn St. L7: Liv 7G 59

R

Rabbit La. L40: Burs 2D 20
RABY 2J 101
Raby Av. CH63: Raby M 9A 90
Raby Cl. CH60: Hesw 8N 87
CH63: Raby M 8N 89
WA8: Widnes 6A 80
Raby Ct. CH65: Ell P 2B 112
Raby Dell CH63: Raby M 9A 90
Raby Dr. CH46: More 1L 71
CH63: Raby M 8N 89
Raby Gdns. CH64: Nest 6E 100
Raby Gro. CH63: H Beb 8K 73
Raby Hall Rd. CH63: Brom, Raby M . . . 1L 101
RABY MERE 8N 89
Raby Mere Rd. CH63: Raby, Raby M . . . 2J 101
(not continuous)
Raby Pk. Cl. CH64: Nest 6E 100
Raby Pk. Rd. CH64: Nest 6E 100
Raby Rd. CH63: Raby, Thorn H 9H 89
CH64: Nest 6E 100
Racecourse Retail Pk. 9G 35
Racefield Cl. WA13: Lymm 5F 84
Rachel St. L5: Liv 5C 58
Radburn Cl. L23: Thorn 6A 34
Radburn Rd. L23: Thorn 6A 34
Radcliffe Av. WA3: Cul 7M 53
Raddel La. WA4: H Whi 9D 98
Raddle Wharf CH65: Ell P 7A 104
Raddon Pl. WA4: Westy 5F 82
Radford Av. CH63: Spit 5A 90
Radford Cl. WA8: Widnes 9F 78
Radiant Cl. L11: Crox 7A 46
Radlett Cl. WA5: Penk 5G 80
Radley Ct. PR8: South 8F 6
Radley Dr. CH63: Thorn H 9F 88
L10: Aintr 8H 35
Radley La. WA2: Warr 5E 66
Radley Rd. CH44: Wall 4F 56
Radleys Ct. *L8: Liv* *2E 74*
(off Up. Warwick St.)
Radley St. WA9: St H 2H 63
Radmore Rd. L14: Knott A 6B 60
Radnor Av. CH60: Hesw 6N 87
Radnor Cl. L26: Halew 1J 93
Radnor Dr. CH45: Wall 3J 57
L20: Boot 7D 44
PR9: South 4L 7
WA8: Widnes 6G 78
Radnor Pl. CH43: Oxton 2J 73
L6: Liv 4J 59
Radnor St. WA5: Warr 2N 81
Radshaw Nook L32: Kirkb 4C 46
Radstock Gro. WA9: Sut L 4N 63
Radstock Rd. CH44: Wall 4E 56
L6: Liv 6H 59
Radstock Wlk. *L26: Halew* *1K 93*
(off Romford Way)
Radway Grn. CH66: Gt Sut 9K 103
Radway Rd. L36: Huy 4K 61
Raeburn Av. CH48: W Kir 5D 70
CH62: East 9C 90
CH64: Lit N 7F 100
Raffia Way L9: Faz 6J 45
Raffles Rd. CH42: Tran 3J 73
Raffles St. L1: Liv 9H 5 (1D 74)
Rafter Av. L20: Boot 4D 44
(not continuous)
Raglan Cl. L19: Garst 2A 92
Raglan Ct. WA3: Ris 3N 67
Raikes Cl. WA5: Gt San 2L 81
Railbrook Hey L13: Liv 8M 59
Rail Cl. WA11: Rainf 1C 38
Railside Ct. L5: Liv 4B 58
Railton Av. L35: Rainh 7G 62
Railton Cl. L35: Rainh 8G 62
Railton Rd. L11: Norr G 8K 45
Railway App. L39: Orm 8D 20
Railway Av. PR9: Banks 2D 8
Railway Cotts. CH66: Hoot 5C 102
L25: Hunts X 9G 77
RAILWAY ISLAND 4A 30
Railway Path L39: Orm 1C 28
Railway Rd. L39: Orm 8D 20
WA3: Golb 1C 52
WN8: Skel 3N 29
Railway St. L19: Garst 2A 92
PR8: South 1N 11
WA10: St H 6L 49
WA12: Newt W 7K 51
Railway Ter. PR8: South 1N 11
Railway Vw. L32: Kirkb 8A 36
WA2: Padg 8G 67
Railyard, The L7: Liv 7N 5 (9F 58)
Rainbow Cl. WA8: Widnes 5F 78
Rainbow Dr. L26: Halew 8J 77
L31: Mell 7N 35
Raines Cl. CH49: Grea 4M 71
RAINFORD 4D 38
Rainford Av. L20: Boot 5D 44
Rainford By-Pass 2A 38
Rainford Gdns. L2: Liv 5F 4
Rainford Hall Cotts. WA11: Crank 9J 39
Rainford Ind. Est. WA11: Rainf 7F 38
(not continuous)
RAINFORD JUNCTION 1C 38
Rainford Rd. L39: Bic 6L 29
WA10: St H, Windle 3F 48
WA11: Rainf 6L 29
WA11: Windle 3F 48
(not continuous)
WN5: Bil 6L 39
Rainford Sq. L2: Liv 5E 4 (8B 58)
Rainford Station (Rail) 1C 38
Rainham Cl. L19: Aller 8A 76
RAINHILL 6F 62
Rainhill Rd. L35: Rainh 5F 62
WA9: St H 5F 62
Rainhill Station (Rail) 6F 62
RAINHILL STOOPS 8H 63
Rainhill Trials Exhibition 6F 62
Raithby Dr. WN3: Wigan 1J 41
Rake, The CH62: Brom 7B 90
Rake Cl. CH49: Upton 4A 72
Rake Hey CH46: More 9J 55
Rake Hey Cl. CH46: More 9K 55
Rake La. CH2: Chor B, Lit Stan 7B 112
CH45: New B, Wall 2H 57
CH49: Upton 4A 72
WA6: Dun H 6M 113
WA6: Hel 1F 114
(Hawkstone Gro.)
WA6: Hel 8C 106
(Lordship La.)
Rake M. CH49: Upton 4A 72
Rakersfield Ct. CH45: New B 1J 57
Rakersfield Rd. CH45: New B 1J 57
Rakes La. L29: Seft 5B 34
Raleigh Av. L35: Whis 7A 62
Raleigh Cl. WA5: Old H 8M 65
WA12: Newt W 9L 51
Raleigh Rd. CH46: Leas 5A 56
CH64: Nest 5F 100
Raleigh St. L20: Boot 9A 44
Ralph's Wife's La. PR9: Banks 1C 8
Rambaldi Sq. *WA8: Widnes* *7L 79*
(off Cross St.)
Rame Cl. L10: Faz 4N 45
Ramford St. WA9: St H 8N 49
Ramilies Rd. L18: Moss H 3L 75
Ramleh Pk. L23: Blun 8G 33
Rampit Cl. WA11: Hay 3H 51
Ramsay Cl. WA3: Birchw 6M 67
Ramsbrook Cl. L24: Speke 3G 93
Ramsbrook La. L24: Hale 2N 93
WA8: Hale B 2N 93
Ramsbrook Rd. L24: Speke 3G 93
Ramsbury Dr. L24: Speke 3F 92
Ramsey Cl. L19: Aller 8B 76
L35: Whis 6B 62
WA8: Widnes 5A 80
WN4: Ash M 9K 41
Ramsey Ct. CH48: W Kir 8C 70
Ramsey Rd. CH65: Ell P 4A 112
L19: Aller 8B 76
Ramsfield Rd. L24: Speke 3L 93
Ramsons Cl. L26: Halew 7J 77
Randall Cl. WA12: Newt W 6K 51
Randall Dr. L30: Neth 9B 34
Randle Av. WA11: Rainf 3B 38
Randle Brook Ct. WA11: Rainf 3B 38
Randle Cl. CH63: Spit 5N 89
Randle Hgts. L11: Crox 5C 46
Randle Mdw. CH66: Gt Sut 3L 111
Randle Mdw. Ct. *CH66: Gt Sut* *3L 111*
(off Randle Mdw.)
Randle M. WA8: Widnes 7L 79
Randles Rd. L34: Know 5E 46
Randolph St. L4: W'ton 2E 58
Randon Gro. WA10: St H 6J 49
Ranelagh Av. L21: Lith 2N 43
Ranelagh Dr. PR8: Ainsd 7M 11
Ranelagh Dr. Nth. L19: G'dale 8M 75
Ranelagh Dr. Sth. L19: G'dale 8M 75
Ranelagh Ho. L1: Liv 6H 5
Ranelagh Pl. L3: Liv 5H 5 (8D 58)
Ranelagh St. L1: Liv 6G 5 (8C 58)
Ranfurly Rd. L19: G'dale 9N 75
Range La. L37: Form 4C 24
Rangemoor Cl. WA3: Birchw 3A 68
Rangemore Rd. L18: Moss H 7M 75
Rankin Hall L18: Moss H 6K 75
Rankin St. CH44: Wall 7G 57
Rankin Way CH62: Brom 6D 90
Ranleigh Dr. WN8: Newb 4D 22
Ranmore Av. WN4: Garsw 7F 40
Rannoch Cl. CH66: Gt Sut 2L 111
Ranslett Ct. L37: Form 1G 24
Ranulph Ct. WA6: Frod 7M 107
Ranworth Cl. L11: Norr G 7K 45
Ranworth Dr. WA3: Low 3F 52
Ranworth Gdns. WA9: St H 3G 63
Ranworth Pl. L11: Norr G 7K 45
Ranworth Rd. WA5: Gt San 2G 81
Ranworth Sq. L11: Norr G 7L 45
Ranworth Way L11: Norr G 7L 45
Rappart Rd. CH44: Wall 6K 57
Rashid Mufti Ct. L8: Liv 2F 74
Ratcliffe Pl. L35: Rainh 5E 62
Rathbone Hall L17: Aig 4K 75
Rathbone Rd. L13: Liv, Wavtr 9L 59
L15: Wavtr 9L 59
L38: Hight 8F 24
Rathlin Cl. WA8: Widnes 5A 80
Rathmell Cl. WA3: Cul 7M 53
Rathmore Av. L18: Moss H 5M 75
Rathmore Cl. CH43: Oxton 5G 73
Rathmore Cres. PR9: South 4N 7
Rathmore Dr. CH43: Oxton 4G 73
Rathmore Rd. CH43: Oxton 4G 73
Raven Cl. L6: Liv 2N 5 (6F 58)
Ravendale Cl. CH43: Noct 4D 72
Ravenfield Cl. L26: Halew 8J 77
Ravenfield Dr. WA8: Widnes 5F 78
Ravenglass Av. L31: Mag 1J 35
RAVENHEAD 8H 49
Ravenhead Av. L32: Kirkb 3C 46
Ravenhead Bus. Pk. WA10: St H 8J 49
Ravenhead Dr. WN8: Uph 5K 31
Ravenhead Pk. WA9: St H 9K 49
Ravenhead Rd. WA10: St H 9H 49
Ravenhead Row WA10: St H 9H 49
Ravenhead Way WN8: Uph 6J 31
Ravenhill Cres. CH46: Leas 5N 55
Ravenhurst Ct. WA3: Ris 4N 67
Ravenhurst Way L35: Whis 8A 62
Ravenmeols Hills Local Nature Reserve 3A 24
Raven Meols La. L37: Form 2E 24
Ravenna Rd. L19: Aller 8B 76
Ravens, The L37: Form 3F 24
Ravenscourt *WA13: Lymm* *5F 84*
(off Pepper St.)
Ravenscroft L37: Form 2F 24
Ravenscroft Av. L39: Orm 9C 20
Ravenscroft Rd. CH43: Oxton 3J 73
Ravensdale Cl. WA2: Warr 6E 66
Ravenshaw Cl. CH42: Tran 4K 73
Ravensthorpe Grn. L11: Norr G 7L 45
Ravenstone Cl. CH49: Upton 1N 71
Ravenstone Dr. WA9: St H 2N 63
Ravenstone Rd. L19: Aller 8N 75
Ravenswood Av. CH42: Rock F 8M 73
Ravens Wood Brow WN5: Bil 6A 40
Ravenswood Rd. CH61: Hesw 5A 88
L13: Liv 6M 59
Raven Way *L20: Boot* *7B 44*
(off Strand Shop. Cen.)
Rawcliffe Cl. WA8: Widnes 4J 79
Rawcliffe Rd. CH42: Tran 3K 73
L9: W'ton 6E 44
Rawdon Cl. WA7: Pal F 8C 96
Rawlings Cl. WA3: Birchw 6N 67
Rawlinson Ct. *PR9: South* *7J 7*
(off Rawlinson Rd.)
Rawlinson Cres. L26: Halew 8M 77
Rawlinson Gro. PR9: South 6K 7
Rawlinson Rd. L13: Liv 6L 59
PR9: South 7J 7
Rawlins St. L7: Liv 6J 59
Rawson Cl. L21: Sea 3M 43
Rawson Rd. L21: Sea 2M 43
Raydale Cl. L9: W'ton 7F 44
WA3: Low 1F 52
Raymond Av. L30: Neth 1F 44
WA4: Stockt H 7E 82
Raymond Pl. L5: Liv 5C 58
Raymond Rd. CH44: Wall 6J 57
Raymond Way CH64: Lit N 7G 100
Raynham Rd. L13: Liv 7L 59
Rayrig Fold WA11: Rainf 5C 38
Reach, The L3: Liv 2F 4 (6C 58)
Reade Cl. CH63: Spit 6N 89
Reading Cl. L5: Kirkd 2C 58
Reading St. L5: Kirkd 2C 58
Reads Ct. L9: W'ton 4E 44
Reaper Cl. WA5: Gt San 2M 81
Reapers Way L30: Neth 7F 34
Rear Comn. Pas. L6: Liv 6J 59
Reay Ct. CH44: Wall 6L 57
Reay St. WA8: Widnes 6M 79
Rebecca Gdns. WA9: St H 2M 63
Recreation Av. WN4: Ash M 7M 41
Recreation Dr. WN5: Bil 6A 40
Recreation Rd. PR9: Banks 4H 9
Recreation St. WA9: St H 6M 49
Rector Rd. L6: Liv 2H 59
Rectory Av. WA3: Low 2D 52
Rectory Cl. CH42: Tran 4K 73
CH60: Hesw 8N 87
WA2: Winw 3C 66
Rectory Dr. L26: Halew 7K 77
Rectory Gdns. WA9: St H 3M 63
WA13: Lymm 5E 84
Rectory La. CH1: Cap 4E 110
CH60: Hesw 8M 87
WA2: Winw 3B 66
WA13: Lymm 6E 84
Rectory Rd. CH48: W Kir 7C 70
PR9: South 6M 7
WN4: Garsw 6F 40
Redacre Cl. WA4: Dutt 3J 109
RED BANK 9N 51
Red Bank WA12: Newt W 9N 51
Red Bank Av. WA12: Newt W 9A 52
Redbank Cl. L10: Faz 2L 45
Red Barnes L37: Form 8F 16
Red Barn Rd. WN5: Bil 5L 39
Redbourne Av. L26: Halew 1K 93
Redbourne Dr. WA8: Widnes 4E 78
Redbourn St. L6: Liv 3H 59
Redbrook Cl. CH62: Brom 9C 90
Redbrook Rd. M31: Part 7L 69
Redbrook St. L6: Liv 3H 59
Red Brow La. WA4: Dares 7G 96
WA7: Murd 7G 96
Redbrow Way L33: Kirkb 7C 36
Redburn Cl. L8: Liv 4F 74
Redcap Cl. CH45: Wall 1E 56
Redcar Cl. PR8: South 3E 12
Redcar Dr. CH62: East 1C 102
Redcar M. L6: Liv 3G 59
Redcar Rd. CH45: Wall 3D 56
Redcar St. L6: Liv 3H 59
Red Cat La. L40: Burs 6J 15
WA11: Crank 7H 39
Redcliffe Av. L25: Gate 3E 76
Redcliffe Gdns. L39: Augh 1C 28
Redcote Ct. CH48: W Kir 7B 70
Redcroft CH49: Grea 5K 71
Red Cross St. L2: Liv 6D 4 (8B 58)
Red Cut La. L33: Kirkb 2J 47
Red Dale CH60: Hesw 6N 87
Red Delph La. WA11: Rainf 2A 38
REDDISH 3G 84
Reddish Cres. WA13: Lymm 4F 84
Reddish La. WA13: Lymm 4E 84
(not continuous)
Redditch Cl. CH49: Grea 4K 71
Reddy La. WA14: L Boll, M'ton 9N 85
(not continuous)
Redesdale Cl. WA2: Warr 7F 66
Redfearn Wlk. WA2: Warr 1D 82
Redfern St. L20: Kirkd 1B 58
Redfield Cl. CH44: Wall 5K 57
Red Fold L39: Augh 1A 28
Redford Cl. CH49: Grea 4K 71
Redford St. L6: Liv 3H 59
Red Gables WA4: App T 4J 99
Redgate L37: Form 2G 25
L39: Orm 8B 20
Redgate Av. L23: Crosb 7N 33
Redgate Dr. L37: Form 2H 25
WA9: St H 7N 49
Redgate Rd. WN4: Ash M 5K 41
Redgrave Cl. L20: Boot 8B 44
Redgrave St. L7: Liv 7H 59
Redhill Av. L32: Kirkb 2D 46
Redhill Cl. WA5: Gt San 2K 81
Redhill Dr. PR8: South 3E 12
Red Hill Rd. CH63: Store 2H 89
Redhills M. CH65: Ell P 8N 103
Redhillswood Cl. CH65: Ell P 7N 103
Redhouse Bank CH48: W Kir 5B 70
Redhouse La. CH48: W Kir 5B 70
Redington Rd. L19: Aller 8B 76
Redland Ct. WN2: Bam 4N 41
Redland Rd. *L9: Aintr* *2G 44*
(off Lyncot Rd.)
Red La. WA4: App 8C 82
WA6: Frod 6M 107
Red Lion Cl. L31: Mag 2H 35
Red Lion La. CH66: Lit Sut 7H 103
Red Lion Shop. Cen. 2H 35
Red Lomes L30: Neth 6C 34
Redmain Gro. WA3: Low 2F 52
Redmain Way L12: Crox 8D 46
Redmayne Cl. WA12: Newt W 6K 51
Redmere Dr. CH60: Hesw 7D 88
Redmires Cl. L7: Liv 9G 59
Redmont St. CH41: Tran 4L 73
Redmoor Cres. L33: Kirkb 6C 36
Redoaks Way L26: Halew 7M 77
Red Pike CH66: Lit Sut 6J 103
Redpoll Gro. L26: Halew 6J 77
Redpoll La. WA3: Birchw 5M 67
Red Rocks Marsh Nature Reserve 4A 70
Red Rock St. L6: Liv 5G 58
Red Rum Cl. L9: Aintr 2J 45
Redruth Av. WA11: St H 3N 49
Redruth Cl. WA7: Brook 9E 96
Redruth Rd. L11: Crox 5B 46
Redsands L39: Augh 1B 28
Redshank Cl. PR9: Banks 2E 8
WA12: Newt W 6L 51
Redshank La. WA3: Birchw 5N 67
Redshanks, The CH47: Hoy 1D 70
Redstart Cl. WA3: Low 2F 52
Redstone Cl. CH47: Meols 9E 54
Redstone Dr. CH60: Hesw 6K 87
Red Stone Hill WA6: Hel 1F 114
Redstone M. CH47: Meols 9E 54
Redstone Pk. CH45: Wall 1F 56
Redstone Ri. CH43: Noct 2D 72
Redstone Way L35: Whis 4D 62
Redtail Cl. WA7: Run 4J 95
Redvales Ct. WA3: Birchw 5K 67
Redvers Av. CH66: Hoot 4F 102
Redvers Dr. L9: W'ton 4E 44
Redwald Cl. L33: Kirkb 5D 36
Redwing Ct. CH64: P'gte 7D 100
Redwing La. L25: Gate 4E 76
Redwing Way L26: Halew 6H 77
Redwood Av. L31: Lydi 9H 27
Redwood Cl. CH43: Oxton 6F 72
L25: Gate 3G 76
WA1: Wools 2M 83
Redwood Ct. *L8: Liv* *4F 74*
(off Byles St.)
Redwood Dr. CH2: Elt 1N 113
CH66: Gt Sut 4L 111
L39: Orm 9B 20
WA11: Hay 5B 50
Redwood Gro. *L20: Boot* *6B 44*
(off Strand Rd.)

Redwood Rd.—Rivington Dr.

Redwood Rd. L25: Gate 3F 76
Redwood Way L33: Kirkb 5C 36
Reedale Cl. L18: Moss H 4M 75
Reedale Rd. L18: Moss H 4M 75
Reedgate La. CW9: Ant 7M 99
Reed La. CW9: Ant 9J 99
Reedmace Rd. L5: Liv 3E 58
Reeds, The L39: Orm 7B 20
Reeds Av. E. CH46: Leas 6N 55
Reeds Av. W. CH46: Leas 6N 55
Reeds Brow WA11: Rainf 3E 38
Reed's La. WA11: Rainf 7B 38
Reeds La. CH46: Leas, More 5N 55
Reedsmere Cl. WA4: Stockt H 6F 82
Reeds Rd. L36: Huy 5J 61
Reedville CH43: Oxton 3H 73
Reedville Gro. CH46: Leas 7N 55
Reedville Rd. CH63: Beb 2M 89
Reel Cinema
Widnes 9L 79
Rees Pk. L40: Burs 1K 21
Reeve Ct. Village WA9: St H 3F 62
Reeves Av. L20: Boot 5D 44
Reeves St. WA9: St H 7A 50
Reeve St. WA3: Low 2J 53
Reflection Ct. WA10: St H 7J 49
Regal Cl. CH66: Gt Sut 2K 111
Regal Ct. PR8: Ainsd 9K 11
Regal Cres. WA8: Widnes 8E 78
Regal Dr. WA10: Windle 5F 48
Regal Rd. L11: Crox 7A 46
Regal Wlk. L4: W'ton 2E 58
Regency Ct. *CH42: Rock F 7N 73*
(off Rock La. W.)
PR9: South 6J 7
Regency Gdns. PR8: Birkd 2L 11
Regency Pk. WA8: Widnes 5H 79
Regency Sq. WA5: Warr 1A 82
Regent Av. L14: Brd G 7C 60
L30: Neth 8E 34
WA1: Padg 9H 67
WA11: Hay 3D 50
WN4: Ash M 6H 41
Regent Cl. PR8: Birkd 2M 11
Regent Ct. PR9: South 7H 7
Regent M. PR8: Birkd 2M 11
Regent Pk. L36: Huy 4J 61
Regent Rd. CH45: Wall 3D 56
L3: Liv 5M 43
L5: Kirkd, Liv 5M 43
L20: Boot, Kirkd 5M 43
L23: Crosb 7K 33
PR8: Birkd 2L 11
WA8: Widnes 7L 79
Regents Cl. CH61: Thing 1B 88
Regents Fld. L37: Form 8D 16
Regents Rd. WA10: St H 8F 48
Regent St. CH65: Ell P 9L 103
L3: Liv 5A 58
WA1: Warr 3B 82
WA7: Run 4K 95
WA12: Newt W 7J 51
Regents Way CH63: H Beb 8K 73
Regiment Way L12: W Der 2B 60
Regina Av. L22: Wloo 9J 33
Reginald Rd. WA9: St H 3A 64
Regina Rd. L9: W'ton 4F 44
Reid Av. WA5: Warr 9A 66
Reid Ct. CH66: Lit Sut 7H 103
Reigate Cl. L25: Woolt 5G 77
Reins Cft. CH64: Nest 5E 100
Rembury Pl. WA4: Dutt 3H 109
Renacres La. L39: Hals 9D 12
Renaissance CH64: Nest 6F 100
Renaissance Way L24: Halew 2H 93
Rendal Cl. L5: Liv 4F 58
Rendcombe Grn. L11: Norr G 7L 45
Rendel Cl. WA12: Newt W 8M 51
Rendelsham Cl. CH49: Upton 3M 71
Rendel St. CH41: Birke 1K 73
Rendlesham Cl. WA3: Birchw 3B 68
Renfrew Av. CH62: East 1D 102
WA11: St H 3N 49
Renfrew Cl. WN3: Wigan 1J 41
Renfrew St. L7: Liv 3N 5 (7F 58)
Renfrey Cl. L39: Orm 5C 20
Renlake Ind. Est. WA9: St H 3B 64
Rennell Rd. L14: Knott A 6A 60
Rennie Av. WA10: St H 6F 48
Rennie Dr. WA4: Westy 5J 83
Renown Cl. WA3: Ris 5L 67
Renown Way L24: Speke 1E 92
Renshaw St. L1: Liv 6H 5 (8D 58)
Renton Av. WA7: Run 5N 95
Renville Rd. L14: Brd G 7A 60
Renwick Av. L35: Rainh 5D 62
Renwick Rd. L9: W'ton 5F 44
Renwick Sq. WN4: Ash M 8H 41
Repton Gro. L10: Aintr 9H 35
Repton Rd. CH65: Ell P 1B 112
L16: Child 9B 60
Reservoir Rd. CH42: Tran 7H 73
L25: Woolt 5D 76
Reservoir Rd. Nth. CH42: Tran 6H 73
Reservoir St. L6: Liv 5F 58
WA9: St H 2F 62
Rest Hill Rd. CH63: Store 2H 89
Retford Rd. L33: Kirkb 9D 36
Retford Wlk. L33: Kirkb 9D 36
Reva Rd. L14: Brd G 6D 60
Revesby Cl. WA8: Widnes 6G 79
Rex Cohen Ct. L17: Aig 3K 75
Rexmore Rd. L18: Moss H 6M 75
Rexmore Way L15: Wavtr 1K 75
Reynolds Av. WA3: Ris 4M 67
WA9: St H 8D 50
Reynolds Cl. L6: Liv 5F 58
Reynolds St. WA4: Westy 5F 82
Reynolds Way L25: Woolt 6E 76
Rhiwlas St. L8: Liv 3F 74
Rhodesia Rd. L9: Aintr 4G 45
Rhodes St. WA2: Warr 1D 82
Rhodesway CH60: Hesw 8B 88
Rhona Cl. CH63: East 2B 102
Rhona Dr. WA5: Gt San 2G 80
Rhosesmor Cl. L32: Kirkb 3D 46
Rhosesmor Rd. L32: Kirkb 4D 46
Rhuddlan Cl. L13: Liv 7L 59
Rhuddlan Ct. CH65: Ell P 3B 112
Rhum Cl. CH65: Ell P 4A 112
Rhyl St. L8: Liv 3E 74
WA8: Widnes 9J 79
Rialto Cl. L8: Liv 1E 74
Rib, The L37: Form, Gt Alt 8M 17
Ribble Av. L31: Mag 1K 35
L35: Rainh 6F 62
PR9: South 3A 8
Ribble Cl. WA3: Cul 8N 53
WA8: Widnes 5B 80
Ribble Cres. WN5: Bil 8M 39
Ribbledale Rd. L18: Moss H 4M 75
Ribble Ho. L25: Gate 4G 76
Ribble Rd. L25: Gate 5G 76
Ribbler's La. L34: Know 6M 47
Ribblers La. L32: Kirkb 3B 46
Ribblesdale CH65: Whit 2N 111
Ribblesdale Av. L9: Aintr 3G 44
Ribblesdale Cl. CH62: East 1E 102
Ribble St. CH41: Birke 8F 56
Ribchester Gdns. WA3: Cul 7N 53
Ribchester Way L35: Tar G 1L 77
Rice Hey Rd. CH44: Wall 4J 57
Rice La. CH44: Wall 4J 57
(not continuous)
L9: W'ton 7E 44
Rice Lane City Farm 6E 44
Rice Lane Station (Rail) 5F 44
Rice St. L1: Liv 8J 5 (9D 58)
Richard Allen Way *L5: Liv 5E 58*
(off Netherfield Rd. Sth.)
Richard Chubb Dr. CH45: Wall 3K 57
Richard Cl. WA7: Cas 6C 96
Richard Gro. L12: W Der 4C 60
Richard Hesketh Dr. L32: Kirkb 9A 36
Richard Kelly Cl. L4: W'ton 1J 59
Richard Kelly Dr. L4: W'ton 8J 45
Richard Kelly Pl. L4: W'ton 1J 59
Richard Martin Rd. L21: Ford 1B 44
Richard Reynolds Ct. *M44: Cad 3L 69*
(off Dean Rd.)
Richard Rd. L23: Blun 6G 32
Richards Gro. WA9: St H 6A 50
Richardson Rd. CH42: Rock F 7L 73
Richardson St. L7: Liv 1H 75
WA2: Warr 9D 66
Richbell Cl. M44: Irlam 2L 69
Richland Rd. L13: Liv 4L 59
Richmond Av. L21: Lith 2N 43
L40: Burs 2J 21
WA4: Grap 5K 83
WA4: Westy 4G 83
WA7: Run 5A 96
WA11: Hay 3D 50
Richmond Cl. CH63: Beb 1N 89
L38: Hight 1F 32
WA3: Cul 6L 53
WA10: Ec'stn 6D 48
WA13: Lymm 4H 85
Richmond Ct. CH65: Ell P 2B 112
L6: Liv 4F 58
(off Richmond Ter.)
L21: Lith 3A 44
(off Delta Rd.)
L40: Burs 2J 21
WA4: Westy 5H 83
WA8: Widnes 4N 79
Richmond Cres. L30: Neth 8E 34
Richmond Dr. WA13: Lymm 4H 85
Richmond Gdns. WA12: Newt W 8L 51
Richmond Gro. L31: Lydi 9K 27
Richmond M. L40: Burs 2K 21
Richmond Pk. L6: Liv 3G 59
Richmond Rd. CH63: Beb 1M 89
L23: Crosb 6L 33
PR8: Birkd 4M 11
WN4: Ash M 6H 41
Richmond Row L3: Liv 1H 5 (6D 58)
Richmond St. CH45: New B 9H 43
L1: Liv 5F 4 (8C 58)
WA4: Westy 5H 83
WA8: Widnes 7M 79
Richmond Ter. L6: Liv 4G 58
Richmond Way CH61: Hesw 5N 87
CH61: Thing 9A 72
L35: Tar G 1L 77
Rich Vw. CH43: Oxton 5H 73
Rickaby Cl. CH63: Brom 7B 90
Rickerby Ct. PR9: South 7H 7
Rickman St. L4: Kirkd 2C 58
Rickman Way L36: Huy 9K 61
Ridding La. WA7: Brook 1D 108
Riddings, The CH65: Whit 1N 111
Riddock Rd. L21: Lith 5A 44
Rides, The WA11: Hay 4F 50
Ridge, The CH60: Hesw 5L 87
Ridgebourne Cl. WA5: Call 7M 65
Ridge Cl. PR9: South 2A 8
Ridgefield Rd. CH61: Pens 2N 87
Ridgemere Rd. CH61: Pens 2N 87
Ridgetor Rd. L25: Woolt 5D 76
Ridgeview Rd. CH43: Noct 3D 72
Ridgeway WA3: Low 3G 52
Ridgeway, The CH47: Meols 1F 70
CH60: Hesw 8B 88
CH63: H Beb 8K 73
L25: Woolt 5E 76
WA6: Frod 2H 115
WA7: Murd 9F 96
WA8: Cron 2F 78
Ridgeway Cl. CH66: Gt Sut 3H 111
Ridgeway, The (Country Holiday Pk.)
WA6: Frod 3K 115
Ridgeway Dr. L31: Lydi 8J 27
Ridgewell Av. WA3: Low 2D 52
Ridgewell Cl. L21: Lith 3N 43
Ridgewood Dr. CH61: Pens 3M 87
WA9: St H 3M 63
Ridgewood Way L9: W'ton 3F 44
Ridgmont Av. L11: Norr G 8L 45
Ridgway Gdns. WA13: Lymm 5D 84
Ridgway St. WA2: Warr 1E 82
Riding Cl. L39: Down 9E 18
WA9: Clock F 5M 63
Ridingfold L26: Halew 6H 77
Riding Hill Rd. L34: Know 8H 47
Riding Hill Wlk. L34: Know 8H 47
Riding La. L39: Down 9C 18
WN4: Ash M 5N 41
Ridings, The CH43: Noct 3D 72
PR9: South 4M 7
Ridings Hey CH43: Noct 4D 72
Riding St. L3: Liv 4K 5 (7E 58)
PR8: South 9G 6
Ridley Dr. WA5: Gt San 4L 81
Ridley Gro. CH48: W Kir 5B 70
Ridley La. L31: Mag 2J 35
Ridley Rd. L6: Liv 6H 59
Ridley St. CH43: Oxton 3J 73
Ridsdale WA8: Widnes 8F 78
Ridsdale Lawn L27: N'ley 5L 77
Riesling Dr. L33: Kirkb 6B 36
Rigby Dr. CH49: Grea 6L 71
Rigby Rd. L31: Mag 9G 27
Rigbys La. WN4: Ash M 8M 41
(not continuous)
Rigby St. L3: Liv 3C 4 (7A 58)
WA3: Golb 2B 52
WA10: St H 7J 49
(Clock Twr. St.)
WA10: St H 6J 49
(Henry St.)
WN4: Ash M 8J 41
Rigby St. Sth. *WA10: St H 7J 49*
(off Nth. John St.)
Riley Av. L20: Boot 5C 44
Riley Bank M. WA6: Frod 4L 115
Riley Dr. WA7: Run 7K 95
Rilston Av. WA3: Cul 7L 53
Rimington Av. WA3: Golb 1D 52
Rimington Cl. WA3: Cul 7M 53
Rimmer Av. L16: Child 8E 60
Rimmerbrook Rd. L25: Gate 1F 76
Rimmer Cl. L21: Lith 3A 44
Rimmer Grn. PR8: South 5J 13
Rimmer Gro. WA9: St H 7A 50
Rimmer's Av. L37: Form 7E 16
PR8: South 9G 6
Rimmer St. L3: Liv 3J 5 (7D 58)
Rimmington Rd. L17: Aig 6K 75
Rimrose Bus. Pk. L20: Boot 6N 43
Rimrose Rd. L20: Boot 5N 43
Rimrose Valley Country Pk. 7A 34
Rimrose Valley Rd. L23: Crosb 8N 33
Rimsdale Cl. L17: Aig 9K 75
Ringcroft Rd. L13: Liv 6N 59
Ringley Av. WA3: Golb 1A 52
RING O' BELLS 3M 21
Ring O'Bells La. L40: Lath 3M 21
Ringo Starr Dr. L6: Liv 6G 59
Ring Rd. CH1: Back 6L 111
CH2: Lit Stan 5B 112
CH66: Back 6L 111
Ringsfield Rd. L24: Speke 5L 93
Ringtail Ct. L40: Burs 1F 20
Ringtail Ind. Est. L40: Burs 2F 20
Ringtail Pl. L40: Burs 2F 20
Ringtail Retail Pk. 3F 20
Ringtail Rd. L40: Burs 1E 20
Ringway CH64: Nest 4E 100
CH66: Gt Sut 1K 111
Ringway Rd. L25: Gate 4G 77
WA7: Run 5N 95
Ringways CH62: Brom 4C 90
Ringwood CH43: Oxton 5G 72
Ringwood Av. L14: Brd G 7D 60
Ringwood Cl. WA3: Birchw 4B 68
Rio Ct. L34: Presc 2A 62
Ripley Av. L21: Lith 1A 44
Ripley Cl. L31: Mag 2K 35
Ripley St. WA5: Warr 1N 81
Ripley Way WA9: St H 5J 63
Ripon Av. CH66: Lit Sut 9H 103
WA3: Low 2E 52
Ripon Cl. L30: Neth 1E 44
L36: Huy 6L 61
PR8: South 3E 12
WA12: Newt W 6L 51
Ripon Dr. WN4: Ash M 9M 41
Ripon Rd. CH45: Wall 3E 56
Ripon Row WA7: Run 9N 95
Ripon St. CH41: Tran 4L 73
L4: W'ton 9E 44
Risbury Rd. L11: Norr G 8L 45
Rishton Cl. L5: Liv 4F 58
Rishton St. *L5: Liv 4F 58*
(off Tynemouth Cl.)
RISLEY 3M 67
Risley Employment Area WA3: Ris 2N 67
Risley Moss Local Nature Reserve 5B 68
Risley Moss Vis. Cen. 4A 68
Risley Rd. WA3: Ris 4N 67
Ritchie Av. L9: Aintr 4H 45
Ritherup La. L35: Rainh 5F 62
Ritson St. L8: Liv 2G 74
Rivacre Brow CH66: Ell P 7K 103
Rivacre Bus. Cen. CH66: Ell P 9K 103
Rivacre Pk. 5H 103
Rivacre Rd. CH62: East 1F 102
CH65: Hoot 4H 103
CH66: Ell P, Hoot 4H 103
Rivacre Valley Country Pk. 6J 103
Riva La. CH60: Hesw 5M 87
Rivenhall Sq. L24: Speke 3F 92
Rivenmill Cl. WA8: Widnes 3M 79
Rivenmill Pl. WA8: Widnes 3M 79
Rivenmill Way WA8: Widnes 3N 79
River Avon St. L8: Liv 1H 75
(not continuous)
Riverbank Cl. CH60: Hesw 9N 87
Riverbank Rd. CH60: Hesw 9M 87
CH62: Brom 3D 90
L19: G'dale 9M 75
Riverbend Technology Cen.
M44: Irlam 3N 69
River Cl. L37: Form 3H 25
River Gro. CH62: New F 8A 74
River La. M31: Part 5M 69
Rivermeade PR8: South 2C 12
Riverpark Gdns. *L8: Liv 2D 74*
(off Hyslop St.)
River Rd. WA4: Warr 5C 82
(not continuous)
Riversdale WA1: Wools 1N 83
WA6: Frod 5M 107
Riversdale Ct. L19: Aig 8L 75
Riversdale M. L19: Aig 8L 75
Riversdale Rd. CH44: Wall 5K 57
CH48: W Kir 6B 70
L19: Aig 9L 75
L21: Sea 3M 43
WA7: Hal 6A 96
Riverside CH48: W Kir 8C 70
CH62: Port S 2A 90
L12: W Der 9C 46
L38: Hight 8F 24
Riverside Bowl 9H 43
Riverside Cl. L20: Boot 5N 43
WA1: Warr 4D 82
Riverside Ct. CH62: New F 7A 74
Riverside Dr. L3: Liv 5D 74
L17: Aig 6F 74
Riverside Gro. WA9: St H 2N 63
Riverside Holiday Pk. PR9: Banks 5H 9
Riverside Ho. CH41: Birke 8M 57
Riverside M. L36: Huy 3G 61
Riverside Retail Pk. 4D 82
Riverside Trad. Est. WA5: Penk 7F 80
Riverside Vw. L17: Aig 7H 75
Riverside Wlk. CH64: Lit N 9D 100
L3: Liv 3C 74
(Atlantic Way)
L3: Liv 8C 4 (9A 58)
(The Colonnades)
PR9: Banks 4H 9
Riverslea Rd. L23: Blun 9H 33
River St. CH41: Birke 2K 73
Riversview PR9: Banks 5H 9
River Vw. *CH41: Tran 4L 73*
(off Marquis St.)
CH62: New F 8B 74
L22: Wloo 9J 33
Riverview CH49: Wdchu 7A 72
Riverview Bus. Pk. CH62: Brom 5E 90
Riverview Gdns. CH42: Rock F 6M 73
River Vw. Res. Cvn. Pk.
WA8: Widnes 8M 79
Riverview Rd. CH44: Wall 6L 57
CH62: Brom 4E 90
CH64: Lit N 9F 100
Riverview Wlk. *L8: Liv 4E 74*
(off Cockburn St.)
River Wlk. *WA7: Pal F 8B 96*
(within Halton Lea Shop. Cen.)
River Way L25: Gate 5G 76
Riverwood Rd. CH62: Brom 6E 90
Riviera Dr. CH42: Rock F 7K 73
L11: Crox 6A 46
Rivington Av. CH43: Noct 4E 72
WA3: Golb 1D 52
WA10: St H 4H 49
Rivington Cl. PR8: Birkd 3N 11
Rivington Ct. WA1: Wools 9M 67
Rivington Dr. L40: Burs 2J 21
WN8: Uph 5M 31

Rivington Gro.—Rosthwaite Cl.

Rivington Gro. M44: Cad . . . 3K 69
Rivington Rd. CH44: Wall . . . 6K 57
CH65: Ell P . . . 9A 104
WA7: Pres B . . . 3H 109
WA10: St H . . . 7G 49
Rivington St. WA10: St H . . . 8G 48
RIXTON . . . 7G 68
Rixton Av. WA5: Warr . . . 9A 66
Rixton Claypits Local Nature Reserve . . . 7F 68
Rixtonleys Dr. M44: Irlam . . . 1N 69
Rixton Pk. Homes WA3: Rix . . . 7F 68
Roadside Ct. WA3: Low . . . 2D 52
Roadwater Cl. L25: Gate . . . 1F 76
Robarts Rd. L4: W'ton . . . 3G 58
ROBBINS BRIDGE . . . 7K 27
Robbins Bri. L31: Lydi . . . 7K 27
Robeck Rd. L13: Liv . . . 8N 59
Robert Dr. CH49: Grea . . . 5M 71
Robert Gro. L12: W Der . . . 4C 60
Roberts Av. WA11: Hay . . . 5C 50
Roberts Ct. WA7: Pal F . . . 9B 96
Roberts Dr. L20: Boot . . . 3D 44
Roberts Fold WA3: Birchw . . . 5L 67
Robertson St. L8: Liv . . . 3D 74
Roberts St. L3: Liv . . . 2B 4 (6A 58)
Robert St. CH41: Birke . . . 1K 73
WA5: Warr . . . 2A 82
WA7: Run . . . 5M 95
WA8: Widnes . . . 7L 79
Robina Rd. WA9: St H . . . 1N 63
Robin Cl. WA7: Murd . . . 8F 96
ROBIN HOOD . . . 2L 23
Robin Hood La. WA6: Hel . . . 4E 114
WN6: Wright . . . 2L 23
Robin La. WN8: Parb . . . 1F 22
Robins Bri. Mdws. L39: Augh . . . 7L 27
Robins Cft. CH66: Gt Sut . . . 3L 111
Robin's La. WA11: Kings M . . . 3K 39
Robins La. WA3: Cul . . . 8L 53
WA9: St H . . . 1M 63
Robinson Pl. WA9: St H . . . 7N 49
Robinson Rd. CH65: Ell P . . . 1C 112
L21: Lith . . . 1B 44
Robinsons Barn L40: Lath . . . 6H 21
Robin Way CH49: Wdchu . . . 6B 72
L6: Liv . . . 5G 58
Rob La. WA12: Newt W . . . 6N 51
Robsart St. L5: Liv . . . 4D 58
Robson Gro. WA1: Warr . . . 2E 82
Robson St. L5: Liv . . . 2E 58
L13: Liv . . . 8M 59
WA1: Warr . . . 2E 82
Robson Way WA3: Low . . . 2G 52
ROBY . . . 7G 61
Roby Cl. L35: Rainh . . . 5F 62
Roby Ct. L36: Roby . . . 8H 61
Roby Gro. WA5: Gt San . . . 2J 81
ROBY MILL . . . 1L 31
Roby Mill WN8: Roby M . . . 9L 23
Roby Mt. Av. L36: Roby . . . 7H 61
Roby Rd. L14: Brd G . . . 8D 60
L36: Roby . . . 7E 60
(not continuous)
Roby Station (Rail) . . . 7G 60
Roby St. L15: Wavtr . . . 1K 75
L20: Boot . . . 6B 44
WA10: St H . . . 9G 48
Roby Well Way WN5: Bil . . . 6N 39
Rocastle Cl. L6: Liv . . . 2N 5 (6F 58)
Rochester Av. L30: Neth . . . 1E 44
Rochester Cl. WA3: Golb . . . 2B 52
WA5: Gt San . . . 3L 81
Rochester Dr. CH65: Ell P . . . 2B 112
Rochester Gdns. WA10: St H . . . 9G 49
Rochester Rd. CH42: Rock F . . . 6N 73
Rock, The WA6: Hel . . . 3E 114
Rock Av. CH60: Hesw . . . 6N 87
Rock Bank CH49: Upton . . . 3A 72
Rockbank Rd. L13: Liv . . . 4L 59
Rockbourne Av. L25: Woolt . . . 3D 76
Rockbourne Grn. L25: Woolt . . . 3D 76
Rockbourne Way L25: Woolt . . . 3D 76
Rock Cl. CH42: Rock F . . . 6M 73
Rock Ct. WA6: Frod . . . 5L 107
Rock Dr. WA6: Frod . . . 5M 107
Rockfarm Cl. CH64: Lit N . . . 8G 101
Rockfarm Dr. CH64: Lit N . . . 8G 100
Rockfarm Gro. CH64: Lit N . . . 8G 100
ROCK FERRY . . . 7N 73
Rock Ferry By-Pass . . . 5N 73
Rock Ferry (Park & Ride) . . . 6M 73
Rock Ferry Station (Rail) . . . 6M 73
Rockfield Cl. WA8: Widnes . . . 6G 79
Rockfield Dr. WA6: Hel . . . 3F 114
Rockfield Gdns. *L31: Mag* . . . *1H 35*
(off East Meade)
Rockfield M. WA4: Grap . . . 6G 83
Rockfield Rd. L4: W'ton . . . 2E 58
Rockford Av. L32: Kirkb . . . 3C 46
Rockford Cl. L32: Kirkb . . . 3C 46
Rockford Gdns. WA5: Gt San . . . 9J 65
Rockford Wlk. L32: Kirkb . . . 3C 46
Rock Gro. L13: Liv . . . 6M 59
Rockhill Rd. L25: Woolt . . . 6F 76
Rockhouse St. L6: Liv . . . 4H 59
Rockingham Cl. WA3: Birchw . . . 3C 68
Rockingham Ct. L33: Kirkb . . . 7D 36
Rockland Rd. CH45: Wall . . . 2F 56
L22: Wloo . . . 9L 33
Rocklands, The CH43: Noct . . . 2D 72
Rocklands Av. CH63: Beb . . . 9N 73
Rocklands La. CH63: Thorn H . . . 7J 89
Rock La. L31: Mell . . . 5L 35
WA8: Widnes . . . 5H 79
Rock La. E. CH42: Rock F . . . 7N 73
Rock La. W. CH42: Rock F . . . 7M 73
Rocklee Gdns. CH64: Lit N . . . 8G 100
Rockley St. L4: Kirkd, W'ton . . . 1D 58
(not continuous)
Rocklis Grange *CH64: Nest* . . . *6E 100*
(off Tannery La.)
Rockmount Cl. L25: Woolt . . . 5D 76
Rockmount Pk. L25: Woolt . . . 5D 76
Rockmount Rd. L17: Aig . . . 7L 75
Rock Pk. CH42: Rock F . . . 6N 73
(not continuous)
Rock Pk. Rd. CH42: Rock F . . . 7A 74
Rockpoint Av. CH45: New B . . . 2J 57
Rock Retail Pk. . . . 3L 73
Rock Rd. WA4: Westy . . . 4F 82
ROCKSAVAGE . . . 1M 107
Rocksavage Expressway . . . 1N 107
Rocksavage Way WA7: Run . . . 1K 107
Rockside Rd. L18: Moss H . . . 7M 75
Rock St. L13: Liv . . . 6M 59
WA10: St H . . . 1F 62
Rock Vw. L31: Mell . . . 7M 35
Rockville Rd. L14: Brd G . . . 8A 60
Rockville St. CH42: Rock F . . . 6M 73
Rockwell Cl. L12: W Der . . . 1B 60
Rockwell Rd. L12: W Der . . . 1B 60
Rocky Bank Rd. CH42: Tran . . . 5K 73
Rocky La. CH60: Hesw . . . 7N 87
L6: Liv . . . 4H 59
L16: Child . . . 9A 60
Rocky La. Sth. CH60: Hesw . . . 7A 88
Roderick Rd. L4: W'ton . . . 8F 44
Roderick St. L3: Liv . . . 2J 5 (6D 58)
Rodgers Cl. WA6: Frod . . . 5L 107
Rodick St. L25: Woolt . . . 6D 76
Rodmell Rd. L9: Aintr . . . 4G 44
Rodney St. CH41: Birke . . . 3K 73
L1: Liv . . . 8J 5 (9D 58)
WA10: St H . . . 7H 49
Roe All. L1: Liv . . . 6G 4
Roeburn Way WA5: Penk . . . 5F 80
Roedean Cl. L25: Woolt . . . 7F 76
L31: Mag . . . 1J 35
Roehampton Dr. L23: Blun . . . 5J 33
WA7: Pal F . . . 8A 96
Roe La. PR9: South . . . 7K 7
Roemarsh Cl. L12: W Der . . . 8N 45
Roemarsh Ct. WA7: Pal F . . . 9A 96
Roe Pk. M. PR9: South . . . 7J 7
Roe St. L1: Liv . . . 5G 4 (8C 58)
Roften Works Ind. Est. CH66: Hoot . . . 5C 102
Roger Arden Ct. L20: Boot . . . 6C 44
Rogers Av. L20: Boot . . . 5D 44
Rogersons Grn. L26: Halew . . . 6J 77
Rokeby Av. WA3: Low . . . 1E 52
Rokeby Cl. L3: Liv . . . 1J 5 (6D 58)
L20: Boot . . . 3D 44
Rokeby Ct. WA7: Manor P . . . 2F 96
Rokeby St. L3: Liv . . . 1J 5 (6D 58)
Rokeden WA12: Newt W . . . 6M 51
Roker Av. CH44: Wall . . . 6G 57
Rokesmith Av. L7: Liv . . . 9H 59
Roklis Bldg. *CH44: Wall* . . . *5K 57*
(off Liscard Rd.)
Roklis Ct. *CH49: Upton* . . . *4A 72*
(off Rake La.)
Roland Av. CH63: H Beb . . . 1K 89
WA7: Run . . . 5J 95
WA11: St H . . . 3M 49
Rolands Wlk. WA7: Cas . . . 6B 96
Roleton Cl. L30: Neth . . . 7G 34
Rollesby Gdns. WA9: St H . . . 3H 63
Rolleston Dr. CH45: Wall . . . 2F 56
CH63: Beb . . . 3N 89
Rolleston St. WA2: Warr . . . 2B 82
Rolling Mill La. WA9: St H . . . 1B 64
Roman Cl. WA7: Cas . . . 5A 96
WA12: Newt W . . . 8L 51
Roman Ct. CH64: Lit N . . . 7F 100
Roman Rd. CH43: Pren . . . 8G 72
CH47: Meols . . . 8E 54
CH63: Store . . . 8G 73
WA4: Stockt H . . . 7D 82
WN4: Ash M . . . 6J 41
Roman Way L33: Kirkb . . . 8E 36
Rome Cl. L36: Huy . . . 6H 61
Romer Rd. L6: Liv . . . 6H 59
Romford Way L26: Halew . . . 1K 93
(not continuous)
Romiley Dr. WN8: Skel . . . 2C 30
Romiley Rd. CH66: Ell P . . . 8K 103
Romilly St. L6: Liv . . . 2N 5 (6G 58)
Romley St. L4: W'ton . . . 9E 44
Romney Cl. CH64: Lit N . . . 7E 100
WA8: Widnes . . . 6A 80
Romney Cft. CH64: Lit N . . . 7F 100
Romney Way CH64: Lit N . . . 7F 100
Romsey Av. L37: Form . . . 2H 25
Romsey Gro. WN3: Winst . . . 1F 40
Romulus St. L7: Liv . . . 7J 59
Rona Av. CH65: Ell P . . . 4A 112
Ronald Cl. L22: Wloo . . . 1M 43
Ronald Dr. WA2: Fearn . . . 7J 67
Ronald Rd. L22: Wloo . . . 1M 43
Ronald Ross Av. L30: Neth . . . 8E 34
Ronaldshay WA8: Widnes . . . 6A 80
Ronald St. L13: Liv . . . 6L 59
Ronaldsway CH49: Upton . . . 2N 71
CH60: Hesw . . . 9N 87
L10: Faz . . . 3M 45
L23: Thorn . . . 5N 33
L26: Halew . . . 8L 77
Ronan Cl. L20: Boot . . . 6N 43
Ronan Rd. WA8: Widnes . . . 2H 95
(not continuous)
Rone Cl. CH46: More . . . 9L 55
Rookery, The WA12: Newt W . . . 6M 51
Rookery Av. WN4: Ash M . . . 9K 41
WN6: App B . . . 5N 23
Rookery Dr. L19: Aig . . . 8L 75
WA11: Rainf . . . 5D 38
Rookery La. WA11: Rainf . . . 6D 38
Rookery Rd. PR9: South . . . 6K 7
Rookley Cl. L27: N'ley . . . 4K 77
Rooks Way CH60: Hesw . . . 7M 87
Rooley, The L36: Huy . . . 8H 61
Roome St. WA2: Warr . . . 1D 82
Roosevelt Dr. L9: Aintr . . . 2G 45
Roper's Bri. Cl. L35: Whis . . . 7A 62
Ropers Ct. L34: Presc . . . 4A 62
Roper St. L8: Liv . . . 3E 74
WA9: St H . . . 6M 49
Ropewalk, The CH64: P'gte . . . 5C 100
Ropewalks Sq. L1: Liv . . . 7H 5
Ropeworks Cl. L20: Boot . . . 5C 44
Rosalind Av. CH63: H Beb . . . 9L 73
Rosalind Way L20: Kirkd . . . 9C 44
Rosam Ct. WA7: Pal F . . . 9A 96
Rosclare Dr. CH45: Wall . . . 3F 56
Roscoe & Gladstone Hall L17: Aig . . . 4K 75
Roscoe Av. WA2: Warr . . . 9E 66
WA12: Newt W . . . 7N 51
Roscoe Cl. L35: Tar G . . . 1L 77
Roscoe Cres. WA7: West P . . . 8H 95
Roscoe La. L1: Liv . . . 7H 5 (9D 58)
Roscoe Pl. L1: Liv . . . 7H 5 (9D 58)
Roscoe Rd. M44: Irlam . . . 1L 69
Roscoe St. L1: Liv . . . 8J 5 (9D 58)
WA10: St H . . . 7G 49
Roscommon St. L5: Liv . . . 5D 58
Roscommon Way WA8: Widnes . . . 5H 79
Roscote, The CH60: Hesw . . . 8N 87
Roscote Cl. CH60: Hesw . . . 8N 87
Roseacre CH48: W Kir . . . 5B 70
Roseacre Gdns. L40: Ruf . . . 3M 15
Roseate Ct. CH45: Wall . . . 1E 56
Rose Av. L20: Boot . . . 3B 44
M44: Irlam . . . 1M 69
WA9: St H . . . 2M 63
WA11: Hay . . . 4G 51
Rose Bailey Cl. L11: Norr G . . . 6N 45
Rose Bank WA13: Lymm . . . 5E 84
Rose Bank Rd. L16: Child . . . 1B 76
Rosebank Rd. L36: Huy . . . 4G 60
M44: Cad . . . 5J 69
Rosebank Way L36: Huy . . . 4G 61
Rosebay Cl. L37: Form . . . 1G 24
Roseberry Rd. WN4: Ash M . . . 6J 41
Rosebery Av. CH44: Wall . . . 5J 57
L22: Wloo . . . 9J 33
Rosebery Gro. CH42: Tran . . . 6H 73
Rosebery Rd. WA10: St H . . . 5G 48
Rosebery St. L8: Liv . . . 1F 74
PR9: South . . . 9M 7
Rosebourne Cl. L17: Aig . . . 6H 75
Rose Brae L18: Moss H . . . 4N 75
Rosebrae Ct. CH41: Birke . . . 1M 73
CH60: Hesw . . . 6A 88
Rosebrae Walkway CH41: Birke . . . 1N 73
Rose Brow L25: Woolt . . . 4E 76
Rose Cl. L26: Halew . . . 9L 77
WA7: Murd . . . 1F 108
Rose Ct. CH41: Birke . . . 2K 73
L15: Wavtr . . . 1K 75
Rose Creek Gdns. WA5: Gt San . . . 2K 81
Rose Cres. PR8: Ainsd . . . 3J 17
WA8: Widnes . . . 9J 79
WN8: Skel . . . 3B 30
Rosecroft CH62: Brom . . . 9B 90
Rosecroft Cl. L39: Orm . . . 7C 20
Rosecroft Ct. CH47: Hoy . . . 2B 70
Rosedale Av. L23: Crosb . . . 7L 33
WA1: Wools . . . 1K 83
WA3: Low . . . 3D 52
Rosedale Cl. L9: W'ton . . . 6G 45
Rosedale Rd. CH42: Tran . . . 5L 73
L18: Moss H . . . 4N 75
Rose Dr. WA11: Rainf . . . 6D 38
Rosefield Av. CH63: H Beb . . . 9L 73
Rosefield Rd. L25: Woolt . . . 7G 76
Rose Gdns. CH64: Lit N . . . 8F 100
Rosegarth Grn. *L13: Liv* . . . *5N 59*
(off Black Horse La.)
Roseheath Dr. L26: Halew . . . 9K 77
ROSE HILL . . . 4H 41
Rose Hill L3: Liv . . . 1G 5 (6C 58)
PR9: South . . . 9J 7
Rosehill Av. WA9: Bold . . . 4D 64
Rosehill Bus. Pk. PR9: South . . . 9J 7
Rosehill Ct. L25: Woolt . . . 4E 76
Rosehill Dr. L39: Augh . . . 2A 28
Rosehill Vw. WN4: Ash M . . . 4H 41
Roseland Cl. L31: Lydi . . . 8G 27
Roselands Ct. CH42: Rock F . . . 7L 73
Rose La. L18: Moss H . . . 5L 75
Rose Lea Cl. WA8: Widnes . . . 4K 79
Roselea Dr. PR9: South . . . 3A 8
Roselee Ct. CH42: Rock F . . . 7N 73
Rosemary Av. WA4: Stockt H . . . 6F 82
WA7: Beech . . . 2B 108
Rosemary Cl. CH43: Bid . . . 9E 56
L7: Liv . . . 7N 5 (9F 58)
WA5: Gt San . . . 2L 81
Rosemary Dr. WA12: Newt W . . . 7N 51
Rosemary La. L37: Form . . . 1E 24
L39: Down . . . 8F 18
Rosemary Wlk. *M31: Part* . . . *7M 69*
(off Broom Rd.)
Rosemead Av. CH61: Pens . . . 3N 87
Rosemere Dr. CH1: Back . . . 6L 111
Rosemont Rd. L17: Aig . . . 6L 75
Rosemoor Dr. L23: Crosb . . . 6N 33
Rosemoor Gdns. L11: Norr G . . . 8M 45
WA4: App . . . 2G 98
Rose Mt. CH43: Oxton . . . 5H 73
WA2: Winw . . . 1C 66
Rosemount Cl. CH43: Oxton . . . 5G 73
Rose Mt. Dr. CH45: Wall . . . 3G 57
Rosemount Pk. CH43: Oxton . . . 4G 73
Rose Path L37: Form . . . 2G 24
Rose Pl. CH42: Tran . . . 4K 73
L3: Liv . . . 1G 5 (6C 58)
(not continuous)
L39: Augh . . . 2B 28
WA11: Rainf . . . 6D 38
Roseside Dr. L27: N'ley . . . 2K 77
Rose St. L1: Liv . . . 4G 5 (8C 58)
L25: Woolt . . . 6D 76
WA8: Widnes . . . 9J 79
Rose Ter. L18: Moss H . . . 4M 75
Rose Va. L5: Liv . . . 5D 58
(not continuous)
Rose Vw. Av. WA8: Widnes . . . 6K 79
Rose Vs. L15: Wavtr . . . 1L 75
Rose Wlk. M31: Part . . . 6L 69
Rosewarne Cl. L17: Aig . . . 6G 75
Roseway Av. M44: Cad . . . 4L 69
Rosewood *PR9: South* . . . *5L 7*
(off Cambridge Rd.)
Rosewood Av. WA1: Warr . . . 1F 82
WA6: Frod . . . 7N 107
Rosewood Cl. L27: N'ley . . . 3J 77
L28: Stockb V . . . 2F 60
Rosewood Dr. CH46: More . . . 9J 55
Rosewood Farm Ct. WA8: Widnes . . . 4H 79
Rosewood Gdns. L11: Norr G . . . 9N 45
Rosewood Gro. WA8: Widnes . . . 8E 78
Roseworth Av. L9: W'ton . . . 3F 44
Rosina Cl. WN4: Ash M . . . 5H 41
Roskell Rd. L25: Hunts X . . . 9G 76
Roslin Ct. CH43: Oxton . . . 4H 73
Roslin Rd. CH43: Oxton . . . 4H 73
CH61: Irby . . . 1L 87
Roslyn St. CH41: Tran . . . 5M 73
CH42: Tran . . . 5M 73
Rossall Av. L10: Aintr . . . 8J 35
Rossall Cl. L24: Hale . . . 5B 94
Rossall Ct. CH46: Leas . . . 7N 55
Rossall Gro. CH66: Lit Sut . . . 8J 103
Rossall Rd. CH46: More . . . 8N 55
L13: Liv . . . 7N 59
WA5: Gt San . . . 4K 81
WA8: Widnes . . . 6N 79
Ross Av. CH46: Leas . . . 5C 56
Rossbank Rd. CH65: Ell P . . . 7M 103
Rosscliffe Rd. CH65: Ell P . . . 7M 103
Ross Cl. L34: Know . . . 7H 47
WA5: Old H . . . 1M 81
WN5: Bil . . . 5A 40
Rosscourt Vw. CH42: Rock F . . . 6N 73
Ross Dr. CH66: Gt Sut . . . 9H 103
Rossendale Cl. CH43: Noct . . . 4D 72
Rossendale Dr. WA3: Birchw . . . 3A 68
Rosset Cl. WN3: Winst . . . 1F 40
Rossett Av. L17: Liv . . . 2K 75
Rossett Cl. WA5: Call . . . 7N 65
Rossett Rd. L23: Crosb . . . 8J 33
Rossett St. L6: Liv . . . 4H 59
Rossfield Rd. CH65: Ell P . . . 7M 103
Rossington Gdns. WA9: St H . . . 4J 63
Rossini St. L21: Sea . . . 4N 43
Rossiter Dr. CH43: Bid . . . 2C 72
Rosslyn Av. L31: Mag . . . 3G 35
Rosslyn Cres. CH46: More . . . 9M 55
Rosslyn Dr. CH46: More . . . 9M 55
Rosslyn Pk. CH46: More . . . 1M 71
Rosslyn St. L17: Aig . . . 5G 74
Rossmore Bus. Pk. CH65: Ell P . . . 7N 103
Rossmore Bus. Village CH65: Ell P . . . 7N 103
Rossmore Ct. CH66: Ell P . . . 8K 103
Rossmore Gdns. CH66: Lit Sut . . . 8J 103
L4: W'ton . . . 1H 59
Rossmore Ind. Est. CH65: Ell P . . . 7M 103
(not continuous)
Rossmore Rd. E. CH65: Ell P . . . 7L 103
Rossmore Rd. W. CH66: Ell P, Lit Sut . . . 7J 103
Rossmore Trad. Est. CH65: Ell P . . . 8M 103
Rossmount Rd. CH65: Ell P . . . 8M 103
Ross Rd. CH65: Ell P . . . 8M 103
Ross St. WA8: Widnes . . . 7L 79
Ross Twr. Ct. CH45: New B . . . 1J 57
Rosswood Rd. CH65: Ell P . . . 8M 103
Rostherne Av. CH44: Wall . . . 6G 57
CH66: Gt Sut . . . 1K 111
WA3: Low . . . 2E 52
Rostherne Cl. WA5: Warr . . . 4M 81
Rostherne Cres. WA8: Widnes . . . 6G 78
Rosthwaite Cl. WN3: Wigan . . . 1J 41

Rosthwaite Gro.—St Annes Gdns.

Rosthwaite Gro. WA11: St H 1L 49
Rosthwaite Rd. L12: W Der 3A 60
Rostron Cres. L37: Form 3E 24
Roswell Ct. L28: Stockb V 3F 60
Rosyth Cl. WA2: Fearn 6G 67
Rothay Dr. WA5: Penk 5F 80
Rothbury Cl. CH46: More 9K 55
WA7: Beech 9A 96
Rothbury Ct. WA9: Sut M 7L 63
Rothbury Rd. L14: Knott A 3D 60
Rother Dr. CH65: Ell P 7M 103
Rother Dr. Bus. Pk. CH65: Ell P 7M 103
Rotherham Cl. L36: Huy 5K 61
Rotherwood CH43: Noct 3D 72
Rotherwood Cl. CH63: H Beb 1K 89
Rothesay Cl. WA7: Cas 5B 96
WA11: St H 3A 50
Rothesay Ct. CH63: Beb 3M 89
Rothesay Dr. CH62: East 2D 102
L23: Crosb 8L 33
Rothesay Gdns. CH43: Pren 7F 72
Rothley Av. PR8: Ainsd 1G 17
Rothsay Cl. L5: Liv 5E 58
Rothwell Cl. L39: Orm 8B 20
Rothwell Dr. L39: Augh 2N 27
PR8: Ainsd 9G 11
Rothwell Rd. WA3: Golb 1D 52
Rothwells La. L23: Thorn 5A 34
Rothwell St. L6: Liv 5F 58
Rotten Row PR8: South 1L 11
Roughdale Av. L32: Kirkb 3D 46
WA9: Sut M 5L 63
Roughdale Cl. L32: Kirkb 3D 46
Rough La. L39: Bart 4K 17
Roughlea Av. WA3: Cul 6L 53
Roughley Av. WA5: Warr 4M 81
Roughley Ho. *CH41: Birke* *1M 73*
(off Bridge St.)
Roughsedge Ho. L28: Stockb V 1F 60
Roughwood Dr. L33: Kirkb 8D 36
Roundabout, The WA8: Cron 2G 78
WN8: Skel 3N 29
Round Hey L28: Stockb V 1E 60
Round Meade, The L31: Mag 1G 35
Round Thorn WA3: Croft 1H 67
Roundway, The L38: Hight 9F 24
Roundwood Dr. WA9: St H 9L 49
Routledge St. WA8: Widnes 7L 79
Row, The CH47: Hoy 1C 70
Rowan Av. L12: W Der 9D 46
WA3: Low 3G 52
Rowan Cl. L40: Burs 8K 15
WA5: Gt San 2H 81
WA7: Run 8M 95
WA11: Hay 5B 50
WA11: St H 3N 49
Rowan Ct. CH49: Grea 6J 71
CH63: H Beb 1K 89
Rowan Dr. L32: Kirkb 8A 36
Rowan Gro. CH63: H Beb 3L 89
L36: Huy 9H 61
Rowan Ho. WA6: Kgswd 6N 115
Rowan La. WN8: Skel 9E 22
Rowans, The L39: Augh 5M 27
WA8: Widnes *4N 79*
(off Hampton Ct. Way)
Rowan Tree Cl. CH49: Grea 5J 71
Rowan Wlk. M31: Part 6L 69
Rowena Cl. L23: Crosb 7M 33
Rowen Ct. L17: Aig 6K 75
Rowland Cl. WA2: Fearn 6H 67
Rowlings Way *L32: Kirkb* *2D 46*
(off Park Brow Dr.)
Rowsley Gro. L9: Aintr 3G 45
Rowson Ct. *CH45: New B* *1H 57*
(off Pickering Rd.)
Rowson Dr. M44: Cad 3K 69
Rowson St. CH45: New B 9H 43
L34: Presc 2A 62
Rowswood Ctyd. WA4: H Walt 1N 97
Rowthorn Cl. WA8: Widnes 8H 79
Rowton Cl. CH43: Oxton 5F 72
Roxborough Cl. WA5: Burtw 3J 65
Roxborough Wlk. L25: Woolt 5G 76
Roxburgh Av. CH42: Tran 6K 73
L17: Aig 5H 75
Roxburgh Rd. CH66: Lit Sut 8E 102
Roxburgh St. L4: Kirkd 8D 44
L20: Boot 8D 44
Royal, The CH47: Hoy 2A 70
Royal Av. WA8: Widnes 8E 78
Royal Birkdale Golf Course 5K 11
Royal Cl. L37: Form 3G 24
Royal Ct. *CH42: Rock F* *7N 73*
(off Rock La. W.)
Royal Court Theatre
Liverpool 4G 4 (8C 58)
Royal Cres. L37: Form 3G 24
Royal Cft. L12: W Der 5N 59
Royal Gro. WA10: St H 9G 49
Royal Liverpool Golf Course 3B 70
Royal Liverpool Philharmonic Hall 7K 5 (9E 58)
Royal London Bus. Pk. WA5: Westb 6N 65
Royal Mail St. L3: Liv 5H 5 (8D 58)
Royal Mersey Yacht Club 6N 73
ROYAL OAK 8D 28
Royal Pk. PR8: Birkd 2L 11
Royal Pl. WA8: Widnes 8E 78
Royal Quay L3: Liv 8E 4 (9B 58)
Royal Shop. Arc. 6E 100
Royal Standard Way CH42: Tran 5M 73
Royal St. L4: W'ton 2D 58
Royal Ter. PR8: South 8F 6
Royden Av. CH44: Wall 4K 57
M44: Irlam 1M 69
WA7: Run 7J 95
WN3: Wigan 1J 41
Royden Cres. WN5: Bil 6A 40
Royden Rd. CH49: Upton 2M 71
WN5: Bil 6A 40
Royden Way L3: Liv 5D 74
Royleen Dr. WA6: Frod 8N 107
Roysten Gdns. WA9: St H 8N 49
Royston Av. WA1: Padd 1H 83
Royston Cl. CH66: Gt Sut 2L 111
WA3: Low 2F 52
Royston St. L7: Liv 8G 58
Royton Cl. L26: Halew 1K 93
Royton Rd. L22: Wloo 9M 33
Rozel Cres. WA5: Gt San 4K 81
Rubbing Stone CH48: Caldy 1E 86
Ruby Cl. L21: Lith 2B 44
Ruby St. L8: Liv 5E 74
(not continuous)
Rudd Av. WA9: St H 8D 50
Ruddington Rd. PR8: South 4D 12
Rudd St. CH47: Hoy 1C 70
Rudgate L35: Whis 7B 62
Rudgrave M. CH44: Wall 4K 57
Rudgrave Pl. CH44: Wall 4K 57
Rudgrave Sq. CH44: Wall 4K 57
Rudheath La. WA7: Nort 4F 96
Rudley Wlk. L24: Speke 5K 93
Rudloe Ct. WA2: Padg 8G 66
Rudstone Cl. CH66: Lit Sut 9G 103
Rudston Rd. L16: Child 9A 60
Rudyard Cl. L14: Knott A 6A 60
Rudyard Rd. L14: Knott A 6A 60
Ruecroft Cl. WN6: App B 5N 23
Ruff La. L39: Orm 9D 20
L40: Westh 9D 20
RUFFORD 2N 15
Rufford Av. L31: Mag 9K 27
Rufford Cl. L10: Faz 1L 45
L35: Presc 4C 62
WA8: Widnes 6F 78
Rufford Ct. WA1: Wools 9M 67
Rufford Dr. PR9: Banks 2D 8
Rufford New Hall L40: Ruf 1M 15
Rufford Old Hall 1N 15
Rufford Pk. La. L40: Ruf 1L 15
Rufford Rd. CH44: Wall 6J 57
L6: Liv 6H 59
L20: Boot 5B 44
PR9: South 4A 8
WA11: Rainf 4C 38
Rufford Station (Rail) 2N 15
Rufford St. WN4: Ash M 6H 41
Rufford Wlk. WA11: St H 4A 50
Rugby Dr. L10: Aintr 1K 45
Rugby Rd. CH44: Wall 5F 56
CH65: Ell P 2A 112
L9: Aintr 2G 44
Rugby Wlk. CH65: Ell P 2B 112
Ruislip Cl. L25: Woolt 6G 77
Ruislip Ct. WA2: Padg 8G 66
Rullerton Rd. CH44: Wall 5G 56
Rumford Pl. L3: Liv 4C 4 (7B 58)
Rumford St. L2: Liv 4D 4 (7B 58)
Rumney Pl. L4: Kirkd 1D 58
(not continuous)
Rumney Rd. L4: Kirkd 1D 58
Rumney Rd. W. L4: Kirkd 1C 58
RUNCORN 4K 95
Runcorn Bus Station 4K 95
Runcorn Docks Rd. WA7: Run 5H 95
Runcorn East Station (Rail) 8F 96
Runcorn Golf Course 8K 95
Runcorn Hill Local Nature Reserve 7J 95
Runcorn Hill Vis. Cen. 7J 95
Runcorn Rd. WA4: H Walt, Moore 3H 97
Runcorn Ski & Snowboard Cen. 8D 96
Runcorn Spur Rd. WA7: Run 5L 95
Runcorn Station (Rail) 5J 95
Runcorn Swimming Pool 4L 95
Rundle Rd. L17: Aig 6K 75
Runic St. L13: Liv 7L 59
Runnel, The L39: Hals 3G 18
Runnell, The CH64: Nest 3D 100
Runnell's La. L23: Thorn 6B 34
Runnymede L36: Huy 5H 61
WA1: Wools 1L 83
Runnymede Cl. L25: Woolt 4E 76
Runnymede Ct. *WA8: Widnes* *7M 79*
(off William St.)
Runnymede Dr. WA11: Hay 4C 50
Runnymede Gdns. *WA8: Widnes* *7M 79*
(off Cliffe St.)
Runnymede Wlk. *WA8: Widnes* *6M 79*
(off William St.)
Runton Rd. L25: Gate 3G 77
Rupert Dr. L6: Liv 1M 5 (5F 58)
Rupert Rd. L36: Huy 6G 61
Rupert Row WA7: Cas 7C 96
Ruscar Cl. L26: Halew 6J 77
Ruscolm Cl. WA5: Gt San 1F 80
Ruscombe Rd. L14: Knott A 4D 60
Rushbury Ct. L15: Wavtr 9L 59
Rushden Rd. L32: Kirkb 1E 46
Rushes Mdw. WA13: Lymm 3H 85
Rushey Hey Rd. L32: Kirkb 9C 36
Rushfield Cres. WA7: Brook 1D 108
Rush Gdns. WA13: Lymm 4G 84
RUSHGREEN 4G 84
Rushgreen Cl. CH43: Bid 1C 72
Rushgreen Rd. WA13: Lymm 4F 84
Rushlake Dr. L27: N'ley 3H 77
Rushmere Rd. L11: Norr G 9M 45
Rushmoor Av. WN4: Ash M 7N 41
Rushmore Dr. WA8: Widnes 5J 79
Rushmore Gro. WA1: Padd 1H 83
Rusholme Cl. L26: Halew 1L 93
Rushton Av. WA12: Newt W 6K 51
Rushton Cl. WA5: Burtw 2H 65
WA8: Widnes 5J 79
Rushton Pl. L25: Woolt 6E 76
Rushtons, The CH66: Lit Sut 7H 103
Rushton's Wlk. L30: Neth 6C 34
Rushy Vw. WA12: Newt W 6J 51
Ruskin Av. CH42: Rock F 7M 73
CH44: Wall 6G 57
WA2: Warr 7D 66
WA12: Newt W 6L 51
Ruskin Cl. L20: Boot 7B 44
Ruskin Dr. CH65: Ell P 2B 112
WA10: St H 6G 49
Ruskin Health & Fitness
Eccleston 5G 48
Ruskin St. L4: Kirkd 9D 44
Ruskin Way CH43: Noct 5E 72
L36: Huy 8H 61
Rusland Av. CH61: Pens 3N 87
Rusland Rd. L32: Kirkb 2D 46
Russeldene Rd. WN3: Wigan 1G 40
Russell Av. PR9: South 8M 7
Russell Ct. PR9: South 3N 7
WA8: Widnes 4L 79
Russell Pl. L19: Garst 1A 92
Russell Rd. CH42: Rock F 5M 73
(not continuous)
CH44: Wall 4E 56
L18: Moss H 3L 75
L19: Garst 1A 92
L36: Huy 7M 61
M31: Part 6N 69
PR9: South 8M 7
WA7: Run 6H 95
Russell St. CH41: Birke 1L 73
L3: Liv 4J 5 (8D 58)
Russet Cl. L27: N'ley 3J 77
WA10: St H 5J 49
Russian Av. L13: Liv 4L 59
Russian Dr. L13: Liv 4L 59
Rutherford Cl. L13: Wavtr 8K 59
Rutherford Rd. L18: Moss H 2N 75
L31: Mag 4K 35
WA10: Windle 4F 48
Rutherglen Av. L23: Crosb 9M 33
Ruth Evans Ct. L35: Rainh 5D 62
Ruthin Cl. WA5: Call 6N 65
Ruthin Ct. CH65: Ell P 2B 112
WA7: Cas 5C 96
Ruthin Wlk. WA6: Hel 4D 114
Ruthven Ct. L21: Lith 3N 43
Ruthven Rd. L13: Liv 8N 59
L21: Lith 3N 43
Rutland Av. L17: Liv 2J 75
L26: Halew 8K 77
WA3: Low 3E 52
WA4: W'ton 8C 82
Rutland Cl. L5: Liv 4F 58
Rutland Cres. L39: Orm 6B 20
Rutland Dr. WN4: Ash M 7L 41
Rutland Ho. L17: Aig 3J 75
L23: Blun 8H 33
Rutland Rd. M31: Part 7L 69
M44: Cad 4K 69
PR8: South 1C 12
Rutland St. L20: Boot 6C 44
WA7: Run 5J 95
WA10: St H 5J 49
Rutland Way L36: Huy 6M 61
Rutter Av. WA5: Warr 7A 66
Rutter St. L8: Liv 3D 74
Ryburn Rd. L39: Orm 1B 28
Rycot Rd. L24: Speke 3F 92
Rycroft Rd. CH44: Wall 6J 57
CH47: Meols 9F 54
L10: Faz 2K 45
Rydal Av. CH43: Noct 3C 72
L23: Crosb 9M 33
L34: Presc 3C 62
L37: Form 1D 24
WA4: Warr 6B 82
Rydal Bank CH44: Wall 5J 57
CH63: Beb 9N 73
Rydal Cl. CH61: Pens 3N 87
CH64: Lit N 8F 100
CH65: Ell P 3A 112
L10: Aintr 9L 35
L33: Kirkb 7B 36
WN4: Ash M 7L 41
Rydal Gro. WA6: Hel 4E 114
WA7: Run 7L 95
WA11: St H 3K 49
Rydal Rd. L36: Huy 8J 61
Rydal St. L5: Liv 3F 58
WA12: Newt W 7L 51
Rydal Way WA8: Widnes 7F 78
Rydecroft L25: Woolt 6D 76
Ryder Cl. L35: Rainh 5D 62
L39: Augh 2A 28
Ryder Ct. L35: Rainh 3E 62
Ryder Cres. L39: Augh 3A 28
PR8: Birkd 6L 11
Ryder Rd. WA1: Wools 9K 67
WA8: Widnes 4L 79
Rydinge, The L37: Form 7G 16
Ryding's La. PR9: Banks 1H 9
Rye Cl. WA9: Clock F 5M 63
Ryecote L32: Kirkb 3C 46
Ryecroft CH2: Elt 2M 113
L21: Ford 8A 34
Ryecroft Av. WA3: Low 1F 52
Ryecroft Rd. CH60: Hesw 8C 88
Ryedale Cl. L8: Liv 1G 74
Ryefield La. L21: Ford 8A 34
Ryegate Rd. L19: G'dale 8N 75
Ryeground La. L37: Form 8G 16
Rye Gro. L12: W Der 3C 60
Rye Hey Rd. L32: Kirkb 9C 36
Rye Moss La. L37: Gt Alt 4N 25
Ryfields Village WA2: Warr 9E 66
Rylance Rd. WN3: Winst 2F 40
Ryland Pk. CH61: Thing 2A 88
Rylands Dr. WA2: Warr 1D 82
Rylands Hey CH49: Grea 4L 71
Rylands St. WA1: Warr 3C 82
WA8: Widnes 8L 79
Ryleys Gdns. L2: Liv 4E 4
Rylock Cl. WA1: Warr 1D 82
Rymer Gro. L4: W'ton 9F 44
Rymers Grn. L37: Form 9E 16
Rynet Ct. WA2: Warr 1D 82

S

Sabre Cl. WA7: Murd 8F 96
Sackville Rd. WA10: Windle 4F 48
Saddle Cl. L9: Aintr 2J 45
Saddlers Ri. WA7: Nort 7E 96
Saddlers Wlk. WA4: Westy 5H 83
Saddlestone Gro. L8: Liv 3D 74
Sadler's La. WA11: Windle 3B 48
Sadler St. WA8: Widnes 7M 79
Saffron Cl. WA2: Padg 8J 67
WA3: Low 2F 52
Saffron Gdns. WA9: St H 8N 49
Saffron M. L23: Thorn 5A 34
Saffron Wlk. *M31: Part* *7M 69*
(off Cross La. W.)
Sagar Fold L39: Augh 4B 28
Sage Cl. WA2: Padg 7K 67
Sage Dr. L11: Norr G 9M 45
St Aelreds Dr. WA12: Newt W 6M 51
St Agnes Rd. L4: Kirkd 1C 58
L36: Huy 7J 61
St Aidan's Cl. WN5: Bil 5A 40
St Aidan's Ct. CH43: Clau 2F 72
St Aidans Ct. WA9: Clock F 6A 64
St Aidans Dr. WA8: Widnes 2J 79
St Aidan's Gro. L36: Huy 2G 61
St Aidan's Ter. CH43: Clau 2F 72
St Aidan's Way L30: Neth 8C 34
St Alban Rd. WA5: Penk 3G 81
St Albans L6: Liv 4G 58
St Albans Cl. WA11: Hay 3H 51
St Albans Ct. L5: Liv 4B 58
St Alban's Rd. L20: Boot 7B 44
St Albans Rd. CH43: Clau 1G 72
CH44: Wall 5H 57
St Alban's Sq. L20: Boot 8B 44
St Alexander Cl. L20: Kirkd 9C 44
St Ambrose Ct. *WA4: Warr* *6C 82*
(off Boswell Av.)
St Ambrose Cft. L30: Neth 7D 34
St Ambrose Gro. L4: W'ton 3G 59
St Ambrose Rd. WA8: Widnes 7M 79
St Ambrose Way *L5: Liv* *5D 58*
(off Everton Brow)
St Andrew Rd. L4: W'ton 3G 58
St Andrews Av. L12: W Der 3C 60
St Andrews Cl. WA2: Fearn 5H 67
St Andrew's Ct. L22: Wloo 2L 43
PR8: South 9G 6
St Andrews Ct. CH43: Noct 2D 72
CH65: Ell P 3C 112
St Andrew's Dr. L36: Huy 2G 61
St Andrews Dr. L23: Blun 5J 33
St Andrews Gdns. L3: Liv 4J 5 (7D 58)
St Andrew's Gro. L30: Neth 8B 34
St Andrews Gro. WA11: St H 4L 49
St Andrew's Pl. PR8: South 9G 6
St Andrews Pl. *L17: Aig* *5H 75*
(off Normanton Av.)
St Andrew's Rd. CH43: Oxton 2H 73
CH65: Ell P 2B 112
L23: Blun 5H 33
St Andrews Rd. CH63: Beb 3N 89
L20: Boot 4B 44
St Andrew St. L3: Liv 5K 5 (8E 58)
St Andrews Vw. L33: Kirkb 5C 36
St Anne's Av. WA4: Grap 6J 83
St Anne's Av. E. WA4: Grap 6J 83
St Anne's Cl. L37: Form 7F 16
St Annes Cl. CH41: Birke 1K 73
St Anne's Cotts. *L14: Knott A* *6A 60*
(off Rudyard Cl.)
St Anne's Ct. L13: Liv 6L 59
L17: Aig 7K 75
St Annes Ct. L3: Liv 1H 5
St Annes Gdns. L17: Aig 7L 75

St Annes Gro.—Salisbury Pk.

St Annes Gro. CH41: Birke 9J 57
L17: Aig 7K 75
St Anne's Ho. *L20: Boot 8C 44*
(off University Rd.)
St Anne's Path L37: Form 7F 16
St Anne's Pl. CH41: Birke 9J 57
St Anne's Rd. L17: Aig 7L 75
L36: Huy 8J 61
L37: Form 7F 16
L39: Orm 9B 20
PR9: South 3L 7
St Annes Rd. WA8: Widnes 6L 79
St Annes Ter. CH41: Birke 9J 57
St Anne St. CH41: Birke 1J 73
(Livingstone Gdns.)
CH41: Birke 1K 73
(Robert St.)
CH41: Birke 9J 57
(St Anne's Pl.)
L3: Liv 1H 5 (5D 58)
St Annes Way CH41: Birke 1K 73
St Ann Pl. L35: Rainh 5F 62
ST ANNS 8G 48
St Ann's Rd. WA10: St H 7F 48
St Anselms Pl. WA5: Warr 8A 66
St Anthony Pl. WA2: Winw 3C 66
St Anthony's Cl. L39: Huy 2G 61
St Anthony's Gro. L30: Neth 8C 34
St Anthony's Rd. L23: Blun 6H 33
St Asaph Dr. WA5: Call 6M 65
St Asaph Gro. L30: Neth 1E 44
St Asaph Rd. CH66: Gt Sut 5K 111
St Augustine's Av. WA4: Westy 4G 82
St Augustine St. L5: Liv 4C 58
St Augustine's Way L30: Neth 7C 34
St Austell Cl. CH46: More 8J 55
WA5: Penk 5G 81
WA7: Brook 9D 96
St Austells Rd. L4: W'ton 8D 44
St Austins La. WA1: Warr 4C 82
St Barnabas Pl. WA5: Warr 2N 81
St Bartholomew Rd. L3: Liv 1F 4 (6C 58)
St Bartholomews Ct. L36: Huy 7G 60
St Bedes Cl. L39: Orm 1B 28
St Bedes Vw. WA8: Widnes 7K 79
St Bees Cl. WA10: St H 3J 49
St Benedict's Cl. WA2: Warr 1C 82
St Benedict's Gro. L36: Huy 2G 61
St Benet's Way L30: Neth 8D 34
St Bernard's Cl. L30: Neth 8C 34
St Bernards Cl. L8: Liv 1G 74
St Bernard's Dr. L30: Neth 8C 34
St Brendan's Cl. L36: Huy 2G 61
St Brides Cl. WA5: Penk 5G 80
St Bride's Rd. CH44: Wall 4K 57
St Bride St. L8: Liv 8L 5 (9E 58)
St Bridget's Cl. WA2: Fearn 6G 66
St Bridgets Cl. WA8: Widnes 2K 95
St Bridget's Gro. L30: Neth 8C 34
St Bridget's La. CH48: W Kir 7C 70
St Brigid's Cres. *L5: Liv 4B 58*
(off Silvester St.)
St Catherine's Cl. L36: Huy 8J 61
St Catherines Gdns. CH42: Tran 4K 73
St Catherine's Rd. L20: Boot 7B 44
St Chad's Dr. L32: Kirkb 9C 36
St Chads Pde. L32: Kirkb 9C 36
St Christopers Dr. L36: Huy 2G 61
St Christopher's Av. L30: Neth 7C 34
St Clair Dr. PR9: South 6M 7
St Columba's Cl. CH44: Wall 4K 57
St Cuthbert's Cl. PR9: South 5M 7
St Cuthberts Cl. L12: Crox 7C 46
St Cuthbert's Rd. PR9: South 5M 7
St Cyrils Cl. L27: N'ley 2G 77
St Cyril's Ct. L27: N'ley 2G 77
St Damian's Cft. L30: Neth 8D 34
St David Rd. CH43: Clau 2G 72
CH62: East 9F 90
St David's Cl. L35: Rainh 5F 62
St David's Dr. WA5: Call 7N 65
St Davids Dr. CH66: Gt Sut 5L 111
St David's Gro. L30: Neth 9C 34
St Davids La. CH43: Noct 3D 72
St David's Rd. L14: Knott A 4F 60
St Davids Rd. L4: W'ton 3G 58
St Domingo Gro. L5: Liv 3F 58
St Domingo Rd. L5: Liv 2D 58
St Domingo Va. L5: Liv 3E 58
St Dunstan's Gro. L30: Neth 8C 34
St Edmond's Rd. L20: Boot 8B 44
St Edmunds Ho. CH65: Ell P 1C 112
St Edmund's Rd. CH63: Beb 2M 89
St Edwards Cl. CH41: Birke 9H 57
St Edwards M. *CH41: Birke 9H 57*
(off Old Bidston Rd.)
St Elizabeth Av. L20: Boot 4B 44
St Elmo Rd. CH44: Wall 4K 57
St Elphins Cl. WA1: Warr 3D 82
St Elphin's Vw. WA4: Dares 5N 97
St Gabriel Cl. WN8: Roby M 1L 31
St Gabriel's Av. L36: Huy 7L 61
St George's Av. CH42: Tran 6K 73
WA10: Windle 5F 48
St Georges Av. CH66: Gt Sut 5L 111
St Georges Cl. WA4: App 4F 98
St Georges Ct. L31: Mag 3J 35
WA8: Widnes 8G 79
St George's Gro. CH46: More 9L 55
L30: Neth 9C 34
St George's Hall 4G 5 (7C 58)
St George's Hill L5: Liv 4E 58
St George's Mt. CH45: New B 1H 57
St George's Pk. CH45: New B 1H 57
St George's Pl. L1: Liv 4G 5 (7C 58)
PR9: South 8G 7
St George's Rd. CH45: Wall 3E 56
L36: Huy 4J 61
L37: Form 9E 16
L38: Hight 7F 24
St Georges Rd. WA10: St H 8G 48
St George's Way CH63: Thorn H 8G 89
L1: Liv 5G 5
St Gerard Cl. L5: Liv 3C 58
St Gregory's Cft. L30: Neth 7D 34
ST HELENS 7K 49
St Helens Bus Station 7K 49
St Helens Central Station (Rail) 7L 49
St Helens Cl. CH43: Clau 2H 73
WA3: Rix 6H 69
St Helens Crematorium 3F 48
St Helens Junction Station (Rail) 2B 64
St Helens Linkway L35: Rainh 8J 63
WA9: Rainh, St H 8K 49
St Helens Retail Pk. 7L 49
St Helens RLFC 8L 49
St Helens Rd. L34: Presc, Eccl P 2A 62
L39: Orm 8D 20
WA11: Rainf 9E 38
WN7: Leigh 2J 53
St Helens Theatre Royal 7K 49
St Hilary Brow CH44: Wall 5F 56
St Hilary Dr. CH45: Wall 4F 56
St Hilda's Dr. WA6: Frod 5M 107
St Hilda St. L4: W'ton 1D 58
St Hugh's Cl. CH43: Clau 2H 73
St Hugh's Ho. L20: Boot 8B 44
St Ives Cl. CH43: Clau 1G 72
St Ives Gro. L13: Liv 6L 59
St Ives Rd. CH43: Clau 2G 72
St Ives Way L26: Halew 8K 77
St James Cen. *CH41: Birke 9F 56*
(off Laird St.)
St James Cl. CH49: Grea 4L 71
L40: Westh 1G 28
WA6: Frod 5M 107
St James' Cl. L12: W Der 3M 59
St James Ct. *CH45: New B 1H 57*
(off Victoria Rd.)
St James' Ct. WA4: Warr 4C 82
St James Dr. L20: Boot 6A 44
St James Ho. L39: Augh 2B 28
St James M. L20: Boot 6A 44
St James Mt. L35: Rainh 7F 62
St James Pl. L8: Liv 1D 74
St James Rd. CH43: Birke 9F 56
CH45: New B 1H 57
L1: Liv 9J 5 (1D 74)
L35: Rainh 7F 62
L36: Huy 9J 61
WN5: Orr 8N 31
St James' Rd. L34: Eccl P, Presc 2B 62
St James St. L1: Liv 9G 4 (1C 74)
PR8: South 9G 7
St James Way *L30: Neth 7C 34*
(off St Nicholas' Dr.)
St Jerome's Way L30: Neth 7D 34
St Joans Cl. L20: Boot 5N 43
St John Av. WA4: Warr 6C 82
St Johns Av. L9: W'ton 5F 44
St Johns Brow WA7: Run 4L 95
St John's Cen. L1: Liv 5G 4 (8C 58)
St John's Cl. CH47: Meols 9E 54
St John's Ct. L22: Wloo 1K 43
WA1: Warr 1G 82
(off Grantham Av.)
St Johns Ct. PR8: Ainsd 1K 17
St John's Ho. L20: Boot 7C 44
St Johns Ho. CH65: Ell P 9C 104
St John's La. L1: Liv 4G 4 (7C 58)
St John's Pavement CH41: Birke 2K 73
St John's Pl. L22: Wloo 1K 43
St John's Rd. CH45: Wall 4E 56
CH62: East 1F 102
L20: Boot, Kirkd 8A 44
L22: Wloo 1K 43
L36: Huy 8K 61
PR8: Birkd 5M 11
St John's Sq. CH41: Birke 2K 73
L1: Liv 5G 5
St John's Ter. *L20: Boot 9A 44*
(off St John's Rd.)
St John St. CH41: Birke 2K 73
WA7: Run 4L 95
WA10: St H 1G 63
WA12: Newt W 7J 51
St Johns Vs. WA8: Widnes 6G 79
St John's Way L1: Liv 5G 5
St Joseph's Cl. L36: Huy 2G 61
WA5: Penk 3G 80
St Josephs Cl. *WA9: St H 9M 49*
(off Cleveland St.)
St Josephs Cres. L3: Liv 2H 5 (6D 58)
St Jude's Cl. L36: Huy 2G 61
St Julien Dr. L6: Liv 5G 58
St Katherines Way WA1: Warr 3E 82
St Kevin's Dr. L32: Kirkb 7C 36
St Kilda Cl. CH65: Ell P 4A 112
St Kilda's Rd. CH46: More 1M 71
St Laurence Cl. CH41: Birke 1K 73
St Laurence Dr. CH41: Birke 1K 73
St Laurence Gro. L32: Kirkb 2D 46
St Lawrence Cl. L8: Liv 4F 74
St Lawrence Rd. WA6: Frod 7L 107
St Leonard's Cl. L30: Neth 7C 34
St Lucia Rd. CH44: Wall 4K 57
St Luke's Av. WA3: Low 2E 52
St Luke's Church
(The Bombed Out Church) 7J 5 (9D 58)
St Lukes Chu. Rd. L37: Form 2C 24
(not continuous)
St Lukes Cl. L14: Knott A 3D 60
St Luke's Ct. L4: W'ton 8F 44
St Luke's Cres. WA8: Widnes 4L 79
St Luke's Dr. WN5: Orr 8N 31
St Lukes Dr. L37: Form 2C 24
St Luke's Gro. *L30: Neth 7C 34*
(off Dartmouth Dr.)
PR9: South 8K 7
St Lukes Ho. WN4: Ash M 7L 41
St Lukes Pl. L1: Liv 7H 5 (9D 58)
St Luke's Rd. L23: Crosb 7K 33
PR9: South 9J 7
WA10: St H 7G 48
St Luke's Way L36: Huy 2G 61
WA6: Frod 5L 107
St Margaret's Av. WA2: Warr 8E 66
St Margaret's Gro. L30: Neth 9B 34
St Margaret's Rd. CH47: Hoy 2B 70
St Marks Ct. CH43: Oxton 3H 73
St Marks Cres. CH66: Gt Sut 5L 111
St Mark's Gro. L30: Neth 7B 34
St Mark's Rd. L36: Huy 8K 61
St Mark's St. WA11: Hay 4C 50
St Martins Dr. CH66: Gt Sut 3J 111
St Martins Gro. L32: Kirkb 3D 46
St Martin's Ho. L20: Boot 7B 44
St Martin's La. WA7: Murd 8F 96
St Martins M. L5: Liv 5D 58
St Mary's Arc. *WA10: St H 7K 49*
(within St Mary's Mkt.)
St Mary's Av. CH44: Wall 5H 57
L4: W'ton 8F 44
WN5: Bil 7M 39
St Mary's Cl. L13: Liv 8L 59
L20: Boot 7A 44
L24: Hale 5A 94
WA4: App 1D 98
St Mary's Ct. CH49: Upton 4A 72
WA3: Low 1J 53
St Marys Ct. L25: Woolt 6E 76
WA4: Warr 4D 82
(off St Mary's St.)
St Marys Gdns. PR8: Ainsd 7M 11
St Mary's Ga. CH41: Birke 2M 73
St Mary's Grn. WA1: Warr 3D 82
St Mary's Gro. L4: W'ton 8F 44
L30: Neth 8B 34
St Mary's La. L4: W'ton 8F 44
St Mary's Mkt. WA10: St H 7K 49
St Mary's Pl. L4: W'ton 8F 44
St Mary's Rd. L19: Garst, G'dale 9N 75
L22: Wloo 1M 43
L36: Huy 7J 61
WA5: Gt San, Penk 3H 81
St Marys Rd. WA7: Hal 6B 96
WA8: Widnes 3K 95
St Mary's St. CH44: Wall 5H 57
L25: Woolt 6E 76
WA4: Warr 4D 82
St Mary's Tower
Birkenhead 2M 73
St Mathews Cl. L4: W'ton 8J 45
L36: Huy 6K 61
St Matthew's Av. L21: Lith 2B 44
St Matthews Cl. WA4: App 9E 82
St Matthews Gro. WA10: St H 1F 62
St Mawes Cl. WA8: Widnes 6H 79
St Mawes Way WA10: Windle 4E 48
St Mawgan Ct. WA2: Padg 7G 66
St Michael Rd. L39: Augh 6L 27
St Michael's Chu. Rd. L17: Aig 5G 75
St Michael's Cl. PR9: South 4L 7
WA8: Widnes 9F 78
St Michaels Cl. L17: Aig 6H 75
St Michaels Ct. L36: Huy 6J 61
St Michael's Golf Course
Widnes 9H 79
St Michael's Gro. CH46: More 9L 55
L30: Neth 8B 34
St Michaels Gro. L6: Liv 5G 59
St Michaels Hall L17: Aig 6G 75
ST MICHAEL'S HAMLET 6G 74
St Michael's Ind. Est. WA8: Widnes 9F 78
St Michaels Pk. CH62: Port S 1A 90
L39: Augh 5M 27
St Michael's Rd. L17: Aig 6G 75
L23: Blun, Crosb 6H 33
WA8: Widnes 9F 78
St Michaels Rd. WA9: St H 6K 63
St Michael's Station (Rail) 6G 74
St Michael's Vw. WA8: Widnes 9G 78
St Monica's Cl. WA4: App 9F 82
St Monica's Dr. L30: Neth 7C 34
St Nicholas' Dr. L30: Neth 7C 34
St Nicholas Gro. WA9: St H 2N 63
St Nicholas Pl. L3: Liv 5B 4 (8A 58)
(not continuous)
St Nicholas Rd. L35: Whis 8A 62
WA3: Low 1H 53
St Nicholas' Rd. CH45: Wall 4D 56
St Oswald's Av. CH43: Bid 8C 56
St Oswalds Cl. WA2: Winw 3C 66
St Oswald's Ct. L30: Neth 8E 34
St Oswald's La. L30: Neth 8E 34
St Oswald's M. CH43: Bid 8C 56
St Oswald's Rd. WN4: Ash M 9J 41
St Oswald's St. L13: Liv 7M 59
St Paschal Baylon Blvd. L16: Child 9D 60
St Patrick's Cl. L33: Kirkb 6C 36
St Patricks Cl. WA8: Widnes 2K 95
St Patrick's Dr. L30: Neth 7C 34
St Paul's Av. CH44: Wall 7L 57
St Paul's Cl. CH42: Rock F 6L 73
St Pauls Cl. L33: Kirkb 6B 36
WA7: Run 7H 95
St Pauls Gdns. CH66: Lit Sut 7G 102
St Pauls Mansion PR8: South 9F 6
St Paul's Pas. *PR8: South 9F 6*
(off St Paul's St.)
St Pauls Pl. L20: Boot 8C 44
St Paul's Rd. CH42: Rock F 6M 73
CH44: Wall 7K 57
WA8: Widnes 9K 79
St Paul's Sq. L3: Liv 3C 4 (7A 58)
(not continuous)
PR8: South 9F 6
St Paul's St. PR8: South 9F 6
St Paul St. WA10: St H 7H 49
St Paul's Vs. CH42: Rock F 6M 73
St Peter's Av. L37: Form 9D 16
St Peter's Cl. L37: Form 9D 16
WA13: Lymm 4G 84
St Peters Cl. CH60: Hesw 8N 87
L33: Kirkb 6B 36
WA9: St H 6B 50
St Peter's Ct. CH42: Rock F 7N 73
L17: Aig 4G 75
WA2: Warr 2C 82
St Peter's Ho. L20: Boot 8C 44
St Peter's M. CH42: Rock F 7A 74
St Peter's Rd. CH42: Rock F 7N 73
L9: Aintr 3H 45
PR8: Birkd 3N 11
St Peters Row L31: Mag 5J 35
St Peter's Sq. L1: Liv 7H 5
St Peter's Way CH43: Noct 4C 72
WA2: Warr 2C 82
St Peters Way WA9: St H 6B 50
St Philip's Av. L21: Lith 2B 44
St Richards Cl. L20: Kirkd 9C 44
Saints Cl. L13: Liv 7N 59
St Seiriol Gro. CH43: Clau 2G 72
St Stephen Rd. WA5: Gt San, Penk 3H 81
St Stephen's Av. WA2: Warr 6C 66
St Stephens Cl. CH60: Hesw 9C 88
L25: Gate 3G 76
PR9: Banks 1E 8
St Stephen's Ct. CH42: Tran 7H 73
St Stephen's Gro. L30: Neth 8C 34
St Stephen's Pl. L3: Liv 2F 4 (6C 58)
St Stephen's Rd. CH42: Tran 6H 73
L38: Hight 8F 24
St Teresa's Cl. L11: Norr G 8L 45
St Teresa's Rd. WA10: St H 6G 48
St Thomas Cl. WA10: St H 4G 48
WN4: Ash M 9K 41
St Thomas Ct. WA8: Widnes 7G 79
St Thomas More Dr. PR8: Ainsd 8L 11
St Thomas's Ct. WN8: Uph 5M 31
St Thomas's Dr. L30: Neth 8C 34
St Thomas' Vw. CH65: Whit 1N 111
St Vincent Rd. CH43: Clau 2G 72
CH44: Wall 4K 57
WA5: Penk 3H 81
St Vincents Cl. L12: W Der 3C 60
St Vincent St. L3: Liv 4J 5 (7D 58)
St Vincent's Way PR8: Birkd 2N 11
St Vincent Way L3: Liv 4J 5
St Werburgh's Sq. CH41: Birke 2L 73
St Wilfreds Rd. WA8: Widnes 4A 80
St Wilfrid's Dr. WA4: Grap 7K 83
St William Rd. L23: Thorn 6A 34
St William Way L23: Thorn 5A 34
St Winifred Rd. CH45: New B 2H 57
L35: Rainh 4E 62
St Wyburn Ct. *PR8: Birkd 1M 11*
(off Westcliffe Rd.)
Saker St. L4: W'ton 2E 58
Salacre Cl. CH49: Upton 4B 72
Salacre Cres. CH49: Upton 4A 72
Salacre La. CH49: Upton 3A 72
Salacre Ter. *CH49: Upton 3A 72*
(off Salacre La.)
Salcombe Dr. L25: Hunts X 9F 76
PR9: South 2M 7
Salem Vw. CH43: Oxton 5H 73
Salerno Dr. L36: Huy 5H 61
Salesbury Way WN3: Wigan 1J 41
Saleswood Av.
WA10: Ec'stn 7D 48
Salford Ct. PR8: Ainsd 9J 11
Salford Rd. PR8: Ainsd 9J 11
Salhouse Gdns. WA9: St H 3G 63
Saline Cl. L14: Knott A 3E 60
Salisbury Av. CH48: W Kir 6B 70
L30: Neth 1F 44
Salisbury Cl. CH66: Gt Sut 5L 111
Salisbury Ct. CH42: Rock F 7L 73
Salisbury Dr. CH62: New F 9A 74
Salisbury Hall L18: Moss H 6L 75
Salisbury Ho. L20: Boot 6A 44
Salisbury Pk. L16: Child 3B 76

Salisbury Rd.—School La.

Salisbury Rd. CH45: New B 1G **57**
L15: Wavtr 1J **75**
L19: G'dale 1M **91**
L20: Boot 6A **44**
WA11: Hay 2G **50**
WN4: Ash M 6J **41**
Salisbury St. CH41: Birke 3K **73**
L3: Liv 1J **5** (5E **58**)
L34: Presc 3A **62**
PR9: South 9M **7**
WA1: Warr 2E **82**
WA3: Golb 2B **52**
WA7: Run 6K **95**
WA8: Widnes 8L **79**
WA10: St H 7K **49**
Salisbury Ter. L15: Wavtr 9L **59**
Salkeld Av. WN4: Ash M 8H **41**
Sallowfields WN5: Orr 7N **31**
Sally's La. PR9: South 5M **7**
Salop St. L4: W'ton 1E **58**
Saltash Cl. L26: Halew 8J **77**
WA7: Brook 9D **96**
Saltburn Rd. CH45: Wall 4D **56**
Saltergate Rd. L8: Liv 4F **74**
Saltersgate CH66: Gt Sut 3L **111**
Salthouse Quay L3: Liv 7D **4** (9B **58**)
Saltney St. L3: Liv 5A **58**
Salton Gdns. WA5: Warr 1N **81**
Saltpit La. L31: Mag 2K **35**
Saltwood Dr. WA7: Brook 1E **108**
Saltworks Cl. WA6: Frod 4N **107**
Salvia Way L33: Kirkb 6B **36**
Salvin Cl. WN4: Ash M 8M **41**
Salwick Cl. PR9: South 2L **7**
Samaria Av. CH62: New F 9B **74**
Sambourn Fold PR8: Ainsd 9G **11**
Samphire Gdns. WA9: Bold 2D **64**
Samuel St. WA5: Warr 4N **81**
WA9: St H 2G **62**
Samwoods Ho. *WN4: Ash M* *6J **41***
(off Whitledge Grn.)
Sanbec Gdns. WA8: Cron 3G **78**
Sandalwood L23: Crosb 7K **33**
WA7: Nort 6D **96**
Sandalwood Cl. L6: Liv 4G **58**
WA2: Warr 7E **66**
Sandalwood Dr. CH43: Noct 4D **72**
Sandalwood Gdns. WA9: St H 2M **63**
Sandbanks CH47: Hoy 1B **70**
Sandbeck St. L8: Liv 5E **74**
Sandbrook Ct. CH46: More 9M **55**
Sandbrook Gdns. WN5: Orr 7N **31**
Sandbrook La. CH46: More 9M **55**
Sandbrook Rd. L25: Gate 9E **60**
PR8: Ainsd 2K **17**
WN5: Orr 7M **31**
Sandbrook Way PR8: Ainsd 2J **17**
Sandcliffe Rd. CH45: Wall 1E **56**
Sandcross Cl. WN5: Orr 8N **31**
Sandeman Rd. L4: W'ton 1J **59**
Sanderling Dr. PR9: Banks 2E **8**
Sanderling Rd. L33: Kirkb 8E **36**
WA12: Newt W 6L **51**
Sanders Hey Cl. WA7: Brook 1C **108**
Sanderson Cl. WA5: Gt San 2F **80**
Sandfield L36: Huy 7H **61**
Sandfield Av. CH47: Meols 8E **54**
Sandfield Cl. CH63: H Beb 1K **89**
L12: W Der 4A **60**
WA3: Low 2F **52**
Sandfield Cotts. L39: Augh 2B **28**
Sandfield Ct. WA6: Frod 6L **107**
Sandfield Cres. L35: Whis 4D **62**
WA10: St H *7J **49***
(off Liverpool Rd.)
Sandfield Golf Course 9L **113**
Sandfield Hey *L12: W Der* *3A **60***
(off Sandfield Pk. E.)
SANDFIELD PARK 4N **59**
Sandfield Pk. CH60: Hesw 7L **87**
L39: Augh 2B **28**
Sandfield Pk. E. L12: W Der 3A **60**
Sandfield Pl. L20: Boot 6A **44**
Sandfield Rd. CH45: New B 2H **57**
CH49: Wdchu 6B **72**
CH63: H Beb 1K **89**
L20: Boot 8C **44**
L25: Gate 4F **76**
WA10: Ec'stn 5D **48**
Sandfields WA6: Frod 6L **107**
Sandfield Ter. CH45: New B 2H **57**
Sandfield Wlk. L13: W Der 5N **59**
Sandford Dr. L31: Mag 1J **35**
Sandford Rd. WN5: Orr 7M **31**
Sandford St. CH41: Birke 1L **73**
Sandforth Cl. L12: W Der 3M **59**
Sandforth Ct. L13: W Der 4M **59**
Sandforth Rd. L12: W Der 4M **59**
Sandgate Cl. L24: Speke 3F **92**
Sandham Gro. CH60: Hesw 7C **88**
Sandham Rd. L24: Speke 3L **93**
Sandhead St. L7: Liv 9J **59**
Sandhey Rd. CH47: Meols 9D **54**
Sandheys CH64: P'gte 5C **100**
Sandheys Av. L22: Wloo 1J **43**
Sandheys Cl. L4: W'ton 2D **58**
Sandheys Dr. PR9: South 6L **7**
Sandheys Gro. L22: Wloo 9J **33**
Sandheys Rd. CH45: New B 2H **57**
Sandheys Ter. L22: Wloo 1J **43**
Sandhills L38: Hight 9F **24**
Sandhills, The CH46: Leas 6M **55**
Sandhills Bus. Pk. L5: Kirkd 3B **58**
(not continuous)
Sandhills La. L5: Kirkd 2A **58**
Sandhills Station (Rail) 3B **58**
Sandhills Vw. CH45: Wall 4D **56**
Sandhill Ter. WA4: Warr 5F **82**
Sandhurst L23: Blun 7J **33**
Sandhurst Cl. L21: Sea 3M **43**
L37: Form 3C **24**
Sandhurst Dr. L10: Aintr 9K **35**
Sandhurst Rd. L26: Halew 1L **93**
L35: Rainh 4D **62**
Sandhurst St. L17: Aig 5G **74**
WA4: Westy 5G **83**
Sandhurst Way L31: Lydi 7G **27**
Sandicroft Cl. WA3: Birchw 4K **67**
Sandicroft Rd. L12: Crox 8D **46**
San Diego Dr. WA5: Gt San 2K **81**
Sandilands Gro. L38: Hight 9F **24**
Sandino St. L8: Liv 2E **74**
Sandiway CH47: Meols 8E **54**
CH63: Brom 9B **90**
L35: Whis 7A **62**
L36: Huy 8K **61**
Sandiway Av. WA8: Widnes 7D **78**
Sandiway Ct. PR9: South 7K **7**
Sandiways L31: Mag 2K **35**
Sandiways Av. L30: Neth 9F **34**
Sandiways Rd. CH45: Wall 3E **56**
Sandlea Pk. CH48: W Kir 6B **70**
Sandlewood Gro. L33: Kirkb 7D **36**
Sandmoor Pl. WA13: Lymm 6G **85**
Sandon Cl. L35: Rainh 5E **62**
Sandon Ct. *L22: Wloo* *1K **43***
(off Sandon St.)
Sandon Cres. CH64: Lit N 9E **100**
Sandon Gro. WA11: Rainf 5D **38**
Sandon Ind. Est. L5: Kirkd 3A **58**
Sandon Lodge *L21: Sea* *4N **43***
(off Seaforth Rd.)
Sandon Pl. WA8: Widnes 7N **79**
Sandon Prom. CH44: Wall 5L **57**
Sandon Rd. CH44: Wall 5L **57**
PR8: Birkd 5M **11**
Sandon St. L8: Liv 8L **5** (9E **58**)
L22: Wloo 1K **43**
Sandon Way L5: Kirkd 3A **58**
Sandown Av. L14: Brd G 7B **60**
Sandown Cl. WA3: Cul 6N **53**
WA7: Run 9M **95**
Sandown Ct. L15: Wavtr 9L **59**
PR9: South 7H **7**
Sandown La. L15: Wavtr 9L **59**
SANDOWN PARK 8L **59**
Sandown Pk. Rd. L10: Aintr 8K **35**
Sandown Rd. L15: Wavtr 8L **59**
L21: Sea 3M **43**
Sandpiper Cl. CH49: Upton 2L **71**
WA12: Newt W 6L **51**
Sandpiper Gro. L26: Halew 7J **77**
Sandpipers Ct. CH47: Hoy 1C **70**
L22: Wloo *9J **33***
(off Bridge Rd.)
Sandra Dr. WA12: Newt W 7M **51**
Sandridge Rd. CH45: New B 2H **57**
CH61: Pens 2N **87**
Sandringham Av. CH47: Meols 9D **54**
L22: Wloo 2L **43**
WA6: Hel 2E **114**
Sandringham Cl. CH47: Meols 1D **70**
CH62: New F 9N **73**
L33: Kirkb 6C **36**
Sandringham Ct. *PR9: South* *7G **7***
(off Gordon St.)
WA3: Low *3F **52***
(off Thurlow)
Sandringham Dr. CH45: New B 1G **57**
L17: Aig 4G **74**
WA5: Gt San 4L **81**
WA9: St H 3M **63**
Sandringham Gdns. CH65: Ell P 3B **112**
Sandringham Ho. L39: Augh 2B **28**
Sandringham M. CH47: Meols 1D **70**
Sandringham Rd. L13: Liv 3K **59**
L22: Wloo 2L **43**
L31: Mag 3H **35**
L37: Form 3E **24**
PR8: Ainsd 9J **11**
PR8: Birkd 3L **11**
WA8: Widnes 4K **79**
Sandrock Cl. CH45: New B 2H **57**
Sandrock Rd. CH45: New B 2H **57**
Sands Rd. L18: Moss H 4L **75**
Sandstone CH45: Wall 4J **57**
Sandstone Cl. L35: Rainh 8F **62**
Sandstone Dr. CH48: W Kir 6F **70**
L35: Whis 4D **62**
Sandstone M. WA8: Widnes 4H **79**
Sandstone Rd. WN3: Winst 1G **40**
Sandstone Rd. E. L13: Liv 5M **59**
Sandstone Rd. W. L13: Liv 5L **59**
Sandstone Wlk. CH60: Hesw 8A **88**
Sandwash Bus. Pk. WA11: Rainf 7E **38**
Sandwash Cl. WA11: Rainf 7E **38**
Sandway Cres. L11: Norr G 8M **45**
Sandwith Cl. WN3: Wigan 1K **41**
Sandy Brow La. L33: Kirkb 3J **47**
WA3: Croft 8F **52**
Sandy Cl. WN8: Newb 3C **22**
Sandy Ct. WN7: Leigh 1H **53**
Sandy Grn. L9: Aintr 4H **45**
Sandy Gro. L13: Liv 3L **59**
Sandy Ho. L21: Sea 3M **43**
Sandy Knowe L15: Wavtr 8M **59**
Sandy La. CH45: Wall 3E **56**
CH48: W Kir 8C **70**
CH60: Hesw 6A **88**
CH61: Irby 9K **71**
CH64: Lit N 7G **100**
CW9: Ant 6L **99**
L9: Aintr 4G **45**
L13: Liv 3L **59**
L21: Sea 3N **43**
(not continuous)
L31: Lydi 6G **27**
L31: Mell 6M **35**
L38: Hight 8G **24**
L39: Augh 6N **27**
L40: H'wood 1G **15**
L40: Lath 6G **21**
WA2: Warr 6C **66**
(not continuous)
WA3: Croft 1H **67**
WA3: Golb 2A **52**
WA3: Low 1H **53**
WA4: Stockt H 8E **82**
WA5: Penk 4J **81**
WA6: Hel 3E **114**
WA7: Pres B 9H **97**
WA7: Run, West P 8G **95**
WA8: Cron, Widnes 3G **79**
WA8: Widnes 2C **80**
WA11: St H 1H **49**
WA13: Lymm 3H **85**
WN5: Orr 8N **31**
WN8: Newb 4C **22**
WN8: Skel 3A **30**
(not continuous)
Sandy La. Cen. WN8: Skel 3A **30**
Sandy La. Nth. CH61: Irby 9K **71**
Sandy La. W. WA2: Warr 6B **66**
SANDYMOOR 4F **96**
Sandymoor La. WA7: Nort 3F **96**
(Kings Ct.)
WA7: Nort 4F **96**
(Lady Richeld Cl.)
Sandymount Dr. CH45: Wall 2G **56**
CH63: Beb 3M **89**
Sandy Rd. L21: Sea 2M **43**
Sandyville Gro. L4: W'ton 1K **59**
Sandyville Rd. L4: W'ton 1J **59**
Sandywarps M44: Irlam 1N **69**
Sandy Way CH43: Oxton 3G **72**
L40: H'wood 2H **15**
Sanfield Cl. L39: Orm 7C **20**
Sangness Dr. PR8: South 3D **12**
SANKEY BRIDGES 4M **81**
Sankey Bridges Ind. Est.
WA5: Gt San 4L **81**
Sankey for Penketh Station (Rail) 2H **81**
Sankey Grn. WA5: Warr 3N **81**
Sankey La. WA4: Hatt 6A **98**
Sankey Mnr. WA5: Gt San 2H **81**
Sankey Rd. L31: Mag 4J **35**
WA11: Hay 5B **50**
Sankey St. L1: Liv 8H **5** (9D **58**)
WA1: Warr 3B **82**
WA3: Golb 2B **52**
WA8: Widnes 1K **95**
WA9: St H 8N **49**
WA12: Newt W 7J **51**
Sankey Valley Country Pk. 6C **50**
Sankey Valley Country Pk. Vis. Cen. 4A **50**
Sankey Valley Ind. Est.
WA12: Newt W 8J **51**
Sankey Valley Pk. 2N **81**
Sankey Way WA5: Gt San, Warr 3J **81**
Santa Rosa Blvd. WA5: Gt San 1J **81**
Santon Av. L13: Liv 4K **59**
Santon Dr. WA3: Low 2F **52**
Sanvino Av. PR8: Ainsd 9K **11**
Sapphire Dr. L33: Kirkb 6C **36**
Sapphire St. L13: Liv 8L **59**
Sarah's Cft. L30: Neth 8D **34**
Sark Av. CH65: Ell P 4N **111**
Sark Rd. L13: Liv 5L **59**
Sarsfield Av. WA3: Low 2E **52**
Sartfield Cl. L16: Child 9C **60**
Sarum Rd. L25: Gate 1E **76**
Sarus Ct. WA7: Manor P 3D **96**
Satinwood Cl. WN4: Ash M 8H **41**
Satinwood Cres. L31: Mell 8M **35**
SAUGHALL MASSIE 2K **71**
Saughall Massie La. CH49: Upton 3M **71**
Saughall Massie Rd. CH48: W Kir 5E **70**
CH49: Grea, Upton 5E **70**
Saughall Rd. CH46: More 1K **71**
CH49: Upton 1K **71**
Saunby Cl. L19: Garst 2A **92**
Saunders Av. L35: Presc 5A **62**
Saundersfoot Cl. WA5: Call 7N **65**
Saunders St. PR9: South 6G **7**
Saunderton Cl. WA11: Hay 3E **50**
Savannah Pl. WA5: Gt San 1L **81**
Saville Av. WA5: Warr 1A **82**
Saville Rd. L13: Liv 7N **59**
L31: Lydi 9H **27**
Savon Hook L37: Form 3G **25**
Savoylands Cl. L17: Aig 6H **75**
Sawdon Av. PR8: South 2D **12**
Sawley Av. WA3: Low 1E **52**
Sawley Cl. WA3: Cul 8N **53**
WA7: Murd 8G **96**
Sawpit La. L36: Huy 7K **61**
Sawpit St. WA13: Warb 1N **85**
WA14: Dun M 1N **85**
Sawyer Dr. WN4: Ash M 8M **41**
Saxby Rd. L14: Knott A 4E **60**
Saxenholme PR8: Birkd 1M **11**
Saxon Cl. L6: Liv 5G **58**
WA4: App 2C **98**
Saxon Ct. WA10: St H 5H **49**
Saxonia Rd. L4: W'ton 8G **44**
Saxon Lodge PR8: Birkd 1M **11**
Saxon Rd. CH46: More 8N **55**
CH47: Meols 9D **54**
L23: Crosb 8K **33**
PR8: Birkd 1M **11**
WA7: Run 5L **95**
Saxon Ter. WA8: Widnes 7L **79**
Saxon Way CH66: Gt Sut 5L **111**
L33: Kirkb 5C **36**
Saxony Rd. L7: Liv 4N **5** (7F **58**)
(not continuous)
Sayce St. WA8: Widnes 7L **79**
Scafell Av. WA2: Warr 6D **66**
Scafell Cl. CH62: East 3C **102**
CH66: Ell P 7L **103**
Scafell Lawn L27: N'ley 5L **77**
Scafell Rd. WA11: St H 2J **49**
Scafell Wlk. L27: N'ley 4L **77**
(not continuous)
Scaffold La. L38: Ince B 6H **25**
Scape La. L23: Crosb 6L **33**
Scarborough Dr. WA12: Newt W 8J **51**
Scargreen Av. L11: Norr G 7L **45**
SCARISBRICK 7J **13**
Scarisbrick Av. L21: Lith 3A **44**
PR8: South 8F **6**
WN8: Parb 3F **22**
Scarisbrick Bus. Pk. L40: Scar 2A **20**
Scarisbrick Cl. L31: Mag 9K **27**
Scarisbrick Ct. PR8: South 9H **7**
Scarisbrick Cres. L11: Norr G 7J **45**
Scarisbrick Dr. L11: Norr G 7J **45**
Scarisbrick Ho. *L39: Orm* *8D **20***
(off Abbotsford)
Scarisbrick Marina L40: Scar 1L **19**
Scarisbrick New Rd. PR8: South 9H **7**
Scarisbrick Pk. L40: Scar 8M **13**
Scarisbrick Pl. L11: Norr G 8J **45**
Scarisbrick Rd. L11: Norr G 8J **45**
WA11: Rainf 4C **38**
Scarisbrick St. L39: Orm 7C **20**
PR9: South 8G **7**
Scarsdale Rd. L11: Norr G 9L **45**
SCARTH HILL 2F **28**
Scarth Hill La. L39: Augh, Orm 3C **28**
L40: Westh 2F **28**
Scarth Pk. WN8: Skel 5F **30**
Sceptre Cl. WA12: Newt W 7J **51**
Sceptre Rd. L11: Crox 6A **46**
Sceptre Wlk. L11: Crox 7A **46**
Scholars' Ct. *CH64: Nest* *6E **100***
(off Cross St.)
Scholars Grn. La. WA13: Lymm 5F **84**
Scholes, The WA10: St H 2E **62**
Scholes Cft. *WA9: St H* *2G **62***
(off Scholes La.)
Scholes La. WA9: St H 2E **62**
WA10: St H 2E **62**
Scholes Pk. WA10: St H 2E **62**
Schomberg St. L6: Liv 1N **5** (6F **58**)
School Av. CH64: Lit N 8F **100**
L37: Form 1F **24**
School Brow WA1: Warr 3D **82**
WN5: Bil 6A **40**
School Cl. CH46: More 8N **55**
L27: N'ley 1G **77**
L39: Augh 3N **27**
PR8: Birkd 4A **12**
School Dr. WA13: Lymm 3J **85**
WN5: Bil 6A **40**
Schoolfield Cl. CH49: Wdchu 6B **72**
Schoolfield Rd.
CH49: Wdchu 6B **72**
School Hill CH60: Hesw 8N **87**
School Ho. Grn. L39: Orm 8D **20**
School Ho. Gro. L40: Burs 9H **15**
SCHOOL ISLAND 2A **30**
School La. CH2: Elt 2L **113**
CH43: Bid 8C **56**
CH44: Wall 4E **56**
CH45: Wall 5E **56**
CH47: Hoy 1C **70**
(not continuous)
CH47: Meols 8E **54**
CH61: Thurs 1J **87**
CH62: New F 9A **74**
CH63: H Beb 1K **89**
CH64: Lit N 8F **100**
CH64: Nest 4H **101**
CH64: P'gte 5B **100**
CH66: Chil T 5E **102**
L1: Liv 6F **4** (8C **58**)
L10: Aintr 9J **35**
L21: Lith 2A **44**
L21: Sea 3N **43**
L25: Woolt 9E **76**
L31: Mag 1M **35**
L31: Mell 6M **35**
L34: Know 4E **46**

School La. L35: Rainh 7J **63**	**Seaforth Nature Reserve** 3J **43**	**Sefton St.** L3: Liv 2C **74**
(not continuous)	**Seaforth Rd.** L21: Sea 5N **43**	L8: Liv 2C **74**
L36: Huy 7L **61**	**Seaforth Va. Nth.** L21: Sea 4N **43**	L21: Lith 2A **44**
L37: Form 1F **24**	**Seaforth Va. W.** L21: Sea 4N **43**	(not continuous)
L39: Down 1E **26**	**Seagram Cl.** L9: Aintr 2H **45**	PR8: South 2A **12**
L40: Burs, Lath 9J **15**	**Sealand Av.** L37: Form 2D **24**	WA12: Newt W 7H **51**
L40: Westh 2H **29**	**Sealand Cl.** L37: Form 2D **24**	**SEFTON TOWN** 7C **34**
M44: Cad 4K **69**	WA2: Padg 9F **66**	**Sefton Vw.** L21: Lith 2A **44**
WA3: Ris 4C **68**	**Sea La.** WA7: Run 5N **95**	L23: Crosb 7N **33**
WA3: Rix 7G **68**	**Sealy Cl.** CH63: Spit 6N **89**	WN5: Orr 7N **31**
WA4: H Whi 9E **98**	**Seaman Rd.** L15: Wavtr 1K **75**	**Segar's La.** L39: Hals 1M **17**
WA6: Frod 7M **107**	**Seaport St.** L8: Liv 2G **74**	PR8: Ainsd 9K **11**
WA6: Manl 8K **115**	**Sea Rd.** CH45: Wall 1F **56**	**Seiont Ho.** L8: Liv 3E **74**
WA7: Hal 7B **96**	**Seascale Av.** WA10: St H 1E **62**	**Seized! Gallery** 7D **4** (9B **58**)
WA8: Bold H 1A **80**	**Seasons, The** WA7: Run 6J **95**	**Selborne** L35: Whis 7C **62**
WN4: Garsw 8E **40**	**Seath Av.** WA9: St H 6A **50**	**Selborne Cl.** L8: Liv 1F **74**
WN8: Roby M 1L **31**	**Seathwaite Cl.** L23: Blun 8H **33**	CH45: New B 9M **5** (1E **74**)
WN8: Skel 2A **30**	WA7: Beech 1A **108**	L20: Boot 8A **44**
WN8: Uph 5M **31**	**Seathwaite Cres.** L33: Kirkb 7B **36**	**Selbourne Cl.** CH49: Wdchu 5C **72**
School Rd. CH65: Ell P 9N **103**	**Seaton Cl.** L12: Crox 7E **46**	**Selby Cl.** WA7: Nort 3G **97**
L38: Hight 8F **24**	**Seaton Gro.** WA9: St H 3G **62**	WA10: St H 8G **49**
WA2: Warr 8D **66**	**Seaton Pk.** WA7: Nort 4G **96**	**Selby Dr.** L37: Form 2H **25**
School St. WA3: Golb 2B **52**	**Seaton Pl.** WN8: Skel 1B **30**	**Selby Grn.** CH66: Lit Sut 9G **103**
WA4: Warr 4C **82**	**Seaton Rd.** CH42: Tran 4J **73**	**Selby Gro.** L36: Huy 6M **61**
WA11: Hay 4B **50**	CH45: Wall 3G **57**	**Selby Pl.** WN8: Skel 1A **30**
WA12: Newt W 7K **51**	**Seaton Way** PR9: South 2M **7**	**Selby Rd.** L9: W'ton 4F **44**
WN4: Ash M 6M **41**	**Seattle Cl.** WA5: Gt San 1K **81**	**Selby St.** CH45: Wall 4H **57**
School Ter. WA3: Golb 2B **52**	**Sea Vw.** CH64: Lit N 9E **100**	WA5: Warr 3N **81**
School Way L24: Speke 4F **92**	**Seaview** CH47: Hoy 1C **70**	(not continuous)
WA8: Widnes 5N **79**	**Seaview Av.** CH45: Wall 4G **57**	**Seldon St.** L6: Liv 2N **5** (6G **58**)
Schooner Cl. WA7: Murd 9F **96**	CH61: Irby 1L **87**	**Select Security Stadium** 8J **79**
Schubert Cl. CH66: Gt Sut 1K **111**	CH62: East 9G **90**	**Selina Rd.** L4: W'ton 8E **44**
Schwartzman Dr. PR9: Banks 1E **8**	**Seaview La.** CH61: Irby 1L **87**	**Selkirk Av.** CH62: East 2D **102**
Science Pk. Nth. WA3: Birchw 3L **67**	**Sea Vw. Rd.** L20: Boot 6N **43**	WA4: Westy 5H **83**
Science Pk. Sth. WA3: Ris 4L **67**	**Seaview Rd.** CH45: Wall 3G **57**	WN4: Garsw 7F **40**
Science Rd. L24: Speke 3G **93**	**Seaview Ter.** L22: Wloo 1J **43**	**Selkirk Cl.** CH66: Lit Sut 9E **102**
Scilly Cl. CH65: Ell P 4A **112**	**Seawood Gro.** CH46: More 1L **71**	**Selkirk Dr.** WA10: Ec'stn 5E **48**
Scone Cl. L11: Crox 7A **46**	**Secker Av.** WA4: Warr 6E **82**	**Selkirk Rd.** L13: Liv 6L **59**
Score, The WA9: St H 3K **63**	**Secker Cres.** WA4: Warr 6E **82**	**Sellar St.** L4: Kirkd 2D **58**
(not continuous)	**Second Av.** CH43: Bid 2B **72**	**Selsdon Rd.** L22: Wloo 9J **33**
Scorecross WA9: St H 9L **49**	L9: Aintr 4K **45**	**Selsey Cl.** L7: Liv 9G **59**
Score La. L16: Child 8A **60**	(First Av.)	**Selside** WN3: Wigan 1K **41**
Scoresby Rd. CH46: Leas 6B **56**	L9: Aintr 3J **45**	**Selside Lawn** L27: N'ley 5L **77**
Scorpio Cl. L14: Knott A 4E **60**	(Third Av.)	(off Selside Wlk.)
Scorton St. L6: Liv 4H **59**	L23: Crosb 7K **33**	**Selside Wlk.** L27: N'ley 5L **77**
Scotchbarn La. L34: Presc 3B **62**	L35: Rainh 5E **62**	**Selston Cl.** CH63: Spit 5N **89**
L35: Presc 3B **62**	WA7: Pal F 7B **96**	**Selworthy Dr.** WA4: Thel 5L **83**
Scoter Rd. L33: Kirkb 9D **36**	**Sedbergh Av.** L10: Aintr 8H **35**	**Selworthy Grn.** L16: Child 2B **76**
Scotia Av. CH62: New F 1A **108**	**Sedbergh Gro.** WA7: Beech 1A **108**	**Selworthy Rd.** PR8: Birkd 3K **11**
L30: Neth 1D **44**	**Sedbergh Rd.** CH44: Wall 4F **56**	(not continuous)
Scotia Rd. L13: Liv 5M **59**	**Sedburgh Gro.** L36: Huy 6G **60**	**Selwyn Cl.** WA8: Widnes 5A **80**
Scotia Wlk. WA3: Low 2G **52**	**Sedburn Rd.** L32: Kirkb 3E **46**	WA12: Newt W 5K **51**
Scotland Rd. L3: Liv 2G **4** (6C **58**)	**Seddon Cl.** WA10: Ec'stn 7C **48**	**Selwyn Jones Sports Cen.** 4L **51**
L5: Liv 5C **58**	**Seddon Pl.** WN8: Skel 1B **30**	**Selwyn St.** L4: Kirkd 9D **44**
WA1: Warr 3C **82**	**Seddon Rd.** L19: Garst 1A **92**	**Senate Bus. Pk.** L30: Neth 2E **44**
Scott Av. L35: Whis 6C **62**	WA10: St H 1E **62**	**Senator Point** L33: Know I 2G **46**
L36: Huy 8L **61**	**Seddons Ct.** L34: Presc 3A **62**	**Senator Rd.** WA9: St H 2G **63**
WA8: Widnes 8J **79**	**Seddon St.** L1: Liv 7F **4** (9C **58**)	**Seneschal Ct.** WA7: Pal F 9A **96**
WA9: Sut M 6K **63**	WA10: St H 3J **49**	**Sennen Cl.** WA7: Brook 1D **108**
Scott Cl. L4: W'ton 2E **58**	**Sedgefield Cl.** CH46: More 9A **56**	**Sennen Rd.** L32: Kirkb 2D **46**
L31: Mag 2J **35**	**Sedgefield Rd.** CH46: More 9A **56**	**Sentinel Way** L30: Neth 2F **44**
Scott Dr. L39: Orm 6D **20**	**Sedgeley Wlk.** L36: Huy 4K **61**	**Sephton Av.** WA3: Cul 7M **53**
Scotton Av. CH66: Lit Sut 9G **103**	**Sedgemoor Rd.** L11: Norr G 7K **45**	**Sephton Dr.** L39: Orm 6D **20**
Scott Rd. WA3: Low 1E **52**	**Sedgewick Cres.** WA5: Burtw 3G **65**	**Serenade Rd.** L6: Liv 4H **59**
Scotts Pl. CH41: Birke 1F **72**	**Sedley St.** L6: Liv 3G **59**	**Sergeant Dr.** WA1: Padg 1G **83**
Scotts Quays CH41: Birke 8L **57**	**Sedum Gro.** L33: Kirkb 6B **36**	**Sergeant Rd.** L12: W Der 2C **60**
Scott St. CH45: Wall 4H **57**	**Seeds La.** L9: Aintr 2H **45**	**Sergrim Rd.** L36: Huy 6G **61**
L20: Boot 5A **44**	**Seeley Av.** CH41: Birke 1G **72**	**Serin Cl.** L14: Knott A 3E **60**
PR9: South 8M **7**	**Seel Rd.** L36: Huy 7K **61**	WA12: Newt W 7L **51**
WA2: Warr 2C **82**	**Seel St.** L1: Liv 6G **4** (8C **58**)	**Serinhall Dr.** L9: Faz 6L **45**
Scott Wlk. WA12: Newt W 9L **51**	**SEFTON** 4E **34**	**Serpentine, The** L19: G'dale 8M **75**
Scribe Pl. M44: Irlam 3L **69**	**Sefton Av.** L21: Lith 3A **44**	L23: Blun 7G **32**
Scroggins La. M31: Part 5M **69**	WA8: Widnes 5K **79**	L39: Augh 4B **28**
Sculthorpe Cl. WA10: St H 7F **48**	WN5: Orr 7N **31**	**Serpentine Nth., The** L23: Blun 7G **32**
Scythes, The CH49: Grea 4K **71**	**Sefton Bus. Pk.** L30: Neth 2F **44**	**Serpentine Rd.** CH44: Wall 4J **57**
L30: Neth 7G **34**	(not continuous)	**Serpentine Sth., The** L23: Blun 7H **33**
Scythia Cl. CH62: New F 8B **74**	**Sefton Cl.** L32: Kirkb 8A **36**	**Serpentine Wlk.** WA12: Newt W 2M **51**
Seabank Av. CH44: Wall 4J **57**	WN5: Orr 7N **31**	**Servia Rd.** L21: Lith 3A **44**
Seabank Cott. CH47: Meols 7F **54**	**Sefton Dr.** L8: Liv 3H **75**	**Servia Cl.** L22: Wloo 9J **33**
Seabank Ct. CH48: W Kir 7B **70**	L10: Aintr 9K **35**	**Servite Cl.** L25: Woolt 8G **76**
Seabank Rd. CH44: Wall 1H **57**	L23: Thorn 4N **33**	**Servite Ho.** L17: Aig 4G **74**
CH45: New B, Wall 1H **57**	L31: Mag 3F **34**	**Sessions Rd.** L4: Kirkd 1D **58**
CH60: Hesw 9M **87**	L32: Kirkb 8A **36**	**Seth Powell Way** L36: Huy 3G **61**
PR9: South 7G **7**	**Sefton Fold Dr.** WN5: Bil 6N **39**	**Seven Acre Rd.** L23: Thorn 6A **34**
Seabury St. WA4: Westy 5H **83**	**Sefton Fold Gdns.** WN5: Bil 6N **39**	**Seven Acres La.** CH61: Thing 1A **88**
Seacole Cl. L8: Liv 2G **75**	**Sefton Gdns.** L39: Augh 5B **28**	**Sevenoak Gro.** L35: Tar G 1M **77**
SEACOMBE 8K **57**	**Sefton Gro.** L17: Aig 4H **75**	**Sevenoaks Av.** PR8: Ainsd 9H **11**
Seacombe Dr. CH66: Gt Sut 2K **111**	**Sefton Ho.** L9: Aintr 3G **44**	**Sevenoaks Cl.** L5: Liv 4D **58**
Seacombe Prom. CH44: Wall 5L **57**	L40: Burs 2K **21**	**Seven Row** CH64: Lit N 9E **100**
(not continuous)	**Sefton La.** L31: Mag 3F **34**	**Seventh Av.** L9: Aintr 3J **45**
Seacombe Vw. CH44: Wall 7L **57**	**Sefton La. Ind. Est.** L31: Mag 3F **34**	(Lakes Rd.)
Sea Ct. CH45: Wall 2F **56**	**Sefton Mill Ct.** L29: Seft 4E **34**	L9: Aintr 3J **45**
Seacroft Cl. L14: Knott A 3E **60**	**Sefton Mill La.** L29: Seft 4E **34**	(Sixth Av.)
Seacroft Cres. PR9: South 2N **7**	**Sefton Mills** L29: Seft 4E **34**	**Severn Cl.** WA2: Warr 7F **66**
Seacroft Rd. L14: Knott A 3E **60**	**Sefton Moss La.** L30: Neth 8C **34**	WA8: Widnes 5B **80**
Seafarers Dr. L25: Gate 4E **76**	**Sefton Moss Vs.** L21: Lith 8C **34**	WA9: Sut L 4M **63**
Seafield L37: Form 2G **25**	**SEFTON PARK** 4K **75**	WN5: Bil 8N **39**
Seafield Av. CH60: Hesw 9M **87**	**Sefton Pk. Ct.** L17: Aig 4K **75**	**Severn Rd.** L33: Kirkb 5D **36**
L23: Crosb 8L **33**	(off Aigburth Va.)	L35: Rainh 6E **62**
Seafield Dr. CH45: Wall 2G **56**	**Sefton Pk. Palm House** 4J **75**	WA3: Cul 8N **53**
Seafield Rd. CH62: New F 8A **74**	**Sefton Pk. Rd.** L8: Liv 2G **75**	WN4: Ash M 6N **41**
L9: W'ton 5E **44**	**Sefton Rd.** CH42: Rock F 7N **73**	**Severn St.** CH41: Birke 8G **56**
L20: Boot 6A **44**	CH45: New B 2H **57**	L6: Liv 3E **58**
(off Cleary St.)	CH62: New F 8N **73**	**Severnvale** CH65: Whit 2N **111**
PR8: Ainsd 8J **11**	L9: Aintr 3J **45**	**Severs St.** L6: Liv 5G **58**
Seaford Cl. WA7: Wind H 6F **96**	L9: W'ton 6F **44**	**Sewell St.** L34: Presc 3A **62**
Seaford Pl. WA2: Warr 5B **66**	L20: Boot 5C **44**	WA7: Run 5L **95**
Seafore Cl. L31: Lydi 8G **27**	L21: Lith 2A **44**	(Perry St.)
SEAFORTH 3M **43**	L37: Form 2E **24**	WA7: Run 5L **95**
Seaforth & Litherland Station (Rail) 3N **43**	WN4: Ash M 5H **41**	(Union St.)
Seaforth Dr. CH46: More 1M **71**	WN5: Orr 7N **31**	**Sextant Cl.** WA7: Murd 9F **96**

Sexton Av. WA9: St H 8D **50**	
Sexton Way L14: Brd G 7D **60**	
Seymour Ct. CH42: Tran 4L **73**	
L14: Brd G 8B **60**	
WA7: Manor P 4E **96**	
Seymour Dr. CH66: Ell P 8K **103**	
L31: Mag 9K **27**	
WA1: Padd, Padg 1H **83**	
Seymour Pl. E. CH45: New B 1J **57**	
Seymour Pl. W. CH45: New B 1H **57**	
Seymour Rd. L14: Brd G 7B **60**	
L21: Lith 3A **44**	
(off Bridge Rd.)	
Seymour St. CH42: Tran 4L **73**	
CH45: New B 1H **57**	
L3: Liv 4J **5** (7D **58**)	
L20: Boot 8A **44**	
Seymour Ter. L3: Liv 4J **5**	
Shacklady Rd. L33: Kirkb 7E **36**	
Shackleton Av. WA8: Widnes 4M **79**	
Shackleton Cl. WA5: Old H 9L **65**	
Shackleton Rd. CH46: Leas 5B **56**	
Shadewood Cres. WA4: Grap 6J **83**	
Shadowbrook Dr. L24: Speke 1G **92**	
Shadwell St. L5: Liv 4A **58**	
Shaftesbury Av. L33: Kirkb 6C **36**	
PR8: Birkd 6N **11**	
WA5: Penk 6G **80**	
Shaftesbury Gro. PR8: Birkd 5N **11**	
Shaftesbury Rd. L23: Crosb 7K **33**	
PR8: Birkd 6N **11**	
Shaftesbury St. L8: Liv 2D **74**	
Shaftesbury Ter. L13: Liv 6M **59**	
Shaftesbury Way WA5: Burtw 2H **65**	
Shaftway Cl. WA11: Hay 3H **51**	
Shakespeare Av. CH42: Rock F 7M **73**	
L32: Kirkb 2B **46**	
Shakespeare Cen., The PR8: South 1A **12**	
Shakespeare Cl. L6: Liv 5F **58**	
Shakespeare Gro. WA2: Warr 7D **66**	
(not continuous)	
Shakespeare Rd. CH44: Wall 7K **57**	
CH64: Nest 5E **100**	
WA8: Widnes 7K **79**	
WA9: Sut M 6K **63**	
Shakespeare St. L20: Boot 5N **43**	
PR8: South 1A **12**	
Shalcombe Cl. L26: Halew 9L **77**	
Shaldon Cl. L32: Kirkb 2E **46**	
Shaldon Gro. L32: Kirkb 2E **46**	
Shaldon Rd. L32: Kirkb 3E **46**	
Shaldon Wlk. L32: Kirkb 2E **46**	
Shalem Ct. CH63: H Beb 1K **89**	
Shalford Gro. CH48: W Kir 6E **70**	
Shallcross L6: Liv 5F **58**	
(off Shallcross Pl.)	
Shallcross Pl. L6: Liv 5F **58**	
Shallmarsh Cl. CH63: H Beb 2K **89**	
Shallmarsh Rd. CH63: H Beb 2K **89**	
Shalom Ct. L17: Aig 2K **75**	
Shamrock Rd. CH41: Birke 1F **72**	
Shand St. L19: Garst 3A **92**	
Shanklin Cl. WA5: Gt San 2E **80**	
Shanklin Rd. L15: Wavtr 8L **59**	
Shannon Gro. WA8: Widnes 6H **79**	
Shannon Ho. CH46: Leas 5M **55**	
Shannons La. L34: Know 9G **46**	
Shannon St. CH41: Birke 6E **56**	
Shard Cl. L11: Crox 5N **45**	
Shard St. WA9: St H 2A **64**	
Sharon Pk. Cl. WA4: Grap 7K **83**	
Sharpeville Cl. L4: Kirkd 2C **58**	
Sharples Cres. L23: Crosb 7M **33**	
Sharp St. WA2: Warr 1C **82**	
WA8: Widnes 8K **79**	
Sharrock St. PR8: South 8G **6**	
Sharwood Rd. L27: N'ley 4K **77**	
Shavington Av. CH43: Oxton 5F **72**	
Shawbury Av. CH63: H Beb 9K **73**	
Shawbury Gro. WA1: Padg 9H **67**	
Shaw Cl. CH66: Gt Sut 1L **111**	
L39: Hals 8F **12**	
Shaw Cres. L37: Form 9H **17**	
Shawell Ct. WA8: Widnes 6A **80**	
Shaw Entry L35: Whis 9C **62**	
Shaw Hall Cvn. Pk. L40: Scar 1N **19**	
Shaw Hill St. L1: Liv 4F **4** (7C **58**)	
Shaw La. CH49: Grea 6K **71**	
L35: Presc, Whis 5A **62**	
L39: Bart 7C **18**	
Shaw Rd. L24: Speke 2G **93**	
Shaws All. L1: Liv 8F **4** (9C **58**)	
Shaw's Av. PR8: Birkd 5N **11**	
WA2: Warr 9C **66**	
Shaws Dr. CH47: Meols 9E **54**	
Shaws Gth. L39: Hals 8F **12**	
Shaw's Rd. PR8: Birkd 5N **11**	
Shaw St. CH41: Birke 3K **73**	
CH47: Hoy 1C **70**	
L6: Liv 1K **5** (5E **58**)	
WA3: Cul 7N **53**	
WA7: Run 5J **95**	
(not continuous)	
WA10: St H 7L **49**	
WA11: Hay 4G **51**	
WN4: Ash M 6K **41**	
Shawton Rd. L16: Child 9B **60**	
Shearer Av. WA9: St H 9N **49**	
Shearman Cl. CH61: Pens 3A **88**	
Shearman Rd. CH61: Pens 3A **88**	
Shearwater Cl. L27: N'ley 4K **77**	

Sheen Rd.—Smithy Ct.

Sheen Rd. CH45: New B .2J 57
Sheepfield Cl. CH66: Lit Sut .7H 103
Sheerwater Cl. WA1: Padg .1G 82
Sheffield Cl. WA5: Gt San .3L 81
Sheffield Row
WA12: Newt W .1M 65
Shefford Cres. WN3: Winst .1E 40
Sheila Wlk. L10: Faz .4N 45
Sheilings, The WA3: Low .2G 52
Sheil Pl. L6: Liv .6H 59
Sheil Rd. L6: Liv .5H 59
Shelagh Av. WA8: Widnes .7K 79
Sheldon Cl. CH63: Spit .6N 89
M31: Part .6M 69
Sheldon Rd. L12: W Der .1B 60
Sheldrake Gro. CH64: Lit N .9E 100
Shelley Cl. L36: Huy .8K 61
Shelley Ct. L32: Kirkb .2B 46
Shelley Dr. L39: Orm .7B 20
Shelley Gro. PR8: South .9L 7
WA4: Westy .4G 83
Shelley Pl. L35: Whis .6C 62
Shelley Rd. WA8: Widnes .7K 79
Shelley St. L20: Boot .6A 44
(not continuous)
WA9: Sut M .7L 63
Shelley Way CH48: W Kir .8C 70
Shellfield Rd. PR9: South .4M 7
SHELL GREEN .7A 80
Shell Grn. WA8: Widnes .7A 80
Shell Grn. Est., The WA8: Widnes .8A 80
Shell Grn. Ho. WA8: Widnes .8A 80
Shellingford Cl. WN6: Shev .6N 23
Shellingford Rd. L14: Knott A .5E 60
Shellway Rd. CH65: Ell P .2D 112
Shelmore Dr. L8: Liv .4E 74
Shelton Cl. L13: Liv .7M 59
WA8: Widnes .5B 80
Shelton Dr. PR8: Ainsd .1G 17
Shelton Rd. CH45: Wall .3G 56
Shenley Cl. CH63: Beb .1M 89
Shenley Rd. L15: Wavtr .9A 60
Shenley Way PR9: South .2B 8
Shenstone St. L7: Liv .8G 58
Shenton Av. WA11: St H .4N 49
Shepcroft La. WA4: Sttn .5D 98
Shephard Cl. CH65: Ell P .8B 104
Shepherd Cl. CH49: Grea .4K 71
Shepherds Fold Cl. L8: Liv .2F 74
Shepherd's La. L39: Hals .8J 19
Shepherds Row WA7: Cas .5B 96
Shepherd St. L6: Liv .3L 5 (7E 58)
Sheppard Av. L16: Child .9E 60
Shepperton Cl. WA4: App .1F 98
Shepsides Cl. CH66: Gt Sut .2H 111
Shepston Av. L4: W'ton .9F 44
Shepton Rd. CH66: Gt Sut .3K 111
Sherborne Av. L25: Hunts X .8H 77
L30: Neth .7D 34
Sherborne Cl. WA7: Nort .4H 97
Sherborne Rd. CH44: Wall .4F 56
Sherborne Sq. L36: Huy .7J 61
Sherbourne Rd. CH65: Ell P .2B 112
Sherbourne Way WA5: Burtw .3H 65
Sherbrooke Cl. L14: Knott A .5C 60
Sherburn Cl. L9: Aintr .2J 45
Sherdley Bus. Pk. WA9: St H .9L 49
Sherdley Ct. L35: Rainh .5F 62
Sherdley Pk. .2L 63
Sherdley Pk. Dr. WA9: St H .2M 63
Sherdley Pk. Golf Course .2K 63
Sherdley Rd. WA9: St H .9L 49
(Delphwood Dr.)
WA9: St H .3J 63
(Welwyn Cl., not continuous)
Sherdley Rd. Cvn. Site WA9: St H .1K 63
Sherdley Rd. Ind. Est. WA9: St H .9L 49
Sherford Cl. L27: N'ley .4K 77
Sheridan Av. WA3: Low .3E 52
Sheridan Pl. WA2: Winw .4B 66
Sheridan Way WA7: Nort .5F 96
Sheri Dr. WA12: Newt W .8M 51
Sheriff Cl. L5: Liv .5D 58
Sheringham Cl. CH49: Upton .1A 72
WA9: St H .7N 49
Sheringham Rd. WA5: Gt San .2G 81
Sherlock Av. WA11: Hay .3G 50
Sherlock La. CH44: Wall .7G 57
(not continuous)
Sherman Dr. L35: Rainh .8G 63
Sherrat St. WN8: Skel .3A 30
Sherringham Rd. PR8: Birkd .4L 11
Sherry Ct. L17: Aig .3K 75
Sherry La. CH49: Wdchu .6A 72
Sherwell Cl. L15: Wavtr .8M 59
Sherwood Av. CH61: Irby .9K 71
L23: Crosb .6K 33
L39: Augh .2A 28
WN4: Ash M .7L 41
Sherwood Cl. L35: Rainh .4E 62
WA8: Widnes .7F 78
Sherwood Ct. L12: Crox .7D 46
L36: Huy .7K 61
Sherwood Cres. WA5: Burtw .3G 65
Sherwood Dr. CH63: H Beb .9L 73
L35: Whis .7C 62
WN8: Skel .1G 30
Sherwood Gro. CH47: Meols .9G 54
WA6: Hel .2D 114
Sherwood Ho. PR8: Ainsd .9J 11
Sherwood Lodge PR8: Birkd .1M 11
Sherwood Rd. CH44: Wall .6J 57
CH47: Meols .9G 55
L23: Crosb .6J 33
Sherwood Row L26: Halew .1J 93
(off Honey Hall Rd.)
Sherwood's La. L10: Faz .2L 45
Sherwood St. L3: Liv .5A 58
Sherwyn Rd. L4: W'ton .1H 59
Shetland Cl. WA2: Fearn .5F 66
WA8: Widnes .5A 80
Shetland Dr. CH62: Brom .7D 90
CH65: Ell P .4A 112
Shevington Cl. WA8: Widnes .5A 80
WA9: St H .2M 63
Shevington's La. L33: Kirkb .6B 36
Shevington Wlk. WA8: Widnes .5A 80
Shewell Cl. CH42: Tran .4K 73
Shiel Rd. CH45: New B .2H 57
Shiggins Cl. WA5: Gt San .2M 81
Shillingford Cl. WA4: App .2F 98
Shimmin St. L7: Liv .6N 5 (8F 58)
Shipley Wlk. L24: Speke .3H 93
Ship St. WA6: Frod .5L 107
Shipton Cl. CH43: Pren .7E 72
L19: Aller .8N 75
WA5: Gt San .9K 65
WA8: Widnes .5G 78
Shirdley Av. L32: Kirkb .3D 46
Shirdley Cres. PR8: Ainsd .2J 17
SHIRDLEY HILL .8F 12
Shirdley Wlk. L32: Kirkb .3D 46
Shirebourne Av. WA11: St H .3L 49
Shirebrook Cl. WA9: St H .4H 63
Shireburn Rd. L37: Form .8C 16
Shiregreen WA9: St H .3M 63
Shires, The WA10: St H .8H 49
Shirley Dr. WA4: Grap .6H 83
Shirley Rd. L19: Aller .8A 76
Shirley St. CH44: Wall .6L 57
Shirwell Gro. WA9: Sut L .5M 63
Shobdon Cl. L12: Crox .6D 46
Shones Cft. CH64: Ness .9G 101
Shop La. L31: Mag .2H 35
Shop Rd. L34: Know .6G 47
Shore Bank CH62: New F .8B 74
Shore Dr. CH62: Port S .1B 90
Shorefields CH62: New F .8B 74
Shorefields Ho. CH62: New F .9B 74
Shorefields Village L8: Liv .5E 74
Shoreham Dr. WA5: Penk .5J 81
Shore La. CH48: Caldy .9D 70
Shore Rd. CH41: Birke .1M 73
CH48: Caldy .9D 70
L20: Boot .5M 43
PR8: Ainsd .8F 10
Shore Road Pumping Station .1M 73
Shore Wood Rd. CH62: Brom .5E 90
Short Cl. WA12: Newt W .7G 51
Short Cft. La. L37: Gt Alt .3K 25
Shortfield Rd. CH49: Upton .4A 72
Shortfield Way CH49: Upton .4A 72
Short St. WA3: Golb .1C 52
WA8: Widnes .2K 95
WA11: Hay .4G 50
WA12: Newt W .7G 51
Short Wlk. M31: Part .7L 69
Shortwood Rd. L14: Knott A .6D 60
Shorwell Cl. WA5: Gt San .1E 80
Shottesbrook Grn. L11: Norr G .7L 45
SHOTWICK .9A 110
Shotwick Helsby By-Pass .9B 110 (5N 111)
Shotwick La. CH1: Shot, Woodb .9A 110
Showcase Cinema
Liverpool .6M 45
Shrewsbury Av. L10: Aintr .8H 35
L22: Wloo .8K 33
Shrewsbury Cl. CH43: Clau .2F 72
Shrewsbury Dr. CH49: Upton .2A 72
Shrewsbury Pl. L19: Garst .1A 92
(off Shrewsbury Rd.)
Shrewsbury Rd. CH43: Clau, Oxton .1F 72
CH44: Wall .4F 56
CH48: W Kir .7B 70
CH60: Hesw .6A 88
CH65: Ell P .9A 104
(off Norfolk Rd.)
L19: Garst .1A 92
Shrewsbury St. WA4: Warr .5E 82
Shrewton Rd. L25: Gate .1E 76
Shropshire Cl. L30: Neth .7F 34
WA1: Wools .2M 83
Shropshire Gdns. WA10: St H .8J 49
Shropshire Rd. CH2: Lit Stan .2D 112
Sibford Rd. L12: W Der .4B 60
Sibley Av. WN4: Ash M .7M 41
Siddeley Dr. WA12: Newt W .7H 51
Siddeley St. L17: Aig .5H 75
Sidgreave St. WA10: St H .7H 49
Siding Ct. WA8: Widnes .9K 79
Siding La. L33: Simsw .5G 37
WA11: Rainf .2N 37
Sidings, The L7: Liv .7N 5
Sidings Ct. WA1: Warr .2D 82
Sidlaw Av. WA9: St H .7B 50
Sidlaw Cl. CH66: Lit Sut .8F 102
Sidmouth Cl. WA5: Penk .4F 81
WA10: Windle .4F 48
Sidmouth Gro. WN3: Wigan .1G 41
Sidney Av. CH45: New B .1G 57
Sidney Cl. CH64: Nest .5F 100
Sidney Ct. CH42: Tran .5L 73
Sidney Pl. L7: Liv .6N 5 (8F 58)
Sidney Powell Av. L32: Kirkb .9A 36
Sidney Rd. CH42: Tran .4L 73
CH64: Nest .5F 100
L20: Boot .8C 44
PR9: South .7L 7
Sidney St. CH41: Birke .1L 73
WA10: St H .6G 49
Sidney Ter. CH42: Tran .5L 73
Sidwell St. L19: Garst .1A 92
Siemens Rd. M44: Irlam .4L 69
Sienna Cl. L27: N'ley .2G 77
M44: Irlam .3L 69
Signal Works Rd. L9: Aintr, Faz .2K 45
Silcock's Funland .7F 6
Silcock St. WA3: Golb .2B 52
Silcroft Rd. L32: Kirkb .2C 46
Silk Ct. L39: Orm .9E 20
Silkhouse Ct. L2: Liv .4D 4
Silkhouse La. L3: Liv .4D 4
Silkstone Cl. L7: Liv .9G 59
WA10: St H .7G 49
Silkstone Cres. WA7: Pal F .8D 96
Silkstone St. WA10: St H .7G 49
(not continuous)
Silsden Av. WA3: Low .2J 53
Silver Av. WA11: Hay .5C 50
Silverbeech Av. L18: Moss H .4N 75
Silverbeech Rd. CH44: Wall .6J 57
Silver Birch Av. PR9: Banks .4H 9
Silverbirch Gdns. CH44: Wall .4E 56
Silver Birch Gro. WN4: Ash M .6J 41
Silver Birch Way L31: Lydi .7G 27
Silverbirch Way CH66: Whit .5L 111
Silver Blades
Widnes .9L 79
Silverbrook Rd. L27: N'ley .1H 77
Silverburn Av. CH46: More .8M 55
Silverdale Av. L13: Liv .4K 59
Silverdale Cl. L36: Huy .9J 61
WA6: Frod .7M 107
Silverdale Ct. PR8: Birkd .2L 11
PR8: South .2E 12
Silverdale Dr. L21: Lith .2C 44
Silverdale Gro. WA11: St H .2K 49
Silverdale Rd. CH43: Oxton .4G 72
CH63: H Beb .9M 73
WA4: Warr .6C 82
WA12: Newt W .6K 51
Silverlake Cl. L4: W'ton .7F 44
Silver La. WA3: Ris .2M 67
(not continuous)
Silverlea Av. CH45: Wall .4H 57
Silver Leigh L17: Aig .7J 75
Silverlime Gdns. WA9: St H .2F 62
Silverne Dr. CH65: Whit .3M 111
Silverstone Dr. L36: Roby .9H 61
Silverstone Gro. L31: Lydi .7G 26
Silver St. WA2: Warr .2C 82
Silverthorne Dr. PR9: South .6L 7
Silverton Rd. L17: Aig .8K 75
Silverwell Rd. L11: Crox .5B 46
Silverwell Wlk. L11: Crox .5B 46
Silverwing Ho. L19: Aig .9L 75
Silvester St. L5: Liv .4B 58
Simkin Av. WA4: Westy .4G 82
Simmons Cl. WA10: St H .3J 49
Simms Av. WA9: St H .7A 50
SIMM'S CROSS .8L 79
SIMM'S LANE END .6D 40
Simm's Rd. L6: Liv .3J 59
Simnel Cl. L25: Gate .2F 76
Simon Ct. CH48: W Kir .6B 70
Simonsbridge CH48: Caldy .1E 86
Simons Cl. L35: Whis .9A 62
Simon's Cft. L30: Neth .8B 34
Simonside WA8: Widnes .6F 78
Simons La. WA6: Frod .8L 107
Simonstone Gro. WA9: St H .2N 63
SIMONSWOOD .5E 36
Simonswood Ind. Pk. L33: Simsw .5F 36
Simonswood La. L33: Kirkb .1E 46
L39: Bic .8D 28
Simonswood Wlk. L33: Kirkb .9E 36
Simply Gym
Runcorn .8A 96
Simpson Pl. CH49: Upton .5N 71
Simpson's Pl. PR8: South .9G 7
Simpson St. CH41: Birke .2K 73
L1: Liv .9F 4 (1C 74)
Sim St. L3: Liv .2J 5 (6D 58)
Sinclair Av. L35: Presc .4C 62
WA2: Warr .7C 66
WA8: Widnes .8J 79
Sinclair Cl. L35: Presc .3C 62
Sinclair Dr. L18: Moss H .2N 75
Sinclair St. L19: Garst .2A 92
Sinclair Way L34: Presc .4N 61
Sineacre La. L33: Simsw .3J 37
L39: Bic .3J 37
Singleton Av. CH42: Tran .5J 73
WA11: St H .5N 49
Singleton Cl. PR9: South .3M 7
Singleton Dr. L34: Know .7H 47
Singleton Rd. CH65: Gt Sut .1L 111
Sirdar Cl. L7: Liv .9G 59
Sir Howard St. L8: Liv .8L 5 (9E 58)
Sir Howard Way L8: Liv .8L 5
Sir Thomas St. L1: Liv .4F 4 (7C 58)
Siskin Cl. WA12: Newt W .7L 51
Siskin Grn. L25: Gate .4E 76
Sisters Way CH41: Birke .2K 73
Six Acre Gdns. WA4: Moore .2J 97
Six Acre La. WA4: Moore .2H 97
Sixpenny La. L39: Bart .5L 17
Sixpenny Wlk. WA1: Warr .2D 82
Sixteen Acre La. L37: Form .7G 16
Sixth Av. L9: Aintr .3K 45
(Broadway)
L9: Aintr .3J 45
(Seventh Av.)
Skeffington L35: Whis .7B 62
Skelhorne St. L3: Liv .5H 5 (8D 58)
SKELMERSDALE .3E 30
Skelmersdale Concourse Bus Station .3E 30
Skelmersdale Rd. L39: Bic .5L 29
WN8: Skel .5L 29
Skelton Cl. WA11: St H .3L 49
Skelton St. WN4: Ash M .5H 41
Skerries Rd. L4: W'ton .3F 58
Skiddaw Cl. WA7: Beech .2C 108
Skiddaw Rd. CH62: Brom .5D 90
Skipton Av. PR9: South .1A 8
Skipton Cl. WA7: Cas .6B 96
WA12: Newt W .8H 51
Skipton Dr. CH66: Lit Sut .1H 111
Skipton Rd. L4: W'ton .2G 59
L36: Huy .6M 61
Skirving Pl. L5: Liv .3C 58
Skirving St. L5: Liv .3D 58
Skitters Gro. WN4: Ash M .7G 41
Skull Ho. La. WN6: App B .4M 23
Skull Ho. M. WN6: App B .5M 23
Skye Cl. CH65: Ell P .4A 112
WA8: Widnes .5A 80
Skyes Cres. WN3: Winst .2E 40
Skyhawk Av. L19: Speke .3C 92
Skylark Cl. PR9: Banks .1E 8
Sky Lark Ri. WA9: St H .7C 50
Skyline Dr. WA5: Gt San .8F 64
Sky Pk. Ind. Est. L24: Speke .4F 92
Slackey's La. PR9: South .3A 8
Slackswood Cl. CH65: Ell P .7N 103
Slade La. CH63: Thorn H .8H 89
Slag La. WA3: Low .2E 52
WA11: Hay .2D 50
(not continuous)
Slaidburn Cl. WN3: Wigan .1J 41
Slaidburn Cres. PR9: South .2M 7
WA3: Golb .1A 52
Slaidburn Ind. Est. PR9: South .2M 7
Slate La. WN8: Skel .1N 29
Slater Pl. L1: Liv .7G 5 (9C 58)
Slater St. L1: Liv .7G 5 (9C 58)
WA4: Warr .4D 82
Slatey Rd. CH43: Oxton .2H 73
Sleaford Rd. L14: Knott A .4F 60
Sleepers Hill L4: W'ton .2E 58
Slessor Av. CH48: W Kir .5E 70
Slim Rd. L36: Huy .6J 61
Slingsby Dr. CH49: Upton .4A 72
Sluice La. L40: Ruf .4L 15
Slutchers La. WA1: Warr .4B 82
Smallacres CH65: Ell P .7L 103
Small Av. WA2: Warr .7D 66
Small Cres. WA2: Warr .7D 66
Smallholdings, The L31: Mag .9L 27
Small La. L39: Augh .1M 27
L39: Orm .9D 20
L40: Scar .6C 14
Small La. Nth. L39: Hals .3J 19
Small La. Sth. L39: Hals .8H 19
Smallridge Cl. CH61: Pens .3M 87
Smallshaw Cl. WN4: Ash M .9J 41
Smallwood M. CH60: Hesw .5M 87
Smeaton St. L4: Kirkd .9D 44
(not continuous)
Smethick Wlk. L30: Neth .7F 34
Smethurst Hall Pk. WN5: Bil .1M 39
Smethurst Rd. WA11: Kings M .2L 39
WN5: Bil .1M 39
Smilie Av. CH46: More .8K 55
Smith Av. CH41: Birke .9H 57
Smith Cres. WA2: Warr .9E 66
Smithdown Gro. L7: Liv .7N 5 (9F 58)
Smithdown La. L7: Liv .9G 58
(Malt St.)
L7: Liv .5M 5 (8F 58)
(Paddington)
Smithdown Pl. L15: Wavtr .3M 75
Smithdown Rd. L7: Liv .1H 75
L15: Wavtr .1H 75
Smith Dr. L20: Boot .5D 44
WA2: Warr .9E 66
Smithfield St. L3: Liv .3E 4 (7B 58)
WA9: St H .8N 49
Smithford Wlk. L35: Tar G .1M 77
Smithills Cl. WA3: Birchw .4L 67
Smith Pl. L5: Kirkd .3C 58
Smith Rd. WA8: Widnes .9J 79
Smith St. L5: Kirkd .2D 58
L34: Presc .3B 62
WA1: Warr .3C 82
WA9: St H .2A 64
WN8: Skel .3A 30
SMITHY BROW .2G 66
Smithy Brow WA3: Croft .2G 66
WN8: Newb .4D 22
Smithy Cl. CH64: Ness .9G 101
L37: Form .9H 17
WA8: Cron .3F 78
Smithy Ct. CH66: Lit Sut .8H 103

Smithy Grn.—Springfield Pl.

Smithy Grn. L37: Form 9H **17**
Smithy Heritage Cen. 5E 48
Smithy Hey CH48: W Kir 6D **70**
Smithy Hill CH63: Thorn H 9G **89**
Smithy La. CH64: Will 6N **101**
CH66: Lit Sut 8H **103**
L39: Augh 6L **27**
L39: Bart 7F **18**
L40: H'wood 9N **9**
L40: Scar 1M **19**
M31: Part 6M **69**
WA3: Croft 1H **67**
WA6: Hel 9F **106**
WA8: Cron 2F **78**
SMITHY LANE ENDS 8A 14
Smithystone Cl. L15: Wavtr 1M **75**
Smithy Wlk. L40: Burs 9J **15**
SMM Bus. Pk. CH41: Birke 7J **57**
Smock La. WN4: Garsw 7E **40**
Smollett St. L6: Liv 6G **58**
L20: Boot 4A **44**
Smugglers Way CH45: Wall 1E **56**
Smythe Cft. PR9: South 5M **7**
Smyth Rd. WA8: Widnes 6N **79**
Snab La. CH64: Ness 9F **100**
Snabwood Cl. CH64: Lit N 9E **100**
Snaefell Av. L13: Liv 4K **59**
Snaefell Gro. L13: Liv 4K **59**
Snaefell Ri. WA4: App 9D **82**
Snapdragon Way L11: Norr G 9L **45**
SNAPE GREEN 5J 13
Snape Grn. PR8: South 6J **13**
Snave Cl. L21: Lith 5A **44**
Snowberry Cl. WA8: Widnes 4A **80**
Snowberry Cres. WA5: Warr 5M **81**
Snowberry Rd.
L14: Knott A 3E **60**
Snowberry Wlk. *M31: Part* *6L 69*
(off Wood La.)
Snowberry Way CH66: Whit 5L **111**
Snowden Rd. CH46: More 9K **55**
Snowdon Cl. CH66: Lit Sut 8F **102**
WA5: Gt San 2G **81**
Snowdon Gro. WA9: St H 2M **63**
Snowdon La. L5: Liv 4B **58**
Snowdon Rd. CH42: Tran 6K **73**
Snowdrop Av. CH41: Birke 9F **56**
Snowdrop Cl. WA7: Beech 2B **108**
Snowdrop M. L21: Lith 4A **44**
Snowdrop St. L5: Kirkd 2C **58**
Soane Cl. WN4: Ash M 8M **41**
Soapstone Way M44: Irlam 1N **69**
Soho Pl. L3: Liv 2J **5** (6D **58**)
Soho St. L3: Liv 1J **5** (6D **58**)
(not continuous)
Solar Rd. L9: Aintr 4G **44**
Solly Av. CH42: Rock F 6L **73**
Solomon St. L7: Liv 7G **59**
Solway Cl. WA2: Fearn 5G **67**
WN4: Ash M 7J **41**
Solway Gro. WA7: Beech 1N **107**
Solway St. CH41: Birke 8G **56**
Solway St. E. L8: Liv 1G **75**
Solway St. W. L8: Liv 1G **74**
Soma Av. L21: Lith 2B **44**
Somerford Ho. L23: Blun 8H **33**
Somerford Rd. L14: Knott A 5E **60**
Somerford Wlk. WA8: Widnes 5A **80**
Somerley Cl. L12: W Der 1B **60**
Somerset Cl. M44: Cad 3K **69**
Somerset Dr. PR8: Ainsd 3J **17**
Somerset Pl. L6: Liv 4J **59**
Somerset Rd. CH45: Wall 4E **56**
CH48: W Kir 5D **70**
CH61: Pens 3M **87**
L20: Boot 6C **44**
L22: Wloo 9J **33**
Somerset St. WA9: St H 8N **49**
Somerset Way WA1: Wools 9J **67**
Somerton St. L15: Wavtr 9K **59**
Somerville Cl. CH63: Brom 9A **90**
CH64: Lit N 9E **100**
Somerville Cres. CH65: Ell P 1A **112**
Somerville Gro. L22: Wloo 9K **33**
Somerville Rd. L22: Wloo 9K **33**
WA8: Widnes 8G **79**
Somerville Wlk. *WA5: Gt San* *1L 81*
(off Boston Blvd.)
Sommer Av. L12: W Der 2M **59**
Sonning Av. L21: Lith 1N **43**
Sonning Rd. L4: W'ton 8J **45**
Sophia Dr. WA5: Gt San 8H **65**
Sorany Cl. L23: Thorn 5N **33**
Sorbus Cl. CH2: Elt 2N **113**
Sorby Rd. M44: Irlam 2M **69**
Sorogold Cl. WA9: St H 7M **49**
Sorogold St. WA9: St H 7M **49**
Sorrel Av. L11: Norr G 9M **45**
Sorrel Cl. CH43: Noct 3D **72**
WA2: Padg 7K **67**
Sorrel Way WA9: Clock F 6N **63**
Sougher's La. WN4: Ash M 5G **41**
Sth. Albert Rd. L17: Aig 4G **75**
Southampton Dr. L19: Garst 1N **91**
Southampton Way WA7: Murd 9G **96**
Sth. Atlantic Av. L30: Neth 1E **44**
South Av. L34: Presc 3M **61**
WA2: Warr 9C **66**
WA4: Stockt H 7D **82**
South Bank CH43: Oxton 5H **73**
Sth. Bank Rd. L7: Liv 7J **59**
Southbank Rd. L19: G'dale 9N **75**
PR8: South 9G **7**
Sth. Bank Ter. WA7: Run 4J **95**
Sth. Barcombe Rd. L16: Child 1C **76**
Sth. Boundary Rd. L33: Know I 2F **46**
Southbourne Rd. CH45: Wall 4D **56**
Southbrook Rd. L27: N'ley 2G **77**
Southbrook Way L27: N'ley 2G **77**
Sth. Cantril Av. L12: W Der 2D **60**
Sth. Chester St. L8: Liv 2E **74**
Southcroft Rd. CH45: Wall 4D **56**
South Dale WA5: Penk 3H **81**
Southdale Rd. CH42: Rock F 6L **73**
L15: Wavtr 9L **59**
WA1: Padd 1H **83**
Southdean Rd. L14: Knott A 3F **60**
SOUTHDENE 2D 46
Southdene WN8: Parb 3E **22**
South Dr. CH49: Upton 3A **72**
CH60: Hesw 8A **88**
CH61: Irby 2K **87**
L12: W Der 4M **59**
L15: Wavtr 9L **59**
WN6: App B 3M **23**
Southern Cres. L8: Liv 3D **74**
Southern Gateway L24: Speke 2G **92**
Southern Rd. L24: Speke 5J **93**
PR8: South 9F **6**
Southern's La. WA11: Rainf 5D **38**
Southern St. WA4: Stockt H 7D **82**
Southey Cl. WA8: Widnes 8J **79**
Southey Gro. L31: Mag 5J **35**
Southey Rd. WA10: St H 1F **62**
Southey St. L15: Wavtr 1K **75**
L20: Boot 6A **44**
(not continuous)
Sth. Ferry Quay L3: Liv 2C **74**
Southfield Rd. CH66: Lit Sut 8H **103**
L9: W'ton 4E **44**
Southfields Av. WA5: Gt San 3H **81**
South Front L35: Whis 8B **62**
Southgate Cl. L12: Crox 7C **46**
Southgate Rd. L13: Liv 6N **59**
South Gro. L8: Liv 4F **74**
L18: Aller 7A **76**
Sth. Hey Rd. CH61: Irby 2L **87**
Sth. Highville Rd. L16: Child 2B **76**
South Hill PR8: South 9F **6**
Sth. Hill Gro. CH43: Oxton 5H **73**
L8: Liv 4F **74**
Sth. Hill Rd. CH43: Oxton 4J **73**
L8: Liv 5E **74**
Sth. Hunter St. L1: Liv 7K **5** (9E **58**)
Sth. John St. L1: Liv 6E **4** (8B **58**)
WA9: St H 7M **49**
Sth. Lancashire Ind. Est.
WN4: Ash M 5K **41**
Southlands Av. WA5: Penk 5H **81**
Southlands Ct. *WA7: Run* *7J 95*
(off Southlands M.)
Southlands M. WA7: Run 7J **95**
South La. WA8: Widnes 4A **80**
Sth. La. Entry WA8: Widnes 4B **80**
Sth. Mnr. Way L25: Woolt 7G **76**
South Meade L31: Mag 2G **35**
Southmead Gdns. L19: Aller 9C **76**
Southmead Rd. L19: Aller 9C **76**
Sth. Mossley Hill Rd.
L19: Aig, G'dale 7M **75**
Southney Cl. L31: Mell 8N **35**
South Pde. CH48: W Kir 6B **70**
CH64: P'gte 6C **100**
L23: Crosb 8M **33**
L24: Speke 4J **93**
L32: Kirkb 9C **36**
WA7: West P 8G **94**
South Pk. Ct. *CH44: Wall* *6L 57*
(off Demesne St.)
L32: Kirkb 8A **36**
South Pk. Rd. L32: Kirkb 8N **35**
Sth. Parkside Dr. L12: W Der 2A **60**
Sth. Parkside Wlk. *L12: W Der* *1N 59*
(off Parkside Dr.)
South Pk. Way L20: Boot 8C **44**
Sth. Pier Rd. CH65: Ell P 7B **104**
SOUTHPORT 8G 7
Southport & Ainsdale Golf Course 8K 11
Southport & Birkdale Sports Club 3L 11
Southport Argyle Lawn Tennis Club 5K 7
Southport Bus. Cen. *PR9: South* *8G 7*
(off Lord St.)
Southport Bus. Pk. PR8: South 3C **12**
Southport Crematorium 4G **12**
Southport Eco Vis. Cen. 8D 6
Southport Ent. Cen. PR9: South 9M **7**
Southport FC 1D 12
Southport Little Theatre 8G 7
Southport Model Railway Village 8F 6
Southport Municipal Golf Links 6H 7
Southport New Pleasureland 8E 6
Southport New Rd. PR4: Mere B, Tarl 5K **9**
PR9: Banks 2C **8**
Southport Old Links 7N 7
Southport Old Rd. L37: Form 6H **17**
Southport Pier 6E 6
Southport Pier Tram 7E 6
Southport Res. Parkhomes
PR8: South 4F **12**
Southport Rd. L20: Boot 4D **44**
L23: Thorn 3N **33**
L31: Lydi 4F **26**
Southport Rd. L37: Form 8G **17**
L39: Bart 7F **18**
L39: Orm 7C **20**
L40: Scar 2M **19**
PR8: South 3F **12**
Southport Sailing Club 6G 6
Southport Station (Rail) 8G 7
Southport St. WA9: St H 7C **50**
Southport Theatre & Convention Cen. 7F 6
Southport Watersports Cen. 7G 6
South Quay L3: Liv 9E **4** (1B **74**)
Southridge Rd. CH61: Pens 2A **88**
South Rd. CH42: Tran 5J **73**
CH48: W Kir 7B **70**
CH65: Ell P 9D **104**
(Bridges Rd.)
CH65: Ell P 2A **112**
(Malvern Av.)
CH65: Hoot 3H **103**
L9: Aintr 4J **45**
L14: Brd G 6B **60**
L19: G'dale 1M **91**
L22: Wloo 2K **43**
L24: Halew 3J **93**
WA7: West P 8G **94**
Sth. Sefton Bus. Cen. L20: Boot 7A **44**
South Sta. Rd. L25: Gate 3F **76**
South St. L8: Liv 3F **74**
WA8: Widnes 8L **79**
WA9: St H 2G **62**
Sth. Sudley Rd. L19: Aig 7M **75**
South Ter. L39: Orm 9C **20**
South Vw. CH62: Brom 2C **90**
L8: Liv *4F 74*
(off Dentwood St.)
L22: Wloo 2L **43**
L36: Huy 7M **61**
South Vw. Ct. L22: Wloo 2L **43**
South Vw. Ter. WA5: Cuerd 5C **80**
South Vs. CH45: New B 2H **57**
Southward Rd. WA11: Hay 3J **51**
Southwark Gro. L30: Neth 1E **44**
Southway L15: Wavtr 9N **59**
WA7: Pal F 8B **96**
(not continuous)
WA8: Widnes 8G **78**
WN8: Skel 4E **30**
(not continuous)
Southway Av. WA4: App 9E **82**
Southwell Cl. WA3: Low 2D **52**
Southwell Pl. L8: Liv 3D **74**
Southwell St. L8: Liv 3D **74**
Southwick Rd. CH42: Tran 5L **73**
Southwold Cres. WA5: Gt San 2F **80**
Southwood Av. WA7: Wind H 5E **96**
Southwood Cl. L32: Kirkb 2E **46**
Southwood Rd. CH62: Brom 6E **90**
L17: Aig 6G **74**
Southworth Av. WA5: Warr 9A **66**
Southworth La. WA2: Winw 2E **66**
WA3: Croft 2E **66**
Southworth Rd. WA12: Newt W 7N **51**
Sovereign Cl. WA3: Low 3F **52**
WA7: Murd 8F **96**
Sovereign Ct. WA3: Birchw 5K **67**
Sovereign Hey L11: Crox 7A **46**
Sovereign Rd. L11: Crox 7A **46**
Sovereign Way CH41: Birke 8K **57**
L11: Crox 7A **46**
Spaceport 7M 57
Spa Fold L40: Lath 9L **21**
Spa La. L40: Lath 9L **21**
Spark Hall Cl. WA4: Sttn 5F **98**
Spark La. WA7: Hal 6B **96**
Sparks Cft. CH62: Port S 1B **90**
Sparks La. CH61: Thing 1A **88**
Sparling St. L1: Liv 9F **4** (1C **74**)
(not continuous)
SPARROW HALL 6L 45
Sparrow Hall Rd. L9: Faz 6L **45**
Sparrowhawk Cl. L26: Halew 7J **77**
WA7: Pal F 8C **96**
Sparrow Hill WN8: Parb 3J **23**
Spawell Cl. WA3: Low 1F **52**
Speakman Av. WA12: Newt W 5L **51**
Speakman Rd. WA10: St H 4G **49**
Speakmans Dr. WN6: App B 7M **23**
Speakman St. WA7: Run 4J **95**
Speakman Way L34: Presc 4A **62**
Speedwell Cl. CH60: Hesw 7C **88**
WA3: Low 2F **52**
Speedwell Dr. CH60: Hesw 7C **88**
Speedwell Rd. CH41: Birke 1F **72**
SPEKE 5J 93
Speke Blvd. L24: Speke 3F **92**
L26: Halew 3F **92**
Speke Chu. Rd. L24: Speke 4F **92**
Speke Hall Av. L24: Speke 4E **92**
Speke Hall Garden & Estate 5D 92
Speke Hall Ind. Est. L24: Speke 4E **92**
Speke Hall Rd. L24: Speke 2E **92**
L25: Hunts X 2E **92**
Speke Ho. L24: Speke 5L **93**
Spekeland Rd. L7: Liv 9H **59**
Speke Rd. L19: Garst 2A **92**
L24: Speke 2B **92**
L25: Hunts X, Woolt 6F **76**
L26: Halew 1B **94**
WA8: Widnes 1B **94**
Speke Town La. L24: Speke 3F **92**
Spellow La. L4: W'ton 1E **58**
Spellow Pl. L3: Liv 4C **4**
Spence Av. L20: Boot 5C **44**
Spencer Av. CH46: More 8A **56**
Spencer Cl. L36: Huy 9K **61**
Spencer Gdns. WA9: St H 1N **63**
Spencer La. L40: Ruf 2L **15**
Spencer Pl. L20: Boot 3C **44**
Spencer's La. L31: Mell 9K **35**
L39: Hals 2B **18**
WN5: Orr 5N **31**
Spencers La. WN8: Skel 4E **30**
Spencer St. L6: Liv 5E **58**
Spenders La. WA7: Aston 5F **108**
Spennymoor Ct. WA7: Pal F 8A **96**
Spenser Av. CH42: Rock F 7M **73**
Spenser Cl. WA8: Widnes 7J **79**
Spenser Rd. CH64: Nest 5E **100**
Spenser St. L20: Boot 6A **44**
Sphynx Tennis Club 2D 12
Spicer Gro. L32: Kirkb 9C **36**
Spice St. L9: Aintr 4G **45**
Spike Island Vis. Cen. 2K 95
Spilsby Sq. WN3: Wigan 1J **41**
Spindle Cl. L6: Liv 5E **58**
Spindle Hillock
WN4: Garsw 6F **40**
Spindrift Ct. CH48: W Kir 7B **70**
Spindus Rd. L24: Speke 4E **92**
Spinnaker Cl. WA7: Murd 9F **96**
Spinnakers, The L19: Aig 9L **75**
Spinner M. L39: Orm 8E **20**
Spinners Dr. WA9: St H 1B **64**
Spinners Pl. WA1: Warr 2D **82**
Spinney, The CH48: W Kir 6F **70**
CH49: Upton 2A **72**
CH60: Hesw 1C **100**
CH63: Spit 4A **90**
CH64: P'gte 5D **100**
L28: Stockb V 2F **60**
L34: Presc 2N **61**
L37: Form 8G **17**
WA11: Rainf 4C **38**
Spinney Apts. WN8: Uph 3M **31**
Spinney Av. WA8: Widnes 7D **78**
Spinney Cl. L33: Know I 2G **47**
L39: Orm 1B **28**
WA9: Clock F 5M **63**
Spinney Cres. L23: Blun 5H **33**
Spinney Dr. CH66: Gt Sut 3J **111**
Spinney Gdns. WA4: App T 3J **99**
Spinney Grn. WA10: Ec'stn 7D **48**
Spinney Rd. L33: Know I 2H **47**
Spinney Vw. L33: Know I 2H **47**
Spinney Wlk. WA7: Cas 6C **96**
Spinney Way L36: Huy 6G **60**
Spion Kop WN4: Ash M 8J **41**
Spire Grn. L9: W'ton 4F **44**
Spires, The WA10: Ec'stn 6D **48**
Spires Gdns. WA2: Winw 2B **66**
Spires Vw. WA1: Warr 3D **82**
SPITAL 4A 90
Spital Heyes CH63: Spit 4A **90**
Spital (Park & Ride) 5A 90
Spital Rd. CH62: Brom, Spit 4N **89**
CH63: Spit 4N **89**
Spital Station (Rail) 4A 90
Spitfire Rd. L24: Speke 1D **92**
Spofforth Rd. L7: Liv 9J **59**
Spooner Av. L21: Lith 3B **44**
Sports Direct Fitness
Formby 3G 25
Liverpool 5M 75
Sprainger St. L3: Liv 5A **58**
Sprakeling Pl. L20: Boot 3D **44**
Spray St. WA10: St H 6H **49**
Spreyton Cl. L12: W Der 8A **46**
Sprig Cl. L9: Aintr 2J **45**
Spring Av. CH66: Lit Sut 8H **103**
Spring Bank WN6: App B 5M **23**
Springbank Cl. WA7: Run 9L **95**
Springbank Gdns. WA13: Lymm 3H **85**
Springbank Rd. L4: W'ton 4G **58**
Springbourne WA6: Frod 8N **107**
Springbourne Rd. L17: Aig 6G **75**
Springbrook WA4: W'ton 8B **82**
Springbrook Cl. WA10: Ec'stn 6D **48**
Springburn Gdns. WA1: Wools 1N **83**
Spring Cl. L33: Kirkb 6E **36**
PR8: Birkd 1N **11**
Spring Ct. WA7: Run 5L **95**
Springcroft CH64: P'gte 5C **100**
Springdale Cl. CH46: More 8A **56**
L12: W Der 2A **60**
Springfield L3: Liv 2H **5** (6D **58**)
(not continuous)
WA11: Rainf 1B **38**
Springfield Av. CH48: W Kir 5F **70**
L21: Lith 2B **44**
WA1: Padg 9G **67**
WA3: Golb 2A **52**
WA4: Grap 5J **83**
WA6: Hel 2E **114**
WA13: Lymm 3H **85**
Springfield Cl. CH49: Wdchu 6C **72**
L37: Form 2C **24**
L40: Burs 2H **21**
WA10: St H 1F **62**
Springfield Cres. L36: Huy 3G **61**
Springfield La. WA10: Ec'stn 5D **48**
Springfield Pk. WA11: Hay 3E **50**
Springfield Pl. CH44: Wall 5K **57**

Springfield Rd.—Stockbridge La.

Springfield Rd. L39: Augh 7L 27
WA8: Widnes 8D 78
WA10: St H 1F 62
Springfields WA6: Hel 2E 114
Springfield Sq. L4: W'ton 1E 58
Springfield St. WA1: Warr 3B 82
Springfield Way L12: W Der 1C 60
Spring Gdns. CH66: Lit Sut 8H 103
L31: Mag 3K 35
Spring Gro. L12: W Der 3A 60
Springhill Av. CH62: Brom 9C 90
Springhill Ct. L15: Wavtr 2M 75
Springholm Dr. WA4: App 4E 98
Spring La. WA3: Croft 3J 67
WA13: Lymm 5L 85
Springmeadow Rd. L25: Gate 3E 76
Springmount WA3: Low 2F 52
Springmount Dr. WN8: Parb 1F 22
Springpool WA9: St H 2N 63
WN3: Winst 1D 40
Springs Cl. *L20: Boot* *6C 44*
(off Davies St.)
Springside Cl. L36: Huy 3G 61
Spring St. CH42: Tran 5M 73
WA8: Widnes 1K 95
SPRINGVALE 3D 38
Spring Va. CH45: Wall 2E 56
Springvale Cl. L32: Kirkb 1B 46
Springville Rd. L9: Aintr 3H 45
Springwell Av. L36: Roby 7G 61
Springwell Rd. L20: Boot 3B 44
Springwood Av. L19: Aller 8B 76
L25: Woolt 8B 76
Springwood Ct. *L19: Aller* *9B 76*
(off Brocklebank La.)
Springwood Crematorium 8D 76
Springwood Dr. L40: Ruf 1L 15
Springwood Gro. L32: Kirkb 3D 46
Springwood Way CH62: New F 8N 73
Sprint Way L24: Speke 2D 92
Sprodley Dr. WN6: App B 3L 23
Spruce Cl. CH42: Tran 4K 73
WA1: Wools 1M 83
WA3: Low 3G 52
Spruce Gro. L28: Stockb V 2F 60
Spruce Way L37: Form 1C 24
Sprucewood Cl. L6: Liv 4G 58
Spunhill Av. CH66: Gt Sut 2H 111
Spur, The L23: Crosb 8K 33
Spur Cl. L11: Crox 7A 46
Spurgeon Cl. L5: Liv 4E 58
Spurling Rd. WA5: Burtw 3H 65
Spurriers La. L31: Mell 3A 36
Spurstow Cl. CH43: Oxton 5F 72
Spymers Cft. L37: Form 7G 16
Square, The CH2: Ince 9L 105
WA13: Lymm 5E 84
Square Ho. La. PR9: Banks 1F 8
Square La. L40: Burs 2J 21
Squibb Dr. CH46: Leas 7A 56
Squires Av. WA8: Widnes 7J 79
Squires Cl. WA11: Hay 4D 50
Squires M. M31: Part 6L 69
Squires St. L7: Liv 6N 5 (8F 58)
Squirrel Grn. L37: Form 8C 16
Stable Cl. CH49: Grea 4L 71
Stables, The L23: Crosb 6N 33
Stables Bus. Cen., The *L13: Liv* *2K 59*
(off Larkhill La.)
Stables Ct. *WA9: St H* *8M 49*
(off Appleton Rd.)
Stableyard Cotts. WA11: Crank 9H 39
Stackfield, The CH48: W Kir 5G 70
Stadium Ct. CH62: Brom 5E 90
Stadium Rd. CH62: Brom 4D 90
Stadt Moers Pk. 7M 61
Stadt Moers Vis. Cen. 7N 61
Staffin Av. CH65: Ell P 5N 111
Stafford Cl. L36: Huy 5L 61
Stafford Gdns. CH65: Ell P 9N 103
Stafford Moreton Way L31: Mag 2H 35
Stafford Rd. PR8: Birkd 5N 11
WA4: Warr 6D 82
WA10: St H 9G 48
Staffordshire Cl. L5: Liv 3D 58
M31: Part 7L 69
Stafford St. L3: Liv 3J 5 (7D 58)
WN8: Skel 2A 30
Stage La. WA13: Lymm 4H 85
Stag Rd. L24: Speke 1C 92
Stainburn Av. L11: Norr G 7L 45
Stainburn Cl. WN6: Shev 7N 23
Stainer Cl. L14: Knott A 4D 60
WA12: Newt W 5K 51
Staines Cl. WA4: App 2F 98
Stainforth Cl. WA3: Cul 6L 53
Stainmore Cl. WA3: Birchw 3B 68
Stainton Cl. L26: Halew 8J 77
WA11: St H 2L 49
Stairhaven Rd. L19: Aller 7N 75
Stakes, The CH46: Leas 6M 55
Stalbridge Av. L18: Moss H 3L 75
Stalbridge Dr. WA7: Nort 3H 97
Staley Av. L23: Crosb 8M 33
Staley Dr. L20: Boot 4C 44
Stalisfield Av. L11: Norr G 8M 45
Stalisfield Pl. L11: Norr G 8M 45
Stalmine Rd. L9: W'ton 6F 44
Stamford Ct. L20: Boot 7C 44
Stamfordham Dr. L19: Aller 8A 76
Stamfordham Gro. L19: Aller 9B 76
Stamfordham Pl. L19: Aller 9B 76
Stamford Rd. PR8: Birkd 3A 12
WN8: Skel 2A 30
Stamford St. CH65: Ell P 9M 103
L7: Liv 7H 59
Stanbridge Cl. WA5: Gt San 2K 81
Stanbury Av. CH63: Beb 1N 89
Standale Rd. L15: Wavtr 9L 59
Standard Rd. L11: Crox 6A 46
Standedge Way L14: Knott A 3E 60
Standen Cl. WA10: St H 6H 49
Stand Farm Rd. L12: Crox 7D 46
Standhouse La. L39: Augh 2A 28
Standingwood Rd.
CH65: Ell P 7N 103
Standish Av. WN5: Bil 6A 40
Standish Ct. WA8: Widnes 8G 78
Standish Dr. WA11: Rainf 4D 38
Standish St. L3: Liv 2F 4 (7C 58)
WA10: St H 6K 49
Stand Pk. Av. L30: Neth 9E 34
Stand Pk. Cl. L30: Neth 9E 34
Stand Pk. Rd. L16: Child 2B 76
Stand Pk. Way L30: Neth 8D 34
Standring Gdns. WA10: St H 1E 62
Standside Pk. WN8: Skel 4A 30
Stanedge Gro. WN3: Wigan 1K 41
Stanfield Av. L5: Liv 4E 58
Stanfield Dr. CH63: Beb 4M 89
Stanford Av. CH45: New B 2H 57
Stanford Cres. L25: Hunts X 7H 77
Stangate L31: Mag 1G 35
Stanhope Dr. CH62: Brom 6C 90
L36: Huy 6G 60
Stanhope St. L8: Liv 2C 74
(not continuous)
WA10: St H 5J 49
Stanier Way L7: Liv 8H 59
Staniforth Pl. L16: Child 8B 60
Stanlaw Abbey Bus. Cen.
CH65: Ell P 3B 112
Stanlawe Rd. L37: Form 7E 16
Stanlaw Rd. CH65: Ell P 1A 112
STANLEY 7K 59
Stanley Av. CH45: Wall 3D 56
CH63: H Beb 8H 73
PR8: Birkd 3M 11
WA4: Stockt H 6G 82
WA5: Gt San 1F 80
WA11: Rainf 4B 38
Stanley Bank Rd. WA11: Hay 3C 50
Stanley Bank Way WA11: Hay 4B 50
Stanley Bungs. L34: Know 7G 47
Stanley Cl. CH44: Wall 7L 57
L4: Kirkd 2C 58
WA8: Widnes 6M 79
Stanley Cotts. L29: Thorn 2B 34
Stanley Ct. CH42: Tran 5M 73
L1: Liv 4E 4
L40: Burs 9J 15
Stanley Cres. L34: Presc 3N 61
Stanley Gdns. L9: W'ton 5E 44
STANLEY GATE 5J 29
Stanley Ho. L20: Boot 6A 44
Stanley Ind. Est. WN8: Skel 1B 30
STANLEY ISLAND 2B 30
Stanley La. CH62: East 2E 102
STANLEY PARK 1B 44
Stanley Pk.
Walton 1F 58
Stanley Pk. L21: Lith 1N 43
Stanley Pk. Av. Nth. L4: W'ton 9G 45
(not continuous)
Stanley Pk. Av. Sth. L4: W'ton 1G 59
Stanley Pl. WA4: Stockt H 6G 82
Stanley Pct. L20: Boot 7B 44
Stanley Rd. CH41: Birke 8F 56
CH47: Hoy 3A 70
CH62: New F 8N 73
CH65: Ell P 7A 104
L5: Kirkd, Liv 1C 58
L20: Boot, Kirkd 5B 44
L22: Wloo 2L 43
L31: Mag 5H 35
L36: Huy 7J 61
L37: Form 7E 16
WN8: Uph 5L 31
Stanley St. CH44: Wall 7L 57
L1: Liv 4E 4 (7B 58)
L7: Liv 6K 59
L19: Garst 3B 92
L39: Orm 8D 20
PR9: South 8G 6
WA1: Warr 4C 82
WA7: Run 4L 95
WA12: Newt W 7J 51
Stanley Ter. CH45: New B 2H 57
L8: Liv 9L 5
L18: Moss H 5M 75
Stanley Theatre 5L 5 (8E 58)
Stanley Vs. WA7: Run 6J 95
Stanley Way WN8: Skel 1B 30
STANLOW 1G 113
Stanlow & Thornton Station (Rail) 9J 105
Stanlowe Vw. L19: G'dale 1L 91
Stanmore Pk. CH49: Grea 5J 71
Stanmore Rd. L15: Wavtr 2N 75
WA7: Run 5N 95
Stannanought Rd. WN8: Skel 1F 30
(not continuous)
Stanner Cl. WA5: Call 7M 65
Stanney Cl. CH62: East 3D 102
CH64: Nest 7E 100
Stanney La. CH2: Back 9A 112
CH2: Lit Stan 4C 112
CH65: Ell P 1N 111
(not continuous)
Stanney Mill Ind. Est. CH2: Lit Stan 2D 112
Stanney Mill La. CH2: Lit Stan 4D 112
Stanney Mill Rd. CH2: Lit Stan 2D 112
Stanney Oaks Annex 3A 112
Stanney Woods Av. CH65: Ell P 5A 112
Stanney Woods Local Nature Reserve 5N 111
Stannyfield Cl. L23: Thorn 5A 34
Stannyfield Dr. L23: Thorn 5A 34
Stansfield Av. L31: Mag 2L 35
WA1: Warr 2G 82
Stansfield Dr. WA4: Grap 9H 83
Stanstead Av. WA5: Penk 5H 81
Stanton Av. L21: Lith 1N 43
Stanton Cl. L30: Neth 6C 34
WA11: Hay 4E 50
WN3: Wigan 1K 41
Stanton Ct. CH64: Nest 6E 100
Stanton Cres. L32: Kirkb 9A 36
Stanton Rd. CH63: Beb 4L 89
L18: Moss H 3L 75
WA4: Thel 5L 83
Stanwell Ho. CH65: Ell P 1N 111
Stanwood Cl. WA10: Ec'stn 7C 48
Stanwood Gdns. L35: Whis 6B 62
Stanza Ct. L5: Liv 4D 58
Stapehill Cl. L13: Liv 7N 59
Stapeley Gdns. L26: Halew 1L 93
Staplands Rd. L14: Brd G 7B 60
Stapleford Ct. CH66: Ell P 6L 103
Stapleford Rd. L25: Gate 2G 76
Staplehurst Cl. L12: Crox 7C 46
Staplehurst Dr. CH42: Rock F 7N 73
Stapleton Av. CH49: Grea 4L 71
L24: Speke 4H 93
L35: Rainh 5F 62
WA2: Warr 9E 66
Stapleton Cl. L25: Gate 1F 76
L35: Rainh 5F 62
Stapleton Ct. WA6: Frod 6M 107
Stapleton Rd. L35: Rainh 4E 62
L37: Form 3D 24
Stapleton Way WA8: Hale B 2E 94
Stapley Cl. WA7: Run 6J 95
Starbeck Dr. CH66: Lit Sut 8G 102
Starkey Gro. WA4: Westy 4G 82
Star La. WA13: Lymm 4C 84
Starling Cl. WA7: Murd 8F 96
Starling Gro. L12: W Der 9D 46
Starling Way L30: Boot 2C 44
Star St. L8: Liv 2D 74
Startham Av. WN5: Bil 8N 39
Starworth Dr. CH62: New F 9B 74
STATHAM 4D 84
Statham Av. WA2: Warr 7D 66
WA13: Lymm 5C 84
Statham Cl. WA13: Lymm 5D 84
Statham Dr. WA13: Lymm 5D 84
Statham La. WA3: Rix 1B 84
WA13: Lymm 3B 84
Statham Rd. CH43: Bid 9C 56
WN8: Skel 9A 22
Statham Way L39: Orm 9C 20
Station App. CH46: More 7M 55
CH47: Meols 9F 54
L39: Orm 8D 20
L40: Burs 9J 15
(not continuous)
Station Av. CH66: Lit Sut 7H 103
WA6: Hel 1E 114
WN5: Orr 7N 31
Station Cl. CH2: Ince 1L 113
CH64: Nest 7F 100
L25: Hunts X 9G 76
Station Cotts. M31: Part 5N 69
Station Ct. CH66: Lit Sut 7H 103
Station Grn. CH66: Lit Sut 7H 103
Station Ho. WA2: Warr 2C 82
Station La. CH3: L Barr 9A 114
Station M. L32: Kirkb 8A 36
WA8: Widnes 7E 78
WN4: Garsw 8F 40
Station Pas. *L9: W'ton* *6F 44*
(off Walton Pk.)
Station Rd. CH1: Lea B 9N 111
CH2: Elt 1M 113
CH2: Ince 9L 105
CH3: Moul 9K 115
CH41: Birke 8F 56
CH44: Wall 5G 56
CH47: Hoy 2C 70
CH60: Hesw 9N 87
CH61: Barns 2D 88
CH61: Thurs 3G 87
CH63: Store 2D 88
CH64: Nest 7E 100
(not continuous)
CH64: P'gte 6C 100
CH65: Ell P 8A 104
(not continuous)
CH66: Lit Sut 8H 103
L25: Gate 3E 76
L31: Lydi 6F 26
L31: Mag 3K 35
L31: Mell 8N 35
Station Rd. L34: Presc 3A 62
(not continuous)
L35: Rainh 6F 62
L36: Roby 7G 60
L39: Bart 6C 18
L39: Orm 7D 20
L40: Ruf 2N 15
M44: Irlam 2L 69
PR8: Ainsd 9J 11
PR9: Banks 2C 8
WA2: Padg 8H 67
WA4: Warr 6F 82
WA5: Gt San 3H 81
WA5: Penk 5F 80
WA7: Run 5J 95
WA7: Sut W 2D 108
WA8: Widnes 4M 79
WA9: St H 2A 64
WA11: Hay 4E 50
WA14: Dun M 3N 85
WN4: Garsw 8E 40
WN8: Parb 3F 22
Station Rd. Blvd. L34: Presc 4A 62
Station Rd. Ind. Est. WA4: Warr 6G 82
Station Rd. Nth. WA2: Fearn 7H 67
Station Rd. Sth. WA2: Padg 8H 67
Station St. L35: Rainh 6F 62
Statton Rd. L13: Liv 8N 59
Staveley Av. L40: Burs 1J 21
Staveley Rd. L19: G'dale 8N 75
PR8: Ainsd 1K 17
WN8: Skel 1B 30
Stavert Cl. L11: Norr G 7N 45
Staverton Pk. L32: Kirkb 1A 46
Stavordale Rd. CH46: More 8N 55
Steble St. L8: Liv 3E 74
Steel Av. CH45: Wall 3J 57
Steel Ct. L5: Liv 4B 58
Steel St. WA1: Warr 1E 82
Steeple, The CH48: Caldy 1E 86
Steeplechase Cl. L9: Aintr 2H 45
Steeple Ct. CH64: Nest 7E 100
Steeple Vw. L33: Kirkb 6C 36
Steers Cl. WA4: Westy 4J 83
Steers Cft. L28: Stockb V 1D 60
Steetley Dr. WA9: St H 5H 63
Stein Av. WA3: Low 2F 52
Steinberg Ct. L3: Liv 5B 58
Steley Way L34: Presc 4A 62
Stella Nova L20: Boot 7B 44
Stella Pct. L21: Sea 4N 43
Stenhills Cres. WA7: Run 5M 95
Stephens Gdns. CH66: Lit Sut 8G 102
Stephen's Gro. WA6: Hel 3E 114
Stephens La. L2: Liv 4E 4
Stephenson Ct. *L7: Liv* *8H 59*
(off Crosfield Rd.)
Stephenson Gro. L35: Rainh 5D 62
Stephenson Ho. L7: Liv 7N 5 (9F 58)
Stephenson Rd. L13: Liv 7M 59
WA12: Newt W 8L 51
Stephenson's Sankey Viaduct 8H 51
Stephenson Way L13: Wavtr 8K 59
L37: Form 1H 25
Stephens Ter. CH66: Lit Sut 8G 102
Stephen St. WA1: Warr 2E 82
Stephen Way L35: Rainh 4E 62
Stepney Gro. L4: W'ton 9F 44
Steppingstone M. WA8: Widnes 4N 79
Sterling Way L5: Kirkd 3C 58
Sterndale Cl. L7: Liv 9G 59
Sterrix Av. L30: Neth 9B 34
Sterrix Grn. L21: Lith 9B 34
Sterrix La. L21: Lith 9B 34
L30: Neth 9B 34
Stetchworth Rd. WA4: W'ton 7C 82
Steuber Dr. M44: Irlam 4M 69
Steve Biko Cl. L8: Liv 1G 75
Stevenage Cl. WA9: St H 2J 63
Stevens Ct. WA9: St H 1G 62
Stevenson Cres. WA10: St H 6G 49
Stevenson Dr. CH63: Spit 4M 89
Stevenson St. L15: Wavtr 9L 59
Stevens Rd. CH60: Hesw 8C 88
Stevens St. WA9: St H 1G 62
Steventon WA7: Nort 3G 96
Steward Ct. L35: Presc 4C 62
Stewards Av. WA8: Widnes 8J 79
Stewart Av. L20: Boot 6D 44
Stewart Cl. CH61: Pens 4N 87
Stickens Lock La. M44: Irlam 1N 69
Stile Hey L23: Thorn 6A 34
Stiles, The L39: Orm 8C 20
Stiles Rd. L33: Kirkb 5D 36
Stillington Rd. L8: Liv 4F 74
Stiperstones Cl. CH66: Lit Sut 8F 102
Stirling Av. L23: Crosb 8L 33
Stirling Cl. WA1: Wools 1M 83
Stirling Ct. CH65: Ell P 2B 112
PR9: South 5M 7
Stirling Cres. WA9: St H 3L 63
Stirling Dr. WN4: Garsw 7F 40
Stirling La. L25: Hunts X 9H 77
Stirling Rd. L24: Speke 4F 92
Stirling St. CH44: Wall 7H 57
Stirrup Cl. WA2: Fearn 6H 67
Stirrup Fld. WA3: Golb 2B 52
STOAK 6E 112
Stoak Lodge CH65: Ell P 1A 112
Stockbridge La. L36: Huy 4F 60
(not continuous)

Stockbridge Pl.—Sutton Rd.

Stockbridge Pl. L5: Liv 4F 58
Stockbridge St. L5: Liv 4F 58
STOCKBRIDGE VILLAGE 1E 60
Stockdale Cl. L3: Liv 2E 4 (6B 58)
Stockdale Ct. WA5: Gt San 1G 81
Stockdale Dr. WA5: Gt San 1G 81
Stockham Cl. WA7: Hal 7C 96
Stockham La.
WA7: Brook, Hal, Murd, Pal F 7C 96
(not continuous)
Stockley Cres. L39: Bic 6J 29
Stockley La. WA4: H Whi, L Stret 8G 98
Stockmoor Rd. L11: Norr G 7L 45
Stockpit Rd. L33: Know I 9G 37
Stockport Rd. WA4: Grap, Thel 6K 83
Stocks Av. WA9: St H 7A 50
Stocks Ct., The WA3: Low 2E 52
Stocks La. WA5: Gt San, Penk 3F 80
Stockswell Farm Ct. WA8: Widnes 4H 79
Stockswell Rd. WA8: Widnes 4C 78
Stockton Cres. L33: Kirkb 5B 36
Stockton Gro. WA9: St H 3G 63
STOCKTON HEATH 7E 82
Stockton La. WA4: Grap 7F 82
Stockton Vw. WA4: Warr 6C 82
Stockton Wood Rd. L24: Speke 4G 92
Stockville Rd. L18: Moss H 4C 76
Stoddart Rd. L4: W'ton 8F 44
Stoke Cl. CH62: East 3D 102
Stoke Gdns. CH65: Ell P 1A 112
Stoker Way L9: W'ton 5F 44
Stokesay CH43: Noct 2D 72
Stokesay Ct. CH65: Ell P 2C 112
Stokes Cl. L26: Halew 7L 77
Stokesley Av. L32: Kirkb 9A 36
Stokes St. WA3: Ris 4M 67
Stoke St. CH41: Birke 9H 57
Stoke Wlk. CH65: Ell P 1A 112
Stoneacre Gdns. WA4: App 3F 98
Stonebank Dr. CH64: Lit N 8G 100
Stonebarn Dr. L31: Mag 9H 27
Stone Barn La. WA7: Pal F 9C 96
Stonebridge La. L11: Crox 5N 45
Stoneby Dr. CH45: Wall 2G 56
Stonechat Cl. L27: N'ley 4J 77
WA3: Low 2F 52
WA7: Beech 1A 108
Stone Ct. WA11: Hay 4D 50
Stonecrop L18: Moss H 3C 76
WN6: App B 4N 23
Stonecrop Cl. WA3: Birchw 5K 67
WA7: Beech 2B 108
Stone Cross Dr. WA8: Widnes 3H 79
Stonecross Dr. L35: Rainh 8G 62
Stone Cross La. Nth. WA3: Low 3D 52
Stone Cross La. Sth. WA3: Low 5D 52
STONE CROSS PARK 3C 52
Stonedale Cres. L11: Crox 6N 45
Stonedale Pk. L11: Crox 6M 45
Stonefield Rd. L14: Knott A 5D 60
Stonefont Cl. L9: W'ton 7F 44
Stonegate Dr. L8: Liv 4E 74
Stone Hall La. WN8: Dalt 9J 23
Stonehaven WN3: Winst 1F 40
Stonehaven Cl. L16: Child 9D 60
Stonehaven Dr. WA2: Fearn 6H 67
Stone Hey L35: Whis 8A 62
Stonehey Dr. CH48: W Kir 7D 70
Stonehey Rd. L32: Kirkb 2C 46
Stonehey Wlk. L32: Kirkb 2C 46
Stonehill Av. CH63: Beb 1N 89
L4: W'ton 3G 58
(off Stonehill St.)
Stonehill Cl. WA4: App 3E 98
Stonehills Ct. WA7: Run 5M 95
Stonehills La. WA7: Run 5M 95
Stonehill St. L4: W'ton 3G 58
Stonehouse M. L18: Aller 5B 76
Stonehouse Rd. CH44: Wall 4E 56
Stonelea WA7: Wind H 6D 96
Stoneleigh Cl. PR8: Ainsd 1J 17
Stoneleigh Ct. *WA4: Grap 7L 83*
(off Cliff La.)
Stoneleigh Gdns. WA4: Grap 7L 83
Stoneleigh Gro. CH42: Rock F 8M 73
Stone Mason Cres. L39: Orm 8E 20
Stonemasons Ct. *L25: Woolt 5E 76*
(off Clay Cross Rd.)
Stonemill Ri. WN6: App B 6N 23
Stone Pit Cl. WA3: Low 1G 52
Stone Pit La. WA3: Croft 8G 52
Stoneridge Ct. CH43: Bid 9C 56
Stone Sq. L20: Boot 5D 44
Stone St. L3: Liv 5A 58
L34: Presc 3A 62
Stonethwaite Cl. WN3: Wigan 1J 41
Stoneville Rd. L13: Liv 5M 59
Stoneway Ct. CH60: Hesw 6N 87
Stone Yd. Cl. L39: Orm 8D 20
Stoney Brow WN8: Roby M 1L 31
STONEYCROFT 5M 59
Stoneycroft L12: W Der 5N 59
Stoneycroft Cl. L13: Liv 4M 59
Stoneycroft Cres. L13: Liv 4M 59
Stoneygate La. WN6: App B 3L 23
Stoney Hey Rd. CH45: New B 2G 57
Stoneyhurst Av. L10: Aintr 8H 35
Stoney La. L35: Rainh, Whis 5C 62
WN6: Wright 1F 22
WN8: Parb 1F 22
Stoney La. Ind. Est. L35: Rainh 6D 62
Stoney Vw. L35: Rainh 6E 62
Stonham Cl. CH49: Upton 3M 71
Stonyfield L30: Neth 6D 34
Stony Holt WA7: Nort 7E 96
Stonyhurst Cl. WA11: St H 3L 49
Stonyhurst Cres. WA3: Cul 5L 53
Stonyhurst Rd. L25: Woolt 7F 76
Stopford St. L8: Liv 4E 74
Stopgate La. L9: Aintr, Faz 6J 45
L33: Simsw 5E 36
Store St. L20: Kirkd 9C 44
STORETON 2H 89
STORETON BRICKFIELDS 2E 88
Storeton Cl. CH43: Oxton 5H 73
Storeton La. CH61: Barns 4C 88
Storeton Rd. CH42: Tran 5H 73
CH43: Oxton 5H 73
Stormont Rd. L19: Garst 9N 75
Storrington Av. L11: Norr G 7N 45
Storrsdale Rd.
L18: Moss H 5N 75
Stour Av. L35: Rainh 6F 62
Stourcliffe Rd. CH44: Wall 5G 56
Stour Ct. CH65: Ell P 7N 103
Stourport Cl. CH49: Grea 4K 71
Stourton Rd. L32: Kirkb 2C 46
PR8: Ainsd 1J 17
Stourton St. CH44: Wall 7J 57
Stourvale Rd. L26: Halew 9K 77
Stowe Av. L10: Aintr 9K 35
Stowe Cl. L25: Hunts X 9E 76
Stowell St. L7: Liv 7K 5 (9E 58)
Stowford Cl. L12: W Der 8A 46
Strada Way L3: Liv 2K 5 (6E 58)
Stradbroke Cl. WA3: Low 3H 53
Stradbroke Rd. L15: Wavtr 2M 75
Strafford Dr. L20: Boot 6D 44
Straight Length WA6: Frod 6G 107
Straker Av. CH65: Ell P 8L 103
Strand, The L2: Liv 5D 4 (8B 58)
WN4: Ash M 7K 41
Strand Av. WN4: Ash M 7K 41
Strand Rd. CH47: Hoy 1C 70
L20: Boot 7N 43
(not continuous)
Strand Shop. Cen. 7B 44
Strand St. L1: Liv 6D 4 (8B 58)
L2: Liv 6D 4 (8B 58)
Strand Vw. L20: Boot 7N 43
Strange Rd. WN4: Garsw 8F 40
Stratford Cl. PR8: Ainsd 8G 11
Stratford Rd. CH64: Nest 8D 100
L19: Aig 8L 75
Strathallan Cl. CH60: Hesw 5M 87
Strathcona Rd. CH45: Wall 3J 57
L15: Wavtr 1K 75
Strathearn Rd. CH60: Hesw 9N 87
Strathlorne Cl. CH42: Tran 5M 73
Strathmore Av. WN4: Ash M 6J 41
Strathmore Dr. L23: Crosb 8L 33
Strathmore Gro. WA9: St H 3M 63
Strathmore Rd. L6: Liv 5H 59
Stratton Cl. CH45: Wall 3J 57
L18: Aller 6C 76
WA7: Brook 9D 96
Stratton Dr. WA9: St H 3G 62
Stratton Pk. WA8: Widnes 3J 79
Stratton Rd. L32: Kirkb 1A 46
WA5: Gt San 3K 81
Stratton Wlk. L32: Kirkb 1A 46
Strauss Cl. L8: Liv 2G 75
Strawberry Cl. WA3: Birchw 5K 67
Strawberry Cross CH1: Back 5M 111
Strawberry Dr. CH66: Whit 5M 111
Strawberry Field 5C 76
Strawberry Grn. CH66: Whit 5M 111
Strawberry La. CH1: Moll 8H 111
Strawberry Pk. CH66: Whit 5M 111
Strawberry Rd. L11: Norr G 8K 45
Strawberry Way E. CH1: Back 5M 111
Strawberry Way W. CH1: Back 5M 111
Streatham Av. L18: Moss H 3L 75
Street Hey La. CH64: Will 4A 102
Stretford Cl. L33: Kirkb 6C 36
STRETTON 5E 98
Stretton Av. CH44: Wall 5G 57
WA3: Low 3F 52
WA9: St H 7B 50
WN5: Bil 6A 40
Stretton Cl. CH43: Oxton 5E 72
CH62: East 3D 102
L12: Crox 7E 46
Stretton Dr. PR9: South 7L 7
Stretton Grn. Distribution Pk.
WA4: App T 3L 99
Stretton Rd. WA4: App T, Sttn 5E 98
Stretton Way L36: Huy 9M 61
Strickland Cl. WA4: Grap 9H 83
Strickland St. WA10: St H 5L 49
Stringer Cres. WA4: Westy 4F 82
Stringhey Rd. CH44: Wall 4J 57
Stroma Av. CH65: Ell P 5N 111
Stroma Rd. L18: Aller 7N 75
Stromford Cl. WA8: Widnes 2K 79
Stromness Cl. WA2: Fearn 6J 67
Stroud Cl. CH49: Grea 5K 71
Stroud Ct. CH45: New B 2H 57
Stuart Av. CH46: More 8N 55
L25: Hunts X 9G 76
Stuart Cl. CH46: More 9A 56
Stuart Cres. WN5: Bil 6N 39
Stuart Dr. L14: Brd G 6C 60
WA4: Stockt H 6G 82
Stuart Gro. L20: Kirkd 9C 44
Stuart Rd. CH42: Tran 5K 73
L4: W'ton 8D 44
L22: Wloo 9L 33
L23: Crosb 9L 33
L31: Mell 8N 35
WA7: Manor P 3D 96
WA10: Windle 4F 48
Stuart Rd. Nth. L20: Boot 7D 44
Stubbs La. CH43: Noct 5E 72
Stub La. L40: Burs 3E 20
STUBSHAW CROSS 6M 41
Studholme St. L20: Kirkd 2B 58
Studland Rd. L9: Faz 6K 45
Studley Ct. PR9: South 5J 7
Studley Rd. CH45: Wall 3E 56
Sturdee Rd. L13: Liv 8N 59
Sturgess Cl. L39: Orm 6D 20
Sturgess St. WA12: Newt W 7H 51
Sturton Av. WN3: Wigan 1G 41
Suburban Rd. L6: Liv 3H 59
Sudbrook Cl. WA3: Low 2F 52
Sudbury Cl. L25: Woolt 6H 77
WN3: Wigan 1K 41
Sudbury Gdns. WA9: St H 3F 62
Sudbury Rd. L22: Wloo 9H 33
Sudell Av. L31: Mag 1L 35
Sudell La. L31: Lydi 6J 27
L39: Augh 6J 27
Sudley Grange L17: Aig 7K 75
Sudley House 6L 75
Sudworth Rd. CH45: New B 2G 57
Suez St. WA1: Warr 3C 82
WA12: Newt W 7J 51
Suffield Rd. L4: Kirkd 1C 58
Suffolk Av. CH65: Ell P 9M 103
Suffolk Cl. WA1: Wools 2M 83
Suffolk Pl. WA8: Widnes 9F 78
Suffolk Rd. PR8: Birkd 6N 11
Suffolk St. L1: Liv 8G 4 (9C 58)
L20: Boot 6C 44
WA7: Run 4J 95
Suffton Pk. L32: Kirkb 1A 46
Sugarbrook Dr. L11: Faz 5L 45
Sugar La. L34: Know 7G 47
WA6: Manl 8G 115
Sugar St. L9: Aintr 5G 44
Sugar Stubbs La. PR9: Banks 3G 9
Sugnall St. L7: Liv 8K 5 (9E 58)
(not continuous)
Sulby Av. L13: Liv 4K 59
WA4: Warr 5C 82
Sulby Cl. PR8: Birkd 3M 11
Sulgrave Cl. L16: Child 8A 60
Sullington Dr. L27: N'ley 2J 77
(not continuous)
Sullivan Av. CH49: Upton 4N 71
Sullivan Rd. WA8: Widnes 9N 79
Sullivans Way WA9: St H 1L 63
Sumley Cl. WA11: St H 5N 49
Summer Cl. WA7: Hal 6B 96
Summercroft Cl. WA3: Golb 3B 52
Summerfield CH62: Brom 5C 90
Summerfield Av. WA5: Warr 7A 66
WA10: Ec'stn 7C 48
Summerford Cl. CH42: Tran 5L 73
Summerhill Dr. L31: Mag 4L 35
Summerhill Pk. L14: Brd G 8C 60
Summer La. WA4: Dares, Hatt, Pres H . . . 9J 97
WA7: Hal 6B 96
Summer Rd. L20: Boot 5B 44
Summers Av. L20: Boot 6D 44
Summer Seat L3: Liv 1F 4 (5C 58)
L20: Boot 7N 43
Summers Rd. L3: Liv 3C 74
Summer St. WN8: Skel 1C 30
Summertrees Av. CH49: Grea 4L 71
Summertrees Cl. CH49: Grea 4L 71
Summertrees Rd. CH66: Gt Sut 3K 111
Summerville Gdns. WA4: Stockt H 7G 83
Summerwood CH61: Irby 9L 71
Summerwood Gdns. L39: Hals 5H 19
Summerwood La. L39: Hals 4H 19
Summit, The CH44: Wall 4J 57
Summit Cl. WA4: L Stret 6F 98
Summit Way L25: Woolt 5D 76
Sumner Av. L39: Down 9E 18
Sumner Cl. L5: Liv 4B 58
L35: Rainh 8G 62
Sumner Gro. *L33: Kirkb 6D 36*
(off Mossdale Rd.)
Sumner Rd. CH43: Bid 9F 56
L37: Form 1F 24
Sumners Farm Ct. WA4: Pres H 9J 97
Sumner St. WA11: Hay 4C 50
Sunbeam Cl. WA7: Run 4J 95
Sunbeam Rd. L13: Liv 6M 59
Sunbeam St. WA12: Newt W 7L 51
Sunbourne Rd. L17: Aig 6G 75
Sunbury Dr. PR8: Ainsd 1H 17
Sunbury Gdns. WA4: App 9F 82
Sunbury Rd. CH44: Wall 6J 57
L4: W'ton 2G 58
Sunbury St. WA10: St H 1F 62
Suncourt PR8: Birkd 9E 6
Suncroft Cl. WA1: Wools 1M 83
Suncroft Rd. CH60: Hesw 8C 88
Sundale Av. L35: Presc 3C 62
Sundene Lodge L22: Wloo 3L 43
Sundew Cl. L9: W'ton 3E 44
Sundial Ho. WA3: Cul 7N 53
Sundridge St. L8: Liv 4F 74
Sunfield Cl. CH66: Gt Sut 2J 111
Sunfield Rd. CH46: More 7N 55
Sunfield Vw. PR9: Banks 4E 8
Sunflower Cl. CH49: Wdchu 4B 72
WA9: Bold 2C 64
Sunflower Dr. WA5: Warr 5M 81
Sunlight St. L6: Liv 4H 59
Sunlight Way CH62: Brom 3B 90
Sunloch Cl. L9: Aintr 2J 45
Sunningdale CH46: More 9A 56
Sunningdale Av. WA8: Widnes 7E 78
Sunningdale Cl. L36: Roby 8G 61
WA5: Burtw 2H 65
Sunningdale Dr. CH61: Thing 2A 88
CH63: Brom 9A 90
L23: Blun 5J 33
Sunningdale Gdns. L37: Form 1E 24
Sunningdale Rd. CH45: Wall 1F 56
L15: Wavtr 9L 59
Sunningdale Way CH64: Lit N 9E 100
Sunniside La. WA7: Nort 3G 97
Sunny Bank CH63: H Beb 1K 89
Sunnybank CH49: Upton 2N 71
Sunnybank Av. CH43: Noct 4D 72
Sunnybank Cl. WA12: Newt W 6L 51
Sunny Bank Rd. L16: Child 1B 76
Sunnydale L35: Rainh 6G 63
Sunnyfields L39: Orm 8E 20
WN3: Winst 1E 40
Sunnygate Rd. L19: G'dale 8M 75
Sunnymede Dr. L31: Lydi 9J 27
Sunny Rd. PR9: South 5M 7
Sunnyside CH46: More 7L 55
CH65: Ell P 8A 104
L8: Liv 3G 74
L39: Augh 5A 28
PR8: Birkd 3M 11
WA5: Gt San 2G 81
Sunnyside Ct. PR9: South 6H 7
Sunnyside Rd. L23: Crosb 8J 33
WN4: Ash M 5H 41
Sunrise Cl. L19: G'dale 9N 75
Sunsdale Rd. L18: Moss H 3M 75
Sunset Blvd. WA5: Gt San 2K 81
Sunset Cl. *L33: Kirkb 6E 36*
(off Freckleton Dr.)
Sunset Cotts. CH64: Ness 9G 100
Superbowl UK
Widnes 9L 79
Superior Cl. L27: N'ley 3J 77
Surby Cl. L16: Child 9C 60
Surlingham Gdns. WA9: St H 3H 63
Surrey Av. CH49: Upton 3M 71
Surrey Cl. PR9: South 2A 8
Surrey Dr. CH48: W Kir 8D 70
Surrey St. CH44: Wall 6G 57
L1: Liv 8F 4 (9C 58)
L20: Boot 6C 44
WA4: Warr 5E 82
WA7: Run 5K 95
WA9: St H 7N 49
Susan Dr. WA5: Penk 3F 80
Susan Gro. CH46: More 9L 55
Susan St. WA8: Widnes 6M 79
Susan Wlk. L35: Whis 4C 62
Sussex Cl. CH61: Pens 3M 87
L20: Boot 6C 44
Sussex Gro. WA9: St H 8N 49
Sussex Rd. CH48: W Kir 5D 70
L31: Mag 4J 35
M31: Part 7L 69
M44: Cad 3J 69
PR8: South 9J 7
PR9: South 8H 7
Sussex St. L20: Boot 6C 44
L22: Wloo 9J 33
WA8: Widnes 7N 79
Sutch La. L40: Lath 1M 21
WA13: Lymm 5G 84
Sutcliffe St. L6: Liv 6G 59
Sutherland Ct. WA7: Run 5L 95
Sutherland Dr. CH62: East 2C 102
Sutherland Rd. L34: Presc 3B 62
SUTTON 1B 64
Sutton Av. CH64: Nest 8E 100
WA3: Cul 6M 53
Sutton C'way. WA6: Frod 4A 108
Sutton Cl. CH62: East 3D 102
Sutton Fields Golf Driving Range 2E 108
Sutton Fold WA9: St H 1N 63
Sutton Fold Ind. Pk. WA9: St H 1A 64
SUTTON GREEN 2H 111
Sutton Hall Dr. CH66: Lit Sut 8F 102
Sutton Hall Gdns. CH66: Lit Sut 8F 102
Sutton Hall Golf Course 3C 108
SUTTON HEATH 2J 63
Sutton Heath Rd. WA9: St H 3H 63
SUTTON LEACH 4N 63
Sutton Leisure Cen. 3L 63
SUTTON MANOR 7L 63
Sutton Manor 7M 63
Sutton Moss Rd. WA9: St H 1B 64
Sutton Oak Dr. WA9: St H 9N 49
Sutton Pk. Dr. WA9: St H 2M 63
Sutton Quays Bus. Pk. WA7: Sut W 3A 108
Sutton Rd. CH45: New B 2H 57
L37: Form 3E 24
WA9: St H 9M 49

Sutton's La.—Tetchill Cl.

Sutton's La. L37: Gt Alt 2L 25
Suttons La. WA8: Widnes 9L 79
Sutton St. L13: Liv 4K 59
WA1: Warr 4D 82
WA7: Run 5L 95
Suttons Way *L26: Halew* *7J 77*
(off Betony Cl.)
Sutton Way CH65: Gt Sut, Whit 9L 103
CH66: Gt Sut 1J 111
SUTTON WEAVER 3D 108
Sutton Wood Rd. L24: Speke 4G 92
Suzanne Boardman Ho.
L6: Liv 4H 59
Swainson Rd. L10: Faz 3L 45
Swale Av. L35: Rainh 6F 62
Swaledale Av. L35: Rainh 6G 62
Swaledale Cl. CH62: East 1D 102
WA5: Gt San 1H 81
Swalegate L31: Mag 1H 35
Swale Rd. CH65: Ell P 7M 103
Swallow Cl. L12: Crox 7D 46
L27: N'ley 3K 77
L33: Kirkb 4C 36
WA3: Birchw 5N 67
Swallow Ct. WA10: St H 7G 48
Swallowfield Gdns. WA4: App 2G 98
Swallow Flds. L9: Faz 6L 45
Swallowhurst Cres.
L11: Norr G 8M 45
Swallowtail M. WA4: Warr 7C 82
Swanage Cl. WA4: Stockt H 6F 82
Swan All. *L39: Orm* *8C 20*
(off Burscough St.)
Swan Av. WA9: St H 8C 50
Swan Cl. CH66: Gt Sut 3J 111
L40: Scar 5N 13
Swan Ct. CH43: Pren 6F 72
Swan Cres. L15: Wavtr 9N 59
Swan Delph L39: Augh 2A 28
Swanfield Wlk. *WA3: Golb* *1A 52*
(off Walters Grn. Cres.)
Swan Gdns. WA9: St H 3H 63
Swan Hey L31: Mag 4K 35
Swan La. L39: Augh 6K 27
Swanpool La. L39: Augh 3A 28
Swan Rd. WA12: Newt W 6F 50
Swansea Cl. L19: Garst 1N 91
SWANSIDE 6C 60
Swanside Av. L14: Brd G 6C 60
Swanside Pde. L14: Knott A 6C 60
Swanside Rd. L14: Brd G 6C 60
Swanston Av. L4: W'ton 9F 44
Swan St. L13: Liv 6L 59
Swan Wlk. L31: Mag 4K 35
Sweden Gro. L22: Wloo 1K 43
Sweet Briar Ct. WA9: Clock F 7N 63
Sweetfield Gdns. CH66: Lit Sut 7J 103
Sweetfield Rd. CH66: Lit Sut 7J 103
Sweeting St. L2: Liv 5E 4 (8B 58)
Swift Cl. WA2: Warr 6F 66
Swift Gro. L12: Crox 6D 46
Swift's Cl. L30: Neth 7C 34
Swifts Fold WN8: Skel 4A 30
Swifts La. L30: Neth 7C 34
Swift St. WA10: St H 5K 49
Swift's Weint *CH64: P'gte* *5B 100*
(off Coastguard La.)
Swinbrook Grn. L11: Norr G 7L 45
Swinburne Cl. L16: Child 9D 60
Swinburne Rd. WA10: St H 5G 48
Swinburn Gro. WN5: Bil 2N 39
Swindale Av. WA2: Warr 6C 66
Swindale Cl. L8: Liv 1G 74
Swinden Cl. WA7: Wind H 5F 96
Swinderby Dr. L31: Mell 8N 35
Swindon Cl. CH49: Grea 4K 71
L5: Kirkd 2C 58
Swindon St. L5: Kirkd 2C 58
Swineyard La. WA16: High L 3N 99
Swinford Av. WA8: Widnes 6A 80
Swinhoe Pl. WA3: Cul 7L 53
Swireford Rd. WA6: Hel 3E 114
Swisspine Gdns. WA9: St H 2F 62
Swiss Rd. L6: Liv 6H 59
SWITCH ISLAND 6G 35
Switch Island Leisure Pk. L30: Neth 8F 34
Sword Cl. L11: Crox 7A 46
Swordfish Cl. L40: Burs 1F 20
Sword Meanygate PR4: Tarl 2M 9
Sword Wlk. L11: Crox 7A 46
Swynnerton Way WA8: Widnes 3L 79
Sybil Rd. L4: W'ton 2F 58
Sycamore Av. CH49: Upton 1L 71
L23: Crosb 5M 33
L26: Halew 1K 93
WA3: Golb 1B 52
WA8: Widnes 6L 79
WA11: Hay 5C 50
WA12: Newt W 7L 51
Sycamore Cl. CH49: Upton 1L 71
L9: W'ton 7H 45
PR9: Banks 1F 8
WA10: Ec'stn 6E 48
Sycamore Ct. *L8: Liv* *4F 74*
(off Weller Way)
WA7: Manor P 3F 96
Sycamore Cres. WA3: Rix 7H 69
(not continuous)
Sycamore Dr. CH66: Whit 4L 111
L33: Kirkb 8D 36
WA7: Sut W 2C 108
Sycamore Dr. WA13: Lymm 4D 84
WN3: Winst 1D 40
WN8: Skel 2B 30
Sycamore Gdns. WA10: St H 4H 49
Sycamore Gro. L37: Form 3C 24
Sycamore La. WA5: Gt San 2K 81
(not continuous)
Sycamore Pk. L18: Aller 6B 76
Sycamore Ri. CH49: Grea 6K 71
Sycamore Rd. CH42: Tran 4K 73
L22: Wloo 9L 33
L36: Huy 9J 61
M31: Part 6K 69
WA7: Run 7M 95
Syddall St. WA10: St H 3J 49
Sydenham Av. L17: Liv 3H 75
Sydenham Ho. L17: Aig 3J 75
Syder's Gro. L34: Know 7G 47
Sydney Av. WN7: Leigh 1L 53
Sydney St. L9: Aintr 4F 44
WA7: West P 8G 95
Syers Ct. WA1: Warr 1F 82
Sylvan Ct. L25: Woolt 7F 76
Sylvandale Gro. CH62: Brom 5C 90
Sylvania Rd. L4: W'ton 8F 44
Sylvia Cl. L10: Faz 4N 45
Sylvia Cres. WA2: Warr 8E 66
Synge St. WA2: Warr 1D 82
Syren St. L20: Kirkd 1B 58
Syston Av. WA11: St H 4M 49
Sytchcroft CH64: Nest 6E 100

T

Tabby Nook PR4: Mere B 6K 9
Tabby's Nook WN8: Newb 4D 22
Tabley Av. WA8: Widnes 6F 78
Tabley Cl. CH43: Oxton 6F 72
Tabley Gdns. WA9: St H 3G 62
Tabley Rd. L15: Wavtr 1J 75
Tabley St. L1: Liv 9F 4 (9C 58)
Tace Cl. L8: Liv 1E 74
Tadlow Cl. L37: Form 3C 24
Taggart Av. L16: Child 2B 76
Tagus Cl. L8: Liv 2G 75
Tagus St. L8: Liv 2G 75
Tailor's La. L31: Mag 3K 35
Talaton Cl. PR9: South 2M 7
Talbot Av. CH63: Brim 6G 88
CH64: Lit N 8F 100
Talbot Cl. CH64: Lit N 8F 100
WA3: Birchw 6M 67
WA10: St H 6J 49
Talbot Ct. CH43: Oxton 4G 73
L36: Huy 8J 61
Talbot Dr. PR8: South 9G 6
Talbot Gdns. CH64: Lit N 8F 100
Talbot Rd. CH43: Oxton 4G 72
CH66: Gt Sut 2L 111
WA6: Dun H 6B 114
Talbot St. PR8: South 1N 11
WA3: Golb 2B 52
Talbotville Rd. L13: Liv 8A 60
Talgarth Way L25: Gate 1E 76
Talisman Cl. WA7: Murd 8G 96
Talisman Way L20: Boot 6N 43
Talland Cl. L26: Halew 7J 77
Tallarn Rd. L32: Kirkb 9N 35
Tallow Way M44: Irlam 1N 69
Tall Trees WA9: St H 1L 63
Talman Gro. WN4: Ash M 8M 41
Talton Rd. L15: Wavtr 1J 75
Tamar Cl. L6: Liv 5F 58
Tamar Gro. CH46: More 9L 55
Tamarisk Gdns. WA9: St H 2F 62
Tamar Rd. WA11: Hay 4E 50
Tame Ct. WA8: Widnes 3K 79
Tamerton Cl. L18: Aller 6C 76
Tamneys, The WN8: Skel 3C 30
Tam O'Shanter Urban Farm 1E 72
Tamworth St. L8: Liv 3D 74
WA10: St H 6H 49
WA12: Newt W 7J 51
Tanar Cl. CH63: Spit 4A 90
Tanat Dr. L18: Moss H 4N 75
Tancaster WN8: Skel 3B 30
Tancred Rd. CH45: Wall 4G 56
L4: W'ton 2F 58
Tanfield Nook WN8: Parb 3F 22
Tanfields WN8: Skel 3C 30
TANHOUSE 3G 30
Tanhouse WA7: Hal 6A 96
Tan Ho. Cl. WN8: Parb 2F 22
Tan Ho. Dr. WN3: Winst 1E 40
Tan Ho. La. WA5: Burtw 5H 65
WA8: Widnes 8M 79
WN3: Winst 1E 40
WN8: Parb 3F 22
Tanhouse Rd. L23: Thorn 6A 34
WN8: Skel 4F 30
Tankersley Gro. WA5: Gt San 3J 81
Tanner's La. WA3: Golb 2B 52
Tanners La. WA2: Warr 2B 82
Tannery Ct. WA2: Warr 2C 82
Tannery La. CH64: Nest 6E 100
WA5: Penk 5E 80
Tanning Ct. WA1: Warr 4C 82
Tan Pit Cotts. WN3: Winst 1F 40
Tan Pit La. WN3: Winst 1F 40
Tansley Cl. CH48: W Kir 6F 70
Tanworth Gro. CH46: More 8J 55
Tanyard M. WA13: Lymm 4F 84
Tapestry Gdns. CH41: Birke 8F 56
Tapley Pl. L13: Liv 7L 59
Taplow Cl. WA4: App 1F 98
Taplow St. L6: Liv 3G 59
Tapton Way L13: Wavtr 8L 59
Tara Pk. Cvn. Site L3: Liv 1C 4 (6A 58)
TARBOCK GREEN 4N 77
TARBOCK INTERCHANGE 9N 61
Tarbock Rd. L24: Speke 3H 93
L36: Huy 8H 61
Tarbot Hey CH46: More 9K 55
Tarbrock Ct. *L30: Neth* *6C 34*
(off Great Hey)
Target Rd. CH60: Hesw 7J 87
Tariff St. L5: Liv 4C 58
Tarleton Cl. L26: Halew 9J 77
TARLETON MOSS 1M 9
Tarleton Rd. PR9: South 7M 7
Tarleton St. L1: Liv 5F 4 (8C 58)
TARLSCOUGH 5G 15
Tarlscough La. L40: Burs 5G 15
Tarlswood WN8: Skel 3C 30
Tarlton Cl. L35: Rainh 4D 62
Tarnbeck WA7: Nort 8E 96
Tarn Brow L39: Orm 1A 28
Tarncliff L28: Stockb V 1G 60
Tarn Cl. WN4: Ash M 6K 41
Tarn Ct. WA1: Wools 1N 83
Tarn Gro. WA11: St H 2L 49
Tarnmere Cl. L4: W'ton 7F 44
Tarnrigg Cl. WN3: Wigan 1G 40
Tarn Rd. L37: Form 1D 24
Tarnside Rd. WN5: Orr 6N 31
Tarnway WA3: Low 3G 52
Tarporley Cl. CH43: Oxton 5F 72
WA10: Ec'stn 7E 48
Tarporley Rd. CH66: Gt Sut 1K 111
WA4: Sttn, L Whit, Nor B 5E 98
(not continuous)
Tarragon Cl. L23: Thorn 6A 34
Tarran Dr. CH46: More 7L 55
Tarran Rd. CH46: More 7L 55
Tarrant Cl. WN3: Winst 1F 40
Tarran Way E. CH46: More 7L 55
Tarran Way Nth. CH46: More 7L 55
Tarran Way Sth. CH46: More 7L 55
Tarran Way W. CH46: More 6L 55
Tarves Wlk. L33: Kirkb 9D 36
Tarvin Cl. CH65: Ell P 1A 112
PR9: South 2B 8
WA3: Low 3F 52
WA7: Run 9M 95
WA9: Sut M 5L 63
Tarvin Rd. CH62: East 2E 102
WA6: Alv, Frod 3G 115
WA6: Manl 9K 115
Tasker Ter. L35: Rainh 5F 62
Tasman Cl. WA5: Old H 9L 65
Tasman Gro. WA9: St H 2H 63
Tate Cl. WA8: Widnes 6G 79
Tate Liverpool 7C 4 (9A 58)
Tate St. L4: W'ton 1E 58
Tatham Gro. WN3: Winst 2F 40
Tatlock Cl. WN5: Bil 6A 40
Tatlocks Grange L39: Orm 7B 20
Tatlock St. L5: Liv 5B 58
Tattersall Pl. L20: Boot 8A 44
Tattersall Rd. L21: Lith 3N 43
Tattersall Way L7: Liv 7K 59
Tatton Ct. WA1: Wools 9L 67
Tatton Dr. WN4: Ash M 6H 41
Tatton Rd. CH42: Tran 3K 73
L9: W'ton 4F 44
Tatton Way WA10: Ec'stn 7E 48
Taunton Av. WA9: Sut L 4N 63
Taunton Dr. L10: Aintr 9K 35
Taunton Rd. CH45: Wall 3E 56
L36: Huy 7M 61
Taunton St. L15: Wavtr 9K 59
Taurus Pk. WA5: Westb 5M 65
Taurus Rd. L14: Knott A 5E 60
Tavener Cl. CH63: Brom 1B 102
Tavington Rd. L26: Halew 7L 77
Tavistock Dr. PR8: Ainsd 8H 11
Tavistock Rd. CH45: Wall 3E 56
WA5: Penk 4G 80
Tavlin Av. WA5: Warr 8A 66
Tavy Rd. L6: Liv 5F 58
TAWD BRIDGE 5F 30
Tawd Rd. WN8: Skel 4F 30
Tawd St. L4: Kirkd 1D 58
Tawny Cl. L10: Faz 4M 45
Tawny Ct. WA7: Pal F 8A 96
Tayleur Ter. WA12: Newt W 8M 51
Taylforth Cl. L9: W'ton 5F 44
Taylor Av. L39: Orm 8E 20
Taylor Bus. Pk. WA3: Ris 8N 53
Taylor Cl. WA9: St H 1A 64
Taylor Pl. CH43: Clau 2F 72
Taylor Rd. WA11: Hay 4G 51
Taylors Cl. L9: W'ton 7D 44
Taylor's La. PR4: Tarl 4N 9
WA5: Cuerd 6C 80
Taylors La. L9: W'ton 7D 44
Taylor's Meanygate PR4: Hesk B, Tarl 1L 9
Taylors Row WA7: Run 5M 95
Taylor St. CH41: Birke 1L 73
WA3: Golb *1D 52*
(off Lowton Rd.)
Taylor St. WA4: Warr 7B 82
WA8: Widnes 7M 79
WA9: St H 1A 64
WN8: Skel 3N 29
Teakwood Cl. L6: Liv 4G 58
Teal Bus. Pk. WA8: Widnes 8M 79
Teal Cl. L39: Augh 2A 28
WA2: Warr 6F 66
WA11: St H 4L 49
Teal Gro. L26: Halew 7J 77
WA3: Birchw 6N 67
Teals Way CH60: Hesw 7L 87
TeamSport
Warrington 4A 82
Tears La. WN8: Newb 5C 22
Teasville Rd. L18: Moss H 4C 76
Tebay Cl. L31: Mag 1L 35
Tebay Rd. CH62: East 7D 90
Teck St. L7: Liv 4N 5 (7F 58)
Tedburn Cl. L25: Gate 4G 77
Tedbury Cl. L32: Kirkb 2C 46
Tedbury Wlk. L32: Kirkb 2C 46
Tedder Av. PR9: South 8M 7
Tedder Sq. WA8: Widnes 8G 78
Teddington Cl. WA4: App 2F 98
Teehey Cl. CH63: H Beb 1K 89
Teehey Gdns. CH63: H Beb 1K 89
Teehey La. CH63: H Beb 1K 89
Tees Cl. L4: Kirkd 9D 44
Tees Ct. CH65: Ell P 7M 103
Teesdale Cl. WA5: Gt San 1H 81
Teesdale Rd. CH63: Beb 3L 89
WA11: Hay 3E 50
Teesdale Way L35: Rainh 4F 62
Tees Pl. L4: Kirkd 9D 44
Tees St. CH41: Birke 8F 56
L4: Kirkd 9C 44
Teign Cl. L6: Liv 5F 58
Teignmouth Cl. L19: Garst 1N 91
Teilo St. L8: Liv 3F 74
Telary Cl. L5: Liv 4B 58
Telegraph Ho. L23: Crosb 6L 33
Telegraph La. CH45: Wall 4C 56
Telegraph Rd. CH48: Caldy 9G 71
CH60: Hesw 9G 71
CH61: Thurs 9G 71
Telegraph Way L32: Kirkb 9C 36
Telford Cl. CH43: Oxton 4H 73
WA4: Westy 5J 83
WA8: Widnes 4G 78
Telford Ct. CH1: Dunk 7J 111
L7: Liv 8G 58
Telford Dr. WA9: St H 2B 64
Telford Rd. CH65: Ell P 1C 112
Telford's Quay CH65: Ell P 7B 104
Telletholme Ind. Est. L40: Burs 2F 20
Tempest Hey L2: Liv 4D 4 (7B 58)
Temple Ct. L2: Liv 5E 4 (8B 58)
WA3: Ris 3M 67
Templehill Cl. L14: Knott A 5D 60
Temple La. L2: Liv 4E 4 (7B 58)
Templemartin *WN8: Skel* *2C 30*
(off Thorpe)
Templemore Av. L18: Moss H 5M 75
Templemore Rd. CH43: Oxton 4G 73
Temple Rd. CH42: Tran 6J 73
Temple St. L2: Liv 4E 4 (7B 58)
Templeton Cres. L12: W Der 9N 45
Templeton Dr. WA2: Fearn 6H 67
Tempsford Cl. WA7: Nort 4G 97
Tenbury Cl. WA5: Gt San 9J 65
Tenbury Dr. WN4: Ash M 7H 41
Tenby WN8: Skel 2B 30
Tenby Av. L21: Lith 1N 43
Tenby Cl. WA5: Call 7A 66
Tenby Dr. CH46: More 9N 55
WA7: Run 5N 95
Tennis St. WA10: St H 5H 49
Tennis St. Nth. WA10: St H 5H 49
Tennyson Av. CH42: Rock F 7M 73
Tennyson Dr. L39: Orm 7B 20
WA2: Warr 7D 66
WN5: Bil 2N 39
Tennyson Rd. CH65: Whit 1M 111
L36: Huy 9L 61
WA8: Widnes 7K 79
Tennyson St. L20: Boot 5A 44
WA9: Sut M 7K 63
Tennyson Way L32: Kirkb 1B 46
Tenpin
Ellesmere Port 4B 112
Tensing Cl. WA5: Gt San 9K 65
Tensing Rd. L31: Mag 2J 35
Tenterden St. L5: Liv 5C 58
Tenth Av. L9: Aintr 3J 45
Terence Av. WA1: Padd 2G 83
Terence Rd. L16: Child 2B 76
Terminus Rd. CH62: Brom 4C 90
L36: Huy 4F 60
Tern Cl. L33: Kirkb 4C 36
WA8: Widnes 4L 79
Ternhall Rd. L9: Faz 6L 45
Ternhall Way L9: Faz 6L 45
Tern Way CH46: More 8J 55
WA10: St H 2D 62
Terrace Rd. WA8: Widnes 2K 95
Terret Cft. L28: Stockb V 2F 60
Tesla Way L37: Form 4E 24
Tetbury St. CH41: Birke 3J 73
Tetchill Cl. CH66: Gt Sut 3J 111
WA7: Nort 7F 96

Tetlow St.—Torwood

Tetlow St. L4: W'ton 1E 58
Tetlow Way L4: W'ton 1E 58
Teulon Cl. L4: W'ton 1E 58
Teversham WN8: Skel 2C 30
Teviot WN8: Skel 2B 30
Tewit Hall Cl. L24: Speke 4G 93
Tewit Hall Rd. L24: Speke 4G 92
Tewkesbury *WN8: Skel* *2B 30*
(off Tenby)
Tewkesbury Cl. CH66: Gt Sut 5K 111
L12: Crox 6D 46
L25: Woolt 6H 77
Tewkesbury Rd. WA3: Golb 2C 52
Teynham Av. L34: Know 6H 47
Teynham Cres. L11: Norr G 8L 45
Thackeray Cl. L8: Liv 2E 74
Thackeray Ct. *L8: Liv* *2E 74*
(off Pomfret St.)
Thackeray Gdns. L30: Boot 2C 44
Thackmore Way L19: Aller 7B 76
Thackray Rd. WA10: St H 1G 62
Thames Av. WN7: Leigh 1N 53
Thames Cl. WA2: Warr 7E 66
Thamesdale CH65: Whit 2N 111
Thames Gdns. CH65: Whit 2M 111
Thames Rd. WA3: Cul 8N 53
WA9: Sut L 3M 63
Thames Side CH65: Whit 2N 111
Thames St. L8: Liv 2G 74
Thames Trad. Cen.
M44: Irlam 2M 69
Thanet WN8: Skel 2C 30
Thatchers Mt. WA5: Coll G 9F 50
THATTO HEATH 1H 63
Thatto Heath Rd. WA9: St H 1G 62
WA10: St H 1G 62
Thatto Heath Station (Rail) 1G 62
The
Names prefixed with 'The' for example 'The Academy' are indexed under the main name such as 'Academy, The'
Thealby Cl. WN8: Skel 2B 30
THELWALL 5L 83
Thelwall La. WA4: Warr, Westy 5G 82
Thelwall New Rd. WA4: Grap, Thel 5H 83
Thelwall New Rd. Ind. Est. WA4: Thel 4K 83
Thelwall Rd. CH66: Gt Sut 1K 111
Thermal Rd. CH62: Brom 3C 90
Thermopylae Ct. CH43: Noct 2D 72
Thermopylae Pas. CH43: Noct 2D 72
Thetford Rd. WA5: Gt San 2G 81
Thewlis St. WA5: Warr 3N 81
Thickwood Moss La. WA11: Rainf 6C 38
THINGWALL 1A 88
Thingwall Av. L14: Knott A 7B 60
Thingwall Dr. CH61: Irby 1A 88
Thingwall Grange CH61: Thing 1B 88
Thingwall Hall Dr. L14: Brd G 7B 60
Thingwall La. L14: Knott A, Brd G 6B 60
Thingwall Recreation Cen. 1B 88
Thingwall Rd. CH61: Irby 1L 87
L15: Wavtr 1N 75
Thingwall Rd. E. CH61: Thing 1A 88
Third Av. CH43: Bid 2B 72
L9: Aintr 3J 45
(Fourth Av.)
L9: Aintr 3K 45
(Meres Rd.)
L23: Crosb 7K 33
WA7: Pal F 7B 96
Third St. WN2: Bam 4N 41
Thirlmere Av. CH43: Noct 2C 72
L21: Lith 2C 44
L37: Form 2G 25
WA2: Warr 6D 66
WA11: St H 2K 49
WN4: Ash M 7L 41
WN8: Uph 5L 31
Thirlmere Cl. L31: Mag 1K 35
WA6: Frod 6N 107
Thirlmere Ct. *L5: Liv* *4F 58*
(off Harding Cl.)
Thirlmere Dr. CH45: Wall 4H 57
L21: Lith 2C 44
PR8: Ainsd 2H 17
WA13: Lymm 5F 84
Thirlmere Grn. L5: Liv 4F 58
Thirlmere M. L38: Hight 8G 24
Thirlmere Rd. CH64: Nest 8E 100
CH65: Whit 3N 111
L5: Liv 4F 58
L38: Hight 8G 24
M31: Part 5L 69
WA3: Golb 1D 52
Thirlmere Wlk. L33: Kirkb 7B 36
Thirlmere Way WA8: Widnes 8F 78
Thirlstane St. L17: Aig 5G 75
Thirsk WN8: Skel 2C 30
Thirsk Cl. WA7: Run 9M 95
Thirty Acre La. L37: Form 8K 17
Thistle Ct. L40: Burs 8J 15
Thistledown Cl. L17: Aig 5F 74
Thistledown Dr. L38: Hight 8F 24
Thistle Sq. M31: Part 7L 69
Thistleton Av. CH41: Birke 9F 56
Thistleton Cl. WA9: St H 6A 50
Thistleton M. PR9: South 7H 7
Thistle Wlk. *M31: Part* *7L 69*
(off Thistle Sq.)
Thistlewood Rd. L7: Liv 7K 59
Thistley Hey Rd. L32: Kirkb 9D 36
Thomas Cl. CH65: Whit 3N 111
L19: Garst 2A 92
Thomas Ct. CH43: Oxton 3J 73
WA7: Pal F 8B 96
Thomas Dr. L14: Brd G 7A 60
L35: Presc 5N 61
Thomas Jones Way WA7: Run 5K 95
Thomas La. L14: Brd G, Knott A 5B 60
Thomason's Bri. La. WA4: H Walt 1N 97
Thomas Steers Way L1: Liv 7E 4 (8B 58)
Thomas St. CH41: Birke 3L 73
WA3: Golb 2B 52
WA7: Run 4L 95
WA8: Widnes 9K 79
Thomaston St. L5: Liv 3D 58
(not continuous)
Thomas Winder Ct. *L5: Kirkd* *3C 58*
(off Sterling Way)
Thompson Av. L39: Orm 8E 20
WA3: Cul 7M 53
Thompson Cl.
WA12: Newt W 9L 51
Thompson St. CH41: Tran 4L 73
WA3: Ris 4M 67
WA10: St H 9G 48
WN4: Ash M 7M 41
Thomson Rd. L21: Sea 3M 43
(not continuous)
Thomson St. L6: Liv 5G 58
Thorburn Cl. CH62: New F 8A 74
Thorburn Ct. CH62: New F 7A 74
Thorburn Cres. CH62: New F 8A 74
Thorburn Dr. L7: Liv 8G 59
Thorburn Lodge
CH62: New F 7A 74
Thorburn Rd. CH62: New F 8A 74
Thoresby Cl. WN3: Wigan 1G 41
Thorlby Rd. WA3: Cul 7N 53
Thorley Cl. L15: Wavtr 8M 59
Thornaby Gro. WA9: St H 3G 62
Thornbeck Av. L38: Hight 9F 24
Thornbeck Cl. L12: Crox 7D 46
Thornbridge Av. L21: Lith 2C 44
L40: Burs 2J 21
Thornbrook Cl. L12: W Der 2B 60
Thornbury WN8: Skel 2C 30
Thornbury Av. WA3: Low 3F 52
Thornbury Rd. L4: W'ton 2H 59
Thornbush Cl. WA3: Low 1F 52
Thornby WN8: Skel 2C 30
Thorncliffe Rd. CH44: Wall 6G 56
Thorn Cl. WA5: Penk 5H 81
WA7: Run 8M 95
Thorncroft Dr. CH61: Barns 3B 88
Thorndale WN8: Skel 2C 30
Thorndale Lawn Tenris Club 4G 56
Thorndale Rd. L22: Wloo 9K 33
Thorndyke Cl. L35: Rainh 8H 63
Thorne Dr. CH66: Lit Sut 9G 103
Thorne La. CH44: Wall 4F 56
Thornes Rd. L6: Liv 6G 58
Thorness Cl. CH49: Grea 6K 71
Thorneycroft Dr. WA1: Warr 2D 82
Thorneycroft St. CH41: Birke 9G 56
Thornfield Cl. CH46: More 9A 56
WA3: Golb 2D 52
Thornfield Hey CH63: Spit 5N 89
Thornfield Rd. L9: W'ton 5E 44
L23: Thorn 5N 33
Thornham Av. WA9: St H 1M 63
Thornham Cl. CH49: Upton 1A 72
Thornhead La. L12: W Der 3B 60
Thornhill L39: Augh 3N 27
Thornhill Cl. L39: Augh 4N 27
Thornhill Rd. L15: Wavtr 1M 75
WN4: Garsw 7E 40
Thornhurst L32: Kirkb 3C 46
Thornleigh Av. CH62: East 3E 102
Thornleigh Dr. CH66: Ell P 8K 103
Thornley Cl. WA13: Lymm 5C 84
Thornley Rd. CH46: More 1K 71
WA13: Lymm 5C 84
Thorn Rd. WA1: Padd 9H 67
WA7: Run 8M 95
WA10: St H 7F 48
Thorns, The L31: Mag 1G 35
Thorns Dr. CH49: Grea 6K 71
Thornside Wlk. L25: Gate 4F 76
THORNTON 5N 33
Thornton WA8: Widnes 8H 79
WN8: Skel 2C 30
Thornton Av. CH63: H Beb 8K 73
L20: Boot 3C 44
Thornton Cl. L40: Ruf 2N 15
WA3: Low 1H 53
WN4: Ash M 7H 41
WN7: Leigh 1N 53
Thornton Comn. Rd.
CH63: Raby M, Thorn H 8H 89
Thornton Crematorium 5B 34
Thornton Cres. CH60: Hesw 9B 88
Thorntondale Dr. WA5: Gt San 1G 81
Thornton Dr. WA12: Newt W 8H 51
Thornton Grn. La. CH2: Thorn M 3J 113
Thornton Gro. CH63: H Beb 8K 73
THORNTON HOUGH 9H 89
THORNTON-LE-MOORS 3J 113
Thornton M. CH66: Chil T 6G 102
Thornton Rd. CH45: Wall 3G 56
CH63: H Beb 8K 73
CH65: Ell P 1B 112
Thornton Rd. L16: Child 8C 60
L20: Boot 5B 44
(not continuous)
PR9: South 8L 7
WA5: Gt San 4K 81
Thornton St. CH41: Birke 9G 56
L21: Lith 4A 44
Thornton Way L36: Huy 3H 61
Thorn Tree Cl. L24: Hale 6B 94
Thorntree Cl. L17: Aig 5F 74
Thorntree Grn. WA4: App T 2J 99
Thorn Wlk. M31: Part 7L 69
Thornwood WN8: Skel 2C 30
Thornwood Cl. L6: Liv 4G 58
Thornwythe Gro. CH66: Gt Sut 1K 111
Thornycroft Rd. L15: Wavtr 1J 75
Thoroughgood Cl. L40: Burs 3H 21
Thorpe WN8: Skel 2C 30
Thorpe Bank CH42: Rock F 8M 73
Thorstone Dr. CH61: Irby 9K 71
Thorsway CH42: Rock F 6M 73
CH48: Caldy 8E 70
Threadneedle Ct. WA9: St H 1B 64
Three Acres Cl. L25: Woolt 5C 76
Three Butt La. L12: W Der 3L 59
Three Crowns WA8: Widnes 7J 79
THREE LANES END 3J 71
Three Oaks Cl. L40: Lath 3M 21
Three Pools PR9: South 4A 8
(not continuous)
Three Sisters Ent. Pk., The
WN4: Ash M 5K 41
Three Sisters Race Circuit 4L 41
Three Sisters Rd. WN4: Ash M 5K 41
Three Tuns La. L37: Form 1F 24
Threlfalls La. PR9: South 5L 7
Threlfall St. L8: Liv 4F 74
Thresher Av. CH49: Grea 4K 71
Threshers, The *L30: Neth* *7G 34*
(off Reapers Way)
Throne Rd. L11: Crox 7A 46
Throne Wlk. *L11: Crox* *6A 46*
(off Throne Rd.)
Thurcroft Dr. WN8: Skel 2B 30
Thurlby Cl. WN4: Ash M 7M 41
Thurlow WA3: Low 3F 52
Thurne Way L25: Gate 2E 76
Thurnham St. L6: Liv 4H 59
Thursby Cl. L32: Kirkb 2D 46
PR8: Ainsd 2H 17
Thursby Cres. L32: Kirkb 1D 46
Thursby Dr. L32: Kirkb 1D 46
Thursby Rd. CH62: Brom 5D 90
Thursby Wlk. L32: Kirkb 2D 46
THURSTASTON 2J 87
Thurstaston Common Local Nature Reserve
8H 71
Thurstaston Rd. CH60: Hesw 6M 87
CH61: Irby, Thurs 2J 87
Thurston WN8: Skel 2B 30
(not continuous)
Thurston Av. WN3: Wigan 1K 41
Thurston Billiard & Snooker Mus.
2H 5 (6D 58)
Thurston Cl. WA5: Gt San 2M 81
Thurston Rd. L4: W'ton 3G 59
Thynne St. WA1: Warr 4B 82
Tibb's Cross La. WA8: Bold H 9N 63
Tiber St. L8: Liv 2G 75
Tichbourne Way L6: Liv 2L 5 (6E 58)
Tickford Bank WA8: Widnes 6H 79
Tickle Av. WA9: St H 7N 49
Tidal La. WA1: Padg 9G 67
Tideswell Cl. L7: Liv 9G 59
Tide Way CH45: Wall 1E 56
Tiger Ct. L34: Presc 4L 61
Tilbey Dr. WA6: Frod 6K 107
Tilbrook Dr. WA9: St H 3N 63
Tilbury Gro. WN6: Shev 6N 23
Tilbury Pl. WA7: Murd 9G 96
Tilcroft WN8: Skel 2B 30
Tildsley Cres. WA7: W'ton 9J 95
Tilia Rd. L5: Liv 3F 58
Tilley St. WA1: Warr 3D 82
Tillotson Cl. L8: Liv 3D 74
Tilman Cl. WA5: Gt San 9J 65
Tilney St. L9: W'ton 4F 44
Tilstock Av. CH62: New F 8A 74
Tilstock Cl. L26: Halew 6L 77
Tilstock Cres. CH43: Pren 7F 72
Tilston Av. WA4: Westy 4H 83
Tilston Cl. L9: Faz 7J 45
Tilston Rd. CH45: Wall 3G 56
L9: Faz 6J 45
L32: Kirkb 9A 36
Timberland Cl. L25: Gate 1E 76
Timberscombe Gdns. WA1: Wools 2M 83
Time Pk. L35: Whis 4C 62
Timmis Cl. WA2: Fearn 6H 67
Timmis Cres. WA8: Widnes 7K 79
Timms Cl. L37: Form 8F 16
Timms La. L37: Form 8F 16
Timon Av. L20: Boot 6D 44
Timor Av. WA9: St H 1H 63
Timperley Av. WA4: Westy 4H 83
Timperley Ct. *WA8: Widnes* *8L 79*
(off Alfred St.)
Timpron St. L7: Liv 9H 59
Timway Dr. L12: W Der 1C 60
Tinas Way CH49: Upton 3A 72
Tinling Cl. L34: Presc 3B 62
Tinsley Av. PR8: South 3D 12
Tinsley Cl. L26: Halew 6J 77
Tinsley's La. PR8: South 5E 12
Tinsley St. WA4: Westy 5G 82
Tintagel WN8: Skel 2A 30
Tintagel Cl. WA7: Brook 9E 96
Tintagel Rd. L11: Crox 5B 46
Tintern Av. WN4: Ash M 8M 41
Tintern Cl. WA5: Call 7N 65
Tintern Dr. CH46: More 9M 55
L37: Form 2H 25
Tiptree Cl. L12: Crox 6D 46
Titchfield St. L3: Liv 5B 58
L5: Liv 5B 58
Tithebarn Cl. CH60: Hesw 8N 87
Tithebarn Dr. CH64: P'gte 4B 100
Tithebarn Gro. L15: Wavtr 1M 75
Tithebarn La. L31: Mell 6M 35
L32: Kirkb 1B 46
Tithebarn Rd. L23: Crosb 7M 33
L34: Know 6G 47
PR8: South 9J 7
WN4: Garsw 9E 40
Tithebarn St. L2: Liv 4D 4 (7B 58)
WN8: Uph 5L 31
Titherington Way
L15: Wavtr 2J 75
Tithings, The WA7: Run 6A 96
Tiverton Av. CH44: Wall 5G 57
WN8: Skel 2B 30
Tiverton Cl. L36: Huy 6M 61
WA8: Widnes 5F 78
Tiverton Rd. L26: Halew 1J 93
Tiverton Sq. WA5: Penk 4G 81
Tiverton St. L15: Wavtr 9K 59
TMAS Health & Fitness *6K 49*
(off Tolver St.)
Tobermory Cl. WA11: Hay 5C 50
Tobin Cl. L5: Liv 5B 58
Tobin St. CH44: Wall 5K 57
Tobruk Rd. L36: Huy 5H 61
TOBY ISLAND 1E 30
Todd Rd. WA9: St H 7L 49
Todd's La. PR9: Banks 1E 8
Toft Cl. WA8: Widnes 7J 79
Toft St. L7: Liv 7H 59
Toftwood Av. L35: Rainh 8G 63
Toftwood Gdns. L35: Rainh 8G 63
Tokenspire Pk.
L33: Know I 3F 46
Toleman Av. CH63: Beb 2N 89
Toll Bar Pl. *WA2: Warr* *5B 66*
(off Poplars Av.)
Toll Bar Rd. WA2: Warr 6B 66
Tollemache Rd. CH41: Birke 1F 72
CH43: Bid 1F 72
CH43: Clau 1F 72
Tollemache St. CH45: New B 1J 57
Tollerton Rd. L12: W Der 3L 59
Tollgate Cl. L25: Gate 2D 76
Tollgate Cres. L40: Burs 2G 20
Tollgate Rd. L40: Burs 3F 20
Tolpuddle Rd. L25: Woolt 5D 76
Tolpuddle Way L4: Kirkd 1C 58
Tolver Ho. *WA10: St H* *6K 49*
(off Tolver St.)
Tolver Rd. WN4: Ash M 5J 41
Tolver St. WA10: St H 6K 49
Tomlinson Av. WA2: Warr 9E 66
Tom Mann Cl. L3: Liv 3G 5 (7C 58)
Tommy Gent Way L31: Mag 3J 35
Tonbridge Cl. L24: Speke 3F 92
Tonbridge Dr. L10: Aintr 8J 35
Tongbarn WN8: Skel 2B 30
TONTINE 7N 31
Tontine WN5: Orr 7M 31
Tontine Rd. WN8: Uph 6M 31
Toothill Cl. WN4: Ash M 6K 41
Tootle La. L40: Ruf 3K 15
Top Acre Rd. WN8: Skel 5F 30
Topaz Cl. L4: W'ton 8D 44
Topcliffe Gro. L12: Crox 7E 46
Topgate Cl. CH60: Hesw 7B 88
Topham Dr. L9: Aintr 9G 35
Topham Ter. L9: Aintr 2G 45
Top Pk. Cl. WA13: Warb 8L 69
Topping Ct. WA3: Birchw 5K 67
Top Rd. WA6: Frod 9N 107
Top Sandy La. WA2: Warr 6C 66
Topsham Cl. L25: Gate 4G 77
Torcross Cl. PR9: South 2M 7
Torcross Way L25: Gate 4G 77
L26: Halew 7J 77
Tordelow Cl. L6: Liv 5F 58
Toronto Cl. L36: Huy 2H 61
Toronto M. CH45: Wall 3E 56
Toronto St. CH44: Wall 6L 57
Torpoint Cl. L14: Knott A 3E 60
Torquay Dr. WN5: Bil 3A 40
Torr Dr. CH62: East 8F 90
Torridon Gro. CH66: Gt Sut 2L 111
Torrington Dr. CH61: Thing 1B 88
L26: Halew 9J 77
Torrington Gdns. CH61: Thing 9B 72
Torrington Rd. CH44: Wall 5G 57
L19: G'dale 9N 75
Torrisholme Rd. L9: Aintr 7J 45
Torus Rd. L13: Liv 5M 59
Torver Cl. WN3: Wigan 1J 41
Tor Vw. L15: Wavtr 2M 75
Torwood CH43: Noct 1D 72

Total Fitness—Ulverston Av.

Total Fitness
Bootle 7G 34
Prenton 8D 72
Wigan 1H 41
Totland Cl. L27: N'ley 4K 77
WA5: Gt San 1E 80
Totnes Av. L26: Halew 7K 77
Totnes Dr. PR9: South 2M 7
Totnes Rd. L11: Crox 5A 46
Tourist Info. Cen.
Liverpool 4H 5 (7D 58)
Liverpool John Lennon Airport 5G 92
Runcorn 4K 95
Southport 8G 6
Warrington 3C 82
Tourney Grn. WA5: Westb 7J 65
Towcester St. L21: Lith 4A 44
Tower Bldgs. PR9: South 7H 7
(off Gordon St.)
Tower End L37: Form 8C 16
Tower Gdns. L3: Liv 5D 4 (8B 58)
TOWER HILL 5D 36
Tower Hill CH42: Tran 5K 73
L39: Orm 8E 20
Tower Hill Rd. WN8: Uph 7J 31
Towerlands St. L7: Liv 5N 5 (8G 58)
Tower La. WA7: Nort 8E 96
WA13: Lymm 6F 84
Tower Nook WN8: Uph 7K 31
Tower Prom. CH45: New B 9J 43
Tower Quays CH41: Birke 9L 57
Tower Rd. CH41: Birke 9L 57
CH42: Tran 7H 73
(Reservoir Rd.)
CH42: Tran 5K 73
(Tower Hill)
Tower Rd. Nth. CH60: Hesw 5M 87
Tower Rd. Sth. CH60: Hesw 6N 87
Towers, The CH42: Tran 6L 73
Towers Av. L31: Mag 1J 35
Towers Ct. WA5: Warr 1N 81
Towers La. WA6: Alv, Hel 5D 114
Towers Rd. L16: Child 2A 76
Tower St. L3: Liv 3C 74
Tower Vw. Cl. L40: Burs 6E 20
Tower Way L25: Woolt 5E 76
Tower Wharf CH41: Birke 9L 57
Towneley Ct. WA8: Widnes 7K 79
TOWN END 2F 78
Town End Cl. L39: Orm 9B 20
Townfield Av. WN4: Ash M 9K 41
Townfield Cen. CH43: Oxton 5E 72
Townfield Cl. CH43: Oxton 5E 72
Townfield Gdns. CH63: H Beb 9M 73
Townfield La. CH1: Moll 9J 111
CH43: Oxton 5E 72
CH63: Beb 9M 73
CH63: Beb, H Beb 9M 73
WA2: Winw 4B 66
WA6: Frod 7M 107
WA13: Warb 9H 69
Townfield Rd. CH48: W Kir 6C 70
WA7: Wind H 5E 96
Town Flds. CH45: Wall 3E 56
Townfields WN4: Ash M 8J 41
Townfield Vw. WA7: Wind H 5E 96
Townfield Wlk. WA12: Newt W 6K 51
Townfield Way CH44: Wall 5H 57
Towngate Bus. Cen. WA8: Widnes 9E 78
TOWN GREEN
L39 4A 28
WN4 8M 41
Town Grn. Ct. L39: Augh 4A 28
Town Grn. Gdns. L39: Augh 4A 28
Town Grn. La. L39: Augh 4A 28
Town Green Station (Rail) 5A 28
Town Hall Dr. WA7: Run 6L 95
Town Hill WA1: Warr 3C 82
Town La. CH63: H Beb 1K 89
CH64: Lit N 8F 100
L24: Hale 6A 94
PR8: South 2C 12
Town La. (Kew) PR8: South 3B 12
Townley Ct. CH47: Hoy 1C 70
(off Seaview)
Town Mdw. La. CH46: More 9J 55
TOWN OF LOWTON 5C 52
Town Rd. CH42: Tran 5K 73
Town Row L12: W Der 2N 59
Townsend Av. L11: Norr G 7K 45
L13: Liv 1K 59
Townsend La. L4: W'ton 3G 59
L6: Liv 3G 59
L13: Liv 3G 59
Townsend St. CH41: Birke 8E 56
L5: Kirkd 3B 58
Townsend Vw. L11: Norr G 7K 45
L21: Ford 9A 34
Townshend Av. CH61: Irby 2L 87
Townson Dr. WN7: Leigh 1N 53
Town Sq. WA7: Pal F 8B 96
(within Halton Lea Shop. Cen.)
Town Vw. CH43: Oxton 3J 73
Town Vw. M. CH43: Oxton 3J 73
Town Wlk. WA7: Pal F 8B 96
(within Halton Lea Shop. Cen.)
Towson St. L5: Liv 3E 58
(Adam St.)
L5: Liv 3F 58
(Hartnup St.)
TOXTETH 4E 74
Toxteth Gro. L8: Liv 4F 74
Toxteth St. L8: Liv 3E 74
(not continuous)
Tracks La. WN5: Bil 9N 31
Tracy Dr. WA12: Newt W 7N 51
Tradewind Sq. L1: Liv 8G 5
TRAFALGAR 3N 89
Trafalgar Av. CH44: Wall 4K 57
Trafalgar Ct. PR8: Birkd 3M 11
WA8: Widnes 1K 95
Trafalgar Dr. CH63: Beb 3N 89
Trafalgar Rd. CH44: Wall 4J 57
PR8: Birkd 4L 11
Trafalgar St. WA10: St H 6H 49
Trafalgar Way L6: Liv 2L 5 (6E 58)
Trafford Av. WA5: Warr 1N 81
Trafford Cres. WA7: Run 9M 95
Tragan Dr. WA5: Penk 5F 80
Tramway Rd. L17: Aig 5H 75
M44: Irlam 2M 69
TRANMERE 5M 73
Tranmere Ct. CH42: Tran 4K 73
Tranmere Recreation Cen. 6J 73
Tranmere Rovers FC 6J 73
Trap Hill L37: Form 2C 24
Trapwood Cl. WA10: Ec'stn 7E 48
Travanson Cl. L10: Faz 4N 45
Travers' Entry WA9: Bold 2C 64
Traverse St. WA9: St H 7M 49
Travis Dr. L33: Kirkb 6D 36
Travis St. WA8: Widnes 8L 79
Trawden Way L21: Ford 7B 34
Traynor Ct. CH43: Oxton 3G 73
(off Beresford Rd.)
Treborth St. L8: Liv 3F 74
Trecastle Rd. L33: Kirkb 7E 36
Tree Bank Cl. WA7: Run 7K 95
Treen Cl. PR9: South 1N 7
Treesdale Cl. PR8: Birkd 2M 11
Treetop Ct. L6: Liv 5H 59
Treetops CH64: Lit N 9E 100
Treetops Cl. WA1: Padg 1G 82
Treetops Dr. CH41: Birke 8D 56
Treetop Vs. PR9: South 3L 7
Tree Vw. Ct. L31: Mag 3K 35
Trefoil Cl. L8: Liv 2E 74
WA3: Birchw 4K 67
Treforris Rd. CH45: Wall 2F 56
Trefula Pk. L12: W Der 3M 59
Trelawney Cl. L25: Gate 2F 76
Tremore Cl. L12: W Der 9N 45
Trenance Cl. WA7: Brook 1E 108
Trendeal Rd. L11: Crox 5B 46
Trent Av. L14: Brd G 6D 60
L31: Mag 1L 35
Trent Cl. L12: Crox 7B 46
L35: Rainh 6E 62
L40: Burs 9K 15
WA3: Cul 8N 53
WA8: Widnes 4L 79
WA9: Sut L 4M 63
Trentdale CH65: Whit 2N 111
Trentham Av. L18: Moss H 3L 75
Trentham Cl. WA8: Widnes 4L 79
WA9: St H 4J 63
Trentham Rd. CH44: Wall 6J 57
L32: Kirkb 1A 46
Trentham St. WA7: Run 4J 95
Trentham Wlk. L32: Kirkb 1A 46
Trent Pl. L35: Rainh 6E 62
Trent Rd. L35: Rainh 6E 62
WN4: Ash M 6N 41
WN5: Bil 7M 39
Trent St. CH41: Birke 8F 56
L5: Kirkd 3B 58
Trent Way CH60: Hesw 9B 88
L21: Lith 1N 43
Tresham Dr. WA4: Grap 8H 83
Tressel Dr. WA9: Sut M 6K 63
Tressell St. L9: W'ton 7E 44
Treswell Rd. L14: Brd G 7C 60
Trevelyan Dr. WN5: Bil 2N 39
Trevelyan St. L9: W'ton 7E 44
Treviot Cl. L33: Kirkb 5B 36
Trevor Dr. L23: Crosb 8M 33
Trevor Rd. L9: W'ton 4F 44
L40: Burs 1H 21
PR8: Ainsd 1J 17
Triad, The L20: Boot 6B 44
Trident Bus. Pk. WA3: Ris 3M 67
Trident Ind. Est. WA3: Ris 2M 67
Trident Pk. WA7: Pal F 8A 96
Trimley Cl. CH49: Upton 3M 71
Tring Cl. CH49: Upton 1A 72
Trinity Ct. CH47: Hoy 1C 70
WA3: Ris 4N 67
Trinity Gdns. CH43: Oxton 3F 72
CH47: Hoy 1C 70
PR8: South 9F 6
WA6: Frod 5M 107
WN4: Ash M 7H 41
Trinity Gro. L23: Blun 8H 33
Trinity Ho. WA6: Frod 5M 107
Trinity La. CH41: Birke 1L 73
Trinity M. PR9: South 8H 7
Trinity Pl. L20: Boot 7C 44
WA8: Widnes 9L 79
Trinity Rd. CH44: Wall 4H 57
CH47: Hoy 1C 70
CH65: Ell P 1B 112
L20: Boot 8B 44
Trinity St. CH41: Birke 1J 73
WA7: Run 4L 95
WA9: St H 6M 49
Trinity Wlk. L3: Liv 2J 5
Trispen Cl. L26: Halew 8J 77
Trispen Rd. L11: Crox 6B 46
Trispen Wlk. L11: Crox 6B 46
(off Trispen Rd.)
Tristram's Cft. L30: Neth 8C 34
Triumph Trading Pk., The L24: Speke 1D 92
Triumph Way L24: Hunts X, Speke 1D 92
Troon Cl. CH63: Brom 1B 102
L12: W Der 3C 60
WA11: Hay 5C 50
Trooper Cl. L12: W Der 2C 60
Trossach Cl. WA2: Warr 7F 66
Trotwood Cl. L9: Aintr 2J 45
Troutbeck Av. L31: Mag 1K 35
WA5: Warr 1A 82
WA12: Newt W 6G 51
Troutbeck Cl. CH49: Wdchu 6A 72
WA7: Beech 1C 108
Troutbeck Gro. WA11: St H 9L 39
Troutbeck Rd. L18: Moss H 3B 76
WN4: Ash M 6L 41
Trouville Rd. L4: W'ton 2H 59
Trowbridge St. L3: Liv 5J 5 (8D 58)
Trueman Cl. CH43: Bid 9C 56
Trueman St. L3: Liv 3F 4 (7C 58)
Truman Cl. WA8: Widnes 5J 79
Trumans La. CH66: Lit Sut 7H 103
Trundle Pie La. L39: Hals 6H 19
Truro Av. L30: Neth 7E 34
PR9: South 2N 7
Truro Cl. CH66: Gt Sut 5L 111
WA1: Wools 9J 67
WA7: Brook 9E 96
WA11: St H 3N 49
Truro Rd. L15: Wavtr 2M 75
Truscott Rd. L40: Burs 1H 21
Tryfan Way CH66: Ell P 7L 103
Tucana Cl. WA5: Westb 7K 65
Tudor Av. CH44: Wall 7L 57
CH63: Beb 4N 89
L14: Knott A 4F 60
Tudor Cl. CH66: Gt Sut 5L 111
L7: Liv 6L 5 (8E 58)
WA4: Grap 6H 83
WA11: Rainf 3B 38
Tudor Ct. L19: G'dale 9M 75
(off Dugdale Cl.)
WA4: Stockt H 7F 82
Tudor Gdns. L38: Hight 8F 24
Tudor Grange CH49: Grea 5L 71
Tudor Gro. WN3: Winst 1G 40
Tudor Mans. PR8: South 9E 6
Tudor Rd. CH42: Tran 5L 73
L23: Crosb 8K 33
L25: Hunts X 9G 76
PR8: Ainsd 8H 11
WA7: Manor P 4D 96
Tudor St. Nth. L6: Liv 6G 59
Tudor St. Sth. L6: Liv 6G 59
Tudor Vw. L33: Kirkb 6C 36
(not continuous)
Tudorville Rd. CH63: Beb 2M 89
Tudor Way CH60: Hesw 7B 88
TUE BROOK 3K 59
Tue La. WA8: Cron 2E 78
Tuffins Cnr. L27: N'ley 3H 77
Tulip Av. CH41: Birke 1F 72
Tulip Gro. WA5: Warr 5N 81
Tulip Rd. L15: Wavtr 1N 75
M31: Part 7L 69
WA11: Hay 4H 51
Tulketh St. PR8: South 8G 7
Tullimore Rd. L18: Moss H 7M 75
Tullis St. WA10: St H 8H 49
Tulloch St. L6: Liv 6G 58
Tully Av. WA12: Newt W 7G 51
Tulsa Gdns. WA5: Gt San 1J 81
Tumeric Rd. L11: Norr G 9M 45
Tumilty Av. L20: Boot 6D 44
Tunbridge Cl. WA5: Gt San 9J 65
Tundra Cl. L4: W'ton 8F 44
Tunnage Sq. L1: Liv 7G 4
Tunnel End WA4: Dutt 2J 109
Tunnel Rd. CH41: Birke 3M 73
L7: Liv 9G 59
Tunnel Top Nth. WA4: Dutt 9H 97
WA7: Pres B 9H 97
Tunstall Cl. CH49: Upton 3M 71
Tunstall St. L7: Liv 1H 75
Tunstalls Way WA9: Clock F 5N 63
Tupelo Cl. L12: Crox 6D 46
Tupman St. L8: Liv 3E 74
Turbine Rd. CH41: Tran 4M 73
Turmar Av. CH61: Thing 1B 88
Turnacre L14: Brd G 6C 60
L37: Form 7G 17
Turnall Rd. WA8: Widnes 9E 78
Turnberry WN8: Skel 2A 30
Turnberry Cl. CH46: More 8J 55
L12: W Der 3D 60
L36: Roby 8G 61
WA13: Lymm 4C 84
Turnberry Way PR9: South 2B 8
Turnbridge Rd. L31: Mag 9H 27
Turner Av. L20: Boot 3D 44
Turner Cl. L8: Liv 5F 74
WA8: Widnes 5G 78
Turner Dr. WA9: St H 9N 49
Turner Gro. L33: Kirkb 5C 36
Turner Home, The L8: Liv 4G 74
Turners Ct. L25: Gate 5G 76
Turner St. CH41: Birke 3J 73
Turners Vw. CH64: Nest 4D 100
Turners Yd. WN5: Orr 7N 31
Turney Rd. CH44: Wall 5G 56
Turnill Dr. WN4: Ash M 9K 41
Turning La. PR8: South 6F 12
Turnpike Cres. L40: Burs 6E 20
Turnpike Rd. L39: Augh 2M 27
Turnstone Av. WA12: Newt W 6L 51
Turnstone Bus. Pk. WA8: Widnes 9M 79
Turnstone Cl. L12: Crox 7C 46
Turnstone Dr. L26: Halew 7J 77
Turret Hall Dr. WA3: Low 2F 52
Turret Rd. CH45: Wall 3G 57
Turriff Dr. CH63: East 2B 102
Turriff Rd. L14: Knott A 4E 60
Turrocks Cl. CH64: Lit N 9E 100
Turrocks Cft. CH64: Lit N 9E 100
Turton Cl. L24: Hale 6A 94
WA3: Birchw 4K 67
Turton St. L5: Kirkd 3C 58
WA3: Golb 2B 52
Tuscan Cl. WA8: Widnes 3L 79
Tuson Dr. WA8: Widnes 4J 79
Tutor Bank Dr. WA12: Newt W 7M 51
Tweed Cl. L6: Liv 5H 59
Tweedsmuir Cl. WA2: Fearn 5H 67
Tweed St. CH41: Birke 8G 56
Twenty Acre Rd. WA5: Old H 9L 65
Twickenham Dr. CH46: Leas 6N 55
L36: Roby 8G 61
Twickenham St. L6: Liv 3G 59
Twigden Cl. L10: Faz 2L 45
Twig La. L31: Mag 2K 35
L36: Huy 6G 61
TWISS GREEN 6M 53
Twiss Grn. Dr. WA3: Cul 6M 53
Twiss Grn. La. WA3: Cul 6L 53
Twist Av. WA3: Golb 2D 52
Twistfield Cl. PR8: Birkd 1M 11
Two Acre Gro. CH66: Gt Sut 4L 111
Two Butt La. L35: Whis, Rainh 4D 62
Twomey Cl. L5: Liv 5B 58
TWO MILLS 5D 110
Two Saints Retail Pk. 8C 20
Twyford Av. L21: Lith 1A 44
Twyford Cl. L31: Mag 2K 35
WA8: Widnes 4L 79
Twyford La. WA8: Widnes 1M 79
Twyford Pl. WA9: St H 7M 49
Twyford St. L6: Liv 3G 59
Tyberton Pl. L25: Hunts X 1G 92
Tyburn Cl. CH63: Spit 5M 89
Tyburn Rd. CH63: Spit 5M 89
Tyle St. L20: Kirkd 2A 58
Tyndall Av. L22: Wloo 2M 43
Tyne Cl. L4: Kirkd 1D 58
WA2: Warr 7F 66
WA9: St H 3G 63
Tynemouth Cl. L5: Liv 4F 58
Tynemouth Rd. WA7: Murd 9E 96
Tynesdale CH65: Whit 2N 111
Tyne St. CH41: Birke 8F 56
Tynron Gro. CH43: Noct 4D 72
Tynville Rd. L9: Aintr 3H 45
Tynwald Cl. L13: Liv 4L 59
Tynwald Cres. WA8: Widnes 3J 79
Tynwald Dr. WA4: App 8D 82
Tynwald Hill L13: Liv 5L 59
Tynwald Pl. L13: Liv 5L 59
Tynwald Rd. CH48: W Kir 6B 70
Tyrer Gro. L34: Presc 2B 62
Tyrer Rd. L39: Orm 6D 20
WA12: Newt W 9L 51
Tyrers Av. L31: Lydi 7G 27
Tyrers Cl. L37: Form 2F 24
Tyrer St. CH41: Birke 8F 56
L1: Liv 5G 4 (8C 58)
Tyrer Wlk. WA3: Low 2G 52
Tyrrell Way WA7: Cas 5C 96

U

U-boat Story 1N 73
Uldale Cl. L11: Norr G 8M 45
PR8: Ainsd 2H 17
Uldale Way L11: Norr G 8M 45
Ullapool Cl. CH66: Lit Sut 8E 102
Ullet Rd. L8: Liv 4G 74
L17: Aig 4G 74
Ullet Wlk. L17: Aig 3J 75
Ullswater Av. CH43: Noct 2D 72
WA2: Warr 6D 66
WA11: St H 2K 49
WN4: Ash M 7K 41
Ullswater Cl. L33: Kirkb 7B 36
Ullswater Gro.
WA7: Beech 1N 107
Ullswater Ho. L17: Aig 6J 75
WA3: Golb 1D 52
Ullswater Rd. CH65: Ell P 3A 112
WA3: Golb 1D 52
Ullswater St. L5: Liv 3F 58
Ulster Rd. L13: Liv 6N 59
Ulverscroft CH43: Oxton 4F 72
Ulverston Av. WA2: Warr 6C 66

Ulverston Cl.—Village Rd.

Ulverston Cl. L31: Mag 1K 35
WA11: Hay 4C 50
Ulverston Lawn L27: N'ley 4K 77
Underbridge La. WA4: H Walt 1N 97
Undercliffe Ho. WA4: App 8E 82
Undercliffe Rd. L13: Liv 5M 59
Under Hill Cl. PR8: Ainsd 8L 11
Underhill Rd. WA10: St H 8G 49
Underley Ter. CH62: New F 9A 74
Underway, The WA7: Hal 7B 96
Underwood Dr.
CH65: Ell P, Whit 3N 111
Unicorn Rd. L11: Crox 6A 46
Unicorn Way CH41: Tran 3M 73
Union Bank La. WA8: Bold H 8L 63
Union Ct. L2: Liv 5E 4 (8B 58)
Union Sq. WA5: Gt San 9J 65
Union St. CH42: Tran 5M 73
CH44: Wall 5K 57
L3: Liv 4C 4 (7A 58)
PR9: South 7H 7
WA1: Warr 3C 82
WA7: Run 5L 95
WA10: St H 5K 49
Union Ter. CH45: New B 9H 43
Unit Rd. PR8: Ainsd 9K 11
Unity Bldg. L3: Liv 4C 4
Unity Gro. L34: Know 5E 46
Unity Theatre 7J 5
University of Chester
Warrington Campus 6J 67
University of Chester C of E Academy Sports Cen. 1N 111
University of Liverpool
Cambridge St. 7L 5 (9E 58)
Central Campus 6L 5 (8E 58)
North Campus 4L 5 (8E 58)
Peach St. 6L 5 (8F 58)
School of Veterinary Science, Leahurst Campus 6K 101
University of Liverpool Library 7M 5
University of Liverpool Sports Cen. 6L 5 (8E 58)
University Rd. L20: Boot 8C 44
Unsworth Av. WA3: Low 1F 52
Unsworth Ct. WA2: Padg 8G 66
Upavon Av. CH49: Grea 5J 71
Upchurch Cl. L8: Liv 4E 74
UP HOLLAND 5L 31
Upholland Rd. WN5: Bil 8N 31
Upholland Station (Rail) 8J 31
Upland Cl. WA10: St H 1E 62
Upland Dr. WN4: Ash M 7M 41
Upland Rd. CH49: Upton 2N 71
WA10: St H 1E 62
Uplands, The CH43: Oxton 4E 72
WA7: Pal F 8B 96
Uplands Rd. CH62: Brom 6B 90
Up. Aughton Rd. PR8: Birkd 1N 11
Up. Baker St. L6: Liv 1N 5 (6F 58)
Up. Beau St. L5: Liv 1H 5 (5D 58)
Up. Beckwith St. CH41: Birke 9H 57
UPPER BIDSTON VILLAGE 8C 56
Up. Brassey St. CH41: Birke 9F 56
Upperbrook Way L4: Kirkd 2C 58
Up. Bute St. L5: Liv 5D 58
Up. Duke St. L1: Liv 8H 5 (9D 58)
Up. Essex St. L8: Liv 3E 74
Up. Flaybrick Rd.
CH41: Birke 1E 72
Up. Frederick St. L1: Liv 8F 4 (9C 58)
(not continuous)
Up. Hampton St. L8: Liv 9L 5 (1E 74)
Up. Harrington St. L8: Liv 2D 74
Up. Hill St. L8: Liv 2D 74
(not continuous)
Up. Hope Pl. L7: Liv 7K 5 (9E 58)
Up. Huskisson St. L8: Liv 9M 5 (1F 74)
Up. Mann St. L8: Liv 2D 74
(not continuous)
Up. Mason St. L7: Liv 5N 5 (8F 58)
Up. Mersey Rd. WA8: Widnes 2K 95
Up. Mersey St. CH65: Ell P 7A 104
Upper Newington L1: Liv 6H 5 (8D 58)
Upper Pk. St. L8: Liv 3E 74
Up. Parliament St. L8: Liv 9K 5 (1D 74)
Up. Pitt St. L1: Liv 8G 5 (9C 58)
(not continuous)
Up. Pownall St. L1: Liv 8F 4 (9C 58)
Up. Raby Rd. CH63: Raby 4G 101
CH64: Nest 4G 101
Up. Rice La. CH44: Wall 4J 57
Up. Stanhope St. L8: Liv 1D 74
(not continuous)
Up. Warwick St. L8: Liv 2E 74
Up. William St. L3: Liv 5A 58
Uppingham WN8: Skel 3A 30
Uppingham Av. L10: Aintr 9K 35
Uppingham Rd. CH44: Wall 4F 56
L13: Liv 4L 59
UPTON
CH49 3A 72
WA8 5E 78
Upton Av. PR8: Ainsd 8H 11
Upton Barn L31: Mag 1H 35
Upton Bridle Path WA8: Widnes 4J 79
Upton By-Pass CH49: Upton 2M 71
Upton Cl. CH49: Upton 3N 71
L24: Speke 4J 93
WA3: Low 2E 52
WA9: St H 4J 63
Upton Ct. CH49: Upton 2A 72
Upton Dr. WA5: Penk 3H 81
Upton Grange WA8: Widnes 5G 79
Upton Grn. L24: Speke 4J 93
Upton La. WA8: Widnes 4H 79
Upton Locks Local Cen. WA8: Widnes 5H 79
Upton Mdw. CH49: Upton 4N 71
Upton Pk. Dr. CH49: Upton 2A 72
Upton Rd. CH41: Birke 3C 72
CH43: Bid, Noct 3C 72
CH46: More 9M 55
CH66: Gt Sut 1J 111
UPTON ROCKS 5J 79
Upton Rocks Av. WA8: Widnes 4H 79
Upton Rocks M. WA8: Widnes 4H 79
Upton Station (Rail) 3C 72
Upwood Rd. WA3: Low 3E 52
Ure Ct. CH65: Ell P 7M 103
Urmson Rd. CH45: Wall 4H 57
Urmston Av. WA12: Newt W 5K 51
Ursula St. L20: Boot 9C 44
Utkinton Cl. CH43: Oxton 5F 72
Utting Av. L4: W'ton 2G 58
Utting Av. E. L11: Norr G 9K 45
UVECO Bus. Cen. CH41: Birke 8H 57
Uxbridge St. L7: Liv 8G 59
(not continuous)

V

Vahler Ter. WA7: Run 5M 95
Vale, The WN6: App B 5N 23
Vale Av. WA2: Warr 9C 66
Vale Ct. *L21: Sea 4N 43*
(off Seaforth Va. Nth.)
WA4: Dutt 3J 109
Vale Cres. PR8: Ainsd 3J 17
Vale Cft. WN8: Uph 6K 31
Vale Dr. CH45: New B 2J 57
Vale Gdns. CH65: Whit 1N 111
WA6: Hel 1E 114
Vale Gro. L32: Kirkb 1E 46
Vale La. L40: Lath 9A 22
(not continuous)
Vale Lodge L9: W'ton 6E 44
Valencia Gro. L34: Eccl P 2D 62
Valencia Rd. L15: Wavtr 9M 59
Valentia Rd. CH47: Hoy 2B 70
Valentine Gro. L10: Aintr 1K 45
Valentine Rd. WA12: Newt W 7H 51
Valentines Bldg. L9: Aintr 1H 45
Valentines Way L9: Aintr 9H 35
Vale Owen Rd. WA2: Warr 8E 66
Valerian Rd. CH41: Birke 1F 72
Valerie Cl. L10: Faz 4N 45
Vale Rd. CH65: Whit 1N 111
L23: Crosb 7K 33
L25: Woolt 5C 76
Valescourt Rd. L12: W Der 4A 60
Valiant Cl. L12: Crox 8E 46
WA2: Padg 7G 66
Valiant Ho. CH41: Birke 2M 73
Valiant Way CH41: Tran 4M 73
Valkyrie Rd. CH45: Wall 4G 57
Vallance Rd. L4: W'ton 2H 59
Valleybrook Gro. CH63: Spit 5A 90
Valley Cl. L10: Aintr 1L 45
L23: Crosb 7A 34
Valley Community Theatre 3H 77
Valley Ct. WA2: Padg 8G 66
Valley Dr. CH66: Gt Sut 9J 103
Valley Rd. CH41: Birke 7D 56
CH62: Brom 7C 90
L4: W'ton 3F 58
L32: Faz, Kirkb 3M 45
Valley Rd. Bus. Pk. CH41: Birke 8E 56
Valley Vw. CH66: Gt Sut 9J 103
WA12: Newt W 8K 51
Vanbrugh Cres. L4: W'ton 2H 59
Vanbrugh Rd. L4: W'ton 1H 59
Vancouver Rd. L27: N'ley 3J 77
Vanderbilt Av. L9: Aintr 2G 45
Vanderbyl Av. CH62: Spit 5B 90
Vandries St. L3: Liv 1B 4 (5A 58)
Vandyke St. L8: Liv 1H 75
Vanguard Ct. *WA3: Ris 5L 67*
(off Renown Cl.)
Vanguard St. L5: Liv 3E 58
Vanguard Way CH41: Tran 5M 73
Vanilla Cl. L11: Norr G 9L 45
Vardon St. CH41: Birke 9K 57
Varley Rd. L19: Aig 7M 75
WA9: St H 6M 49
Varlian Cl. L40: Westh 1G 28
Varthen St. L5: Liv 3F 58
Vaudrey Dr. WA1: Wools 1L 83
Vaughan Cl. L37: Form 9D 16
Vaughan Rd. CH45: New B 1J 57
PR8: Birkd 2A 12
Vaughan St. CH41: Birke 9F 56
Vaux Cres. L20: Boot 5C 44
VAUXHALL 5B 58
Vauxhall Bus. Cen. L3: Liv 1D 4
Vauxhall Cl. WA5: Penk 4H 81
Vauxhall Motors FC 5H 103
Vauxhall Rd. L3: Liv 1E 4 (6B 58)
L5: Liv 6B 58
Vaux Pl. L20: Boot 5C 44
Vela Cl. WA5: Westb 7K 65
Venables Cl. CH63: Spit 6A 90
Venables Dr. CH63: Spit 5N 89
Venables Way CH65: Ell P 8N 103
Venice St. L5: Liv 3E 58
Venmore St. L5: Liv 3E 58
(not continuous)
Venns Rd. WA2: Warr 9E 66
Ventnor Cl. WA5: Gt San 1E 80
Ventnor Rd. L15: Wavtr 9L 59
Ventura Dr. WA5: Gt San 1K 81
Venture Ct. CH41: Birke 3L 73
Venture Flds. WA8: Widnes 9L 79
Venture Point CH2: Lit Stan 3D 112
Venture Point W. L24: Speke 2F 92
Venture Works L33: Know I 1G 46
Verbena Cl. M31: Part 6M 69
WA7: Beech 2B 108
Verbena Dr. L11: Norr G 8M 45
Verdala Pk. L18: Moss H 6A 76
Verden Ct. WA5: Gt San 2K 81
Verdi Av. L21: Sea 4N 43
Verdi St. L21: Sea 4M 43
Verdi Ter. L21: Sea 5M 43
Vere St. L8: Liv 3D 74
Vermont Av. L23: Crosb 7K 33
Vermont Cl. L33: Kirkb 4B 36
WA5: Gt San 1L 81
Vermont Rd. L23: Crosb 7K 33
Vermont Way L20: Boot 6B 44
Verne Wlk. WN4: Ash M 8M 41
Verney Cres. L19: Aller 8A 76
Verney Cres. Sth. L19: Aller 8A 76
Vernon Av. CH44: Wall 7K 57
CH66: Hoot 4F 102
Vernon Ct. PR8: South 1C 12
Vernon Rd. PR9: South 7M 7
Vernon St. L2: Liv 4E 4 (7B 58)
WA1: Warr 4C 82
WA9: St H 6M 49
Verona St. L5: Liv 3E 58
Veronica Cl. L12: Crox 7C 46
Veronica M. WA8: Widnes 7G 79
Veronica Way CH66: Lit Sut 7J 103
Verulam Cl. L8: Liv 9N 5 (1F 74)
Verulam Rd. PR9: South 4N 7
Verwood Cl. CH61: Irby 9L 71
Verwood Dr. L12: Crox 7E 46
Veryan Cl. L26: Halew 7K 77
Vescock St. L5: Liv 5C 58
Vesta Rd. L19: Garst 3B 92
Vesty Bus. Pk. L30: Neth 2F 44
Vesty Rd. L30: Neth 2F 44
Vesuvian Dr. L19: Garst 3B 92
Vesuvius Pl. L5: Kirkd 3C 58
Vesuvius St. L5: Kirkd 3C 58
Vetch Cl. WA3: Glaz 4H 69
Viaduct St. WA12: Newt W 7J 51
Vicarage Cl. CH42: Tran 7H 73
L18: Moss H 6N 75
L24: Hale 6B 94
L37: Form 9D 16
L40: Westh 1F 28
Vicarage Dr. WA11: Hay 3C 50
Vicarage Gdns. L40: Burs 9H 15
WN5: Orr 8N 31
Vicarage Gro. CH44: Wall 4J 57
Vicarage Hill WA6: Hel 1F 114
Vicarage La. CH1: Shot 9A 110
L40: Westh 1F 28
PR9: Banks 1D 8
WA6: Frod 7M 107
WA6: Hel 1F 114
Vicarage Lawn L25: Gate 3G 76
Vicarage Pl. L34: Presc 3N 61
Vicarage Rd. L37: Form 9D 16
WA8: Widnes 9K 79
WA11: Hay 3C 50
WN4: Ash M 9J 41
WN5: Orr 8N 31
Vicarage Wlk. L39: Orm 8C 20
WA4: Stockt H 8D 82
(off Southern St.)
Vicar Rd. L6: Liv 2H 59
Viceroy Ct. PR8: South 9F 6
Viceroy St. L5: Liv 3E 58
Vickers Dr. WN8: Skel 4H 31
Victoria Av. CH60: Hesw 9N 87
L14: Brd G 7B 60
L15: Wavtr 9L 59
L23: Blun 7J 33
WA4: Grap 6H 83
WA5: Gt San 2F 80
WA8: Widnes 5K 79
WA11: St H 2K 49
Victoria Bri. Rd. PR8: South 9H 7
Victoria Bldgs. L37: Form 8E 16
Victoria Cl. L17: Aig 5K 75
Victoria Ct. CH42: Rock F 7N 73
L15: Wavtr 9M 59
L17: Aig 4G 75
(off Lit. Parkfield Rd.)
PR8: Birkd 2M 11
(not continuous)
WN8: Skel 3A 30
(off Ormskirk Rd.)
Victoria Dr. CH42: Rock F 7N 73
CH48: W Kir 6B 70
L9: W'ton 4E 44
Victoria Falls Rd.
L27: N'ley 4K 77
Victoria Flds. CH42: Tran 4J 73
Victoria Gallery & Mus. 5L 5 (8E 58)
Victoria Gdns. CH43: Oxton 4H 73
WA4: Westy 5G 83
(off Kingsway Sth.)
Victoria Gro. WA8: Widnes 5K 79
Victoria Hall L2: Liv 3E 4
Victoria Hall Wlk.
CH63: H Beb 1K 89
Victoria Ho. L34: Presc 3A 62
Victoria La. CH43: Oxton 4H 73
Victoria Leisure & Fitness
Southport 7G 6
(off Promenade)
Victoria M. *CH65: Ell P 9N 103*
(off Victoria Rd.)
PR9: South 8J 7
Victoria Mt. CH43: Oxton 4H 73
Victoria Pde. CH45: New B 9J 43
VICTORIA PARK
L15 9M 59
L20 3D 44
Victoria Pk.
St Helens 4J 49
Westy 4F 82
Victoria Pk. WN8: Skel 3N 29
Victoria Pk. Arena 4E 82
Victoria Pk. Glasshouses 7K 79
Victoria Pk. Rd. CH42: Tran 6K 73
Victoria Pl. CH44: Wall 7M 57
L35: Rainh 6F 62
WA4: Stockt H 7D 82
(off Victoria Sq.)
Victoria Prom. WA8: Widnes 3K 95
Victoria Rd. CH42: Tran 4J 73
CH45: New B 1G 57
CH48: W Kir 7B 70
CH63: H Beb 1K 89
CH64: Lit N 8F 100
CH65: Ell P 9N 103
L13: Liv 3K 59
L17: Aig 5K 75
L22: Wloo 2L 43
L23: Crosb 7K 33
L36: Huy 7K 61
L37: Form 8B 16
L38: Ince B 9L 25
L39: Augh 1A 28
WA4: Grap 6G 83
WA4: Stockt H 7E 82
WA5: Gt San 4K 81
WA5: Penk 4F 80
WA7: Run 5K 95
(not continuous)
WA8: Widnes 9K 79
WA12: Newt W 6L 51
WN4: Garsw 8F 40
Victoria Rd. W. L23: Blun 7J 33
Victoria Sq. WA4: Stockt H 7D 82
WA8: Widnes 9K 79
WA10: St H 6K 49
Victoria St.
CH62: Port S 2A 90
L1: Liv 5E 4 (8B 58)
L2: Liv 5E 4 (8B 58)
L35: Rainh 6F 62
L40: Burs 9J 15
PR9: South 7G 6
WA1: Warr 3D 82
WA8: Widnes 9L 79
WA10: St H 5K 49
WA11: Rainf 4C 38
Victoria Ter. *L15: Wavtr 2M 75*
(off Prince Alfred Rd.)
L35: Rainh 6F 62
Victoria Trad. Est. *L35: Rainh 6F 62*
(off Victoria St.)
WA8: Widnes 1K 95
Victoria Vw. CH45: New B 1G 57
Victoria Vs. L35: Rainh 6F 62
Victoria Way L37: Form 8D 16
PR8: South 8E 6
Victor St. L15: Wavtr 9J 59
Victory Av. PR9: South 8M 7
Victory Cl. L30: Boot 2D 44
Victory Rd. M44: Cad 5J 69
Vienna St. L5: Liv 3E 58
Viennese Rd. L25: Gate 2F 76
View 146 L5: Liv 4D 58
Viewpark Cl. L16: Child 1D 76
View Rd. L35: Rainh 7F 62
Viking Cl. L21: Lith 3N 43
PR8: Birkd 2N 11
Viking Ct. *WA8: Widnes 9K 79*
(off Vine St.)
Village, The CH63: Beb 1N 89
Village Cl. CH45: Wall 3E 56
WA4: Thel 4M 83
WA7: Cas 7C 96
WN8: Skel 4A 30
Village Ct. CH43: Oxton 4G 73
CH61: Irby 1L 87
L17: Aig 6H 75
Village Courts L30: Neth 6E 34
Village Grn. Ct. CH43: Bid 9C 56
Village M. CH45: Wall 3E 56
CH63: H Beb 1K 89
Village Nook L10: Aintr 9K 35
Village Rd. CH43: Oxton 4G 72
CH48: W Kir 7C 70
CH60: Hesw 8N 87
CH63: H Beb 1K 89
WA6: Dun H 8B 114

Village Row—Wasdale Rd.

Village Row PR8: Ainsd 9J 11
Village Sq. CH64: Will 6M 101
(off Buckley La.)
Village Sq., The WA7: Cas 5C 96
Village St. L6: Liv 5E 58
WA7: Nort 5G 96
Village Vw. WN5: Bil 6A 40
Village Way CH45: Wall 4E 56
L38: Hight 8F 24
WN8: Skel 4A 30
Villa Gloria Cl. L19: Aig 8M 75
Villars St. WA1: Warr 3E 82
Villas Rd. L31: Mag 1N 35
Villiers Ct. L34: Know 5F 46
Villiers Cres.
WA10: Ec'stn 5C 48
Villiers Rd. L34: Know 4F 46
Vincent Cl. WA5: Old H 9K 65
Vincent Ct. L1: Liv 8G 4 (9C 58)
Vincent Naughton Ct.
CH41: Birke 3L 73
Vincent Rd. L21: Lith 1B 44
L35: Rainh 5E 62
Vincent St. CH41: Birke 2K 73
L13: Liv 8M 59
WA10: St H 6K 49
Vine Cl. L26: Halew 9K 77
Vine Cres. WA5: Gt San 2H 81
Vine Ho. L21: Sea 4N 43
Vineries, The L25: Woolt 5C 76
Vine Rd. CH66: Gt Sut 4L 111
Vineside Rd. L12: W Der 4B 60
Vine St. L7: Liv 8M 5 (9F 58)
WA7: Run 5K 95
WA8: Widnes 9K 79
Vine Ter. WA8: Widnes 6D 78
Vineyard St. L19: Garst 2C 92
Vineyard Way WA8: Widnes 8M 79
Vining Rd. L35: Presc 3C 62
Vining St. L8: Liv 2E 74
Viola Cl. L33: Kirkb 6B 36
Viola St. L20: Boot 9B 44
Violet Cl. WA3: Birchw 5K 67
Violet Cft. CH63: Beb 3M 89
Violet Rd. CH41: Birke 1F 72
L21: Lith 4A 44
Violet St. WA8: Widnes 9K 79
WN4: Ash M 9K 41
Virgil St. L5: Liv 5D 58
WA10: St H 6H 49
Virginia Av. L31: Lydi 9J 27
Virginia Gdns.
WA5: Gt San 9K 65
Virginia Gro. L31: Lydi 9H 27
Virginia Rd. CH45: New B 9H 43
Virginia St. PR8: South 9H 7
Virginia Ter. CH66: Chil T 6F 102
Virgin's La. L23: Thorn 4M 33
Viscount Cen. L24: Speke 2H 93
Viscount Ct. WA8: Hale B 3D 94
Viscount Dr. L24: Hale 5J 93
Viscount Rd. WA2: Padg 7F 66
Vista, The M44: Cad 5J 69
Vista Av. WA12: Newt W 6J 51
Vista Rd. WA7: Run 7K 95
WA11: Hay 3J 51
WA12: Newt W 3J 51
Vista Way
WA12: Newt W 6J 51
Vitesse Rd. L24: Speke 1D 92
Vittoria Cl. CH41: Birke 1K 73
Vittoria Ct. CH41: Birke 1K 73
Vittoria St. CH41: Birke 1J 73
Viva Way CH65: Ell P 8M 103
Vivian Av. CH44: Wall 7L 57
Vivian Dr. PR8: Birkd 4N 11
Vixen Gro. WA8: Widnes 4J 79
Voce's La. L39: Bic 9F 28
Voelas St. L8: Liv 2F 74
Vogan Av. L23: Crosb 8N 33
Volans Dr. WA5: Westb 7K 65
Volunteer St. WA6: Frod 5N 107
WA10: St H 6J 49
Vose Cl. WA5: Gt San 2M 81
Vronhill Cl. L8: Liv 2F 74
Vue Cinema
Birkenhead 2L 73
Ellesmere Port 3B 112
Southport 7E 6
Vulcan Cl. CH41: Birke 9F 56
L19: Garst 3A 92
WA2: Padg 7G 66
WA12: Newt W 9L 51
Vulcan Ct. PR9: South 8H 7
Vulcan Pk. Ct. WA12: Newt W 9L 51
Vulcan Pk. Way
WA12: Newt W 9L 51
Vulcan Sports Facility 8M 51
Vulcan St. CH41: Birke 9F 56
L3: Liv 5A 58
L20: Boot 6N 43
PR9: South 8H 7
VULCAN VILLAGE 1L 65
Vyner Cl. CH43: Noct 2E 72
Vyner Ct. CH43: Noct 2E 72
Vyner Cft. CH43: Clau 2E 72
Vyner Pk. CH43: Noct 2E 72
Vyner Rd. CH45: Wall 4F 56
Vyner Rd. Nth.
CH43: Bid 1D 72
L25: Gate 3E 76
Vyner Rd. Sth. CH43: Bid, Noct 2D 72
L25: Gate 3F 76
Vyrnwy St. L5: Liv 3F 58

W

WADDICAR 7M 35
Waddicar La. L31: Mell 8M 35
Waddington Cl. WA2: Padg 8G 66
WA3: Low 2G 53
Wade Av. WA4: Warr 6D 82
Wadebridge Rd. L10: Faz 4N 45
Wadeson Rd. L4: W'ton 8J 45
Wadeson Way WA3: Croft 2J 67
Wadham Pk. L20: Boot 8C 44
Wadham Rd. L20: Boot 9B 44
Wagon La. WA11: Hay 6D 50
Waine Gro. L35: Whis 4D 62
Waine St. WA9: St H 6N 49
WA11: Hay 4B 50
Wainfleet Cl. WN3: Winst 1G 40
Wainwright Cl. L7: Liv 9H 59
Wainwright Cl. WA2: Warr 7D 66
Wainwright Gro. L19: Garst 1A 92
Wakefield Dr. CH46: Leas 5N 55
Wakefield Rd. CH66: Gt Sut 4K 111
L30: Neth 9F 34
Wakefield St. L3: Liv 2H 5 (6D 58)
WA3: Golb 3B 52
Walby Cl. CH49: Wdchu 6C 72
Walcot Pl. WN3: Wigan 1H 41
Walden Cl. WA4: Thel 5L 83
Walden Dr. CH1: Woodb 5C 110
Walden Rd. L14: Knott A 6A 60
Waldgrave Pl. L15: Wavtr 8N 59
Waldgrave Rd. L15: Wavtr 8M 59
Waldorf Cl. WN3: Winst 1F 40
Waldron WN8: Skel 4A 30
Waldron Cl. L3: Liv 2E 4 (6B 58)
Walford Cl. CH63: Spit 5M 89
Walford Rd. WN4: Ash M 8L 41
Walk, The L24: Speke 5D 92
L28: Stockb V 2G 60
(off Dannette Hey)
PR8: Birkd 2N 11
Walkden Ho. WN4: Ash M 6H 41
Walker Art Gallery 3G 5 (7C 58)
Walker Av. WA9: Sut M 6L 63
Walker Cl. L37: Form 2F 24
Walker Dr. L20: Boot 3B 44
Walker Hgts. CH42: Tran 5K 73
(off Walker St.)
Walker M. CH42: Tran 5K 73
Walker Pl. CH42: Tran 5K 73
Walker Rd. L21: Lith 3N 43
M44: Irlam 1M 69
Walker's Cft. CH45: Wall 4F 56
Walkers La. CH66: Lit Sut 8H 103
WA5: Penk 5G 80
WA9: Sut M 6K 63
Walker St. CH42: Tran 5K 73
CH47: Hoy 1C 70
CH62: Port S 1A 90
L6: Liv 2M 5 (6F 58)
WA2: Warr 2B 82
Walker Way L9: W'ton 4E 44
Wallace Av. L36: Huy 5L 61
Wallace Dr. L36: Huy 5K 61
WA10: St H 4J 49
Wallace St. L9: Aintr 4F 44
WA8: Widnes 8K 79
Wallacre Rd. CH44: Wall 5E 56
WALLASEY 4E 56
Wallasey Bri. Rd. CH41: Birke 8F 56
Wallasey Golf Course 2D 56
Wallasey Grove Road (Park & Ride) 3E 56
Wallasey Grove Road Station (Rail) 3E 56
Wallasey Rd. CH44: Wall 5F 56
CH45: Wall 5F 56
Wallasey Village CH44: Wall 3E 56
CH45: Wall 3E 56
Wallasey Village Station (Rail) 4E 56
Wallbrook Av. WN5: Bil 2N 39
Wallcroft CH64: Will 7N 101
Wallcroft St. WN8: Skel 4B 30
Waller Cl. L4: Kirkd 2D 58
Waller St. L20: Boot 4A 44
Wallgarth Cl. WN3: Winst 1G 40
Wallgate Rd. L25: Gate 2D 76
Wallgate Way L25: Gate 2D 76
Wallingford Rd. CH49: Upton 4N 71
Wallis Dr. WA8: Widnes 5M 79
Wallis St. WA4: Warr 5C 82
Wallrake CH60: Hesw 8N 87
Wallsend Ct. WA8: Widnes 5J 79
Wall St. L1: Liv 6E 4 (8B 58)
Walmer Ct. PR8: Birkd 2M 11
Walmer Rd. L22: Wloo 2L 43
PR8: Birkd 3N 11
Walmesley Dr. WA11: Rainf 6D 38
Walmesley Rd. WA10: Ec'stn 5D 48
Walmsley St. CH44: Wall 4J 57
L5: Liv 4B 58
WA8: Widnes 8M 79
WA12: Newt W 6M 51
Walney Rd. L12: W Der 1M 59
WN3: Winst 1F 40
Walney Ter. L12: W Der 1M 59
Walnut Av. L9: W'ton 7H 45
Walnut Cl. WA1: Wools 1M 83
Walnut Gro. CH66: Whit 4L 111
L31: Mell 8M 35
WA9: St H 1L 63
Walnut Rd. M31: Part 6K 69
Walnut St. L7: Liv 6L 5
PR8: South 2B 12
Walnut Tree La. WA4: App 3G 99
Walpole Av. L35: Whis 6C 62
Walpole Gro. WA2: Warr 7D 66
Walpole Rd. WA7: Run 9L 95
Walro M. PR9: South 4M 7
Walsham Gdns. WA9: St H 3H 63
Walsh Cl. L5: Liv 5B 58
WA12: Newt W 5L 51
Walsh Rd. L14: Brd G 7A 60
Walsingham Ct. CH44: Wall 6K 57
(off Liscard Rd.)
Walsingham Dr. WA7: Nort 5F 96
Walsingham Rd. CH44: Wall 6K 57
L16: Child 8C 60
WA5: Penk 3H 81
Walter Beilin Ct. L17: Aig 3K 75
Walter Gro. WA9: St H 2B 64
Walter Leigh Way WA3: Low 1H 53
WN7: Leigh 1H 53
Walters Grn. Cres. WA3: Golb 1A 52
Walter St. L5: Liv 4A 58
WA1: Warr 1F 82
WA8: Widnes 7N 79
WN4: Ash M 6M 41
Waltham Ct. WA7: Nort 3G 97
Waltham Rd. L6: Liv 3H 59
WALTHEW GREEN 1M 31
Waltho Av. L31: Mag 2K 35
WALTON
L4 8G 45
WA4 8B 82
Walton Av. WA5: Penk 3G 80
Walton Breck Rd. L4: W'ton 2E 58
Walton Hall Av. L4: W'ton 8F 44
L11: Norr G 7J 45
Walton Hall Gdns. 9B 82
Walton Hall Golf Course 9A 82
Walton Hall Rd. L4: W'ton 8G 44
Walton Heath Rd. WA4: W'ton 7C 82
Walton La. L4: W'ton 2E 58
WA3: Ris 4M 67
Walton Lea Crematorium 9B 82
Walton Lea Rd. WA4: H Walt 9A 82
(not continuous)
Walton New Rd.
WA4: Stockt H, W'ton 8C 82
Walton Pk. L9: W'ton 6F 44
Walton Rd. L4: W'ton 2D 58
WA3: Cul 7N 53
WA4: Stockt H 8D 82
WA10: St H 4G 49
Walton Station (Rail) 6E 44
Walton St. CH41: Birke 2L 73
PR9: South 7H 7
WA7: Run 5K 95
Walton Va. L9: W'ton, Aintr 4F 44
Walton Village L4: W'ton 8E 44
Wambo La. L25: Gate 3G 76
Wandsworth Rd. L11: Norr G 9L 45
Wandsworth Way WA8: Widnes 2J 95
Wanes Blades Rd. L40: Lath 1B 22
Wango La. L10: Aintr 1K 45
Wanisher La. L39: Down 8F 18
Wansfell Pl. WA2: Warr 6B 66
Wantage Vw. L36: Roby 9G 61
Wapping L1: Liv 8E 4 (9B 58)
Wapping Quay L3: Liv 9E 4 (1B 74)
Wapshare Rd. L11: Norr G 9K 45
Warbler Cl. L26: Halew 6H 77
Warbreck Av. L9: W'ton, Aintr 3F 44
Warbreck Moor L9: Aintr 4G 44
WARBRECK PARK 3F 44
Warbreck Rd. L9: W'ton 4F 44
Warbrook Rd. L36: Roby 7G 61
WARBURTON 9H 69
Warburton Bri Rd. WA3: Rix 8G 68
Warburton Bri Rd. WA13: Warb 8G 68
Warburton Cl. WA13: Lymm 4G 84
Warburton Hey L35: Rainh 5E 62
Warburton La. M31: Part 5M 69
M31: Part, Warb 1K 85
WA13: Warb 1K 85
Warburton St. WA4: Stockt H 7E 82
Warburton Vw. WA3: Rix 7G 69
Ward Av. L37: Form 2D 24
Ward Cl. WA5: Gt San 8K 65
Warden St. L4: W'ton 1D 58
Wardgate Av. L12: Crox 7C 46
Ward Gro. CH42: Rock F 8M 73
Wardley Rd. WA4: W'ton 7C 82
Wardour St. WA5: Warr 2N 81
Ward Rake L30: Neth 7C 34
(off Granams Cft.)
Ward Rd. L23: Blun 6G 32
Ward St. L3: Liv 4H 5 (7D 58)
L34: Presc 2A 62
WA10: St H 6K 49
Ware Cl. WN4: Ash M 7M 41
Wareham Cl. WA1: Wools 9K 67
WA11: Hay 3E 50
Warehouse Studios WA3: Cul 8L 53
Wareing Rd. L9: Aintr 4H 45
Waresley Cres. L9: Faz 6K 45
WARGRAVE 7L 51
Wargrave M. WA12: Newt W 9L 51
Wargrave Rd. WA12: Newt W 7K 51
Warham Rd. L4: W'ton 2H 59
Waring Av. CH42: Tran 6K 73
WA4: Westy 3G 83
WA9: St H 8D 50
Warkworth Cl. L36: Huy 9L 61
WA8: Widnes 5F 78
Warkworth Ct. CH65: Ell P 2C 112
Warmington Rd. L14: Knott A 6A 60
Warminster Gro. WN3: Winst 1F 40
Warmwell Cl. L24: Speke 4F 92
(off Cartwrights Farm Rd.)
Warner Dr. L4: W'ton 1H 59
Warnerville Rd. L13: Liv 8N 59
Warnley Cl. WA8: Widnes 5G 79
Warper's Moss Cl. L40: Burs 9K 15
Warper's Moss La. L40: Burs 9K 15
Warpers Way L39: Orm 8E 20
Warren, The CH49: Upton 3B 72
WA12: Newt W 7J 51
Warren Ct. CH66: Gt Sut 2J 111
PR8: Birkd 1L 11
WA6: Frod 8N 107
Warren Cft. WA7: Nort 8E 96
Warrender Dr. CH43: Bid 9F 56
Warren Dr. CH43: Bid 2C 72
CH45: Wall, New B 1F 56
CH66: Ell P 7K 103
WA4: App 8D 82
WA12: Newt W 6A 52
Warren Golf Course
Wallasey 2F 56
Warren Grn. L37: Form 9D 16
Warren Hey CH63: Spit 6N 89
Warrenhouse Rd. L22: Wloo 9H 33
L33: Kirkb 7E 36
Warren Hurst CH45: New B 1G 56
Warren La. CH62: Brom, East 6E 90
(not continuous)
WA1: Wools 9L 67
Warren Pk. CH45: Wall 2F 56
Warren Point CH45: Wall 1F 56
Warren Rd. CH47: Hoy 1B 70
L23: Blun 6G 33
PR9: South 7M 7
WA2: Warr 8E 66
WA4: App 9D 82
Warren St. L3: Liv 5J 5 (8D 58)
Warren Way CH60: Hesw 6L 87
WARRINGTON 3C 82
Warrington Av. CH65: Whit 3N 111
Warrington Bank Quay Station (Rail) 4A 82
Warrington Bri. WA1: Warr 4C 82
Warrington Bus. Pk. WA2: Warr 8D 66
Warrington Bus Station 3B 82
Warrington Central Station (Rail) 2C 82
Warrington Central Trad. Est.
WA2: Warr 2B 82
Warrington Golf Course 2E 98
Warrington La. WA13: Lymm 5K 85
WA14: L Boll 5K 85
Warrington Mus. & Art Gallery 4B 82
Warrington New Rd. WA9: St H 7L 49
Warrington Rd. L34: Presc 3A 62
L35: Presc, Rainh, Whis 3A 62
WA3: Birchw, Cul, G'bury, Ris 6K 67
WA3: Golb 3B 52
WA4: Hatt, H Walt 2N 97
WA5: Penk 4G 80
WA7: Cas 6A 96
WA7: Manor P 3C 96
(not continuous)
WA8: Bold H 9J 63
WA8: Widnes 8M 79
WA12: Newt W 5B 52
WA13: Lymm 5A 84
WN3: Wigan 2H 41
WN4: Ash M 9K 41
Warrington Sports Club 9B 82
Warrington St. CH41: Tran 4L 73
Warrington Wolves RLFC 2B 82
Warton Cl. L25: Woolt 6G 77
WA5: Penk 5J 81
Warton St. L20: Boot 4A 44
Warton Ter. L20: Boot 4A 44
Warwick Av. L23: Crosb 8K 33
WA5: Gt San 1F 80
WA5: Warr 1A 82
WA12: Newt W 8M 51
WN4: Ash M 9M 41
Warwick Cl. CH43: Oxton 3J 73
CH64: Nest 9E 100
L36: Huy 6L 61
PR8: South 2A 12
Warwick Ct. CH65: Ell P 3C 112
L8: Liv 2F 74
(off Gwent St.)
WA1: Warr 1F 82
Warwick Dr. CH45: Wall 3J 57
CH48: W Kir 8D 70
Warwick Gro. WA7: Cas 6B 96
Warwick Rd. CH49: Upton 3M 71
L20: Boot 6C 44
L36: Huy 6L 61
M44: Cad 4K 69
Warwick St. L8: Liv 2D 74
PR8: South 2A 12
WA10: St H 7G 48
Wasdale Av. L31: Mag 1L 35
WA11: St H 2L 49
Wasdale Rd. L9: W'ton 5F 44

Washbrook Av.—Wentworth Dr.

Washbrook Av. CH43: Bid 9C 56
Washbrook Cl. WA10: Ec'stn 6E 48
Washbrook Way L39: Orm 9C 20
WASH END 2J 53
Wash End WA3: Low 2J 53
Washington Cl. WA8: Widnes 5J 79
WA9: St H 5H 63
Washington Dr. L33: Kirkb 5B 36
WA5: Gt San 1L 81
Washington Pde. L20: Boot 6B 44
Washington Rd. L27: N'ley 4K 77
Wash La. WA4: Warr 6F 82
Washway La. WA10: St H 3J 49
WA11: St H 3J 49
Wasley Cl. WA2: Fearn 6H 67
Wastdale Ct. CH46: More 8K 55
Wastdale Dr. CH46: More 8K 55
Wastdale M. CH46: More 8K 55
Wastdale Rd. WN4: Ash M 3J 41
Wastle Bri. Rd. L36: Huy 4J 61
Watchfield Cl. *L24: Speke* 4F 92
(off Cartwrights Farm Rd.)
Watchyard La. L37: Form 1G 25
Waterbridge Ct. WA4: App 8E 82
WA13: Lymm 5B 84
Waterbridge M. WA7: Cas 5C 96
Water Bus. Pk. CH65: Ell P 7B 104
Waterdale Cres. WA9: St H 2N 63
Waterdale Pl. WA9: St H 2N 63
Waterfall Dr. L4: W'ton 7F 44
Waterfield Cl. CH63: H Beb 2K 89
Waterfield Way L21: Lith 1N 43
Waterfoot Av. PR8: Ainsd 2H 17
Waterford Dr. CH64: Lit N 7G 100
Waterford Rd. CH43: Oxton 3F 72
L27: N'ley 2G 77
Waterford Way WA7: Murd 9E 96
Waterfront WA4: Pres H 9H 97
Waterfront, The PR9: South 7F 6
Waterfront Bus. Area L8: Liv 1D 74
Waterfront Bus. Area Parliament St. Nth.
L1: Liv 1D 74
(off New Bird St.)
L1: Liv 9G 4
(Simpson St.)
Waterfront Bus. Area Parliament St. Sth.
L8: Liv 2D 74
(off Stanhope St.)
Waterfront Dr. WA4: Westy 5J 83
Watergate La. L25: Woolt 6F 76
Watergate Way L25: Woolt 6F 76
Waterhouse Cl. L6: Liv 3G 59
Waterland La. WA9: St H 8B 50
Water La. L35: Tar G 4N 77
PR9: South 2B 8
WATERLOO 1L 43
Waterloo Cl. CH65: Ell P 9A 104
L22: Wloo 2K 43
Waterloo Ct. CH63: Beb 1N 89
L22: Wloo 2L 43
Waterloo Dock L3: Liv 1B 4 (6A 58)
Waterloo La. WA6: Frod, Kgswd 4M 115
WATERLOO PARK 1M 43
Waterloo Pl. CH41: Birke 3L 73
Waterloo Quay L3: Liv 2B 4 (6A 58)
Waterloo Rd. CH45: New B 9H 43
L3: Liv 1B 4 (5A 58)
L21: Sea 4L 43
L22: Wloo 2L 43
PR8: Birkd 4L 11
WA7: Run 4J 95
(not continuous)
WA8: Widnes 2K 95
Waterloo Station (Rail) 1L 43
Waterloo St. L15: Wavtr 1M 75
WA10: St H 7J 49
Waterloo Warehouse L3: Liv 1B 4 (6A 58)
Watermead Dr. WA7: Pres B 1H 109
Watermede WN5: Bil 9N 31
Waterpark Cl. CH43: Pren 7F 72
Waterpark Dr. L28: Stockb V 1D 60
Waterpark Ho. *CH42: Tran* 6H 73
(off Storeton Rd.)
Waterpark Rd. CH42: Tran 7F 72
CH43: Pren 7F 72
Waterperry Dr. L5: Liv 3F 58
Waters Edge WA4: Warr 7C 82
Watersedge WA6: Frod 4N 107
Watersedge Apts. *CH45: New B* 9J 43
(off Egerton St.)
Watersedge Dr. L40: Ruf 2N 15
Waterside L30: Neth 6D 34
WA4: App 8E 82
WA9: St H 6L 49
Waterside Bus. Pk. L40: Burs 9F 14
Waterside Ct. WA7: Run 4H 95
WA9: St H 6L 49
Waterside Dr. WA6: Frod 4M 107
Waterside La. WA8: Hale B 2F 94
Waterside Pk. L36: Roby 8H 61
Waters Rd. CH65: Ell P 7B 104
Waterstone Cl. L11: Norr G 7N 45
Water St. CH41: Birke 2M 73
CH44: Wall 5K 57
CH62: Port S 2B 90
L2: Liv 5D 4 (8B 58)
L3: Liv 5C 4 (8A 58)
L22: Wloo 2L 43
(off Brunswick Pde.)
L23: Thorn 5A 34
WA7: Run 4K 95
Water St. WA8: Widnes 1K 95
WA10: St H 7J 49
WA12: Newt W 6L 51
Water Twr. Rd. CH64: Nest 5E 100
Waterway Av. L30: Neth 8G 34
Waterways WA5: Gt San 2M 81
Waterworks Dr. WA12: Newt W 6A 52
Waterworks La. CH66: Hoot 5D 102
WA2: Winw 3C 66
Waterworks Rd. L39: Orm 7E 20
Waterworks St. L20: Boot 7C 44
Waterworth Dr. L7: Liv 8G 59
Watery Ct. WA9: St H 1B 64
Watery La. WA2: Winw 3N 65
WA6: Frod 8A 108
WA9: St H 1A 64
WA10: Windle 3D 48
WA11: Windle 3C 48
Watford Rd. L4: W'ton 2G 58
Watkin Cl. L30: Neth 1G 44
Watkins Av. WA12: Newt W 7H 51
Watkinson St. L1: Liv 9F 4 (1C 74)
Watkinson Way WA8: Widnes 9J 63
Watkin St. WA2: Warr 1C 82
Watling Av. L21: Lith 1N 43
Watling Way L35: Whis 3D 62
Watmough St. L5: Liv 1J 5 (5D 58)
Watson Av. WA3: Golb 1A 52
WN4: Ash M 8L 41
Watson Ct. *CH41: Birke* 1M 73
(off Argyle St.)
Watson St. CH41: Birke 1K 73
Watton Beck Cl. L31: Mag 1L 35
Watton Cl. L12: Crox 8E 46
WA4: Thel 5K 83
Watts Clift Way WA9: St H 7L 49
Watts Cl. L33: Kirkb 7E 36
Watts La. L20: Boot 3C 44
Wauchope St. L15: Wavtr 9K 59
Wavell Av. PR9: South 8N 7
WA8: Widnes 8F 78
Wavell Cl. PR9: South 8N 7
Wavell Rd. L36: Huy 5J 61
Waverley WN8: Skel 3A 30
Waverley Av. WA4: App 8E 82
Waverley Ct. WN3: Winst 1F 40
Waverley Cres. L33: Kirkb 9E 36
Waverley Dr. L34: Presc 4K 61
Waverley Gro. CH42: Tran 6J 73
Waverley Ho. L19: Aig 9L 75
Waverley Rd. CH47: Hoy 1D 70
L17: Aig 4H 75
L23: Blun 8J 33
WA3: Low 1E 52
Waverley St. L20: Boot 7A 44
PR8: South 8F 6
Waverly Ct. WA9: St H 9M 49
Waverton Av. CH43: Oxton 6E 72
Waverton Rd. CH66: Gt Sut 9K 103
WAVERTREE 9L 59
Wavertree Av. L7: Liv 8K 59
L13: Wavtr 8K 59
WA8: Widnes 8J 79
Wavertree Blvd. L7: Liv 8J 59
Wavertree Blvd. Sth. L7: Liv 8K 59
Wavertree Bus. Pk. L15: Wavtr 1L 75
Wavertree Bus. Village L13: Wavtr 8L 59
Wavertree Ct. CH66: Ell P 7L 103
Wavertree Gdns. *L15: Wavtr* 1L 75
(off Prince Alfred Rd.)
WAVERTREE GREEN 1N 75
Wavertree Grn. L15: Wavtr 1M 75
Wavertree Ho. *L13: Liv* 8M 59
(off Binns Rd.)
Wavertree Nook Rd. L15: Wavtr 8A 60
Wavertree Retail Pk. 8H 59
Wavertree Rd. L7: Liv 8G 58
Wavertree Sports Pk. 1L 75
Wavertree Technology Pk. L7: Liv 8J 59
L13: Wavtr 8K 59
Wavertree Technology Park Station (Rail)
8L 59
Wavertree Va. L15: Wavtr 9J 59
Wayfarers Arc. PR8: South 8G 6
Wayfarers Dr. WA12: Newt W 8N 51
Wayford Cl. WA6: Frod 5L 107
Wayford M. WA6: Frod 5L 107
Waylands Dr. L25: Hunts X 9F 76
Waymark Gdns. WA9: Sut M 6L 63
Wayside Cl. WA13: Lymm 6D 84
Wayville Cl. L18: Moss H 6N 75
Waywell Cl. WA2: Fearn 6G 67
Weald Dr. CH66: Lit Sut 8F 102
Weardale Rd. L15: Wavtr 2K 75
Wearhead Cl. WA3: Golb 3B 52
Weaste La. WA4: Thel 7L 83
Weates Cl. WA8: Widnes 5A 80
Weatherstones Bus. Cen.
CH64: Nest 6J 101
Weatherstones Cotts. CH64: Nest 6K 101
Weaver Av. L33: Kirkb 5D 36
L35: Rainh 6E 62
L40: Burs 9K 15
Weaver Ct. L25: Gate 5G 76
Weaver Cres. WA6: Frod 5N 107
Weaver Gro. WA9: St H 7C 50
Weaver Ho. *L25: Gate* 5G 76
(off Ribble Rd.)
Weaver Ind. Est. L19: Garst 3A 92
Weaver La. WA6: Frod 4L 107
Weavermill Pk. WN4: Ash M 9L 41
Weaver Pk. Ind. Est. WA6: Frod 4N 107
Weaver Rd. CH65: Ell P 2A 112
WA6: Frod 5N 107
WA7: W'ton 9K 95
Weaver Sailing Club 4N 107
Weavers Fold WA1: Warr 2D 82
Weaverside Av. WA7: Sut W 2B 108
Weavers La. L31: Mag 5L 35
Weaver St. L9: W'ton 7E 44
Weaver Vw. WA7: Clftn 2M 107
Webb Cl. L7: Liv 8H 59
Webb Dr. WA5: Burtw 3H 65
Webber Estates L33: Know I 9G 36
Webber Rd. L33: Know I 1F 46
Webb St. L7: Liv 1H 75
WA9: St H 9N 49
Web Complex, The L33: Know I 2G 46
Webster Av. CH44: Wall 4K 57
L20: Boot 6D 44
Webster Ct. WA5: Westb 7K 65
Webster Dr. L32: Kirkb 9C 36
Webster Rd. L7: Liv 1J 75
Websters Holt CH49: Upton 2N 71
Websters La. CH66: Gt Sut 3L 111
Webster St. L3: Liv 3F 4 (7C 58)
L21: Lith 4A 44
Weddell Cl. WA5: Old H 1M 81
Wedge Av. WA11: Hay 5C 50
Wedgewood Gdns. WA9: St H 3E 62
Wedgewood St. L7: Liv 7G 59
Wedgwood Dr. WA4: Warr 6D 82
WA8: Widnes 4L 79
Wednesbury Dr. WA5: Gt San 2H 81
Weedon Av. WA12: Newt W 5K 51
Weightman Gro. L9: Aintr 4F 44
Weint, The WA3: Rix 6H 69
Weir La. WA1: Wools 2M 83
WA4: Warr 4E 82
Weirside WA9: St H 3N 63
Weir St. WA4: Warr 7B 82
Welbeck Av. L18: Moss H 3L 75
WA12: Newt W 8M 51
Welbeck Ct. *L22: Wloo* 1K 43
(off Mt. Pleasant)
Welbeck Rd. PR8: Birkd 2M 11
WN4: Ash M 6L 41
Welbeck Ter. PR8: Birkd 2N 11
Welbourne WN8: Skel 4A 30
Welbourne Rd. L16: Child 8A 60
Weldale Ho. PR8: Birkd 2M 11
Weld Blundell Av. L31: Lydi 8G 27
Weld Dr. L37: Form 9D 16
Weldon Dr. L39: Orm 9D 20
Weldon St. L4: W'ton 8E 44
Weld Pde. PR8: Birkd 2M 11
Weld Rd. L23: Blun 8J 33
PR8: Birkd 1L 11
Welford Av. CH43: Pren 6F 72
WA3: Low 3D 52
Welford Cl. WA9: St H 2N 63
Welland Cl. L26: Halew 1J 93
Welland Gdns. WA12: Newt W 8L 51
Welland Rd. CH63: H Beb 2K 89
WN4: Ash M 6N 41
Wellbank Dr. L26: Halew 7L 77
Wellbrae Cl. CH49: Upton 3L 71
Wellbrook Cl. L24: Speke 3H 93
WA7: Brook 1E 108
Wellbrooke Cl. WN4: Ash M 8L 41
Wellbrook Grn. L24: Speke 4H 93
Wellbrow Rd. L4: W'ton 8F 44
Well Cl. CH64: Ness 9G 100
Wellcroft Gdns. WA13: Lymm 6G 84
Wellcroft Rd. L36: Huy 5J 61
Wellcross Rd. WN8: Uph 6L 31
Wellens Wlk. WA10: St H 7F 48
Weller St. L8: Liv 3E 74
Weller Way L8: Liv 4F 74
Wellesbourne Cl. CH64: Nest 8D 100
Wellesbourne Pl. L11: Norr G 8M 45
Wellesbourne Rd. L11: Norr G 7M 45
Wellesley Av. CH65: Ell P 9A 104
Wellesley Cl. WA12: Newt W 5K 51
Wellesley Gro. CH63: Beb 1N 89
Wellesley Rd. CH44: Wall 5H 57
(not continuous)
L8: Liv 4F 74
Wellesley Ter. L8: Liv 4F 74
Wellesley Wlk. *CH65: Ell P* 9A 104
(off Wellesley Av.)
Well Farm Cl. WA1: Wools 9L 67
Wellfarm Cl. L9: Aintr 7J 45
Wellfield WA7: Pres B 1G 108
WA8: Widnes 5K 79
WA11: Rainf 7D 38
Wellfield Av. L32: Kirkb 1C 46
Wellfield La. L40: Westh 1G 28
Wellfield Pl. L8: Liv 4F 74
Wellfield Rd. L9: W'ton 6F 44
WA3: Cul 6M 53
Wellfield St. WA5: Warr 2N 81
(not continuous)
Wellford Ho. L14: Brd G 7B 60
Wellgreen Rd. L25: Gate 1D 76
Wellgreen Wlk. *L25: Gate* 1E 76
(off Wellgreen Rd.)
Wellingford Av. WA8: Hale B 2E 94
Wellington Av. L15: Wavtr 2J 75
Wellington Cl. CH63: Beb 1N 89
CH65: Ell P 9A 104
L10: Aintr 8H 35
Wellington Cl. WA2: Padg 7G 66
WA12: Newt W 7J 51
WN8: Skel 4H 31
Wellington Ct. *CH65: Ell P* 9A 104
(off Arthur Av.)
Wellington Employment Pk. Sth.
L5: Kirkd 3B 58
Wellington Flds. L15: Wavtr 2J 75
Wellington Gdns. *L22: Wloo* 1K 43
(off Mason St.)
WA12: Newt W 7J 51
Wellington Ga. L24: Hale 5A 94
Wellington Gro. L15: Wavtr 9K 59
Wellington Mans. *CH45: New B* 9G 43
(off Atherton St.)
Wellington Rd. CH43: Oxton 3G 72
CH45: New B 1G 56
CH63: Beb 1N 89
CH65: Ell P 1N 111
(not continuous)
L8: Liv 4E 74
L15: Wavtr 1K 75
L21: Lith 3N 43
Wellington Rd. Nth. CH65: Ell P 9A 104
Wellington St. L3: Liv 1F 4 (6C 58)
L19: Garst 1A 92
L22: Wloo 1K 43
PR8: South 9F 6
WA1: Warr 3D 82
WA7: Run 4K 95
WA8: Widnes 1K 95
WA12: Newt W 7J 51
Wellington St. Ind. Est. *WA8: Widnes* 1K 95
(off Wellington St.)
Wellington St. Workshops *WA1: Warr* 3D 82
(off Wellington St.)
Wellington Ter. CH41: Birke 3K 73
L8: Liv 3F 74
WA10: St H 5K 49
Well La. CH42: Rock F, Tran 5K 73
CH49: Grea 5K 71
CH60: Hesw 9A 88
CH63: H Beb 1K 89
CH64: Ness 9F 100
L16: Child 1D 76
L20: Boot 7C 44
L25: Gate 1D 76
L39: Bart 7D 18
WA4: L Stret 7F 98
WA5: Penk 5G 81
(not continuous)
WA6: Manl 9J 115
Well La. Gdns. L20: Boot 7C 44
Wells Av. WN5: Bil 5N 39
Wells Cl. CH66: Gt Sut 5K 111
WA1: Wools 9J 67
Wells St. L15: Wavtr 1L 75
Wellstead Cl. L15: Wavtr 9M 59
Wellstead Rd. L15: Wavtr 9M 59
Wellstead Wlk. *L15: Wavtr* 9M 59
(off Wellstead Rd.)
Wellswood Rd. CH66: Ell P 7K 103
Wellwood Cl. CH65: Ell P 7N 103
Welsby Cl. WA2: Fearn 6G 66
Welshampton Cl. CH66: Gt Sut 3J 111
Welshpool Cl. WA5: Call 6M 65
Welsh Rd. CH1: Woodb 9B 110
CH66: Chil T, Led, Lit Sut 4C 110
Welton Av. CH49: Upton 3N 71
Welton Cl. L24: Speke 4H 93
Welton Grn. L24: Speke 4H 93
Welton Rd. CH62: Brom 5C 90
Welwyn Av. PR8: Ainsd 8L 11
Welwyn Cl. WA4: Thel 5K 83
WA9: St H 3J 63
Wembley Gdns. L9: W'ton 4E 44
Wembley Rd. L18: Moss H 4N 75
L23: Crosb 8M 33
Wendell St. L8: Liv 1H 75
Wendlebury Cl. WN7: Leigh 1M 53
Wendover Av. L17: Aig 5H 75
Wendover Cl. CH43: Noct 4D 72
WA11: Hay 3F 50
Wendron Rd. L11: Crox 5B 46
Wenger Rd. WA8: Widnes 3L 79
Wenlock Cl. WA1: Padg 9H 67
Wenlock Ct. L26: Halew 9J 77
Wenlock Dr. L26: Halew 9J 77
Wenlock Gdns. CH66: Gt Sut 3L 111
Wenlock La. CH66: Gt Sut 3L 111
Wenlock Rd. L4: W'ton 2G 59
WA7: Beech 2C 108
WN7: Leigh 1M 53
Wenning Av. L31: Mag 1K 35
Wennington Rd. PR9: South 7L 7
(not continuous)
Wensley Av. L26: Halew 9K 77
Wensleydale L9: W'ton 3F 44
Wensleydale Av. CH62: East 1D 102
L35: Rainh 6G 62
Wensleydale Cl. L31: Mag 1G 35
WA5: Gt San 9H 65
Wensley Rd. L9: W'ton 3F 44
WA3: Low 3F 52
Wentworth Av. CH45: New B 2H 57
WA1: Wools 1J 83
Wentworth Cl. CH43: Noct 4D 72
PR8: Ainsd 1J 17
WA8: Widnes 3K 79
Wentworth Dr. CH63: Brom 1B 102
L5: Liv 5E 58

Wentworth Gro.—White Friars

Wentworth Gro. L36: Huy 7F 60
Wentworth Rd. WN4: Ash M 6J 41
Werburgh Cl. WA13: Warb 9J 69
Wernbrook Cl. CH43: Noct 4D 72
Wernbrook Rd. L4: W'ton 2H 59
WERVIN 9E 112
Wervin Cl. CH43: Oxton 6E 72
Wervin Mobile Home Pk. CH2: Wer 9E 112
Wervin Rd.
CH2: Crou, Stoak, Upton, Wer 8E 112
CH43: Oxton 6E 72
L32: Kirkb 1B 46
Wesley Av. CH44: Wall 4J 57
WA11: Hay 3H 51
Wesley Cl. CH64: P'gte 6D 100
Wesley Gro. CH44: Wall 6L 57
Wesley Hall Gdns. WA9: St H 3G 62
Wesley Pl. L15: Wavtr 9L 59
Wesley St. L22: Wloo 2K 43
PR8: South 8G 6
Wessex Cl. WA1: Wools 1M 83
W. Albert Rd. L17: Aig 4G 75
W. Alfred Ct. *CH43: Oxton* *3J 73*
(off Alfred Rd.)
West Allerton Station (Rail) 7N 75
West Av. WA2: Warr 9C 66
WA3: Golb 1C 52
WA4: Stockt H 7D 82
WEST BANK 3K 95
Westbank Av. CH45: New B 2J 57
W. Bank Dock Est. WA8: Widnes 2H 95
Westbank Rd. CH42: Tran 5J 73
L7: Liv 7K 59
W. Bank St. WA8: Widnes 2K 95
Westbourne Av. CH48: W Kir 6C 70
L23: Thorn 5A 34
Westbourne Gdns. PR8: Birkd 2K 11
Westbourne Gro. CH48: W Kir 6C 70
Westbourne Rd. CH41: Birke 3J 73
CH43: Oxton 3J 73
CH44: Wall 5F 56
CH48: W Kir 6B 70
PR8: Birkd 2K 11
WA4: Stockt H 9C 82
Westbridge M. WA1: Padd 1G 83
WESTBROOK 7K 65
Westbrook Av. L34: Presc 3M 61
WA4: Warr 6E 82
Westbrook Cen. WA5: Westb 8K 65
(not continuous)
Westbrook Cres. WA5: Gt San, Westb 8K 65
(not continuous)
Westbrook Rd. CH46: More 1K 71
L25: Gate 3G 77
Westbrook Way WA5: Westb 8J 65
W. Brow Gdns. CH43: Bid 9C 56
Westbury Av. WN3: Winst 1F 40
Westbury Cl. L17: Aig 7H 75
L25: Hunts X 8H 77
WA1: Padg 9H 67
Westbury St. CH41: Tran 4L 73
West Cheshire Sailing Club 2D 56
Westcliffe Ct. PR8: Birkd 1M 11
WA8: Widnes 4L 79
Westcliffe Rd. L12: W Der 2M 59
PR8: Birkd 1L 11
Westcliff Gdns. WA4: App 4F 98
West Cl. CH43: Noct 3D 72
L34: Eccl P 2D 62
Westcombe Rd. L4: W'ton 2H 59
Westcott Rd. L4: W'ton 3G 58
Westcott Way CH43: Noct 4D 72
Westdale Rd. CH42: Rock F 6L 73
L15: Wavtr 9L 59
WA1: Padd 1H 83
Westdale Vw. L15: Wavtr 9L 59
Westdene PR9: South 6K 7
WN8: Parb 3E 22
WEST DERBY 2N 59
West Derby Golf Course 3C 60
W. Derby Rd. L6: Liv 1M 5 (6F 58)
(Low Hill)
L6: Liv 4J 59
(Orphan Dr.)
L13: Liv 3L 59
W. Derby St. L7: Liv 4L 5 (7F 58)
W. Derby Village L12: W Der 2N 59
West Dr. CH49: Upton 3A 72
CH60: Hesw 8A 88
CH64: Nest 8D 100
WA5: Gt San 4K 81
W. End Gro. WA11: Hay 4B 50
W. End Rd. WA11: Hay 4B 50
W. End Ter. *PR8: South* *8F 6*
(off West St.)
Westenra Av. CH65: Ell P 8L 103
Westerdale Dr. PR9: Banks 2F 8
Westerhope Way WA8: Widnes 5J 79
Western Approaches - Liverpool War Mus.
(Underground Wartime Mus.)
4D 4 (7B 58)
Western Av. CH62: Brom 4C 90
L24: Speke 5G 93
L36: Huy 6E 60
Western Dr. L19: G'dale 9M 75
Westerton Rd. L12: W Der 3C 60
Westfield Av. L14: Brd G 7C 60
WN4: Ash M 7J 41
Westfield Cres. WA7: Run 6H 95
Westfield Dr. L12: Crox 8C 46
Westfield M. WA7: Run 6J 95
Westfield Rd. CH44: Wall 8K 57
L9: W'ton 4D 44
WA7: Run 6H 95
Westfields Dr. L20: Boot 3E 44
Westfield St. WA10: St H 7J 49
(not continuous)
Westfield Wlk. L32: Kirkb 9N 35
W. Float Ind. Est. CH41: Birke 7H 57
Westford Rd. WA4: Warr 7B 82
Westgate WA8: Widnes 9E 78
WN8: Skel 3A 30
Westgate Dr. WN5: Orr 7N 31
Westgate Ind. Est. WN8: Skel 4A 30
Westgate M. *WN8: Skel* *3A 30*
(off Westgate)
Westgate Rd. CH62: Port S 3A 90
L15: Wavtr 3M 75
WEST GILLIBRANDS 4N 29
West Gro. CH60: Hesw 7N 87
Westhaven Cres. L39: Augh 3A 28
Westhaven M. WN8: Skel 1G 30
Westhay Cres. WA3: Birchw 4A 68
WESTHEAD 9J 21
Westhead Av. L33: Kirkb 9D 36
WA3: Low 1F 52
Westhead Cl. L33: Kirkb 1E 46
Westhead Wlk. L33: Kirkb 9D 36
W. Heath Gro. WA13: Lymm 4C 84
West Hill PR8: South 9F 6
Westholme Ct. PR9: South 6H 7
Westhouse Cl. CH63: Brom 1B 102
West Hyde WA13: Lymm 5C 84
WEST KIRBY 6B 70
West Kirby Concourse (Leisure Cen.) 5B 70
W. Kirby Rd. CH46: More 2K 71
West Kirby Station (Rail) 6B 70
West Knowe CH43: Oxton 4F 72
West Lancashire Crematorium 4D 20
West Lancashire Golf Course 5G 33
W. Lancashire Investment Cen.
WN8: Skel 6C 30
West Lancashire Yacht Club 6F 6
Westland Dr. WA2: Padg 8F 66
Westlands Cl. CH64: Nest 5F 100
West La. L37: Form 7F 16
WA7: Pal F 8A 96
WA13: Lymm 9J 85
WA16: High L 9J 85
Westleigh Pl. WA9: Sut L 4M 63
W. Lodge Dr. CH48: W Kir 5B 70
West Mains L24: Speke 4L 93
West Meade L31: Mag 1G 35
Westminster Av. L30: Neth 7D 34
Westminster Bri. CH65: Ell P 9A 104
Westminster Chambers *L1: Liv* *4F 4*
(off Crosshall St.)
Westminster Cl. L4: Kirkd 1D 58
WA4: Grap 6K 83
WA8: Widnes 8E 78
Westminster Ct. CH43: Oxton 3F 72
Westminster Dr. CH62: Brom 8C 90
PR8: Ainsd 9G 11
WA11: Hay 3H 51
Westminster Gro. CH65: Ell P 8A 104
L34: Presc 4L 61
Westminster Ind. Pk. CH65: Ell P 8L 103
Westminster Pl. *WA1: Warr* *3C 82*
(off Winwick St.)
Westminster Retail Pk. 8B 104
Westminster Rd. CH44: Wall 5H 57
CH65: Ell P 8A 104
L4: Kirkd 9C 44
Westmoreland Rd. CH45: New B 2J 57
PR8: South 1B 12
Westmorland Av. L30: Neth 8B 34
WA8: Widnes 7L 79
Westmorland Dr. L3: Liv 2E 4 (6B 58)
Westmorland Pl. L5: Liv 4C 58
Westmorland Rd. L36: Huy 7J 61
M31: Part 7L 69
Westmount Pk. CH43: Noct 2E 72
Westmount Pl. CH43: Noct 2E 72
W. Oakhill Pk. L13: Liv 7M 59
WESTON 9J 95
Westonby Ct. WN4: Ash M 8M 41
Weston Ct. L23: Blun 8H 33
WA7: W'ton 8J 95
Weston Cres. WA7: W'ton 9J 95
Weston Gro. L26: Halew 1L 93
L31: Mag 5J 35
WESTON POINT 8G 95
Weston Point Docks
WA7: West P 8G 94
Weston Point Expressway 6H 95
Weston Rd. WA7: Run, W'ton 7H 95
Weston Vw. WA7: Clftn 2N 107
W. Orchard La. L9: Aintr 2J 45
Westover Cl. L31: Mag 2H 35
Westover Rd. L31: Mag 2H 35
WA1: Padg 1G 83
WEST PARK 8G 49
West Pk. PR9: South 6J 7
West Pk. Cl. WN8: Skel 4A 30
West Pk. Dr. CH66: Gt Sut 5L 111
West Pk. Gdns. CH43: Bid 9C 56
West Pk. Rd. WA10: St H 8G 49
WEST PIMBO 8G 31
Westport Bus. Pk. L20: Kirkd 2B 58
West Quay L3: Liv 9E 4 (1B 74)
W. Quay Rd. WA2: Winw 6A 66
Westridge Ct. PR9: South 7J 7
West Rd. CH43: Noct 3D 72
CH65: Ell P 2A 112
CH65: Ell P, Hoot 3H 103
L14: Brd G 7A 60
WA7: West P 8G 94
Westry Cl. CH46: More 9J 55
West Side WA9: St H 8M 49
W. Side Av. WA11: Hay 4C 50
Westside Ind. Est.
WA9: St H 8M 49
West St. CH45: Wall 4H 57
L34: Presc 3N 61
PR8: South 8F 6
WA2: Warr 1C 82
WA10: St H 9G 48
West Twr. L3: Liv 3C 4
WESTVALE 9A 36
West Va. CH64: Nest 8E 100
West Vw. CH41: Tran 4M 73
CH66: Chil T *6F 102*
(off Orchard La.)
L36: Huy 7M 61
L39: Orm 8D 20
WA2: Padg 8H 67
WN8: Parb 3E 22
West Vw. Av. L36: Huy 7M 61
West Vw. Cl. L36: Huy 7M 61
Westview Cl. CH43: Noct 4D 72
Westward Ho CH48: Caldy 1E 86
Westward Vw. L17: Aig 5F 74
L22: Wloo 9H 33
Westway CH43: Noct 4D 72
CH46: More 8M 55
CH49: Grea 4L 71
CH60: Hesw 9N 87
L15: Wavtr 9N 59
L31: Mag 1H 35
L38: Hight 8F 24
WA7: Pal F 8A 96
Westway Sq. CH46: More 8M 55
Westwick Pl. L36: Huy 6F 60
Westwood WA7: Wind H 6E 96
Westwood Cl. PR8: South 3D 12
Westwood Ct. CH43: Oxton 3F 72
CH64: Nest 4E 100
Westwood Gro. CH44: Wall 5G 56
Westwood Rd. CH43: Bid 2C 72
L18: Aller 8A 76
WESTY 4G 82
Westy La. WA4: Westy 4F 82
Wet Ga. La. WA13: Lymm 4J 85
Wetherby Av. CH45: Wall 4E 56
WA4: Warr 6D 82
Wetherby Cl. WA12: Newt W 5L 51
Wetherby Ct. L36: Huy 4G 60
Wetherby Way CH66: Lit Sut 8G 102
Wethersfield Lodge CH43: Noct 4E 72
Wethersfield Rd. CH43: Noct 5E 72
Wetstone La. CH48: W Kir 7D 70
Wetton La. CW8: Act B 9N 109
Wexford Av. L24: Hale 5A 94
Wexford Cl. CH43: Oxton 4E 72
WA11: Hay 3F 50
Wexford Rd. CH43: Oxton 4F 72
Wexwood Gro. L35: Whis 7C 62
Weybourne Cl. CH49: Upton 1A 72
Weybridge Cl. WA4: App 9F 82
Weyman Av. L35: Whis 6B 62
Weymoor Cl. CH63: Spit 5M 89
Weymouth Av. WA9: St H 9B 50
Weymouth Cl. L16: Child 9D 60
WA7: Murd 9G 97
Weymouth Rd. WA5: Burtw 3H 65
Whaley La. CH61: Irby 1N 87
Whalley Av. WA10: St H 3H 49
WA11: Rainf 5C 38
Whalley Cl. WN3: Wigan 1J 41
Whalley Ct. L30: Neth 7C 34
Whalley Dr. L37: Form 2G 24
L39: Augh 4A 28
Whalley Gro. WA8: Widnes 5N 79
Whalley Rd. CH42: Tran 3K 73
WHALLEYS 8E 22
Whalleys Farm Cl. WN8: Dalt 8E 22
Whalleys Rd. WN8: Skel 8D 22
Whalley St. L8: Liv 4E 74
WA1: Warr 2D 82
Wharf, The WA7: Pres B 9H 97
Wharfdale Cl. WA5: Gt San 1J 81
Wharfedale WA7: Pal F 9D 96
Wharfedale Av. CH42: Tran 6H 73
Wharfedale Dr. CH62: East 1E 102
L35: Rainh 6G 62
Wharfedale Rd. CH45: Wall 3F 56
Wharfedale St. L19: Garst 2C 92
Wharfe La. CH65: Ell P 7M 103
Wharf Ind. Est. WA1: Warr 4D 82
Wharford La. WA7: Nort 4G 97
Wharf Rd. WA12: Newt W 8G 51
Wharfside Ct. WA4: App 7F 82
Wharf St. CH62: Port S 2B 90
WA1: Warr 4C 82
Wharmby Rd. WA11: Hay 4G 50
Wharncliffe Rd. L13: Liv 6M 59
Wharton Cl. CH49: Upton 2L 71
Wharton St. WA9: St H 9L 49
Whatcroft Cl. WA7: Run 9N 95
Wheatacre WN8: Skel 4B 30
Wheatcroft Cl. WA5: Gt San 2L 81
Wheatcroft Rd. L18: Aller 6A 76
Wheatear Cl. L27: N'ley 4J 77
Wheatfield Cl. CH46: More 1N 71
CH66: Gt Sut 2H 111
L30: Neth 8G 34
Wheatfield Rd. WA8: Cron 3F 78
Wheatfield Vw. L21: Ford 9A 34
Wheathill Rd. L36: Huy 1J 77
Wheathills Ind. Est. L27: N'ley 2H 77
Wheatland Bus. Pk. CH44: Wall 7K 57
Wheatland Cl. WA9: Clock F 5M 63
Wheatland La. CH44: Wall 6K 57
Wheatland Rd. CH60: Hesw 8C 88
Wheatlands WA7: Run 6A 96
Wheat La. L40: Lath 2L 21
Wheatlea Ind. Est. WN3: Wigan 2H 41
Wheatlea Rd. WN3: Wigan 1H 41
Wheatley Av. L20: Boot 5D 44
WA12: Newt W 5L 51
Wheatsheaf Av. WA9: Sut L 3N 63
Wheatsheaf M. L40: Ruf 3M 15
Wheatsheaf Wlk. *L39: Orm* *8C 20*
(off Burscough St.)
Wheatstone Rd. L37: Form 4E 24
Wheeler Dr. L31: Mell 8N 35
Wheelwrights Wharf L40: Scar 1L 19
Whelan Gdns. WA9: St H 3H 63
Wheldon Rd. WA8: Widnes 1C 94
Wheldrake Cl. CH66: Lit Sut 9G 103
Whelmar Ho. WN8: Skel 3F 30
Whernside WA8: Widnes 6F 78
Whetstone Ct. *CH41: Birke* *3K 73*
(off Whetstone La.)
Whetstone Hey CH66: Gt Sut 9J 103
Whetstone La. CH41: Birke 3K 73
Whickham Cl. WA8: Widnes 5J 79
Whimbrel Av. WA12: Newt W 7L 51
Whimbrel Cl. WA7: Beech 1B 108
Whimbrel Pk. L26: Halew 7J 77
Whinberry Dr. L32: Kirkb 1B 46
Whinbury Ct. WA9: Clock F 5M 63
Whinchat Av. WA12: Newt W 6L 51
Whinchat Cl. WA3: Low 3F 52
Whinchat Dr. WA3: Birchw 6N 67
Whincraig L28: Stockb V 2F 60
Whinfell Gro. WA7: Beech 1A 108
Whinfell Rd. L12: W Der 4A 60
Whinfield Rd. L9: W'ton 4E 44
L23: Thorn 5N 33
Whinhowe Rd. L11: Norr G 8N 45
Whinmoor Cl. CH43: Noct 2D 72
Whinmoor Rd. L10: Faz 3M 45
L12: W Der 4A 60
Whinney Gro. E. L31: Mag 5H 35
Whinney Gro. W. L31: Mag 5H 35
WHISTON 6B 62
WHISTON CROSS 6A 62
Whiston La. L36: Huy 5L 61
WHISTON LANE ENDS 7B 62
Whiston Station (Rail) 6B 62
Whitbarrow Rd. WA13: Lymm 4C 84
Whitburn WN8: Skel 3A 30
Whitburn Cl. WN4: Garsw 7F 40
Whitburn Rd. L33: Kirkb 7E 36
WHITBY 1M 111
Whitby Av. CH45: Wall 4E 56
PR9: South 1B 8
WA2: Warr 7E 66
Whitby Cl. WA12: Newt W 8H 51
WHITBYHEATH 3L 111
Whitby Rd. CH1: Back 5M 111
CH65: Ell P, Whit 1N 111
(not continuous)
WA7: Run 6K 95
Whitby St. L6: Liv 3J 59
Whitchurch Cl. WA1: Padg 9H 67
Whitchurch Way WA7: Run 9N 95
Whitcroft Rd. L6: Liv 6J 59
Whitebeam Av. CH66: Gt Sut 4L 111
Whitebeam Cl. L33: Kirkb 5D 36
WA7: Wind H 6E 96
Whitebeam Dr. L12: Crox 7B 46
Whitebeam Gdns. WA9: St H 3F 62
Whitebeam Wlk. CH49: Grea 6J 71
White Bri. Rd. CH62: Port S 2B 90
White Broom WA13: Lymm 4H 85
Whitechapel L1: Liv 5F 4 (8C 58)
White Clover Sq. WA13: Lymm 6G 85
Whitecroft Av. WA3: Low 1F 52
Whitecroft Rd. CH66: Gt Sut 3K 111
WN3: Wigan 1J 41
Whitecroft Vs. M31: Part 7L 69
White Cross Cl. WA12: Newt W 6K 51
Whitecross Rd. WA5: Warr 3N 81
Whitefield WA13: Lymm 4G 85
Whitefield Av. L4: Kirkd 1D 58
WA12: Newt W 8A 52
Whitefield Cl. CH49: Wdchu 5B 72
L38: Hight 1F 32
L40: Ruf 3N 15
WA3: Golb 2B 52
WA13: Lymm 3G 85
Whitefield Ct. WA3: Ris 8N 53
Whitefield Dr. L32: Kirkb 9N 35
Whitefield Gro. WA13: Lymm 4G 85
Whitefield La. L35: Tar G 3L 77
Whitefield Rd. L6: Liv 5G 58
WA4: Stockt H 8C 82
WA10: St H 5G 48
Whitefields CH2: Elt 2M 113
WHITEFIELDS CROSS 5B 80
Whitefield Way L6: Liv 5F 58
White Friars WA10: Ec'stn 6D 48

Whitegate Av.—Windermere Ter.

Whitegate Av. WA3: Cul 8N 53
Whitegate Cl. L34: Know 6H 47
Whitegates Cl. CH64: Will 5L 101
Whitegates Cres. CH64: Will 6L 101
Whitehall Av. WN6: App B 5N 23
Whitehall Cl. L4: Kirkd 9D 44
Whitehall Pl. WA6: Frod 6M 107
(not continuous)
Whitehart Cl. L4: W'ton 9G 44
Whitehaven Cl. PR8: Ainsd 2H 17
Whitehaven Rd. L5: Liv 3E 58
Whiteheath Way CH46: Leas 6N 55
Whitehedge Rd. L19: Garst 9N 75
Whitehey WN8: Skel 4B 30
WHITEHEY ISLAND 4B 30
Whitehey Rd. WN8: Skel 4B 30
WHITEHOUSE 2H 109
White Ho., The WA4: Warr 6D 82
Whitehouse Av. L37: Form 1G 24
White Ho. Cl. WA11: Hay 4D 50
White Ho. Dr. WA1: Wools 1M 83
Whitehouse Expressway 9A 96
Whitehouse Ind. Est.
WA7: Pres B 2G 109
(not continuous)
White Ho. La. L40: Scar 5A 14
Whitehouse La. CH60: Hesw 6C 88
CH63: Brim 6C 88
L37: Form 1G 24
Whitehouse Rd. L13: Liv 7N 59
Whitehouse Va. Ind. Est.
WA7: Pres B 1H 109
Whitelands Mdw. CH49: Upton 3M 71
Whiteledge Rd. WN8: Skel 5E 30
Whiteleggs La. WA13: Lymm 7H 85
Whiteley's La. L40: Westh 2H 29
White Lodge Av. L36: Huy 6H 61
White Lodge Cl. CH62: Brom 1C 102
White Lodge Dr. WN4: Ash M 7M 41
Whitely Gro. L33: Kirkb 5E 36
White Mdw. Dr. L23: Thorn 6N 33
Whitemere Ct. CH65: Ell P 7A 104
WHITE MOSS 5B 30
Whitemoss Bus. Pk. WN8: Skel 6B 30
White Moss Rd. WN8: Skel 5N 29
White Moss Rd. Sth. WN8: Skel 5N 29
White Oak Lodge *L19: G'dale* 9L 75
(off Beechwood Rd.)
White Otter Cl. PR8: Ainsd 8L 11
Whiterails Dr. L39: Orm 7B 20
Whiterails M. L39: Orm 7B 20
White Rock St. L6: Liv 5G 58
Whitesands Rd. WA13: Lymm 4C 84
Whiteside Av. WA11: St H 5A 50
Whiteside Cl. CH49: Upton 4A 72
L5: Liv 4C 58
Whiteside Rd. WA11: Hay 4D 50
Whitestocks WN8: Skel 4B 30
Whitestone Cl. L34: Know 8G 47
White St. WA1: Warr 3B 82
WA4: Stockt H 7D 82
WA8: Widnes 2K 95
Whitethorn Av. WA5: Gt San 3H 81
Whitethorn Dr. L28: Stockb V 1F 60
Whitethroat Wlk. WA3: Birchw 6N 67
Whitewell Dr. CH49: Upton 2N 71
Whitewood Cl. WN4: Ash M 5J 41
Whitewood Pk. L9: Aintr 4J 45
Whitfield Av. WA1: Padd 1G 83
Whitfield Ct. CH42: Tran 4K 73
Whitfield Gro. WA11: Hay 4C 50
Whitfield La. CH60: Hesw 5A 88
Whitfield Lodge WA9: Sut L 5N 63
Whitfield Rd. L9: W'ton 5F 44
WHITFIELDS CROSS 5A 80
Whitfield St. CH42: Tran 4K 73
Whitford Rd. CH42: Tran 4J 73
Whitham Av. L23: Crosb 8M 33
Whithill Wlk. WN4: Ash M 6J 41
Whithorn St. L7: Liv 9J 59
Whitland Rd. L6: Liv 6J 59
Whitledge Grn. WN4: Ash M 6J 41
Whitledge Rd. WN4: Ash M 6J 41
Whitley Av. WA4: Westy 4H 83
Whitley Cl. WA7: Run 7J 95
Whitley Dr. CH44: Wall 4K 57
WHITLEY REED 7L 99
Whitley Rd. WN8: Roby M, Uph 1M 31
Whitley St. L3: Liv 5A 58
Whitlow Av. WA3: Golb 1A 52
Whitlow Rd. L5: Liv 3F 58
Whitman St. L15: Wavtr 1K 75
Whitmoor Cl. L35: Rainh 8H 63
Whitney Pl. L25: Woolt 6G 76
Whitney Rd. L25: Woolt 5G 76
Whitstable Pk. WA8: Widnes 4H 79
Whitstone Cl. L18: Aller 6C 76
Whitstone Dr. WN8: Skel 5G 31
Whittaker Av. WA2: Warr 7E 66
Whittaker Cl. L13: Liv 8L 59
Whittaker St. WA9: St H 9N 49
Whittier St. L8: Liv 1H 75
Whittington Ho. *L21: Lith* 3N 43
(off Beach Rd.)
Whittle Av. WA5: Gt San 9H 65
WA11: Hay 5C 50
Whittle Cl. L5: Kirkd 3D 58
Whittle Ct. WN3: Winst 1G 40
Whittle Dr. L39: Orm 6C 20
Whittle Hall La. WA5: Gt San 2H 81
Whittle La. WN6: Wright 1H 23
Whittle St. L5: Kirkd 3D 58
WA10: St H 9G 48
Whittlewood Cl. WA3: Birchw 4A 68
Whittlewood Ct. L33: Kirkb 7D 36
Whitwell Cl. WA5: Gt San 1F 80
Whitworth Cl. WA3: Birchw 6M 67
Whitworth Ct. WA7: Manor P 3F 96
Wholesome La. L40: Scar, Burs 4A 14
Wicket Cl. L11: Crox 5B 46
Wickham Cl. CH44: Wall 7K 57
Wicklow Cl. CH66: Lit Sut 8F 102
Wicks Cres. L37: Form 9C 16
Wicks Gdns. L37: Form 1E 24
Wicks Grn. L37: Form 1C 24
Wicks Grn. Cl. L37: Form 9C 16
Wicks La. L37: Form 1C 24
(not continuous)
Wicksten Dr. WA7: Run 5M 95
Widdale Av. L35: Rainh 6G 62
Widdale Cl. WA5: Gt San 1H 81
Widgeons Covert CH63: Thorn H 1F 100
Widmore Rd. L25: Gate 4G 76
WIDNES 8L 79
Widnes Crematorium 5K 79
Widnes Eastern By-Pass 1L 95
Widnes Golf Course 7J 79
Widnes Rd. WA5: Cuerd, Penk 6B 80
WA8: Widnes 9K 79
(not continuous)
Widnes Shop. Pk. 8L 79
Widnes Station (Rail) 5K 79
Widnes Tennis Academy 6J 79
Widnes Trade Pk. WA8: Widnes 9M 79
Widnes Vikings RLFC 8J 79
Widney Cl. L7: Liv 9G 59
Wiend, The CH42: Rock F 7K 73
CH63: Beb 2N 89
Wigan Rd. L39: Orm 8D 20
L40: Westh 9J 21
WN4: Ash M 3H 41
WN5: Bil 4B 40
WN8: Skel 3C 30
Wigeon Pl. PR9: Banks 2E 8
Wiggins La. L40: H'wood 1E 14
Wigg Island Community Pk.
Local Nature Reserve 3N 95
Wight Cl. CH65: Ell P 4A 112
Wightman Av. WA12: Newt W 5L 51
Wightman St. L6: Liv 6G 58
Wight Moss Way PR8: South 3C 12
Wigmore Cl. WA3: Birchw 3A 68
Wignall Cl. L32: Kirkb 3C 46
Wignalls Mdw. L38: Hight 9F 24
Wigsey La. WA13: Warb 1G 84
WIGSHAW 8L 53
Wigshaw Cl. WN7: Leigh 1N 53
Wigshaw La. WA3: Cul 8K 53
Wigston Cl. PR8: Ainsd 1H 17
Wilberforce Rd. L4: W'ton 9G 45
Wilbraham Pl. L5: Liv 4C 58
Wilbraham St. CH41: Birke 2L 73
L5: Liv 4C 58
WA9: Clock F 6A 64
Wilburn St. L4: W'ton 9E 44
Wilbur St. WA9: St H 2A 64
Wilcock Cl. L5: Liv 4C 58
Wilcock Rd. WA11: Hay 2J 51
Wilcote Cl. WA8: Widnes 4M 79
Wilcove WN8: Skel 3C 30
Wild Arum Cl. WA3: Low 2F 52
Wildbrook Dr. CH41: Birke 8D 56
Wildcherry Gdns. WA9: St H 2E 62
WILDERSPOOL 6D 82
Wilderspool C'way. WA4: Warr 4C 82
Wilderspool Cres. WA4: Warr 7C 82
Wilderspool Pk. WA4: Warr 6D 82
Wilde St. L3: Liv 3H 5 (7D 58)
Wilding Av. WA7: Run 5L 95
Wildings Old La. WA3: Croft 1H 67
Wilding Way CH43: Bid 9D 56
Wild Pl. L20: Boot 3D 44
Wildwood Gro. WA1: Padd 1J 83
Wilfer Cl. L7: Liv 9H 59
Wilfred Owen Dr. CH41: Birke 1E 72
Wilkes Av. CH46: Leas 6B 56
Wilkie St. L15: Wavtr 1K 75
Wilkinson Av. WA1: Padd 2G 83
Wilkinson Cl. WA8: Widnes 2K 95
Wilkinson Ct. *L15: Wavtr* 9J 59
(off Willow Rd.)
Wilkinson St. CH41: Birke 3J 73
CH65: Ell P 8N 103
WA2: Warr 1D 82
Wilkinson St. M. *CH65: Ell P* 8A 104
(off Wilkinson St. Nth.)
Wilkinson St. Nth. CH65: Ell P 8A 104
Wilkin St. L4: Kirkd 2D 58
Willan St. CH43: Oxton 4H 73
Willard Av. WN5: Bil 9N 31
Willard Dr. L20: Boot 4B 44
WILLASTON 6M 101
Willaston Dr. L26: Halew 1L 93
Willaston Grn. M. CH64: Will 6M 101
Willaston Rd. CH46: More 8L 55
CH63: Raby, Thorn H 9K 89
L4: W'ton 9G 44
Willedstan Av. L23: Crosb 8L 33
William Beamont Way *WA1: Warr* 3B 82
(off Ebenezer Pl.)
William Brown St. L3: Liv 4G 4 (7C 58)
(not continuous)
William Ct. CH64: Nest 4F 100
William Harvey Cl. L30: Neth 8E 34
William Henry St. L3: Liv 1J 5 (6D 58)
L20: Boot 8A 44
William Jessop Way L3: Liv 3B 4 (7A 58)
William Johnson Gdns.
CH65: Ell P 8N 103
William Morris Av. L20: Boot 5D 44
William Penn Cl. WA5: Penk 3G 81
William Rd. WA11: Hay 5B 50
William Roberts Av. L32: Kirkb 9A 36
Williams Av. L20: Boot 5D 44
WA12: Newt W 5L 51
Williamson Art Gallery & Mus. 3H 73
Williamson Av. WA9: St H 6M 49
Williamson Ct. L25: Woolt 7G 76
L26: Halew 7L 77
Williamson Sq. L1: Liv 5F 4 (8C 58)
Williamson St. L1: Liv 5F 4 (8C 58)
Williamson Student Village L7: Liv 5N 5
Williamson Tunnels Heritage Cen. 6N 5
Williams St. L34: Presc 3A 62
William St. CH41: Birke 2L 73
CH44: Wall 7L 57
WA8: Widnes 6M 79
WA10: St H 6K 49
Williams Way WA6: Frod 6K 107
William Wall Rd. L21: Ford 9A 34
William Way WN7: Leigh 1J 53
Willingdon Rd. L16: Child 8C 60
Willington Av. CH62: East 3D 102
Willink Rd. WA11: St H 3M 49
Willis Cl. L35: Whis 7A 62
Willis La. L35: Whis 7A 62
Willis St. WA1: Warr 2E 82
Williton Rd. L16: Child 3C 76
Willmer Rd. CH42: Tran 3J 73
L4: W'ton 2G 58
Willoughby Cl. WA5: Old H 8L 65
Willoughby Dr. WA10: St H 1E 62
Willoughby Rd. CH44: Wall 5F 56
L14: Brd G 7C 60
L22: Wloo 1L 43
Willow Av. L32: Kirkb 8A 36
L35: Whis 6B 62
L36: Huy 9J 61
WA8: Widnes 6L 79
WA12: Newt W 6M 51
Willow Bank CH44: Wall 7H 57
L40: Westh 9J 21
PR9: Banks 4H 9
(off Main Av.)
WA6: Alv 3G 115
WA12: Newt W 7A 52
Willowbank Cl. L36: Huy 4G 61
Willowbank Holiday Home & Touring Pk.
PR8: Ainsd 3H 17
Willowbank Rd. CH42: Tran 5K 73
CH62: New F 1A 90
Willow Brook L39: Hals 8F 12
Willowbrow Rd. CH63: Raby 2J 101
Willow Cl. CH44: Wall 7H 57
L14: Brd G 7C 60
WA7: Run 8L 95
WA13: Lymm 4E 84
Willow Ct. CH63: H Beb 1K 89
WA2: Winw 6A 66
WA9: Clock F 5N 63
(off Clock Face Rd.)
WA12: Newt W 6M 51
Willow Cres. L40: Burs 8K 15
WA1: Padg 9J 67
WA4: Moore 9J 81
Willowcroft Rd. CH44: Wall 7J 57
Willowdale WA12: Newt W 7N 51
Willowdale Rd. L9: W'ton 6F 44
L18: Moss H 3L 75
Willowdale Way CH66: Gt Sut, Whit 4L 111
Willow Dr. WA4: Stockt H 7F 82
WN8: Skel 3B 30
Willow End L40: Burs 1K 21
Willowfield Gro. WN4: Ash M 9J 41
Willow Grn. L25: Woolt 4D 76
L39: Orm 8D 20
(off School Ho. Grn.)
L40: Ruf 3L 15
PR9: South 3A 8
Willow Gro. CH2: Elt 2L 113
CH46: More 1L 71
CH66: Whit 4M 111
L15: Wavtr 9M 59
L35: Presc 4B 62
L37: Form 9F 16
PR8: South 8K 7
PR9: Banks 3E 8
WA3: Golb 1B 52
WN4: Ash M 6N 41
Willowherb Cl. L26: Halew 6H 77
Willow Hey L31: Mag 4K 35
WN8: Skel 3C 30
Willowhey PR9: South 3L 7
Willow Ho. L21: Sea 4N 43
Willow La. CH63: Raby 3K 101
WA4: App 3E 98
Willow Lea CH43: Oxton 4G 72
Willowmeade L11: Norr G 7N 45
Willow Moss Cl.
CH46: More 7A 56
Willow Pk. CH49: Grea 4K 71
PR8: South 1N 11
Willow Ri. L33: Kirkb 8D 36
Willow Rd. L15: Wavtr 9K 59
M31: Part 7L 69
WA10: St H 7F 48
WA11: Hay 3G 50
WA12: Newt W 6N 51
Willows, The CH45: Wall 2E 56
M31: Part 6M 69
PR8: South 9E 6
(off Beechfield Gdns.)
WA5: Gt San 3H 81
WA6: Frod 6M 107
WA9: Clock F 5M 63
Willow Tree Av. WA9: Sut L 5N 63
Willow Tree Ct. WA8: Widnes 6N 79
Willow Tree Pk. WA13: Lymm 6B 84
Willow Wlk. WN8: Skel 9E 22
Willow Way CH46: More 9N 55
L11: Crox 5B 46
L23: Crosb 6L 33
Wills Av. L31: Mag 1H 35
Willsford Av. L31: Mell 8N 35
Wilmcote Gro. PR8: Ainsd 1H 17
Wilmere La. WA8: Widnes 3K 79
Wilmot Av. WA5: Gt San 2H 81
Wilmot Dr. WA3: Golb 3A 52
Wilmslow Av. CH66: Gt Sut 9K 103
Wilmslow Cres. WA4: Thel 4L 83
Wilmslow Dr. CH66: Gt Sut 9K 103
Wilne Rd. CH45: Wall 3G 57
Wilsden Rd. WA8: Widnes 7E 78
Wilsford Cl. WA3: Golb 1C 52
Wilson Av. CH44: Wall 5L 57
Wilson Bus. Cen. L36: Huy 8L 61
Wilson Cl. WA4: Thel 5L 83
WA8: Widnes 7N 79
WA10: St H 7H 49
Wilson Gro. L19: Garst 1A 92
Wilson La. WA3: Ris 4M 67
Wilson Patten St. WA1: Warr 4B 82
Wilson Rd. CH44: Wall 5L 57
L35: Presc 6A 62
L36: Huy 7K 61
Wilson's La. L21: Lith 2A 44
Wilsons La. CH65: Whit 2M 111
Wilson St. WA5: Warr 1B 82
Wilstan Av. CH63: H Beb 2K 89
Wilstone Cl. L6: Liv 5E 58
Wilton Grange CH48: W Kir 4B 70
Wilton Gro. L13: Liv 7M 59
Wilton La. WA3: Cul 5H 53
Wilton Rd. CH42: Rock F 7N 73
L36: Huy 8H 61
Wilton's Dr. L34: Know 7G 47
Wilton St. CH44: Wall 5H 57
L3: Liv 2J 5
WN4: Ash M 5J 41
Wiltshire Cl. WA1: Wools 1L 83
Wiltshire Dr. *L30: Neth* 8C 34
(off Simon's Cft.)
Wiltshire Gdns. WA10: St H 8J 49
Wiltshire Rd. M31: Part 7L 69
Wimbald Cl. L25: Gate 3G 77
Wimbledon St. CH45: Wall 4H 57
L15: Wavtr 1K 75
WIMBOLDS TRAFFORD 8K 113
Wimborne Av. CH61: Thing 2A 88
Wimborne Cl. L14: Knott A 3F 60
WA5: Warr 3N 81
Wimborne Pl. L14: Knott A 4F 60
Wimborne Rd. L14: Knott A 3E 60
Wimborne Way CH61: Irby 9L 71
Wimbrick Cl. CH46: More 9N 55
L39: Orm 9B 20
Wimbrick Ct. CH46: More 9N 55
Wimbrick Cres. L39: Orm 1B 28
Wimbrick Hey CH46: More 9N 55
Wimpole St. L7: Liv 7G 59
Winchcombe Cl. WN7: Leigh 1M 53
Winchester Av. CH65: Ell P 1B 112
L10: Aintr 8J 35
L22: Wloo 9J 33
WA5: Gt San 3L 81
WN4: Ash M 8J 41
Winchester Cl. L25: Woolt 9F 76
Winchester Dr. CH44: Wall 5G 56
Winchester Pl. WA8: Widnes 8F 78
Winchester Rd. L6: Liv 3H 59
WA11: Hay 1G 50
WN5: Bil 1N 39
Winchfield Rd. L15: Wavtr 2L 75
Windbourne Rd. L17: Aig 6G 75
Windermere Av. WA2: Warr 6D 66
WA8: Widnes 4L 79
WA11: St H 2K 49
Windermere Cl. CH64: Lit N 7F 100
Windermere Ct. *CH41: Birke* 3J 73
(off Penrith St.)
Windermere Cres. PR8: Ainsd 2J 17
Windermere Dr. L12: W Der 9A 46
L31: Mag 1K 35
L33: Kirkb 7B 36
WA11: Rainf 1C 38
Windermere Ho. L17: Aig 6J 75
Windermere Pl. WA11: St H 2K 49
Windermere Rd. CH43: Noct 2C 72
CH65: Ell P 3A 112
L38: Hight 8G 24
WA11: Hay 4D 50
Windermere St. L5: Liv 3F 58
WA8: Widnes 4L 79
Windermere Ter. L8: Liv 3G 75

Woodlands Rd.—Zircon Cl.

Woodlands Rd. L17: Aig . . . 6K 75
L36: Huy . . . 7F 60
L37: Form . . . 2D 24
WA11: St H . . . 4L 49
Woodlands Sq. *L27: N'ley* . . . *4L 77*
(off Wood La.)
Woodland Ter. M31: Part . . . 6L 69
Woodland Vw. CH66: Chil T . . . 6G 102
L23: Thorn . . . 4N 33
Woodland Wlk. CH62: Brom . . . 6B 90
Wood La. CH45: Wall . . . 3E 56
CH49: Grea . . . 3L 71
CH64: P'gte . . . 4C 100
CH64: Will . . . 5N 101
L27: N'ley . . . 3K 77
L34: Presc . . . 4M 61
L36: Huy . . . 7M 61
L37: Down, Gt Alt . . . 3B 26
L40: Lath . . . 1B 22
M31: Part . . . 6K 69
WA4: App . . . 8F 82
WA7: Beech, Sut W . . . 1B 108
WA7: Murd . . . 9E 96
WN8: Parb . . . 3G 22
Wood Lea L12: Crox . . . 7C 46
Woodlea Cl. CH62: Brom . . . 1C 102
PR9: South . . . 2B 8
Woodlee Rd. L25: Gate . . . 4G 77
Woodleigh Cl. L31: Lydi . . . 7G 27
Woodley Fold WA5: Penk . . . 5H 81
Woodley Pk. Cen. . . . 9E 22
Woodley Pk. Rd. WN8: Skel . . . 9E 22
Woodley Rd. L31: Mag . . . 5H 35
Woodmoss La. L40: Scar . . . 4J 13
Woodnook Rd. WN6: App B . . . 5N 23
Woodpecker Cl. CH49: Upton . . . 3L 71
L12: W Der . . . 9D 46
WA3: Birchw . . . 5N 67
Woodpecker Dr. L26: Halew . . . 6J 77
Woodridge WA7: Wind H . . . 6E 96
Wood Rd. L26: Halew . . . 9J 77
Woodrock Rd. L25: Woolt . . . 6F 76
Woodrow WN8: Skel . . . 4B 30
Woodrow Dr. WN8: Newb . . . 4C 22
Woodrow Way M44: Irlam . . . 2M 69
Woodruff St. L8: Liv . . . 4E 74
Woodruff Wlk. M31: Part . . . 6M 69
Woods Cl. L39: Down . . . 9E 18
Woodside CH65: Whit . . . 3A 112
Woodside Av. CH46: More . . . 1L 71
PR8: Ainsd . . . 2H 17
WA6: Frod . . . 7N 107
WA11: St H . . . 2J 49
WN4: Ash M . . . 3J 41
Woodside Bus. Pk. CH41: Birke . . . 1M 73
Woodside Bus Station . . . 1M 73
Woodside Cl. L12: W Der . . . 1N 59
WN8: Uph . . . 4M 31
Woodside Ferry App. CH41: Birke . . . 1M 73
Woodside Gdns. *M31: Part* . . . *5M 69*
(off Lock La.)
Woodside La. WA13: Lymm . . . 7H 85
Woodside Rd. CH61: Irby . . . 1M 87
WA5: Gt San . . . 1H 81
WA11: Hay . . . 3G 51
Woodside St. L7: Liv . . . 8G 59
Woodside Walkway CH41: Birke . . . 1M 73
Woodside Way L33: Kirkb . . . 6D 36
Woods La. WN4: Ash M . . . 6L 41
Woodsome Cl. CH65: Whit . . . 4N 111
Woodsome Dr. CH65: Whit . . . 4N 111
Woodsome Pk. L25: Gate . . . 5G 76
Woodsorrel Rd. CH41: Birke . . . 1F 72
L15: Wavtr . . . 1N 75
Wood Sorrel Way WA3: Low . . . 2F 52
Woods Rd. M44: Irlam . . . 1M 69
Woodstock Av. WA12: Newt W . . . 8M 51
Woodstock Cl. WN7: Leigh . . . 1M 53
Woodstock Dr. PR8: Birkd . . . 6M 11
Woodstock Gdns. WA4: App . . . 1G 98
Woodstock Gro. WA8: Widnes . . . 6G 79
Woodstock Rd. CH44: Wall . . . 6G 57
Woodstock St. L5: Liv . . . 4C 58
Wood St. CH41: Birke . . . 1K 73
CH47: Hoy . . . 1C 70
CH62: Port S . . . 2A 90
L1: Liv . . . 6G 4 (8C 58)
L19: Garst . . . 1A 92
L21: Lith . . . 3A 44
L34: Presc . . . 3A 62
WA1: Warr . . . 2E 82
WA3: Golb . . . 2C 52
WA8: Widnes . . . 7M 79
WA9: St H . . . 6M 49
Woodthorn Cl. WA4: Dares . . . 3H 97
WOODVALE . . . 2J 17
Wood Va. WA9: St H . . . 3H 63
Woodvale Cl. CH43: Bid . . . 9C 56
WA2: Padg . . . 8F 66
Woodvale Ct. *CH49: Wdchu* . . . *7A 72*
(off Childwall Grn.)
PR9: Banks . . . 2E 8
Woodvale Dr. WA3: Low . . . 1F 52
Woodvale Rd. CH66: Lit Sut . . . 8J 103
L12: Crox . . . 7D 46
L25: Woolt . . . 6F 76
PR8: Ainsd . . . 3J 17
Woodvale Sidings PR8: Ainsd . . . 4K 17
Woodview L34: Know . . . 7H 47
Woodview Av. CH44: Wall . . . 7L 57
Woodview Cl. WN3: Winst . . . 2F 40
Woodview Cres. WA8: Widnes . . . 8D 78
Woodview Rd. L25: Woolt . . . 4D 76
WA8: Widnes . . . 8D 78
Woodville Av. L23: Crosb . . . 8K 33
Woodville Pl. WA8: Widnes . . . 7G 78
Woodville Rd. CH42: Tran . . . 4J 73
Woodville St. WA10: St H . . . 6L 49
(not continuous)
Woodville Ter. L6: Liv . . . 4G 58
Woodward Rd. CH42: Rock F . . . 8N 73
L33: Know I . . . 7G 37
Woodway CH49: Grea . . . 4L 71
Woodway Ct. CH62: Brom . . . 5D 90
Woodyear Rd. CH62: Brom . . . 8D 90
Woolacombe Av. WA9: Sut L . . . 4M 63
Woolacombe Cl. WA4: Warr . . . 6E 82
Woolacombe Rd. L16: Child . . . 2C 76
Woolage Cl. L14: Knott A . . . 5D 60
Woolden Rd. M44: Cad . . . 2G 69
Wooler Cl. CH46: More . . . 9K 55
Woolfall Cl. L36: Huy . . . 5F 60
Woolfall Cres. L36: Huy . . . 5F 60
WOOLFALL HEATH . . . 4H 61
Woolfall Heath Av. L36: Huy . . . 4G 60
Woolfall Ter. L21: Sea . . . 4N 43
Woolhope Rd. L4: W'ton . . . 8G 44
Woollam Dr. CH66: Lit Sut . . . 7J 103
Woolley Cl. WA6: Frod . . . 4N 107
Woolmer Cl. WA3: Birchw . . . 3B 68
Woolmoore Rd. L24: Speke . . . 1G 92
WOOLSTON . . . 1J 83
Woolston Grange Av. WA1: Wools . . . 7K 67
WA2: Padg . . . 7K 67
Woolston Hall WA1: Wools . . . 1L 83
Woolston Neighbourhood Hub . . . 1L 83
Woolston Rd. WA11: Hay . . . 3E 50
WOOLTON . . . 6F 76
Woolton Cl. WN4: Ash M . . . 6H 41
Woolton Ct. CH66: Ell P . . . 6L 103
Woolton Golf Course . . . 8F 76
WOOLTON HILL . . . 5C 76
Woolton Hill Rd. L25: Woolt . . . 4C 76
Woolton M. *L25: Woolt* . . . *6E 76*
(off Quarry St.)
Woolton Mt. L25: Woolt . . . 5E 76
WOOLTON PARK . . . 4E 76
Woolton Pk. L25: Woolt . . . 4E 76
Woolton Pk. Cl. L25: Woolt . . . 5E 76
Woolton Picture House . . . 6E 76
Woolton Rd. L15: Wavtr . . . 1M 75
L16: Child . . . 2A 76
L19: Aller, Garst . . . 1A 92
L25: Aller . . . 9B 76
L25: Woolt . . . 3C 76
Woolton St. L25: Woolt . . . 6E 76
(not continuous)
Woolton Views L25: Hunts X . . . 8H 77
Worcester Av. L13: Liv . . . 2J 59
L22: Wloo . . . 9K 33
WA3: Golb . . . 2C 52
Worcester Cl. WA5: Gt San . . . 3L 81
WA10: St H . . . 8J 49
Worcester Ct. L20: Boot . . . 7C 44
Worcester Dr. L13: Liv . . . 2J 59
Worcester Dr. Nth. L13: Liv . . . 2J 59
Worcester Rd. CH43: Bid . . . 9D 56
L20: Boot . . . 6C 44
Worcester St. CH65: Ell P . . . 8A 104
Worcester Wlk. CH65: Ell P . . . 8A 104
Wordsworth Av. CH42: Rock F . . . 7M 73
WA4: Warr . . . 5C 82
WA8: Widnes . . . 8J 79
WA9: Sut M . . . 6K 63
WN5: Bil . . . 2N 39
Wordsworth Cl. L39: Orm . . . 7B 20
Wordsworth Ct. L32: Kirkb . . . 2A 46
Wordsworth St. L8: Liv . . . 1H 75
L20: Boot . . . 5N 43
Wordsworth Wlk. CH48: W Kir . . . 8C 70
Wordsworth Way CH66: Gt Sut . . . 4K 111
L36: Huy . . . 8K 61
World Mus. Liverpool . . . 3G 4 (7C 58)
World of Glass, The . . . 7K 49
Worrow Cl. L11: Norr G . . . 7N 45
Worrow Rd. L11: Norr G . . . 7N 45
Worsborough Av. WA5: Gt San . . . 3K 81
Worsley Av. WA4: Westy . . . 4G 82
WORSLEY BROW . . . 1A 64
Worsley Brow WA9: St H . . . 1A 64
Worsley Cl. WA7: Cas . . . 5C 96
Worsley Rd. WA4: W'ton . . . 7C 82
Worsley St. WA3: Golb . . . 2B 52
WA5: Warr . . . 1A 82
WA11: Hay . . . 4B 50
Worthing Cl. PR8: Birkd . . . 3M 11
Worthing St. L22: Wloo . . . 9J 33
Worthington Av. M31: Part . . . 6M 69
Worthington Cl. WA7: Pal F . . . 8C 96
Worthington Way WN3: Wigan . . . 1G 41
Wortley Rd. L10: Faz . . . 2K 45
Wotton Dr. WN4: Ash M . . . 8M 41
Wray Av. WA9: Clock F . . . 5N 63
Wrayburn Cl. L7: Liv . . . 9H 59
Wray Ct. WA9: Clock F . . . 5N 63
Wrekin Cl. L25: Woolt . . . 7F 76
Wrekin Dr. L10: Aintr . . . 9K 35
Wrenbury Cl. CH43: Oxton . . . 6F 72
WA7: Sut W . . . 2B 108
Wrenbury St. L7: Liv . . . 7H 59
Wren Cl. WA3: Birchw . . . 5N 67
WA7: Pal F . . . 9C 96
Wrenfield Gro. L17: Aig . . . 6H 75
Wren Gro. L26: Halew . . . 7J 77
Wrexham Cl. WA5: Call . . . 7N 65
Wright Cl. WA10: St H . . . 3J 49
Wright Cres. WA8: Widnes . . . 2K 95
WRIGHTINGTON . . . 1M 23
WRIGHT'S GREEN . . . 1H 99
Wright's La. WA5: Burtw . . . 5G 65
Wrights La. WA5: Cuerd . . . 6B 80
Wrights Ter. L15: Wavtr . . . 1M 75
PR8: Birkd . . . 3A 12
Wright St. CH44: Wall . . . 5K 57
L5: Liv . . . 4C 58
PR9: South . . . 8G 7
WN4: Ash M . . . 5H 41
Wright Tree Vs. M44: Cad . . . 4K 69
Wrigley Rd. WA11: Hay . . . 4G 50
Wrigleys Cl. L37: Form . . . 8F 16
Wrigleys La. L37: Form . . . 8F 16
Wroxham Cl. CH49: Upton . . . 3A 72
WA6: Hel . . . 1E 114
Wroxham Ct. *CH49: Upton* . . . *3A 72*
(off Wroxham Cl.)
Wroxham Dr. CH49: Upton . . . 4A 72
Wroxham Rd. WA5: Gt San . . . 2F 80
Wroxham Way CH49: Upton . . . 3A 72
Wryneck Cl. WA10: St H . . . 1E 62
Wrynose Rd. CH62: Brom . . . 7D 90
Wulstan St. L4: Kirkd . . . 2C 58
Wyatt Gro. WN4: Ash M . . . 8M 41
Wychelm Rd. M31: Part . . . 6M 69
Wycherley Rd. CH42: Tran . . . 5K 73
Wycherley St. L34: Presc . . . 3A 62
Wychwood CH49: Upton . . . 3N 71
Wychwood Av. WA13: Lymm . . . 5C 84
Wychwood Cl. L14: Knott A . . . 5B 60
Wycliffe Rd. CH65: Gt Sut . . . 2L 111
L4: W'ton . . . 2H 59
WA11: Hay . . . 3G 51
Wycliffe St. CH42: Rock F . . . 6M 73
Wye Cl. CH42: Rock F . . . 5M 73
Wyedale CH65: Whit . . . 2N 111
Wyedale Rd. WA11: Hay . . . 3E 50
Wye St. L5: Liv . . . 3E 58
Wyke Cop Rd. PR8: South . . . 2J 13
PR9: South . . . 2J 13
Wykeham St. L4: Kirkd . . . 2C 58
Wyke La. PR9: South . . . 7A 8
Wyken Gro. WA11: St H . . . 5M 49
Wyke Rd. L35: Presc . . . 4B 62
Wyke Wood La. PR9: South . . . 7D 8
Wyllin Rd. L33: Kirkb . . . 9E 36
Wylva Av. L23: Crosb . . . 8N 33
Wylva Rd. L4: W'ton . . . 3F 58
Wyncroft Cl. CH65: Whit . . . 2N 111
WA8: Widnes . . . 9F 78
Wyncroft Rd. WA8: Widnes . . . 9F 78
Wyncroft St. L8: Liv . . . 4F 74
Wyndale Cl. L18: Moss H . . . 5N 75
Wyndcote Rd. L18: Moss H . . . 3N 75
Wyndham Av. L14: Brd G . . . 7E 60
Wyndham Cl. CH62: East . . . 8F 90
Wyndham Cres. CH66: Gt Sut . . . 3K 111
Wyndham Rd. CH45: Wall . . . 4D 56
Wyndham St. L4: W'ton . . . 8E 44
Wynne Rd. WA10: St H . . . 5H 49
Wynnstay Av. L31: Lydi . . . 9J 27
Wynnstay St. L8: Liv . . . 2F 74
Wynstay Rd. CH47: Meols . . . 9D 54
Wynton Cl. WN7: Leigh . . . 1M 53
Wynwood Pk. L36: Roby . . . 8G 60
Wyoming Cl. WA5: Gt San . . . 2L 81
Wyre Rd. L5: Liv . . . 2E 58
Wyrescourt Rd. L12: W Der . . . 4B 60
Wyresdale Av. PR8: South . . . 2C 12
WA10: St H . . . 3H 49
Wyresdale Rd. L9: Aintr . . . 3G 44
Wyrevale Gro. WN4: Ash M . . . 8L 41
Wysall Cl. WA11: St H . . . 5N 49
Wyswall Cl. L26: Halew . . . 7J 77
Wythburn Cres. WA11: St H . . . 2L 49
Wythburn Gro. WA7: Beech . . . 1A 108
Wyvern Rd. CH46: More . . . 9M 55

X

X Building L3: Liv . . . 3D 4 (7B 58)
XL Bus. Pk. WN8: Skel . . . 1N 29

Y

Yanwath St. L8: Liv . . . 1G 75
Yarcombe Cl. L26: Halew . . . 7K 77
Yardley Av. WA5: Warr . . . 9A 66
Yardley Cen. L33: Know I . . . 9G 36
Yardley Dr. CH63: Spit . . . 6N 89
Yardley Rd. L33: Know I . . . 1G 46
Yarmouth Rd. WA5: Gt San . . . 2G 81
Yarn Cl. WA9: St H . . . 1B 64
Yarrow Av. L31: Mag . . . 1L 35
Yates Cl. WA5: Gt San . . . 3L 81
Yates Ct. L34: Presc . . . 4A 62
Yates Rd. CH2: Thorn M . . . 4J 113
Yates St. L8: Liv . . . 3D 74
Yeadon Wlk. L24: Speke . . . 4G 92
Yeald Brow WA13: Lymm . . . 5B 84
Yellow Ho. La. PR8: South . . . 9G 6
Yellow Submarine . . . 5G 92
Yelverton Cl. L26: Halew . . . 7K 77
Yelverton Rd. CH42: Tran . . . 5L 73
L4: W'ton . . . 2H 59
Yeoman Cl. L5: Liv . . . 1J 5 (5D 58)
Yeoman Cotts. CH47: Hoy . . . 2D 70
Yeoman Way CH66: Gt Sut . . . 4K 111
Yeovil Cl. WA1: Wools . . . 9K 67
Ye Priory Ct. L25: Aller . . . 7C 76
Yew Bank Rd. L16: Child . . . 1B 76
Yewdale WN8: Skel . . . 3D 30
Yewdale Av. WA11: St H . . . 1L 49
Yewdale Dr. CH66: Whit . . . 4L 111
Yewdale Pk. CH43: Oxton . . . 4H 73
Yewdale Rd. L9: W'ton . . . 6G 44
WN4: Ash M . . . 4J 41
Yew Tree Av. WA9: St H . . . 3M 63
WA12: Newt W . . . 6J 51
Yew Tree Cl. CH2: Thorn M . . . 4J 113
CH49: Wdchu . . . 6A 72
L12: W Der . . . 3D 60
L33: Kirkb . . . 7C 36
WA13: Lymm . . . 4E 84
Yewtree Cl. CH64: Lit N . . . 7F 100
Yew Tree Ct. CH60: Hesw . . . 7A 88
WA3: Ris . . . 9M 53
Yew Tree Grn. L31: Mell . . . 7N 35
Yew Tree La. CH48: W Kir . . . 6C 70
L12: W Der . . . 4C 60
WA4: App T . . . 2K 99
Yew Tree Rd. CH46: More . . . 7N 55
CH63: H Beb . . . 3L 89
L9: W'ton . . . 6E 44
L18: Aller . . . 5B 76
L25: Hunts X . . . 8G 77
L36: Huy . . . 9H 61
L39: Orm . . . 6C 20
Yew Tree Trad. Est. WA11: Hay . . . 2H 51
Yew Tree Way WA3: Golb . . . 3C 52
Yew Wlk. M31: Part . . . 7L 69
Yew Way CH46: More . . . 8N 55
Yorkaster Rd. L18: Aller . . . 7A 76
York Av. CH44: Wall . . . 6K 57
CH48: W Kir . . . 8C 70
L17: Liv . . . 2J 75
L23: Crosb . . . 7K 33
PR8: South . . . 1N 11
WA3: Cul . . . 8N 53
WA5: Gt San . . . 1G 80
York Cl. L30: Neth . . . 6E 34
L37: Form . . . 7F 16
WA10: St H . . . 6J 49
York Cotts. L25: Gate . . . 4F 76
York Ct. *WA4: Stockt H* . . . *7F 82*
(off Limetree Av.)
York Dr. WA4: Grap . . . 6H 83
York Gdns. PR8: Birkd . . . 1N 11
York Ho. L17: Aig . . . 3J 75
York Mnr. L37: Form . . . 1F 24
PR8: Birkd . . . 1N 11
York Pl. WA7: Run . . . 5L 95
York Rd. CH44: Wall . . . 7K 57
CH65: Ell P . . . 9A 104
L23: Crosb . . . 7L 33
L31: Mag . . . 4J 35
L36: Huy . . . 6L 61
L37: Form . . . 1F 24
M44: Cad . . . 4K 69
PR8: Birkd . . . 2M 11
WA4: Grap . . . 6H 83
WA8: Widnes . . . 8F 78
WN4: Ash M . . . 8K 41
York Rd. Sth. WN4: Ash M . . . 9L 41
Yorkshire Gdns. WA10: St H . . . 8J 49
Yorkshire Rd. M31: Part . . . 7L 69
York St. CH62: Brom . . . 2C 90
L1: Liv . . . 7F 4 (9C 58)
L9: W'ton . . . 7E 44
L19: Garst . . . 3A 92
L22: Wloo . . . 2K 43
WA3: Golb . . . 1B 52
WA4: Warr . . . 4D 82
WA7: Run . . . 5K 95
York Ter. L5: Liv . . . 3D 58
PR9: South . . . 7H 7
York Way L19: Garst . . . 3B 92
L36: Huy . . . 6L 61
Youatt Av. L35: Presc . . . 5B 62
Youens Way L14: Knott A . . . 5C 60
Youth Court
Liverpool . . . 6E 4
Yoxall Dr. L33: Kirkb . . . 6B 36
Yvonne Cl. WN4: Ash M . . . 6M 41

Z

Zander Gro. L12: Crox . . . 7E 46
Zante Cl. L5: Liv . . . 3D 58
Zara Ct. WA11: Hay . . . 3E 50
Zenith Wlk. L25: Gate . . . 1E 76
Zetland Rd. CH45: Wall . . . 2F 56
L18: Moss H . . . 3L 75
Zetland St. CH41: Birke . . . 3K 73
PR9: South . . . 8J 7
Zig Zag Rd. CH45: Wall . . . 3H 57
L12: W Der . . . 4B 60
Zinnia Dr. M44: Irlam . . . 1L 69
Zircon Cl. L21: Lith . . . 2B 44

HOSPITALS, HOSPICES and selected HEALTHCARE FACILITIES covered by this atlas.

N.B. Where it is not possible to name these facilities on the map,
the reference given is for the road in which they are situated.

AINTREE UNIVERSITY HOSPITAL 4K **45**
Longmoor Lane
LIVERPOOL
L9 7AL
Tel: 0151 525 5980

ALDER HEY CHILDREN'S HOSPITAL 5A **60**
Eaton Road
West Derby
LIVERPOOL
L12 2AP
Tel: 0151 228 4811

ARROWE PARK HOSPITAL 7A **72**
Arrowe Park Road
WIRRAL
CH49 5PE
Tel: 0151 678 5111

ASHTON HOUSE HOSPITAL 4H **73**
26 Village Road
Oxton
PRENTON
CH43 5SR
Tel: 0151 488 8100

ASHWORTH HOSPITAL 9M **27**
Parkbourn
LIVERPOOL
L31 1HW
Tel: 0151 473 0303

BMI SEFTON HOSPITAL *4K* **45**
University Hospital Aintree
Lower Lane
LIVERPOOL
L9 7AL
Tel: 0151 330 6551

BROADGREEN HOSPITAL 7A **60**
Thomas Drive
LIVERPOOL
L14 3LB
Tel: 0151 706 2000

CHESHIRE & MERSEYSIDE NHS TREATMENT CENTRE 9B **96**
Earls Way
RUNCORN
WA7 2HH
Tel: 0151 928 701777

CHRISTOPHER GRANGE CENTRE FOR ADULT BLIND 4C **60**
Youens Way
East Prescot Road
LIVERPOOL
L14 2EW
Tel: 0151 220 2525

CLAIRE HOUSE CHILDREN'S HOSPICE 6K **89**
Clatterbridge Road
WIRRAL
CH63 4JD
Tel: 0151 334 4626

CLATTERBRIDGE CANCER CENTRE, THE 6K **89**
Clatterbridge Road
WIRRAL
CH63 4JY
Tel: 0151 334 1155

CLATTERBRIDGE HOSPITAL 6K **89**
Clatterbridge Road
Bebington
WIRRAL
CH63 4JY
Tel: 0151 334 4000

CLOCKVIEW HOSPITAL 7E **44**
2a Oakhouse Park
LIVERPOOL
L9 1EP
Tel: 0151 330 7200

ELLESMERE PORT HOSPITAL 3M **111**
114 Chester Road
Whitby
ELLESMERE PORT
CH65 6SG
Tel: 01244 362986

FAIRFIELD INDEPENDENT HOSPITAL 9H **39**
Crank Road
Crank
ST. HELENS
WA11 7RS
Tel: 01744 739311

HALTON GENERAL HOSPITAL 9B **96**
Hospital Way
RUNCORN
WA7 2DA
Tel: 01928 714567

HALTON HAVEN HOSPICE 1E **108**
Barnfield Avenue
Murdishaw
RUNCORN
WA7 6EP
Tel: 01928 712728

HESKETH CENTRE, THE 6H **7**
51-55 Albert Road
SOUTHPORT
PR9 0LT
Tel: 01704 383110

HOLLINS PARK HOSPITAL 3A **66**
Hollins Lane
WARRINGTON
WA2 8WA
Tel: 01925 664000

HOSPICE OF THE GOOD SHEPHERD 9N **111**
Gordon Lane
Backford
CHESTER
CH2 4DG
Tel: 01244 851091

HOUGHTON HALL (STEP DOWN UNIT) 7F **66**
Greenwood Crescent
WARRINGTON
WA2 0DT
Tel: 01925 858970

ISIGHT PRIVATE 9E **6**
Drayton House
2 Lulworth Street
SOUTHPORT
PR8 2AT
Tel: 01704 563279

LIVERPOOL HEART & CHEST HOSPITAL 7A **60**
Thomas Drive
LIVERPOOL
L14 3PE
Tel: 0151 600 1616

LIVERPOOL WOMEN'S HOSPITAL 8N **5** (9F **58**)
Crown Street
LIVERPOOL
L8 7SS
Tel: 0151 708 9988

MARIE CURIE CENTRE, LIVERPOOL 6F **76**
Speke Road
Woolton
LIVERPOOL
L25 8QA
Tel: 0151 801 1400

**MINOR INJURIES UNIT
(VICTORIA CENTRAL HOSPITAL)** 5H **57**
Victoria Central Hospital
Mill Lane
WALLASEY
CH44 5UF
Tel: 0151 514 2888

MOSSLEY HILL HOSPITAL 5K **75**
Park Avenue
Mossley Hill
LIVERPOOL
L18 8BU
Tel: 0151 4730303

NEWTON COMMUNITY HOSPITAL 8K **51**
Bradlegh Road
NEWTON-LE-WILLOWS
WA12 8RB
Tel: 01925 222731

NHS CHILDREN'S WALK-IN CENTRE (SMITHDOWN) ..2J **75**
Smithdown Road
LIVERPOOL
L15 2LF
Tel: 0151 285 4820

NHS WALK-IN CENTRE (BIRKENHEAD) 9G **57**
31 Laird Street
BIRKENHEAD
CH41 8DB
Tel: 0151 652 6077

NHS WALK-IN CENTRE (EASTHAM) 2E **102**
31 Eastham Rake
WIRRAL
CH62 9AN
Tel: 0151 327 3061

NHS WALK-IN CENTRE (KNOWSLEY HALEWOOD) 9K **77**
Halewood Centre
Roseheath Drive
LIVERPOOL
L26 9UH
Tel: 0151 281 4041

NHS WALK-IN CENTRE (KNOWSLEY - HUYTON) 7J *61*
Nutgrove Villa
Westmorland Road
Huyton
LIVERPOOL
L36 6GA
Tel: 0151 244 3150

NHS WALK-IN CENTRE (KNOWSLEY - KIRKBY) 9C *36*
St Chad's Clinic
57 St Chad's Drive
LIVERPOOL
L32 8RE
Tel: 0151 244 3180

NHS WALK-IN CENTRE (LITHERLAND TOWN HALL) 2A **44**
Hatton Hill Road
LIVERPOOL
L21 9JN
Tel: 0151 475 4840

**NHS WALK-IN CENTRE
(LIVERPOOL CITY CENTRE)** 6G **4** (8C **58**)
6 David Lewis Street
LIVERPOOL
L1 1HU
Tel: 0151 247 6500

NHS WALK-IN CENTRE (LIVERPOOL - OLD SWAN) 7M **59**
Old Swan Health Centre
Crystal Cl.
LIVERPOOL
L13 2GA
Tel: 0151 247 6700

NHS WALK-IN CENTRE (MORETON) 9M **55**
8-14 Chadwick Street
Moreton
WIRRAL
CH46 7XA
Tel: 0151 522 0099

NHS WALK-IN CENTRE (NEW FERRY) 8A **74**
Parkfield Medical Practice
Sefton Road
New Ferry
WIRRAL
CH62 5HS
Tel: 0151 644 0055

NHS WALK-IN CENTRE (ST HELENS) 7L **49**
Millennium Building
Bickerstaffe Street
ST. HELENS
WA10 1DH
Tel: 01744 627400

NHS WALK-IN CENTRE (SKELMERSDALE) 3E **30**
116-118 The Concourse Shopping Centre
SKELMERSDALE
WN8 6LJ
Tel: 01695 588640

NHS WALK-IN CENTRE (SOUTH LIVERPOOL) 1A **92**
Church Road
Garston
LIVERPOOL
L19 2LW
Tel: 0151 295 9010

NHS WALK-IN CENTRE (WIRRAL) 6H **57**
Victoria Central Hospital
Mill Lane
WALLASEY
CH44 5UF
Tel: 0151 514 2888

NHS WALK-IN CENTRE (WIRRAL ARROWE PARK) 7A **72**
Arrowe Park Hospital
Arrowe Park Road
WIRRAL
CH49 5PE
Tel: 0151 678 8496

OAKDENE UNIT 5M **53**
Jibcroft Brook Lane
WARRINGTON
WA3 4TH
Tel: 01925 765335

ORMSKIRK & DISTRICT GENERAL HOSPITAL 9E **20**
Wigan Road
ORMSKIRK
L39 2AZ
Tel: 01695 577111

PEASLEY CROSS HOSPITAL .9M **49**
Marshalls Cross Road
ST. HELENS
WA9 3DE
Tel: 01744 458459

QUEENSCOURT HOSPICE 2E **12**
Town Lane
SOUTHPORT
PR8 6RE
Tel: 01704 544645

RATHBONE HOSPITAL 7M **59**
Mill Lane
Old Swan
LIVERPOOL
L13 4AW
Tel: 0151 471 7810

RENACRES HOSPITAL 9G **13**
Renacres Lane
Halsall
ORMSKIRK
L39 8SE
Tel: 01704 841133

ROYAL LIVERPOOL UNIVERSITY DENTAL HOSPITAL
. . . . .4L **5** (7E **58**)
Pembroke Place
LIVERPOOL
L3 5PS
Tel: 0151 706 2000

ROYAL LIVERPOOL UNIVERSITY HOSPITAL 3L **5** (7F **58**)
Prescot Street
LIVERPOOL
L7 8XP
Tel: 0151 706 2000

ST CATHERINE'S HOSPITAL (BIRKENHEAD) 4K **73**
Church Road
BIRKENHEAD
CH42 0LQ
Tel: 0151 678 7272

ST HELENS HOSPITAL (MERSEYSIDE) 9M **49**
Marshalls Cross Road
ST. HELENS
WA9 3DA
Tel: 01744 26633

ST JOSEPH'S HOSPICE 3M **33**
Ince Road
LIVERPOOL
L23 4UE
Tel: 0151 924 3812

ST ROCCO'S HOSPICE 1N **81**
Lockton Lane
WARRINGTON
WA5 0BW
Tel: 01925 575780

SMITHDOWN HEALTH PARK .2J **75**
Smithdown Road
LIVERPOOL
L15 2HE
Tel: 0151 300 8290

SOUTHPORT & FORMBY DISTRICT GENERAL HOSPITAL
. . . . .2D **12**
Town Lane
SOUTHPORT
PR8 6PN
Tel: 01704 547471

SPIRE CHESHIRE HOSPITAL .6E **98**
Fir Tree Close
Stretton
WARRINGTON
WA4 4LU
Tel: 0845 602 2500

SPIRE LIVERPOOL HOSPITAL 3L **75**
57 Greenbank Road
LIVERPOOL
L18 1HQ
Tel: 0151 733 7123

SPIRE MURRAYFIELD HOSPITAL 2D **88**
Holmwood Drive
Heswall
WIRRAL
CH61 1AU
Tel: 0845 600 2110

ST. MARY'S HOSPITAL 8C **66**
Floyd Drive
WARRINGTON
WA2 8DB
Tel: 01925 423300

URGENT CARE CENTRE (ORMSKIRK) 9E **20**
Ormskirk and District General Hospital
Wigan Road
ORMSKIRK
L39 2AZ
Tel: 01695 577111

VICTORIA CENTRAL HOSPITAL 6H **57**
Mill Lane
WALLASEY
CH44 5UF
Tel: 0151 678 7272

WALTON CENTRE, THE 3K **45**
Lower Lane
LIVERPOOL
L9 7LJ
Tel: 0151 525 3611

WARRINGTON HOSPITAL 2A **82**
Lovely Lane
WARRINGTON
WA5 1QG
Tel: 01925 635911

WHISTON HOSPITAL 5C **62**
Warrington Road
PRESCOT
L35 5DR
Tel: 0151 426 1600

WILLOWBROOK HOSPICE 2D **62**
Portico Lane
Eccleston Park
PRESCOT
L34 2QT
Tel: 0151 430 8736

WINDSOR HOUSE 9K **5** (1E **74**)
Up. Parliament St.
LIVERPOOL
L8 7LF
Tel: 0151 473 0303

WIRRAL HOSPICE ST JOHN'S 6L **89**
Mount Road
Higher Bebington
WIRRAL
CH63 6JE
Tel: 0151 334 2778

WOODLANDS HOSPICE 4J **45**
Longmoor Lane
LIVERPOOL
L9 7LA
Tel: 0151 529 2299

WRIGHTINGTON HOSPITAL .3N **23**
Hall Lane
Appley Bridge
WIGAN
WN6 9EP
Tel: 01942 244000

YORK CENTRE 2J **75**
Smithdown Health Park
Smithdown Road
LIVERPOOL
L15 2HP
Tel: 0151 330 8056

ZOE'S PLACE BABY HOSPICE 4C **60**
Yew Tree Lane
LIVERPOOL
L12 9HH
Tel: 0151 228 0353

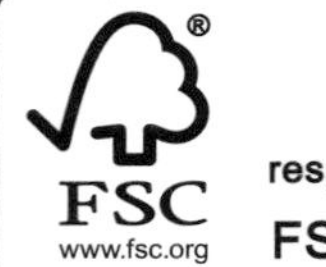

SAFETY CAMERA INFORMATION

PocketGPSWorld.com's CamerAlert is a self-contained speed and red light camera warning system for SatNavs and Android or Apple iOS smartphones/tablets. Visit www.cameralert.com to download.

Safety camera locations are publicised by the Safer Roads Partnership which operates them in order to encourage drivers to comply with speed limits at these sites. It is the driver's absolute responsibility to be aware of and to adhere to speed limits at all times.

By showing this safety camera information it is the intention of Geographers' A-Z Map Company Ltd. to encourage safe driving and greater awareness of speed limits and vehicle speed. Data accurate at time of printing.